THE NEW ENGLISH BIBLE

COMPANION TO THE NEW TESTAMENT

THE NEW ENGLISH BIBLE

COMPANION TO THE NEW TESTAMENT

BY

A. E. HARVEY

OXFORD UNIVERSITY PRESS

CAMBRIDGE UNIVERSITY PRESS

1979

INTERNATIONAL STANDARD BOOK NUMBERS

HARD COVERS 0 19 826160 8 OXFORD UNIVERSITY PRESS
0 521 07705 2 CAMBRIDGE UNIVERSITY PRESS
PAPERBACK 0 19 21322 9 OXFORD UNIVERSITY PRESS
0 521 50539 9 CAMBRIDGE UNIVERSITY PRESS

FIRST PUBLISHED 1970
REPRINTED 1971 1973
FIRST PAPERBACK EDITION 1979

Printed in Great Britain at the
University Press, Cambridge

CONTENTS

PREFACE

In this Companion I have been concerned with questions which anyone may be expected to ask who approaches the New Testament in general, and the New English Bible translation of it in particular, without any previous introduction. These questions are not always the same as those which occupy professional scholars; yet it is mainly their research which has made it possible to attempt to answer them. All that I have learnt from them I gratefully acknowledge; and I am aware that there are countless things I have still failed to learn.

This book could not have been written at all had it not been for the generosity of the Governing Body of Christ Church, Oxford, which readily accepted that I should devote to this work the main part of my time as a Research Student of the House. It would also hardly have been completed had it not been for the stimulus of eight months spent in Jerusalem in 1966–7, which again I owe to the liberality of Christ Church, as well as to the hospitality of the Right Revd Campbell MacInnes, then Archbishop in Jerusalem, and of others in St George's Close, Jerusalem. I am also deeply indebted to the École Biblique and its Director for permission to make use of its magnificent library during my stay in Jerusalem.

I should not have presumed to offer so ambitious a book for publication had it not first received the scrutiny of men wiser and more learned than myself. Chief among these is the Revd Dr C. H. Dodd, who was one of the first to conceive the project of a book such as this, who constantly encouraged me while I was writing it, and who patiently read and weighed every word of the typescript. After him, I owe the greatest debt of gratitude to the Revd Professor C. F. D. Moule, who read more than half the book in typescript and helped me with a large number of suggestions.

Others who have read parts of the typescript and made valuable comments are Père P. Benoit O.P., the Very Revd Dr Henry Chadwick, Professors J. Duncan M. Derrett and E. R. Dodds, Mr E. W. Gray, the Revd J. L. Houlden, Mr Kenneth Pearce, Mr C. H. Roberts and Dr G. Vermes. Besides these, there are many others without whose help the work could hardly have been done: my colleagues at Christ Church, who patiently responded to my insistent questions on matters lying within their special competence; my pupils, who helped me to keep my mind fresh on the basic questions which confront any student of the New Testament; and finally some of the students at St Augustine's College, Canterbury, who helped me with the proofs.

Two men, who in their different ways helped me most, died before the book was published. One was Dr C. A. Simpson, Dean of Christ Church, who read much of the typescript, made characteristically candid and thoughtful comments on it, and sustained me through this long task with his warm-hearted encouragement. The other was my father: the small share which I may have inherited of his integrity, his powers of analysis, and his unusual ability to ask searching questions about what others take for granted, is largely responsible for any originality which this book may have. I have tried throughout to ask the questions which he would have asked and to seek the answers which he would have regarded as honest. The book, indeed, was written for him, and owes more to him than he ever knew.

To the memory of these two men I gratefully dedicate this Companion to the New Testament.

A. E. H.

St Augustine's College, Canterbury
March 1970

NOTE: The English text referred to throughout is that of the New English Bible (Second Edition) with the notes in the Library Edition. Where this differs significantly from the First Edition, attention is drawn to the point in a footnote. The Index makes no pretence to being a complete concordance to the New Testament: it is merely intended to guide the reader to the pages on which each item is discussed at any length.

THE NEW TESTAMENT

THE NEW TESTAMENT

The word TESTAMENT is a technical term with a long history. Strictly speaking, the English word, like the Latin word from which it is derived, means a legal document, a "will"; and the same was true of the Greek word, *diathēkē*, of which TESTAMENT is a translation. But it is obvious that what has been known since the early centuries of the church as the New Testament is not a legal document, and has little in common with a will. That it bears this name is the result of a particular turn in the fortunes of the Greek word.

When, in the third century B.C., a group of Jewish scholars translated the Hebrew scriptures into Greek for the use of the Greek-speaking Jews in Alexandria, they found themselves confronted by a number of words in the original which had no equivalent in the Greek language. One of these was the Hebrew word *berith*, of which the usual English translation is "covenant". This word was an exceedingly important one in the history and religion of the Jewish people: it expressed one of their most fundamental convictions about the relationship between God and man. God, they believed, had shown in the distant past his readiness to protect and care for his own people. He had miraculously rescued them from bondage in Egypt and settled them in a land of their own. He had undertaken to continue this relationship with them, so long as they, for their part, observed in their lives and in their worship those principles which he had revealed to them at the beginning of their history, and which were known to them as the Law of Moses. All this was often described in the Jewish scriptures as the "covenant" into which God had entered with his people. Indeed, the Jews' conception of this covenant embraced their deepest convictions about the faithfulness, the justice and the mercy of God. In rendering this important word by the Greek word *diathēkē*, the translators virtually gave a new meaning to a familiar legal term. Thereafter, any Greek-speaking person who was familiar with the Hebrew scriptures knew that *diathēkē*, though it normally meant "will" or "testament", was also a technical term for that "covenant" which the Jews believed God had made with his own people.

The documentary evidence, so to speak, for this covenant consisted in a collection of sacred books which had been formed gradually over the centuries and which, by the time of Christ, had already been complete for about two hundred years. This collection was not homogeneous. It consisted of books originally written at different times for different purposes. The Jews distinguished three broad divisions: first, the Law (the five books attributed to Moses); then the Prophets (which included most of the historical books); and finally the remaining books, which they called simply the Writings. The first of these divisions, since it included the code of religious and civil laws under which they lived, they regarded as the most important. Consequently, when they wished to refer to the whole collection, they sometimes called it "the Law". Otherwise, they called it "the Holy Writings", "the scriptures". These scriptures were regarded by the Jews with the greatest veneration. Elaborate precautions were taken to prevent the smallest alterations to the text, and the leather scrolls on which they were written were reverently preserved in the temple and the synagogues. It was not just that they were more important or more authoritative than other books. They were in a class by themselves. They were believed to have been inspired by God, and they formed the basis of all worship, all education and all justice in every Jewish community.

The first Christians, being Jews, inherited the same reverence towards the scriptures. When they referred to them, it was sufficient to call them simply "Scripture" or "the scriptures". No other writings had any importance for them. It would not have occurred to them to think that the scriptures had in any way lost their unique authority merely because a new way of understanding them had been made possible by Christ. On the contrary, they continued to take it for granted that the scriptures contained the authentic record of God's dealings with men, and (following the example of Jesus himself) they soon began to find in them numerous prophecies and oracles which seemed to have come alive for the first time in the light of their new faith in Christ. Christianity, they realized, was the crowning chapter of an old story. In Christ, God had done something absolutely new for men, yet it was something which complemented rather than superseded the historic faith of Israel. The matter was neatly expressed by Paul in one of his letters. God's previous relationship with men should be called, no longer "the covenant", but "the old covenant"; for now God had made a new covenant through Christ (2 Corinthians 3). The documents of the old covenant were the scriptures. Paul, indeed, on one occasion called the scriptures themselves 'the old covenant' (2 Corinthians 3.14), in order to help Christians (who now had a new covenant) to place them in the right perspective. But the terminology seems to have stuck. By the end of the second century A.D. the church had grown used to calling the original Jewish scriptures the "old covenant" (the Old Testament), in contrast to which the formative writings of the Christian faith inevitably began to be known as the "new covenant" (the New Testament).

For Paul, of course, no authoritative Christian writings existed. Indeed, he made much of the contrast between the old covenant which was expressed in written documents, and the new covenant which was expressed 'not in a written document, but in a spiritual bond' (2 Corinthians 3.6). The first generation of Christians drew their faith, not from a book, but from a living experience. They may even have shared something of the Jews' distrust for the idea of any religious writing apart from the Old Testament. Nevertheless, circumstances made them into writers. Paul himself travelled constantly, and kept in touch with the widely scattered churches which he had founded by writing them letters in which he strengthened their faith and discussed important points of doctrine. These letters are the earliest Christian writings in existence, and they were followed by others from other Christian leaders, who may or may not always have been in Paul's position of needing to communicate with a distant church, but who adopted the form of an apostolic letter in order to consolidate the faith of their fellow-Christians. At the same time, the need began to be felt to preserve in written form the sayings of Jesus and the events of his life. To meet this need several Christians, probably in different parts of the church, composed the books which we now call the gospels. These relate the story of Christianity from its very beginning; but they appear to have been composed later than Paul's letters, towards the end of the first century A.D. One of them was completed by a second volume (Acts of the Apostles) which carried the story on into the history of the early church.

Thus the first Christian writings were the result of particular circumstances and particular needs encountered during the early decades of the church's existence. Christians did not need to rely on a new "holy book"; their faith was sustained by the spirit active among them, and their teaching was based, partly on the Old Testament, and partly on facts and traditions which were remembered by their elders and which could be traced back to Jesus or to his immediate followers. But in the course of the second century A.D., as living contact with this first age of Christianity began to die out, it became necessary to assemble whatever writings still survived from that period in order to provide a solid and authentic basis for Christian teaching, and also in order to have some standard of Christian truth to appeal to against the attacks and innovations of heretical thinkers. The task was complicated by the fact that there were already books in circulation which purported to have been written by one of the original apostles, but which were in fact the work of later imitators. The church had to decide which of these writings were authentic. In theory, it had a simple criterion: only those which had been written by an apostle could be accepted. In practice, the matter was not so easy, since some of the books were originally anonymous, and some that were attributed to an apostle were plainly imitations. But in general it appears that only those were regarded as "apostolic" which were written during the first seventy years or so of the church's existence, and which seemed always to have held a firm place in the esteem of Christians. In essentials, the selection was settled by the end of the second century A.D., though the inclusion or exclusion of a few books continued to be debated for much longer. On the evidence available, it can be said that the church did its work well. Almost all the writings in the New Testament belong unmistakably to the first century A.D. and have a note of authenticity which is absent from other surviving documents which the church might have been tempted to include.

As soon as the selection was established, it inevitably changed its character. By the end of the second century A.D. the New Testament came to be regarded, like the Old, as Scripture. Its various writings, regardless of the original differences between them, were all treated as equally authoritative documents of the Christian faith. Christianity became, like Judaism, a religion of a book. The methods which had long been used to find the Word of God in any verse of the Old Testament began to be used on the New. The New Testament, along with the Old, began to be called "the Bible", which means simply "the Books". This Bible, like the Old Testament before it (which it still included), became in its turn a book different from all other books, to be interpreted in a special way and possessing in its every part a unique degree of authority and truth.

It was only in comparatively recent times that it began to be realized that this approach does violence to the original diversity and vitality of the individual writings which make up the Old and New Testaments. To regard them as deriving all their authority from the fact that they bear the common name of Scripture is to do them an injustice. This Companion is written in the conviction that the New Testament gains in life and cogency when it is taken for what it originally was, that is, a collection of writings each of which was produced under particular circumstances. Sometimes these circumstances are lost beyond recall; but often it is possible to reconstruct them with reasonable certainty, and so to recapture something of the urgency and authority which these writings possessed for their first Christian readers.

All the books of the New Testament have come down to us in Greek. It is possible that some of them, or small parts of them, originally existed in Aramaic, the language spoken by Jesus himself, and were translated within a few years into Greek; but as we have it, the New Testament is written in the language which was understood by the majority of people in the eastern half of the Roman empire in the first centuries of our era. To understand it we need to know something of the culture of what is loosely called the Hellenistic world, that is, that part of civilization which, since the time of Alexander the Great, had come progressively under the influence of Greek ideas and Greek institutions, even though its political centre had passed to Rome. But Christianity was born in the one part of the Roman empire where there had been determined resistance to the influence of Greek civilization. The great majority of the Jews in the world spoke Greek, but their culture remained essentially Jewish. In Palestine itself they spoke for the most part Aramaic, a language which had spread over much of the Middle East since the days of the Persian empire, and their lives were still regulated by the pattern laid down in their scriptures. Even in the Dispersion they kept themselves at a certain distance from the ideals and institutions of Greek culture, and were allowed to dissociate themselves completely from Greek religion. The society of which we read in the New Testament is therefore not that of the Hellenistic world in general, but of that particular part of it which jealously retained its national religion and culture and way of life.

It happens that not many documents have survived which are evidence for this particular section of the population of the Roman empire. Very few non-Jewish writers had any interest in it; and the Jews in Palestine, for reasons already given, were far from being prolific writers. The recent discovery of the Dead Sea Scrolls has done something to dispel the darkness. They reveal in considerable detail the life and beliefs of a particular religious movement that was flourishing in Palestine in the time of Jesus. Our only other contemporary record is that of Flavius Josephus, a Jewish aristocrat who was involved in the fighting in the Jewish War of A.D. 66–70, and who subsequently wrote both a history of that war and a complete history of the Jewish people, in the hopes of gaining sympathy at Rome for the Jewish cause. Another Greek-speaking Jewish writer, Philo of Alexandria, was meanwhile devoting his life to interpreting the Jewish scriptures in terms that would be familiar to people educated in Greek philosophy. By temperament and circumstances Philo was remote from the concerns of the Jews in Palestine. Yet his writings were intended for readers of similar background to those addressed by early Christian writers, and they can occasionally be usefully compared with passages in the New Testament.

Apart from this, there is very little indeed. A few Jewish writings of a visionary and symbolic character (known as "apocalyptic"), which were subsequently suppressed by the Jewish authorities, were preserved in translation by the Christian church. Otherwise, the characteristic Jewish distrust of any authoritarian writings apart from the scriptures continued right into the second century A.D., and it was only in about the middle of that century that the Jewish rabbis began to write down and codify the traditions which had been handed down to them. These rabbinic writings became voluminous in the centuries that followed, and often contain genuine recollections of customs, events and doctrines of first-century Palestinian Judaism. But their evidence is always fragmentary and often misleading. The picture they present is frequently idealized beyond recognition.

In this respect the New Testament stands very much by itself. Much of it is first-hand evidence for conditions and events of which we should otherwise be totally ignorant. Where we can check it against independent sources of information, it is usually faithful to the facts. Where we cannot, we have to judge it on its merits. On the whole, the historical evidence it provides is consistent and plausible, and for reconstructing the circumstances in which any part of it was written the most important information is usually to be found within the New Testament itself. Yet it is still necessary (and this is one of the objects of this Companion) to supplement this information so far as possible from the little we know about the history, religion and culture of the Jewish people in Palestine and in the Dispersion during the first century A.D.

Not that the Christians were ever merely Jews, or Christianity simply a form of Judaism. The Christian religion and the Christian church represented something new and unique in the ancient world. Yet Jesus was a Jew, and so were all his first followers and all the founders of the first churches. Christianity stood closer to Judaism than to any other religion or philosophy of life, and its history and its beliefs were written in predominantly Jewish terms. The clearest instance of this is the constant use of the Old Testament which is made by nearly every New Testament writer. Sometimes whole passages are quoted, sometimes just a word or a sentence, sometimes there are subtle allusions, and sometimes a writer seems deliberately to imitate the style of the Old Testament without actually quoting it. There is nothing surprising in this. The only form of literature with which most of these writers were familiar was either Scripture itself, or else some kind of commentary upon it; and it was natural that they should see their own work in the same light, however new the message was that they had to convey. To us their use of Scripture, and the interpretation they placed on particular passages, often seems recondite and artificial. It presupposes a long tradition of Jewish scholarly interpretation which was based on principles very different from those which would be acceptable today. But this does not alter the fact that the Old Testament was the most important single element in the background shared by all the New Testament writers.

The NEB, unlike most editions of the New Testament, seldom gives the reader any indication when a passage of Scripture is being quoted. But even if it did, it would not always be easy to turn up the relevant passage of the Old Testament and identify it with the quotation in the New. Most English translations of the Old Testament are based on a Hebrew text which did not become fully standardized until the early centuries of our era. In the time of Christ it is unlikely that every synagogue and religious group in Palestine used an identical text of the scriptures. Moreover, although in Palestine they were read in Hebrew, the reading was usually followed by a translation into Aramaic; and throughout the Dispersion the Jews read and listened to the scriptures in a Greek translation. The most famous of these Greek translations, the Septuagint (so called because of the legend that it was compiled by a team of 70 translators), was made in Egypt in the third century B.C. and had a wide circulation. It still exists, and by comparing it with the quotations which occur in the New Testament we can tell that this was the translation most frequently used by Christian writers. But they did not always use exactly the translation which we now possess. Sometimes their Greek version seems to have been different from that of the Septuagint, sometimes they seem to have quoted a version based on an Aramaic translation, and occasionally they may have made their own translation from the Hebrew. If all these translations had been strictly accurate by modern standards, this would not much matter. But in fact they show striking variations from each other. Sometimes the translators misunderstood the original, sometimes they rephrased it to make it (as they thought) more comprehensible or more edifying to their readers. In addition to this, the Septuagint included more books than were subsequently admitted into the Hebrew text which has survived. These books, having been "hidden away" by the Jewish scholars of Palestine on the grounds that they were not sufficiently important or authoritative to be included, have since the Reformation been printed separately in Protestant Bibles under the title Apocrypha (literally, "hidden books").

For all these reasons, quotations of the Old Testament in the New are not always easy to recognize and identify, and their function in the argument is often difficult to follow. In this matter as in others, this Companion represents an attempt to enter the minds of these writers, and so to bring out the tremendous importance which the Old Testament held for them as a prime source of inspiration and truth. Even the title, THE NEW TESTAMENT, can hardly be understood apart from that other term, "The Old Testament", from which it was originally derived.

THE GOSPEL

THE GOSPEL

To the modern reader, the word GOSPEL denotes the kind of book which has come down to us under the names of Matthew, Mark, Luke and John. But in the early church it was some time before the word took on this meaning. It is clear from the letters of Paul that "the Gospel" existed before any of the "gospels" came to be written down. *Euangelion*, "gospel", was a technical name given by the first generation of Christians to the message they had to impart. Literally, it meant "the good news".

When this message was first preached, it appears to have consisted of a fairly brief summary of those facts about Jesus of Nazareth which had caused his followers to believe that the Messiah, or Christ, of Jewish expectation had now come. For the purpose of convincing their Jewish hearers, the first preachers needed to concentrate primarily upon the fact of Jesus' resurrection, and on the consequences of that fact for faith and conduct. But as time passed, and as the membership of the church began to embrace more and more people of different backgrounds, it became necessary to give flesh to the bare bones of this simple proclamation. New questions were being asked. For example, Christians found themselves caught in a tense controversy with the Jews. What had been Jesus' own attitude to this people? They suffered occasional persecution from the officials of the Roman empire. How far had Jesus himself provoked the hostility of the Roman occupying power in Palestine? They were confronted with problems about life and discipline within the Christian community. Had Jesus left any instructions that were relevant? These and many other questions inevitably arose in the course of the early decades of the church's existence. To answer them, it was necessary to recall the life and teaching of Jesus. His sayings, and the main events of his life, were doubtless reverently preserved in the memories of his followers. We do not know how soon they began to be written down and gathered into collections of sayings or consecutive narratives. But between about A.D. 65 and 100, four books were written in Greek which gathered together much of what was still remembered about the life and work of Jesus. In point of literary form these books were unlike anything that had been written before. They were not biographies, since they omitted a great deal which the reader of a biography would expect to be told; but equally they were not religious treatises. What they contained was the original "Gospel" proclaimed by the church, though cast in extended narrative form. It seemed simplest to refer to them simply by the title of the message they embodied (THE GOSPEL) and to distinguish between them by adding "according to" Matthew, Mark, Luke or John.

These four names do not tell us very much. They were almost certainly intended to stand for four men who appear in the New Testament under the names of 'Matthew', 'John Mark', 'Luke the doctor', and 'John'. But it is only a tradition of the church, going back to the second century A.D., which attributes the gospels to these men; the books themselves are anonymous, and the environment they reflect is not, for the most part, that which one would have expected if they had been written by men who were among the earliest members of the church. Nevertheless, there must have been some reason for preserving these names; two of them (Mark and Luke) are not even the names of apostles. It may well be that at some stage the traditions contained in the gospels passed through the hands of the men whose names they bear.

More significant is the relationship between the four, and in particular between the first three. The gospels according to Matthew, Mark and Luke all tell what is essentially the same story, and sometimes they tell it in almost identical language, while at other times they diverge widely from each other. Usually they agree, sometimes they disagree; and each of the three preserves some material which is absent from both the others. Mark is the shortest of the three, and contains very little which does not appear in Matthew or Luke or both. On the other hand, Matthew and Luke have a number of passages in common which do not appear in Mark. In short, the relationship between the three is close, but very complicated. Evidently they originated in different places, for use in different churches: no church would have needed a second or third one so similar to the first, and it can only have been when they began to be circulated more widely that they were bound up together in the same book. On the other hand, they cannot all have been written quite independently of each other. The occurrence of almost identical passages in two different gospels is explicable only if one writer had the work of the other before him.

There is no completely convincing explanation of all these facts. The most popular hypothesis in modern times has been that Mark was composed first, and was used by both Matthew and Luke; that Matthew and Luke also used another document, now lost, consisting chiefly of sayings of Jesus (hence the appearance of passages common to both of them but absent from Mark); and that each of them had access to traditions not available to either of the others, which they worked as best they could into the narrative framework provided by Mark. To account for all the facts this explanation needs considerable refinement, and it cannot be said to have been proved correct. Nevertheless, as a working hypothesis it has probably aided the study of the first three gospels more than any of the other possible combinations, and it is adopted in this Companion, not because it can be taken for granted as true, but because it is impossible to make sense of the evidence without some explanation of this kind. Moreover, it would have been a waste of space and of the reader's time to provide a full commentary on the same passage each time it appears in different gospels. It was therefore a matter of convenience, as well as a deliberate exploitation of the most widely held hypothesis, to make the commentary on Mark more detailed than any of the others. Any passage which occurs in Mark and in one or more of the other gospels is fully discussed in its context in Mark. The commentary on a parallel passage in another gospel is confined to pointing out significant differences. Further, where a passage occurs in both Matthew and Luke, the discussion will normally be found under Matthew—though this is merely for the reader's convenience: it is not intended to suggest that Luke had read the gospel according to Matthew (although this, theoretically, is also possible).

However, more important consequences follow from adopting this hypothesis than the arrangement of a commentary. If Matthew and Luke used Mark, Mark must have been written first. It seems unlikely, for various reasons, that any of the gospels were written as early as the lifetime of Paul, or later than the end of the first century A.D. To allow time for Mark to have been circulated and then rewritten by Matthew and Luke, it seems sensible to place Mark near the beginning of that period—say between 65 and 70—and the other two a decade or two later. John's gospel seems to reflect external conditions and a stage in the development of Christianity which are somewhat later than those reflected in the other three. It is therefore usually dated between A.D. 90 and 100. But there is virtually nothing by which to check these dates—even the catastrophic event of the fall of Jerusalem in A.D. 70 is not certainly alluded to in any of the New Testament writings.

There is another consequence of accepting this hypothesis which bears more directly on the interpretation of the gospels themselves. When a passage occurs in Mark and in one or two other gospels, it is necessary to account for the changes, sometimes very slight, sometimes quite substantial, which have been made in Matthew or Luke. By studying these changes, one can often see a certain pattern beginning to emerge: it is as if each gospel writer had a particular approach of his own to the material he was recording, an approach which he expressed by subtle editorial changes or careful rearrangement of the episodes. The case is clearest when we come to John, whose gospel, at first sight, tells a story very different from the others, and in a distinctive style of its own. It is possible that John, like Matthew and Luke, used Mark, but used it much more freely than they did. But he clearly also had other sources of information, and may indeed preserve traditions which are older than Mark's gospel. In any event, it can hardly be doubted that he was consciously recasting his material in a form which he felt expressed better the genius of Jesus' teaching and the significance of Jesus' life and work. Sometimes his narrative is incompatible with that in the other gospels, and we have to make a choice between the two. It is usual to regard Mark's gospel (assuming it is the earliest) as providing the most reliable historical information. But we do not possess the material which Mark himself may have been editing and adapting to his own purpose. It is possible that he, like John, imposed a certain pattern on his sources in order to bring out the significance of the events he was recording. There is no good reason to think that one gospel more than another was ever intended merely to present a bare chronicle of Jesus' life, death and resurrection.

Detailed analysis of the gospels has shown that much of the material out of which they were composed originally consisted of small independent units, sometimes amounting only to a single saying, sometimes running to the length of a complete episode. It was the writers of the gospels who put these units together in the form of a coherent narrative. The NEB sub-headings are intended to indicate the broad shape which the story assumed at their hands; and to this extent a commentary which tries to elucidate the particular style and concerns of each writer is in line with the translators' purpose. But it does not follow from this approach that it is impossible to get behind the gospels and discover the original sayings and actions of Jesus. On the contrary, the individual contribution of each of the gospel writers is very slight and subtle; to present the message in their own way, each had to be content with comparatively small touches. It is as if the material they had to work on, having been reverently preserved by their fellow-Christians, set a strict limit to their editorial freedom. At any point the reader must be prepared to detect their hand; but it seems never to have been a free hand. There is an essential element in the works which have come down to us under the names of Matthew, Mark, Luke and John which the writers could never have created themselves.

Even this does not necessarily take us back to Jesus himself. By the time the gospel writers set to work, the traditions they possessed about Jesus had already been collected and preserved by the church and put to use in preaching, teaching, and defending the faith. They had also at some stage been translated into Greek, with all that that implies of subtle accommodation to a different culture. The gospels as we have them often betray the marks of this process. The circumstances and needs of the early church are discernible in the form in which Jesus' sayings and the events of his life have been preserved. Yet once again there is an essential element in the traditions so preserved which the church could not have created itself. It is this element which makes it possible to say with confidence that the gospels, despite the mysterious and complicated history of their compilation, still preserve an authentic recollection of the life and teaching of Jesus of Nazareth.

THE GOSPEL ACCORDING TO MATTHEW

The coming of Christ

This innocent-looking heading has been placed by the translators at the beginning of each of the gospels; but neither of the terms which it contains is as simple as it looks. In the first place when, and in what sense, did Christ "come"? The New Testament writers themselves were by no means agreed on the point at which the gospel story began. Mark, for example, followed what we may believe to have been the oldest pattern of Christian preaching: he began with Jesus' baptism, and recorded nothing before this except the activity of John the Baptist, Jesus' immediate precursor. Matthew felt it important to record the circumstances of Jesus' birth and parentage, and Luke went back still further to the birth of John the Baptist. John's "beginning" is on another time-scale altogether: Christ had existed with God the Father since the birth of time, and his "coming" was really a "becoming", the appearance of a pre-existent divine being at a certain moment and place in history. These differences of approach and emphasis are characteristic of each gospel; and the similarity of the headings in the NEB should not obscure the fact that for each of these writers the word *coming* might have borne a different meaning.

Secondly, *Christ*. The Greek word *Christos* stands for the Hebrew word *Messiah*, "the Anointed One". This was an old title, originally used of the first kings of Israel. But in the time of Jesus it was reserved for a divinely appointed figure whom (it was widely believed) God would soon send into the world to inaugurate a new and blessed age for the benefit of his elect. Was Jesus this Messiah, this Christ? His work and teaching were such that the question was bound to be constantly raised. In public, he never gave an altogether unambiguous answer to it, and during his lifetime his name remained simply the not uncommon Hebrew name *Yeshua*, represented in Greek as Jesus. It was only after the resurrection that his disciples became completely convinced that he was the Christ. They then began to refer to him as Jesus "the Christ", and soon simply as Jesus Christ.

Many different beliefs were held by Jesus' contemporaries about the exact nature and function of this Messiah; but it was common ground to most of them that he would be a descendant of King David. Jesus apparently fulfilled this qualification: he had a family tree which could be traced back to David; and this is one reason why Matthew begins his gospel with a

1. 1 **table of the descent of Jesus Christ.** But it may not be the only reason. Jewish writers were fond of establishing the genealogies of their heroes, and of showing them to be descendants of great figures of the past, and Matthew in fact takes the genealogy back, not just to David, but further still, to Abraham. Abraham, for any Jewish thinker, was the decisive figure in the story of God's concern for mankind; and Matthew's genealogy serves to knit Jesus firmly into this story. Moreover, the series of three groups of
17 **fourteen generations** (which is somewhat artificially imposed upon the list of names) is probably intended to suggest that divine providence had been at work in bringing Jesus into the world at this exact moment of history.

The list itself is demonstrably inaccurate in certain details, but is not
2–12 necessarily entirely untrustworthy. From Abraham to Zerubbabel the genealogy runs through the well-known leaders of the Jewish people. Where it can be checked against similar lists in the Old Testament (such as in the first chapters of 1 Chronicles), it shows certain discrepancies and errors; but it is certain that no single and authoritative genealogy of the leading families in Jewish history existed in Matthew's time, and it need cause no surprise that Matthew's list differs slightly from others, particularly since it had
12–16 to be adjusted a little to fit into a fourteenfold pattern. After Zerubbabel, the line branches off from the main stem in order to reach the immediate ancestors of Jesus, and from this point we have no means of checking it. It is quite different from Luke's table; but this does not necessarily prove either of the tables to be a fiction. The evangelists may have had access to family papers such as many Jewish families possessed, recording one or more family trees (perhaps through different parents or grandparents) and proving that Joseph was among the descendants of David.

But Joseph was not Jesus' father. This difficulty, which was felt suffi-
16 ciently acutely in antiquity to cause some variants in Matthew's text (see the footnote in NEB), arose out of the fact that Matthew had two apparently incompatible things to say about Jesus: first that he was (as the Messiah was expected to be) a descendant of David, and secondly that he was born in a unique way, without a human father. But Jewish law and custom offered a solution to this difficulty. If a Jew formally named and adopted a child, that child became his son. This is the theme of the following paragraph.

18 **This is the story of the birth of the Messiah.** The birth was miraculous: it was God, and no human father, who caused Mary to conceive. In the Old Testament, the creative power of God was called his "spirit"; and it may still have come naturally to a Jewish writer such as Matthew to use the same language: **she was with child by the Holy Spirit.** But Matthew does not linger over the miracle itself; he goes straight on to its human

consequences. Mary was **betrothed to Joseph**, which meant under Jewish law that she was fully committed to marrying him: the contract had already been signed, and it only remained for the marriage ceremony to take place and for the bride to take up residence in her husband's house. Her pregnancy, if suddenly discovered at this stage by the bridegroom, was therefore
a potential source of scandal. **Being a man of principle**, Joseph could 19
not possibly condone it: he must either bring his fiancée publicly before a court in order to prove her guilty, or else repudiate the marriage contract (which he was entitled to do at any time) and leave the question of Mary's shame to be resolved by her family. But a further divine intervention, related this time in the form of a dream and an angel, made him take responsibility himself. If the world believed that he had had intercourse with his betrothed before their marriage, it would not greatly matter: this was not regarded as a serious sin in Jewish society; and by adopting and naming the child, he took him formally into his own family and ensured that Jesus,
like himself, could be rightfully called a '**son of David**'. 20

However, Matthew is not only concerned to settle these practical details. He compresses into this short paragraph some important clues to the wider
significance of Jesus' birth. The name itself, Jesus, meant **Saviour**, and 21
described something of Jesus' destiny; and the manner of Jesus' birth had a striking parallel in Old Testament prophecy. One of Matthew's particular contributions to the gospel story was to demonstrate that not merely the suffering, death, and resurrection of Jesus but also many other episodes were foretold or prefigured in Scripture. In doing this his methods were not always such as modern scholarship would countenance, though they would have aroused no scruples among Jewish scholars of his time. Here, for example,
the original Hebrew of Isaiah 7.14 has, not '**the virgin**', but 'a young 23
woman', and it is unlikely that Isaiah, in this prophecy of future abundance and divine favour, meant to predict anything so miraculous as a virgin birth. But in the Greek translation of the Old Testament, which Matthew used, the word could (though it did not necessarily) mean 'virgin', and so to Matthew's mind the text provided a startlingly exact prophecy of the event he had just recorded.

Jesus was born at Bethlehem in Judaea during the reign of Herod. 2. 1
Herod the Great died, after a long reign, in about 4 B.C. Matthew's narrative implies that Jesus was born not less than two years before this (verse 16), but also not much more (verse 19)—say, 7–6 B.C. This is somewhat earlier than the traditional date (between 1 B.C. and A.D. 1), but the idea of dating world history by the birth of Christ was only invented five hundred years later, and the date which was then chosen was the result of a mistaken calculation. Matthew's date is not improbable in itself; the only difficulty is to reconcile it with the chronology in Luke (see below on Luke 2.1).

In any country where astrology was taken seriously (as it was in most countries in the ancient world, and particularly in those which lay immediately to the east of Palestine) a new star, or a notable conjunction of stars, would quickly attract attention, presaging an important new turn in human affairs. Conversely, it was believed that it was the very regularity of the stars which guaranteed the orderly course of history, and it followed that any really significant event must necessarily be accompanied by some striking phenomenon in the heavens. The birth of Jesus was such an event, and if the following story reads more like legend than history, it is easy to see how such a legend could have originated, particularly since similar legends were told in Jewish folklore about the birth of Moses, and it is arguable that Jesus was regarded by Matthew as, in some sense, a second Moses. On the other hand, the story is by no means incredible. The visitors from the east are called in the Greek *Magi*. The word came originally from Persia, where it denoted influential religious leaders; but in ordinary Greek usage it meant sorcerers or magicians. What does it mean here? These men were certainly not "three kings of Orient"—that is a later legend [a]; and they may not have been quite as dignified as "wise men". But one kind of knowledge they did possess—astrology; and it is certainly correct (though it may not be the
2 whole truth) to call them, with the NEB, **astrologers.** Their observation
of the star had satisfied them that some change was impending in the west,
that is to say, in Palestine; and they felt sure enough of their interpretation
to put to Herod a specific question, '**Where is the child who is born to be
king of the Jews?**'. Herod, who doubtless intended to make his own
arrangements about the succession to the throne, preferred to regard the star
as a sign of that other "king" whom the Jews were awaiting, the Messiah.
Many passages of the Old Testament pointed forward to this figure, and it
was to be expected that the religious leaders of the Jews, and particularly
4 the **lawyers** (who were the professional expositors of the Old Testament,
the law of the Jewish people) would be able to answer the astrologers'
question. Their answer could by no means be taken for granted: many
opinions were abroad about the place and circumstances in which the
5, 6 Messiah would appear. But there was a **prophecy** in Micah 5.2 [b] which was
understood by some as an oracle about the birthplace of the Messiah. In Matthew's story the function of the prophecy is to direct the astrologers to the village five miles south of Jerusalem where they would find what the star had led them to expect; but in the wider context of the gospel its apparent fulfilment serves to strengthen Jesus' claim to be both Messiah and "son of David" (for Bethlehem had been David's home).

[*a*] Based on an application of the prophecy in Isaiah 60.3.

[*b*] Matthew quotes this in a version a little different from that in either the Hebrew or the Greek of the Septuagint, and combines with it a few words from 2 Samuel 5.2: this may have been one of a collection of texts which the early Christians used to prove that Jesus had fulfilled Old Testament prophecy.

The purpose of the astrologers in seeking the child was to **pay him** 2
homage. When they found him, they **offered him gifts: gold, frank-** 11
incense, and myrrh—traditional products of the wealth and luxury of the
east (compare Isaiah 60.6 for gold and frankincense, Song of Solomon 3.6
for frankincense and myrrh); their gifts showed that they recognized him
as the "king" of whom the star was a sign, and theirs was the first testimony
to him who was to be crucified as "king of the Jews". Herod's interest,
however, was more practical: to eliminate one who might grow up to be, if
not a pretender to the throne, at least a cause of dissension in Judaea. It
would be in keeping with what we know of the character of Herod that **he** 16
fell into a passion, and gave orders for the massacre of all suspect
children. His reign, especially in its closing years, was marked by many
atrocities. But Matthew may not mean that he killed all the children in
Bethlehem of two years or less. The phrase, **corresponding with the time**
he had ascertained from the astrologers (which refers back to verse 7
above), suggests that he limited the slaughter to the babies born at the
exact season of the star's appearing in the previous two years—possibly quite
a small number. Matthew's concern, in any case, was not so much to portray
the savagery of Herod as to discern the significance of the episode. He saw
it, first, as a direct fulfilment of a prophecy of Jeremiah (31.15), **'A voice** 18
was heard in Rama . . . it was Rachel weeping for her children'.
In Jeremiah, Rachel, the wife of Jacob and mother of two of the "tribes"
of Israel, is imagined as weeping over her descendants who are being
deported by the Assyrian conquerors past the northern frontier-town of
Rama. Matthew evidently imagines her lamenting near Bethlehem, perhaps
because there was an old tradition (Genesis 35.19), which is still preserved
by a monument today, that Rachel's tomb was close to Bethlehem. Secondly,
Herod's massacre was the motive for the flight of Jesus' parents into Egypt,
and this too placed Jesus in the line of a great national tradition: God had
"called his son"—the people of Israel—"out of Egypt" (Hosea 11.1). 15
Jesus, who was "God's son" *par excellence*, lived through a similar exile
and a similar return.

He settled in a town called Nazareth. Matthew's explanation of the 23
move from Bethlehem to Galilee is not very cogent: Galilee was ruled by Herod Antipas, another of Herod's sons, and the danger might have been as great there as in Bethlehem. In practice, however, Nazareth was probably much safer. It was a small and rather isolated town in the hills of Galilee, with none of the Davidic traditions of Bethlehem. Indeed, no one would have expected a native of Nazareth to make any mark in history (John 1.46, 'Can anything good come from Nazareth?'). Jesus, at any rate, became known as **'a Nazarene'** and indeed Christians were for many years called "Nazarenes" in Palestine. One of Matthew's purposes in the whole of this chapter has been to show how this Nazarene was nevertheless born in

Bethlehem, as a true descendant of David should be. Even in the name "Nazarene", however, Matthew finds some significance. But here we are at a loss. The Old Testament does not contain the words '**He shall be called a Nazarene**'. The nearest phrase occurs in the narrative of the birth of Samson: Samson was to be a "Nazarite" (Judges 13.5), which means an ascetic under vows to God. But Matthew may have had in mind a more subtle allusion to the Hebrew word *netser*, "branch", which occurs in various biblical texts that were held in his time to be prophecies of the Messiah.[a]

3. 1 **About that time.** Literally, "in those days", a phrase which is perhaps deliberately imprecise. Many years have passed in the little gap between chapter 2 and chapter 3. Jesus has grown up. Judaea is now under direct Roman rule, the reign of Archelaus, Herod's successor, having quickly come to an ignominious end (A.D. 6); while the northern and eastern parts of the country, Galilee and Peraea, are still under the more or less independent rule of another of Herod's sons, Herod Antipas. It is in connection with Herod Antipas that **John the Baptist** makes a brief appearance in the pages of another writer nearly contemporary with the author of this gospel, the Jewish historian Josephus. Josephus' interest in him is more political than religious, but his account agrees in the basic facts. John's movement appeared to Herod Antipas as a threat to peace, and in due course Herod imprisoned him.

When Mark introduces John the Baptist he concentrates entirely (apart from a few words devoted to the nature of his baptism) on his rôle as the herald and forerunner of Jesus. Matthew, though he quotes the same
3, 1 prophecy from Isaiah (40.3), presents him at the outset **as a preacher,** making his proclamation in the manner of an Old Testament prophet. John, in any case, resembled a prophet, both by his clothes (compare the description of Elijah in 2 Kings 1.8), and also by his appearance in **the Judaean wilderness.** Large tracts of Palestine, one of them reaching right up to the neighbourhood of Jerusalem, were bare and uncultivable, as against the densely inhabited farmlands of Galilee or the vineyards of other parts of Judaea. Traditionally, a prophet was a man who pondered his message in an austere environment, away from the amenities of sophisticated life. John conformed to this tradition; and his message was correspondingly
2 simple and direct. '**Repent**': the word meant not so much personal remorse as a corporate re-orientation, away from the subtleties of contemporary political and religious life, towards a single-minded attention to the commands of God. '**For the kingdom of Heaven**': this is the same concept as "the kingdom of God", only in somewhat more pious Jewish dress (the Jews liked to avoid using God's name, and preferred to speak of "heaven",

[*a*] Especially Isaiah 11.1. **Nazarene** is actually the form used by Mark, and sometimes by Luke. Elsewhere, including this passage, the actual form of the word is "Nazoraean".

"angels" and the like). It means God's rule, that longed-for state of affairs
when men will willingly and spontaneously do the will of God. '**Is upon
you**': literally, the Greek means "has drawn near". How near? From the
Greek word alone, it is impossible to tell. But it is clear from what follows
that John is giving urgent warning of coming judgement. All Jews expected
this some time in the future. John proclaims that it is very near indeed: his
word (like that of Jesus, whose preaching, in this gospel, begins in exactly
the same way) is meant to drive the point home: it is no longer in the
uncertain future, it is '**upon you**'.

Among the crowd were **Pharisees and Sadducees**. (It does not strictly 7
follow from the Greek that they came **for baptism**. They may simply have
been there to watch.) These people represented a higher level of society than
(presumably) the rest of the throng, and in Matthew's account (unlike
Luke's) they are singled out for attack by John the Baptist just as, later in
this gospel, they are consistently criticized by Jesus. The ground on which
they are attacked here is that they claimed a certain immunity from the
coming judgement: "**We have Abraham for our father**".[a] John—with 9
words also used by Jesus (7.19)—sweeps aside this suggestion of divine
favouritism, and returns to the arresting element in his proclamation.
The **one who comes** is certainly (as in Mark) a person greater than himself, 11
and his baptism will be not just a ritual washing with water but a personal
experience of the power of **the Holy Spirit**: he is also an Elijah-figure (the
language recalls Malachi 4, Ecclesiasticus 48), a man of **fire**, bringing 12
immediate judgement.

We know, and Matthew's first readers knew, who it was for whom John
was preparing a way. It was Jesus. But we should not necessarily read this
knowledge back into the narrative. For in many respects Jesus does not fit
the portrait given here. Jesus himself still expected and proclaimed the
coming judgement, he did not immediately precipitate it; and as for an
Elijah-figure, Jesus regarded John, not himself, as Elijah (11.14). Matthew, in
any case, does not state here that John recognized Jesus as the Man of Fire.
All that John recognized was some exceptional quality in Jesus which 14
seemed to make it inappropriate to baptize him "confessing his sins". It
looks, indeed, as if this was a difficulty felt by Matthew's readers. They
knew that Jesus had been baptized by John, and they knew that John's
baptism was 'for the forgiveness of sins' (Mark 1.4). But Jesus did not
commit sin; why therefore was he baptized? This passage may have been
moulded to suggest an answer: **to conform . . . with all that God requires.** 15
The translation is rather free (the literal sense is "to complete all righteousness"), but gives at least a possible meaning: just as Jesus came to "complete" the Law, by endorsing its inner meaning and laying a new form of it
on his followers (5.17), so he submitted to John's baptism and, by his action,

[a] This classic argument of the Jew is criticized by Paul in Romans 2; see below, p. 509.

validated the rite for all future generations of Christians. The account of Jesus' baptism follows Mark closely (Mark 1.9–11). The same combination
17 of scriptural texts **was heard** (though possibly only by Jesus—the Greek has simply, "a voice from heaven saying"); but even this did not conclusively identify Jesus as the one whom John was expecting. Indeed, John was still in doubt some time later (11.2–3).

4. 1 **Jesus was then led away.** Mark, at this point, simply records a period of
contest with the devil in the wilderness. Matthew and Luke evidently knew
a fuller version of the story, and one which puts it in a somewhat different
light. In Mark, one has to imagine a sustained struggle between Jesus and
the devil, Jesus being meanwhile aided and fed by angels. Here, Jesus first
undergoes a prolonged fast (he is only afterwards waited on by the angels,
3 verse 11) and is then approached by the devil in the character of **the tempter,**
3–4 and exposed to three "temptations", or tests. The first of these tests was
a natural consequence of his hunger, and could have taken place on the spot.
5 The other two are also vividly set in Palestinian scenery—the **parapet of
the temple** is usually thought to be the south-east corner of the immense
terrace constructed by Herod the Great around the temple in Jerusalem,
from which there was a sheer drop of some 150 feet into the Kedron valley
below; and many hill-tops in the Judaean desert offer immense views over
the Jordan valley and the mountains beyond which could well be described as
8 a microcosm of **the kingdoms of the world in their glory.** But the actual
tests could not have been carried out in one region of the Judaean desert;
they must have taken place in Jesus' mind. In which case it must be asked,
in what sense is it likely that the story represents a historical episode in the
life of Jesus? One feature in the story bears on this question. All of Jesus'
4 replies are quotations from the Book of Deuteronomy: Deuteronomy 8.3,
7, 10 6.16 (in answer to the devil's quotation of Psalm 91.11–12) and 6.13.
Furthermore, these verses in Deuteronomy are set in the context of
the period of "testing" which the people of Israel underwent in the wilderness. It is clear that the biblical narrative has influenced the form, and perhaps the content, of the story recounted by Matthew and Luke: Jesus was re-enacting, in his own person, the formative experience of the desert generation. But this, of course, is not to say that Jesus did not experience something of this kind. The disciples could well have been aware that Jesus treasured these verses of Deuteronomy and had come to realize their significance during his period of retreat in the wilderness. The remaining details would not have been hard to fill in.

12 **When he heard that John had been arrested.** Like Mark, Matthew regards the moment of John's arrest—which he can assume his readers know all about, and which he only describes later on—as the point in time at which Jesus appeared in Galilee. But he is a little more specific than Mark

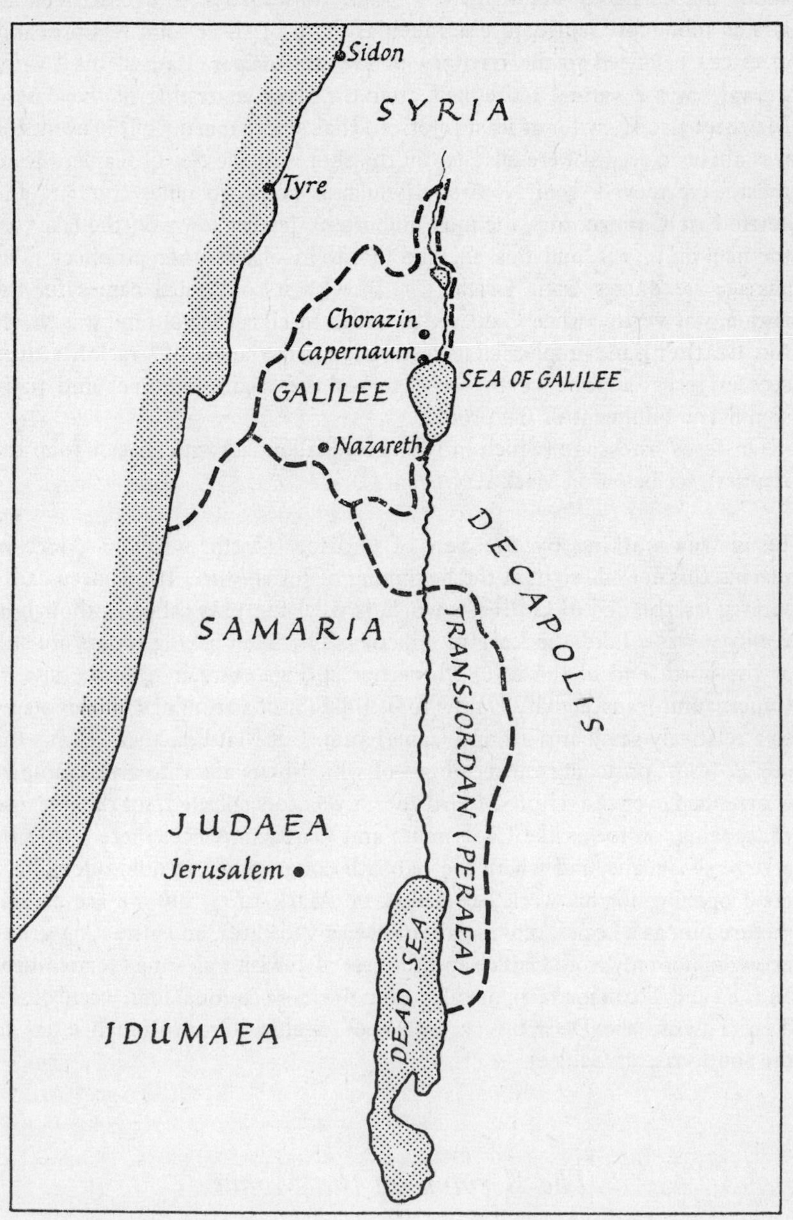
Sidon
SYRIA
Tyre
Chorazin
Capernaum
SEA OF GALILEE
GALILEE
Nazareth
DECAPOLIS
SAMARIA
TRANSJORDAN (PERAEA)
JUDAEA
Jerusalem
DEAD SEA
IDUMAEA

about the details. **Jesus withdrew**—not, presumably, to avoid the same
fate as John; for Galilee, just as much as Peraea (where John was probably
arrested) belonged to the territory of Herod Antipas. Rather, his "withdrawal" was a natural retirement after the rigorous testing of the desert.
Matthew also knew (or at least inferred) that since so many of the events he
was about to record were enacted on the shores of the Sea of Galilee, Jesus
must have moved from Nazareth (which is some 30 miles from it) and
13 **settled at Capernaum**, the most important Jewish town on the lake (see
the map on p. 25); and this enabled him to invoke another prophecy. The
15–16 passage he quotes from Isaiah (9.1–2), with its old tribal names for the
region, was written when Galilee was under foreign control (and was therefore **heathen**), and prophesied its restoration to the people of Israel. Matthew
sees in Jesus' appearance by the **Way of the Sea** a different and more
significant fulfilment of the prophecy.

17 On Jesus' **message** (which in Matthew is identical with that of John the
Baptist), see below on Mark 1.15.

18 **Jesus was walking by the Sea of Galilee.** Matthew follows Mark in
placing this episode right at the beginning of Jesus' work. It was necessarily
located by the **Sea of Galilee**—which is what the Jews called it, though in
reality it was a **lake**, the Lake of Tiberias. The main fishing waters are still
at the north end of the lake, where hot springs enter it near the site of
Capernaum. Jesus' activity is thus to be thought of as confined, at this stage,
to a relatively small area around Capernaum. But Matthew then widens the
scene. Jesus' preaching and healing—of which he is about to give examples
23 —extended over **the whole of Galilee.** It was concentrated, for the purpose
of teaching, on towns like Capernaum and Chorazin, where there would be
a large synagogue, and where the Sabbath congregations would offer him a
good opening for his work (see below on Mark 1.21); but we are also to
25 picture him as a healer, moving about over a wide area, and attracting **great
crowds**, not only from Galilee and the rest of Jewish Palestine (**Jerusalem,
Judaea and Transjordan**), but also from the more cosmopolitan world of the
Ten Towns (the Decapolis, a league of wealthy Greco-Roman cities to
the south-east of Galilee).

The Sermon on the Mount

This is the title by which the next three chapters of Matthew's gospel have
been known since at least the time of Augustine. The NEB adopts the old
5. 1 title, but in verse 1 it replaces "mount" with a more colloquial word, **when
he saw the crowds he went up the hill.** This rendering makes one want to

ask, what hill? But the original Greek is probably less precise, and means "up into the hill-country",[a] that is, away from the populous coast of the lake into the more lonely foothills to the west and north, and Jesus' purpose in thus going "up the hill" was usually simply to get away from the crowds in order to pray (Matthew 14.23) or to talk privately with his disciples
(Mark 3.13). Accordingly, the opening of his discourse here is specifically
addressed to his **disciples** (who are mentioned here for the first time, and 2
may be assumed to be a group which has grown out of such episodes as
Simon's and Andrew's decision to "follow" Jesus, 4.18–20), and the traditional picture of Jesus standing on a high place addressing the multitudes is unwarranted by these opening verses. However, at the end of the discourse (7.28) we find that 'the people (literally, "the crowds") were astounded at his teaching'. If we are to accept these chapters at their face value as the record of a historical occasion, we shall have to assume that the crowds caught up with Jesus while he was talking, and that what began as the giving of **teaching** to a group of disciples ended, by force of circumstances, as a "sermon" addressed to a large congregation.

This is a possible explanation; but the apparent change in the audience between the beginning and the end is not the only indication that these chapters are not quite what they seem. Some of the sayings they contain must have been originally intended for the disciples, some for the crowds; some of them are found in other gospels in quite different contexts, and some, by the time Matthew wrote them down, seem to have been slightly altered by the early church into a form which it found more relevant to its own situation. Moreover, the discourse as a whole hardly constitutes a "sermon" in the modern sense. There is a logical development of the argument in certain sections, but there is no clear theme, and it is hard to imagine the discourse being delivered on a single occasion and listened to by a single audience. In short, it seems to fit the facts better if we regard these chapters as a collection made by Matthew (or the source he was using) of Jesus' ethical teaching, arranged under certain headings, and provided with an introduction and a conclusion which (since these occur also in the "sermon" in Luke's gospel, 6.20–49) may well reproduce a pattern which Jesus was accustomed to use in his teaching. Such a collection would obviously have been useful for teaching purposes in the early church, and this may be one of the reasons why Matthew incorporated it in his gospel. Another reason may be that Matthew saw Jesus as, in some respects, a new Moses: Jesus' teaching on the mount corresponded to, and was indeed the necessary fulfilment of, Moses' proclamation of the Law on Sinai.

These possibilities must be borne in mind throughout the next three chapters. But they do not necessarily affect our estimate of the "sermon". For however it came into existence, it remains the most comprehensive

[a] The same words are translated 'up to the hills' in Matthew 15.29.

discourse of Jesus of which we have any record. It was regarded by the author of the gospel as a fair summary of what Jesus taught (this follows from the prominent position he assigned to it near the beginning of his narrative), and even if we can at times detect evidence of subsequent editing and retouching by Matthew or by the tradition which he preserves, and although we may suspect that on some points Jesus may originally have expressed himself differently or have had specific situations in mind which are no longer remembered, yet we shall never in fact replace this discourse by something different, nor are we likely to find a better picture of Jesus' ethical teaching than that which Matthew gives us. These are the words through which we must still hear the voice of Jesus; this is the *Sermon on the Mount* which, down the centuries, has left its mark on the church and on the world.

Jesus' teaching begins with a series of "beatitudes". What kind of people are "blest"—that is to say, what are the conditions which a person must fulfil if he is to enter upon the rewards which are promised by religion?

3 **'How blest are those who know their need of God'**. Here the NEB rendering is a bold paraphrase. Literally, the Greek means, "Blest are the poor in spirit", a phrase which sounds unnatural in Greek, and can only be understood in the light of a characteristic Old Testament conception of poverty. In the corresponding passage of Luke's gospel (6.20) Jesus is reported as saying, 'How blest are you who are in need', where there can be little doubt that 'in need' means literally poor. In many ancient cultures, including the Jewish, this would have sounded like nonsense: riches, not poverty, showed that a man was blest. But there was one strain of Jewish piety (represented particularly by some of the psalms) which saw the matter differently. In this tradition, "the poor" had become a religious as well as a social term. As opposed to the rich, the influential, the extortionate and the oppressive, "the poor" were those who, by keeping intact their own righteousness and piety, could be sure that, however much they appeared to be the victims of society, they would ultimately be rewarded and vindicated by God. This tenacious faith of "the poor man" was decisively endorsed by Jesus: the compromises and injustices into which men are inevitably led by wealth and position are incompatible with the integrity demanded by God. Consequently, "Blest are the poor". But of course they are not blest merely because they are poor. There was a spirit of poverty which went with physical poverty, and it was this spirit which was important. The corresponding Hebrew phrase, "poor in spirit", actually occurs in the Dead Sea Scrolls, and was doubtless current in Palestine in the time of Jesus. Matthew was probably trying to put this into Greek when he wrote the words, "poor in spirit". Poor meant literally poor: but it also implied an attitude of simplicity, integrity, and dependence upon God—an attitude which is spelled out in

more detail in the beatitudes which follow. It is this attitude which the NEB has tried to define by the paraphrase, **those who know their need of God.** [a]

'How blest are the sorrowful; they shall find consolation'. The 4
NEB translation makes this sound a little philosophical, as if it expresses the truth that there is a way of bearing sorrow which enables one to "find" consolation. But the Greek is more direct: "they shall be consoled". It was one of the great truths of the Gospel that it gave men true "consolation" (see below on 2 Corinthians 1). And the condition of obtaining that blessing was, again, not the complacency and satisfaction of those who are insulated by their possessions from the general suffering of mankind but —sorrow.

'How blest are those of a gentle spirit'. Almost identical words occur 5
in Psalm 37.11. This "gentleness" (which is the mark, in the Old Testament, of one who accepts his humble status without bitterness) is one of the characteristic notes of "the poor"; and the confidence that it would be rewarded had already found expression in one tradition of Jewish piety.

'How blest are those who hunger and thirst to see right prevail'. 6
Luke, again, preserves a more radical version: 'How blest are you who now go hungry'. The social context is still the same. Those who are poor and oppressed are blest, even though they may in fact go hungry; but the reason why they are blest is not merely that they go hungry—they do not swerve from what is right; and here too Matthew may have added the single word "righteousness" (of which the NEB has brought out the meaning by a paraphrase, **to see right prevail**) in order to fill in another of the "spiritual" characteristics of the traditional "poor man" of Jewish piety.

After this first group of four beatitudes, three of which are more decisive and radical than anything which is to be found in the Old Testament or in
contemporary Jewish piety, the series continues with three more which seem 7–9
rather to recommend certain virtues than to propound a new scale of values. These, which can be paralleled in Jewish literature, are lacking in Luke's more radical version; and they give the opening of the Sermon a distinctly more ethical character than do the abrupt statements in the first beatitudes.
Only the last—**'How blest are those who have suffered persecution** 10
for the cause of right'—returns to the decisive tone of the opening. There had been many in Jewish history who had "suffered persecution for the cause of right". Religious men trusted and prayed that, despite their

[a] In the First Edition of NEB the first beatitude is rendered, "How blest are those who know that they are poor". This is more open to criticism. Any Greek philosopher might have agreed that a man who "knows that he is poor" has made important progress in self-knowledge, and is consequently more "blest" than one who takes a complacent view of his worldly possessions. But for the purpose of achieving this self-knowledge it did not much matter whether one were rich or poor; the important thing was to cultivate a philosophic detachment from whatever wealth one happened to possess. It is unlikely that Jesus was recommending merely this philosophical detachment. His teaching is always concerned as much with people's actual circumstances as with their frame of mind.

apparent humiliation, these martyrs had been accepted and would one day be vindicated by God. Jesus, again, gave his authoritative endorsement to this faith.

Such people, then, are blest. But what does this blessedness consist of? Jewish religion conceived of it as a future state of felicity in a new order which would soon be brought into being by God; and most of Jesus' beatitudes similarly have a future tense: the blessedness cannot be expected in this world, but Jesus promises it, with the full weight of his authority, for the life in heaven. But what of the first and last in the series of beatitudes,
3, 10 which end, **'the kingdom of Heaven is theirs'**? Should these also be
understood as future, or is there a sense in which the kingdom is already present? This is a question which runs right through the gospel. It is raised by Jesus' very first words, 'The kingdom of Heaven is upon you' (see above on 3.2). For the present, it is important to bear in mind that Jesus saw himself (or at least was seen by the earliest Christians) as fulfilling the prophecy, "The Spirit of the Lord is upon me because the Lord has appointed me to bring good tidings to the poor . . . to comfort all who mourn". (Isaiah 61.1–2). The coming of Jesus inaugurated a new situation, in which many of the world's accepted values would be reversed.

11 **'How blest you are'**. The language suddenly becomes personal: no longer the broad sweep of a religious teacher pronouncing general truths, but the direct address of a master to his disciples. It seems early yet to think of those who had so recently begun to follow Jesus suffering **insults and persecution and every kind of calumny**. It was the church, after Jesus' death and resurrection, which first began to experience these things, and will have gratefully remembered (if indeed it did not adapt to its own situation) Jesus' warning and Jesus' promise. Similarly, the metaphors which follow clearly apply, not to any casual listeners, but to those who have committed themselves to discipleship.

13 **'You are salt to the world'**. We now use salt mainly for flavouring, and so the metaphor suggests to us a small but necessary element in that total mixture which is human civilization (and this, in fact, is precisely what many would say the Christian contribution to history has been). But in antiquity salt was equally important for preserving food; and the metaphor may be similar to that used by a Christian writer of the second century, "Christians are the soul of the world"—for they are responsible for its continuance in life. But how does salt become **tasteless**? Chemically, it can never lose its saltness. But in the various kinds of use to which it was put in Palestine it could become progressively less and less pure, until finally it was useless—and then nothing could be done to "restore its saltness".

14 **'Light for all the world. A town that stands on a hill'**. The two metaphors probably belong together. Isaiah had declared it to be the destiny

of Israel to be "a light to the nations" (49.6); and the symbol of this destiny
was the city of Jerusalem set **on a hill**, to which the peoples of the world
would come to worship the one true God. Jesus' disciples were to become
the new Israel, and could be described in the same imagery. (For a note on
the **meal-tub**, see below on Mark 4.21.) 15

'Do not suppose that I have come to abolish the Law and the 17
prophets'. Jesus' ethical teaching was by no means entirely new but,
like the teaching of his contemporaries, took as its point of departure the
systematic code of behaviour contained in the books of the Old Testament
attributed to Moses (which the Jews in fact observed not merely as a moral
code but as a legal code, and referred to as **the Law**), and also the great
moral insights contained in the writings of **the prophets**. Sometimes his
teaching was so radical that it seemed a direct contradiction of the Law of
Moses—and some of the first Christians were quick to draw the conclusion
that Christianity completely superseded the moral and legal code of the
Jews. But Matthew was anxious to show that even where Jesus' teaching
seemed most at variance with normal Jewish practice, it was still a direct
development of the original Law: **I did not come to abolish, but to**
complete.[a] Consequently Jesus' followers, whatever their enemies might
say (and we can probably overhear this debate at several places in Matthew's
gospel), were as committed to "keeping the Law" as the Jews themselves.
To demonstrate this, Matthew arranged the first section of his collection of
Jesus' teaching in the form of a new interpretation of the Law of Moses—
and indeed Jesus himself is likely to have given his teaching in this form;
it was one of the regular patterns followed by Jewish moral teachers in his
day. **The Pharisees**, and those **doctors of the law** who shared their 20
convictions, devoutly believed that the Law of Moses, though originally
formulated many centuries before, was still valid in their own day as a
comprehensive guide to conduct; and in order to bring it up to date (so to
speak) they evolved certain rules of interpretation by which its provisions
could be shown to apply to present-day circumstances. Jesus' quarrel with
these men (and again this is a debate which we can often overhear as the
gospel progresses) was that their interpretation had become so subtle and
casuistical that it often frustrated the original intention of the Law. But in
offering his own interpretation, he had no idea of taking the Law less
seriously than they did. He too regarded it as unalterable down to the
smallest **letter** or **stroke** of a letter, and as of eternal validity: and as regards 18
the keeping of its detailed provisions, his followers must show themselves
better men even **than the Pharisees and the doctors of the law.** 20
This, at least, seems to have been Matthew's view of the relation between

[a] The word translated complete can also mean "fulfil", or even (perhaps) "establish". Its exact meaning here must depend upon the way in which the whole passage is understood.

Jesus' teaching and the Law of Moses. But the question was not an easy one, nor was it always answered in the same way by different New Testament writers.

21 **'You have learned that our forefathers were told'.** The phrase is repeated, with slight variations, six times in this chapter. In each case, it refers to a well-known provision of the Law of Moses, and prepares for a new interpretation; and it is likely that this form of argument was one that was frequently used in Jesus' time in learned debates about the application of specific laws. **'Do not commit murder'** is the sixth of the Ten Commandments. But the rest of the sentence, **'anyone who commits murder must be brought to judgement'** is not in fact to be found in the Old Testament (though it is of course implied in it), but is the kind of addition which the doctors of the law made to the original text in order to show its practical application. When Jesus pronounced that anger and abuse were as serious as murder in the eyes of God, many of his contemporaries would have agreed with him—in theory; for the Old Testament said as much itself. But in practice there was a difference: a man who had committed murder could be brought before a court, a man who had merely expressed anger could not—and this difference inevitably made the one seem much less serious than the other. If human justice were perfectly to mirror the judgement of God (as the Jewish law was claimed to do) this difference
22 should not exist: **anyone who nurses anger against his brother** should be as accountable in a human court as a murderer is; for in the divine court both will be sentenced to **the fires of hell.**

23–6 Before the series is continued, two practical examples are given, which in a general way illustrate the same point. Both examples are vividly drawn
23–4 from daily life.[a] In the temple at Jerusalem one of the commonest sights will have been that of individual Jews bringing beasts or birds to be sacrificed at the great altar in the central court. Some of these sacrifices were laid upon them by the Law on certain occasions (Luke 2.24), some were offered voluntarily as thank-offerings or as offerings to atone for some transgression. From the point of view of the temple cult, a personal grievance would have seemed a small matter compared with the due completion of the sacrifice; but from Jesus' statement that any offence against one's brother is as serious as murder, it followed that personal reconciliation must be of infinitely more importance than any ritual act.

25 **'If someone sues you'.** This again seems drawn from life. It follows
26 from the end of the saying (**'you will not be let out till you have paid the last farthing'**) that Jesus was thinking of someone who was really in

[a] The details of private sacrifice, so far as we can discover them, do not fit in too well with Jesus' words: the animal was normally killed by the layman not far from the altar, and the blood then poured on the altar by the priest. But the idea of individual sacrifices was so familiar from the Old Testament that perhaps Jesus did not need to be precise about the details.

debt, and who was ultimately sued by his creditor. In the east, it would be natural (though of course sometimes risky) to play for time by pretending that the debt did not exist, and even to allow the matter to come to court. But this natural litigiousness was an offence against Jesus' moral standard. It was only right (as well as prudent) to come to some agreement about
repayment **on your way to court.** 25
'You have learned that they were told, "Do not commit adultery"'. 27
Jesus' interpretation of the Law is resumed, this time with the Seventh
Commandment, interpreted in the light of the Tenth ("You shall not covet
your neighbour's wife"). Some of Jesus' contemporaries took much the same
view, though none of them, so far as we know, stated the principle in quite
such an uncompromising way. The metaphor of the **right eye** and the 29
right hand, being embedded in the same context, seems to refer to sexual 30
behaviour—and so it has often been taken in Christian history; but in Mark
the saying occurs in a more general context, and it may originally have had
nothing to do with adultery. **'They were told, "A man who divorces his** 31
wife must give her a note of dismissal"'. This same text (Deuteronomy
24.1) is interpreted by Jesus in a later discussion with the Pharisees. It is
significant that here an exception is allowed: **for any cause other than** 32
unchastity (see below on 19.3–9, Mark 10.1–12).
'Again, you have learned that they were told, "Do not break your 33
oath", and, "Oaths sworn to the Lord must be kept"'. These quotations do not occur as they stand in the Old Testament, but they doubtless represent a standard way of summarizing the laws on swearing. Oaths were a serious matter; in principle, they had to be taken on the name of God (Deuteronomy 6.13 and elsewhere). Not surprisingly, many teachers, from the Old Testament onwards, discouraged swearing as much as possible (though it remained necessary on certain occasions, such as in law-courts). But some saw another way of avoiding the extreme seriousness of oaths, that of swearing by lesser things, such as heaven or earth. Jesus exposes the casuistry of this. Swearing is swearing, and nothing will make it less serious. Better to avoid it altogether.
"Eye for eye, tooth for tooth". This basic principle of elementary 38
justice was written into the Old Testament (e.g. Leviticus 24.19), and was still theoretically in force, though more civilized ways of applying the principle had been evolved. In a primitive society, it brought the instinct of revenge under control by limiting the compensation which could be demanded for an injury; but later the Jews, with their reverence for the letter of the law, were apparently somewhat embarrassed by it, and it was only by ingeniously stretching their interpretation of the words that they were able to use it as a rough criterion for assessing damages in court. Jesus doubtless had this debate in mind; but instead of contributing to it himself, he allowed the principle to stand in all its severity, and simply

told his followers not to invoke it. Humiliation should be willingly suffered, service should be willingly offered; there should be no threats of recourse to the law.

43 **"Love your neighbour, hate your enemy."** Only the first phrase stands in the Old Testament: "Love your neighbour" (Leviticus 19.18). But, as we know from Luke's gospel (10.29) as well as from Jewish writings, people asked, Who is my neighbour? And the answer given was usually, Any fellow-Jew, with the addition (in some more liberal quarters) of certain particularly deserving Gentiles. The rest of the world (since it consisted, by definition, of Gentiles and idolaters, God's "enemies") could be treated with something considerably less than love (which is all that a Semitic language like Hebrew or Aramaic, which tends to call things either black or white, need mean by "hating"). **"Hate your enemy"** was therefore the kind of implication which many of Jesus' contemporaries may have seen in the command to love your neighbour. [a] And it was in opposition to this that Jesus offered his own interpretation.

44 No: you must **love your enemies**—and this becomes, either in Jesus' mouth or in the tradition of the early church, no longer a matter of Jews' attitude to non-Jews, but of the individual's attitude towards his personal enemies, a Christian's attitude towards his persecutors. The injunction in Leviticus, which was taken by most Jews as a guide to the proper attitude of their nation, was translated by Jesus into the universal realm of personal
46 ethics. Yet the teaching is still expressed in typically Jewish idioms: **tax-gatherers**, being somewhat ostracized from Jewish society, tended to "love
47 each other" out of a natural sense of solidarity; and **the heathen**, whatever their other faults (in Jewish eyes), certainly extended hospitality and courtesy to each other. But the followers of Jesus must thrust aside all such social barriers, and fulfil the command, Love your neighbour, in the total and uncompromising sense in which it was intended by God. The Jews were accustomed to being told to imitate God; but since they believed that God extended to their own race a favour and compassion which he withheld from the Gentiles, it seemed to follow that they should show a similar partiality themselves. But in reality a truer picture of God is given by the
45, 48 proverb, He **makes his sun rise on good and bad alike**. God's **goodness knows no bounds**, he makes no distinctions. In the same way, **there must be no limit to** the goodness of his followers.[b]

[*a*] We now know of one Jewish sect—the community which produced the Dead Sea Scrolls—which enshrined this implication in a maxim and may, for all we know, have taken it quite literally.

[*b*] Literally, "you must be perfect, as your heavenly Father is perfect". In Greek thought, perfection consisted in an advance towards higher levels of knowledge and understanding. To the Jews, it meant a wholehearted and uncompromising conformity to the ethical standards and practical provisions of the Law. The Greek meaning occurs in Paul: but here only the Jewish meaning is appropriate. The translation "goodness" must therefore be understood, not in a philosophical sense of general moral goodness, but in the completely

'Be careful not to make a show of your religion before men.' Just as 6. 1
Jesus did not attack the Law of Moses as such, but only the way in which
it was being interpreted in his time, so he did not reject the religious practices of his contemporaries, but only criticized the attitude with which these
were often performed, particularly by those who most insisted upon them,
the Pharisees (to whom Jesus—or subsequently the church—seems to have
given what became almost a nickname: **the hypocrites**). "Acts of charity" 2
were very highly regarded by the Jews, and with this Jesus agreed. But it
had become the custom to announce any substantial gift at the meeting
of the congregation either **in synagogue**, or at an open-air service **in the**
streets. By contrast, **'your good deed must be secret'**. Again, the Jews 4
regularly prayed (**standing up**) at certain times of day: either **in synagogue**, 5
or else wherever they happened to be. This too gave opportunities for
ostentation, particularly if one chose out **street-corners** for the purpose.
Again, there was a tendency to admire anyone who knew and could recite
especially long prayers (and here there is a sideways glance at heathen 7
worship as well as the synagogue); by contrast, Jesus prescribed a very
short and condensed prayer for his followers. Finally, fasting was a recog- 16–18
nized practice, and was becoming more widely observed in Jewish circles
at the time this gospel was written. Christians were also to fast, but their
fasting must be secret.

'This is how you should pray.' Into this series of contrasts between 9
Jewish and Christian religious practices is slipped the Lord's Prayer. It is possible that this prayer was originally taught by Jesus in deliberate opposition to traditional Jewish forms of prayer (though Luke offers a quite different reason, 11.1); and certainly, although many of its clauses belonged equally to Jewish spirituality, its brevity presents a striking contrast to the more elaborate prayers which every Jew was supposed to recite daily. It is given twice in the New Testament, once here in Matthew, and once in Luke (11.2–4). In each case the basic elements of the prayer are the same, but Luke's version is considerably shorter. Jesus may, of course, have taught the prayer in both forms; but it is not difficult to think of reasons why, in the different churches for which Luke and Matthew wrote, two different versions of the same prayer should have existed. If, for instance, Luke's version is original, Matthew's version could be an early expansion of it under the influence of other Jewish prayers; while if Matthew's is original, Luke's could be an abbreviation of it for the benefit of a church less accustomed to Jewish forms of prayer. In any case, it is the longer form which since very early times has become standard in the church. The NEB offers

practical sense of a total and extraordinary conformity to the Law as interpreted by Jesus. This kind of goodness must be learnt from the goodness (the perfection) of God himself. God is not called "perfect" anywhere in Jewish literature. But there was a tendency to regard him as the model for any human virtue. The prototype for such a comparison is Leviticus 19.2, "Be holy, as I am holy".

a new translation, and attempts to convey some of the extreme brevity and directness of the original Greek. The more polished and rhythmical phrases of the King James version will probably always come more naturally to most people in their prayers; but the importance of grasping the precise meaning of each petition justifies this new rendering of familiar words.

9 "**Our Father in heaven.**" Prayers written exclusively for private use are a comparatively modern invention. Jesus' prayer, like all formal Jewish prayers, was primarily intended to be used in corporate worship by a congregation. This gives content to the word **our**. In most religions of the world God is at one time or another addressed as Father, but not always with the same meaning. For the Greeks, God was "father" in the sense of creator: he was therefore everyone's father. From this we inherit such ideas as the universal fatherhood of God and brotherhood of man. The Jews, on the other hand, thought of God as Father in a much more particular way: God was "father" to Israel, in that he had a special relationship with his people, and guided and protected them "like a father". To the Jew, therefore, he was "our" father in a highly exclusive sense. What then could Jesus have meant by '**Our Father**'? There is no evidence in the gospels that he endorsed the Greek view of God's universal fatherhood; and he certainly did not accept the exclusive attitude of the Jews that only they were the true "sons" of God. Jesus' own attitude lies somewhere between. He himself was the Son of God, and God was in a unique way his Father. Moreover, those who followed him became, along with him, God's "sons", and were entitled to address God with that singularly intimate Aramaic word which passed at once into the praying of the earliest Christians, *Abba*, "Father".[a] "Our Father" therefore takes on its meaning from those who use it. It is the distinctive prayer of the community whose members, through Jesus Christ, have become "sons of God".

"**Thy name be hallowed.**" The translators have kept the archaic word, which is probably known to most people only through its occurrence in the Lord's Prayer. To "hallow" is to separate from all that profanes. There is a part of creation where God's name is already perfectly hallowed—**in heaven**; the prayer is that this hallowing should be extended to earth, that the whole of creation should become consonant, instead of discordant, with the divine nature. Two implications of this are drawn out in the next two
10 clauses. "**Thy kingdom come.**" Much of Jesus' teaching in the gospel concerns this "kingdom". God is king—that is axiomatic. But his reign is not yet universally acknowledged. Jesus often draws attention to those

[*a*] See below on Romans 8.15. Luke's version of the prayer, which begins with the single word "Father", probably reflects an original which began with this distinctive word *Abba*. Such apparently easy familiarity with God would have seemed shocking to the Jewish mind, and it may have been as a concession to Jewish feelings that Matthew's version had the solemn phrase (which can be paralleled from contemporary writings), **Our Father in heaven.**

moments in the present—often quite unexpected ones—when an individual's response to an ordinary human situation makes this reign actual; but he also constantly looks ahead to the time when God, by his own act, will make his kingdom universal. The prayer presumably envisages both kinds of "coming". "**Thy will be done.**" The meaning of this, again, follows from the "hallowing" of God's name. It does not express (as it might in some religions) a resigned acquiescence in an inscrutable providence, but a longing for God's purposes to be accomplished **on earth as in heaven.**

"**Give us today our daily bread.**" This is unlikely to be a metaphor: 11
most Jewish prayers included a petition for bread, and no formal Jewish meal
would ever be eaten without thanksgiving to God who provides food for
the use of men. But the clause says, not just bread, but **daily bread.** The
adjective is strange. This particular Greek word occurs nowhere else in
literature, and we can only guess at its meaning here. Still less can we
recover the Aramaic word which Jesus originally used. It is true that a
"religious" interpretation is possible. Bread came to have a special significance for Jesus: the bread which he broke became a means of communion;
and it is possible that, apart from the satisfaction of hunger, this petition
with its mysterious adjective contains a reference to the supernatural
nourishment given by Jesus to those who worship him. [a] But even if this
meaning is present, it can hardly be the whole meaning. Bread is still bread,
and the adjective must define the amount that is asked for. This is a remarkable limitation. Men usually pray for a steady supply of bread to last through
the year. But a Christian, it seems, is to ask only for what is necessary today 11
(or, at most, tomorrow). [b] We need bread today, because the present weighs
upon us, life is to be lived and we have work to do. But tomorrow—next
week, next year—is in the hands of God.

"**Forgive us the wrong we have done.**" Literally, "our debts"—a 12
rendering which has prevailed in some English versions of the Lord's Prayer, as it has in the traditional Latin version (*debita nostra*). But "debt" was a strongly religious concept in Hebrew culture: God had laid obligations on his people, and, in so far as they had failed to fulfil them, they felt themselves in debt to God. So our "debts" amount, in fact, to the **wrong we have done** (and in Jesus' own language of Aramaic the same word was used for both). To be released from this debt was the ultimate, if barely attainable, object of Jewish religion, and a constant burden of Jewish prayers. Jesus taught that this release was an immediate possibility —on condition that one had already extended a free pardon in one's own

[*a*] For this reason, "super-substantial" has been one of the translations current in the Roman Catholic church since the time of Jerome (about A.D. 400).

[*b*] The alternative translation in the footnote has been suggested since the second century. It would permit the Christian to ask for bread "for the morrow"—but still not for the whole year!

circle. So the clause is added (and the perfect tense is a correct translation of the Greek), "**as we have forgiven those who have wronged us**".

13 "**And do not bring us to the test.**" **Test** here replaces the familiar word "temptation", and is probably a more faithful rendering. Temptation is a psychological concept, suggesting a struggle within the individual between good and bad impulses. But this kind of psychological analysis was not characteristic of Hebrew thinking. The nearest corresponding Hebrew concept was that of "testing". In the Old Testament, many of the afflictions suffered by the people of Israel, and many personal catastrophes which befell pious individuals, were understood as a "test" imposed by God. How one would ultimately be judged by God would depend on how one survived this "test"; and the more urgently that judgement was expected (and Christians soon began to expect it in their own lifetime), the more reason there was to dread any decisive moment which might bring out the true worth of the individual and so determine God's final verdict.

"**The evil one.**" The Greek word can mean either "evil" or "the evil one", and translators have to make their choice. Perhaps in the long run it makes little difference whether a personal devil is seen behind the phenomena of evil. In Jesus' time it was natural to think in this way; today it may seem less so. But the reality of evil, with which the follower of Jesus is in perpetual conflict, is acknowledged either way.

Traditionally, the prayer ends with an ascription of glory to God, "For thine is the kingdom and the power and the glory, for ever. Amen". These words are absent in most early manuscripts, and were almost certainly added, under the influence of Jewish prayers, when the prayer began to be used in public worship. The original prayer taught by Jesus contains no liturgical elaborations; indeed the most striking thing about it is the directness and simplicity of its petitions.

14 Just one of these petitions is singled out for comment: '**For if you forgive others the wrongs they have done**'—and here a Greek word is used which does literally mean "wrongs". There is a very similar saying (in a quite different context) in Mark 11.25.

So far, the teaching of the sermon seems to have been in conscious opposition to the most prominent religious party among Jesus' contemporaries. It now becomes more general, and continues a tradition that goes back to Old Testament writings such as Proverbs or Ecclesiasticus: the tradition of Hebrew "wisdom", which consisted of an intensely practical attitude to life combined with firm religious values. Accordingly the object of attack is no
19 longer the Jewish 'hypocrites', but 'the heathen'. '**Do not store up for yourselves treasure on earth**'—this advice was already centuries old, and was usually taken as an encouragement to generous almsgiving. In Jesus'

mouth it has a strongly Palestinian flavour: the "treasure" is not the gold
of a rich man locked away in a strongroom, but the cherished possessions
of country people, like clothes and carpets,[a] stored in a corner of a mud-
brick house, so that thieves could easily **break in**[b] through the walls. '**The** 22
lamp of the body is the eye.' It was quite natural in Greek to call the eye a
"light", and the sentence may have been a proverb already. But the elaboration of this in the following metaphors is more puzzling. There may be an
allusion to an idiom known in both Hebrew and Greek, according to which
the bad eye is a term for meanness, and therefore the "sound eye" for
generosity. But the saying can also be taken as a small parable: just as the
body moves in darkness if the eyes are bad, so a person lives in spiritual darkness unless his whole personality is trained upon the source of all true light.
'**No servant can be the slave of two masters.**' It was a commonplace that 24
a slave who had to take his orders from two different members of a household, say from both father and son, was in a luckless position. With his usual
radical approach to worldly possessions, Jesus declares that any attempt to
combine the service of God with a concern about money is equally
impossible.

'**Therefore I bid you put away anxious thoughts.**' The word **anxious** 25
occurs four times, and is the key-word of the paragraph. The imagery
belongs again to the Palestinian countryside. '**Look at the birds of the air**' 26
—and Jesus makes his point with a certain humour, conjuring up the absurd
picture of birds carrying bags of seed and reaping-hooks. '**Consider how** 28
the lilies grow in the fields.' For a few brief weeks in the spring, the fields
are a mass of colour, to be compared with the proverbial splendour of
Solomon. **Lilies** is the traditional translation, but we do not know
exactly which wildflower Jesus was thinking of.[c] However the image is
clear enough. A few days of hot sun, and the flowers and bushes (**the grass** 30
in the fields has a falsely European sound) turn brown and dry, and the
peasant can gather them to burn in his baking-oven or under his cooking-
pot.[d] God has no less concern for mankind than for birds and flowers.
Moreover God has given men a more serious concern—to work for his
kingdom and his justice. '**Each day has troubles enough of its own**'— 33, 34
which is not the sigh of a man who has become resigned to misfortune, but
a programme of action. There is plenty of work to be done today, combating
and overcoming the evil around us. We are not to take on in addition a
useless burden of anxiety about the evil which will have to be faced tomorrow.

('**Is there a man of you who . . . can add a foot to his height?**' As it 27

[*a*] If **rust** is a correct translation, presumably one must add things like metal implements. But the meaning of the word is uncertain. It may denote other destructive insects.
[*b*] The Greek word means literally "dig through".
[*c*] Many suggestions have been made. A plausible one is the Anthemis, or Easter daisy.
[*d*] If Palestinian peasants had "stoves", they certainly did not use brushwood as fuel for them. The Greek word probably means "oven".

stands, this seems to be making rather a different point. But the Greek word translated **height** can also mean age, and a **foot** may be metaphorical (see footnote in NEB). Compare Psalm 39.5, "Thou hast made my days a few handbreadths". If so, anxiety about prolonging one's life would fall naturally into series with anxiety about food and clothing.)

7. 1, 2 **'Pass no judgement, and you will not be judged . . . whatever measure you deal out to others will be dealt back to you.'** One of the most powerful generators of proverbs is the old belief that there is a law of retribution in human affairs, and that what you do to others will be returned upon your own head. But Jesus' sayings, even if they have the same proverbial sound, go a good deal deeper. Here, it is not stated whom you may be judged by: but every Jew would have known what was meant. The unexpressed subject is God, the judgement is the verdict God will one day pass on every man, and you are not to anticipate it (as an individual, or a community, or a church) by initiating proceedings yourself. The same goes for the measure that **will be dealt back to you**—not by your fellow-men, but by God. As for the hypocrisy of criticizing others before you look carefully at yourself, the world's literature is full of proverbs about it. Jesus' example is
3 characteristic of him, in that it is almost grotesquely exaggerated—a **great plank** and a **speck of sawdust.**

6 **'Do not give dogs what is holy.'** Proverbial again, and with a perfectly general sound. But perhaps there was originally a sharper edge to it. "Dogs" and "pigs" were words of abuse which the Jews were accustomed to use of Gentiles. Jesus himself used this language (Mark 7.27), but here he presumably meant, not Gentiles in general, but unbelievers.

7 **'Ask, and you will receive.'** The efficacy of prayer was taken for granted, but (since prayers often appear to go unanswered) it was felt that a prayer must fulfil all sorts of conditions (sincerity, humility, etc.) in order to qualify for an answer. Jesus' teaching, by contrast, appears to be quite unconditional, and proceeds from the premise (which also underlies the Lord's Prayer) that God, being Jesus' own father, is therefore also Father of all who follow Jesus. And if God is the Christian's Father, then he will treat his children as a human father does—but tempering his discipline with infinitely more patience and generosity.

12 **'Always treat others as you would like them to treat you'**—the Golden Rule. A somewhat similar moral rule-of-thumb was current among the Jews in Jesus' time, and was indeed thought to sum up the **Law and the prophets.** But it took the negative form, "Do not do to others what you would not wish them to do to you". This is significantly different from Jesus' rule, not just because avoiding evil is a colourless concept compared with doing good, but because there is a totally different presupposition. Beneath the negative form there is an implied threat: Do not do to others

what you would not wish them to do to you, otherwise they will retaliate. But there is no such threat in Jesus' rule. Always treat others as you would like them to treat you, otherwise—what? Otherwise they may not do for you all you wish they would? But no one ever expected they would! There is no "otherwise". Jesus' teaching is not prudential at all, but an absolute principle: this is how you are to treat others—regardless!

'**Enter by the narrow gate.**' Moralists in antiquity often represented the 13
choice between good and bad as a decision between "two ways", the
narrow, difficult path of virtue, and the easy road of licentiousness. Jesus
stands in the same tradition, but he seems to use the metaphor somewhat
differently. He combines the image of a road with that of a gate—one
should perhaps imagine oneself in a walled city, with its principal gate
leading on to a main road, while a small side gate leads to a mountain path;
moreover, he does not seem to be drawing just the usual moral—not many
are virtuous, but make sure you are yourself. By **the gate that leads to life**
he means the path of Christian discipleship; and it has been true ever since
the beginning of Christianity that, relatively speaking, **those who find it
are few.**

'**Beware of false prophets.**' We know nothing of such people in the time 15
of Jesus; but we do know that during the first century or so of the church's
existence "false prophets" constituted a practical problem. Christian
"prophecy" was highly esteemed, and itinerant "prophets" were warmly
received when they visited local churches. But this hospitality could easily
be abused. It was not difficult to play the part of a prophet, and the churches
soon had to devise some means of "testing" the inspiration of their visitors.
The tests they used are described in various early Christian writings (there
is an example in 1 John 4.1); and here it looks as if a general principle of
moral judgement—**you will recognize them by their fruits**—which was 20
spoken by Jesus in various contexts (Matthew 12.33, Luke 6.43) came to be
applied to the specific problem of **false prophets** in the church. Much the
same goes for the following paragraph. Jesus was hardly addressed as
"**Lord, Lord**" in his lifetime; but in the church it was an article of faith 21
that Jesus was "Lord", and Christians were by definition those who
acknowledged "the Lord Jesus". But was it enough simply to make this
confession of faith? Was it enough even to speak inspired words and perform 22
miraculous cures and exorcisms "in his name"? Were such people necessarily Christians, and would they be accepted by Christ at the final judgement? By no means. **When that day comes**, it will be by a man's adherence
to the kind of teaching given in the Sermon, more than by his professions
of faith or his psychic powers, that he will be judged worthy of entering the
kingdom of Heaven.

The Sermon ends, like other discourses of Jesus, with a brief parable. 24–7
Two houses may look outwardly the same; but one, foolishly built on the

sandy bed of a *wady*, is suddenly inundated by a deep raging torrent which, after a few days of Palestinian rain, will rush down the valley, sweeping all before it. Outwardly, two men's lives may look much the same. But when the moment of testing comes, all the pretensions of one of them will collapse into ruin.

Teaching and healing

Matthew, Mark and Luke all give a picture of Jesus' activity in Galilee in which the two principal elements are *Teaching and healing*. Matthew, by placing the Sermon on the Mount so early in his narrative, gives special prominence to the teaching. He now devotes a few paragraphs to examples
8. 2 of the healing, and begins with the cure of **a leper**. This episode, in Mark (1.40–5), is told in greater detail and with an eye to its social and religious implications; but Matthew omits everything except the bare narrative. The only emphasis he appears to lay on the story is not (as in Mark) on the behaviour of the leper who has been cured, but on Jesus' anxiety to conform
4 with the Law: **make the offering laid down by Moses for your cleansing.**
5 **When he had entered Capernaum.** The next episode is evidently recorded for the sake of the conversation between Jesus and a military officer. Much of the point of the conversation lies in the fact that the man who **came up to ask** Jesus for **his help was a centurion** (the Roman title for a junior officer in charge of about a hundred men). This does not reveal his nationality: whether he was in the service of Rome or of one of the vassal kings (Herod Antipas or Philip), he could have been recruited from any part of the eastern empire. But one thing about him is almost certain: he was not a Jew (for Jews did not normally serve in any army in Palestine). The episode is therefore one of the very few in the gospel which illustrate Jesus' attitude towards the Gentiles. The conversation is almost identical in both Matthew and Luke, though the two evangelists seem quite independent of each other when it comes to narrating the episode in which this conversation took place.
6 **'A boy of mine'.** The translators have successfully caught the ambiguity of the Greek phrase: it could mean one of the centurion's children, or one of his servants. Matthew probably intended it to mean his son, in which case the urgency of his request needs no explanation (Luke took a different view, 7.2). Jesus' immediate response to this request by a foreigner was apparently
7 favourable:[a] **'I will come and cure him'.** But the soldier, sensing the

[*a*] A different punctuation would turn Jesus' reply into a question, as in the footnote in NEB; since early Greek manuscripts had no punctuation, this could equally be correct. In which case Jesus' response will have been initially, not favourable, but unfavourable: "Am I to come and cure him?", i.e. "Do you expect me, a Jew, to defile myself by entering a Gentile's house?"

impropriety of having a Jew of Jesus' renown entering his house (or else out
of pure diffidence) requested Jesus merely to **say the word**, and made a 8
comparison (which is the other main point of the story) between the
authority of himself as an officer and the authority of Jesus. Just as he, being
under orders[a] himself, had soldiers under him, and in his own small way 9
could get his will done by his subordinates, so, he believed, Jesus had supreme authority over those powers of evil which caused such things as the paralysis of his son. Jesus surely did not need to go and encounter the particular demon concerned; he had only to **say the word**, and the whole regiment of the devil would obey him. To credit Jesus with such authority over the entire realm of evil spirits (unlike ordinary exorcists, who could only take them on one by one) was a sign of remarkable faith; and Jesus was led to comment on the contrast between such implicit faith and the much
more reserved and sceptical attitude which he had encountered[b] **in Israel.** 10
'Many, I tell you, will come from east and west.' This saying occurs in 11
a different context in Luke (13.28–9), and was doubtless remembered for its own sake, apart from any particular occasion. It is added here as a general comment on the episode which has just taken place. The Jews looked forward to a future age of glory, often pictured as a heavenly feast, presided over by the great patriarchs of the past. In the language of those prophets who wrote when the Jewish nation was exiled far away from Jerusalem (e.g. Isaiah 49.12), there would at the same time be a great coming together of people **from east and west**—but these, of course, would be Jews, people
born to the kingdom. Jesus here turns this conventional imagery on its 12
head: it is Gentiles who will flock in to enjoy the promised kingdom, while the Jews who so confidently look forward to it will be driven out into **the dark, the place of wailing and grinding of teeth.**

Two brief paragraphs follow which appear to be borrowed from Mark's gospel (1.32–4), with slight abbreviation. In Mark, the events are included in his account of a complete day's activity, and since that day was a Sabbath,
the words **when evening fell** are significant: only after the Sabbath ended 16
at sunset was it permissible to travel any distance or to perform more than the most necessary tasks for the sick. Matthew, by his rearrangement, has robbed this of its significance. Characteristically, he sets Jesus' activity in
relation to a prophecy of Isaiah (53.4). This comes from a chapter which 17
the church rapidly came to see as one of the key Old Testament passages bearing on the person of Jesus; but Matthew quotes the text in an unusual

[*a*] This phrase is strange: one would expect, not "under orders", but "in a position to give orders", and it is possible that our present text is at fault on these words. But perhaps it comes to the same in the end. An officer, if he is to have authority over his men, must be under a higher authority himself.

[*b*] Or rather: was to encounter. This may be a saying which Jesus in fact uttered much later on. But the story had come to be associated with the beginning of Jesus' activity in Galilee.

version which appropriately makes it apply, not to salvation from sin (its usual sense), but to healing from disease.

Two sayings on discipleship follow, which seem on the face of it to make the demands of Jesus almost impossibly exacting: not only must the disciple do without the security of a home, but he must even be prepared to neglect what was for the Jews (as for most people) one of the most sacred of all family duties, that of providing an honourable burial for one's father. It is true that Jesus often seems to have called men to a break with their previous lives so radical that these demands can be seen as a consistent part of his teaching on discipleship. On the other hand, each of Jesus' replies has something of the ring of a proverb, and may originally have been spoken in a
20 somewhat different context. Thus, '**the Son of Man has nowhere to lay**
his head' sounds oddly inappropriate immediately after the welcome given to Jesus in Peter's house (verses 14–15 above), and since no teaching has yet been given about the Son of Man it is hard to see how, at this stage, anyone could have understood what Jesus meant. But later on, when Jesus had finally turned his back on his own country and was on his way to meet humiliation, suffering and death in Jerusalem, the saying could well have been one of those in which he tried to convey to his disciples the darker side
22 of his destiny as Son of Man. Again, '**leave the dead to bury their dead**'
is understandable enough as an invitation to leave the ranks of those whose minds are closed to new possibilities of life and to become, through the gospel, really "alive"; and it may only be Matthew (or the tradition he was reproducing) who, by taking the phrase literally and introducing a circumstantial little story to illustrate it, has made Jesus appear so ruthlessly insensitive to the most precious family ties of his would-be disciples.

23 **Jesus then got into the boat, and his disciples followed.** The word
followed is a little odd in this sentence: "his disciples went with him" would be more natural. But "following" was the disciples' *métier*, and was the vocation of the church which came after them; and this may be the first of the subtle alterations and adjustments to the story as we know it from Mark (4.35–41) by which Matthew appears to have adapted it to the needs of a Christian community that was struggling against persecution like a small boat caught in a storm, apt to imagine that its Protector was asleep. This record of Jesus' magisterial words to the raging elements may have been intended to reassure the church that its destiny was, after all, in safe hands.

28 **When he reached the other side, in the country of the Gadarenes.**
It is likely that a small strip of the southern shore of the lake belonged to the important Greco-Roman city of Gadara (which lay about seven miles away), and to this extent Matthew's correction of Mark's 'Gerasenes' somewhat eases the geographical difficulty of the story (for Gerasa lay much further away); at the same time, the name of the city, as well as the presence

of a herd of pigs, still gives the impression of a predominantly non-Jewish
environment. The story clearly reproduces that given by Mark (5.1–10),
but is told more briefly, and in a much less sensational form. The man
possessed by a whole legion of unclean spirits becomes (unexpectedly) **two**
men **possessed by devils** of considerable violence; and the enormous herd
of two thousand pigs becomes simply **a large herd**. Moreover the emphasis 30
here is quite different. In Mark's version the interest is focused upon the
state of the man before and after the exorcism, and upon the crowd's reaction
to the cure. But here the two sufferers are barely mentioned more than
once. The scene is played out entirely between Jesus and the devils, who
(as always) recognize him as the Son of God, and expect from him an unwelcome anticipation of that punishment which (according to popular
Jewish mythology) the devil and all his company were to receive at the end
of time. They beg to be allowed to make a spectacular demonstration of their
power before yielding (a common feature of exorcism stories), and this duly
takes place in the destruction of the herd of pigs. The consequence is very
different from that in Mark's version: instead of a vociferous witness being
left behind in gentile territory to spread the word of Jesus' greatness, there
was a unanimous reaction of hostility: **all the town . . . begged him to** 34
leave the district. According to Matthew, Jesus' work at this stage aroused
no response among the Gentiles.

And now some men brought him a paralysed man. The story is told 9. 2
more fully by Mark (2.1–12) and Luke (5.17–26), and the men's exploit in
lowering the stretcher through the roof (which is not mentioned by Matthew)
seems a necessary presupposition of the story if the words **seeing their**
faith are to make good sense. Jesus' first words to the paralytic perhaps
bring out the true sequence of events more clearly than in the parallel
versions. **'Take heart, my son; your sins are forgiven'**. Since, it was
believed, God must forgive a man his sins before he could recover from an
illness, this was sufficient reason for saying **'take heart'**: if the paralytic's
sins were really forgiven, he could now expect to recover. But the unspoken
accusation of blasphemy incited Jesus (as in the other accounts) to make a
demonstration of his authority to pronounce forgiveness of sins by miraculously performing an instant cure. **The people**, in Matthew, were not
merely stunned by the miracle, but appreciated, perhaps, that it was a
decisive answer to the charge of blasphemy. Jesus' act proved that God
had indeed granted him **such authority**. 8

As he passed on from there. In Mark (2.13–14) and Luke (5.27–28) the 9
name of the customs official is Levi; here it is **Matthew**. There can be no
doubt that this is the same incident as in the other two gospels; all the main
features of this and the following paragraphs (down to verse 17) are the same.
The only important difference is the name of the disciple. One reason for

the change is probably that Levi does not occur in any of the lists of the Twelve, and the writer of this gospel (or indeed a later hand, if it was desired to bring the reputed author of the gospel into the narrative) wished to attach this story to one of the names which certainly appeared in the list, and which subsequently appears (10.3) as 'Matthew the tax-gatherer'.

The narrative continues exactly as in Mark (2.15–17), save that Jesus'
13 reply to his critics includes a quotation from Hosea (6.6), "**I require mercy,
not sacrifice**". Possibly Matthew was dissatisfied with Jesus' brusque and proverbial reply to the Pharisees, and deliberately introduced the quotation from Hosea, which was a classic formulation of the superiority of spontaneous acts of compassion and generosity over the fulfilment of the temple ritual, and which Jesus (at least according to Matthew), also used on another occasion (12.7 below). In this way Jesus could be portrayed as meeting the Pharisees on their own ground. '**Go and learn what that text means**' was, incidentally, a characteristic phrase in Jewish scholarly arguments.

In verses 14–17 Matthew runs very close to Mark (2.18–22), but adds a characteristic touch at the end. The drift of these sayings in Mark, and still more in Luke, is that Jesus' new message is incompatible with the old observances. But for Matthew this must have seemed too bald a statement. Christianity was a new interpretation, but it by no means superseded the
17 Jewish Law: so he adds, '**then both are preserved**'.

A short section follows devoted to miracle stories, which are told very briefly, but in such a way as to bring out the fact that the miracles were performed in
18 response to a gesture of faith. In Mark's version (5.21–43) the **president of
the synagogue** (who is actually called simply "a ruler" in Matthew's text, but the translators have filled in his title from the parallel accounts in Mark and Luke) came to Jesus when his daughter, though critically ill, was still alive: he asked only for a healing miracle, and it was Jesus who took the initiative once it was known that the child was dead. But here the child is already dead, and the man's faith in Jesus is demonstrated in that he believes from the outset that Jesus can perform the miracle, exceptional even in Jesus' activity, of restoring the dead to life. Similarly, the story of the woman with haemorrhages is much shortened, but is told in such a way as to bring out the woman's faith and Jesus' approval of that faith. Nevertheless, even within this brief scope, Matthew adds two touches of what we would now call local colour which are not found in Mark. Jesus' garment had
20 an **edge**, which in the Greek is a technical word for the tassels which Jews
were bidden to wear on each corner of their cloak (Numbers 15.38); and the
23 house of bereavement had already attracted **flute-players**, whose profession
it was to attend mourners.

The gospels contain a number of stories of Jesus curing the blind. There is one in both Matthew (20.29–34) and Luke (18.35–43) which follows the

story as told in Mark 10.46–52. But here, Matthew has an additional version,
told more briefly than the others but preserving two typical features: first,
that the blind recognize Jesus as **Son of David** (which, all the evangelists 27
agree, was correct in a sense, but was not normally discerned by those with
whom Jesus came into contact: there may be something symbolic in the fact
that it is only the blind who "see" this); and secondly, Matthew on each
occasion unexpectedly introduces not one but two blind men, just as, in 8.28,
he equally unexpectedly introduces two madmen. In this very brief account
Matthew is careful, once again, to emphasize the men's faith: '**As you have** 29
believed, so let it be'. The injunction is added, which is more characteristic
of Mark's gospel than of Matthew's, '**See that no one hears about this**'. 30
Matthew perhaps understood the matter like this: the fame of Jesus' miracles
was bound to have spread whatever happened; but the particular intuition
which the blind men had about Jesus' true identity (**Son of David**) ought
not, at this stage, to be revealed.

The last in the series of miracles, the exorcism of a devil from a dumb 32–3
man, is told only in barest outline. Since Jesus is dealing here, not with the
patient, but with a devil which has assumed control over the patient, there
can be no question of the individual's faith. Instead, the interest of the story
is shifted to the reaction of the onlookers.

The kernel of the following section is to be found in Mark (6.7–13). Jesus, at some stage in his work in Galilee, commissioned his disciples to go out independently of him as missionaries and healers, and the instructions and advice which he gave them are recorded in each of the first three gospels. But it was perhaps inevitable that the early church, when it meditated on these sayings, was more interested in their application to its own circumstances and problems than in the actual historical situation in which Jesus originally pronounced them. There was consequently a tendency, both to collect together scattered sayings of Jesus which seemed to have a bearing on church life, and to hand them down in language that was appropriate to the time. This tendency, which is present even in Mark's much briefer collection, has clearly influenced this section of Matthew. In the first place, the setting of the discourse has become artificial. In Mark (6.7, 30) and Luke (9. 2, 10), the disciples are sent out on a mission, and when they return they give some account of their exploits. In Matthew, too, they are "sent out" (10.5); but it is never said that they actually go, and there is no reference to their return: Matthew has characteristically allowed the importance he attaches to Jesus' discourse to crowd out the details of the circumstances which inspired it. In the second place, the conditions prevailing in the church when Matthew wrote are clearly discernible in the form in which some of the sayings are recorded (especially 10.17–20, 40–2). And in the third place, Matthew has added to the original collection a number of sayings about the future which lies ahead of the Christian community, sayings which occur in a quite different context in other gospels and which have little relevance to the situation of twelve disciples supposedly about to depart on a missionary tour. In short, Matthew has edited his material in such a way that it has become, not so much the report of words which Jesus may have spoken on a particular occasion in his life, as a manual of Jesus' sayings relevant to the work and witness of the church.

Before proceeding to the task of the disciples, Matthew introduces two similes to characterize, first the people among whom they would work, and secondly the urgency of the mission on which they would be sent. The
36 people were **like sheep without a shepherd**—a well-remembered comparison recorded in another place in Mark (6.34), but serving here to fix in the mind one of the commonest designations of Christian ministers: they
37 were to be "shepherds". The disciples, moreover, were to be like **labourers** when **the crop is heavy**; and the church must pray that God would liberally increase the number of men called to this urgent task—or so Matthew understood the saying. But just as the 'fishers of men' metaphor (Mark 1.17) probably had a different meaning before it became a commonplace in the church, so with the harvesting metaphor. The harvest was one of the commonest biblical images for the Last Judgement; and the Greek phrase,
38 "Lord of the harvest", though it could perhaps mean simply the **owner** of a farm (as it is translated here), would naturally lead the mind to the divine Judge himself. The labourers, at this ultimate harvest, were traditionally to be the angels (as they are, for instance, in the Revelation); but the followers of Jesus were to have their place on the tribunal at this judgement, and might also have their share in the harvesting. **'Beg the owner to send labourers to harvest his crop'**, on Jesus' lips, was doubtless a command to pray for the immediate beginning of the Judgement, hastened by the efforts of his followers.

10. 1 **Then he called his twelve disciples.** We have not been told that he had twelve; but the existence of the Twelve was so taken for granted in the church that it was hardly necessary to introduce them: they were simply **his twelve disciples.** Just as there were twelve legendary tribes of Israel, so there were to be twelve leaders of the new People of God. Matthew's list is much the same as Mark's (3.16–19). But only a few of the names are known personalities. The important thing was that the group existed, and
2 consisted of **apostles** (which means men "sent out" on a particular mission) whom the church subsequently recognized as its immediate founders. It
5 followed that the **instructions** given to them were given, through them, to the church.

'Do not take the road to gentile lands'. By the time Matthew's gospel was written, Gentiles outnumbered Jews in the church, and the Christian message had penetrated deep into non-Jewish lands. This com-

mand of Jesus, recorded only by Matthew, is therefore extremely puzzling. It is true that Jesus himself did not extend his work into **gentile lands**, but quite apart from the specific command which, after his resurrection, he gave to 'make all nations my disciples' (Matthew 28.19) there are numerous hints in his teaching that he thought of his message and his mission as something far wider than a religious movement within Judaism. Why then is he here reported as limiting the scope of the mission to **the house of Israel** (by which Matthew, like other Jewish writers, means the Jewish population of Palestine)? Only two solutions seem possible, and neither is entirely satisfactory. Either the command was (or was subsequently understood to have been) a temporary limitation, which was removed after the resurrection; or else perhaps the church Matthew knew was one engaged in a difficult mission to the Jewish people, tempted to abandon the task and join the more successful mission to the Gentiles, but needing to be recalled to its first duty by the recollection of some stern words that Jesus had once
uttered: **'Go rather to the lost sheep of the house of Israel'.** 6
'As you go proclaim the message'. The task of the missionaries was 7
to continue the preaching and healing work of Jesus. Sufficient examples of this work are given in the course of the gospel, and little space is devoted to it here. Instead, the discourse is concerned with the way these missionaries
are to live. **You received without cost; give without charge.** Some of 8
the powers which the disciples were to exercise—such as healing and exorcizing—were possessed by others in the ancient world, who accepted payment and hoped to make a living by their exceptional gifts. But Christian missionaries were to use their powers as freely as they had received them.
Their bearing, it seems, must be one of complete poverty—**no pack for the** 10
road, either for provisions or for accepting alms (see on Mark 6.8); not even shoes and stick (which are allowed in Mark, but forbidden in Matthew), either as a sign of more extreme asceticism, or else because coat, stick and begging-pouch (**pack**) was the uniform of the many wandering philosophers who accepted a beggar's reward in return for their wisdom. How then were they to live? **The worker earns his keep.** However Jesus originally meant this proverb, the early church soon made a clear principle out of it. As in other religious societies, the travelling preacher was to be given hospitality in believers' houses, bringing with him only the customary greeting of peace
(though this was not a mere formality: it could be revoked if necessary!). 12
The readiness to hear and receive was a test of ultimate salvation: if a house
or a town failed to pass it, the traveller, by "shaking the dust off his feet", 14
would demonstrate that it would have no part in the kingdom—just as a Jew, entering Palestine, would shake off the dust of gentile countries which could not share the sacred destiny of the Holy Land. Its punishment, said Jesus, would be worse even than that of the proverbially sinful cities, Sodom and Gomorrah. Doubtless Jesus was thinking of the serious condemnation

brought upon themselves by those who gave no hearing to the first preaching of the gospel; but possibly the church, when it remembered these words, was thinking of the experience of its own members in inhospitable Jewish towns.

However this may be, the sayings which follow plainly reveal a perspective different from that of twelve men sent out on a brief preaching tour. Matthew, in fact, has drawn into this discourse a number of sayings which Mark and Luke place considerably later in the narrative. In those gospels, the sayings are prophecies of the sufferings which Christians will have to endure, and describe some of the traditional tribulations (such as strife within families) which will presage the approaching end. In Matthew, they refer equally clearly to the period, not of Jesus' lifetime (when there is no evidence and little probability that the disciples suffered persecution) but of the church; and they are grouped here for convenience, even though they hardly fit the
16 context. Apart from the opening warning ('**be wary as serpents, innocent
as doves**'), which sounds like an old proverb, the next few verses all occur
23 in Mark 13. But Matthew adds a startling new saying at verse 23: '**before
you have gone through all the towns of Israel the Son of Man will have come**'. The "coming" of the Son of Man is a phrase which usually seems to stand for the moment when world history will come to an end, the Last Judgement begin, and the righteous be finally vindicated; and the saying looks at first sight like a prophecy of Jesus which was soon proved false. Yet Matthew, half a century later, deliberately included this saying in his "manual for the church". Was he writing for a community of Christians engaged in the difficult task of preaching in Jewish cities, and encouraging them to persevere, despite discouragement and persecution, on the grounds that there were still plenty of towns for them to work through before the end? Or did he understand the figure of the Son of Man in a more sophisticated way, as he in whom the righteous were represented and, in a sense, already vindicated? If so, in so far as Christianity had already been widely accepted, it could be said that the Son of Man had "come". As in other passages, we must beware of imagining that Jesus, when he used the language in which his contemporaries speculated about the future, was indulging in predictions as naïve as theirs. [a]

24 '**A pupil does not rank above his teacher.**' There is a similar proverb
in the sermon in Luke (6.40). Here it is applied to persecution of the dis-
25 ciples, who can have nothing worse to endure than their master did. (On
26 Beelzebub, see below on Mark 3.22.) '**There is nothing covered up that**

[a] This verse was the basis of Albert Schweitzer's famous view that Jesus expected the end to take place before the disciples returned from their journey. This view is not widely accepted today, mainly because it appears that the discourse as a whole is an artificial composition by Matthew, and that the sayings it contains were not necessarily spoken on the historical occasion of the disciples' departure for their mission. See below on Jesus' similar prophecy in Mark 9.1.

will not be uncovered'—another proverb, usually somewhat pessimistic:
acts which one is ashamed of and hopes to leave concealed, will be known, if
not in one's lifetime, certainly at the Judgement. But perhaps there is a
larger thought here (as probably also in Mark 4.22): the gospel, in its
beginnings, was essentially a mystery, something **covered up** and **hidden,**
known only to a few. But Christians need not be discouraged: one day there
would be "revelation", a full manifestation to the whole world, and in the
strength of this promise they should meanwhile **shout from the house-tops.** 27
The worst that could happen to them would be physical death; while to fail
in their mission would expose them to the judgement of God, who alone
is able to destroy both soul and body in hell. God's concern for them 28
was as certain as for the sparrows that are sold as poor men's food in the
market—so long as they were faithful. But **whoever disowns** Jesus **before** 33
men loses the right to call God his Father: Jesus will no longer admit him
as a brother, and therefore God will no longer be his Father.

'You must not think that I have come to bring peace to the earth'— 34
and yet, 'how blest are the peacemakers' (5.9)! The solution of the paradox
probably lies, again, in the fact that this saying originally belonged in the
context of Jesus' predictions about the time immediately before the end.
One of the terrors of that time (it was traditionally believed) would be inter-
necine fighting and the reversal of family loyalties (see below on Mark 13.12).
Jesus, by precipitating this climactic period of history, would be bringing not
peace **but a sword**—and the early church, seeing families divided by the
new faith (for Jewish communities were evidently as intolerant of conversions
to Christianity in the first century as they were subsequently), saw here a
clear sign of the approaching end.

In view of this, loyalty to Jesus must take precedence over all other
loyalties—Luke expresses this even more strongly (14.26)—and the sayings 37-9
which follow take on their full meaning in the light of the subsequent
experience of the church (see below on Mark 8.34-6). In verses 40-2 one
can even overhear something of the church's structure and nomenclature.
Travelling "prophets" were frequent visitors to each local church and (so 41
long as they were genuine) it was the Christian's duty to give them hospitality. **A good man** seems, for a time at least, to have been a name used by
Christians for Christians; and **one of these little ones** was a familiar way 42
of referring to the poor and the gentle, the "little flock" out of which the
church was characteristically composed (see below on Mark 9.42). In short,
the theme of this short paragraph is the same as that which is worked out
on a grand scale in the parable at the end of chapter 25: 'anything you did
for one of my brothers here, however humble, you did for me'.

John, who was in prison. The circumstances of John the Baptist's **11.** 2
imprisonment are related below, 14.3-12. We learn here for the first time

that he had a following of **disciples**: he evidently had a great deal of teaching to give on moral questions (we can glean scraps of this from the various New Testament references to him), but his main importance, at least in Christian eyes, lay in his rôle as precursor. His message was centred upon one who was to come after him, whom he thought of as a Man of Fire, bringing universal judgement; or as the Elijah who (according to Jewish mythology) was to return in supernatural form shortly before the end of the world; or perhaps even as the Messiah who was to inaugurate a New Age. Now Matthew's account of the first meeting between John and Jesus makes it appear that John recognized in Jesus at least some marks of the Person whom he had been announcing. But since then, Jesus' activity, though clearly something out of the ordinary, scarcely measured up to the sensational programme outlined by John. To this extent his question is under-
3 standable: **'Are you the one who is to come?'**

Jesus' answer (as so often when he was questioned about his true nature) was somewhat ambiguous. There were prophecies in the Old Testament (see especially Isaiah 35. 5–6; 61.1) which foretold a time when physical infirmaties would be cured and social evils righted; and the usual interpretation of these passages was that this golden age would begin with the coming of the Messiah. Jesus' miracles had already fulfilled the spirit of these prophecies. This meant, at the very least, that a new age was dawning. But how far Jesus himself corresponded to the popular image of the inaugurator of that new age was another matter: John must draw his own conclusions. In particular, Jesus was certainly not the man of unlimited power whom the populace expected. His activity raised questions rather than compelled allegiance. Men had to make up their minds for or against him, and might find him
6 challenging too many of their presuppositions. Hence—'**happy is the man who does not find me a stumbling-block**'.

7 **Jesus began to speak to the people about John.** There were many different versions current of the programme which popular Jewish speculation envisaged for the end of history and the dawning of the promised new age. They tended to revolve around some supernatural Person, be it an Elijah *redivivus* or a Messiah. But they did not normally make room for two such figures: and therefore, given the fact that Jesus was such a person, it was something of a problem (doubtless for subsequent generations of Christians as much as for the contemporaries of these events) to fit in John the Baptist as well. Jesus sharpened this question for his hearers. When they went out **to the wilderness**, what had they expected to find? Not, obviously, something as ordinary as **a reed-bed swept by the wind** (which may or may not be metaphorical: either an actual reed-bed—or reed, as the Greek can also mean—or a man as feeble as a reed); nor yet something as crudely supernatural as a splendidly dressed figure in the depths of the desert. A desert preacher was likely to be one thing only: **a prophet**. But

this prophet was unique, in that he was a **herald**—the prophecy which
fitted him (Malachi 3.1) is given here exactly as at the opening of Mark's 10
gospel. The new state of affairs which he heralded was being even now
brought about by Jesus; and if you could accept that, then you could accept
that John was after all the great herald of popular expectation, **the destined** 14
Elijah, the last figure in the old era of the Law and the prophets. But to
recognize this, you had to be able to recognize what was unique in Jesus,
and this insight was not given to everyone, just as not everyone could grasp
Jesus' parables. And so here (as several times in connection with parables):
'If you have ears, then hear'. 15

Two very difficult sayings are worked into this section. (i) John was of
quite exceptional importance and greatness; **'yet the least in the kingdom** 11
of Heaven is greater than he.' Why? Perhaps because all human priorities
in the kingdom are turned upside down, so that, by definition, the least
become the greatest, the first last. Or else perhaps because John the Baptist
only announced the kingdom and came too soon actually to belong to it. It
is true that Jesus nowhere else suggests that you have to belong to a particular
time or place to enter it. But there are a number of his sayings which do
imply that the appearance of Jesus had opened an entirely new chapter in
world history, and that the least of his disciples enjoyed a privilege which
had been denied to the greatest of the figures of the past (see below, 13.17).
(ii) **'Ever since the coming of John the Baptist the kingdom of Heaven** 12
has been subjected to violence and violent men are seizing it.' The
Greek is capable of more than one meaning (see the footnote in NEB), and
the sentence itself appears to be a riddle to which we no longer have the key.
The arrival of John the Baptist was a turning-point, so much is clear; but
why this should have given their chance to men of violence (who might be
over-enthusiastic adherents of Jesus, like zealots, or else ruthless opponents)
remains mysterious.

'How can I describe this generation?' The little parable that follows 16
presupposes two groups of children playing a game of marriages and funerals.
One group makes the appropriate music, the other goes through the appropriate actions. Both John and Jesus, in their different ways, had sounded a
call to repentance; but their hearers, like sulky children, had answered,
"You are not playing it right". **'Yet God's wisdom is proved right by its** 19
results.' The Greek has simply "wisdom"; but it would seem a trite proverb
if it meant merely "it pays to be clever", and quite irrelevant to what has
preceded. "Wisdom", in the sense of philosophy, was not much prized
among the Hebrews. For them, "wisdom" usually meant God's wisdom—
the divine plan which underlies the universe and which is reflected in the
righteous deeds of men. John and Jesus were conspicuous agents of that
divine plan. Their conduct might seem wrong to some, but the **results** of
their work would prove them to be right. (Luke 7.35 has a slightly different

version of this saying, which in any case is obscure, and may not have been understood even by the time the gospels were written.)

20 **Then he spoke of the towns in which most of his miracles had been**
21 **performed. Chorazin** lies a few miles inland from Capernaum. It was a smaller and less pretentious town (to judge from the surviving remains), and this is the only indication in the gospels that Jesus worked there. A miracle at **Bethsaida** is recorded in Mark 8.22–6. Jesus here gives high importance to his miracles: the sight of them should have moved people to repentance. According to the gospels, the impression they create is normally favourable, in that people come for more and praise God for what they have seen; but we also hear of frank opposition and scepticism on the part of certain individuals, and in fact (in view of this saying of Jesus) the reaction of most people may have been a good deal less positive than the gospel
21–4 writers suggest. Jesus uses the tones of an Old Testament prophet: Amos (1.9–10), Isaiah (23), Ezekiel (26–28) and Zechariah (9.2–4) had all made of **Tyre and Sidon** a classic example of cities which deserved the imminent wrath of God; Isaiah (14.13–15) had said of Babylon that, even if it thought
23 of itself as **exalted to the skies**, it would soon be **brought down to the depths**; and **Sodom**, since the book of Genesis, was the sinful city *par excellence*. But even these cities were excusable compared with the impenitent witnesses of Jesus' miracles.

25 **At that time Jesus spoke these words.** Verses 25–30 have a solemn ring. Whether or not the sayings they contain originally belonged together, they are cast in a form which was quite frequently used by great teachers in antiquity. The last chapter of Ecclesiasticus (a book that was written about two centuries before the time of Christ) is composed on much the same pattern (thanksgiving for benefits received, verses 1–12; claim to special knowledge, 13–22; invitation to others, 23–30) and contains many phrases which are startlingly similar to the words of Jesus. Similarly, the Stoic philosopher Epictetus, not many years after Jesus' death, appealed to others to follow his manner of life in a sentence of exactly the same structure as
28 **'Come to me . . . and I will give you relief.'** Therefore if Jesus, at some stage, made a general appeal to the public to come to him for instruction, this was a natural way for him to do it (or for an early editor of his sayings to picture him doing it); and the understandable modern reaction, that such an encomium would have come better from a follower of Jesus than from Jesus himself, probably fails to take account of the literary conventions of the time.

25 **'I thank thee, Father'.** Since the nineteenth century this saying has been called "a meteor from the Johannine sky". Certainly Jesus' intimacy with God, as that of a son with his father, is a leading theme of the fourth gospel, and these words of Jesus, which come as something of a surprise here,

would hardly be noticed in John. Nevertheless the ideas they express belong to Matthew's gospel as much as to any other. The contrast between the misguided learning of the Pharisees and the truer insight of the least of Jesus' followers underlies many episodes in the gospel, and the claim that Jesus was to God as son to father, and that his followers, through their solidarity with him, come to share his sonship and thereby to address God as Father, runs through much of the Sermon on the Mount, and is a presupposition of the Lord's Prayer. Terms such as "knowing", "hiding" and "revealing" suggest at first sight the kind of religion in which the mystical "knowledge" of God is the main object, to be obtained by initiation into successive degrees of intellectual illumination. Almost from the beginning, there were tendencies to assimilate Christianity to this kind of mysticism (see below on Colossians, p. 646); and these verses have often been regarded as evidence for similar influences. But the terminology also has its home in Jewish thought. To the Jew, God was not "known" to the man who searched unaided for religious truth: God "chose" to reveal himself to his people, whom he "knew", in the sense that he had chosen and identified them. In return, his people "knew" God, in the sense that they gave him their allegiance, and were the recipients of his self-revelation. The same deliberate self-revelation was still in progress: but the vehicle of this revelation was now Jesus, and its recipients no longer the historical people of the Jews but those who were "chosen" by Jesus to share in the privilege of Sonship, and to enter into the son's intimate "knowledge" of the Father.

'**Come to me, all whose work is hard, whose load is heavy.**' Any 28
religious leader lays a "yoke" on his followers, just as any king lays a yoke on his subjects. Men's allegiance can only be expressed in acts of submission and obedience. Moreover, to encourage that allegiance, any ruler or teacher will certainly promise "relief" to those who are under the yoke, and the extent to which that relief seems worth having will depend, in part, on the severity of the previous régime. Now it was a common figure of speech that the Law of Moses by which the Jews were obliged to live, despite the many blessings and privileges which it conferred, was nevertheless a "yoke" which had to be borne with discipline and patience; and one of Jesus' complaints against the Pharisees was that with all their efforts to make the Law fully applicable to present-day conditions they had only succeeded in making the yoke more oppressive. At least a part of what Jesus meant by his "yoke" must be understood in this context: even though he expected from his followers an obedience to the Law as great as that of the most exacting of his contemporaries, yet by returning to the spirit of the Law instead of the letter, by giving assurance that prayers were heard and answered, and by promising blessings both now and in the future to those whom society had traditionally victimized, he was able to say
'**My yoke is good to bear, my load is light**'. But at the same time, the 30

saying has a generality and a nobility which transcend this particular con-
29 trast. **'I am gentle and humble-hearted'**. These words do not merely describe Jesus' moral character; they define the kind of king which Jesus was—one 'who comes to you in gentleness' (21.5), one who 'humbled himself' (Philippians 2.8). His kingship was so new, his rule such a reversal of the usual structures of authority, that his yoke had nothing to do with oppression. Paul, indeed, was to call it freedom.

Controversy

The first main topic of *Controversy* in Matthew, as in Mark and Luke, is the observance of the Sabbath. The principal exponents of correct Sabbath observance were the Pharisees, and Jesus' criticism of some of the restrictions which beset what was intended to be a day of goodwill and rejoicing, and his own and his disciples' comparative freedom with regard to these restrictions, naturally became a serious issue between himself and the Pharisees. Matthew, in the next two episodes, follows much the same tradition as Mark (2.23–3.6) and Luke (6.1–11), but in each case introduces a somewhat more technical argument which shows Jesus meeting the Pharisees on their own ground.
In the first, after referring his opponents (as in Mark) to the difficult but
12. 3–4 indecisive case of David, Jesus adds (using a technical formula of scholarly
5 discussion, **have you not read in the Law**) a logically more powerful
argument. It was agreed that the necessities of the temple service made it
necessary for the priests to break a Sabbath regulation—for instance, they
still had to reap a sheaf for the ritual on the second day of Passover, even
6 if this happened to be a Sabbath. *A fortiori*, if **there is something greater
than the temple here** it will provide exemption for other kinds of "reap-
7 ing". An appeal to the general principle expressed in Hosea 6.6, that mercy
(which includes charitableness) is superior to ritual observances, rounds off
the argument. The validity of this reasoning depends of course ultimately
on the authority which Jesus claims for himself. So here (as in Mark and
8 Luke): **'For the Son of Man is sovereign over the Sabbath'**.

9–14 In the second episode the challenge to Jesus is answered, in Mark and
Luke, by a simple counter-challenge: 'Is it permitted to do good or to do
evil on the Sabbath?' Here, Jesus' reply takes the form of another argument
a fortiori. It was admitted that it was permissible to rescue a sheep on the
12 Sabbath. How much more then **to do good** to a man!

15–21 The following paragraph appears to offer an explanation of certain rather puzzling statements which are found in Mark. Mark records that, while Jesus was performing cures, the unclean spirits by which some of the sufferers were possessed shouted out who he was, and Jesus 'insisted that

they should not make him known' (3.11–12). Matthew uses exactly the same
language (**he gave strict injunctions** renders the same Greek word as 16
'he insisted' in Mark) but omits all reference to the spirits. What in Mark
takes the form of a dialogue with supernatural powers appears in Matthew
as a simple command given to the crowds. Nevertheless, the question still
remains as puzzling in Matthew's version as it does in Mark's: why did
Jesus insist on this secrecy? Matthew seems to hint, by his introductory
words (**Jesus was aware of it and withdrew**) that Jesus' motive was 15
simply prudence: he wished, for the time being, to avoid further controversy
with the Pharisees. But he also has a more profound explanation to offer.
One of the Old Testament passages which seemed to Matthew (and doubtless to the early church) both to foretell Jesus' coming and to explain his
destiny was the opening of Isaiah 42—the prophecy of a "servant" who
would establish justice in the world. An allusion to this prophecy seems to
underlie the words heard at Jesus' baptism (3.17 above); here Matthew 18–21
quotes it in full. His version does not exactly follow either the Hebrew text
or the Greek version of the Septuagint, but is a curious combination of the
two, suggesting that the verses had already been much pondered in the
church and had been slightly modified in the process. But the point which
was important for Matthew here was the silence and modesty of this servant:
He will not strive, he will not shout, nor will his voice be heard in the 19
streets. It was in conformity with this prototype, Matthew suggests, that
Jesus maintained his mysterious secrecy.

The following episode is told by Matthew and Luke in a form somewhat
different from that which it has in Mark (3.22–30). It begins with a brief
account of an exorcism, which aroused in the bystanders a reaction of considerable expectancy: **the word went round: 'Can this be the Son of** 23
David?' It was widely believed among the Jews that God would at any
moment bring into being the New Age by means of a divinely appointed
Person (a Messiah), who would be the true successor of King David, and
who was therefore often called (not because of his genealogy, but because
of his destiny) **the Son of David**. This Person, it was said, existed already,
but his identity would remain unknown until the time for his appearing
should come. When that moment came, he would manifest himself with
signs and wonders. Jesus' miracles naturally gave rise to the question,
'Can this be the Son of David?'

The Pharisees were ready with an alternative explanation: **'It is only by** 24
Beelzebub prince of devils that this man drives the devils out'. Jesus
shows this to be sophistry. His argument is here very close to that in Mark's
account (3.22–6) but has an additional point of some interest. It shows that 27
there were exorcists about whom the Pharisees approved of; therefore the
argument used against Jesus would apply equally to them. No, the Pharisees

were wrong, and the people (in a sense) were right. Jesus' exorcisms were a
28 sign of the new age: '**the kingdom of God has already come upon you.**'
29 The comparison with the **strong man's house** is almost exactly as in
30 Mark (3.27); the saying in verse 30 is a proverb, expressing the challenge
presented by Jesus' teaching (Jesus appears to say the opposite in Mark 9.40,
but the inconsistency is probably only apparent: see below on that passage).
The saying about the slander against the Spirit is as difficult here as it is in
Mark (3.28–30), even though Matthew, like Luke, has the additional words,
32 '**any man who speaks a word against the Son of Man will be forgiven.**'
It is possible that the experience of the early church has influenced this
formulation. It was one thing, out of ignorance or perversity, to misunderstand the church's teaching about the nature of Jesus Christ (i.e. "to speak against the Son of Man"). But if, confronted by the manifest activity of the Spirit in the church, men still reviled and persecuted, then there seemed no further hope for them **either in this age or in the age to come** (as Matthew puts it, borrowing a standard Jewish idiom).

33 '**Either make the tree good and its fruit good.**' This is essentially the
same saying as in the Sermon on the Mount (7.16–20). There it was applied
to the problem of discriminating between true and false prophets; here it is
part of an attack on the hypocrisy of the Pharisees, whom Jesus (in Matthew)
34 treats with great asperity ('**vipers' brood**'). Their words cannot be (as they
claim) "good" when their actions are evil—and the theme of "words"
seems to explain the addition of another completely general saying. That a
36 **thoughtless word** will have consequences on the day of Judgement
is a conclusion reached by any thinker who takes God's judgement seriously; but Jesus' contemporaries would not normally have expressed the matter so uncompromisingly.

38 '**Master, we should like you to show us a sign**'. This request occurs
in Mark (8.11), and is there refused without any reason being given. Here
39 the refusal is expanded by a reference to **Jonah**. The book of Jonah was one
of the most popular of the Old Testament. It contained a message both of hope and of warning. All the other Old Testament prophets had met resistance, unbelief, even outright rejection; but Jonah had preached and (much to his discomfiture!) the whole city of Nineveh had attended to him and repented. This was the hopeful side of the message: repentance was always possible, and God would reward the penitent as he had rewarded Nineveh. But Nineveh was a gentile city! This was the note of warning: was there anything in Jewish history to compare with Nineveh's repentance?
41 And the warning is taken up by Jesus here: '**when this generation is on
trial, the men of Nineveh will appear against it**'—a moral that could
42 also be drawn from that other great Old Testament story of the visit of the
Queen of Sheba to Solomon (1 Kings 10). But Matthew (unlike Luke) has worked in another motif from the legend of Jonah. The decisive "sign"

which Jesus ultimately did give to "that generation" was the resurrection,
and the church (whether or not there was originally a saying of Jesus on
these lines) very soon came to see Jonah's legendary sojourn in **the sea-** 40
monster's belly as a prefigurement of Jesus' brief period of physical death.

When an unclean spirit comes out of a man. Given the naïvely realistic 43
language of an age which believed implicitly in spirit-possession, this was, and remains, a valid description of what we would now call a psychological danger, that of removing an obsession without putting anything positive in its place. So Luke (11.24–6) understands it; but Matthew records it as a parable, and it is hard to be sure what it was supposed to illustrate. Perhaps the idea was that "that generation", after an imperfect repentance provoked by Jesus' teaching, would soon be exposed to the dangers of still worse religious and political leaders than they had before.

The scene which closes the section is given almost exactly as in Mark 46–50
(3.31–5).

Matthew now devotes a further chapter to the teaching of Jesus; but this
time it is teaching of a new kind. So far, it has taken the form of rules and
precepts for the conduct of life. But it was well known that Jesus also **spoke** 13. 3
to them in parables, and Matthew (who follows very closely the account given in the corresponding chapter of Mark) now presents a collection of these parables, and at the same time casts Jesus in a new rôle: that of an inspired teacher of divine mysteries.

The collection begins with a parable of sowing, told almost exactly as in Mark. Just as, however good the harvest, there will always be some wastage, so, despite the apparent success of Jesus' work, there would always be some who opposed it and so excluded themselves from the kingdom. But if this was how the parable was intended by Jesus to be understood (see below on Mark 4.1–10), it was not for this reason that Matthew set it down here. Matthew, in common with Mark, possessed another and much more recondite interpretation; and this led him to see Jesus' parables, not as illustrations intended to make his meaning clearer (which was the most common sense of the Greek word), but as cryptic sayings fully intelligible only to the initiated (which was one of the meanings of the Hebrew word corresponding to "parable"). There was good precedent for an inspired thinker clothing his teaching in mysterious imagery. From time to time visionaries appeared among the Jews who believed that they had been vouchsafed glimpses of the destiny which God had in store for the world, and it was to be expected that they would express the content of their visions in cryptic form; for they were, in effect, divulging "mysteries" or secrets, the full manifestation of which was reserved for the future. Meanwhile, it was only to themselves, and to the privileged few who had the knowledge and understanding to grasp the meaning of their cryptic discourses, that these things were

revealed. An example of this kind of writing is the Revelation of John; another is the long series of Jewish "apocalypses" which begins with the Book of Daniel and runs on at least to the end of the first century A.D. Jesus himself was remembered to have conformed to this tradition when he gave some teaching on the "last things" (see below on Matthew 24 and Mark 13); and in Matthew the parables are regarded as part of the same kind of teaching. In the centre of the picture stand the disciples, a privileged group to
11 whom it has been granted **to know the secrets of the kingdom of**
17 **Heaven.** Even the **prophets and saints** of the Old Testament, for all their remarkable insight and vision, did not reach that point of initiation into the purposes of God which the disciples have already reached—and they will go further still: Matthew applies to them a saying of Jesus which
12 stands isolated in Mark (4.25), **'the man who has will be given more'.** The disciples, unlike the people of Israel of old, have been given "eyes to see and ears to hear" (Deuteronomy 29.4), and this makes of them a uniquely privileged class, in sharp contrast to the bemused crowds who are straining to catch the import of Jesus' teaching from the shores of the lake. But what then of these crowds? Why is their fate so different from that of
10 the privileged few? This is the sense of the disciples' question, **'Why do you speak to them in parables?'** (which, in Mark, appears as a question about the nature of the parables themselves). And the answer is that here, once
14–15 again, is a fulfilment of prophecy. Matthew quotes (at far greater length than Mark or Luke) from Isaiah 6.9–10, and his quotation follows word for word the Septuagint version of the Greek Bible, which gives a somewhat different sense from the Hebrew. Jesus is not likely to have used a Greek version, but it does not follow from this that he did not on occasion make use of the same passage in Hebrew (see below on Mark 4.11–13)—only that Matthew has been at work editing his material. The word in the passage which has
14 caught Matthew's imagination is **understand.** It is not opposition, or indifference, or perversity, which has kept the crowds from salvation, but a lack of **understanding**; and Matthew has subtly altered the interpretation of the parable (an interpretation which, for various reasons, is unlikely to go back to Jesus himself: see below on Mark 4.14–20) in order to make the
23 point that the reward belongs to the man who hears the word **and understands it.**

24–30 The second parable also describes the ordinary cultivation of the fields but, unlike the first, contains something of a story. The farming described is again perfectly normal. It was to be expected in any cornfield that there
25 would be weeds, and one of the most troublesome was that species of **darnel** which, in its early stages, is almost indistinguishable from the young blade
26 of corn. Nothing could be done about it, therefore, until the corn **sprouted and began to fill out**: by then (in fact, somewhat before then) it would be easy enough to distinguish the darnel. There were then two possible courses

of action, both of which were quite common practice, but each of which had
disadvantages. Either the darnel could be pulled out when the corn was still
green—but it had strong roots, and there was a danger of pulling up the
corn at the same time; or else it could be left **till harvest**—but then it had 30
either to be carefully separated out in the reaping (which was done, not by
the farmer's own labourers alone, but by a force of specially hired men), or
else sieved out in the threshing; for the seeds of darnel are poisonous. In the
parable, the farmer is made to choose the second course; and if the parable
originally existed (like the parable of sowing) in the form of a straightforward description of familiar farming methods, with the emphasis on the
words, **let them both grow together**, then we can guess at the point Jesus
was making. Do not judge before the time, do not try to weed out your
ranks and form a sect of "holy men". There will be time enough for this
at the Last Judgement (for which "harvest" was a familiar symbol).

But, in the present form of the parable, a familiar scene is turned into an
anecdote by the addition of a curious feature. The presence of weeds in the field
would not normally surprise anyone; it was the commonest of the farmer's
difficulties. But here a different explanation is given: "**This is an enemy's** 28
doing". This is not necessarily improbable in itself. Stories are told of village
feuds being carried on in this way. On the other hand it does not add anything
to the point of the parable, which appears to lie in the wheat and the darnel
both "growing together" till harvest. The detail of the **enemy** becomes significant only if the parable is in reality something quite different, that is, a
cryptic discourse in which each term stands for something else. As has just been
said, the "harvest" is a conventional image of the Last Judgement. The description of the harvesting in verse 30 is difficult to visualize in terms of wheat and
darnel, but is apt enough if the real material being harvested is a cross-section of
good and bad human beings; and in this case, the **enemy** is a necessary
character, since it is the devil who prompts the evil deeds committed by men.

In this form (which may or may not be the form in which Jesus originally
spoke it) the parable fits appropriately into its context in Matthew's gospel.
The story, like the previous one, is deliberately mysterious, and only the
privileged few have the key to its meaning. Moreover, since its theme is the
Last Judgement, it falls naturally into place in the teaching of one who had
a special vision of the future to impart to his chosen disciples. As in the case
of the previous parable, Matthew has an esoteric interpretation to offer. The 36–43
interpretation, again, has a number of features more characteristic of
Matthew's editing than of Jesus' own idiom, and uses terms which are
conventional elements in Jewish descriptions of the Last Judgement. There
are thus serious reasons for doubting whether it can go back to Jesus himself.

No clue is given for interpreting the next two parables. If they were 31–3
intended to receive the same kind of esoteric interpretation, then each
element in them would presumably have to be a cryptogram for something

else; and given one correspondence (the kingdom of Heaven is like a mustard-seed, or like yeast) one would have to ask what, for instance, the man who sowed, or the woman who baked, stand for. But it is unlikely that Jesus meant them to be taken in this sense. The phrase, '**the kingdom of Heaven is like . . .**', does not necessarily (or at least did not, in the language that Jesus spoke) mean that the kingdom corresponded to just one person or thing in the parable, but that it was illustrated by the parable as a whole (thus the same Greek phrase is translated in 13.24 'The kingdom of Heaven is like this', and in 13.45 as 'Here is another picture of the kingdom of Heaven'). The point of comparison in each case seems to be simply the contrast: the tiny seed and the huge full-grown plant, or the small amount of yeast with which a baker can leaven a whole day's baking.

34 **In all this teaching to the crowds Jesus spoke in parables; in fact**
he never spoke to them without a parable. The word **never** has been
inserted by the translators and needs qualifying. Matthew, of course, does
not mean that Jesus never spoke to the crowds at all without a parable—after
the Sermon on the Mount this would be nonsense. But in his rôle as a
revealer of the secrets of providence, his speech to the crowds (Matthew
wishes us to understand) was always cryptic, and only his disciples were
given the key to his meaning. Matthew again finds a scriptural model for this.
35 The passage he quotes is Psalm 78.2, with a slight modification of the
second line: **things kept secret since the world was made** is a phrase
which describes the kind of revelation being given by Jesus better than the
literal text in either the Greek version or the Hebrew. Although it is from a
psalm, it could legitimately be regarded as a **prophecy**: Jesus himself
found things in the psalms which were prophetic in the sense that they were
still awaiting fulfilment. But why some manuscripts of Matthew's gospel
give **Isaiah** it is impossible to say. It is conceivable that Matthew took the
text from an anthology of quotations in which it stood next to a passage of
Isaiah; otherwise it must be simply a mistake.

44–6 The next pair of parables obviously belong together, and presumably
make the same point: the total personal commitment demanded by the kingdom of Heaven. To buy a field, the man in the first parable had to sell everything he had: he was therefore a poor man, doubtless working in the field
as a hired labourer. Having found the treasure, he was not necessarily
obliged to report it, but he could not expect to be allowed to acquire it
45 unmolested until he became the owner of the field. The **merchant** of the
second parable would have been a far more prosperous person. He is to be
imagined passing through Galilee on his way from the pearl-fishing seas of
the east. On his last journey he was able to acquire an exceptional pearl, for
which he willingly surrendered his entire stock, knowing that it would make
his fortune when he brought it to the dealers in the big cities.

47 The last parable is drawn from one of the commonest scenes on the lake

(here called the **sea**, which was the way the local inhabitants referred to the 47
Lake of Tiberias). The point about the drag-net is that it catches **fish of every kind**, which are only sorted out afterwards—and this presumably (as in the case of the wheat and the darnel) was the original point of the parable. Do not try to sort out the good from the bad in this life by forming a little sect of specially pious men and despising all who will not join you: all the sorting necessary will be done by God at the Last Judgement. The interpretation added by Matthew does not conflict with this, but it shifts the emphasis from the present to the future, and treats the parable primarily as a cryptic description of the Last Judgement. This is consonant with Matthew's picture of Jesus in his rôle of an expounder of the secrets of the future to a privileged few, but may, once again, represent a later understanding of the parables themselves.

Mark's parable chapter ends with a summary of the way in which Jesus addressed the crowds (4.33–4). Matthew slightly alters this by focusing attention on the disciples, who alone have the privilege of "understanding".
The ordinary Jewish **teacher** of the law, in the course of his training, built up 52
an immense store of **the old**—that is, of knowledge of the scriptures themselves and of the traditional interpretations of them that were handed down and elaborated by generations of scholars. But the training of Jesus' disciples, as sketched in this chapter, gave them something altogether **new** to offer as well.

Matthew's account of Jesus' visit to Nazareth follows Mark closely (6.1–6), and only two slight changes have significance: Jesus is called, not the carpenter,
but **the carpenter's son**—perhaps Christians hesitated to acknowledge that 55
Jesus had actually been a tradesman; and Mark's 'he could work no miracle
there' is altered to **he did not work many miracles there.** Matthew was 58
not prepared to concede that Jesus was less than omnipotent.

Prince Herod. Mark calls him 'king', which is doubtless what he was **14.** 1
popularly called; but Matthew, more precisely, gives him his official title of *tetrarch*, or **Prince.** The tetrarchy of Herod Antipas included the whole of Galilee, and this was the ruler with whom Jesus had to reckon until he travelled up to Jerusalem. Herod's attitude to religious movements of the kind started by John the Baptist and Jesus was clearly an important factor in the story. It is for this reason that Matthew, who has already alluded to John's arrest in 4.12, now introduces the full story (the context in Mark is more contrived). Herod is made to see in Jesus a visitation of his guilty conscience about John the Baptist, and this gives the cue for the story of John's 3–12
execution, told exactly as in Mark (6.14–29), with the omission of a few details.

The news of this execution also sets in motion the sequence of events which 13–27
follows (the context in Mark is again slightly different). The narrative closely follows that in Mark (6.45–56), leaving out a few details, and showing

21 only a slight tendency to enhance the miracles (**to say nothing of women**
24 **and children . . . some furlongs from the shore**) and to present the
28–33 disciples in a better light. Peter's venture upon the water, however, is told only by Matthew. It is a vivid illustration of a theme Matthew is fond of: the importance of faith in a disciple. It is also a perfect illustration of the impulsiveness of Peter's character and his failures at moments of crisis—traits which had serious consequences during the trial of Jesus.

The next episode justifies the title under which this section stands,
15. 1 *Controversy*. A critical question from some **Pharisees and lawyers from**
Jerusalem provokes Jesus into a violent counter-attack, which the Pharisees
12 have no difficulty in recognizing as a deliberate challenge to their principles. When Mark comes to this incident (7.1), he elucidates it for non-Jewish readers by adding an explanation of the Jewish customs alluded to. Matthew omits these notes. Presumably his readers would have known
2 at once that the Pharisees' comment, '**They do not wash their hands before meals**', touched a question, not of hygiene, but of ritual purity. Precisely what the **ancient tradition** was which Jesus was attacking, and what the target was of Jesus' counter-attack on the Corban-oath (the technical word is omitted by Matthew, but the argument is the same as in Mark), are questions of some difficulty (see below on Mark 7.1–13); but the
6, 9 underlying tendency of Pharisaic tradition to overlay **God's law** with **the commandments of men** is neatly summed up in the quotation from
8–9 Isaiah 29.13 (which Matthew, like Mark, quotes according to the Greek version), and is here, as elsewhere, made the object of Jesus' criticism. No
12 wonder the Pharisees took **great offence**! But Jesus, in the presence of his disciples, went further still. The religious leaders of the Jews prided themselves on being 'guides to the blind' (Romans 2.19). Jesus casts this back
14 in their teeth by calling them **blind guides** themselves, and denies that they have any part in the ordained process of God's self-revelation.

10–11 Woven into this controversy is a saying which appears in Mark (7.15) in a completely general form: 'nothing that goes into a man from outside can defile him; no, it is the things that come out of him that defile a man'. This saying certainly sounded a little mysterious, and needed interpretation; and the interpretation added by Mark in fact made it apply to the question (much discussed in the early church, but of less apparent topical interest in the Jewish environment of Galilee) of ritually permissible foods. Matthew, by adding the words **into his mouth**, robs the original saying of its generality, and makes it into one which could have no application except to food. As a
15–20 result, it hardly needs interpretation. But Matthew, who is obviously using Mark as his model, none the less gives the same detailed explanation for the
16 benefit of the **dull** disciples, and then, with a slight twist at the end, brings
20 it round to the point from which the section started: the washing of hands.

Jesus and his disciples

It is true that the interest of the narrative soon begins to shift from Jesus and the crowds to the more intimate episodes concerning only *Jesus and his*
disciples; but there is first a section in which the disciples play little part, and 21–8
which is of some interest in view of the subsequent history of the church. The question to which the passage offers an answer is, What was Jesus' attitude to Gentiles? There can be little doubt that Matthew knew of Mark's version of this story, but he may well have felt that it left the question somewhat in the air. According to Mark (7.24–30), Jesus seemed both to endorse the usual Jewish attitude of exclusiveness towards all non-Jews, and at the same time to make an unexplained exception for the benefit of a woman who was 'a Phoenician of Syria by nationality'. Matthew endeavours to bring more logic into the story by adding a few details which may be in part his own invention, in part drawn from another source of the same story.
The woman came **from those parts**—that is (in all probability) from some 22
village at the north end of the Jordan valley, where the administration was carried out from the coastal cities of Tyre (and perhaps even Sidon), but the population was still mainly Jewish. She is here called a **Canaanite**, which is a piece of antiquarianism on the part of Matthew: Canaanite is the Old Testament word for those inhabitants of Palestine, such as the Phoenicians, whom the people of Israel found already in occupation. But it serves to underline the apparent exclusiveness and scriptural correctness of Jesus'
reply, **I was sent to the lost sheep of the house of Israel, and to them** 24
alone. More clearly than the lively, and perhaps slightly humorous, dialogue which follows, this first reply leaves no doubt of Jesus' attitude towards Gentiles: his mission was not to them. But Matthew also makes clear the reason (which Mark does not) why an exception was made for the Canaanite woman: she had faith. As in the case of the Roman centurion (8.5–10), so here: non-Jews, if they have faith enough, can qualify for the privileges up to now possessed by the Jews alone. Whether or not this was originally Jesus' attitude, it certainly soon became that of the early church. It governs the thought, for instance, of the first few chapters of Paul's letter to the Romans.

Matthew continues to follow closely the order of events in Mark's gospel,
but gives them a more logical sequence. What in Mark is a single miracle 29–31
(the healing of a deaf and dumb man, 7.31–7) becomes in Matthew a whole series of miracles. The effect is the same: the prophecy of Isaiah 35.5 is seen
to be fulfilled (the three words **dumb, lame** and **blind** all occur in that 30
passage), and the people, doubtless recognizing the significance of these
events, give **praise to the God of Israel**. But the episode in Matthew's 31
version, with the crowds flocking to Jesus where he was seated somewhere

29, 32–9 in **the hills**, also sets the scene neatly for the feeding-miracle which follows.
The same considerations apply to this narrative as to the version in Mark
(8.1–10); Matthew has made only slight alterations, perhaps partly to increase
32 the impression of Jesus' mastery of the situation ('**I do not want to send**
them away unfed' for Mark's 'If I send them away', the enlargement of
38, 39 the crowd by the addition of **women and children**). The **neighbourhood**
of Magadan is Matthew's alteration of Mark's 'Dalmanutha'. But from our
point of view this is no improvement: Magadan is also completely unknown.

16. 1–4 Matthew has already given a full report of the question of the "sign" (12.38–9), doubtless drawn from a source other than Mark; but here, for all that, he continues to follow Mark's order and relates it again, closely following the version in Mark (8.11–12), but avoiding Mark's reference to Jesus' emotion and adding an allusion to **the sign of Jonah** which was mentioned in the earlier conversation.

5–12 Matthew's treatment of the next episode is highly significant. He normally
presents the disciples as a privileged group of men, constantly in the company of their Teacher and, in contrast to the multitudes, in a unique position
to grasp the meaning of Jesus' teaching. This picture is rudely shattered if
we turn to the parallel passage in Mark (8.14–21); for there this episode is
the occasion for the severest criticism ever made by Jesus of the disciples'
obtuseness and lack of understanding. It is therefore not surprising to find
that Matthew gives the incident a different turn. The elements are the same:
6 the saying on **the leaven of the Pharisees and Sadducees**, and the crossing of the lake without a provision of bread. But Matthew's combination of
them is different. Instead of concentrating on the disciples' total incomprehension of the feeding miracles, Matthew shifts the emphasis on to
Jesus' admittedly somewhat enigmatic saying about leaven. It was this
which the disciples had failed to understand. Matthew even suggests that
12 they were trying to take it literally, as a warning against the **baker's leaven**.
But of course the saying, like the parables, had a deeper meaning and, by excluding (with a reference to his feeding miracles) the naïve literal meaning, Jesus led them to understand that it was a warning **against the teaching of the Pharisees and Sadducees.** Once more, the disciples are shown to be in possession of an esoteric interpretation of a saying of Jesus. Whether this was the interpretation intended by Jesus is perhaps doubtful. In Mark, the relevant phrase is 'the leaven of the Pharisees and the leaven of Herod', and can hardly mean anything but the common desire of both the religious and political authorities to do away with Jesus. In Matthew, Herod is replaced by the Sadducees. This party certainly had its own **teaching**, to which Jesus was openly opposed. But it was an aristocratic party, more political than religious, and would hardly have been interested in trying to influence men at the social level of Jesus' disciples. It is difficult to see why they should have had to be **on their guard** against the Sadducees' teaching.

The territory of Caesarea Philippi, to the extreme north of Galilee, is 13
the scene (as in Mark) of an important moment in the unfolding of the true
nature of Jesus. But this moment, in Matthew's treatment, becomes also a
means of drawing attention to one of the disciples, who has so far usually
been mentioned only along with the others, but now begins to become
prominent in the story (not always to his credit) and who was subsequently
a leading figure (if not *the* leading figure) in the early church: Simon Peter.

Who do men say that the Son of Man is? This is a strangely oblique 13
way of speaking,[a] but there can be no doubt that Jesus' question is really
about himself: the sequel makes this plain—and in any case the question is
clearly not just a theoretical one about that mythological figure who
appeared in Jewish speculation as the "Son of Man". The stage reached in
the popular estimate of Jesus was that of moderately tense expectancy: he
seemed to be bringing the promised kingdom appreciably nearer, and therefore he might well be one of those Old Testament figures who, it was
popularly believed, would return to earth as a herald of the impending new
age. Indeed, John the Baptist himself had appeared to fulfil so faithfully the
traditional rôle of an Old Testament prophet, and had at the same time
proclaimed such an urgent message, that Jesus might even be a reincarnation
of him. But Simon Peter had advanced to a further stage in understanding
who Jesus was: **'You are the Messiah, the Son of the living God'.** That 16
Jesus was in fact these things was of course taken for granted by the church
when Matthew was writing; and by relating that Peter offered and Jesus
accepted these titles, Matthew incidentally allowed his readers to feel that
the language they were accustomed to use of their Lord had been endorsed
by Jesus himself. But the significance of the narrative is mainly the light it
throws on Peter. Matthew has inserted a saying of Jesus which occurs in 17–19
no other gospel. So far, he has represented the disciples as a group of men
who are given the unique privilege of private and esoteric teaching, while
the crowds who listen to Jesus are left in doubt and bewilderment about his
real meaning. One of them, however, has now shown that he has advanced
further still, to the point where he can receive a direct revelation from God.
His recognition of the true nature of Jesus is something not to be learnt
from mortal man: it is the very highest type of knowledge imparted by 17
God alone to those who are **favoured indeed**—and it is doubtless implied
by Matthew that all those Christians who come to acknowledge the same
truth for themselves are similarly **favoured** (the word is the same as that
which is translated 'blest' at the beginning of the Sermon on the Mount).

But if Peter is up to this point the prototype of all Christians who confess
Jesus to be Christ and Son of God, the next part of the saying sets him apart
in a position by himself. **'You are Peter, the Rock.'** Matthew has already 18

[*a*] A way which puzzled some copyists, hence the alternative reading in the footnote.

said more than once that Simon was 'called Peter', and Mark states that it was Jesus who gave him the name. Unlike, for instance, the name given to two other disciples ('Boanerges'), Simon's name stuck to him, and he is known throughout the gospels indifferently as Simon or Peter (or its Aramaic equivalent, Kephas). Jesus' intention in so naming Simon is here explained for the one and only time in the New Testament: Peter (in Greek *Petros*, in Aramaic *kephas*) means "stone" or "rock"; and in true Hebrew fashion the full significance of the name is worked out, giving its bearer an apparently unique rôle to play in the subsequent history of the church.

Since it is clear from the New Testament that Peter was in fact not, or at any rate not for long, the universally acknowledged leader of the church; and since, on the other hand, it has been of primary concern to one whole section of Christendom for many centuries past to assert the absolute supremacy of Peter and of his successors over the church at large, the authenticity and meaning of this saying have become a subject of longstanding controversy. Further, the word **church** is very rare in the gospels (it occurs only here and at 18.17, where it is translated 'congregation'), and even though the concept of a community of followers may be implied in Jesus' teaching as a whole, it remains surprising to find him using the actual word **church**, and it is tempting to think that it was only after the church had come into existence that such a saying could have assumed its present form. On the other hand the building metaphor, as applied to the church, seems to have been used from very early times by Christians: it is taken for granted, for instance, by Paul. The metaphor is not unparalleled in Jewish writings; but it remains a striking one, and it is only reasonable to assume that it goes back to Jesus himself. Moreover, if Jesus gave Simon a name which means "stone" or "rock", it need not surprise us if at some moment he put the two ideas together and ascribed to this disciple an important function in the "building" which was to come. To this extent, the saying may well go back to Jesus, even if the subsequent evolution of a Christian "church" has modified the form in which we now possess it.

18 **'The powers of death shall never conquer it.'**[a] Again, it is easier to
understand the birth of this saying after the resurrection than before it;
for it was the resurrection which assured Christians that they no longer had
anything to fear from the powers of death. Yet if Jesus did in fact make
predictions about the community which was soon to arise, these predictions
19 could well have included some form of this saying. The expression, **the keys
of the kingdom of Heaven**, appears to be explained in the sentence which

[a] Literally, "The gates of hell will not prevail over it". This suggests a more concrete image: when men die, the gates of "hell" (understood in the ordinary Greek sense, not as a place of torment, but as the shadowy dwelling-place of all the dead) close irrevocably behind them. But for Christians, death is not irrevocable. The church (in a sense) can pass back and forth through the gates. This is the sense of the alternative rendering in the NEB footnote.

follows. The Greek means literally, "what you bind . . . and what you loose", and the NEB rendering, **what you forbid . . . and what you allow**, represents a possible interpretation of the words. A qualified lawyer had the authority to decide, in disputed matters, precisely what was "allowed" by the Law and precisely what was "forbidden" by it. Similarly, it could perhaps be said of Peter (and, if of him, possibly of other leaders of the church) that he would have the authority to decide what was, and what was not, permissible for Christians. This authority would doubtless imply the decision when to excommunicate a member of the church (which is another possible meaning of "bind" and "loose"); and it is not altogether easy to reconcile this responsibility of Peter's (or of any single church leader) with the more democratic procedure described in chapter 18 below. The precise interpretation of these words depends, once again, on whether it is thought credible that Jesus should have made detailed predictions about the organization of the church, and on whether it is admitted that the subsequent practice of the church may have influenced the form in which the sayings have been handed down.

The remainder of the section reproduces the corresponding passage in 24–8
Mark (8.34–8) with only a few alterations. The final saying, on the coming
of the kingdom, has been modified significantly. One of the rôles of the Son
of Man (suggested by the Son of Man passage in Daniel 7) was to assist at
the final Judgement, when each man would receive '**the due reward for** 27
what he has done.' So far, the saying merely endorses what was probably
a current Jewish belief. But the sequel, '**there are some of those standing** 28
here who will not taste death before they have seen the Son of Man coming in his kingdom', is more startling. It appears to predict (erroneously) the coming of the end of the world in the lifetime of Jesus' own generation. Matthew, unlike Mark, made the saying turn on the figure of the Son of Man, and in so doing was perhaps trying to reconcile it with the experience of the church; for there was a sense in which Christians had already seen **the Son of Man coming in his kingdom**—compare Stephen's vision in Acts 7.55–6. Nevertheless, the saying remains a puzzling one: see below on Mark 9.1.

He was transfigured. Matthew's account of the Transfiguration follows **17.** 1
closely that in Mark (9.2–8), and the details, as in Mark, frequently suggest a symbolical interpretation, even if (again as in Mark) they do not necessarily demand it. The small changes made by Matthew nevertheless indicate a slightly different understanding of the scene. Moses comes before Elijah, so that the two figures are clearer symbols of the Law and the prophets; and certain small touches, such as the radiance of Jesus' face, the brightness of the cloud, and the prostration of the disciples after (instead of before) the heavenly voice, bring the experience of Moses on Mount Sinai more vividly

to mind (Exodus 34.29–35). These details perhaps show Matthew at work, deliberately presenting Jesus as the new Moses, the definitive lawgiver. The scene is followed, as in Mark, by the disciples' question about Elijah,
10 **'Why then do our teachers say that Elijah must come first?'** The **teachers** are the "doctors of the law", whose traditional interpretation of the prophecy in Malachi 4.5 (that Elijah was to come "before the day of the Lord") had given to this Elijah-figure an ever greater rôle, so that he was
11 now popularly believed to be one who would **set everything right.** Matthew, compared with Mark, somewhat simplifies Jesus' reply. Elijah's rôle was compatible (contrary to popular belief) both with remaining unrecognized and with suffering execution. Similarly, the Son of Man (again contrary to
12 popular belief) was **to suffer.** That such could be the destiny of Elijah (who was now at last recognized by the disciples in the figure of **John the Baptist**) should help them to understand how such too could eventually be the destiny of the Son of Man.

14–18 The exorcism which follows is related more briefly in Matthew than in Mark (9.14–29), and there is here no dialogue on the subject of faith. Nevertheless, Matthew makes faith the point of the story. To the question, why did Jesus' disciples (and presumably also the early Christians) not always succeed in their exorcisms, the answer, in Mark, is: they do not pray
20 enough! The saying of Jesus given here suggests a different answer: they have not sufficient faith!

A further prediction of the fate in store for the Son of Man is recorded here in Matthew as it is in Mark and Luke, but with a characteristic difference. In the other gospels the disciples failed to understand; but here they under-
23 stood so well that **they were filled with grief.**

24 **'Does your master not pay temple-tax?'** It was an almost universal custom among the Jews, not only in Palestine but all over the Roman empire, to pay an annual tax of a "half-shekel" or (in Greek money) a "double drachma" for the upkeep of the temple in Jerusalem. The amount of this tax was relatively small: it was just twice the labourer's wage for a day's work (20.2), and the obligation to pay it was taken for granted by rich and poor alike. But in fact it is doubtful whether any legal sanctions attached to it, and it was the view of the Sadducees, for example, that since the only description of the tax in the Law of Moses (Exodus 30.11–16) made no mention of it as a recurrent tax, the institution must be a product of a later "tradition", and was therefore not binding. The question of the collectors did not therefore necessarily amount to asking whether Jesus was a law-abiding person in this respect, but implied that Jesus, as a new religious teacher, might possibly have a view of his own on the matter.

25 Jesus answered with a simple analogy. **'From whom do earthly monarchs collect tax or toll?'** The **monarchs** of whom the Jews had

experience were those lesser kings whom the Romans allowed to administer parts of Palestine under the general jurisdiction of the Roman empire. The **tax** which these princes exacted was a capitation tax levied on all subject peoples; the "tolls" were customs dues. Roman citizens were exempt from both these; but all others—**aliens** from the Roman point of view—were subject to them. Jesus' answer implied that, just as Roman citizens were exempt from taxes, so Jews should have a similar immunity with regard to taxes for their own institutions. This might give the impression that Jesus was opposed to the institution of the temple as such; but this is not borne out by his attitude at other times, and is indeed contradicted by his approval of free-will offerings to the temple treasury (Mark 12.41–4). What he objected to was probably the notion of a formal obligation to pay the tax,
instead of spontaneous offerings. '**But as we do not want to cause offence** 27
. . .' This was clearly not the moment to make an issue out of it, and Jesus complied with the collectors' demand.

The story of how he did so is reminiscent of many folk tales, and is often thought to be an example of the kind of legend which very soon attached itself to the person of Jesus: similar stories came to be told of other famous Jewish rabbis, by way of emphasizing their exceptional holiness. Alternatively, some saying of Jesus—a parable or a simile—may in the course of telling have been changed into a story about Jesus himself. The **silver coin** in the fish's mouth was a *stater*, which corresponded to four drachmas, or two persons' temple-tax. Matthew alone records this story; it may have been preserved (and possibly modified) in a Jewish-Christian church because of its bearing on what may have been a delicate question for Palestinian Jews converted to Christianity: should they or should they not continue to pay the temple-tax? They may have found their answer in the words, '**we do not want to cause offence**'.

At that time the disciples came to Jesus and asked. Matthew calls **18.** 1
Jesus' long answer a 'discourse' (19.1), and the chapter constitutes one of the five substantial discourses with which this gospel is punctuated. It is addressed specifically to **the disciples**; but the topics it deals with are unmistakably those which were later to arise in the life of the church.

'**Who is the greatest in the kingdom of Heaven?**' The question looks innocent enough; but the context in Mark (9.33–4) reveals why it was originally asked—the disciples had been discussing 'who was the greatest' among them. We can probably detect in Matthew's handling of this his desire to present the disciples in a more favourable light: he simply omitted the disreputable argument which was the original cue for the question. Whether or not the church was interested in the order of precedence which may have obtained among Jesus' first disciples, it was intensely interested in the order of precedence which should be observed among its own members, and in the problems of organizing its community life; and it doubtless found all the sayings of Jesus which are collected here relevant to these questions.

2 **He called a child, set him in front of them, and said.** In the narrative in Mark (9.36), Jesus answers the disciples' question with the same gesture: he makes them concentrate their attention on a mere child, and declares himself present even in such an insignificant member of the community.
5 Matthew repeats this: '**Whoever receives one such child in my name**
3 **receives me**', but he adds to it other children-sayings. '**Unless you turn round and become like children**'. **Turn** is a synonym (with more of an Old Testament than a New Testament feeling: compare Mark 4.12, where it occurs in a quotation from Isaiah) of the more common "repent". In what respect must they become like children? What Jesus' original meaning may have been is a deep question; but in the immediate context given to the saying by Matthew—that of order and priority in the church—the
4 point is probably quite simple. As the text goes on to say, '**Let a man humble himself till he is like this child**', not so as to become child-like (for children are not necessarily humble), but so as willingly to occupy a child's humble place in the community.

In the corresponding passage of Mark, sayings about children lead on to sayings about 'little ones' (9.42), but there are signs that this is a superficial connection: 'little ones' was a name given to the weaker members of the Christian fellowship. The case is even clearer here. The notion of a small child "having faith in Jesus" is a modern one; in antiquity, children were deemed simply to go along with their parents. A man became a Christian 'with his household', and nobody asked questions about the quality of his children's "faith". Therefore, when Matthew presents us with the phrase,
6 **one of these little ones who have faith in me**, we must beware of
7 assuming that the discourse is still about children. In the church, **causes of stumbling** were bound to appear, in the form of persecutions, heresies and betrayals—the ever-active devil would see to that. But deliberately to add to these causes by making life still more difficult for the "weaker brethren" would be a very serious matter—and one which had a natural place in this discourse about the life of the church.

8 '**If your hand or your foot is your undoing**'. Almost the same saying occurs in the Sermon on the Mount (5.29–30) in the context of personal renunciation. Why does Matthew repeat it here? Possibly because he found it in the corresponding passage in Mark (9.42–7); or perhaps he saw a new meaning for it in this context. The church is the "body" of Christ. Offensive members must be thrown out rather than the whole community be corrupted.
10 By contrast, the **little ones** must never be despised, for **they have their guardian angels in heaven**. The function of angels in Jewish literature was twofold. First, they constituted the court of God in heaven, offering him unceasing praise and worship; secondly, they acted as the messengers

and agents through which God intervened in the affairs of men (there are a number of examples of this in the early chapters of Matthew and Luke). Popular belief also ascribed a third function to them, that of **guardian angels** of individuals and nations (this is clear from Acts 12.15, and became officially recognized in Jewish writings in the following centuries). But these guardian angels were not excused their duties in heaven: they still had their place in the heavenly court. As to the order of precedence of these angels: it was usually thought that only a very few actually had the privilege of standing in God's presence and (to use a court metaphor) of "looking continually on his face". If the guardian angels of **these little ones** had this dignity, what must be the worth in God's sight of the individuals whom they guarded!

'Suppose a man has a hundred sheep'—an easy supposition: this was a 12
reasonable-sized flock for a single-handed shepherd; and if one strayed, he would not necessarily abandon it just to stay close to the rest of the flock. But the parable is given a quite different application from the more famous one it has in Luke's gospel. There, all the emphasis is on the joy of the shepherd that the "lost" sheep is found; here, it is on the duty of the shepherd not to let a "straying" sheep get lost. The lesson for the leaders of the church is obvious.

'If your brother commits a sin'. These sentences are not (like what has 15
gone before) mere exhortation, they lay down a strict procedure to be
followed. From the language it is possible almost to date the words to a
particular phase in the growth of Christianity. There was already a **con-** 17
gregation [a]—that is to say, there is no pretence that the words were applicable to the disciples in Jesus' lifetime. But this congregation was still completely Jewish: it shared, with an exclusiveness that was hardly characteristic of Jesus, the attitude that all whose nationality or occupation disqualified them from membership of the Jewish people were incapable of salvation. Hence, it treated its own recalcitrants as the Jewish community treated a **pagan or a tax-gatherer**. Nevertheless, the actual procedure it followed was by no means characteristically Jewish. It is true that the Dead Sea sect had a very similar procedure (and the similarity between these verses and a passage in the Scrolls shows, at the very least, that at this stage the Palestinian church was in touch with ideas that had shaped other communities); but the patience which Christians were to show towards a sinner (expressed
in its most radical form in Jesus' reply to Peter about forgiving **seventy** 22
times seven times) is very different from the normal procedure of the synagogue, where excommunication normally followed the commission of certain sins automatically. Nevertheless, moments would come when the leaders of the church would have to apply the ultimate sanction of exclusion.

[a] This word can also be translated "church". Apart from 16.18 above, this is the only occurrence of the word in the gospels.

When this happened, there was a saying of Christ (see above on 16.19) which
18 authorized them to act: **'Whatever you forbid on earth shall be forbidden in heaven, and whatever you allow on earth shall be allowed in heaven'.**

19 **'If two of you agree on earth'.** This "agreement" was the united prayer of the church, for the church was the place where two or three individuals were gathered together "in Christ's name"; and just as a later Rabbi could say, "When two sit occupied with the words of the Law, the divine glory is in the midst of them", so the fact of being united in the worship of Christ guaranteed his presence among them.

23 **'The kingdom of Heaven, therefore, should be thought of in this way'.** The parable is clearly intended to be an illustration of the teaching which has just been given about forgiveness, and makes its point, as so often, by a touch of exaggeration. The scene is the court of **a king**: Jesus may have been thinking of one of the sons of Herod the Great who ruled as vassals of Rome, or else of a more distant and perhaps legendary oriental monarch. Among the men who served this king were officials entrusted with the taxation of his realm, or perhaps local governors set over certain areas
24 of the kingdom. **There appeared before him a man whose debt ran into millions.** Here is the first touch of exaggeration. Ten thousand talents (the sum named in the Greek) would have been more than the total tribute paid by Galilee to Rome in 15 years—an immense sum, but it would be just conceivable for a local governor to fall into arrears to this extent; if he did, he would presumably enrich himself enormously by so doing, and the king could hope to recoup much of the revenue by confiscating the man's
27 property. However, out of **pity** the king **remitted the debt**—that is (in practical terms) he wrote off the revenue or at least postponed the date when payment would be due.[a] By contrast, another official owed the first
28 **a few pounds**, and the first had every right to bring him to court and, if convicted, have him jailed; but the affair, as being between court officials,
31 was noticed by **the other servants** (or courtiers[b]), with the consequences described. At the end of the story there is another touch, if not of exaggera-
34 tion, at least of the exotic: the Jews did not practise **torture**, and did not normally suffer it at the hands of the Romans; but they had all heard vaguely of the methods used by oriental despots, and torturing was in any case the obvious way of forcing a debtor to reveal what assets and credits he really had. Jesus' parable describes a situation which is by no means impossible but which, by being slightly larger than life, makes the point all the more cogently.

[*a*] Literally, the Greek means "remitted the loan", which may be meant to imply that the king turned the servant's debt into a loan repayable at some future date.

[*b*] In an eastern court no distinction would be made between a king's "servants" and his officials. Both could easily be slaves.

He left Galilee. The geography, both here and in Mark (10.1), is some- **19.** 1
what obscure. One of the pilgrims' routes from Galilee to Jerusalem crossed the Jordan south of the lake, followed the east side of the valley through "Transjordan" (i.e. Peraea, which like Galilee was part of the territory of Herod Antipas) and then recrossed the Jordan to Jericho. If Jesus took this route, it would effectively have taken him **across Jordan**; and since Peraea was predominantly Jewish, the presence, for instance, of
some Pharisees need cause no surprise. The difficulty is that Matthew 3

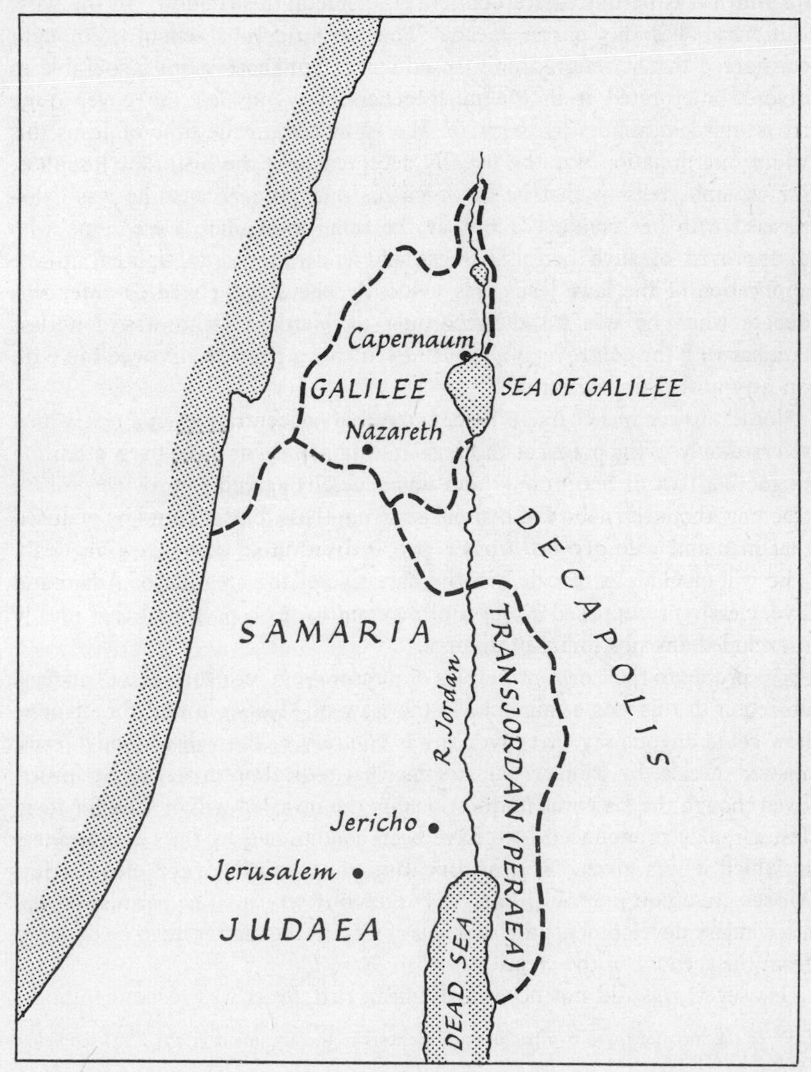

1 appears to call this part of the country **the region of Judaea.** Strictly speaking, Judaea (the area administered by a Roman procurator) lay on the west side of the Jordan; but the word was sometimes used as a name for Jewish Palestine generally.

The Pharisees' question reflects a controversy which certainly existed in the time of Jesus. The relevant passage in the Law of Moses runs (Deuteronomy 24.1): "When a man has married a wife, but she does not win his favour because he finds something shameful in her, and he writes her a note of divorce..." Divorce, in this passage, is taken for granted; and the grounds on which it is permitted are defined as "something shameful" in the wife. But what does this phrase mean? The most rigorous school of thought considered that it referred only to adultery; but those more favourable to divorce interpreted it in the most general way possible, to cover quite trivial misdemeanours by the wife. We know that in the time of Jesus this wider interpretation was the usually accepted one: the historian Josephus, for example, tells us that he divorced his own wife because he was "displeased with her conduct"; but at the same time there were some who disapproved of such permissiveness and endeavoured to tighten up the application of the law. Jesus was evidently being challenged to enter this debate when he was asked (according to Matthew, who was doubtless
3 familiar with the controversy), **'Is it lawful for a man to divorce his wife on any and every ground?'**

Jesus' answer was characteristic. Instead of concentrating on a text which
4–5 referred only to the practical and legal question of divorce, he drew attention to another part of Scripture which was generally agreed to provide positive teaching about the nature of marriage.[a] From these texts it could be deduced
6 that man and wife **are no longer two individuals: they are one flesh.** The will of God, as revealed in the narrative of the creation of Adam and Eve, clearly presupposed a union of man and wife so profound that ideally it excluded any possibility of divorce.

According to their own principles of interpreting Scripture, the Pharisees' objection to this was a fair one. If the Law of Moses allowed for divorce, how could anyone say that divorce was contrary to the will of God? Jesus' answer reveals, by comparison, a somewhat radical approach to Scripture. Even though the Law was unquestionably the revealed will of God for men, Jesus frankly pronounced it to have been conditioned by the circumstances
8 in which it was given. **'It was because your minds were closed that Moses gave you permission to divorce your wives.'** The permission was a secondary development; the real will of God in the matter must be deduced from the account of the creation.

However, this did not necessarily mean that Jesus was recommending a

[a] For the force of these two passages of Genesis in the argument (1.27; 2.24) see below on Mark 10.1–12.

new law on divorce. It was an agreed principle among legal experts that no
rules of conduct were legally binding that could not be deduced from explicit
commandments in Scripture. Principles deduced from statements of fact—
such as that **the two shall become one flesh** (Genesis 2.24)—could never 5
be more than morally binding. And in fact Jesus' answer reads more like
a moral judgement than a legal one. '**If a man divorces his wife . . .** he 9
commits adultery.' Adultery was regarded by the Jews as a very serious
sin. Jesus' words show that he regarded divorce as just as serious. Ideally,
it should never occur.

Yet his answer also reveals his attitude to the practical debate about the permissible grounds for divorce. It contains the exception, **for any cause other than unchastity**. By this, Jesus showed that he sided with those of his contemporaries who interpreted the law on divorce as strictly as possible. In allowing this exception, he implicitly acknowledged that the relevant clause of the Law of Moses, with its recognition of the principle of divorce, was still in force; but by appealing to the narrative of creation he demonstrated that divorce itself was something deserving the very strongest moral condemnation. It is characteristic of Matthew's gospel that Jesus should be represented as taking part in a technical dispute of this kind. Mark's gospel, by contrast, records only Jesus' general moral condemnation of divorce as such—which is indeed the more striking part of his teaching on the subject (Mark 10.1–12).

The meaning of the following short paragraph depends on how much of it goes back to a historical conversation between Jesus and his disciples, and how much is an addition by the church in the interests of making Jesus' ethical teaching more practicable. That the sequence of thought is due to Matthew is suggested at once by a comparison with the corresponding passage in Mark (10.10–12). There, Jesus' pronouncement on marriage is followed by a private conversation with the disciples about the practical implications of it. Matthew follows the same pattern, but gives it a quite different content: the disciples' question is a more pointed one, and Jesus' answer to it leads into a fresh saying altogether. It appears, therefore, to be Matthew who has taken advantage of the change of scene recorded in Mark in order to add an important piece of ethical teaching, ostensibly for the benefit of the disciples, but in reality of greater relevance to the life of the church.

Seen in this light the disciples' comment, though banal, is quite natural.
Jesus' teaching on marriage seemed to the church to set an impossibly high
standard: might it not be better **not to marry** at all? The answer given 10
was a saying of Jesus about the renunciation of marriage which seemed, by
implication, to accept the point of view of the disciples, and to concede
that his teaching could not be literally carried out by more than a few.
Marriage without divorce, he seemed to be saying, is indeed an impossible

11 ideal. The only safe way is to renounce marriage—but of course **that is something which not everyone can accept.** Thereby, the church might well feel authorized to countenance divorce among its own members: Jesus' absolute teaching about marriage was never intended to be taken literally except by those few who could be sure of not transgressing it—by renouncing marriage altogether.

This, in view of palpable assimilation in certain parts of Matthew's gospel to conditions prevailing subsequently in the church, is a possible reading of the passage. However, if we assume that the dialogue is historical, and transpose it back into the context of first-century Palestine, we get a very different result. Among the Jews, one matter on which there could be absolutely no question was that a man had an unqualified obligation to marry and beget children. "Be fruitful and multiply" (Genesis 1.28) was regarded as a command binding on every Jew; and only certain extremist sects, which regarded ritual pollution caused by intercourse with women as a still more serious matter than the command to bring up children, ever thought of recommending a celibate life. Against this background, the disciples'
10 objection takes on a very different sense. **'If that is the position with husband and wife, it is better not to marry'.** But (in view of God's clear command) it cannot ever be better not to marry; therefore that cannot "be the position": marriage without the possibility of divorce is absurd. Read in this way, the disciples' objection is a real one: it seeks, by a *reductio ad absurdum*, to show that Jesus' teaching cannot hold; the divorce permitted by Moses must belong to the nature of things. Jesus' reply [a] then goes some way to meet the point: to most people it will seem like this, but there will be some (and here doubtless the disciples are in mind and those followers of Christ who are their successors) who, by God's appointment, can accept it. It is God's will that some, at least, should be able to fulfil the nature of marriage as God originally intended it to be.

The discussion (at least as Matthew presents it) runs on into a saying
12 about those who are **incapable of marriage.** The original character of the saying is a little obscured by the NEB rendering. A more literal translation would run:

"For some are eunuchs because they are born so,
And some are eunuchs because they were made so by men,
And some have made eunuchs of themselves for the sake of the kingdom of Heaven."

The saying, in fact, is concerned, not with those who are **incapable of marriage** (for it was by no means unknown for a sexually impotent man to

[*a*] In the Greek, the words 'That is something which not everyone can accept', can refer equally to (i) the saying in verse 9, (ii) the disciples' remark in verse 10, (iii) the implication of their remark that celibacy is desirable, or even (iv) the saying in verse 12. The translators settled, without complete conviction, for the third of these possibilities.

marry) but with those who are incapable of consummating a marriage. Jewish society recognized two classes of impotent men, those who were **born so**, and those who became so by accident or the action of enemies. But "eunuchs", in the sense of men who had been deliberately and willingly castrated, represented something utterly foreign to their culture, a repellent phenomenon which they took to be explicitly forbidden in the Law (Deuteronomy 23.1). In a Jewish setting, the first two lines of Jesus' saying would have seemed to exhaust the possibilities; and one would have expected the third line of the epigram to be a statement about men other than eunuchs, or else an expression of utter condemnation of those who have "made eunuchs of themselves". Hence the extreme originality of Jesus' saying. The meaning is of course metaphorical: the last class of "eunuchs" are those who have voluntarily and decisively **renounced marriage**. But by setting this class in series with those who were genuinely eunuchs,[a] Jesus was expressing in a forcible and almost paradoxical way his opposition to the contemporary Jewish view that procreation was an absolute duty laid on every male who was capable of it. This too (like riches further on in the chapter) was something which it might be proper to renounce **for the sake of the kingdom of Heaven.**

From this point to the end of the chapter Matthew follows Mark closely (10.13-31), and it is only necessary here to draw attention to certain small changes he has introduced.

They brought children for him to lay his hands on them with 13
prayer. Mark writes simply 'for him to touch': Matthew makes it clear
from the start that what they wanted was a blessing such as a parent or
respected teacher would often be asked for. He omits one of the sayings
recorded by Mark, but retains the essential one for the sake of which the
incident was doubtless remembered: '**the kingdom of Heaven belongs to** 14
such as these'.

And now a man came up. Matthew appears to have inferred from the 16
enthusiasm of his approach (as described by Mark) that he was a **young** 20
man; but he has eliminated some of Mark's more striking details. In
particular, instead of the pointed exchange, 'Good Master . . .' 'Why do
you call me good?', he makes the conversation open with the very ordinary
question, '**What good must I do to gain eternal life?**' (which makes 16
Jesus' answer, '**One alone is good**', appear a little irrelevant). Good works, 17
particularly almsgiving, were generally regarded as a qualification for a
reward in heaven, and the young man may have desired some direction on
what kind of munificence he should aspire to. Jesus directed him instead to
keep the commandments, mentioning some of the Ten Commandments, 17

[*a*] It is just possible that Jesus was criticized by his enemies for not marrying, and that the saying was originally his answer to insulting insinuations that he was a "eunuch". If so, Matthew, or his source, has given it an entirely different context, that of private instruction to the disciples.

and adding the very general commandment from Leviticus (19.18) to
19 **love your neighbour as yourself**, which he himself regarded as a summary
of the Law. But he attached no value, apparently, to any extra works of piety
which his questioner may have had in mind. The only alternative he gave
21 him was **to go the whole way**, a new ethic altogether demanding a decisive
break with the past.

28 The reply to Peter on the question of rewards gives a specially privileged
place to the disciples in a way characteristic of Matthew. The imagery of
the saying about **thrones** stems from the book of Daniel (7.9–14): "As I
looked, thrones were placed . . . the court sat in judgement . . . and behold,
with the clouds of heaven there came one like a son of man". The significance
of Jesus' title, 'Son of Man', in Matthew's gospel is concentrated in the rôle
which this figure was to play in the final Judgement, and those of Jesus'
followers who were admitted to know the 'secrets of the kingdom' (13.11)
would also play their part in the same drama. **The twelve tribes of Israel**
was an archaic title that could be used for the contemporary Jewish nation.
A possible meaning of the saying (which has a totally different context in
Luke 22.28) is that the nation as a whole would be "judged" by those few
individuals who had accepted Jesus as Lord. But **the twelve tribes of
Israel** was also a way of describing the New Israel constituted by the
Christian church (see below on Revelation 7.4–8); and the saying could
equally well mean that the disciples were to "judge" the church, in the
sense (which followed the Old Testament concept of "judging") of assuring
29 its members of their rightful reward. This second sense leads more naturally
into the following saying, which is again concerned with rewards in heaven.
Matthew is still apparently following Mark (10.29–31); but he smooths out
the apparent materialism of Mark's version by omitting the words, 'in this
age'.

20. 1 **'The kingdom of Heaven is like this.'** The setting of the parable is
vintage-time in Palestine, the only time in the year when unskilled labourers
would be needed in a vineyard. Normally the **landowner** would hire all
the men he needed first thing in the morning; but the story required that he
should have miscalculated and taken the rather unusual step of engaging
6 further labourers right up to **an hour before sunset**. At the end of the day,
he was bound by law (Leviticus 19.13) to pay the stipulated wage to those
who had done a day's work; but, with regard to the rest, he could either wait
till they came again the next day and made up the full time (this was the
4 usual procedure) or else, if the work were finished, pay **a fair wage** for the
number of hours worked. On this occasion he instructed his steward to
8 settle the men's wages, **beginning with those who came last**—that is to
say, the eleventh-hour men were not to be allowed to go home and return
in the morning, but were to be paid off at once. The surprise came in the
9 fact that they **were paid the full day's wage.**

Matthew has shown how he understood the parable by enclosing it in the motto, 'the first will be last and the last first' (19.30 and 20.16), a motto which was highly relevant to the subject in hand, namely the correct ordering of the Christian community. But it is clear that this is not really the point of the parable: the fact that the last to be employed were paid first is an unimportant one in the story; the emphasis is on their being given, not first treatment, but equal treatment with the others. What was the original point of the parable? We may guess that the question which caused Jesus to tell it was not that of priorities in the church of the future, but of his own converse with 'tax collectors and sinners'. According to strict justice, those who had devoted their whole lives to observing the law in all its detailed provisions (especially the Pharisees) deserved a reward far greater than the men and women who, after lives of irresponsibility or even immorality, had responded at the eleventh hour to the preaching of Jesus. The logic of the parable was intended to force Jesus' hearers to see the question of ultimate rewards from the point of view of a God who is not only just but generous.

Challenge to Jerusalem

Jesus was journeying towards Jerusalem. During his activity in Galilee, 17
Jesus' activity could be characterized by the heading *Teaching and healing*, which gave rise, not so much to overt opposition, as to *Controversy*. This was followed by an itinerant period, when the bulk of what Matthew records was in the nature of private instruction to Jesus' immediate followers (*Jesus and his disciples*). But on his arrival at Jerusalem, Jesus' actions were such as to make an official reaction inevitable, and the heading consequently changes to *Challenge to Jerusalem*, even though there are still a few sections to come which consist of teaching addressed to the disciples.

Matthew here follows Mark closely (10.32–52), but makes a few changes
of detail. As so often, he appears to have been unwilling to present the
disciples in an unfavourable light, and the blame for ambitious sentiments
is laid, not on James and John themselves, but on their mother. (The 20
difficult saying in Mark about 'a baptism' is also omitted.) The miracle-
story is a doublet of the one already told earlier (9.27–31). The blind man of 29–34
Mark has for some reason again become **two blind men**, and the theme of 29
faith, which was kept in the previous version (9.29), is omitted here.

When they reached Bethphage at the Mount of Olives. Matthew has 21. 1
the most exact geography here of any of the gospels. The road from Jericho, just before it reached the crest of the Mount of Olives, had a turning off to the left leading to the small village of Bethphage and after that to Bethany.

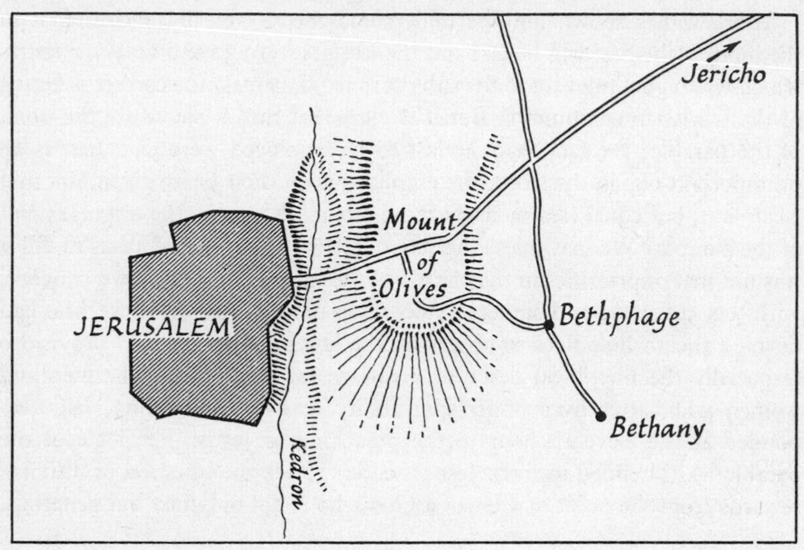

It was the natural place for Jesus to pause while obtaining a mount for his entry into Jerusalem. All the gospel accounts see this episode as a symbolic act and interpret it with reference to Old Testament prophecies of the coming Messiah, in particular Zechariah 9.9 (see below on Mark 11.1–10).
4 Matthew characteristically makes this correspondence quite explicit—**this was to fulfil the prophecy**—and quotes the verse from Zechariah in full, prefacing it with a phrase from Isaiah (62.11), **'Tell the daughter of Zion'.**
2 However, he also adds a curious detail: there were two beasts, **a donkey tethered with her foal beside her.** It is true that the prophecy of Zechariah
5 has a double description of the animal—**riding on an ass, riding on the foal of a beast of burden**—but this was simply a common idiom of Hebrew poetry, which often, in the two halves of a single line, likes to say the same thing in slightly different words. So far as we know, no Jewish interpreter ever thought of reading Zechariah's words as if they meant two animals; but Matthew appears to have done so—unless, of course, he knew of a tradition that Jesus entered Jerusalem with two mounts, and then offered a literal interpretation of Zechariah to explain it. But he offers no
7 explanation of how Jesus actually used the two animals: **they laid their cloaks on them and Jesus mounted** is a translation which smooths out the awkwardness. The Greek has "Jesus mounted *them*".
9 **'Hosanna to the Son of David!'** The relevant words of Psalm 118.25–6 are as follows:

> "Save us, we beseech thee (*Hosanna*), O Lord . . .
> Blessed be he who enters in the name of the Lord."

The psalm was used at a number of annual festivals, and in the course of its liturgical use the Hebrew word *Hosanna* seems to have lost its literal meaning, "save us now", and to have become a general cry of acclamation or shout of praise. The Septuagint version of the Old Testament translates the word into Greek; but both Matthew and Mark are content to leave it as it stands, without offering any explanation of its meaning. The reason must be that this was one of the Hebrew words (*Amen* is another) which the Greek-speaking church had taken over into its worship, so that it would have been already familiar to Matthew's readers.

Matthew makes one significant change to the text of the psalm. He adds: **to the Son of David.** It is an important theme of the gospel that Jesus' Messiahship was confirmed by his physical ancestry, which could be traced back to David. Indeed, **Son of David** is Matthew's distinctive title for the Messiah. The crowds, therefore, if they shouted out this title, must have recognized that Jesus was the Messiah, and this would explain Matthew's
comment that **the whole city went wild with excitement.** Jesus' entry, 10
according to Matthew, was not directly into the temple area, but by way of a detour through the city. But, curiously, the recognition that here at last was the awaited Messiah was not sustained. Once in the city, the crowd seems to have dropped the portentous title **Son of David**, and given to inquirers the
much less sensational reply, '**This is the prophet Jesus, from Nazareth** 11
in Galilee'.

It seems likely, therefore, that Matthew has allowed the subsequent faith of the church, which thought of Jesus as riding triumphantly into Jerusalem as the awaited Christ, the Son of David, to colour his description of the scene. At any rate, the status of Messiah is hinted at much less obviously in
what follows. (On the details of Jesus' action **in the temple precincts**, 12
see below on Mark 11.15–17.) The healing of **blind men and cripples** 14
could be interpreted, by those who wished, as the breaking in of the Messiah's kingdom, but equally it could be regarded as of no decisive
significance. This was the view of **the chief priests and doctors of the** 15
law. Matthew contrasts them, not with the crowds (whose attitude had now become uncertain), but with **the boys in the temple** who continued the cry started on the Mount of Olives, '**Hosanna to the Son of David!**' Matthew has said elsewhere (19.14) that it is children who are closest to the kingdom; and the fact that these boys intuitively recognized Jesus as the Messiah is
explained in the words of a psalm (8.2): "**Thou hast made children and** 16
babes at the breast sound aloud thy praise". In the Hebrew, the last word of this text is, not "praise", but "strength". Matthew's quotation is according to the Greek version, and fits the situation perfectly. But the Hebrew or Aramaic text known to Jesus would have been less appropriate: and our impression is thereby strengthened that Matthew has written up this section fairly freely, to bring out the ambiguity of Jesus' reception in Jerusalem.

23 Matthew somewhat abbreviates the story of the fig-tree, but follows Mark
closely in verses 23–7 (see below on Mark 11.20–33). He then inserts a
28 parable not found elsewhere. **A man had two sons.** The story itself is
perfectly clear; and its immediate application by Jesus is plausible enough:
31 **'tax-gatherers and prostitutes are entering the kingdom of God
ahead of you.'** These were the two classes of people whose way of life most
30 flagrantly (in the view of strict Jews) expressed a clear "**I will not**" to the
commands of God, but for whom Jesus consistently kept open the possibility of "changing their mind"; whereas the Pharisees, for all their
profession of obedience, remained obstinately inactive in the things that
really mattered. Thus far, the point is clear enough; but Matthew has
added (at least so it would appear from the fact that Luke (7.29–30) records
a similar saying in a quite different context) a second saying about John the
Baptist, which is a little difficult to relate to the preceding parable, and is
32 perhaps better understood separately. **John came to show you the right
way to live.** This is a rather free translation, and takes the sense differently
from most English versions. Linguistically, it may be correct; but John the
Baptist's message, apart from a few ethical rules given in Luke's gospel
(3.10–14), is usually presented as more concerned with preparation for a
coming event than with instructions about the **right way to live**. An alternative rendering would be, "When John came on his mission to you, he
lived in strict observance of the Law; but even so you did not believe him".
In this case there would of course be an implied contrast between John,
whose austerity made it almost impossible to criticize him for breaking any
ritual regulation, and Jesus, whose way of life showed notorious freedom
with regard to the detailed provisions of the Law.

33 **'Listen to another parable.'** The problems this parable raises are discussed in detail below on Mark 12.1–12. Except for a slight change in the
number of servants, the details of the story are exactly as in Mark. But if,
in Mark, the story shows signs of having had an interpretation imposed upon
it by the early church, in Matthew this is very much clearer. The passage of
Isaiah (5.1) on which the opening words are based, continues (verse 3): "And
now, O inhabitants of Jerusalem and men of Judah, judge, I pray you,
between me and my vineyard." Hence, perhaps, the extra dramatization in
40 Matthew, when Jesus puts the question to his hearers, **'How do you think
he will deal with those tenants?'** The reply, at any rate, shows a clear
tendency to interpret the parable. The main crime of the tenants is of course
their maltreatment of the owner's servants and their murder of the son; but
Matthew makes it sound as if their real guilt was that they did not let the
41 owner **have his share of the crop**. This, applied to the Jewish people, was
a constant theme of Jesus' preaching (at least in Matthew's gospel): they had
failed to bring forth fruit (or "a crop"—the word is the same in the Greek)
comparable with the blessings God had bestowed upon them. Consequently

(and Matthew draws out a consequence which was in fact only slowly
realized by the church), '**the kingdom of God will be taken away from** 43
you, and given to a nation that yields the proper fruit'—that is, the
Gentiles! The parable thus becomes, in Matthew, an attack on the Jewish
people as a whole; and it is perhaps by a slight oversight that he reproduces
from Mark the statement that the chief priests and Pharisees **saw that he** 45
was referring to them.

'**The kingdom of Heaven is like this**'. A parable occurs in Luke's gospel **22.** 2
so similar to this one that both must go back to the same original. But in
Matthew the story is considerably less lifelike, and sometimes appears even
far-fetched, whereas in Luke it seems to spring (like most of Jesus' parables)
straight from Palestinian daily life. It is tempting to see here an instance of
what was originally a straightforward story with a single point having been
transformed, in the course of telling, into an elaborate piece of allegory. The
setting is a royal wedding-feast. Invitations had been sent out to the notables
among the city-dwellers, and when the day came the king, following the
courteous custom of the time, **sent his servants** to inform the guests that 3
all was ready and to conduct them to the palace. But—**they would not**
come! No reason is given for their rude and disloyal behaviour; and at this
point the story becomes frankly implausible. Why should the king, after
receiving the first affront, have demeaned himself still further by sending a
second set of servants with a renewed invitation? And why should the
invited guests have then **attacked them brutally, and killed them**? As a 6
story, the sequence of events is fantastic; but as an allegory, it has a logic of
its own. A wedding-feast was a familiar image for the kingdom of glory
promised to the elect people of God. "Servants"—the prophets—had been
repeatedly sent to invite the guests to prepare themselves, but had been
ignored, or maltreated, or killed. As a result, Jerusalem (as the prophets
themselves had foretold) had been taken and destroyed—once by the
Assyrians centuries before, and now, shortly before Matthew's gospel was
written, by the Romans. The story so far is clearly an allegory of these
things. But what of the wedding-feast? Was God's purpose now frustrated,
and his promise void? Regardless of factual verisimilitude, the story continues as if only an hour had passed. "**The guests I invited did not** 8
deserve the honour", but there are others to whom it can be offered
instead. "**Go out to the main thoroughfares**". The Greek means 9
literally the places where the narrow city streets debouch into public squares
and open country places, that is, the places where people congregate. It was
a fact, both of Jesus' own practice and of the missionary experience of the
church, that the gospel, after its rejection by the Jewish leaders, was offered
to a much wider public, **good and bad alike.** 10

'**When the king came in to see the company at table.**' The story goes 11

on, but the sequel is again quite implausible. How could those who had just been "collected" from the streets have been expected to provide themselves with wedding clothes? There is no evidence for the solution sometimes proposed that a festal garment was issued to each guest on arrival; and even if this had been the case, the refusal of one guest, to put it on would be incomprehensible. To make sense of it, we have to assume that another, and originally separate, piece of allegory has been added by Matthew, and somewhat inexpertly welded into a single story. The kingdom of Heaven is like a royal wedding-feast: and woe to him who comes not properly prepared (with repentance? with righteous deeds?). The penalty will be exclusion; and on the last day the consequence will be hell, in all its traditional horror.
14 The essential thing is to be among the **few who are chosen.**

15 **Then the Pharisees went away and agreed on a plan.** The four questions
and answers which follow are very much the same as in Mark (12.13–37),
but Matthew builds up a slightly more dramatic setting for them by presenting them as a series of attacks by different sections of Jesus' opponents, while
the people stand by in amazement. The scene culminates in a devastating
46 counter-attack by Jesus, after which **no one dared ask him another
question.** Within the conversations themselves, it is only in the third that
34–40 Matthew's hand can be seen at work. In Mark, Jesus' interlocutor is a
'lawyer', who appears to ask the question about the greatest commandment
in perfectly good faith, and is then warmly commended by Jesus on his own
attitude to the Law. But in Matthew the question has a different tone. The
speaker is one of the Pharisees (which is often Matthew's way of saying, an
35 enemy of Jesus) who **tested him with this question.** The question, we
know, was one which was earnestly discussed in Pharisaic circles; but in
what sense was it a "test" for Jesus? Did his enemies want to see whether
Jesus had the technical skill and knowledge to take part in their debates? Or
did they hope to lead him down the path (a dangerous one, as they saw it)
of calling some laws more important than others—a position which would
imply a lack of respect for some provisions of the Law? In Mark's version,
the question, in the course of the conversation, becomes a fundamental one
of moral principles. But Matthew, who was more familiar than Mark with
the rules of Palestinian scholarship, reports Jesus' reply in a form that would
40 have been regarded as technically correct. '**Everything in the Law and the
prophets hangs on these two commandments**' implies that Jesus understood the question as an academic one and answered it in the same terms. The words could not be construed as emphasizing some parts of the Law at the expense of others; they merely stated that all the rest of the Law (and indeed the regulative utterances of the prophets) could be deduced from these two commandments. In saying this, Jesus was making precisely the kind of judgement his opponents made themselves; and the scene contri-

butes to Matthew's careful portrait of Jesus as a perfectly correct (even though sometimes startlingly original) interpreter of the Law.

Jesus then addressed the people and his disciples. The discourse which 23. 1
follows consists of a sustained attack on **the doctors of the law and the** 2
Pharisees. In the time of Jesus, these two groups were by no means identical. The **doctors of the law** (the "scribes" of older versions) were a professional class, who underwent a formal and exacting training in the interpretation of the Law of Moses, and were then qualified to undertake the education of others, to sit as justices in the law-courts, and to give their ruling on questions of law and conduct. For these services they received no payment, and most of them followed another profession at the same time; but since the Law of Moses was determinative in Jewish society for both religious and civil matters, their learning gave them considerable authority, and they were beginning to displace the old landed aristocracy of the Jewish nation as the most influential class in society. The Pharisees, on the other hand, had no official status as such. The origin of their name is obscure, but their emergence as a distinctive party can be dated to the time of the Maccabean revolution (second century B.C.), when, under the name of "Hasideans", they were "volunteers in the cause of the Law" (1 Maccabees 2.42), and became the most devoted and intransigent defenders of the traditional Jewish way of life against Hellenistic influences. Their successors, the Pharisees of Jesus' day, were thus not so much a professional class as a school of thought. Their original concern to preserve the ancestral Law uncontaminated by foreign influences had developed into a distinctive approach to the Law itself. They found in Scripture not only a code of law sufficient for the civil and religious ordering of the community, but a detailed and comprehensive system of commandments which (given their own subtle methods of interpretation) could be shown to govern every aspect of an individual's life. To demonstrate this, these men formed themselves into fellowships whose members were committed to carrying out every detail of the law according to its distinctive Pharisaic interpretation, and to keeping themselves ritually "pure" by shunning the society of all non-Pharisees. These fellowships did not consist only of scholars; indeed the majority of their members were laymen. But they formed an increasingly important and exclusive element in Jewish society, and both in their lives and in their teaching the Pharisees treated Scripture with a seriousness and a determined obedience which far exceeded that of society as a whole.

The natural way for Pharisaism to extend its influence was through the administration of justice and through education; and in fact in the time of Jesus many of the doctors of the law belonged to the Pharisees' fellowships. Nevertheless the two groups remained distinct: the doctors of the law were qualified professionals, the Pharisees were exponents of an unofficial idea;

and not all the lawyers were Pharisees. Consequently, though both had failings which came under sharp criticism from Jesus, these failings were not necessarily the same in each case. The lawyers, though required to be professionally competent in the Law, were not thereby committed to make their lives morally superior to other people's, and as a class they may often have deserved the charge of oppressing others while keeping on the right side of the law themselves. The Pharisees, on the other hand, aimed at a very high standard of moral conduct, and strove to bring their lives into conformity with a detailed and comprehensive interpretation of the Law. Their distinctive failing was that of allowing an elaborate system of outward legal observances to obscure the original humanitarian basis of the Law and to lead them into an exclusiveness which ignored the real needs of their fellow-men. It was for this reason that Jesus so often called them 'hypocrites'.

Why then in this chapter of Matthew (as often in Luke, though not in Mark or John) are the two classes grouped together as the object of Jesus' attacks? Some of the charges brought against them fit the lawyers, some the Pharisees, but not all fit both. Moreover, Luke's gospel (especially 11.37–52) makes a distinction between those of Jesus' criticisms which were aimed at the lawyers and those which were aimed at the Pharisees. The reason may be simply some confusion in the tradition. But it must also be remembered that by the time Matthew's gospel came to be written, towards the end of the first century, conditions in Palestine were no longer what they had been in the days of Jesus. Jerusalem had fallen; and in the dispersed and disorganized Jewish population authority and influence had passed to a "school" of learned men which had recently been founded at Jamnia, on the coastal plain west of Jerusalem. These men were Pharisees; and from then on there ceased to be any real distinction between them and the lawyers; for, in their efforts to consolidate and codify the traditions and observances of the old Jewish nation, the Pharisees gained complete control over the administration of justice and education. The Judaism with which Christianity was confronted when Matthew wrote his gospel was therefore becoming increasingly Pharisaic; and we can probably overhear, in these attacks of Jesus which Matthew records against **the doctors of the law and the Pharisees**, something of the polemic which was being carried on by Christians against the leaders of neighbouring synagogues.

2 **'The doctors of the law and the Pharisees sit in the chair of Moses'.** This may not be pure metaphor. An imposing stone seat has been found in the ruins of several ancient synagogues, placed in the centre of the rear wall facing the congregation. This may have been called **the chair of Moses**. But in any case the name describes the function of him who sits there. Moses both promulgated the law and acted as judge. His successors were those who interpreted the law and gave judgement on transgressions of it. Christians, as much in Jewish as in Gentile communities, were to be law-abiding: **'do**

what they tell you'. But these professional judges were not to be regarded
as models of behaviour: their knowledge of the intricacies of the law enabled
them to discover exemptions and saving clauses which greatly eased the
burden of keeping it personally, and so it could be said of them that '**they** 3
say one thing and do another.' The law, to the ordinary layman, was a
burden, and could be made oppressive by judges who elaborated its application but had the skill to circumvent it themselves.

'**Whatever they do is done for show.**' This refers to a custom that was 5
widespread among pious Jews. The two passages referred to in the NEB
footnote (Deuteronomy 6.8–9 and Exodus 13.9) were commonly interpreted
as instructions to wear short texts from the Law bound on to forehead or
wrist, and many Jews in fact carried such texts on their persons in little
leather boxes. These boxes looked, of course, very similar to the amulets or
charms carried by those who believed in magic, and when, in Matthew, they
are called **phylacteries** (which means "charms"), this looks like a
deliberately derogatory description of them. There appears, in any case, to
have been a practice of carrying especially **broad** and ostentatious ones, and
of wearing especially **large tassels** on one's robes (for all Jews, following
Deuteronomy 22.12, wore distinctive tassels at the corners of their outer
garment): and these affectations, along with a desire for **places of honour** 6
and for public respect (which is singled out also in Mark's gospel, 12.38–9),
were characteristic of a profession that was becoming increasingly conscious
of its influence, and offering increasingly attractive rewards to the vain and
the ambitious.

'**You must not be called "rabbi"**'. "Rabbi" became a technical title 8
for an ordained doctor of the law in the period after the fall of Jersualem
(A.D. 70) when authority in religious matters was concentrated in the school
of Jamnia. In the time of Jesus it was simply a term of respect, given spontaneously to distinguished teachers. While the disciples had Jesus, their
"master", with them, it is unlikely that anyone would have thought of
addressing them as "rabbi"; but later, when the leaders of the Christian
community began to exercise authority in a way somewhat similar to the
leaders of the local synagogues, there may have been a tendency to follow
the Jews in introducing the technical title, "rabbi". But the Christian
community, if it were to remain faithful to Jesus' teaching, must be in
important respects distinct from the Jewish community, and must eschew
such titles. (A slightly different point seems to underlie the saying, '**Do not** 9
call any man on earth "father"'. This time it is not an injunction to the
disciples to avoid such titles themselves, but a warning to dissociate themselves from a particular Jewish doctrine. When the Jewish people talked
about their "fathers", they meant the patriarchs (and, in more recent times,
distinguished rabbis). They held that the virtues of these men laid up a kind
of treasury of merit for the nation in the eyes of God. This saying seems to

be an attack on the whole conception; compare the treatment of the characteristic Jewish claim, 'We have Abraham for our father', 3.9; John 8.33.)
10 **'Nor must you be called "teacher"'**. The Greek word here is an unusual
one: perhaps it was a title being tried out in the church when Matthew
wrote, perhaps it was simply the Greek equivalent of "rabbi". But it came
under the same condemnation: Christians (for this saying can hardly have
been spoken in its present form by Jesus, who never referred to himself
without explanation as "the Messiah") **have one Teacher, the Messiah.**
Only one principle could properly obtain in the church, one which Jesus
11 laid down on several different occasions (20.26; Mark 9.35); **'the greatest
among you must be your servant'**. And this in turn depended on a
principle of God's dealings with men which had already found expression
12 in the Old Testament (Proverbs 29.23; Job 22.29 etc.): **'whoever exalts
himself will be humbled'**.

13 **'Alas, alas for you'**. Seven of these "woes" follow, still aimed indiscriminately at the lawyers and Pharisees, and perhaps again influenced by
the strained relations existing in Matthew's time between the church and
the new leaders of Judaism. **'You shut the door of the kingdom of
Heaven in men's faces'**. Jesus himself proclaimed the coming of the
kingdom, and his opponents could hardly keep people away from it; but
later, when the Christian community was thought of as an (at least partial)
realization of God's kingdom on earth, it was a cause of deep concern to
Christians that the Jews not only refused to join, but stopped others from
joining. Moreover, some sections of Judaism believed in vigorous proselytizing, and this often happened in direct competition with the Christian
mission. We can probably detect the language of very strained relations when
15 one side calls the other **'fit for hell'**.

16 **'Blind guides'**. Jesus called his opponents this more than once (15.14; Luke 6.39), and the phrase became part of the language of Christian polemic against the Jews (Romans 2.19). The point of attack here is similar to that in the Sermon on the Mount (5.33–7): no casuistry can mitigate the seriousness of oaths and vows, which are all, even if they do not seem so, sworn by the name of God—and perhaps we should supply the same conclusion as Jesus draws in the Sermon, 'you are not to swear at all'.

23 **'You pay tithes of mint and dill and cummin'**. This was a typical Pharisaic elaboration of the law (Deuteronomy 14.22–3) that all Israelites must pay tithes of their grain, wine and oil: the Pharisees extended this even to herbs, and although none of them would have admitted to overlooking **the weightier demands of the Law**, the burden of Jesus' attack on them was that this excessive attention to detail caused them to lose sight of the great general principles upon which the whole law was based. This and the following accusation must both have originally been directed specifically against the Pharisees (as indeed they are in Luke 11.39–42).

'You clean the outside of cup and dish'. The ritual cleansing of 25
vessels used in the worship of the temple was being extended by the Pharisees
to apply even to the cups and dishes of daily household use, and in the
following centuries they developed an astonishingly complicated system of
rules applying to almost any household utensil. Jesus saw in this tendency
(for there is no reason to doubt that this saying at least goes right back to
Jesus) material for a trenchant simile: all this attention to the outside of
crockery vessels was like their attention to the externals of religion. But what
were they like **inside**? If they would begin there, the externals would look
after themselves. The same thought continues in the next simile. **'You are** 27
like tombs covered with whitewash'. Jewish tombs were mostly hewn
out of rock, and if they were whitewashed it was not for display but (as Luke
rightly sees, 11.44) to mark the spot. Jesus was probably thinking of the
conspicuous pagan tombs, built of white marble or perhaps of whitewashed
stone, which were to be seen near the Greco-Roman cities of Palestine. All
this exterior show made no difference to the fact that the contents of
the tomb were, to the Jewish way of thinking, repugnant and ritually
unclean.

Nevertheless, the Jews did raise up monuments to the memory of the
great figures of their history. **'You build up the tombs of the prophets'.** 29
We know nothing of any "prophets' tombs" in the neighbourhood of
Jerusalem. The so-called "Tomb of Zechariah" which still stands in the
Kedron valley is Hellenistic, and was not associated with the prophet before
the Christian era. But we do know that legends were growing up in this
period about the lives, deaths and burial places of the Old Testament
prophets; and at Hebron there were certainly famous monuments which
were (and still are) reputed to be the tombs of Abraham, Isaac and Jacob, the
saints of the remote past. But this did not alter the fact that the ancestors of
Jesus' contemporaries (and this last "woe" seems to apply to the Jewish
nation as a whole, rather than to the lawyers and Pharisees in particular) had
taken part **in the murder of the prophets.** Only one such murder is men- 30
tioned in the Old Testament, that of a certain Zechariah (2 Chronicles
24.20–2); but Jewish legend had added five more of the great prophets to the
list of national martyrs. Jesus, who was in some sense a "prophet", doubtless
saw his own impending death as part of the same tradition, and these words
challenge his opponents to play their appointed part in the grim drama. **'I** 34
send you therefore prophets, sages, and teachers'. An old theme of
Scripture is adapted to the destiny of the Christian church. Just as God
"sent prophets among them" (the same passage from 2 Chronicles), so Jesus
is made to say **'I send'** the men who were to become the leaders of Christian
communities, among whom there would be **prophets** (see above on 10.41),
sages and teachers. Their fate would follow a pattern which filled the Old
Testament from cover to cover: the death of Abel was the first murder in the

book of Genesis (4.8), that of Zechariah [a] the last in 2 Chronicles, which was at that time the last of the books in the canon of Hebrew scriptures.
37 **'O Jerusalem, Jerusalem'.** Jerusalem was not in fact, or even in legend,
the place where many of the prophets met their death; yet it was the
symbolic centre of a religion which again and again had rejected the prophetic
voice. Jesus, to end this discourse of condemnation, once again assumes the
rôle of a prophet destined to suffer a similar fate, upbraiding the city which
should have accepted his message, using the classic metaphor of the pro-
tective wings of a bird (Deuteronomy 32.11; Isaiah 31.5 etc.), and prophesy-
38 ing, as if he saw it before his eyes, the day when the great temple [b] in the
midst of it would be made meaningless by the departure of God from its
sanctuary and by the destruction of its magnificent buildings. It was not for
Jesus to reverse this terrible destiny by compelling the inhabitants to repent.
On the contrary, their very recognition of him would be delayed until such a
time (perhaps at his final vindication in glory) as there rose spontaneously to
39 their lips that traditional phrase of acclamation (Psalm 118.26), "**Blessings
on him who comes in the name of the Lord**".

Prophecies and warnings

24. 1 **Jesus was leaving the temple.** The setting for the discourse of *Prophecies
and warnings* is as vivid and realistic as in Mark (13.1–3). The immense scale
of Herod the Great's architectural achievement on the temple mount
2 evoked both the disciples' admiration and Jesus' prophecy that **not one
stone will be left upon another**; and Jesus' long answer to the disciples'
astonished question about this prophecy was appropriately delivered on the Mount of Olives, which commanded a magnificent view of the whole temple area. The elements of this answer are the same as in Mark's version, and Matthew has made only a few rearrangements and additions. The catastrophes and tribulations which were normal in history were to be intensified, the faithful would be put to a severe test; but these things would be no mere accidents, they would be signs that the end was about to come. The disciples' question (in Matthew) invited such an answer. They did not wish to know merely when the temple would be destroyed: they realized that such a staggering reversal of Jerusalem's present splendour must be a presage of still

[a] In 2 Chronicles 24.20 Zechariah is called "son of Jehoiada". It is only in the Book of Zechariah that the prophet (who may or may not be the same person) is called **son of Berachiah**. The confusion here may have existed in many minds in Jesus' time; it may be a mistake of Matthew's; or the words **son of Berachiah** may even be the addition of a well-meaning but misguided copyist not long after Matthew wrote.

[b] The Greek may mean, either the **temple**, or else, more generally, the place where God makes his dwelling with his people. See the footnote in NEB.

more significant events; and the only two events which they could envisage
as being on the required scale were the **coming** of Jesus in glory and **the end** 3
of the age. They realized (with that deeper insight which Matthew, unlike
the other evangelists, ascribes to the disciples) that all these things must be
related; and they asked Jesus for further precision.

The reply includes conventional elements: the danger of being **misled,** 5
the intensification of warfare, **famines,** and **earthquakes.** The persecution 7
of the faithful also belonged to the picture of the bitter period before the end
(which Matthew, like Mark, calls by the technical name, **the birth-pangs** 8
of the new age); but Matthew has already recorded sayings about this in an
earlier discourse (chapter 10) and includes only brief allusions to it here;
whereas more space is given to the implications of a period in which, inevitably, **lawlessness spreads.** 12

And then the end will come. The reader is disconcerted to find that it 14
does not, but that other calamities are still to be recorded which clearly
belong to the time before the end. But it is a feature of the kind of literature
to which this chapter belongs (of which we possess numerous Jewish
examples, such as 2 Esdras in the Apocrypha, and also one Christian example,
the Revelation) that the drama is not made to unfold in an orderly progression, but the description keeps turning back on itself to fill in details
belonging to an earlier phase. So here: the next events predicted (whatever
the precise meaning of the cryptogram from **the prophet Daniel**—see 15
below on Mark 13.14) are not those of the end at all, but of an incursion of
military strength into Palestine on a scale that makes immediate flight the
only sensible course; and, since mainly Jews will be affected, Matthew adds
that it will be as well if it does not happen on the **Sabbath,** when all journey- 20
ing is forbidden, and fugitives will have a crisis of conscience to contend
with as well as their other troubles.

The danger from impostors is made precise. The fanatics who proclaimed themselves divinely inspired leaders and attempted to lead a nationalist
rising did in fact often begin by gathering a following **in the wilderness**; 26
alternatively they might form a conspiracy in an **inner room.** But the coming
of the Son of Man (as the next verses make clear) will be totally different:
it will be as quickly and clearly recognized by all as a corpse is spotted by 28
vultures (if this is the sense of the proverb inserted at verse 28). The language
used of it is like that of the Old Testament prophets when they looked
forward to the "day of the Lord": disorder among the heavenly bodies 29
(Isaiah 13.10; 34.4), **lamentation** among the peoples, a **sign** (which is 30
probably an ensign, Isaiah 11.12), a **trumpet blast** (Isaiah 27.13, Joel 2.1), 31
and the gathering of the **chosen from the four winds** (Zechariah 2.6;
Deuteronomy 30.4). All these conventional features are gathered round
Daniel's description of the coming of the **Son of Man** (Daniel 7.13, 14).

With the simile of the fig-tree the discourse moves (as in Mark) from 32

description to exhortation: this must be your posture in the face of all these
developments, neither scepticism because of the apparent delay of the end,
36 nor agitated preoccupation with the exact day and hour (which **only the**
42 **Father** knows). The watchword (as in Mark) is **'keep awake'**.

Matthew goes on to illustrate this lesson of wakefulness with a series of
parables and similes, which emphasize (at least in Matthew's presentation of
them, if not in their original form) the suddenness with which the end must
be expected, and the error of not taking seriously the teaching which has just
37 been given. **'As things were in Noah's days'**. The narrative in Genesis
concentrates entirely upon Noah and his family. Apart from the brief statement (6.11–13) that "the earth was corrupt" and that God had "determined
to make an end of all flesh", nothing is said about the behaviour of all those
who were doomed to destruction. But as the Jews meditated upon this story
they began to be impressed by the attitude of Noah. Even though there
were no signs in advance of the coming deluge, he put such trust in the word
of God that he unhesitatingly set about the immense and apparently absurd
task of building a great ship on dry land. He became, in fact, one of the
classic examples, along with Abraham, of those who unhesitatingly put their
whole faith in God (Hebrews 11.7). If Jesus mentioned him in his teaching,
one would have expected him to have drawn the same moral: When I preach
to you, be like Noah, who believed the message of God, and not like those
39 others who, since they neither heard nor believed—**they knew nothing**—
were consigned to destruction. But here, all the emphasis is not on Noah but
37 on the men and women of **Noah's days**, who showed by their manner of
living that they had no idea of the calamity which threatened them. How
different must be the lives of Christians (this seems to be the moral) who are
aware of what is impending! There will be no time for last-minute repent-
41 ance. Suddenly, in the midst of daily occupations, **one will be taken** (to
join the company of the elect) **the other left** (to face the Judgement).

45 The parable of **the trusty servant** may have had a somewhat different
point when Jesus first told it from the simple lesson of vigilance which it is
used to illustrate here. The background to it is one of the many estates in
Palestine which were owned by foreign magnates and managed in their
absence by stewards or agents. The **household staff**, which included all
who worked on the estate, will normally have consisted of slaves, and the
landlord's agent will also probably have been a slave (this was quite usual,
and the Greek word translated **servant** also means "slave") since his
reward was to be, not higher wages, but a position of still greater respon-
48 sibility in his master's establishment. Similarly, if he turned out to be a **bad**
servant he could be punished, not just with dismissal, but with death—but
at this point the details become blurred. "Cutting in pieces" was not unknown as a punishment, but seems unnecessarily brutal here (it is possible
that Jesus used an Aramaic idiom "divide out to him" (his punishment)

which was subsequently misunderstood as "divide him"); and by the end of
the parable the landlord seems to have become the divine Judge, and the
slave's punishment the punishment which will be meted out to all **hypocrites** 51
on the Last Day. Clearly the parable, at some stage in its progress from the lips of Jesus to the written page of the gospel, has been adapted to yield teaching about the proper behaviour of Christians in view of the impending return of their Lord: all the emphasis is now on the suddenness of the master's home-coming. But the natural structure of the story, with its balanced contrast between a trust deserved and a trust betrayed, points in a different direction. Who, among Jesus' contemporaries, had been set over God's household? The Jewish leaders, the lawyers and Pharisees. Now the hour of reckoning had come, and they had been found unworthy of their trust!

'When that day comes, the kingdom of Heaven will be like this'. 25. 1
Another parable follows, which Matthew evidently saw as a further illustration of the same theme of watchfulness and preparedness for the last day.
It ends with the same message—**keep awake then**—and the detail that the 13, 5
bridegroom was late in coming suggests the context in which the parable may have been used in the church. The Last Day, and the coming of Jesus, was being delayed longer than expected: those who relaxed their vigilance would be like the girls who failed to reckon with the possibility of delay, and were not ready for the moment when it came. But it can be seen at once that this interpretation of the parable is somewhat forced. If five of the girls had fallen asleep, and the other five had remained awake and ready, the
moral—**keep awake then**—would have been exactly right. But in the story
they all dozed off to sleep, and there is no suggestion that there was 5
anything wrong about doing so. The error of the five foolish girls was not that they fell asleep, but that they did not allow for the possibility of delay. Was the original point of the parable therefore to warn Jesus' followers that they must be prepared for a longer period of waiting than they thought?

We are unfortunately not in a position to fill in the background of the story with any certainty. Marriage customs vary from place to place, and from one period to another, and we possess no independent description of marriage festivities in Palestine in the first half of the first century A.D.: in particular, we hear nowhere else about a procession at night, or about attendants with lamps. On the other hand, one of the high-points of marriage festivities all over the ancient world was the moment when the bridegroom was escorted, either to the house of the bride, or (with his bride) to his own house. This was a moment for singing and dancing; and when the procession got indoors the guests would sit down to the wedding feast. In broad outline the story of the ten girls fits well enough into this pattern. The story is
about **ten girls who took their lamps and went out to meet the bride-** 1

groom. [a]The **lamps** one usually thinks of are the small domestic oil lamps used all over the ancient world, which consist simply of a shallow container of oil and a wick fitted into a hole in one end. But it is difficult to imagine how such lamps could have been used on this occasion. For one thing, they would instantly blow out when taken out of doors; for another, they were quite inappropriate for carrying about; and thirdly, they would normally have lasted all night without being refilled. Some kind of hurricane lamps are another possibility; but the Greek word used here never (so far as we know) meant this, and anyway, being made of horn, they would have given out a very subdued and unfestive light. Far the most likely kind of lights for the girls to have used (and this is what the Greek word normally means) were torches—the only lights which could be carried by anyone running or dancing, and which were certainly the normal thing for any procession at night. But torches usually consisted of long cones of wood coated with pitch; if this was what the girls were carrying, they cannot possibly have needed oil as well. The only convincing solution which has yet been found to this mystery is a custom which has been observed in comparatively modern times in Palestine. This consists of wrapping the head of the torch with some material impregnated in olive oil. The torch will then burn for a short time, say a quarter of an hour, but will need soaking in oil again if it is to be made to blaze up suddenly or to last for a longer time. If this is what the girls were to carry, the fault of the foolish ones was not that they did not allow for the delay, but that they came at the beginning without an essential part of their equipment; and having slept during the time they might have put this right, they had no chance to make good their negligence when the critical moment came. The bridegroom went in to **the wedding** (probably the wedding feast) with the girls who had lighted his way; but he was not going to admit some more girls whom he had never seen until the moment they came to the door.

If this is the true explanation—and it cannot claim, in the present state of our knowledge, to be much more than a conjecture—then it gives a very different point to the parable. The moral which Matthew himself draws—
13 **keep awake then**—has already been shown not to fit the parable; and the
suggestion that the original emphasis was on the unexpected delay of the bridegroom now fares no better: the fault of the foolish girls was not that they had brought too little oil, but that they had forgotten to bring any oil at all. The parable in fact falls into place beside that of the man without a wedding garment. The new life promised to believers (often described in the image of a feast) is freely offered to all—but on condition that they prepare themselves (presumably with repentance, or perhaps with good deeds). Those who take this condition lightly must expect to be turned away.

[a] The first four verses must be in the nature of an introduction, setting the scene for the story itself, which begins at verse 5, "As the bridegroom was late in coming". Otherwise, we would be left with the very improbable circumstance that the girls fell asleep out of doors.

'It is like a man going abroad'. Precisely what is like this is not said: as 14
with many parables of Jesus, the original application was not preserved, though Matthew (as we shall see) found reason to include this one in the general context of teaching about the Last Things. The parable reflects commercial conditions in Palestine. Jews were not permitted to practise usury among themselves; therefore the **man going abroad** could not simply invest his capital in someone else's business. He had to find agents whom he could trust to initiate and carry on commercial enterprises on his behalf. It was natural that he should choose **his servants** for this. These would not have been slaves (who had not sufficient rights at law to carry on a business), but salaried men whom he had been employing as agents or administrators while he lived in Palestine. Among these servants, some would have proved themselves more capable than others, and it was natural to
divide up the capital, not into equal parts, but to each **according to his** 15
capacity: he would not risk losing a large sum by giving it as working capital to an inexperienced or incompetent agent. The sums involved were substantial, and reckoned by *talents* (the NEB has translated this **bags of gold**, which well describes the way in which such large sums of money were in fact transferred from one owner to another). A *talent* was equivalent to 6,000 standard silver coins (*denarii*), which, by the scale of values adopted in the NEB, would have been worth about £600. In the story, therefore, the capital sums involved were (very roughly) £3,000, £1,200 and £600. If the servants went bankrupt, they probably had to compensate their master out of their own pockets for up to half the capital sum. If they made a profit (and high rates of profit and interest were normal in antiquity), most of this, as well as the original capital, would be due to be repaid to their master; for the servants were still his agents, they had not been set up in business on their own. It followed that although they had to take a part of the risk for losses they could not expect to enrich themselves by their profits. Their principal reward would be the prospect of promotion in their master's employment.

So much for the setting; now for the characters. Two of them are vividly drawn, the master and the third servant. This servant, compared with the two others, was given only a small capital to work with: clearly he was not regarded as very competent. But a small capital is more difficult to trade with than a large one; he could not expect a large profit, and there was always the risk of loss. So he buried the money—this was regarded as the safest way of minding a deposit. And when he had to settle accounts with his master, he
stood up to him firmly. **"I knew you to be a hard man"**, that is, one who 24
expected the maximum return on his money (and so would leave little or nothing of any profit to his servants), and who made as small an outlay as possible (by way of "sowing" or "scattering" his money for the benefit of his agents or his debtors) and pressed for the highest possible rate of return.

The servant feared the risk of losing the capital more than that of forfeiting his own exiguous share of any possible profit. We see him, not only as a timid and incompetent businessman, but as a servant with a sense of grievance towards his master.

The description of the master is equally vivid. Far from denying the
27 servant's description of him, he proceeds to substantiate it. "**You ought to have put my money on deposit**". In modern terms this makes good sense: a deposit account at a bank is a safe and painless way of securing a small increase of capital. But in antiquity one did not normally deposit money for interest, but only for safety. It is possible that a more literal translation gives a better sense: "you should have given my coins to the money-changers". Gold and silver coins were minted outside Palestine, and money-changers charged a small commission for exchanging them for the local bronze coinage. The suggestion seems to be that the servant with a substantial capital of such coins could at least have gone into nominal partnership with a money-changer and secured some interest that way. At any rate the master, true to character, could not accept the servant's point that, with a small capital, it is better to be safe than sorry.

28 '**Take the bag of gold from him, and give it to the one with the ten bags**'. This was no punishment: he was due to pay back the capital in any case; and it was only logical for the master to add it to the capital of the servant who had shown himself the most efficient businessman. But, as we read the parable in Matthew, this comparatively trivial detail becomes the most important point in the story. For it appears to be a perfect illustration
of a saying of Jesus that is recorded also (though without any particular
29 context) in Mark's gospel: '**the man who has will always be given more . . . and the man who has not will forfeit even what he has**'. Precisely what Jesus originally meant by this saying (which was probably a proverb drawn from the market—see below on Mark 4.25) we do not know. But Matthew seems to have seen in it a commentary on the rewarding of a man's
spiritual resources at the Last Judgement; for he goes on to consign the
30 **useless servant** to hell (for which **the place of wailing and grinding of teeth** is his favourite expression), and we are left in little doubt that, as he tells the story, the return of the master has turned into a symbol of Christ's final Coming, and that the reward of the "good" servants has been deliberately spiritualized, so that they are not merely given a position of greater
21 responsibility on earth, but are invited to share their **master's delight**—that is (as the striking Greek phrase suggests), to enter into the joy of the heavenly kingdom. In Matthew's hands, if not before, the parable has become an allegory of the Last Judgement.

Was this the original meaning? It seems hardly likely that Jesus would have given the main figure in the parable the character of a hard and unscrupulous businessman if he had intended him to stand for the divine Judge himself! The parable is probably best understood alongside that of the 'trusty servant' (24.45–51). The theme, again, is trust. Even an extortionate capitalist could justly blame an agent who did nothing at all with the capital entrusted to him. And what had Jesus' opponents done with the immense capital of their ancestral religion which had been entrusted to them?

The discourse ends with a grand tableau of the Last Judgement, built up
out of a number of separate images. **When the Son of Man comes in his** 31
glory is the language of Daniel's prophecy (7.13–15) describing the solemn
moment of divine judgement, when **all the nations** would become subject 32
to the righteous Son of Man and the elect whom he represented. **As a**
shepherd separates the sheep from the goats is a simile of judgement as
old as Ezekiel (34.17): the Palestinian shepherd would pasture his flocks of
sheep and goats together, but at some stage he would **separate** the one from
the other; the white sheep were a natural symbol for the pure apparel of the
righteous, the black goats for the dark deeds of the wicked. And finally, a
king on his throne was one of the commonest of images for the God of 34
justice who would one day bring all men to account for the "acts of kindness"[a] which they had done or failed to do. All these elements, including
even the dialogue between the king and those who appear before him, are conventional enough. But the way these elements are combined and exploited
is unique and arresting. That Jesus was himself the Son of Man who would
"come in glory" has already been intimated several times in the gospel, and
it followed from the title itself, and from the destiny traditionally connected
with it, that he would play an important part in the Last Judgement. But
here the thought is taken a step further—he becomes the Judge himself, the
King who gives sentence—though still in some way subordinate to God the
Father ("**You have my Father's blessing**"). This represents a greater 34
concentration of attributes in the person of the Son than appears anywhere else in the gospels, and if these are to be taken literally, rather than as a poetic accumulation of images, they confront the interpreter with difficult problems about the true nature and status of Christ. But the real originality of the passage, as well as its beauty and symmetry, lies in the dialogue. That men would be richly rewarded for their acts of kindness was taken for granted by Jesus' contemporaries; and that these acts (rather than the fact of belonging to the Jewish race, or the fact of having faithfully observed the Law) would serve as the principal basis of distinction between the blest and the damned was a point of view that many would have been prepared to accept. But the reason given here must have seemed revolutionary: it was not just that acts of this kind are specially meritorious, but that in doing them to certain people one is doing them to Jesus himself. Who are these people in whom lurks the Son of Man? It is tempting to answer, All who are in need.

[a] See below on Mark 14.3–9. The only act listed here which does not occur in similar Jewish lists is visiting prisoners.

40 But this is not what is said here. "**Anything you did for one of my brothers here, however humble, you did for me**". "Brothers", in this gospel (and indeed throughout the New Testament) is almost a technical name for Christians; moreover, Jesus called his "brothers", not mankind in general, but those who, with him, have God as their father. In short, the reward
46 of **eternal life** is promised here to those who show kindness to Christians, for it is in the Christian community that Jesus lives on, bringing men face to face with the ultimate issues of life and death, reward and condemnation, just as he did when he preached and worked on earth.

The final conflict

From this point on Matthew follows the account in Mark very closely, and it will be sufficient to notice a few details which he has changed or added.
26. 2 **'You know that in two days' time it will be Passover'**: This is exactly
the same chronology as in Mark, but here, in Jesus' own mouth, the dating
takes on deeper meaning: Jesus knows in advance that this particular Passover will be unique as being the exact moment when the **Son of Man is to**
be handed over for crucifixion—and the stage is set for this "handing
3 over" at a meeting, which only Matthew mentions, **in the palace of**
the High Priest, Caiaphas (whom we know to have held this office from
A.D. 18 to 36). Already there is conflict: Jesus is prophesying his crucifixion
during the Passover, while his enemies are endeavouring to avoid exactly
5 this. **'It must not be during the festival,' they said.**

6 **Jesus was at Bethany**. Compared with Mark's account (14.3–9), Matthew's
is less startling. Instead of breaking the neck of the bottle and emptying the
7 entire contents over Jesus' head, the woman merely **began to pour it**, and
the value of the ointment is not the very large figure of thirty pounds (which
9 Mark gives) but merely a **good sum**. Any reader who still found in Mark's
version of the story, despite its symbolic meaning, an unnecessarily wasteful gesture, would have been considerably less shocked when reading Matthew, where almsgiving and this particular act of charity are kept more in proportion with each other.

14 **Then one of the Twelve**. Matthew alone gives the details of the bargain made between Judas and the chief priests. How did he know the exact figure? Possibly some Christian was able to find it out afterwards, and passed on the information; but possibly Matthew inferred it from a passage of the Old Testament which he regarded as a prophecy of the events he was recording. Zechariah 11.12 runs, "they weighed out as my wages thirty

pieces of silver". In Zechariah's time these silver pieces were doubtless shekels; in the time of Jesus the equivalent was the tetradrachm, which was the largest silver coin in currency, and which had been minted all over the Greek-speaking world since the time of Alexander the Great. The sum of money would therefore amount to 120 Roman *denarii*, or (according to the scale adopted by the NEB) twelve English pounds. There is slight doubt whether the verb in the Greek means that the chief priests paid Judas at
once ("weighing out" the coins in case any should be under weight) or 16
merely promised to pay (as Mark has it). But the rendering adopted in the main text comes closer to the meaning in Zechariah and is not improbable in itself.

On the first day of Unleavened Bread. Strictly speaking this is 17
inaccurate: it was the afternoon (as Mark makes clear) preceding the evening which, by Jewish reckoning, began the new day of 15th Nisan, the first day of Unleavened Bread. But a non-Palestinian reader, counting the days as we do from midnight to midnight, would not have been misled. The miraculous details in Mark's account of the finding of a room are omitted by Matthew, who evidently assumed that the matter was prearranged. This was
Jesus' **'appointed time'**, the Passover which would be the signal for his 18
crucifixion.

Matthew's additions to Mark's account of the supper (14.17–25) are very 20–9
small. The traitor is explicitly identified as Judas—though perhaps not so clearly and unambiguously that anyone but Jesus and Judas himself would have realized what was going to happen. It is not said when Judas left the company to carry out his plot; but this point (i.e. after verse 25) is the most likely one; and if the traitor was then out of the room, the slightly greater emphasis in this account (compared with Mark's) on the privileged circle of
the disciples (**'Drink from it, all of you'** . . . **'when I drink it new with** 27, 29
you') is understandable. There is one further addition of significance: the
blood is shed **for the forgiveness of sins.** To the image of the old covenant, 28
sealed by the blood of a sacrifice, is added that of the "new covenant", foreseen by Jeremiah (31.31–4), which would be brought into effect by God's forgiveness of his people's sins.

Jesus then came with his disciples to a place called Gethsemane. 36
This episode is told almost exactly as in Mark (14.32–42): Matthew has merely modified some of Mark's more forcible expressions and clarified a
few obscurities—adding, however, a fresh one. Jesus' reply to Judas, **'Friend,** 50
do what you are here to do' is a puzzling piece of Greek. Jesus certainly returned Judas' greeting, but in just what tone of voice we cannot tell (see the footnote in NEB). Matthew makes one significant addition to the narrative. The scuffle which led to the High Priest's servant losing an ear is only mentioned in passing by Mark, but in Matthew it leads to two sayings

52 of Jesus. The first, **'All who take the sword die by the sword'**, sounds
like a proverb—possibly, like another proverb used by Jesus, originating in a
reaction against the violent tactics of fanatical rebels against the Roman
régime (see below on Mark 9.40): Jesus made a point of dissociating himself
from any movement of that kind. The second raises the conflict to a different
level. As Luke puts it, this moment was 'the hour when darkness reigns',
which is not just a metaphor, but a clear indication of the way the crisis
presented itself to the gospel writers (and doubtless to Jesus). The contest was
not merely between Jesus and the secular powers. Behind this was raging a
supernatural battle against Satan and all the evil powers. We now know
from the Dead Sea Scrolls how this battle was imagined in the time of Jesus:
huge detachments of angels arrayed in military order were lined up against
each other in readiness for the final conflict. The discipline and organization
of the Roman occupying army were projected by these writers into the scene
53 of heavenly warfare; hence Jesus' somewhat surprising expression, **'twelve
legions of angels'**.

57 **Jesus was led off under arrest to the house of Caiaphas the High
Priest**. Matthew, unlike Luke and John, follows exactly the same order of
events as Mark: immediately after Jesus' arrest there was a formal session of
the Sanhedrin, not in its usual meeting place, but in the house of Caiaphas,
59 who was probably president of the court. The court consisted of other **chief
57 priests, the lawyers** (who were mainly Pharisees) and **elders** (who were
probably influential and aristocratic laymen). There was nothing unusual in
members of the court themselves presenting evidence against the accused.
But for any charge to be substantiated, it was necessary for two witnesses
independently to give consistent evidence, and this seems to have been the
61 court's first difficulty. **Finally two men alleged**. It seems that valid
evidence was obtained on only one point, a saying of Jesus which in fact
John's gospel records in another context (2.14). Matthew's version of the
saying is a little milder than Mark's: not, 'I will pull down the temple',
but **'I can pull down the temple'**—a form which will have troubled subsequent Christians less, since it did not raise the question (as Mark's perhaps
more original version does) of when and how this promise was fulfilled.
Nevertheless, the allegation was serious. "Prophesying against the temple"
had once nearly cost Jeremiah his life (Jeremiah 26) and was the kind of
thing which, if uttered in the precincts of the temple, could doubtless be
regarded as blasphemy. Here, *prima facie*, was damning evidence; and when
Jesus refused to speak a word in his own defence, a case seemed to have been
made out. The critical point which proceedings had reached is marked by
62 the fact that **the High Priest rose**; but before passing judgement he had
one further question to put which would explain and confirm the evidence
so far given. It was generally expected that when the Messiah came one of

the marks of his reign would be a period of new holiness and new splendour
in the temple in Jerusalem. Could it be that Jesus' saying was not just
blasphemous arrogance, but was a sign that he believed himself to be the
Messiah? If so, this would by no means lessen his guilt, since it must have
seemed obvious to the court that their silent prisoner could not possibly be
the glorious deliverer expected by the whole Jewish people; but it would
make Jesus' saying about the temple intelligible and give the judges a more
substantial case to pronounce on. Jesus was therefore put on oath to answer
the question, **'Are you the Messiah, the Son of God?'** (where **Son of** 63
God would be understood, not in the deep sense propounded by the early
church, but simply as a successor to the long line of Old Testament figures
who, by virtue of their divine commission, were called Sons of God).

Jesus' reply to the specific question seems, as usual, to have been ambiguous: to have accepted without qualification the title of Messiah would
perhaps have been to accept too many of the secular and superficial ideas
which his contemporaries attached to it. But, by means of allusions to two
Old Testament passages (Daniel 7.13; Psalm 110.1) which described a
personage honoured and glorified by God, Jesus affirmed that at least one
of the implications of the title was true of himself. **'From now on'**—not in 64
some theoretical future, but by an immediate reversal of fortune—Jesus
would be seen to be vindicated and given a unique status **at the right hand**
of God. Matthew doubtless saw this claim as having been fulfilled by the
resurrection and ascension of Jesus: the church did in fact come to know
and experience its Lord as glorified and vindicated. But to the judges such
a claim seemed merely to aggravate the original blasphemy. **'He is guilty,'** 66
they answered; 'he should die.'

But, under the Roman administration, the Jewish court had apparently
lost the power to carry out the death penalty, and further measures were
necessary to secure Jesus' execution. Meanwhile, in a scene of brutality,
Jesus' claim to be Messiah was put to the test. The Messiah would have the
gift of prophecy—for instance, he would know who people were without
being told. It was a fair test: **'Now, Messiah, if you are a prophet, tell** 68
us who hit you'. But Jesus offered no such spectacular confirmation of the
possibility that he was the Messiah.

Meanwhile Peter was sitting outside. Here Matthew has rearranged 69
Mark's narrative very little, omitting only the curious feature of two separate
cock-crows. The story of Peter's denial occurs in all the gospels: see below
on Mark 15. 66–72.

When morning came. Does Matthew mean to record a second formal **27.** 1
session of the Sanhedrin? A meeting in the morning would certainly
harmonize better with the accounts in Luke and John, but after the proceedings which Matthew had just described, taking place during the night

and ending with a verdict and a sentence, a further session seems superfluous. All that remained to be done was **to plan the death of Jesus**—in the sense that, since the court was not competent to carry out its own sentence, it was necessary to have Jesus sentenced also by the Roman governor. Deciding on their tactics need not have taken the judges very long, nor required another formal session; in any case it was necessary for them to hand Jesus over to
2 **Pilate, the Roman Governor**, as early as possible, so as to catch him when he would be available.

At this point Matthew inserts an episode which is recorded in none of the other gospels (though it is mentioned in Acts 1.18–19): the death of Judas.
3 It comes in a little awkwardly, for **the chief priests and elders** are at this
moment at Caiaphas' house, whereas Judas' gesture of returning the money
5 presupposes that he is **in the temple**—that is to say, at least in one of those courtyards of the temple where there were arrangements for receiving money (see below on Mark 12.41–4). Matthew, in fact, is adding an excursus on the working-out of Judas' destiny, without too much concern for its connection with the main narrative (a modern writer would probably use a footnote for the purpose). It is clear that the interest of the early Christians was not merely biographical. There were other reasons for the tradition being preserved. One was that the Christian community in Jerusalem came to associate a particular spot with Judas' sinister death. They named it, in Aramaic,
8 Akeldama (Acts 1.19), which meant '**Blood Acre**'; but to everyone else it
7 was known as **the Potter's Field**. The site of it is fairly certain. The "Potter's Gate" of Jerusalem lay at the extreme south-east corner of the city, at the mouth of the ill-famed valley of Gehinnom. Nearby were tombs cut into the rock: the whole area, with its smoking industries, its sinister historical associations, and the ritual uncleanness which belonged to any cemetery, was a fit place to bear the memory of the death of the traitor. Precisely what the connection was between Judas and this place was perhaps (by the time the gospel was written) no longer remembered, and it was necessary to work back from the name the Christians themselves had given it. A quite different explanation is given in Acts (1.18–19); here, an inference is drawn which at least shows Matthew's expert knowledge. The area belonged to the temple authorities and was used **as a burial-place for foreigners** (for whom, of course, the associations of the place were less sinister—in later centuries it became an honoured burial-place for Christian pilgrims). How did they acquire it? What better explanation than that they used Judas' money which, being blood-money, could not be put into **the**
6 **temple fund**? These details are quite correct. Deuteronomy 23.18 runs: "You shall not bring the hire of a harlot or the wages of a sodomite into the house of the Lord your God". *A fortiori*, blood-money could not be put into **the temple fund** (literally *Corban*, another technical term).

But there was also a more fundamental reason for this interest in the circumstances of Judas' death. His treachery did not present itself to the first Christians as something demanding a psychological explanation: it was intended and destined by God. But things which had long been prepared in the purposes of God might be expected to be alluded to in prophecy. Sure enough, Zechariah 11.12–13 runs as follows:

> "They weighed out my wages, thirty pieces of silver. The Lord said to me, Throw it back into the treasury. I took the thirty pieces of silver—that noble sum at which I was valued and rejected by them—and threw them into the house of the Lord, into the treasury."

This text was always somewhat obscure and widely different versions of it exist. Moreover, it had a curious variant. Only certain versions gave "throw it into the treasury"; the original Hebrew appears to mean, "cast it to the potter". It looks as if Matthew knew both these interpretations and he was also able to exploit the fact that, when translated into Greek, the word meaning "I took" was identical with the word meaning "they took". Consequently, it only needed a little skilful manipulation of the original (which scholars in his time took very much for granted) to yield an impressive prophecy of the events of Judas' suicide. Only one problem remains: why does Matthew say
Jeremiah instead of Zechariah? It is true that there were two well-known 9
passages of Jeremiah in which the prophet "went to the house of the potter" (18.3) and "bought a field" (29.9); but even if these lay at the back of Matthew's mind, it was Zechariah, not Jeremiah, that he was quoting. The most likely answer is that this was simply a mistake. It is in any case likely that early Christian writers, when quoting from the Old Testament, used, not a complete copy, but a collection of short prophecies which the church had found particularly relevant to the proclamation and defence of the Christian faith; and it is quite possible that these short passages were not always correctly arranged under their respective authors (for another example, see below on Mark 1.2-3).

Jesus was now brought before the Governor. After this digression, 11
Matthew returns to the hearing before Pilate, and his account closely follows
that of Mark, though it presupposes on the part of his readers less familiarity
with the original circumstances than Mark's does. Mark's readers were
evidently expected to have heard of Barabbas; but here he is introduced
with the slightly more precise name, **Jesus Bar-Abbas,**[a] and the scene is 16
given a new element of drama by the confrontation of two criminals called
Jesus—**Jesus Bar-Abbas, or Jesus called Messiah.** Matthew has two new 17
details to add to the narrative. One is the intervention of Pilate's wife. 19

[a] That Barabbas had the first name **Jesus** is the evidence of a number of early manuscripts, and also of the third-century writer Origen. It would be more understandable that the piety of later generations suppressed a second Jesus than that their fantasy invented one, and the NEB translators have therefore adopted this reading. Bar-Abbas (if that is the correct division of the syllables) is not an uncommon name. It means "father's son".

Roman provincial governors had recently begun to take their wives with them when on foreign service. Her dream is very much the kind of portent which ancient historians often recorded before a battle or a crisis. The
24 other detail is Pilate's gesture of washing his hands **in full view of the people.** The gesture would be intelligible in any culture, but it was also a classical biblical way of expressing innocence (Deuteronomy 21.6; Psalm 73.13). By recording it, Matthew emphatically attaches the blame for what followed to the Jewish people as a whole.

27 **Pilate's soldiers then took Jesus into the Governor's headquarters.**
Matthew is still following Mark very closely—and the fact that he uses the
32 same rather uncommon word (said to be of Persian origin) for **pressed him into service** is one of the detailed pieces of evidence which show that he must have had a copy of Mark's gospel in front of him.[a] He leaves out the names of Simon of Cyrene's sons (which Mark gives as Alexander and Rufus), since these men, who must have been known to the Christians who first read Mark's gospel, were presumably of no interest to Matthew's readers. At the same time he adds or alters certain details. When the soldiers
28 mocked Jesus, they **dressed him in a scarlet mantle**—not the royal purple of Mark's version, but the Roman Emperor's colour: there may be a touch of historical precision here, for it would have been difficult for the soldiers to procure purple, but they could perhaps have borrowed the scarlet mantle of one of the official attendants of Pilate (who was the Emperor's
34 representative). It is not clear why Matthew substitutes **wine mixed with gall** for Mark's 'drugged wine': possibly a recollection of Psalm 69.21 (which, in the Greek version, contains the words "for my food they gave me gall") influenced him. In any case, the point is the same. The drink was a narcotic, such as was normally provided by the Jews for prisoners who were about to be executed. To the description of the mockery to which Jesus was
39-40 subjected, Matthew adds a further touch, drawn again from the repertory of Old Testament poetry describing innocent suffering. The closest parallel is Psalm 22.8 (the psalm which provides the most impressive precedent for and commentary on the details of Jesus' crucifixion):

> " 'He committed his cause to the Lord; let him deliver him,
> let him rescue him, for he holds him dear.' "

But there is another passage which must also have been in Matthew's mind. The first chapters of the Wisdom of Solomon are concerned precisely with the problem of the righteous sufferer, and in chapter 2 the mockery of the

[*a*] For many centuries it was believed that the dependence is the other way round, and that Mark is simply an abridged edition of Matthew; hence the comparative neglect of Mark's gospel until recent times. But it is now generally thought that the differences between the two gospels are easier to explain on the hypothesis that Mark's gospel was written first. See the introductory note to THE GOSPEL, p. 14.

unrighteous is described. The following phrases (from verses 13–18) will show how closely Matthew's account conforms to what had already become a classical model in Jewish literature: "He styles himself 'the son of the Lord' . . . he boasts that God is his father . . . let us test the truth of his words . . . for if the just man is God's son, God will stretch out a hand to him and save him."

Matthew diverges significantly from Mark's account only when it comes to
the moment of Jesus' death. At this point (15.38) Mark mentions one event
which he must have regarded as supernatural: the tearing of the curtain of
the temple. In this Mark is probably making use of an ancient and somewhat
oriental convention: the reference to miraculous events accompanying a
person's death is an element of commentary on the significance of the
moment rather than of meticulous historical reporting. Matthew takes this
somewhat further, and thereby starts a trend which produces a mass of
increasingly improbable miracles in the accounts of the later apocryphal
gospels. The symbolism may have in fact begun with the **curtain of the** 51
temple itself. This huge piece of tapestry was a famous sight. It was hung
in front of the doors of the main temple building, and could be seen even by
non-Jews when they looked through the gateway of the Court of the Israelites towards the temple entrance. Embroidered upon it was the firmament
of heaven. The most obvious symbolism in the tearing of this curtain **from**
top to bottom was the end of the importance of the temple in religious life
and the removal of the barrier which had hitherto excluded non-Jews from
the worship of the true God. But a further meaning may have been suggested
by the picture woven upon it. Not the curtain only, but the heavens themselves, were rent asunder (one of the traditional signs of the Day of the Lord);
and this was answered on earth by an **earthquake**. To this extent Matthew's 52
miracle-commentary on the moment of Jesus' death is of a piece. That **the**
graves opened is more strange; but resurrection was also an element of the
Day of the Lord, even though, as Matthew admits, the time for such a
miracle was really **after his resurrection**. 53

'Truly this man was a son of God'. This is a total reversal of the 54
mockery of a few minutes earlier. At the very moment of Jesus' death, God
had acted to vindicate his righteous servant, and even the foreigners standing
by—**the centurion and his men**—were moved to recognize something
divine in Jesus. In Mark it is Jesus' bearing at his death which impresses
the centurion; here it is the accompanying portents which overwhelm the
whole group of soldiers. Their confession was valid: it was as "Son of God"
that the church soon began to worship Jesus. But if we are to ask what the
phrase could have meant in the mouths of the soldiers, the answer, in
Matthew, is quite clear: Jesus was one of those so-called "sons of God"
who would work miracles and whose death would appropriately be marked
by an earthquake.

55 **A number of women were also present.** Matthew mentions the same
56 names as Mark, except that he seems to identify Mark's Salome with **the
mother of the sons of Zebedee.** But only two of them remain to witness
the burial, and only two return on Sunday morning to the tomb, Mary of
Magdala and the other Mary (28.1). Joseph of Arimathaea, too, has undergone
a significant change at Matthew's hands. In Mark, he is presented as a devout
and influential Jew, whose main motive in undertaking the burial of Jesus
was probably that of saving the city and its surrounding country from the
defilement of an unburied corpse. But in Matthew his motive is quite
57 different: he is a man who **had himself become a disciple of Jesus** (which
might have been difficult if, as Mark says, he was a member of the Sanhedrin: Matthew omits this detail), and his action is that much more devoted
60 in that he lays Jesus **in his own unused tomb.** What in Mark was a hasty
burial perfunctorily performed by a stranger has become in Matthew a work
of charity undertaken by an influential disciple.

62 **Next day, the morning after that Friday.** Matthew alone reports this
episode, which accounts for the presence (in his account) of soldiers at the
tomb, and so makes the events of Sunday morning still more miraculous.
It is a little surprising to find the Jewish authorities taking action of this kind
on the Sabbath, and in any case one would have thought that they should
have taken the precaution as soon as Jesus was buried. However, Pilate
65 provided a **guard** (Matthew uses the Latin word *custodia*, suggesting a
contingent from the Roman army, not from the Jewish temple police), and
the Jews, as an additional precaution, placed some kind of seal on the stone
so that any unauthorized opening could be detected.

28. 1 **The Sabbath was over.** The scene is recognizably the same as that in
Mark, but is told with less detail and a greater emphasis on the supernatural.
2 The **earthquake**, the description of **the angel of the Lord**, and the
paralysed fear of the guards, are all features that belong less to a factual
narrative of the discovery that the tomb was empty than to an imaginative
description of a supernatural experience. Such importance as the empty tomb
itself may have had is still further played down when the vision of the angel
is immediately followed by an encounter with the risen Jesus. This brings
the women's experience into line with that of the church as a whole. It was
not the empty tomb, but the appearances of Jesus himself, which gave them
9 confidence to proclaim the resurrection. The women were the first to
worship him in his risen state. **Clasped his feet, falling prostrate before
him,** are signs of the deepest reverence.

11–15 Matthew has his own explanation to offer (different from Mark's) of why
the discovery that Jesus' tomb was empty was not immediately seized upon
and proclaimed by the church: a counter-story was deliberately put about
by the Jews; and since the Christian version of the matter rested only on the

testimony of two women (whose evidence would not have been admitted in a Jewish court), this could presumably never have had much force in disputes (such as we can frequently overhear in Matthew's gospel) between the Christian church and its Jewish opponents. Matthew simply reports the two versions of the facts and leaves the reader to decide between them.

The eleven disciples made their way to Galilee. Matthew, like Mark, 16
has faithfully recorded (26.32) the somewhat puzzling statement of Jesus that after the resurrection he would 'go on before' his disciples to Galilee. The promise has just been repeated by the angel at the tomb (28.7) and by the risen Jesus himself (28.10); and Matthew ends his gospel by recounting its fulfilment. The mention of **the eleven disciples** sounds deliberately precise. The 'twelve' were last mentioned at the Passover supper (26.20). Since then Judas had defected and killed himself; but although Peter had denied Jesus, and the rest had deserted him, these eleven were still evidently (at least to Matthew's way of thinking, if not in historical fact) the only appropriate group to receive the final revelation of Jesus' authority and commission. Matthew reports that they **made their way to Galilee.** This contradicts Luke's account, according to which all Jesus' last appearances took place in or near Jerusalem. But it is possible that Matthew was more interested in the symbolic significance of the setting than in the geographical spot where the vision was actually seen. In his gospel, Matthew has said nothing of a
mountain where Jesus had told them to meet him: this phrase does 16
not help us to locate the scene. On the other hand, the greatest moments of Jesus' self-revelation, whether of his true nature (the Transfiguration) or of his moral demands (the Sermon on the Mount), were conceived of as taking place on a mountain, and just as the definitive revelation of God in the Old Testament took place on Mount Sinai, so Matthew may well have taken it for granted that the scene he was about to relate must have taken place on a mountain, and therefore that Jesus must previously have arranged this meeting-place with his disciples.

They fell prostrate before him. The appearance of Jesus is not de- 17
scribed, and has to be inferred from the disciples' reaction. On meeting the earthly Jesus, their greeting would have been respectful, certainly—that of disciples to master; but they would hardly have prostrated themselves, for this was regarded as a subservient action only appropriate to the great monarchs of the east. The only reason for prostration would have been some vision of the supernatural—and this is clearly what is intended here, though not a word is used to describe what the disciples saw. **Some were doubtful.** Possibly the vision was ambiguous: the figure was certainly Jesus, but there was not such a radiance in his person that all those who saw him were led to recognize that they were in the presence of a divine being. Nevertheless, their doubt at this stage seems surprising—particularly since Matthew is usually careful to present the disciples so far as he can as models

of Christian discipleship. This may perhaps be Matthew's momentary admission of the fact, which is clearly stated in Luke and John, that some of the disciples took time to be convinced of the reality of the resurrection.

18 **'Full authority in heaven and on earth has been committed to me.'**
This is the fulfilment of the destiny of the Son of Man—"Sovereignty and glory and kingly power were given to him, so that all people and nations of every language should serve him" (Daniel 7.14). The words provide the answer to the question, What was Jesus' status after the resurrection? He was the one to whom supreme power had been given under God. The church had various ways of expressing this, one drawn from Psalm 110—"You shall sit at my right hand, until I make your enemies the footstool under your feet"—and others besides. But most appropriate to the triumphant end of the story of the suffering Son of Man were these words from Daniel; and the following sentences offer a commentary on the **authority** which was now exercised by the risen Jesus. It was effective, not when men were blindly
19 subservient, but when they became Jesus' **disciples**, by accepting baptism and by observing his teaching. However much Jesus may have limited the range of his disciples' mission during his life on earth, their task was now world-wide. Indeed, by the time Matthew's gospel was written, Christianity had spread so far round the civilization of the Mediterranean that it seemed already to have reached **all nations**. For the language of these sentences is the language of the early church: baptizing and instructing were the main activities of Christian ministers, and it is of a piece with the emphasis which, throughout his gospel, Matthew lays upon Jesus' ethical teaching that Jesus
20 should say, **'teach them to observe all that I have commanded you'**.
Doubtless the conviction of the first generations of Christians that this was their task and mission, and that the risen Christ was perceptibly "with them", went back to an assurance of Jesus, given in the course of an experience such as Matthew here describes. But plain reporting cannot do justice to such experiences; an author has to add what personal touches he can to draw out their meaning. And we can hardly be wrong in detecting, in the last words of the gospel, an allusion to one of the very first things which Matthew reports about Jesus (1.23): 'He shall be called Emmanuel—a name which means "God is with us."'

THE GOSPEL ACCORDING TO MARK

The coming of Christ

Here begins the Gospel. When a messenger brought news of a victory in 1. 1
war or of some stroke of personal good fortune, the correct Greek word for his tidings was *euangelion*, "good news". In the Roman empire, happy events of this kind were ascribed to the apparently superhuman power of the reigning Emperor. It was the Emperor's genius which gave men victory, peace and prosperity. The Emperor was the saviour of mankind, and the news of a new Emperor's birth or accession was therefore the most important *euangelion* of all. The essence of the Christian message was that a new Saviour had now appeared among men and had ascended his throne in heaven. It was no stretch of language to call this message a *euangelion*, and the word soon became a technical term in the Christian vocabulary. The equivalent, in English, has always been the Anglo-Saxon word **Gospel.**

The content of this Gospel concerned **Jesus Christ the Son of God.** At least a generation before Mark wrote (as is evident from Paul's letters) the title **Son of God** had become attached to Jesus. Nevertheless in the gospels it is used only sparingly, and its occurrence here in the very first verse of Mark's gospel is significant: evidently one of the main purposes of Mark's work was to demonstrate that Jesus was in fact the Son of God. To feel the force of this claim, it is important to know what the title would have suggested to Mark's first readers. Among Greek-speaking people, the phrase **Son of God** denoted nothing very much out of the ordinary. The many miracle-workers and men of exceptional psychic or ascetic powers who moved about the ancient world were often so described; and the citizens of the Roman empire had become accustomed to the Emperor being called "son of a god". But (as is clear from the temptation stories in Matthew and Luke) Jesus vigorously rejected any connotations of this sort. If he was the Son of God, this did not mean that he was just one among the many "sons of God" of the ancient world; for he was unique. The meaning of the title for the earliest Christians (and perhaps for Jesus himself) must therefore be looked for, not in the secular language of Greece and Rome, but in Jewish religion; and here it is clear that the title was much more specific. It meant one who was specially singled out by God for an important rôle in the unfolding of the destiny of his people. In the past, certain kings and prophets had had such a vocation. But in recent times no comparable person had appeared, and hopes were concentrated instead on a single, almost legendary figure, the Messiah (in Greek, the Christ) who was to appear at the end of the present age. Tentatively before the resurrection, and confidently after it, the disciples recognized that Jesus was indeed this Christ (albeit a very different Christ from that of Jewish expectation). Similarly they were led to the point, by the life, death and resurrection of Jesus, of seeing in him **the Son of God**—though, once again, the title when applied to Jesus meant a great deal more than it ever had in the Old Testament: Jesus was not merely the chosen instrument of God, he was uniquely related to God with the intimacy which a son has with his father. That any man should claim such intimacy with God was a source of scandal to the religious men of Palestine, and was one of their reasons for securing Jesus' execution. But the disciples had intimations during Jesus' life on earth that this intimacy was a fact; and they saw the resurrection as decisive proof of it. Thereafter they could talk confidently of **Jesus Christ the Son of God**. It is one of the themes of Mark's gospel that this sonship was already apparent, to those few who could discern it, during Jesus' life on earth.

The writers of the gospels each chose a different point at which their story could be said to "begin". Mark starts later than any of them with the appearance of John the Baptist—which is in fact where early Christian sermons seem often to have begun (Acts 10.37). Here John is introduced with an Old Testament prophecy; but only the second part of the quotation
2–3 (**A voice crying aloud** etc.) can be found in **the prophet Isaiah** (40.3);
the first part appears to be a combination of Malachi 3.1 and Exodus 23.20. It is possible that Christians had come to see references to John the Baptist in all these texts from Scripture, and that after they had been quoted together a few times they were thought of as a single passage of prophecy and attributed as a whole to **the prophet Isaiah**. In any case the prophecy serves here to stress that element in the mission of John which was of supreme importance for Christians: John was the immediate forerunner of Jesus.

4 **And so it was.** The prophecy simply announced a "herald". Mark now fills out the picture of the historical figure, John, who fulfilled the prophecy. He appeared **in the wilderness**. This, for anyone who knew Palestine, was a sufficient indication: although a large part of the country was desert, it was the arid and wild mountainous area which begins dramatically just below the Mount of Olives and stretches down to the Jordan valley over 3,000 feet below which was the "wilderness" any local inhabitant would think of at once. John's appearance there doubtless helped to emphasize the austere and challenging message which he had come to proclaim (see above on Matthew 3.1–6). It was also close to the Jordan, where John carried out his characteristic work of **baptism**. This baptism was something quite new. The Jews practised many forms of ritual washing as part of the ceremonies needed to remove the impurities of sin, and we now know (from the Dead Sea Scrolls) that in one Jewish sect at least such washing was the principal

rite by which it was felt that men could be made morally "clean". But nothing in such practices prepares us for the baptism of John. Admittedly John's baptism was also **in token of repentance, for the forgiveness of sins.** But it was clearly not intended to be understood merely as a new supplement to existing institutions. It was proclaimed as something quite decisive, an act which everyone should submit to, regardless of their religious upbringing; it was a necessary preparation for a new state of affairs which was shortly to come into being. Some of the implications of this radically simple message are worked out in the narratives of the other gospels. Here it seems to have been sufficient to indicate the barest elements of the scene: a new rite of moral cleansing, readily undergone by a great multitude of people, performed by an austere preacher in the wilderness of the Jordan valley, far from the usual holy places and institutions of the Jewish religion. The essence of it was that the people, however scrupulously they had been abiding by the moral and ceremonial laws of their religion,
came **confessing their sins.** John's baptism, like the teaching of Jesus, 5
marked a new stage in the progress of religion from a system of observances to an attitude of uncompromising moral sincerity.

The quotation from Malachi (3.1), "Here is my herald whom I send on ahead of you", has already prepared the reader to think of John as Elijah; for Elijah was not merely a great figure of the past: it was prophesied that he would one day return (Malachi 3.23). The description of John's clothes reinforces this impression: in 2 Kings 1.8 Elijah is described as "a man wearing a garment of hair cloth and a leather belt". Moreover the returning Elijah was to herald the day of the Lord; John heralded not only one who
was **mightier** than himself, but one whose baptism would be of a different 7
order altogether.

The readers of the gospel knew who this was, and Mark spends no time on the questions which worry the other evangelists, such as whether John recognized Jesus, or whether it was appropriate for Jesus to be baptized.
He relates the important facts in a single sentence and proceeds at once to 9
interpret the significance of Jesus' baptism. The **dove** appears to be a visible 10–11
symbol of what was essentially an invisible event: Jesus' endowment with the Holy Spirit. The voice from heaven, given in words drawn from Ps. 2.7 or Isaiah 42.1 (or both), serves to justify the title given to Jesus in the first
sentence of the gospel: **Son of God.** 1

Matthew and Luke each give a full account of the "temptation" of Jesus. According to them, it consisted of certain choices suggested to Jesus by Satan. Mark's account is so brief that we cannot be sure whether he intended the same interpretation. The details are more or less traditional.
Forty days was a biblical round number, the time Moses spent on Mount 13
Sinai (Exodus 24.28), the time Elijah spent on his pilgrimage to Horeb (1 Kings 19.8); and **the angels waited on him** (provided him with food)

exactly as they did on Elijah (1 Kings 19). All the meaning of the passage is concentrated in the words **tempted by Satan.** If we do not supply the details from the other accounts we need not think of this as a succession of specific "temptations" so much as a trial of strength between the Son of God and the powers of evil—a contest which remains present in the background of many other episodes as the gospel progresses.

In Galilee: success and opposition

14 **After John had been arrested, Jesus came into Galilee.** Mark's readers evidently were expected to be familiar with the story of John's arrest (which Mark in fact tells later on, 6.17–29): it is mentioned here simply in order to mark the moment at which Jesus' work in Galilee could properly be said to have begun—that is, not immediately after the baptism and temptation, but after a certain interval. What Jesus was doing in that interval (whether, for instance, he remained in company with John the Baptist) is not explained by Mark, who is less concerned to fill the gaps in his biography than to divide the narrative into clearly marked sections. For him (contrast, for example, John's gospel) the activity of Jesus has two main phases: first in Galilee, where Jesus has both *Success and opposition*—though the emphasis is on the success rather than on the opposition; and secondly in Jerusalem, where *The final conflict* leads to his death. This simple arrangement of the material concerning Jesus is logical and plausible, and is followed with only slight modification by Matthew and Luke. But the fact that John's gospel follows a different pattern, weaving together Jesus' activity in Galilee and Jerusalem, suggests that Mark's arrangement may be schematic rather than historical; and there are hints even in Mark's narrative that Jesus made more journeys to Jerusalem (as a pious Jew living in Galilee would normally do) than the single one which he records. However this may be, Mark clearly intends Jesus' appearance in his home country to mark the beginning of the first period, that of preaching, healing and controversy in Galilee. He devotes the next few chapters to giving some typical examples of these activities.

14 **Proclaiming the Gospel of God.** The modern reader is curious to know what Jesus' message was like, and will probably find Mark's summary of it somewhat disappointing. In this respect Matthew, who places the Sermon on the Mount right at the beginning of his account of Jesus' work, may seem much more satisfactory. The reason why Mark was content with such a brief summary is probably that when he used the phrase **the Gospel of God** he could be sure that his first readers would be thoroughly familiar with what was meant by it. The Gospel was the preaching which they

themselves had heard and responded to when they became Christians; and
Mark gives here, not the content which Jesus must have given to this Gospel
when he first preached it, so much as the tone in which he preached, and in
which indeed the message was still preached in the church.

'The time has come.' Every Jew would have known what this meant. 15
History as recorded in the Old Testament was all preparation for a consummation that still lay in the future; Jesus was proclaiming that the time
of preparation was at last over. **'The kingdom of God is upon you.'** Again,
the meaning of the phrase **the kingdom of God** was one which Mark's
readers would have come to grasp for themselves. It could not be easily
defined; it would only gradually be demonstrated in the teaching and destiny
of Jesus and in the new experience of the church. The point here is that it
was **upon you**: unlike his predecessors, Jesus did not merely teach about
the kingdom, he proclaimed its imminent arrival. **'Repent, and believe the
Gospel.'** It will have made no difference that Jesus' hearers already professed a religion in which repentance played an important part. It will have
been no good answering, "But we repented yesterday". For Jesus' appearance was the irruption of something new, and the urgency of his preaching
demanded (as the next two paragraphs will show) a single-minded and
immediate response, a turning away from old habits, and a total commitment
to a new standard and a new master. Christian preaching doubtless had this
urgent and demanding tone in Mark's time and continued to have it for a
long time. Mark is showing here that it had the same tone when first
formulated by Jesus.

Jesus was walking. Mark has now set the scene: Jesus is in Galilee 16
proclaiming the Gospel by his deeds, as we shall see, as much as by his
words. The next events hardly fall into a biographical sequence: they are
presented as typical examples of Jesus' activities, somewhat loosely strung
together. The first such event is Jesus' summons to two pairs of brothers to
accompany him. How much they knew of Jesus beforehand, and how much
they were prepared for this sudden call, are details which Mark does not
trouble to record. The only important point for him (as doubtless it was the
important point also for the young church, when it reflected upon the
experience of conversion) was the immediacy of the disciples' response.
They were fishermen: not peasants (for Zebedee employed **hired men**) but 20
partners in a family fishing business. Jesus said he would make them **fishers** 17
of men. The metaphor is obvious enough in the context of the life of the
church, where "fishing for men" meant drawing them in from the pagan
world outside into the security of the "net" of the church. But when Jesus
used the phrase, he probably meant something different. The fishing net in
the teaching of Jesus (as in the Old Testament) is usually a symbol of the
Last Judgement: when that judgement comes, men and women will be
caught up into it inescapably. Simon and Andrew, James and John, are to

share in Jesus' work of confronting men with a judgement which is already beginning and which (like a fishing net) they cannot evade.

21 **They came to Capernaum.** Jesus, Mark has informed us, came from Nazareth: but the centre of his teaching was to be Capernaum, some 30 miles away from Nazareth and some 1,500 feet lower in altitude—a different world altogether from that of his native highland village. Capernaum was the largest town on the lake, it had a brisk commercial life (it was situated on the important trade route from Damascus to the Mediterranean) and was an important centre of the fishing industry. Its synagogue would certainly have been (as the existing ruins show it to have been in the following century) one of the largest in the country, and here Jesus went **on the Sabbath** for the normal service of prayer, readings from the Old Testament, and exposition. It was normal for the president of the synagogue to invite a qualified layman to give the teaching, and it was natural that Jesus, who was exceptionally well versed in Scripture, should receive such an invitation. Indeed we find him often (like the apostles after him) seizing just such an opportunity to proclaim his message. Mark does not say what the teaching was: but we may assume that (as in Luke 4) it took the usual form of exposition of Scripture. But it was nevertheless something very different from the
22 ordinary run of Sabbath sermons. **Unlike the doctors of the law, he taught with a note of authority.** It is possible that the Galilean congregation would have been equally impressed by the **authority** of, say, a learned scholar from Jerusalem, compared with the less highly qualified local **doctors of the law** (the "scribes" of older versions) to whom they were accustomed: but Mark, who has already stated that Jesus was the Son of God, doubtless has a more significant kind of authority in mind, something which would invest Jesus' words with a greater weight than would proceed from the mere scholarship of an expert. He proceeds to illustrate this, not by an example of Jesus' teaching, but by what we would call a "miraculous cure". By calling it this, we misdescribe it. Mark sees it as another encounter between Jesus and the forces of evil, and the onlookers are made to have the same interest. They are impressed by the fact, not that the sufferer is cured,
27 but that **even the unclean spirits submit.** Popular belief in Palestine—as indeed in many parts of the ancient world—was inclined to find demons and spirits (as agents of the devil) operative in many spheres of life. A fairly obvious case of their activity was felt to be any kind of mental or physical illness, such as epilepsy or some forms of schizophrenia, in which the
23 sufferer behaved as if controlled from outside, i.e. **possessed.** Furthermore, if (as was usually the case) this condition compelled the victim to commit acts which made him ritually "unclean", then the agent possessing him was called an **unclean spirit.** The proper technique for dealing with this condition was exorcism, and the power to perform exorcisms was by no means uncommon (Matthew 12.27; Acts 19.13). The normal procedure was

to make the spirit confess who or what it was and then to invoke the name of a mightier power in order to drive it out. Clearly (at least in Mark's understanding) Jesus had no need to invoke any authority apart from his own: the spirit instantly recognized him and submitted (with the usual final manifestation of its power—in this case **convulsions**). The episode falls naturally 26
into place. After the trial of strength with the devil himself (1.12–13) Jesus shows his mastery of the devil's agents. The people, impressed both by the authority of his teaching and the effectiveness of his exorcism, rapidly spread abroad the news.

The case of **Simon's mother-in-law** is told quite simply and is one of 29–31
the passages in Mark which seems most likely to go back to the personal testimony of the apostles.

That evening after sunset. Mark is very precise about the timing. The 32
Sabbath ended at sunset, and only then would it have been lawful to bring (if that meant carrying) **all who were ill** out of their own houses to the house where Jesus was: they came in fact at the first possible moment after Jesus' appearance in the synagogue that morning. Jesus **drove out many** 34
devils, presumably in much the same way as in the story recorded a few verses earlier. The devils had to submit **because they knew who he was.** But Jesus was evidently anxious to keep his true nature dark—a motive which is characteristic of Mark's presentation of Jesus.

Very early next morning. The phrase in the original is rough and vivid: 35
"very early, it was still night". Mark does not say what Jesus' motive was—whether simply to gain time for prayer, or to escape from the pressure of the crowds in Capernaum. The episode marks the transition from Jesus' initial appearance in Capernaum to his wider activity **all through** 39
Galilee.

Once he was approached. Mark has been giving a sequence of events 40
that fill out the picture of Jesus' first twenty-four hours in Capernaum, culminating in his departure to undertake a wider field of work. From now on it is clear that the episodes are less carefully linked together and are more in the nature of a selection of Jesus' activities, which perhaps came into Mark's possession without any clear order or sequence. The healing of the **leper** is a typical instance of these activities. It is not at all certain that the biblical disease of leprosy was the same as the terrible paralysis, anaesthesia and rotting of limbs which bears that name today. Descriptions of it in the Bible (see especially Leviticus 13–14) suggest a variety of skin diseases which were certainly severe and difficult to cure, but which cannot have been regarded as totally incurable, as modern leprosy would have been: for there are elaborate directions both in the Old Testament (Leviticus 14) and in later Jewish literature about the formalities of ritual cleansing which must be performed by the patient when he recovered. The real terror of the disease was seen, not in the physical suffering which it involved, but in the

ritual "uncleanness" which was imposed upon the sufferer. Strictly speaking (though it is possible that the severity of these rules was partially relaxed in the time of Jesus) a leper was allowed no physical contact with the persons or the houses and possessions of other Jews, and this social ostracism was inspired not so much by the fear of contagion as by the ritual "contamination" which was believed to be involved in any such contact. There is
41 therefore significance in the detail that Jesus **touched him**, and the **warm indignation**[a] which accompanied the act may have been a feeling aroused by the inhumanity of the social regulations which added so much suffering to the physical condition of lepers. Jesus seems to have been careless of the implications for himself of having touched him—indeed, it is just possible
45 that this was the reason why Jesus **could no longer show himself in any town**: as a result of contact with the leper, he would have been ritually unclean. Nevertheless, he instructed him to conform to the regulations governing recovery. Anyone whose leprosy healed had to go and show
44 himself **to the priest** who would examine him; if the priest confirmed that the recovery was complete, he would allow him to be readmitted to the community after making the prescribed **offering** (all these regulations can be found in Leviticus 14 and were still in force). Only the completion of this ritual would **certify the cure** and allow him to resume normal social
43 contacts. The vehemence with which Jesus **dismissed him** and told him, **'Be sure you say nothing to anybody'**, was perhaps due simply to the desire to avoid making a stir; Jesus was anxious not to become known at this stage for an activity which could be regarded as a threat to the authority of the priests. But the subject of the cure, even if he subsequently travelled to Jerusalem to fulfil his ritual obligations, clearly did not wait before mingling freely with others and spreading the news of the miracle.

2. 1 **The news went round that he was at home.** The scene of the next episode is once again Capernaum, where Jesus seems to have made his home with the family of Simon (1.29). It should not be imagined that such a house would have been large enough for Jesus to preach to a great number of people inside (though Luke (5.18–19), who was more familiar with the larger houses of the west, evidently pictured the whole scene as taking place indoors). Rather he will have stood in front of the door and addressed the
2 crowd in the street or open space outside—though even[b] that space **was not big enough to hold them.** Because of the press of people, the four men carrying the paralysed man could not force their way through; so they must have found a way up to the roof of the house, perhaps at the side or at the back. Small houses in Palestine normally had flat roofs: one would have

[a] This is not certainly the correct reading: the majority of manuscripts give "sorry for him"; but in **warm indignation**, being more difficult, was thought by the translators more likely to be original.

[b] The word "even" is in the Greek, but has been omitted by the translators.

thought it would have been easier for them to have let down the stretcher from the edge of it, directly in front of Jesus. But presumably the closely packed throng of people made even this impossible; so they broke through the roof (which would have been of dried mud and wattle, and of no great thickness) and lowered the stretcher on to the only spot where there would have been any room, inside the house, behind Jesus. Their faith was that Jesus must ultimately turn back into the house and would then be forced to attend to the sufferer.

When Jesus saw their faith, he said to the paralysed man, 'My son, 5
your sins are forgiven'. It was widely believed among the Jews that illness
came to men as a direct punishment for sin. This theory was obviously
inadequate to explain the whole problem of suffering (and Jesus certainly
did not accept the theory unreservedly); nevertheless no one denied that
there was a close connection between sin and sickness, and to be forgiven
by God was regarded as an essential precondition of recovery. Now, since
people did certainly recover, it followed that God must often forgive them
their sins, either of his free mercy or in view of their repentance and their
meritorious acts. But God could not be forced to forgive them: he retained
his sovereign freedom to give or to withhold forgiveness, and no man (unless
perhaps he was a prophet to whom God had given intimations of the future)
could presume to know whether God would forgive or had forgiven until
unmistakable signs of physical recovery could be seen. Jesus' unequivocal
statement, **your sins are forgiven**, therefore embodied a striking claim. He
was not just speaking with the voice of a prophet (who might have claimed
to know that the man was about to recover, and who could have said, in
virtue of this knowledge, that it must be the case that the Lord had forgiven
him). Jesus declared outright that the man was forgiven, and so implicitly
claimed the authority (which of course Mark's readers knew that he possessed) to dispense God's forgiveness himself. The **lawyers** with their 6
professional knowledge of Scripture were naturally quick to recognize the
implication as blasphemous. **'Who but God alone can forgive sins?'** 7

Jesus' claim was certainly blasphemous—unless it was true. Could it be proved true? How (since a man's forgiveness was entirely a concern between him and God) could it ever be known whether he had been forgiven? If it was a simple blasphemy, it was a singularly "easy" one to utter, since there could be no evidence to show that it was false. If on the other hand the claim was true, it was a stupendous one. It was no "easier" to make such a declaration than to effect immediately the physical improvement which, if the forgiveness was authentic, could be expected to follow in any case in due course. Jesus therefore authenticated his claim by what we now call a miracle: by giving the man an immediate recovery from his paralysis, he demonstrated that his declaration "your sins are forgiven" had been effective. Mark does not say whether the lawyers were convinced. This is just the beginning of a long series of events which built up the tension between Jesus and the religious authorities. Instead, he brings the story to a close by describing the impression made on the crowd, who were less interested in the theological point at issue than in the unprecedented evidence of a supernatural power at work among them.

10 This is the first use of the title **Son of Man** in the gospel. It occurs again, perhaps with a somewhat different meaning, later in the chapter, but otherwise its occurrences are all concentrated in the second half of the gospel. The title appears never to have established itself in the early church as a formal title of Jesus, but the evidence of the gospels is unanimous that Jesus frequently used it himself. Why did Jesus refer to himself in this cryptic way, and how did he intend the title to be understood? In his own language (Aramaic), the equivalent must have been *bar nasha*, "son of a man"; and just as the frequent biblical phrase, "sons of men", often means nothing more than "men", so this idiom may have been used in certain circumstances to mean simply "a man" or "a certain man". It is therefore possible that there are some instances in the gospels where Jesus originally used the expression, not of anyone in particular, but of men in general. But these instances are the exception; normally it is quite clear that when Jesus talked about the Son of Man he was referring to a particular individual. There are reasons for thinking that in Aramaic the idiom was sometimes understood as a deliberately enigmatic and oblique way of referring to oneself. If so, Jesus' use of it may have been of a piece with his characteristic manner of speaking: instead of making explicit claims for himself, he challenged his hearers to make up their own minds whether or not he was a person about whom such claims could be made. Nevertheless, his use of the expression had far-reaching implications. It suggested, for instance, not just "a man", but "the Man", that is to say, a particular man who had been singled out by God to perform an important and perhaps representative rôle in the destiny of his people or of mankind at large. There was much speculation in the ancient world about the appearance or return of the perfect Man, who would restore mankind to its pristine glory and inaugurate a new age. But the only form in which such speculation is likely to have impinged on the society in which Jesus moved was that which stemmed from some verses in the book of Daniel. "I was still watching in visions of the night, and I saw one like a son of man coming with the clouds of heaven; he approached the Ancient in Years and was presented to him. Sovereignty and glory and kingly power were given to him . . ." (7.13–14). This "son of man" in Daniel is again a little mysterious—the book was deliberately written in cryptic imagery—but certain things can be said about him with reasonable certainty. The context in Daniel shows that he appeared before God (the "Ancient of Years") at the moment when the divine judgement of the world was about to begin. He was in some sense a representative figure: he stood for the righteous men

who (at the time the book of Daniel was written) were being brutally oppressed by a foreign power; and Daniel's vision was that in God's judgement their destiny would be reversed: they would be vindicated, and there would be given to them that ascendancy among the peoples of the world which was being denied them at the present time. We know that this Son of Man figure fired the imagination of the Jews and enjoyed some popularity in later writings. Unfortunately we cannot say for certain how far the idea had been embellished in Jesus' day or what the popular image of the Son of Man would have been. But certain elements in it must have been constant. In particular, the Son of Man was always a personage who was (or would be) vindicated at God's final judgement, and he always had some connection—whether as representative or as leader—with those who suffered on account of their faith. When therefore Jesus used the expression—which he did most frequently (at least according to Mark) in connection with his own impending sufferings—he must have been understood by at least some of his hearers to be tacitly claiming that, whatever his present humiliations, he was destined to be vindicated by God; and also that he had a unique degree of solidarity, if not with all mankind, at least with those whom God regarded as righteous.
Now Jesus healed the paralysed man to convince those who accused him of
blasphemy that **the Son of Man has the right . . . to forgive sins.** These 10
lawyers will have known that the Son of Man was a person to whom there would ultimately be given **authority** (this was an implication of the word "sovereignty" in Daniel). The conclusion forced upon them by Jesus' words and actions will have been twofold: first, that Jesus was in some sense the person prefigured in the prophet's vision of the Son of Man; and secondly, that the authority given to this person included **the right** (which is the same word as **authority** in the Greek) **on earth to forgive sins**, and therefore to heal the sick.

As he went along. The exact locality of the call of Levi is left vague by 14
Mark, except that it was in the neighbourhood of the Lake; but we can fill in the details from the geography of Galilee. Capernaum, which was built on the northern shore of the lake, was a station on the important "road to the sea" which carried trade between the cities of the Decapolis and the Mediterranean ports. It was also close to the frontier between the territories of Herod Antipas and Philip, and was the centre of the fishing industry on the lake. It was the obvious place for a **custom-house**; and since Jesus had already become well known in Capernaum there is no reason to suppose that Levi did not have time to ponder the message of Jesus before he responded to Jesus' summons. Curiously, Levi does not appear in the list of the Twelve in 3.14–19 below (although his brother James does): this is perhaps the reason why in Matthew's gospel the same story is told, not of Levi, but of one who was known to have been one of the Twelve: Matthew.

The social status of Levi can be inferred from the next paragraph. His

house[a] was large enough to accommodate a fair number round the table; he
was therefore probably a senior customs officer in the service of Herod
15 Antipas. But the profession of **tax-gatherers** (including customs officials)
was one of those which was very severely judged by Jewish society. It was
assumed that it invariably involved extortion and dishonesty—for how else
could these officials make a good living?—and it was usually exercised on
behalf of a foreign power. Morally speaking such people were thought to be
no better than thieves and criminals. They were therefore shunned by the
stricter members of society and were even denied certain civic and religious
rights. They tended consequently to make their friends mainly among themselves and with members of similarly "disreputable" professions; and a
group of such people would be looked upon as by definition **bad characters**.

At the other extreme of society were the Pharisees, who not merely
avoided contact with all such people but constituted a closed society of their
own, observing a code of moral obligations and ritual observances more
elaborate than that accepted by the majority of Jews. They would naturally
have expected a religious teacher such as Jesus to observe the same rule of
life as themselves, and this was doubtless an initial cause of tension between
Jesus and the Pharisees. But now Jesus was behaving in a way that scandal-
16 ized them still more. It happened that some of them who were also **doctors
of the law** (with whom Jesus had already had some controversy) observed
him not merely conversing with these disreputable members of society but
15 actually sitting **at table** with them, which according to Jewish custom was
the principal way in which a man could express his solidarity with his
friends. And not only this: Jesus, like many teachers of his time, had
now gathered a number of "disciples" around him (**for there were many
who followed him**: Mark has recounted the call of only five disciples,
and he hastily makes good his omission here), and he was allowing
16 these also to associate with **bad company**. In reply to their scandalized
comments, Jesus quoted a familiar proverb and then boldly applied it to his
17 own rôle in contemporary society. **'I did not come to invite virtuous
people, but sinners.'** This saying will have been understood by the church
of Mark's time in a general and spiritual sense: it will have been their
experience that Christ's invitation had come to them, not as specially
"virtuous people", but as "sinners"; and it is possible that their understanding of this saying has influenced the form in which it has come down to
us. Nevertheless the application of Jesus' words to the social conditions of
his time is still intelligible and is borne out by one of the most characteristic
features of his activity: he found himself constantly in opposition to those
who were widely regarded as the most **virtuous** people in society, and

[*a*] In the Greek, as in the translation, verse 15 is ambiguous: it could mean Levi's house or Jesus' house. But Jesus had no house in Capernaum; he apparently stayed in that of Simon's family. Luke at any rate understood the house to be that of Levi (5.29).

sought out those who were shunned as **sinners.** It was these people whom he came **to invite**—that is, these were the people with whom he expressed solidarity by offering them a place at that heavenly banquet which (in traditional Jewish imagery) was the destined reward of the righteous.

Once, when John's disciples and the Pharisees were keeping a fast. 18
Fasting was an obligation laid on all the Jewish people on one day of the year; but stricter religious sects tended to lay upon themselves additional fast days. This was certainly true of the Pharisees (Luke 18.12) and Mark says that it was true of their **disciples** (though strictly speaking they were a closed society and did not have disciples, except in so far as some of them were "doctors of the law" and therefore had students). We are not surprised to hear that it was also true of the religious movement initiated by John the Baptist. Seeing Jesus surrounded by disciples, people naturally expected it to to be true also of his "sect", and when they found that he laid down no such practices for his followers, they asked the reason. Jesus replied with a comparison. It was the task of the **bridegroom's friends** at a wedding banquet 19
to contribute gaiety to the proceedings. Fasting—which meant of course doing without drink as well as food—would be quite out of place and was in fact waived even by the Pharisees on such occasions. **'As long as they have the bridegroom with them, there can be no fasting.'** By this it is clearly meant that Jesus' presence with his disciples was a time of rejoicing: fasting was appropriate to a time of waiting and preparation, but now the awaited moment had come, and the old observances had lost their meaning. Jesus was not merely initiating a variant of the Jewish religion, he was proclaiming something entirely new which the old forms of religion could not contain.
Two similes help to make the point: old material will not take the strain of a 21
new patch that pulls on it when it begins to shrink; and new wine (which 22
was poured off from the vats into jars or skins before it had finished fermenting) needed new and supple wineskins, not old and brittle ones which would burst under the pressure.

Thus understood, these verses form a connected and intelligible whole. But the sequence is interrupted by a verse which appears to say something
quite different: **'But the time will come when the bridegroom will be** 20
taken away from them, and on that day they will fast.' Jesus, we have said, appears to have been answering the question about fasting by showing in three short similes that the new dispensation which he had come to proclaim superseded all older observances. Why then did he prophesy a time when they would be resumed? Furthermore it was the firm belief of the church, expressed in words attributed to Jesus himself (e.g. Matthew 28.20, 'I am with you always, to the end of time'), that the Lord was always, and always would be, present among those who acknowledged him. What moment then can be in mind when Jesus is reported as saying, **'the time will come when the bridegroom will be taken away from them'**? Was

Jesus already hinting at the dark days between the cruciflxion and the resurrection? If so, the hint comes a long time before Jesus (at least in Mark's gospel) makes any clear allusion to his destiny in Jerusalem. Alternatively, is this a saying which was invented or adapted by the early church to justify its observance of days of fasting? The verse remains mysterious.

23 **One Sabbath he was going through the cornfields.** A short sequence of sayings and episodes follows which illustrates Jesus' attitude to the most fundamental and widely observed of all Jewish institutions, the Sabbath. The Sabbath was regarded as one of God's greatest gifts. It was the privilege of the Jew to observe it and to hand down the tradition of its observance from generation to generation. Much of this tradition was of a very positive character: the Sabbath was a day for rest, for rejoicing, for family gatherings, and of course for worship in the synagogue. But it had also its negative side. The simple direction in the Law of Moses, "Thou shalt do no manner of work", had been elaborated into a long series of complicated and often oppressive prohibitions, and it is with these petty restrictions—which were insisted upon most vigorously by the Pharisees—that Jesus is shown frequently taking issue in the gospels. One of the pettiest is illustrated by the first episode. **His disciples, as they went, began to pluck ears of corn.** It was expressly allowed in Jewish law for anyone to satisfy his hunger by taking a handful of fruit or corn from someone else's field (Deuteronomy 23.24–5). Normally this would offend no one. But on the Sabbath, according to the Pharisees' point of view, such an action must be regarded differently: it fell in the same category as reaping, which was "work", and therefore
24 **forbidden.** Jesus, in reply, appealed to a passage of Scripture which the rigorists themselves had some difficulty in explaining. The story about David is told in 1 Samuel 21: David was being pursued by Saul, and coming
26 to the sanctuary (**the House of God**) which then existed at Nob demanded food for himself and his men. (The priest concerned was actually Ahimelek and not his son **Abiathar**; but Abiathar was one of the two most famous priests in the time of David, and the error, whether it be Mark's or Jesus', is trivial.) It happened that the only bread available consisted of the **sacred bread** which was placed each week before the sanctuary, and which could afterwards be eaten only by the priests (Leviticus 24.5–9). Jewish scholars were in some embarrassment to explain how it could have been right for David and his men to eat this bread. Jesus, in recalling the incident, may simply have been trying to silence his critics by pointing to an instance where their own technique of interpretation left them in difficulties; but there may also be an unspoken implication (made explicit in Matthew's account, 12.1–8) that "a greater than David was here" who, even more than David, had the authority to exempt his followers from particular regulations of the law.

27 **He also said to them.** This is one of Mark's ways of binding into the context of his narrative a saying of Jesus which may originally have been

remembered in isolation. The saying adds a further touch to Mark's portrait of Jesus' attitude to the Sabbath. Even the Pharisees were prepared to concede that, if a human life were in danger, it was allowable to ignore a Sabbath restriction in order to save it; and they would have agreed that **the Sabbath was made for the sake of man**, in the sense that it conferred a great blessing on those who observed it. But they would certainly not have agreed with the much more liberal attitude which doubtless underlay Jesus' use of these words. It is possible that verse 28 should be understood in the same
way. It was pointed out above that in the Greek the phrase **Son of Man** 28
may sometimes be a mistranslation of an expression which in Jesus' own language of Aramaic meant simply "man". If this is the case here, Jesus will have been saying that, not just when life is in danger, but in countless other cases besides, man is **sovereign even over the Sabbath** and not the Sabbath over man. On the other hand, if Mark has here correctly recorded Jesus' use of the title Son of Man, then Jesus must be once again understood as making a particular claim for himself: by virtue of his unique status he could legislate even on such matters as the observance of the Sabbath.

On another occasion. Mark adds one more dispute between Jesus and 3. 1
the Pharisees over the Sabbath, this time leading up to a clear breach between them. The presence of **a man in the congregation who had a withered arm** constituted a test case; for although it was permissible on the Sabbath to save a life that was in danger, it was generally forbidden to perform services for the sick on the grounds that, apart from the danger of infringing minute regulations about permitted work and movement, too much concern for those who were ill would be incompatible with the sense of joy and well-being which a Jew should feel on the Sabbath. It seems to have been, once again, the sheer inhumanity of such an interpretation of the Sabbath which
moved Jesus to **anger and sorrow at their obstinate stupidity** and 5
caused him to make a public issue out of an act of healing. This was sufficient, according to Mark, to set in motion a plot against his life, the Pharisees
making common cause with the **partisans of Herod**. These men, who 6
reappear later (12.13), were presumably influential citizens who gave their support to the administration of Herod Antipas and saw in Jesus' movement a threat to the peace of the district.

Jesus went away to the lake-side. The scene changes from an ordinary 7
Sabbath congregation in a synagogue to a huge gathering on the shore of the lake. Mark's list of the districts from which Jesus' hearers had come seems to include all the main areas of Jewish population in Palestine. So far, the movement had been confined to Galilee; but now the whole of the Jewish nation in Palestine came to hear him: from **Judaea and Jerusalem** in the south (omitting of course Samaria, which was regarded as a hostile and alien
district) and, still further south, from **Idumaea**, the Edom of the Old 8

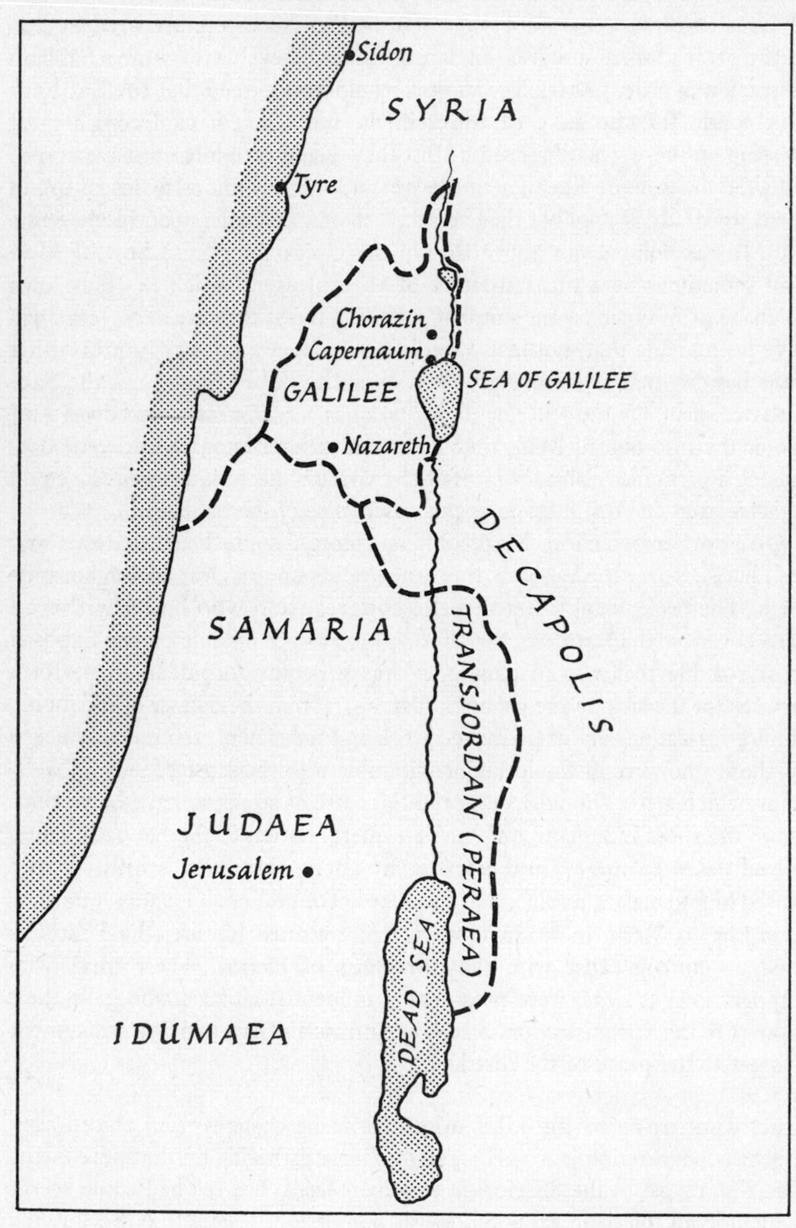
Sidon
SYRIA
Tyre
Chorazin
Capernaum
SEA OF GALILEE
GALILEE
Nazareth
DECAPOLIS
SAMARIA
TRANSJORDAN (PERAEA)
JUDAEA
Jerusalem
DEAD SEA
IDUMAEA

Testament; from **Transjordan**, that is, the narrow strip of valley and the
highlands immediately to the east of the Jordan (officially called Peraea); and
from the **neighbourhood of Tyre and Sidon**, to the north-west of Galilee,
where there were substantial communities of Jews. It was, it seems, Jesus'
reputation as a healer which brought the crowds. Healing involved exorcism,
and therefore contact with spirits who knew (as Mark and his readers knew,
but as the crowds did not know) that Jesus was the **Son of God**. But once 11
again Jesus refused to allow his true status to be known to the multitudes who
came for healing.

He then went up into the hill-country. Steep and therefore unin- 13
habited country lay not far from the lake, and was an appropriate setting for
a moment which demanded quiet and privacy. **He appointed twelve as his** 14
companions, a statement which becomes more significant a moment later
in the form **he appointed the Twelve.** Mark's readers knew, not just that 16
Jesus had had a certain number of **companions** entrusted with specific tasks
during his work in Galilee, but that he had left behind him a group of men
known as the Twelve, who (or at least some of whom) constituted an essential
link between Jesus' work on earth and the continuing existence of the church.
Some members of this group were well known to Mark and his readers,
either because of the part they played in the gospel narrative, or because of
their subsequent rôle in the church: this goes for the first four in the list,
and of course for Judas Iscariot. But the rest seem to have been little more
than names, and the lists given in different parts of the New Testament do
not always agree with each other. The important thing was evidently not
the name and character of each, but the fact that there were **twelve**, symbolizing perhaps that the new people of God was in important respects the
successor of the old Israel with its legendary Twelve Tribes.

To Simon he gave the name Peter. The name means "a stone", as is 16
explained in John's gospel (1.42); and a reason for the name is suggested by
a passage in Matthew (16.18). The name **Boanerges** is mysterious. We do 17
not know precisely what these letters are supposed to represent in Aramaic or
Hebrew, nor what Jesus intended by renaming the two brothers. Mark tells us
that the name meant **Sons of Thunder.** This may be right, but it does not
take us much further; nor is there any record of these two disciples ever having
been called by this name subsequently. **Thaddaeus** occurs only in Mark's list, 18
replaced in Matthew (10.3) by Lebbaeus,[a] in Luke (6.16) by 'Judas the son
of James'. **Simon** (as the NEB makes explicit)[b] was a **member of the**
Zealot party. Not much is known of the Zealot party before the beginning 19
of the Jewish War (60–66 A.D.), when its members became champions of
revolt against the Roman occupying forces; but there is no reason to doubt

[a] Some manuscripts give Thaddaeus also in Matthew's list.
[b] The Greek has *kananaios* ("Canaanite"), which probably, though not certainly, bears this technical meaning here. Luke calls him 'Simon who was called the Zealot' (6.15).

that this fanatical anti-Roman movement was active during the previous decades, especially in Galilee, and Simon seems to have been a member of it.

Up to this point in Mark's narrative, such opposition as Jesus had encountered (which first comes to the surface in 3.6) had been created by his attitude to Sabbath regulations. The next two episodes illustrate the beginnings of a deeper antagonism. That the activity of Jesus should have collected
21 a large crowd inevitably suggested to some[a] **that he was out of his mind**,
and that the crowds had been attracted by mere curiosity. Consequently his
family (who are to be imagined a day's journey away in Nazareth) **set out to**
take charge of him. Meanwhile Jesus was being confronted with a more
22 menacing accusation. The **doctors of the law**—whom Mark probably
assumes to have **come down** to Galilee from Jerusalem specially to investigate the reports about Jesus—admitted the reality of Jesus' exorcisms but gave them a sinister explanation. The power by which Jesus drove out the demons and spirits that caused (it was believed) so much of people's illness, was not a good power, but was a worse power still. '**He drives out devils by the prince of devils.**' The man who professed to cure those who were "possessed by devils" was in a worse case himself—he was **possessed by Beelzebub**,[b] who was, if not the devil in person (as Matthew states, 12.24), at least a prince among devils. Jesus showed this up as sheer sophistry. It was one thing to believe (as Jesus and his contemporaries certainly believed) that there was an objective and personal force of evil abroad which could enter a man and make him act in a way untrue to his nature; and it made sense, on this view of the matter, to talk of devils, spirits, demons and so forth in the plural: these were all different manifestations of the same supernatural power. But it was quite another thing to infer from this terminology that different "devils" could be played off against each other for the benefit of
human beings. Evil was ultimately one single power, and to talk of evil being
25 **divided against itself** was a contradiction in terms. It was as silly as saying
24 that "Satan could drive out Satan".

23 Jesus put his answer in the form of two **parables**. To see what a parable
is one must look at the parables of Jesus: it was he who made the form immortal. But the word itself did not necessarily mean anything so extended and elaborate as most of Jesus' stories. In Greek it meant any "comparison" or "simile"; and the Hebrew word to which this corresponded had an even
wider range of meanings—proverbs, riddles, illustrations and stories. Thus
24–7 Jesus' answer here consists of two quite simple and obvious illustrations.

[*a*] Perhaps indeed to his own family—the Greek reads as easily in this sense. See the footnote in NEB.

[*b*] The name occurs nowhere outside the New Testament and its origin and meaning are unknown. An old theory is that it is a form of Baalzebub, "the God of Ekron" (2 Kings 1.2), and in view of this theory many Latin versions and the older English translations, followed by NEB, reproduce the name in the form *Beelzebub*. But all Greek manuscripts have the still more mysterious name *Beelzebul* (or, in some cases, *Beezebul*).

The only deeper meaning which may possibly be present lies in the phrase
the strong man. According to contemporary Jewish mythology, the mon- 27
strous power of evil was due to be "bound" for a period before the end of the world (see below on Revelation 9.1); so that underneath the comparison may lie a claim of Jesus to be stronger than the devil himself and to be the person destined to bring evil into subjection.

On any interpretation the saying which follows is hard to understand. The first part of it fits easily enough into the general pattern of Jesus' teaching. Some Jewish thinkers had drawn up a whole list of sins which in their view put the sinner outside the range of divine forgiveness and deprived him of his share (as they put it) in the life to come. Jesus' teaching stands at the opposite extreme to such legalism: it is open to anyone to repent and be
forgiven. '**No sin, no slander, is beyond forgiveness for men.**' Why then 28
does he make the severe exception which follows? And what does it mean, to "slander the Holy Spirit"? Mark indicates the way he understands this
himself: **He said this because they had declared that he was possessed** 30
by an unclean spirit. Confronted, that is to say, by a clear instance of the defeat of evil powers (which in Mark's theology indicated that the Holy Spirit was at work), they had rejected this clear evidence of God's activity. Mark may have wished his readers to infer that, since no clearer case could be given them of the presence of the Spirit, nothing further could happen which would lead them to repentance, and therefore there was no chance that they would adopt the attitude necessary to obtain forgiveness. In the wider context of a doctrine of God's mercy, this is a hard saying. But Mark's concern is a more limited one. He has to explain how it happened that men crucified the Son of God. If they were capable even of "slandering" the clearest manifestations of his divine power, then it was understandable that they would not stop short of destroying Jesus. Nothing would move them to repentance: therefore nothing could qualify them for forgiveness.

Then his mother and his brothers arrived. We were told in verse 21 31
that they were setting out from Nazareth to 'take charge' of Jesus. Mark does not say what happened when they tried to do so; their arrival in Capernaum simply gives him the cue for recording a saying of Jesus which was perhaps remembered apart from any particular context (it appears to be
alluded to by Paul in Romans 8.29): '**Whoever does the will of God is my** 35
brother, my sister, my mother.' The word **brothers** is less precise in Greek than in Hebrew: it could mean half-brothers (i.e. sons of Joseph by another wife) or even cousins. It does not follow from this passage (even if it seems likely for other reasons) that Mark knew nothing of the tradition that Jesus was born of a virgin.

On another occasion. But it was clearly, in Mark's view, an important **4.** 1
occasion. Just as Jesus' fame as a healer had drawn such crowds that he had

to have a boat ready to 'save him from being crushed' (3.9), so too his teaching drew a crowd **so large that he had to get into a boat.** Mark evidently intended to set the two scenes in parallel, and just as in the first he gave some notable examples of Jesus' works of healing, so now, for the first time in his gospel, he gives a specimen of Jesus' teaching, introduced by a word which would have had solemn overtones for Jewish listeners, since it stood at the beginning of a formula which they used every day in their
3 prayers ("Listen O Israel, the Lord is our God, the Lord is one"): **'Listen'.**

In fact however this sample of Jesus' teaching can hardly have been typical. Admittedly it consists mainly of "parables", which were one of Jesus' most characteristic figures of speech; but the point of these particular parables is not so much to convey new religious or ethical truths as to illustrate how Jesus' teaching as a whole was to be understood. In this they continue an important theme from the previous chapter. Just as Jesus' works of healing had provoked opposition as well as admiration, with the result that his opponents, having "slandered the Holy Spirit", had now lost all chance of repenting and being forgiven, so his teaching was such as to arouse different reactions among his hearers, some of whom would inevitably be
9 deaf to his message—God would not give them **ears to hear** (a phrase which evokes Deuteronomy 29.4, and recalls the pristine obstinacy of the people of Israel in the face of the spectacular benefits they received at the time of the Exodus). What was the explanation of this? Why was the teaching of the Son of God ignored or rejected by some of those who heard it? In the case of the acts of healing, Mark was able to give two reasons for this opposition: some thought Jesus was mad, others that he was inspired by the devil. Neither of these reasons would account for the mixed reception given to his teaching; and so Mark opens his collection of Jesus' sayings with a discourse which bears upon this very question.

3 **'A sower went out to sow.'** The first of the parables describes what we know to have been usual farming practice in Mediterranean lands in antiquity, and its freshness comes more from Jesus' vivid and poetic observation than from any intrinsic interest in the narrative. After the harvest (around June) the farmer would probably plough his fields at least once, perhaps several times, during the dry summer months, both to prevent the dry earth from becoming hard and to keep it free of weeds. In November or December (the time of the first heavy rains, when there was enough moisture in the ground to allow the seed to germinate) the field would be sown, the sower casting the seed by hand and probably varying the quantity of seed according to the quality of the soil. Very soon after the sowing, the seed would be ploughed in to protect it from the birds. In these circumstances a certain amount of wastage was inevitable. The field would be bounded at least on
4 one side by a path. Some seed would naturally fall on it, but since the farmer would not plough over the path, it would remain on the surface and

be eaten by the birds. Some would fall **on rocky ground**, that is to say, 5
places where the limestone rock which underlies the soil in Galilee came close
to the surface. Probably the farmer would not expect much of a crop from
it: the soil would be too shallow to hold moisture, and the fierce heat of the
sun would quickly scorch the plant as soon as it began to grow. But he would
not for that reason leave such patches completely unsown. Some seed would
fall among **thistles**, which could never be completely eradicated from the 7
soil and which were always a serious nuisance to the farmer. But this amount
of wastage was only what was to be expected. Most of the seeds sown would
grow to fruition, often producing several side-shoots. A return of thirty to
sixty grains from each plant was normal, a return of a hundred was exceptional (though not unheard of)—Jesus was fond of a touch of exaggeration.

The parable then is a description of ordinary farming practice with which Jesus' hearers will have been perfectly familiar. Nevertheless it dwells on a number of details which would not normally come to mind. From the farmer's point of view the wastage would be negligible: it would hardly occur to him to pay much attention to it, or to censure the sower for allowing a few seeds to fall on the path. But Jesus, by recounting three different ways in which the grain might be lost, drew attention to the fact that even when the harvest was good some wastage was inevitable, some seeds would come to nothing. Similarly: however successful his own work might appear to be, it was perfectly natural that there should be some wastage, some indifference, even some opposition.

If this is the natural interpretation of the parable, it is also one that is
entirely consistent with Jesus' understanding of himself and his work: he
presented an unavoidable challenge, and it was inevitable that some would
react against him. But Mark evidently saw a further meaning in the parable,
and knew of a more subtle interpretation of it. Consequently, before going on
with the scene of Jesus teaching the crowds, he recorded some conversation
which Jesus had in private with **the Twelve and others who were round** 10
him. This change of scene puts the matter in a different perspective. The
emphasis in the parable was on the small but necessary amount of wastage:
a few will always remain unfruitful even though the main harvest develops
normally. But now it is the other way round. The phenomenon being
explained is no longer the small (though potent) opposition to Jesus' teaching,
compared with the crowds who press in to hear it. It is those who accept
who are now a small and privileged minority, and what has to be explained
is the fact that the great majority remain **outside**. 11

At this stage of his work, Jesus had had more *success* than *opposition*. He was more aware of the crowds who strained to see and hear him than of the enemies who were already plotting against him. But for the early church things were very different. The Christians were a small movement set in the midst of a large and (particularly on the Jewish side) hostile world;

and to account for this hostility they were glad to find an explanation in a
prophecy of Isaiah (6.9–10). That great prophet had been entrusted with the
authentic word of God. Yet the people would not listen. Why? It must have
been because God himself had intended it that way and dulled their under-
12 standing—**that they may look and look, but see nothing**—and it was
this which was preventing them from turning to God and obtaining his
forgiveness. Paul used the same text when confronted by the opposition of
fellow-Jews in Rome (according to Acts 28.26–7); and doubtless the prophecy
helped many Christians in the early days of the church to understand their
own position and the attitude of their neighbours.

Did Jesus quote this text himself? Mark says that he did, and there is no
good reason to doubt it: there will have been many occasions later on when
it may have helped him to understand and interpret the massive opposition
which he encountered. But it is hardly appropriate to the context here, where
Jesus has more admirers than opponents; and it looks as though Mark (or
the source from which he derived his narrative) introduced it in order to
explain a somewhat different sense of the word "parable" from that which is
exemplified by the story of the sower. The word parable (or its Hebrew
equivalent) could mean a variety of figures of speech, including riddles and
enigmatic sayings. The parables of Jesus, though they may have been
perfectly clear to those who first heard them, were often inspired by the
circumstances and context in which they were delivered, and there may soon
have come a time when, since their original setting had been forgotten, the
parables themselves could no longer be understood: they then became
"parables" in the sense of mysterious, enigmatic utterances. In which case
the fact that Jesus taught in "parables" could be held to explain why some
(indeed the majority, as it seemed to the first Christians) did not accept his
teaching: they did not understand it! It was only to his intimate disciples (so
this explanation ran), and through them to the church, that Jesus had given
11 the clue—**the secret of the kingdom of God**. As one example of the kind
of esoteric understanding which (on this view) was necessary in order to
grasp the meaning of Jesus' teaching, Mark appends a detailed interpretation
of the parable of the sowing. He attributes the interpretation to Jesus, and it
may well have come down to Mark along with the parable itself. But there are
serious reasons for doubting whether Jesus was the author of it. While the
parable bears some traces of the idioms of the language (Aramaic) which
Jesus spoke, the interpretation contains many expressions which do not occur
elsewhere in the gospels but are characteristic of the preaching of the Greek-
speaking church. Further, the circumstances which prevent the proper
reception of the word (**trouble, persecution, false glamour of wealth**)
belong more to the experience of the church than to that of the crowd which
first listened to Jesus' teaching in Galilee. Most significant of all: the psychological analysis of different kinds of unbelief, profound though it may be,

does not spring from the parable itself (as the meaning springs from most of
Jesus' parables). It has to be read into it. Mark was right: if this was the way
in which the parables were intended to be understood, then they would
indeed be mysterious to anyone who did not possess the clue. If Jesus taught
like this, no wonder that only a few followed him. Mark indeed goes on to
suggest that Jesus' parables were all like this. '**You do not understand this** 13
parable? How then are you to understand any parable?' And at the end
of the chapter he explicitly makes the same point: the disciples were privately 33–4
given the key to all the teaching which to everyone else remained simply
"parables"—mysterious and perplexing. This is one of Mark's answers to a
question which runs through his gospel: why was Jesus not universally
recognized as the Son of God? Because he deliberately gave his teaching in a
form which few could understand. Mark develops this idea here, at the
expense of breaking into the scene of Jesus' public teaching—which is
resumed without apology at verse 21.

He said to them. Clearly the section containing private instruction to the 21
disciples is finished, and the scene is once again the lake-side, with the crowds
straining to hear Jesus' teaching, just as on a previous occasion they had
pressed upon him to witness his powers of healing. According to Mark, the
parables were such as to mystify all except those who belonged to the
privileged circle of the disciples and were given the clue to their interpretation. He now gives some examples of precisely this kind of enigmatic parable.
All but one of them (that of the seed scattered on the land) reappear in
Matthew and Luke, who, by placing them in a certain context, or by making
minor alterations, often give some hint as to how they understood them. But
Mark neither gives an esoteric explanation of them (as he does for the
parable of the sowing) nor offers by his editing any suggestion about their
meaning. He evidently intends the sayings to remain mysterious, as an
illustration of what he has just said about their effect on their hearers. It may
well be that the point of them was already obscure to him.

The sayings themselves are characteristically vivid, drawn from life, and
often with the ring of proverbs. The **lamp** is the ordinary oil-lamp that has 21
been found by thousands among the ruins of the ancient world, shaped like
a small flattened teapot with the wick in the spout. To light a room, it would
have to be put on a **lamp-stand**, not underneath one of the pieces of furni-
ture in the room such as **the bed** or the **meal-tub** (there is a little evidence
that this part of the equipment of a peasant house might be mounted on legs;
otherwise we should have to think of the tub being placed upside down over
the lamp in order to extinguish it, which is a rather different idea). Proverbially, anything hidden away (the meaning of the parables? the true nature of
Jesus? the infant church in the world?) will be brought into view one day.
The two proverbs in verses 24 and 25 seem drawn from the bazaar: the fair 24, 25
and generous merchant does better in the end, but (as in all economies) the

poor get poorer, the rich richer (in understanding the parables? in understanding the gospel? in faith?). The seed is sown, the farmer continues his
normal activities, and does nothing to it until the moment comes for
the decision to harvest (judgement will be sudden and unprepared?—
the harvest, at all events, was a biblical symbol of the Last Judgement
29 often used by Jesus, and the words **he plies the sickle, because harvest-**
31 **time has come** are a quotation from Joel 3.13). The **mustard-seed**
was proverbially the smallest seed in the ground, and by comparison the
plant which sprang from it (which grows over six feet tall in Galilee) was
prodigious—though Jesus was once again exaggerating when he used language about it which in Daniel (4.12) and Ezekiel (17.23; 31.6) is applied
to a massive tree (small beginning of the gospel? of the church? of faith in
26, 30 the human heart?). These last two parables are said to illustrate **the king-**
dom of God—but what aspect of the kingdom remains mysterious. Mark
has kept faithfully to his programme of showing that Jesus' teaching was
likely to be unintelligible to the mass of his hearers.

Miracles of Christ

So far Jesus' activity had all been situated on the west side (or rather in the
north-west corner) of the Lake of Tiberias. Now Jesus crossed over to the
37 east side, and the **heavy squall** which his boat encountered was of the kind
for which the lake is notorious, and which can take even the most experienced
fisherman by surprise. It is a little curious that the crossing should have been
35 undertaken **in the evening**. Jesus would then have reached the other side
two or three hours later, long after nightfall; but the events which immediately followed his landing clearly took place in daylight. We cannot be
sure that Mark was really concerned about such details; but if he was, then
he must have envisaged the crossing as being combined with an all-night
fishing expedition, during which it would have been natural for Jesus to take
the opportunity to get some sleep. The episode is told quite simply, with
some details which are usually thought to suggest the use of an eye-witness
account (the other boats, the cushion, the disciples' almost reproachful cry
to Jesus, and Jesus' words which, in the Greek, recall the way he spoke
to devils). It is interesting to compare the accounts in Matthew and
Luke, who see a more symbolic meaning in the story (Matthew 8.23–7;
Luke 8.22–5).

5. 1 **So they came to the other side of the lake, into the country of the**
Gerasenes. Gerasa was one of the most important of the group of Greco-
Roman cities which lay for the most part on the eastern side of the Jordan
and which, though subject to Rome, constituted a league known as the

Decapolis (**the Ten Towns**). Later in the century Gerasa began an 20
ambitious building programme and became one of the most splendid Roman
cities of the east. But even before that, those of Mark's readers who knew
little about Palestine were likely to have heard of it. This may be the reason
why Mark calls the scene of this episode the **country of the Gerasenes**: 1
with the name, and with the detail of a herd of pigs (which was unthinkable
in Jewish territory), he will have succeeded in conveying an impression of the
very different Greco-Roman world in which Jesus set foot when he crossed
over the lake. But as a matter of geographical detail his description creates
difficulties. The scene is laid by the shore, not too far from a town (verse 14).
Gerasa lay some thirty miles away from the lake, more than a day's walk
across the mountains, and no part of the shore could properly be called "the
country of the Gerasenes". A few Greek manuscripts, following the version
of the story in Matthew, give "Gadarene": Gadara was another city of the
Decapolis, somewhat closer than Gerasa, in the hills within sight of the lake;
but even this city was too far away to fit the details of the story. Either the
name conceals that of an unknown smaller town near the lake, or else Mark,
for the reason suggested, was more anxious to give the area a pagan atmosphere than to be precise about geographical details (of which in any case he
may have been ignorant).

Just as the area was exceptional for Jesus' activity, so too the case of
possession is described as an exceptional one. The **unclean spirit** gave its 2
victim superhuman strength, and its name, **Legion** (a Roman military unit 9
of over six thousand men), put it in a class apart from the more common
cases of possession by, say, seven demons. Yet on seeing Jesus it reacted just
as other unclean spirits had: it recognized him by his name (**Jesus**) and his 7
real nature (**son of the Most High God**), and acknowledged his superiority.
And it was doubtless to illustrate Jesus' power even over such a demon, and
even in gentile surroundings, that Mark recorded the story. But there are
some further details which make the story unlike any other in the gospels.
The first is Jesus' conversation with the spirit. Usually he simply commands
it to come out. Here he also asks its name (which was standard exorcists'
technique, though it was normally done before, not after, the command to
come out, as a way of getting control of the spirit). The second is the occurrence of the title, **Most High God**, which was not a Jewish phrase, but
belonged to the common vocabulary of many Hellenistic cults—another
detail which gives a non-Jewish tone to the whole scene. The third
is the destruction of the pigs. It was to be expected in an exorcism that
the devil would make a final demonstration of its power before leaving
its victim. This usually took the form of a paroxysm in the victim himself, though stories were told of other violent manifestations (such as a
statue being overturned near by). In this way the onlookers would be
assured that the spirit had been decisively overcome. A herd of two

thousand pigs can hardly have been a common sight, and their loss would
have been a major calamity for their owner. But neither the interest of
the narrator nor, it seems, of the crowd which soon collected was attracted
by this aspect of the matter. The miracle, in the eyes of all, was the
recovery of one who had been possessed by so formidable a spirit. It was
15 because of this that **they were afraid** and begged such a potent exorcist
16 **to leave the district.** Nevertheless, since Jesus would not allow the subject
of the cure to go with him, the evidence of the miracle, in the person of
a notorious demoniac suddenly restored to health, was soon widely
acknowledged in an area far outside the normal range of Jesus' activity.

The two miracles which follow are woven into each other in a way which
suggests the hand of an expert narrator (Mark was particularly adept at this).
22 The **president** of a synagogue was in charge of the maintenance and worship
of the synagogue, and was necessarily one of the dignitaries of any Jewish
community.[a] That he should have appealed to Jesus was therefore a clear
sign that Jesus had by now achieved considerable fame as a miracle-worker.
But although the present section of Mark's gospel contains a group of
miracles which give substance to this reputation, Mark is careful not to tell
the stories as mere miracles. It was said of a number of people in antiquity
that contact even with their clothes could heal diseases (compare Acts 5.16;
19.12); and this was explained in terms of a magical "power" going out of
them. Mark does not reject this explanation, but he makes it clear that the
34 cure was nevertheless much more than magic: '**My daughter, your faith
has cured you**'. Similarly with the restoring to life of a little girl who had
just died. This was of course the supreme miracle for anyone to perform—
though Jesus was by no means the only miracle-worker of his time to be
credited with it. The story is told with vivid detail, down to the actual words
41 spoken by Jesus in his own language, Aramaic; and in outline it could be
regarded as a typical miracle story. But again, Mark preserves a dimension
36 which raises it above mere miracle: '**Do not be afraid; only have faith.**'
And (though this can hardly be conveyed in a modern English translation)
the words used of the girl's recovery are full of deeper meaning. For those
(Jews and Christians alike) who believed in a future resurrection, the
39 righteous who had died were in reality **asleep**, waiting for the great moment
41–2 of awakening; and the words translated **get up, got up**, are those which the
first Christians always used of the raising of Jesus himself from the dead.
The miracle did not merely bring the girl back to life; it was a demonstration
of the wonderful fact, known to faith, of resurrection from the dead. Even so,
Mark hastens to add, the demonstration could not yet be made fully public,

[*a*] The Greek means literally "one of the synagogue-presidents". There was only one effective president of each synagogue, but there is some evidence that the title was also an honorary one, so that the text does not necessarily imply (as the NEB translation does) that there was more than one synagogue in the town.

but was deliberately veiled by Jesus: **he gave them strict orders to let no** 43
one hear about it.

This (at least according to Mark) was Jesus' one visit **to his home town** 6. 1
(Nazareth). Jesus followed his regular practice of attending the synagogue on the Sabbath and making use of an invitation to preach in order to spread his teaching. As always, he made an impression; but the dominant reaction of his audience was sceptical. How could one who had grown up among them and practised a trade,[a] and whose family was still well known to them, pretend to speak as if he had had all the training and authority of a professional expositor of Scripture? Their incredulity was an obstacle—it prevented them from accepting his authority and believing in him. The translation,
they fell foul of him, is an English colloquialism suggesting the break-up 4
of a partnership. But the word in the Greek is not colloquial at all; it was a technical expression, drawn from the Greek Old Testament, for the shattering of religious faith. The incredulity of Jesus' hearers was an obstacle, a snare (*skandalon*), which prevented them from accepting his authority and believing in him. Jesus, presumably detecting the intransigence of their attitude, replied to them with a familiar proverb. Apparently the strong feeling against him prevented him from performing the miracles which usually went with his appearance in synagogue.

On one of his teaching journeys. At some stage in his activity in Galilee 7
(Mark evidently did not know at what stage) Jesus enlarged the scope of his work by sending out his disciples as missionaries. They had the double task of calling for repentance and of carrying on Jesus' onslaught against the powers of evil in the form of the **unclean spirits.** This mission was very similar to that which was subsequently entrusted to the church, and there can be little doubt that, at least in some of the gospel accounts, the practice and experience of early Christian missionaries have influenced the record of Jesus' instructions to his disciples (see above on Matthew 10). It is hard to
be sure, for instance, whether the detail of anointing the sick **with oil** (which 13
is not mentioned anywhere else in connection with Jesus' activity) is an authentic element of the disciples' mission or is a reflection of the subsequent practice of the church (James 5.15). In either case it is clearly not thought of as a medicinal treatment (for which indeed oil was often used, as in Luke 10.34) but as an instrument or sign of supernatural power over disease. But even if such details are uncertain, there is no reason to doubt either that Jesus, on at least one occasion,[b] sent his disciples out on a mission, or that his charge to them was faithfully remembered. The way they were to

[a] The alternative reading 'son of the carpenter and Mary' is probably an assimilation to Matthew's version. It was a repugnant idea in some quarters that Jesus should actually have been a carpenter.

[b] Luke records two: see below on Luke 10.1.

proceed is vividly drawn: apart from what was basically necessary for any-
8–9 one walking across the country—sandals and stick—they were not to take any of the provisions of food, clothes and money with which a prudent traveller always equipped himself before a long journey. (There may also be the implication that they were not to go as beggars—the word translated **pack** can mean the pouch in which a beggar put what was given to him.) The reason for travelling so light was probably twofold. In the first place, the mission seems to have taken place in Galilee, which was densely populated: the distance between one town or village and the next was never so great as to warrant serious preparations. Secondly (and this is more important), they were to expect hospitality (as any traveller could who had a good reason for his visit) and to accept it. They were not to exploit this by moving from house to house in turn: their work was presumably too urgent, and time too precious. On the other hand, the kind of reception they had would be a clear sign of people's readiness to hear them. If it were unfavourable, they were to perform a gesture which was a characteristic Jewish way of emphasizing the holiness of Palestine: after being abroad, or in any place regarded as "unclean", Jews would shake the dust from their feet before they stepped in the holy land, so as not to contaminate it. The disciples' gesture could be interpreted only in one way: the place which did not receive them could have no part in the coming kingdom.

Mark separates the departure of the disciples from their return by a narrative which bears only indirectly on the theme of the gospel. It is certainly true that John the Baptist was put to death by Herod Antipas: the fact is recorded by Josephus. It is also true that, just as John's preaching was the forerunner of Jesus' preaching, so his death prefigured Jesus' death, and perhaps for that reason won a place in the gospel story. But the vivid
17–28 details of Mark's account are clearly there for their own sake. The story as told in Mark is somewhat different from Josephus' account: according to Josephus, Herod's motive was political. But it is perfectly consistent with what is known of Herod's character; and although it is told more in the manner of a *raconteur* than of a serious historian, it may well have a basis in history.

14, 15 **People were saying . . . others said.** The kind of rumours to which Jesus' activity gave rise all tended in one direction. There was no special
16 reason to think that a man who had been **raised from the dead** would be capable of performing miracles; on the other hand, it was a widespread popular belief that the new age, which the Jews confidently expected in the near future, and which would be marked by a miraculous triumph of good over evil, would be ushered in by the return of one of the great Old Testa-
15 ment figures, Moses, Elijah or **one of the old prophets**. In so far, then, as the activity of Jesus seemed to betoken the arrival of the new age, it was natural to identify him with one of these; and following the same line of

thought, it might even have seemed possible that John the Baptist himself had been a person in the same tradition who would "come again" at the appointed time, and Mark, by way of introducing the following story, makes Herod think the same.

This same Herod. Herod Antipas had been tetrarch (and doubtless 17
known locally as **king**) of Galilee and Transjordan (Peraea) since the death 14
of his father, Herod the Great, in 4 B.C. He had recently, while returning from a visit to Rome, fallen in love with Herodias, the wife of his brother. This brother did not possess a kingdom of his own at the time, which may be one of the reasons why Herodias left him and was prepared to marry Herod Antipas. So far as we know, the brother's name, like his father's, was simply Herod: that Mark calls him **Philip** is perhaps no more than a mistake. Herod Antipas then prepared to divorce his first wife (who anticipated him by returning to her father's court at Petra) and duly married Herodias, who brought with her the child of her first marriage, Salome (Josephus gives us her name). The girl would have been around twenty years old. All sorts of unfortunate results followed from this marriage, including, predictably enough, a war with the Nabataean king of Petra, the father of Herod Antipas' first wife. But in the eyes of strict Jews there was a further reason for disapproval in that it was unlawful to marry a brother's wife while the brother was still alive. This is the background to John the Baptist's remonstrances and Herodias' grudge against him. According to Josephus the scene of John's imprisonment and execution was Machaerus, Herod's frontier stronghold east of the Dead Sea. The gospel narrative is not incompatible with this, although Herod's luxurious palace in Tiberias on the Sea of Galilee would certainly have been a more appropriate setting for the story of the fatal banquet.

The apostles now rejoined Jesus. For the first and only time in Mark's 30
gospel the disciples, on their return from their mission, are called **the apostles**. The word, which means literally "one who is sent out", was a technical one used by the Jews for a messenger entrusted with an official mission; but in the early church it had only one significance: it meant the select group of disciples who, having witnessed the Resurrection, were entrusted with the task of founding the church. It is a striking fact that this title is seldom read back into the gospel narrative; but there is perhaps reason for it here in that the disciples had just acquitted themselves of the kind of task which was subsequently to be the particular mission of the apostles.

Jesus' reaction to the crowds who had just frustrated his intention of
sailing **to some lonely place** was that they were **like sheep without a** 31, 34
shepherd. This biblical expression (Numbers 27.17, Ezekiel 34.5) was more than a picturesque metaphor for an aimless multitude. It evoked the whole history and destiny of Israel. God himself had shepherded his people, keeping them as one flock in the face of all disintegrating pressures and

leading them into their own land towards the fulfilment of that ideal of perfection which their religion constantly held before them. But God had also deputed this shepherding to the people's own political and religious leaders, who had again and again failed to discharge their responsibility—the classic description of this failure is in Ezekiel 34. And it was the same in the time of Jesus. The religious leaders—particularly the Pharisees and the doctors of the law—had failed to give the guidance expected of them (this is a recurring motif in Jesus' discourses). And it was because of this failure that Jesus' heart went out to the crowd—**they were like sheep without a shepherd**. But there is more still in this phrase: it was promised in the Old Testament (and the hope was still alive in later Jewish writings) that God would send a leader who would be a true shepherd. Jesus knew himself to be this shepherd; and he deliberately began to fulfil the rôle by showing,
34 first that **he had much to teach them**, and secondly that he was aware of
their physical needs.

The four gospels between them give no less than six accounts of a feeding miracle of this kind, and clearly the church cherished the memory of it. Just as, in Mark at least, the healing miracles are not presented merely as the feats of a wonder worker, so the miracle of the feeding has a deeper significance. The scene is not a picnic but a formal meal: the men are made to sit in an orderly way as for a banquet;[a] and Jesus proceeds, like a devout Jewish host, to say the blessing and break the bread himself. The crowd is thus brought into table fellowship with him—the most expressive symbol the Jews knew of solidarity between one man and another; and the whole scene could hardly fail to be remembered when in later years the Christian church began to meet together for that eucharistic meal by which they were still miraculously fed and at which their Lord was still somehow present as host.

The traditional site of this miracle is a small and very luxuriant plain in the north-west corner of the lake, which appears not to have been populated in the time of Christ and which lay about an hour's walk west of Capernaum. If this was in fact the place, and if Mark or the tradition he was making use of was sufficiently familiar with the country for us to be able to rely on the details—and both these assumptions are open to question—then the course of the following events is to be imagined as follows. It had been quite possible for the crowds to gather on the shore from the neighbouring towns before the boat reached the spot: the boat had therefore clearly not crossed the lake from one side to the other (which would have been a much quicker way of crossing than walking all the way round), but had simply moved some
31 distance westward along the shore in order to reach **a lonely place**. If it

[*a*] **A hundred rows of fifty each** gives the required total of five thousand: but it is the translators' idea. The traditional translation "by hundreds and by fifties" may equally well be right.

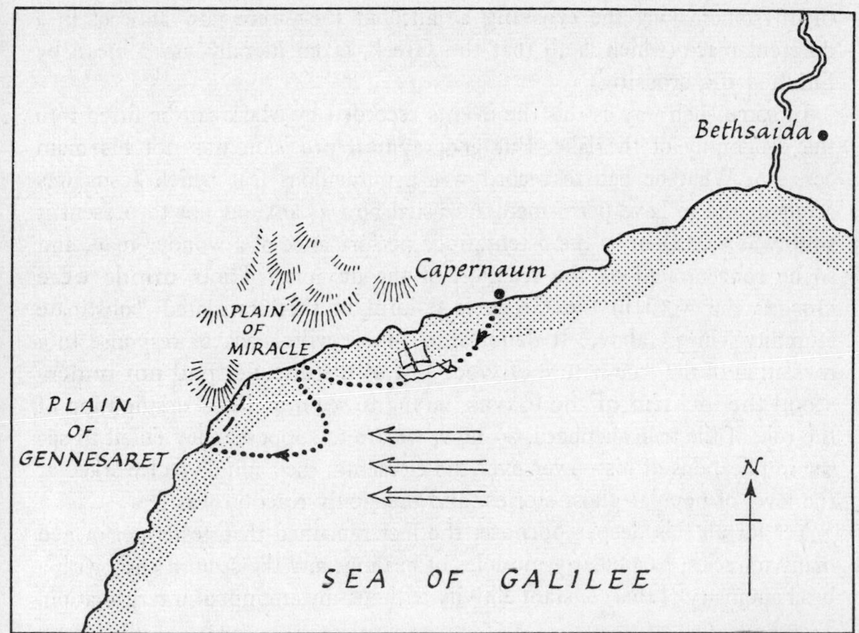

started from Capernaum (which was the centre of Jesus' activities) then the traditional site of the feeding miracle would be about the right distance away. After the miracle Jesus apparently intended to do what the crowds had done, that is to say, to walk round on foot while the boat returned the way it had come.

Thus, **he made his disciples embark and cross to Bethsaida ahead** 45
of him. Bethsaida was in fact a few miles further east than Capernaum on
the other side of the mouth of the Jordan. However, the disciples found
themselves rowing **against a head-wind** so powerful that by the early hours 48
of the morning (Mark uses the Roman reckoning, "the fourth watch of the
night") they had not merely made no headway but were actually (we must
suppose) drifting in the opposite direction. Seeing this, Jesus turned west
to meet them and apparently struck out across the water. [a] **He was going to**
pass them by, presumably because he wished to get to the land in time to
meet them. But once they had seen him he joined them in the boat. **So they** 53
finished the crossing and came to land at Gennesaret. The plain of
Gennesaret lay still further to the west, and they were now further from
home than when they had set out. The contrary wind had in fact prevented

[*a*] The plain of the feeding miracle and the plain of Gennesaret are separated by a rocky hill which runs right up to the shore of the lake. Normally Jesus would have had to walk round it or climb over it, so losing sight of the boat. This could explain why he chose to cut across over the water.

them from making the **crossing** at all; but they were now at least in a different place (which is all that the Greek, taken literally, need mean by **finished the crossing**).

In some such way as this the events recorded by Mark can be fitted into the geography of the lake. But geographical precision was not his main concern. What he had to record was a miraculous feat which Jesus was remembered to have performed. As usual he was anxious not to present it simply as a freak or as the ostentatious performance of a wonder-man, and
52 so he concentrated on the reaction of the disciples. **Their minds were closed**: the word in the Greek is a form of that translated "obstinate stupidity" in 3.5 above. It denotes an almost wilful lack of response to a revelation of the true nature of God. Just as the disciples **had not understood the incident of the loaves**, failing to see in it Jesus' assumption of the rôle of the true shepherd, so now, we are to suppose, they failed to see the implications of his power over the elements: their minds still worked at the level of popular ghost-stories, and their only reaction was fear.

Yet for all this deeper purpose, the fact remained that Jesus performed
53-6 many miracles, particularly miracles of healing; and the section ends with a brief summary of this constant activity without any attempt at interpretation.

Growing tension

7. 1 **A group of Pharisees, with some doctors of the law.** Almost from the beginning of the gospel these men have been constantly in the background, representing a sinister and powerful opposition to Jesus. Not only were they allied to the civil authorities in Galilee (the 'Herodians'), but they were in touch with the religious leaders in Jerusalem (some of these lawyers **had come from Jerusalem**, perhaps for the express purpose of reporting on Jesus' activities). So far, conflict with them had been sporadic and inconclusive, and had been focused mainly on specific questions of Sabbath observance. But now the antagonism came further into the open, beginning with some criticism made of Jesus' disciples on a technical question of purity, but developing into a fierce counter-attack by Jesus against the whole principle on which his opponents' religious practices were based.

The dispute began because some of Jesus' disciples were observed to be
2 **eating their food with 'defiled' hands—in other words, without washing them.** It is known that a hundred years later (if not earlier) it was indeed a strict rule among orthodox Pharisaic Jews to wash their hands before eating, in order to avoid the risk of contaminating their food with any ritually "unclean" substance which might be on their hands; and since this
3 rule was not to be found in Scripture they appealed to **an old-**

established tradition. But strangely enough there is no evidence for this having been a general rule in the time of Jesus, and the most that can be said is that at a formal meal it was normal for guests to wash their hands (Luke 11.38), and that some exceedingly strict Jews of Pharisaic tendencies may already have been regarding hand-washing as essential for the ritual purity of the ordinary layman in his daily life, just as it was for the priest in the performance of his temple duties. In support of this they may have appealed to a traditional interpretation of some passage of Scripture. Mark's comment, in any case, which is clearly intended for readers unfamiliar with Jewish customs, is certainly an exaggeration in so far as it attributes this kind of scrupulousness to **the Jews in general**; and in other respects it offers information which is barely credible for Palestine in the time of Jesus. It may, however, reflect the conduct of Jewish communities in a city such as Rome where the risks of ritual "defilement" through contact with pagan
institutions were so much greater.[a] Moreover, the passage from Isaiah 6
(29.13) is quoted according to the Greek version of the Septuagint, which is somewhat different from the original Hebrew text. Jesus himself could not have used this version, but the church did so, and indeed in Colossians 2.22 we find the passage quoted in the same form as in Mark, again in the context of a discussion about ritually permissible food. It may well be that discussion of this kind between Jews and non-Jewish Christians has left its traces upon the gospel; consequently we have to go behind it to reach the nerve of the original controversy as it would have been conducted between Jesus and the Pharisees.

If it is not true that **the Jews in general** observed this rule about the 3
washing of hands, the offence given by Jesus' disciples must have been similar to their failure to fast: they were not adopting those practices of extra piety which were expected of any serious religious movement within Judaism. Jesus' reply, assuming that he quoted from the Hebrew text of Isaiah, would have ended: "their religion is but a precept of men, learned by rote". He was endorsing, in fact, the prophet's criticism of any religious practice which diverted the pious from their basic moral obligations; and
he was applying it directly to his critics with the words, **'You neglect the** 8
commandment of God, in order to maintain the tradition of men'. The many detailed observances which the Pharisees regarded as binding were based, not on the Law of Moses itself, but on a traditional interpretation of the law which sought to make all injunctions relevant to the conditions of contemporary life. The sheer complexity of these observances made the mastery of them a matter which seemed at times to crowd out any

[*a*] The details are also somewhat obscure. We know of no rules about washing after visiting a "market-place" (which was the name for the civic centre of any Greco-Roman city), and the phrase "washing the hands with the fist", which appears in the best manuscripts and ought probably to be kept in the text, has baffled interpreters. A recent suggestion is that it means holding the hands out, not flat, but cupped.

balanced understanding of the spirit in which the divine law had been given; and it is on this point that Jesus' most characteristic attacks against the Pharisees were made. Their attempt to secure perfect obedience to the law by fencing it round with a mass of detailed regulations had resulted in an actual neglect of the original commandments.

But Jesus, in Mark's narrative, carried his attack a stage further. The
9 Pharisees not merely distracted attention from **the commandment of God** by the mass of their detailed applications of it, they actually **set aside** commandments by developing traditions which were incompatible with them. This was a serious charge indeed. The particular example chosen by Jesus is surprising at first sight. From all we know of Pharisaic tradition, it is
10 clear that they placed very high value on the commandment **Honour your father and your mother** (Exodus 20.12 and the negative form of it, Exodus 21.17), and were prepared to waive all sorts of other obligations in order to ensure that it would be observed. The case envisaged by Jesus is
11 that of a son who, in a moment of anger, says "**Corban**". Literally, this **meant set apart for God**. But the word had become an element in a very common form of oath. What the son said amounted to the oath: "I swear you shall have no benefit from anything of mine" (literally, "If I give you anything, it will have to be set apart for God and paid into the temple treasury"). Now the Jews, like many people in antiquity, took oaths very seriously: it was laid down in their law that a man must fulfil his oath (Deuteronomy 23.21), and fearful consequences were expected if he failed to do so. Therefore it made no difference if, when the moment had passed, the son repented of his precipitate words. He was now bound by an oath which prevented him from fulfilling his normal duties to his parents. Clearly such a use of oaths had the makings of a serious abuse. It is true that the Pharisees attempted to remedy it by arguing that a large number of popular ways of swearing were not valid oaths at all and therefore constituted no excuse for failing to observe a clear commandment of the law. Nevertheless, we know from the Dead Sea Scrolls as well as from later rabbinical writings that abuses of this kind flourished in the time of Jesus, and it was fair to attack the Pharisees for having countenanced them. It was their own thoroughly casuistical interpretation of the law which had given the word "Corban" the status of an oath, and so had made it possible for a man to evade his clear duty to his parents simply by uttering the word. This was
13 a good example of their **own tradition** having made an important article of **God's word null and void.**

14 **On another occasion he called the people**. This introductory sentence is so general that it gives no hint of Jesus' motive in making the pronounce-
15 ment which follows. On the face of it, the saying, '**Nothing that goes into a man from outside can defile him**', is of a piece with Jesus' prophetic criticisms of the religion of his day: outward observances are valueless

compared with the pure intentions of the heart. But there is no clue to its
precise application; and we can understand why it was subsequently thought
of as an enigmatic saying (which is one of the meanings of the word **parable**). 17
Following the pattern which he used when explaining the parable of sowing
in chapter 4, Mark appends an interpretation that was given privately to
the disciples. This interpretation makes the saying apply specifically to
regulations about food; but is this the point which Jesus originally had in
mind? The topic was not particularly appropriate to Jesus' work among the
Jewish population of Galilee. It was clearly stated in the Old Testament
(Leviticus 11, Deuteronomy 14) that certain kinds of meat and fish were not
to be eaten, and no Jew would ever have thought of doing so. It was only in
a mixed community of Jews and non-Jews that the question became urgent.
Moreover, the list of evil deeds and vices is more typical of the conventional 21–2
language of Hellenistic ethics than of the teaching of Jesus. The principle
given here was certainly accepted in the church by the time this gospel was
written; but there is abundant evidence, both in Acts (10.15; 15.29) and in
Paul's letters (Galatians 2.11–14; 1 Corinthians 8 and elsewhere) that the
traditional Jewish scruples over "unclean" foods continued to cause divisions of opinion among Christians. Jesus' general statement doubtless
implied a liberal attitude towards food; but the implication may not have
been worked out by the church until the whole question of the application
of Jewish ordinances to Christians had been settled. **Thus he declared all** 19
foods clean appears to be a comment by Mark himself, reflecting the
position on this matter at last reached by the church.

Then he left that place and went away into the territory of Tyre. 24
The predominantly Jewish region of Galilee was bounded on most sides by
territories that were mainly gentile. To the west, the plain lying between the
mountains of Galilee and the Mediterranean sea belonged to the Roman
province of Syria, and its inhabitants were called "Phoenicians of Syria" to 26
distinguish them from the Phoenician settlers who founded Carthage, in
Libya. The principal Phoenician cities in Syria were Tyre and Sidon, which
were both cosmopolitan Mediterranean ports; but there is some evidence
that politically the **territory of Tyre** extended eastwards over the mountains 24
as far as the upper reaches of the Jordan, and therefore included an area
where the population was still mainly Jewish. Mark's meaning therefore
may be that Jesus travelled to the extreme north of the Jordan valley (where
he would have been still among his fellow-countrymen), and not that he took
the more drastic step of crossing the mountains into the completely non-Jewish environment of the coastal plain.

Nevertheless the point of the following story was that it put to the test for the first time Jesus' attitude to Gentiles. What would he do when accosted by a gentile woman? Was he prepared to extend his miraculous and compassionate powers to pagans? Jesus' first response, though a little cryptic

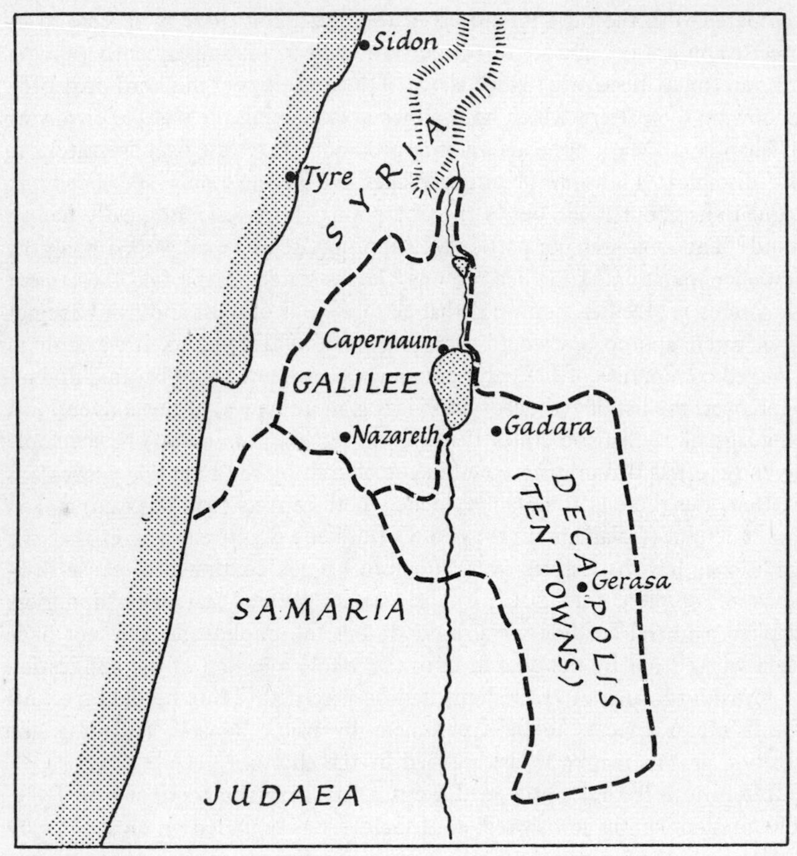

and perhaps spoken with sufficient humour not to give offence, was discouraging: everyone knew that the Jews, themselves in a special sense the
27 '**children**' of God, were not above referring to non-Jews as '**dogs**'; and
Jesus seemed to be endorsing the usual Jewish attitude. But the woman, instead of protesting at this order of priority, accepted that Jesus' mission was primarily to his own people, but surmised (with a prophetic insight which may well have seemed significant to Mark and to the many non-Jews in the church to which he wrote) that its effect could not be limited to the Jewish race. For this insight she was rewarded by a rare miracle: exorcism from a distance.

31 Jesus' **return journey from Tyrian territory** is exceedingly puzzling. Assuming that Mark intended to continue the series of episodes which took place in the outposts of Jewish territory, it is reasonable that Jesus' destination should have been that part of the Sea of Galilee which lay in **the territory of the Ten Towns** (the Decapolis, a league of Greco-Roman cities to

the east and south of Galilee), and it is just intelligible to describe the journey there as having been **through** this territory, even though this territory was the last he came to. Jesus' route would then have kept to a direction roughly south-east. But **Sidon** (and its territory which, like that of Tyre, extended far inland) lay considerably to the north. If Jesus went literally **by way of Sidon**, he must have made an immense detour, and his journey would have taken several weeks. If he went even into the territory of Sidon at its nearest, he must have gone substantially out of his way, and it seems preferable to assume, either that Mark was ignorant of the geography, or else that Sidon is mentioned only because, since early times, it was customary to refer to it in the same breath as Tyre.

The cure of the man **who was deaf and had an impediment in his** 32
speech is described in some detail, and Jesus' procedure conforms closely
to that of miracle-healers in many parts of the world: the touch, the spittle,
and the solemn word of command (for **Ephphatha** probably represents the 34
Hebrew form of the word, and Jesus would have used Hebrew as a sacred
language) are all typical details; and the raising of the eyes to heaven and the
sigh can also be paralleled from magical techniques (though they may of
course also indicate something of Jesus' emotion on this occasion). But Mark
characteristically avoids giving the impression of a mere miracle. He adds
once again Jesus' curious injunction forbidding them **to tell anyone**; and 36
he records the very strong impression made on the crowds in words which 37
suggest that they saw the miracle as a sign of greater things to come. For had
not Isaiah prophesied (35.5) that in the promised new age "the ears of the
deaf shall be unstopped and the tongue of the dumb shout aloud"?

There was another occasion. Mark seems to have had no information **8.** 1
about the place or the time of this miracle; and it is of no help to us when he
records that the place Jesus went to immediately after it was **Dalmanutha,** 10
since nothing whatever is known about this place.[a] Nor has he attempted to
read a deeper meaning into the story, as he did for the remarkably similar
incident in 6.30–44. He simply presents the miracle as a notable feat of Jesus,
motivated this time (unlike the previous one) by the sheer physical necessity
of the people who had followed him: they were now too far from civilization
to procure themselves food, and could have come to serious harm unless
something were done. It is true that the words **after giving thanks to God,** 6
he broke the bread recall Jesus' institution of the eucharist; but they do
not in themselves provide a satisfactory explanation why Mark, whose gospel
contains on the whole a highly economical selection of Jesus' words and deeds,
records two such similar episodes, even if there were in fact (as both Mark

[a] This is the reason why some manuscripts offer the variants Magedan (which is the name, equally unknown, given in Matthew's gospel) or Magdala, which can be identified with a town on the west side of the lake.

and Matthew relate) two such feeding miracles in the course of Jesus' work in Galilee.

11 **They asked him for a sign from heaven.** Coming straight after the report of some remarkable miracles, this request may seem puzzling. What more impressive "signs" could be given than the feats which Jesus had been performing? But from the point of view of sophisticated and sceptical onlookers like the Pharisees, the vital question about Jesus could not be so easily settled. However much deeper meaning the miracle-stories may have possessed (and Mark takes care to show that most of them were more than mere miracles), they were never entirely cogent or unambiguous. Jesus' exorcisms, it was suggested, were carried out in collusion with the devil himself; his healings used recognized techniques of magic; his apparent control of the forces of nature could be accounted for in terms of harnessing powers considerably inferior to that of God himself. There were too many miracle-workers about for it to be prudent to give one's allegiance to any particular one of them without very careful "testing". Moreover Jesus' teaching constituted a direct challenge to existing institutions and traditional piety. If the Pharisees were to own his authority, they would be forced to abandon much of what they stood for. If indeed it were true, as Jesus was proclaiming, that 'the kingdom of God is at hand', then a decisive response of penitence and self-preparation could no longer be postponed. Naturally the Pharisees (and doubtless many others) were unwilling to draw such disturbing conclusions from their encounters with Jesus unless they had a clear and unambiguous "sign" that he had full authority to say what he said and do what he did. What would they have regarded as such a sign? Here we can only speculate; but parallels from the Old Testament and from later Jewish sources suggest that a dramatic fulfilment by Jesus of a specific prophecy, or a miraculous confirmation of one of his own predictions, would have confronted them with a challenge which they could no longer evade.

12 Jesus **sighed deeply to himself.** The signs of emotion which, to a notable extent in this gospel, are attributed to Jesus seem to be provoked by impatience with the religious observances and attitudes by which he was surrounded. So here: the religious mentality which will not yield its allegiance without first being given what it will recognize as unassailable evidence makes Jesus impatient. He sees his questioners as representatives of a whole **generation** which, like the "generation" of Israelites in the wilderness, is too obstinate to recognize the source and implications of the wonders done in its midst.

15 **'Be on your guard against the leaven of the Pharisees and the leaven of Herod.'** These words are not elucidated by the story in which they occur, and since they are found in a quite different context in Luke (12.1) it is likely that they were remembered as an isolated and somewhat

enigmatic saying of Jesus which Mark thought it appropriate to work in at this point. Leaven, because of its impressive power of transforming a mass of dough many times greater than itself, was often used metaphorically. Sometimes good things were compared to it (Matthew 13.33), sometimes bad (1 Corinthians 5.6). The only clue to its meaning here is that it must have been something which the Pharisees and Herod had in common; and this (particularly since an alliance of Pharisees and Herodians on the very point is recorded in 3.6 above) can hardly have been anything but a common disposition to suppress Jesus and his movement. Jesus' warning, in fact, was entirely practical.

But the story in which the saying is embedded (and in which it plays
virtually no part) has a very different point. It gives Jesus an opportunity
to castigate his disciples severely for their still unenlightened response to
the great things he is doing in their presence. He repeats the condemnation
of them already recorded by Mark after the first of the two feeding miracles
(6.52). Their **minds** were **closed**—a biblical phrase suggesting that they 17
were still in that state of obtuseness which, in the face of divine revelation,
had characterized the people of Israel throughout its history; indeed Jesus
goes so far as to apply to his disciples those fatalistic words of Isaiah (6.9) 18
which (at least according to Mark) he used of the crowds at large when they
failed to understand his parables (4.11–12). The distinction between the
disciples and the crowds is here at vanishing point: Mark, unlike Matthew,
makes no attempt to portray them in a favourable light. Their moment of
glory came later, after Easter, and belonged not to the gospel story but to
the history of the church. Meanwhile, even after witnessing Jesus' feeding
miracles, they remained blind. The sections which follow show Jesus taking
steps to penetrate their blindness.

For Jesus could heal the physically blind. It may be in order to point to a
deliberate contrast between his power over blindness and the continuing
obtuseness of the disciples that Mark inserts here a second healing story
remarkably similar to that given at the end of the previous chapter (the two
stories have in common the privacy of the cure, the use of touch and spittle,
and the injunction to secrecy, and what was said above about the conventional traits of this kind of miracle applies with equal force here). This one
takes place at **Bethsaida**, which was on the far side of the Jordan, in the 22
tetrarchy of Herod Antipas' brother Philip. Philip had begun to found a new
city on the site, named Julias after Augustus' daughter Julia; but, since very
little is heard about this "city", and since no buildings of any pretension
have ever been found on the site, it may be that his plans never got very far,
and Mark may not be altogether inaccurate in calling it a **village**; in any 23
case, there is no reason to think that its population must have been much less
Jewish than that of, say, Capernaum, or that Mark intends us to imagine
that the blind man was a Gentile. The unique feature of the cure is that it was

gradual. If a parallel was intended between the man's blindness and the disciples' obtuseness, it is possible that it was this detail which led Mark to place the story here: the next three chapters relate the gradual (and in fact only partial) enlightenment of the disciples.

From Bethsaida, a day's walk northward through the territory of Philip
27 would have been more than sufficient to reach the **villages of Caesarea Philippi**, a town which had been refounded by Philip as a Hellenistic city, without presumably much affecting the character of the villages round it. The
28 beginning of the conversation is a little contrived: Jesus presumably did not need to ask the disciples for information about what people were saying; and their answer to Jesus' question has already been given once by Mark in connection with Herod (6.14). But it serves to point up the significance of the disciples' reply. The people at large had certainly come to see in Jesus more than a mere miracle-worker: he appeared to be a sign that God's promises to his people were about to be fulfilled, and they therefore inclined to identify him with one of those prophetic figures of the past who, it was believed, would return to earth as a herald of the new age. But since the world around them still remained very much the same as it was, they did not take the further step of identifying Jesus with that unique person, the Messiah, who would be the central figure in the inauguration of a new age. The new age, it seemed, had not yet come, even though there might be signs of its dawning in the liberating activity of Jesus. Moreover Jesus himself had not openly admitted to the title of Messiah. Now all the Christians for whom Mark's gospel was written knew that Jesus was in fact the Messiah: indeed they had come to call him, as a matter of course, Jesus "Christ". Mark here relates that even before the resurrection the disciples (for whom Peter appears simply as the spokesman, since Jesus' response to what he says seems on each occasion to embrace all the disciples) had come to recognize
29 the same truth: '**You are the Messiah**' (the Christ).
30 This truth however was not yet to be openly revealed. The injunction to silence continues the series of such injunctions which (particularly in Mark's gospel) Jesus often gives after the performance of a miracle. It is debatable whether these injunctions go back to Jesus (in which case they may have been motivated by a desire for privacy, an anxiety to avoid conflict with the government, or a sense that a popular following was a form of temptation to be resisted), or whether they were (at least in part) inserted by Mark in order to explain the comparatively small following which Jesus obtained in Galilee. But here the injunction makes a clear distinction between the disciples and the people in general: the disciples are shown to have advanced, despite their previous failures, to the point of recognizing Jesus as Messiah, whereas this is something which must still be concealed from the crowd.

Their progress however does not go very far. Jesus immediately gives

them some further teaching which finds no response in them whatever. **The** 31
Son of Man was a phrase which suggested a glorious and vindicated figure; but he was to come into this state of glory only after he, or the righteous people whom he represented, had suffered, and even been martyred, for their faith. It was perhaps natural that popular thought should concentrate more on the glory to come than on the necessary condition that the righteous people of God (of whom everyone hoped to be a member) should first undergo severe tribulation; and the effect of Jesus' words here is to correct this bias and to emphasize the things which have got to happen first, before glory and vindication can be contemplated. He does this in some detail; and the details are an unmistakable description of his own rejection, death and resurrection. According to Mark, therefore, Jesus both identifies himself completely with the Son of Man and gives a detailed forecast of his own destiny. How near we stand to historical truth at this point is a tantalizing question. On the one hand it was only be to expected that the words in which the church was accustomed to recite the bare facts of Jesus' life, death and resurrection should have influenced at least the form in which Jesus' prophecy was remembered (and there are vestiges of this process in the Greek text of Mark). On the other hand it is difficult to make sense of Jesus' mission unless it is granted that he had at least a premonition of the fate in store for him, and some consciousness of his destiny.

He spoke about it plainly. Much of his teaching was in parables, much 32
of it enigmatic; the disciples had as much difficulty in understanding it as anyone else unless, as sometimes happened, Jesus gave them a clue to his meaning. But on this occasion Mark relates that Jesus talked to them **plainly**, that is, in a way they could not possibly misunderstand. Their reaction, for all that, was no more enlightened than usual. Instead of their usual bewilderment, they registered frank opposition to the idea that Jesus (and perhaps also themselves, as members of the people whom the Son of Man would represent) should suffer rejection and execution. This amounted to a frank substitution of human preferences for obedience to the divine purpose. It was a manifestation, in the very circle of Jesus' own disciples (for whom, again, Peter stands as spokesman), of the seductive power of the devil with which Jesus had already had to wrestle in the "temptation" with which his work began.

Since the disciples were unresponsive to this message of suffering, Jesus
called the people to him for some more general teaching on the same theme 34
—or so, at least, Mark or his source arranged this group of Jesus' sayings: the whole difficulty of this passage is to determine how far the later experience of the church has influenced the record of this important moment in Jesus' self-revelation. That there has been some influence is difficult to deny. **'He must take up his cross'**, for example, is a phrase which can hardly have had much meaning before the crucifixion of Jesus. Crucifixion was the

Romans' normal method of executing those of their subjects in Palestine who were convicted of causing sedition; but before Jesus' own passion and crucifixion set the pattern for his followers, the call to "take up one's cross" could hardly have been understood except as an invitation to risk one's life in acts of resistance or rebellion against the Roman occupying power—which is hardly likely to have been Jesus' intention. Again, whatever teaching
34 Jesus may himself have given about the necessity to **leave self behind** (which is the NEB translators' interpretation of the Greek phrase "to deny
36 oneself") and to maintain one's **true self** at all costs (which is an attempt to bring out the double sense of the word "life" in the original phrase, "whoever shall lose his life . . . shall save it"), there can be no doubt that these sayings take on far more relevance and significance if they are read in the context of a Christian community which is being persecuted. The same goes
38 for the final sentence. There may have been moments in Jesus' life (such as Peter's denial of him) when this saying would have been relevant; but it reads more easily as a subsequent warning to the church that anyone who is **ashamed** of Jesus and his followers[a]—that is, who has not the courage to confess his allegiance in the face of persecution—cannot expect to be numbered among those who will share the Son of Man's glorious vindication at the end of history.

9. 1 **He also said.** This is one of Mark's usual ways of adding a saying of Jesus which did not originally belong to the context. The saying presents great difficulty because (taken in its plainest sense) it was soon proved false; but equally, since no one would have thought of attributing to Jesus an apparently unfulfilled prediction if he did not make it himself, it is almost certain to be authentic. In the context both of Jesus' own teaching and of contemporary Jewish expectation, **the kingdom of God . . . come in power** could only have meant one thing: the moment when God would bring the present course of world history to an end and institute a new order which would be unmistakably his **kingdom.** If this is what Jesus in fact predicted in the lifetime of his hearers, then he was mistaken; and many interpreters have felt bound to accept this clear limitation of Jesus' understanding of the future, particularly since it is clear from the New Testament letters that the early Christians in general expected the end to come within their own generation. On the other hand a number of decisive events, of less finality than the end of the world, but of considerable significance in the working out of the divine purpose, did in fact take place before the passing of Jesus' generation. One was the destruction of Jerusalem by the Romans in A.D. 70 which seemed to many to symbolize God's final judgement passed on the Jewish religion;

[*a*] Jesus had no "followers" (people whom he could call **mine**) in the sense of a steady community of which a wavering member might be **ashamed**, until after the resurrection. This would be clear evidence that the saying took its present form not on the lips of Jesus but in the church, were it not that it is far from certain that this is the correct manuscript reading. See the footnote in NEB.

another was the vindication of Jesus (the Son of Man) by the resurrection; a third was the manifest power released in the church which caused the gospel to be accepted on a scale beyond all human expectation, and seemed a clear foretaste of the **kingdom of God already come in power**. It is possible that Jesus' prediction originally referred to one or more of these events; in addition to which, the kingdom of God in Jesus' teaching was never a concept confined to the future: his message was that, though the consummation was still to come, vital things were happening and vital decisions were being asked of men even now in the course of his own activity. Since all his teaching about the coming of the kingdom was thus a great deal richer in meaning than the simple prophecies of doom or glory made by some of his contemporaries, it is reasonable to think that the saying here, whatever its original form, was neither so naïve nor so misguided as it now appears.

The episode which follows is traditionally known as the Transfiguration,
transfigured being derived from the Latin word which corresponds most 2
nearly to the Greek *metemorphōthē*, "changed his form". The account is
brief and succinct; but the difficulty is to know whether it is intended simply
to report an eyewitness account or whether some of the details derive from a
symbolical interpretation of the event. **Elijah . . . and Moses with him**, 4
for example, are clearly not just extras on the stage, but are intended by their
presence to point to the nature of him with whom they are conversing. But
what on this occasion do they stand for? Are they symbols of the Law and
the prophets which Jesus was destined to fulfil and supersede? Elijah was
commonly thought of as the first of the prophets, and Moses was of course
the lawgiver (though it is surprising to find him in second place after Elijah:
it is just possible that he was added later to the original story to fill out the
symbolism). Or does Elijah appear in his usual rôle of precursor of the
Messiah? In which case Moses is presumably there for the same reason: and
it may well be that there was a belief in the time of Jesus (as there certainly
was at a later date) that Moses, as well as Elijah, would return at the inauguration of the new age. **Shall we make three shelters**? Again, this could be a 5
purely practical suggestion of Peter's, an effort to offer hospitality on the
mountain to the disciples' distinguished guests—and Mark himself notes
how inappropriate the suggestion was: **he did not know what to say**. But 6
equally the **shelters** (the word means literally "tents") could be an allusion
to the fact that in the earliest history of Israel it was in a "tent" that God
came to meet his people (Exodus 33.7–11), and the image of a tent continued
to serve as a description both of the actual temple in Jerusalem and also of
the true sanctuary of God in the heavens (Hebrews 9.1–14). After this,
however, the symbolism of the details becomes apparent: the **cloud** was a 7
traditional sign of the presence of God (Exodus 16.10; 19.9, and many other
Old Testament passages); and, since the extinction of the prophetic spirit
with the death of the last of the Old Testament prophets, the **voice** from

heaven was the most frequent of the ways in which God was believed to reveal himself to men. The words spoken by the heavenly voice are identical with those spoken at Jesus' baptism; the significant difference here is that they are addressed to the disciples, who are henceforward (though their behaviour might seem to belie such knowledge) in possession of the key to Jesus' true nature. One more clue to the mystery of Jesus may lie in the final phrase, '**listen to him**'. Deuteronomy 18.15 reads (Moses is speaking): "The Lord your God will raise up for you a prophet like me from among you, from your brethren—listen to him." Jesus (it is doubtless implied) is this prophet.

The vision, then, is cast in a Jewish mould: some if not all the details take on their significance from traditions that originate in the Old Testament. All the more striking therefore is the one verse in the section which describes,
3 in language of an almost peasant simplicity (**with a whiteness no bleacher on earth could equal**), the transfiguration of Jesus himself. To this there is no parallel in Jewish literature: to find anything comparable one has to go to Greek myths, where gods often enough assume human form and then suddenly, by their dazzling appearance, betray their real nature. The vision is unparalleled for good reason. Jewish religion, unlike Greek religion, did not conceive of another and more glorious reality lying in some sense "behind" the physical world and occasionally breaking through to the senses of men. The Jews thought of this other world not metaphysically but temporally. It lay, not in the present behind the outward appearance of things, but in the future: it was the content of God's promises to his people and would one day, by an act of God, be fully revealed to them. The substance of Jewish religious visions was therefore 'what must happen hereafter' (Revelation 4.1), and it may be that Jesus' transfiguration should in part be understood in this sense: the "glorification" of Jesus lay in the future, it was the state he would assume after the resurrection, and what the three privileged disciples were being vouchsafed was a glimpse of that which was to come. But clearly the vision was more than this. Jesus was already Son of God and Messiah; therefore he was already (for those who could see it) a figure of glory. In his transfiguration, as in his preaching of the kingdom and in his power over the forces of evil, Jesus brought decisively into the present things which until then all Jewish religious thinkers had reserved for the future.

In Mark, any spectacular action of Jesus is very often followed by an injunction to secrecy. The transfiguration evidently falls into the same category of things not, or not yet, to be revealed. Jesus refers to himself
9 again (as in 8.31) as **the Son of Man**, and places for the first time a limit to
the period of secrecy—until he **had risen from the dead**. The NEB offers
10 an entirely original translation of the following phrase: **They seized upon
those words**. The sense is excellent, making a smooth transition to the

question about **'rising from the dead'**. But it is doubtful whether the Greek can mean this: it is normally translated "They observed his commandment" or (following a different punctuation) "they kept these things to themselves". In any case their question about rising from the dead arose out of the last words of Jesus' injunction. It was not of course a question about the meaning of "resurrection" itself, for this concept was part of everyone's stock of religious knowledge. One of the most widely held beliefs in Palestine was that at the end of the world all men would "rise from the dead" in order to receive judgement and just reward. What presumably puzzled them about Jesus' saying was that it implied that the Son of Man would rise from the dead, not at, but before the general resurrection. If so, his rising would doubtless (according to the accepted scheme) be a signal for the speedy coming of the end; and this accounts (if strict logic is to be applied to this somewhat jerky paragraph) for their second question: if the end was to come so soon, why had not all things yet come to pass which were due to happen first?

'Why do our teachers say that Elijah must come first?' These 11
teachers are the "lawyers" of a few verses further on, those whose profession it was to determine, by reference to their own tradition of interpretation, the precise bearing upon any matter of conduct or belief of a given passage of Scripture. The passage in question here was Malachi 4.5–6: "Look, I will send you the prophet Elijah before the great and terrible day of the Lord comes. He will reconcile fathers to sons and sons to fathers..." The original prophecy was straightforward enough: before the day of the Lord a new prophet would appear who would be none other than the first of the prophets, who had in fact never died (but had been taken up to heaven) and who would return to establish peace in the families of Israel before the end came. But from earliest times there was a tendency to elaborate the rôle of this future Elijah. The Septuagint Greek version of the Old Testament (by adding the words, "and a man to his neighbour") had already extended the area of his peacemaking from family life to the life of the nation as a whole, and Ecclesiasticus 47.13 gives him further tasks. By the time of Christ he had become an important figure in the scheme of the Last Things, and his rôle had grown from that of domestic peacemaking to that of restoring all things
to their pristine perfection (**to set everything right** is a colourless and not 12
entirely accurate translation). Whether he was to be a precursor of the Messiah, or himself to fulfil part of the traditional task of the Messiah, was a matter on which opinions were probably divided. But in any case it was inconceivable that the end could take place without the previous appearance of this Elijah-figure; and the words of Jesus, which seemed to bring the end sensationally close at hand, naturally raised the question in the disciples' minds how, in Jesus' scheme of things, Elijah could be fitted in.

Jesus' reply is somewhat obscure. The correctness of a traditional inter-

pretation of a passage of Scripture could be established or refuted by reference to another passage, and this seems to be Jesus' technique here.
12 Prophecies that the Son of Man himself was **to endure great sufferings and to be treated with contempt** are frequently appealed to in the New Testament, but are not easy to find: Isaiah 53 is usually thought to come nearest to what is required, and doubtless the Son of Man passage itself in Daniel 7 implies that the now vindicated and glorious figure had recently (in the persons of the saints) suffered persecution. But such prophecies seemed to conflict with the Elijah traditions, for the Son of Man unquestionably belonged to the final act of the drama, and if Elijah had already **set everything right**, it was hard to see what would be left to cause **great sufferings**
13 for the Son of Man. For the true answer, Jesus appeals to another prophecy which stated that Elijah too was to suffer at the hands of men. No such prophecy occurs in the Old Testament or the surviving Apocrypha; but we must assume that it occurred in some writing now lost which was sufficiently reputable for Jesus to quote it in the same breath as "the scriptures" (it is just possible that this tradition underlies the passage in Revelation 11 which is concerned with two suffering "witnesses"). If this prophecy was to be preferred to the tradition of a glorious and well-nigh omnipotent Elijah, then the disciples could look among their own contemporaries for a man who fulfilled this rôle. If we turn to Matthew (11.14), his account makes explicit what is doubtless implicit in Mark. They need not look far: the person in question was John the Baptist.

15 **As soon as they saw Jesus the whole crowd were overcome with awe.** The last phrase in the sentence is a strong one, a little stronger perhaps in the translation than it is in the Greek, which could mean simply that the crowd was "astonished" to see Jesus arriving at the precise moment when his presence was required. But **overcome with awe** may be correct. When Moses came down from Mount Sinai "the skin of his face shone" (Exodus 34.30), and the people were "afraid to come near him". Since the story of the transfiguration itself is full of Old Testament allusions, this may well be one more: Mark thought of a reflection of glory still visible in Jesus, as in Moses, some hours after the event, and producing awe in those who saw him.

The argument seems to have started with the disciples' failure to perform an exorcism. That they were empowered to exorcize is stated in 6.7; but that they should have occasionally failed is not surprising in itself (for some spirits were stronger than others) and must also have given the story a particular interest for the early church, in which exorcism was still practised but doubtless not always with success. What was the reason for these failures? Surely the disciples, and the Christians after them, either had the power or did not have it? A possible answer lay in words attributed to Jesus and added here by Mark as a piece of private instruction to the disciples:

'There is no means of casting out this sort but prayer'. If they failed, 29
it must be because they did not pray enough![a]

The exorcism, the last recorded by Mark, concerns a severe case of what we would now call epilepsy or hysteria, but was then ascribed to the activity of a spirit. The episode contains elements which allow Mark to present it, not as a mere miracle, but as a characteristic manifestation of the power and true nature of Jesus. Jesus' reaction to the all too human scene which met him on his descent from the mountain recalls the impatience and resignation of an Old Testament prophet: in the face of the signal acts of God performed before their eyes, the people remained (as so often in their history: the words
clearly evoke Deuteronomy 32.5) **an unbelieving and perverse genera-** 19
tion. The justification for such severe language is immediately provided by
the tentative approach of the boy's father: **'if it is at all possible for you'**. 22
This showed a clear lack of faith in Jesus' power, only partly made good by
his impassioned appeal, **'I have faith... help me where faith falls** 24
short' (literally "help my lack of faith"); for it was apparently the approach of the crowd, rather than the singularly candid confession of the father, which spurred Jesus to perform the exorcism, and cure the boy, not just of
his present fit, but of his illness altogether: **'come out of him and never** 25
go back'. Nevertheless it was doubtless because of these words about faith, and because of Jesus' statement which formed part of the dialogue and which must have been a source of great encouragement to Mark's readers—
'everything is possible to one who has faith'—that Mark included this 23
exorcism story in his gospel. It is possible also (as his use of the technical Greek words for "rising from the dead" may suggest) that in the very lifelike
details of the boy looking **like a corpse**, and in the judgement of **many** that 26
he was dead, Mark saw a prefigurement of that victory over death which was to be accomplished in Jesus' resurrection and shared by all who had faith in him.

He was teaching his disciples. Mark now devotes a section explicitly 31
to Jesus' instruction of his disciples. The main burden of this teaching was the prediction of the fate in store for the Son of Man, which is here repeated in very much the same terms as before (8.31); and just as on that
occasion the disciples refused to accept it, so now **they did not understand** 32
what he said, and were afraid to ask. For us, who have come to regard
the Son of Man simply as a title for Jesus, the teaching seems to be a 31
straightforward statement of what was going to happen, and we find it hard to believe that anyone could have failed to understand it. But **Son of Man** to Jesus' contemporaries meant (so far as we can now establish its meaning) a figure who was first and foremost vindicated and glorified; he embodied

[a] Many manuscripts add the words "and fasting". This looks like an early Christian addition giving a further reason for failure: they did not fast enough!

the splendid destiny to which God's righteous and elect people could confidently look forward. The disciples may not have found any difficulty in Jesus' use of the title as such, for they saw in him a person of unique power and authority; but the teaching which Jesus was giving them about the rôle which suffering was to play in the destiny of this figure (and doubtless in the destiny of that community of righteous and elect men whom the Son of Man represented) was apparently too much for their preconceptions.

Nevertheless the teaching—or at least that part of the teaching which concerned what would be demanded of the community, and which gave guidance to that community in times of stress—was remembered; and it is possible that we can detect in the apparently illogical sequence of these paragraphs one of the ways in which it was in fact held in the memory. For these sayings were clearly not originally spoken in the order, or even necessarily in the context, in which we have them. There is little apparent logical connection between them; and several of them occur in Matthew or Luke in quite different (and sometimes more appropriate) surroundings. On the other hand, one saying often contains a word or an idea which occurs again in the next, so that the memory would be assisted in moving from one to the other. Thus, **in my name** in the saying about children (verse 37) is picked up by **in your name . . . in my name** in the saying about non-Christian exorcists; **is a cause of stumbling** in verse 42 is picked up by **is your undoing** (which is the same word in the Greek) in verse 43; **fire** in connection with hell leads on to **everyone will be salted with fire**; and this again leads on to two further sayings about **salt** (verse 50). It is even possible that the word **servant** in verse 35 represents a word in Jesus' own language (Aramaic) which also meant **child**, in which case a further link would be established between the saying about greatness (35) and the saying about receiving children (37). In short the easiest explanation of the inconsequential character of this paragraph is that it reproduces a kind of crude mnemonic system used by teachers in the early church.

To understand these sayings it is therefore necessary to take them separately.

35 (i) The saying, **'If anyone wants to be first, he must make himself last of all and servant of all'** occurs again at 10.43–4 and in various other places in Matthew and Luke, and the context is always that of Jesus' instruction to the circle of his disciples; but the saying was clearly remembered as one of Jesus' most fundamental pieces of teaching about human relationships.

37 (ii) **'Whoever receives one of these children'**. Two presuppositions seem to underlie this saying. First, to maltreat an accredited envoy is to maltreat him who sent him (the idea was as much taken for granted in antiquity as it is now); and secondly, Jesus is in some way present in the poor and needy to whom one gives, or refuses, hospitality, help and service (this is worked out in Matthew 25.31–46). But neither of these presuppositions

explains why the saying is about **children**. It is true that Jesus had an unusual (for his time) interest in children as such (10.13–16). But it is also possible that the original saying was, like verse 42, about 'little ones who have faith', that is, the weaker and more humble of the followers of Jesus, and that at some stage the expression 'little ones' was taken too literally and turned into **children**.

(iii) Part of the ordinary technique of exorcism was to find out the name 38
and so the power of the devil concerned, and then to invoke by name a
stronger power with which to cast the devil out. There is nothing surprising
in the report that a contemporary exorcist, hearing of Jesus' power over a
large number of "unclean spirits", should have been using his name without
any sense of obligation to join Jesus' following. The reaction of Jesus'
disciples is human and understandable: that of Jesus suggests that he was
anxious to avoid forming any kind of militant and exclusive sect. To make
the point, he used what was almost certainly a proverb: **'he who is not** 40
against us is on our side'. The proverb was presumably a political one,
and represented the attitude of a liberal and conciliatory party, as opposed
to that of the more fanatical nationalist sects which were continually spring-
ing up under the Roman administration in Palestine. The fact that Jesus
appears to say the opposite in Matthew 12.30, Luke 11.23, is probably again
because the proverb existed in reverse, "He who is not with us is against us".
This would have been the watchword of the more fanatical parties; and
there were certainly aspects of Jesus' teaching which had a certain exclusiveness, and which he (or an evangelist) may have found it appropriate to
express by this severer version of the same proverb.

(iv) **'I tell you this'**—one of Mark's characteristic ways of adding an 41
isolated saying of Jesus. The saying occurs in Matthew (10.24) in the context of instructions about the reception to be given to Christian missionaries.

(v) **'As for the man who is a cause of stumbling to one of these little** 42
ones'. The **little ones** are doubtless the weaker members of the community of followers of Jesus, and a commentary on this saying can be found in Romans 14; indeed it may have been the kind of situation described there which caused this saying to assume its present form.

(vi) The necessity for sacrifice and single-mindedness is described with all 43–8
Jesus' usual vividness and lack of compromise. Cutting off **hand or foot** was certainly intended as a metaphor; and since the language is metaphorical, the saying should not be pressed for teaching about hell and eternal punishment. Jesus accepted and used the language of his contemporaries about these things. In the Greek, the word for **hell** in this passage is *Gehenna*, the precipitous valley on the south side of Jerusalem which was of baneful memory in Old Testament history ("Hinnom" in 2 Kings 23.10, Jeremiah 7.31 etc.) and was in the time of Jesus smoking with the refuse of the city. It was in common use as a name for "hell", and other conventional touches

43 are added, like the **unquenchable fire** and the phrase (which is a quotation
48 from Isaiah 66.24) **where the devouring worm never dies and the fire is not quenched.**

49 (vii) **'For everyone will be salted with fire.'** Salt preserves; and that which will make Jesus' disciples worthy of eternal life and preserve them in a state of preparedness for it will be the fire of persecution. (This at least is one possible meaning of this difficult sentence.)

50 (viii) **'Salt is a good thing.'** It is clear from the form given to this saying by Matthew in the Sermon on the Mount that it is the followers of Jesus who are to be like salt. For the rest, see above on Matthew 5.13.

50 (ix) **'Have salt in yourselves.'** This appears to come close to the Greek idiom in which salt means sharpness of mind and speech—'never insipid' as the very similar phrase is translated in Colossians 4.6.[a]

10. 1 **On leaving those parts he came into the regions of Judaea and Transjordan.** The journey was destined to be of the greatest significance. Jesus was leaving the comparative freedom of the somewhat provincial territory of Galilee and would soon be facing a direct confrontation with the religious leaders in Jerusalem. On the way, however, there was no reason why things should be any different for him, since the populations and political conditions through which he passed would have been much the same as they were in Galilee. The shortest route from Galilee to Jerusalem was due south along the mountain ridge on the west side of the Jordan. But this meant going through Samaria, and since relations between the Jews and the Samaritans were exceedingly strained at this period, Jewish travellers sometimes preferred to cross the Jordan south of the lake and proceed down the east side of the valley through territory which was also, like Galilee, under the administration of Herod Antipas and in which the population was predominantly Jewish. This territory was called Peraea (rendered in the NEB as **Transjordan**). They would then re-cross the Jordan in order to reach Jericho, and by so doing enter **Judaea**, having skirted both Samaria and most of the Decapolis, and having remained for almost the entire journey on what could reasonably be described as Jewish soil. Mark's description of the route is a little vague, and is often thought to be an indication that he had no first-hand knowledge of the geography of Palestine; but whether or not this is so, his words suggest one of the routes which were normally taken by Jewish travellers and pilgrims to Jerusalem.

2 **The question was put to him: 'Is it lawful for a man to divorce his wife?'** It is not easy to be sure what prompted this question. There was considerable discussion in the time of Jesus on the question of what constituted adequate grounds for divorce, for the relevant text of Scripture

[*a*] "Sharing salt" was also an expression for giving hospitality: hence the possible rendering in the footnote.

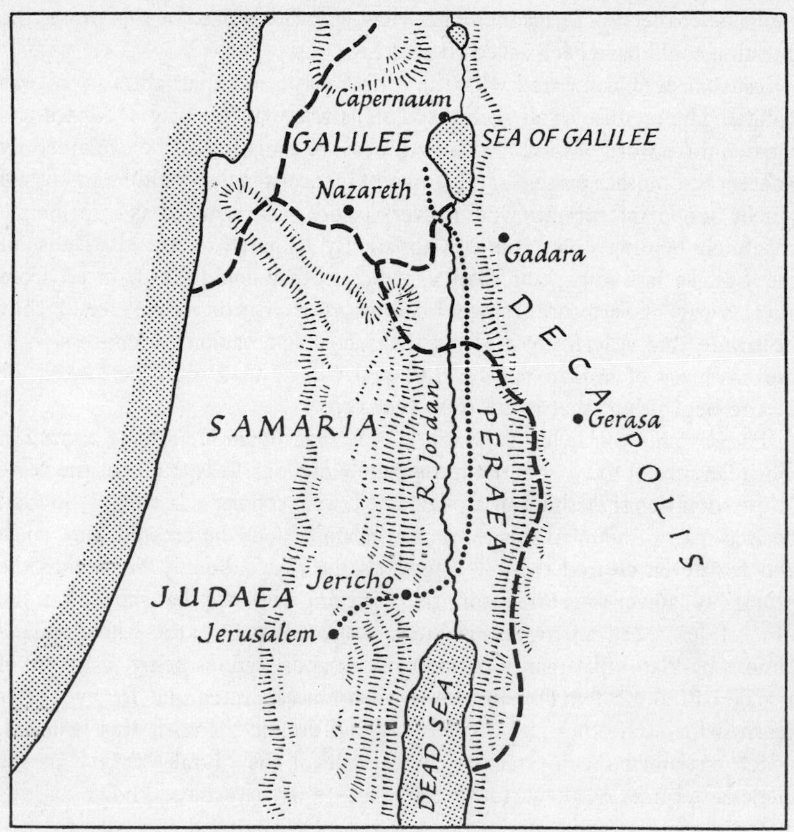

(Deuteronomy 24.1–4) was not precise, and the opinions of the professional interpreters (the 'doctors of the law') were divided, some taking a strict view, some a more permissive one. Matthew, who had greater familiarity than Mark with conditions in Palestine, set Jesus' sayings on marriage and divorce in the context of such a discussion (19.3–9). But in Mark the question is more general: not, Under what circumstances is divorce permissible? but, Is it lawful at all? On the face of it, this question could hardly have arisen in a Jewish community, for there was a passage in the Law of Moses (again Deuteronomy 24.1) which expressly sanctioned divorce. The only practical question was the definition of the grounds on which a divorce could be obtained. Nevertheless, there was at least one Jewish sect in Palestine which disapproved of divorce as such; but anyone who held this extreme view had then to explain away the explicit sanction of divorce in Deuteronomy 24.1. If Mark is correct, and the question was put to Jesus in this general form (and not in the more technical form recorded in Matthew), it must have been because it was thought he would take an extreme view on the matter, and

could be challenged to reconcile his view with Scripture. In this sense, the
2 question could have been asked **to test him.**

Jesus' answer, compared with the ordinary run of expert discussion, was radical. The premise of all such discussions was that the Law of Moses was the definitive word of God to man. An obscure clause could be explained by reference to another passage, and apparent inconsistencies could be smoothed out by subtle interpretation; but every clause was regarded as in principle absolutely binding. But Jesus was apparently prepared to regard a clause of the Law as less important than a principle that could be deduced from
5 another part of Scripture. **It was because your minds were closed that**
he made this rule for you. Moses' dispensation was only a concession to
the obstinacy of human nature. The real will of God must be looked for
6 **in the beginning**, that is, **at the creation.**

To prove his point, Jesus quoted two passages from Genesis (1.27; 2.24). The relevance of the first is not immediately obvious. It is true that the verse in question was something of a puzzle to Jewish scholars. It runs: "So God created man in his own image, in the image of God he created him; male and female he created them." Why does the text suddenly break into the plural? Whatever the real reason, there is some evidence that scholars in the time of Jesus had an ingenious interpretation based on the legend (made famous by Plato) that man was originally an androgynous being, made up of a male half and a female half, which then got separated and for ever after yearned for each other. It was this original double being, it was believed, which explained the mysterious appearance of the plural "them" in the Genesis account of the creation of man. Jesus may have known of this interpretation; in some circles the text was certainly used in order to propound a somewhat mystical view of the true nature of marriage. In any case,
7 the argument becomes clearer with the second quotation. The words, **for**
this reason, are part of the quotation, and immediately follow the account of
the creation of the woman from the rib of the man. The biblical explanation
8 of the fact that man and wife become **one flesh** is rather similar to Plato's
legend: originally, woman was actually a part of man's flesh. By the institu-
9 tion of marriage, God simply **joined together** what originally belonged
together. On the basis of this passage, Jesus could argue that divorce as such
is contrary to the will of God.

10 **The disciples questioned him about this matter.** The disciples may
simply not have understood this somewhat sophisticated piece of reasoning,
or else they were puzzled (as Christians have been puzzled ever since) about
11 its practical implications. But Jesus' reply to them was quite uncompromis-
ing. He was not, it seems, offering an interpretation of the law as it stood; for in theory (though this seldom happened in practice) Jewish law permitted polygamy, and therefore a prohibition of divorce would hardly have affected the position of the husband: he was permitted to have more than one wife in

any case. Rather, Jesus was making a judgement on divorce in general. Adultery was one of the acts which Jews regarded with the greatest abhorrence and punished very severely: its prevalence among non-Jews was one of their most constant complaints against gentile society. By calling the remarriage of divorced persons **adultery**, Jesus condemned it in very strong
terms indeed. As for the second part of Jesus' reply, it is difficult to see how 12
it could possibly have had this form in Palestine, where a wife had no right to institute divorce proceedings, and where consequently the words **if she divorces her husband** would have made little sense. She might however ask her husband for a divorce, and if he gave it to her the law permitted her to marry another man;[a] this may originally have been the point of Jesus' saying.

They brought children for him to touch. Their purpose (as Matthew 13
explains, 19.13) was to obtain his blessing: it was something very commonly asked of a religious teacher. Why the disciples objected is left to our imagination; but Jesus' reaction, as described by Mark (who hesitated less than any of the evangelists to ascribe expressions of emotion to him), was a strong one:
he was indignant. What was the quality in children which Jesus prized so 14
highly? We have to clear our minds of all those concepts of children's innocence, freshness of vision and spontaneity of motive which have come to be taken for granted in the west only since the Romantic movement, and have probably never had much currency in the east. The child, in antiquity, was valued not for his childishness but only for the promise in him of adult manhood; and the "blessing" of a parent or a teacher would be in effect a prayer that the promise would be fulfilled: it was a blessing entirely for the future. It is therefore a new and curiously modern tone which we hear in Jesus' voice when he appears to value children as children, in the present and not the future. It is possible, of course, that he was not doing anything of the sort. **Children** in this passage may be simply symbols for the poor and meek and humble of heart, a nickname for Christians (as perhaps in 9.37); or the episode may even (as some maintain) owe its form, if not its origin, to disputes in the early church about the propriety of baptizing infants. But
neither of these explanations does full justice to the saying, '**the kingdom of** 14
God belongs to such as these', which implies a clear recognition that there is something in children, as children, of real religious importance. The nearest the Bible (or indeed any ancient literature) comes to this is a passage such as Psalm 131.2—"I have calmed and quieted my soul like a child quieted at its mother's breast"—where the total dependence of a small child on its parents is an image of the dependence, trust and humility a man should feel before God. We can only guess how much more than this was intended by Jesus, or would have been understood by his hearers.

[*a*] A manuscript reading exists (not noted in NEB) which, since it gives "departing from her husband" instead of "divorcing him", is compatible with Jewish law. It is possible that this is what Mark originally wrote and that the text was subsequently changed to correspond with Roman law.

17 **A stranger ran up, and, kneeling before him, asked, 'Good Master . . .'** This scene, which contains some notably vivid details, has also a striking beginning. It was not customary for one Jew to kneel to another—the gesture was associated more with the cringing behaviour expected in the presence of an oriental monarch—and '**Good Master**' was a form of address so unusual that Jesus was moved to comment on it. This is hard to convey in English, for in a phrase like "Good Sir" the word "good" is nothing more than an expression of courtesy. The same was true to some extent in Greek society, and a Greek reader would probably have found the phrase, '**Good Master**,' as innocuous as a modern English reader does. But in Jewish conversation this polite idiom was unknown. To say of someone that he was "good" would not even have been understood as a professional compliment: a Jew would not have said that Jesus was "good" in the sense of being a good teacher, better than other teachers. To call someone "good" was to use the word in all seriousness of his moral character and personal conduct. Furthermore it was to use of a human being an absolute term that was proper to God alone. Hence Jesus' objection. It has often been felt (as it appears to have been felt by Matthew, who altered the sense of the remark) that the objection came oddly from Jesus: surely he, if anyone, merited the title "good"? But it may be that Jesus was objecting less to the word itself, which might in fact have been appropriate to him, than to the attitude of his questioner, who was prepared to use so serious a concept as a term of courtesy or even flattery.

17 '**What must I do to win eternal life?**' The question was a standard one. After death, at the general resurrection, men would be judged on their record, and those whose good deeds and way of life had merited it would **win eternal life** while the rest would be consigned to hell. This, at any rate, was the usual way of looking at the matter in the time of Jesus and in the circles in which he moved, and the ultimate purpose and goal of religious life and moral conduct was to "gain a share in the world to come" or to **win eternal life**. In broad terms the Jews were agreed on the way this could be achieved. God's will for man was revealed in the Law of Moses, and those who kept this law would automatically qualify for their promised share in the life to come. Did the stranger expect from Jesus some kind of practical precision and elaboration of the Law in answer to his question, or did he hope for a new ethic altogether, superseding the old? His words alone do not tell
us, though the eagerness of his approach suggests that he expected some-
19 thing quite new. Jesus' reply was almost brusque. **'You know the commandments'**. Jesus simply referred him back, without any refinements of
interpretation, to that basic section of the Ten Commandments which
20 governs conduct towards one's neighbour. **'But, Master', he replied, 'I
have kept all these since I was a boy'**. This reply was not pretentious. A
devout Jew treasured his consciousness of living correctly by the law, and it

was only the immense elaboration introduced into the observance of the law
by certain schools of Pharisaic thought which made scrupulous souls such as
Paul despair of keeping the law in its entirety. Jesus at any rate did not
criticize his reply; on the contrary, **his heart warmed to him.** Perhaps he 21
valued especially the man's dissatisfaction with a moral achievement which
would have seemed adequate to most men of his circumstances (for we learn
at the end that **he was a man of great wealth**). The obvious advice to give 22
him would have been to recommend a drastic increase in his almsgiving,
for this was valued by the Jews as one of the most meritorious acts of all, a
sure way of amassing **riches in heaven**; and the rich were regarded as 21
fortunate in having the resources to do this on a large scale. But Jesus pushed this far beyond the limit that would have been thought desirable by most of his contemporaries (some of whom actually discouraged excessive almsgiving, on the grounds that a man had a duty not to impoverish himself). The man must give away everything. Only total "giving to the poor" would answer to his situation. And to the question, What should he do then, as a pauper? Jesus had an answer ready: **'Come, follow me'.**

The story is one of a personal encounter between Jesus and a particular wealthy man. The question must immediately have been raised (as it has been raised ever since), Would the same apply to every rich man? The normal Jewish view (which was shared by all but the most sophisticated thinkers in antiquity) was that a man's riches were a sign of God's blessing, and that he could turn his wealth to a source of still greater blessing by generous acts of charity. The obverse of this, of course, was that the poor were not blest; and in a society like the Jewish, where throughout their history the rich were few and the poor were many, a more refined view had developed, according to which the poor had other virtues and opportunities of service which they could cultivate, and other evidence in their lives of God's blessing upon them, which compensated for their lack of wealth and privilege. Jesus very strongly endorsed this attitude. He went so far as to say, without qualification, 'How blest are you who are in need' (Luke 6.20). But it would not necessarily have occurred to his listeners to draw the conclusion which Jesus drew, 'Alas for you who are rich', for this would have drastically upset their presuppositions. When therefore Jesus generalized the case of this particular rich man by
saying, **'How hard it will be for the wealthy to enter the kingdom of** 23
God', the reaction of his disciples was one of bewildered astonishment.

'It is easier for a camel to pass through the eye of a needle.' The 25
almost grotesque disproportion of the simile is characteristic of Jesus' speech: there is no reason to think (as some have thought) that the original saying in his own language was misunderstood when it came to be translated into Greek. It is possible indeed that the saying was originally even more general and paradoxical than it appears; for the reading of the majority of manuscripts (as given in the NEB text as opposed to the footnote) gives in

24 verse 24 **'how hard it is to enter the kingdom of God'**, without any
mention of riches, and it is possible that all these sayings were originally quite general: the possibility of anyone entering the kingdom of God is one created only by God; no human qualifications (let alone riches) make any difference.

28 **At this Peter spoke.** The disciples had responded to the challenge which
the rich man had failed to meet. Could they at least be sure of their reward? Jesus' reply should probably be understood as that of a man who was even now leading a small group of impoverished disciples towards an uncertain destiny. A religious leader with political aspirations (and there were several
30 in first-century Palestine) would naturally promise **in this age** material
rewards, as well as **in the age to come eternal life.** On the other hand, a teacher whose concern was entirely with religious truth would be likely to content himself with promising his followers spiritual benefits after death. Jesus' rôle was clearly of the second type, and that part of the saying which promises **eternal life** seems the more characteristic of him. But it was also a feature of his teaching that much of what was normally reserved for the promised future life, Jesus brought startlingly into the experience of the present. It is therefore perhaps not surprising that part of Jesus' answer to Peter's question should have dealt with the question of rewards **in this age.** Nevertheless the apparently unashamed materialism of these promises comes as a shock, only slightly mitigated by the addition that there would be **persecutions besides.** Jesus may have been speaking metaphorically; but the saying is none the less puzzling, and it is possible (particularly in view of the conflicting evidence of a number of manuscripts) that some confusion crept in soon after the saying was written down.

31 **'But many who are first will be last and the last first.'** This saying
occurs in a different context in each gospel (compare Matthew 20.16, Luke 13.30), and was evidently remembered as an isolated dictum, to be inserted by the evangelists into their narratives wherever it fitted best. Its setting in Luke's gospel seems the most appropriate.

Challenge to Jerusalem

32 **They were on the road, going up to Jerusalem.** They were about to
come to Jericho, whence the road begins the long steep climb up to Jerusalem. The summit of the Mount of Olives could already be seen, some four thousand feet above. They were therefore, in the most literal sense, **going up to Jerusalem.** But "going up" meant more than this. It was the expression used of going to Jerusalem as a pilgrim on one of the great festivals (and the road may already have been crowded with pilgrims on their way to join in the

Passover); and the deliberate and public confrontation which Jesus seemed to be seeking with the centre of religious authority in the land may be a sufficient explanation of the awe of his disciples and the fear of **those who followed behind**. Nevertheless, the awed reaction of his followers, though understandable under the circumstances, remains a little strange. Mark may have deliberately anticipated, at this point, something of the dark drama which was soon to begin. He has certainly done this, in any case, in his report of Jesus' pronouncement to the Twelve. The two previous predictions of the destiny awaiting the Son of Man (8.31; 9.31) were in general terms, and could well have been spoken out of Jesus' awareness of the nature of the part he had soon to play. But this third prediction includes details drawn directly from the history of Jesus' subsequent trial; and unless we wish to credit Jesus with the most literal kind of second sight, we must recognize the hand of the narrator, writing up this saying of Jesus in the light of its fulfilment a few days later.

On the two previous occasions, the disciples had failed to understand how
the glorious title, Son of Man, could be compatible with so menacing a
future. Here, this failure is not mentioned; but the request of James and John
perhaps indicates that understanding had still not dawned. '**Grant us the** 37
right to sit in state with you'. They may have imagined that in Jerusalem
Jesus would become a real king, and that they would be his chief courtiers;
or they may have been looking forward to the supernatural transformation of
things in the age to come—the Greek phrase translated **in state** means
literally "in glory". In either case, they were making the disciples' usual
mistake of looking ahead to the future glory without reckoning on the tribulations which must come first, both for the Son of Man and for those whom
he represented. Jesus' reply, once again, insisted on this necessary preliminary. '**Can you drink the cup that I drink, or be baptized with the** 38
baptism I am baptized with?' Cup and baptism were soon to have their
own specific place in Christian worship, and this may have influenced the
form in which Jesus' saying has come down to us; but it is possible to attach
meaning to the saying without reference to the later technical meaning of
these words. The **cup** was an obvious symbol for a destiny of suffering (as in
14.36), and was a standard Old Testament expression for the severe judgement of God; and to be **baptized** was probably (though there are too few
instances in ancient literature for us to be sure) a not uncommon metaphor,
meaning to be overwhelmed by a wave of afflictions. Jesus was in effect
challenging the two disciples to share in that destiny of suffering which must
precede his own ultimate glorification. They accepted the challenge, and so
qualified for a share in the Son of Man's glory. But the further privilege of
absolute precedence in the court of heaven was not so readily granted. [a]

[a] There are grounds for believing that John died of old age in Ephesus; but another tradition relates that he was martyred at the same time as James (Acts 12.2). This is

43 **'Whoever wants to be great must be your servant'.** This radical
teaching on personal relationships is repeated here (after its appearance
already at 9.35) as Jesus' response to signs of ambition among his disciples;
but this time it is firmly based upon the example of Jesus himself. The Son
45 of Man, in Daniel 7.14, is indeed exalted to a position where he is **to be**
served "by all peoples". But that lies in the future, when he will be glorified.
Meanwhile (and this is the side of the Son of Man's destiny upon which
Jesus lays special stress in these chapters) his rôle is the exact opposite: he
has come **to serve**; and since he is a representative figure, it follows that each
44 of those who throw in their lot with his must also be the **willing slave of all**.
The full extent of the service which is to be demanded of Jesus is defined in
45 the words which follow: **'to give up his life as a ransom for many'**.
At first sight this somewhat technical phrase looks more like the later language of the church than that of Jesus himself. But although there are passages, in Paul for instance, which use similar language (Romans 3.25, Colossians 1.14 and elsewhere), there is no other instance in the New Testament of this precise phrase, and there is nothing in the phrase itself which would necessarily have been strange to Jesus' own way of thinking. The idea of a **ransom** was a common metaphor in the Old Testament: God's interventions on behalf of his people were often described as acts by which he "ransomed" his people from their enemies; and since, in the time of Jesus, people thought of themselves as under the power, not merely of the occupying Roman forces, but (in a deeper sense) of the forces of the devil and indeed of the only too obvious consequences of their own sins, the metaphor of being rescued from all this by the payment of a **ransom** was very much alive. But how could the death of one man have such a result? The explanation is often sought in Isaiah chapter 53, where the exiled prophet seems to have had some intimation that the death of a righteous man could atone for "the sin of many" (53.12). But, apart from the word **many**, the saying of Jesus is barely reminiscent of this passage, and it may not be necessary to look so far for the origin of the idea of a vicarious and atoning death. Not long after the time of the Maccabees, some two centuries previously, the deaths of those who were martyred for their loyalty to the Jewish religion were regarded as an expiation for the misdeeds of their nation (2 Maccabees 7.37–8); and it appears that many Jewish thinkers soon came to take the same view of the vicarious effect of the martyrdom of a righteous man. If Jesus expressed the significance of his own death in such terms as these, there is no reason to think that the idea would have been altogether strange to his hearers.

46 **They came to Jericho.** The last healing miracle recorded in this gospel

unlikely to be correct; if it were, it would lend support to the view that Jesus' words are a prophecy of the two martyrs' death, a prophecy perhaps attributed to Jesus soon after. The reason why they were denied the two places of honour is sometimes thought to be that it was Peter, and then James "the Lord's brother", and not the sons of Zebedee, who subsequently emerged as the leaders of the church.

is told with much circumstantial detail. The place of it was remembered as
the road which led out of Jericho towards Jerusalem; there was a crowd
around Jesus, probably of pilgrims who, like him, were "going up to
Jerusalem" for the Passover, but who were possibly already curious about
Jesus himself and ready, if given the signal, to proclaim him their leader;
and a third detail, which is unusual in Mark, is that the subject of the cure is
named: **Bartimaeus** (which simply means **son of Timaeus** as Mark
explains). Perhaps the fact that after his cure he **followed** Jesus **on the road** 52
caused his name to be remembered. A further touch of colour suggests that
the story goes back to an eyewitness account: when Bartimaeus speaks to
Jesus he uses the Aramaic word *Rabbuni*, which is a particularly respectful
form of the title "Rabbi". In John 20.16 the Aramaic word is both recorded
and translated. Here Mark simply reproduces it, without translating it: his
readers, even if they knew little about Palestine, were evidently expected to
understand it (the NEB aids the reader, but eliminates the local flavour of
the words, by writing **Master**). On the other hand, there are two elements 51
which betray Mark's usual concern to reveal that the cure was more than a
mere miracle. '**Son of David**' is a title which has not been used before in 47
this gospel. It does not mean that Bartimaeus knew anything about Jesus'
physical ancestry. It was simply one of the names by which it was natural
to refer to the person who (it was popularly believed) was destined to restore
the fortunes of Israel: the Messiah, or Christ. The following which Jesus had
gathered, and the air of expectancy which surrounded his approach to
Jerusalem, were doubtless sufficient to suggest to Bartimaeus that **Jesus of
Nazareth** was this Messiah. And since a well-known prophecy (Isaiah 61.1),
which was usually held to refer to the coming of the Messiah, promised that
he would bring "recovery of sight to the blind", Bartimaeus' excitement
needs no further explanation. But, from the point of view of the narrator,
his cry had a further significance: Jesus *was* the Christ. So far only his
disciples had recognized the fact; now a blind man had come to the same
decisive realization, and it was in response to this that Jesus opened his eyes:
'**your faith has cured you**'. If there is any symbolism in the previous 52
cure of a blind man (8.22–6), the same implication is doubtless intended here:
after a series of attempts to open the eyes of the disciples to his true nature
and destiny, Jesus demonstrates that even the physically blind can be made
to see.

When they reached Bethphage and Bethany, at the Mount of Olives. **11.** 1
These two villages did not lie on the direct route from Jericho to Jerusalem,
but would have been reached by turning off southwards just before the road
began to climb over the crest of the Mount of Olives. It is not clear why Mark
mentions both the villages, which lay at least a mile apart; but if Jesus had
in fact reached the crossroads from which the road straight on led to Jerusa-

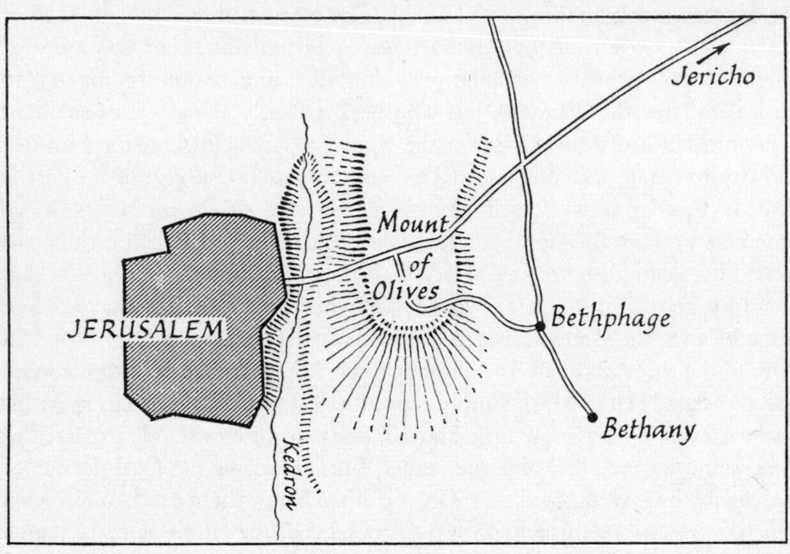

lem, while that to the left went through the small village of Bethphage to the larger village of Bethany, it is not difficult to imagine him sending two
2 disciples '**to the village opposite**' to fetch a colt.

The details of the episode are all capable of a thoroughly prosaic interpretation. Jesus could have made prior arrangements about the colt, in which case there is nothing surprising in the way it was provided for him; and the acclamation and the brushwood may have an equally simple explanation. It is often thought likely, for other reasons, that Mark may have been wrong in stating that Jesus entered Jerusalem only once, at Passover-time. At two other annual festivals it was customary for people to gather green branches from the countryside and bring them into Jerusalem; and on one of them
9 Psalm 118 (from which the words '**Hosanna**...' are a quotation) was one of
the prescribed liturgical songs. It is therefore perfectly possible that the story in the gospels has grown out of an almost accidental involvement with a crowd of pilgrims on the road. This would incidentally explain why the procession had no immediate consequences, and apparently provoked no official counter-measures.

However, even if this was the origin of the story, it was not the way any of the evangelists understood it. Mark's account is the simplest; but even so the details are evidently intended to carry a deeper significance. One point which is crucial to the story, and which tells against a too rationalistic interpretation of it, is that Jesus, having travelled the whole way from Jericho on foot, chose to ride into Jerusalem. Pilgrims were expected to enter the

city on foot. Thus Jesus' action was a deliberate gesture, intended to draw attention to himself. Furthermore, the manner in which he acquired his mount is narrated in great detail. It is true that the matter could have been pre-arranged by Jesus, but it is unlikely that Mark would have recorded it so carefully if he had thought of it simply as a detail of organization. For him, and for those who first remembered and recorded the episode, it must almost certainly have appeared as an instance of Jesus' supernatural prescience. There is significance, too, in the animal he rode on. Mark and Luke use a word for it which, in ordinary Greek, would normally mean a horse's
colt. But this was also the word which the Septuagint translators of the Old 2
Testament used to represent the Hebrew word meaning "foal of an ass". Two Old Testament texts in particular use this Hebrew expression. One is Genesis 49.11, a rather mysterious oracle about someone who would some day come to rule over Judah and over "all the nations", and would "tether his ass to the vine and his ass's foal to the red vine". This oracle was certainly interpreted as a prophecy of a coming Messiah in the time of Jesus. The other text is Zechariah 9.9: "Your king is coming to you . . . humble and mounted on an ass, on a foal, the young of an ass"; and this again was regarded as a prediction of the Messiah who was to come. Matthew and John, by quoting the text from Zechariah, make it quite clear that they understand Jesus' mount to be "the foal of an ass", and Jesus' ride into Jerusalem to be the fulfilment of a prophecy about the advent of the Messiah. The matter is not so clear in Mark: but certain details point in the same direction. The colt was **tethered**, as in Genesis 49.11; and it was one **which no one has yet ridden**—a fact about it which would hardly have struck the disciples when they went to fetch it; but it was axiomatic that any beast used for a sacred purpose must never have been ridden, and in fact the Septuagint Greek version of Zechariah adds the detail that the foal the king was riding was "new". Thus the details of Mark's account seem to imply that, like Matthew and John, he thought of the **colt**, not as a young horse, but as the symbolic and sacred "ass's foal" on which people expected the Messiah to ride.

Jesus' deliberate and ostentatious ride from the Mount of Olives (a spot which also had a place in Zechariah's prophecies of the ultimate coming of the Lord, Zech. 14.4) was therefore staged in such a way as to alert those who could interpret it to the fact that he was himself the promised Christ. But, just as throughout Mark's gospel it had only been a very few who had recognized Jesus for what he really was, so here there was no open and unmistakable declaration of his true nature; and the response of the crowds, though it had all the enthusiasm to be expected in view of Jesus' reputation,
does not give anything away. Their cry '**Hosanna**' (which originally meant 9
"save now" but had probably become a very general word of religious acclamation), '**Blessings on him who comes in the name of the Lord**', was a quotation from a psalm (118.25–6) that was particularly associated with

the carrying of green branches at religious festivals, and the evocation of the
10 **coming kingdom of our father David** was a sign, certainly, of a lively
expectation of the Messiah, but did not necessarily single out Jesus as the
Messiah himself. Mark's readers knew who Jesus was and would have found
many hints of his true nature in the narrative; but it is nowhere stated that
the crowds who thronged round Jesus recognized him for what he really was.

11 **He entered Jerusalem and went into the temple.** "Going up to
Jerusalem" reached its goal when the pilgrim descended the west side of the
Mount of Olives, crossed the Kedron valley, and climbed up the other side
to the tremendous terrace on which Herod the Great had built the temple.
The terrace formed part of the city wall, and one gate on this side led straight
into the immense area of colonnaded porches, open courtyards and subsidiary buildings which surrounded the temple itself. To look **at the whole
scene,** Jesus could well have spent some time there; but he soon retired for
the night to Bethany, where (if we may supply details from the other gospels)
he had friends and the assurance of hospitality.

The story of Jesus cursing the fig-tree is odd in so many respects that it is
widely believed to have been misreported by the gospel writers. Why should
12 Jesus have **felt hungry** on the short walk (barely two miles in all) from
Bethany to Jerusalem? How can he have expected to find fruit on the tree
13 if **it was not the season for figs**? And is not his curse on the tree both quite
unreasonable in the circumstances and also out of character? Of all these
oddities, the greatest is the detail that **it was not the season for figs.** If this
phrase were removed, the story, though still puzzling, would at least be
plausible; and it is possible to think of reasons why the phrase may not
belong to the original version. If it was the case (as John's gospel maintains,
and as certain details in Mark's account make us suspect) that Jesus went up
to Jerusalem at other festivals besides this Passover, then the story may have
belonged originally to one of his earlier visits at a different time of year (say
for the autumn feast of Tabernacles, when figs would be ripe). But Mark, or
the source he was using, recounts only one visit to Jerusalem, at Passover-
time, that is to say March–April, too early by some two months for any ripe
figs to be found on the trees. The story could not be inserted anywhere else
in the gospel, since it was set in the neighbourhood of Bethany; and either
Mark, or else some scribe working over the manuscript not long after it was
written, may have added the words, **for it was not the season for figs.** In
the framework of Mark's narrative this was correct: but unfortunately it
made nonsense of the story.

Even if this explanation is accepted, the story is still puzzling. Why did Jesus curse the tree? Two possibilities are often suggested. One is that the story was originally a parable told by Jesus to express the point that a husbandman's patience could not be expected to last for ever, and that the parable subsequently became confused with an actual event in Jesus' life;

the other is that the action was symbolic, in the tradition of the Old Testament prophets: for all its early promise, the "tree" of Israel had failed to produce any fruit, and the time had come for its destruction. The literal withering of the fig-tree could have been intended as a lesson for the Jewish people of Jesus' time.

Jesus **began driving out those who bought and sold in the temple.** 15
The **temple** comprised not only the sanctuary itself and the central buildings connected with the cult, but also a series of large colonnaded courts, one of which, since it was open to non-Jews, was known as the Court of the Gentiles. The whole precinct was sacred, and subject to ritual regulations which were enforced by Jewish temple police; nevertheless there is no reason to doubt that people came to the outer courts for many purposes. It was here, under Herod's colonnades, that Jesus 'taught day after day in the temple' (14.49), and here that crowds gathered to hear him. But the target of Jesus' action on this first day after his arrival in Jerusalem was apparently quite specific: **those who bought and sold . . . the tables of the money-changers and the seats of the dealers in pigeons.** The curious thing here is that these seem to have been necessary and (granting the whole principle of the temple's existence and function) unobjectionable institutions. Contributions to the temple treasury, whether the annual temple tax or offerings for other purposes, had to be made in the purest and most exact coinage known in Palestine, the silver coins minted in Tyre. These could be obtained from money-changers, who charged a small commission on the exchange; and at least at one time of year (a short period ending about a fortnight before the Passover) these money-changers were officially permitted to have their **tables** (or banks) inside the temple precincts. This is all we know about such trading in the temple; and if this is what Jesus objected to, then it is not easy to interpret his action. If he had wanted to attack the whole temple system, we should have expected some gesture directed at the priests and administrators, not at such a small and comparatively harmless part of the organization as was represented by the money-changers. On the other hand, it is not at all unlikely that, out of this small beginning, a considerable amount of commercial business had developed. The money-changers may have combined their technical function of providing the ritual silver coins with full-scale commercial banking (there are many parallels to this in the ancient world: the comparative security of a shrine made it the natural place for a bank); the necessary dealing in birds and animals for sacrifices, which should have been confined to markets outside the temple area, seems, from Mark's reference to **dealers in pigeons**, to have made its way into the temple courts; and for all we know, trading of other kinds may have followed in its wake. Jesus' protest, in this case, will have been against an abuse which had grown up with the connivance, but presumably without the official sanction, of the temple authorities; and if the practices he was attacking were

technically illegal, this would explain why the temple police did not imme-
16 diately intervene. His action in not allowing anyone **to use the temple court as a thoroughfare for carrying goods** will have been of exactly the same kind. There is some evidence that this too was technically prohibited, and Jesus may have found that the prohibition was not being enforced.

So far Jesus' action (if this is the correct interpretation of it) reads like that of a reformer anxious to stamp out abuses which the authorities had complaisantly allowed to creep into the administration of the temple. It reflects an extreme reverence for the sanctity of the place and for the importance of the ritual which took place there. But the saying with which Jesus is recorded to have interpreted his action sets it in a different light. It consists
17 of two quotations. The first, "**My house shall be called a house of prayer for all the nations**" (Isaiah 56.7) is drawn from a well-known Old Testament prophecy that the worship of the God of Israel would one day be shared by men of all nationalities, who would therefore have free access to the temple. In Jesus' time, non-Jews were admitted into the so-called Court of the Gentiles, but were very strictly prohibited from penetrating any further; and the natural target of such a saying would have been the prominent notices which were set up to warn Gentiles from trespassing any further. The second quotation is from Jeremiah 7.11: the prophet was attacking the people of Jerusalem for assuming that, because they maintained the worship of the temple, the violence, injustice and idolatry of the city's life would be condoned by God. On the contrary, argued Jeremiah, the presence of such people in the temple showed that they thought of it simply as some sort of protection against the consequences of their unlawful behaviour, rather like a **robbers' cave**. The translation of this phrase in the NEB reads, at first sight, like a poor substitute for the traditional rendering, "den of thieves"; for if the object of Jesus' attack was the presence of extortionate traders in the holy place, then the description of their offices as a "den of thieves" is as apt as one could wish. But the old translation in fact begs the question. Nothing in the account so far has suggested that the bankers and dealers were dishonest, and moreover the original phrase, both in the Hebrew of Jeremiah and in the Greek translation used by Mark, does not mean anything of the sort. The essence of a "thief" is that he acts surreptitiously; but the word used here means, not a surreptitious thief, but a man of violence, an armed robber or brigand. In the time of Jesus the word became almost a technical word for fanatical rebels against the Roman régime, who conducted guerrilla warfare, terrorized peaceable citizens, and very often had their hideouts in the caves which are to be found in the mountains all over Palestine. The NEB translation is thus a great deal more accurate than the traditional one—if indeed it goes far enough: "brigands' cave" would probably come still nearer to the meaning the phrase would have conveyed to Jesus' contemporaries. Clearly, the quotation cannot have

been intended as a comment on ordinary commercial transactions: it implies that the temple had become a place of violence, or at least a meeting-place of violent men.

It seems necessary, therefore, to assume that Jesus' saying on this occasion has nothing to do with his action in turning out the bankers and traders, but is a separate piece of teaching directed against the exclusive Jewishness of the temple and perhaps also against incidents of violence which had taken place within it (such as Josephus tells us took place quite frequently at this period), or at any rate at the hands of those who frequented it. If so, we must ask what was the intention of this whole sequence of actions and sayings which marked Jesus' first complete day in the temple. On the face of it, they appear as a protest against abuses of the proper function and sanctity of the temple. But a further meaning may lie in the background. On the previous day, Jesus had entered Jerusalem in a manner calculated to suggest that a prophecy in Zechariah about the coming Messiah was even now being fulfilled. The same book ends, "When that time comes, no trader shall again be seen in the house of the Lord of Hosts" (14.21). Moreover, it was a traditional belief, inspired by the visions of the prophet Ezekiel (40–8), that in the days of the Messiah the temple would be renewed. All these thoughts will have been present in the minds of Mark's first readers; and Mark may have wished it to be understood that the same inferences could have been drawn by those who actually witnessed the scene, had they had eyes to see and ears to hear.

Early next morning. The miraculous sequel of the cursing of the fig-tree 20
gives Mark the cue to introduce three sayings about prayer which, since two
of them occur in other gospels in a quite different connection (Matthew 22–5
6.14–15; Luke 17.6), were presumably remembered separately. The form
of the first saying was proverbial. "Moving mountains" was nearly as
common an expression for doing the apparently impossible as it is now.
Nevertheless, the Mount of Olives would have been a singularly striking
setting for the saying. From it the Dead Sea can be seen nearly four thousand
feet below, and a cataclysm which "lifted it from its place" would naturally 23
be thought of as "hurling it into the sea". There may also be in the background (at least of Mark's consciousness) a final echo of Zechariah (14.4): "On that day . . . the Mount of Olives . . . shall be cleft in two by an immense valley running east and west."

'Believe that you have received it and it will be yours'. This sounds 24
a little like permission to use the power of prayer for any purpose whatever, along with a hint on how to do it. But Jesus was fond of exaggerations and striking simplifications. The point is surely, as so often in Mark's gospel, and doubtless also in Jesus' original teaching, the critical importance of faith. The same point is made explicit in Matthew (21.22), and is related to other aspects of Christian spirituality by Paul (1 Corinthians 13.2). There is perhaps a commentary on it in 1 John 5.14–15.

25 The third saying, besides being a characteristic element of Jesus' teaching, reads like a commentary on the Lord's Prayer. Mark, unlike Matthew and Luke, does not include the Lord's prayer in his gospel; but this saying, and the phrase, **your Father in heaven**, strongly suggest that he knew it.

27 **They came once more to Jerusalem.** According to Mark's scheme, this
was the second full day of Jesus' activity in Jerusalem. It was taken up with
controversy between himself and the Jewish authorities, whose supreme
council, the Sanhedrin, had its meeting-place and offices in or near the
temple precincts. The members of this body are often described in the gospels
as **the chief priests, lawyers, and elders**, and it was therefore probably
in their official capacity as members of the Sanhedrin that they accosted
28 Jesus **as he was walking in the temple court.** Their question, '**By what
authority are you acting like this?**' was one to which it was important
for the Sanhedrin to have an answer. Jesus was attracting crowds by his
teaching (11.18), and much of his teaching took the form of a new exposition
of Scripture. But the exposition of Scripture was the prerogative of professionally qualified "lawyers". Did Jesus have the necessary qualification?
Their question may also have concerned Jesus' reforming actions the day
before (11.15–17). Had the High Priest (who was the ultimate authority for
the conduct of temple affairs) sanctioned this?

Regarded as a matter of official qualifications and sanctions, the question had a straightforward factual answer: Jesus had received no authority. This was doubtless the answer the deputation hoped to extract. But Jesus (or Mark, or the tradition he used) chose to see the question as a far more searching one. He had not merely assumed the privilege of a qualified lawyer or official representative of the temple authorities; he had acted as a prophet, a preacher and a miracle-worker. For such activity it was meaningless to ask for human authorization. It was either inspired by God or it was not, and a witness of these things had to make up his own mind. Taking the question in this sense, Jesus was justified in returning it to his questioners. It was ultimately the same question as was posed by the person of John the Baptist; and the presence of a crowd of people more ready to see the hand of God in the preaching of a John or a Jesus than in the policies of the official religious leaders put Jesus' questioners at a temporary disadvantage.

12. 1 **He went on to speak to them in parables.** The word "parable" was one with a wide range of meanings (see above on 3.23). Sometimes it was an illustration intended to make the speaker's meaning clearer; sometimes it was riddling and enigmatic, leaving its hearers guessing. What was the meaning here? In the chapter devoted to Jesus' parables earlier in the gospel (chapter 4), Mark seems deliberately to have represented them as obscure and enigmatic to all but those who were specially privileged to understand them. But

here Mark allows that the point was more obvious. Jesus' enemies **saw that** 12
the parable was aimed at them.

'A man planted a vineyard'. At first sight the opening of the story is in 1
the characteristic style of Jesus' parables: the stage is set with a careful description of a familiar scene. The essential features of a Palestinian vineyard are mentioned: **a wall** built all round to protect the precious vines from the depredations of men and of beasts; **a winepress**, which was usually constructed over a trough that had been "hewn out" of rock; and a **watch-tower** which was essential for guarding the vineyard, particularly at vintage time. But this straightforward beginning leads into a story which (unlike most of Jesus' parables) appears to be singularly implausible, and the beginning itself turns out to be not at all what it seems. Compare the following verses from Isaiah (5.1–2):

> "My beloved had a vineyard
>   high up on a fertile hill-side.
>   He trenched it and cleared it of stones
>   and planted it with red vines;
> he built a watch-tower in the middle
> and then hewed out a winepress in it."

The details of the watch-tower and the winepress are identical; and in the Septuagint Greek version of Isaiah (which Mark, but not Jesus, may have used) the **wall** occurs also. Now in Isaiah the vineyard is an allegory for the people of Israel. If Jesus began his parable in words so closely reminiscent of this well-known text, his listeners must have been prepared to find the same kind of allegory in it.

But if the vineyard stood for Israel, then it was to be expected that other features of the story would be equally symbolic. And along these lines the interpretation of the story is so obvious that one ceases to ask whether such a thing could have happened in real life. The owner of the vineyard is God; his servants are the prophets (the prophets are often called "God's servants" in the Old Testament), who were consistently maltreated by the people to whom they were sent; and the only son is Jesus himself. The question, Whom do the **vine-growers** stand for? is answered by Mark himself. Jesus'
interlocutors were the religious leaders of Jerusalem; and **they saw that the** 12
parable was aimed at them. The only remaining doubtful point is to
determine who were the **others** to whom the vineyard would be given. 9
Reading the story after the event, we have to answer: the Christian church.

On this reading of the parable, it would be beside the point to ask for a plausible explanation of the apparently absurd expectation of the vine-growers that they would acquire the property by murdering the heir, or of the imprudence of the owner in sending his son into such a dangerous situation. The course of events would have been dictated, not by the conditions of real life, but by the relationship of God with his people which the characters in the story were intended to illustrate. But there are considerable difficulties involved in taking the parable in this way. Could Jesus have foreseen his own condemnation by the Sanhedrin and his subsequent execution so clearly that he worked it into an allegory? Did he ever refer to himself as the "only son" of God, and would he have been understood by a Jewish audience if he had? Moreover, since his parables are usually entirely realistic stories, is it likely that he would have made up one that was quite improbable in order to illustrate what was about to happen? These questions are difficult to answer with any degree of certainty, but, once raised, they suggest two other approaches to the parable. (i) Since the allegorical interpretation fits more easily into the thinking of the early church than that of Jesus (for it was the church which recognized Jesus to be the only Son of God, it was the church which saw in the crucifixion the decisive climax of God's dealings with his people, it was the church which clearly represented those "others" to whom the inheritance would pass—even if these truths were implicit in the teaching of Jesus), then the parable may have been invented altogether after Jesus' death, or at least (if Jesus told some such story) so modified and adapted by the church that we can no longer recover the original story. (ii) Alternatively, even if some of the details have been altered under the pressure of a later interpretation, it may still be possible to reconstruct the circumstances of the story in such a way that it ceases to be implausible and takes its place alongside the precise and vivid scenes of real life with which Jesus usually illustrated his teaching. The following reconstruction can only be tentative, but may help the reader to choose between these possibilities.

Planting a vineyard was a long-term investment. In the long run it could be highly lucrative, but for the first few years expenses were liable to exceed profits. No fruit could be gathered at all for the first three years; but during that time the new vines would need constant and expert tending. The owner, being a man of property with other more urgent interests abroad, would naturally commit the care of the vineyard for these first years to experienced vine-growers. No return could be expected from the vines; but it was normal to plant them sufficiently far apart to allow vegetables to be grown between, and the profits on these might be sufficient to pay the wages of the vine-growers and perhaps a nominal interest to the owner. During these first
2 three years, it was sufficient to send **a servant** to collect the nominal rent;
but if the vine-growers had been unable to make a profit on the vegetables, the servant's arrival could well have led to a dispute and ended in blows. In the parable, this scene is repeated at the end of each of the first three years.[a]

[a] In verse 2, the First Edition of NEB has "the vintage season", which is incompatible with this interpretation. But in the Greek the word means simply **the season**, as it is translated in the Second Edition.

In the fourth year matters would be different. For the first time there would be a vintage. This, being "first-fruits", was subject to ritual regulations, and the profit could be appropriated freely only in the fifth year. Nevertheless, it was important for the owner, or his accredited representative, to be present—Jews were even excused military service for the purpose (Deuteronomy 20.6). Moreover, the owner in the parable had special reason to take personal action. His tenants, three years in succession, had refused to pay rent; and since he had received no rent, he had nothing but the title deed to prove he was the owner. If (as was possible in Jewish law) the tenants were contemplating claiming ownership of the vineyard on the basis of three years' undisputed possession, he would be in a weak position, since servants (if they were slaves) were not admitted as legal witnesses, and he would have no evidence that he had attempted to collect his rent during the last three years. It was therefore essential that in the fourth year he should come himself or, if his other interests kept him abroad, that he should send a reliable representative. In fact he sent his son.[a]

The tenants could not of course have acquired the vineyard simply by killing the heir of the owner. But they may have argued that if they repudiated the claims of the owner's representative—if necessary by force—they would by now have a fairly strong case in a court of law; and that if the owner no longer had an heir who would benefit from the investment in the vineyard, he might not think it worth his while to return to Palestine to press his claim. They therefore allowed the son's arrival to develop into a fight—they could say it was self-defence—which resulted in the death of the son. With an eye
on future developments, they flung the body unburied **out of the vineyard** 8
as evidence of the battle (and possibly also to avoid having to forfeit the vines as being ritually polluted by a corpse). But if they had been counting on the continued absence abroad of the owner, and on the strong points of their case if meanwhile it came into a Jewish court, they were rudely disillusioned. The owner unexpectedly arrived with a strong following and punished their resistance with death.

Such a reconstruction would make the parable plausible as a story. It may seem unduly complicated; but if there had recently been a well-known case of such a thing in Palestine, Jesus' hearers would have had no difficulty in following it. The church, however, might have very soon lost the original point, and seized upon the allegorical meaning implicit in the vineyard, the servants and the son; with the result that when it came to retell the story it concentrated on these details and omitted many others. If the above reconstruction is anywhere near the mark, the parable will fall into place as one of those which illustrate the folly of prevaricating with God: now is the time

[*a*] See the footnote in NEB. The Greek word means literally **dear son**, but often meant "only son", and was particularly used in the early church of Jesus Christ, God's "only son". This is another detail which may be due to a later interpretation of the original parable.

to recognize the messengers of God and repent! If so, Mark may well be
12 right in saying that the religious leaders saw **that the parable was aimed at them.** Not much help is to be gained from the following quotation of
10 Psalm 118.22–3. It follows exactly the existing Greek version of the Old Testament; if Jesus quoted it, he will have done so in Hebrew. '**Can it be that you have never read this text?**' Of course they had; but they did not necessarily know how to interpret it. Some said it referred to Abraham, some to David; in the early church (which had become accustomed to the idea of the Messiah being **rejected**) it was unhesitatingly used of Christ (Acts 4.11; 1 Peter 2.6–8). It has no obvious relevance to the parable; but Jesus, conscious of the opposition gathering against him, may well have used it of himself on some such occasion; and the evangelist may have placed it in this position as a hint that the death of the "son" was by no means the end of the story.

13 **A number of Pharisees and men of Herod's party.** These two groups were mentioned earlier (3.6) as being in league together against Jesus, doubtless seeing in him a threat alike to the religious and the political *status quo*. (It is a little surprising to find representatives of Herod's party in Jerusalem, for Jerusalem lay outside the dominions of any of the Herods and was ruled directly by a Roman procurator. It is possible therefore that the story originally belonged to Jesus' activity in Galilee.) They now hoped **to trap him** by extracting from him a declaration of disobedience towards
14 political authority. The **taxes** in question consisted of the annual poll-tax levied on every citizen of Palestine and paid direct into the treasury of **the Roman Emperor.** The question was a subtle one. The tax was imposed by the Romans, and no Jew who was liable to pay it could refuse to do so without being prosecuted. At first sight, therefore, the question, '**Are we or are we not permitted to pay taxes?**' sounds academic: they had in practice no option. But, after addressing Jesus somewhat fulsomely as someone who had a special insight into **the way of life that God requires,** the questioners hoped perhaps that he would produce some proof from Scripture to show that paying tax to a foreign power was contrary to the **way of life** which God had laid down for his people the Jews. If he did so, he would align himself decisively with those extreme nationalists who regarded the tax as an intolerable symbol of subordination, and it would then be easy to have him arraigned before the Roman authorities. But the trap was cleverly laid; for if Jesus produced no learned argument against payment, his reply would amount to an expression of acquiescence in the tax. And since the tax was by all accounts exceedingly unpopular, such a reply might discredit him in front of the crowd.

15 '**Fetch me a silver piece**'. Coins minted in Palestine—for instance by the Herods—took account of Jewish sensitivity to portraits and pagan

images, and the small coins in any man's pocket would probably have little on them to remind him that his country was ruled by a foreign and heathen power. But only copper coins were minted in Palestine; the silver coins in circulation were all—apart from the special Phoenician pieces used for the temple treasury—the standard coinage of the empire, bearing on one side the head of the reigning Emperor. One of these silver coins—called a *denarius*, which is the word used here in the Greek[a]—was equivalent to a day's wage, or to half the annual tax which every Jew paid to the temple. The Roman tax must have amounted to at least this sum, and the Roman silver coinage will have been the usual, if not the obligatory, currency in which to pay it. When Jesus therefore asked his questioners to "fetch a silver piece" he was in effect casting the question back at them. If they possessed such a piece, it meant that they used the Emperor's coinage, and if they used his coinage, they implicitly accepted his authority, and if they accepted his authority, then they could have no grounds to refuse to pay his
taxes. His reply has a brilliance and a finality which caused **astonishment** 17
at the time, and has inevitably influenced all subsequent discussions about the relationship of church and state; but it must never be forgotten that when he made it his interlocutors were holding in their hands a piece of coinage which already committed them to the same answer. The Romans probably did not think of their coinage as minted for the convenience of their subjects throughout the empire. Its primary purpose was to be a means of paying the army in any part of the world; and in theory it was expected that the coins, after being spent abroad, would be recovered through taxation. In this sense, a silver coin bearing the image of the Roman Emperor was literally **due to Caesar**. By analogy, a human being, made in the image of God, could be said to be **due to God**.
Next Sadducees came to him. The Sadducees represented an important 18
party. Most of the high priests and other important officials belonged to their number; and in matters of scriptural interpretation they were sharply opposed to the teaching of the Pharisees. Jesus, with his expertise in the law and his authority as a teacher, will have appeared to them as likely to share the views of the Pharisees; and so they presented him with a question calculated to cast ridicule on a specifically Pharisaic belief.

Apart from the Sadducees, the great majority of Jews in the time of Jesus believed in the future resurrection of the dead. But this doctrine was a comparatively new one. It had become generally accepted only during the last two centuries, and the Old Testament contained at most some faint intimations of it. To prove it, the Pharisaic interpreters of Scripture had to resort to a rather subtle use of texts, and to appeal more to their own tradition on the subject than to any clear proof from the Old Testament. It was

[a] The old translation, "a penny", which now suggests a bronze coin, has become entirely misleading.

precisely for this reason that the Sadducees differed from them on the question. They denied the validity of the Pharisees' "tradition", and held that, since the Old Testament makes no mention of it, **there is no resurrection.**

But their question shows them taking a stronger position than this: not merely does the Old Testament make no mention of resurrection, it contains provisions which make the idea absurd. The particular provision of the Law
19 of Moses referred to here is in Deuteronomy 25.5–6—the institution of so-called "Levirate marriage". This institution belonged to an early stage of Israel's history, when it was regarded as a desirable way of keeping property in one family and of keeping the family name alive. But it could only flourish in a polygamous society, and although attempts had been made to give it a higher moral significance (the Book of Ruth was probably one such attempt) it is unlikely that it was often put into practice in the time of Jesus. Nevertheless, the commandment stood in the Law, and may still have occasionally been observed, and the Sadducees were perfectly justified in quoting it to make their point, and in weaving a story around it.

23 **'At the resurrection, when they come back to life, whose wife will she be?'** The absurdity of the conclusion was probably a fair point in view of the crudity with which the belief in resurrection was often held. Writings have come down to us from this period in which the future life is portrayed with the naïvest materialism as a mere continuation, under beatific conditions, of ordinary human existence. Such crude beliefs deserved the Sadducees' ridicule. At the same time there were many thinkers who were ready to formulate the doctrine in a much more sophisticated and spiritual form; against them, the Sadducees' argument would have had no force. Jesus
25 aligned himself with this more developed view: **'When they rise from the dead, men and women do not marry; they are like angels in heaven.'**

Jesus then attacked the Sadducees' own position by quoting a passage from Exodus (3.6). Since it was recognized that the Old Testament provides no clear proof of the resurrection, how was this text going to carry his point? Was he going to give it a new and subtle interpretation, in the manner of the Pharisees? Jesus' commentary on it is so brief that it is not easy to say. But his usual procedure with Old Testament texts was very different from that of the Pharisees. Instead of manipulating the literal sense of the words, he liked to reveal their underlying purpose, and this may be his technique here.
26 The phrase, **the God of Abraham, the God of Isaac, and the God of Jacob**, which occurred in the Jews' daily prayers and was one of their characteristic ways of referring to "the God of Israel", carried a heavy load of meaning. God was the God of these patriarchs in the sense that he had led them, protected them, and above all promised to them that he would be eternally concerned for their descendants. In early centuries this promise was understood as being fulfilled in the prosperity and (at times) glorious history of the people of Israel. But in the time of Jesus, when that history

had become anything but glorious, and when, in any case, religious interest
had at last become focused upon the destiny of the individual as much as of
the nation, the promise had to be understood differently. Since so many
generations of pious Israelites had died without seeing any material evidence
of the fulfilment of God's promises, either these promises were false (which
was inconceivable) or else they would have to be fulfilled for every righteous
Jew in a future life. God had not made his promises to **the dead** but to **the** 27
living. By such reasoning, the Old Testament as a whole could be seen to
imply the resurrection, even if it did not actually state it. The Sadducees, in
short, had failed to understand both the true sense of the **scriptures** and the 25
power of God who, despite the apparent finality of human death, was still
able to fulfil his promises.

Then one of the lawyers . . . asked him. The question was not neces- 28
sarily asked in order to embarrass Jesus, for it was one which we know to
have been a subject of discussion among **lawyers** in the time of Jesus. But
the question was probably intended in a rather technical sense. '**Which
commandment is first of all?**' sounds to us like a question about the
most important principle by which to direct one's life. But in the mouth of
the questioner it must have meant something different. For a professional
expounder of the law, there could be no question of one part of the law, or
one principle contained in it, being more important than the rest. A Jew
was strictly obliged to keep the whole law—all the 613 commandments of it
(as the Rabbis were soon to calculate the number), and the question, **Which
commandment is first of all?** could not have been a question about what
part of the law one ought particularly to observe (for one had to observe all
parts of it equally). It could only have been the more academic question,
from what part of the law (if any) could the rest of the law be deduced? Or,
in any systematic arrangement of the many individual laws, which law
should come at the head of the list? We know that this question was debated
(even though some disapproved of the debate, thinking that it might tempt
people to concentrate on some laws at the expense of others and so fail to
do their duty by the whole law); and the lawyer may well have been
genuinely interested to know what Jesus' own position was.

Jesus' reply keeps well within the usual bounds of such a discussion. The
first phrase, "**Hear, O Israel: The Lord our God is the only Lord**" 29
sounds at first inappropriate, since it is not a "commandment" at all, but is
in the nature of a statement of faith. But in fact it is the beginning of a text
(Deuteronomy 6.4–5) which was a basic part of Jewish devotion. It was
recited by everyone twice a day, and there was general agreement that it did
in fact sum up the essentials of the Jewish faith and the Jewish life. Therefore it was not inappropriate for Jesus to preface his answer with this introduction: it served to put the first great "commandment" in the perspective
of the Jew's daily profession of faith. To complete his answer, Jesus somewhat 31

unexpectedly added a second "commandment", taken from Leviticus 19.18, "**Love your neighbour as yourself**".

Thus far, the conversation had run on lines which would have caused no surprise in scholarly circles. Both the first and the second of these commandments were quite often quoted as being basic to the whole structure of the Law of Moses, and even though we do not happen to know of any other teacher who explicitly paired these two commandments together as Jesus did, it does not follow that, simply by putting them together, Jesus was doing anything startlingly original. Indeed, Matthew in his version (22.40) ends the episode at this point, and uses it precisely in order to reveal Jesus in the rôle of an authoritative Jewish teacher. Luke attaches to it the parable of the Good Samaritan, in order to illustrate Jesus' radical interpretation of the commandment to "love your neighbour". Mark alone allows the conversation with the lawyer to develop in such a way as to throw a new light on the sense in which Jesus understood the "commandments".

32 '**Well said, Master.**' The lawyer agreed with Jesus; but his commentary
on Jesus' answer set it in a totally different light. The keeping of these two
33 commandments was **far more than any burnt offerings or sacrifices.** At
a stroke, this phrase turned the question from an academic one into a practical
one. Instead of being an attempt to subsume all other laws (including those
concerning burnt offerings and sacrifices) under one or two general principles, Jesus' answer became, in the lawyer's commentary (what it was
doubtless always intended to be) a clear statement that the spirit and basic
motivation of the law was **more important** than the observance of its
detailed ritual provisions. We can infer, from other parts of Jesus' teaching,
that this was in fact Jesus' view. Mark here allows it to be expressed by a
member of that party which was normally opposed to him; and Jesus, to
show how closely this formulation came to his own teaching, reversed his
34 usual judgement on the lawyers, and said of this one, '**You are not far from
the kingdom of God**'—the highest compliment he ever paid to anyone.

There is a further point to notice about the narrative. The liberal view of the law which is implied in the lawyer's answer was certainly not an orthodox one at the time; but we cannot say for certain that a professional lawyer could not have held it, and we ought probably to leave open the question whether this conversation actually took place as Mark (unlike Matthew and Luke) records it, or whether Mark deliberately constructed it in order to bring out Jesus' understanding of the Jewish law. On the other hand, there are certain details which suggest that at some stage the story has been edited to suit a different *milieu.* When the Jewish faith was being presented to educated Greeks, it tended to be formulated somewhat differently from the way in which it was discussed among Jews in Palestine. It was proclaimed, first and foremost, as the one great monotheistic religion of the world (as compared with the many deities of Greek, Roman and oriental

religions); secondly, greater stress was laid on its intellectual content than
came naturally to traditional Jewish psychology; and thirdly, there was a
tendency to play down the ritual side of it, particularly the sacrificial system
of the temple, which struck the Greeks as crude and unnecessary. In Mark's
narrative it is noticeable, first, that the lawyer's paraphrase of the Jewish
confession of faith reads remarkably like a conscious defence of monotheism;
secondly, that an intellectual term, **mind**, is added to **heart, soul** and 30
strength (the three terms which stand in the Hebrew text of Deuteronomy);
and thirdly, that the conversation ends with a depreciation of **burnt** 33
offerings or sacrifices. From this, one conclusion suggests itself. This was
the language Mark had often heard being used by Greek-speaking Jews
while commending their faith to pagans. If he allowed it to influence his
composition of the dialogue between Jesus and a lawyer in the temple at
Jerusalem, it was because he realized that the liberal Judaism being preached,
say, at Rome or Alexandria was in essence an approximation to the teaching
of Jesus: it was **not far from the kingdom of God**. 34

The last of this series of questions is asked by Jesus himself, and in form it
is the kind of question that was much discussed at the time: given such and
such a doctrine, which we infer from the Old Testament, how is a certain
text, which seems at first sight to contradict that doctrine, to be reconciled
with it? The doctrine concerned was that **the Messiah is "Son of David"**. 35
On this subject, **the teachers of the law** could hardly maintain anything
else. It is true that the Old Testament itself does not say in so many words
that the coming Messiah would be a physical descendant of David—though
some passages come very near it (Isaiah 11.1–9; Jeremiah 33.14–18); but
that this would be so had become a very widely held belief, and the gospels
themselves, when they show Jesus to be a descendant of David, presuppose
that this was regarded as one reason for claiming that he was the Messiah.
It is very unlikely, therefore, that Jesus meant to cast doubt on this doctrine.
Rather, his question (in the manner of such discussions) drew attention, not
to any uncertainty about the doctrine itself, but to a text which had not
previously been brought into harmony with it. This text (Psalm 110.1) was
subsequently used by the early church as an important prophecy of the
ascension and exaltation of Christ (Acts 2.34; 1 Corinthians 15.25 and elsewhere). Here, Jesus apparently quoted it to bring a new element into the
usual understanding of what was meant by a Messiah who was "Son of
David". The psalm, which was almost certainly written later, and possibly
many centuries later, than David's time, was nevertheless found by Jesus'
contemporaries among the collection of the "Psalms of David", and it would
have occurred to none of them to question its authorship. Moreover, it
occurred in the sacred scriptures, every part of which was **inspired by the** 36
Holy Spirit, and must therefore be taken seriously as a word of God. In the
first line, **The Lord** clearly meant God, and **my** meant David's; but who

was David's "**Lord**"? There was nothing in the psalm to say; and this was just the kind of ambiguity in the sacred text which later scholars came to regard as full of deeper meaning. "David's Lord" must be a kind of cryptogram for some other important person in the present or future destiny of Israel. Some two centuries after the date of this conversation, there is evidence that this person was thought by Jewish scholars to be the awaited Messiah. The Christian church evidently drew the same conclusion when, soon after the death and resurrection of Jesus, it began using the psalm as a prophecy about the risen Christ. Was "David's Lord" popularly thought to be the Messiah even earlier? This narrative, if it was not composed after the event (as some believe it was) seems to presuppose that he was; and in an age in which expectation of a coming Messiah was a marked feature of many Jews' religion, it would not be at all surprising if the cryptogram was popularly interpreted in this way. But if so, it raised a difficulty: how could the Messiah, whom all agreed must be David's "son", be addressed by his father as if he was a superior being—"Lord"? This was the difficulty which Jesus wanted to emphasize: it would not do to use this somewhat grandiose verse as a prophecy about the Messiah without thinking out its implications. Could someone who was human enough to be called David's "son" also be "lordly" enough to sit at God's right hand? Jesus did not offer an answer to this at once: the answer (so at least the first Christians believed) was given, not in a single word, but by the whole life, death and resurrection of Jesus.

38 **'Beware of the doctors of the law'.** In both Matthew and Luke a substantial section is devoted to an attack on the Pharisees and upon the professional experts in the law. In Mark, even though no secret is made of the opposition between Jesus and these people, only three verses (38–40) are devoted to an explicit attack on their character. Yet perhaps more is implied than is actually said. The real reason to **beware** of them was not, of course, the rather trivial signs of petty ambition and ostentation which are mentioned here, but the hypocrisy of which these things were a symptom and which Jesus attacks elsewhere (7.6–8) as being their really serious fault. This fundamental hypocrisy proceeded from their whole understanding of religion; and it was presumably as particularly striking manifestations of this hypocrisy that Jesus singled out certain instances of arrogant behaviour of which, perhaps, only a few were guilty. Similarly with verse 40: the con-
40 demnation of **men who eat up the property of widows** was as old as the prophets (e.g. Isaiah 10.1–2), and one which religious groups often used as ammunition against each other. The obligation laid on wealthy women to give hospitality to travelling teachers could have given rise to such an abuse, though it is doubtful whether many lawyers were guilty of it, any more than Jesus' own acceptance of hospitality could be regarded as reprehensible. But if there were even a few cases of it they were sufficient to make Jesus' point: saying **long prayers for appearance' sake** made these acts of injustice into

particularly scandalous examples of that same hypocrisy of which the lawyers, as a class, were guilty.[a]

Once he was standing opposite the temple treasury. It is not possible 41
to reconstruct this scene with any certainty. There were a large number of "treasuries" in the temple, and contributions (some obligatory, some voluntary) were made for many different purposes. Clearly the story is about free-will offerings and not about taxes; and it is usually thought that the scene must have taken place in the Women's Court of the temple, where thirteen trumpet-shaped receptacles were set up for receiving various kinds of contributions. But it is superfluous to press the details: how, for instance, Jesus could have seen how much money everyone gave is an unanswerable question. The narrative, in fact, is in the style of a story deliberately told to point a moral, and it is even possible that it was originally told by Jesus as a story and subsequently projected back as an episode in his life—for the story itself has parallels both in Jewish tradition and in the religious literature of other cultures. Its moral is obvious enough, and only one vivid detail requires
comment. **Two tiny coins**: the Greek word (*lepton*) was used for the 42
smallest coin in currency in Palestine. It was little more than a quarter of an inch in diameter, and 128 of them went to the silver *denarius*. In Rome it was unknown; the smallest coin there was the *quadrans*, which was twice the size of the widow's coin, and Mark may have had his non-Palestinian readers in mind when he added the explanation, **together worth a farthing** (*quadrans*).

'Look, Master, what huge stones.' This is still the visitor's reaction 13. 1
today. The buildings of Herod the Great can be recognized anywhere in Palestine by the immense rectangular blocks of beautifully hewn stone with which their walls are constructed. The temple, with its surrounding buildings and colonnades, was the greatest of his building enterprises, and not the least spectacular part of it was the huge substructure by which the top of the sacred hill had been extended to form a terrace of some 35 acres. The great east wall of this substructure, which rose vertically from the floor of the valley over 100 feet below, is in position today and still excites admiration. On the occasion of Jesus' visit it will have been quite recently completed. The exclamation of Jesus' disciples as they left the temple area and passed through the gate in this gigantic wall is exactly what one would expect. Indeed, the setting for the long discourse which follows is vivid and
plausible. From the Mount of Olives, **facing the temple**, one could look 3
down across the steep valley between, and the whole of the temple area, perhaps the most grandiose and impressive architectural achievement of

[*a*] The alternative rendering in the footnote is perhaps a smoother translation of the Greek, but gives the last saying a much more general application. If it was not aimed at the Pharisees and lawyers, it was a sentiment any pious Jew might have uttered.

antiquity, lay spread out before one's eyes. That it should ever be totally destroyed must have seemed almost unimaginable; yet this is what Jesus had just prophesied. No wonder then that Jesus was **questioned privately** about it by some of his disciples.

Yet however realistic the setting, Jesus' answer, which is the longest continuous discourse recorded by Mark, shows signs of being an artificial composition. When a master gave "private teaching" to his disciples, it might be merely a matter of clarifying for their benefit difficult or enigmatic points made in public (Mark 4—the parable chapter—provides a good example of this). But another type of private teaching consisted of esoteric truths about the ultimate destiny of the world and of instructions on correctly reading the signs of the times. To impart teaching of this kind, Jewish writers had to hand a well-developed literary form, the so-called "apocalypse" or "revelation". They described the approaching end of the world in terms of a supernatural drama, in which the main events were fairly constant, but to which new details were added according to the particular vision of each writer; and these details could often be interpreted, by those sufficiently instructed to do so, as cryptic references to persons and events of their own time. In the time of Jesus, and particularly also in the second half of the first century A.D. (the period when the gospels were written) a number of these "apocalypses" were composed by visionaries who were inspired to see, in contemporary events, clues to the shape of that final cosmic drama which (they earnestly believed) God was about to initiate. If Jesus gave some teaching of this kind, it need cause no surprise that he utilized some of the elements of traditional apocalypses; and it would be still less surprising if, when that teaching came to be written down, it became further assimilated to the pattern of contemporary apocalyptic writings.
14 There is one clear instance of this process in the present chapter. **Let the reader understand** is an admonition which could not possibly have occurred in a spoken discourse of Jesus; but it is just the kind of hint by which a visionary writer of the period was accustomed to indicate that a phrase or image he had just used was a symbol or a cryptogram for some familiar person, place or event. It shows that at some stage Jesus' teaching on the future has been assimilated to the conventions of a written apocalypse.

Not only the form but also the content of Jesus' discourse has been influenced by these conventions. Speculations about the future tended to assume that the ultimate act of the drama, when God would finally manifest his sovereignty and save his elect, would be preceded by a period of exceptional calamity and tribulation, when the powers of evil would be unleashed to an unheard-of degree, and all but the most faithful and courageous of the saints of God might be tempted to despair. This dark period before the end
8 came to be known in some circles as the **birth-pangs of the new age** (this almost technical expression occurs in Mark's narrative); and moreover it had

a purpose: it would prepare for the impending judgement by putting men to a decisive test. Those whose faith was already wavering would lose heart,
and those whose grasp of the truth was insecure would be **misled** (again 6
an almost technical word in this context) by various manifestations of a spirit of deliberate deception. But, severe though the ordeal would be, the righteous could take courage. '**For the sake of his own, whom he has**
chosen,' God '**has cut short the time**'—another feature which, if it was not 20
already conventional, was soon to occur regularly in Jewish apocalypses; for the ultimate purpose of these writers was to encourage and sustain their readers. Once these calamitous events had got under way, the final act could not be long delayed, and the righteous could begin to look forward to their promised reward. The important thing was to be able to recognize what stage the drama had reached.

For these reasons, it has become customary to refer to this chapter as a "little apocalypse", with the implication that, since an "apocalypse" is essentially a literary creation, the teaching it contains can hardly have been given by Jesus in anything like its present form. But at the same time it is important to notice the difference between this discourse and a typical "apocalypse". In the Revelation, for example (which is a true Christian apocalypse), the basic pattern is the same—a period of intensified tribulation, followed by the judgement, the new age, and the reward of the righteous; but the treatment is totally different. The tribulations are not the kind of ordinary catastrophes which might be encountered in the course of history: they consist of altogether supernatural upheavals in the processes of nature, accompanied by—or rather caused by—desperate conflicts between cosmic and mythological powers; and the climax to which the book builds up is the establishment of a new order by God, in which his chosen people will at last take their rightful place. In short, the setting is throughout mythological, the powers at work supernatural. The style is that of poetry, not of prose. By contrast, the greater part of Jesus' discourse is set firmly within history. The events predicted are little larger than life, the warnings which accompany the predictions are meant to be serious and practical, and very little space is devoted to the scene which is in fact the *raison d'être* of an "apocalypse"—the final phase of judgement and glory. For the most part, the nearest parallels are to be found, not in the Book of Daniel (the first of the Jewish apocalypses), but in the Old Testament prophets; and the discourse as a whole is more concerned with interpreting the significance of contemporary history (which is the main part of what the Bible means by "prophecy") than with painting a mythological picture of the age to come.

The question the disciples put to Jesus was in any case not a general one about the future of the world, but was quite specific. After Jesus' astounding
prophecy of the total destruction of the temple, they asked, '**When will this** 4
happen?' In the course of his reply, Jesus gave an equally specific answer:

30 **'the present generation will live to see it all.'** And he was right. In A.D.
70 (shortly after the date when this gospel is likely to have been written) the
Jewish revolt, which had begun four years earlier, was finally crushed. The
Romans captured Jerusalem, set fire to the temple, and subsequently
levelled it to the ground. That events were already moving in this direction
some forty years before must have been clear to a man of Jesus' prophetic
insight.

But the essence of prophecy was not merely to discern the course which
history was taking, but to set these events in the wider context of God's
judgement upon his people, and to prepare men to see in them the signs of
a greater providence. The discourse is an essay in reading the signs of the
times, and weaves together predictions of actual events or circumstances
which Jesus foresaw (or which the next generation of Christians filled in from
their experience) with some of the traditional elements which the prophets
had incorporated in their descriptions of the impending climactic phase of
history. To take each detail as it comes:

6 (i) **'Many will come claiming my name.'** Fanatics who claimed to
have divine authority to lead the Jewish people in revolt against the Romans
had already appeared in Jesus' lifetime and were to appear again before A.D.
70. This was the historical form in which the mythological "spirit of deception" was to appear in the final period before the end. Possibly Jesus' own
appearance and death would accentuate the danger: men might claim to be
Jesus himself, returned from the dead with power.

7 (ii) **'The noise of battle . . . the news of battles.'** An intensification of
the political upheavals of which Palestine had always been a victim was a
8 standard feature expected in the last days. Verse 8 is only a slight adaptation
of Isaiah 19.2.

9 (iii) **'You will be handed over to the courts.'** How far the experience
of the early church has coloured these verses we cannot tell. For instance,
they would serve as an accurate description of the things which Paul had to
endure; but equally it would not have been difficult for Jesus to foresee that
his followers had these trials ahead of them. **Governors and kings** do not
necessarily shift the scene outside Palestine: "governor" was a usual word
for a senior Roman administrator, and those of Herod's sons who still ruled
over parts of Palestine by leave of the Roman empire were commonly known
as "kings". On the other hand, a wider perspective than was usual in Jesus'
10 teaching is opened up in the words, **'the Gospel must be proclaimed to
all nations.'** It soon became a firm conviction of Paul's that this must happen
before the end (literally, "first"); but it took the church as a whole some
time to accept the proposition that the Gospel was intended, not merely for
the Jews and their immediate neighbours, but for the whole Greco-Roman
world; and if Jesus made such a clear statement about it, we must assume
30 that the church did not at first take it as a practical commission, but assumed

that he was predicting some supernatural proclamation which would be
made immediately before the end.

(iv) '**Brother will betray brother to death**'. This prophecy occurs in 12
Micah (7.6). The Jews set particular store by the solidarity of family and of
race, and this desecration of family ties was, in their eyes, one of the most
horrifying features of the terrible last days.

(v) '**But when you see the "abomination of desolation"**'. The 14
phrase is as meaningless in the Greek as it is in English. It was the
deliberately cryptographic translation which the Greek version of the Old
Testament offered for a subtle piece of Hebrew invective. In 168–167 B.C.
Antiochus Epiphanes set up a statue of Zeus in front of the temple in
Jerusalem (1 Maccabees 1.54). The author of the book of Daniel (9.27 and
elsewhere), by a kind of word-play on the Hebrew equivalent to the title
"Olympian Zeus", called this "the abominable thing which desolates".
Anyone who came across the phrase, either in Greek or in Hebrew, would
automatically think of this notorious case of deliberate desecration; and he
would be led to look for a similar meaning here by the unexpected parenthesis, **let the reader understand**. It is probably useless to speculate on
precisely what kind of desecration Jesus would have had in mind, if indeed
he used this particular cryptogram at all. Possibly he imagined the ensigns of
the Roman legions, which were regarded by the Jews as idolatrous, being
set up as a sign of victory and conquest in the temple precincts. But by the
time Mark wrote one event had taken place which may have suggested how
the oracle was likely to be fulfilled. In A.D. 40 the Emperor Gaius (Caligula)
attempted to have a statue of himself placed in the temple, thereby nearly
causing an insurrection. It may be the memory of this which led Mark to
make the idol sound like a live person (at the expense, in the Greek, of
correct grammar): **usurping a place which is not his.**

'**Then those who are in Judaea must take to the hills**'. The event
just mentioned was clearly meant to be regarded as a real possibility. When it
happened, the only course would be immediate flight to the caves and
inaccessible places in the mountains where no victorious soldiers were likely
to follow up fugitives. The haste required is described with conventional
but vivid details drawn from life in Palestine. Inside staircases to the roof 15
of one-storied houses were not usual. If a man were on the roof (where many
domestic tasks were done), he would have to come down outside before going
into his house—and there would not be time for him to go in. Work in the 16
countryside was done without a coat on—and there would not be time for
him to go and fetch it. The winter in Palestine sometimes brings rains so
heavy that travel is virtually impossible—so **pray that it may not come in** 18
winter. Those days will bring distress, the kind of distress the Jews had 19
so often endured at the hands of conquering or marauding armies, but this
time of an intensity so great that it could only be the fulfilment of well-known

prophecies about the great tribulation immediately preceding the end (the language of verse 18 is an almost exact quotation from Daniel 12.1).

21 (vi) "**Look, here is the Messiah**". Another instance of the manifestation of the spirit of deception, calculated **to mislead**, similar to (i) above.

24 (vii) '**The sun will be darkened**'. At this point one might get the impression that the discourse moves from the realm of reality to that of mythology, from events which can be imagined as taking place in history to cataclysms which mark the end of all history. But the words (which are in any case a tissue of allusions to Isaiah 13.10 and 34.4—the imagery was quite conventional) would not necessarily have suggested, as they do to us, a general disintegration of the universe. The sun, the moon and the stars were thought of as being much the same size as they look; and the main function of them
25 (and of the spirits or powers which were thought to control them, the **celestial powers**) was to maintain life on earth in an orderly system. The sun and the moon assured the orderly procession of night and day, the stars (by the principles of astrology, which were widely accepted) regulated, not only the seasons, but the destinies of men. Even a minor dislocation (such as an eclipse was thought to be) was regarded as the sign of some extraordinary portent or disaster. *A fortiori*, disorganization in heaven would unleash chaos on earth.

26 (viii) '**Then they will see the Son of Man**'. This, at last, is the final moment towards which the whole process has been tending. The language again is conventional: compare Daniel 7.13, Zechariah 2.6, and also Paul's description of the same scene in 1 Thessalonians 4.16 (a passage which perhaps gives the clue to the final phrase: the chosen who are to be gathered
27 from **the farthest bounds of heaven** may be those of the faithful who have died). The manifestation of the Son of Man will be the climax of the whole drama.

28 '**Learn a lesson from the fig-tree.**' The discourse, which has mainly consisted of prophecies of what is to happen, now becomes concerned with the proper attitude which men should have in face of the impending future. Two dangers very soon presented themselves in the early church: first, that of assuming that since the end had not come at once it would not come at all, and that vigilance could be relaxed; secondly, that of becoming distracted with all kinds of speculation about exactly "what day or what hour" these things would happen. Jesus, like other Jewish teachers, seems to have had these two dangers in mind. The end would be preceded by signs, just as certainly as summer is preceded by spring. In England we would probably express the simile differently (and Luke may have been adapting it to European conditions when he wrote (21.29) 'look at the fig-tree or any other tree'): for us, spring is the time of the return of green life after the dead colours of winter. But in Palestine the winter, with all its rains, is the one time when the mountains look green: greenness as such is not a sign that

summer is near. But the fig-tree, which is one of Palestine's few deciduous trees, stands strikingly bare in the winter, and only puts on fresh green leaves in the spring. The transition between winter and summer is short: it is completed between March and early May; and the appearance of leaves on the fig-tree is a sure sign that this rapid period of change is beginning.

'In the same way'. How exactly is the simile to be applied? What in the 29
previous discourse corresponds to the sign of spring and what corresponds to the summer? **'When you see all this happening, you may know that the end is near'**. As the NEB footnote shows, the Greek is ambiguous: it does not say just what it is which will be near. Further, the phrase **'all this'**
is vague, and the next saying, **'the present generation will live to see it all'**, 30
only increases the obscurity; for it is clear that there are many things in the previous discourse which the generation contemporary with Jesus did not live to see. We are confronted once again by the same difficulties as are presented by 9.1 (on which see above), and many have inferred that Jesus was in error, or was misunderstood, or even that he never said anything of the kind. In fact, the same considerations apply here as there. Many of the things which Jesus predicted actually happened "in that generation"—civil strife, a famine, persecution of Christians, and a terrible war culminating in the siege and destruction of Jerusalem. Moreover, there was a sense in
which Christians did in fact see **the Son of Man coming in the clouds** 26
with great power and glory: this was one of their ways of expressing the conviction that Jesus had risen from the dead and was now at the right hand of God (Acts 7.56). But one thing did not happen: the final judgement at the end of history. Jesus may have been in error or have been misunderstood about the temporal relation between this ultimate culmination and the catastrophes and trials which those who heard him would have to endure; but this in any case may not have been the main point which he was making. He was speaking in the tones of ancient prophecy. The course of events which he so clearly foresaw was not meaningless, but predetermined and significant. Men would be able to read from them the lesson that God's purpose was being accomplished, and the universal judgement of mankind brought nearer. What might seem like senseless suffering and catastrophe was an essential precondition of the coming of that state of affairs for which men longed, and was therefore, if rightly interpreted, a cause for encouragement rather than despair. The discourse was an exercise in correctly reading the signs of the times.

'Heaven and earth will pass away; my words will never pass away.' 31
If the consummation were delayed, men might cease to believe in it, and find history once again bitter and meaningless. Jesus, in effect, refuses to admit any excuse for this attitude. Whatever time world history may take, its conclusion will always be the same. And against the opposite danger of fussy
speculation about the exact timing of **that day or that hour**, he stresses 32

that no human calculation can reveal it. God is free to choose the moment. Surprisingly, even **the Son** is excluded from the secret. (This is the one occasion in this gospel on which Jesus explicitly claims unique sonship of God. Significantly, he does so in the context, not of his divine power, but of his human limitations.)

Between these two attitudes—the one of ceasing to believe, the other of
33 agitated preoccupation—is the true one. **'Be alert, be wakeful.'** Another
brief simile illustrates it, similar to many others which Jesus uses for the same theme (and perhaps, in the telling, this one has been slightly contaminated by those others: there seems no reason why it should be only **the door-keeper** who has to keep awake and not the other servants, unless the master of the house is expected at night. But in the east a traveller on a long journey seldom travelled by night; the task of a door-keeper was to be awake to open to him only if he returned late from dinner, or to detect the entry of a thief—and Jesus used these similes too). With that, the discourse, which began as private instruction to three disciples, is now declared to be
37 destined for the whole community of Jesus' followers: **'What I say to you,
I say to everyone: Keep awake'.**

The final conflict

14. 1 **Now the festival of Passover and Unleavened Bread was only two days off.** This sentence gives, or appears to give, a precise date; and indeed, from this point on, events move rapidly, and in a fairly strict chronological sequence. Passover was a springtime festival, at which the slaughter of lambs before the temple and the eating of them by household groups was understood as a re-enactment of one of the great moments of the Exodus from Egypt (Exodus 12). The Festival of Unleavened Bread, on the other hand, which involved removing all old leaven from the house and eating only unleavened bread for the following week, must have been originally connected with the renewal of life at the beginning of each New Year. Long before the New Testament period, these two festivals had been combined, and the order of events was as follows. The main preparations were made on the 14th day of the month Nisan (which normally fell between March and May, though the Jewish calendar, being lunar and not solar, had constantly to be adjusted). Search was made for leaven and leavened food in all houses, and all that was found was destroyed; and in the afternoon the Passover lambs were slaughtered according to a prescribed ritual at the great altar in front of the temple. After sunset (which, for the Jews, meant the beginning of a new day, so by their reckoning we must now call it 15th Nisan) the people assembled by families or small groups to make a solemn meal of roasted lamb, one lamb having been brought to the altar by each group that afternoon. At this meal (since the festival of Unleavened Bread was now combined with Passover) all the bread and cakes were unleavened; and the festival continued for a further week, during which all bread was prepared without leaven.

Which of these days is Mark referring to when he speaks of **the festival**? Properly speaking neither Passover nor Unleavened Bread began until after sunset, which by Jewish reckoning was a new day, 15th Nisan; but if Mark was reckoning in the Roman manner (midnight to midnight) and not in the Jewish manner (sunset to sunset), both the preparation in the afternoon and the ritual meal in the evening will have appeared to him as happening on the same "day", the first day of the festival. It is likely, therefore, though by no means certain, that Mark was counting back from that day, which, as we shall see, he believed to be a Thursday. But how far did he count back? **Two days off** suggests to us the previous Tuesday; but when Greeks and Romans counted days, they tended to include the day they started counting from. If today is Tuesday, tomorrow is the second day, and so Wednesday, not Thursday, is **two days off**. For all these reasons, we cannot be sure whether Mark meant to place these events on the Tuesday or the Wednesday of the week of *The final conflict*.

Apart from this uncertainty, the chronology in Mark is clear, and appears to be followed by Matthew and Luke. Jesus celebrated the Passover meal with his disciples in the evening, was tried during the following night and early morning, and was executed the same day, which was a Friday. It follows that the Passover festival, properly speaking, took place after sunset on the Thursday, which was therefore the beginning of 15th Nisan by Jewish reckoning. But against this has to be set the clear evidence of John's gospel that in that year the festival fell one day later, that is to say, that the Thursday evening was only the beginning of the preparation day, 14th Nisan, and that the Jews did not eat the Passover meal until after sunset on the Friday, by which time Jesus had been crucified. This difference between John's gospel and the other accounts prevents us from accepting Mark's time-scheme uncritically; and certain details in Mark's own narrative also fit in a little awkwardly. Not the least significant of these details is the
attitude of the chief priests and the doctors of the law. **'It must not be** 2
during the festival', they said.[a] But, according to Mark's account, "during the festival" was exactly the moment when the betrayal and arrest took place.

Meanwhile an episode is introduced which has no exact date. **Jesus was** 3
at Bethany, in the house of Simon the leper. The story, or one like it, occurs in all the gospels. In Matthew, its position in the narrative and most

[a] It is just possible that the Greek was intended to mean, instead of "not during the festival", "not in the festival crowd". This would considerably ease the difficulty.

of its details are the same; but Luke places a somewhat similar story much earlier in his gospel and gives it a totally different application; and John tells a similar story (though many of the details are different) not two, but six days before the Passover. Evidently the story circulated in more than one form, and it is likely that Mark himself chose to introduce it at this point and placed his own interpretation upon it.

It was customary to anoint face, hands and feet with olive oil, especially before any kind of social occasion, and those who could afford it mixed a little perfume with the oil. Perfume was expensive, and was sold in bottles of alabaster or pottery with long narrow necks, so that it would pour very slowly. But the woman **broke it open**, that is, she broke off the neck, and poured out the entire contents at once. This was extravagant. 300 *denarii*
5 (**thirty pounds** in the NEB) was perhaps the total which a labourer might
4 earn in a year. The reaction of **some of those present** was perfectly
understandable.

Jesus' reply is perhaps illuminated by the contemporary Jewish attitude to "good works". Giving alms to the poor was always praiseworthy, and was indeed constantly expected of all who could afford it. But still more praiseworthy were certain exceptional acts of kindness, such as hospitality to strangers. (There is a list of these acts of kindness in a parable in Matthew 25.35–6.) One of these acts was that of giving decent burial to a friend; and it seems that decent burial was held to include anointing the corpse. Compared, then, with an unremarkable act of almsgiving, the woman's gesture
7 was seen by Jesus as a highly praiseworthy act of kindness—'**It is a fine**
thing she has done for me'; and whatever the original meaning of her
action (Luke gives a different explanation, John offers none) Mark evidently
understood it as the fulfilment in advance of an act of kindness which he
8 would soon have no one else to perform for him—'**anointing my body for**
9 **burial. I tell you this:**' the saying which follows has a perfectly obvious
meaning. The woman's act was so remarkable that some mention of it was bound to be made wherever the story of Jesus was told. Nevertheless, it is curious that the woman has no name (only in John's version is she called Mary)—it is odd to perpetuate the memory of a good deed but not to record the name of the person who did it; and the phrase, **wherever in all the world the Gospel is proclaimed**, sounds a little strangely in Jesus' mouth (for it is hard to understand why it took the church so long to accept the necessity of a world-wide mission if Jesus had so clearly predicted it, see above on Mark 13.10). Therefore an alternative translation is sometimes suggested: "When the Gospel is proclaimed to all the world (i.e. at the end of the world), then what she has done will be told (at the Last Judgement) so that God may remember her with favour."

After this interlude, the narrative continues from the point reached in
1 verse 2. Jesus' enemies were **trying to devise some cunning plan to seize**

him; one of the twelve disciples listed in 3.13–19 was ready to betray him. It was not in Mark's manner to give reasons for Judas' treachery. Jesus had predicted that he would be betrayed, and here was Judas fulfilling the prediction. Such things happened according to the secret providence of God; there was no need to enquire about human motives as well.

Now on the first day of Unleavened Bread, when the Passover lambs 12
were being slaughtered. By Jewish reckoning, these were two different days. The festival of Unleavened Bread began only after sunset (a new day according to the Jewish calendar, so 15th Nisan) whereas the Passover lambs were slaughtered earlier on the same afternoon (14th Nisan). But Mark's expression, though technically inexact, is quite unambiguous: he means the afternoon of 14th Nisan, which (according at least to his information) fell that year on a Thursday, and was the time when each family or group of pilgrims made their preparations for celebrating the festival. These preparations included bringing a lamb to the temple to be slaughtered by the priests in the proper ritual manner. Jesus and his disciples had come to Jerusalem along with the thousands of pilgrims who travelled from all over Palestine to attend the festival; and his disciples took it for granted that he would be observing the festival like everyone else: **'Where would you like us to go and prepare for your Passover supper?'**

The first necessity was to find a room. In earlier times the Passover lamb had been roasted and eaten by all male Israelites over 20 years old in the precincts of the temple; but by now it had become a more domestic festival, and the meal was held in private houses. Nevertheless, although the practice had changed, the theory remained the same: on Passover night, the whole city of Jerusalem was deemed, by a special dispensation, to form part of the temple precincts. This meant that those who lived in Jerusalem could hold the meal in their own homes; but those who came as pilgrims from outside had to find a room in the city where they could do the same. It appears to have been expected of the residents that they should lend the upstairs rooms in their houses for this purpose; and in this way even the many thousands of pilgrims were apparently accommodated. Nevertheless, finding a room was an urgent matter, and the disciples were naturally anxious to press on with it. To the modern reader, it sounds as if Jesus had already made arrangements. It was probably as unusual then as it is now in Palestine to see **a man**, 13
instead of a woman, carrying an earthenware **jar of water**, and the signal could easily have been prearranged. But the episode is remarkably similar to the requisitioning of an ass at the beginning of chapter 11; and it is likely that Mark regarded both that and the finding of the room as instances of Jesus' miraculous foresight.

A large room upstairs, set out in readiness. Since all who possessed 15
a large enough spare room were bound to have it filled on that evening, it is

not surprising that this one should have been already **set out in readiness** with the necessary tables and couches (for on special occasions such as this the Jews followed the Greek and Roman custom of reclining on couches, leaning on their left arm). But this would still leave the two disciples with many things to be **prepared for Passover**. A lamb would have to be bought, taken to the temple for slaughter by the priests, skinned and prepared for roasting; besides this, unleavened bread, herbs and wine would have to be obtained.

17 **In the evening he came to the house with the Twelve.** The number of people who shared the same Passover meal followed from the number for whom one lamb would provide sufficient meat. It was normally not less than ten, nor more than twenty. These groups might be family groups: married women and male children over 12 years old were allowed to take part (Luke 2.41–2). But equally, men who had come to Jerusalem as pilgrims could make up "fellowships" for the purpose. The lamb was then slaughtered in the name of each member of the fellowship, and from that moment no further members could be admitted. So long as the meal lasted, the members of such a "fellowship" felt themselves to be intimately bound together by the fact of having shared it; when it was over, they were free to separate. Jesus and his twelve disciples formed an appropriate group to observe the celebration together.

18 **As they sat at supper.** This is good modern English, but conveys a false
impression: they were not sitting but reclining, as was the custom on special
occasions. **'One of you will betray me—one who is eating with me'.**
Since table-fellowship was a particularly strong expression of solidarity
between individuals, the betrayal of one who had shared a meal had long
been regarded as a particularly base form of treachery: "Even the friend
whom I trusted, who ate at my table, exults over my misfortune" (Psalm
41.9, a passage which is clearly alluded to here). On this occasion, the traitor
20 was one who was **dipping into the same bowl** with Jesus. Particularly in
the Passover meal, but also at other meals, pieces of bread or vegetable were
dipped into a bowl of sweet sauce. Judas must have been lying fairly close
to Jesus to use the same bowl; but the point of the saying was probably not
to help the disciples to identify the traitor, so much as to emphasize the
table-solidarity which the traitor was breaking. As a sin, that was already
serious enough; but again, the narrative does not permit us to be sentimental
21 about it. **'The Son of Man is going the way appointed for him in the
scriptures'** (an allusion doubtless to the darker side of the destiny of the
Son of Man, and of the righteous people whom he represented, that is hinted
at in Daniel 7.21). It was God, not Judas, who was guiding events along their
predestined course.

22 **During supper.** It may seem surprising that Mark's description of the meal makes no mention of its central feature, the eating of the lamb. But his

concern was not to provide a consecutive account of the details of a Jewish observance, but to record certain acts and words of Jesus which, though they may have been prompted by the original character of the meal, were in themselves something entirely new. The Christian "Lord's Supper", in almost every one of its various manifestations, has from its inception centred round these acts and words, and when Mark came to record them he can hardly have failed to be influenced by the recital of them which took place every time the Supper was celebrated in the Christian community. It is understandable, therefore, that he should have omitted those details of the Jewish rite which had no interest for his Christian readers. Nevertheless, he preserves sufficient indication of the sequence of events during the meal for
us to be able to place Jesus' innovations in their original context. **During** 22
supper he took bread. It is significant that the breaking of bread took place after the meal had begun. Almost all formal meals among the Jews began with the host saying the blessing and breaking a loaf of bread, which he then divided out among the guests. This was the beginning of the meal: unless it was a luxurious occasion, when hors d'œuvres might first be eaten in another room, nothing would have been eaten until this moment. But there was one exception to this. At the Passover, the supper began with "bitter herbs"—lettuce and the like—which were dipped into a dish of sweet sauce. This was the moment for the Judas episode which has just been narrated. The breaking of bread seems to have had no important rôle in the meal, and certainly did not take its usual place at the beginning. To this extent, it is intelligible that Jesus' action should have been **during supper**, though so far as we know the **blessing** (which took a form such as, "Blessed be thou who bringest forth bread from the earth") and breaking, though usual on any other occasion, normally played no special part in the Passover meal.

'Take this; this is my body.' Another feature of the Passover meal, which certainly goes back to the time of Jesus (though it was much elaborated in later times) was that the host—or the father, if it was a family group—had to explain the significance of the special food that was being eaten. The whole meal was to be seen as a re-enactment of the exodus of the Jews out of Egypt (Exodus 12); and the explanation took the form of a commentary on a passage such as Deuteronomy 26.5–9, where these events are summarized. For instance, the Passover lamb stood for the original sacrifice made in Egypt; its blood for the blood which was painted on the Israelites' doorposts so that the punishment of the Lord should "pass over" them (Exodus 12.27); and the bitter herbs for the days of bitter slavery which God's people had undergone in Egypt. But what did the unleavened bread stand for? This (since it probably did not belong to the original festival) was more difficult, and differing answers were given. It may have been in this context that Jesus pronounced the words, **'this is my body.'**

What do the words mean? The question can only be fully answered out of the subsequent reflection and experience of the church. Here it is sufficient to ask how the disciples would originally have understood them. They would have been accustomed, at every formal meal, to the head of the household breaking a loaf of bread with a prayer of thanksgiving to God (a "blessing"), and when each person at the table received and ate a piece of this loaf as it was given to him, he thereby associated himself with the blessing which had been spoken. To this extent, when Jesus **took bread, and having said the blessing he broke it,** the disciples, when they ate the bread he gave them, were doing something entirely familiar: they were expressing their solidarity with Jesus and saying Amen to his blessing. But when Jesus added the words, '**this is my body**', he went far beyond the meaning of an ordinary family blessing. The only "body" which it would make sense to them to "eat" was the body of an animal which had been offered as a sacrifice—like the lamb which was doubtless (though it is not mentioned here) the main element of the meal which Mark is describing, and which had been ritually slaughtered earlier the same afternoon at the altar before the temple. When Jesus called the bread "his body", his disciples are likely to have grasped that he was likening himself to a sacrificial victim; and when he said, '**take this**', he was inviting them to share in the benefits which would flow from the sacrifice being offered.

23 **Then he took a cup.** If the meal was following the usual course of a Passover, some time will have elapsed since the breaking of bread: the lamb itself will have been eaten, and the prescribed explanation given of the meaning of the special food that was served. But the Christian community had no interest in these details (though an echo of them survives in Paul's phrase, 'he took the cup after supper', 1 Corinthians 11.25), and Mark goes straight on to the moment, at the end of the meal, when the host took a cup of wine in his hands and **offered thanks to God** in much the same way as he had said the blessing over the bread. Once again, the disciples would have found it natural to associate themselves with Jesus in this by immediately drinking with him, and it is likely (though this cannot be proved from the evidence available) that they would have been used to passing round a common cup on such an occasion. But, once again, Jesus went far beyond this ordinary
24 ceremony by adding the words, '**This is my blood, the blood of the covenant, shed for many.**' This, more clearly than the saying over the bread, was the language of sacrifice. The most important moment in the ritual slaughter of a victim at the altar in Jerusalem was the shedding of its blood. It was by virtue of the blood poured upon the altar that the sacrifice was deemed effective. Certain sacrifices made by the priests were moreover made **for many** (though Jesus probably had in mind a larger section of humanity than would have been envisaged at a normal Jewish sacrifice); and on one occasion the blood of a sacrifice had been sprinkled upon the whole

people of Israel to seal **the covenant** made with them by God (Exodus 24.8). The Old Testament looked forward to a "new covenant" of an inner, spiritual kind (Jeremiah 31.31–4), and the work of Jesus was soon to be understood by Christians as the inauguration of this new covenant. The wine, therefore, which the disciples were to drink[a] was interpreted by Jesus as the blood of himself as a sacrificial victim, whose death would be on behalf of many and would seal a new covenant between God and men.

'I tell you this: never again shall I drink from the fruit of the vine'. 25
As it stands here (the meaning is different in Luke), the saying appears to be a simple prophecy by Jesus that he would not live to partake of any further meals at which wine was drunk; and since the narrative implies that he was by now certain of his impending death, it can be taken as one more solemn prediction of what was about to happen. But the saying does not stop there. It continues with a rich sequence of biblical ideas: **'until that day when I drink it new in the kingdom of God'.** The **kingdom of God** was often described as a heavenly banquet, at which the Messiah would preside, and all things would be made **new**; and Jesus seems to have been deliberately relating the meal he had just shared with his disciples to the heavenly reality which, he prophesied, would shortly come to pass. The one was a foretaste of the other, just as the traditional Jewish Passover meal was often interpreted as an anticipation of the coming redemption which God had promised to his people.

After singing the Passover Hymn. The Passover meal ended with the 26
singing of part of the so-called *Hallel*, which consisted of Psalms 113–18. The Greek says simply, "after singing a hymn", but the translators are doubtless right that this special **Passover Hymn** is meant. **They went out to the Mount of Olives.** It was obligatory upon all who kept the festival to remain in Jerusalem until sunrise; but in view of the very large number of pilgrims, a technical dispensation had been introduced under which, for this one night, "Jerusalem" was deemed to embrace a number of outlying areas, including the Mount of Olives, but not including Bethany, where Jesus had been spending the night during the earlier part of the week. We can assume, therefore, that it was long before sunrise when Jesus left the city, crossed the Kedron valley and approached the lower slopes of the
Mount of Olives. His prediction, **'you will all fall from your faith'**, is 27
supported by a quotation from Zechariah 13.7 (in a form slightly different from that of any version which has come down to us). It is remarkable that in the gospels no attempt is made to conceal or mitigate the failure of the disciples to stand by Jesus; on the other hand, it may have helped them to live it down, so to speak, when they remembered an Old Testament prophecy

[*a*] Presumably red wine, to make the symbolism obvious. But all wine looks dark red when drunk out of pottery cups, and the "blood of grapes" was a common metaphor for wine in Hebrew poetry.

which made their conduct seem predestined. In any case, all Jesus' predictions seem to presuppose that he knew he was to suffer alone. What may have made the realization all the more poignant is that this denial and desertion took place even before the end of the night, during which he and his disciples should have been particularly closely bound together by their table-fellowship. As on previous occasions in this gospel, Peter is singled out from the disciples, but apparently only to represent them all in their apo-
30 stasy: '**You will all fall from your faith**' applies to them all, '**you . . . will disown me**' is the particular way in which Peter will fulfil the prediction. '**Before the cock crows twice**'. In the east there is often a remarkably regular cock-crow, the first soon after midnight, another about an hour later, and a third one an hour later still, leaving two or three hours of silence before the chorus at dawn. Certainly, the third of the four "watches" into which the Romans divided the night (and this way of reckoning the parts of the night now prevailed in Palestine, as can be seen from 13.35) was popularly called "cock-crow", as was the bugle-blast with which a Roman military garrison would announce it. Whatever therefore Mark meant precisely by the cock crowing **twice**, the moment referred to was one which was going to be easy to recognize, well before dawn.

28 The section contains one very curious prophecy. '**Nevertheless, after I am raised again I will go on before you into Galilee.**' After the flock has been scattered through the striking down of the shepherd, it will once more gather behind its leader as he moves away northward into Galilee. This, at any rate, is the natural meaning of the Greek words, which are repeated below at 16.7; and the difficulty is to see in what way, if any, they were fulfilled. After the resurrection, Jesus appeared to the disciples in Jerusalem, and the fact that there are two traces in the gospels of an appearance in Galilee (Matthew 28.16–20 and John 21) does not really affect the fact that the church began its life, not following its master back to Galilee, but waiting upon his appearances and the manifestations of his power in Jerusalem. On the other hand, the church did soon find itself in movement, being guided by the Holy Spirit from its centre in Jerusalem to all parts of the civilized world. Jesus, in his lifetime, barely went further from the centre of Jewish life than Galilee; but Galilee, compared with Jerusalem, already represented an excursion into a partly non-Jewish world. Moreover, "Galilee" itself was a symbolic name: in its Old Testament form, it meant "land of the heathen" (as in Matthew 4.15). It is just possible that by this prophecy Jesus meant that after the resurrection he would lead his church far beyond the confines of the Jewish world. And this indeed took place.

32 **When they reached a place called Gethsemane.** The name is likely to mean "oil-press". John's gospel calls it a 'garden' on the far side (from Jerusalem) of the Kedron valley which separates Jerusalem from the Mount

of Olives. All the gospel accounts imply that it was somewhere on the Mount of Olives itself. The traditional site, not far from a cave on the slope of the mount facing Jerusalem, fits these data as well as any, and we should visualize a secluded and perhaps enclosed spot not far from the road that led over the Mount of Olives to Bethany. Jesus' purpose in coming to it was to pray, for which he usually preferred to be alone; but on this occasion he allowed near him the three privileged disciples who had earlier been witnesses of his transfiguration.

From this perfectly natural and quiet beginning, two altogether unexpected sequences of events unfold. First, Jesus' steady resolution and apparent foresight of what was to happen suddenly forsook him. For no
reason that the gospels explain, **horror and dismay came over him**, and 34
his prayer, which we may suppose normally took the form of intimate communion with his Father, was on this occasion an anguished mixture of rebellion and resignation. It may be asked, did Jesus really pray like this? Were his actual words heard and remembered (despite the fact that the only witnesses fell asleep), or did a subsequent tradition compose the kind of prayer which Jesus is likely to have prayed, just as ancient historians, from Thucydides on, freely composed the speeches which generals or statesmen were likely to have made on critical occasions? Not all these words of Jesus
are (in the modern sense) original: '**My heart is ready to break with** 34
grief' is not an exact quotation, but it recalls both the tone of a psalmist whose faith in God is tested to breaking point (Psalm 42.6), and also the exclamation of the prophet Jonah, when the most recent turn of events had made him feel that it would be better that he should die rather than attempt
any longer to fulfil his vocation (Jonah 4.9). '**Abba**', an intimate Aramaic 36
word for '**Father**', was the way in which the first Christians believed they should now address their prayers to God (very likely following Jesus' own example). '**Not what I will, but what thou wilt**' is a clear allusion to the Lord's Prayer itself. In short, the materials for composing the prayer lay ready to hand in the spirituality of the Old Testament and of the early church; and if it is thought unlikely that any reliable record of Jesus' words could have been preserved, there is no difficulty in seeing how the first Christians, meditating on Jesus' last hours of solitude in Gethsemane, may have composed and attributed to him a prayer of this nature. Moreover, however surprising it may seem that Jesus underwent such agony, both the Letter to the Hebrews (5.7) and the Gospel according to John (12.27) offer apparently independent testimony to some experience of Jesus comparable with that recorded here; and the episode is so unexpected that it is difficult to see how it could have been invented by the church.

The second unexpected sequence of events concerns the disciples. At the
outset Jesus merely bade them, without explanation, to **stay awake**. If we 34
are to understand that Jesus was still deliberately observing the customs of

Passover night, then the injunction is natural: if one of the group which had
eaten the supper together fell asleep, the table-fellowship was deemed to have
been broken. For the sake of their solidarity with him, Jesus may have
warned them to **stay awake**. But there is no hint of this in the narrative.
And when Jesus found that they had nevertheless fallen asleep (for it was by
38 now doubtless late in the night), he urged them again to **'stay awake'**, and
this time gave the reason: **'pray that you may be spared the test'**. What
test? The prayer, again, sounds like a reminiscence of the Lord's Prayer:
Christians are always to pray, 'Do not bring us to the test' (Matthew 6.13).
But clearly a special "test" is in mind here with which the disciples were
threatened. Was there a danger that they would be arrested and executed
along with Jesus? Or was it precisely the temptation to flee danger and deny
Jesus which constituted their "test", and about which they ought to be
praying just as Jesus was praying about his own greater test? We are not
told; nor do we know in what tone of voice Jesus commented on their
38 failure **to stay awake for one hour: 'The spirit is willing, but the flesh
is weak.'** Was this a proverb, wryly appropriate to the situation? Or an
indulgent comment, made by one who suffered no weakness of the flesh
himself? Or a general observation on human psychology? We do not know.
Once again, it is true that "stay awake" became a very common moral
exhortation in the early church, that "do not bring us to the test" was a
prayer which Christians uttered every day, and that the power of the spirit
and the weakness of the flesh became a familiar contrast in the experience
of the first Christian communities. Moreover, **'the spirit is willing, but
the flesh is weak'** is the kind of balanced antithesis more characteristic of
literary Greek than (so far as we know) of spoken Aramaic, and is hardly
likely to have been said by Jesus in exactly this form. In short, there is no
difficulty in detecting signs that the subsequent reflection of the church may
have influenced or even created the narrative. But equally, if the disciples
did not in fact fall asleep, it is difficult to see why anyone in the church
should have wanted to cast discredit on them by making up the story; and
if the story of their failure to stay awake is true, the rest flows from that. We
are left with an account which, though puzzling in its details, is vivid,
moving and apparently authentic.

41 **'Still sleeping? Still taking your ease?'** The force of these words
depends on the punctuation, and since, when the gospels were first written,
punctuation signs were not much used, we can only tell from the context
whether here Jesus was giving a command ("Go on sleeping!"), making an
exclamation ("Still asleep!") or asking a question ("Still sleeping?"). Most
older translations take the words as a command; more recent ones, like the
NEB, take them as a comment on the disciples' repeated failure to stay
awake. This has the advantage of making better sense with what follows,
though there is still considerable obscurity about the Greek word translated

'Enough!'.[a] At any rate, the tone is now abrupt and commanding. Jesus knows that **the hour has come.**

Suddenly, while he was still speaking. It is difficult, in translation, to 43
reproduce the finer points of an author's style without falling into pedantry. But here there is some significance in the exact word which Mark uses to introduce the next episode. It means, not **suddenly**, but "at once" (as it is translated in verse 45), and is Mark's favourite way of joining one episode to another. The detail is important, because it is at this point that the narratives of all four gospels converge and begin to move forward together along very similar lines; and this convergence is most easily explained if, in the early church, the account of Jesus' arrest, trial and crucifixion was the first part of the gospel narrative to assume a fairly standardized form, leaving each evangelist little freedom to rearrange it. If such a common tradition existed, it apparently began with Jesus' arrest. In Mark's gospel, however, the arrest seems to be so closely linked with what goes before (**suddenly, while he was still speaking**) that it looks at first sight improbable that a new chapter, so to speak, originally began at this point; but the word "at once" (**suddenly**) betrays Mark's editorial hand: it was he who joined up the episodes into a single sequence.

The characters in the scene are clearly identified. **Judas, one of the Twelve**: there seems to be a deliberate emphasis (as in verse 10 above) on the fact that Jesus was betrayed by one of his own disciples; the fact that he was to be "handed over" to his enemies was one which Jesus constantly mentioned when he predicted his own death, and we are left in no doubt that this was the way it turned out. The **crowd armed with swords and cudgels** might sound like an unofficial gang of ruffians were it not that it is explicitly said that they were **sent by the chief priests, lawyers, and elders.** These three classes of people made up the supreme Jewish Council known as the Sanhedrin, which was actually assembling at this moment (verse 53). This Council, though many of its civil powers had been taken over by the Roman administration, exercised legal authority in all religious matters, and maintained some kind of police or body of armed men to ensure that its authority was observed. It was these men, according to Mark, who arrived with Judas to arrest Jesus.

Now the traitor had agreed with them upon a signal. The kiss 44
strikes us as a particularly repellent gesture of betrayal, but this may be a modern reaction. It was customary for a pupil to greet his master with a kiss:
when Judas kissed Jesus and called him **'Rabbi'**, he was using the ordinary 45
form of greeting, and at the same time identifying, for the benefit of the armed band, the one man in the group who could be addressed in this way. One thing which is clear from his action is that the authorities had no inten-

[*a*] A further possible rendering might be mentioned, which would give the sense: "Your untimely sleep has its reward: we are caught!"

tion of arresting Jesus' disciples. If they had, they would have needed no
signal from Judas: it would have been sufficient to arrest the whole group
and identify Jesus afterwards. Therefore we probably should not make too
50 much of the fact that the disciples **all deserted him and ran away.**
Physical resistance to the armed party was presumably both out of the
question and also contrary to Jesus' wishes; John's gospel states that Jesus
actually intended them to escape. Their desertion, in fact, may have been more
in accord with Jesus' wishes than the preliminary scuffle. Indeed, Mark seems
47 a little embarrassed by this incident when he says that it was caused by **one of
the party.** The Greek word is vague (see the alternative translation in the
footnote), as if the perpetrator might have been some casual onlooker. But
in fact, apart from Jesus' disciples, there is unlikely to have been anyone
there.

48 **Then Jesus spoke.** His words are recorded, with slight variations, in all
49 the gospels, and show that he had no thought of resistance. **'Let the scriptures be fulfilled'** summarizes his attitude. With **the scriptures,** perhaps
he had in mind those passages of the Old Testament which seemed to point
to a Messiah who must suffer, or perhaps he was thinking of a particular
prophecy like that which is given in Luke's version (22.37) "And he was
counted among the outlaws" (Isaiah 53.12). Despite his resignation, he
49 allowed himself the irony of saying, **'day after day I was within your
reach as I taught in the temple'**—words which present a critical problem,
since according to Mark's narrative Jesus had spent at most three days
teaching in the temple. This is another small hint that Mark's chronology
of these last days may be artificial.

51 Mark alone mentions the **young man with nothing on but a linen
cloth.** The Greek says simply "linen", and means that his only outer
garment was made of linen—a sign that he was not poor. The detail is so
vivid and unexpected that it has often been suggested that Mark put it in
because the young man was none other than the writer of the gospel himself.
But this is pure speculation.

53 **Then they led Jesus away to the High Priest's house.** There follows a
hearing before the **chief priests, elders, and doctors of the law.** These
were the people of influence in Jerusalem, and members of these three classes
composed the supreme Jewish judicial Council (the Sanhedrin). There can
be little doubt that Mark believed that it was before this Council, or a committee of it, that Jesus appeared. But compared with what we know of the
usual procedure of the Council, the hearing has some unusual features. The
Council's official meeting place was a building inside (or at least close to)
the temple precincts, but on this occasion it met in the High Priest's house.
Sittings were permitted only during the day, but this one took place in the
middle of the night. Capital sentences required confirmation by a further

sitting not less than twenty-four hours after the first, and no capital case could be heard on the eve of a Sabbath or feast day; but on this occasion the judges proceeded immediately to secure the carrying out of the sentence, the following day was a Sabbath, and the night of the hearing was the beginning of the Passover festival. However, it is only fair to say that almost all our information about the procedure of the Sanhedrin is unreliable, in the sense that it was first written down and codified over a century after Jerusalem had been destroyed and the Council, at any rate as a judicial authority with civil powers, had ceased to exist. These later Jewish sources provide us with a picture which may well be idealized and artificial. In the troubled period which preceded the Jewish revolt, it must often have been necessary to improvise and adapt; and the gospel accounts should not be suspected merely because they fail to conform with all the details of a procedure which was worked out theoretically some time later.

However, if the hour and the place are unusual, the hearing itself follows the usual pattern of Jewish legal proceedings. Witnesses were called; but the only way in which a charge could be sustained was by securing two witnesses who, when examined independently (and out of each other's hearing), gave
identical evidence. This **the chief priests and the whole Council** failed 55
to do: **many gave false evidence against him, but their statements** 56
did not tally. One accusation is mentioned which, if substantiated, would have been very damaging. The temple was the holiest possession of the Jews, the central shrine of the national religion, the place where, above all, God
was felt to be present among his people. The threat, "**I will pull down this** 58
temple", could presumably have been interpreted as blasphemy—and we read in John's gospel (2.19) that Jesus did in fact say something about building a new temple to replace the old (though we may be sure that he did
not mean literally to destroy the existing temple).[a] **But even on this point** 59
their evidence did not agree. Apparently, on this point like the others, no two people could be found whose independent evidence was sufficiently consistent to form the basis of a charge.

In the absence of witnesses, the only course left to the Council was to try to get Jesus to incriminate himself. The High Priest's first attempt was
simply to put Jesus on the defensive: '**Have you no answer to the charges** 60
that these witnesses bring against you?' But, since no charge had been substantiated, Jesus had nothing to gain by replying. **He kept silence**. The first attempt was a failure.

Surprisingly, the second attempt was successful. **Again the High Priest** 61
questioned him: '**Are you the Messiah, the Son of the Blessed One?**' When Mark called Jesus 'Son of God' (as in the first sentence of his gospel) he intended the full range of meanings which, by the time he wrote, the church had come to associate with the title. But in the mouth of the High

[a] For other versions of this accusation, see Matthew 26.61; Acts 6.14.

Priest the same title (**the Blessed One** stands for God: the Jews preferred to avoid using the divine name) clearly meant the same as **Messiah**, that is, the supernaturally endowed figure whom the Jewish people expected to institute a new age, and who would necessarily stand in the line of those great figures of the Old Testament who were called "Sons of God". Would Jesus admit to being that figure? So far, Jesus had always avoided making any public declaration of his Messiahship. At most he had given hints of it, and his understanding of the title was clearly very different from that of his contemporaries. But asked point blank, he now gave an unequivocal answer,
62 **'I am'**,[a] and, by means of two Old Testament allusions, proceeded to draw out one of the implications of his answer. In the course of Daniel's vision (7.13), these words occur: "I saw one like a son of man coming with the clouds of heaven; he approached the Ancient of Years and was presented to him." The scene was the Last Judgement, and the meaning of the vision was that this Son of Man was then to be given a position of the highest honour and authority. Similarly, Psalm 110 was currently interpreted as a prophecy that One was to come who would have supremacy next only to God:[b] "The Lord says . . . sit at my right hand". By means of these two allusions, Jesus accredited himself not merely with a unique mission and with unique power, but with a unique status in all creation.

64 **'You have heard the blasphemy'**. Exactly what constituted blasphemy is not defined in the Old Testament, and we do not know what definitions were in use in the time of Jesus. On the face of it, Jesus' words were not blasphemous in themselves, unless the claim they expressed was obviously false; and it may be that the fact that they were uttered by one who, far from being a person of glory and power, was actually a prisoner of the court, was sufficient for the judges to dismiss Jesus' claim out of hand. At any rate the
63 High Priest **tore his robes** (the action which was required of anyone who heard words of blasphemy) and the rest of the court signified its agreement. Jesus had uttered blasphemy; and blasphemy, according to Jewish law (Leviticus 24.16) was punishable by death.

However, in a province governed by a Roman magistrate, it would have been unusual for a local court to have had the power to impose the death penalty. This power was normally kept firmly in the hands of the Roman governor. John's gospel explicitly informs us that the Sanhedrin refused to carry out the sentence for this reason (18.31), and although there is little independent evidence for Judaea at this period, there is no convincing reason for doubting what John says. The Jews could not execute Jesus themselves, and had to take the further measures which are described in the next chapter. Meanwhile they vented their feelings in a scene of mockery and

[*a*] The answer is less decisive in Matthew and Luke, and also in some manuscripts of Mark.
[*b*] "The Power" (see footnote in NEB) was another Jewish periphrasis for God.

insult. The gospels all offer slightly different accounts at this point, and it is difficult to be sure what really happened, but certain ideas seem always to be in the background. The main feature of the scene, in all three accounts, is the
sarcastic command, '**Prophesy!**' If Jesus was truly the Messiah, then the 65
easiest proof he could give would be to show that he possessed the "spirit" promised to the Messiah, a spirit which would surely manifest itself especially through the gift of prophecy—and the fact that Jesus did not, there and then, give a demonstration of prophecy may have confirmed his judges in their view that he was an impostor. In addition, there seems to have been an element of teasing cruelty in the blindfolding of Jesus. And a third point which doubtless influenced the narrative was a prophecy of Isaiah (50.6),

> "I offered my back to the lash . . .
> I did not hide my face from spitting and insult"

—one of those passages about a "suffering servant" of the Lord which Christians very soon came to see as having been fulfilled in the destiny of Jesus.

Meanwhile Peter was still below in the courtyard. The High Priest's 66
house must be imagined as a substantial building round a courtyard, with the principal rooms (of which one was large enough to hold **the whole Council**) on the first floor, the ground-floor rooms presumably accommodating servants and guards. Peter, we are told in verse 54, had penetrated right into this courtyard—John's gospel (18.16) provides the explanation that another of the disciples was well known there and was able to get him
admitted. He was **sitting among the attendants, warming himself at** 54
the fire. There it was light enough (either because of the fire, or because of
torches) for him to be recognized by **one of the High Priest's serving-** 66
maids, and after a stammering denial he retreated **outside into the porch**, 68
that is to say, out of the courtyard, to the street side of the main door of the
house where, despite the hour, there were some **bystanders** who had 69
perhaps been attracted by the news of the unusual sitting of the Council. But the serving-maid noticed him still lingering near the house, and passed on her suspicions to others in the throng. Finally, Peter was identified as a
Galilean, perhaps by his accent (as Matthew reports), perhaps by his 70
clothes. This was more incriminating than the maid's personal suspicion,
and Peter became vehement: **At this he broke out into curses.** "May 71
God destroy me if I know the man" is the kind of language the phrase
suggests. **Then the cock crew a second time.** We cannot be sure whether 72
Mark mentioned the first cock-crow: only some manuscripts give it (at the end of verse 68), and if Peter had heard it, why did he not notice it and realize what he was doing? At any rate, the cock crowing **a second time** brings the scene into harmony with Jesus' prediction (14.30); and Peter

burst into tears (if that is what the very difficult Greek word means: "He rushed out and wept" would be another possible rendering, but in the present state of our knowledge the NEB translation is as likely to be correct as any).

15. 1 **As soon as morning came.** The position at this point was that the Sanhedrin had found Jesus guilty on a capital charge, but not having the power to carry out the sentence they had either to let him off with a flogging or else bring the matter before the Roman governor in the hope that he would arrive at the same verdict and authorize the death penalty. The time for approaching a senior Roman official was the very early morning. The working day of a Roman gentleman began at dawn or even earlier; later in the morning he would have finished his official work and have been unavailable. Consequently the Council **having made their plan**[a]—that is, having decided on an approach to the Roman governor and on the kind of case to put before him—lost no time after their night session but immediately **put Jesus in chains . . . led him away and handed him over to Pilate.** Pilate was the governor of Judaea from A.D. 26 to 36. He had a bad record of tactless and provocative actions aimed at the Jews, but there is nothing in the following narrative to suggest that he acted irregularly. Under Roman law, his task, in a case of this kind, was simply to take note of the charges being brought, make sure that the accused was given opportunity to defend himself, decide what law, if any, the accused's conduct contravened, give his verdict, declare the sentence, and give orders for it to be carried out. Mark does not attempt to give a systematic account of this procedure; but the points which he records all fit into it well enough.

2 **Pilate asked him, 'Are you the king of the Jews?'** From this question we can infer (what Luke, for instance, makes explicit) that the "plan" of the Jewish authorities consisted in bringing Jesus before Pilate on a political charge. A Roman governor, as we can guess from similar hearings in Acts, would not have felt willing or qualified to give a decision on a matter of Jewish law; and the only charge against Jesus which had so far been substantiated was that of blasphemy, the definition of which was entirely a matter for Jewish jurists. To justify their action in bringing Jesus before Pilate, it was necessary to present a different charge. Jesus had admitted to being the Messiah, and this could be represented as a claim to be **the king of the Jews** (which, taken literally, was of course an act of sedition). We must assume that the **many charges** they brought against him before Pilate's tribunal centred round this one accusation.

Now there was certainly a sense in which one who was the Messiah must

[*a*] The NEB does not indicate the fact that at this point a number of manuscripts offer a reading which would almost certainly mean not, **having made their plan** but, "having convened a meeting". If this is the correct reading, we must allow for the possibility that Mark knew of two sessions, one before and one after dawn. This becomes important when his account is compared with those of Luke and John.

also be "the king of the Jews". The Messiah was to be the successor of King David, and some kind of kingship was inseparable from his status. Therefore
Jesus once again, when asked point blank, did not deny that there was truth 2
in the allegation (though his answer in the Greek is too ambiguous—perhaps intentionally so—for us to be able to say that he actually affirmed
it). But it is clear from a later remark of Pilate—'**Why, what harm has he** 14
done?'—that this admission was not such as to make Jesus appear as a dangerous revolutionary: Pilate must have understood—and in the account in John's gospel Jesus explains this to him—that Jesus' aspirations to kingship were not primarily political, and he was presumably not convinced by the allegations of ambition, amounting to sedition, which the prosecutors were able to bring forward. Nevertheless, he did not omit the regular
procedure of giving the accused an opportunity to make his defence. **But, to** 5
Pilate's astonishment, Jesus made no further reply. This silence of Jesus, both here and in the earlier proceedings before the Council, is much insisted on in all the gospel accounts. It is true that, once again, since the prosecution had apparently failed to make out a case, Jesus had little to gain by trying to defend himself. But there is probably more to it than that. In the first place, his silence was a fulfilment of one of the "suffering servant" passages of Isaiah which the first Christians (and possibly Jesus himself) regarded as an important clue to the meaning of these events:

> "He was afflicted, he submitted to be struck down
>   and did not open his mouth;
> he was led like a sheep to the slaughter
> like a ewe that is dumb before the shearers,
> and he would not open his mouth." (Isaiah 53.7)

In the second place, his refusal to say a word in his own defence was so unusual and so unexpected that it doubtless stuck in the mind of anyone who witnessed it. It is not surprising that it is one of the best-attested facts of Jesus' trial.

The Governor used to release one prisoner. We have no other 6
evidence of this custom in Judaea, but it is not inherently improbable. The custom provided Pilate with the possibility of an easy solution; if the people requested the release of Jesus, he would be relieved of the task of making
a decision in the case. But there was another prisoner **in custody** whom 7
apparently the crowd knew well, and indeed Mark introduces him as if both the man and his past were well known to his readers. Barabbas is not a distinctive name—indeed rather the opposite if it represents Bar-Abbas, "Father's son"; and Mark does not trouble to tell us who the other **rebels** were and what **the rising** was they had taken part in (and we know nothing about this from any source outside the gospels). He seems to assume that the whole episode was well known, and it presumably had nothing to do with

8 Jesus' trial that **the crowd appeared**[a] **asking for the usual favour.** This
early-morning "office hour" of Pilate was the right time for the crowd to
present their request, just as it was for the members of the Sanhedrin to bring
to Pilate's notice the case of Jesus of Nazareth. Pilate evidently knew that
Jesus was more popular with the people than with the Jewish authorities, and
10 that he had been brought before him **out of malice.** Consequently, the
fortuitous arrival of people who might be expected to support Jesus seemed
9 to give him his opportunity: **'Do you wish me to release for you the king
of the Jews?'**

However, under the influence of the chief priests, the people kept to their original purpose of asking for the release of Barabbas. It is not clear why Pilate then drew them into Jesus' case. Possibly he hoped that, if they showed themselves sympathetic to Jesus, they would provide him with further reasons for releasing a man who (he was now satisfied) was not a source of political danger; and this would give him the satisfaction of disappointing
the Jewish leaders whom (as we know from other sources) he disliked and
13 despised. But **they shouted back, 'Crucify him!'** Again Mark gives no
explanation. Up to now the crowd had been on Jesus' side. Why this sudden animosity against him? It may be simply that the presence of the chief priests was sufficient to make them change their mind (though we should not have guessed, otherwise, that the chief priests had so much influence with the populace). Alternatively, Pilate's question was understood—and perhaps intended—as a test of their loyalty. Here was a man who called himself "king of the Jews". On the face of it, this meant that he was an insurrectionary. In the presence of the Roman governor, what would be the reaction of the crowd? To acclaim Jesus as king, and expose themselves to the same charge of attempted insurrection? Or to demand the appropriate punishment under Roman law for a public enemy? These were the alternatives. Understandably they chose the second: **'Crucify him!'** Without more ado (for in such cases the Governor was not bound to any precise legal procedure) Pilate pronounced Jesus guilty and sentenced him to crucifixion, the penalty prescribed for action taken "against the Roman people". As usual, the
sentence was to be carried out straight away; and it was normal for the
15 condemned man first to be **flogged,** probably to weaken him so that he
would die more quickly on the cross.

16 **Then the soldiers took him inside the courtyard.** When the Roman
governor came up to Jerusalem from his capital (the port of Caesarea), he normally brought with him his own **company** of troops; the word used here was the technical Greek name for a Roman cohort, consisting of between two hundred and six hundred men. These he will have lodged in the building

[a] Literally "went up" (according to the most probable reading of the manuscripts). Both the sites which have been suggested for the Praetorium were on high ground: see below on John 19.13.

he used as his **headquarters** (*praetorium*), [a] and it is no surprise to find them
here ready to carry out the sentence passed on Jesus. The soldiers themselves
are unlikely to have been either Jews (who were not enlisted for military
service in Palestine) or Romans (who were reserved for the regular legions of
the Roman army), but non-Jewish local men recruited from Palestine and
Syria for the auxiliary forces. They will therefore have had some idea of the
religious and political pretensions of a man who called himself "king of the
Jews", and their mockery of the prisoner was a natural consequence. **They** 17
dressed him in purple—this was the distinctive mark of a monarch in the
eastern part of the empire; **and plaiting a crown of thorns, placed it on**
his head—not a crown in the modern sense, but an insulting travesty of a
wreath such as the Emperor's head always bears on Roman coins. So
dressed, they greeted Jesus with a parody of a royal acclamation, **'Hail,** 18
King of the Jews!'

Then they took him out to crucify him. Crucifixion, though generally 21
regarded as a cruel and barbarous form of execution, was a common enough
sight in Palestine under the Roman administration, since it was the usual
punishment for those who committed violence and insurrection. The **two** 27
bandits (the word was often used for members of armed resistance movements) who were crucified along with Jesus were typical victims of it, and the
fact that Jesus received this penalty proclaimed, as clearly as the inscription
placed on his cross, that the charge against him was political: he had claimed
to be **'The king of the Jews'**. Few details are given in the gospels about 26
how it was carried out, but the traditional representation of the scene is
probably roughly correct: the cross might be in the shape of a T or a †, the
prisoner was fastened to it either with cords or with nails (John 20.25
proves that Jesus' hands and feet had scars from nails). A peg was driven
into the upright of the cross to support the body either between the legs or
under the feet. Elsewhere in the empire the victims were stripped naked;
but in Judaea the Romans may have respected the Jewish abhorrence of
nakedness and allowed a loincloth. All executions, whether Jewish or
Roman, took place outside the city walls (**they took him out** could mean 21
out of the praetorium, or out of the city), but since crucifixions were intended
to be a warning example, they usually took place not far from a city gate, so
that many people would be compelled to see them on their way in or out of
the city (John 19.20 confirms that the place was 'near to the city'). The
traditional site of Jesus' crucifixion, where in the fourth century Constantine
built his great church, is at a spot which, until new city walls were built some
ten years later, would have lain just outside one angle of the walls, a few
hundred yards from one of the gates, in an area which had once been a
quarry but which now held some tombs. A rocky mound jutted up from

[a] On the question where this was, see below on John 19.13.

this area (and still exists inside the present church) which, by its shape,
22 could have suggested the name **'Place of a skull'**; of this name, **Golgotha**
(more correctly *Golgoltha*) is the Aramaic equivalent, and Calvary (*Calvarium*)
the traditional Latin translation. The identification of this spot with the site
of Jesus' crucifixion is by no means certain, but recent archaeological
research has made it seem increasingly probable. In any case, the few details
which are given by the gospels are entirely consistent with what we know
otherwise both about the ancient city of Jerusalem and about the customary
procedure at executions in the Roman empire.

21 **A man called Simon, from Cyrene.** Mark seldom gives the name of
the subsidiary characters in his story, but here he gives not only his name but
his country of origin. There were substantial Jewish settlements in North
Africa, and Simon may have been a Jew who either owned land in Palestine
(and so could be **on his way in from the country**) or who had come up
to Jerusalem for the festival.[a] Mark reveals his reason for naming Simon
when he adds that he was **the father of Alexander and Rufus.** These
names mean nothing to us, but they must have been known to Mark's first
readers. That is to say, the gospel must have been written for use in a
community which counted among its members the children of one of the
witnesses of the crucifixion. If Rufus could be shown to be the same Rufus
as Paul mentions in his letter to the Romans, we could go further and locate
this community at Rome; but the name is fairly common, and Simon's sons
could just as well have belonged to the church in North Africa (which is
another place where Mark's gospel is often thought to have been composed).
They pressed him into service to carry his cross. Criminals on their way
to execution were normally made to carry the cross-beam of their cross
themselves (which is how John's gospel represents Jesus on the way to
Golgotha), but Jesus may already have been too exhausted to carry it the
22 whole way—indeed the Greek word translated **they brought him** is a
rather physical one, and suggests that Jesus was dragged or helped along
rather than simply led under escort.

Two more details are given which again correspond with normal practice.
23 **He was offered drugged wine.** This was an anaesthetic, and was normally
given to Jews before execution; indeed, in view of Proverbs 31.6 ("Give
strong drink to him who is perishing, and wine to those in bitter distress"),
it was thought meritorious to do so, if not actually obligatory, and it was
doubtless Jews—and very likely Jewish women—who offered the anaesthetic
24 to Jesus. On the other hand, those who **divided his clothes among them**
were the soldiers of the execution squad, who had a customary right to them.

[*a*] It is often argued that travelling was not permitted on the first day of the Feast any more than on a Sabbath, and that this detail is a sign that Mark's chronology is artificial, and that (as in John's gospel) the Passover had not yet begun. But "from the country" need not mean a longer distance than was permitted; and in any case, Simon may not have been a Jew at all.

That they should have cast lots **to decide what each should have** sounds perfectly natural; but Mark's language shows that he had in mind a precedent. The author of Psalm 22, writing out of a situation very similar to that of Jesus—that of an innocent man brought to the last degree of suffering and humiliation by his enemies—included the same detail in his description of his own abject circumstances (verse 18):

> "They share out my garments among them
> and cast lots for my clothes."

The hour of the crucifixion was nine in the morning. This trans- 25
lation is correct, but suggests greater precision than perhaps Mark intended. The day was divided into twelve hours between sunrise and sunset (and in a country such as Palestine where the length of the days does not vary more than two or three hours between mid-summer and mid-winter this worked well enough). Ordinary citizens did not use a water-clock or hour-glass to tell which "hour" it was; they looked at the sun, and observed when it was noon (the "sixth hour"), when it was mid-morning (the "third hour"), and when mid-afternoon (the "ninth hour")—and these are the three hours which are in fact most frequently mentioned in the New Testament. The last two were of course approximations: one cannot have more than a rough idea when the sun has got half-way between sunrise and noon, or noon and sunset. Here, Mark says it was "the third hour". If anyone was taking the trouble to find out the correct time by a clock, then this would certainly be equivalent to **nine in the morning**. But there is no reason to think that Mark intended such accuracy. He meant that Jesus was crucified in the middle of the morning, and died in the middle of the afternoon (verse 33). That is to say, Mark spread the main events of Good Friday evenly over the day. John follows a slightly different scheme, and places the crucifixion at midday.

The passers-by hurled abuse at him. Classic descriptions of mockery 29
can be found in the Old Testament. Sometimes it was Jerusalem in ruins which was the object of scorn—"All those who pass by . . . hiss and wag their heads at you" (Lamentations 2.15); sometimes it was a stricken man who had claimed to be pious and good—"All who see me jeer at me, make mouths at me, and wag their heads" (Psalm 22.7); "I have become the victim of their taunts; when they see me, they toss their heads" (Psalm 109.25). Mark uses the conventional vocabulary, but for the content of the taunts he has drawn on earlier scenes from his own narrative—the saying on the temple (14.58), Jesus' "saving" (i.e. healing) of the sick, his assertion that he was the Messiah (14.62). Jesus was subjected in full measure to the insults received by the righteous sufferers of Old Testament poetry.

At midday a darkness fell over the whole land. An eclipse of the sun 33
would have been impossible at full moon, but a dust-storm could have made the day unusually dark—if indeed it was a natural phenomenon that Mark

meant to describe; but the notion that the sun is "darkened" at a great king's death was so common in antiquity, and the expectation that the heavenly bodies would leave their regular courses at a moment of universal crisis, occurred so often in Jewish imaginative writing that we cannot be sure whether Mark was intending to give a literal description of the weather, or a
34 symbolic clue to the unique significance of Jesus' death. The cry, '*Eli, Eli,*
lema sabachthani', represents a quotation from the first line of Psalm 22. The last two words are in Aramaic—and Mark preserves other sayings of Jesus in his own language. *Eli* is more difficult: it certainly means 'My God', but it sounds more like the original Hebrew of the psalm than its Aramaic equivalent (which would be *Elāhi*, when the *ā* might have a sound rather like the "a" in "law", and so be transliterated *Eloi*).[a] On the other hand, this Hebrew form of the word for God is likely to have come quite naturally even to Aramaic-speakers who (unlike Jesus) knew no Hebrew; and if Jesus' cry was mistaken for Elijah (*eliyya*), then it is clear that the one sound that was clearly heard by everyone from his lips was *eli*. Elijah was a figure as much of popular folk-lore as of serious religion. Having been "caught up to heaven" instead of undergoing death, it was widely believed that he was still alive and capable of supernatural interventions in human affairs. A common
35 criminal might well have been thought to be **calling Elijah**. But a disciple
with sharper ears, or a more inspired imagination, explained the cry in a different way. Jesus was entering into the depths of the desolating experience undergone by many righteous sufferers in the Old Testament. Their predicament was a result of the religious presuppositions of their time. (i) God was just, and therefore bound to reward those who served him in perfect uprightness. (ii) This reward must take some visible form, such as health, prosperity and honour: the absence of these could be interpreted by others only as a sign that God was punishing the sufferer for some misdeed. (iii) The reward must be given in this life; after death it would be too late. If a man was convinced of his own innocence before God, and yet found himself in extreme misfortune; if, in addition, he fell ill and knew himself to be in danger of death—then, on these presuppositions, his predicament became agonizing. Everyone around him was drawing the obvious conclusion that he must have somehow deserved his fate. He knew this to be false, but unless God acted soon, his faith in himself, and even in the God whom he served, would be unable to bear the strain, and his mockers and persecutors would have the last word—and there was not much time left: something must happen very soon! This predicament of the righteous sufferer was in

[*a*] Most manuscripts of Mark give the first word in the form *eloi*; but the translators evidently thought that, although Jesus is more likely to have quoted the line as a whole in Aramaic than in Hebrew (which would give *lămā azaphtani*), he must have pronounced the first word *eli* for his cry to be mistaken for *eliyya*. They therefore adopted the reading of a group of manuscripts which gives the same text as in Matthew 27.46, continuing the Hebrew word *Eli* with the remaining words in Aramaic.

fact the classic way in which the problem of evil presented itself to a reflective Jew of the Old Testament period, and it finds one of its most eloquent and agonized expressions in the twenty-second psalm, which describes a whole range of emotions, from near-despair to a triumphant confidence that, despite everything, God would yet bring good out of the present evil. It was the conviction of some witness of the crucifixion that when Jesus uttered the cry '*Eli*' he was experiencing the deepest strain of what we would now call the problem of evil, and confronting it with the spirituality he had inherited from the religious tradition of his own people. He was praying, in his own
language, the prayer of the psalmist, '**My God, my God, why hast thou** 34
forsaken me?'.[a]

A man ran and soaked a sponge. This seems to have been another effect 36
of Jesus' cry. The **sour wine** was probably the cheap drink which soldiers and labourers carried about with them, and it was presumably a soldier who offered it. We cannot be sure what his motive was. The soldiers employed by the Romans in Palestine, though they were not Jews, were probably recruited locally. There would therefore be nothing surprising in this one sharing the popular belief about Elijah and, seeing that Jesus was about to die, endeavouring to prolong his life with a drink in order to see '**if Elijah will come to take him down**'. Alternatively, he may have simply interpreted Jesus' cry as one of physical agony, and had an impulse of pity. There is no reason to doubt that the episode took place; at the same time, when recording it Mark certainly had in mind a verse from another of the "righteous sufferer" psalms (69.20–1):

> "I looked for consolation and received none,
>   for comfort and did not find any.
> They put poison in my food
> and gave me vinegar when I was thirsty."

Then Jesus gave a loud cry and died. And the curtain of the temple 37, 38
was torn in two from top to bottom. The rending of the curtain, like the three hours of darkness, seems to add a touch of the supernatural to what is otherwise a sober and factual account. Admittedly a natural explanation is possible. If the darkness was caused by the *hamsin* wind, which frequently blows in from the desert during April and can bring with it such clouds of dust that there is even a kind of 'darkness over the whole land', then a gust of the same wind (which sometimes reaches gale force) could have split the heavy curtain which was hung over the main eastern porch of the temple.[b] That is to say, it is possible that someone familiar with Palestine

[*a*] That Jesus should have had this experience evidently seemed inconceivable to some Christians at an early period, who altered the text to the form given in the footnote.

[*b*] There was in fact another curtain—a double one—hung over the entrance of the Holy of Holies itself. Mark gives no clue which curtain he means.

would have seen nothing extraordinary about these two events. On the other hand, Mark was not writing for Palestinians, and he nowhere mentions the wind, so that no one who did not know the country could possibly have understood how these things were supposed to have happened. Moreover, we know from the Letter to the Hebrews (10.19–20) that the **curtain of the temple** had symbolic value for Christians: that which separated the Jewish sanctuary (that is, the special dwelling-place of God) from the eyes of all non-Jews was now destroyed by the death of Jesus, who had opened up a direct way to the presence of God for Jews and Gentiles alike. This was certainly one of the ways in which the significance of Jesus' death was very soon understood. It is more foreign to the western mentality than to the eastern to confuse fact with symbol, and it seems to us difficult to take two apparently factual statements ("Jesus died" and "the curtain was torn") in two quite different ways, as if one was prose and the other poetry. But when Jewish tradition reported, for instance, that at the death of a certain famous rabbi "the stars became visible in broad daylight", the statement was meant neither to deceive the credulous nor to be dismissed as a scientific impossibility. It was the author's way of describing the significance of the life and death of the rabbi. So with Mark: he gives, in the guise of a bare fact, a hint of the meaning of Jesus' death on the cross.

39 **The centurion who was standing opposite** was the officer in charge of the execution squad. Again, he was certainly not a Jew, but he may still have been a Palestinian. The manner of Jesus' death elicited from him the comment, '**Truly this man was a son of God.**' "A son of God" has a very different sound (in English) from the phrase with which Mark describes Jesus in the very first sentence of his gospel, 'The Son of God'. In the mouth of the ordinary Greek-speaking citizen of the empire, "son of God" was a way of describing any man (particularly a ruler) who seemed endowed with supernatural powers or blessed with exceptional marks of the divine favour; and the way in which Jesus met his death may have brought this expression to the mind of the centurion. Nevertheless, although the English translation quite legitimately makes the centurion say "a son of God" and not "the Son of God", the Greek words so translated are exactly the same as those with which Mark prefaces his gospel.[a] The saying thus takes on a stronger meaning. That Jesus was the Son of God had become a central article of faith in the church when Mark's gospel was written; but the fact was recognized immediately after his death—by a Gentile.

40 **A number of women were also present.** Mary of Magdala (Magdala being an identifiable site on the north-west shore of the Lake of Galilee) is known to us from Luke 8.2; nothing is known of the other two women named, but it is interesting that Mark identifies them for his readers by connecting

[a] See the footnote in NEB (Second Edition).

them with two other names which were presumably familiar in the Church where his gospel was read. **James the younger** could be James the son of Alphaeus (5.18)—distinguished perhaps by his age from James the son of Zebedee—but there is no proof. **Salome** appears to be identified by Matthew (27.56) as 'the mother of the sons of Zebedee'.

Preparation-day could equally well be translated Friday, the day before 42
the Sabbath. As soon as darkness fell, it would no longer be permitted to do any kind of work, and in strict Jewish eyes the land would be "defiled" (Deuteronomy 21.23) if the body of a Jew was allowed to remain in the place of execution unburied until the next day. A pious and public-spirited Jew
(for whom **a man who looked forward to the kingdom of God** would be 43
a perfectly appropriate description: the phrase itself certainly does not suggest that he was a clandestine Christian,[a] even though Matthew assumes that he was) might understandably be anxious that consciences should not be scandalized by the sight of Jesus' dead body so close to the city. Moreover, the Jews attached great importance to burial: it was esteemed a work of great charity to perform the last duties for a man whose own relatives were not present to do it. **Joseph of Arimathaea** (which was probably, though not certainly, a town about twenty miles north of Jerusalem) therefore **bravely went in to Pilate and asked for the body**. We do not know how far, if at all, the Roman administration was in the habit of accommodating Jewish scruples in such a matter. The usual Roman practice was to leave the dead bodies exposed, and refuse them proper burial. Moreover, victims of crucifixion often took two or three days to die, and indeed **Pilate was surprised** 44
to hear that Jesus **was already dead**, and made certain of the fact before taking any action. However, Joseph's request was granted, and Mark gives a
reason why: he was **a respected member of the Council**. A less influential 43
person (say, a relative of Jesus) might have had no success.

So Joseph bought a linen sheet. The Jews did not bury in coffins, but 46
wrapped the corpse firmly and laid it in one of the numerous rock tombs to be found outside any town in Palestine. Usually the tombs were family tombs, a large chamber in the rock having a number of small cavities carved out of it; and the **entrance** would often be sealed by a massive stone (in more pretentious tombs shaped like a mill-stone and rolling into place along a groove in the rock) that was rolled **against the entrance**. Jesus could not be buried in a family tomb: according to Jewish law, the bones of a criminal defiled those of others; and it was presumably too late in the day to convey him right away from the city to one of the common tombs reserved for criminals. So Joseph gave him a rapid burial in a tomb that happened to be empty near by.

That Jesus rose from the dead on "the third day" (that is to say, by the inclusive reckoning generally used in the ancient world, on the Sunday

[a] Luke uses a similar phrase in 2.38, where it cannot possibly mean "Christian".

following the Friday on which he was put to death) was the central point in all the preaching of the early church; and we can tell from the sermons and the summaries of the Christian faith which are recorded in the New Testament (especially 1 Corinthians 15.3–6) that they based this startling assertion on the evidence of those who had actually seen the risen Christ, either on that first Sunday, or on one of the days which followed. This was the evidence on which the first Christians rested their faith: after his crucifixion and his burial, Jesus was seen by a number of reliable witnesses under circumstances which made them say, not that they had seen a ghost, or that Jesus had "come back" from the dead, or even that his death had been an illusion, but that he had now entered upon a new and glorious mode of existence of which they had had visible and tangible evidence, and which, using contemporary religious language, they described in terms of Jesus having "risen from the dead". Now it is true that, to the Jew, "resurrection" meant the calling back to life of a person complete with his mortal body—transformed, no doubt, and adapted to a supernatural existence, but still recognizably his own. It followed that, if Jesus had indeed "risen from the dead", his body must already have undergone this transformation, and that his tomb would be empty. But the absence of Jesus' body from the tomb was apparently never regarded as the main evidence for the resurrection—it was, after all, capable of other explanations: the body might have been removed, or stolen. The whole weight of the Christians' case was placed upon the testimony of those who had actually seen that Jesus was alive, "risen from the dead"; and this short paragraph in Mark's gospel is the earliest reference in Christian literature to the fact that, on Sunday morning, the tomb was found to be empty.

Why was this fact not immediately seized upon and proclaimed? The
gospel writers seem to have been conscious of this question, and to have
16. 8 suggested different answers. Mark says that the women kept it a secret: **they
said nothing to anybody, for they were afraid.** Luke says that, on the
contrary, they told the disciples, but were not believed (Luke 24.11).
Matthew says that the authorities tried to cover up the fact by spreading the
story that the body had been stolen (Matthew 28.11–15). And a further
reason can be suggested: the first Christians rested their case on the evidence
of witnesses, and in a Jewish court women were not permitted to give
evidence. The report brought back from the tomb by the three women
would have been of little use to them as a formal proof of Jesus' resurrection.

Moreover, Mark's narrative contains some peculiar details. First: it was
1 probably a regular custom to **anoint** a corpse as part of the preparation for
burial, and this was doubtless omitted by Joseph of Arimathaea, who had no
time to give Jesus more than a hasty burial. But thirty-six hours had passed
since Jesus' death. It was too late to do it now. Secondly: the time of their
2 arrival is a little obscure. **Very early on the Sunday morning** ought to

mean before sunrise (**the Sabbath was over** at sunset the previous evening), 1
and **just after sunrise** appears to be a somewhat clumsy correction. 2
Thirdly: since they knew that the tomb was closed by a heavy stone, their
whole enterprise sounds curiously unrealistic. On the other hand, the scene
which Mark goes on to describe can easily be imagined taking place in a
typical Jewish tomb. Once the **stone . . . had been rolled back** along the 4
vertical face of the rock, an aperture would have been revealed. Through this,
the women **went into the tomb**—a large rock chamber, with small tunnels 5
opening out of it for individual burials. They would not have known which
of these openings was used for Jesus' burial; but the angel (conventionally
described as **a youth . . ., wearing a white robe**) pointed it out to them: 6
'Look, there is the place where they laid him'. The angel then repeated
Jesus' prediction about Galilee (see above on 14.28), and the scene ends with
the understandable **terror** of the women. 8

For they were afraid. These words, according to a number of important
manuscripts, are the last words of the gospel. It is certain that the following
paragraphs, which occur in some manuscripts, are not by the same author.
Even in English, the phrase, **the sacred and imperishable message of** 8
eternal salvation is recognizably un-Marcan: it belongs to the theological
language of the later church, and is quite unlike the idiom of Mark's sober
narrative; and the longer ending (verses 9–20) is mainly a summary of episodes that are reported in other places, and betrays in its details the hand of a later editor.[a]

Did Mark intend to end his gospel on this note of fear and uncertainty, or has the original ending of his book been accidentally lost? On this question opinion is still divided, and there is no evidence to support a decision. One point can be made: we know how books normally ended in the ancient world, and if Mark meant to finish his work with the words, **for they were afraid,** he was doing something very unusual. But then this would not be the only respect in which his gospel is a very remarkable book.

[*a*] Verses 9–11: cf. John 20.14–18; Luke 24.11. Verses 12–13: cf. Luke 24.13–35. Verse 14: cf. Luke 24.36–43. Verse 15: cf. Matthew 28.16–20. Verse 16 suggests a later conception of baptism (and the confession of faith which accompanies baptism) as a guarantee of salvation. Verses 17–18: casting out devils and healing the sick are powers given to the disciples in the gospels (Mark 6.12–13), speaking in strange tongues is referred to in Acts and the letters of Paul, handling snakes is reminiscent of Acts 28.3–6, and drinking poison without coming to harm occurs in a number of second-century legends. Verses 19–20 are a general summary of the first chapters of Acts.

THE GOSPEL ACCORDING TO LUKE

1. 1 **The Author to Theophilus.** With this introductory phrase (which does not stand, as such, in the Greek original) the NEB allows one to see at a glance that the first four verses of this gospel are what we should now call a preface. It is the preface to the writings of the author whose name tradition has preserved as Luke, and who may in fact (though we cannot be sure of it) have been the same person as 'Luke the doctor' (Colossians 4.14), the friend and companion of Paul. Then as now, writing a preface was a literary convention. But the books of the New Testament were written for religious, not literary purposes; it is only here, and at the beginning of Acts (which is the second part of Luke's work), that any kind of preface occurs. Immediately, Luke presents himself to us as someone unusual among the New Testament writers: a conscious literary stylist (this opening paragraph is a smooth and polished piece of Greek prose), ready to make use of the conventions of the world of letters.

Greek historians took it for granted that their work should begin with a
preface explaining the writer's purpose and methods; and Luke, who certainly felt himself to be writing a chapter of world history, followed the same
convention. Moreover, however wide a readership a book was intended for,
it was customary to dedicate it to a personal friend or an influential acquaintance. Luke's preface, though it is shorter and less fulsome than most, is
entirely in the spirit of his age. But this conformity to convention also makes
it impossible for us to draw any precise conclusions from his language.
Theophilus could be almost anyone—Greek, Roman or Jew, pagan or
3 Christian, senior civil servant or private gentleman (**your Excellency**
suggests a person of some rank, but the Greek word was a very general term
1 of respect). **Many writers** could be a rhetorical exaggeration of the fact that
Mark, and possibly Matthew, had already completed their gospels; or it
could be an indication that far more accounts of the gospel story were
current in Luke's day than have survived to ours. And Luke's own decision
3 **to write a connected narrative** of these events could be due to a desire to
improve on the work of his predecessors, an anxiety to refute false information that had been coming to the ears of inquirers such as Theophilus, or
simply a sense that there was a need for a third "gospel" based, as such
2 history ought to be, on **the traditions handed down to us by the original**
eyewitnesses. The language of the preface does not allow us to decide
between these possibilities. But the fact that Luke wrote such a preface at all,
and moreover that he extended his work (through his "Acts of the Apostles")

to embrace the story of the spread of Christianity from Jerusalem to Rome, shows that he was aware of tackling a more ambitious task than the other gospel writers, and that, unlike them, he had at his disposal many of the techniques and the literary conventions of the professional Greek historian.

The coming of Christ

In the days of Herod king of Judaea. By contrast with the Hellenistic 5
polish of the preface, and indeed with the historical precision Luke shows
elsewhere (see especially 3.1), the narrative begins in a way more reminiscent
of the Old Testament than of contemporary history books. Herod the Great
reigned for over thirty years, and died in 4 B.C. So Luke's indication of date
is extremely vague. On the other hand, "in the days of so-and-so king of
Judah" is a standard Old Testament formula for introducing an episode in
the history of the Jewish kingdoms, and this is only the first of many touches
by which Luke, in these first two chapters, gives an Old Testament atmosphere to his narrative.[a]

**There was a priest named Zechariah, of the division of the priest-
hood called after Abijah.** The ritual of the temple in Jerusalem was performed by members of all the families which could trace their ancestry back
to Aaron and who formed the priestly class in Jewish society. Twenty-four
such families had returned from the exile, each tracing its descent back to one
of the grandsons of Aaron (one of whom was **Abijah**), and each of these
families (or "divisions of the priesthood") still existed as a distinct clan in
some part of Judaea and Galilee, and twice a year took responsibility for a
week's duty in the temple. The whole clan took up residence in Jerusalem
for its week's duty, and the several families of the clan each took responsibility
for one day of the week, casting lots on the morning of the day to determine
the duty of each individual. Luke was evidently well acquainted with this
system, and was able to show how it came about that Zechariah was offici-
ating in the temple on a particular day. **It was the turn of his division,** 8
that is, it was one of the two weeks in the year when his clan attended the
temple; **he was there to take part in divine service,** that is, it was the day
appointed for the family to which he belonged; and **it fell to his lot** to be 9
the individual who on that day received the coveted privilege **to enter the
sanctuary of the Lord and offer the incense.**

[a] Most of these touches are linguistic, and can hardly be reproduced in translation. Sometimes, indeed, the idioms are more Semitic than Greek, and many believe that Luke's infancy narratives are a translation of a Hebrew or Aramaic original. But phrases thoroughly characteristic of Luke also occur, and it is at least as likely that Luke, who could in any case write in more than one style, is here composing the story in language modelled mainly upon the Greek translation of the Old Testament.

Twice a day, morning and evening, a lamb was sacrificed and burnt at the
10 altar before the temple. **The hour of the incense offering** came just before
this sacrifice in the morning, and just after it in the evening (we cannot tell
whether morning or evening is meant here): it was the moment when the
chosen priest left his two assistants outside by the altar and entered **the
sanctuary.** This was the first room in the temple proper, being a kind of
anteroom to the Most Holy Place (which only the High Priest could enter,
and that only on one day of the year). Here stood a small altar for burning
incense; and the mysterious sanctity of the place, combined with the smoke
of the incense and the complete solitude of the priest, made this moment a
particularly likely one for visions and intimations of the divine. Certainly
many stories are told in Jewish literature of similar experiences in the temple;
so much so, that **the people** who were waiting outside (who were probably
laymen from the district where the clan lived, come to worship with their
own priests) had little doubt what had happened when Zechariah stayed so
long inside and was unable to give them the customary blessing when he
22 emerged from the sanctuary: **they realized that he had had a vision.**
13 **'Your prayer has been heard'.** A divine intervention, granting the birth
of a child to a woman who had been barren and was now past the age of
childbearing, was a feature of many Old Testament stories; and these stories
often included the apparition of an angel and a supernatural intimation of the
name which the child was to bear. Almost all the details of Luke's narrative
(and much of the actual language) can be found in one or other of these Old
Testament stories, and a comparison of these shows how deeply Luke was
influenced by such precedents.[a] But this is not to say that his own combination of these conventional elements was simply due to his imagination;
for certain known facts about the subsequent life of John the Baptist, if not
a reliable tradition about the circumstances of his birth, must have suggested
to him that it would be true of John (as it had been true of Samson and
15 certain other Old Testament persons[b]) that he would be sworn **never to
touch wine or strong drink**; that, like an Old Testament prophet, he
would be **filled with the Holy Spirit,** and this **from his very birth;**[c]
and that he would be a figure fulfilling many of the prophecies and
17 expectations which had gathered round the name of **Elijah** (see above on
Mark 9.11).
19 Again, that the angel was **Gabriel** (the angel-messenger *par excellence*
since his appearance in the Book of Daniel), that Zechariah asked for a sign
18 (**'How can I be sure of this?'**), and that he was rewarded (or punished)

[*a*] Compare especially Genesis 17.15–21; 18.4–15 (the promise of the birth of Isaac to Abraham and Sarah), Judges 13 (Samson), 1 Samuel 1 (Samuel).
[*b*] Such as Rechabites (Jeremiah 35) and Nazirites (Numbers 6).
[*c*] The Greek is a biblical idiom, which can mean from the moment of conception. Luke may have seen the stirring of the baby in the womb (1.41) as the first proof that John was filled with the Spirit.

with temporary loss of speech, are all typical elements of this kind of story;[a]
but this hardly affects the question whether Luke's story is legend or truth.
Experiences of this kind, whether true or fictitious, tend to fall into a certain
pattern. Some eye witness may well have remembered the vivid moment
when Zechariah **stood there making signs to them, and remained** 22
dumb, even if the rest of the story is the writer's attempt to make explicit
what was essentially an incommunicable experience.

Failure to bear children was keenly felt by Jewish women as a cause of
'reproach among men', and Elizabeth's thankful reaction is the same as 25
that of Rachel when, after years of barrenness, she gave birth to Joseph: "God
has taken away my reproach" (Genesis 30.23). Why did Elizabeth then live
in seclusion for five months? We know of no custom that would have 24
obliged her to do so; but her seclusion gives added point to the surprise of the
meeting which took place between her and Mary **in the sixth month.** 26

Woven into the story of the strange circumstances of John the Baptist's
birth is the story of the birth of Jesus. This too comprises a supernatural
message and a miraculous birth, but it no longer recalls the stories of Jewish
literature and folklore, since it culminates in a happening which was unique
and unparalleled, [b] the birth of a child whose mother was a virgin. Matthew
and Luke are the only New Testament writers who explicitly mention this.
Matthew simply states it in a single sentence, with very little comment. Luke,
on the other hand, devotes a whole paragraph to it, and his account is clearly
intended to give some explanation of its meaning. He introduces the scene
very carefully. Mary was **a girl betrothed to a man named Joseph.** The 27
Greek word translated **girl** has traditionally been translated "virgin", and
it is true that it often meant this; but it was also one of the commonest words
for "girl", and there is no reason to think that Luke intends to stress Mary's
virginity at this stage of the story. Mary is introduced simply as a young
fiancée, already legally committed to her future husband, but not yet living
with him. Unlike Zechariah, who received his vision when performing a
ritual act in a holy place, Mary is no one in particular and has done nothing
special, and the words of the angel's greeting seem to recognize this: **'most** 28
favoured one'—the phrase shows that God has regarded her with exceptional favour, not that there is necessarily anything in her to have drawn the
favour upon herself. How will this divine favour be shown? The angel's
answer still holds back the critical point: for the present, he simply promises
to Mary a son who will be qualified to bear the titles and attributes of many

[*a*] Asking for a sign: Genesis 15.8. Dumbness: Daniel 10.15. Paul was similarly struck blind for a while, Acts 9.9. Compare the temporary blindness of Elymas, Acts 13.11.

[*b*] In Greek mythology there are numerous stories of unions between an immortal God and a mortal woman. But Luke's account shows no traces of influence from such sources. The setting is entirely Jewish, and Jewish traditions knew nothing of such things. Any miraculous birth always involved a human father. So far as Luke and his readers were concerned, Jesus' birth was absolutely unique.

of the great figures of Old Testament history and prophecy, and who will be
32 a worthy successor of **his ancestor** (through Joseph) **David.** (The angel's
words are a tissue of scriptural allusions: compare especially Genesis 16.11,
Isaiah 9.7, Micah 4.7.) Such promises had been made to women in the past.
34 **'How can this be?' said Mary; 'I am still a virgin.'** Mary's reaction
is puzzling. She is about to be married, and can expect to have a son; and it
is necessary to read a good deal into the text if we are to find there some
reason for Mary thinking it impossible that she should give birth to a child.[a]
However, the difficulty disappears if we ask, not why Mary should have said
these words, but why Luke placed them in her mouth. From the story-teller's
point of view, the question has a clear purpose: it is the cue[b] for the angel's
35 decisive declaration that the child is to have no human father at all. **'The
Holy Spirit will come upon you, and the power of the Most High will
overshadow you'.** Matthew says simply that Mary became 'with child by
the Holy Spirit'. Luke uses some more poetic and suggestive idioms to convey
the proposition that God would himself take the place of a human father,
and that the child would therefore be, in a unique and literal sense, "Son of
God". Mary's apparently naïve question is the key to the whole mystery:
to have this child she will not need, physically, to cease being a virgin.
36 **'Moreover . . .'** In the Old Testament, the recipients of divine promises
commonly ask for a "sign". Mary does not ask; but a sign is given. **'Your
kinswoman[c] Elizabeth has herself conceived a son in her old age.'**
When Mary has seen this, she will have no difficulty in believing that for her,
37 as for Elizabeth, **'God's promises can never fail'** (a phrase from Exodus
13.12).
39 In response, Mary went **straight** (the Greek implies haste and determination) to visit Elizabeth. **A town in the uplands of Judah** is probably
intentionally vague, Judah being the old tribal name for the mountainous
area around Jerusalem; it implies no more than that Mary took the angel's
message seriously enough to make a three days' journey south from Galilee.
Her purpose was presumably to confirm the angel's words by seeing for
45 herself that Elizabeth was pregnant. This, at least, was proof of her **faith
that the Lord's promise would be fulfilled,** and would have been sufficient
to elicit Elizabeth's blessing. But the coincidence of the baby stirring in
Elizabeth's womb at the moment of Mary's arrival gave the scene a new turn.
41 **Elizabeth was filled with the Holy Spirit**—Luke's way of describing a
sudden gift of prophecy—and declared that her baby had not merely stirred,

[*a*] It has been suggested that Mary had made a vow of virginity; or that she understood the angel to mean that she was to conceive immediately. But there is no support for such explanations in the text.

[*b*] Luke is fond of introducing such "cues". Compare 13.23; 17.37; 3.10, 14 and elsewhere.

[*c*] The word is very vague. It could mean belonging to the same nation, or the same tribe within the nation, or the same family within the tribe. We do not know what the relationship was.

it had **leapt for joy**. The Greek word used for **joy** here was rich with scrip- 44
tural overtones: it suggested the joy of the people of God in the presence of their long-awaited Lord, the Messiah.

And Mary said. The narrative is interrupted by a song of praise. There 46
was good precedent for this. In Old Testament narratives, when a barren woman was granted her prayer for a child, she was often found to break out in a cry of joy and thanksgiving. The finest example is in 1 Samuel 2: when Hannah was at last blest with a son, she uttered a song which fills a whole page of text, and which is so similar in tone to Mary's song that the one can hardly be regarded as completely independent of the other. Yet Hannah's great song is anything but personal; it is mostly a hymn on the justice and the mercies of God, with barely a word that bears upon Hannah's own situation—so much so, that it is quite possible that the verses originally had an independent existence, and were only subsequently inserted into the story of Hannah. Very much the same is true of Mary's song here. The greater part of it is concerned with themes which occur again and again in the psalms and in later Hebrew poetry: the fidelity of God to his people, and the ultimate vindication of the cause of the poor and oppressed against the proud and the rich. Almost every phrase occurs at one place or another in the Greek translation of the Old Testament, there is not a word in it that is distinctively Christian, and barely a sentence which is characteristic of Luke. To all intents and purposes, the song is a beautiful example of a Jewish psalm. As such, there is no reason why it should not have risen spontaneously to the lips of the joyful mother-to-be. But equally (if one concedes that Luke was writing up the scene fairly freely), it could have been inserted by the writer to comply with the convention that the apparently miraculous gift of a child should be answered by a cry of praise.

But who sang the song? It was Elizabeth, not Mary, who was in the classic situation of one whose "reproach" of barrenness had been taken away, and some manuscripts actually give her name in this verse. Moreover, there is one point at which the song seems to become personal, and to spring from the events which have just been narrated:

> **'so tenderly has he looked upon his servant,** 48
> **humble as she is.'**

This last phrase could mean literally, "her humiliation". And who has been "humiliated"? Not Mary, but Elizabeth, who has borne the reproach of barrenness all her life. In short, were no name given in the text for the singer of the song (which may indeed originally have been the case, later copyists adding one name or the other as they thought best), we should probably not hesitate to ascribe it to Elizabeth, and to regard those few manuscripts which give her name in verse 46 as having correctly divined the original intention of the writer.

However, the last of these arguments is double-edged. "Humiliation" is a correct translation in verse 48, but so is "humility", and in so far as the song is a typical utterance of that strain of Jewish piety which fervently believed in the blessedness and ultimate vindication of the poor, the meek and the humble, the speaker could just as well be anyone (or any group of people) who belonged to that class. Mary, just as much as Elizabeth, is to be imagined as an upright and "humble" person to whom God had shown particular favour; therefore the translators (though not without hesitation) decided to abide by the traditional ascription of the song to Mary. The song is throughout in general but fervent terms. If it does not allude specifically to this moment in Mary's life, it is nevertheless a fine expression of what she may have been feeling. Its spirituality, though entirely Jewish in origin, has a universal quality which, since early centuries, has won for it a firm place in the worship of the Christian church.

57 **Now the time came for Elizabeth's child to be born.** Luke is very soon
to recount the circumstances surrounding the birth of Jesus: but the way he
has chosen to weave together the strands of the two stories makes it necessary
for him to balance this by first working in the birth of John. The main interest of this story lay in the apparently inexplicable agreement of the child's
parents to call him John. This was a miracle, sufficient for those who wit-
65 nessed it to be **struck with awe.** The impressiveness of the story is marred
by the banality of the language in the NEB translation. Luke is here still
writing in the idiom of the Greek Old Testament, and thus imparting more
solemnity to these events than the English version conveys.

59 **On the eighth day.** This was the normal time for circumcision (Leviticus
12.3), but it is a little surprising to find a Jewish family at this date naming
the child (as the Greeks did) when a week or so old instead of at birth. It was
by no means invariable to call a child after its father, even in a priestly
family; in fact it was more common to call it after its grandfather. But
60 doubtless if the name **John** (which had been fairly popular since the time of
the Maccabees) had never been given to a member of this family, the sudden
consensus of mother and father must have seemed striking, particularly since
the narrator seems to assume that, since his vision in the temple, Zechariah
had been not just dumb, but deaf and dumb. (In Greek, a single word meant
deaf-and-dumb, and was often used for either affliction.)

67 **And Zechariah his father was filled with the Holy Spirit and uttered
this prophecy.** Another song of praise, this time with rather more allusion
to the events of the gospel, and therefore justly called a **prophecy**—prophesying was regarded by Luke, as by Jewish writers of the period, as the characteristic manifestation of **the Holy Spirit.** Perhaps it makes little difference whether the words go back to Zechariah's own inspiration, whether they were composed for the purpose by Luke, or whether they

originally had an independent existence as a hymn and were incorporated and perhaps adapted by Luke. This song, like Mary's, is a typical example of Jewish religious poetry, with only small touches added to bring it into line with Christian experience in general and with the story of John the Baptist in particular. Its style, accumulating clause upon clause with little regard for logic or syntax, is reminiscent of some of the psalms in the Bible, and still more of the psalms composed during the century before the birth of Christ and known as the "Psalms of Solomon". Its language, like that of Mary's song, is impregnated with scriptural idioms. Its content departs little
from the mainstream of Jewish piety. Thus the first stanza[a] is a typical 68–9
expression of the old Jewish hope that God would "raise up" a deliverer.
For Luke's readers, this hope had now been fulfilled by Jesus in a startlingly
unexpected form; but the language used here is still perfectly traditional. The
second and third stanzas dwell on God's promises that he would guarantee 70–5
to his own people a land of their own in which they would dwell in safety
and peace. And the last stanza returns to the theme of the promised Messiah
(for whom **the morning sun from heaven** had become an almost technical 78
expression). Only verses 76–7 bear on John the Baptist, who was to be **the** 76
Lord's forerunner, and to baptize for **the forgiveness of . . . sins.** 77

As the child grew up. Luke had nothing further to record between 80
John's infancy and his public appearance some thirty years later. But he could infer that John, being a prophet, must during that time have become **strong in spirit** (for prophecy was a gift of the Spirit of God), and also that his appearance in the wilderness was prepared for by a long ascetic apprenticeship **in the wilds.**[b]

In those days a decree was issued by the Emperor Augustus. One of 2. 1
the innovations of Augustus was to replace the existing somewhat haphazard
system of taxation in the provinces of the Roman empire by a uniform
system based on a census of the population in each province. This policy
gradually became effective **throughout the Roman world**; but we happen
to know, independently of Luke's gospel, when it was applied to Judaea.
Archelaus, one of Herod the Great's sons, ruled over Judaea from his father's
death until A.D. 6, when he was banished by Augustus and his kingdom
became part of the Roman province of Syria. This was the moment to introduce the new system of taxation, and it fell to **Quirinius,** who became 2
governor of Syria in that year, to carry it out. This imposition of direct
taxation was exceedingly unpopular, and actually caused a minor revolt. It

[a] According to the NEB arrangement; but many arrangements are possible. The Greek text has no clear divisions.

[b] There is a certain similarity between the teaching and activity of John and the ideals of the community which produced the Dead Sea Scrolls; but beyond this there is no evidence that he was in any way associated with that community. It is quite possible that during his years in the wilds he came in contact with it; but this remains pure speculation.

was the **first registration of its kind** in Judaea, and it was not liable to be quickly forgotten (Luke in fact refers to it again in Acts 5.37).

If, therefore, Luke intended to provide his narrative at this point with a date (as he does at the beginning of chapter 3), then there can be no doubt that the date in question was A.D. 6–7. But this date causes difficulties. In the next chapter (3.23) Luke says that Jesus was "about 30 years old" in A.D. 28–9. This is probably only approximate; nevertheless, if Jesus was born in A.D. 6–7 he would have been only twenty-two in 28–9, which is rather young for him to be described as "about thirty". Moreover Matthew places Jesus' birth in the lifetime of Herod the Great (that is, before 4 B.C.), and Luke himself states that John the Baptist, who was only six months older than Jesus, was born 'in the days of Herod king of Judaea' (1.5). Luke's date here (A.D. 6–7) seems about ten years too late.

But it is far from certain that Luke is concerned to specify a date at this point. At the beginning of this paragraph he is still using scriptural language:
1 the vague phrase, **in those days**, is typical of the style. His interest in
chronology begins only with the very elaborate dating in the next chapter (3.1–2). Here he mentions the census in order to explain how it came about that Jesus of Nazareth, a Galilean, was born at Bethlehem, a village situated in another part of the country altogether. His explanation is at first sight quite plausible. Although a census of this kind was normally based upon people's actual place of residence, not on their ancestral town, at least one other part of the Roman empire is known where subjects had to register according to their place of birth; and this may have been the case in Judaea. And the explanation may have appealed to Luke on other grounds also: it enabled him to establish a direct connection between the birth of Jesus and an act of the supreme ruler of the Mediterranean world—the gospel story is presented, right from the start, as a chapter of world history. But was there in fact such a census at the time when Jesus was born? There are reasons for doubting whether it could have taken place while Herod the Great or his son Archelaus still ruled Judaea; there is no other record of a census before that of A.D. 6–7, and it is not at all easy to fit Quirinius into the picture some ten years before his only recorded governorship of Syria. If Luke is writing serious history at this point, we ought perhaps to be ready to take his word for all this; but if he is merely working a memory of Quirinius' famous census into his narrative in an attempt to explain the circumstances of Jesus' birth, we must be prepared to admit that, from a historical point of view, he has fallen into error.

7 **She wrapped him in his swaddling clothes, and laid him in a manger.** The manger is the pivot of the story. Already in the gospel there have been two interventions by angels, and each of them has ended with the promise of a sign. This third intervention follows exactly the same pattern, and the sign consists in the new-born baby being found **wrapped in his**

swaddling clothes (i.e. in a tight little bundle, as is still the custom of Arab
women), **in a manger.** Why was the baby in such an unusual place? Luke
offers a thoroughly practical reason: **because there was no room for them** 7
to lodge in the house. The words, **to lodge,** do not occur in the Greek, and
may give a misleading impression. In the east, it is unlikely that travellers
would have been refused "lodging", either in a private house or in an inn;
but it is possible that all the houses were too crowded to offer Mary a room
to herself for having her baby, in which case a shed or a cave[a] used for
sheltering cattle might have been the best the village could provide—thus
giving fulfilment to the angel's "sign". For what really impressed the
shepherds was this miraculous confirmation of the angel's words: **it had all** 20
happened as they had been told. It is only by the way that Luke works in
some deeper comment on the event. The angel proclaimed that the baby
would be **deliverer** (saviour), **Messiah,** and **Lord,** titles which Jesus hardly 11
bore in his lifetime on earth, but which the church was soon to ascribe to him;
and the event (like the fulfilment of each of the previous "signs") was the
cue for another song of praise, this time quite brief and sung by the angels.
One of the main blessings of the age of the Messiah—so it was believed—
would be **on earth his peace,** to be enjoyed by all those whom God had 14
chosen to benefit from it. To Jewish readers this would have meant the Jews;
but Luke was writing for Christians, who now knew that there existed a
much wider company of **men on whom his favour rests.**[b]

Eight days later. Luke shows himself to be thoroughly conversant with 21
everything that was **customary under the Law** for Jewish parents after 27
the birth of a first male child, and he seems to lay great emphasis (by stating
it three times, verses 22, 27 and 39) on the fact that Jesus' parents meticu-
lously fulfilled all the legal requirements. First, after eight days, came circumcision and naming (as with John the Baptist, 1.59). Then, forty days after
childbirth (during which she remained at home awaiting her **purification**)[c] 22
the mother had to offer a sacrifice of a lamb (which, in the case of poorer
people, was remitted to **a pair of turtle doves or two young pigeons,** 24
Leviticus 12.8), after which the priest declared her "clean". A further
obligation arose when the child was the mother's first-born and a male; for

[*a*] There is a tradition, dating back to at least the second century, that Jesus was born in a cave. Constantine's great church at Bethlehem was also built over a cave, but this is indecisive: caves very commonly attracted such traditions anyway. A certain cave on the mount of Olives soon became associated with many episodes in the life of Jesus.

[*b*] The traditional rendering, "goodwill towards men", is of a manuscript reading which is less likely to be original (see NEB footnote). "Men of goodwill" is a possible, but unlikely, translation.

[*c*] **Their purification** is puzzling. Luke's phrase is taken straight from the Old Testament (Leviticus 12.6), where it means, "when the days of (i.e. preliminary to) purifying were completed". The difficulty is in Luke's addition of the word **their.** It was only to the mother that these requirements applied. On the other hand, Joseph and the baby could be regarded as ritually "unclean" through contact with her, and their presence at the temple sacrifice may have been necessary.

23 it was a very old and strong religious principle in Judaism that '**every first-**
born male shall be deemed to belong to the Lord' (Exodus 13.2). In
primitive times this probably meant that every family had its own priest; but
later it was applied literally only to the descendants of Aaron and Levi (the
priests and the Levites), and all other families "redeemed" their first-born
sons from temple duties by paying a tax of five silver pieces (Numbers 18. 15–
16). But Luke mentions no such payment here; instead, the parents of Jesus
22 **brought him up to Jerusalem to present him to the Lord.** It looks as if
Luke is offering a special interpretation of the rule about first-born males:
23 this particular baby was '**to belong to the Lord**' in a unique sense. It was
therefore inappropriate to "redeem" him from the Lord's service by a payment: he must on the contrary be taken to the temple to be "presented" to
27 the Lord. Thus everything was done **as prescribed in the law**—but with a
highly significant difference.

25 **There was at that time in Jerusalem a man called Simeon.** Two
further witnesses are called (so to speak) to give their evidence that the birth
of Jesus was of unique significance. The first was a man **upright and devout,**
qualified by his blameless life, like Zechariah and his wife (1.6), to play a
small part in these critical events. He was also **one who watched and**
waited for the restoration of Israel, that is to say, he believed with an
exceptional earnestness and eagerness that the glorious destiny which God
had promised for his people (the Greek word meaning "consolation" was
almost a technical term for this, and so may perhaps be translated **restora-**
tion) was shortly to come to pass, and like many of his contemporaries he
25, 26 expected the herald of this to be **the Lord's Messiah. The Holy Spirit was**
upon him, giving him, not just guidance and supernatural knowledge, but
above all the gift of prophecy; and when he recognized that the moment
had come for which he had been living, he gave his prophetic testimony in
the form of the last of the songs with which Luke adorns this part of his
gospel. The song begins quite personally: the sight of the baby gives Simeon
29 his **discharge,** and he can now die **in peace.** But to describe what the baby
31 is, language and imagery are borrowed from Isaiah: the promised **deliver-**
ance (Isaiah 40.5) is not only for Israel, but will shine forth far beyond the
32 confines of the Jewish religion as **a light that will be a revelation to the**
heathen (Isaiah 42.6). Yet this Messiah by no means conforms to the
popular image of a figure of glory and power: the story is to have its darker
35 side. Simeon adds some enigmatic oracles addressed to the parents, which
Luke doubtless intends the reader to solve for himself as the gospel unfolds.

36 The second witness is a **prophetess.** The official view in Judaism was
that the gift of prophecy had ceased with the last of the Old Testament
prophets, and would only be revived in the new age with the coming of the
Messiah. But in Jesus the Messiah had come; and so Luke presents the

revival of prophecy as one of the signs accompanying his birth. What this
meant was by no means clear to all; but those **who were looking for the** 38
liberation of Jerusalem (another almost technical expression for this new
age) would have been alive to the significance of Anna's prophetic words
about the child.

When he was twelve. Nothing is said in any of the other gospels about 42
the years which Jesus spent in Nazareth. But Luke, who has just hinted at
the kind of training received by John the Baptist (1.80), provides an anecdote
which does the same for Jesus. To anyone familiar with Greek culture, it was
axiomatic that these early years would be devoted to education: accordingly
Luke reports that Jesus grew **full of wisdom,** and the story of Jesus' 40
precocity can be paralleled from the biographies of many famous figures of
antiquity. But Jesus' learning was of an entirely Jewish character. In Hebrew
culture "wisdom" consisted of an understanding of the ways of God as
revealed in Scripture, and there can be no doubt that the questions being
discussed by the twelve-year-old boy and **the teachers** in one of the colon- 46
naded courts of the temple turned upon the interpretation of certain passages of the Old Testament: Jesus had already learned enough in the local
synagogue in Nazareth to be able to hold his own with the scholars of the
capital. The occasion was a Passover pilgrimage to Jerusalem, which was
often made in family groups; but Jesus' answer already betrays a loyalty
stronger even than to his family. For him, the temple was not just "God's
house", it was **'my Father's house'.**[a] But addressing God as one's own 49
"Father" made little sense to ordinary people. Even his parents **did not** 50
understand what he meant.

There is now a lapse of time; and in the manner of a professional historian
Luke carefully fixes the date at which his story comes within the range of
world history. The commonly received system of dating throughout the
Roman empire was by the year of the reigning Emperor. So here: **in the** 3. 1
fifteenth year of the Emperor Tiberius, A.D. 28–9. This sounds, to
modern ears, as precise and reliable an indication as one could wish. But in antiquity an accurate chronology was a great deal more difficult to obtain than it is now, and historians often liked to provide some chronological cross-references at the beginning of their work. Luke's list is not exceptional, though it is unusually detailed, and it also serves to fill out the picture of the political conditions of the time. After the death of Herod the Great (4 B.C.) his kingdom had been divided into four, each part being governed by a *tetrarch*, which means "ruler of a fourth part". It was this word *tetrarch* (always translated **prince** in the NEB) which perhaps led Luke to specify, for the sake of completeness, the ruler of each of the four parts. Judaea, after

[a] The old translation, "about my father's business", is much less likely to be the meaning of the Greek phrase, though this is admittedly imprecise.

the unsuccessful reign of its first tetrarch, Archelaus, had come directly
under Roman rule in A.D. 6 and was governed by a Roman official called,
first, a *praefectus* and subsequently a *procurator*. Pontius Pilate held this
office from A.D. 26 to 36, and Luke gives him the general title that was used
in Greek for such officials, **governor. Herod** (Antipas, son of Herod the
Great) became tetrarch of Galilee and Peraea ('Transjordan') at his father's
death, and remained in power until A.D. 39. Philip, another of Herod's sons,
ruled his tetrarchy in the north-east until A.D. 33. **Abilene,** the northernmost
part of Herod's original kingdom, lay in the Lebanon, and we know little
about its history; but there is no serious reason to doubt Luke's statement
that its ruler's name was **Lysanias.** Luke then completes the picture with
2 the **high-priesthood.** Only one high priest held office at a time: he normally
presided over the supreme Jewish Council (the Sanhedrin) in Jerusalem. The
high priest in this year was Caiaphas; but Annas, his father-in-law, had also
held the office from A.D. 6 to 15, and he probably still exercised so much
influence that Luke may have thought it right to couple his name with that of
Caiaphas.

2 **The word of God came to John.** The phrase is an Old Testament one,
appropriate to a prophet (compare Jeremiah 1.1). It is one of the touches by
4–6 which Luke fills in the prophetic side of John's ministry. The quotation from
Isaiah (40.3) is common to the accounts in all the gospels, though it is given
7–9 at greater length by Luke; and John's first speech (except that it is delivered
generally to the crowds and not to the Pharisees and Sadducees) runs closely
parallel with the version in Matthew (3.7–10). But after this Luke's narrative
takes a different course. From the other gospels the impression might easily
be gained that John's preaching consisted entirely of an announcement of
the Coming One and an urgent call to repent and be baptized. But it is clear,
both from other passages in the gospels and Acts, and from the fact that his
movement lasted long after the appearance of Jesus, that he must also have
12 given moral teaching. The people, indeed, addressed him as **Master,** a form
of address which was often used when speaking to Jesus, and which implied
11 that John, too, was regarded as a teacher. Luke gives a sample of John's
teaching here. Sharing food and clothing with the needy was recognized as a
social obligation and as a highly meritorious act throughout the history of
Judaism. John's attitude to tax-gatherers and soldiers, however, was more
liberal than that of his contemporaries, who regarded these professions as
incompatible with a strict observance of the law, and excluded them from the
true community of Israel. John by contrast (and here his attitude was closer
to that of Jesus) accepted these people, only warning them against the special
temptations of their professions. Yet even he showed a certain intolerance
12 towards **tax-gatherers**: if they had done what he said, they would have
deprived themselves altogether of their source of livelihood (see below on
18.9–14).

The people were on the tiptoe of expectation. Luke gives the Baptist's 15
proclamation of the Coming One in much the same terms as Matthew, but
characteristically sets the scene for it a little more carefully and vividly. Any
prophetic figure preaching a radical message in the wilderness was liable to
arouse expectations about the promised Deliverer, and indeed we know that
there were a number of pretenders to this rôle during the century, culminating in the figure of Bar Kochba, who led the last revolt of the Jews against
the Romans in A.D. 135. It was against this background that John announced
the coming of a greater successor, not so much relaxing the expectation of the
people as turning it away from himself to another who was still to come.

The subsequent fate of John is recounted by Mark and Matthew in some
detail at a later stage in their gospels (Mark 6, Matthew 11). Luke is content 18–20
merely to summarize it (the story was presumably well known to his readers)
and, with perhaps a historian's concern to round off a story and draw a moral,
he places his summary here. After this, John does not appear again in his
gospel: the stage is left clear for Jesus.

During a general baptism of the people. Jesus was last mentioned 21
growing up in Nazareth. Here it is simply taken for granted that he was
among the crowd who came to be baptized, and the vision which accompanied his baptism serves to bring him out of obscurity and indicates that he
is from now on the protagonist of the story. Who was this Jesus? Luke's
previous chapters have given, so to speak, his divine parentage—but this
was only recognized by the faithful. Who was he in the eyes of ordinary
people? Luke answers, **the son, as people thought, of Joseph,** and 23
impressively proceeds to trace his ancestry right back to **Adam, son of God.** 38
A similar genealogy in Matthew (though it offers a quite different list of
names for Jesus' immediate ancestors) serves to answer the question, How
was Jesus a son of David? But Luke's interest seems to be simply that of a
historian: this is who Jesus was. (On the genealogy itself, see above on
Matthew 1.1–17).

Luke's account of Jesus' temptation is very similar to that of Matthew
(4.1–11), except that the episodes are in a different order. There are some
slight differences of detail which suggest that Luke was less familiar with
Palestine than Matthew and Mark, and found it harder to visualize the setting of Jesus' experience. **Jesus returned from the Jordan.** Did Luke **4.** 1
think that the wilderness was in a different part of the country? In fact it
began close to the edge of the Jordan valley, and Mark and Matthew are
much more convincing when they say that Jesus entered it straight after his
baptism. **Next the devil led him up and showed him in a flash all the** 5
kingdoms of the world. According to Matthew, Jesus was taken 'to a very
high mountain'. In the wilderness of Judaea there are many such mountains
which command an immense view over the Jordan valley and would have

offered an appropriate setting for Jesus' temptation. But Luke prefers to think of the experience as an inner vision: Jesus saw all the kingdoms of the world **in a flash.**

In Galilee: success and opposition

Success and opposition describes Jesus' progress through Galilee as aptly in Luke's narrative as it does in Mark's. But Luke, unlike the other evangelists, places a notable case of opposition (recounted more briefly in Mark and Matthew) right at the beginning, perhaps seeing in it a foretaste of Jesus' ultimate destiny at the hands of his fellow-countrymen. He was doubtless familiar with the tradition which made Jesus' activity in Galilee open with a number of "successes", and he makes a brief allusion to these in verse 15. But he does not linger over them; instead he hurries on to the main episode, which serves to lay down the pattern of Jesus' subsequent activity.

16 **So he came to Nazareth, where he had been brought up.** Matthew
and Mark call it simply his 'home town', but Luke is careful to maintain
consistency with the account he has given of Jesus' infancy. Strictly speaking,
Nazareth was not Jesus' 'home town', it was only **where he had been**
brought up. No followers were with him, as they are in Matthew's and
Mark's narratives; but in those two gospels the episode comes later in the
story, whereas here the disciples have not yet been called. He **went to**
synagogue on the Sabbath day as he regularly did—and what follows
is consistent with what we know from Jewish sources about the order of
service in a synagogue on a Sabbath morning. After prayers came a reading
from the Law of Moses (the first five books of the Bible). After that, a member of the congregation was invited to stand and read a lection from one of
the prophets, and then to sit and expound it. Jesus had already made a
reputation by his teaching, and when he visited a town it was natural that he
should be asked to give the exposition. Indeed it is likely that he (like the
apostles after him) eagerly accepted these opportunities of proclaiming his
message, and the exposition which he gave on this occasion was doubtless
15 typical of his teaching **in their synagogues** in many other places. The
18 passage chosen by Jesus (Isaiah 61.1–2, with the addition of a phrase from
Isaiah 58.6) was originally a prophecy that, after the exile in Babylon, the
Jewish people would once again be free to return to Jerusalem and celebrate
19 the "jubilee year" (Leviticus 25.10), **the year of the Lord's favour.** But
in the time of Jesus it was certainly understood as a still unfulfilled prophecy
of the new age to which the Jews looked forward. Luke gives the quotation
at length (following the Septuagint version of the Greek Bible, which gives a
slightly different sense from the Hebrew text which Jesus is likely to have

used), but offers only the barest summary of Jesus' sermon ('**Today...in** 21
your very hearing this text has come true'). Yet the weight of Jesus'
words is vividly captured. In referring Isaiah's prophecy to himself he was
making a prodigious claim. This claim at first excited admiration; but doubt
and disbelief crept in with the remark, '**Is not this Joseph's son?**'—for so, 22
'as people thought' (3.23), he was. Mark, in his account of this scene (6.1–6),
goes on to describe the effects of this scepticism: Jesus 'could work no
miracle there'. Luke implies the same consequence, even though he does not
state it; for the same picture of Jesus unable to perform miracles or to gain
acceptance among his own kinsfolk is what gives point to the harsh sayings
which follow. Nevertheless, Jesus' words seem to apply, not just to the people
of Nazareth, but to the Jewish people as a whole. "**Physician, heal your-** 23
self!" There was no obvious reason at this stage why anyone should have
cast this well-known proverb in Jesus' teeth, but these were exactly the terms
in which the Jews taunted Jesus at the crucifixion (Matthew 27.42)—Luke is
again using the scene as a foretaste of the treatment received by Jesus, not
just at Nazareth, but (in a wider sense) **in his own country**. Again, Jesus' 24
saying, '**no prophet is recognized in his own country**' is not seen by Luke
(as it is by Mark and Matthew) merely as a comment on his treatment at
Nazareth. It is a paradigm of the progress of his entire mission (and indeed
of the subsequent mission of the church). And the Old Testament examples
which follow are relevant, not so much to the matter in hand, as to what was
to become the recurring pattern of Jesus' work, seeking out either those
whose profession or way of life was thought to disqualify them from membership of the holy people of God, or else even those who were not Jews at all.
The story of Elijah and the widow of Sarepta is found in 1 Kings 17, that of 25
Naaman in 2 Kings 5. The implication of both these stories was that, in 27
God's saving purpose, it could happen that foreigners might be more
favourably placed than Jews; and the result of Jesus quoting them was that
the whole congregation were infuriated. They evidently intended to put 28
him to death by throwing him down a cliff (and there are many steep places
in the neighbourhood of Nazareth, even though the village was not built on
a hill, but rather in a hollow among hills). Luke evidently saw something
miraculous in Jesus' escape: **he walked straight through them all, and** 30
went away.

Coming down to Capernaum, a town in Galilee. The phrase is typical 31
of Luke, who does not expect his readers to be familiar with Palestine, and is
careful to explain that what to Greek ears was nothing but a barbarous collection of syllables (*Kapharnaoum*) was **a town in Galilee.** Luke may not have been familiar with Galilee himself, but he probably knew that Capernaum was on the lake, and he is accurate when he says that Jesus must have "come down" to it from the mountain village of Nazareth. From this point to the end of the chapter his narrative closely follows Mark (1.21–34). The

only notable difference is that the fever of Simon's mother-in-law is per-
39 sonified: Jesus **rebuked the fever** as he had rebuked the devil in the
previous incident. By this touch Luke perhaps wishes to make the whole
paragraph into a series of encounters with devils, culminating in the devils'
41 recognition that Jesus was **the Son of God** and **the Messiah.** Jesus' retreat
42 next morning **to a lonely spot** serves, as in Mark, to make the transition
44 from Capernaum to a wider field of work. Luke places this wider field **in the synagogues of Judaea.** Strictly speaking, Judaea was a long way to the south of Galilee, and if Luke means this literally he is in conflict with the other gospels.[a] But, along with other Greek and Latin writers, Luke sometimes uses "Judaea" to mean Palestine in general, and his intention here is probably only to say that Jesus' preaching extended far over Jewish lands.

By this time, in the other gospels, Jesus had gathered disciples round him. Luke has not yet mentioned this; but he now tells the story of how he was joined by Simon, James and John (who were of course so well known to Luke's readers that they needed no introduction). In Matthew and Mark, this was a simple summons, followed by an immediate response. But Luke leads up to it with a story which is clearly intended to offer some explanation of the disciples' instant decision to follow Jesus—and which also incidentally gives early prominence to Simon Peter among Jesus' followers. Both Mark
(4.1–2) and Matthew (13.1–3) record that Jesus, when teaching by the
5. 1 **Lake of Gennesaret** (a more precise name for the lake which the Jews
usually called the "Sea of Galilee"), liked to put out a little from the shore
in a boat. Luke takes the story on from there. The details are entirely lifelike.
The best time for fishing in the lake was (and still is) at night; and the co-
operation of two boats to bring in a heavy haul of fish was regular practice.
10 The sequel was Jesus' word (here addressed only to Simon), **'from now on you will be catching men'.** The story finds a suggestive echo in John 21, where Jesus (this time after the resurrection) again enables Simon to make an exceptional haul. Both the stories appear to have been freely written up by the evangelists to bring out a symbolic meaning, and both may go back to what was perhaps originally a single event.

12–14 The narrative of the healing of a leper follows Mark (1.40–5) very closely,
only omitting Mark's references to Jesus' anger and sternness (which were
perhaps as puzzling to Luke as they are to us). Jesus, indeed, moves more
gently in this gospel: instead of being forced to leave the town by the numbers of those who were pressing upon him (Mark 1.45), it is merely said that,
16 on his own initiative, **from time to time he would withdraw to lonely places for prayer.**

17–25 The next scene (the healing of a paralysed man) reproduces the actual
words of Jesus almost verbatim from the account in Mark (2.1–12), but

[a] This apparent conflict caused early copyists to make the alteration in the manuscripts which is noted in the NEB footnote.

shows considerable freedom in the narrative. In part, Luke appears simply
to have written the scene in a more polished Greek style—'**You would** 26
never believe the things we have seen today' is, in the original, a fluent
and idiomatic expression compared with Mark's 'Never before have we
seen the like' (2.12); in part also, he makes it easier for the non-Palestinian
reader to visualize: he sets the story inside one of the large tiled houses of
western cities, instead of outside the flat-roofed, baked mud houses of the
east. But in essential points his narrative follows the tradition preserved in
Mark.

In the events and sayings following the call of Levi, Luke has again made 27–39
only minor alterations to the details—he interprets Jesus' "invitation" to
sinners as being, not to a metaphorical banquet (as in Mark), but to **repent-** 32
ance; and he explains the observance of fasting among John's disciples and
the Pharisees as an aid to **the practice of prayer.** But whereas in Mark 33
(2.13–22) there is only a loose and general connection between each paragraph, Luke has neatly worked them into the setting of Levi's **big reception** 29
and, by slight editorial touches to Jesus' sayings, has made them all relevant
to the Pharisees' complaint that his disciples, instead of following the usual
austerities of a strict religious sect, could be seen to **eat and drink.** The 33
comparison with the wedding feast fits this context just as well as the context 34–5
given to it in Mark, and Luke makes no significant alteration to it (the
presence of verse 35 here is just as puzzling as the corresponding verse in
Mark). But the following parables are given a different slant. The point is no 36
longer, as in Mark, that the sheer novelty of Jesus' message demands an
altogether new medium of expression—this would have no relevance to the
question of the presence of the disciples of Jesus at Levi's reception. The
point is now that any attempt to combine the new with the old (the new
freedom of Jesus' message with the old practices of fasting) is fatal to both.
And Luke adds a further saying, which is in fact an old proverb, and seems 37–9
to fit a little awkwardly here. Once you have tasted the superior quality of
old, matured wine, you cannot go back to cheap, new stuff (or perhaps: you
are prejudiced against anything new). The complaints of the Pharisees were
based on assumptions which were now superseded. To have tried to combine
them with Jesus' new principles would have been to render both meaningless.

The two Sabbath stories run even closer to Mark (2.23–36). In the first, **6.** 1–5
Luke characteristically adds a detail which makes the story easier to visualize:
the disciples **were plucking the ears of corn, rubbing them in their** 1
hands, and eating them; and he also omits, as Matthew does, one of the
general sayings about the Sabbath ('the Sabbath was made for the sake of
man', etc.) recorded by Mark—perhaps, like us, he found it difficult to
understand. In the second story the changes are even more trivial, unless it is 6–11
significant that Luke does not mention Jesus' 'anger' on this occasion: such
an emotion did not fit into Luke's portrait of Jesus as it did into Mark's.

12 **During this time.** Luke now begins to set the stage for a major discourse
17 of Jesus. The discourse itself, though it takes place **on level ground**, is
clearly a version of the same collection of teaching as Matthew presents in
his Sermon on the Mount and, as in Matthew, it presupposes a double
audience: an inner group of disciples, and a large crowd. Luke's narrative,
while still running close to that of Mark (3.7–19) is arranged so as to account
for the presence of these two groups. The sequence begins with Jesus spend-
12 ing **the night in prayer**—Luke insists far more on the importance of prayer
in Jesus' life than any of the other evangelists. Jesus then, out of an existing
group of disciples (the presence of which was presupposed in chapter 5)
13 **chose twelve and named them Apostles.** Even in the less portentous
account in Mark, these twelve are clearly mentioned for the sake of their part
in the subsequent history of the church. Luke makes this even more explicit,
by recording that Jesus actually called them **Apostles** (the title by which
the founders of the early church came to be known), and by subsequently
referring to them by this title four times in his narrative. His list corresponds
to that in Mark and Matthew, except that the Thaddaeus of Mark, or the
16 Lebbaeus of Matthew, is replaced by a mysterious **Judas son of James**—a
name also apparently known to John (14.22).

The inner group of listeners being now identified, Luke brings Jesus down
17 to **level ground** (which he presumably thought more appropriate as a setting
for a sermon than a hill—he seems to have reserved hills for supernatural
experiences) and accounts for the presence of a crowd by the spread of Jesus'
fame far to the south and the north of Galilee. It was not merely that he had
19 been known to perform miraculous cures; there was **power** in him (recognized also by Mark, 5.30) which could be released if a sick person so much as
touched him.

20 **Then turning to his disciples he began to speak.** Luke, like Matthew, places a long discourse of Jesus early in his narrative, and if we compare Matthew's Sermon on the Mount, we see at once that here is another version of the same thing. Both begin with "beatitudes" and end with a parable; Luke's version, though it is much shorter, contains only a few verses which are not in Matthew's; and there is even the same indeterminacy of audience: at the beginning Jesus is speaking 'to his disciples', at the end (7.1) we hear that he has been 'addressing the people'—exactly as in Matthew. Yet Luke's "sermon" is not merely an abridged version of Matthew's. It has its own distinctive tone, and in certain details it presents Jesus' teaching in a somewhat different light.

20 **'How blest are you who are in need'.** The first and most striking difference between these beatitudes and those in Matthew is that they are all in the second person: they presuppose an audience of people who were actually in need, hungry, weeping and reviled. And this goes with a second

difference. In Matthew (5.3), the needy are 'those who know their need of God' (literally, "poor in spirit"), the hungry are those who 'hunger and thirst to see right prevail'. In other words, the blessing is pronounced as a reward for a certain moral and religious disposition. But here, the needy are really needy, the hungry really hungry; and the promise is that their condition will be reversed **on that day**, that is, at the future coming of the king- 23
dom of God. Doubtless many of the religious connotations of poverty and hunger, which are spelled out in Matthew's version (particularly in those beatitudes which Luke omits), are also present here; but the emphasis is on the dramatic reversal of fortune which awaits those who are literally poor and in need.

The same emphasis runs through the "woes" ('**Alas for you**') with which 24–6
Luke balances each of the beatitudes (these do not occur in Matthew's Sermon on the Mount, though rather similar woes appear at another place in
his gospel, 23.13–30). '**Alas for you who are rich.**' This is the logical corol- 24
lary of 'how blest are you who are in need', but although there was a strong strain in Jewish piety which was prepared to find a blessing in poverty, it would have come hard to deny that there was also a blessing in riches. Yet this was Jesus' teaching, embodied here in an unambiguous condemnation of whole classes of society which recalls the manner of an Old Testament
prophet. One other detail characterizes those who were to be blest: like the 26
prophets (as a Jewish tradition had begun to say—see above on Matthew 23.31) they would be persecuted for their faith; and their persecutors would be the descendants of those who had persecuted the prophets—not the world in general, but the Jews.

'**But to you who hear me I say**'. The rich and prosperous were not in the 27
audience, and little time is spent over denunciations of the world at large: the sermon is for those who will follow Jesus. The next sayings are placed
under a single bold heading, '**Love your enemies**'. In the Sermon on the 28
Mount, this radical injunction developed out of Jesus' interpretation of the familiar commandment, Love your neighbour; here it is bluntly stated as a distinctive ethical principle, and illustrated by a series of examples. The examples are familiar from Matthew (5.39–48), but Luke has added touches
of his own. '**When a man takes your coat**': evidently a robber who tears off 29
the first garment he can get hold of, not a litigant (as in Matthew) who is
prepared to take a shirt as a pledge before he insists on a coat. '**Even sinners** 33
love those who love them.' Matthew contrasts the conduct of Christians with that of the outcasts of Jewish society (tax-collectors) or of "the heathen". Luke is more general: **sinners** are simply non-Christians. In Matthew, impartiality is inculcated on the grounds that God dispenses sun and rain impartially to just and unjust. Luke sharpens this, so that loving your
enemies can be seen to be a way of imitating the God who is **kind to the** 35
ungrateful. Similarly, God is to be imitated not (as in Matthew) because

he is 'perfect', but—and this is more relevant in the present context—
36 because he is **compassionate.**

37 **'Pass no judgement, and you will not be judged.'** In Matthew's version
(7.1–2), the judgement is the Last Judgement, the rewards are other-worldly.
The same doubtless goes for these sentences (which, if taken as this-worldly
38 advice, would sound like either opportunism or wishful thinking). The **good
measure** of a truly generous corn-merchant is an image of the reward which
awaits the generous giver in heaven.

39 **He also offered them a parable.** The word often means "a riddle",
and these two sayings, which both have the ring of proverbs, are certainly
enigmatic. (Matthew (15.14) applies the first to the Pharisees, and there is
40 an echo of it in a similar context in Romans 2.19. The second, **'A pupil is not
superior to his teacher,'** is made into a rule of discipleship in Matthew
10.24; but Luke has a different ending, and the meaning is mysterious.)

41–2 Other parables follow: the speck of sawdust and the plank almost exactly
43–5 as in Matthew, the fruit-metaphor much more generalized so that it becomes
a test, not of the authenticity of a prophet (as in Matthew), but of whatever
46 goes on in the heart. Generalized too is the saying about calling Jesus **"Lord,
Lord"**—it is not a question of deciding who is and who is not a Christian
(as in Matthew) but of relating the worship of Christ to a sincere intention to
perform his exceedingly exacting ethic.

47–9 And so, with the same parable of two houses as in Matthew (though Luke perhaps imagines a house near a European river like the Tiber rather than near a Palestinian *wady*), the sermon comes to an end. It contains much less teaching than Matthew's sermon (though much of what is omitted here appears elsewhere in Luke's gospel), but its tone is both sharper and more general—sharper, because the most radical elements in it are presented without qualification or interpretation; more general, because the debate between Christians and Jews, which is so prominent in Matthew, can hardly be overheard in Luke, and the ethic stands alone as a guide for life under any circumstances whatever. Whether Matthew and Luke themselves were responsible for these two different versions, or whether two different collections of Jesus' moral teaching already existed before these gospels came to be written, is a tantalizing question. But both versions reflect a teacher of outstanding originality, whose influence has disturbed not only those of his first followers who undertook to write down his words, but the many generations of Christians who, in a great variety of ways, have endeavoured to bend their lives to his teaching.

7. 1 **He went to Capernaum.** As in Matthew, so in Luke, the great sermon is immediately followed by a petition addressed to Jesus by a Gentile. In both gospels, the dialogue between Jesus and the centurion is virtually identical; but Luke presents the episode itself somewhat differently. In Matthew, the

sufferer is 'a boy of mine'—which is ambiguous. Matthew apparently takes
it to mean the centurion's son; but Luke chooses the other alternative, **a** 2
servant. However, he then has to explain why the officer was so anxious
about this particular servant, and so he adds the explanation: **whom he**
valued highly. In Matthew, again, the point of the episode, with the
dialogue it contains, is the comparison between the authority of a military
officer over his men and that of Jesus over the world of spirits; but in Luke
this point is almost incidental (and indeed fits somewhat awkwardly into the
story). All the stress is on the character and behaviour of the centurion; he
was "a friend of the Jewish nation", he was so respected by the Jews that
some of their **elders** were willing to press his case, and at the same time he 3
had too much humility to approach Jesus in person. No Gentile could have
been better qualified to gain his petition from Jesus; and Luke doubtless
saw all these moral excellences comprised in the **faith** which Jesus promptly 9
rewarded.

Afterwards Jesus went to a town called Nain. The site of this town is 11
known: it lies just off one of the roads leading from the lake to the coast, on the side of a steep hill. As Jesus approached it from the main road he would have had before him the principal gate of the town. Out of this gate was coming a funeral procession. The Jews normally buried within a few hours of death. The body, wrapped in a linen cloth, was carried from the house on a bier (for coffins were not used) to a family grave cut in the rock; and since graves were always outside the walls of a town, the procession had at some stage to pass through the gate. This was the moment at which Jesus intervened, and performed what was regarded as the greatest of all miracles, that of bringing a dead person back to life. Two such miracles are recorded in the gospels apart from this one: Jairus' daughter (Luke 8.40, Mark 5.21, Matthew 9.18) and Lazarus (John 11). Here the story is told quite simply, and there is little to distinguish it from similar stories told about other miracle-workers in antiquity. On the other hand, the reaction of the bystanders was conditioned by their religious beliefs. '**A great prophet has arisen among** 16
us'. Elijah and Elisha, the first great prophets, had performed similar miracles (1 Kings 17; 2 Kings 4): Jesus must be another of the same calibre. Moreover, raising from the dead was a sign of the new age that was to come: '**God has shown his care for his people**'—the same phrase as is translated 'has turned to his people' in Zechariah's prophetic song (1.68). The miracle was evidence of a new relationship beginning between God and man.

John too was informed of all this by his disciples. This episode, with 18
its sayings about John the Baptist, occurs in Matthew 11, where it reads like
a digression. By placing it immediately after the account of two notable
miracles, and by inserting the note that **there and then** Jesus **cured many** 21
sufferers, Luke knits the same material more neatly into his narrative. In
other respects his version is much the same, apart from verses 29–30. This 29–30

comment, which draws a clear distinction between Jesus' supporters and opponents, occurs only in Luke's gospel (though it is possibly echoed, in a quite different context, in Matthew 21.32). The only difficulty is to know (since Greek manuscripts originally had no inverted commas) whether the comment is that of the narrator or is to be attributed to Jesus himself (see the footnote in NEB).

36 **One of the Pharisees invited him to eat with him**—evidently a formal
meal, since the word translated **took his place at table** literally means "lay
on a couch", and it was only on more formal occasions that the Jews adopted
the Greek and Roman custom of reclining, instead of sitting, at table. Moreover, an ordinary family meal might have been held in private; but any kind
of larger dinner-party always attracted visitors other than the invited guests
(whether people simply wishing to listen to the conversation or beggars
37 hoping for scraps of food). It was only on such an occasion that **a woman
who was living an immoral life in the town** could have gained admission
to a Pharisee's house and, finding the guests reclining on couches with their
legs stretched out behind them, could have discreetly ministered to Jesus,
taking **her place behind him, by his feet.** Jesus' host evidently had certain
presuppositions about his guest. He assumed that, like himself, Jesus would
be particular about who touched him, in order to remain ritually "clean"
(particularly before a meal); and he was interested to see whether Jesus had
the prophetic gift of knowing intuitively about the personal lives of those
40 with whom he came in contact. Jesus ignored the first point, but **took him
41–3 up** on the second. First, he told a brief and pointed parable, and then he drew
attention to the signs of powerful emotion in the woman. Washing a
guest's feet or anointing him with oil and perfume were not courtesies
normally offered to guests at a banquet; they were part of a specially careful
toilet which a guest might make before he left home. Jesus therefore was not
criticizing his host on the subject of his hospitality, but pointing out that
these attentions from a woman were clear signs of her feelings. He did not
need to be a prophet to see that her actions expressed a love and gratitude
towards himself which could only be due to the fact that she was indeed a
"sinner", but now knew herself to have been forgiven. By contrast, the
47 formal hospitality of the Pharisee expressed no such emotion. **'Where little
has been forgiven, little love is shown'.**

To this extent, the point of the dialogue is clear: Jesus wins his point against the Pharisee. But there is evidently far more to the story than this; and as soon as it is examined more carefully, difficulties and uncertainties appear. A somewhat similar story (set in the house of a certain 'Simon the leper', Mark 14.3) occurs in the other gospels shortly before the narrative of the passion. Luke has no such story in that place: has he adapted it to a different purpose here, or were there originally two episodes which both involved a woman with a flask of ointment? Did Jesus originally speak the

parable on this occasion, or has Luke added it to his story? Do the final verses
belong to the original story, or is it Luke's own explanation that the woman
had been forgiven because of her **faith** in Jesus, perhaps as a result of his 50
preaching earlier in the day? If the paragraph seems less than perfectly
coherent, the reason may be that all its parts did not originally belong
together. At the same time, the episode is bound together by a very strong
association of ideas. Sins, in Jewish teaching, were often described as debts
—this links the parable firmly to the dialogue; and the English word **love**
must not mislead us into thinking that the scene is intended to offer an analysis
of deep emotions. In Jesus' own language, such words meant, not lasting
affection, but the outward expression of loyalty and gratitude; indeed, the
same word was used for "love" and "thank". The generous gestures of the
woman and the response of the pardoned debtors would have been described
by the same word, only imperfectly represented by *agapē* in Greek or **love**
in English.

After this he went journeying. This marks a new stage in the narrative: **8.** 1
Jesus left the area around Capernaum, where he could count on the hospitality of friends, and became an itinerant preacher, moving at first from town
to town without any clear sense of direction, and then 'setting his face
resolutely towards Jerusalem' (9.51). Luke (alone of the evangelists) allows
us a glimpse of the way in which Jesus and his disciples were provided for:
women who had been cured by him offered **their own resources.** Luke's 3
list of names overlaps with that in other gospels (Matthew 27.55–6; Mark
15.40–1), in so far as they all include **Mary of Magdala. Joanna** reappears 2
below (24.10), **Susanna** is otherwise unknown. It is interesting (and was 3
doubtless of interest to Luke, with his concern for connections with secular
history) that Jesus' following extended to the household of **Herod** Antipas,
the tetrarch of Galilee.

At this point in the narrative both Mark (chapter 4) and Matthew (chapter
13) introduce a section devoted to Jesus' parable-teaching, and offer some
hints on the place of this teaching in Jesus' work as a whole. Luke follows the
same tradition, but (perhaps because he has so many other parables to put in
later on) he makes much less of it. **He said in a parable**: only the parable 4
of sowing is given, followed by two short sayings; and although Luke retains
the difficult quotation from Isaiah 6.9 (**so that they may look but see** 10
nothing, hear but understand nothing), he gives it in the briefest possible
form, and softens the contrast between the disciples to whom it has been
granted **to know the secrets of the kingdom of God** and those who are
not so privileged, whom indeed he vaguely calls **the others.** Some, perhaps
many, may have reacted with the stubborn obstinacy foretold by Isaiah, but
no clear line is drawn. The disciples are not singled out again, nor does Luke
suggest that they are given any private instruction. He reserves his full

treatment of the Isaiah passage until the very end of his two-volume work (Acts 28.26–7), where he identifies the people from whom God has withheld understanding with that majority of the Jewish race who, though given the first opportunity to hear and accept the gospel message, have persistently rejected it. Meanwhile, the possibility of Jesus' hearers coming to a full understanding of his teaching remains open. Luke accordingly sums up the paragraph with words which represent a slight but significant alteration of the saying which is given in Matthew and Mark (4.24), and which are clearly
18 addressed to the crowds at large: **'Take care, then, how you listen'.**

For the details of the parables, see above on Mark 4. Luke has made only slight changes. He appears to have thought that the seed on the footpath
5 would fail to grow because it was **trampled on,** and for that reason would ultimately be eaten by the birds. The interpretation of the parable only differs from the parallel versions in that it introduces still more of the
12 language of the Greek-speaking church, such as **believe and be saved,**
13, 15 **time of testing** and, most striking of all, **a good and honest heart,** which is a cliché of classical Greek ethics.

Some incidents follow which, in Mark, are carefully woven into the narrative but which appear to be assembled together by Luke without much concern for a proper sequence. The parable-teaching which has just finished was clearly given out of doors; but, when Jesus' family arrives (and no reason is given for their visit, as it is in Mark 3.21), he seems suddenly to be indoors,
20 and is told that his mother and brothers **are standing outside.** Similarly,
22 the crossing of the lake is given no context: it simply happens **one day,** though in other respects the paragraph seems to be a straightforward rewriting of the version in Mark (4.35–41), omitting extraneous details and considerably softening the severity with which Jesus reproves his disciples
26–39 for their lack of faith. The following story also runs closely parallel to Mark (5.1–12), and the differences are no more than might be expected from Luke's attention to stylistic detail. He places the episode (according to the testimony
26 of a number of important manuscripts), in the **country of the Gergesenes.** Matthew and Mark give the names of two cities, Gadara and Gerasa, neither of which is close enough to the lake to give any clear indication of the locality. Gergesa (if this is what Luke meant) is totally unknown; all we can say for sure is that Luke correctly understood the place to have been on the east side of the lake, **opposite Galilee**—that is to say, in predominantly gentile territory. The devils however (as in Matthew 8.29) use the language of
31 Jewish mythology: **the Abyss** was the place in which the powers of evil were destined to be imprisoned at the end of time (Revelation 20.1–3).

40–56 In the two interwoven episodes which follow, Luke is faithful to the account in Mark (5.21–43). The few changes he has made are only those which a writer might be expected to introduce in order to make a story his own.

The departure and return of the Twelve are separated, as in Mark 6, by the
device of a brief change of scene to the court of Herod. But Luke, though he
follows Mark's arrangement, has greatly abbreviated it. The words, '**As for** 9. 9
John, I beheaded him myself', are all that is left of the well-known story
of Salome's dance. Herod himself is also presented in a more sophisticated
light. He is called (as in Matthew) by his correct title of "tetrarch" (**Prince**) 7
and not (as in Mark) by the popular name of 'king', and he is not made to
share the somewhat naïve view (which is more characteristic of Jewish folklore than of a Hellenistic ruler) that Jesus might be John the Baptist **raised**
from the dead. His reaction is more pragmatic: after disposing of John he
now finds himself with another religious leader to come to terms with. His
desire to see Jesus for himself is referred to again in 23.8.

In other respects the narrative in Mark is clearly the model for Luke's
account, and the differences are unimportant. '**Neither stick nor pack**' 3
agrees with Matthew (10.9–10) against Mark (6.9) in forbidding even a stick
—perhaps because the main use of the travellers' stick was self-defence, and
this was felt inappropriate for the peace-loving disciples of Jesus. The only
serious discrepancy in Luke is the mention of **Bethsaida.** This village, 10
which lay on the east side of the mouth of the Jordan, and therefore in the
jurisdiction of the tetrarch Philip, had recently been rebuilt as a town of some
pretensions. It was hardly a place to choose for withdrawing privately, and
the miracle which follows can hardly have been in its vicinity, since it 10–17
presupposes **a lonely place.** By introducing the name, Luke has made the 12
scene extremely hard to visualize. On the other hand, his approach to the
geography of Galilee is rather different from that of the other evangelists.
He mentions very few place-names, and is usually content to situate the
various incidents quite vaguely in the countryside. He is about to omit a
series of episodes recorded in Mark, which end with one at Bethsaida (Mark
8.22). His concern may simply have been to bring the general course of
Jesus' progress roughly into line with the narratives he was using as his
sources, without much attention to the exact setting of any particular episode.

One day when he was praying alone in the presence of his disciples. 18
The translators have made no attempt to soften the contradiction contained
in this sentence, and it is Luke who must bear the blame. What appears to
have happened is that Luke liked to represent important experiences in the
life of Jesus as taking place when Jesus was at prayer: see, for example, the
baptism (3.21) and the transfiguration (9.28). But it was also necessary to
have the disciples present for the sake of the conversation which follows.
Hence, **praying alone in the presence of his disciples.** Luke omits much
of the detail of this conversation (compared with Mark (8.27–30), whose
narrative he seems now to pick up again, having passed over the contents of
several pages, and compared still more with Matthew (16.13–20), who has
some altogether original material to insert at this point). He preserves only

20 the two most significant points: Peter's recognition that Jesus is **God's Messiah** (and Luke for once follows Mark in reporting Jesus' injunction
22 to secrecy on the matter), and the prophecy that '**the Son of Man has to undergo great sufferings**'.

23 **And to all he said.** There is again little attention paid to actual circumstances. If Jesus was 'praying alone' there can have been no **all** within earshot to whom Jesus could have addressed his teaching. But the sayings which (following Mark) Luke had now to record were obviously not part of Jesus' private instruction to his disciples, and so the presence of a larger audience had simply to be taken for granted. '**Day after day he must take up his cross**': the expression, "taking up" (or "carrying") one's cross is one which must have been formulated after Jesus' execution (see above on Mark 8.34); and Luke adapts it still more to the purpose of strengthening the resolve of Christian congregations by making it sound like a constant spiritual exercise —**day after day.** In other respects, the sayings stand much as they are in
27 Mark, including the most difficult of them, '**there are some of those standing here who will not taste death before they have seen the kingdom of God.**' Only Mark's final words, 'already come in power', are omitted; and this omission perhaps made the oracle easier for Luke's readers to interpret. The **kingdom of God,** so long as it did not involve a manifestation of power on a cosmic scale, was a reality already sometimes present in the activity of Jesus, and certainly now experienced in the life of the church. To this extent, Jesus' prediction had come true.

One should not properly use the word "transfiguration" as the name of
29 the next episode in Luke. Instead of 'he was transfigured', Luke writes **the appearance of his face changed,** and his account of the scene, while it
32 retains an emphasis on the supernatural **glory** of Jesus and the two figures who appeared with him, nevertheless adds a few touches to make the sequence of events more credible and logical, at the expense of the symbolic meanings present in Mark (9.2–8) and Matthew (17.1–8). Thus: the disciples **had been in a deep sleep**; only on waking did they see the three resplendent figures. Peter's suggestion of making shelters was motivated by the fact that the
33 figures **were moving away**, and he hoped (somewhat inappropriately, Luke admits) to detain them; the disciples' fear was caused, not by the vision (which should not have been particularly frightening) but by their being suddenly enveloped in a cloud. Yet despite these touches of rationalization, the scene in Luke retains its other-worldly quality, and has a clear message
31 to give. Moses and Elijah spoke of Jesus' **departure, the destiny he was to fulfil in Jerusalem.** The Greek word is *exodos*, which certainly meant **departure,** but was also used as a euphemism for "death", and was furthermore a word which Luke could hardly have chosen to use if he had not intended his readers to be reminded of the Exodus of Israel from Egypt. Moses had had an *exodos*, a "destiny", to fulfil, and had died before it was

completed; and the force of the disciples' vision was not only (as in Matthew)
that Jesus was a new Moses, and that (as in Mark) he would shortly be
clothed with a glory which was even now momentarily visible in his person,
but that meanwhile there was a **destiny he was to fulfil in Jerusalem,**
which would involve his "departure" (or death)—that is, an *exodos*. The
disciples, according to Luke, needed no injunction to secrecy: they **told** 36
nobody anything of what they had seen.

Next day. It is just possible that Luke thought of the vision as having 37
taken place at night (hence the 'deep sleep' of the disciples), in which case he
may have deliberately added this note of an interval in time. His account
of the exorcism is otherwise a much-abbreviated version of that in Mark
(9.14–29), but has a different ending: **they were all struck with awe at the** 43
majesty of God. This atmosphere of **general wonder** is built up still
more in the next phrase, and provides the setting for the solemn announcement which Jesus makes to his disciples. The announcement is introduced in 44
strikingly biblical language, a point which is lost in this translation. According
to Mark (9.32), the disciples 'did not understand what he said and were
afraid to ask him'. Mark offers no reason for their incomprehension. But
Luke has a simple (if somewhat artificial) explanation. Judging by their
subsequent conduct, the disciples had clearly not grasped Jesus' unambiguous prediction. The reason must have been that they were not intended to
grasp it: **it had been hidden from them.** 45

To conclude the section, Luke makes a very brief selection from the 46–50
sayings recorded at this point by Mark (9.34–41), without apparently attempting to bring them into a more logical order.

Journeys and encounters

The NEB inserts a new heading at this point; and certainly the next ten chapters form a section sufficiently distinct to deserve its own title. In the narrative of Mark (10.1), Jesus now begins his decisive journey from Galilee to Jerusalem, and in both Mark and Matthew it is possible, at least approximately, to plot this journey on the map. In Luke, Jesus also begins his journey shortly after the episode of the transfiguration; but the journey is so packed with sayings and events that it becomes quite impossible to visualize the progress made by the travellers or to be sure which route from Galilee to Jerusalem they are supposed to have taken. The journey, in fact, which would normally have taken three or four days at most, and which is recorded quite briefly in Mark, becomes a whole series of *Journeys and encounters*, lasting perhaps several weeks.

If Luke were a little more precise about Jesus' route, and offered some

indication, as the journey progressed, of the places Jesus had reached, we might conclude that he was better informed about this part of Jesus' activity and was therefore in a position to expand his account of the journey. But in fact he is so vague on these points that a different explanation seems preferable. Practically none of the material in these chapters appears in Mark, and only some of it (in other contexts) in Matthew. We must imagine that Luke had received a substantial amount of information about Jesus' teaching and activities which had no fixed place in any connected narrative, and which he had to work in as best he could. He knew that, at a certain point, Jesus travelled from Galilee to Jerusalem; and it occurred to him to fill out the picture of Jesus as a travelling teacher (a picture which his Greek and Roman readers will have found familiar, since such teachers were a common phenomenon in the Hellenistic world) by inserting into this journey most of the extra material which he possessed. It did not greatly matter exactly what route Jesus took; all that was necessary was to remind his readers from time to time that Jesus was on the road, and to help them to visualize the itinerant
58 life of one who had said that he had **nowhere to lay his head.**

There may also be another reason why Luke, though he devotes so much space to the journey, is vague about the route which was actually taken. He may not have known the country; and reliable maps did not exist. He knew that Galilee was a separate region from Judaea, and he was well informed about the political differences between each region. But both regions were essentially Jewish; and he may not have known that they were in fact separated by the alien territory of Samaria, so that to go from one to the other it was necessary to go either through Samaria or round it. He may have visualized Galilee and Judaea (as the Roman geographer Pliny appears to have done) as a continuous stretch of country, with Samaria lying alongside. He knew that Jesus must have entered Samaria at some stage, since one or two episodes clearly belonged there; but whereas in fact a traveller who took the route through Samaria would soon have left Galilee far behind him, Luke may have imagined that Jesus could have crossed the border at any time during his journey and then have crossed back to continue through Galilee to Judaea. If so, he would have felt free to work in the Samaritan episodes at almost any point he liked.

In any case, it was no ordinary journey. For Jesus, it was a necessary
51 prelude to being **taken up to heaven** (Acts 1.2,11), and it fixed his course
as being from now on directed inexorably towards Jerusalem. All this Luke expresses in a sentence rich in scriptural overtones; his language leaves no doubt that a new chapter is beginning in the story of Jesus. At the same time, one of these overtones sounds right through the first of these "encounters". One Old Testament figure in particular—Elijah—had been "taken up into heaven" (2 Kings 2.11). Many thought that Jesus must be this same Elijah,
54 now returned to earth; and **the disciples James and John** (appropriately

called 'Sons of Thunder', Mark 3.17) were probably simply echoing this popular view when they expected Jesus to do what Elijah had done to his enemies (2 Kings 1.10) and **burn them up** by calling down fire from
heaven. The scene took place in **a Samaritan village.** For several centuries 52
the Samaritans had been something of a race apart from the rest of the Jewish nation. They possessed a different version of the Old Testament (consisting of only the first five books) and regarded Mount Gerizim, near their own capital, as the "chosen place" where God should be worshipped, believing this, and not Jerusalem, to be the true site of the temple. More recently, Samaria had been brought under the same administration as Judaea; but relations between the two races were still strained, and little more than twenty years before Jesus' visit the Samaritans had caused a crisis by deliberately defiling the temple in Jerusalem at the time of the Passover. It was not unknown for them to attack pilgrims on their way through Samaria from Galilee to Jerusalem; and when Jesus tried to make the same journey,
the Samaritan villagers were behaving true to form when they **would not** 53
have him because he was making for Jerusalem. The disciples' reaction was probably equally typical of Jews; but Jesus (as several stories in this section show) dissociated himself altogether from the traditional animosity between the two races.

Jesus (as Luke will be constantly reminding us) was on the road; and **the** 57
road is the cue for three sayings about "following". Two of these occur also 57–60
in Matthew (8.18–22), and what was said of them there may apply equally
here: the sayings themselves (including the third, added by Luke) have a 61–2
general and proverbial sound, and it may have been only later that a little anecdote was added to each, thereby making the sayings more particular and more radical.

After this the Lord appointed a further seventy-two. It is clearly **10.** 1
stated in each of the first three gospels that Jesus had a distinct group of twelve disciples and that on one occasion he sent them out on an independent mission; and in the early church the existence of this original Twelve was taken for granted. Luke alone mentions **a further seventy-two** and a further mission; but he says practically nothing to explain the function of this second group. The instructions given to them are almost exactly the same as those in his own (9.1–5) or Matthew's (10) version of the charge to the Twelve (the only addition here is that they are to travel so hastily that
they must **exchange no greetings on the road**—oriental courtesies con- 4
sume a lot of time!); and after their return they play no further part in the story. What is their significance? Luke was a historian: he knew the importance of the mission to non-Jews in the subsequent history of the church, and he knew that this had been conducted by apostles who were not members of the original Twelve. He may have wished to justify the credentials of this
larger circle of apostles by mentioning the **further seventy-two** in the 1

gospel. Alternatively, seventy-two (or seventy: there was constant oscillation between the two) was an important round number in Jewish legend and history. Moses commissioned 72 (or 70) elders (Numbers 11); 70 (or 72) elders had translated the Old Testament into Greek under divine inspiration. Any of these motives may have been in Luke's mind: more we cannot say.

13 **'Alas for you, Chorazin!'** This condemnation of cities of Galilee occurs
(more appropriately in a Galilean context) in Matthew 11.20–4; and the
16 final words to the seventy-two ('**whoever listens to you listens to me**')
are evidently another version of the saying at the end of the charge in Matthew (10.40), which appears also, in a slightly different form and in another context, in Mark 9.37.

17 **The seventy-two came back jubilant.** The mission and return of this larger group conforms to the pattern of that of the Twelve (9.1,10), who had also been given 'power and authority to overcome all the devils' (9.1). Invocation of the **name** of Jesus could effect an exorcism, even if the exorcist was not a follower of Jesus (9.49). The reason was Jesus' victory over Satan.
18 **'I watched how Satan fell'.** Jesus' vision of this victory is in terms
19 of Jewish mythology (Isaiah 14.12), his promise to the disciples of **power to
tread underfoot snakes and scorpions** (of which Luke later gives an
instance in the case of Paul, Acts 28.6) is a fulfilment of Psalm 91.13. The
20 idea of names **enrolled in heaven**—meaning a secure place in the age to
come—is a commonplace in the Bible.

21 **At that moment Jesus exulted in the Holy Spirit.** The startling saying
21–2 that follows occurs in Matthew 11.25–7. Here perhaps it is better in place,
since the scene concerns only Jesus and his disciples; and if Luke was
thinking of the seventy-two as the prototypes of subsequent apostles, then he
23–4 may have found in this saying (and in the next, which in Matthew occurs in
the parable-chapter, 13.16–17) a validation of their authority: they were
22 **those to whom the Son may choose to reveal** the Father.

25 **A lawyer came forward to put this test question to him.** It is the same question as was put to Jesus on another occasion (18.18; Mark 10.17), and the answer is the same as that given to a slightly different (and perhaps more "testing") question in Mark 12.28, Matthew 22.34. This dialogue in Luke may be a record of a different occasion altogether, or it may be a conflation of the others; in either event, it shows Jesus and the professional lawyer in
complete agreement—at least so far as general principles were concerned.
29 But on the practical application of these principles—'**And who is my
neighbour?**'—Jesus had something quite new to say.

30 **'A man was on his way from Jerusalem down to Jericho.'** The long steep descent through the mountains, winding along the courses of the *wadys*, was a notorious haunt of robbers until quite recent times. The robbery was nothing out of the ordinary; the interest of the story turns entirely upon the

response of the three other travellers. We may feel that the response of the first two was strangely inhuman; but their conduct was probably due, not to any lack of human feelings, but to a deliberate choice between conflicting obligations. On the one hand, there was a clear commandment to help any "neighbour" (normally interpreted as any fellow-Jew) whose life was in danger; on the other hand, if the victim were already dead (which, by his appearance, this one presumably might have been) both a priest and a Levite would incur ritual defilement by touching or even by approaching the corpse, and this might prevent them from fulfilling their duties in the temple, or from collecting the tithes to which they were entitled. It would probably not have surprised Jesus' contemporaries to hear that in this case caution
overcame charity: they decided to avoid all risk of defilement and **went past** 32
on the other side.

We know what Jesus thought of such an attitude: just as it was absurd to invoke rules about the keeping of the Sabbath as a pretext for refusing to cure a sick man, so it was indefensible to regard rules about ritual purity as more binding than the needs of a human sufferer. But if this were the point which Jesus intended here, we should expect the third traveller to have been an ordinary Jewish layman, whose simple understanding of the law would put to shame the casuistry of the professional religious classes. The element of surprise in the story consists in the fact that the third traveller was, of all
things, **a Samaritan.** It is true that the Samaritans, according to their own 33
version of the Law of Moses, were also commanded to "love their neighbour as themselves"; and it is true that there was a familiar story in the Old Testament about the mercifulness of certain Samaritans (2 Chronicles 28). But at the time when Jesus told this story, Jews and Samaritans hated each other with great bitterness. The Samaritan had every reason for not regarding the wounded Jew as his "neighbour". Yet he did for him all—if not more than all—that one Jew would feel obliged to do for another.

'**Go and do as he did**'. It is tempting to regard these words as permission 37
to use the parable as a moral tale, and to make the Samaritan into an example of how one should behave when one finds oneself, say, at the scene of a road accident. But this can hardly be what Jesus intended. The Samaritan's behaviour was only what, at their best, human beings can be expected to do for each other. It did not need a parable of Jesus to inculcate such an ideal: people already knew that this was what one ought to do, and doubtless Jesus' listeners each hoped that, in a similar situation, he would have done as much himself. Nevertheless, they would have had more sympathy than we have with the priest and the Levite, whom they would have realized to be in the grip of conflicting obligations; and they would have been virtually forced by their Jewish upbringing to regard the concept of "neighbour" in a very narrow sense, and to feel no obligation to come to the help of any of the traditional enemies of the Jewish race, such as the Romans, the Samaritans

or indeed most Gentiles. The example of the Samaritan, who was prepared
36 to regard his worst traditional enemy as his **neighbour**, was designed to shock them out of this attitude. '**Go and do as he did**' meant, treat anyone, of any race and background, as your neighbour, with all in the way of help and charity which the word implies. The parable found its target in the exclusive nationalism of the Jewish people in the time of Jesus; but there has never yet been a society or a civilization in which it would have no relevance.

38 **A woman named Martha made him welcome in her home.** Hospitality was offered to a visiting preacher as a matter of course; but we are rarely given a glimpse of the domestic strains which it caused. Jesus' hostess
40 was **distracted** by her many tasks (the word meets us often in harassed private letters of the period), while her sister took up the position of a listener at the teacher's feet. Jesus' reply speaks for itself: it is an application of the old adage that it is better to concentrate on one thing than to dissipate one's energies on many (compare Ecclesiasticus 11.10). But what the moral was for Jesus' contemporaries or for Luke's readers is a harder question. Simple fare for visiting teachers? The rights of women in the Christian church? Or simply the very modern tension between domestic chores and "the things that matter"? We cannot tell. For Luke's readers, in any case, the whole
39 point probably lay in the one phrase, **listening to his words.** "Listening
42 to Jesus' words" was the "best part" that anyone could possibly choose.

11. 1 **Once, in a certain place, Jesus was at prayer.** In Matthew (6.5–13) the Lord's Prayer is deliberately contrasted with the lengthy and ostentatious prayers of Jews and pagans. Luke gives it in a different context. Jesus was a man of prayer (a point which Luke likes to emphasize), and his disciples naturally wished to imitate him: '**Lord, teach us to pray.**' Modern instruction on prayer usually concentrates on mental and psychological techniques for becoming aware of the presence of God. But, whatever experience and methods the religious men of antiquity may have had, their teaching on prayer had a slightly different function: it defined the relationship which the worshipper had to God, the rewards and benefits which his faith justified him in praying for, and the conditions he must fulfil if his prayer was to be accepted. It was in this sense that the Pharisees and other religious groups in Judaism "taught their disciples to pray": they each used distinctive prayers to formulate their doctrine of the relationship of God and man and of the destiny which God had promised to his chosen people. We learn from this passage that John the Baptist had composed such prayers; and we are now given Jesus' own instruction, which can be regarded, from one point of view, as a succinct summary of his teaching.

The version in Luke is even briefer[a] than that in Matthew. It is also less

[*a*] There was a tendency for copyists to fill out Luke's version with clauses from Matthew's. Later manuscripts therefore offer a text very similar to that in Matthew, and this is why

Jewish, in the sense that the additional clauses in Matthew can all be paralleled from Jewish prayers of the period, and that some of the phrases would have been easier for a non-Jew to understand in Luke's version than in Matthew's. Whether this makes Luke's text more likely to represent the prayer which Jesus originally taught is open to question; but it certainly lays bare, even more starkly than Matthew's, the radical economy of Jesus' teaching.

"**Father**". Even in Greek, this sounds strikingly direct and intimate, and 2
there can be little doubt that it represents the Aramaic word *Abba*. This was
a child's familiar name for its father; it was Jesus' own way of addressing his
heavenly Father; and it became a distinctive mark of the praying of Christians: through Jesus, Christians are admitted to an intimate relationship with
God, such as sons have with their father. The directness of the opening in
Luke, compared with Matthew's more formal address, expresses that new
boldness in prayer which we know to have been characteristic of Christians
from earliest times (see below on Romans 8.15). The next change is Luke's
each day for Matthew's 'today': the meaning of **daily bread** is still obscure 3
but, in Luke, life seems a little less provisional; we can look forward to
praying for bread **each day** rather than confining ourselves to 'today' and
leaving the future entirely to God. And thirdly, Luke uses the natural Greek
word for **sins** (instead of "debts"), though he brings back the Hebraic 4
concept of debt in the next words: **all who have done us wrong** (literally,
"all our debtors").

'**Ask, and you will receive.**' This apparently unconditional affirmation 9
that a Christian's prayer is always heard is illustrated, as in Matthew (7.7–11),
by the analogy of an earthly father: if God is your father—and that he is so
is a premise of the Lord's prayer and of all Christian praying that begins
Abba, "Father"—how much more will he grant the prayers of his children!
But what prayers? Luke may have been conscious of the obvious question:
surely God does not answer all prayers? In Matthew's version of the saying,
the promise seems quite general: God will give 'good things' to those who
ask him. According to Luke, there is only one prayer that will certainly be
answered, the prayer for **the Holy Spirit.** Luke also gives another small 13
parable. '**Suppose one of you has a friend**'. The scene is a Palestinian 5
one-room house, with the family all in bed; the conflict is between the rules 7
of hospitality that would be normal in village life in the east, and the trouble
caused to a whole family by such an appeal at midnight. The moral seems to
be: a pressing request (even if it looks like **shamelessness**) makes a man 8
give a friend **all he needs.** How much greater the efficacy of even an
apparently shameless prayer, given the overwhelming "friendship" of God!

older translations such as the Authorized Version (which was based on late manuscripts) offer virtually the same text in Luke as in Matthew (see the footnotes in NEB). But it is certain that Luke originally had a much briefer prayer than Matthew.

14 **The people were astonished, but some of them said.** The only substantial difference between Luke and Matthew (12.22–30) in this paragraph
is that in Luke the objectors are, not the Pharisees, but one section of the
crowd: the scene represents, not a deliberate attack by opponents, but a
puzzled reaction on the part of some of Jesus' listeners. Luke has also changed
20 one or two details. **'If it is by the finger of God'.** Matthew has, 'by the
Spirit of God'. Luke's phase is more biblical: "finger of God" occurs in
Exodus 8.19, "hand of God" frequently in the Old Testament; and these
are evidently equivalent expressions for "spirit" (compare Ezekiel 8.1 and
21 3). In verse 21 Matthew's 'strong man in his house' has become **'a strong
man fully armed . . . on guard over his castle'.** We should probably
think of a local prince, such as one of the sons of Herod the Great: many of
their palaces were heavily fortified against insurgents or against belligerent
27 neighbours from the east. **'Happy the womb that carried you'.** This brief
exchange occurs only in Luke. **Happy** is the word translated 'Blest' at the
beginning of the Sermon on the Mount. The woman's blessing is in perfectly
conventional language. Jesus caps it with another, which would have again
been unremarkable on the lips of any Jewish teacher. But the reader who was
28 aware of the uniqueness of Jesus and of the **word of God** which he preached
would have seen that the saying had a special point for the disciples and their
successors.

For the remaining details, see the comments on the parallel passages in
15–19, 24–6 Mark and Matthew: Beelzebub, Mark 3.22–7; the unclean spirit, Matthew
29–30, 33–6 12.43–5; the sign of Jonah, Matthew 12.38–42 and Mark 8.11–12; the sayings
about a lamp, Mark 4.21 and Matthew 6.22–3.

The two following sections are a striking example of Luke's way of arranging
and editing his material. The setting, a meal in a Pharisee's house, is due to
Luke (and appears to be quickly forgotten as the chapter progresses). The
38–41 background of the discussion about inner and outer cleansing is drawn from
Mark 7.1–9, and the various accusations against the Pharisees and lawyers
53–4 are all found (though in a different order) in Matthew 23. The section ends
with a summary account of Jesus' controversies which is, like the opening,
apparently due to Luke.

41 In the details, Luke's changes are very slight. **'Let what is in the cup be
given in charity'** is an obscure expansion of the simpler phrase in Matthew
(23.25). The NEB footnote suggests a possible alternative rendering, which
would involve a pun on a Greek word which can mean both "what is inside"
and "what is possible" but it may be that the Aramaic original has been
44 misunderstood. **'Alas, alas, you are like unmarked graves over which
men may walk without knowing it.'** The Jews took elaborate precautions
to avoid the defilement which followed walking over a grave: Luke's version
of this saying has an authentic Palestinian ring. So also has his introduction

of a quotation from Scripture (which however we cannot place exactly,
though it is close to 2 Chronicles 24.19) with the phrase, '**the Wisdom of** 49
God said'. The Jews were fond of referring to God in this kind of oblique
way. By contrast, the '**key of knowledge**' is an expression more at home in 52
the world of Greek religious speculation than of Jewish controversy. On the
whole, Luke shows himself to be expert on political and social conditions in
Palestine, and his recognition that only some of Jesus' accusations were
applicable equally to the Pharisees and the lawyers corresponds to the facts
better than Matthew's more simplified picture.

Meanwhile, when a crowd of many thousands had gathered. Luke **12.** 1
slightly changes the setting, but continues to offer a selection of sayings
(occurring in different contexts in other gospels), some of which are addressed
to the disciples, some to the crowd. The scene with which the previous
chapter closed—the Pharisees submitting Jesus to intensive cross-questioning
—is the cue for the first saying about **the leaven of the Pharisees.** In Mark
(8.15) the phrase is unexplained, but seems to refer to political activity. In
Matthew (16.5–12) the 'leaven' is the teaching of the Pharisees and Sadducees.
Here, it becomes the **hypocrisy** of the Pharisees: what lies behind their
profession of piety will be revealed at the Judgement—and Luke sets in this
context (of the darker things of the soul being one day brought to light) a
saying which in Matthew (10.26–7) has a quite different application. 2, 3
'**To you who are my friends I say**'. **Friends** is a new word, but clearly 4
refers to an inner ring of already loyal followers rather than to the crowd
outside, and introduces a series of sayings intended to give encouragement 4–12
under persecution. Down to verse 9, the sequence is the same as in Matthew
10.26–33. The only significant difference is that the saying in verses 8–9
introduces the figure of **the Son of Man**: here he is not a figure of glory and 8
triumph (as in Mark 8.38) so much as an "advocate" at the heavenly assize
that will be held by God with his **angels.** Verse 10 (on slandering the Holy
Spirit) is an abbreviated version of Matthew 12.31–2 (Mark 3.28–30).
Verses 11–12 correspond to Matthew 10.19–20 (Mark 13.11).
'**Master, tell my brother to divide the family property with me**'. 13
In Palestine, disputes about inheritance were complicated by the fact that
wills had to be made in accordance with detailed provisions in the Law of
Moses which defined the rights of eldest sons and of other members of the
family. At the same time there was a strong instinct to keep the family property so far as possible intact, and not to **divide** it among a number of inheritors. The lawyers who dealt with such disputes needed, in this as in other matters, to be experts in the interpretation of Scripture. Jesus had proved himself an expert, and it was perhaps natural for **a man in the crowd** to assume that he could be appealed to as a qualified judge. Jesus was reluctant; and the exchange led (at least in Luke's editing) to a general discourse about

15 **greed of every kind.** The parable which illustrates it is unusually philo-
16–21 sophical for Jesus. Instead of pressing upon its hearers the demands of a new situation (like most of the parables), it appears to be simply an illustration of the age-old truth that man proposes and God disposes. Its vividness comes more from the style of telling (the debate of the man with himself, the dramatic divine summons) and from the unexpected use of some of the catch-
19 words of popular philosophical debate ("**eat, drink, and enjoy yourself**",
20 "**You fool**") than from the intrinsic interest of the story. The moral—that true riches are of another kind—is also an old one. There is a rather similar expression of it in Ecclesiasticus 11.14–19.

22 **'I bid you put away anxious thoughts.'** These warnings against anxiety occur, in much the same words, in the Sermon on the Mount (Matthew 6.25–34). Luke, who is particularly interested in the degree of actual renunciation and poverty required in the followers of Jesus, focuses the same teaching upon every kind of preoccupation with worldly posses-
33–4 sions and, in the saying about thieves and moths, makes a little more of the contrast (again a cliché of popular philosophy) between material wealth and
33 **never-failing treasure** than is present in the more poetically balanced
32 version in Matthew (6.19–21). Jesus' followers are **a little flock**, the new elect people of God. They correspond to that faithful remnant of Israel whom Isaiah sought to strengthen in terms very similar to these words of Jesus
33 (41.8–20; 43.1–7). **'Sell your possessions and give in charity'.** Luke is clear about the distinctive way of life demanded of this small group of followers, and he is to show how it was put into practice at the very beginning of the history of the church (Acts 2.44–6).

35 **'Be ready for action'.** A Christian must be constantly alert: this theme occurs in all the gospels, and is illustrated here by several variations on the theme of a servant who is not taken by surprise when his master unexpectedly returns. In Matthew and Mark these illustrations occur when Jesus is explicitly teaching about the imminent but still unpredictable hour of general judgement which is to come upon the whole world; and in Matthew (25.1–13) the parable of the 'ten girls' (whatever its original significance may have been) is offered as an illustration of the same theme. Echoes of that parable may perhaps be heard here also. But in this chapter of Luke very little is said about the future. It looks as if Luke has deliberately shifted the emphasis of this teaching from the prediction of future woes and rewards to the inculcation of the right attitude in the present. Whether the culmination of all things was far or near (and perhaps it was beginning to seem farther than nearer by the time Luke wrote), the same vigilance and alertness were still demanded of Jesus' followers. Of course it remained true that, when the great Day finally came, there would be a stupendous reversal of accepted values: the poor, not the rich, would be blest, the last would be first, the least would be greatest. In such an age, one could even imagine the master and the servants

changing places at supper. But again, this was not only a matter of the future.
In the Christian church, the paradox had already been experienced in the
present. Their Master had come to serve (Mark 10.45) and actually **wait on** 37
them (John 13). At this point the master–servant illustration leaves the
world of ordinary experience and points unmistakably to him whom the
church came to recognize as its Servant-Lord.

Peter said. Luke makes the next paragraph (which is almost identical with 41, 42–6
Matthew 24.45–51) depend on a question of Peter's. The question is not
directly answered; but the illustration (as in Matthew) points to the Last
Judgement. The vigilance shown now will be one of the criteria by which it
will then be known whether any individual belongs to **us** or to **everyone,**
whether **he will find his place** among the faithful or **among the**
faithless.

'The servant who knew his master's wishes'. Another servant illustra- 47
tion, this time preserved only by Luke. Its point seems to be different from
the others, but we are given no clue how to interpret it. The situation it fits
best is the debate which was soon to begin between Jews and Christians.
The Jews, since they possessed the Law of Moses, claimed that they knew
their **master's wishes.** This, they believed, assured them of salvation.
Most of them shaped their lives in such a way as to **carry them out** (or so
they thought). Even those who **made no attempt** to do so could still perhaps
be saved through their solidarity with a race which was committed, as a
whole, to observing the revealed will of God. On the other hand the Gentiles
(they argued) did not know the **master's wishes**; they did not possess the
Law of Moses. The verdict on them would surely be infinitely more severe.
But suppose Jesus' merciless analysis of their way of life was right; suppose
that the Jews did not in fact succeed in keeping the Law. They might find it
was the Gentiles, not themselves, who were judged **less severely.** 48

'I have come to set fire to the earth'. Fire: a symbol of the Last 49
Judgement and an attribute of the Elijah-figure whom John the Baptist had
predicted and who was to precipitate the final phase of history. The saying is
one of those which show Jesus in this rôle of inaugurating a new and critical
epoch, and it suggests (as does the baptism saying in Mark 10.38) that he
knew that he too would be near-submerged by it—for **baptism,** in this 50
saying, is probably correctly understood by the translators as an **ordeal,**
rather than as an anticipation of the sacrament of the church. **For from now** 52
on: this note of time is Luke's most significant addition to Matthew's version
of the saying (10.34–6). **Division** within families was an outrage to Jewish 51
morals, but it was one of the features of that period of intensified evil which
(it was believed) would immediately precede the end. Jesus had said (so at
least Luke presents the matter) that such division would occur **from now**
on; and when the church found that the new faith was in fact tearing families
apart, it knew how to interpret these tragedies: they were signs of the critical

54 age which had begun, as surely as, in Palestine, clouds **in the west** mean
55 rain, and a **wind . . . from the south** brings parching heat.

58 **'When you are going with your opponent to court'**. The saying, in the Sermon on the Mount (Matthew 5.25–6), is a simple everyday illustration of the kind of conduct demanded by Jesus. Luke may simply have added it here for want of a better place; or he may have seen a rather different point in it. The **opponent** could be understood as the Christian's persecutor: in view of the urgency of the times, it was better not to get involved with him at all!

13. 1 **At that very time**: Luke was a conscious historian, and this is another instance of his concern to tie his story in with contemporary events. Unfortunately the allusions are lost on us: the historian Josephus does not mention these events, and we have to reconstruct them as best we can from the little Luke says about them. If Galileans were sacrificing in Jerusalem the occasion must have been a Passover, when thousands of pilgrims came in and slaughtered their lambs in the temple. We know that this was often an occasion for civil disorders, and it is quite possible that Pilate had to use
4 force to restore order even in the temple area. It is less surprising that the disaster at Siloam is not mentioned by Josephus. The south-east corner of the city walls of Jerusalem stood on high ground looking over the Pool of Siloam. Some repairs to one of the towers were doubtless the occasion for this accident, which may have been very much in the news in the last year of Jesus' life, but would have been completely forgotten a few years later had not Jesus commented upon it. The contemporary Jewish explanation of why such calamities befall individuals was very simple (though it was often made more plausible by some subtle refinements): they must have sinned, and this was their punishment. Jesus did not altogether reject this solution; there were certainly occasions on which he seems to have regarded illness as a consequence of sin. But here he offers a more prophetic explanation: these catastrophes are warnings, they are typical of the fate which awaits you all
5 —**'unless you repent.'**

6 **He told them this parable**—and its theme is the same: repentance. Fruit and vegetables were grown in vineyards alongside the vines, but clearly a tree had to yield fruit if it were to justify the amount of good it took out of the soil. Manuring a fig-tree would be a somewhat exceptional measure. So too the activity of Jesus was exceptional, and gave his hearers an exceptional opportunity to repent.

10 **One Sabbath he was teaching in a synagogue**—a typical instance of a Sabbath controversy provoked by a miracle of healing. Luke has already recorded one such episode (6.6–11), and this one (which has no exact parallel in the other gospels) follows the same pattern, but with slightly different
11 details. The sufferer was **bent double**. In modern terms, we would say her

condition was one of physical deformity; but it was apparently quite natural to think of this, no less than an obviously mental disorder like epilepsy, as a case of being **possessed by a spirit.** The miracle, then, was an exorcism; and there is considerable play, throughout the paragraph, on the words "binding" and "freeing" (though this can hardly be reproduced in an English translation). We can detect, below the surface, a whole mythology of evil: Satan "binds" his victims, but when he himself is "bound" by one who is stronger (see above on Mark 3.27), his victims are "freed". However,
the real interest of the story lies in the dialogue between Jesus and **the presi-** 14
dent of the synagogue. Granted their own premises, it is a little difficult to
see why Jesus' opponents should have been **covered with confusion.** In 17
the following centuries, careful regulations were made which permitted Jews to do what was necessary for their animals without infringing the Sabbath rest; and doubtless some such regulations were already in force. If so, they could well have answered that they did not neglect the needs of their animals, but they still kept the Sabbath, and a permanently crippled woman could just as well have been healed another day. In his attack on them, Jesus seems
to have argued *ad hominem*. The woman is called a **daughter of Abraham** 16
—an appeal to the solidarity of the Jewish race—and a rather artificial parallel is drawn between loosing an animal from a manger and loosing a person from Satan. But if the argument seems thin, the point was gained in any case by the miraculous cure: only blinkered legalists could regard such an action as wrong, even on the Sabbath.

The two brief parables of mustard-seed and yeast occur (without any 18–20
interpretation) in the parable-chapters of Matthew and Mark (Matthew 13.31–3; Mark 4.30–2).

He continued his journey. So much has happened since Luke told us that 22
Jesus had begun his journey from Galilee to Jerusalem that we need to be reminded of it; for the journey is in reality little more than the literary framework for a collection of otherwise disconnected sayings and episodes. In this section, as so often, Luke gets the dialogue moving with a question from one of Jesus' listeners. The reply, and the sayings which follow it, are all familiar from Matthew's gospel, but appear in a strangely different combination. The
'narrow gate' of Matthew 7.13 has become a **narrow door**, and the difficulty 24
is not to find it (Matthew 7.14) but, having found it, **to enter**—for there is a danger of being too late, and the door may be shut (as it is in the parable in Matthew 25.10). Those who are too late are greeted only with a fierce
dismissal—"**Out of my sight, all of you, you and your wicked ways!**" (a 27
quotation from Psalm 6.8)—regardless of their apparent right to enter. Here again Luke offers a different application from that in Matthew (7.22–3), where those excluded are spurious Christian prophets. Here they are Jesus' own society and nation, the Jews—and this leads to the strongly anti-Jewish

29 picture of Gentiles having precedence over Jews in the coming **feast in the kingdom of God**, almost exactly as in Matthew (8.11–12), and complete with a phrase which is otherwise entirely confined to Matthew's gospel,
28 **wailing and grinding of teeth.**

31 **At that time a number of Pharisees came to him.** Mark says (3.6) that the Pharisees were in league with the partisans of Herod. Were they now plotting an ambush together, or had the Pharisees suddenly become anxious to save Jesus' life? We do not know—though it is interesting that in Acts Luke represents the Pharisees as initially sympathetic to Christianity. In any case Jesus' reply was doubtless remembered for its own sake, and not for the light it threw on his relations with Herod and the Pharisees. It also shows that Luke imagined Jesus' journey to be still through the territory of Herod
32 Antipas, that is to say, through Galilee or Transjordan. **He replied, 'Go and tell that fox'.** To the Greeks, as to us, the fox was a by-word for cunning; but in Hebrew writings it more often stood simply for a puny creature, and Jesus may have been saying, "Go and tell your little king". His reply, nevertheless, was very much to the point. Herod wished to put an end to Jesus' activity of **casting out devils and working cures.** But he did not need to trouble himself. **On the third day**—three days was a natural way of describing any short space of time (e.g. Jonah 1.17)—it would all be brought to an end by the will of a power far greater than Herod's, and Jesus would have reached his **goal.** The Greek word here is as ambiguous as the English, and leads on to a saying about the geographical "goal" of Jesus'
33 journey, Jerusalem. **'It is unthinkable for a prophet to meet his death anywhere but in Jerusalem.'** This seems to put it very strongly: it was only a fairly recent tradition which asserted that most of the prophets had in fact been killed in Jerusalem.[a] But for Luke, with a historian's bird's-eye view of religious developments in Palestine, any other destiny for Jesus may well have seemed **unthinkable.** And there follows, with great appropriate-
34–5 ness, a lament over Jerusalem in virtually the same words as in Matthew 23.37–9.

14. 1 **One Sabbath he went to have a meal.** The main meal on a Sabbath took place after the morning service in the synagogue, and guests were often invited. Perhaps Jesus had been preaching, and was invited to the meal afterwards; in any case, his presence on such an occasion **in the house of a leading Pharisee** (that is to say, probably a leading member of the community who also happened to be a Pharisee) was perfectly natural—and Luke makes it the occasion for a number of sayings to do with feasts and banquets. But first, there was a healing miracle to record. Jesus' question,
3 **'Is it permitted to cure people on the Sabbath or not?'** probably had a perfectly clear-cut answer in the teaching of the lawyers and the Pharisees:

[a] See above on Matthew 23.29.

it was permitted when it was a question of saving life, but otherwise not. The man with dropsy was not in immediate danger, therefore it was not permitted to treat him. But possibly the sheer inhumanity of this principle when there was a prospect of an immediate miraculous cure reduced them to silence,
and **they said nothing.** If the Law permitted them (as it did) to save even 4
an animal's life on the Sabbath, how could they be so casuistical as to regard it as wrong to heal a man?

Elsewhere, Jesus explicitly criticizes the lawyers and Pharisees for their
tendency to seek **the places of honour** (for at any formal meal the seating 7
at table was strictly by seniority). Here, he contrasts this fashion with a rule of his own—which is what, in this instance, the word **parable** seems to
mean.[a] The rule itself ('**Do not sit down in the place of honour**') was an 8
old one (Proverbs 25.6–7) and was not strange to Jesus' contemporaries; and even the motive Jesus gave for it was not unmixed modesty but a desire that
the **fellow-guests will see the respect in which you are held.** However, 10
a saying is added (perhaps by Luke, for it occurs also in other contexts, Luke 18.14, Matthew 23.12) which makes the rule into a **parable** in another sense: it is an illustration of that great reversal of values which will be a
feature of the kingdom of God. '**Whoever humbles himself will be** 11
exalted'.

Then he said to his host. Another rule, this time based on Jesus' 12
distinctive principle (6.33) that one must do good without expecting any return. Jewish culture was very conscious of the curse of poverty, and when any large party was given it was not done to exclude paupers and beggars who might be fed on what was left over. Moreover, many devout Jews made a point of keeping open house to the poor. Jesus' rule only goes further than this in that the poor were to be invited, not in addition to the usual guests, but instead of them.

One of the company, after hearing all this. Practical questions 15
about hospitality led the mind naturally to the **feast in the kingdom of God.** This was an image which, ever since Old Testament times, the Jews loved to use for the promised reward which awaited the just and devout of their nation. '**Happy the man who shall sit at the feast**' was a typical "beatitude": a Jewish teacher might well use it to encourage his students to greater virtue. But Jesus' beatitudes struck a different note: 'how blest are those in need' (6.20); and the story that follows illustrates the contrast. The story itself runs more smoothly in Luke than in Matthew (22.1–14), whether because of Luke's more careful editing or because he had access to a purer version of it. It faithfully reflects Palestinian customs; but at the same time it has one or two touches which point to a subsequent adaptation of the story to the needs of the church. It was a normal courtesy to send a servant to
inform the invited guests when the dinner was ready; but if it was a **big** 16

[*a*] On the wide range of meanings of this word, see above on Mark 3.23.

dinner party, one servant could hardly have managed the task alone.
Matthew, more plausibly, makes the host send 'his servants', but Luke's
single servant may be intended to help the reader to think of Jesus, sent by
God with the final summons to the kingdom. The first two excuses (which
are here made more explicit than in Matthew) are entirely plausible: the
last hour of daylight, after the day's work was finished, was the natural time
to complete a purchase of land or livestock, and since large dinner parties
normally lasted well into the night, the guest would normally lose nothing by
giving his apologies to the servant and arriving somewhat later. For this
21 seems to be the point of the story. Instead of keeping these guests' places for
them (as would have been usual) the indignant host sent his servant **out
quickly** to bring in all the beggars who could be found, so that those whom
he had invited (who were men of considerable substance if they could afford
five yoke of oxen) would suffer the indignity of arriving at the house and
15 being turned away because there was no room for them. '**Happy the man
who shall sit at the feast in the kingdom of God!**' Yes, but (Jesus
replies) this happiness may be enjoyed by those whom you least expect. It is
the poor who are **happy** (or "blest", the same word in the Greek). The
24 others, by putting it off, have missed their chance: '**I tell you that not one
of those who were invited shall taste my banquet**'. However, two
further details suggest how this story was used in the early church. First, the
20 third excuse: "**I have just got married and for that reason I cannot
come**". There is no hint of this in Matthew's version, and it fits awkwardly
into the story; for unlike the others, who could have come late, a newly
married man could not have come at all, and it is difficult to see how he could
have accepted the invitation in the first place. On the other hand, some
Christians soon came to see marriage, as well as possessions, as an obstacle
to following the call of Jesus (the servant), and this, as well as artistic symmetry (for most good stories contain groups of three) may have helped this
extra detail to come into the story. Secondly, the servant is commanded to go,
21 not only into **the streets and alleys** (as in Matthew) but also **on to the
23 highways and along the hedgerows.** This is perfectly plausible; beggars
were to be found outside cities on the roads, especially in the shelter of a
wall that enclosed some estate or vineyard (there were no **hedgerows** in
Palestine: the Greek word here means a wall or a fence). But it is also a
perfectly intelligible symbol for those who were "outside" the Jewish
nation—the Gentiles. The subsequent history of the church was to demonstrate that it was these people, not the Jews, who got in first.

26 **'If anyone comes to me and does not hate his father and mother'.**
Matthew (10.37) has 'who cares more for father or mother', and this is
clearly the meaning; Luke's more violent version may nevertheless be closer
to Jesus' own language (see above on Matthew 5.43). Moreover, the saying
in Matthew is addressed to those who are already disciples. Luke, by bringing

in **great crowds**, has given this and the following sayings a rather different 25
meaning: this is what you must be prepared for if you are contemplating
following me. '**None of you can be a disciple of mine without parting** 33
with all his possessions'. This extreme implication of Jesus' teaching about poverty and detachment occurs only in Luke; and it is a question in which Luke seems to be particularly interested, both when recording Jesus' sayings and when relating the church's attempt to put the principle into practice (Acts 2.44; 5.1–12). It comes in here as the corollary of two little
illustrations which seem to have the moral: Count the cost first! But, though 28–32
the paragraph hangs together well enough, the examples of the man building a tower and the king planning a campaign do not quite do what is expected of them; for their natural meaning is that one should not begin at all unless one is sure one can finish. This seems an unlikely thing for Jesus to have
said about Christian discipleship in general. But if the sayings were originally 34
intended, not for the crowds (as here), but for the small group of disciples who were steeling themselves to face whatever lay ahead of Jesus, then they would make good sense if they were spoken by way of encouragement at a moment when the disciples were faltering: you cannot give up now, you should have counted the cost before you began following me!

'**This fellow**', **they said**, '**welcomes sinners and eats with them**'. **15.** 2
Several other episodes have illustrated the offence Jesus gave by consorting with **sinners**—that is, with those whose profession or way of life excluded them from the privileged position which all law-abiding Jews claimed to possess in the economy of God. It was clearly expected of him, as the leader of a new religious movement, to be as careful about the company he kept as the highly exclusive fellowships of the Pharisees. The defence Jesus made on this occasion involved a small but very important difference between himself and his opponents. It could not be said of the Pharisees, or indeed of Jewish religious thinkers generally, that they did not value repentance. On the contrary, they took it for granted that a truly penitent man was accepted by God, and they made no objection to welcoming a "sinner" into their company if he had shown genuine signs of repentance. But it was essential that the sinner should take the initiative: he must first repent, and only then could he be "welcomed", either by God or by his fellow-men. There was no question of having anything to do with him until he showed signs of renouncing his old ways. Jesus' offence consisted in not waiting for these signs.

On this occasion, Jesus justified his initiative with a group of parables (the first of which occurs also in Matthew 18.12–14, but with a quite different point). Luke, compared with Matthew, dwells a little more on the moment
of finding: the shepherd lifts the sheep **on to his shoulders** (the only way 5
of carrying an injured or exhausted animal), the woman (and also, less appropriately, the shepherd) invites friends and neighbours in to celebrate

8 the find—she is evidently very poor, for the value of the **ten silver pieces**
(Luke gives them the name of the equivalent Greek coins, *drachmas*) only
amounts to a pound by NEB values. All the emphasis is on the joy which
follows finding what was lost; and if it is true that the sinner is also someone
who is "lost", it is legitimate to read off from these simple illustrations
7 something of the **joy in heaven over one sinner who repents.** It follows
that repentance is not (as the Pharisees would probably have put it) just a
way of making amends for past misdeeds and rejoining the ranks of the just.
It belongs to a different order of things altogether.

11–32 The third parable (for which "The Prodigal Son" is perhaps not the best
title, since all the emphasis is on the behaviour of the father) illustrates the
same point, but takes it a great deal further. The opening reflects actual
conditions in Palestine. A father could either bequeath his property in his
will (in which case it was laid down by law how he must divide it between his
heirs), or else make a gift of it before he died, in which case he was free to
dispose of it as he wished, but was entitled to the produce or the interest
until his death. The younger son's request was quite normal: the main part
of the property would in any case go to his elder brother, and he could expect
13 to do better by turning **his share into cash**[a] and setting himself up in
business among the Jews of the Dispersion in some foreign city, than by
trying to live on a small-holding in the over-populated farmland of Palestine.
14 However, his taste for **reckless living,** combined with **a severe famine**
(which would have sent up the price of food) soon brought him to total
poverty. He hired himself out to a gentile employer (and minding pigs would
have been a job particularly repugnant to a Jew), but even so his wages were
not sufficient to buy himself food (at least in famine conditions), and he
16 would have been content even with the pauper's diet of carob-tree pods—
had he been able to get them, but they were jealously guarded for the pigs.
In despair, he decided to return home.

So far, the story is a typical rake's progress. But the reaction of the father
20 is new and arresting. **He ran to meet him**—which was very much beneath
the dignity of the head of a family—and instead of listening to his son's
22 request or testing his penitence, he invested him in the **robe** reserved for an
honoured guest, and showed, with the gift of **ring** and **shoes,** how far he was
17 from treating the prodigal as one of his **paid servants.** The welcome, the
presents, the feast were all tokens of his joy at finding one who was lost. The
story, thus far, is a humanly convincing example of that same joy which is
the point of the preceding two parables. But, if it is legitimate to read off
from it a general lesson about the nature of God's forgiveness (and it is
irresistible to do so, since it yields such riches in the process), one point in
particular seems relevant to Jesus' controversy with his opponents. They laid

[*a*] This is probably, but not certainly, what the Greek phrase means. Older versions have "gathered all he had together", which is also possible.

down all kinds of conditions (genuineness, lastingness, a will to make reparation, etc.) which a sinner's repentance had to fulfil if it were to be accepted. But in the parable, it was sufficient for the son simply to return to his father. Similarly, it was not necessary for the "sinners" with whom Jesus consorted to prove their penitence: it was sufficient that they sought his company.

This already provided part of the answer to those who were criticizing
Jesus for consorting with sinners. But the parable goes on. From the point
of view of strict fairness, the elder son had a genuine grievance: while he
had **slaved** for years to work his father's estate, and had gone on working it 29
for his father's benefit even after it had become legally his own, his brother,
by squandering his inheritance, had deprived his father of the interest due
to him. Surely, therefore, the rewards given to the younger brother were
inappropriate and unfair. Once again, the father acted with striking generosity.
Instead of waiting until his elder son approached him (as fitted his dignity),
he **came out and pleaded with him. "Everything I have is yours".** 29, 31
This was technically true: the original gift of the entire property to the elder
son was a sign of much greater esteem than the killing of the fatted calf for
the younger. But the main force of the appeal depended, not on technicali-
ties, but on humanity: **"How could we help celebrating this happy** 32
day?" Jesus' strongest argument against his critics likewise depended, not
on technical definitions of repentance, but on those ultimate principles of
humanity which are a sure guide to the nature of God's dealings with men.

'There was a rich man who had a steward'. The situation must have 16. 1
been a common one in Palestine, where there were many large estates, owned
by absentee landlords, and administered by a **steward.** But the story itself
is puzzling. On the face of it, the steward's action was dishonest and unscrupulous, and we are astonished to read at the end that **the master** 8
applauded the dishonest steward. It is true that this last sentence is
ambiguous. The Greek words for **the master** could also mean "the Lord".
The sentence might therefore be, not a continuation of the story, but a
comment on it by Luke: "Jesus applauded the dishonest steward". But this
does not make the matter any easier. Why should Jesus, any more than the
rich man in the parable, have **applauded** a blatant case of dishonesty?

However, the situation presupposed in the parable may not be quite what
it seems at first sight. The steward had been accused of **squandering the** 1
property. What does this mean? Simply helping himself to more than his
due from the revenues would hardly have constituted **squandering**—the
word is that used of the younger son of the previous parable who 'squandered' his whole fortune in reckless living. More likely, the steward had been trying to enrich himself by lending out at a high rate of interest large sums from his master's fortune, to the detriment of the proper management of the estate. In Jewish circles, this was strictly illegal (for usury was forbidden); but there were many ways round this prohibition, and a steward who behaved

8 in this way, though he would certainly be morally **dishonest**, might nevertheless succeed in keeping on the right side of the law. It is true that there is
1 not a word in this parable to say that this was the kind of **squandering** involved;[a] but if we suppose that it was, then the negotiations with the debtors become more plausible. The amount they owed was very large—too large, surely to represent arrears of rent payable by tenants to a landlord; and the steward is hardly to be imagined as having paid large sums on account to merchants who had then failed to honour their contracts (for this was not the usual way of doing business and could anyway hardly be described as **squandering**). On the other hand, if the debtors were borrowers, the situation immediately becomes intelligible. Repayment in kind was regular practice (and incidentally provided many loopholes for avoiding the technical prohibition of usury). The difference between a thousand and eight hundred bushels of wheat represents interest at twenty-five per cent (a normal rate), and the difference between a thousand and five hundred gallons of olive oil represents interest at one hundred per cent, which sounds very high, but is not without parallel in antiquity, since oil was a much riskier commodity than wheat. This interest the steward had hoped to receive as personal profit; the rest represented what had to be repaid to his master. But in view of his imminent dismissal, he decided to forgo the profit, and by voluntarily liquidating the original contracts and replacing them with bare statements of the amount of the original loan, he earned the gratitude of the debtors and the approbation of society at large—for easing or remitting the repayment of a loan was regarded by the Jews as a singularly meritorious act.

8 **The master applauded the dishonest steward for acting so astutely.** If this explanation of the parable is on the right lines, the comment becomes intelligible. The master had not been cheated as a result of the steward's hasty transactions. On the contrary, the steward, seeing where his true interests lay, had abandoned his own chances of immediate profit, and the master had quickly recovered his capital. The steward offered a commendable example of radical action in the face of a crisis. This may well have been the point Jesus wished to make, here as elsewhere. Judgement was imminent: no time must be lost in remitting debts, forgiving offences, and preparing oneself for the kingdom of God.

Nevertheless, in the form in which it has come down to us, the parable is exceedingly obscure. A great many details have to be read into it in order to make it yield an acceptable sense. What did Luke think was the moral?

He appears to offer no less than three, but two of these are unfortunately
8 as obscure as the story itself. (i) '**The worldly are more astute than the other-worldly in dealing with their own kind**'. The steward was certainly **astute** (this is strongly emphasized in the parable); but if this saying

[a] Though the word used for "squandering" is the same as that translated 'scattered' in Matthew 25.24, and there it does seem to carry the meaning, "lending out for interest".

is to be seen as anything more than a cheap comment on unpractical pietists, it is necessary to find something admirable in his astuteness. If in fact it consisted of the praiseworthy act of freely remitting debts then, even if his motives were astute and self-regarding, his conduct could be held up as an example to Christians who, with their infinitely more altruistic ideals, could hardly afford to be less generous than a **dishonest steward.** But does **the other-worldly** mean Christians? Literally, the phrase means "the sons of light", which is as unusual an expression for religious people as **the worldly** (literally, "the sons of this age") is usual for the irreligious. It appears to be a phrase which some religious sects (if we may judge from the Dead Sea Scrolls) liked to use of their own members. It is quite likely that at some stage the Christian community began to use similar language about itself. (ii)
'Use your worldly wealth to win friends for yourselves'. This again 9
clearly refers back to the parable. The steward had "made friends" by his prompt action (verse 4). Christians are to do the same, though in a more lasting sense, in that instead of procuring for themselves hospitable homes on earth they are to obtain **an eternal home** in heaven. But how is **worldly wealth** to be used for this purpose? If the steward of the parable was dishonest all along the line, it is hard to draw any moral; but if he genuinely remitted debts to his own disadvantage, then again he can serve as an example to Christians, who are to secure their ultimate reward by renouncing every kind of monetary gain. (The phrase translated **worldly wealth** is a curious one, and means literally "unrighteous mammon". This may correspond to a Hebrew expression meaning any kind of financial profit which, strictly
speaking, was forbidden under the Law.) (iii) **'The man who can be** 10
trusted in little things can be trusted also in great'. This group of 10–12
sayings simply commends trustworthiness, and would be a more appropriate comment on the parable of the pounds (19.11–27) than on this one; but perhaps it also serves here as a warning against taking the dishonest steward as an example of the wrong kind of "astuteness".

There is no obvious connection between the sayings which follow, and all 13–18
except one of them have parallels in different parts of Matthew or Mark: verse 13 = Matthew 6.24, verse 16 = Matthew 11.12–13, verse 17 = Matthew 5.18, verse 18 = Mark 10.11–12 (and, with a significant variation, Matthew
5.32). Verses 14–15 however are found only in Luke. **The Pharisees, who** 14
loved money. It is unlikely that the Pharisees as a class were wealthy; indeed we know of several learned Pharisees who were very poor. But there were certainly some who were not above turning their reputation for sound learning to financial advantage, and even the strictest of them found means of accommodating their interpretation of the law to the necessity of commercial transactions. Much as they praised the virtue of alms-giving, they regarded it as positively undesirable to impoverish oneself by too much generosity, and their attitude to money was a great deal less radical than that

of Jesus. Jesus' criticism of them here is a variation of his usual attack on
their "hypocrisy". Their outward show of strict observance is a cloak, not
just for a lack of humanity, but for a preoccupation with worldly gain. The
social position they achieve by these means puts them in the category of
those who must expect a reversal of fortune: as it is expressed in Mary's song
at the beginning of the gospel (1.51), 'the arrogant of heart and mind God
15 has put to rout'. Or, still more drastically, **'What sets itself up to be**
admired by men is detestable in the sight of God'.

19 **'There was once a rich man'**—unnamed, like most of the characters
in the parables (though in the course of time he has acquired a name, Dives,
which is simply the Latin for "rich man"). Surprisingly, the poor man has
20 a name: **Lazarus** (the Greek form of a common Jewish name, Eleazar). The
contrast is carefully drawn: purple and fine linen and daily feasting were
marks of the greatest luxury, while the beggar was a cripple (he **lay**) who
had no one even to keep the dogs from trying to slake their thirst by licking
his sores (as they would in a dry summer, when water was far too precious
21 to give to dogs). It is true that it was unusual not to allow beggars **the scraps**
from the table, but nothing is said by way of moral judgement on either the
rich man or Lazarus. All we are told is that one was very rich, the other very
poor. In the next scene the contrast is equally vivid, though the setting is
drawn from contemporary Jewish folklore and popular religion. Whatever
might be said in theory about a general resurrection and a universal Last
Judgement, ordinary people in Palestine certainly believed (as ordinary
people have always believed in many parts of the world) that immediately
after death some go to heaven and some go to hell. Clearly Jesus was not
using the parable as an opportunity to give new teaching about the after-life.
22 On the contrary, **the angels** escorting Lazarus, the presence of **Abraham**
24 in heaven, the **fire** in hell, and the glimpse given to the damned of the better
lot they might have had, were all standard features of popular Jewish belief.
Again there is no moralizing. It is a simple contrast; one is very happy, the
other very unhappy, not because of their virtues and vices, but because of a
necessary reversal of fortunes. Thus far, the parable is a pictorial statement
of that great change in values proclaimed in Jesus' beatitudes: 'How blest
are you who now go hungry; your hunger shall be satisfied' (Luke 6.21);
'how blest are the sorrowful; they shall find consolation' (Matthew 5.4).

'Blest are you who are in need', 'Alas for you who are rich' (Luke 6.20, 24).
The message is stark and clear (especially in Luke's gospel). But can nothing
be done, cannot the rich still be saved? Certainly not after death: it will be
26 too late then, **there is a great chasm fixed.** But suppose a messenger were
sent to the rich who are still alive, to warn them? The parable goes on to
deny even this possibility—and here it seems to point to the very heart of
Jesus' understanding of himself and the people among whom he worked.
29 **'They have Moses and the prophets'.** The Jews were uniquely privileged

in having, in the Old Testament, an authoritative guide to the conduct required of them by God. But even to this they could be indifferent—they "hear and hear but understand nothing" in the words of Isaiah quoted by Jesus on another occasion (Mark 4.12)—so much so that they could still tolerate extremes of riches and poverty in their own society. No further prompting by God would help these "children of Abraham" (like the rich man of the parable) to live worthily of their inheritance, not even if someone
should rise from the dead—and the parable ends with tantalizing allusions 31
to another Lazarus who did "rise from the dead" (John 11—did Luke know of this?), and to Jesus himself, whose own resurrection at first aroused incredulity and even mockery (Acts 17.32).

'Causes of stumbling are bound to arise'. The phrase is barely English, 17. 1
and in the original it is barely Greek. The reason is that **causes of stumbling** is an expression so loaded with meaning from the Old Testament that it almost serves as shorthand for a number of distinctive Jewish beliefs. The underlying metaphor is of a snare into which one falls or an obstacle over which one stumbles. To us, the metaphor suggests the kind of things which cause accidents. But the Hebrews seldom thought of things happening by accident: either someone had deliberately laid a snare, or else it was intended by God that a person should be tripped. And so the metaphor was used of all sorts of catastrophes or dangers which God laid in the path of his people or of an individual in order to test or to punish them (Isaiah 8.14; Jeremiah 6.21; Ezekiel 3.20). Jesus' followers would not be immune from such trials: there would be persecutions from outside and heresy and schism from within. Such things were **bound to arise**. But this would be no excuse for any member of the community willingly precipitating further trials by thoughtless or malicious behaviour.

By the **little ones** who must not be made to stumble, Jesus may originally 2
have meant small children: he was exceptionally interested in them for a religious teacher of his time. Children must always have been following him about, as they still do any unusual person in the east; and Jesus took notice of them instead of ignoring them. But the church was more interested in its own "little ones", the weaker brethren who might stumble over the radical implications of Jesus' teaching; and this is probably how Luke (like Matthew, 18.6) understood the phrase here.

'If your brother wrongs you'. Compare Matthew 18.15, 21–2, where the 3
same rule is given as part of the order of the church. **Seven times in a day** is 4
equivalent to Matthew's 'seventy times seven'—an unlimited number of times.

The apostles (seldom so called in the gospels, see above on 6.13) **said** 5
to the Lord—a typically Lucan introduction to a saying also recorded in
Mark (11.23) and Matthew (17.20). Luke replaces 'mountain' by **mulberry-** 6
tree, we do not know why.

7 **'Suppose one of you has a servant'.** The application of this little
parable is built into it from the start. It was a common idiom of religious
speech to call oneself "God's servant", and what was true of the relationship
of master and servant could be seen to be true, in important respects, of that
between God and man. If the relationship described in the parable sounds
austere, it must be remembered that the word **servant** meant literally a
slave. The master here is of modest means, having only one slave both to
work on his farm and to look after the house. He is under no obligation to
put his slave's comfort before his own. Equally, the slave is in no position
10 to take credit [a] for completing his usual routine. **'So with you: when you
have carried out all your orders'.** Men's **orders** from God were the
detailed commands and prohibitions of the Law of Moses. There were many
of Jesus' contemporaries who believed they "deserved credit" for their
meticulous observance of them, and failed to realize that the demands of God
upon man are far more fundamental than can be expressed in any set of
orders.

11 **He was travelling through the borderlands of Samaria and Galilee.**
On the map this makes little sense (and the translation **through the borderlands** is itself a simplification of a puzzling Greek phrase). By now—since
Jesus' "journey" has lasted through eight chapters—he should have left
Galilee far behind. But Luke may have had a rather different picture of the
geography and imagined that much of Jesus' journey lay close to the Samaritan frontier (see above, p. 250). If so, he would have seen nothing inappropriate in placing a story involving a Samaritan at this stage in the journey.

12 **Ten men with leprosy.** On the disease and its social consequences, see
above on Mark 1.40–5. The lepers were necessarily on the edge of the
village, and **stood some way off** to avoid contact. Jesus' reply to their appeal
14 took the unexpected form of a command to **'go and show yourselves to
the priests'.** The command occurs in Mark's story (1.44) of the cleansing
of a single leper, and we can see the point of it from Jesus' point of view: he
did not wish to come into conflict with the priests by trespassing on their
prerogatives. But, in Luke's story, what sort of answer was it to the lepers'
appeal? They must have known that, in their present state, they had no hope
of being certified **clean** by a priest—otherwise they would have gone for
examination long ago. Jesus' answer could only mean that, if they went now,
they would be well enough by the time they arrived at the temple to be
certified clean—which is just what happened. We can assume that nine of
them were Jews, and had to go to Jerusalem for the purpose; but the tenth,
being a Samaritan, must have gone to the ruins of the Samaritan temple on
15 Mount Gerizim in Samaria. Precisely when he **turned back** (whether before
or after he had seen a priest) is not stated; nor is it clear exactly what the

[*a*] The translation, **deserve no credit,** is probably correct, though the usual meaning of the word is that given by older translations, "unprofitable".

others ought to have done. But these details probably did not trouble the narrator, who saw in the story a clear illustration of two points he had already made elsewhere: first, even a Samaritan can be an example to a Jew; secondly,
a man's **faith** is more important than the race he belongs to. 19

The Pharisees asked him, 'When will the kingdom of God come?' 20
Given the earnest expectation for a new order of things which (at least in Palestine) ran right through the Jewish religion, and given the fact that this new order was expected to come, not by gradual evolution, but by a sudden act of God, the question was an obvious one to put to Jesus, and was asked by friends and enemies alike. When asked by the Pharisees, the question may have been intended to elicit a reply which (if it were at all naïve or literal) would bring Jesus into ridicule; but Jesus avoided the trap. **'You cannot tell by observation'**—the word suggests particularly astrological observation, calculations from the conjunctions of stars with historical events—and Jesus showed that he agreed with all those learned and responsible Jews who tried to discourage this kind of fanciful speculation about
the future. **'There will be no saying, "Look, here it is!"'**, as if it were 21
likely to be something doubtful and ambiguous, needing careful inspection to check its authenticity. Jesus then went on to add a positive answer of his own to the question—but exactly what that answer was is obscured from us by the imprecise Greek in which it is recorded. **'The kingdom of God is among you'** (or within you, or within your grasp—see the footnote in NEB). Several meanings are possible—and it may be that the preposition in Jesus' own language was equally ambiguous, since Jewish scholars themselves debated what was meant by saying that God was "among them": did it mean, God saw that they were clothed and fed, or that God knew their innermost thoughts? Older translations of Jesus' saying have mainly preferred "within you". But this suggests an inner spiritual experience, which is something very different from what the Jews—and, it appears, Jesus—meant by the kingdom of God. Jesus seems to have talked of the kingdom both as a future consummation and as an already perceptible reality. Something of his new and rich understanding of the old Jewish phrase probably lurks in this difficult saying.

He said to the disciples. Luke changes the setting, even though the 22
subject is still the same: the culmination of history in the Last Judgement and the inauguration of a new age. Jesus projected himself into this drama in the rôle of the Son of Man; and Christians, therefore, looked forward to it as **one of the days of the Son of Man.** Perhaps, when Luke wrote, there was already a disappointed longing for this "day", and this saying seemed to offer an antidote; certainly there was for a long
time a temptation to abandon ordinary occupations and **go running off in** 23
pursuit of anything which seemed to promise the advent of the new era.

There were sayings of Jesus to discourage this (compare Matthew 24.26–7); there were also sayings about the darker side of the destiny of the Son of Man which should have corrected a one-sided preoccupation with his ultimate glory (see above on Mark 8.31).

26 **'As things were in Noah's days'.** The rest of the chapter inculcates the
27–37 attitude of vigilance and readiness for immediate action which must be maintained in the face of what is to come. The sayings are almost all found (somewhat differently arranged) in Matthew 24. Luke adds to the example of Noah that of Lot (the two were often paired together—see 2 Peter 2.5–6 for
32 another example), and gives us the proverb, **'Remember Lot's wife'.** The two biblical stories not only warn against neglecting the signs of the times. It is also fatal (doubtless in the Christian life in general, as well as at the last critical moment) to look back!

18. 1 **He spoke to them in a parable.** One of the characters in this little story is
6 called **the unjust judge,** and this has given its name to the parable. But it is important to see in what sense he was **unjust.** The setting was a small town.
3 **A widow**—which was a byword for someone reduced to poverty through no fault of her own—had been the victim of some fraud or sharp practice, and in order to recover her money she had to go to law. In such cases, this did not involve a formal sitting of a court; it was sufficient for the parties to agree upon a qualified lawyer to arbitrate between them. The little town, in any case, may have possessed only one such lawyer; if so, the widow's only hope of redress lay in persuading this lawyer to attend to her case. Now it was a fundamental principle of Jewish justice that a judge received no payment. There was therefore only a moral obligation for the lawyer to attend to all the cases brought before him. This particular lawyer was not
2 sensitive to his moral obligations—he **cared nothing for God or man;** possibly he waited until litigants brought him a present before he concerned himself with their affairs. But the widow, by again and again thrusting her papers in front of him, finally got her way.

6 The **unjust judge,** therefore, was not necessarily guilty of perverting justice; indeed it might be less misleading to call him "the unrighteous judge",[a] since it was his unreadiness to do his duty and hear cases brought before him which was reprehensible. The justice of the widow's claim is taken for granted; the point is the difficulty she had in getting it attended to. The application of the parable follows easily. Christians needed to have no doubts about the rightness of their cause; but, in the face of calumny and persecution, they longed for vindication. This was expected to take the form of a reversal of present values, a bringing to light of the things known

[a] This is an equally faithful translation of the original, which probably represents a Hebrew idiom, "judge belonging to the world of unrighteousness, the world of inadequate observance of the Law".

only to faith, and the visible establishment of the Christian community as
the chosen people of God—in short, the end of the present order, the judgement, and the new age. Those things were taking longer to come than perhaps
the earliest generation of Christians expected (a disappointment which may
underlie the difficult phrase, **while he listens patiently to them**; an 7
alternative rendering is given in the NEB footnote—"while he delays to help
them"—which would make this clearer). But they must **keep on praying** 1
for them. If even a neglectful human judge yielded at last to constant
entreaties, how much more certainly would God **vindicate his chosen**! 6
But that moment of vindication would always involve judgement. Anyone
who had lost faith (perhaps because of the delay) would have reason to fear
it. **'When the Son of Man comes, will he find faith on earth?'** 8

And here is another parable that he told. The scene this time is set 9
in the main inner quadrangle of the temple at Jerusalem at the hour of the
morning or evening sacrifice. At these two times in the day every Jew was
bidden to pray, either in the synagogue or else wherever he happened to be;
but if he was near by, he **went up to the temple** for the purpose, and 10
joined the crowd of those who were present at the sacrifice. The Pharisee's
prayer probably sounded a great deal less objectionable then than it does to
us now. He was not necessarily priding himself on his virtues; rather, he was
thanking God for the privilege of leading a life which, both in public and in
private, laid him open to no charge of rapacity, failure to observe the law,
or adultery. For example: far from ever failing to observe the annual fast-day
of the Jews, he followed the pious practice of the stricter groups and fasted
twice a week. Far from ever failing to pay the necessary tithes on his agri- 12
cultural produce, he paid tithes on everything in his possession. In short, his way of life was that of a Pharisee, it was an example of one of the most sustained efforts any Jewish group had ever made to observe the law in every detail—and he thanked God for it: thanksgiving, it was said, was the most precious of all forms of prayer. The tax-gatherer, by contrast, was committed to a way of life which made any such prayer impossible for him. He lived by raising slightly more taxes from his fellow-citizens than he was bound to pay to the government, and the fundamental dishonesty inherent in his profession branded him, in the eyes of Jewish society, as one who was for ever "outside the law". It was beyond his power to make the kind of amends (say, giving away most of his profits) which would alone be regarded by his fellow-citizens as a sign of true repentance and allow him to be re-admitted to the society of the just. His prayer was despairing and simple—but not new: it echoed the opening of Psalm 51; and later in that psalm come the words, "A broken and humbled heart, O God, thou wilt not despise". Jesus' parable is a vivid illustration of that wonderful document of Hebrew spirituality. Luke says,
it was aimed at those who were sure of their own goodness and looked 9
down on everyone else. Certainly, the Pharisees believed (and not only

they) that their way of life assured them of salvation to a greater extent than that of any of their contemporaries; and this was one of the instances of human pretension which was destined to be exposed by that great reversal of values which Jesus proclaimed. In the words of a saying that occurs in a
14 number of different contexts, '**everyone who exalts himself will be humbled**'.

15 **They even brought babies for him to touch.** At this point Luke
returns to the order of events in Mark, and reproduces Mark's narrative
15–30 (10.13–31) with only a small amount of rewriting. The children who are
brought to Jesus for his blessing become **babies** in Luke; and the 'rich man'
of Mark's narrative (who is inferred by Matthew to be 'young') becomes **a**
18 **man of the ruling class,** which is logical enough: riches secure social
position.

Challenge to Jerusalem

31 '**We are now going up to Jerusalem**'. After the long section of *Journeys and encounters* which, though Jerusalem was given at the outset as the ultimate destination, gave little feeling of actual progress southward, the narrative now begins to move again. As in Mark (10.33–4), the disciples are once more taken into Jesus' confidence about the impending destiny of the Son of Man. The rejection and humiliation of this figure, who was traditionally thought of as vindicated and glorified, was something the disciples found it hard to accept, and Mark makes no secret of their bewilderment. But Luke presents the matter more from the point of view of a church historian. The early church must have momentarily felt the same difficulty in reconciling the glorified Christ of their faith with the humiliated Jesus of their memory. How did they overcome it? They went back to the Old Testament and found evidence there (doubtless in such passages as Isaiah 53) that this was what had to happen: **all that was written by the prophets** had **come true for the Son of Man.** But the disciples did not yet realize this: the true interpretation of these prophecies was only revealed to them later (24.27). Meanwhile, their failure to grasp Jesus' prediction—a failure demonstrated by their subsequent conduct—could only be explained (as Luke also suggests,
34 9.45) as part of God's purpose: **its meaning was concealed from them.**
Luke has omitted from Mark's account (10.46–52) the name of the beggar (Bartimaeus) and the word of Aramaic with which he addressed Jesus (*Rabbuni*), but in other respects he has followed Mark closely, except for adding a conclusion which he seems to have felt appropriate to a number of
43 Jesus' miracles, **And all the people gave praise.**

19. 1 **Entering Jericho.** The Jordan valley between the Lake of Tiberias and the Dead Sea consists of a long narrow plain which is for the most part

parched and treeless. But at Jericho, which lies toward the southern end of
this plain close to the mountains of Judaea, there is a spring which irrigates
the fields and orchards and makes the town a veritable oasis in the desert. In
the time of Jesus it was a prosperous city, rich in date-palms and balsam
trees, and the home of a well-to-do Jewish community. It was also the
principal eastern frontier town of Judaea; Herod the Great had built a winter
palace there, and it had a large traffic of merchants and travellers. **There was** 2
a man there named Zacchaeus. This is the Greek form of a common Jewish name, Zakkai. The man was a Jew, a wealthy **superintendent of**
taxes. This does not mean a civil servant in the employment of the government; for the government did not collect its own taxes, but offered the job
to any firm of tax-collectors which could offer to return the highest revenue
from a given area. These firms made their money, partly by exacting a
slightly higher rate of taxation than they returned to the government, partly
by investing the revenues in business interests before paying over the total
assessment. Zacchaeus is to be imagined as the head of one of these com-
panies. In this profession he had enriched himself; but he had also incurred
social disapproval, since the principles upon which tax-collectors made their
living could be regarded as extortionate and usurious, and as therefore
incompatible with Jewish law. In the eyes of strict Jews, at least, such a
man was **a sinner,** and excluded from the society of those who maintained 8
a careful observance of the law. Hence the **general murmur of disapproval** 7
when Jesus deliberately sought lodging with him. But on this occasion Jesus'
action was spectacularly vindicated. It was always possible for a tax-collector
to repent and rejoin the society of the righteous, so long as he made restitu-
tion to all from whom he had exacted more than was due. It was recognized
that it was probably impossible for him to identify and repay more than a
small number of those whose taxes he had collected, and it was considered
adequate if he made up the rest by making a proportionate contribution to
the public good. The result of Jesus' visit was that Zacchaeus resolved to do
all this—and more. He **stood there**—the word suggests that he was making 8
a public declaration—and promised to give away half his possessions (which
was more than would have been considered adequate), and to anyone who
could prove he had been **cheated** in the tax collection to pay back the
difference, not merely plus twenty per cent (as the Jewish Law required,
Leviticus 6.1), but plus 400 per cent. After this, no one could call Zacchaeus
a sinner again; he and his family would recover their full rights in the 7
Jewish community—'**Salvation has come to this house today**'. But this 9
had happened because Jesus, instead of shunning him as his pious contemporaries did, had deliberately sought his company.

They thought the reign of God might dawn at any moment. This 11
is Luke's introduction to a parable which, in its main features, is familiar
from Matthew's gospel (25.14–30), where it is told as an allegory of the Last

Judgement. Whatever people thought of Jesus, there was inevitably a temptation to see in one who gave such notable signs of miraculous power the harbinger of that new age—**the reign of God**—which the majority of Jews earnestly awaited; and Jesus' arrival at the Holy City must have seemed to many a likely moment for the promised new age to begin. Such crude expectations were politically dangerous to Jesus in his lifetime; but they lived on after his death and resurrection, and we know (from the letters of Paul, for example) that Christian leaders had strenuously to discourage those who tried to contract out of all the normal responsibilities of daily life because **they thought the reign of God might dawn at any moment.** The question, at any rate, was still very much alive in Luke's day, and by
12 subtly emphasizing certain details in the parable (the **long journey abroad**
17 of the king, the necessity to be **trustworthy in a very small matter**), Luke
made the parable teach a lesson of patience and responsible social conduct. But Luke's version also has some original features which suggest that the parable had already had a complicated history before it came into his hands. It now contains a by-plot; the capitalist who starts his servants in business
12 is also **a man of noble birth** who has hopes of being **appointed king.** This
supplies the destination of his **journey.** All "kings" in Palestine held their kingdoms by appointment of the Roman Emperor; and in fact one of Herod the Great's sons, Archelaus, acquired his right to rule over Judaea by making the journey to Rome in circumstances exactly similar to those described here, so much so that Jesus' story may well be an allusion to this actual event (4 B.C.). But what has this political episode to do with the story of the three servants? On the face of it, very little; indeed the two fit together so badly that it seems likely that (as in Matthew 22.1–10) what were originally two separate stories have somehow been combined into one. Nevertheless, the political setting of the by-plot has influenced the telling of the main story; for the capitalist is now also a king, and is able to reward his servants, not just with more capital and more responsibility, but with governorships over cities. And this introduces a new point into the story: these glittering rewards seem out of all proportion to the very modest commercial successes of the servants, all the more so since the sizeable capital sums mentioned by Matthew
13 ('talents') appear in Luke as the almost unworkably small assets of a few
pounds.[a] This makes the detail of giving the third servant's capital to the first servant seem slightly grotesque—he had by now become a provincial
25 governor! Hence, perhaps, the protest, "**he has ten already**". But it con-
siderably heightens the point which Luke saw in the parable: your attention now to small and humble things will gain you a reward out of all proportion in the kingdom of God. One further detail sharpens the point. In Matthew,

[*a*] The NEB translators seem to have abandoned their own principles here. The Greek *mina* (which is the sum in the text) was worth 100 *denarii*, and the NEB normally makes ten denarii equivalent to a modern pound. The servants had the equivalent of roughly ten pounds sterling to trade with.

the third servant buried his money in the ground, which was regarded as the
most prudent way of keeping it safe. But here, he put it away **in a handker-** 20
chief, which was improvident and dangerous. At Luke's hands he has
become a typical example of one who is definitely not **trustworthy in a very** 17
small matter.

The **ascent to Jerusalem** from Jericho was a walk of some twenty miles up 28
a road which climbed nearly four thousand feet from the plain to the crest
of the Mount of Olives. Luke follows Mark in mentioning **Bethphage and** 29
Bethany (which lay just off the road to the south), but prefers an alternative
(and possibly more exact) name for the Mount of Olives, **the hill called**
"olive plantation" (which in Latin is *olivetum*, hence **Olivet**).

The details of the narrative of finding the colt follow Mark closely 29–35
(11.1–10). As in Mark, the episode is doubtless meant to be understood as a miraculous confirmation of Jesus' authority, not as a piece of prior organization. But Luke gives Jesus' ride a slightly different interpretation. The branches and greenery, with their Jewish festival associations, disappear; instead, the disciples throw their cloaks on the ground in front of Jesus, which is the gesture of acclaiming a king. The Zechariah prophecy, "Here is your king, who comes to you in gentleness, riding on an ass", which is implicit in Mark's account and is expressly quoted in Matthew, is no more
than distantly suggested here; but the word **king** is deliberately introduced 38
into the cry of the disciples (who take the place of the crowds in the other versions). Their cry, as in the other accounts, uses the words of Psalm 118.25–6. But Luke has made it sound somewhat less Jewish, omitting the Hebrew word Hosanna, and adding words reminiscent of the angels' song at Jesus' birth. Jesus' entry thus becomes, no longer an uncertain recognition by the crowds of the nearness of the Messiah, but a proclamation by Jesus' own disciples that he is a divinely commissioned king. And Jesus accepts the proclamation. Using a familiar proverb, he tells those who question his
right to the title, **'If my disciples keep silence the stones will shout** 40
aloud'.

As soon as the procession had come over the saddle of the Mount of Olives the whole city of Jerusalem would have appeared before their eyes, spread out on the opposite side of the valley, with the immense and magnificent buildings of the temple in the foreground and Herod's citadel commanding the city from its highest point behind. According to popular etymology,
the name Jerusalem meant "vision of peace". In the manner of a prophet, 41–4
Jesus based his lament over the city upon the name itself and, foreseeing the inevitable course which events were taking and which his own intervention would do nothing to deflect, he prophesied, not peace, but siege and destruction. By the time Luke wrote, these things had in fact taken place (A.D. 70); but the details of Jesus' prophecy have not necessarily been rewritten in the

light of subsequent history. They can all be found in the Old Testament (see especially Isaiah 37.33; Psalm 137.9; and the description of Nebuchadrezzar's siege of Jerusalem in Jeremiah 52); they were already conventional terms for describing a besieged and conquered city. There is no reason to doubt that Jesus foresaw such a fate coming upon Jerusalem as clearly as Isaiah had before him. It must indeed have been clear to any man of vision that the increasing turbulence of Jewish nationalist groups under the Roman administration could only lead to disaster. Nothing short of a change of
44 heart could avert it. The moment—**God's moment**—for such a change of heart had arrived in the person of Jesus. But the opportunity had been, and would be, rejected.

45 **Then he went into the temple and began driving out the traders.** The episode, told in full by Mark (11.15–19) and Matthew (21.12–13), is no more than briefly summarized by Luke, and is also detached from Mark's strict chronological scheme; for whereas, in Mark, it is placed in the last week in Jesus' life, in Luke it forms only the beginning of a substantial
47 period of activity in Jerusalem: **Day by day he taught in the temple.**

20. 1 **One day.** The question about Jesus' authority, which in Mark (11.20–5) follows close upon his violent action in the temple, is recorded by Luke as having been put to him in the course of his daily teaching, and so becomes a
2 question specifically about his authority as a teacher. '**Acting like this**' must mean, "setting yourself up as a qualified expounder of Scripture". The only authority his questioners were prepared to recognize was that which they conferred themselves; but Jesus was in effect questioning all their presuppositions when he returned their challenge with reference to John the Baptist: John had received no **authority** from them to baptize; was his activity therefore invalid?

9–16 The parable of the vineyard is told very much as in Mark (12.1–12), and Luke's only changes (such as the reduction of the number of servants to one each time) are signs of literary artistry rather than of any different understanding of the story. But there can be little doubt that in the son of the story he saw Jesus himself. The slight alteration (made also by Matthew) that
15 the son was **flung out of the vineyard** before being killed is perhaps deliberately intended to suggest Jesus' crucifixion outside Jerusalem; and the two texts which follow the parable, though they have no very clear application to the story, have much to say about the destiny of the Son of
17 God. "**The stone which the builders rejected has become the main corner-stone**" (Psalm 118.22) was originally an image for the miraculous restoration by God of the fortunes of any righteous man who had seemed to his enemies ruined and God-forsaken, and it was an image which the early church eagerly added to the complex series of building metaphors with which it strove to express the idea of the Christian community as God's new

temple. But here it expresses a straightforward claim that Jesus, though now
to be rejected and killed, will subsequently be vindicated and glorified. The
continuation (found only in Luke), '**Any man who falls on that stone will** 18
be dashed to pieces' is not a logical sequel, but another stone-saying which
Luke felt it appropriate to insert at this point. It is not an exact quotation: the idea, and some of the wording, is drawn from Daniel 2.34—where a great stone smashes an idolatrous statue—with possibly also a hint of Isaiah 8.14 (the "rock of stumbling"). Later Jewish scholars interpreted the Daniel passage as a prophecy about the Messiah, and this interpretation may have been current in Jesus' time. But in any case, in its context here it clearly expresses the reverse side of the Son's coming glorification: all who do not accept him now will then experience, not the thrill of his glory, but the severity of his judgement.

The following sections follow Mark (12.13–44) very closely. Luke, like 19-**21.** 4
Matthew, has simply added a few narrator's touches in order to keep the
action moving. In particular, he connects the question about paying taxes
with one of the accusations actually made against Jesus later on (23.2). One
point of detail is corrected. Jesus' answer to the Sadducees in Mark 12.25
('When they rise from the dead, men and women do not marry; they are like
angels in heaven') could conceivably have been misunderstood as a promise
of heaven to everyone, good and bad, without distinction. Luke removes the
ambiguity: Jesus was talking only of **those who have been judged worthy** 35
of a place in the other world.

Some people were talking about the temple. The new temple, begun 5
by Herod the Great in 20 B.C., was still not entirely completed; but it was already one of the most spectacular pieces of architecture in the ancient world. Like the great pagan temples which could be seen everywhere in the Roman Empire, the temple building itself had a façade of brilliant white marble, and its appearance was enriched by **votive offerings,** among which was a great golden vine set up over the door by Herod the Great himself. It is these features, which would have been of a kind familiar to any Greek reader, rather than the exceptional size of the masonry (which only those who had seen it could appreciate) that Luke (unlike Mark) singles out for mention.

The same concern to give, for his Greek readers, a less alien character to a discourse which in Mark (chapter 13) is expressed in a thoroughly Jewish idiom, accounts for some of the detailed alterations which Luke has made in this chapter. But there are also some more significant changes. It is possible that Luke was combining the material in Mark with some other source; but at the same time certain deliberate touches which he gave to the discourse show that he had an editorial policy of his own. He wrote his gospel a decade or two later than Mark, and the church, though still firmly believing in the

impending end of the world, had nevertheless had to revise its idea of the course which history was going to follow. In Mark, the disciples' question ('When will this happen?') was elicited by Jesus' startling prophecy that the massive temple buildings were to be totally destroyed; and Jesus answered that all this would take place within their own generation, but that it must be understood in a wider context of world history: it would be no isolated catastrophe, but only one of the events in that turbulent period which must necessarily precede the end. These prophecies were spoken, and perhaps also written down by Mark, before Jerusalem was in fact taken and the temple desecrated and destroyed by the Roman army in A.D. 70. Naïve Christians, up to that time, may well have thought that the end of the world would follow immediately. But as the years passed, and history continued as before, a more sophisticated interpretation was placed on Jesus' words. A part of what he had prophesied—in particular the fall of Jerusalem and the persecution of Christians—had already been fulfilled; but the climax presaged by these events—the Last Judgement and the glorious coming of the Son of Man—still lay in the future. To be precise (and this appears to be
9 Luke's own formulation of the matter): **'These things are bound to happen first; but the end does not follow immediately'**.

This concern to present a slightly more sophisticated and less esoterically Jewish version of Jesus' discourse appears in a number of small details. The setting itself is different in Luke. In Mark, the discourse is a piece of private instruction given to four disciples as they sit on the Mount of Olives overlooking the temple; but here, it is a part of Jesus' general teaching given in
7 the temple itself. The audience are all those who call him **'Master'**, and the words are clearly destined, in Luke's account, for the encouragement of subsequent generations of Christians. Those Christians have experience, not
8 of political agitators in Palestine who claimed to be the Messiah (**saying, "I am he"**), but of over-enthusiastic preachers in the church who unsettle their congregations by proclaiming "**The Day is upon us**" (a phrase which
12 occurs only in Luke). **Before all this happens**—that is to say, in the continuing experience of the church—those same Christians are to suffer persecution; and in their frequent appearances in law-courts (**synagogues** both in Palestine and elsewhere were constituted as judicial bodies) they are
14 **not to prepare** their **defence beforehand** (Luke uses the technical
16 language of a Greek court). **'Some of you will be put to death'**: doubtless this had already happened when Luke wrote; but there was a saying of
18 Jesus, **'not a hair of your head shall be lost'**. How was this saying to be reconciled with the fact that Christians had already been martyred? Perhaps along the lines, suggested more clearly by the NEB translation than by the Greek text, that Jesus was talking, not of physical safety and physical death,
19 but of **true life** and true death.

20 **'But when you see Jerusalem encircled by armies.'** The historical

event around which Jesus' prophecies turned was the siege and destruction
of Jerusalem. In Mark and Matthew it is referred to, in the conventionally
cryptic language of apocalyptic writing, as the 'abomination of desolation'.
Luke drops the convention, and makes Jesus refer explicitly to the siege. If
Mark was written before the event, and Luke after it, this might seem a
sufficient explanation of the difference between them. But Luke's procedure
is by no means just to write an account of the siege as it happened and to
put this into Jesus' mouth as a prophecy. He does not mention any of the
things which (as we know from the contemporary historian Josephus) were
particularly notable in the siege of Jerusalem; his language is entirely that
which the Old Testament prophets used in their premonition of a similar
event, and which, therefore, Jesus may well have used himself when prophesying the fate of Jerusalem. Moreover, the catastrophe is not merely prophesied, it is also interpreted, and interpreted in a fully Old Testament manner:
it will be '**the time of retribution, when all that stands written is to be** 22
fulfilled' (Deuteronomy 32.35; Hosea 9.7; Jeremiah 5.29); and its consequences will fulfil other oracles, Zechariah 12.3 (where the Septuagint Greek 24
version is much closer to the text of Luke than to its Hebrew original) and
Isaiah 63.18. Only the last words are mysterious: **until their day has run
its course.** The foreigners, it would seem, cannot be destined to trample on
Jerusalem indefinitely. Jerusalem (even if only metaphorically) has still a
part to play in the salvation of mankind—a hint, perhaps, of that view of
history which is worked out by Paul in Romans 9–11.

'**Portents will appear.**' All the calamities described so far, however severe, 25
were the kind of thing which could happen in the ordinary course of history.
Even the fall of Jerusalem must not be regarded as so unexampled that it
was necessarily a sign of the imminence of the end (Luke, as a historian, and
indeed many of his non-Palestinian readers, were doubtless able to keep a
sense of proportion about it). Nothing, in short, which the church had
experienced so far was to be interpreted as an immediate presage of the last
things. These would be heralded by events of another order, by a serious
break in the continuity and orderliness of the physical world. The portents
to be looked for would be in the sky: if the heavenly bodies lost their regularity—and still more if the **celestial powers** which controlled those bodies 26
were **shaken**—then chaos must be expected on earth (for most people took
a certain amount of astrology for granted: it was the regular movement of
sun, moon and stars which guaranteed the regular succession of cause and
effect on earth). **The roar and surge of the sea**, too, means more than an 25
ordinary storm. It was believed that only God's firm hand held the sea back
from engulfing dry land; if this were relaxed, a great tidal wave would make
men not know **which way to turn.** It would be signs such as these, and not
the familiar vicissitudes of history, which must be read as heralding the
coming of the Son of Man. But that coming would also put an end to the

28 tribulations of the church; therefore it would be the moment to **hold your heads high.**

The tone of this is comparatively optimistic: as soon as things get really severe, Christians may take courage because their **liberation is near.** But
31 it is still necessary to utter warnings. Although **the kingdom of God** (so
Luke fills out the cryptic blank left by Mark and Matthew—see above on
Mark 13.29) will follow the portents as surely as summer follows the budding
29 of the fig-tree (**or any other tree,** as Luke adds for the benefit of his
European readers, see above on Mark 13.28), nevertheless in the meantime
the apparent delay of these things must not lead either to scepticism or to
32 moral laxity. Jesus had authoritatively predicted that **the present genera-**
tion would **live to see it all,** and when it came it would not just be a
cataclysm in Palestine (as the purely Jewish language in which Christians
35 tended to describe it might make others think) but **the whole world over.**
34 **Dissipation and drunkenness and worldly cares**—which Luke perhaps
saw already taking hold of some Christian communities—would only dull
the mind in the face of this prospect: in this state, men would fail to read the
signs and would be caught **suddenly like a trap.** They must pray for
strength, so that, whether or not they died before the end, they would at all
36 events win the right to **stand in the presence of the Son of Man.** Luke
has written this final exhortation in such a way that it could serve as the end of a sermon to the church at any time, whether or not the "portents" had begun to appear. In a subtle way, he has adapted material that was originally all conditioned by expectation of an immediate end to the needs of a church which was beginning to accept the indefinite continuation of the present.

37 **His days were given to teaching in the temple.** Luke has not yet fallen in with the careful time-scheme propounded by Mark, but allows an indefinite number of days to elapse before *The final conflict*. To **spend the night on the hill called Olivet** does not necessarily imply camping out. The village of Bethany, where (according to Mark) Jesus lodged during these days, lay on the far slopes of the Mount of Olives.

The final conflict

22. 1 **Now the festival of Unleavened Bread, known as Passover, was approaching.** Luke's narrative of the Supper follows the outlines of Mark's version, but also diverges from it at a number of points. Either he was rewriting the passage somewhat freely, or else he was drawing on a different tradition. In either event, the resultant picture is a new one. The introduction seems aimed, as so often in Luke, at giving a slightly more consequential account of events. There is no attempt to offer a date (as in Mark): the

festival was simply **approaching**, and this gave urgency to the schemes of
the authorities to do away with Jesus. It is not quite clear from the other
gospel accounts how Judas' treachery in fact helped them; but Luke makes
this explicit: Judas' task was **to betray him . . . without collecting a** 6
crowd, at a time when Jerusalem was packed with pilgrims. He effectively
did so by leading the authorities to a spot where he knew that Jesus would go
for solitude during the night. He acted, Luke says, under the impulsion of
Satan. Whereas we might now be tempted to speculate on Judas' motives, 3
the first-century approach was less psychological: the events of *The final
conflict* were set in motion by supernatural powers, who used human beings
as the instruments of their purpose. [a]

The preparations for the Passover supper, on the afternoon **on which the** 7
Passover victim had to be slaughtered, are told almost exactly as in
Mark; and it follows that Luke, like Mark and Matthew, thought of this supper as a celebration of the Passover meal, with its special dishes of bitter herbs, roasted lamb and unleavened bread, and its recital of the miraculous deliverance of Israel out of captivity. This meal was always a formal one. The people in each group which shared it were bound together by table-fellowship, which they signified by partaking of the bread and the wine which their host had blessed. Like Mark and Matthew again, Luke does not trouble to mention all the normal details of this meal, but singles out certain words and actions of Jesus which made this celebration exceptional; and it is precisely in the words and actions which he reports that Luke shows how differently he understands the occasion.

'How I have longed to eat this Passover with you before my death!' 15
The Greek, like the English, is ambiguous (see the footnote in NEB): did
Jesus eat with them or did he not? The phrase in the following verse, **'never** 16
again shall I eat it', sounds less ambiguous, and seems on the face of it to
settle the matter: Jesus shared this Passover with his disciples, but would do so **never again**—a prophecy which occurs in similar terms in Matthew and Mark. But the words **never again** occur only in certain manuscripts (see the footnote); indeed the majority of the most authoritative manuscripts omit the word in question, and give simply "I shall not". In itself, this does not settle the matter. The text in the NEB may still be the right one. But we must keep open the possibility that Jesus' saying was not a prophecy at all but a vow of abstinence. He had longed to share this Passover with his friends, but when it came to the point he may have refused to partake of it. If so, his abstinence would certainly have been surprising. Not only do Matthew and Mark give no hint of it [b] (the most they suggest is that after the cup of blessing Jesus refused any further wine: the final "cup" of the formal

[*a*] Nevertheless, the story recorded in Matthew (26.14–16) may be intended to supply a human explanation: Judas betrayed Jesus for money.

[*b*] Unless Jesus' refusal to accept wine just before the crucifixion was connected with such a vow of abstinence (Mark 15.23).

meal was waived, not only for himself, but probably also for his disciples), but it would have been odd in itself on such a solemn occasion.[a] Could Luke really have meant this? In view of the ambiguities already mentioned, it is hard to be sure; but there is one further point which bears on it. Both Matthew and Mark lay some emphasis on the fact that Judas' act of betrayal was an instance of that basest form of treachery which consists in betraying someone with whom one has become intimate through the solidarity of table-fellowship: Jesus was betrayed by one who had 'eaten with him' (Mark 14.18; Matthew 26.23). But if Luke believed that Jesus himself ate nothing at this meal, he would have needed to make some change at this
point; and sure enough we find that Judas is not identified as one who "ate
21 with" Jesus, but as one whose "hand was with his on the table"; there is no
mention of eating together.

However this may be, the point serves to focus attention on one respect in
which Luke's account is different from any other. Few words are spoken in
16, 18 explanation of the cup and the bread; but twice over Jesus uses the present
meal to point forward to a greater reality, that of the **kingdom of God**, in
16 which the Old Passover ritual will find **its fulfilment**. The coming "Mes-
sianic Age"—that is to say, the paradise which (it was confidently expected) God would one day create for his elect by the agency of his Messiah—was often described in the imagery of a banquet; and the principal interpretation placed, in Luke's account, on the disciples' Passover supper is that it was the last that would be celebrated in the old manner. Soon—indeed very soon, if Jesus' sayings are intended to be taken as an indication of his intention to fast until this came about—it would be superseded by an experience which would reveal the coming of the kingdom of God. The purpose of this present meal was to foreshadow something greater in the near future.

19 Little else is added by way of interpretation except the words, **'This is my
body'**, which follow the blessing and breaking of the bread. The saying points in the direction of the longer versions in Mark and Matthew, where Jesus calls the bread his body because he sees himself as a victim about to be sacrificed, and his disciples can appropriate the benefits of this sacrifice by partaking of the victim's flesh. But Luke gives us no explicitly sacrificial imagery. The saying stands in complete isolation, and could just as well be interpreted as John interprets it in his gospel: Jesus gives men, in his body, the bread of eternal life.

It can now be seen how differently Luke presents the Passover supper. It is not merely that he reverses the order of the cup and the bread—the breaking of the bread had no fixed place in the Passover ritual, and his account can be fitted into its Passover context as well as the others. More

[a] It was for some centuries the practice of a part of the church to fast during the Jewish Passover as a religious act performed on behalf of the Jews. It has been suggested that this provides an explanation of Jesus' fast: he fasted on behalf of his own people.

striking is the fact that, instead of offering an interpretation of Jesus' words over the bread and the wine, Luke appears to concentrate on the significance of the whole meal as a foretaste of the greater realities of the coming kingdom of God. Only at the very end, with the words '**This is my body**', does he come near the sacrificial imagery that occurs in Mark and Matthew. This is, in fact, the only vestige in his narrative of that understanding of the bread and wine which was adumbrated by Mark and Matthew, was slightly elaborated by Paul, and then became normative in the church at large.

Or so, at least, the matter stands as the main text runs in the NEB. But this is by no means the only, or even the best-attested, text. The majority of manuscripts give a longer text which brings the narrative much closer to that in Matthew and Mark, and also reproduces some details from Paul's account in 1 Corinthians 11.24–5. If this text is adopted, many of the peculiarities of Luke's account disappear: the usual order is restored of the cup following the bread, and an interpretation is given of Jesus' sayings over the bread and wine which corresponds closely with that in the other accounts. Even so, certain oddities remain, in particular the extra cup of wine shared by the disciples before the breaking of bread; and the critic is left with the very difficult task of explaining how the shorter version ever came into existence. Many believe that it is easier to explain the longer text as a subsequent amplification of an original shorter one than to explain why an original longer one should ever have been abbreviated; and it is for this reason that the NEB translators decided to relegate the longer version to a footnote.

Then a jealous dispute broke out. It is natural, in the light of sub- 24
sequent Christian devotion, to think of the breaking of bread and the sharing of a cup as the most important, if not the only important, features of this meal. But this was not Luke's view. Luke saw the Passover supper as the occasion for a farewell speech by Jesus to his disciples. Such farewell speeches were one of the conventional devices used by ancient historians; Luke himself provides another example in Paul's farewell to the elders of Ephesus (Acts 20.18–35), and the gospel of John considerably extends the convention in reporting a long discourse of Jesus to his disciples on the night before his death. For the content of the speech, Luke draws partly on sayings which are recorded in other gospels in different contexts. In particular, the question, **Who among them should rank highest**, was raised, according to Mark (10.41) and Matthew (20.24), as a result of the indiscreet request of the two sons of Zebedee on the way up to Jerusalem. The answer given by Jesus here is very similar to the one recorded in those accounts. A new
detail is the word "**Benefactors**". Some of the Hellenistic kings of the east 25
liked to adopt this title (*Euergetēs*): by their wealth (however acquired) and by the peace they procured for their kingdoms (however precarious) they were pleased to characterize their rule (however tyrannical) as a benefaction to their subjects. The use of the word here is perhaps ironical; at any rate

26 **the highest** among Jesus' disciples must have no such pretensions. As in
the versions in Mark (10.42–5) and Matthew (20.25–8), the image invoked
27 for this reversal of ordinary precedence is that of **the one who sits at table**
or the servant who waits on him; but Jesus' final word, '**Yet here am I**
among you like a servant', though it rings true in a general sense, seems
a little inappropriate in its setting here, where Jesus is to be imagined
reclining at the head of the table. Did Luke know anything of the tradition
in John's gospel that, before the meal began, Jesus washed his disciples' feet?
28 '**You are the men who have stood firmly by me in my times of trial**'.
This surprising description stands in the place of the simple phrase, 'you my
followers', in Matthew's version of the same saying (19.28). It is difficult to
see to what moments in Jesus' life it can refer. The disciples were not present
when he was "tempted" (the same word, in the Greek, as "tried") in the
wilderness; and there are few occasions in the main part of Luke's narrative
on which it could be said that the disciples distinguished themselves by
their constancy in moments of trial. Moreover, in the "trials" that were
about to begin, they first fell asleep when they might have supported Jesus
in his suffering, and then forsook him altogether. The description, therefore,
seems hardly appropriate—unless it is a reminiscence of some **times of trial**
which happen not to be recorded in the gospels. On the other hand, after the
resurrection, when the church was subjected to severe "trials", and Christians were notably "standing firm", the phrase will have sounded particularly apt; and since, in Luke's gospel, the disciples often stand as representative figures for Christians in general, we may suspect here a certain amount
of reading back into the lifetime of Jesus the subsequent experience of the
29 church. '**And now I vest in you the kingship**'. This translation is not quite
accurate, and fails to evoke the associations present in the Greek word. In
Matthew and Mark, Jesus calls the wine shared by the disciples at the
Passover 'my blood of the covenant'. Luke says nothing of this, but it may
be significant that he makes up for it by introducing the word "covenant"
here. Jesus is not, at this moment, "vesting" his disciples with a kingship
that will begin at once, but (to take the Greek word literally) "covenanting"
or "bequeathing" to them a status which they will enjoy, not immediately,
but after his death and resurrection. The symbol of this is one which has been
30 used a few verses before—the coming heavenly banquet; and, in slightly
uneasy juxtaposition,[a] a further image is added belonging not to the festivities of the new age but to the Judgement which will inaugurate it. Exactly
as in Matthew's version of the saying (19.28), the disciples are promised a
30 part to play at the coming Judgement: they will '**sit on thrones as judges**'.
31 '**Simon, Simon, take heed.**' All the gospels record Jesus' prediction of
Peter's threefold denial. Matthew and Mark place it a little later, on the

[a] Though feasting in full view of one's humiliated enemies was traditionally one of the rewards to which the righteous looked forward: Psalm 23.5.

walk out of the city to Gethsemane; Luke and John set it in the context of
Jesus' farewell discourse. Luke, moreover, introduces it with some words
which seem, like the rest of the speech, to look further forward into the
future. Peter would indeed (by the time this gospel was written) have gone
to prison and death; and there would certainly be times when it was the 33
responsibility of any church leader, in times of stress, to **lend strength** to 32
his brothers ("brother" became almost a technical term for "fellow-
Christian"). Jesus could have foreseen these things. But in any case there was
a severe test to be undergone in the near future. We have seen that, instead of
speculating about Judas' motives in betraying Jesus, the tradition ascribed
the cause of his action to Satan (22.3). In the same way, there is no psychological reflection in the gospels about the disciples' behaviour in forsaking
Jesus at his arrest. This too happened through the intervention of Satan. But
this time Satan was not permitted to destroy his instruments; he was merely
given leave to put them to the test (as he was given leave to torment Job; 31
see Job 1.12; 2.6). The metaphor used is a strange one (though well in the
manner of Jesus). Wheat is either sifted in a coarse sieve to separate it from
the chaff and other rubbish (in which case the wheat falls through), or else,
after threshing, in a fine sieve to separate it from smaller seeds and impurities
(in which case the wheat remains in the sieve). Either way, it is tested and
separated out. What the disciples were about to undergo was an equally
rigorous test; but because of Jesus' prayer, and with the aid, apparently, of
Peter's timely recovery (**when you have come to yourself** is only one of 32
the possible meanings of the Greek word), they would—unlike Judas—
survive the ordeal.

The last section of Jesus' speech bears more closely still on what was 25–37
about to happen. All the gospels record that when Jesus was arrested in
Gethsemane at least one of those who were with him was carrying a sword
and attempted to use it (John's gospel actually gives the name of the slave
who was wounded). This appeared to be incompatible with the instructions
which Jesus had previously given to his followers (10.3–4), quite apart from
being contrary to the spirit of Jesus' teaching, and from carrying with it the
danger of trouble with the Roman authorities. Luke explains the circumstance by recording a saying of Jesus which seemed (if it was really spoken
on this particular occasion) to authorize exceptional preparations. '**We have** 38
two swords here'—certainly not enough for serious resistance, but enough
(as perhaps Luke was the first to notice) to give **fulfilment** to an important 37
prophecy. One of the first clues which the early church found to the meaning
of Jesus' person and work (a clue which may indeed have been given by
Jesus himself) was the "suffering servant" of Isaiah 53. But one verse of that
prophecy ran, "**He was counted among the outlaws**" (53.12). How could
this be true of Jesus? In what sense could his disciples be regarded as "outside the law" or "transgressors of the law" (both nuances are present in the

word translated **outlaws**)? A possible answer lay in the firm tradition that one of them had used a sword in Jesus' defence. From the strict Jewish point of view simply carrying a sword on the Sabbath (and so, *a fortiori*, on a festival such as the Passover) was probably forbidden, and from the Roman point of view its use in resisting arrest would have incurred severe penalties. If two of Jesus' disciples had swords on that particular night, this would have been **enough** to make the prophecy, "**he was counted among the outlaws**", seem to have come true.

39 **Then he went out and made his way as usual to the Mount of Olives.**
Luke has a version of the following scene which is rather different from that
of Matthew and Mark. The main elements are the same—the words of Jesus'
40 prayer, the disciples falling asleep, and the warning about '**the hour of
testing**'. But all this is told more briefly, as if it were already well known to
Luke's readers. Luke does not mention Gethsemane by name; he simply calls
it **the place**, and suggests (rather to our surprise, since Matthew and Mark
give the impression of a unique occasion) that Jesus made a habit of going
39 there (**as usual**)—which perhaps explains how Judas was able to find him.
Further, the sequence of events in Mark's version is drastically shortened;
only a summary of Jesus' hours of prayer is given, and much less is said about
the disciples—indeed their falling asleep is made to seem less culpable: Luke
45 suggests they could not stay awake because they were **worn out by grief.**

But in return, Luke offers a description of Jesus at prayer which is quite
41 unparalleled. To pray, Jesus **knelt down**, an unusual attitude (Jews usually
stood to pray, sometimes prostrated themselves, only occasionally knelt). He
43 received a vision of an **angel from heaven bringing him strength**: angels
appear often enough in Luke's narrative, but nowhere in a rôle quite like
this. Evidently the struggle was exceptionally severe (Luke probably
thought of it as a struggle between Jesus and the devil rather than as
a psychological struggle within Jesus himself), and despite the angel's help,
44 Jesus underwent **anguish of spirit.** The Greek word so translated is *agōnia*,
from which our word "agony" is derived. It means, not so much an acute
conflict of emotions, as an intense anxiety about what is going to happen.
Jesus, we must suppose, was in suspense whether Satan would after all
prevail, and Luke, by using the violent metaphor of "bloody sweat", [a]
leaves his readers in no doubt of the reality of Jesus' agitation.

47 **While he was still speaking.** Once again, the main points of Mark's
narrative are here, but are much more briefly told; on the other hand, Luke
48 adds one or two new details. The **kiss**, for Matthew and Mark, was simply

[*a*] **Like clots of blood falling to the ground** is a bizarre image (sweat can hardly be compared to bits of *congealed* blood) and, though accurate, is probably an over-pedantic translation. Luke doubtless meant "drops" of blood. The metaphor occurs in Greek literature from the time of Homer.

the signal pre-arranged between Judas and the armed band; here it is the
cue for outraged comment by Jesus. The momentary resistance of **his** 49
followers is placed, perhaps more logically, before the arrest of Jesus instead
of after it, and is followed by a miracle of healing (which only Luke mentions,
perhaps to indicate that Jesus did not intend his instructions about carrying 36
swords to have such bitter consequences). The flight of the disciples is not
mentioned (Luke seems to be avoiding anything which would discredit
them); on the other hand, point is given to Jesus' reply to his captors by
bringing on to the scene people of some responsibility—not just servants
and police, but some of the **chief priests** and **elders** themselves (represent- 52
ing the Sanhedrin), and **officers of the temple police** who were responsible
for public order in the temple area, and would have been the men to take
action had Jesus' conduct been in any way irresponsible when, **day after** 53
day, he was **in the temple. 'But this is your moment—the hour when**
darkness reigns'. It was no good arguing. It was not just that Jesus and his
followers were utterly outnumbered; behind the crowd of armed men were
supernatural forces of evil which were to be allowed a temporary victory.
Satan (euphemistically called **darkness**) had already claimed Judas (22.3),
though he was to be denied the other disciples (22.32); he still had more to
gain before the end.

They brought him to the High Priest's house. Luke arranges the 54
next events somewhat differently from Mark and Matthew. If we had only
his account we should not suspect that there were any legal proceedings
during the night. Jesus seems to have been brought to Caiaphas' house
simply for safe detention until the morning session, and this period of
waiting provided a natural context for the stories of Peter's denial and the
mocking of Jesus. **They lit a fire in the middle of the courtyard** for 55
warmth and light. Peter, sitting in the group gathered round it, was three
times identified. Jesus, meanwhile, was presumably held by the guards
somewhere in the courtyard where he could turn and look at Peter—which, 62
in Luke, is the climax of the episode,[a] and we are left to imagine Peter's
feelings. The mockery and insults heaped on Jesus are described as the
guards' way of passing the time—not, as in Mark and Matthew, as a deliberate test of Jesus' Messiahship.

At this point Luke's account is quite different from Mark's and is, in many
ways, more plausible. **When day broke.** The session of the Sanhedrin (of 66

[*a*] Most manuscripts add, after verse 61, "He went outside and wept bitterly". These words are exactly as in Matthew's account, though different from Mark. If Luke wrote them here, it would seem to follow that he was making use, not only of a source of his own and of Mark, but also of Matthew. But on other grounds it is not very likely that he knew Matthew's gospel, at least in its finished Greek form; and it is perhaps easier to assume, as the NEB translators do, that the words crept into most manuscripts of Luke through assimilation with Matthew.

which **the elders of the nation, chief priests, and doctors of the law**
together made up the membership) is described as taking place, not at night,
but at the more normal time of early morning—official business, even at
Rome, and still more in the east, was done between dawn and midday—and
for all Luke says may have been held, not in the High Priest's house, but in
the usual assembly chamber of the Council. No witnesses were called, no
evidence presented. The object of the session seems to have been simply to
establish from Jesus' own lips whether he admitted to being the Messiah
70 and therefore (in that sense at least) **the Son of God.** Jesus' reply was
67 guarded, but for good reason. **'If I tell you . . . you will not believe me;
and if I ask questions, you will not answer'.** Jesus could not admit to
being the Messiah without qualification; to give a truthful answer, he would
need opportunity to explain and define, and this was being denied him.
However, the judges took this reserve as tantamount to a confession.

As soon as the council was satisfied that Jesus admitted to being (at least in
23. 1 some sense) the Messiah, **they brought him before Pilate:** Jesus was a
threat to public order, and it was the governor's responsibility to deal with
him. In this, they were acting as proper citizens of a country governed by
Rome. A Roman official did not normally institute proceedings against
criminals and troublemakers, but received charges brought by a third party
against them. Having heard the charges and questioned the witnesses and
the accused, it was for him to decide upon the legal nature of the alleged
offence, and to pronounce the verdict and the sentence. Luke gives fuller
details than the other gospels do of the charges that the Jewish authorities
brought against Jesus. These charges appear as deliberate but entirely
credible misrepresentations of events which are actually recorded in the
gospel. Pilate seized upon Jesus' admission that he was the Messiah, which
2 implied, in some sense at least, the claim to be **a king.** If Jesus seriously
claimed to be "king", then there might well be grounds for a charge of
sedition against Rome. So Pilate questioned Jesus on this point. But he
evidently did not regard Jesus' reply as sufficiently incriminating to proceed
with the matter.

Jesus' accusers then slightly changed their tactics, and picked up in more
5 detail one of their earlier charges. **'His teaching is causing disaffection
among the people all through Judaea. It started from Galilee and
has spread as far as this city'.** Galilee was in the jurisdiction of the
tetrarch Herod Antipas, and Pilate immediately remitted the prisoner to him
(an episode which Luke alone records). It is unlikely that Pilate was obliged
to do this merely because Jesus' country of origin lay outside his own
jurisdiction: the misconduct of which Jesus was accused had come to a head
in Jerusalem, and he had a perfect right to deal with it himself. On the other
hand, the accusers of Jesus were now alleging charges which arose out of
events in Galilee and which Pilate had no means of verifying, and he could

well have felt that this part of the case would be much better heard by the
local ruler, who happened to be available in Jerusalem at that time. In
addition, the remission of Jesus to Herod was perhaps intended as a courtesy.
Luke says that it was anyhow received as such, and healed the strained
relations between the two men. We have no other evidence that there had
been **a standing feud between them**; but it is not improbable that the 12
Roman administrator had frequent causes of difference with the part-Jewish
ruler in the adjoining territory. Herod Antipas apparently had some influence
with the Emperor at Rome—it was not for nothing that he had named his
capital Tiberias, after the reigning Emperor. Pilate's gesture towards his
influential neighbour is perfectly understandable.

We know from Josephus where Herod would have been: not in the great
palace built by his father, for this was now the Roman governor's *praetorium*,
but in the older palace built by the Hasmoneans, close to the walls of the
temple area. **When Herod saw Jesus he was greatly pleased.** Hints of 8
Herod's interest in Jesus were given earlier in the gospel (9.9; 13.31); but
the hearing does not seem to have advanced matters, and it ended once again
in a scene of mockery. Presumably the question of kingship was still the main
charge against Jesus. Herod obviously regarded it as preposterous, and **sent** 11
him back to Pilate dressed in a glorious robe.

Pilate now called together the chief priests, councillors, and people. 13
Neither Pilate nor Herod having found Jesus guilty **on a charge of sub-** 14
version, Pilate now publicly delivered his considered decision. He would
let Jesus off with a warning, probably accompanied by a light **flogging** (which 16
was usual enough in such cases (Acts 22.25), though here the Greek word is
a general one and could mean a "warning" alone). But at this point the crowd
intervened to upset the normal course of justice. Mark and Matthew provide
the explanation (which has found its way into many ancient manuscripts of
Luke, but is probably not part of the original text) that it was customary for
Pilate to release a prisoner at the festival—which also explains incidentally
what the crowd was doing there: they had come to claim their prisoner. Luke
merely represents the crowd as demanding that if any prisoner were to be
released it should be, not Jesus, but a certain Barabbas, who, because of his
connection with **a rising** against the Romans, was perhaps understandably 19
the more popular of the two. Not merely this, but they clamoured for Jesus'
crucifixion, even though neither the Jewish authorities, nor Herod, nor
Pilate, had **found him guilty of any capital offence.** The result of their 22
clamour, in Luke's account, was a total miscarriage of justice. **Their shouts** 24
prevailed and Pilate decided that they should have their way. There
was no pretence at a fair trial or a regular verdict: it was the rule of the mob,
connived at by the Roman governor. Luke, by this means, reaches the same
conclusion as Matthew and Mark: it was the Jews who were guilty of Jesus'
death, even though the punishment—crucifixion—was one that could only

have been inflicted by the Roman authorities. But his presentation, if it exculpates Pilate from direct responsibility for Jesus' death, leaves him with a strange reputation for the administration of justice in his province, and also has the implication that it was not just the Jewish leaders, but the people of Jerusalem as a whole, who secured Jesus' condemnation.

26 By a very slight change, Luke has made the episode of **Simon from Cyrene** carry a load of symbolic meaning. Simon does not just "carry Jesus' cross" as in Matthew and Mark; he walks **behind Jesus carrying it,** and so becomes the first to fulfil the condition of discipleship, 'he must take up his cross, and come with me' (9.23).

27 **Great numbers of people followed.** Luke's interest, throughout the
gospel, in the **people** as a whole, and particularly in the group of women
who followed Jesus, was perhaps his reason for mentioning this; and it
28 gave him a cue for recording a further saying of Jesus. **'Daughters of**
Jerusalem'. The tone is prophetic, both in its language and in its intention.
The women were weeping, ostensibly for Jesus. But the real meaning of
their tears (this is how the Old Testament prophets worked, giving the true
interpretation of signs that were misread by their contemporaries) was that
they presaged the fate of Jerusalem. Jesus had already prophesied about the
future: 'Alas for women who are with child in those days, or have children at
the breast' (21.23). Here the same thing is expressed in different words, and
an oracle from Hosea is added, which showed that the impending catastrophe
must not be regarded as a transient disaster, but as the decisive judgement
30 of God. Rather than face that, people would **'start saying to the moun-**
tains, "Fall on us", and to the hills, "Cover us"' (Hosea 10.8). Jesus
31 ends his speech with a proverb. **'If these things are done when the wood**
is green, what will happen when it is dry?' To give the proverb its most
immediate application (though we cannot be sure that this is what Jesus
intended): if this sort of thing can happen even to a harmless preacher, what
may not happen when there are real revolutionaries at work? This prophecy,
at least, was gruesomely fulfilled during the Jewish rebellion against the
Romans, A.D. 66–70.

34 **'Father, forgive them; they do not know what they are doing.'** Luke is the only evangelist to record this saying.[a] In its setting, the prayer appears to be for the executioners who were acting under Roman orders: they knew nothing of the issues involved, and they must not be held to bear the blame for the crucifixion any more than Pilate himself. But Luke doubtless saw more in the saying than this. The unconditional and radical character of God's forgiveness is often stressed in his gospel; and in Acts he makes it clear that this pardon was available even for the Jews, who through ignorance

[a] And not all manuscripts of his gospel contain it (see NEB footnote) so that we cannot be sure that it is authentic.

and failure to understand (Acts 13.26) had crucified their own Messiah (Acts 2.36–8). Even they had the excuse that "they did not know what they were doing". Even they could be forgiven.

In his gospel Luke often abbreviates an episode we know from Mark and Matthew, and then adds a new element of his own. So here: the mockery is told more economically, but a new light is thrown on it by the reactions of
the two criminals. To one criminal, as to all the mockers, Jesus was a false 39
pretender: his impending death proved the absurdity of his claims. But the
other criminal accepted that Jesus would, nevertheless, "come to his throne" 42
—that is, that there was some sense in which the title over Jesus' head would be shown to be true. This could doubtless only happen in that hoped-for age when the Messiah would inaugurate the glorious kingdom of his elect people. The criminal begged that, through Jesus' "remembrance" of him, he too would have a place in that kingdom. "He got more than he asked for" is an old comment on this passage. Whatever theoretical picture the Jews officially held of the after-life (involving first a period of waiting, then the moment of general resurrection, judgement, and apportioning of reward), there was another far simpler way of talking about life after death which perhaps the majority of people in Palestine tended to adopt and which Jesus himself felt able to make use of (for instance, in the parable of the rich man and Lazarus): immediately after death, the individual expected to be judged by God and awarded his appropriate punishment or reward. It is this more popular way
of seeing the matter that seems to be reflected in Jesus' reply to the criminal,
'Today you shall be with me in Paradise.' As in all languages and 43
cultures, there were many names for the reward of the just (as for the condemnation of the wicked). **Paradise** was originally the sumptuous garden of a Persian monarch. When the Jews used the word, they probably thought of the Garden of Eden. Jesus' promise to the criminal was in language he could easily understand: God would grant him the reward of the just. His faith that Jesus was after all a "king" made him the first to inherit the glorious destiny of all who acknowledged Jesus as their Lord.

The sun's light failed. This was Luke's explanation of the darkness. If 45
he meant that there was an eclipse (which is the usual meaning of the Greek word he uses),[a] his explanation was physically impossible: there can be no eclipse of the sun at full moon (the Passover was always at full moon), and in any case an eclipse lasts only a few minutes. But Luke certainly regarded the darkness as a miracle, and these objections will hardly have occurred to him; one way or another, he was convinced that **the sun's light failed.** Mark and Matthew both report that Jesus died with a cry, Luke alone informs us what
it was: a verse from a psalm, **'Father, into thy hands I commit my** 46
spirit' (Psalm 31.6). Perhaps someone heard it, perhaps it was an early Christian intuition that Jesus had made his own this serene Old Testament

[a] It is so translated in the First Edition of NEB.

prayer (drawn from another of the "righteous sufferer" psalms) and prefaced
it with his characteristic address to God, '**Father**'. The last word rests (as
47 in Mark and Matthew) with **the centurion.** What impressed him was
evidently Jesus' bearing on the cross (and not the supernatural portents
which accompanied his death, as in Matthew's version). But his exclamation
is given in a form which would perhaps have come more naturally to such a
man than the theologically pregnant confession ('Son of God') attributed to
him by Mark and Matthew. '**Beyond all doubt', he said, 'this man was
innocent.'** [a]

At this the mood of the onlookers seems to change from mockery to
48 sympathy or remorse. With the rather stylized literary expression, **beating
their breasts,** the crowd is described as already perhaps regretting its part
in the crucifixion of Jesus and preparing for the repentance which (as Luke
will soon describe in his second volume) will be induced in many of them by
the preaching of the apostles.

49 Jesus' **friends,** and **the women who had accompanied him from
Galilee,** showed their loyalty by remaining near by until the end. And
Joseph of Arimathaea, out of sympathy with Jesus' cause, obtained from Pilate
the body for burial. Luke tells this episode in his own way. In Mark, Joseph's
motive seems to be one of ordinary Jewish piety: no dead body must be left
exposed after nightfall. In Matthew, Joseph is a secret disciple, and acts out
of loyalty to the master. But in Luke, Joseph takes his place among the other
51 pious Jews (men who **looked forward to the kingdom of God**) on the
fringe of the gospel story who, without being disciples, were **good** and
upright (like Zechariah and Elizabeth, 1.6, and Simeon, 2.25); and his
goodness and uprightness were shown precisely in that he dissociated himself
from the action of the Council, and wished to make some kind of amends—in
other words, Luke characteristically offers a moral explanation for Joseph's
action which, in its main details, he records exactly as it stands in Mark.

54 **It was Friday, and the Sabbath was about to begin.** This is a very
precise note of time: [b] the Sabbath began at sunset on what non-Jews would
naturally call "Friday evening". Luke is carefully building up his effect:
the women evidently meant to return, and we are told exactly how they spent
24. 1 the intervening time, and why they came back only **on the Sunday morning**
—if they had come earlier they would have broken the Sabbath command-

[a] Literally, "just" or "righteous". But the point of the sentence was not to pass a relative moral judgement on Jesus, but to show which side the centurion had taken: guilty or innocent, blasphemer or man of God, false or true. The translation "innocent" catches this well enough.

[b] The Greek word means, not "about to begin", but "dawning", and is an odd way of saying that the Sabbath *evening* was beginning. But the translation given, which assumes that the word could be used very loosely, seems the only way to make sense of Luke's sentence. There is some evidence that contemporary Jewish writers used a similar idiom, which may have been translated literally into Greek at an early stage of the gospel tradition.

ment. In what follows, the details (including the improbable one that they still thought of anointing Jesus' body with **spices**) are as in Mark, but the emphasis is slightly shifted. The main fact in the story is still that the tomb
was empty; but this only put the women **utterly at a loss.** The important 4
element is now the declaration of the angels (two angels have taken the place of one in Mark, but the effect is the same: the essential thing is the angelic vision, not the number of angelic beings). No more than an echo remains of the puzzling promise that Jesus will meet his disciples in Galilee (Mark 16.7; Matthew 28.7). Galilee is only mentioned as the place where Jesus uttered a prophecy of his resurrection. And the resurrection was now proved to have taken place, not so much by the empty tomb, as by the realization that the prophecy had been fulfilled. It was this realization which the women hastened to tell the apostles. Luke does not name them until this point. His list agrees with that of Mark and Matthew, except that Joanna (see above on 8.2) takes the place of Salome. Like both Mark and Matthew, he has his own explanation of why their experience did not pass straight into the proclamation of the first Christians: they were not believed.

That same day. This story occurs only in Luke; indeed, all the gospels, 13
after having run closely together in their accounts of the trial and execution, diverge markedly when they come to the circumstances of the resurrection, and it is impossible to fit their accounts together into a single coherent scheme. The reason for this may well be that the conviction that Jesus had "risen from the dead" was not reached at the same time and in the same way by all the disciples, and many different stories about these critical days must have been current (we know in any case from 1 Corinthians 15.5–7 that there were more appearances of the risen Christ than are recorded in the gospels). Each evangelist will have chosen to narrate the particular experiences which seemed to bring out most clearly the meaning of this almost unimaginable event—
something **too good to be true**, as the NEB expresses it with perhaps 41
unnecessary banality—and we can expect to find a vein of deliberate teaching in each of the episodes. Luke's story, even though the mysterious stranger and his mysterious disappearance give it at first a slightly fairy-tale atmosphere, is nevertheless precise in its details. The name of the village is given, and its distance from Jerusalem; and though there are certain difficulties
in identifying it, there is every reason to believe that it existed.[a] One of the 18

[a] The present village of *Amwas* stands on the site of the important Roman town of Nicopolis, some eighteen miles north-west of Jerusalem. In the third century this town was firmly believed to be the Emmaus of the gospel, and there are the remains of a large Byzantine basilica there. But the distance does not agree with Luke's figure of "60 stades" (**seven miles**). Consequently the Crusaders built a church exactly 60 stades along the same road, and thereby started a second tradition. A third possibility is a village which was called *Koloniyeh* after the Romans had planted a "colony" there, but which in Jesus' time was certainly called Emmaus. This lies on the Jaffa road, some four miles north-west of Jerusalem. If this is the true site, the discrepancy of Luke's **seven miles** is not serious.

two disciples is also named: Cleopas (short for Cleopatros, a not uncommon name: he may have been the Clopas who was the husband of a certain Mary, John 19.25). Presumably his home was at Emmaus; and the disciples' offer of hospitality to the stranger rings true for the east: by early afternoon the main part of the day is thought to be over. The stranger made the proper show of reluctance—**he made as if to continue his journey**—but no one liked to be still on the road too late in the day (for darkness falls very rapidly in Palestine), and he soon gave in and stayed for a meal. At his sudden departure the disciples could still have had an hour or two's daylight in which to walk back rapidly to Jerusalem.

The significance of the story is concentrated in two points. First, Jesus
27 **explained to them the passages which referred to himself in every part of the scriptures.** The various beliefs which Jesus' contemporaries held about the coming Messiah were all based on passages of Scripture which could be interpreted as prophetic references to him. But the picture which was usually obtained from these sources was of a glorious and powerful figure who would immediately inaugurate a new age. In the course of his teaching, Jesus had frequently tried to modify this picture by replacing the central figure with another, the Son of Man, and by insisting on the suffering which must precede glorification, both for himself and for those who followed him. Nevertheless, he had not succeeded in preparing his disciples for the apparent catastrophe of the crucifixion, which they found quite impossible to reconcile with any of their existing ideas of what a Messiah should be. Nevertheless, after the resurrection, they came to see that Jesus' humiliation and death did in fact "fulfil" Scripture as much as his glorification; or (to put it the other way round) that the many passages in the Old Testament about a Righteous Sufferer pointed to the same person as those which were more usually quoted in support of the expectation of a divinely sent Deliverer. Thus Christianity very soon gave to its adherents a distinctive approach to the Old Testament quite different from that current among the Jews; and Jesus is here shown to have given his authority to this method of interpretation.

31 The other point of significance is the moment at which **their eyes were**
30 **opened, and they recognized him. Jesus took bread . . . said the blessing . . . broke the bread**—the precise actions of his solemn last supper three days previously. That last supper was continued by Christians whenever they met together for the Eucharist. It was their experience that when they did this the Lord was there. The meal was the right and inevitable moment for the two strangely blinded disciples to recognize the risen Christ.

34 They returned to Jerusalem and found that meanwhile Jesus had **appeared to Simon**—that is, to Simon Peter: this is confirmed by Paul (1 Corinthians 15.4) though it is not narrated in any of the gospels. Jesus' next appearance
37 is also clearly recorded for a purpose. **They thought they were seeing a**

ghost; and the emphasis on their being able to touch Jesus, and on his human appetite, was meant to show them that this was not a ghost-story. But not only them: doubtless there were still many people when this gospel was written who thought they could explain away the resurrection (and so discredit Christianity) by suggesting that the disciples had only seen a ghost. The evidence of Jesus' tangibility continued to be important long after the first Easter day.

Then he opened their minds to understand the scriptures. Jesus' 45
magisterial lesson in the right understanding of the Old Testament is
repeated—but with an important addition: all this was **to be proclaimed** 47
to all nations. How this came to be fulfilled is the subject of Luke's next
volume, Acts of the Apostles, and there is no real break in the story. Nevertheless, the narrative up to this point has been a "gospel", like the other gospels, and needs to end, as they do, with Jesus' last appearance on earth. So a brief summary is given of the events which fill the first chapters of Acts,[a] and the gospel ends, as it began, in the temple at Jerusalem. But this
is not really the end. The disciples only **begin from Jerusalem.** Luke has 48
still to tell the story of how Christianity reached Rome.

[*a*] Some manuscripts make this summary correspond more closely to the account of the Ascension in Acts 1. See the footnote in NEB and below on Acts 1.1–10.

THE GOSPEL ACCORDING TO JOHN

The coming of Christ

The purpose of the Gospel according to John is declared, not at the beginning, but at the end: 'in order that you may hold the faith that Jesus is Christ, the Son of God' (20.31).

To anyone (other than a Christian) who understood what was meant by the term "Christ" (Messiah, Anointed One), it would have come as a surprise that a book should have to be written for this purpose. "Christ", by definition, was a figure of power and glory. When he came, it would be impossible not to be aware of the fact. His destiny was to restore a kingdom of unprecedented splendour and justice to God's elect people among the Jews. Once his reign had begun, it would hardly be necessary to write a book to prove that he had come.

Nevertheless, Christians were not deterred from calling Jesus "Christ", even though the fact that the Christ had come was not recognized by the majority of the human race, not even by the Jews, who for centuries had been praying for his coming. This technical term of Jewish religion seemed the natural way to describe one who had actually been among them on earth, who was now at God's right hand in heaven, and who was the source of new life for his followers. They were able to find Old Testament texts which not only prophesied his glory but also implied a destiny of suffering and rejection; and the more they reflected on the life and teaching of Jesus, the better they began to understand the mysterious necessity that 'the Christ was bound to suffer' (Luke 24.26) and that his reign was to be, at least for the present, unrecognized by all but a few.

However, they soon came to realize that Jesus was more than this. He had power, not only over the hearts of men, but over the elemental and demonic forces of the universe; he gave meaning, not only to human life, but to the whole created order; he belonged, not only to time, but to eternity. But if so, then the problem of his rejection became more acute than ever. If Jesus belonged to the very structure of the world, why did the world not accept him? How could one possibly explain the bitter reality of the crucifixion?

John's gospel is an attempt to tackle the wider implications of this problem. The technical terms of Jewish religious expectation which are found in the other gospels—Christ, Son of God, Son of Man—were no longer adequate to describe the depth and universality of the Christian's understanding of Jesus. Accordingly, John uses a new vocabulary. Jesus is light, and life, and truth: words which belong more to religious poetry than to the prosaic language of doctrine, and which set Jesus in a much larger frame than could be provided by the traditional categories of the Jewish religion. These words need no explanation, though they take on new depths of meaning as they are put to work in the course of the gospel.

The distinctive character of John's gospel is apparent in the way it begins. The other gospels, confining themselves to a more modest programme, and mainly concerned to show that Jesus was—in some sense—the Christ of Jewish expectation, were each content to describe some of the circumstances in which this Christ made his appearance among men. But John, having so greatly enlarged the scale on which he proposed to tackle his subject, could not regard the story as beginning only with the birth or the first public appearance of Jesus. He needed some way of describing Jesus which would show him to have been an integral element in the created universe from the beginning. For this purpose he chose another suggestive term which featured in the vocabulary of both religion and philosophy: **the Word.**

No single English word conveys the associations which the word *logos* would have had for an educated Greek. It meant far more than a mere unit of spoken language: it included any articulate thought, any logical and meaningful utterance; it was that which gave order and shape to the process of thinking—proportion in mathematics, rational intelligibility in the study of the natural world, an ordered account of human affairs. It was almost equivalent to "rationality". As such, it was a convenient tool for philosophy: the Stoics, indeed, used the word *logos* for the immanent rational principle of the whole universe, the single divine system which (according to their philosophy) underlay the multiplicity of the visible world; and doubtless their use of the word had already begun to influence the everyday speech of many Greek-speaking people who had never troubled to explore the theoretical implications of Stoicism.

To a Greek-speaking Jew, the word had a still wider range of meanings. In the Bible, God's "word" was not only the means by which (as it might be through a prophet) God communicated with men and brought them into obedience to his Law; it was also the expression of his relationship with the whole created universe: God said . . . and there was, God spoke . . . and it was done. "My word . . . shall not return to me fruitless without accomplishing my purpose" (Isaiah 55.11). God's word was an expression of his creative power.

A term which embraced so many ideas could be put to many uses. For Philo of Alexandria, whose life was devoted to the task of expressing the essence of the Jewish religion in terms borrowed from contemporary philosophy, the *logos* became a philosophical entity in its own right, and seemed to offer the key to understanding the relationship between the transcendent God of the Bible and the world that is known to the human senses. But there is no reason to think that John was addressing his gospel to readers who were accustomed to any particular or technical use of the word *logos*: they spoke Greek, and therefore shared the usual Greek understanding of it as a word with a wide range of meanings to do with the rational use of the intellect; but they were also familiar with Jewish traditions, and knew something of the power and vigour associated in the Old Testament with the Word of God. They were therefore prepared for this *logos* of John to mean a great deal more than can be expressed in English by "word"; and it was for John to show, by some specimen phrases, in exactly what sense he wished to apply it to Jesus Christ. The first eighteen verses of his gospel may be regarded as a kind of poem in which successive stanzas seek to draw out the implications of this single word, *logos*.[a]

1. 1 **When all things began.** In the Greek, the first two words of the gospel are the same as the first two words of the Old Testament; and there can be little doubt that this echo is intentional. The first image brought to mind is the creation. But whereas, in Genesis, the sentence continues with a statement about the first thing that happened—God made the heavens and the earth—here it goes on quite differently: **the Word already was.** It is as if something is being said, not about creation itself, but about the conditions under which creation was brought about. This was in fact an old line of thought: surely God was not to be imagined as personally supervising every detail of the universe that was being brought into being? The omniscient intelligence which could be seen to underlie all created things, and which indeed rendered them intelligible to man's own power of reasoning—this intelligence was surely not identical with God himself (as some philosophers would have said, who denied the existence of any God beyond that which is revealed in the rational system of the universe)? An answer to these questions had been already supplied in some of the later writings of the Old Testament: God was assisted at the creation by the figure of Wisdom.

"The Lord created me when he began his work . . .
When he marked the foundations of the earth
then I was beside him like a master-workman."
(Proverbs 8.22–31)[b]

[*a*] These verses are poetical in the further sense that they are more evocative than precise; hence many of them can be translated in more than one way, as can be seen from the number of alternatives offered in the NEB footnotes. Moreover the sequence of thought seems less than perfectly logical; and it is possible (as some have supposed) that the writer did not in fact compose the poem himself but found it already in existence and, in adapting it to his purpose, made changes and additions which interrupted its continuity and disturbed its logic. On the other hand, it is not to be expected of poetry—and certainly not of poetry inspired by the Old Testament—that it should say things in perfectly logical order, any more than that each of the concepts it uses should be capable of exact definition.

[*b*] This translation follows, not the Hebrew text, but the Septuagint Greek version. It was this version that John's readers were familiar with; and it contains certain small changes in the sense which make it seem to bear more directly on the part played by Wisdom at the creation.

"With thee is wisdom who knows thy works
and was present when thou didst make the world."
(Wisdom 9.9)

No Jew would ever have been tempted to think of this "wisdom" as a separate deity, usurping the honour of the one true God. On the contrary, wisdom provided a way of speaking of God with greater respect, avoiding the somewhat crude and anthropomorphic idea of God actually at work on the details of his creation, and yet conceding that, in the last analysis, wisdom was nothing other than God, though it was God conceived under the particular aspect of the physical and moral laws of the universe. Nevertheless, it was the way of religious poetry to allow this figure of wisdom to take on almost a life of its own. Wisdom was "beside" God (Proverbs 8.30), it "went forth to make its dwelling among the children of men, and found no dwelling" (Enoch 42.2—an apocryphal Jewish scripture compiled during the second and first centuries B.C.). John clearly stands in this tradition when, in his opening verses, he says similar things about the Word. Only, by using that term (instead of "Wisdom") he brings this old image of Jewish religious poetry within reach of a more philosophical reader. The Jesus who can be described in such terms is not a figment of the Hebrew imagination, but has to do with those essential and rational principles of the universe that must
have existed from the beginning: **no single thing was created without** 3
him.

By a progression which is again more poetical than logical, two further
ideas are associated with the Word: **life,** and **light.** Both of these are 4
developed as the gospel proceeds; but the second serves to lead into the next
great theme of the prologue. **The light shines on in the dark**: the concept 5
of light presupposes its opposite; light would not be recognized as light if there were no darkness with which to compare it. A scientist would doubtless express the matter differently; but a poet speaks naturally of a light that shines **in the dark,** and goes on from there to imagine a kind of contest between the light on the one hand and the darkness on the other, the darkness surrounding the light and trying to quench it. This image is the first hint of the mystery with which the gospel is concerned: the rejection of Christ by mankind. Christ is the Word, an agent of creation, a principle of the universe. As such he is eternal, he can never be **mastered** or "quenched",[a] as a light can; but, just as light presupposes darkness, so the Word presupposes a world which does not understand and acknowledge. It need be no more paradoxical

[a] **The darkness has never mastered it** is a brilliant rendering, suggested also by R. A. Knox in his own translation (1945), of an ambiguous Greek expression. The words can mean either, "the darkness has never quenched it" (NEB, First Edition), or "the darkness has never understood it", an interpretation which became popular in the Middle Ages, and has found its way into many English versions. Linguistically, the first of these meanings is more probable; but John may well have intended a *double entendre*. In 12.35 the same word is translated 'overtake'.

to say that the divine Word was not received than that a light is surrounded by darkness.

But this admission raises a new question. If it was of the nature of this Word that, although integral to the created order, it could yet be ignored and rejected by men, what assurance was there that it would ever be recognized and acclaimed at all? The answer was that there must be "witnesses" to it, men and women whose lives, by being dedicated to the Word and entirely determined by it, would be powerful arguments for its existence and power. Here was a way to understand that strange figure who always stood on the
6 first page of the Christian story. **There appeared a man named John**—the sentence is suddenly in the style of the Old Testament, and we are reminded at once of the other gospels, where it is as a man in the tradition of the Old Testament prophets—an ascetic preacher of the desert, with something of Elijah about him—that John the Baptist makes his appearance. He fulfils prophecies, he revives the long-silent gift of prophetic speech, he foretells his greater successor and places him in the flaming scenery of the Last Judgement—in short, a figure only comprehensible in a culture shaped by the Bible and conditioned by urgent expectation of a new world-order that is about to come. The writer of this gospel suggests a different and less esoteric
7 rôle for him: **he came as a witness to testify to the light.**

9 **The real light which enlightens every man was even then coming into the world.** A strictly chronological scheme would yield a different order: Jesus' birth would come before John the Baptist's preaching. But this is poetry, not history: John's sequence of ideas reflects, not the passage of time, but a movement of thought, a movement from the metaphysical implications of the Word which was present with God 'when all things began', to that moment in time when there was on earth a person—Jesus—whose appearance challenged mankind to accept the Word. The description of that unearthly presence on earth is the climax of the prologue; but lest it should be supposed that the splendour of that moment commanded the assent of all who saw it, John first reminds his readers of the point already made: there was darkness around the light, the Word was inevitably not
10 received, it needed witnesses to commend it. **The world, though it owed its being to him, did not recognize him.** That was true of the world in general; but certain people did recognize him, and these—that is, Christians,
12 **those who have yielded him their allegiance**—experienced a relationship with God which could be described as that of the **children of God** (for a new appreciation of the personal fatherhood of God was one of the distinctive marks of early Christianity).

14 **So the Word became flesh.** John makes no attempt to soften the harshness of this terrific proposition. The man Jesus was now at the right hand of God: that was an easy way of putting it, given the limitations of such naïvely pictorial language (it was the way most early Christians did put it). But this

"Christ" was also—had always been—part of the structure of the universe, something that is essential to understanding the created order; and all this was somehow concentrated in one individual who fully shared the human condition. John had no alternative but to bring into one sentence words which would normally seem to belong to totally different worlds of discourse: **the Word became flesh.**

He came to dwell among us. The man Jesus was also the Word. An easier way to conceive of this double aspect of Jesus' person is that adopted by most New Testament writers: the two aspects are assigned to two different periods of time. After (and perhaps also before) his life on earth, Jesus was a figure of glory, seated at the right hand of God, superior to all heavenly and earthly powers. But when he was literally 'among us', he was simply man—a unique and exceptional man, no doubt, but so far as his humanity went indistinguishable from other men. By contrast, John makes no such clear distinction between Jesus in heaven and Jesus on earth. Throughout his gospel he invests Jesus with something of the divinity and the glory which belongs to the Word, even though this Word became absolutely flesh, even though Jesus was absolutely human; and so here, his brief description of the manner in which Jesus was **among us** contains more than a hint of a presence that was all the time something more than merely human, merely 'flesh'. **He came to dwell.** The translation is as correct as any English rendering can be; but the Greek word has far more overtones than its English equivalent. Originally it meant "dwell in a tent": it was in a "tent" that God had dwelt when he first accompanied his people in their travels across the desert. Moreover, the same Greek word was reminiscent of a Hebrew expression for the glory of God "dwelling" on earth. **He came to dwell among us** is therefore a phrase which, with its Old Testament associations, already suggests a more than human side to the period of Christ's humanity. The following words—**glory, grace, truth**—are equally charged with meaning by their use in the Old Testament, where they belong to the vocabulary of God's care for his people; yet almost all these words are ones which will take on new meaning as the gospel unfolds. For the present, they serve as a summary of what it could be said that **we saw**—that is, not the subjective impressions of one man or of a group of people, but the essential double aspect of Jesus' life on earth to which witness was borne by the whole community of those who had actually acknowledged him, whether after seeing him themselves, or after hearing the testimony of others.

Here is John's testimony to him. The synoptic gospels present a 15
simpler view of John the Baptist's work: John prophesied that a greater than
himself would come, and a greater did come. But in this gospel John is not
so much a prophet as a witness: he was the first to recognize and give testimony that a greater *had* come. Jesus' appearance was such as, in a sense, to
put one off the scent. It was John who was drawing the crowds; Jesus only

came **after** (perhaps as a disciple, perhaps simply later in time). On the face of it, it was John who marked the arrival of something new. But his real importance was in the testimony he gave that, despite appearances, Jesus was of superior **rank**, of another order altogether: '**before I was born, he already was**'.

17 **The Law was given through Moses.** This was one of the basic premises of Jewish religion. From this flowed the tremendous benefits and privileges which the Jewish people believed they had received from God: the Law was the expression and guarantee of the 'grace and truth' with which God had consistently treated his people. John boldly corrects this ancient belief: **grace and truth came through Jesus Christ.** But of course it was not just a matter of Jesus having replaced Moses as the bearer of the same benefits as before. The 'grace' received through Jesus Christ was greater than anything received through the Law of Moses: it was **grace upon grace.**

18 **No one has ever seen God.** Pagan religions might speak lightly of gods appearing to men; but the seriousness with which the Jews took the idea of God forbade any such fantasy. God was far too terrible to be 'seen' by men; at most they might expect to have to face him at the moment of Judgement. Therefore the Jesus whom men had "seen", despite all the near-divine titles given to him, was not in every sense identical with God.[a] He revealed God only to the extent that men could bear it. John uses what in Greek was almost a technical term for the inspired activity of one who imparted truths about God: **he has made him known.** Men did not literally "see" God in Jesus: this would have been inconceivable. Through Jesus, they came to "know" God.

19 **This is the testimony which John gave.** Jesus' work and message burst upon the Jews of Palestine as something entirely new and original; but it was immediately preceded by a movement which was itself quite out of the ordinary, that of John the Baptist. The gospels differ among themselves in the picture they give of him, and drop occasional hints that there was a good deal more to him than they have chosen to record; and the contemporary historian Josephus also sketches a portrait of him which is recognizably of the same person, and yet is seen from a quite different point of view. The main question to which Christian writers had to address themselves was this: the movement of John and the movement of Jesus was each in its own way unique; yet the one came immediately before the other, and there were

[*a*] As can be seen from the footnote in NEB, the evidence of the manuscripts is divided on this point. Since the exact relationship of Christ to God was one of the most burning questions which agitated the church in the early centuries, it is perhaps not surprising that a verse which had such bearing on it as this one should have been quoted in different versions by theologians of different persuasions. The version given in the text is that which seems to give the best sense. But the much more difficult reading, which calls Jesus "himself God", is offered by our earliest papyrus manuscripts, and must therefore have been current within a century of the writing of the gospel.

clear points of contact between them, so much so that it was impossible to tell the story of Jesus without first referring to the story of John. What then was the relationship between the two? Out of what was clearly a mass of tradition about John, the writers of the other gospels selected three points in particular which seemed to point towards an answer. First, John fulfilled an
Old Testament oracle about **a voice crying aloud in the wilderness** 23
(Isaiah 40.3) which clearly cast him in the rôle of a person preparing for an event of universal importance; secondly, he was the precursor of someone infinitely greater than himself—he had used words like those of the humblest
of servants about his master, **'I am not good enough to unfasten his** 27
shoes'; and thirdly (the most obvious point of contact) he had baptized Jesus.

John's gospel, where it uses the same material, uses it in a quite different way. The quotation from Isaiah, the sayings about the superiority of the
Baptist's successor, and the description of **the Spirit coming down from** 32
heaven like a dove (one of the phenomena accompanying the baptism of Jesus, according to the other gospels) are all phrased, not as news, but as reminiscences. They describe, not what John did, but what he said. They are his **testimony**. Accordingly, no interest is shown in what was, after all, his main activity—baptizing. This (as we know both from Josephus and from the other gospels) was a ritual of great significance: it was 'for the forgiveness of sins' (Mark 1.4). But for this writer it had only one meaning: it was the prototype—the first inkling, as it were—of that infinitely more profound experience offered by Jesus to his followers, baptism **in Holy Spirit.** In itself, it was unimportant: this writer does not even mention that John baptized Jesus. For him, the whole importance of John lay, not in his being a "baptist", but in his being the first "witness" to Jesus Christ.

This is subtly emphasized at the beginning. John, while working at a
place[a] called **Bethany beyond Jordan,** was confronted by **the Jews of** 28, 19
Jerusalem—that is to say, by that element in the total Jewish population which was to show itself consistently opposed to Jesus: the men of influence in Jerusalem. Here, they are represented first by some of those concerned with the administration and worship of the temple (**priests and Levites**), and subsequently by more learned men whose interests extended particularly
to the interpretation of the Law—**some Pharisees.** His reply to them is 24
introduced by a curious phrase: **He confessed without reserve and** 20

[a] The site of this Bethany had been forgotten even by the time Origen looked for it early in the third century A.D., and there was a tendency to insert into the manuscripts the name *Bethabara*, the site of which could still be identified. But a possible derivation for the name Bethany is *bet aniyyah*, House of the Boat—a very plausible name for a small place on the bank of the river which subsequently disappeared. At any rate, an early tradition fixed the place of John's baptism on the east bank of the Jordan, near the ford closest to Jericho, just below the small mountain which was believed to be the place where Elijah ascended into heaven—for John had much about him which seemed deliberately to recall the figure of Elijah, even though he is here said to have denied that he was Elijah.

avowed. In the Greek, as in the English, this sentence appears cumbrous and over-emphatic. But the emphasis of the words is surely deliberate: John's "testimony" to Jesus demanded, in the first place, that he should make it absolutely clear that his own rôle, though unique and significant, did not detract in any way from the weight of the titles which would soon be suggested for Jesus. (On Jesus' reaction to a similar question, and on the titles themselves, see above on Mark 8.28.)

However, John's "testimony" does not consist only of statements familiar
26 from the other gospels. **'Among you, though you do not know him,**
stands the one who is to come after me'. This is something new. One
of the many current beliefs about the coming Messiah was that he already
existed, and might even be already on earth, but that he was to remain
"unknown" until the day when he would be revealed. This idea was rich in
11 possibilities for explaining the paradox that Jesus, 'the Word', **entered his**
own realm, and his own would not receive him. Jesus conformed to the
traditional type of a hidden Messiah; it was only the way in which he was
revealed which was totally different from what his contemporaries expected.
31, 33 He was hidden, at first, even from his first witness: John says twice over, **'I**
did not know him'. There is evidence in the other gospels that John continued for some time to be in doubt about him. But here, he has now seen
34 enough to give his precious evidence: **'I have borne witness. This is God's**
Chosen One'. [a]

29 **'There is the Lamb of God'.** This too is something quite new; but it is hard to know how to interpret it. By the time the gospel was written, the phrase had a rich store of meanings: the death of Jesus, occurring as it did in the course of the Passover festival, could be described as the sacrifice of a Passover lamb (1 Corinthians 5.7); and his glorious ascension into heaven as Messiah is represented in the Revelation as the exaltation of a slaughtered Lamb in heaven. If John the Baptist used this phrase about Jesus, he can hardly have foreseen all this, and the only clue to his meaning is in the sequel, **'it is he who takes away the sin of the world'.** There was nothing in the Jewish sacrificial system about a "lamb" which could have such atoning power; but the words, **takes away the sin of the world,** are reminiscent of just one passage in the Old Testament, which describes a Servant of God who was "led like a sheep to the slaughter", and who "bore the sin of many" (Isaiah 53.7,12). It is even possible that the original Aramaic word used by John the Baptist was one which meant both "lamb" and "servant"; if so, John may have been the first to recognize in Jesus the mysterious Servant prophesied in Isaiah 53. However that may be, this is

[a] Another Old Testament title, probably derived, like "Beloved" in Mark 1.11 and Matthew 3.17, from Isaiah 42.1: "... my chosen in whom I delight; I have bestowed my spirit upon him". Here, as in Mark and Matthew, the reading of some manuscripts gives the much less technical and allusive title, "Son of God".

only the first of a series of related images in this gospel: here Jesus is the lamb, later he is the door of the sheepfold, and finally he is the shepherd himself.

After John the Baptist, the gathering of disciples—an episode which
necessarily stands near the beginning in all the gospels. John again has a
particular interest in it—not so much in the fact that certain disciples
decided to follow Jesus, or in the reasons why they did so, but because they
too could be called as early "witnesses" to the true nature of Jesus. The
first two, for instance, called him '**Rabbi**' **(which means a teacher)**, and 38
their question '**where are you staying?**' showed what they meant by it:
a man of fixed abode, who gathered a group of pupils—a kind of "school"
—around him. True, Jesus certainly deserved the title Rabbi, and much of
his work consisted of teaching; and the prosaic question about his lodging
received a prosaic answer. But his pupils were soon to find that he was a
great deal more besides. Indeed, one of these two, Andrew, immediately
went on to give a more significant testimony: '**We have found the Messiah**' 41
(John characteristically both offers the original Hebrew word and explains
that its Greek equivalent is '**Christ**'). This led to the adherence of Simon
Peter. In the other gospels, the call of these two men takes place beside the
Sea of Galilee. Here the setting is quite different; but John's account includes
one of the most certain facts in the New Testament: that Jesus gave Simon
the name **Cephas**, of which the Greek equivalent is **Peter, the Rock.** 42

Philip appears in the lists of the Twelve given in the other gospels. His 43
testimony is much the same as Andrew's: '**we have met the man spoken** 45
of by Moses in the Law, and by the prophets'—the person, that is to
say, to whom so many passages of the Old Testament were believed to point
forward, the Messiah, the Christ. It was not in itself implausible that this
Messiah should turn out to be identical with a particular man **Jesus**, of
known family (**Joseph**) and home (**Nazareth**): many believed that the
Messiah would first appear *incognito*. But what the next disciple, Nathanael,
found hard to accept was that the incognito should be so complete. Nazareth
was a small, remote place, without even a mention in the Old Testament to
give a clue to its future distinction. '**Can anything good come from** 46
Nazareth?' Nevertheless, his initial doubt soon yielded to recognition, and
he gave the most important testimony so far: '**You are the Son of God;** 49
you are king of Israel'. Like the titles already given, these will be shown
to be true (in a sense) as the gospel proceeds.

Nathanael is not in any surviving list of the Twelve, and in fact it is not 45
said here that he became a disciple. He is brought in, again, entirely because
of the value of his testimony. But there was reason to place him as the last
and most decisive witness in the series. Jesus said, '**Here is an Israelite** 47
worthy of the name; there is nothing false in him'. He was, in short,
the exact opposite of Jesus' Jewish opponents in Jerusalem: he was a true

Israelite, one whose Jewish nationality and upbringing were to yield their proper fruit in making him a man who recognized and acclaimed Jesus for what he was. But how did Jesus know this about him? Was it a guess? Or had he a true gift of prophecy? This time it was Jesus' turn to be a witness. If you wished to give evidence about a scene you had witnessed, you could be asked about the exact place and time. The question might take the form (as in Daniel and Susanna 51–8), "What kind of tree did it happen under?"
Jesus passed the test; he then went on to cap the series of testimonies with
51 a startling statement of his own: **'You shall see heaven wide open,
and God's angels ascending and descending upon the Son of Man.'**

Here again, the synoptic gospels preserve elements out of which this saying could have been constructed. At Jesus' baptism, the heavens were 'torn open' (Mark 1.10); immediately after, in the temptation story, 'angels waited on him' (Mark 1.13); and there are a number of places where Jesus appears to refer to himself in this same oblique way as **the Son of Man.** But even if these elements were the original material out of which this saying in John's gospel was composed, the result suggests a quite different picture. "Jacob dreamt that he saw a ladder, which rested on the ground with its top reaching to heaven, and angels of God were going up and down upon it" (Genesis 28.12). Grammatically, the last word in the Hebrew could equally well mean "upon him", that is, on Jacob; and in due course Jewish scholars came to be attracted by the possibility. Jacob, after all, was Israel, and the Israel on earth had surely some kind of spiritual counterpart in heaven; might it not be that the verse in Genesis was intended to illustrate the relationship of the earthly and the heavenly Israel? We do not know how much of this kind of speculation was going on in John's day, but it is tempting to see a similar train of thought here: when Nathanael saw Jesus it was as if the true Israelite saw the true Israel in heaven, and his true counterpart on earth. At any rate, the allusion to the Jacob story is unmistakable, and the picture is one which emphasizes what (at least for John) was an essential feature of the mythological title, Son of Man: it meant a figure whose destiny was to be played out both on earth and in heaven.

Christ the giver of life

2. 1 **On the third day there was a wedding.** We can fill in a few of the details. The wedding took place in a small town, Cana, which was about nine miles north-east of Nazareth.[a] It was the home-town of Nathanael (21.2) and a

[a] The modern *Khirbet Kana*, now a mound of ruins. Another possible site is *Kefar Kenna*, rather closer to Nazareth on the road to Tiberias. Here, two churches have been built to commemorate the miracle; but the tradition that this was Cana-in-Galilee seems not to be older than the Middle Ages.

place, according to this gospel, visited more than once by Jesus. Certainly,
his family was well known there, for the mother of Jesus was present at the
festivities, helping with the domestic arrangements (for only men were
invited to the actual meal). **Jesus and his disciples were guests also**: 2
whether he was invited because of a family connection, or out of a new respect
for him as a teacher, it would have been normal and courteous to include in
the invitation those who had begun to form a regular group of disciples
around him. Five have been mentioned: there may already have been more.
They will have gone, not merely to receive hospitality, but to assist the
bridegroom in the formalities and the entertainment which were a necessary
part of the wedding and which usually went on for several days.

On the face of it, the story describes how Jesus spared his host a serious
social embarrassment. It is possible that Jesus had been partly responsible
for the crisis (hence his mother's unexpected approach to him to tell him of
the alarm felt in the domestic quarters). He had arrived with a large party,
but without bringing the kind of contribution expected of such guests—food
and wine. If so, his deed may have been originally understood as a miraculous
resourcefulness in the face of an obligation which his chosen way of life made
it impossible for him to meet out of his own resources (the story of the
tribute-money found in a fish's mouth—Matthew 17.24–7—is on the same
lines). In any case, he acted with great discretion. The other guests were
spared the shock of knowing anything about it, and even **the steward of** 8
the feast (who was probably a kind of head waiter or master of ceremonies)
was not in the secret.

Reduced to these simple terms, the story yields no very obvious moral:
like many of the stories which must have circulated about Jesus, it could only
qualify to stand in a gospel if it could be shown to contain some deeper
meaning. John describes it as one of **the signs by which Jesus revealed** 11
his glory, and characteristically places a load of significance upon some of
the most banal details. In the brief dialogue, for instance, between Jesus and
his mother the sentence, '**Your concern, mother, is not mine**', can bear 4
more than one meaning. The tone is a little formal ('**mother**' translates the
Greek word meaning "woman", and would have been the correct form of
address on such an occasion) and the idiom is the same as that used by the
demons to Jesus in Mark 1.24 and 5.7 ('what do you want with me?'). At its
simplest level, it need be no more than an expression of surprise and slight
annoyance that his mother should have come in to interrupt his attention to
the festivities. But (as the NEB rendering suggests) a further meaning is
possible: "you are worried about the supply of wine, but my concern is with
more important things". Again, the **six stone water-jars** were nothing out 6
of the ordinary, and their impressive size simply underlines the miraculous
abundance created by Jesus; but when John adds the detail that they were
of the kind used for Jewish rites of purification, we can be sure that we

are intended to draw a moral: the ritual observances of the Jews had given
10 place to the spiritual sacraments of the Christians. Finally, the comment of the steward, which rounds off the episode, sounds like a trite piece of convivial small talk; but for Christian readers it bears more than a hint of those sayings of Jesus in which the old wine of the Jewish religion is shown to be infinitely inferior to the new wine of the gospel.

12 **After this he went down to Capernaum.** John gives a quite different picture of Jesus' movements from that in the other gospels. There, Jesus makes Capernaum his base for much of his work in Galilee; here, Jesus makes Cana (if anywhere) his base, and only makes one brief visit to Capernaum. Again, in the other gospels Jesus (after his baptism) makes only one pilgrimage to Jerusalem, the pilgrimage which ends in his death; all the Jerusalem episodes are therefore concentrated in the last few days of Jesus' life. But in John's gospel Jesus makes several journeys to Jerusalem (a fairly frequent pilgrimage for the great festivals was customary for such a person), and his drastic action with regard to the temple is accordingly placed near the beginning of the gospel instead of towards the end. If we wish to know in what order things actually happened, we have to make our choice between the two versions, and allow for the fact that one or the other (or both) may have been deliberately rearranged in order to bring out better the significance of each period of Jesus' life.

15 **Jesus made a whip of cords.** This is one of the small details by which John succeeds in conveying a slightly different and more agitated picture than the other gospels. Jesus' action was not just a prophetic gesture: he effectively drove the animals out of the precincts with his whip, causing chaos among the money-changers, and finally ordering out the **dealers in pigeons** with their caged birds. What was his reason for this action? In the other gospels, the question is a complicated one (see above on Mark 11.15–
16 19); here, there is a simpler answer. **'You must not turn my Father's house into a market'.** This is a fairly plain allusion to the last words of Zechariah (14.21), "There shall no longer be a trader in the house of the Lord of hosts on that day": Jesus was deliberately fulfilling this oracle, and his deed proclaimed the imminence of that "day of the Lord" which the prophet had foretold. For the disciples, on the other hand, the episode came
17 to have another meaning. **'Zeal for thy house will destroy me'** is a quotation from Psalm 69.9—and the subject of that psalm is one of the nameless righteous sufferers of the Old Testament: even the devotion and piety of the man towards the temple had been held against him. These **words of Scripture** seemed to fit Jesus perfectly.

18 **The Jews challenged Jesus.** As in the other gospels, the action inevitably provoked a controversy. The reply of Jesus is a saying that is reported by the New Testament writers in different forms and contexts. Speaking sacri-

legious words against the temple could have been a serious offence, possibly even punishable by death; and a charge of this kind was evidently brought against Jesus at his trial. It caused the evangelists some embarrassment: could Jesus really have threatened to destroy the temple? Various solutions are suggested in the gospel accounts (see above on Mark 14.58). Here, the saying (as John reports it) is not so much an attack on the temple, as a claim that, if it were destroyed, Jesus could rebuild it in three days. With characteristic irony, John makes the Jews take this quite literally: the temple had been begun by Herod the Great in 20–19 B.C., and was not in fact finished
until A.D. 63, though the main work may have been completed after **forty-six** 20
years—by, say, A.D. 27, which is about the time this conversation could have taken place. It is pedantic to ask whether John knew that work was still in progress a generation later: the point is simply to contrast the immense labours of the builders with Jesus' grandiose claim to accomplish something comparable in three days. The claim was absurd—taken literally; but that its literal meaning was absurd or sacrilegious was (according to John) quite
beside the point. **The temple he was speaking of was his body**—a hidden 21
meaning which could only be grasped in the light of the resurrection and of the many scriptures which were thereby fulfilled.

Many gave their allegiance to him. The response to Jesus' 'signs' was 23
positive. How could it be said, therefore, that 'his own would not receive him' (1.11)? The full answer lay in the sequel; but in the meantime a
sufficient reason could be found in the attitude of Jesus himself: he **would** 24
not trust himself to them. He knew men so well.

There was one of the Pharisees named Nicodemus. He was evidently 3. 1
more sympathetic to Jesus than most of the influential people in Jerusalem:
he recognized Jesus as a **teacher** (like himself) and acknowledged that the 2
signs he performed indicated that he had a divine mission on the level at least of one of the great figures of the Old Testament. Nevertheless, though
a **famous teacher of Israel**, this Pharisee could not advance to any real 11
understanding of Jesus. He was a case in point of a man who was ready to "give his allegiance" to Jesus, but to whom, because of the limitations of his understanding, Jesus could not 'trust himself'.

So far as the narrative goes, this Nicodemus has a humble function. He simply provides the questions and comments that are needed to draw out a discourse from Jesus, and his contribution is of a kind that occurs again and again in this gospel: by understanding a saying of Jesus in its most literal and
banal sense ('**how is it possible...for a man to be born when he is** 4
old?') he gives the dramatic cue for a more subtle explanation from Jesus. Indeed, the whole episode is characteristic of the way in which the writer of this gospel presents the teaching of Jesus, a way which is quite different

from that of the other gospels. In them, Jesus' teaching takes the form of brief and memorable sentences, usually evoked by some question or incident, sometimes running over into a parable or illustration, but never offering a systematic development of a particular line of thought. Even where we find substantial paragraphs entirely devoted to teaching (as in the Sermon on the Mount, or in the discourse on the future), they turn out to consist of collections of sayings, many of which were remembered separately and were only later brought together into a composite discourse. But in this gospel the style of teaching is quite different. Starting from a particular episode, or question, or comment, Jesus develops his thought on a given subject, and ranges over a wide field of ideas. Sometimes his words are reminiscent of sayings recorded elsewhere; but more often they are expressed in the more sophisticated and philosophical idiom which is characteristic of this gospel. Theoretically, it is possible that Jesus actually spoke like this, and that we have here an authentic style of teaching which is unaccountably missing from the other gospels. But this is hardly the most likely explanation. The sayings in the other gospels are pungent, poetic and easily memorable: many of them are in exactly the form to be expected of teaching given in a Semitic language, and there is no difficulty in imagining how they could have been preserved in people's memory until they came to be written down. The discourses in John, on the other hand, are literary and artificial. They are cast in the form of dialogues or monologues such as are familiar from some of the philosophical literature of the time; they are carefully composed around a group of concepts which occur again and again, with different variations, as the gospel proceeds; and they seem to presuppose a writer meditating in his study rather than a teacher responding spontaneously to the questions of his hearers. In other words, Jesus did not deliver the discourses that are attributed to him in this gospel. But nor (in all probability) did he deliver the "Sermon on the Mount" in the form in which Matthew has recorded it. The gospels present us with different attempts to gather the teaching of Jesus into a form which would bring out its meaning and meet the needs of subsequent generations of Christians. The author of this gospel has done this in a more systematic way than the others. If, in the process, he has recast it in a somewhat different idiom, it is still possible that he has come at least as near as any other New Testament writer to its essential meaning.

3 **'Unless a man has been born over again he cannot see the kingdom of God'.** This saying, introduced by the solemn and distinctive formula which so often goes with a pronouncement of Jesus in this gospel (**'In truth, in very truth I tell you'**) is the substance of the discourse; the rest, in a sense, is commentary. The idea that, by committing himself to a new religion or philosophy, a man might be "reborn", was not unheard of in antiquity. But what precisely did this mean in Christian terms? In the subsequent experience of Christians, the obvious moment when this "rebirth" took

place was at baptism (in Titus 3.5 baptism is actually called "rebirth"). The
elements of Christian baptism were the **water** which symbolized the washing 5
away of sin, and a new **spirit** which was received; of these, it was the spirit
which (to this writer at least) gave meaning to the notion of rebirth. It has
already been said in the prologue (1.13) that those who accept Jesus as Christ
are born, not 'by fleshly desire', but 'of God himself'. Here the same point
is made by means of the psychology of flesh and spirit (see below on Romans
8.5–8). "Flesh" is the whole of the human person as it were in its crude state,
untouched by God: physical birth in itself can bring forth nothing more.
"Spirit" is that aspect of the personality which is capable of responding to
God, and which is brought to life when the Spirit of God touches it. The
argument is an example of the old philosophical principle that "like begets
like". If Christian baptism was "in spirit", it evidently caused a rebirth in
the spirit of a man: '**it is spirit that gives birth to spirit**'. Jesus may 6
originally have meant something much less technical; but John, in his
commentary, makes sense of the saying about being **born over again** in
terms of Christian baptism.

John's gospel contains only one explicit parable (10.1–6); but there are
occasionally other illustrations which, like the parables in the other gospels,
invite the reader to do some thinking for himself. '**The wind blows where** 8
it wills' is one of these. The point of comparison seems to be the freedom
and unpredictability of the wind: in the same way, Christian "rebirth" is
not tied to physical laws and long processes like physical birth, but is sudden
and unpredictable. Indeed you can take the comparison as far as you like;
it happens that in Greek, as in Hebrew, the same word is used for both wind
and spirit.

However, there is still more to be said about the concept of being "born
again". In Greek the words have a double meaning: "**born over again**"
or "born from above". This second meaning suggests a whole new line of
thought. Baptism is something which happens **on earth**: the spirit is received 12
as an enrichment of the possibilities of human life; it does not follow that it
reveals to the Christian the **things of heaven.** But if rebirth is also "from
above", then it must also introduce him to the divine world above. The clue
to this aspect of it is in Christ himself. Rebirth is faith in Christ; and Christ
is a figure who belongs to both worlds. The title which most clearly brings
this out is **Son of Man.** It has already occurred once (1.51) with precisely 13
this significance of uniting the two worlds. And here are two more Son of
Man sayings which make the same point. This figure is one who is not only
a special and perhaps representative Man on earth, he also has a place on the
right hand of God in heaven. The conception of such a Son of Man belongs
to both worlds; and if Jesus was in fact (as he appears to have claimed in a
number of sayings) the eventual embodiment of this Son of Man conception,
then he was the unique link between the two worlds. '**No one ever went**

up into heaven except the one who came down from heaven, the Son of Man.' And how was the believer helped by this? Many of the Son of Man sayings in the other gospels seemed anything but illuminating. The Son of Man was to suffer and to die: how then could he help the believer to draw near to heaven, and give him a rebirth "from above"? John's version of
14 these sayings (for that is what verse 14 appears to be) is that the **Son of Man must be lifted up.** This had all kinds of possible meanings—lifted up on the cross, lifted up to heaven—which could be said to have been fulfilled in what happened to Jesus. But for the present, we are left to grapple with a single image from the Old Testament. To end an attack of fiery serpents on the people of Israel in the wilderness,

> "the Lord told Moses to make a serpent of bronze and erect it as a standard, so that anyone who had been bitten could look at it and recover. So Moses made a bronze serpent and erected it as a standard, so that when a snake had bitten a man, he could look at the bronze serpent and recover."
> (Numbers 21.8–9)

This serpent, according to later tradition, was "raised on high" by Moses; it was a "token of deliverance" for the people (Wisdom 16.6). The parallel is subtle but illuminating: by "looking at" and believing in Jesus in the various ways in which he was "lifted up", the Christian may find deliver-
15 ance, **possess eternal life**, and so be brought by the Son of Man into heaven.

16 **'God loved the world so much'.** Is Jesus still speaking? The original text, having no inverted commas, leaves the question open, and modern translators have to make a choice. Perhaps in fact it makes little difference. The whole discourse is a commentary on some basic affirmations of Jesus, and is the work of the writer. His task is to show what Jesus meant, not to provide a transcript of his actual words, and it does not much matter how much of the commentary is actually placed in Jesus' mouth. The object of these final paragraphs, in any case, is to get rid of a misconception. Mention of the Son of Man suggests judgement; for, in the classic Old Testament passage about him—Daniel 7—it is at God's final judgement that he makes his triumphant appearance. But if now this Son of Man has already appeared
13 and gone **up into heaven**, does this mean that it is too late for any more rebirth, are men already lined up for judgement, is their fate already sealed? The answer lies in a radical reformulation of traditional beliefs about God's judgement. The old conception was of a moment at the end of time when all men, the living and the dead, would be summoned to appear before the divine tribunal. To some extent that picture may still be valid; but now, much of what was traditionally thought of as belonging to the ultimate
19 future must be realized as taking place in the present. **Here lies the test**—here and now. Judgement has indeed begun, but it consists in the challenge

now presented to mankind by Jesus: men are judged when they declare for or against the light. Rebirth, involving salvation, is still an option for all.
Thus it can be said, '**It was not to judge the world that God sent** 17
his Son into the world, but that through him the world might be saved.'

Jesus . . . baptized. John too was baptizing. This gospel records a period 22–3
when both men were apparently doing identical work simultaneously. Such a period is not mentioned in the other gospels; indeed it seems to be implied that Jesus did not begin his public activity until after John had been imprisoned (Mark 1.14). John's gospel explicitly contradicts this: **This was** 24
before John's imprisonment. There was an initial period when both John and Jesus were "baptists".

Nevertheless, the activity of the two men was quite distinct. First with
regard to geography: **John . . . was baptizing at Aenon, near to Salim.** 23
We cannot locate this precisely. Aenon is probably simply a form of an Aramaic word meaning "springs", and in later centuries travellers were doubtful just where Salim was. But all traditions point to the northern end of that part of the Jordan valley which runs from the Sea of Galilee to the Dead Sea. If this is correct, it is certainly true that **water was plentiful in**

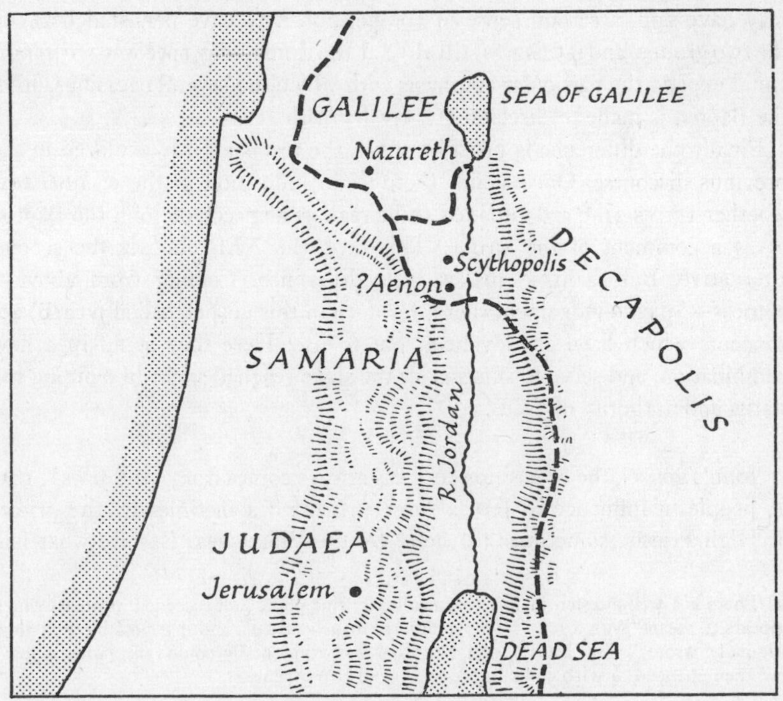

that region; and there is the further point that it lay in the territory of one of the cities of the Decapolis, Scythopolis (Bethshan). There would still have been a substantial Jewish population there, but politically it was outside the jurisdiction either of Herod Antipas or of the Roman governor of Judaea.
22 Meanwhile, Jesus was baptizing in **Judaea**—that is to say, probably lower down the Jordan valley. The two baptizers were some way apart, in different political territories.

Secondly, the two men, even if they were both baptists, were not strictly comparable. This has already been shown by John's 'testimony' (1.26–30), and the reader is given a further reminder of that testimony here, along with
29 a brief parable to illustrate how the two men stood in relation to each other (as the bridegroom's friend to the bridegroom on the wedding day). The
25 conversation arose out of **a dispute with Jews**[a] **about purification.** This is something we hear nothing about elsewhere; there was clearly a great deal more to be known about John the Baptist than the gospels tell us, and this may be a genuine fragment of history. Possibly this gospel recorded it because of the word "purification": John's baptism remained on the level of outward observance and ritual purification, but Jesus, who had turned water intended for Jewish purification into wine, had a baptism which far transcended such things. Furthermore, John the Baptist's followers were evidently looking askance at the success of Jesus. Whatever John himself may have said, a certain sense of competition may have persisted between the two groups, and if this was still alive at the time this gospel was written, it could explain the particular emphasis with which, on several occasions, John the Baptist is made to disclaim any rivalry with Jesus.

Finally the difference is brought out in the terms already explored in the previous discourse. Once again, there is no indication in the original text whether verses 31–6 are intended to be read as a speech of John the Baptist or as a comment of the writer. This time the NEB chooses the second alternative. But again, it makes little difference. Coming from above—
36 witness—Spirit—judgement (here, for once in this gospel, called **wrath**) are concepts which have already been put to use. Here they stand in a new combination, and serve to summarize the stage reached so far in defining the status and authority of Jesus.

In John's gospel, the opposition to Jesus always comes from "the Jews", that is, people of influence in Jerusalem, represented sometimes by the priests
4. 1 or High Priests, sometimes (as here) by the **Pharisees**. Exactly what had

[a] There is a well-attested manuscript reading at this point (not recorded in NEB) which appears to mean "with a Jew". This is hard to make sense of; and it is possible that John originally wrote "with Jesus", and that this was accidentally copied as "with a Jew" and then changed to **with Jews** in order to yield better sense.

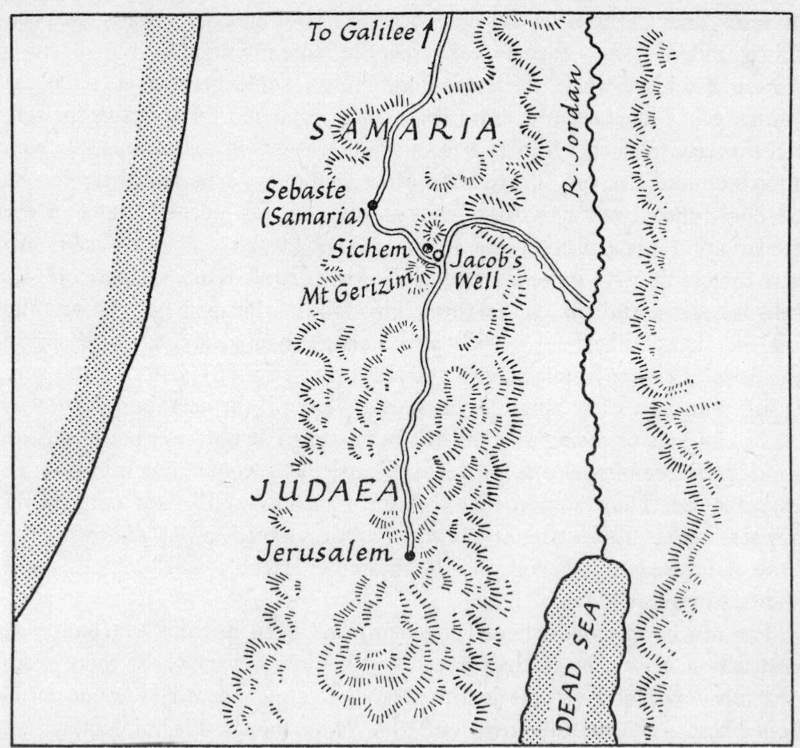

aroused them on this occasion is a little obscure. It has just been said (3.26) that Jesus was baptizing, and crowds were flocking to him; but now a correction is made: **in fact, it was only the disciples who were baptizing and** 2
not Jesus himself. This certainly matches better with the other gospels, where it is taken for granted that Jesus was not a "baptist". But in this gospel Jesus certainly had a "baptist" period, whether or not he did the actual baptizing himself (the correction, in fact, is impossible to reconcile with John's narrative, and may have been added by a later editor to remove the apparent discrepancy with the other gospels). In the face of some sort of threat from the Pharisees, he brought this period to an end, and moved to Galilee, where he was to make use of a different kind of water-symbolism.

He had to pass through Samaria. In practical terms, this was not 4
absolutely necessary: it was possible to travel from the lower Jordan to Galilee without climbing into the Samaritan hill-country. But it was common for Jewish travellers (despite the hostility of the Samaritans) to take the higher road through the mountains of Samaria: walking there was very much easier than in the stifling climate of the Jordan valley. Jesus' route was therefore perfectly normal. Moreover, there are several examples in Luke

of Jesus' attitude towards the feud between Jews and Samaritans; in part, this episode in John's gospel clearly has the same intention.

Near the place where the road which Jesus would have taken from the
Jordan valley joins the mountain road from Jerusalem there is a deep well.
Recent archaeological evidence has shown that it was in continuous use from
1000 B.C. until A.D. 500. There is no other well in the area, and there can be
no doubt that it was here that Jesus stopped on his journey. Later in the
12 conversation it is explained why it was called "Jacob's well": it was '**Jacob
our ancestor, who gave us the well, and drank from it himself, he
and his sons, and his cattle too**'. This too fits the spot. Nearby was the
ancient city of Shechem, which had particular associations with Jacob
(Genesis 33.18–20, Joshua 24.32), and the burial place of Joseph, Jacob's son,
is still venerated a few hundred yards away. Even if the neighbouring towns
all had springs of their own (as they have today), a watering place outside
would have been important for herds of cattle, and would have been kept in
constant use. The tradition that this was "Jacob's well" does not rest on
any text in the Old Testament but was doubtless already a very old one in the
time of Jesus. It was beyond doubt the same "Jacob's well" which is still
shown to visitors today.

The nearby city of Sichem (Shechem) had been in ruins ever since its
destruction in war more than a century before. Nevertheless, there were
certainly towns and villages in the area. We cannot identify the one men-
5 tioned here, **a Samaritan town called Sychar**, though it is quite likely that
its name has survived in the modern village of *Askar*, less than a mile away.

Why should a Samaritan woman have walked out from Sychar (where
7 there was probably a spring) **to draw water** at this well? It is possible that
its water was thought to be especially pure or even medicinal (this was certainly the case as recently as the nineteenth century), given the great depth
and antiquity of the well; but John gives no hint of anything of the kind.
However, from this point on the story fits perfectly into its setting. Jesus
was in Samaria—that is to say, a country of people who, though closely
related to the Jews, had their own customs and religion, and who were liable
to be unfriendly to Jewish visitors. The distrust was mutual, and a generation
later it found expression in a Jewish decree that all Samaritan women must
be regarded by strict Jews as ritually unclean. "Unclean" persons automatically made all their household vessels "unclean". It followed that Jews
who wished to remain ritually clean could not eat or drink from the household
9 vessels of a Samaritan woman: in John's words, **Jews and Samaritans, it
should be noted, do not use vessels in common.** This was true by the
time the gospel was written. That it was true in the time of Jesus is questionable; but the anachronism (if it is one) is not serious. Relations were certainly
strained between the two races, even if the decree about Samaritan women
was not yet in force.

There was therefore some justification for the disciples' astonishment
when they found Jesus **talking with a woman.** There was no Jewish 27
convention forbidding a man to converse with a female stranger. On the
other hand, there was a fairly strong prejudice against the idea of a learned
teacher spending any time giving instruction to women; and the fact that
the woman was a Samaritan must have made the scene which greeted them
seem even odder.

However, the story is not told for this reason, but for the sake of the
conversations which took place. First, the simple request by Jesus for a
drink leads into some teaching about **'living water'**. This expression, in 10
the Greek, can also mean fresh or running water, so that the woman's misunderstanding of Jesus' meaning—though it is an example of John's most
characteristic device for keeping this kind of conversation going—is not
wholly implausible. Her mind remains on the level of wells and buckets;
Jesus is speaking (in words which Jewish writers sometimes liked to use
when describing the Law of Moses) of **'an inner spring always welling** 14
up for eternal life'.

Then the conversation makes a fresh start. Telepathic knowledge (as we should call it) marked a man as a prophet. If a prophet, then perhaps the Messiah himself—an inference which the Samaritans may have been particularly ready to draw, since they accepted only the first five books of the Old Testament, and the only reference there to any Coming One was to a "prophet like Moses" (Deuteronomy 18.18). The reaction of the woman was thus typically Samaritan (though many Jews might have had the same
question): **'Could this be the Messiah?'** 29

But again, some deeper teaching is worked into the conversation. Just as, for the Jews, one of the tasks of the Messiah would be to restore the purity and splendour of the temple worship at Jerusalem, so, according to Samaritan belief, the Messiah would re-consecrate the Samaritan sanctuary which now lay in ruins on Mount Gerizim. This, in fact, was the point of the deepest cleavage between Jews and Samaritans. For the Jews, the place where God "made his name to dwell" (as the Book of Deuteronomy puts it) was unquestionably Jerusalem; for the Samaritans, it was Gerizim, one of the three great mountains of the country, to which the Samaritan woman could have
pointed with a wave of the hand when she referred to **'this mountain'** (she 20
and Jesus were actually at the foot of it). Jesus' attitude to this dispute was
frankly Jewish: the Samaritans' eccentric cult was due to an ignorant interpretation of Scripture. **'You Samaritans worship without knowing what** 22
you worship, while we worship what we know'. However exclusive the Jewish religion seemed for the moment, there could be no question that it provided the only possible basis for a universal religion. **'It is from the Jews that salvation comes'**. For many Jews, Jerusalem itself was doubtless mainly a symbol: it was not the actual city with its temple which was im-

portant, but the deeper realities it stood for. Nevertheless, they felt the need
for some focus for their worship. Their conception of God was transcendent,
yet it was still localized. **Worship** meant turning in the direction of Jerusalem, orientating oneself towards that place on earth which God had made
24 particularly his own. To this, Jesus now opposed the conception of **worship
in spirit and in truth.** The terms have a rich load of philosophical and
religious meaning. There was a sense, for instance, in which any Stoic might
have agreed that **God is spirit** (it was a possible way of defining God's
substance). In the Old Testament, on the other hand, the words would have
meant that there is a spirit which is God's Spirit, and that God therefore has
that freedom and spontaneity which goes with wind or spirit. Here, these
terms serve to hint at the possibilities of a worship which is totally detached
from the limitations of any particular place.

33 '**Can someone have brought him food?**' This time it is the disciples
who keep the conversation going by their prosaic understanding of Jesus'
32 words, '**I have food to eat of which you know nothing**'. But then a few
verses follow which read more like a recollection of some isolated sayings of
Jesus (in the manner of the other gospels) than like the kind of continuous
35 discourse into which this writer usually casts his material. '**Do you not say,
"Four months more and then comes harvest"?**' This sounds like a
proverb (especially in the Greek, which scans like a line of verse): in Palestine
the interval between sowing and harvest was regularly about four months.
'**But look, I tell you**'. Jesus is evidently not just commenting on the actual
season of the year: the **harvest** stands for something else. In the other
gospels, as in the Bible as a whole, it is a constant symbol of the Last Judgement. The same meaning fits here. Men have seldom expected the Last
Judgement to come inconveniently soon: when you sow your corn, harvest
seems a long time ahead; when you look at your moral record, the reckoning
seldom seems imminent. But Jesus, in his own person, brought judgement
into the present. He put an end to the comfortable sense of delay which
belonged to the old way of looking at things. At the same time he brought
the joy of a future heavenly reward within the grasp of human life. This, at
least, seems to be the drift of his words. But we have little to go by, and we
37 are still more at a loss when it comes to the other proverb, "**One sows, and
another reaps**". This was usually said from the point of view of the sower:
it was the expression of a gloomy recognition of the inherent injustice of life.
But here it is said from the point of view of the reaper, and has a cheerful
note. It is possible to think of circumstances in the history of the church to
which the saying might have applied by the time the gospel was written. The
first "toiling" for the gospel in Samaria, for instance, was done by a group of
"Hellenists" (Acts 8.4–13); when the Jerusalem leaders arrived, they simply
38 came in '**for the harvest of their toil**'. But if Jesus used the proverb, he
must have meant something different. '**I sent you to reap**'. That his followers

were to have a part in the "reaping" that was the prelude to the judgement of the world, was something which Jesus certainly hinted at (Matthew 9.37). But who were the mysterious **others** who would have already done the hard work? The Samaritan religious leaders who had prepared their people so well for the coming of a great "prophet"? A group of Samaritans who came to believe in Jesus as a result of this very visit? We cannot tell.

The Samaritan woman had believed in Jesus because of his apparently
psychic powers ('**He told me everything I ever did**'). He was a prophet, 39
and therefore he might well be the awaited Messiah. But after Jesus had
stayed with the Samaritans for two days, **many more became believers** 41
because of what they heard from his own lips. A feat of telepathy was
only the prelude to much more serious pronouncements; and the idea that
Jesus might be the Messiah gave place to the realization that he was a
more universal figure than their religion allowed for: '**the Saviour of the** 43
world'.

A prophet is without honour in his own country. This saying is recorded 44
in all the gospels, but here it has a completely new context. Jesus' "own country", in the most literal sense, was Nazareth, a village in Galilee; and the other three gospels record, as an apt setting for the saying (which was probably in fact already a proverb), an occasion when honour was withheld from Jesus in his home town (Matthew 13.57; Mark 6.4; Luke 4.24). But the literal meaning was not the only possible one, nor even the most plausible one. John took the phrase **his own country** in a much deeper sense: Jesus was sent to the Jewish people, the centre of whose religion and national life was Jerusalem. But "the Jews" (as John usually calls Jesus' influential opponents at Jerusalem, by contrast with the ordinary Jewish inhabitants of Palestine) consistently "dishonoured" him—this was the true application of the proverb. Jesus' **own country** was the place where, above all, he should have been accepted—Jerusalem. In due course, Jesus would deliberately face this hostility; but for the present he returned to the more welcoming **Galileans.** 45

An officer from Capernaum, whose son (or servant) was dangerously ill, is the subject of an episode recorded by Matthew (8.5–13) and Luke (7.1–10). These two accounts each tell the story in a somewhat different way, but both include a dialogue between Jesus and the officer which stresses the officer's exceptional faith; and there is the further point (especially in Luke) that the
officer was a Gentile who showed very marked deference to Jesus. In John,
the story is again different. The **officer** was not necessarily a soldier at all; he 46
was simply **in the royal service**, that is to say, probably an official in the household of Herod Antipas, and therefore just as likely to have been a Jew. Moreover, Jesus' rejoinder to him was reminiscent of the rebuke which Jesus gave to Jewish people in general in Matthew 12.38–9, 'It is a wicked, godless

generation that asks for a sign'; despite which, the boy's father continued to
plead with him. Thus the interest arising from Jesus' first confrontation with
a Gentile, and the whole dialogue that turns on a comparison between the
authority of a soldier and that of Jesus, is absent from John's version. On the
50 other hand, the emphasis is once again on faith. **The man believed what
Jesus said,** and this initial act of faith turned into a whole-hearted acceptance of the gospel: in a phrase curiously reminiscent of the later history of
53 the church as it is recorded in Acts, **he and all his household became
believers.**

5. 1 **Later on Jesus went up to Jerusalem for one of the Jewish festivals.**
In this gospel, unlike the others, Jesus makes frequent visits to Jerusalem
as a pilgrim: the festivals offered the most natural reason for a Galilean
2 teacher to "go up". **Now at the Sheep-Pool in Jerusalem there is a
place with five colonnades.** Archaeology has shown John's information to
be correct. Architecturally, five colonnades is a puzzling number; but Cyril,
a fourth-century bishop of Jerusalem, provides the solution: "four ran
round the sides, but the fifth, where the crowd of sick lay, ran across the
centre". We are therefore to imagine a pool enclosed by a colonnade on
each of the four sides, the pool being in fact a double pool, divided by a
fifth colonnade running down the middle. An arrangement of this kind has been
excavated in the north-east corner of Jerusalem. No colonnades have been
found, though there may well have been some in the time of Jesus; but
water can still be seen in the two largest pools. It may be only an accident
that there is still a sheep market in the vicinity; but there is little reason to
doubt John's statement that this pool was in some way associated with
sheep and was called **Bethesda.** [a]

7 One more piece of information is given by implication. **'I have no one
to put me in the pool when the water is disturbed'.** Evidently the pool
was thought to have miraculous power, and this was connected with a
mysterious "disturbance" of the water. This could have been the result of a
peculiarity of the spring which fed the pools (at least one intermittent spring,
which produced a kind of siphon-action when it failed, has been known to
exist in Jerusalem); and an occasional unexplained eddy in the pool would
have been enough to account for the legend which drew a crowd of sick
people to it. [b]

[*a*] The NEB does not record that the manuscripts offer more than one version of these names. In particular, one very slight variant gives the meaning, "At the Sheep Gate in Jerusalem there is a pool with five colonnades", which fits the archaeological evidence more neatly. Bethesda also appears in some manuscripts as Bethzatha or Bethsaida; but Bethesda (meaning "House of Mercy") is probably correct.

[*b*] Most of this is made explicit in the additional sentences given in the NEB footnote. But these sentences, which occur only in some manuscripts, look like an intelligent inference from John's text, and not a piece of independent tradition.

Jesus' cure of the cripple is told, not just as a spectacular miracle, but as a meaningful encounter between healer and healed. It begins with a searching
question—'**Do you want to recover?**', after which, despite his relatively 6
trivial answer, the man is cured. Subsequently, Jesus adds, '**leave your** 14
sinful ways, or you may suffer something worse.' The other gospels see most of Jesus' cures as exorcisms: when the demon had been driven out of a man, there was always a danger of a worse one coming in, and Jesus was remembered to have made a vivid comment on precisely this danger (Matthew 12.43–5; Luke 11.24–6). Here, it is as if the same idea is translated into terms of a more sophisticated view of disease, though still with the presupposition (which lay deep in Hebrew culture and is sometimes reflected in sayings of Jesus) that disease is the result of sin.

But the story gains its dramatic point from the circumstance that **that day** 10
was a Sabbath. The easiest offence to establish was that of the cripple himself: it was forbidden to carry any burden on the Sabbath, and so **the Jews** (who stand again, evidently, for the authorities) were justified in
saying, '**You are not allowed to carry your bed**', even though the bed in 9
question may have been no more than a stretcher. However, the cripple disclaimed responsibility, and passed the blame on to Jesus. In fact, far more than a case of "carrying" was involved: the healing itself was the real cause of offence. This is exactly the situation so often described in the other
gospels: **it was works of this kind done on the Sabbath that stirred** 16
the Jews to persecute Jesus.

It was certainly arguable that to heal was a form of "work", and therefore prohibited on the Sabbath. Jesus was impatient of this attitude. Sometimes (according to the other gospels) he simply poured contempt on it in the name of sheer humanity, sometimes he found in Scripture a precedent for his exceptional authority to waive the Sabbath regulations. His defence here was
both more subtle and more far-reaching. '**My Father has never yet** 17
ceased his work, and I am working too'. There was certainly debate in Jesus' time on the implications of Genesis 2.2–3: "On the sixth day God completed all the work he had been doing, and on the seventh day he ceased from all his work. God blessed the seventh day and made it holy . . ." This, it was supposed, was the origin of the Sabbath. But could it be the case that God, who is now enjoying his own "Sabbath", does no "work" of any kind? Surely God is still active; how then does he avoid breaking his own Sabbath regulations? Different answers were suggested to this question; but it was generally admitted that there must be some sense in which God is still "working", and that the Sabbath prohibition of work therefore does not apply to God in the same sense that it applies to men. Jesus seems to have been alluding to this debate when he said, '**My Father has never yet ceased his work**'; but when he went on, '**and I am working too**', he clearly implied that the special exemption from the Sabbath rest which

applied to God applied equally to himself. His opponents were quick to see
18 that thereby **he claimed equality with God.**

This was a serious matter, more serious even than breaking Sabbath regulations. The God of the Old Testament was unique and absolute. For any man to compare himself with God was blasphemous: even to claim an attribute like "goodness", which properly belonged only to God, was to show irreverence (Mark 10.18). It was true that the Jews claimed a special relationship with God: in a certain sense, they were his "children", he was their "father". But this did not affect the immense distance which necessarily separated any individual from God. The claim Jesus had just made, and the form in which he had expressed it (**calling God his own Father,** as if he had a special and intimate relationship with him), went far beyond anything a Jew would normally dare to utter. It sounded like a direct assault on the basic monotheism of their faith. Did Jesus claim to be some sort of second "god"? The question could have been a burning one for John's readers as much as for Jesus' original hearers. Jesus' reply was a preliminary answer to it.

19 **'The Son can do nothing by himself'.** In this and the following verse,
it would be perfectly correct (so far as the Greek goes) to write Father and
Son without capital letters. When this is done, the saying reads almost like
one of Jesus' parables in the other gospels: the picture is of a boy appren-
ticed to his father and learning his trade entirely under his father's supervision. But it would be clear, even without the capital letters, that in fact
Jesus was applying the parable to himself: just as a boy-apprentice learns
all his skill and derives all his knowledge from his craftsman-father, so Jesus,
far from claiming "equality" with God, was completely dependent on his
heavenly Father. But that is only one side of the parable's meaning. The
other side is more startling. If Jesus was God's apprentice-son, then Jesus'
work was God's work. This would be innocuous enough if it were meant in
the general sense that all men are doing "God's work" (though some more
than others, and Jesus to an exceptional degree). But the application Jesus
made of it was to a "work" that would normally be thought to be the
21 prerogative of God alone. **'As the Father raises the dead and gives them
life, so the Son gives life to men'.** God (it had always been believed) was
the supreme judge of mankind; but even this had now been learnt and
22 carried on from him by the apprentice: God **has given full jurisdiction
to the Son.** Jesus pretended to no "equality" with God, he was no "second
god" himself; yet in virtue of all that he had learnt from God and which he
23 did with God's authority, **'all should pay the same honour to the Son
as to the Father'.**

Raising the dead and giving them life, judging—these terms belonged to the standard Jewish picture of the destiny which awaits every man after death: at a given moment, God will "raise" all who have died, so that they

may stand before him for judgement; the righteous he will reward with an everlasting life of felicity, the unrighteous he will consign to an appropriate
punishment. To put it in its simplest terms, '**those who have done right** 29
will rise to life; those who have done wrong will rise to hear their doom'. Jesus nowhere explicitly rejects this traditional picture; but in what has just been said he claims to occupy a significant place in it. It appears that he is to take over from God the actual administration of the
final judgement: he is to have **full jurisdiction.** What is the importance of 22
this? Is it simply a redistribution of rôles in that mythological drama which is the way men tend to imagine the judgement of God? Does it mean that in any picture of the last things the traditional representation of the divine Judge at the centre must now be replaced by the figure of Jesus? Doubtless, yes—so long as the old picture is kept at all. But in this gospel Jesus' words, though still using the old language, suggest a different picture altogether.

The furthest possible extremes of human experience are represented by the two words, life and death. If one wants to describe two kinds of living as totally different from each other, one can draw a metaphor from the same antithesis. The old, poor kind of life one can call "death", the new and splendid dimension one can call "life", "real life", or better still, borrowing a term from the traditional picture of the life of the blest after death, "eternal life". In doing this, one is not necessarily denying that the old picture of a final judgement after death is in some sense valid; but one is deliberately using the old imagery to describe the intensity of a new way of life which is now attainable in the present.

This is what John is doing here. His interpretation of Jesus' parable about father and son begins with a preliminary definition of what this new kind of
living consists of: '**anyone who gives heed to what I say and puts his** 24
trust in him who sent me has hold of eternal life, and does not come up for judgement, but has already passed from death to life'. The old imagery is pressed into service to show how radically different this new kind of life is from the old. The traditional concepts are not necessarily cancelled (the restatement of them in verses 28–9 is completely ambiguous: it could be an endorsement of them or a total reinterpretation of them). But now, the "judgement" which matters consists in the way a man reacts to Jesus, **eternal life** is what is experienced as a result of reacting warmly. This is all new; and yet it is an expression of the unchanging justice of the judgement of God: '**I judge as I am bidden, and my sentence is just, because** 30
my aim is not my own will, but the will of him who sent me'.

Reacting warmly to Jesus, however, meant believing him to be what he claimed to be; and it was legitimate to ask (as one would ask in a court of law) what the evidence was for such tremendous claims. In this sense, however compelling some people might find Jesus' own sayings, what he said himself could not count as evidence: to be believed, he must have independent

witnesses. From this strictly legal point of view, it was correct for him to
31 say, '**If I testify on my own behalf, that testimony does not hold good**'. Now in fact two particular kinds of testimony to Jesus have already been mentioned, that of John the Baptist, and that of the scriptures. But both these were cogent only for those already disposed to believe. Most
35 people saw significance in John the Baptist's movement only **for a time**: they failed to see its lasting significance as a testimony to Jesus. And as for
39 the **scriptures,** the duty of studying them **diligently** was recognized by every Jew who took his religion seriously, and no one doubted that this was the surest way of securing the prospect of **eternal life** after death; but the
40 Jews still missed the true meaning of those scriptures (that '**their testimony points to me**'), and so failed to come to him who could offer them '**that life**' here and now. For anyone who was beginning to believe in Jesus, both these kinds of testimony were exceedingly important. About that of John,
34 for instance, Jesus could say, '**I remind you of it for your own salvation**'. But, for those who remained unconvinced, Jesus' ultimate appeal was to a
36 **testimony higher than John's,** a testimony more explicit than that of the scriptures—the testimony of God himself, not in the form of a crude and dazzling appearance of the divine (for the Jews quite rightly thought of
37 God as far too transcendent a figure for anyone to have **heard his voice** or
36 seen **his form**), but expressed in **the works** of Jesus, which testified to the true nature of him who performed them. It is of these "works" and of the testimony they gave to Jesus that John's gospel is principally a record.

41 '**I do not look to men for honour**'. There was of course something else which might have caused people to believe in Jesus. There is normally no difficulty in believing that a certain man is, say, a king: the fact becomes evident from the honour which people pay to him, and from the prestige which he acquires in the performance of his exalted office. The same kind of "honour" could conceivably have been concentrated in the person of Jesus, and so have convinced people of who he was. But "honour" of this
44 kind is a purely human category, something which men receive **from one another.** It could be of no value in attesting Jesus' relationship with God.
41 '**I do not look to men for honour**'. On the other hand, there was a kind of
44 honour which he did possess, '**the honour that comes from him who alone is God**'. Here there is a word-play which can hardly be reproduced in English. When the Hebrew Bible was translated into Greek, the Septuagint translators used the word *doxa*, "honour", to translate the Hebrew expression which in English we usually call "the glory of God". This was an extension of language: it was as if God could be said to have an "honour" which (unlike honour in the ordinary sense) is given to him by no one else, but belongs to him by right, and is an expression of his transcendence and power, his "glory". Jesus' argument (at least as reported in Greek by John) makes deliberate play with this double meaning of the word *doxa*. No human

"honour" would add any weight to Jesus' claims; but if people only had an eye for the kind of *doxa* which is the glory of God, they would realize that this was something which did attach to Jesus and showed him to have been **accredited** by his Father. 43

'Do not imagine that I shall be your accuser'. If everything depends 45
on how a man reacts to Jesus, then it could be expected (given the traditional picture of the Last Judgement, when each man's words and deeds will be held against him) that Jesus himself would be the "accuser", saying to God (in effect), This man did not accept me. But this would be to suggest that Jesus introduced a new criterion of judgement—no longer right or wrong, good or evil, but for or against Jesus. In fact, the criterion is the same as it always was. Rightly understood, the whole of Scripture points to the same criterion. **'Your accuser is Moses'.**

Some time later. A miracle performed by Jesus, in which a great crowd 6. 1
was fed from a small number of loaves and fishes, is told twice over by Mark and Matthew, and once each by Luke and John. In all these accounts, the main elements of the story are the same: the two episodes that are reported in Mark and Matthew differ only in relatively unimportant details, and Luke appears to follow Mark's first account. The version in John, like that of the second miracle in Mark and Matthew, places the episode on **the farther shore of the Sea of Galilee (or Tiberias),**[a] but in other respects it comes closer to the first (Mark 6.33–44). A single well-remembered episode evidently forms the basis of these various accounts (even if Jesus, as Mark and Matthew record, actually repeated the miracle on a second occasion). But John characteristically tells the story in his own way, and, by a slight shift of emphasis, makes it yield a new meaning.

According to all the other accounts of this miracle, the crowd was hungry, the hour was late, the place deserted. A compassionate concern for the pilgrims' needs was the spring of Jesus' action. But John says nothing of
this. Instead, he simply records that **it was near the time of Passover, the** 4
great Jewish festival. Our attention is drawn, not to the urgent need for food,[b] but to the imminence of the one symbolic meal of the Jewish year. The food Jesus was about to provide must not be understood, any more than the Passover lamb, merely as a means of satisfying hunger.

When everyone had had enough. Five thousand men had been satisfied 12

[a] Tiberias is on the west shore of the lake. It was built by Herod Antipas for his capital city, and its name was intended as a compliment to the reigning Emperor, Tiberius. To Gentiles, it would have been natural to call the lake by the same name. But the Jews, who disliked the new pagan city, preferred to call it either by its biblical name, the Lake of Gennesaret (Luke 5.1), or else (as usually in the gospels) the Sea of Galilee.

[b] Most of Galilee, in the time of Jesus, seems to have been about as densely populated and cultivated as modern rural Surrey. Even on the mountains one could never have been far from towns. In this respect, John's account is perhaps more plausible than the others.

with five barley loaves and two small fishes: this was surely a sufficiently
sensational fact to make the narrator pause a moment. But John allows it
13 only a passing reference, and hurries on to another point: they **filled twelve
baskets with the pieces left uneaten of the five barley loaves.** Why was
this so important? On the face of it, it was the feeding that mattered, not what was left over. Admittedly, the detail is mentioned in the other gospels, and it may have seemed to the writer to be almost a necessary part of any story of this kind. A miracle performed by Elisha, for instance, included the same point (and also has other features in common with this one):

> "A man came from Baal-shalisha, bringing to the man of God some of the new season's bread, twenty barley loaves... Elisha said, 'Give this to the people to eat.' But his disciple protested, 'I cannot set this before a hundred men.' Still he repeated, 'Give it to the people to eat; for this is the word of the Lord: "They will eat and leave over"'. So he set it before them, and they ate and left some over, as the Lord had said." (2 Kings 4.42–4)

And there is also something similar in the story of Ruth: "Boaz passed her some roasted grain. She ate all she wanted and still had some left over" (Ruth 2.14). Moreover, when Jesus (according to the other gospels) later alluded to this miracle, he referred deliberately to this point of bread having been left over: 'When I broke the five loaves among five thousand, how many basketfuls of scraps did you pick up?' (Mark 8.19). Gathering up scraps of bread after a meal was certainly an ingrained habit. Bread was eaten with everything. It was the only implement for eating, and was used for wiping the fingers. To leave substantial pieces lying about was dirty, wasteful and irreverent. But on this occasion there was far more to it than that. It is important to visualize the quantities involved. A modern baker's loaf may feed several people; but the loaves of Jesus' time were the small, round, flat ones still used by Semitic peoples. Three of them were needed to give a man a meal (Luke 11.5). Twenty of them, in the Elisha story, seemed
absurdly little to set before a hundred men. Any basket would hold at least
13 a dozen such loaves, if not many more. On this occasion, they **filled twelve
baskets with the pieces left uneaten of the five barley loaves.** In other
words, even after the meal, they were left with many times more than they
started with. We can now see why this detail is the real climax of the story.
How much bread the men needed to eat could not be calculated. Perhaps (a
cynic might have said) they were not very hungry. But this did not matter.
The real evidence for the miracle lay in those twelve baskets full of scraps.
14 This was the **sign that the people saw.** Moreover, it gave John the cue
27 for adding some teaching of Jesus about **food that lasts, the food of
eternal life.** Like the 'water' which is 'an inner spring always welling up
for eternal life' (4.14), the bread which Jesus gives is always there, even after
it has fed multitudes.

The word went round, **'Surely this must be the prophet that was to** 14
come into the world'. The Jewish religion encouraged people to pin their hopes on a figure "who was to come", even though it allowed a wide variety of opinions on what kind of figure this would be. Speculation ranged from a purely human warrior-king to an almost transcendental being who would usher in a new age. One text which was often quoted in this connection was that in which Moses foretold that God would "raise up a prophet from among you like myself" (Deuteronomy 18.15). Moses had miraculously fed the people with manna, and here was Jesus doing much the same thing. It was not difficult for the crowd to guess that Jesus **'must be the prophet'**, and the subsequent dialogue shows that this was the way their minds were working. But this kind of religious excitement could easily spill over into something more practical and dangerous. There were several "prophets" in this period who promised to show an authoritative "sign" and then to lead the Jewish people against their Roman conquerors. It needed no more than
what Jesus had just done for the crowd **to come and seize him to proclaim** 15
him king.

Jesus . . . withdrew. In Matthew and Luke, the possibility of an earthly kingship was one of the "tests" to which Jesus was exposed by the devil. In all the gospels, the point was important when it came to Jesus' trial; and there were many earlier occasions on which his words and actions had political implications. This is the only place in any of the gospels where the possibility of a political movement starting outside Jerusalem is explicitly referred to; but it would have been natural for the evangelists to play down this motif, and John may well preserve something here which the others have passed over. In any case, the danger (as Jesus saw it to be) provides a convincing motive for Jesus separating himself from his followers and for
his disciples taking to their boat—an episode which also comes in this place 16–21
in Mark (6.45–52) and Matthew (14.22–32).

'It is I; do not be afraid'. All the accounts of this episode contain these 21
words; but the story itself is told by John in a rather different way. Matthew and Mark leave the reader in no doubt that Jesus miraculously walked across the water. In John, the details are not so clear: Jesus could have been in shallow water near the edge of the lake. But (as the sequel shows) the writer
certainly believed he was describing a supernatural event. **Next morning** 22
the crowd tried to work out what had happened to Jesus, and found his disappearance inexplicable.[a] When they finally tracked him down in Capernaum, this was the first thing they wanted to ask him. **'Rabbi', they said,** 26
'when did you come here?'

It looked, then, as if the crowd's motives in following Jesus were pure curiosity and a desire for more free bread. Jesus ignored the first and poured

[a] Verses 22–4 are somewhat obscure in the original; but the essential point seems to be that there was originally only one boat, and Jesus was known not to have embarked in it.

scorn on the second. The miracle of the loaves was not intended just to
satisfy their hunger. It was a "sign" of something more important—something the crowd had failed to grasp. To turn the discussion in the right
27 direction, Jesus used a form of words they could easily understand. **'You
must work, not for this perishable food, but for the food that lasts,
the food of eternal life'.**

This was the familiar choice offered by religious teachers: either "perishable food"—that is, the material rewards of a wholly this-worldly life—or
the kind of god-fearing and obedient living which would secure a favourable
judgement on the Last Day and the reward of **eternal life.** Jesus' next
words seemed at first sight to fit into the same picture: **'This food the Son
of Man will give you'.** The Son of Man (in Daniel 7 and also probably in
popular belief) was a figure associated with the Last Judgement. So, missing
the real point of Jesus' saying (which only becomes clear later in the chapter),[a] they asked him the usual question about the way of life which would
secure their acquittal on the day of Judgement and entitle them to receive
28 food from the Son of Man. **'Then what must we do', they asked him,
'if we are to work as God would have us work?'**

This was a stock question. In the other gospels it is put to Jesus in the
form, 'What must I do to inherit eternal life?' (Mark 10.17); and Jesus'
answer is, 'Follow me'. Here, his answer is similar, though "following" has
29 given place to "believing": **'believe in the one whom God has sent'.**

But how were they to believe? Jesus must do something, give some sign,
to show who he was. Of course (John would have us understand) this is
exactly what Jesus had been doing; but the "signs" Jesus gave were too
subtle, and demanded too much readiness of acceptance, to be generally
understood. The crowd was thinking of something more obvious, such as
31 Moses providing the people with manna (Exodus 16; the quotation, "**He
gave them bread from heaven to eat**", does not occur in the Old Testament in precisely this form: it is a recollection of such passages as Psalm
78.24, Nehemiah 9.15). If Jesus were similarly to arrange a miraculous supply
of bread, they would believe in him. Perhaps; but that was not Jesus' way.
Believing in Jesus did not depend on happening to have witnessed a miracle.
'His own would not receive him' (1.11) expressed a greater mystery than
44 this. Ultimately, believing was something given by God. **'No man can
come to me unless he is drawn by the Father who sent me'.** This

[*a*] **'He it is upon whom God the Father has set the seal of his authority'** is a sentence open to many interpretations. The crowd would presumably have understood it as a piece of normal Son of Man doctrine: God had in some sense marked out and chosen the figure who would ultimately be revealed as Son of Man. The metaphor of a "seal" could have been one way of saying this (though it could also perhaps have suggested another popular doctrine about the Son of Man, that he was "hidden"—shut away and kept secure under a seal—until the day when he was to be revealed). But later Christian readers would certainly have understood it quite differently. God "set his seal" on Jesus at any of those moments in his life—perhaps particularly his baptism—which marked him out as someone unique.

sounds like the harshest determinism. But consider how God does in fact
"draw" men: through the revelation of himself in the Bible. Jesus was
witnessed to by Scripture; it was open to anyone to be "drawn". In this
sense, those who came to Jesus were those who read Scripture aright—
'**who . . . listened to the Father**'—and who could be described in the 45
words of a prophecy of Isaiah (54.13), "**And they shall all be taught by
God.**"

'**The truth is, not that Moses gave you the bread from heaven, but** 32
that my Father gives you the real bread from heaven'. The manna
was supernatural bread, certainly, but it did no more than satisfy physical
hunger. Even if Jesus were to provide bread on that supernatural scale
(instead of just once in the mountains beyond the lake), nothing would be
achieved of real significance. What Moses had done in the wilderness was at
most a shadow of what Jesus now proposed to do. He was offering, not the
satisfaction of physical hunger, but **real bread**, real sustenance. '**Whoever** 35
comes to me shall never be hungry'. Jesus' claim was that in his own
person he represented the spiritual values, the authentic experience, the
true goal of existence, which until then had been envisaged only as a gift
which God would give to the righteous after death. The old language of the
after-life was doubtless still valid: '**I will raise him up on the last day**' 40
was a perfectly conventional promise that, at the Last Judgement, Jesus
would secure for his followers a favourable verdict and a share in the
promised blessings. But by now the reader of this gospel has learnt that
after-life language is also a way of talking about a new kind of life in the
present. '**Eternal life**' was attainable here and now, given a certain relationship with Jesus.

At this the Jews began to murmur disapprovingly. Such a claim, 41
from any man who seemed in so many respects like other men, provoked
incredulity and censure. '**Surely this is Jesus son of Joseph; we know** 42
his father and mother.'[a] Jesus recognized this obstacle to belief, and
accepted the consequence that only some would be led to believe. Undeterred,
he went on to give a further turn to the idea of 'real bread' which this time
led **to a fierce dispute among the Jews** and caused many even of his 52
disciples to withdraw from him. '**The bread which I will give is my own** 51
flesh'.

This is the climax of the chapter, the point towards which the discussion has been leading from the beginning. The Christians for whom this gospel was written were already accustomed to holding a solemn supper at which the bread and wine were affirmed to be the body and blood of Christ; and

[a] Did John know (as Matthew and Luke did) that Jesus had no human father, but was conceived 'by the Holy Spirit' (Matthew 1.18)? It is hard to be sure. The most one can say is that Jesus' miraculous birth is fully compatible with John's understanding of his nature. The present passage, in any case, hardly bears upon the question; the Jews merely echo the usual opinion at the time. Jesus was 'the son, as people thought, of Joseph' (Luke 3.23).

they knew that the institution of this new and distinctive act of worship went back to some explicit teaching of Jesus himself. They will have been prepared by a number of hints earlier on in the chapter to expect such teaching here
11, 23 (**Jesus took the loaves, gave thanks, and distributed,** and **the bread over which the Lord gave thanks,**[a] are phrases which are characteristic of the New Testament accounts of the Lord's Supper); and they will have
51 found what they were expecting in the words, '**The bread which I will give is my own flesh; I give it for the life of the world**'. These words are strikingly similar to those used by Jesus in the other gospels' accounts of the last supper, celebrated by Jesus with his disciples on the night before the crucifixion. Here, however different the setting, the substance of the teaching is the same. Indeed, it seems likely that John chose this point in his gospel to
50 gather together all Jesus' teaching on '**the bread that comes down from heaven**', the bread which is Jesus' own body and which gives eternal life. In the context of his narrative, this teaching had the effect of still further shocking those who heard it into belief or disbelief. But for his readers, the whole chapter took on its full meaning only when read in the light of their own experience of the eucharist.

59 **This was spoken in synagogue when Jesus was teaching in Capernaum.** Considering the dramatic series of episodes which led up to the discourse, it seems both unnecessary and inappropriate to suggest that by the end it had become an ordinary synagogue sermon. But perhaps a new point is being made. This, in John's gospel, is Jesus' last public appearance in Galilee; and, just as in the other gospels it was **in synagogue** that the decisive confrontations between Jesus and the religious leaders in Galilee took place, so here it is fitting that Galilee's final judgement on Jesus' words and works should have been passed at the local centre of religious worship and religious education: the synagogue at Capernaum.

62 '**Does this shock you?**' Taken at all literally, Jesus' words about himself as "bread" to be eaten were of course shocking. Jews, in any case, had a horror of consuming the blood of any slaughtered animal. Therefore Jesus'
53 statement, '**Unless you eat the flesh of the Son of Man and drink his blood you can have no life in you**' seemed an almost deliberate affront to their sensibilities, however figurative the language was supposed to be. Jesus does little to soften the shock; but he adds a brief pointer to the way in
62 which his words should be interpreted. '**What if you see the Son of Man ascending to the place where he was before?**' It is not as an ordinary man that Jesus can give his flesh to eat, but as Son of Man, that is, as a person who belongs both to heaven and earth. There have been hints of this

[*a*] This second hint may be due, not to John himself, but to a later copyist anxious to make the symbolism more explicit. If so, this would explain why some manuscripts omit the phrase. See the footnote in NEB.

earlier. The bread—or Jesus himself[a]—**'comes down from heaven'.** He 33
belongs (and is soon to ascend) to the realm above, which is the realm of
spirit. **'The spirit alone gives life; the flesh is of no avail'.** To think only 63
of the flesh of the human Jesus is to fail to see the meaning of the "bread".
The Jesus who feeds others is a person who belongs to heaven, and whose
real nature is therefore **spirit.** Unless one believed this, one could make
nothing of Jesus' teaching.

Nevertheless, the shock remained, and many found it too much for them.
The rejection of Jesus is necessarily a theme of all the gospels, though they
treat it in different ways. Usually there is a clear distinction between the
crowds on the one hand and the disciples on the other. Here, the dividing
line runs right down the group of disciples themselves: the **Twelve** were
only the remnant of a larger number who had once followed Jesus (there may
be a hint of this in Luke 22.28). It was only **from that time on** that there 66
was a sharply defined group of twelve disciples corresponding to the Twelve
of the other gospels.

So Jesus asked the Twelve, 'Do you also want to leave me?' In 67
Mark 8.27–33 (and in the corresponding passages of Matthew and Luke)
there is an important scene in which Peter recognizes Jesus' true nature, and
in which Jesus then predicts what is to befall him in Jerusalem. This brief
dialogue in John contains the same elements. Peter calls Jesus, not 'the
Messiah' (as in Mark), but **the Holy One of God.** Doubtless it came to 69
much the same thing: it was the title given to Jesus by a demon in Mark 1.24,
and the demons knew who Jesus really was. In any case, it was a decisive
confession of faith. It marked out those who were Jesus' "followers" (not
of their own merit, but by Jesus' call)—except, of course, that even in that
small group there was one who **would betray him.** 71

The great controversy

The new heading marks a new stage in the narrative. It was said at the outset that Christ 'entered his own realm, and his own would not receive him' (1.11). What has just been described is the refusal of some to believe, and the defection of others who had begun to believe. But in the story of Jesus, the failure of his own to receive him was to take a much more drastic form than this. It was not merely that they refused to believe in him. In the end they actually put him to death. That they did so was admittedly the result of a combination of circumstances: Jesus' execution followed a formal trial and was ordered, not by 'his own' (the Jews) but by the Roman governor. But this terrible dénouement was not a sudden reversal of fortune. The intention

[a] Verse 33 is perhaps deliberately ambiguous. See the footnote in NEB.

was there from the moment Jesus arrived in Jerusalem: the arrest, trial and
crucifixion were simply the historical form taken by the principle that 'his
own would not receive him'. Much of *The great controversy* which follows
turns on points that have been made earlier; but there is now a more
7. 1 threatening factor. **The Jews were looking for a chance to kill him.**

Why did they not immediately succeed? On a practical level, it might be
said that the appearance of the Son of God was too complicated a phenomenon for that. People who saw and heard Jesus were both attracted and
32 scandalized by him; even the **temple police**, sent by the authorities to
46 arrest him, found it impossible to carry out their orders—**'No man', they
answered, 'ever spoke as this man speaks'.** These alternating reactions
of exasperation and respect provide the dramatic framework of the controversy. But meanwhile there was another reason for Jesus' repeated
escapes from his enemies, a reason of a different kind. Jesus' death, and the
glorification which was to go with it, was something determined in advance
by God. When the time came, it would take place inexorably; but for the
30 present, **his appointed hour had not yet come.**

There was also another side to this alternation of admiration and enmity.
10 It was as if Jesus was not fully showing his hand: he was present, **not
5 publicly, but almost in secret.** To his brothers, who **had no faith in
him,** and therefore represented the attitude of those who did not understand
the nature of Jesus' person and work, it seemed obvious that one must either
be resigned to the obscurity of a provincial existence in Galilee, or else
4 "show oneself to the world" in Jerusalem: **'Surely no one can hope to
be in the public eye if he works in seclusion'.** But again, the presence
of Jesus in the world, the coming of the Word 'into his own realm', was too
complex a phenomenon to be expressed in such simple terms. A certain
secrecy (as is particularly evident in Mark's gospel) was a necessary condition
attached to the appearance of the Messiah. Those who recognized him did
so because they discerned who he really was, not because his real nature was
so apparent that it could not be denied. To evoke true faith, Jesus necessarily
showed the world a face that was challenging and ambiguous. *The great
controversy* provoked by his appearance in Jerusalem consists of a series of
brief dialogues which lay bare different aspects of this essential ambiguity.
The curiously non-committal way in which Jesus makes his pilgrimage to
Jerusalem sets the tone for the conversations which follow.

2 **The Jewish Feast of Tabernacles** was the greatest of the year—and this
may be a sufficient reason for John mentioning it: Jesus went up to Jerusalem
on that occasion in the year when the largest number of Jews regularly made
their pilgrimage. It was an autumn festival, to mark the safe gathering in of
crops and fruit. It involved the setting up of token "tabernacles", or huts
made of branches (the origin of which is uncertain), and there were processions with greenery and fruit; the services and festivities in the temple lasted

for a week. It is true that certain subsidiary rites, such as the ceremonial
pouring of water over the altar, or the lighting of candles in the court outside
the temple, would have provided cues for sayings of Jesus about '**living** 38
water' and '**the light of the world**'. But in John's narrative these allusions **8.** 12
to little-known ceremonies, if they were intentional, would have been very
recondite, particularly since nothing is said of the "tabernacles" themselves, which were the best-known feature of the festival. For the most part, the festival seems merely to provide the occasion for Jesus' sudden appearance in Jerusalem.

Jesus **began to teach**. This immediately raised the question of his authority **7.** 14
to do so. '**How is it', they said, 'that this untrained man has such** 15
learning?' All authority to teach normally came to the pupil from his
master; but Jesus had been to no professional school to study the interpretation of Scripture. So far as anyone knew, he was **untrained**. So where did
he get his authority? Jesus' answer was that his authority lay in no exterior
qualification, but in the teaching itself. Anyone who sincerely had **the will** 17
to do the will of God as it was revealed in the Law of Moses would find
that Jesus' teaching enabled him to understand how to do so. The teaching
authenticated itself: instead of giving **honour** to Jesus, it gave "glory" to 18
God (there is the same play on the meanings of a single Greek word as in 5.41–4 above).

'**Did not Moses give you the Law? Yet you all break it.**' The 19
majority of the Jews did not aspire to observe every detail of the Law of Moses; but the Pharisees, despising this lack of seriousness, set themselves a very rigorous discipline by which they believed they could avoid even an inadvertent transgression. Yet even they were not always successful: the apostle Paul was a Pharisee who ultimately confessed himself defeated by the complexity of the demands which he believed the Law laid upon him. There may have been those standing by who would have personally denied Jesus' charge that they broke the Law; but they would have been ready to admit that the majority of Jews did so in one way or another. Why, in that case, single out Jesus and try to kill him for one transgression?

But of course Jesus' transgression was a serious one: '**Once only have I** 21
done work on the Sabbath', but breaking the Sabbath was an offence against a basic principle of the Jewish religion, and it has already been said (5.16) that it was Jesus' deliberate healing on a Sabbath which aroused powerful opposition. The gospels all contain instances of such Sabbath work by Jesus, and record various lines which he adopted to justify his actions. Here is yet another (of a kind which some Jewish scholars of the time actually used themselves). Some commandments (such as that to circumcise a baby on the eighth day) inevitably conflict occasionally with resting on the Sabbath, but must still be carried out. If circumcision, affecting only one

member of the body, is permissible on the Sabbath, how much more an act
23 giving health **'to the whole of a man's body'**?

27 **'When the Messiah appears no one is to know where he comes
from'.** Popular belief, picturing the coming Messiah, tended to wrap him
in mystery: he would be a person of unknown origin, appearing from some
secret recess of the world at the time appointed for him to perform his great
work. On the face of it, the known facts of Jesus' home and origin did not
fit the conventional picture. Jesus' reply is characteristic of this gospel.
Knowing the village "where Jesus came from" was irrelevant: what mattered was whether (in a much more fundamental sense) he "came from"
God. This was harder to tell. Some judged the claim to be blasphemous,
31 others reflected on the **'signs'** he had done. Once again, there were conflicting reactions to him.

After the event, we can see that this "having come" from God implied
also that Jesus would soon "go to" God. But at the time Jesus' sayings
33 about **going** could well have seemed enigmatic, and have led to speculation
35 that Jesus proposed to leave Palestine (in which, of course, there was an
element of prophetic truth: by the time the gospel was written, it could be
said that a great part of the ultimate purpose of Jesus' work had been to
'teach the Greeks'.)

38 **'If anyone is thirsty let him come to me; whoever believes in me, let
him drink'.** By itself, this belongs naturally to a whole series of sayings in
this gospel in which Jesus likens himself to real food and real drink; but
here, it gains added point from the context in which it is given. John tells
37 us that it was delivered **on the last and greatest day of the festival.** The
festival lasted eight days in all, and it is the way of such religious functions to be best attended at the end; this fact alone would be sufficient to give particular emphasis and solemnity to Jesus' pronouncement. (Exactly what stage had been reached in the ceremonies, and whether it was a day when the ritual of fetching and pouring out water was performed, are questions which John's sketchy indications do not allow us to answer; but his first readers can hardly have been much better informed than we are, and it is not likely that John intended them to be picturing any particular ceremonies when they read Jesus' words.) But his words also had strong Old Testament overtones.[a] It was prophesied in Zechariah 14.8 that "in that day" (that is, at the beginning of a new age) "living water shall issue from Jerusalem"—a prophecy greatly elaborated by Ezekiel (47.1–12), who shared the same vision of the arid hills and valleys of Judaea being watered by a miraculously abundant spring flowing out of the temple itself (a vivid symbol of the place of Jeru-

[*a*] The punctuation of the saying is uncertain, and it is possible that the quotation from Scripture is actually part of it, instead of being a comment on it (see the footnote in NEB). But this yields a meaning which seems to fit less naturally into the sequence of Jesus' teaching.

salem in the religious life of the world). Moreover, when Moses struck a rock at Horeb, water came out for the thirsty people to drink (Exodus 17.6). There is no phrase in Scripture exactly corresponding to the quotation,
'**Streams of living water shall flow out from within him**'; it was 38
probably a composite text, the result of scholars having constantly seen the possibilities of combining the story of the desert Rock with the prophecy of an abundance of water in the temple.

These Old Testament overtones raised questions. Admittedly Christians held the real clue to the interpretation of the saying: water, in Jesus' teaching, was a symbol for **the Spirit**, a gift which they received in abundance 39
when the church came into existence after the resurrection of Jesus. But Jesus' hearers did not have this clue. Thinking more literally of water (and not of that which the water symbolized) they reflected that it was Moses who
found the miraculous supply of water in the desert (and that **the expected** 40
prophet, like Moses, would doubtless do something similar), and that it was **the Messiah** who would initiate the new age when water would flow from
the temple in Jerusalem. '**If anyone is thirsty let him come to me**'—did 38
this mean that Jesus was the Messiah? There seemed to be the fatal objection
that Jesus had '**come from Galilee**', whereas the Messiah, being a succes- 41
sor to David, was expected to come '**from David's village of Bethlehem**'. 42
John's readers doubtless knew the answer to this: Jesus was in fact born in Bethlehem. But Jesus' hearers could not be expected to know this: for them, Jesus both was and was not like the Messiah. This is the theme of the whole scene: the challenge and ambiguity of the person of Jesus. This time, it
caused a split among the people. The Pharisees, however, were quite 43
clear in their own mind: his Galilean origin was fatal to Jesus' claims. No passage of Scripture could be quoted to show that any important figure or prophet would come from there. It made not the slightest difference what ordinary people thought. The Pharisees firmly believed that it was only the members of their own fellowships who made a serious attempt to observe the Law, and many of them regarded their less disciplined fellow-Jews as
undoubtedly beyond salvation. '**As for this rabble, which cares nothing** 49
for the Law, a curse is on them', was typical Pharisees' language.

(In most older translations of the New Testament, *An incident in the temple* 7.53–8.11
follows here, but is almost certainly out of place. See below, p. 395.)

'**I am the light of the world**'. After water, light. Jesus' great affirmations 8.12
about himself use one great poetical concept after another. "Light" and "life" were two of the evocative words used in the prologue: they are about to be explored in the following chapters. Here they simply serve as an example of the kind of thing Jesus was saying about himself. He was making great claims, and the objection of his enemies at this stage was not so much

to the language he was using about himself as to the fact that he was making
13 such claims at all. **'You are witness in your own cause; your testimony
is not valid'.**

When a person made some claim, he normally had to support it with independent evidence. Jesus' enemies were saying, in effect, that to make the kind of claims he was making, Jesus ought to produce some independent evidence. But it could happen that under exceptional circumstances no such evidence was available: suppose, for example, a man's title deeds to a particular property had been lost, and there was no other evidence of his ownership; in that case a judge or arbitrator would have no choice but to decide whether or not to accept the man's "witness in his own cause". This was Jesus' defence. His claim to recognition rested ultimately upon his origin
and his destiny. But the previous dialogue had proved that only Jesus knew
14 what these were. **'I know where I come from, and where I am going.
You do not know'.** His case rested on facts to which only he had access.
He was in the exceptional position of a claimant whose testimony about
himself was the only evidence available. Therefore his testimony was
valid.

15 **'You judge by worldly standards.'** One reason why at this point the
argument becomes hard for us to follow is that we are accustomed to make
a sharp distinction between judging and giving evidence. To us, judges are
utterly distinct from witnesses; their task is to determine impartially whether
the evidence offered by the witnesses is true. But in a Jewish court, if the
witnesses were persons generally accepted as reliable, if they could not be
shown to have lied, and if their testimony agreed, there was no more to be
said: judgement followed automatically. Indeed, since the penalty for
criminal offences was prescribed by the Law, there was no need even for a
judge to pronounce the sentence; the witnesses were entitled to see that it
was carried out themselves. Thus, "judging" might often include framing
an accusation, testifying as a witness, and carrying out the sentence. The
Jews were concerned to "judge" Jesus on his claim to be the light of the
world. Jesus had shown that only he had access to the kind of evidence
which would support such a claim. The Jews had mistaken the nature of the
case when they demanded independent evidence; they were judging **by
worldly standards.** But suppose now the tables were turned. The Jews had
failed to accept Jesus' claims. He could now "judge" them for their dis-
16 belief. True, that was not his purpose. **I pass judgement on no man.** But
suppose he did (**if I do judge**): he accepted, as they did, the basic proposition
of the Jewish law of evidence (Deuteronomy 19.15) that "a charge must be
established on the evidence of two or three witnesses". It followed from this
17 that **the testimony of two witnesses is valid.** If Jesus were bringing a
charge against the Jews, his own evidence would count: he would be one
witness (not quite "in his own cause", as the NEB puts it, for it was now

the Jews who were on trial for refusing to accept Jesus' claims). Where was
the other? '**My other witness is the Father who sent me**'. Taken literally, 18
this would not count—and the Jews, by their question, '**Where is your** 19
father?' showed that they did take it literally. One's own relative could not
normally be produced as an independent witness. But Jesus' real Father was
God; and to call God as a witness was equivalent to swearing an oath that
one's statement was true. Jesus' other **witness** was such that his words had 18
the force of a solemn oath. This put Jesus' opponents in a difficult position.
It was as sinful to disbelieve a statement made on oath as it was to make a
statement on oath that was not true. It was only because they did not
recognize that Jesus' Father was God that the Jews were indifferent to the
consequences of refusing to believe Jesus' testimony.

'**Where I am going you cannot come**'. When Jesus said this earlier 21
(7.34), his opponents could do no better than imagine that he meant he was
leaving Palestine. This time their suggestion was less improbable: '**Perhaps** 22
he will kill himself'—though this was still a total misunderstanding of
Jesus' meaning. Jesus' origin and destiny belonged to a different order of
things. A fairly obvious way of putting it was in terms of **the world above** 23
as opposed to **this world below**. Admittedly this was not quite the language
the Jews were used to: if asked to think of a world more real than this one, they conceived it as something in the future, the "age to come", as opposed to "the present age". Again and again, Jesus used this traditional language of future expectation to describe a present experience: what they believed would come to pass one day was already a reality, even if as yet they had no experience of it. There existed, not just an age to come, but **a world above.** With their present attitude, the Jews could have no part in that world; they remained in **this world below**, the world where death still has its old power, and where there is no escape from sin.

They asked him, 'Who are you?'. A true answer to this question could 25
only have been in terms of the **world above** of which they had no know- 23
ledge. It was therefore impossible for Jesus to give them any answer they
could understand which would not have been misleading. They did not even
grasp what he meant when he talked about himself having been "sent". All
he could do was to offer them an apparently enigmatic phrase, '**I am what** 28
I am'. On the level of grammar this was almost meaningless. But there is a grammar of religion as well as of ordinary speech. In that grammar, the Jews were accustomed to use the future tense. Reality, for them, was something which would come one day: God would act, there would be a Person among them bringing about a new age. But Jesus' grammar was all in the present. '**I am what I am**', whatever else it might mean, at least showed that Jesus was not merely a hint of what was to be, but was a reality already present. Of course, Jesus' words could have meant more than this. If you knew "what he was", you could fill in the meaning from what you knew. But ultimately,

Jesus was of God, and God is essentially indefinable. It is probably no accident that the phrase seems to echo the mysterious words spoken by God to Moses, "I AM; that is who I am" (Exodus 3.14—compare Isaiah 43.10, ". . . know that I am HE"). All this would be easier to grasp (again, for those who could grasp it at all) when the destiny of the Son of Man was fully
28 played out: the "lifting up" of that figure (on the cross, up to heaven) would make a bridge between the two worlds such that it would at last be possible to see how Jesus belonged to both.

31 **Turning to the Jews who had believed in him.** Jesus' words and actions had been evoking varied reactions: while there was strong opposition, nevertheless some were tempted to accept the claims he was making for himself. Suppose, now, that some Jews came to "believe in him". What difference was this going to make to them? In what sense could their ancestral religion be said to be so inadequate and incomplete that it left room for the radical new factor introduced by Jesus? Was not their Jewish inheritance of more ultimate importance than any new teaching that could be added by Jesus? This question, we know, was to be raised in a sharp form by Jewish groups within the early church—Paul's letter to the Galatians is concerned with little else. It may well have occurred to some of Jesus' original followers; but John can hardly have written this paragraph without being aware how relevant it was to the church of his own day.

33 The argument turned on Abraham. '**We are Abraham's descendants**' was the basic premise of the case for the religious superiority of the Jew. Abraham had been a man of exceptional faith, piety and merit. In reward for these qualities, God had made great promises to him about his descendants; on the strength of these promises, the Jews believed that, whatever might be the destiny of the rest of mankind, they themselves could look forward to a privileged place in that new order which God ultimately intended for the universe. It was true, of course, that Jewish thinkers also saw that this could not be entirely automatic: personal integrity and righteousness must always be some kind of precondition for inheriting God's salvation. Nevertheless, it was a very deeply rooted presupposition that, in the last analysis, the fact of being a Jew was the most important factor of all in the judgement which God would pass on human beings. Again and again in the New Testament we meet the same exclusive claim to special consideration: '**We are Abraham's descendants**'. However hard political circumstances might have borne on the Jewish nation (and the occupation of Palestine by the Romans seemed to some of them like virtual slavery), their sense of superiority to all other nations remained: even the Romans showed them exceptional consideration in allowing them to continue the practice of their own religion. In everything that mattered, they felt justified in saying, '**We have never been in slavery to any man**'.

To non-Jewish thinkers, this would have sounded like nonsense. It is

righteousness, self-understanding, self-control, not belonging to a particular
race, which give men confidence and peace of mind. '**The truth will set** 32
you free' . . . '**everyone who commits sin is a slave**'—such phrases were 34
often on the lips of Greek philosophers. It is perhaps a little difficult to
imagine Jesus using such philosophical language himself (though it would
probably have come quite naturally to John). But in essence his protest
against the traditional Jewish attitude was the same as that of any thinker
who took the facts of human sinfulness seriously. Indeed, it was a protest that
was written into the Old Testament itself and had recently found a powerful
spokesman in the person of John the Baptist.

The point would apply in the first instance to Jewish Christians: their new
faith, however much it owed to their old, was concerned with the realities
of an individual's relationship with God, and no appeal to the privileged
history of a particular race was relevant to the one really important question
of a man's own attitude to Christ. But the same point could also be turned
against Jews who were opposed to Christianity—and Jesus seems to continue
with his enemies in mind rather than his friends. '**Abraham is our father.**' 39
This, to the Jews, was a statement of fact. It was their guarantee of special
rights and privileges. But there were other senses, apart from the purely
physical one, in which one could call a great figure of the past one's **father.** [a]
In particular, one could mean by it that one modelled one's conduct on his.
The Jews' present conduct was sufficient to show that they could not be
Abraham's children in this deeper, more ethical sense. They were bent on
killing Jesus. '**That is not how Abraham acted.**' 40

The Jews were ready to accept this more significant sense of "father".
Indeed, this was part of what they meant when they said, '**God is our** 41
father'. They professed to take all instruction on how to live their lives from
God alone. Whether this claim was justified depended of course on how one
conceived of God. If the Jews had had a true understanding of the nature of
God (through their understanding of the Law of Moses), it might have been
arguable that their lives were indeed modelled on his will, and that they were
therefore justified in calling God their "father". But Jesus claimed to have
"come from God", to have been "sent by God". This gave him a unique
position from which to pass judgement on Jewish pretensions. Their failure
to **understand** his **language** showed that they had no true understanding of 43
God. They did not know what they were modelling their lives on. Therefore
they could not be '**God's children**'. 47

'**You are doing your own father's work . . . your father is the devil**'. 41, 44
What in fact were the Jews modelling their conduct on? They were seeking
to kill an innocent man; and they were refusing to listen to a truth which
nevertheless they could not refute. This suggested a "father" from mythology. The devil had been '**a murderer from the beginning**'—he had 44

[a] This is Paul's argument in Galatians 3, on which see below, p. 606.

been the cause of the death of Adam; and one of his most important rôles, especially in the period immediately preceding the Last Judgement, was to be that of misleading men whose faith was weak, and, by deceiving them, of bringing them into condemnation: he was '**a liar and the father of lies**'. An apt "father" for the Jews who opposed Jesus! And in so far as the devil was not merely a figure of mythology but an active and objective force in the world, here was perhaps a partial explanation of the Jews' attitude to Jesus: it was the work of the devil.

48 '**A Samaritan**'—this was a studied insult: the Jews not merely disowned Jesus from membership of their race, they identified him with their bitterest enemies. '**Possessed**'—this time something more than an insult: it was a sinister explanation of Jesus' words and deeds (Mark 3.22). Jesus of course denied the charge; but (here as in the other gospels), by denying that he was 'possessed', he did not thereby take personal credit for what he said and did. By so acting and speaking, he acted for God, he was "honouring his Father"; their reaction to him affected, not Jesus himself, but the judgement God would pass on them. The other gospels go so far as to call this blasphemous
reaction an unforgivable sin. Here the same reality of judgement is expressed
51 the other way round, in its positive form: '**if anyone obeys my teaching he shall never know what it is to die**'.

"Death" and "life" in Jesus' vocabulary had a special meaning. Missing
53 this, the Jews asked the obvious question. '**Are you greater than our father Abraham, who is dead? . . . What do you claim to be?**' This had, in effect, been the question all along. So far, Jesus' answers had been tantalizing and ambivalent; he was now about to make a claim that was absolutely decisive. But before doing so, he made an important reservation. Any answer he could give to the Jews' question would inevitably draw attention to himself, whereas his whole purpose was to draw men, not to himself, but to his Father (there is the same word-play on "honour" and "glory" as before). Whatever answer he gave must be understood as a statement, not about himself, but about God, or at most about himself in relation to God. The Jews' real error was not that they did not recognize Jesus for what he was, but that they did not "know God". And so Jesus made his reply in terms of
that same Abraham whom the Jews believed to be the key to the history of
56 God's relationship with men. '**Your father Abraham was overjoyed to see my day**'. There was a tradition among Jewish scholars (for which there is evidence not long after the date of the writing of this gospel) that Abraham was given a vision of things to come. Whether or not Jesus was referring to this, his meaning is clear: Abraham may have been the key figure in the Jewish national mythology, but that was not to say that he was the last word in God's dealings with men. The form in which Jesus expressed this, if taken literally, suggested that Jesus must have been alive in Abraham's time, many centuries ago. This, as usual, was how the Jews took it: how could a

man, who had not yet even become **old** himself,[a] reach back across the 57
centuries? Understood in this way, the proposition was absurd. But at the
hands of the writer of this gospel, whose first sentence proclaimed that
'when all things began, the Word already was', it was meaningful and true.
'**Before Abraham was born, I am**'. The statement at last brought Jesus 58
into the open: the speaker could belong to no human category. But to the
Jews it seemed axiomatic that only God could make such a statement, and
it followed that Jesus must be blaspheming. Death by stoning, even if dis-
allowed by the Romans, would have been the proper Jewish punishment.
Once again his life was threatened; once again he avoided the threat, though
this time John does not even offer an explanation. Mysteriously, **Jesus was** 59
not to be seen.

Jesus saw a man blind from his birth. Then as now, the spectacle of 9. 1
human suffering posed an acute religious question: how could a good and
just God allow such things? The usual answer given by Jewish thinkers was
that suffering and misfortune must be regarded as punishments for sin; and
if, as in the present case, it appeared that the individual concerned could
hardly have brought it upon himself, then there was still the possibility that
it was the parents who had sinned and that the son or daughter was bearing
the consequences. This somewhat naïve way of looking at suffering needed
considerable refinement if it was to account satisfactorily for all the facts, and
it was by no means held uncritically by everyone. Nevertheless, the natural
Jewish reaction to a case of illness or personal calamity was that the individual
concerned, or possibly his parents, must have committed some sin. The
disciples' question takes this for granted.

In the other gospels, Jesus seems occasionally to work from the same
presupposition. But here he explicitly rejects it. '**He was born blind so that** 3
God's power might be displayed in curing him.' This was certainly a
sufficient explanation in this particular case, and in any other case (such as
that of Lazarus later on, 11.15) when Jesus was there himself to turn tragedy
into joy. But was it relevant to the innumerable other sufferers who could
have no hope of a personal cure by Jesus? The unexpected "we" of verse
4—'**we must carry on the work of him who sent me**'—is perhaps a hint 4
deliberately given by the writer that Jesus' saying applied to more than his
own miracles of healing: it was addressed to "us", that is, the Christian
church which found itself able to exercise something of Jesus' power over
suffering and thereby (whether actual physical healing was involved or not)
to find a meaning in suffering as one of the circumstances under which God
makes himself known to men. At any rate, this healing was "God's work";

[a] The phrase, '**not yet fifty years old**' was understood by many early Christian writers to mean that Jesus was between forty and fifty. But this contradicts Luke's clear statement (3.23) that Jesus was about thirty years old, and in any case does not follow from John's words.

that is to say, it was of a different order from the "work" to which the Jewish Sabbath rules applied (for this, here as in chapter 5, was to be the main cause of Jewish opposition); it could go on being done continuously until that period of **night** when it would seem that the opposition of men had finally
5 extinguished the **light** of Jesus. Meanwhile, Jesus was still '**the light of the world**', of which the curing of a blind man was an apt illustration.
6 **He spat on the ground and made a paste with the spittle.** Outwardly, the procedure was old-fashioned magic. Such treatment would normally be followed by a careful washing or anointing. In Jerusalem there was only
7 one place where fresh spring water could be had, at **Siloam**, the outlet of the only spring which the city possessed. The spring still exists: it runs through the long underground tunnel originally made for it by King Hezekiah, and emerges at the lowest point of the old city, at the south-east corner of the city walls. In this area there has always been a pool (though its exact position has changed over the centuries). Here the blind man went to wash the paste from his eyes. It was the obvious place to do so; but it also had a name which (whatever it really meant) sounded like the Hebrew word for '**sent**'. The symbolism was obvious: the blind man was cured, not by any magical properties of the water, but by Jesus, the man "sent" from God.

14 **It was a Sabbath day when Jesus made the paste.** This, as with the cure of the cripple in chapter 5, was the immediate cause of the controversy. But this time Jesus was absent, and the scene is played out between the man who
13 had been cured and the Jews (mainly represented by **the Pharisees,** who were in fact the authors of much of the detail of the Sabbath regulations). As a result the episode moves more rapidly, and gives the narrator scope for working in some lively repartee on both sides. One detail, perhaps, betrays
22 his hand: it is true that in the time of Jesus individuals were **banned from the synagogue** for specified periods as a punishment for certain offences; but it is unlikely that this rule could have been applied to people who merely held a certain opinion, such as acknowledging **Jesus as Messiah.** It was only at the end of the century that the Jewish leaders revised their rules in such a way as deliberately to exclude Christians, and it looks as if John is here reading back this recent development into the time of Jesus. In other respects his narrative is entirely lifelike.

The point at issue was quite simple. A man born blind had been given his
17 sight. In the popular view this showed that Jesus was, at the very least, '**a prophet**'. There must have been a special reason why God had answered
31 Jesus' prayer: '**It is common knowledge that God does not listen to sinners; he listens to anyone who is devout and obeys his will.**' To ordinary people it was obvious where Jesus "came from"—from God; and there is a hint here that some of the Pharisees were prepared to take the
16 same view. But other Pharisees saw it differently. '**How could such signs**

come from a sinful man?' was not an entirely convincing argument. There were magicians and exorcists about who certainly achieved remarkable feats, but who were very far from being sinless. Moreover, by their own principles, Jesus had been shown to be "sinful": **'This fellow is no man of God; he does not keep the Sabbath'.** No one who deliberately set
aside such an important commandment could possibly be **devout**, let alone 17
a prophet. These uncertainties made it impossible for some of the Pharisees 31
to join in the popular acclamation of Jesus. Their best course seemed to be to try to cast doubt on what had actually happened. When this failed, they
simply resorted to abuse. **'Who are you to give us lessons', they re-** 34
torted, 'born and bred in sin as you are?' This, again, was the authentic Pharisaic tone of voice towards the undisciplined multitude of their fellow-Jews in general, sharpened in this particular case by the fact that they, unlike Jesus, took it for granted that a man born blind must have been **'born and bred in sin'.**

The man's own acceptance of Jesus was as definite as the Jews' rejection—and this is the moral of the whole episode. The person of Jesus brought into the world of the present that divine judgement which men usually conceived of as lying in the remote future. The blind man recovering his sight was symbolic: those who before had no pretensions that they could "see" came to believe in Jesus; those who relied on their "sight" were shown to be
"blind". Jesus' final rejoinder to the Pharisees is full of irony. **'If you were** 41
blind . . . you would not be guilty'. This was the exact reversal of their presupposition that a man, because he was blind, was bound to be guilty. The only form of guilt that mattered now was that of those who could not "see" who Jesus was.

A parable that Jesus told them. In the other gospels, parables are one of **10.** 6
the most distinctive elements in the teaching of Jesus. Of these, some are complete stories, some are simply pointed descriptions of familiar scenes. In this gospel, Jesus' teaching is more discursive, and makes comparatively little use of parables; when it does (and this passage is the only one where an illustration is explicitly called a parable), they belong to the second kind, that is to say, they are brief and memorable descriptions of something already familiar to the hearer, but with an emphasis on certain details which suggests a particular application. So here: the "parable" consists of a straightforward description of Palestinian shepherding. In the evening (or before a storm, or at any other time when protection is necessary) the shepherd may bring
the entire flock into the walled courtyard of a house (the translation **sheep-** 1
fold, suggesting fences or hurdles, is misleading). The street door of this courtyard is kept by a door-keeper, who keeps the door closed against marauders, but opens it to the shepherd when he comes next morning to lead the sheep out to pasture. European shepherds drive their sheep from

behind; but in the east the shepherd usually walks ahead of his flock: he has special calls which his own sheep know and respond to; indeed he knows his flock so well that he has a name for each sheep, just as an English farmer has a name for each of his cows. The flock is exposed to many dangers: on the mountains, there may be wild animals who will attack it; even inside the courtyard, a robber may climb in during the night and open the door from inside. The robber will not be able to lead away the entire flock, for the sheep will not follow him and will scatter as soon as he lets them out; but in fact
10 he comes only **to steal, to kill, to destroy.** If he can get the meat and the
wool of a few, he will have done a good night's work.

The image of a shepherd at the head of his flock occurs again and again in ancient literature. It was an obvious one for the ruler of a people or the general of an army. It occurs constantly in the Old Testament: the leaders of the Jewish people were its "shepherds", and in Ezekiel 34 (a chapter which has many points in common with this parable) those shepherds are subjected to fierce criticism on the grounds of their selfishness and rapacity, and threatened with being replaced by a new shepherd (David, or a descendant of David) who would make the flock into a single one, obedient to its Lord (who is God). Had Jesus' parable been purely in this tradition, it would have contained a thinly veiled attack on the present "shepherds" of Israel, and would doubtless have been easily understood by his hearers. The reason
6 why, on this occasion, **they did not understand what he meant by it,** was
perhaps because it did not exploit the obvious theme of good and bad shepherds, but concentrated on certain small details, accurately observed from real life, which in fact distinguished the real shepherd from a thief: his free access to the courtyard, and his familiarity with the sheep. These details are never mentioned when the shepherd-image is used in the Old Testament; and Jesus' hearers did not immediately grasp what he meant.

The parable is given an interpretation which makes it bear directly upon the person of Jesus. First (somewhat unexpectedly) one small detail is taken
7 from the parable as a clue to Jesus' nature: **'I am the door'**—a pictorial
symbol of the truth he is to make explicit later, 'No one comes to the Father except by me' (14.6), and also a very definite claim that he possesses an authority of a different order altogether from all previous teachers. But there
11 is a far more important point of comparison than this: **'I am the good
shepherd'.** This goes beyond anything in the parable. There, two points have been mentioned which serve to distinguish the shepherd from a thief or impostor: his right of free access to the sheepfold, and the fact that the
14 sheep have got used to him. Jesus refers to one of these again—**'I know my
own sheep and my sheep know me'**—but the thing which fundamentally distinguishes **the good shepherd** from all others is something that has not been mentioned in the parable and possibly would not have occurred to his
11 hearers: he **'lays down his life for the sheep'.** Such heroic conduct in a

sheep-owner faced with the prospect of losing his flock to a wolf was conceivable; applied to the "shepherds" of nations or armies, it was something which might on occasion be called for, say in time of war. But in what sense could it be said of a religious leader-shepherd that it belonged to his rôle
deliberately, of his own **free will**, to lay down his life? Christians, after the 18
event, could understand this; they could understand also how Jesus' death
had been of service, not just to those within the Jewish **fold**, but to the 16
Gentiles outside. But Jesus' hearers were as bewildered by the idea as by his
other references to "going away". **These words once again caused** 19
a split among the Jews. Until the story was finished and all the clues fell into place, Jesus' words and deeds continued to display a tantalizing ambiguity.

The festival of the Dedication. Festivals, rather than seasons, offered to a 22
Jewish writer the most natural way of marking the time of year. Like Luke, who dates important events in the history of the early church by reference to the Jewish religious calendar (see below on Acts 2.1), John separates the various episodes of Jesus' life by connecting each with a certain festival. Chapter 6 was dated by Passover to the spring, chapter 7 by Tabernacles to the autumn; and now it is Dedication, a winter festival instituted by Judas Maccabaeus in 164 B.C. to mark the re-dedication of the temple after its profanation by Antiochus Epiphanes. In this eight-day festival there were lights, processions, singing; but John clearly mentions it, not because of anything distinctive about the celebrations, but because it gives the episode an approximate date (we should say, "some time in December"). It was in any case a likely time for Jesus and many other visitors to be in Jerusalem.

It was winter. To a European, this suggests the cold months of December, January and February. But in Palestine, as indeed in most Mediterranean countries, there were only two seasons, that of hot, dry, settled weather (roughly from May to September) and that of periodic rainfall (October to April). In Jerusalem, wintry weather—whether it be snow and frost, wind and rain, hail and thunder—can occur at almost any time during the second of these seasons, between long periods of fine days and warm sun. In this sense, "winter" is half the year. No one would think of dating anything by it. John's words probably mean that it was rough weather; and the
other details he gives would then fall into place. **Solomon's Portico** (on 23
which see below on Acts 3.11) offered protection from rain and wind; but it also gave proceedings a more formal character than the open spaces of **the temple precincts.** Such porticos were regularly used for teaching and disputations in any city where there were philosophers or religious teachers. But they were also used as courts of law; and what follows is no longer a
mere controversy, but is in all but name a trial. **The Jews gathered round** 24
him—in the Greek, the expression is distinctly aggressive, evoking the

picture of an army encircling a besieged city, or of a court like the Sanhedrin
seated in a semicircle around the accused; and the dialogue follows the same
pattern (and indeed uses many of the same words) as that which, in Luke's
gospel (22.67–71), takes place at the formal hearing of Jesus' case before a
Jewish court: Jesus is directly challenged to say whether he is the Messiah,
refuses to give an explicit reply on the grounds of his judges' unbelief, but
then makes a claim (in Luke, to be at the right hand of God, in John to be
30 "one with the Father") which makes him appear guilty of blasphemy and
liable to the death penalty. All this, in the other gospels, takes place in the
course of a formal trial, and leads directly to Jesus' crucifixion. John places
it here, and has no record of a formal trial later (its place is taken by a kind of
private interrogation by the High Priest). That is to say, John uses this
occasion instead of the later one to lay bare the issue between Jesus and the
Jewish authorities. Once again, Jesus' immediate execution is averted only
by the strange elusiveness which he has displayed throughout *The great*
39 *controversy*: **he escaped from their clutches.**

The scene, nevertheless, is worked carefully into the pattern of the whole
section. The parable of the shepherd is developed a little further; and the
25 discussion of Jesus' '**credentials**' is brought to a conclusion. Jesus had made
various claims for himself; but the testimony of his words, even though there
was a sense in which it was legally valid (8.14), had not been accepted.
However, there was still another kind of evidence to be considered. '**My
deeds done in my Father's name are my credentials**'. These were done
32 according to his Father's will and in his **Father's power.** Their purpose is
38 now finally defined: '**that you may recognize and know that the Father
is in me, and I in the Father**'. John's readers were by now prepared for this
kind of language, which belonged to a wider religious culture than that of the
Jews: Jesus' relationship with God could not be described only in terms of
the Jewish concepts of Messiah or Son of God. Indeed, Jewish thinking
tended to draw a sharp line between language appropriate to men and
language appropriate to God. Jesus' description of himself seemed to them
33 to be overstepping that line: '**You, a mere man, claim to be a god.**' To
34 this, Jesus replied, in effect, that they had drawn their line too sharply.
Consider these verses of Psalm 82:

> "God takes his stand in the court of heaven
> To deliver judgement on the gods themselves . . .
> I said: you are gods,
> And all of you sons of the Most High.
> Yet you shall die like mortals . . ."

The psalm was originally written against a background of a lingering belief in heathen gods alongside the one true God of Israel. Later interpreters, anxious to banish the idea that any such "gods" could exist, suggested that

the beings meant were angels, demonic powers, or even men. We do not know what Jesus' hearers thought the psalm meant; but whatever view they took, they would have been bound to concede Jesus' point that it showed that the word "god" could be used of someone who is less than God. If so, then it was not so easy to draw the line between language that was and was
not blasphemous. Jesus could truthfully say, **'I am God's son'**. Even if his 36
adversaries did not admit that it was true, they still could not prove that it was blasphemous.

Victory over death

Jesus withdrew again across the Jordan. For a moment before the final 40
conflict in Jerusalem, the contact with John the Baptist's work is renewed,
and a last tribute is paid to John's "witness" to Jesus, which alone caused
many **to believe in him there.** The interlude also prepares for the next 42
scene; for the drama of Lazarus' death depends on Jesus being **across the** 40
Jordan, a long day's journey from the scene of events.

There was a man named Lazarus who had fallen ill. The characters 11. 1
in this scene are first carefully identified—and we receive an unexpected
reminder that the readers of this gospel were assumed to be already so
familiar with the events of Jesus' life that John could point forward to an 2
episode he had not yet recorded (12.1–8) in order to identify Mary.[a] The
family were friends of Jesus, and it was to be expected that he would use his
undoubted power to cure one of them of an illness. This, in fact, is what
everyone—the two sisters and their friends—assumed would happen; and
they were naturally dejected (verses 21, 32), if not cynical (verse 37), when it
failed to happen. What no one dared to hope was that anything could be
done once Lazarus had died. Raising the dead, though not unheard of, was
a rare and exceptional miracle, and Jesus was not assumed to have the power
to perform it. Jesus, however, saw Lazarus' illness as an occasion for doing
precisely this. **'It has come for the glory of God, to bring glory to the** 4
Son of God.' This was to be the climax of his works of power, and a visible
demonstration of the seriousness of his teaching about life and death. Two
comparable miracles are related in the other gospels (Mark 5.21–43; Luke
7.11–17); but this is by far the most spectacular, and is the only one which
teaches such a clear lesson of Jesus' *Victory over death.*

'This illness will not end in death'. By the time the reader has reached 4
the end of the story, he will have grasped the meaning of this reaction of
Jesus. But it was naturally taken by Jesus' disciples to mean that there was

[a] Two sisters named Mary and Martha had their home in "a village" in Luke 10.38–9. We cannot be certain that they are the same; though the reference below (12.2) to Martha "serving" makes it likely that they were.

nothing further to worry about in Lazarus' illness, and they were therefore
7 surprised when, two days later, Jesus suggested returning to Judaea, and
exposing himself to the danger he had just left behind. Jesus answered them,
9 first, with a parable. '**Anyone can walk in day-time without stumbling**'
—it was a vivid way of saying that even near Jerusalem he would be safe for
the time being: his "hour", his "night", had not yet come (but the tell-tale
phrase, **the light of this world**, shows that the parable, by the time this
gospel was written, had come to mean more than this: the Christian, walking
in the light of Christ, is safe from stumbling). Secondly, Jesus had a positive
11 reason for going back, which he gradually unfolded to his disciples. '**Lazarus
has fallen asleep**'. In Greek, as in English, this was ambiguous. The
4 disciples remembered that Jesus had said, '**This illness will not end in
death**', and seized eagerly on what was apparently hopeful news (known
apparently by intuition to Jesus): falling into a calm sleep was a sign that a
14 fever was passing. **Then Jesus spoke out plainly**: '**Lazarus is dead**'.
Before, the journey seemed pointless because Jesus had said that Lazarus
would not die. Now it seemed pointless because he was already dead. Nothing
but certain death awaited Jesus in Jerusalem. One at least of the disciples
16 made up his mind what was expected of them. '**Let us also go, that we
may die with him.**'

We can reconstruct what had happened. Lazarus had died soon after the
sisters sent their message to Jesus. As was usual, he was buried the same
38 day. The tomb was **a cave, with a stone placed against it.** There are
thousands of such tombs in Palestine: they consist of a rock chamber, with
small horizontal niches or tunnels hewn out of the sides. The corpse was
wrapped in linen and laid on one of these rock shelves. The tomb was then
sealed by a large flat stone placed over the entrance to the cave. The mourning
continued for some days. It was a highly esteemed act of charity to visit
and console the bereaved. Mary and Martha were naturally surrounded by
17 their friends from the city. Moreover, **Jesus found that Lazarus had
already been four days in the tomb.** There is probably a touch of folklore
in this. For three days, it was believed, the soul continued to haunt the body,
and a return to life might still seem just conceivable. After that, decomposition began and death was irrevocable. We are told twice over that Jesus did not arrive until the fourth day. What he was about to do exceeded the bounds even of imagined possibility.

In the main the episode is left to speak for itself. But it contains a charac-
23 teristic piece of dialogue. **Jesus said, 'Your brother will rise again'.**
This sounded like ordinary spiritual comfort: most people believed in a
24 **resurrection on the last day,** and it could be consoling to know that one's
dear ones would be there. But of course, this was not what Jesus meant.
Lazarus was to rise again now; and this would demonstrate in visible form

that the categories of life-after-death were being brought by Jesus into the
present. The quality of living offered by Jesus was such that even physical
death could not impair it. Martha could hardly yet grasp all this; but she
did get so far as to make a correct confession of who Jesus was. Her confession was a limited one: Messiah was no more than a Jewish title. But at
least she knew that the arrival of this Messiah **who was to come into the** 27
world must be the signal for something radically new in the experience of
mankind.

Towards the end, Jesus showed signs of strong emotion, sighing and
weeping. It is possible that he was simply entering into the general grief:
this, at any rate, is what the Jews thought—'**How dearly he must have** 36
loved him!' But we must beware of assuming that they were right. It is a
recurring feature of the style of this gospel that the bystanders are made to
misinterpret the words and actions of Jesus. Moreover, it is clear from the
very beginning of the narrative that Jesus, far from being disconcerted by
Lazarus' death, welcomed it as an opportunity to show forth the glory of
God. It would have been surprising (though perhaps only human) if, when
it came to the point, he felt it to be a calamity to be wept over. Finally, the
Greek word translated **sighed heavily** or **sighed deeply** is one which 33, 38
usually expresses anger or indignation rather than grief—in Mark 14.5 it is
translated 'turned upon her with fury'; in Mark 1.43 it expresses a 'stern
warning'. In all the gospels Jesus has moments of anger, and his anger is
usually provoked by the inhumanity and hypocrisy of people and institutions. The same may well be the case here. All these Jewish people, who professed a belief in the resurrection of the dead, were weeping their eyes out
as if the death of their friend Lazarus was something tragic and final. This
exhibition of superstitious weakness moved Jesus to tears of indignation
(mistaken as sympathy by the Jews). He was to show them how foolish their
weeping had been.

Now many . . . But some . . . Even this most sensational of all Jesus' 45
actions did not convince everyone who saw it. Many **put their faith in him**;
but the continued hostility of others resulted in a meeting of the Council—
the only such meeting recorded in this gospel.

It is possible to question John's account of this scene on points of historical
detail. If the meeting was a formal session of the Sanhedrin, and not just a
hurried conference of influential people (John's words would fit either
interpretation), **the Pharisees** as such would have had no official right to 47
convene it; and John's language about Caiaphas being **High Priest that year** 49
makes one wonder whether he knew that he was in fact High Priest continuously from A.D. 18 to 36. On the other hand, in general the episode is
entirely convincing. All the gospels agree that the arrest and execution of
Jesus was the result of plotting by the Jewish authorities; and one of the

most plausible motives for their action was fear of what the consequences
might be if someone who called himself the Messiah were allowed to gather
48 a considerable following. **'The Romans will come and sweep away our
temple and our nation'.** This had happened by the time the gospel was
written: it could well have happened earlier if a serious insurrectionary
movement had got under way under the leadership of a man such as they
took Jesus to be.

On the face of it, Caiaphas' advice was sound political sense: the judicial
murder of one scapegoat was a small price to pay for avoiding serious trouble.
But what might have been merely the practical wisdom of a political leader
51 was seen by John as an instance of inspired **prophesying** such as might be
expected from a High Priest. Jesus did indeed **die for the nation,** not to
save it from Roman oppression, but to make possible a new kind of life. And
John adds that there were to benefit from this many who did not belong to
"that nation", but would be brought by Christ into a new community of the
52 **children of God.**

In any case, Jesus once more retired from the neighbourhood of Jeru-
54 salem. The other gospels do not mention this withdrawal, and **a town called
Ephraim** occurs nowhere else in the New Testament. It is probably to be
identified with a place some 12½ miles north-east of Jerusalem, on the edge
of the arid range of mountains that fall down to the Jordan valley.

55 **The Jewish Passover was now at hand.** In this gospel, all Jesus' visits to Jerusalem have been associated with a festival. His last, which ends in his death, is placed by all the gospels at the time of the Passover. John opens his narrative with the first influx of visitors: those who, either by living abroad or for some other reason, had made themselves ritually "unclean" and had to be in Jerusalem for seven days in order to complete the rites of purification which would enable them to approach the temple on the day of the festival (see below on Acts 21.26). This was a day or two before the main crowd of pilgrims would arrive. It was the moment for the authorities to make their plans, and for the beginning of popular speculation about Jesus' intentions.

12. 2 **A supper was given in his honour.** A somewhat similar episode is recorded in all the gospels. In Luke (7.36–50) it has nothing to do with Jesus' approaching death; the woman who anoints Jesus' feet, after washing them and wiping them with her hair, is a stranger who intends simply to express her gratitude and love. In Mark on the other hand (14.3–9)—who is followed on most points by Matthew (26.6–13)—the woman's action is presented as a kind of rehearsal for the anointing which should have been administered to the body of Jesus before his burial: as such, it was a notable "act of kindness", and therefore far more meritorious than an ordinary contribution to the needs of

the poor. Most of these elements are present here, but in a slightly different
arrangement. First, the characters are all identified. The scene is once again
Bethany, and of the three people already known to us there each is given a
part: **Lazarus sat among the guests,** Martha was behind the scenes 2
serving (characteristically, if she was the same Martha as appears in Luke
10.40), Mary came into the room to perform her extravagant act of devotion
to Jesus. The shocked reaction which this caused is ascribed to Judas
Iscariot, and gives John an opportunity to fill in a trait of Judas' character
in advance of the betrayal itself: he used **to pilfer the money put into the** 6
common purse, which was in his charge. This precision about the people
involved goes with a vivid telling of the story (**the house was filled with the** 3
fragrance is a touch not found in any of the other accounts). But John has
not made it clear how he understood the story. If he had wished to emphasize
Mary's humble service to Jesus, he would surely have mentioned what was in
fact the main point of a similar service performed by Jesus later—the washing
of the guest's feet. Indeed, had he done so, it would have made his description much clearer. In Luke, the woman washes Jesus' feet with her tears, dries them with her hair, and then anoints them with ointment. John also says that Mary **wiped them with her hair**—but apparently after putting on the ointment! John may in fact mean that (as in Luke) she washed them first, and then dried them before anointing them; but if so, his description is so condensed that he certainly cannot have intended to put any stress on the actual washing. Nor does he make anything of the contrast between giving money to the poor and performing exceptional acts of kindness (which seems to be the main point of the scene in Mark); and as for the point about anticipating Jesus' burial, it is expressed so obscurely that it is impossible to be sure what he thought it meant. [a] We are left with the impression that on this occasion John was content to set down the story for its own sake, without attempting to give it a fully consistent interpretation.

The next day. Jerusalem had now begun to fill up with the great body of 12
pilgrims, who were moved to give Jesus a royal acclamation. The **palm** 13
branches were appropriate for greeting a king; the chanting of a psalm,
'Hosanna! Blessings on him who comes in the name of the Lord!'
(Psalm 118.25–6), though it was primarily a song for a religious festival, was apt enough with the addition of the words, **'God bless the king of Israel!'** On a previous occasion, when there had been an attempt to make Jesus king (6.15), Jesus had hastily withdrawn from the scene. Here, his response was similar to that which he was to make when Pilate questioned him on the

[*a*] **'Let her keep it until the day when she prepares for my burial'** would make sense as an answer to Judas if Mary had not in fact already used it to anoint Jesus; and even so, we should have to reckon with the fact that, at Jesus' burial, it was not Mary's pound of ointment, but Nicodemus' hundred pounds, that were used (19.39).

14 matter: he accepted the title, but in a special sense. **Jesus found a donkey**
and mounted it. A warrior king would have chosen a horse; Jesus' action
15 was that of a man of peace. When Zechariah had prophesied (9.9), '**See, your**
king is coming, mounted on an ass's colt', it was obvious that the prophet
envisaged no ordinary king, but a figure who combined authority with a singular humility—in short, a universal peacemaker, a divinely appointed Messiah. Jesus allowed himself to be acclaimed king only on such terms as these.

The accounts of this episode in the other gospels contain much the same elements, but they leave tantalizing questions unanswered. What did the crowds recognize in Jesus which made them follow the disciples' lead and give him a triumphal entry? And why did the demonstration peter out as suddenly as it had begun? John's version makes it all sound more rational. The crowds acclaimed Jesus because of the sensational raising of Lazarus which they had seen or heard about, and far from petering out, the demonstration went on for as long as was to be expected; for some time it could be
19 said, '**All the world has gone after him!**' This popular emotion was of
course transient and superficial: the crowd would follow Jesus only so long as the impression of Lazarus' resurrection was fresh in their minds. Nevertheless, the episode had a deeper significance: in a certain sense, Jesus was truly a king, although even the disciples (who in the other accounts play a
larger part in the scene, and might have been expected to grasp its real
16 meaning) **did not understand this.** In this gospel, Jesus' triumphant entry
into Jerusalem was one more of those moments when his presence was half-accepted, half-rejected, his true nature at best half-understood.

A festival at Jerusalem not only drew a great crowd of Jewish pilgrims: people of other nationalities, whether they were full proselytes or merely sympathetic to the Jewish religion, also made the journey to visit the holy city. It
20 was convenient to call such people **Greeks**, though they might come from
almost anywhere in the eastern part of the Roman empire. Their common language would be Greek; and the main thing that was meant by the word was that they were not Jews by birth. Some of them expressed a desire to see Jesus—which sounds a simple enough request; but the fact that it
elicited from Jesus a series of exceedingly solemn sayings shows that we must
19 be prepared to look for a deeper significance in it. The Jews had said, 'Why,
all the world has gone after him', meaning simply that Jesus had attracted a crowd. But, taken literally, their words suggested something more sensational. Jesus was attracting, not only his fellow-Jews, but **the world,** that is, strangers and foreigners, people who had no allegiance to the Jewish religion. An example is immediately given in the Greeks who approached Philip. But every reader of the gospel knew that the real fulfilment of these words was the existence of the Christian church, which had by now far out-

grown its Jewish origins and was mainly composed of people who were, not Jews, but "Greeks".

The process by which this was to happen had already begun. '**The hour** 23
has come for the Son of Man to be glorified.' In straight Jewish terms,
this would probably have meant that the person whose destiny it was finally
to unite the two worlds of earth and heaven was now to be endued with
supernatural splendour and lead his people to heaven. But John has been
working out a different meaning for these terms. The "glorifying" of the
Son of Man consisted in his being "lifted up" on the cross, it was the other
side of what appeared to be a dark destiny of condemnation and death. The
reader is helped to understand this first by a brief parable. '**A grain of** 24
wheat remains a solitary grain unless it falls into the ground'. The
parable of a single seed growing into a great fruitful plant occurs in the other
gospels (see especially Mark 4.26–32) as an illustration of spectacular growth
from tiny beginnings. But now a new idea is added: '**if it dies, it bears a**
rich harvest.' The idea that a seed (and indeed nature itself) dies in the
dead season of winter and comes to life again in the spring underlies a great
deal of religious symbolism (it occurs again in 1 Corinthians 15.36–8). The
seed, when it falls into the ground, enters the yearly cycle of death and
rebirth. In this sense, **it dies**; and by this small elaboration, the parable of
a rich harvest from a tiny grain is made to turn on that death—the death of
Jesus which is also his glorification—which must precede the prodigious
growth which is to follow. But this death involves others, it conditions the
way in which men must seek to serve and follow Jesus. In a sequence of ideas
and sayings very similar to those in Mark 8.34–8, the implications for Jesus'
followers are spelled out.

'**Now my soul is in turmoil**'. All the gospels record a moment before 27
The final conflict when Jesus seems suddenly to have had a moment of
irresolution. Here the setting is different from that in the other gospels, but
it is clear that the experience being described is the same. We must beware
of psychologizing. Jesus' words are not chosen because these alone exactly
describe his emotions, but because (being an allusion to Psalm 42) they evoke
a classical expression of the agony of one whose faith in God is stretched to
breaking-point. Both here and on the cross, Jesus uses the traditional
language of Hebrew spirituality to show that he, like countless just men
before him, is in a position where circumstances make it hard to continue
to believe in God. The admission is unexpected: apart from this one moment,
Jesus moves with a serene sense of purpose. It is also short-lived. In the other
gospels, the prayer for deliverance gives place to acceptance: 'not what I
will, but what thou wilt' (Mark 14.36). Here, the same is said in the distinctive idiom of John's gospel. Until now, the glory attending the person of
Jesus (which is God's glory) has been ambiguous and incomplete: it will
be fully realized only in Jesus' death and resurrection. So Jesus' acceptance

27 of his destiny takes the form, '**Father, glorify thy name**'. And the supernatural answer to this prayer (corresponding perhaps to the 'angel from heaven bringing him strength' in Luke's account of Gethsemane, 22.43) is in effect that the glory already attendant upon Jesus is now to be consummated by that supreme act of glorification by which the Son of Man will be
32 **lifted up**, on the cross, to heaven.

Jesus, after his brief moment of hesitation, firmly accepted this uniquely demanding mode of glorification. But for men there was still the great difficulty of seeing the glory in the humiliation, of accepting that Jesus' death was an expression of God's glory on earth. Jesus' teaching had been preparing
30 them for this; now a voice from heaven declared it was so. '**This voice spoke for your sake, not mine**'. Even this, of course, was ambiguous. Most people **said it was thunder.** The events leading up to the crucifixion itself
31 were to be the decisive challenge to declare for or against Jesus: '**Now is the hour of judgement for this world**'. Many would doubtless declare against; but this would not rob the crucifixion of its power. It was a firm Christian belief—supported by a number of Jesus' sayings—that the devil himself ('**the Prince of this world**') was vanquished by the crucifixion (compare Hebrews 2.14); and it was the crucifixion which finally broke through the exclusiveness of the Jewish religion and enabled Jesus to "draw all men to himself".
32 '**Lifted up**'. The expression seems to have been deliberately ambiguous —indeed the macabre pun was apparently quite well known (it is exploited for instance, in Genesis 40.12–19). Its most natural meaning was "exalted"; but it could also mean "lifted up (on the cross) for execution". John puts
33 his readers wise to this second meaning—**This he said to indicate the kind of death he was to die**—and then tells us that this was in fact the meaning which Jesus' listeners seized on, and found inconsistent with their
34 conception of a glorious Deliverer. '**Our Law teaches us that the Messiah continues for ever**'. There were varying interpretations of those passages in the Law which pointed foward to a Messiah; but most interpreters agreed that he must be an eternal figure. Call him what they would—Messiah in their own terminology, or Son of Man (apparently) in that of Jesus—the splendid figure they expected was surely not to be **lifted up**—to die! This of course was the question posed by the gospel right from the beginning: how could the Word be rejected, how could the Son of God be crucified? Jesus, in his last response to this question, simply recalled answers he had given before. Light presupposes darkness, day presupposes night. Rejection by men belongs to the conditions under which the Word can dwell on earth.
36 The essential thing is to make the right response: '**Trust to the light, so that you may become men of light.**'

37 Nevertheless, these people had actually seen **the many signs which Jesus had performed in their presence.** They, of all people, ought surely to

have been prepared to believe. Yet it was the Jews of Jerusalem who were
responsible for Jesus being condemned to death, and at the time this gospel
was written it was still the Jewish nation which was the most unwilling to
accept the Christian gospel. This was the extreme case of the paradox stated
at the beginning, 'He entered his own realm, and his own would not receive
him' (1.11). Concluding this part of his narrative, John offers two more
explanations, the first theoretical, the second practical. The theoretical
explanation was the one which was seized on most eagerly by Christians
right from the beginning, and may indeed go back to Jesus himself: **the** 38
prophet Isaiah's utterance had to be fulfilled. Scripture, rightly interpreted, foretold the rejection of Christ. Isaiah 53, with its description of a
suffering servant who nevertheless bore the sins of many, was one of the
passages most frequently invoked (it opens, '**Lord, who has believed what
we reported . . .**'). Another was Isaiah 6.9, '**He has blinded their eyes . . .**', 40
which in all the gospels (though in a slightly different way in each) is used to
explain the failure of Israel to accept and understand Jesus (see above on
Mark 4.11–12). However mysterious the fact of this rejection, and however
brutal and fatalistic this explanation might sound, it remained true that these
things were predicted in Scripture, and must therefore be the will of God.

The second explanation was quite practical. There was a powerful incen-
tive not to acknowledge Jesus: **fear of being banned from the synagogue.** 42
In this form, the threat was probably more of a reality at the time the gospel
was written than in the time of Jesus (see above on 9.22). But the general
point was valid at any time and could be neatly expressed in a pun that has
already been exploited earlier (see above on 5.41–4). One word meant both
human "honour" and divine "glory". Men are men, and it was only to be
expected they would prefer the former sense of the word: **they valued their** 43
reputation with men rather than the honour which comes from God.

So Jesus cried aloud—but there is no audience, no occasion (Jesus, so 44
far as we have been told, is still in **hiding**). What we have here is a final 36
comment on the argument as it has been unfolding throughout these chapters. This argument has necessarily thrust Jesus into the centre of the
picture. It is the Jesus who did these deeds and spoke these words about
whom men must make up their minds. It is for Jesus or against Jesus that
they must decide. But now comes the corrective. '**When a man believes** 44
in me, he believes in him who sent me rather than in me' . . . '**There** 48
is a judge for the man who rejects me'. The words and ideas have all
occurred earlier; but here the emphasis is all on one point: Jesus is no
independent divinity, no isolated challenge. Declaring for or against Jesus
is nothing more nor less than declaring for or against God.

Farewell discourses

'He entered his own realm, and his own would not receive him' (1.11). The first part of the gospel has been wrestling with this paradox. It has illustrated the ambiguity necessarily involved in the appearance of the Son of God on earth, and the diversity of response which he elicited. It has described the words and actions by which Jesus sought to confront men and women with the challenge of his presence, and it has recorded the strength of the opposition which he aroused. There were certainly many who 'believed in him'; but so far the main emphasis has been on those who rejected him and who were soon to bring him to his death.

Yet the story of Jesus was not only a story of rejection. When this gospel was written, the Christian church had already taken firm root in many parts of the world; and this church traced its origin to those who in Jesus' lifetime had given their undivided allegiance to him. By some, Jesus was accepted. And to them, Jesus gave a great deal in return. As was said in the prologue, 'To all who did receive him . . . he gave the right to become children of God' (1.12). The first Christians possessed in common, not only their faith that Jesus was the Christ, but a conviction of his continuing presence among them, and a relationship with him and with each other which was strong and new. It is to this aspect of Jesus' work that the writer now turns.

The other gospels all contain sections of teaching given privately by Jesus to his disciples, but this teaching is usually spread over the whole course of Jesus' activity. Only in Matthew is there a serious attempt to gather it together into substantial discourses; and even there the discourses occur at intervals throughout the gospel. In John all this teaching comes together at the end, and fills several pages. In part it makes use of ideas already introduced in earlier chapters; but in part it works out a new set of concepts, in particular the 'love' which is to bind Jesus' followers together and the effects of Jesus' "going to his Father" upon the nature of his continuing presence with them on earth.

In form, these chapters are unlike what has gone before: no longer a series of dramatic episodes followed by dialogue, but a long speech of Jesus interrupted only by occasional questions from the disciples. It is of course entirely probable that Jesus devoted much of the last night of his life on earth to talking with his disciples. At the same time, when John came to write this part of his gospel, he was doubtless influenced by the historian's convention of writing up a long parting speech purporting to have been made by the hero shortly before his death. An appropriate occasion for such a speech was a final meal shared with friends. John's is not the only gospel to make use of this convention: in Luke's gospel, Jesus' last supper is also made the occasion for a parting speech to the disciples. But in John, the opportunity to gather together Jesus' private teaching at this point is exploited much more systematically, and that moment in Jesus' life which in Mark and Matthew is described simply as a solemn meal and is made to carry only a few important sayings of Jesus, becomes here an occasion for a series of what may appropriately be called *Farewell discourses.*

In the other gospels this meal is stated to have been a Passover supper,
celebrated by Jesus with his disciples according to Jewish custom; in the
course of it, Jesus spoke certain words over the bread and the wine which
gave the meal an altogether new significance and made it the origin and
prototype of the Christian eucharist. John says nothing of all this (though
he has made clear allusions to the eucharist in chapter 6); indeed the chronology he follows for the last days of Jesus' life makes it impossible for this
supper to have been a regular celebration of the Passover: as he says himself,
it was before the Passover. From the historical point of view this creates 13. 1
difficulties. The meal he describes was no ordinary meal. It was a sufficiently
formal occasion for the guests to be **reclining** on couches around the table; 23
and it was held, not in the afternoon (the usual time for the main meal of the
day), but at **night.** These details would fit a dinner party or a solemn festivity 30
such as a wedding. They would also fit a Passover supper, which is in fact the
only kind of occasion which we should expect Jesus and his disciples to have
marked with such careful formality. But by John's reckoning, Passover
night, when a meal of this character would be enjoyed by all the Jews in
Jerusalem, was the following night. It is not easy to imagine Jesus deliberately holding his own celebration of the festival one day earlier than everyone else. However, behind this historical difficulty lies a real difference of
approach between John's gospel and the other gospels. All the gospels
agree that the crucifixion happened at Passover time: they differ over the
exact significance and timing of this connection. According to Mark (apparently followed by Matthew and Luke), Jesus was crucified on the day following Passover night, and the effect of this coincidence was to give Jesus' last
meal with his disciples the character of a Passover supper. In John, on the
other hand, the Passover came twenty-four hours later, so that Jesus' death
was simultaneous with the slaughter of the lambs on the afternoon before
the Passover supper. This made it possible to understand Jesus' death as
that of a Passover victim; but it necessarily removed any specifically Passover
associations from Jesus' own last supper.

Nevertheless, the meal had its own drama. Part of this drama was caused
(as in the other gospels) by the presence of Judas Iscariot who was about to
betray his master—a betrayal which was made still more horrifying by the
fact that the betrayer had just shared this meal with Jesus and so was to
betray, not just a friend, but the table-fellowship which such a meal was held
to establish between friends. "**He who eats bread with me has turned** 18
against me" (Psalm 41.9) was one of the classic Old Testament formula-

tions of such a betrayal. Jesus was well aware of what was to happen (another
21 sign that he was no ordinary person) and was moved by it to **deep agitation
of spirit.** He then identified the traitor. In all the gospels the question why
Judas did what he did (which we would tend to explore in psychological
2 terms) is answered quite simply: **the devil had already put it into the
mind of Judas.** But John is careful not to give the impression that the devil
held the initiative: it was only after Jesus had deliberately singled out Judas
27 for his sinister role that **Satan entered him**; then, with Jesus' connivance,
Judas slipped away to perform his deed without arousing the other disciples'
suspicions. John allows us to visualize the scene: Jesus lay on his left side
with his head towards the table, and his right arm free to help himself to
food. The disciple on his right was in the same position; his head would have
23 been at about the level of Jesus' chest (which is what the Greek of **reclining
close beside Jesus** actually implies), and he would have been in a better
position than anyone to whisper to Jesus. Jesus' gesture to Judas was entirely
natural. Bread was the main implement used at table: one dipped it like a
spoon into the common dish, and it was polite to do so for a guest. It could
well have escaped the notice of all present except **the disciple he loved** (the
first appearance of this cryptic phrase—see below on 21.24); but it was a
poignant signal for the traitor to begin his work.

But the main element of drama is provided by an action of Jesus which is
recorded only in this gospel (though it may be alluded to in Luke 22.27).
4 Jesus **rose from table, laid aside his garments, and taking a towel,
tied it round him.** This was the uniform of the slave whose special task it
was to carry out the hospitable act of washing the guests' feet before supper.
The act itself was one which a Jew felt to be very much beneath his dignity;
indeed, a Jewish slave was usually spared the task if a gentile slave was
available; otherwise it was performed by a woman (as in Luke 7.38; 1 Timothy 5.10). The shock and surprise caused by Jesus' action was voiced by
6 Peter: **'You, Lord, washing my feet?'** But, as so often in this gospel, this
naïve reaction was merely the cue for Jesus to continue the conversation on
a deeper level.

On this occasion, the deeper meaning is no more than hinted at, and it is
not easy to be sure how these hints should be interpreted. The first hint is
7 one which occurs elsewhere in these discourses: **'You do not understand
now what I am doing, but one day you will'.** One of the themes of these
chapters is the connection between the short period of Jesus' activity on earth and the subsequent life of the church. **'One day'** meant after the resurrection, the time when Jesus' presence would be known mainly through the Spirit. Now in this gospel a constant symbol of the Spirit is water; and it is at once obvious that Jesus' act of washing his disciples' feet is intended to symbolize their possession of the Spirit after his resurrection. But we can probably go further: the rite by which Christians received the Spirit was

baptism; and all the things which Jesus said about his action of washing his
disciples' feet could also in fact be said about the symbolic washing of
baptism. It was baptism which marked the moment when a believer found
himself **in fellowship with** Jesus. Baptism was effective once and for all 8
(the convert needed **no further washing**). And baptism, since it procured 10
forgiveness of sins, made any other purification ceremony (such as the Jews
believed in) entirely unnecessary: after baptism, the Christian was **altogether**
clean. All this teaching about the future rite of Christian baptism was elicited
by Peter's unperceptive reactions to Jesus' wish to wash his feet. Indeed it
could even perhaps be said (in case anyone wondered whether the disciples
themselves had ever been baptized) that this *was* their baptism.

Nevertheless, if the deeper meaning of Jesus' action was to symbolize
Christian baptism, it also had a more direct message: '**I have set you an** 15
example: you are to do as I have done for you.' If Jesus' mastership and
lordship could be expressed by such a startling reversal of the usual conventions, the relationship of Christians to each other must be expected to follow a similarly radical pattern. This, in short, is the first example of Jesus' love for his own. So far, his disciples have been there merely to listen and to question and to make their own decision in the face of the challenge of his work and teaching. But now we are taken far below this surface impression and shown something of the strength of that solidarity which binds Jesus to his followers. When Jesus washes his disciples' feet, we have the first and most striking illustration of a theme which runs right through these discourses: **now he was to show the full extent of his love.** 1

The scene also provides a new application for a proverb-like saying which
elsewhere (both in John 15.20 and Matthew 10.24) is intended to show that
a disciple cannot expect to receive less persecution than his master: '**A** 16
servant is not greater than his master.' Here, it is clearly meant to silence any protest that washing a fellow-Christian's feet is beneath one's dignity. The addition, '**nor a messenger than the one who sent him**' makes the same point, but leads on to a further illustration of the relationship between Jesus and his disciples. It was an old principle that a messenger is equivalent in dignity to him who sent him: to maltreat an ambassador is to dishonour a foreign power, to welcome him is to welcome him whom he represents. Here (as in Matthew 10.40) the analogy is applied to the followers of Jesus who (as will soon be shown) are "sent" by Jesus, just as Jesus was "sent" by his Father.

'**Now the Son of Man is glorified**'. For some time the reader has been 31
prepared for a fulfilment of this saying in a more subtle sense than was suggested by the conventional picture of an individual who, after a period of obscurity, was to be manifest to all, clothed in the visible glory of God. The moment of Jesus' final rejection and deepest humiliation was to be the moment

when in fact this "glorification" would take place, since the crucifixion itself, followed immediately by the resurrection and by the emergence of a church endued with the Spirit, was that which would enable all men to come to God through him. Once again, there is an important proviso: this "glory" attaching to the Son of Man was not intended for his own glorification in competition with God. It must always be remembered that '**in him God is glorified**'.

34 '**Where I am going you cannot come.**' To Jesus' adversaries this had
been a riddle they were unable to answer (7.33–6). They were unable to
understand the sense in which Jesus belonged to another world. But even
for his disciples the saying caused difficulties. It was natural for them to think
that Jesus' progress towards glorification was one on which they would be
privileged to accompany him. A period of separation from him, even if
temporary, was hard to understand. A full explanation was about to be given;
37 but another false answer had to be disposed of first. Peter said, '**Lord . . . I
will lay down my life for you.**' Hints have already been given that Jesus'
departure would involve him in "laying down his life" for others. Why
should not his disciples do the same? The short answer to this was that they
simply were not capable of it. Peter was in fact to deny Jesus (all the gospels
record this prediction, though in somewhat different contexts). No, they
would have to be separated from Jesus. The followers would be left without
their master. What would hold them together then, and how would their
34 allegiance be known? The answer lay in a '**new commandment**' (new, at
least, in the narrative of this gospel, and new in the radical interpretation
Jesus was to put upon it): '**love one another**'.

14. 1 '**Set your troubled hearts at rest. Trust in God always**'. This is the
traditional language of faith: it is the spirituality of many of the psalms in the
Old Testament. But Jesus goes on, '**trust also in me**'. Jesus himself is a
decisive new factor in a man's faith in God. He affects even one's belief in
2 life after death. '**There are many dwelling-places in my Father's
house**'—this much was agreed by most people: the usual picture of the
after-life was of a number of different "places" to which people would be
allotted depending on the virtues or vices they had shown during their life
on earth. But faith in Christ introduced a new element into this picture. The
"place" of Christians would be such that after death they would certainly
be with Christ. As Paul expressed it, 'the Lord himself will descend from
heaven; first the Christian dead will rise, then we who are alive shall join
them, caught up in clouds to meet the Lord in the air. Thus we shall always
be with the Lord' (1 Thessalonians 4.16–17). The formulation in John is
3 more abstract, but expresses the same truth: '**I shall come again and
receive you to myself, so that where I am you may be also**'. What then
must a Christian do to be sure of coming to that "place"? What was his
"way" to get there? One of the disciples, Thomas, is made to ask this

question in a crudely literal form, as if a knowledge of the geography of
heaven were necessary in order to be sure of finding oneself in the right part
of it. Jesus characteristically seizes on this to give a new twist to the metaphor: **'I am the way'.** Solidarity with Jesus here and now is the guarantee 6
of being with him hereafter.

'Lord, show us the Father and we ask no more.' The request was 8
natural: instead of constantly straining to glimpse and understand how God
was brought near to them by Jesus, the disciples yearned for a direct vision
of the Father. But the request only showed how little they had grasped of
what Jesus was. In him, they had seen and known as much of God as man is
capable of knowing in this world. Jesus' **words** and **deeds** constituted the 10, 11
final **evidence** on which a man must base his faith in God. This was to be
true, not only during Jesus' visible presence on earth, but in the subsequent
life of the church. The authority of Jesus' words and deeds was due to his
closeness to his Father: **'it is the Father who dwells in me doing his own** 10
work'. But Christians, through their faith in Christ, would be equally close.
Through prayer, they could do things at least as great as Jesus had done,
which would have the same effect of bringing men to God, **'so that the** 13
Father may be glorified in the Son'.

'Your Advocate'. When (according to the traditional picture) men came 16
before the judgement seat of God, they would find themselves facing formidable charges. Sins which they had forgotten would be brought against them; and the devil would be there, seeking to make them appear in the worst possible light. But there would be certain things on the other side. Good deeds they had committed might speak in their favour, and outweigh all contrary evidence. To borrow a technical term from Jewish legal procedure: they would find that they had a *paraclete*, an advocate (the original word *paraklētos* was Greek, but it had been taken over into Jesus' own language, Aramaic, in the form *paraclete*). In a Jewish court, a plaintiff or a defendant was entitled to enlist the help, not only of witnesses to the facts, but of a person of high standing who might give him personal support before the judge and, by his intervention, make the case appear in a more favourable light. This was not "advocacy" in the western, professional sense: the paraclete influenced the judge's decision, not by his knowledge of the law (for this was the judge's business) but by the weight of his personal authority as a man enjoying the esteem of society. Nevertheless, the nearest word in English is probably "advocate", so long as this is understood in a non-professional sense.

In Jewish writing, the most common metaphorical use of the term *paraclete* was in the context of God's final judgement upon men. The Jews believed that when they came before God they would find they had an Advocate in such things as their own good deeds and the merits of their ancestors. But in John, language that was conventionally used of the Last

Judgement is frequently applied to the present; and it is clear that in this passage Christians are promised an Advocate, not only when they come before God after death, but from the very moment that Jesus has left them. Given that John (alone of the New Testament writers) is using this title for the Holy Spirit, it is not too difficult to see why. Christians had been promised that, when they found themselves on trial for their faith, the Spirit would prompt them with the right words for their defence (Mark 13.11): in this sense, the Spirit was already their **Advocate.** Moreover, John is about to make Jesus depict the present confrontation between Christianity and the world as a trial, in the course of which the Spirit plays its part as the Christians' **Advocate.** But neither of these explanations fully accounts for all the things said of the **Advocate** here—that it will be **the Spirit of Truth,**
26 that it **dwells with you,** that it will **teach you everything,** and **will call**
to mind all that I have told you. It is just possible that John saw a further possibility in the metaphor of a *paraclete.* A man of standing who took up a friend's cause before a judge and obtained favourable terms for him would then find himself in the position of reporting back to his friend and having to persuade him to accept the judgement of the court. He would be in the position of a go-between, interpreting the law, as propounded by authoritative judges, to the individual whose interests were affected. In this rôle, he perhaps furnished to John (or to whatever Christian had previously used this title for the Holy Spirit) an illustration of that continuing relationship between Christ and his followers which is one of the principal themes of
15 these *Farewell discourses.* **'If you love me you will obey my commands'.**
This had been the principle of Jesus' relationship with his disciples from the beginning. His '**commands**' were simply the will of the Father; like an "advocate", he had been commending these commands to them all the
16 time he was with them. When he left them, there would be '**another to be**
26 **your Advocate'** [a] to continue the same work: he would **teach you every-**
thing. In this sense (though only in this rather technical sense) it is possible to understand a different translation of the word *paraklētos* which was adopted by Greek commentators some centuries after John's time and which found its way into most older English versions: "Comforter". The Advocate "comforts" the individual by explaining and so far as possible lightening the judicial "commands" by which the individual is bound. In some such way as this, the lives of Christians would continue to be quite different even after Jesus' departure. Here was one way of realizing the fulfilment of Jesus'
18 promise, **'I will not leave you bereft; I am coming back to you.'**
22 **Judas asked him.** Throughout this chapter, the discourse is kept going by questions from different disciples in turn. A Judas, other than Iscariot, is

[*a*] The Greek means literally "another advocate". There was a sense in which Jesus himself had been, and continued to be, the Christians' "advocate", and the word is actually used of him in 1 John 2.1.

known only from the list in Luke (6.16). **'Lord, what can have happened, that you mean to disclose yourself to us alone and not to the world?'** This was indeed the greatest reversal of their presuppositions which the disciples had to face. They could perhaps understand how it was that the person of Jesus, during his time on earth, presented a humble appearance and provoked indifference or rejection instead of eliciting universal homage. But this period, Jesus had said again and again, was merely a prelude to his "glorification". Their whole notion of a Messiah was of a figure who would finally dispel the doubts and ambiguities of religious faith and present all men with a decisive manifestation of the power of God and the vindication of the righteous. But Jesus' words seemed to suggest a further period—even after his glorification—when things would not be so plain, and when faith still would not have given place to sight. And indeed, after the resurrection, the church found itself with the task of explaining why, since Christ was now glorified and God's kingdom was a reality, the world seemed to be going on exactly as before, and the glory of God was still perceptible only to those who believed. The answer was that God was now present in a new and unique way in the church. The old concept of a glorious Messiah-king, establishing the rule of God by force, had to give place to that of a new relationship
between God and man: **'then my Father will love him, and we will** 23
come to him and make our dwelling with him'.

'Peace is my parting gift to you'. Semitic peoples (and not only they) 27
have always "given peace" to one another at greeting or parting. Jesus' parting from his disciples was not to be an ordinary human one, since he would soon be present with them again. This **peace**, too, was more than a mere word. The disciples would have real peace, **'peace, such as the world cannot give'.**

'Up, let us go forward!' Almost exactly the same words occur in Mark 31
and Matthew just before the arrival of the party sent to arrest Jesus in the garden of Gethsemane. Taken in the same sense here, they suggest that Jesus has done with talking and now resolves to go to meet his fate. This is in fact what happens—but only three chapters later. It is tempting to think that something may have gone wrong with John's text, and that these words appear in the wrong place.[a] Nevertheless, this apparent anomaly is not uncharacteristic of John. In the first place, it is in his manner to add a passage amplifying what Jesus has just said, even though the scene itself has come to an end (compare the concluding paragraph of chapter 3). In the second place, the literal meaning of Jesus' words is often no more than a decoy: the real meaning lies below the surface. Here perhaps a further explanation is being given for the course of Jesus' passion. It was not that the devil was in command, but that Jesus had to show his obedience. He would do so in

[*a*] It is possible to understand the whole sentence in more than one way: see the footnote in NEB. But this does not greatly affect the question.

action a little later: meanwhile, on the spiritual level, his words show that he was prepared for whatever might come.

15. 1 **'I am the real vine'.** Vines grow slowly. In a vineyard in Palestine it was three years before any grapes could be gathered from new plants. They needed constant training and pruning. And any damage done to them could destroy in an hour the patient labour of years. Tending vines (the occupation of countless Palestinian farmers) naturally suggested itself as an illustration of the care with which God tended his people (Jeremiah 2.21; Isaiah 5), and the sudden destruction of a vine was a poignant image for national calamities (Psalm 80.8–16; Ezekiel 19.10–14). It was characteristic of Jesus to use such a familiar example in his own teaching. The other gospels preserve a parable about a vineyard (Mark 12.1–9); but it is only here that anything is made of the actual technique of vine-growing.

The solidarity of Jesus with his disciples (which is the main theme of these chapters) could be expressed as that of the stem with the vine-branches. But everyone knew that there was more to it than just letting the vine grow. Not all the branches would survive: there must be constant tending and pruning. The metaphor was easy to apply. A ruthless politician, for example, could be said to do some "pruning" in the state. So, among Jesus' disciples, God (who is **the gardener**) would do some rigorous selection and training.

But "pruning" really involved two processes: breaking unwanted shoots off the branches, and tending the shoots which remained. This made it possible to use the metaphor in two ways. Some disciples would forfeit their solidarity with Jesus and be pruned off altogether. This would amount to total rejection, for which the reward was loss of all possibility of new life:
6 **'The withered branches are heaped together, thrown on the fire, and burnt'**—a sentence which has more than an echo of the traditional language used of the Last Judgement (and John again and again shows that he understands this Last Judgement as a thing of the present: it is what a man brings upon himself by his attitude to Jesus). Those disciples, on the other hand, who maintained their solidarity with Jesus still needed that further tending which is here called "cleaning" or "cleansing". Precisely what this means is obscured by the fact that the discourse is on two levels. In its context it is addressed to the disciples, who in some sense (though in what sense is not
3 quite clear, either here or in the previous reference, 13.10) had **'already been cleansed'.** But on another level it is addressed to the subsequent church, whose members would certainly need "cleansing", both when they entered it (by baptism) and doubtless thereafter (in a more metaphorical sense). The essential thing, in any case, was the solidarity; and the essence of this solidarity was love and obedience. Given this, Christians would be so much at one with Christ and God that prayer would be answered and the

remaining term of the vine-image would be fulfilled: they would **bear** 8
fruit.

The inspiration for such love could only be the example of Christ himself.
'Love one another, as I have loved you'. And this in turn was inspired 12
by God: **'As the Father has loved me, so I have loved you'**. What such 9
love involved has been illustrated already by the washing of the disciples'
feet: it is about to be seen to its full extent in Jesus' own death. **'There is no** 13
greater love than this, that a man should lay down his life for his friends.' As a general proposition, most people might have agreed with this. But friendship was usually defined in terms of mutual advantage. In what sense could it be said that Jesus had **friends**? The answer could lie only in a new definition of friendship. Jesus had no common interest with his disciples, he did not stand to gain anything by their friendship. He was their master, and it would have been natural to think of them as his pupils or his servants. But now he called them his friends, for no other reason than that he had chosen them to be his friends, and had loved them to 'the full extent of his love' (13.1). Love, friendship—these words took on a new meaning in the light of Jesus' relationship with his disciples. All this was implied in
Jesus' reiterated commandment: **'love one another'**. 17

"A servant is not greater than his master." In 13.16 this saying was 20
put to a new use. Here, it is given the meaning it has in the other gospels: persecution will come as much to the one as to the other. But persecution was never regarded in the early church as an avoidable evil, something which might just blow over. Many Christians saw it in terms which they had inherited from the Jewish way of looking at world history: it was a part of that necessary intensification of evil which would be the prelude to the Last Judgement. But there was also another way of looking at it. Just as the world, far from spontaneously acknowledging Jesus, treated him with such indifference or animosity that it could be said to have actually **hated** him, so it 24
would hate his followers. The manner of his continuing presence among them would provoke exactly the same hostile reaction as he had provoked
during his time on earth. **'If I had not come and spoken to them . . . If I** 22, 24
had not worked among them'. Jesus' words and works were the ultimate criterion: to reject them was to be **guilty of sin.** In view of what was soon to happen, "hatred" of Jesus and the Father was not too strong a word for their attitude; it was also a word used in a psalm which was found again and
again to have been fulfilled in the events of Jesus' life and death: **"They** 25
hated me without reason" (Psalm 69.4). Yet not everyone hated: some believed. How did they come to believe? In Jesus' lifetime, they had been
persuaded by the **witness** of John the Baptist, and (in a certain sense) by the 26
witness of Jesus himself. Such witness would still be available when men were challenged to believe by the disciples. It would be one of the functions of the Spirit (which has already been described as the **Advocate** in 14.16) to

bear witness and to lend weight to the Christians' cause; and the disciples
themselves would be powerful **witnesses**, having been eyewitnesses of
27 Jesus' acts **from the first**.

The other gospels record detailed prophecies by Jesus of the persecutions
and tribulations which would be suffered by the church. John gives only
16. 2 two: **'They will ban you from the synagogue'**—a stiffening of the Jewish
attitude towards Christians which we know to have taken place within a few
decades of Jesus' resurrection; and, **'anyone who kills you will suppose
that he is performing a religious duty'**—again, the Jews did believe that
in certain circumstances it was a religious duty to punish blasphemy with
death, and in due course they certainly came to regard Christians as blas-
phemers. These were the dangers which lay before any Jews who became
Christians. We can glimpse (in the very narrow range of these prophecies
compared with those in the other gospels) the specific readership for which
John's gospel was written: Greek-speaking Christians of Jewish origin,
exposed to hostile pressure from the Jewish communities in the cities where
they lived. The persecution they would be exposed to, like other kinds of
persecution which would fall upon other parts of the church, was all part of
a picture which had been carefully painted by Jesus. To know this was to
1 be guarded against **the breakdown** of one's faith.

6 **'You are plunged into grief because of what I have told you'**. On
the human level, the prospect of Jesus' departure from the disciples on the
eve of this period of troubles was daunting. But in the future, what the followers of Jesus would need most was the conviction that, through all their
vicissitudes, they were in the right and had the truth on their side. Persecution is intolerable if you are not sure of that for which you are being persecuted. This would never happen to Christians because of the reality of
their experience of the Spirit among them. This Spirit, in these discourses,
7 is called the **Advocate**; and the scene of its action is again imagined as a
law-court. Each encounter between the world and the church is like that of
two opposing parties before a judge. The world sets out to show (i) that the
Christians have sinned (done wrong) in adopting their new faith (which,
from the Jewish point of view, involved the blasphemy of using divine titles
of Jesus); (ii) that they cannot be in the right after pinning their faith to one
who ended his life on the cross; and (iii) that Jesus' death itself, secured according to the principles of the Jewish faith, was a clear instance of the proper
course of divine justice. The appearance of the **Advocate** on the Christians'
9 side completely turns the tables on the accusers. (i) **'He will convict them
of wrong'**, in that, by being clearly on the side of the Christians in all they do,
he will show that their faith has been vindicated, and that it is their enemies'
10 refusal to believe which is **wrong**; (ii) **'He will convince them that right
is on my side'**, since he will strengthen and validate the Christians' faith
that Jesus, by his resurrection and glorification, has been shown to be in the

right despite the cross; and (iii) '**he will convince them of divine judge-** 11
ment' by showing that what they took to be the condemnation of Jesus was in reality the condemnation of the devil, **the Prince of this world.** All this fits easily enough into the conventional picture of the Last Judgement. When all the world comes before God to be judged, Christians will certainly have an Advocate who will give decisive evidence in their favour. But this Advocate (in John's presentation of Jesus' teaching) is none other than the Holy Spirit who is present even now in the church. As so often in this gospel, 'now is the hour of judgement for this world' (12.31). The Advocate at the Last Judgement, and the Spirit which is on the Christians' side today, are one and the same.

'**There is still much that I could say to you**'. All the gospels report 12
that Jesus gave his disciples some teaching about the conditions under which they would find themselves exercising their discipleship (conditions, it is explained in John, which were only the logical sequel of those under which Jesus himself made his appearance among men). In Matthew, Mark and Luke, these conditions are interpreted in terms of traditional Jewish expectation: their meaning was to be found in the fact that they formed a part of that great drama of inevitable sufferings which would be the prelude and earnest of the imminent end of the world. Given this traditional picture, it was not difficult to fill in the details of the kind of tribulations which the righteous were to endure. In John, this traditional view of the future is taken less for granted, and it is suggested that Jesus, instead of giving his disciples the conventional blueprint, as it were, of what was in store for them, forbore to overwhelm them with predictions of their sufferings ('**the burden would be too great for you now**'), but promised instead that
they would receive enlightenment when the time came from the **Spirit of** 13
truth. 'He will make known to you the things that are coming'. One of the ways in which the church actually experienced the Holy Spirit was as a spirit of prophecy, speaking through individual Christians and predicting events that were about to happen. But we need not suppose that it is only this literal kind of prophecy which is meant here. The essential thing for Christians was to know, not exactly what was about to happen, but the meaning of what was actually happening (which was in fact the main function of Old Testament prophecy). Jesus gave a certain amount of teaching on the subject. But the Spirit was to bring the same prophetic understanding of events into every situation that would be encountered by the church.

In all this, the phenomenon to be described was the continuing experience of the church that, after Jesus' death, they were nevertheless not bereft. For this purpose, it was necessary to use three apparently personal and distinct terms: Father, Son, and Spirit (or Advocate). This might seem a dangerous way of talking, as if there were more than one separate deity involved. Did

Christianity, after all, ask for a belief in many gods? Did it ask Jews to abandon their fundamental doctrine of the one true God? The answer to these fears was to be found in the intimate relationship between the three; and a
13–15 few words are added here to show how tightly the circle is drawn which includes Father, Son and Spirit.

16 **'A little while'.** Any reader of the gospel who knew what was about to
happen could see one obvious meaning of this pregnant little phrase. In "a
little while" Jesus would be arrested, tried and executed; and "a little
while" after that he would rise from the dead. We read in the other gospels
that Jesus predicted his death and his resurrection on the third day (see
above on Mark 9.9), and that his predictions were simply not understood by
18 the disciples. On the face of it, this is exactly the situation here. **'What
is this "little while" that he speaks of? We do not know what he
means'.**

But this "little while" was also a standard phrase in the vocabulary of any Jewish teacher who professed to have an insight into the future. If you believed (as most Jews did, and as Christians certainly did to an intense degree) that world history was tending towards a climax, and that God was about to act, then at any moment when faith in this cosmic dénouement seemed to be slackening, you would recall your hearers or your readers to a proper pitch of expectation by reminding them that all this must surely come to pass "in a little while". The phrase is in the Hebrew prophets, it is in the Christian book called the Revelation (6.11). Jesus, in this part of his discourse, had been saying something about what the future had in store for his followers. This **"little while"** was just what might have been expected: a cryptic reference to the period before the End, when history would at last be hastening towards its consummation. Teaching of this kind about the pattern of the future necessarily sounded cryptic to outsiders. But the intimate followers of such a teacher would expect to be let into the secret meaning. They would hardly remain content to say, **'We do not know what he means'.**

Nor is this the only hint that the paragraph is cast in the mould of traditional esoteric teaching about the imminent crisis of history. It was commonly accepted (at least within certain circles of Jewish teachers) that the period before the end would be one of intensified violence and tribulation: the joys of the age to come would be heralded by unprecedented sufferings. To describe this period, one of the metaphors which suggested itself was that of a woman giving birth to her first child: the suffering would be such as she had never suffered before, but it would be short-lived, and the memory of it would be swallowed up in the joy which followed it. The metaphor had been worked out already in Isaiah 26.16–18, a passage which has many echoes in this chapter of John; and in the time of Jesus (or at least very soon after)

the 'birth-pangs of the new age' (Mark 13.8) was almost a technical expression for the last period of world history. When, therefore, Jesus, in the context of his teaching about the future, elaborated the metaphor of '**a woman** 21
in labour', and then described a state of affairs in which his disciples would 23
be so close to God that their prayers would be certain of an answer (one of the standard blessings in the age to come), there can be little doubt where
these '**figures of speech**' came from. Jesus, here as in the other gospels, was 25
making use of the traditional repertory of those who claimed to have insight into the coming last days of the world and the new age which was to follow them.

But in John's gospel, when Jesus uses language of this kind, it tends to bear a radically original meaning. What his contemporaries described as belonging to a world of the future, Jesus showed to be realities belonging to a kind of life which men may experience here and now. The whole of this section plays upon new meanings of the old language: both the "little while" of apparent dereliction, and the joy of communion, are simultaneous experiences in the life of the Christian. This actualization of traditional hopes becomes explicit towards the end of the section. According to the traditional scheme, one of the conditions of living in the time before the end was having to be content with partial vision, partial understanding. The signs of the times were puzzling and ambiguous, one got no nearer the truth than **figures of speech**. But when the end came the veil would be lifted, the obscurities would be removed. As Paul puts it, 'Now we see only puzzling reflections in a mirror, but then we shall see face to face' (1 Corinthians 13.12). Figures of speech would give place to **plain words**, the truth would be known, no longer through anxious questioning and dimly understood answer, but by direct communication. Jesus had already talked many times about "going to the Father", but had never been understood, even by his own followers. Now, suddenly, they grasped what he meant, and the truth seemed to burst in upon them. It was as if the perfection of knowledge and clarity of vision which they believed they would have only in heaven was available to them
here and now. '**Why, this is plain speaking; this is no figure of speech.**' 29
Here was an earnest of what Jesus had promised: an experience hitherto conceived as only possible in an imagined future was already breaking into the present.

Jesus answered, 'Do you now believe?' In the Bible, this period of 31
"trouble" for the righteous was an element common to all inspired prophecies about the future. Nothing Jesus had said must be interpreted as if his followers would be spared this trouble. He was still exhorting them to bear it. But traditionally, every exhortation to bear trouble steadfastly was based on the promise of ultimate victory: in "a little while", those who now were oppressed and persecuted would conquer. The new factor in Jesus' exhortation was that he did not have to leave his followers with a mere promise. The

victory had already been won. That which made the trouble worth bearing
33 was already possessed. **'The victory is mine; I have conquered the
world.'**

17. 1 **After these words Jesus looked up to heaven.** It is easy enough to imagine
Jesus concluding this long discourse to his disciples with an act of prayer.
Equally, it is easy to imagine that when John came to arrange and reformulate
the teaching of Jesus he should have thought it appropriate to round it off
with a prayer. In fact, however, this final address of Jesus to his heavenly
Father includes rather more than we normally look for in a "prayer". It
expresses, certainly, the perfect resolution of Jesus to undergo his destiny—
a resolution which had seemed to falter for a moment on a previous occasion
(12.27); and it contains a number of petitions for the welfare of his followers
15 (including what appears to be an allusion to the Lord's Prayer: **'keep them
from the evil one'**). But it also consists (particularly in its opening phrases)
of a solemn summary of what has been said earlier about the nature of Jesus
19 and the faith of his disciples; and with the words, **'I now consecrate
myself'**, it marks the actual moment when Jesus might be said to have
committed himself irrevocably to his act of sacrifice **'for their sake'**. All
this is not quite "prayer" in the sense the word bears today. On the other
hand, it falls well within the function which a prayer was deemed to have in
antiquity, that is, not only supplicating and praising God, but defining carefully those beliefs about God and man which justify us in attempting to
pray at all.

1 **'Glorify thy Son'**. That Jesus' "glorification" was to take place on the
cross is a paradox which has already been hinted at more than once. But here
2 it is related to an image more characteristic of the other gospels: **'For thou
hast made him sovereign over all mankind'**. Jesus was the Son of
Man; and it was prophesied of this Son of Man that he would be installed at
the right hand of God, and that all mankind would be made subject to him.
Eternal life, which elsewhere in this gospel is usually defined in terms of
believing in Jesus Christ, is here described as a matter of "knowing" God
and Christ. To put these ideas together: the Christian is one who "knows"
that the humble Son of Man who was crucified is now sovereign, that the
crucifixion was in reality Jesus' glorification, that to recognize Jesus' glory
is to see God's glory and to enter upon that new quality of living which can
4 be called eternal life. Jesus' **work** on earth has had the purpose of making all
this credible. But it is something which has always been true. This glory of
Jesus, which Christians come to understand through his life and death, has
5 in fact existed (as the very first words of the gospel proclaim) since **before
the world began.**

The main part of the prayer is for the disciples. They have just reached a
8 decisive point in their apprenticeship: **'they have had faith to believe**

that thou didst send me'. They are now to continue in the world in something of the same conditions under which Jesus himself taught and lived, that
is, with the same sense of belonging to two worlds, of being **strangers in** 16
the world. The inherent ambiguity of this relationship with the world sets the tone for the prayer which Jesus now makes for them.

He prays first for their safety. This is not just a matter of physical security: the stakes are higher than that. They must be protected, not so much from the danger of suffering and death, as from the danger of being forced by
these things to renounce their faith and forfeit their new life. '**Protect by** 11
the power of thy name those whom thou hast given me'. God's **name** was an expression used in the Old Testament to describe the fact that God was believed to be present to a particular degree in a particular place: God made his **name** dwell in the temple of Jerusalem. Jesus' presence among his disciples was equivalent to this "power of the name", this presence of God on earth; and Jesus prays that the disciples may continue to have this power[a] to protect them from disaster. If it were objected that Jesus' presence did not in fact protect Judas from his fate, the answer was that Judas was a
special case; he was **the man who must be lost,** a traditional phrase for 12
one who, in the current mythology about the future, would appear as a kind of personification of wickedness (2 Thessalonians 2.3); and his special rôle had been amply foretold by **Scripture** (13.18).

Secondly, Jesus prays that **they may be one.** For Christianity, as for any 22
religious movement, unity among its adherents was of course essential for its survival (and indeed, by the time John wrote, the church had been exposed to serious threats to its unity). Jesus' prayer doubtless embraces this functional unity; but it also envisages something more fundamental. The intense solidarity between Jesus and his disciples has already been expounded. Here
it is developed still further: '**as thou, Father, art in me, and I in thee, so** 21
also may they be in us'. The implication of this relationship between men and God is a new unity among men themselves; and this is to be embodied,
not only in the original disciples, but in subsequent generations of Christians. 20
(Jesus may or may not have foreseen such a long history for his followers; but John already knew at least several generations of them.)

Thirdly, Jesus prays that they may be **consecrated by the truth.** The 19
metaphor belongs to temples and sanctuaries. A priest consecrates himself by separating himself from the ordinary concerns and squalor of the world, in order to make himself a fit person to draw near to the presence of God in ritual and service. The metaphor can of course be refined and spiritualized: consecrating oneself need mean no more than simply committing oneself wholeheartedly to a particular task or form of service. But there is always in

[a] However, the "name" does not necessarily imply power. It might also mean simply the common name shared by all who have a common loyalty. Hence the alternative translation offered in the NEB footnote.

it a hint of separation: consecration implies freeing oneself from certain things in order to be fully available for something else. In this sense, it was an appropriate word for the disciples who, for the sake of Christ, had become
14 **strangers in the world.** But again, their solidarity with Christ implied that they would share something of his consecration, a consecration which amounted to utter self-sacrifice.

The whole of the discourse has been exploring the manner in which Jesus would continue to be present with his disciples after the crucifixion and resurrection. Something of heaven, he has been saying, would attend their life on earth. But one could put it the other way round. It was not only that life in this world would be transformed by influences from another world: human beings, while still in this world, could have an experience of heaven. This was the climax of the possibilities of Christian discipleship, and the
24 final subject of Jesus' great prayer for his followers: **'I desire that these men . . . may be with me where I am, so that they may look upon my glory'.**

The final conflict

This is the heading given by the translators to the last section of all four gospels; and indeed at this point the gospel according to John, which up to now has followed a strikingly different pattern from the others, suddenly begins to run closely parallel to them. The differences no longer lie in the grand design, but in the details.

18. 1 **After these words, Jesus went out with his disciples, and crossed the Kedron ravine.** The name occurs nowhere else in the New Testament; but we know exactly what it stands for: it is the deep river-bed (or *wady*) which separates the hill on which Jerusalem was built from the range of higher hills to the east which includes the Mount of Olives. John tells us, therefore, which side of the city Jesus came out of, and when he goes on to say that **there was a garden there,** it is obvious that he means the place which appears in the other gospels as Gethsemane, on the slopes of the
2 Mount of Olives. The detail (also hinted at in Luke 22.39) that Jesus **had often met there with his disciples** casts Judas in a clear rôle: he was able to pass on information to Jesus' enemies on which they could act. But this, according to John, was the full extent of his treachery. His traitor's kiss is not mentioned: there was no need to identify Jesus, for Jesus immediately identified himself, causing some consternation to his captors. Whether or not they originally intended to arrest Jesus' followers as well (a possibility John leaves open), Jesus insisted that they should let them go, and in so doing gave, as it were, a literal demonstration of the truth of a promise he had made earlier in general terms (6.39), **'I have not lost one of those**

whom thou gavest me'. There is no question in this account of the disciples running away.

Jesus' captors are described as a **detachment of soldiers, and police** 3
provided by the chief priests and the Pharisees. In the other gospels it is clear that they were sent by the Sanhedrin. John's description is less precise. The chief priests *ex officio*, and the Pharisaic party in fact, each formed an influential section of the Sanhedrin, and John doubtless meant the **police** to be understood as coming from that authority. But what about the **detachment of soldiers**? In the Greek, this is the correct term for a Roman cohort, and means a force of several hundred men. Apart from the fact that such a large detachment seems quite inappropriate, it is a surprise to find Roman soldiers involved at this stage. John may have known, independently of the other gospels, that Roman soldiers were in fact present, or he may perhaps have wished to tell the story of Jesus' arrest, trial and execution in such a way as would seem to implicate the Roman administration right from the start. Alternatively, just as in Mark 6.21 the senior officers in Herod's private army could be called 'commanders' (which, in Greek, was the correct title for a tribune in the Roman army), so John may have been using military
language rather loosely, and have meant, both by this phrase and by **the** 12
troops with their commander in verse 12, nothing more than a mixed
force of Jewish armed men. At any rate, the brief scuffle took place just the
same. John gives the names of both the disciple and the slave, and in Jesus'
rebuke—'**This is the cup the Father has given me**'—makes a suggestive 11
allusion to the scene of Jesus at prayer in the garden (Mark 14.36), which he may have known about even though he has omitted it from his own narrative.

They took him first to Annas. This is a significant departure from the 13
account in the other gospels. Matthew and Mark report that Jesus was immediately brought before a meeting specially convened during the night; Luke describes Jesus being held prisoner in Caiaphas' house until dawn. John introduces a new element altogether with the mention of Annas. Annas had been deposed from the office of High Priest, which he had held for ten years, in A.D. 15, but he remained a person of influence, for apart from his son-in-law Caiaphas, who was high priest from A.D. 18 to 36, five of his sons also held the office, and it is not in itself unlikely that he was behind Jesus' arrest and was given an opportunity to conduct the first examination. John, however, combines this new piece of tradition with one that he shares with all the other gospels: the story of Peter's denial. Here too he has a fresh piece of information to give. Peter's presence in the courtyard was made possible by
a disciple **who was acquainted with the High Priest.** We are not told who 15
this was; and the fact that Jesus' following included people with connections of this kind is new to us. It does not look, therefore, as if John was simply rewriting the story from a version like that in Mark. He seems to have had

an independent source of information which allowed him to identify some of the characters in the scene.

19 **The High Priest questioned Jesus about his disciples and about
what he taught.** This suggests, not formal legal proceedings, but an informal interrogation. To the High Priest's questions, Jesus replied (as in the
other gospels he replied to his captors in the garden) that after all his public
20 teaching **in synagogue and in the temple** such a procedure was pointless.
John gives no further details; he is hastening on to a new issue altogether,
that between Jesus and the Roman governor. He pauses only to finish off
the story of Peter, and to give his own very mild and attenuated version
(which hinges on Exodus 22.28 "You shall not revile God, nor curse a ruler
of your people") of the insults suffered by Jesus at the hands of the Jewish
authorities. Here it is no more than a single blow struck by an officer; and
23 Jesus replies by insisting upon the conditions of a fair trial: **'If I spoke
amiss, state it in evidence'.**

24 **So Annas sent him bound to Caiaphas the High Priest.** John has
13 already said that Caiaphas, Annas' son-in-law, was **the High Priest for that
year.** This is correct, in so far as Caiaphas was certainly High Priest at the
time, but misleading in that it suggests that the office was held for one year
only—Caiaphas held it for 18 years. Possibly John was confused by the fact
that a number of high priests did in fact hold office for not more than a year
in the first half of the century. A further complication is that Annas, though
no longer in office as High Priest, was still a member of the class of
"High Priests", and therefore a person of great influence. John is therefore
15 correct, though a little confusing, in referring to him too as **the High
Priest.**

28 **From Caiaphas Jesus was led into the Governor's headquarters.** All
the other gospels give some account of a session of a Jewish court, presided over by Caiaphas the High Priest; during this session, Jesus made a statement which the court judged to be blasphemous and punishable by death. Whether or not such a session actually took place, John makes no mention of it here. He has already recorded (10.22–39) an occasion when Jesus was heard committing blasphemy (as they thought) by the Jewish authorities. Even if John knew that a similar scene took place in the presence of Caiaphas, he had no need to delay his readers by repeating the details here. It was clearly the trial before the Roman authorities to which he wished to give the greatest emphasis in this chapter; and his account of it is a great deal fuller than that of the other gospels.

The trial scene itself is also conceived somewhat differently. Instead of hearing the case of accusers and accused together, Pilate has Jesus held prisoner inside his headquarters, but interviews the Jews outside, so that the prosecution and the defence are heard in different places, and Pilate, as

judge, moves in and out from one to the other. John provides a reason for
this: **the Jews themselves stayed outside the headquarters to avoid** 28
defilement, so that they could eat the Passover meal. From an anti-
quarian point of view, this was probably (though not certainly) correct: the
Jews who celebrated the Passover at Jerusalem, and in particular the priests
who had ceremonial duties to attend to during the afternoon, were obliged
to make themselves ritually "clean" beforehand; and the houses of Gentiles
were regarded as places of possible ritual contamination (there was the
danger, for instance, that there might be a grave underneath, which would
make a Jew ritually "unclean" for a week). To this extent, the reason John
gives for their remaining outside is plausible, though a little recondite. A
more obvious reason would have been that it was customary for a Roman
magistrate to set up his tribunal in a public place, and not inside his house,
and what really needed explaining was, not that the Jews remained outside,
but that Jesus was brought inside. However, the significance of the statement (certainly for us, and probably also for John) is that it clearly dates the
Passover festival to the evening following the crucifixion,[a] whereas the other
gospels equally clearly place it on the evening before. The day of the week
is the same in all accounts: Jesus was crucified on a Friday. But according to
the first three gospels, Friday that year fell on 15th Nisan, the day after the
celebration of the Passover meal, and Jesus' last supper was in fact a Passover
celebration. According to John, on the other hand, the feast fell a day later
that year, and Jesus hung on the cross while the lambs for the feast were
being sacrificed at the temple. Both cannot be right, and a choice has to be
made between them. But each, in its different way, exploits the fact that it
was the season of Passover, in order to set the last events of Jesus' life against
the background of a Jewish religious festival.

It was the duty of the Roman governor to hear charges laid against his
subjects, to check their accuracy, and to decide on the action to be taken
under Roman law. Pilate's first question to the Jews was the normal opening
of this procedure: **'What charge do you bring against this man?'** But 29
their answer was curiously evasive. **'If he were not a criminal', they** 30
replied, 'we should not have brought him before you.' It is not clear
how John means us to understand this; but the fact that they did not immediately bring forward a charge apparently made Pilate assume that the
matter was a technical one of Jewish law which the Jews were not disposed to
explain to him and on which, in any case, he could not be expected to give a
ruling (this, at any rate, was the reaction of the Roman governor of Corinth
on a similar occasion, Acts 18.14–15). But the Jews replied to this that, even
if it was a technical matter of their own law, it was a capital case, and they

[*a*] If the translation given in the footnote were correct, this inconsistency would disappear, since the "Passover season" lasted for a week. But it is very doubtful whether the Greek words can bear this meaning.

31 had no competence to carry out the death penalty. **'We are not allowed to
put any man to death.'**

This statement provides, almost casually, the answer to the main problem posed by the gospel accounts of Jesus' trial and death. Jesus was crucified, a form of execution carried out only by the Romans; but the blame for his condemnation is placed by all the evangelists, not on the Romans, but on the Jews. How were these two facts to be reconciled? The solution offered is that it was indeed the Jews who found Jesus guilty of blasphemy; but that they prevailed upon the Roman authorities, in the person of Pilate, to carry out the execution. And the clue to this surprising procedure is provided by a chance remark made in John's narrative (and nowhere else in any of the gospels) that, at this time, the Jews themselves did not have the power to carry out the death penalty. That this was true is at least probable: we have no decisive evidence, but it is consistent with what we know of the Roman administration of the provinces of the empire. But it has to be admitted that this is the one single reference in the New Testament to a fact which is of critical importance to understanding the trial and execution of Jesus. John
underlines the significance of the fact in his own way. That Jesus was
32 crucified was not merely the result of historical circumstances: it was the
only form of execution which would have been consistent with what Jesus himself had said about the symbolism of his death (12.32). If the Jews had executed him, they would have done it by stoning, and this could never have been described as a "lifting up". To those mysterious obstacles which prevented the Jews from summarily doing away with Jesus earlier (see above, p. 336) is now added a purely technical one: they were not allowed to by the Roman regulations.

We must assume that more passed in the conversation between Pilate and
the Jews than is actually recorded here, for when Pilate went inside to examine
33 the defendant he put to him a specific charge (**'Are you the king of the
Jews?'**) and admitted that the charge was one put forward by the Jews. In the accounts in the other gospels, Jesus' reply to the charge, though he never altogether denied it, was always marked by a certain reserve. Here the same reserve is expanded into a definition of the exact sense in which Jesus claimed
to be a king. This convinced Pilate that, if Jesus' kingship operated only with
38 abstractions such as **truth**, no action need be taken. He consequently
returned outside to inform the Jews of his decision. He also entertained the hope that he could at the same time exploit the situation by making his release of Jesus satisfy the Jews' customary demand for the release of one prisoner at Passover. But in this he was disappointed. Instead of being able to get away with releasing the harmless Jesus, he was forced to release one who was a **bandit**, that is, perhaps a member of one of the armed resistance groups which constantly harried the Roman occupying forces: Barabbas.

19. 1 **Pilate now took Jesus and had him flogged.** Events were still taking a

normal course according to Roman justice. The flogging was the Roman equivalent to "letting him off with a warning"; and the soldiers' mockery, and the public exhibition which followed, may have been a legitimate extension of it. But from this point the proceedings became more political than judicial. By Roman law Pilate had found Jesus innocent—indeed that no case had been made out against him at all. But by Jewish law (the chief
priests maintained) Jesus had been proved to have committed blasphemy ('he 7
has claimed to be Son of God') for which the penalty was death; and
Pilate was now being subjected to pressure to carry out the sentence of a
Jewish court which that court was not competent to carry out itself. At first
Pilate was merely impatient. '**Take him and crucify him yourselves,**' he
said sarcastically, knowing that they had no power even to stone him, let
alone to use the Roman method of crucifixion. But then the strength of the
Jewish agitation seems to have unnerved him; he became **more afraid than** 8
ever, and went inside for a further interview with Jesus, doubtless hoping to
discover at least some reason why the Jews were so anxious to see the death
sentence carried out. His question, '**Where have you come from?**' cer- 9
tainly sounded like the opening of a general interrogation. **But Jesus gave**
him no answer. This motif of Jesus' silence appears in all the gospel
accounts. Here it is made the cue for a brief dialogue about authority, and a
further indication of where the main responsibility lay for Jesus' condemnation.

In Pilate's final interview with the Jewish leaders, the issue once again
entered a new phase. Having failed to get their way so far, the Jews brought
forward something of a threat: '**If you let this man go, you are no friend** 12
to Caesar'. "Friend of Caesar"—*amicus Caesaris*—this is what, under the
empire, every Roman official aspired to be: to have the Emperor's ear, to be
known for one's loyalty. A few years later Pilate was deposed from office at
the instigation of one who was more of a "friend of Caesar" than he. At any
time, the possibility of reports reaching home that he was allowing disloyalty
to Caesar among his subjects in Judaea would have alarmed him. Finally,
therefore, he determined to put the matter to the test: if the crowd showed
that they were prepared to acknowledge Jesus as king, clearly the man was
dangerous after all, and action must be taken. For the first time he brought
the prisoner outside his headquarters to confront his accusers. The scene
is carefully and solemnly set. The Roman governor normally set up his
tribunal for the purpose of giving judgement [a] in a public place outside his 13
residence. John knows the name of the place. Greek-speaking people called
it '**The Pavement**': streets and squares paved with smooth and massive

[a] The phrase, "took his seat on the tribunal", certainly suggests that Pilate is about to give judgement. But in fact he has given judgement already, and what follows is hardly judicial. Another possible translation of the Greek is, "he set Jesus on the tribunal". If this were correct, it would add point and drama to the scene: Pilate would be deliberately challenging the Jews to show their allegiance to a usurper of his own authority.

stone blocks were characteristic of Herodian Jerusalem, and it would not be surprising if there were a particularly fine one outside the Governor's residence (which was formerly Herod the Great's palace).[a] **In the language of the Jews** it was called **'Gabbatha'**, which probably represents a Hebrew or Aramaic word meaning "a high place": and again, in a city built on steep hills, this would be an obvious name for any public square in the higher parts
14 of Jerusalem. John also appears to know the exact time: **It was the eve of Passover,**[b] **about noon.** This conflicts with the other gospels, where Jesus is crucified in the morning. John may have had other information; on the other hand, if he knew that on the eve of Passover the sacrificial lambs were slaughtered at the temple in the early afternoon, and if he wished to make Jesus' death carry some of the symbolic meaning of these sacrifices, he may have deliberately pictured Jesus' final condemnation as taking place at the last moment when work was permissible on the eve of Passover: **about noon.**

15 **Pilate said to the Jews, 'Here is your king.'** This was a direct challenge to the Jews. But the Jews replied with a vigorous protestation of their loyalty to Caesar, and demanded Jesus' execution. The demand may have been unjust, but it could be taken as an expression of allegiance to the power of Rome; and Pilate yielded to it.

To this extent John's narrative permits us to make a possible reconstruction of the original events. At the same time, it is clear that here, as throughout his gospel, John is doing a great deal more than merely recording events as they happened. Like the authors of the other gospels, he has certain points that he wishes to make. Jesus was put to death by the Romans, allegedly as a claimant to the treasonable title, "King of the Jews": this was the basic fact known to anyone who had heard anything about Jesus at all. But two obvious inferences from this fact needed to be corrected. First, the execution was not
12 the Romans' fault; on the contrary, **Pilate tried hard to release him.** It was the Jews, not the Romans, who were mainly responsible. Secondly, Jesus was not a traitor to Rome: his "kingship" was not political, and therefore his followers need not be regarded as disloyal citizens by the Roman authorities (a point of importance by the time John's gospel was written). It

[*a*] An impressive area of such paving has been found on the site of one of Herod the Great's buildings in Jerusalem, the fortress-palace called Antonia which lay next to and dominated the temple area. It is tempting to believe that this was the site of Jesus' trial; but unfortunately this identification is not certain. It is in many ways more likely that Pilate had his headquarters (*praetorium*) in the main palace of Herod the Great that was situated in the highest part of the city (and which it has not yet been possible to excavate), than in the Antonia; and in any case the archaeological evidence suggests that the paving at the Antonia dates from the time of Hadrian, a century after the trial of Jesus.

[*b*] The alternative rendering given in the footnote would eliminate the second of the two statements in John's gospel which show that this author believed the crucifixion to have taken place before, not after, the Jewish Passover (the other is 18.28), and would make it possible to reconcile his chronology with that of the other gospels. But it is very doubtful whether the Greek words could bear the sense proposed.

was true of the trial of Jesus—as it was true of the ensuing trials of Christians in Roman courts—that it was not the Roman administration which was
ultimately to blame: '**the deeper guilt lies with the man who handed** 11
me over to you'.[a] But John's account of the trial, though it is in many ways so similar to that in the other gospels, is at the same time characteristic of him. For he uses it, as he uses many episodes, to explain to the reader the significance of some of the concepts used by Jesus. In particular (since it was known that Jesus was crucified as "king of the Jews") there is a conversation between Jesus and Pilate which, whatever may have passed between them (which John could hardly have had any means of knowing), fills a gap in this gospel's presentation of the person of Jesus by explaining
what Jesus meant by the title. '**My task is to bear witness to the truth.**' **18.** 37

Carrying his own cross. John appears not to know of the tradition (vouched **19.** 17
for by the man's own sons in Mark's account) that a certain Simon of Cyrene was forced to carry the cross for Jesus. It may be, in any case, that Jesus did in fact carry the beam of his own cross at least some of the way, until he had to be relieved of it through exhaustion. John may have known of Jesus' saying that stands in Luke 14.27 in the form, 'No one who does not carry his cross . . . can be a disciple of mine'; if so, he may have deliberately concentrated on the early stages of the procession, during which Jesus was as it were setting an example to his future disciples.

Not far from the city. This detail, given only by John, is exactly what 20
we should expect: the Romans crucified insurrectionists to set a public example, and though custom forbade them to do this in the most public place of all (inside the city), they normally chose a place not far outside, where the victims would be seen by a large number of people. John also gives very plausible details about **the inscription** (which he calls by the technical Latin name, *titulus*). **Hebrew** can mean (as often in the New Testament) the language actually spoken by the inhabitants of Palestine; **Latin** was the native language of the Roman administrators; **Greek** was the common language in fact used for official purposes throughout the eastern part of the empire. Thus publicly displayed, the charge against Jesus could well have seemed to the chief priests a deliberate insult to their nation.

'They shared my garments among them, and cast lots for my 24
clothing'. This quotation (Psalm 22.18) occurs in all the gospel accounts, and indeed the psalm, with its classic description of the predicament of a righteous sufferer, evidently offered a convenient and traditional framework in which to set the remembered details of the crucifixion of Jesus. But John seems to have worked out the exact way in which this text of Scripture

[a] In its context this saying is ambiguous: it could mean Judas or Caiphas. But the vagueness may be deliberate. It would have made it easier for Christians to quote the saying when they found themselves on trial before the Roman authorities.

came true. Even though, in Hebrew poetry, the two halves of a line are often intended to balance each other, and to yield, not two statements, but two ways of making the same statement, nevertheless John takes the whole line quite literally, and appears to ask himself how, if the four soldiers **shared** Jesus' garments by dividing them among themselves, they could also find
23 anything to **cast lots** about. He found the answer in Jesus' **tunic**, which might well have been the one really valuable object among the spoils to which the soldiers were entitled: the tunic (*chitōn*) was the long shirt (usually with short sleeves) which was worn under a cloak. Obviously it would have been silly to "share" this by tearing it up (even if it were not **in one piece throughout,** as John painstakingly assures us it was); therefore they "tossed for it", and thus fulfilled the prophecy to the letter.

25 **That is what the soldiers did.** With considerable artistry John builds up a surrounding frame of onlookers before coming to the centre of the picture, Jesus himself. All the gospels refer to the women who were present at the crucifixion, although they differ in the details: only John reports that they were actually **near the cross,** and that Jesus' mother was among them. We do not know who **her sister** was—the Greek, like the English, is ambiguous, and so far as grammar goes she could be the same person as **Mary wife of Clopas**: but it is perhaps not very likely that two sisters would both have been called Mary. Otherwise, the only woman of the group who can be certainly identified is **Mary of Magdala,** who is known from Luke 8.2. In any case their presence enables John to record a further saying of
26 Jesus, **'Mother, there is your son'**. This is evidently more than a last-minute concern for the welfare of a bereaved mother. If it had been merely
27 this, it would have been sufficient to say to the disciple, **'There is your mother'**; there would have been no need for Jesus to address his mother as well. In any case, the form of address is strange and solemn. Literally, the Greek gives "woman", for which **mother** is only a rough equivalent: the word was not rude (as "woman" would be in English), but it was formal (in a way that "mother" is not). Jesus addressed his mother in the same way at Cana (2.4 above), and on that occasion too his utterance had a solemn and formal ring. Clearly there is a hidden meaning, and subsequent Christian meditation has found the germ of many doctrines about the church, about womanhood, and about Mary herself in this single sentence. One point at least seems fairly certain. The **disciple whom he loved** (whoever he was) stands on this occasion for more than one individual: he represents the whole company of followers of Christ; and the saying falls into line with those great affirmations of Paul that Christians are Christ's "brothers", and share his sonship.

28, 29 **'I thirst'.** All the gospels mention that Jesus was offered **sour wine,** and a verse from Psalm 69 (which was one of the classic descriptions of a righteous sufferer) must have helped to determine the words in which the incident was recorded: "for my thirst they gave me vinegar for drink" (Ps. 69.21). John, too, may well have had this text in mind when he added, **in fulfilment of Scripture.** But he also refashioned the incident in his own way. It would be a little strange if Jesus were really yielding to acute thirst at this point. It would be his only expression of physical suffering in any of the gospel accounts, and it would be surprising if John had chosen to record something so trivial at this critical moment. More probably, Jesus' "thirst" was (characteristically in this gospel) metaphorical: it was an intense longing for God. The word was misunderstood, and taken literally by the soldiers [a]—this again was a favourite device of the writer when he wished to draw attention to the deeper meaning of a saying of Jesus. Its true meaning is given in another psalm (63.1):

> "O God, thou art my God, I seek thee,
> my soul thirsts for thee."

This psalm begins, in Hebrew, *elohim eli*. Mark and Matthew both record that Jesus cried *eli* from the cross, and that this was misunderstood as 'Elijah' by the bystanders. John may have assumed that the cry was a prayer of Jesus based on this psalm and that the misunderstanding consisted in his "thirst" being taken literally.

That Jesus' life and work was a perfect unity, a work to be finished and a destiny to be accomplished, is one of the themes of John's gospel (4.34; 5.36;
17.4). Aptly, John records, as his final cry, **'It is accomplished!'** 30
Because it was the eve of Passover. [b] It was laid down in Deuteronomy 31
that a criminal executed by "hanging on a tree" must be buried before
nightfall. Moreover, the day on which Jesus was crucified was a Friday: the
Sabbath began at dusk, and was a day that must not be profaned by dead
bodies in public places—especially (as John adds, perhaps unnecessarily)
since **that Sabbath was a day of great solemnity**, being the first day of the 31
festival. The request of the Jews was therefore reasonable. The "defilement
of the land" (Deuteronomy 21.23) which would have ensued otherwise
would have been a serious matter for the consciences of strict Jews who had
come to Jerusalem to keep the festival. Execution by crucifixion was a slow
death—sometimes it could take up to thirty-six hours. Breaking the legs of
the victims was a recognized way of hastening death. But Jesus was **already** 33

[*a*] **A javelin** is the translation of the Greek word *hyssos*. The manuscripts all give *hyssōpos*, "marjoram", which makes little sense. It was conjectured in the sixteenth century that John must originally have written *hyssos*, and that an easy slip of an early copyist produced the reading of all our existing manuscripts—except one of the thirteenth century which, perhaps by accident, supports the conjectural reading, "javelin".

[*b*] The translation, "eve of Passover", is a correct inference rather than an exact rendering. The Greek word means simply "Friday"; but it is true that, at least by John's reckoning, the Passover was about to begin at nightfall, and so, in that sense, this Friday was the "eve" of Passover. The alternative translation given in the footnote is a further attempt to harmonize John's dating with that of the other gospels. See above on 18.28 and 19.14.

dead, so they did not break his legs. Why did John mention this? We know that many Jews at this time were beginning to have scruples about deliberately breaking a man's bones (for example, by stoning): might it not affect the victim's chances of bodily resurrection at the last day? Possibly John shared this concern, and thought it necessary to show that Jesus was not
36 affected; or possibly he was impressed by the text, '**No bone of his shall be broken**'. It is not quite certain what text he was referring to. Exodus 12.46 reads (of the lamb eaten at Passover), "You shall not break a bone of it". If John intended his readers to have in mind the fact that Jesus was crucified at the same time as the lambs were being slaughtered in the temple, then this might have been meant as a further detail in the symbolism of Jesus' death. Alternatively, the allusion is to Psalm 34.20, which describes how the Lord protects the righteous: "He keeps all his bones; not one of them is broken".

Instead of having his legs broken, Jesus was stabbed in the side with a
34 lance. **There was a flow of blood and water.** This is said to be physiologically possible—a white fluid could have been released by the wound. But John, who lays great stress on the reliability of his report, obviously saw more in it than a mere physical phenomenon. **Blood** and **water** were both highly significant symbols; at the very least, they suggested the two sacraments of eucharist and baptism. In addition, the whole incident fulfilled
37 another prophecy (quoted also in Revelation 1.7), '**They shall look on him whom they pierced**'. This is certainly a quotation of Zechariah 12.10—and the last chapter of Zechariah provided a number of prophecies which seemed to have been fulfilled in the passion of Jesus.

38 **After that, Pilate was approached by Joseph of Arimathaea.** Different suggestions are made by the evangelists about the motives of this Joseph. In Mark and Luke, he is a pious and influential Jew, anxious to avoid the ritual defilement which would ensue if a dead body were left exposed overnight, or else moved to make some amends for the injustice of the Sanhedrin's action. John comes closer to Matthew's explanation: Joseph was a **secret disciple** and was joined by another person of influence, Nicodemus (3.1), who was doubtless also obliged to keep his discipleship secret. They evidently intended to bury Jesus with the full honours that were customary among the
42 Jews. They were pressed for time: **it was the eve of the Jewish Sabbath**, and once the sun had set their activity would no longer be permissible. They therefore made use of a new tomb that happened to be **near at hand** in a garden.[a] But they did not (as in the other gospels) neglect to anoint the corpse. On the contrary, they brought with them a prodigious quantity of
39 spices for the purpose (**more than half a hundredweight**). Such things

[*a*] The traditional site of the Holy Sepulchre is about twenty yards from the rock of Calvary, and since the area was certainly not built over in the time of Christ, a part of it could well have been under cultivation.

were precious, and were normally packed in small jars with long narrow necks, so that they could be used sparingly; and since it was usual to anoint a corpse with olive oil, one would have expected them simply to mix a little of the perfume with it. John perhaps means to emphasize that the two distinguished Jewish disciples gave Jesus a burial worthy of the 'King of the Jews'.

Early on the Sunday morning. Ultimately, the faith of the first Christians **20.** 1
that Jesus had risen from the dead rested on the conviction that they, or at least certain witnesses whom they had reason to trust, had seen him with their own eyes. But all the gospels tell of a sensational event which preceded any appearance of Jesus: the discovery that the tomb was empty. Exactly how this discovery was made, and why it was not immediately seized upon by the disciples as convincing proof of the resurrection, are questions which receive a different answer in each gospel. Clearly there was some uncertainty in the writers' minds about the importance of the discovery, in view of the fact that it was so soon followed by an encounter with the risen Jesus himself. This gospel, however, seems to present a more considered account. John takes for granted many of the details recorded in the other gospels: his readers are evidently expected to know, without having been told, that Jesus' tomb had been sealed with a massive stone, and they are given no explanation how Mary, having left the tomb in verse 2, is back again weeping there in verse 11. In other words, John is evidently working with a narrative similar to the others; but not only does he offer certain details which are different and add whole episodes which are new to us: he arranges the material in such a way that it shows a clear progression from simple consternation to assured belief.

This is at its clearest in the first paragraph. The first reaction to the discovery that the tomb had not remained as it was left on the Friday was that
of Mary of Magdala (in John she is alone, in the other gospels there is a
group of women). She drew the obvious conclusion: '**They have taken the** 2
Lord out of his tomb', **she cried**, '**and we do not know where they**
have laid him' (the other women of the other gospel accounts seem to
have left their mark in the word we). The second reaction was that of a
disciple, and was much more perceptive. Here there is an elaborate distribution of rôles between Simon Peter and **the other disciple, the one whom** 1
Jesus loved. From a formal point of view, Peter seems to be given precedence (he was, after all, and was intended to be, the chief of the apostles).
But in reality the decisive reaction belonged to the other disciple. He, like
Peter, noticed both the linen wrappings (19.40) and the **napkin** (such as 6
was wrapped round the head of Lazarus 11.44) still lying in the tomb. It was
inconceivable that anyone stealing the corpse should have first unwrapped it
and left the wrappings in a neat pile. Something of a different order altogether must have happened. There were of course prophecies in the scriptures about a "rising from the dead", but **until then** these had been but 9

dimly understood. The disciple now grasped the significance of this puzzling
8 discovery: **he saw and believed.**

This is the only occasion in the New Testament on which it is said that someone believed as a result of the empty tomb. In principle, all the apostles came to believe because they saw the risen Jesus. But subsequent generations of Christians were required to believe on the basis of something far less sensational; their faith was, so to speak, at second-hand. It was for such Christians that this gospel was written; and John shows how much he had
29 them in mind when he records Jesus saying, '**Happy are they who never saw me and yet have found faith**'. This disciple had not yet seen the risen Christ; he had not received that decisive experience which was to give the other disciples their faith in the resurrection. He had merely noticed a strange fact about the wrappings in the tomb. But this was enough for him:
8 **he saw and believed.** We do not know who this disciple was. He appears, again in close company with Peter, both in chapter 13 and in chapter 21. Whether or not he stands for the author of the gospel (see below), he was certainly a person whom the first readers of the gospel knew and whose memory (if he was dead) they revered. His was a powerful example to appeal to; and he, despite such slender and puzzling evidence, had come to that faith in the resurrection which was to be the cardinal belief of the whole church.

However, events moved quickly. According to Matthew and Luke, the discovery of the empty tomb was followed almost at once by supernatural appearances, first to the women, then to the disciples. John faithfully follows the same pattern. Mary of Magdala continues to take the place of the whole group of women, and her vision of angels corresponds to the scene in the other gospels. But this vision leaves her still assuming that there must be some natural explanation of the body's disappearance, so much so that, when Jesus himself appears to her, she immediately (since she does not recognize him) puts the same explanation to the stranger, and asks for his help.

16 **Jesus said, 'Mary!'** That simply addressing her by name was enough to open her eyes is a piece of vivid and convincing reporting. The scene is told with a rare simplicity and economy of words. It is of course possible that John meant his readers to have in mind some words that Jesus had spoken earlier: 'he calls his own sheep by name' (10.3). At any rate, there is some
17 serious teaching in the rest of the dialogue. '**Do not cling to me, for I have not yet ascended to the Father.**' In Matthew, the women who first saw the risen Jesus 'clasped his feet, falling prostrate before him' (28.9). This (John may have felt) was to attach the wrong significance to these appearances of Jesus. They were intended to convince, not to excite homage. The reader must not be given the impression that the women, or in this case Mary, or indeed any disciple, had been given a chance to know and worship the risen Christ in a way more direct, more personal, more privileged than

was given to any subsequent Christian. The Christ whom Christians worshipped was the Christ who had **ascended to the Father.** If this were imagined in spatial terms, it could be said that Mary saw him, so to speak, on his way to heaven. But the truth behind this naïve form of expression was that Mary's experience, though at that particular place and time it was decisive in convincing her and others of the fact of Jesus' resurrection, was in no way more direct or more privileged than all Christians have when they worship their ascended Lord.[a]

'But go to my brothers'. That Jesus' followers are his **brothers** is implied by a saying recorded in the other gospels (Mark 3.35) and is a presupposition of much of his teaching in Matthew's gospel—indeed, in Matthew the risen Jesus actually says to the women who have seen him 'Go and take word to my brothers' (28.10). In this gospel the idea is a new one (though it is perfectly consistent with the teaching so far about Christians being children of God, and friends of Jesus); but even if John was faithfully reproducing some tradition that the risen Jesus had used this very word, he did not miss the opportunity to draw the consequence: God was **'my Father and your Father, my God and your God'.** For all the majesty implied in Jesus' ascension, his followers remained in close solidarity with him. In their relationship with God, they were privileged to be his equals.

Mary of Magdala went to the disciples with her news. Each of the 18
other gospels suggests an answer to the question why this news had no
immediate effect on the disciples (see above on Mark 16.8). John ignores the
question. It is as if he is simply following the traditional pattern of Jesus'
appearances: first he was seen by some women (or Mary of Magdala), then
by the disciples all together. He makes little attempt to link these appearances together in a single coherent narrative. The appearance of Jesus to his
disciples **late that Sunday evening** takes place exactly as if it were the very 19
first of its kind. This, in any case, was doubtless the appearance which was
remembered as the most important and authoritative of all. Paul mentions an
appearance 'to the Twelve' (1 Corinthians 15.5); and Luke also gives an
account of it (24.36–43) which is in many respects similar to this one. John's
version has details which are characteristic of this gospel. **'Peace be with** 20
you' is doubtless intended (as in 14.27) to be understood as more than a
formal greeting; and **'As the Father sent me, so I send you'** belongs to 21
the pattern of Jesus' teaching as it is often presented in the *Farewell discourses*. But the scene as a whole falls into place alongside passages in the

[a] It is impossible to be sure of the exact sense of Jesus' words in the Greek (see the footnote in NEB), and their interpretation must remain uncertain. It is possible that John chose the word "touch" (as it is rendered in the footnote) in order to make a deliberate reference to the eucharist: Christians "touch" the Lord in the bread they share (compare 1 John 1.1), and this is the authentic way of experiencing him. Jesus forbade Mary to "touch" him in a literal sense, pending the time when all Christians would be able to "touch" him in the eucharist.

other gospels. Just as in Luke there is much emphasis on the fact that the
risen Jesus was no mere ghost, so here the apparition, though he enters
19, 20 through **locked doors,** shows the disciples **his hands and his side.** Again,
the ending of the scene represents a formal commission given by Jesus to his
22 disciples. **Then he breathed on them, saying, 'Receive the Holy
Spirit!'** It was the distinctive experience of the earliest Christians that, as soon as the church began its existence, it possessed the gift of the Holy Spirit. This spirit was understood in different ways, and had a variety of manifestations. Moreover, there was evidently some doubt about the exact occasion on which it could be said that this new factor had entered the lives of men and women. But all agreed that the Holy Spirit was a reality in the church, and had been so ever since the church began to exist. To describe how in fact it had been given necessarily involved using highly metaphorical language. In Acts 2, Luke narrates a particularly sensational phenomenon which he saw as the definitive irruption of this new power into human lives. Here, John uses a metaphor straight from the Old Testament. "The Lord God formed a man from the dust of the ground and breathed into his nostrils the breath of life" (Genesis 2.7; compare Ezekiel 37.7–14). "Breath", in Hebrew, is the same word as "spirit": the giving of the Spirit by Jesus lent itself easily to being described in the same terms as the original giving of the breath of life by God.

23 **'If you forgive any man's sins, they stand forgiven'.** It is clear (and not at all surprising) that Jesus was remembered to have given to his disciples—and thereby, it has usually been understood, to their successors—a definite authority over the lives of their fellow-Christians. In Matthew (16.19 and 18.18) this is expressed in terms of "forbidding" and "allowing"—apparently an idiom of Jesus' own language, and one that could have been understood in certain rather technical senses. Here, the saying has the same form, but concerns the disciples' power to pronounce the forgiveness of sins. It is likely that it was in this way that Greek-speaking Christians understood the original saying: in the life of the church, it was necessary sometimes to decide whether the conduct of a member made it necessary to exclude him. Authority to do this was found in a saying of Jesus; and John, although he does not elsewhere show interest in the concept of the forgiving of an individual's sins, nevertheless records that Jesus gave this authority to the disciples.

There are traces elsewhere in the gospels that not all the disciples were
immediately convinced of the resurrection. In Matthew, there is the laconic
statement that 'some were doubtful' (28.17). John, alone of the gospel
24 writers, gives a concrete instance. **Thomas, that is 'the Twin',** has already
been named twice in the course of the gospel (11.16; 14.5); here he is an example of one who refuses to believe without incontrovertible and tangible evidence. When it comes to the point, Jesus' appearance elicits from him

what is probably intended to be the most significant confession of faith that
has been made by anyone in the gospel: '**My Lord and my God**'. Earlier 28
in the narrative this might have been misunderstood: Lord and God were
titles which, in the Old Testament, belonged to God alone, and to address
Jesus so might have seemed like calling him another "god". But by now the
reader knows more of the relationship between Jesus and his Father. Jesus
had even said, 'Anyone who has seen me has seen the Father' (14.9).
Thomas, like the whole church after him, acknowledged Jesus as **Lord**; but
he now understood also that his Lord was (in one sense at least) **God**.
Nevertheless, in this story, Thomas is no more than a foil to the true picture
of the Christian believer. To convince Thomas, Jesus had to make, so to
speak, a special appearance. But John was writing for Christians who had
come to their faith without demanding an impossible confirmation of it.
Fittingly, Jesus' last words are addressed to them: '**Happy are they who** 29
never saw me and yet have found faith.'

There were indeed many other signs . . . which are not recorded in 30
this book. The writer now addresses his readers directly. The signs, in this
gospel, are mostly what we should now call miracles; and from a comparison
with the other gospels it is quite clear that John has recorded only a small
selection of those that were ascribed to Jesus. The same indeed is true of
Mark's gospel (1.34); and it is also true that Mark tended, like John, to
narrate only those miracles which had a bearing upon faith. John now makes
this explicit: **Those here written have been recorded in order that you** 31
may hold the faith that Jesus is the Christ, the Son of God. From our
point of view, the phrase is disappointingly ambiguous.[a] It does not make it clear whether John was writing a missionary book for unbelievers or a treatise for people who were already Christians (an answer to this question can only be given on the basis of the work as a whole). Nevertheless, it effectively sums up the grand purpose for which the gospel was written. The purpose, indeed, was the same as that for which any gospel was bound to be written. Any gospel was, almost by definition, 'of Jesus Christ the Son of God' (Mark 1.1), and it can hardly have had any other purpose than to awaken or to strengthen faith in those who heard it or read it. John's gospel is only different from the others in the way in which he approaches his task. As a summary of the writer's aims, the sentence could stand appropriately at the end of any of the gospels. Only the word **life** is distinctive: almost from the beginning, this has been John's most characteristic and emphatic way of describing the benefits and possibilities which are now open to mankind as a result of the story he has been telling.

Normally, it was only by way of a preface or an epilogue that a writer addressed his readers about his own book. The last verse of chapter 20 is a typical way

[a] It also appears in more than one form in the manuscripts. See the footnote in NEB.

of ending a book; and it is astonishing to find that in fact another chapter
follows. This alone would be sufficient to make one suspect that chapter 21
was added after the main work was finished. But there are other oddities.
21. 1 The scene is set **by the Sea of Tiberias.** Nothing has prepared us for this.
The disciples were last heard of in Jerusalem. Yet we read that Simon Peter
3 said, **'I am going out fishing'**, as if he was living the normal life of a
14 fisherman in Galilee. Apart from a kind of editorial comment—**this makes
the third time that Jesus appeared to his disciples after his resurrection from the dead**—there is nothing to suggest that the episode belongs
to the sequence of events that has just been related. If it is an afterthought
by the author of the whole work, one would have expected him at least to
have worked it in more neatly. The style is very similar (though there are a
few points of detail where one would have expected the writer of the rest of
the gospel to express himself differently), and many of the idioms and ideas
are found elsewhere in the gospel. But the awkwardness of the join is such
that, even though all the manuscripts run straight on from chapter 20 to
chapter 21, it seems almost impossible to resist the apparent implication of
21.24 that someone else has had a hand in writing the end of the gospel.

The episode is made up of a number of different elements. The main plot,
so to speak, is the story of a group of Galilean fishermen who, after a night's
unsuccessful fishing, are told by Jesus to try once more; they then make an
astonishingly large catch. A story of this kind is also told by Luke (5.1–11),
who places it near the beginning of Jesus' activity, and uses it to explain how
Jesus attracted his first disciples. Here it has a more unearthly quality, for
it is placed after the resurrection, and Jesus' sudden appearance is as inexplicable as the catch of fish. It is still a wonder story; but its real significance is in the by-plots. The first of these is a delicate balancing of priorities
7 between Peter and **the disciple whom Jesus loved,** very much as in the
discovery of the empty tomb (20.1–9): Peter took action, but it was the other
disciple who first recognized (and believed) that the figure on the shore was
Jesus. The second by-plot (which is rather loosely integrated into the main
plot, since there is no obvious reason why Jesus should have asked for the
disciples' catch of fish, when he already had other fish laid on the fire) is a
meal shared by the risen Jesus with his disciples. This, again, has a parallel in
Luke (24.30, 36–43), and is described in a way which might well be intended
to make the reader think of the eucharist, for the eucharist, the original meal
13 in which Jesus **took the bread, and gave it to them,** was celebrated again
and again in the church in the conviction that the risen Lord was present.
Besides all this, there is a rich load of symbolism. We are told that the net
11 was **full of big fish, a hundred and fifty-three of them.** The writer
hardly intends us to think that someone present counted and remembered
the exact number: to give an idea of the size of the catch, a round number
would have been at least as impressive. In a culture where the symbolism of

numbers meant far more than it does now, it would have been even more obvious that this number had a secret meaning. It happens that the sum of the numbers 1+2+3+ ... up to 17 is 153; 17=10+7, and ten and seven were each numbers signifying a perfect whole. By such reasoning, 153 could have been understood to stand as a symbol for the whole of something (the whole of mankind, or the whole of the church). Alternatively, the explanation may be that some naturalists (again perhaps influenced by the arithmetical properties of the number rather than by actual observation) allowed for exactly 153 different species of fish—in which case the number would again be a symbol of totality. Whether either of these explanations is correct we shall never know; but we can be fairly sure that the writer intended something of the kind. And when he goes on to tell us another quite unimportant detail —**the net was not torn**—we can hardly be wrong in seeing here another symbolical statement. Again, we cannot be sure what is meant; but if the fish in the net represented the totality of peoples who would be brought into the church then the fact that the net was not torn would stand for the unity of the church: for all the great number and diversity of its members, there was no division, no schism. All this may seem rather recondite. But it was Jesus himself who started the metaphor: 'I will make you fishers of men' (Mark 1.17). The rest is only elaboration of this basic idea.

Jesus said to Simon Peter. Sayings of Jesus which seemed to assign a 15
special place to Peter among the apostles are recorded in Matthew (16.18)
and Luke (22.31–2). At the same time, all the gospels faithfully record
Peter's threefold disowning of Jesus during the trial. Here Peter's threefold
profession of love[a] for Jesus may be intended to balance his threefold denial;
and certainly Jesus' final command to him, **'Follow me'**, seems to refer 19
back to 13.36, where Jesus said, 'You cannot follow me now, but one day
you will'. But the actual form of the commission to Peter is new: **'Feed my** 17
sheep'. Up to now, Jesus has been the only shepherd. In the period of the
church, the shepherding is to be continued by a disciple.

'And further'. What follows has a proverbial ring. To walk any distance, 18
a man must hitch up his long clothes by making a fold over his belt, and then
fasten his belt tighter. A young man is perfectly independent; but an old
man is dependent on others, he can only **stretch out** his **arms** for other
people to arrange his clothes for him and lead him where they will. Taken
by itself, this reads like a pessimistic aphorism, of the kind that is so brilliantly elaborated at the end of Ecclesiastes (12.1–8). What was the application of it for Peter? The writer tells us: **He said this to indicate the man-** 19
ner of death by which Peter was to glorify God—in other words, Peter

[a] Two different Greek words are used in this brief dialogue. One of them (*agapō*) is the one characteristically used in the Gospel and Letters of John for the "love" of Christ and of Christians; the other (*philō*) is the commonest Greek word for human affection in general. This alternation may be just a question of style. But in case a distinction is intended, the footnotes in NEB offer a translation which preserves it.

was to find himself as helpless as an old man in the face of those who would put him to death as a martyr for his faith. This comment was clearly written after the event, and is one of our first pieces of evidence that Peter was in fact martyred (probably in Rome, soon after the middle of the first century A.D.). Tertullian, writing a century or so later, knew (or assumed) that Peter had been crucified (and Origen, later still, says that he was crucified, at his own request, head downwards), and saw a prophetic significance in the words
18 **stretch out your arms** and **bind you fast.** But this interpretation involves a
certain forcing of the Greek words. "Another will do up your belt" is a more accurate translation than **a stranger will bind you fast.** Taken as it stands, the prophecy seems to mean only that Peter would not die a natural death.

On two occasions already in these last chapters, there has been a careful
20 balancing of honours between Peter and **the disciple whom Jesus loved.**
If Jesus had made a prophecy about Peter's death (and at the time of writing
the death of a Christian martyr was much honoured: it was the most esteemed
19 way of all **to glorify God**), had he not also said something to the other
22 disciple? He had: **'If it should be my will that he wait until I come,**
what is it to you?' On the face of it, this was less mysterious. For many
23 years after the resurrection, it was believed by the church (here called **the**
brotherhood, a word more familiar in Acts than in this gospel), that, though some Christians might die, the majority, or at least a certain number, would "wait until the Lord's coming". This disciple, it seemed, was intended to be one of these. But the "coming" of Jesus did not take place in this way—indeed it has been one of the themes of this gospel that such naïve language about the future was in reality only a way of speaking about a new dimension of the present. The disciple died. And it became necessary to draw attention to the oracular ambiguity of what Jesus had said. Correcting this misunderstanding was doubtless one of the objects for which this chapter was added to the
25 completed gospel. The writer then provided a new ending, which is little
more than a rhetorical flourish such as many ancient writers used, and answers somewhat colourlessly to the real ending of the gospel in 20.30–1. The proper conclusion of this chapter is in the previous verse. Peter may
24 have glorified God by his death; but this disciple gave **testimony** of another
kind: **it is this same disciple who attests what has here been written. It is in fact he who wrote it.** We hear the voice now, no longer of an author, but of the community which used and treasured this book. They believed, rightly or wrongly, that they had the clue to the mysterious phrase, 'the disciple whom Jesus loved'. It was the author himself. This meant, moreover, that this chapter at least, if not the whole book, had been written by an eye-witness. In an account of Jesus' life and teaching where so much was said to depend on "witness", **testimony,** here was the ultimate ground for confidence. The author had been there himself. **We know that his testimony is true.**

An incident in the temple

This passage did not form part of the original gospel according to John. In its traditional place (7.53–8.11) it clearly disturbs the sequence of John's narrative; and in any case most of the early manuscripts omit it altogether, and some manuscripts have it in a different place. In style, it is more like a passage from one of the other gospels (especially Luke, to which one group of manuscripts actually ascribes it). What appears to have happened is that an isolated story about Jesus was somehow preserved without having been incorporated into any gospel until it was ultimately slipped in at some point where it did not seem inappropriate.

A great many stories about Jesus circulated in the first few centuries of the Christian era, but were never incorporated in the New Testament, and are preserved in what are called the Apocryphal gospels. Almost all of these can be recognized as being of considerably later date than the New Testament. By contrast, this one falls well into place beside all that we know of Jesus from the New Testament gospels, and seems (so far as we can tell) to reflect the conditions of Jesus' own time. Even if it is impossible to find a place for it in any of the four gospels, there is no reason to doubt that it preserves an authentic memory of an episode in the life of Jesus.

It is necessary to fill in the background of the incident. The immediate result of a woman committing adultery would have been that her husband would be entitled to divorce her without any financial loss, and that the woman would bear the disgrace of the act among her own family. Where there was doubt about whether adultery had been committed, further evidence might be collected, or the woman might be subjected to a primitive kind of ritual test (Numbers 5). But in this case we are told that the woman
was **caught in the very act of adultery**, so that there was presumably no 8.4
doubt about the facts, and the divorce would have followed almost automatically. And there, normally, the affair would have ended. Adultery and divorce in most societies are subjects of civil litigation, and carry no graver consequences; and although laxity in sexual matters was very strongly disapproved of in Jewish society, there was seldom any punishment beyond a certain degree of social disgrace. Nevertheless, in the Law of Moses a more serious view was taken. Adultery was conceived of as something which was both against the will of God and a source of harm to the community as a whole. Consequently the Law (which was still the law by which the Jewish people lived) laid down nothing less than the death penalty (Deuteronomy 22.22). It is unlikely that in more recent times this law was often invoked: adultery, after all, is hard to prove conclusively, and most courts are loth to impose the death penalty unless they have to. On the other hand, there were certainly sections of Jewish opinion which zealously tried to bring the society in which

they lived into full conformity with the Law of Moses, and to eradicate
3 conduct which was inconsistent with its demands. Among **the doctors of
the law and the Pharisees** who make their appearance in this story, there
4 may well have been some who felt that this case of an adulteress **caught in
the very act** offered an opportunity for applying the law in all its rigour.

The situation was complicated by the fact that, under the Roman administration, the Jewish authorities had apparently lost the power to impose the death penalty (John 18.31). Those wishing to see the law enforced in its full severity therefore could not hope to get what they wanted through a public trial. Their only course was to constitute themselves as a court and, after making sure that their action was strictly legal according to the Law of Moses, to see justice done themselves. As for the sentence, the relevant passage of Deuteronomy did not prescribe exactly how this was to be carried out; but death by stoning was one of the standard punishments mentioned in the Law, and it is fairly certain that this was the accepted penalty for adultery in the time of Jesus (though it was later changed to the somewhat more humane one of strangling). It was therefore a fair summary of the
5 situation to say that **'in the Law Moses has laid down that such women
are to be stoned'.**

In this particular case, zeal for the full application of the Law was doubtless combined with a desire to compromise Jesus. It was courteous and reasonable to invite someone who had made a name for himself in expounding the Law to give his judgement in such a matter; but against the background of a growing conspiracy against Jesus, the case seemed to offer a handle to his enemies. If Jesus recommended the Mosaic Law to be enforced, he could be accused to the Roman authorities of interfering in their administration of the province. If he did not, he would be showing that he did not take the Law seriously, and therefore had no right to expound it. In some such way as this,
6 the narrator may be right in saying, **They put the question as a test,
hoping to frame a charge against him.**

Jesus bent down and wrote with his finger on the ground. It is possible that he wrote some Hebrew characters, say the first few words of a text from the Law which bore on the case at issue; the advantage of doing this would have been that it is sometimes possible to read Hebrew words with more than one pronunciation, and so to give them more than one meaning: writing the words, instead of speaking them, would have been a way of pointing out a number of possible meanings in a clause of the Law. Alternatively, Jesus was just thinking—his writing on the ground may simply be a vivid touch by which the narrator tells his readers that, on this occasion, Jesus gave no snap answer.

And no wonder. Not only his own position, but the woman's life, was at stake. When it did come, his answer did not for a moment take lightly the binding force of the law about adultery; but by invoking another basic

principle of the Law, it at once cast the whole matter in a different light. To convict on a capital charge, the evidence of at least two witnesses was necessary. To a certain extent their evidence could be checked by examination in court. But in a Jewish court, what carried weight most was the known character and probity of the witnesses. The judges required, not so much independent proof of their story, as reason to believe that the witnesses were trustworthy. If the court was convinced of this, no more questions need be asked: sentence was given and the witnesses had the right and the duty to throw the first stones (Deuteronomy 17.7). In view of this heavy responsibility of the witnesses, there was a large number of conditions they had to fulfil before their word could be accepted. If their probity was questioned, they had to show that they had not been implicated in any way with the crime they had witnessed nor with any other unlawful proceeding. The penalties for giving and accepting evidence when all these conditions were not fulfilled were heavy: both witnesses and judges would be implicated in the grave sin of bearing false witness. Jesus was in effect challenging those who in this case had claimed to have been witnesses of the **very act** of adultery. It was all very well to insist on a literal application of the Law of Moses in the interests of a high standard of morality. But had these zealous reformers considered that they must also observe an equally high standard
of probity as witnesses and judges? '**That one of you who is faultless** 7
shall throw the first stone.'

Jesus had extricated himself and saved the woman. Under these circumstances, no one had dared pronounce the death sentence, no witness had dared insist on exercising the witnesses' right to cast the first stone. In the absence of the witnesses, Jesus, even if he had wanted to, was in no position to do so himself. '**Do not sin again**'. From a judge, this would have been a significant warning: on a subsequent occasion, the woman would have been that much more obviously guilty. But Jesus was now alone with her. His words were not the decision of a court, but expressed what he really felt. The letter of the Law of Moses was not to be enforced. There would be no punishment. But this made no difference to the seriousness of the woman's offence. '**Do not sin again**'.

ACTS OF THE APOSTLES

ACTS OF THE APOSTLES

The beginnings of the church

This book of the New Testament, like the gospel according to Luke, bears a preface addressed to a certain Theophilus. The preface declares that the
gospel was only **the first part** of the total work; what now lies before us is 1.1
the second part. The author gave no title to this sequel, and its earliest readers were somewhat puzzled to know what to call it. It fitted into no existing literary category. If it was like anything, it was like those popular biographies of famous men which were usually called, "Acts of so-and-so". Consequently, since the second century, this work has been known as ACTS OF THE APOSTLES. The title is not altogether accurate. Only two apostles, Peter and Paul, are prominent in the story, and in the first half of the book neither of them is the centre of interest. The real protagonist is the church; and a better guide to the contents of the book may be found in the NEB sub-headings, of which the first is *The beginnings of the church*.

Greek historians not only wrote a preface to their work as a whole; they often introduced successive books of it by a brief résumé of what had gone before. The preface to Acts is evidently an example of this convention, and serves to tie the two parts of the work together. In fact, that the author of Luke's gospel and of Acts is the same would be clear from the style even if it were not implied by the prefaces.

The end of Luke's gospel had already pointed forward to a subsequent volume. The disciples were instructed to remain in Jerusalem until they were 'armed with the power from above' (Luke 24.49), and the first two chapters of Acts are devoted to describing how this came to pass. But however much Luke may have conceived his two-volume work as a single whole, the fact remained that in the first part he had written a "gospel", that is to say, a book of the same form as the "Gospel according to Mark", of which he had been making use himself. As such, his gospel was bound to be read and used as an independent work, apart from its continuation; and Luke therefore must have felt the need to give it an ending which would not merely point forward to the sequel, but would also stand on its own as a fitting conclusion to his account of the earthly life of Jesus. This he did by recording Jesus' final moments with his disciples: 'he blessed them with uplifted hands; and in the act of blessing he parted from them' (Luke 24.50). For the purposes of the gospel narrative, this brief and solemn description was all that was necessary. But for the purposes of the subsequent history of *The beginnings of the church*, it needed some amplification; and this may be the reason why Luke, after correctly referring back to the point reached at the

2 end of his gospel (**he was taken up to heaven**), here goes on to narrate the same episode again, adding a number of new points and indeed setting the whole scene in a new light.[a]

3 **He showed himself to these men after his death, and gave ample proof that he was alive.** This is the first amplification. The task of the apostles was to bear witness to the resurrection; and lest it should be thought that their testimony was based only on one or two subjective experiences, Luke emphasizes that those appearances of Jesus which he narrated at the end of his gospel were no more than a sample of what took place. The witness of the apostles was based on **ample proof.** Secondly, the 'power from above' which, at the end of the gospel, Jesus promised to the disciples, is now defined more sharply. The 'power' would be the Holy Spirit, which they were shortly to receive in an experience analogous to baptism, so fulfilling the prophecy of John the Baptist, 'I baptize you with water . . . he will baptize you with the Holy Spirit and with fire' (Luke 3.16).

All this represented an incursion of the supernatural into the experience of the disciples such that they (and Christians after them) were bound to ask, was this now that final and climactic stage in history to which Jewish religious faith had so long looked forward? The disciples are made to ask this
6 question in its crudest form, '**Is this the time when you are to establish once again the sovereignty of Israel?**'—as if all that Jesus had taught about the kingdom of God could be equated with a mere political change such as the liberation of Palestine from the Roman occupying forces. Jesus' answer appears to ignore this blatant simplification. First, it emphasizes the impossibility of calculating the date of such an event (the same saying occurs in Mark 13.32, but is omitted by Luke in the corresponding passage of his gospel); it then promises two signs which will show that nevertheless a new and critical age is beginning: the activity of the Holy Spirit and the world-wide mission of the Church.

9 **He was lifted up.** At a certain point the appearances of the risen Jesus came to an end, and the church believed him to be now seated in glory at the right hand of God. The clear impression given by the end of Luke's gospel is that this took place on the same day as Jesus was first seen to have risen
3 from the dead. But here it is stated that there was **a period of forty days** (a conventional round number signifying a substantial period) during which Jesus continued to appear to his disciples, and this is corroborated, not only by the last two chapters of John's gospel (which seem to presuppose some-

[*a*] When placed side by side, the final scene of Luke's gospel and the opening of Acts present a number of discrepancies. The period of **forty days** (1.3) seems impossible to fit into the chronology of Luke 24, and the description of Jesus disappearing in a **cloud** (1.9) is very different from the simple parting with a blessing that is reported in the gospel (24.50). The above explanation presupposes that the two passages stand as the author intended them. But if once it is granted that there may have been some alteration or subsequent editing of the text, numerous other explanations become possible, though none is entirely convincing.

thing more than a week during which the appearances took place) but also by the earliest record of these appearances which we possess (1 Corinthians 15.5), which lists more appearances than could possibly have been witnessed in a single day. It seems that there were in fact two affirmations which the church felt enabled to make after the resurrection of Jesus. First, Jesus was raised bodily from the dead, not to continue his former existence on earth, but in order to assume his destined place at the right hand of God. His resurrection involved his vindication in glory, and his place was henceforward "in heaven". If one were to think of it in terms of space and direction, his "rising from the dead" implied an "ascension into heaven", and most Christian writers in the first decades of Christianity looked upon both as two parts of a single event that was completed on the first Easter Day. But secondly, it was an indisputable fact that, during a certain number of days after that Easter Day, Jesus had appeared to his disciples, both to strengthen their faith and to give them instruction. How was this possible, if he had already "ascended into heaven"? The New Testament writers offer no solution to this question; they simply present the two facts side by side. In any case their philosophy made it impossible to conceive of any intermediate state between resurrection from the dead and a glorious existence in heaven. Jesus had been resurrected with his body. That body was not now present on earth (at least in any ordinary sense), it must therefore have "ascended". Precisely how Jesus was still able to appear on earth to his disciples was a philosophical question which, it seems, they neither asked nor answered.

Nevertheless, one question did demand an answer: Jesus' appearances lasted only for a limited time. At a certain moment they came to an end. Which was the last, and how was it known that there would thenceforward be no more of the same kind? This is the question to which Luke's unpretentious account of what the church came to call "The Ascension" offers an answer. The reporting is very sober. There are none of the spectacular phenomena which accompanied the taking up into heaven of certain Old Testament figures, both in the Bible (2 Kings 2.11) and in subsequent Jewish legend. All the emphasis is on the simple fact of a supernatural
parting; and the function of the angels (**two men in white**, as in the resur- 10
rection narrative, Luke 24.4) is to make clear its finality. Jesus would not "appear again". His next "coming" would be that which he had so often prophesied himself in the words of ancient prophecies about the Son of Man. It would be as manifest and as unmistakable as this parting in a cloud. There would be no need to stand **looking up into the sky**. It would be visible to all, and would be accompanied by the end of the world.

Then they returned to Jerusalem from the hill called Olivet. In 12
Luke 24.50 the parting takes place at Bethany, which lay on the far side of the Mount of Olives from Jerusalem. But there is no real discrepancy here: Luke seems to have thought of Bethany as lying on the Mount of Olives

(which he calls **Olivet**), and the disciples' way **from the hill** was also the way from Bethany. **A Sabbath day's journey** was a technical Jewish term for the distance which it was permitted to travel on the Sabbath—about half a mile. Here, the phrase is simply a piece of local colour.

Jesus has departed; and from this point the centre of the story becomes the church in Jerusalem. The basic composition of this church is revealed in
13 two brief scenes. First, in a **room upstairs**, are the leaders: the original
14 Twelve (now eleven), **a group of women**, and Jesus' **brothers**. All these are familiar from Luke's gospel, and constitute the essential nucleus of
15 Jesus' followers. Secondly, out of doors, there is **the assembled brotherhood, about one hundred and twenty in all**. Nothing in Luke's gospel has prepared us for such a **brotherhood**. Jesus' last hours with the Twelve, his solitary trial and death, and the gradual recovery of faith by those who saw evidence of his resurrection, hardly suggest the existence in Jerusalem of a community of believers of this size. Nevertheless, we know (from 1 Corinthians 15.6) that the risen Christ appeared to a much larger group than Jesus' closest disciples, and in any case such a group was necessary in order to provide the "congregation" of the church which Luke is presenting at the outset of his narrative. The figure of 120 is probably no accident. In Jewish local government, 120 persons constituted the smallest group permitted to have its own council; and the number was a multiple of the inner group of Twelve. Thus Luke presents a picture—perhaps more schematic than strictly historical—of the structure of the earliest Christian church; and such is the importance which he attaches to it that he gives again (though he has already given it once in his gospel, 6.13–16) the names of the original disciples, and then goes on to describe the way in which the place left by Judas Iscariot was filled up.

The way this episode is reported is totally unlike anything in the gospel,
15 but is characteristic of the author's method in Acts. **Peter stood up before the assembled brotherhood . . . and said.** This is a formal speech, the first in Luke's work, but now to be followed by many others. Since the time of Thucydides, Greek historians had taken it for granted that they should work speeches into their narratives. Thucydides himself may have had access to records of speeches that were actually made; where he did not, he freely composed the kind of speech which he believed would have been made in the circumstances. Later historians often adopted this convention uncritically, and made up speeches as they went along to put into the mouths of leaders at appropriate moments: it was a recognized technique for enlivening the narrative and for bringing out the deeper issues underlying historical events. It was not normally expected that these speeches should be based on any surviving record or recollection of what was actually said.

Luke has already shown (by his preface) that he was ready to make use of the conventions of Greek history-writing, and it would not be surprising if he deliberately inserted speeches into his work for the same reason. Moreover, this point in his work was the natural one for such speeches to begin. Previously (almost from the beginning of the gospel) the main speaker had always been Jesus, and Jesus' discourses had consisted of sayings that were reverently preserved in the memory of Christians. The evangelist had no liberty to compose what Jesus might have said; he could only select and edit what people remembered that Jesus did say. But from now on the speakers were the leaders of the church, and it is unlikely that their utterances were preserved with anything like the same fidelity. It is possible, of course, that Luke had access to some records or recollections of their speeches; and he may often have been in a good position to know what points a Christian leader made, or was likely to have made, in his own defence against the Jewish or Roman authorities, or what kind of preaching the earliest preachers adopted when challenged to give an account of their faith. Nevertheless, we must always allow for the possibility that, on any given occasion, Luke had no information to guide him and, following the convention of contemporary historians, simply composed the kind of speech which he believed the speaker would have made.

This first speech of Peter's is a case in point. The Hebrew text of Psalm
109.8 runs, "May another seize his goods". But in the Greek version of the
Septuagint the same verse runs, "**Let another take over his charge**". 20
Peter is unlikely to have known this version, or to have used it when making a
speech (presumably in Aramaic) in Jerusalem. Only Luke (or some Greek-
speaking Christians before him who knew the text in its Greek form) could
have seen in it a prophetic instruction to fill the place of the traitor Judas. To
this extent, it is clear that Peter did not deliver this speech exactly as we now
read it in Acts: the application of Psalm 109 to Judas could have been made
only by Christians who read the Old Testament in Greek. On the other hand,
there is no reason to doubt that this is the kind of speech which Peter might
have made. The treatment of Scripture is entirely characteristic of a Palestinian Jew. It was generally believed that, apart from "the Law" (that is,
the Pentateuch, or Five Books of Moses), which had been delivered directly
to Moses by God, the remaining books that had been received into the Old
Testament were dictated to their writers by the Holy Spirit. The psalms, for
example, were given by the Holy Spirit **through the mouth of David.** 16
Some of these writings, it was recognized, applied only to the original circumstances in which they were written. But the prophets, and many of the psalms, were still open to interpretation. The events they prophesied had not yet occurred, and since it was axiomatic that every **prophecy in Scripture was bound to come true**, it was one of the preoccupations of those who studied Scripture to discern in the present, or to forecast in the future, events which could be shown to be the definitive fulfilment of Old Testament prophecies. Luke has already narrated in his gospel (chapter 24) how the

risen Jesus gave instruction on this to his disciples, and we have here an example of the technique being put to use. Psalm 69 was one of the "righteous sufferer" psalms, and contained several verses which appeared to be startlingly exact prophecies of the execution of Jesus. If so, then the sufferer's enemies in that psalm could be identified as the enemies of Jesus, and the fate which it prophesied for them could be confidently expected to come to pass. The first of Jesus' enemies to perish was the disciple who betrayed him, Judas; and the circumstances of his death were such that it seemed an exact
20 fulfilment of that verse in the psalm which ran, "**Let his homestead fall desolate; let there be none to inhabit it**" (Psalm 69.25).

18 **This Judas, be it noted.** This parenthesis recording the manner of Judas' death appears to be a note added by Luke for the benefit of his readers, rather than by Peter for the benefit of his hearers (for Peter would
19 presumably have said, "your own language", not **their own language**), and the NEB has punctuated it accordingly. It should be compared with the similar note, Matthew 27.3–10. Both accounts give the name 'Blood Acre', but each explains the origin of this name differently. In Matthew, Judas 'hanged himself'; in Acts, he has a more gruesome death, which Luke may have borrowed from other literary accounts of the deaths of notable villains —compare especially Wisdom 4.19; 2 Maccabees 9.5–9.

23 **Two names were put forward.** Both men had common Jewish names; one of them, like many educated Jews, bore a Roman **added name,** Justus. It is implied in verse 21 that both had been disciples of Jesus: it may just be chance that there is no mention of them in the gospels. The result of the incident was that the group of Twelve was reconstituted, and the church began its life with a clear organization. Or so, at least, Luke presents the matter. The letters of Paul, written some decades earlier, offer a less tidy picture.

2. 1 **While the day of Pentecost was running its course.** Pentecost means "the fiftieth day", and was the usual Greek name for the Jewish harvest festival which took place seven weeks after Passover. The festival itself, which involved the presentation of harvest produce at the Temple and a day of general festivity, has no obvious bearing on Luke's narrative, but serves simply to date it by the Jewish calendar. Jesus' crucifixion was at Passover; the church's mission began at the next festival, seven weeks later.

4 **They were all filled with the Holy Spirit.** This was the 'power from above' (Luke 24.49) which they had been told to wait for, the fulfilment of the promise that they would receive the Holy Spirit at a certain moment of time in an experience analogous to baptism (1.4–5). John the Baptist had foretold that Jesus would 'baptize with the Holy Spirit and with fire' (Luke
3 3.16). This was now fulfilled in an experience of **tongues like flames of fire.** The experience marked the moment when the Spirit was first given to the church.

But how could you tell when someone was "filled with the Spirit"? In the experience of Paul and of the later church, the Spirit was responsible for many of the moral and spiritual qualities of Christians, and was therefore a secret and slowly maturing power such that you could not always tell at a glance whether a person possessed it. But it was also responsible for some of the more spectacular gifts with which Christians found themselves endowed. One of these was prophecy (for it was the Holy Spirit which had inspired the prophets of the Old Testament); another was a phenomenon which in Greek was called simply "tongues", and for which the NEB equivalent is usually 'ecstatic utterance' or 'tongues of ecstasy'. We cannot always be sure whether this phenomenon was a succession of unintelligible sounds or an actual utterance in a foreign language unknown to the speaker. Paul's references to it usually suggest the former, whereas Luke's narrative here presupposes the latter, even though it sounded to some just like drunken speech (verse 13). In any case, both were clearly regarded as forms of a miraculous phenomenon called "tongues". It was the combination of this
gift with the gift of prophecy (telling **the great things God has done**) 11
which suddenly overwhelmed the apostles and marked the decisive moment at which the Spirit was received by the church.

So, at any rate, Luke saw the matter. He is the only writer in the New Testament to mention this episode; but that is not in itself a reason to doubt that such a thing happened not many weeks after the resurrection. But was Luke right in thinking that it marked the point at which the Spirit was for the first time given to the followers of Jesus? The author of the fourth gospel would not have agreed. According to him, the Spirit was given on the same day as the resurrection took place (John 20.22). It may be that in fact the first generation of Christians were not greatly interested in the exact moment at which the Spirit was given: it was sufficient for them to know that, after Jesus' resurrection, the Spirit was there, and was passed on through baptism to all who subsequently became Christians. But Luke, by fastening upon this particular manifestation of the Spirit (which may well have been the first of its kind), was able to use it as a kind of precise date for the beginning of the work of the church, a church which had by this time been reconstituted in its ideal form of a council of twelve apostles and a 'brotherhood' of 120 men.

He was also able to present it as significant in another way. Among the people who thronged Jerusalem at the festival season were men whose homes or whose place of upbringing lay in countries on all sides of Palestine, from North Africa to Asia Minor, from the Tigris to the Tiber. All these people were of Jewish origin (unless they were **proselytes**, that is, converts to the Jewish faith), but by living scattered in different countries they had learnt to use the local languages and dialects. It must not be imagined that they therefore could not have understood each other when they met in Jerusalem, for Greek had become an international language that was spoken throughout the countries of the eastern Mediterranean. The miracle was not that the language barrier was momentarily overcome and the curse of Babel removed (for this had been practically accomplished by the Greek cultural revolution started in these countries by Alexander the Great), but that this new message, though still addressed to Jews, seemed already to be clothing itself in the languages spoken in remote parts of the world, and therefore to be destined for world-wide proclamation.

14 **But Peter . . . addressed them.** Again a set speech, but much longer and more elaborate than the first. Its purpose is to explain the meaning of the extraordinary phenomenon which had just been witnessed, and it does so by bringing to bear upon it certain passages of the Old Testament. The first
16 passage is from the prophet Joel, 2.28–32. "**God says, 'This will happen in the last days'**". **God says** is an addition by the NEB translators, to make clear (what would have been taken for granted by Peter's listeners) that the phrase **I will** in the prophecy indicates the declared purpose of God. '**This will happen in the last days**' is also an addition, but this time made by Luke or by whatever source he was using. In the original Hebrew text and in all other versions of it known to us, the prophecy is about a quite indefinite time ("after this"). '**In the last days**' is only a slight verbal change, but it greatly alters the meaning, and makes the prophecy much more specific. Everyone knew what **the last days** meant: it was the climactic period immediately before the end, a time both of miraculous happenings and of severe tribulations, of hope and promise for the elect and of foreboding for the rest of mankind. If the scene which had just been witnessed could be shown to be the fulfilment of Joel's prophecy, then it would follow (from the way in which the quotation is introduced) that the period of the last days had already begun—or rather (since Luke seems anxious to make all this easier to grasp for a non-Jewish reader) that the new epoch which began with the birth of the church was the way in which the esoteric and visionary formulations of Jewish seers were to be given meaning on the plane of history.

The Old Testament nowhere foretold the kind of linguistic miracle which Luke has just described. But the phenomenon had been more than this. In various languages, the apostles had suddenly, with one accord, begun 'telling the great things God has done'. That is to say, they had been seized with the gift of prophecy; and prophecy, for Luke as for most Jewish thinkers, was the characteristic manifestation of the Holy Spirit. Seen in this light, what had just taken place was of a kind to which the Old Testament prophets had certainly looked forward, and the passage of Joel provided a perfect commentary on the apostles' experience. As if to underline its message, a refrain
18 is added by Luke which is not in the original: '**and they shall prophesy**'.

The 'last days', then, had begun, announced by a signal manifestation of the gift of prophecy. What had happened to bring this about? Was this simply the moment which God had mysteriously chosen to inaugurate the

new epoch? Or was there something in the immediate past which, if rightly
interpreted, could be seen to have been leading up to this moment? The
answer was, Yes: **Jesus of Nazareth.** Peter's hearers could hardly pretend 22
they had not heard of him: he had been **a man singled out by God and
made known** to them **through miracles, portents and signs.** But far
from recognizing him as the instrument of God, they had **used heathen** 23
men to crucify and kill him (a neat summary of the complicated division
of responsibility that is implied in Luke's own account of the trial and crucifixion). And that, they might have thought, was the end of the matter. **But** 24
God raised him to life again. The principal evidence for this daring
proposition was the testimony of the apostles ('**as we can all bear witness**'). 32
But it also gained greatly in credibility when it could be shown to be '**accord-**
ing to the scriptures'. This is the cue for the second text, Psalm 16.8–11. 25–28

To modern eyes there is no mystery about this psalm. It is the song of one
who has been providentially delivered from death, and who gives thanks to
the God who "does not abandon his soul to death". But the Jews were
accustomed to seeing more in their scriptures than this. The psalms were
regarded as prophecy—the phrase "**I foresaw**", which is not in the original 25
Hebrew, is a typical alteration produced by this way of looking at Scripture.
Moreover, these psalms were unquestioningly ascribed to David. Now the
indisputable fact of David's death made it impossible to think that he was in
this case prophesying about himself. Therefore it was entirely legitimate to
find in his words a prediction of some future "setting free from the pangs of
death". Such a miraculous event would hardly have happened to an ordinary
person. But David knew (from the prophecy of Nathan, 2 Samuel 7) that his
line would not die out (however much it appeared to in the subsequent
history of Jerusalem), and that it would still come to pass that, in a new order
created by God, **one of his own direct descendants should sit on his** 30
throne. This descendant of David could only be the Messiah. Evidently
then, when David appeared to predict a resurrection, **he spoke with fore-** 31
knowledge of the resurrection of the Messiah. The fact of the resurrection of Jesus did not rest only on the evidence of the apostles: it too, like the
outpouring of the Spirit which had just occurred, had been foretold in
Scripture.

Peter could thus point to two events in the last few weeks which had been dramatic fulfilments of Old Testament prophecies. But what had these two events to do with each other? Was there a real connection between the resurrection of Jesus and the outpouring of the Spirit? The answer was two-fold. First, it was by Jesus himself that the gift of the Spirit—the 'power
from above'—**was promised** (Luke makes this clear both at the end of his 33
gospel and at the beginning of Acts). Secondly, Jesus' status after the resurrection was again prophesied in Psalm 110.1 (that is to say, in an oracle which 35
David clearly did not utter about himself, and which therefore pointed to a

Person of the future). Jesus was now at God's **right hand.** Anything, therefore, which came from God (as the disciples' miraculous gift of prophecy did) now came also from Jesus. These events were all part of the same story, and witnessed to the same truth. It only remained for those who had seen
36 them to draw the correct conclusion: **'Let all Israel then accept as certain that God has made this Jesus, whom you crucified, both Lord and Messiah'.**

37 **'Friends, what are we to do?'** The Jewish public had been confronted with two uncomfortable propositions. First, a small group of Galileans had been the privileged subjects, under their very eyes, of an experience which could plausibly be interpreted as the beginning of a new age; secondly, it followed that the Jewish people as a whole, far from being entitled (as they expected) to enter upon the joys of this new age, had actually forfeited their right to do so by securing the condemnation and execution of Jesus. But Peter's answer (which perhaps also shows traces of Luke's mature reflection upon the deeper implications of this question) was encouraging. On the first point, the prophecy of Joel made it quite clear that the new dispensation
39 would affect a far wider circle than this first group of Christians: **'the promise is to you, and to your children, and all who are far away, everyone whom the Lord our God may call'** (a sentence compounded of Biblical phrases, and drawing also upon the continuation of the text from Joel already quoted). In other words, it was open to the whole Jewish people (and others: the sentence seems to allow already for the future mission to the Gentiles) to receive the same blessing. Secondly, even the complicity of the Jewish people in Jesus' crucifixion was not an insurmountable barrier. For Christian baptism—which is here mentioned for the first time as the rite of
38 initiation into the church—conveyed **forgiveness of sins** (as John's baptism had), and was also the means of receiving **the gift of the Holy Spirit** (which was not the case with John's baptism, but was something new and distinctive). Christianity, in short, was destined to be a universal religion—though one must not read back a modern and liberal universalism into this passage. It was never envisaged that the whole world would become Christian; only that men of every nationality would have the chance of joining the new com-
40 munity of the elect and so of saving themselves **'from this crooked age'** (another biblical phrase: Deuteronomy 32.5).

The response was massive; and in a single day the Christian brotherhood was transformed from a fairly small group of friends into a community to be numbered by thousands. How was this crowd of new members to express its
2 common allegiance? Luke answers by giving a sketch of its **common life.** [a]

[a] The Greek text of this paragraph contains some unusual idioms which suggest that Luke may have been transcribing some earlier description of the church's life, or at least making use of some phrases which had become part of the technical language of the early church. Exactly what is meant by **to share the common life** in this sentence is not clear.

Two points may be noticed. The phrase, **breaking bread,** is repeated, and 46
suggests a technical expression for the Lord's Supper; and the community of goods (about which Luke has more to say later) is an answer to questions very deliberately raised in Luke's gospel with regard to Jesus' teaching on wealth and poverty.

So far the narrative has let the young church appear as a sensational but perfectly legitimate fulfilment of the faith of the Jewish people. The 'last days' foretold by the prophets had begun; the promised outpouring of the Spirit was an undeniable fact; and the way was open for the Jewish people as a whole, despite their complicity in the execution of Jesus, to repent, to join the new community of believers through baptism, and themselves to receive the Spirit. Indeed, the Christians felt themselves to be so perfectly expressing
the true Jewish faith that **they kept up their daily attendance at the** 46
temple. But there was more to it than this. Membership of this new community involved holding certain beliefs about Jesus, who was not just an important figure of the immediate past, but whose "name" was still powerful among them. Specifically Christian (as opposed to Jewish) doctrines began to appear; and it was these which produced conflict between the Christians and the Jewish authorities. The first instance of this arose out of a miraculous case of healing.

One day at three in the afternoon, the hour of prayer. This was the 3. 1
time of the afternoon sacrifice of a lamb at the altar before the temple, and was observed as one of the two "hours" of public prayer. Jews, wherever they might happen to be, would break off their occupations to pray; and those who could do so went to the colonnaded courts of the temple for the purpose. We have just been told (2.46) that the Christian brotherhood did this regularly, and it was as a matter of course that **Peter and John were on their way up to the temple.** Beggars naturally took up their positions at the gates where most people entered. There were eight gates at different points of the wall of the temple enclosure, and two more at the entrances of the two inner courts which only Jews were permitted to enter. None of
these is called '**Beautiful Gate**' in any of the descriptions we possess of the 2
temple. A late tradition gives the honour to the one gate (part of which still exists) on the east side of the temple enclosure;[a] but this, being comparatively little used, would have been an unlikely place for a beggar to choose. A better place would have been one of the two main gates leading into the inner courts. These gates were of some magnificence; and one of them may well have been called '**Beautiful Gate**'.

However, the speech by Peter, which offers a commentary on the miracle,

[*a*] The Greek for **beautiful** is *hōraia*; the Crusaders took this to be the Latin word *aurea*, "golden", and so to this day the gate is pointed out to visitors as "The Golden Gate". In the time of Christ its usual name was Shushan Gate.

11 was given **in Solomon's Portico,** which stretched the whole length of the
temple area on the east side. The crowd had become aware that a miracle
had just taken place; and their natural reaction was to assume that it was an
act of God in reward for the exceptional **godliness** of some individual. Peter
explained that there was now a new power in heaven—but not such as to
infringe in any way the unique sovereignty of the God of the Jewish faith.
13 God was still '**the God of Abraham, Isaac, and Jacob, the God of our
fathers**'; but he had now brought to fulfilment the Old Testament prophecy
(Isaiah 52.12) that his **servant** would be given **the highest honour.** This
servant (with all the destiny of rejection and vicarious suffering which is
spelled out in chapter 53 of Isaiah, a chapter quoted at greater length in
Acts 8) was none other than Jesus, whom the people of Jerusalem knew
mainly as one who had been condemned as a criminal **in Pilate's court,** but
whom the apostles proclaimed to have been raised from the dead. If (as
followed from the apostles' experience) this Jesus had been given by God
the highest honour, it followed that he now had 'the name above all names'
(as Paul puts it, Philippians 2.9). Now the sudden cure of the cripple would
have been commonly understood as an exorcism—the casting out of a spirit
which had kept the sufferer physically captive by paralysis or atrophy of the
limbs. The recognized technique of the exorcist consisted in invoking the
name (and so the power) of a being more powerful than the evil spirit. Jesus
now had the most powerful name in the universe (after that of God himself,
which it was blasphemous to pronounce), and it was by invoking this that
6 Peter had performed the cure: '**In the name of Jesus Christ of Nazareth,
walk**'. Not that this Name could be used mechanically: such a miracle (so at
16 least Luke understood it) demanded **faith**—either the faith of the subject
of the cure, or (as the rather involved Greek sentence could also mean) the
faith of the exorcist who invoked the Name.

17 '**And now, my friends, I know quite well that you acted in ignorance**'. Had their rejection and condemnation of Jesus been carried out in
full knowledge of Jesus' real nature, then clearly their action would have
brought decisive judgement on themselves. But (and this seems to pick up a
saying attributed to Jesus in some manuscripts of Luke 23.34) they **acted in**
18 **ignorance.** Moreover, there was a higher destiny at work. '**This is how
God fulfilled what he had foretold in the utterances of all the prophets: that his Messiah should suffer**'. Where in fact does one find such
prophecies in the Old Testament? It is hard enough to find any explicit
references to a future Messiah at all, and there is certainly none which suggests that this Messiah was to suffer. Moreover, little as we know for certain
about Jewish religious expectations in the time of Jesus, we do know that it
would have been unusual to envisage a suffering Messiah—and the men who
nursed Messianic expectations certainly knew their Bibles. That the **Messiah
should suffer** was not written in so many words anywhere in the Old

Testament. It was an inference first drawn by Christians. What they appear to have done (under the guidance of the risen Jesus, according to the last chapter of Luke's gospel) is to have seen, in the many passages of the Old Testament where a righteous and godly man suffers, a reference to the suffering of Jesus. And since Jesus, they now believed, was the Messiah, it could be said that **all the prophets** had foretold that the **Messiah should suffer.**

Jesus' death, then, had been foretold. It was destined to happen, and those who allowed it to happen were the unwitting agents of the purposes of God. They had done wrong, but the wrong was not irremediable. But now, with the outpouring of the Spirit upon the church, the 'last days' had begun, the end was not far off. To Jewish thinkers in the past, it had often seemed as though the promised consummation of history was a long time in coming. God had promised a new and glorious age for his people: what was preventing it from dawning? One answer was beginning to be suggested at this period: the end could not come until there was sufficient righteousness on earth. Only a national repentance would hasten it. And this seems to provide the clue to Peter's speech. Stung by the enormity of their error in obtaining Jesus' crucifixion, the Jewish people might now at last repent and so bring
nearer **the time of universal restoration** (a somewhat philosophical- 21
sounding term for the new age expected by the Jews). The new age would be
inaugurated by that same Messiah, Jesus, whom God had **already ap-** 20
pointed, and who now occupied the place of honour in heaven. This time,
however, there would be no second chance. Another prophecy which Jesus
had fulfilled was an oracle of Moses (Deuteronomy 18.15), "**The Lord** 22
God will raise up a prophet for you from among yourselves as he
raised me". A second Moses was another figure who (on the basis of
this passage) was fitted by some thinkers into their picture of the time preceding the end. But a stern warning was attached to this figure (Deuteronomy
18.19), made still sterner when combined with a verse from Leviticus (23.29):
"**anyone who refuses to listen to that prophet must be extirpated** 23
from Israel". All these events, along with their critical significance for the
Jewish people, could be found predicted in Scripture (given the true interpretation of the relevant passages). '**So said all the prophets, from** 24
Samuel onwards'.

"**And in your offspring all the families on earth shall find bles-** 25
sing". This promise to Abraham (Genesis 22.18) was a keystone of the self-understanding of the Jewish race: one day the blessing they enjoyed would be so manifest that the rest of the world would acknowledge it and benefit from it. More perceptive spirits, like John the Baptist, had seen that mere membership of the Jewish nation was not enough to guarantee this blessing: there must be repentance as well. The matter had now been brought to a head. They must repent at once, before it was too late—and there is already a hint in Peter's words that otherwise the promise might pass to others, it had

26 only been made to the Jews **first.** It was to be for Paul to turn the same text
of Genesis on its head and prove from it that all along the real inheritors of
the promise were the Gentiles (Galatians 3).[a]

The temple area, in part of which this scene took place, was under the
administration of the reigning High Priest, assisted by a number of senior
4. 1 officials such as the **Controller of the Temple,** all of whom belonged to
the Jerusalem aristocracy of **chief priests.** This aristocracy consisted for the most part of **Sadducees,** who differed from the more learned party of the Pharisees on, among other things, the question of **the resurrection from the dead.** They denied any resurrection—this is stated in the New Testament and is one of the few facts known about them. As such, they were bound to be opposed to the new faith, which vigorously proclaimed **the resurrection from the dead—the resurrection of Jesus.** Luke's narrative, quite plausibly, makes them the first adversaries of the church. Whatever exactly had been happening in Solomon's Portico, it would not have been difficult for them to have Peter and John arrested on the pretext that they were causing a disturbance within the jurisdiction of the High Priest.

However, the court to which these prisoners would be brought next
5 morning consisted not only of the **Jewish rulers** and **elders** who, along
with the chief priests, could be expected to be Sadducees, but also of **doctors**
6 **of the law,** who were usually Pharisees. Luke insists that **the high-priestly**
family were there in force, and actually names four of them (Caiaphas, not **Annas** his father-in-law, was actually High Priest at the time, but Annas was doubtless still influential and still bore the title **High Priest**; we know little about **Jonathan,** who was Caiaphas' immediate successor, and nothing about **Alexander**). But the original complaint of the Sadducees was re-
7 placed, in court, by a much more serious enquiry. **'By what power,' they**
asked, 'or by what name have such men as you done this?' A cure had taken place in the sacred precincts of the temple, and the man who had worked the cure had been heard invoking a **name.** To have pronounced the name of a pagan deity in such a place would have been a serious offence. The evidence certainly justified an **examination** by the court.

8 **Then Peter, filled with the Holy Spirit, answered.** The apostles had
received 'power from above', the Holy Spirit; but this meant, not that they were constantly in an ecstatic or inspired state, but rather (at least as it appears in Acts) that the new power was available to them at moments of need. In his gospel (12.11–12) Luke records a saying of Jesus promising the help of the Holy Spirit to all Christians who would have to defend themselves in court; and here is the first example of it. Peter's answer adds little to what

[a] The above is an attempt to give a consecutive account of the argument of Peter's speech. But the speech contains some unusual expressions and fragments of doctrine, and it may be that it incorporates material which was part of the very early preaching of the church and which fits a little awkwardly into the framework of the speech as edited by Luke.

has already been said in earlier speeches. The '**name**' was not that of any
pagan deity (for Peter, at the end of the speech, showed that he understood
the seriousness of this charge: as a good Jew he recognized that '**there is no** 12
other name under heaven'). It was that of **Jesus Christ of Nazareth.** 10
This Jesus was no new and foreign element in the faith of a Jew. Both his resurrection (which the apostles had witnessed) and his crucifixion (in which the Sanhedrin had been instrumental) were foretold in Scripture; and to bring home to the court that even their own rejection of Jesus was foreordained, Peter makes use of another text that was much used in the church
—'**the stone rejected by the builders . . . has become the keystone**' 11
(Psalm 118.22).

This speech showed **boldness**, but also an ability to interpret Scripture 13
which was surprising in **untrained laymen**, until it was realized that, as **former companions of Jesus**, they would have received instruction from their master. The court was in some difficulty over the case. The defendants had said nothing to incriminate themselves, and they could not proceed
further without witnesses; and although the miracle was now **common** 16
knowledge in Jerusalem, the crowd was in no mood to give evidence
against the apostles; indeed **the people were all giving glory to God for** 21
what had happened. They had no alternative but to let the prisoners off with a caution. This would at least provide stronger grounds for proceeding against them next time, which was a matter of some importance in view of the prisoners' defiant question—the classic question of conscience since the
time of Socrates—'**Is it right in God's eyes for us to obey you rather** 19
than God?'

'**Sovereign Lord**'. The prayer is hardly one which could have been 24
uttered spontaneously by the congregation **as one man.** On the other hand, it does not follow that Luke composed it all: it may well contain phrases of prayers which Luke had heard used in the Christian church. From the earliest period of Greek literature down to the collects in the Book of Common Prayer, formal prayers have tended to fall into a certain pattern. First, the deity is invoked by his name or title, then certain of the deity's attributes are recalled, and only then is the actual petition reached. This is exactly the pattern here. In addition, much of the language is drawn from a prayer in the Old Testament (Isaiah 37.16–20), which Luke has adapted to his purpose. The weight of the prayer lies in the quotation from Psalm 2.1–2, which is shown to have been exactly fulfilled in the events of the Passion. In the time of the Kings of Judah, the reigning king was called the Anointed One (the Messiah), and was regarded as the chosen representative of God's people on earth. To make cause against him was therefore, in a
sense, to set up in opposition **against the Lord** himself. In later times, when 26
there was no longer a king in Jerusalem, the psalm was read as a prophecy about the coming Messiah. Jesus, Christians believed, was that Messiah;

and the other references in the psalm could all be filled out from the gospel
26 story. **The kings of the earth** were represented by Herod (who appears
only in Luke's narrative of the trial: was it Luke's interest in this psalm
which made him include this episode?), **the rulers** by Pontius Pilate; and
the psalm, which proclaimed the futility of this opposition, had been
strikingly fulfilled in a general sense by the resurrection of Jesus.

It was a natural belief of pagan religions (and the idea is found occasionally
in the Bible), that when a deity hears the prayer of his worshippers he expresses his approval by a clap of thunder or an earthquake. Luke was writing
for readers used to this convention. Whether or not the earthquake actually
31 happened, there can be no doubt about Luke's meaning: God had answered
the Christians' prayer.

32 **The whole body of believers was united in heart and soul.** The picture
of the first Christian community, already sketched in 2.44–47, is now
33 presented in greater detail. Two features of it are singled out: the **great
power** which attended the witness of the apostles (which is abundantly
illustrated in the episodes which follow), and the unanimity of the whole
32 community which found expression in the fact that **everything was held
in common.** This sharing of all worldly possessions is never referred to in
the New Testament, apart from this passage and 2.44–5 above, and it is certain that it never became a permanent or widespread institution in the church. Paul's letters, for instance, with their frequent exhortations to give generously, presuppose that members of the church were still in possession of their own property. In his gospel, Luke gives special prominence to sayings of Jesus which seem to lay upon his followers a total renunciation of material wealth, and it is tempting to see here Luke's answer to the question how such an injunction could ever have been carried out in practice. If so, it is proper to ask whether such a radical experiment in communal living ever took place, or whether Luke, in this respect as in others, may not be painting a somewhat idealized picture of the first days of the church. On the other hand, it is unlikely that this first Christian community would have allowed its poorer members to become destitute or to go hungry. The Jewish nation as a whole had a very strong social conscience about poverty, and generosity towards the poor was highly esteemed. It was to be expected that the Christians would take this duty even more seriously; and moreover, the old prophecy in Deuteronomy 15.4, "There will be no needy person among you", which had never yet been fulfilled in the history of the nation, was very naturally taken to apply to the "last days" which had begun with the history of the church. We know from Paul's letters that within a few years the community in Jerusalem became the most impoverished part of the church, and its difficulties may well have begun in the aftermath of a radical effort to make good the poverty of some of its members.

Two anecdotes illustrate the principle. The first introduces a figure who
subsequently plays a prominent part in the story. **Joseph** was a very com- 36
mon name, and it was inevitable that he should have been known by some other name as well; but why Luke says that the apostles surnamed him **Barnabas**, and that this meant '**Son of Exhortation**', we cannot tell. Barnabas was a Semitic name of pagan origin which was becoming not uncommon among the Jews; but so far as we know it did not mean anything like 'Son of Exhortation'.[a] This Barnabas, at any rate, was a **Levite**; that is, he belonged by birth to that particular class of Jews who had the privilege of performing certain lesser duties in the temple.

But there was another man. The second anecdote tells, as it were, the 5. 1
other side of the story, and is to our taste exceedingly shocking. We are at a loss to understand how it could have been right or admirable for Peter, a disciple of Jesus, to have used his new power to carry out summary execution on a defaulter, particularly since this was in flat contradiction to the procedure recommended in Matthew 18.15–17. It is true that the story shows signs of having gained in the telling. Even though burial normally took place shortly after death, it is hardly conceivable that a man could have been buried without his wife being told, and the repetition of the miracle when Sapphira made her appearance strikes us as frankly implausible even if we grant the possibility of Ananias' sudden death. We are tempted to suspect the hand of the story-teller, anxious to heighten the effect of his tale. But even if the original episode was less startling and less shocking, we still have to ask why Luke thought it proper to recount it in its present form.

No fully satisfactory explanation has ever been advanced. Nevertheless, there are certain factors which would have been taken for granted by many of Luke's readers, and would have made their reaction to the story somewhat different from ours. In the first place, we know of two other examples of similar experiments in communal living at about the same period. One was the community at Qumran which produced the Dead Sea Scrolls. Here, anyone who dissembled the value of the property he contributed was punished with temporary exclusion from the community. The other was an experiment in communal farming which (according to Diodorus Siculus, a Greek historian who wrote only a generation before Luke) was carried out in a village in Spain. Here, the punishment for keeping anything back for private use was death. Evidently, this kind of dishonesty was generally regarded as a serious sin. In the second place, even though the cue for the story was the sharing of possessions, the point which it illustrated was the 'great power' (4.33) of the apostles, due to the possession of the Holy Spirit.
Peter was able to represent Ananias' deception as a lie '**to the Holy Spirit**', 3

[a] Another possible meaning of the Greek phrase is "Son of Consolation", and this, curiously enough, is the meaning of another name, Manaen, which is mentioned along with Barnabas in 13.1.

and this made it a weighty matter. From the Old Testament on, the attitude required of men by God was "faith", that is, a readiness to accept wholeheartedly the demands and the promises of God. The opposite attitude was called "putting God to the test": it consisted of questioning whether God really intended a certain demand, or whether he would really fulfil a certain promise. This kind of challenge to God was expressly forbidden in the Law (Deuteronomy 6.16), and Peter was drawing attention to the seriousness of
9 this offence when he said, **'Why did you both conspire to put the Spirit of the Lord to the test?'** The punishment brought about through Peter was proportionate to the gravity of the sin. And in the third place, it is possible that Luke approached the story as it were from the other end. The gift of Christ to his church was a gift of new life, and we know that in early years it was a source of bewilderment to Christians when they found that some of their number had died. The explanation which first gained acceptance was that these people must have committed some serious sin since they joined the church, and that their death was an inevitable punishment. In this connection, Paul suggested that the sin most likely to have caused such deaths was that of not discerning the Body of Christ in the sacrament of the Lord's supper (1 Corinthians 11.29–30). But Luke has recorded a saying of Jesus to the effect that 'for him who slanders the Holy Spirit there will be no forgiveness' (Luke 12.10). It is possible that the story of Ananias and Sapphira began its life as an attempt to explain why two members of the early church died suddenly within a few days of joining the community.

12 **They used to meet by common consent in Solomon's Portico.** These words give a visual picture. Any substantial Greco-Roman city possessed one or more porticos—the Greek word is *stoa*—which consisted of a long building open on one side, the roof supported by rows of columns. These buildings were the natural centre of informal life in the city; they afforded shelter from sun and rain, and were convenient for doing business, conducting discussions, and holding small meetings. Jerusalem too possessed its *stoas*, particularly in the temple area, where there was certainly supervision by the temple police, but where nevertheless they provided a natural meeting place for many different kinds of people. In Greece, it was common to see a small crowd in a *stoa* gathered round a philosopher—indeed the Stoic school of philosophy got its name from its custom of meeting in a certain *stoa* in Athens. A Greek reader will have been able to visualize at once the meetings of the first Christian community **in Solomon's Portico.**

But the church was more than a group of disciples listening to its master. The apostles had miraculous powers (and a sensational attribute of Peter—healing even by his shadow—adds a slightly legendary touch to the description of massive instances of healing). The group could not be entered lightly
14 (witness the story of Ananias and Sapphira), yet **numbers of men and**

women were added to their ranks. These three points all follow from the episodes already narrated. In this brief paragraph they are combined a little awkwardly, and the awkwardness may be evidence that more than one strand of tradition was available to the writer, which he then had to reduce to a single narrative.

Then the High Priest and his colleagues. The action continues to 17
unfold within the temple area of Jerusalem. This area was under the ultimate
control of the High Priest. It was administered by another officer of high-
priestly family, the **Controller,** through a company of **police** who were 24, 22
Levites. The '**Sanhedrin**', which Luke here explains as **the full senate of** 21
the Israelite nation (a solemn and slightly archaic-sounding phrase in the
Greek), was primarily a law-court, with competence to decide on all cases
which came under Jewish law, especially matters affecting religion. Its
meeting place was in, or at least very close to, the temple area; and the
prison was doubtless near by. As on the previous occasion (4.1–3), there was
no difficulty in finding a pretext to have the apostles arrested in this area—
the only obstacle was public opinion (verse 26)—and Luke once again
attributes this action to the **jealousy of the Sadducean party,** who could 17
be presumed to object to any new movement which seemed to give support
to the Pharisees' doctrine of resurrection of the dead. Luke, indeed, seems
to have assumed that the Pharisees, the Sadducees' opponents, were at this
time fairly favourably disposed to the church, and he underlines this by
reporting that the man who was responsible on this occasion for saving the
apostles from a sentence of death was one of the most famous of all Pharisaic
lawyers, **Gamaliel.** 34

But an angel of the Lord opened the prison doors during the 19
night. A supernatural rescue of this kind is described in detail in chapter 12,
and Luke does not spoil the effect by anticipating it here. It was sufficient to
mention briefly the divine assistance the apostles received and the almost
comical embarrassment they caused their captors next morning. The
narrative returns to sober prose when it comes to the serious matter of the
trial. Neither the personal **jealousy** of the Sadducees nor the miraculous 17
events of the night are referred to again. The issue is now one of law and wise
government.

The legal charge has two points. First, the apostles have disregarded the
judicial warning they have received, and are continuing to teach **in that** 28
name which they have been expressly forbidden to pronounce; and secondly,
they have been putting it about that the Jews themselves (and presumably
therefore the supreme Jewish court) have been **responsible for that man's**
death (a vivid touch: the judges deliberately avoid pronouncing the **name**
of Jesus which they have forbidden others to mention). We should now call
such charges "contempt of court", and certainly some such offence as this
existed in the Jewish legal code. But Luke may have been less concerned to

make the charge sound technically convincing than to give Peter the cue for
another direct appeal to the Jewish nation, this time through its leaders. His
reply to the charge of disregarding the court's orders is an epigrammatic echo
30 of the defence he made before (4.19): **'We must obey God rather than
men'**. He then goes on to admit and elaborate the other charge. The Jesus
whose "name" was in question was a person whom the God of the Jews had
raised up. [a] It was no good their saying that, since crucifixion was a Roman
penalty, Jesus' death was no responsibility of theirs. Scripture allowed for
the corpse of a criminal being hung on a **gibbet** (Deuteronomy 21.22); and
if the manner of Jesus' execution was (in a sense) allowed for in Jewish law,
the Jewish leaders could not argue that it was no concern of theirs. But this
31 Jesus had now been exalted to be **leader and saviour,** and (the point with
which almost all Peter's speeches have ended) the words he uttered at the
time of his execution were still valid: 'Father, forgive them; they do not
know what they are doing' (Luke 23.34, in some manuscripts only). If they
denied this, they would have to deny not only the word of the actual
32 **witnesses to all this,** but the manifest power possessed by believers which
proceeded from **the Holy Spirit given by God.**

31 But the Jews, as a nation, refused this offer of **repentance and forgiveness of sins**—this is one of the themes which runs right through Acts; and
33 the reaction of their leaders expressed this with unmistakable finality: **this
touched them on the raw and they wanted to put them to death.**
Moderation was advised by the distinguished Pharisee Gamaliel. Two somewhat similar pretenders had made their appearance in recent history, and
had been effectively dealt with by the Roman occupying forces. The Sanhedrin could safely follow the same policy with regard to Jesus, who had
37 perished in the same way as the others, and whose **following** would doubtless soon also be **scattered.** The idea of the speech is plausible, and Gamaliel
may well have recommended a policy along these lines. **Judas the Galilean**
was well known: he had been the leader of the famous rebellion which had
36 followed the hated census of Quirinius in A.D. 6–7. **Theudas** was equally well
known—by the time Luke was writing; but in this case the rebellion took
place some thirty years after Gamaliel is represented as making this speech.
Luke was fond of linking his narrative to memorable events of contemporary
history; but he had not the means which a modern historian possesses of
checking all his dates.

40 **They sent for the apostles and had them flogged.** This was in itself a
severe penalty (on occasion it resulted in death); but the apostles rejoiced.
41 **To suffer indignity for the sake of the Name** was to be a frequent
experience in the future. These first apostles were the prototypes of many
later generations of Christian leaders.

[a] The Greek word, like its English translation, is ambiguous. It could mean "brought into history" or "raised from the dead". See the footnote in NEB.

The church moves outwards

Up to this point, the history of the church has been presented according to a very simple pattern. We have the picture of a single, homogeneous community, sharing all its resources in a spirit of enthusiastic charity, and meeting regularly under the leadership of the twelve divinely commissioned apostles. But the next events allow us to see that it was not really quite so simple. Those who made up the first Christian congregation in Jerusalem belonged to a number of different social and cultural groups, and the existence of these differences was to prove a significant factor in the process by which "the church moved outwards", first to Jewish or mainly Jewish centres outside Jerusalem, and finally to the great cities of the Roman empire.

Those who spoke Greek and those who spoke the language of the 6. 1
Jews. This is the first indication that the church was far from homogeneous. Literally (as the NEB footnote explains) the two parties are called by Luke "the Hellenists" and "the Hebrews". It is likely that the most obvious difference between them was a difference of language. Although Greek was the official language of the Roman government in Palestine, and although most educated Jews were probably able to speak and understand it, the native language of the Jewish people at this period was Aramaic. But Jewish families who had lived for any length of time abroad had lost the habit of speaking either Aramaic or the sacred language of Hebrew, and had adopted Greek as their first language. When such people returned to Jerusalem they continued to speak Greek, not only in secular life, but also in prayer and worship: they used a Greek translation of the scriptures and attended a synagogue where the service was in Greek. Thus, even though these two groups probably knew enough of each other's language to be able to communicate, there existed in Jerusalem (and doubtless in other cities in Palestine) a clear linguistic division between the Jews who spoke Greek and the Jews who spoke the local dialect of Aramaic. In fact, however, the division probably went deeper than this. With the Greek language went a culture and a habit of thought very different from that of the Old Testament; and the Jews of the Dispersion, though they remained loyally and self-consciously Jewish, inevitably came to understand their ancestral faith in terms somewhat different from those still used by their kinsmen in Palestine. In particular, they can hardly have escaped the influence of the sophisticated Greek philosophical approach to religion (which regarded the images and sacrifices of pagan religions as primitive and irrelevant), and they may well have found the continual slaughter of animals which took place before the temple at Jerusalem, and the emphasis on ritual and ceremonial matters which was characteristic of Palestinian Judaism, difficult to reconcile with the much more ethical and philosophical faith in which they had been brought up. How much

of this cultural and religious cleavage between the two groups was in Luke's mind when he called them "Hellenists" and "Hebrews" we cannot say. But the cleavage was undoubtedly there; and once Christians began to be recruited from both groups it was inevitable that the church would begin to show different lines of development.

However, the first signs of discord arose (according to Luke) out of a purely practical matter. The Christian community, like any Jewish community, had a strong social conscience about those of its members who were
1 **widows** and therefore most likely to be destitute,[a] and had organized a daily distribution. Complaints were made that the Greek-speaking widows were not receiving their share, and the proposal of the Twelve was that the distribution should now be administered more systematically, thereby incidentally lightening the burden upon themselves. Seven men were appointed, and duly commissioned at a ceremony the form of which was clearly inspired by a well-known scene in the Old Testament (Numbers 11): Moses, overwhelmed by the number of cases being brought to him, commissioned seventy elders to assist him, who then received "a portion of his spirit".

Luke does not tell us how this arrangement was intended to heal the dispute, nor whether it was successful. The seven men were all presumably
5 Jews (except one, who is singled out as **a former convert to Judaism**) and all bore Greek names; but Greek names were so common even among Palestinian Jews that we cannot tell which party they belonged to. In any case, the narrative can hardly be regarded as giving an accurate picture of the situation. By Luke's own time, there existed in at least some parts of the church an order of "deacons" such as is described here; and possibly Luke read back into this episode (as the later church certainly did) the moment when this order was instituted. But in what follows, Luke has to admit that two of these new "deacons", Stephen and Philip, by no means limited their activities to "waiting at table", but were as active in preaching and as remarkably endued with miraculous powers as the Twelve themselves (8.26–40; 21.8). Seven, like twelve, was a usual number for the inner council of any Jewish community. We can hardly be wrong if we see in these Seven the leaders of the growing Greek-speaking section of the church, corresponding to the Twelve who presided over the others. Certainly this Greek-speaking group remained sufficiently distinct and sufficiently important to become the victim, independently of the apostles (and presumably the Aramaic-speakers), of the first serious wave of persecution which hit the church.

7 (Luke mentions by the way that **very many of the priests adhered to the Faith.** He seems to have been particularly well informed about priests: see above on Luke 1.5–10.)

[a] See below on 1 Timothy 5 (p. 671) for the social status of these widows.

Some members of the Synagogue called the Synagogue of Freed- 9
men. The scene of action now shifts from the crowd of native Jewish
Christians gathered in the temple to the more cosmopolitan society of Greek-
speaking Jews elsewhere in Jerusalem. After the conquest of Palestine by
Pompey in 63 B.C., many Jewish captives were taken to Rome and sold as
slaves. Subsequently they, or their children, mostly regained their freedom,
either by purchase, or as a reward for faithful service. They then became
known by the technical Latin name (which Luke transliterates into Greek)
of *libertini*, **Freedmen,** and those who returned to Palestine seem both to
have kept the name and to have formed a distinct community with its own
synagogue. Traces of a synagogue which may well have been theirs have been
found in Jerusalem, and the building could easily have become a centre for
Jews from other parts of the world as well. [a] At any rate, it was with cosmopolitan Jews of this kind, speaking Greek and having, perhaps, some of the
presuppositions which went with Greek culture, that Stephen became involved in debate. But the debate soon turned into something more serious,
and Stephen found himself, like Peter and the apostles before him, arraigned
before the Council on a serious charge. Nevertheless, this charge was a 12
very different one from that which had been brought against the apostles.
The apostles had been assiduous in their attendance at the temple, and their
outward behaviour had been entirely correct by Jewish standards. Their
offence had consisted entirely in the fact that they had been heard invoking
a new "name". But Stephen had alarmed even his more cosmopolitan
hearers by his overt criticism of the temple itself and of the prescribed
observance of the Jewish Law. So, at least, **false witnesses** alleged. The 13
charges are very similar to those brought against Jesus himself in the accounts of Jesus' trial before this same Council in Matthew (26.59–61) and Mark (14.57–9). Luke omits them there to bring them in here. Doubtless the charges were distorted in both cases: they were brought by **false witnesses.** But in Jesus' case they appear to have arisen from words he actually used. If we may judge from the speech which follows, the same was also true of Stephen.

To the modern reader, Stephen's long speech is exceedingly puzzling. 7. 1–53
Instead of presenting any kind of defence, it appears to consist almost entirely of a sketch of the history of Israel, drawn in the main from the Old Testament and breaking off unexpectedly when it reaches the time of Solomon. Only a final imprecation directed at the court serves to remind us who has been speaking all this time and what the occasion is. The rest reads like a piece of academic history. But to anyone familiar with Jewish literature and Jewish oratory, the impression given by it might have been quite different.

[a] The Greek of verse 9 is ambiguous, and does not make it clear whether this synagogue "comprised" Jews of other nationalities (as the NEB takes it) or whether these other nationalities also had synagogues of their own.

The main facts of their national history were repeated over and over again by the Jews. Two of the psalms which they used in their worship (105, 106) contain little else, and there are three other similar résumés in the prose books of the Old Testament (Joshua 24, Nehemiah 9, Judith 5). But not all these résumés have the same purpose. Compare Psalm 105 with Psalm 106. The story told in both is much the same; but whereas, in the first, all the emphasis is on the greatness of the favours shown by God to his people, in the second it is on the wilful obstinacy of that people in response to these favours, and to the patience of God who still did not repudiate the promises he had made to them. All depended upon the use which was made of the historical facts, and upon the emphasis placed upon the different phases of the story. When a speaker began to make his own résumé of Jewish history, his hearers would have been quick to notice small points of detail indicating the lesson the speaker wished to draw from it.

In fact, a Jewish audience would have found Stephen's presentation startling. From Abraham to Joseph the story is told quite conventionally; but with the appearance of Moses, who occupies almost the whole of the rest of the speech, a new tone begins to be heard. In the Old Testament, and in Jewish piety generally, Moses was the supreme law-giver through whom the people had received from God the inestimable benefit of the Law by which they lived. But here the point made again and again about Moses is
25 that he and his message were consistently rejected by the Jewish nation. '**He thought his fellow-countrymen would understand that God was offering them deliverance through him, but they did not under-**
35 **stand.**' '**This Moses, whom they had rejected . . . was commissioned**
39 **as ruler and liberator by God himself.**' '**But our forefathers would not accept his leadership.**' These sentences occur nowhere in the biblical narrative, and indeed they could not, for they represent a view of Moses as the rejected emissary of God which is totally strange to the Old Testament. If this was really Moses' destiny, it was a destiny very similar to that of
37 Jesus; and the prophecy in Deuteronomy (18.15), "**God will raise up a prophet for you from among yourselves as he raised me**", which was quoted earlier in a speech of Peter, becomes more clearly than ever a prophecy about Jesus.

From this presentation of the story of the Book of Exodus, as a repeated national rejection of Moses and all that he stood for, radical consequences
41 are drawn. The Israelites' worship of the golden **bull-calf** (Exodus 32), which is made to appear in the biblical narrative as no more than a temporary aberration, here marks the climax of Israel's repudiation of Moses and the
42 worship of the true God. As a result, God **gave them over to the worship of the host of heaven.** We know what this phrase meant to a Greek-speaking Jew: the cult of foreign idolatrous gods, combined with astrology. This, Stephen dares to say, was the character of all Jewish worship subsequent

to their idolatry in the desert; and by way of support he quotes a passage of 42–3
Amos (5.25–7) which in its Hebrew form seemed to emphasize the purity of the worship offered by the desert generation, but which in the Greek Septuagint translation (quoted here)[a] gave colour to the opposite view, that in fact the golden bull-calf was by no means an isolated instance, but that other heathen gods were worshipped as well. From that time onwards (this is Stephen's argument) no one could claim that Jewish worship had ever been according to the will of God.

What then of the temple in Jerusalem, the place where the traditions of Jewish worship were most jealously preserved according to the forms laid down in the first books of the Old Testament? This is the culminating point of Stephen's speech. The building of the temple itself by Solomon was merely another instance of the Jews' idolatry. It ought never to have been
built! The provisional **Tent of the Testimony** which had accompanied 44
their forefathers **in the desert** was all that should ever have been required by way of a shrine; anything more was idolatrous. Some support for this could be found in 2 Samuel 7, where David is dissuaded by the prophet Nathan from undertaking the work himself; but the place to look for overt criticism of the temple was in the great Old Testament prophets. Stephen
chose a passage from Isaiah (66.1–2—a text we now know to have been 49–50
written after Solomon's temple had been destroyed and before another had been built in its place). It came naturally to Jews to quote this passage when attacking the idolatrous temples of the heathen. But their own temple contained no image, no idol. It would hardly have occurred to them that Isaiah's words could be used to attack their own institutions. Yet this is exactly what Stephen did.

'Like fathers, like sons'. The subsequent history of Israel could be 51
summed up in a sentence. It was simply a succession of similar rejections of the Word of God, provoked each time a prophet appeared among them. The point is made sharper by means of two traditional legends which had grown up recently. One was that (however little the scriptures said about it) all the prophets had been persecuted (see above on Matthew 23.29). The other was
that, at Sinai, the Law was given to Moses by **God's angels**, a clear proof 53
of its divine sanction.[b] The Jews had consistently rejected its spokesmen,
from Moses onwards; and now their betrayal and murder of **the Righteous** 52
One (a title for Jesus which very occasionally occurs in the New Testament and subsequent writings) was simply the last and decisive stage in the long
history of a people that had consistently shown itself '**stubborn . . . heathen** 51
. . . at heart and deaf to the truth'.

a] The last word, according to all known versions, should be Damascus. But as a matter of history, the Exile was to Babylon, and the change was a natural one for any speaker to have made.

[*b*] See below on Galatians 3.19, in which passage, however, Paul apparently uses the presence of angels as an argument for the relative inferiority of the law!

It can be seen at once that this is a very different approach from that of Peter, whose speeches always end with a statement that God's pardon was still offered to the Jewish people. Here, by contrast, the Jews are totally condemned, not only for their treatment of Jesus, but for their stubbornness throughout their history. Did Luke deliberately compose speeches of such a very different tenor? Or did he possess some record of the kind of speech Stephen might have made, and incorporate it in his narrative despite its apparently inconsistent doctrine? We have seen that this approach to the temple and to Jewish institutions was something that was to be expected from Jews whose first language was Greek and who had been brought up with some Greek culture. Admittedly Stephen's speech went a great deal further than a Jew (particularly in Jerusalem) would normally have dared to go, so much so that the synagogue took alarm and reported him to the authorities. Nevertheless, the speech represents the kind of thinking which could well have been done by a Christian convert from this comparatively cosmopolitan milieu, and Luke may have heard examples of such preaching. Moreover, it contains a number of words and idioms which are unusual for Luke and suggest that he was drawing upon some source rather than composing freely as he went along. On the other hand, the argument of the speech fits happily into the grand design of Luke's history. First, in the preaching of Peter, pardon and salvation is offered to the Jews; when they refuse it, the gospel is taken to the Gentiles. Stephen's speech marks the turning-point: Peter's appeal gives place to Stephen's polemic. The result is the first persecution of the church and the extension of the mission field outside Jerusalem to Samaria and beyond.

It could still be said that, whether or not Luke composed the speech, it is singularly inappropriate to the moment. This was Stephen's opportunity to make his defence; instead, he made an attack on his accusers so stringent that they gave up all pretence of giving him a fair trial, and delivered him to summary justice. This is true; but it is not only the speech which shows that Luke was not taking the details of the trial too seriously. At the beginning, the Council is described as a court sitting in judgement (6.12, 15); but after the
56 speech, Stephen can see '**a rift in the sky**'; the scene seems to have shifted
58 into the open air, and moves rapidly to its climax when they **set about**
stoning him. Luke apparently knew one of the technical details about stoning: the first stones were cast by the witnesses against the defendant—and these duly appear when Luke mentions that **the witnesses laid their coats at the feet of a young man named Saul.** Luke seems to have
60 visualized Stephen on level ground, sinking down **on his knees** under a
hail of stones. In this he was probably correct. It was only in the following century that the Jewish penalty of stoning began to take the form of throwing the victim down a cliff and then, if he was still alive, hurling large stones on top of him.

Whether or not Luke possessed any accurate information about the circumstances of Stephen's death, we can see the motive which led him to describe it as he did. The death of the first martyr to the faith must follow the same pattern as the death of Jesus; and so we find that Stephen was arraigned before the same court as Jesus, and on the same charges, and
that at the moment of death he uttered the same prayers: **'Lord Jesus,** 59
receive my spirit' (Luke 23.46—except that the prayer is now addressed
to Jesus himself), and **'Lord, do not hold this sin against them'** 60
(Luke 23.34). The wording in each case is different; but these variations are very much in Luke's manner. Since Luke often seems to omit a detail from the gospel narrative if he intends to use it in Acts, it is all the more striking that he includes these prayers on both occasions. The echo is clearly intentional.

One more touch brings the two scenes into line. In Luke's account of Jesus' appearance before the Council, the only statement made by Jesus was, 'From now on, the Son of Man will be seated at the right hand of Almighty God'. In these words, Jesus proclaimed that he was about to be vindicated. It was Stephen's privilege to have a vision of this vindication. To describe it,
he used almost the exact words of Jesus' prediction, including the title, **Son** 56
of Man, which otherwise never occurs outside the gospels.

All except the apostles were scattered. This brief paragraph is highly **8.** 1
impressionistic, and is the writer's way of getting the characters into their
places for the next scenes. **Stephen was given burial** (in a manner again 2
perhaps deliberately reminiscent of the burial of Jesus); **Saul, meanwhile,** 3
was harrying the church—having apparently received startling promotion
from being merely a young bystander at the stoning of Stephen (7.58) to
being entrusted (presumably) with strong executive powers by the Sanhedrin. It was necessary for Luke to find a place to sketch his portrait as a
persecutor of the church before narrating his conversion in the next chapter.
And, most important for leading into the next episode, the **violent persecu-** 1
tion which followed Stephen's death was the immediate cause of the spread of Christianity to places outside Jerusalem, some of the Christians having been **scattered over the country districts of Judaea and Samaria.** The apostles themselves, however, remained in Jerusalem—this is a presupposition of the next episode (verse 14). Luke allows for this by saying that **all except the apostles were scattered,** which is sufficient for his purpose here, but hardly gives a fair picture of what was happening in Jerusalem. Quite apart from the improbability of the leaders being spared while the rank and file were persecuted, we find that in 9.31 and 11.1–2 there is still a church in Jerusalem. Luke has so stressed the unanimity of the church at this stage that he cannot easily allow for different groups within it; but it is fairly clear that the persecution must have been aimed particularly at the Greek-

speaking element of the church which, as a result of Stephen's teaching, could be accused of open opposition to Jewish institutions, whereas the Palestinian element, under the leadership of the apostles, continued to meet in the temple and to follow Jewish customs, so that there was not yet any clear cause for a breach with the authorities.

5 **Philip came down to a city in Samaria.** Just as, to a New Testament
writer, "Galilee" meant a primarily Jewish area of Palestine, despite several purely pagan towns that had grown up in it, so **Samaria** meant the region lived in by the Samaritans, even though its capital (called Samaria in the Old Testament) had been rebuilt by Herod the Great as a secular Hellenistic city, and was now called Sebaste, after the Greek form of the name of the Emperor Augustus. Therefore, wherever precisely Philip began his activity,
6 **the crowds** who **listened eagerly** must be imagined as Samaritans, a race
very close to the Jews in language and religion, but socially and politically opposed to them. They represent the first stage in the advance of Christianity from Jerusalem to Rome.

5 Philip **began proclaiming the Messiah to them**: he is specifically
called 'the evangelist' later on (21.8)—that is, one who proclaimed 'the
6 gospel'. But the side of his work which is emphasized here is his **miracles,**
9 and these brought him into competition with a local magician **named**
Simon. The story which Luke tells of Simon first joining the following of one whom he saw to be more powerful than himself, then trying to obtain, not only this power, but the means of transmitting it to others, and finally repenting of his dishonest ambitions, represents a clear contrast between the magic arts practised by not a few notable magicians in antiquity and the authentic activity of the Holy Spirit, transmitted by the apostles to the
15 church. (This is the point of the intervention of **Peter and John** from
Jerusalem: baptism at this time seems normally to have consisted of a single
16 rite in the course of which converts were immersed in water in **the name of**
17 **the Lord Jesus,** and then **received the Holy Spirit** when the minister
laid his hands on them. But it was important in Luke's presentation of church history that the Jerusalem apostles should be seen to have been responsible for any advance of the church into new territories, and so he suggests that on this occasion the rite as administered by Philip was incomplete, and that the presence of the apostles was necessary before the new converts could receive the Holy Spirit.)

But, just as Philip was more than a miracle worker, so there are at least hints in the narrative that Simon was more than a magician. The people
11, 6 were not merely **carried away by his magic,** they **listened eagerly to**
him. He was himself a teacher, making great claims for himself. The title,
10 "**The Great Power**", is a little mysterious, but it suggests at least that
Simon believed himself to be divine—and this takes us at once into a different kind of world from that of the Jewish Christian preachers and their mono-

theistic Samaritan converts. It was among pagans that one found people claiming to be divine. In any case, we know a little more about this Simon. By the middle of the second century he was widely regarded as the first great heretic of the Christian church, and as the originator of all those complicated combinations of mythology with a dualistic philosophy which are usually called Gnosticism. Doubtless much that was told about Simon a century later is legendary, and many of the doctrines attributed to him were first worked out well after his lifetime. But there is no reason to doubt that this was the same Simon as the one who appears in Luke's narrative; if so, he was a more formidable rival than a mere magician would have been, and alongside the simple contest of supernatural power described by Luke there must have been the makings of a far-reaching philosophical and religious dispute. However, in this narrative Peter is allowed to dispose of him with the kind of malediction a magician might have used himself, full of biblical
phrases. **'You are doomed to taste the bitter fruit and wear the fetters** 23
of sin.' In the original (translated literally in the NEB footnote) this is an almost meaningless formula compounded of phrases from Deuteronomy 29.18 and Isaiah 58.6.

Then the angel of the Lord said to Philip. It was perhaps natural for 26
Luke to go straight on to this second story about Philip, even though it does not quite fit into his design; it appears to let Philip steal a march on the apostles in preaching the gospel outside Jerusalem. But the episode is nevertheless presented as being entirely in accord with the divine plan. It is set in
motion by **the angel of the Lord**, and directed by **the Spirit** (the two seem 29
here to be almost equivalent as bearers of intimations from God); without
this, Philip might hardly have thought of going **'south to the road that** 26
leads down from Jerusalem to Gaza'. Gaza, until its destruction in A.D. 66, was a flourishing city on the trade route to Egypt and lay on the edge of the desert. It had been rebuilt in the previous century not far from the site of the old city, which had been destroyed in 96 B.C. by the Maccabean army so thoroughly that it became almost a byword for a deserted place. For both these reasons, Gaza made one think of "desert", and this may be why Luke adds a note which, translated literally, runs, "This is desert". But it is impossible to be sure which word this phrase is meant to explain. It could be Gaza, which was in some sense "desert": but, as the story which follows is all about the road to Gaza, not Gaza itself, it seems more likely that Luke meant (as it is here translated), **This is the desert road.** The difficulty is that none of the possible routes from Jerusalem to Gaza goes through desert; at most there could have been stretches of the descent through the mountains which were comparatively "deserted"—and this was perhaps all that was necessary to underline the miraculous nature of the encounter between Philip and the foreign traveller. In any case the scene can hardly have been in real
desert, since the travellers soon **came to some water.** 36

The story is vividly told, and there is a strong biblical flavour in the lan-
27 guage. The **Ethiopian** came, not from modern Ethiopia, but from the country to the north of it, lying roughly between Aswan and Khartoum, in the Sudan. This "Ethiopia" represented to the Greeks, and probably to Luke, one of the extreme limits of the world; but its people were well known, through trade and politics, and it is recorded that more than one of its rulers was a queen bearing the title **Kandake.** That the chief finance minister should have been **a eunuch** was to be expected in an oriental court. But why should such a person have **been to Jerusalem on a pilgrimage**? He can hardly have been a Jew; but Luke may have thought of him as one of those sympathetic Gentiles who accepted the main principles of the Jewish religion without actually being admitted into the Jewish community. If so, he was the first Gentile to be converted to Christianity, though the point is not stressed by Luke.

The Ethiopians spoke their own language, but presumably this **high official** also knew Greek, and was reading from a scroll of a Greek version of
28 Isaiah. Everyone in antiquity read **aloud** (silent reading, without at least a
movement of the lips, was very unusual), and Philip, walking beside the
carriage, was able to hear what he was reading. The passage was Isaiah
32–3 53.7–8. This whole chapter, a description of a certain "servant" of the Lord
who was subjected to suffering he had not deserved, and whose manner of
bearing it was said by the prophet to have been "for our sins", was seen by
the early church as a clue to the meaning of Jesus' suffering and death. The
34 eunuch's question, **'who is it that the prophet is speaking about here: himself or someone else?'** is one which has been debated by scholars ever since. But whereas the modern approach is to try to answer the question by analysing the thought of the prophet and determining what his words are likely to have meant at the time that he wrote them, a Jewish scholar of the first century A.D. (and indeed of many later centuries) would have proceeded quite differently. He would have assumed that it was no accident that these verses of Isaiah did not fully explain themselves: they were clearly intended to point forward to—or "to be fulfilled" in—some other great person, through whom God would continue to shape the destiny of the people of Israel. The problem was to find a person, in the past, the present or the future, whom these words exactly fitted. So far as we know, Jewish scholars had not yet arrived at a satisfactory answer. But the church was quick to seize on this passage. Jesus' suffering and death had fulfilled it in remarkable
35 detail. It was, in short, an admirable place to "start from", in order to preach **the good news of Jesus.**

36 **'What is there to prevent my being baptized?'** The eunuch's question was regarded as a serious one as soon as the church began to develop its institutions: candidates had to show their knowledge and conviction of the faith before they could be baptized, and this is probably why some manu-

scripts insert a verse at this point to show that in fact the eunuch fulfilled
these conditions (see the footnote in NEB). But this is not Luke's concern
here. The point is the foreigner's readiness to accept the new faith, sealed by
immediate baptism. We can infer roughly how this took place. The two men
walked down to the bed of a *wady* where water was flowing, and Philip
cupped his hand and poured water over the head of the eunuch, invoking the
name of Jesus Christ. Philip then mysteriously disappeared, and began to
preach in the towns of the coastal plain from **Azotus** in the south to **Caesarea** 40
in the north.

Meanwhile Saul was still breathing murderous threats. Saul ('also 9.1
known as Paul', 13.9) becomes the leading figure in the second half of Acts,
and it is necessary for Luke to prepare for this by working in the story of his
conversion here. The story is recognizably the same as that to which Paul
alludes himself in Galatians 1.16, but it is told here (and in two other places
in Acts) in much more detail. At times it is not easy to reconcile this account
with the facts which Paul mentions in Galatians, and one is forced to ask how
far Luke had reliable sources to go by and how far he was simply filling in the
details as best he could, given the bare facts that Paul was at first a persecutor
of the church, was then suddenly converted, but only paid one brief visit to
Jerusalem in the course of his first fourteen years of activity as a Christian
preacher. On the one hand, Saul's experience (like the visions at the beginning of Luke's gospel) has a number of conventional features, and has clearly
been written up fairly freely by Luke (for how else could an ancient writer
set about recording experiences that are essentially incommunicable? We
should probably now attempt the task in mystical or psychological language;
but for Luke it was more natural to use the traditional apparatus of a dazzling
light and a heavenly voice). On the other hand, there are details which are
not only plausible in themselves, but are confirmed by independent evidence
(such as the basket in which Saul was lowered from the walls of Damascus: 25
Paul mentions this himself in 2 Corinthians 11.33). These details set a limit
to the extent to which Luke's narrative can be regarded as legend or imagination; at the same time, they do not force us to regard the whole narrative as a
strictly literal account of historical events.

Letters to the synagogues at Damascus. Damascus was the oldest of 2
the cities of the Decapolis. It was now a rich Hellenistic city, but contained a
large colony of Jews. We know that local synagogues had legal authority
over the faith and observance of their members; but we have no other
evidence that the High Priest in Jerusalem was in a position to procure the
arrest of members of synagogues of the Dispersion in a city some 200 miles
away from Jerusalem. However, Saul's journey to Damascus was a logical
extension of his attempt in Jerusalem to eradicate Christianity (here intrigu-
ingly called **the new way**—literally, "the way": we do not know the source

of this expression); and we learn incidentally (what we should hardly have guessed otherwise) that the Christian gospel had already made considerable progress outside Jerusalem. This makes it likely (though Luke says nothing about a lapse of time) that Paul's conversion took place at least a few years after the first preaching of the gospel in Jerusalem.

3, 4 The **light** and the **voice** are conventional and plausible features of such
an experience; but whereas the speaker is usually an angel, here, and throughout the episode, it is none other than Jesus himself, the **Lord**. And more than
5 this: **'I am Jesus, whom you are persecuting'**. It was implied in some of
the sayings of Jesus, as well as in the more systematic thinking of Paul, that
Jesus would in some sense be present in his followers and therefore in the
church. Here, this is taken for granted. In persecuting the church, Saul had
been persecuting the very Jesus who was now addressing him. But this Jesus,
he now knew, was **Lord**. To our minds, the shock of this realization would
have been sufficient to account for his temporary blindness and his refusal
to eat or drink. But Luke's reason for mentioning these physical effects was
probably quite different. Some kind of "sign" regularly followed a message
from heaven (Zechariah was similarly struck dumb at the beginning of Luke's
gospel), as if to confirm the authenticity of the experience. In Saul's case this
9 was temporary blindness; and that he **took no food or drink** should be
understood as a penitential fast, indicating the reality of his change of heart.
By the time Luke was writing, a comparable fast was probably undertaken
by all Christian converts immediately before baptism.

10 **There was a disciple in Damascus named Ananias**—the second
person in Acts bearing this not uncommon Jewish name (Hananiah). His
vision—in reality something heard, not seen, but this was the case with
many "visions" in the Old Testament—recalls that of the young Samuel (1
11 Samuel 3). **'Go at once to Straight Street, to the house of Judas'**. These
are precise directions. Damascus, like other Greco-Roman cities in the Middle
East, was intersected by a straight street which ran from one side of the city
to the other. It was a mile long, with avenues of Corinthian columns.
Officially, it was probably named after some Emperor or public figure; but
there is no reason to doubt that, for most people, it was simply **'Straight
Street'**.[a] Judas was a very common name. If Luke had to invent the address,
this would almost have been the obvious one to choose.

13 **Ananias answered, 'Lord, I have often heard about this man'**. This
sounds like an objection, and if Ananias were the principal character in the
story, it would probably be right to ask questions about such a hesitant
reaction to the heavenly summons. But the central figure is still Saul, and

[a] This street is still shown to visitors today. It now looks jagged and narrow, since modern houses and shops have used the Roman paving as foundations, and have encroached on the original surface of the street. But there is little reason to doubt that the line of the street has remained unaltered since the first century A.D.

Luke's purpose in this dialogue is to say a little more about him. First, the
terror he inspired as a persecutor is once again emphasized. Secondly, '**This** 15
man is my chosen instrument': the phrase has a biblical sound, and the
definition of Saul's future task corresponds with the words he was later to
use himself (Galatians 1.16). He was to preach, above all, **before the nations**
(that is, to non-Jews): this was the new and decisive aspect of Paul's divine
commission. Luke adds, '**and their kings**'—a hint of Paul's appearances
before pagans—as well as '**the people of Israel**'—for his mission was never
to be quite divorced from that of the other apostles among the Jewish
people. And finally, there was much '**that he must go through**'. The 16
Greek word means "suffer". The church was now beginning to understand how it could be said that Christ had been 'bound to suffer' (Luke 24.26), and had already had a taste of the kind of suffering which would mark its members as faithful followers of their Lord. Paul, who up to now had assumed the task of inflicting suffering, was henceforward to undergo it no less than the others. This word "suffering" could mean actual death; and Paul had probably died as a martyr by the time Acts was written. But his own letters are sufficient evidence of the actual suffering he bore during his lifetime (see especially 2 Corinthians 11.21–7).

Ananias was sent to Saul to give him recovery, baptism, and the Holy
Spirit. **It seemed that scales fell from his eyes.** The metaphor seems an 18
odd one (and has no basis in ancient or modern medicine), but it occurs also in the story of the healing of Tobit's blindness (Tobit 11.11–13), and there are other hints in Luke's work that he drew on the book of Tobit for the details of miraculous events. Thus, once again, Luke may either have had access to a reliable source which supplied him with this detail; or else he may have used his literary knowledge to fill out the details of the facts which he could infer for himself. There are three such facts here: first, Paul certainly recovered his sight; secondly, he was certainly baptized (for all Christians were); thirdly, his subsequent preaching showed that he had received the Holy Spirit (which was in any case usually an inseparable part of baptism).

He stayed some time with the disciples in Damascus. It is at this 20
point that the narrative begins to diverge from what Paul says himself in Galatians. There we learn that he 'went off at once to Arabia' (1.17). Luke appears to know nothing of this, nor of the fact that it was 'the commissioner of King Aretas' (who was the ruler of the Nabatean kingdom, the nearest part of Arabia to Damascus) who was responsible for the measures taken against Paul in Damascus (2 Corinthians 11.32). But this could be due simply to his lack of information. The discrepancies become more serious in the description of Paul's first visit to Jerusalem. This, Paul tells us, took place three years after his conversion, by which time his story must certainly have been known in Jerusalem, and it can hardly have been necessary for Barnabas to explain matters to the apostles. Moreover, this visit was an entirely private

affair lasting only a fortnight, in the course of which Paul saw only two of the
leaders of the church (Galatians 1.18–20). Luke may have known that Paul's stay
was short, without knowing the reason. If so, it would have been a reasonable
guess on his part that Paul, like Stephen, had come in contact with **the** 29
Greek-speaking Jews, and that he too had quickly aroused so much opposition that he had to leave the city rapidly.

Meanwhile the church, throughout Judaea, Galilee, and Samaria, 31
was left in peace. By means of these brief summaries, Luke allows us to
glimpse the kind of progress the church was making apart from the episodes
he actually records. He has told us nothing about any preaching in Galilee
(though we can imagine that the recollection of Jesus' activity there made it
an obvious place for a mission), but he has mentioned that Philip was
working his way up the coastal plain of Judaea from Azotus to Caesarea (8.40),
and it was presumably to visit these new congregations that Peter made a 32
general tour, including Lydda (the modern Lod) some thirty miles north-
west of Jerusalem, and Joppa, which lay on the coast at the end of the same
road. These visits were remembered for two miracles performed by Peter,
which gave a new impetus to the spread of the gospel in the area (**Sharon** 35
was the name of the coastal plain from Joppa to Caesarea). Both are told on
the model of miracles that had been performed by Jesus. That of the cure 33–
of Aeneas (a Greek name, but one that could easily have been taken by a Jew)
recalls the cure of a paralytic in Luke 5.24; the following story is more subtly 36–
constructed. Bringing a dead person back to life was the most impressive of
all miracles. In the Old Testament, it had been accomplished once by Elijah
(1 Kings 17.17–24) and once by Elisha (2 Kings 4.32–7), and echoes of these
stories can be heard in Luke's narrative. In his gospel, Luke records two
occasions when Jesus performed it (7.11–17; 8.51–6). The second of these
occurs also in Mark; and in Mark's version (5.38–43) the actual Aramaic
words are preserved which Jesus used, *talitha cum*. In Luke's version, only
the translation is given, 'Get up, my child'; but we can hardly doubt that,
when he came to write the story of Peter's miracle, the original words were in
his mind; for, translated back into Aramaic, Peter's '**Get up, Tabitha**', 40
would be *tabitha cum*—the same formula, but for one letter, that was used by
Jesus. Yet there is no question of the miracle having happened simply through
the recitation of a magic phrase. The reason for it (apart from Peter's exceptional power) was a moral one of the kind which very much appealed to
Luke: [a] much emphasis is laid on the fact that Tabitha **filled her days with** 36
acts of kindness and charity.

At Caesarea there was a man named Cornelius. Caesarea, named **10**
after the Emperor Caesar Augustus, was one of Herod the Great's most
spectacular achievements. From a small seaside town he transformed it

[a] See above on the healing of the centurion's servant, Luke 7.1–10.

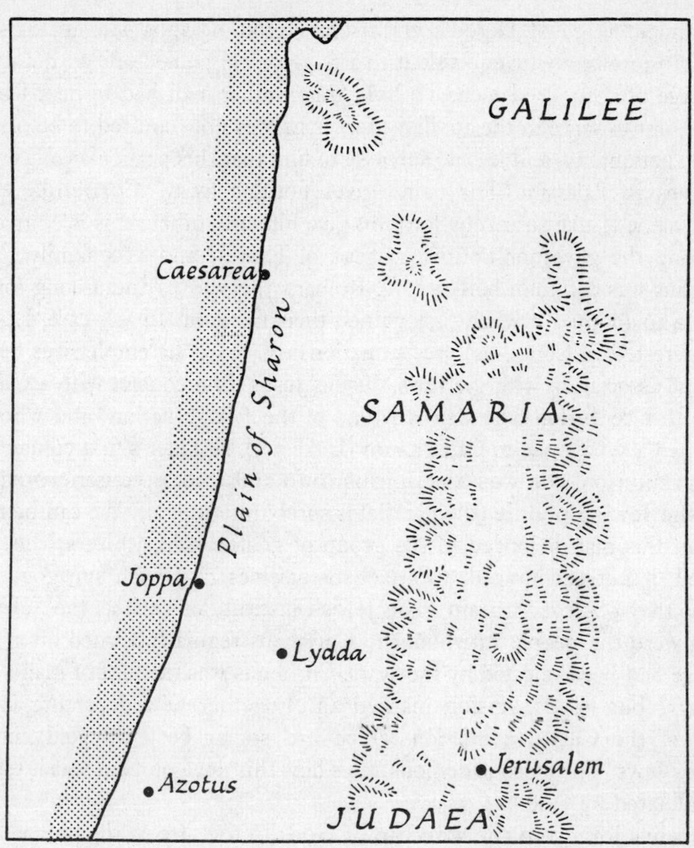

into the most important port on the coast of Palestine; and when the territory came under direct Roman rule in A.D. 6, the city was made the administrative capital of Judaea and the headquarters of the occupying army. It therefore marks an important stage in the progress of the gospel. From its beginnings in Jerusalem, *The church moves outwards* until it reaches the seat of Roman government in Caesarea—just as, in the second half of Acts, Paul advances the gospel from its beginnings in Palestine to the centre of the empire at Rome. Caesarea was politically the most important city that has yet appeared in the story.

Cornelius, a centurion in the Italian Cohort, as it was called. The regular legions of the Roman Army were stationed in Syria; in Judaea, the garrison consisted of auxiliary troops, who were organized in separate "cohorts" of about 500 men. It is known from an inscription that a cohort named *Cohors II Italica* was stationed in Syria later in the century. There is no reason to doubt Luke's word that it was on duty at Caesarea in Judaea somewhat earlier: the only time it cannot have been there is during the

independent reign of Herod's grandson, Herod Agrippa II, A.D. 41–4. A **centurion** was roughly equivalent to a non-commissioned officer, nominally in charge of a hundred men. To hold this rank, a man had to be a Roman citizen, but to serve in the auxiliary forces he was not required to be of pure Roman nationality, and it is no surprise to find that this particular officer had
24 **relatives** in Palestine. His name gives nothing away. **Cornelius** was a family name (Luke strangely does not give him any other: this is equivalent to calling the governor Pontius instead of Pilate); and as a family name, Cornelius was common both among Romans themselves and among former slaves who adopted it when they gained their freedom. In any case, Luke is not interested in Cornelius' precise nationality. What he emphasizes here is his close association with the Jews. Just as Jesus' first contact with a Gentile was with a centurion who was 'a friend of the Jewish nation' and who had presented a synagogue to Capernaum (Luke 7.5), so Peter's first contact was
2 with a centurion who **was a religious man** and who **gave generously to help the Jewish people** (the parallel is surely intentional). We can be more precise: this man belonged to the group of gentile sympathizers who were allowed, if not encouraged, to attach themselves to Jewish synagogues so long as they observed certain basic Jewish institutions such as the Sabbath. These were the people to whom the Christians regularly turned after their message had been rejected by the Jews. Cornelius was the first of many such converts; but his conversion marked an altogether new departure in the policy of the Christian mission which had so far been directed entirely towards Jews. The episode demonstrates how this development was intended and validated by God.

Cornelius **joined in the worship of God**. In the Greek, the phrase has a slightly technical sound, and we can infer what it means: he regularly attended the synagogue, and had adopted some of the Jewish customs, particularly that of saying his prayers at the prescribed hours of the day. One of
3 these hours was **about three in the afternoon.** (Cornelius says himself that
30 he was **saying the afternoon prayers** when the vision took place.) The
4 angel uses a striking Jewish idiom: **'Your prayers and acts of charity have gone up to heaven to speak for you before God'.** It was a common notion of Jewish piety that the function of liturgical prayers and of good deeds was to spur God to gracious action by "reminding" him of the deserts of the individual and of the people. The events which follow are to be seen as immediate proof that a gracious action of God was under way. Luke has presented the centurion as (from the Jewish point of view) the most deserving kind of Gentile imaginable; and he even adds the detail that his household
7 was of the same character: he had **a military orderly who was a religious man.**

The journey from Caesarea to Joppa was about thirty miles. Cornelius' servants may be imagined as having started the same afternoon and covered

a certain distance by nightfall, leaving perhaps fifteen to twenty miles to be
covered the next day between dawn and midday. **About noon Peter went** 9
up on the roof to pray. This is local colour: the flat roof of a Palestine house, perhaps with an awning to give shade, offered cool and solitude in the middle of the day. On the other hand, Peter had no business to be hungry and expect a meal: the Jews ate in the early morning and again in the afternoon. But the Romans ate at midday—and Luke was writing for readers used to the houses of Greek and Roman society. It was important to introduce the vision as coming upon a man who was both hungry and at prayer. To Luke's readers, this could best be conveyed by a time **about noon.**

The background of the vision is Leviticus chapter 11. That chapter makes a distinction between animals that are "clean" and "unclean", and forbids the eating of pork and of the meat of many smaller birds and animals. These prohibitions were regarded as binding by all Jews; and Peter was reacting
like any of his race when he said, **'I have never eaten anything profane** 15
or unclean'. That God should count any of these forbidden creatures **clean** would have seemed an impossible proposition (even though Jesus had said something which came near to it, Mark 7.15). It is not said that Peter attempted to take the vision literally—this would have implied an incredible reversal of lifelong sensibilities. But within a day he was to discover the application of the vision to a matter in which the words "clean" and "unclean" were certainly much used: the relationship of Jews and Gentiles.

The characters in the story continue to move under divine guidance: there is to be no question at the end of it of the decision having been Peter's
own. Peter might well have had some **misgiving** about accepting the mes- 20
sengers' invitation, even though (as Luke emphasizes once again) their master was a man of exceptional piety. Strictly speaking, all social contact with Gentiles was forbidden; but in a city like Caesarea this extreme exclusiveness was impracticable, and in fact many Jews treated their non-Jewish neighbours with great civility. Nevertheless, there was always a certain reserve: to be too much at ease in gentile society was regarded as a dangerous compromise with pagan and idolatrous customs. Peter was doing no more than many of his more liberal and courteous contemporaries when
he gave the messengers a **night's lodging** in his own house: this did not 23
oblige him to eat with them or even to share a room with them. But it was a
different matter when he actually **went in** to Cornelius' house as Cornelius' 27
guest. To be the honoured guest of a pagan meant being ready to accept a pagan's ways. Even if there is a touch of exaggeration in it, Peter's statement well expresses what would have been the normal reaction of a Jew in such a
situation: **'a Jew is forbidden by his religion to visit or associate with** 28
a man of another race.' But Peter had had a vision and was directed by the Spirit; he had divine authority for making this new departure in social relations.

Cornelius, for his part, was inspired by the same deference and humility towards a Jew as his prototype in the gospel who had tried to forestall Jesus with the words, 'it is not for me to have you under my roof' (Luke 7.6). He
25 met Peter outside the house with **deep reverence**: no forwardness on his part was to blur the outlines of Peter's radical decision, a decision prompted entirely by the Spirit. So the scene was set as for a formal disputation:
24 Cornelius with **his relatives and close friends** on one side, Peter with
23 **some members of the congregation at Joppa** on the other.
33 **'All that the Lord has ordered you to say'**. We expect the speech that follows to be an appeal to the Gentiles present to repent and believe in Jesus Christ, along the lines of the speeches which Peter has already made to the Jews in Jerusalem; and in fact many of the same points are made as on previous occasions. But here the tone is strangely different. Instead of culminating in a direct appeal to his hearers, this speech of Peter's seems almost to be addressed to himself and to the Christians who have accompanied him: the important pronoun is not "you" but "us". Moreover, far from proclaiming the "good news" about Jesus, Peter almost apologizes for mention-
38 ing these familiar facts—**'You know about Jesus of Nazareth'**. In the Greek, the whole paragraph is put together in a way that is barely grammatical, and presents an appearance of unexpected roughness in the pages of a writer normally as polished as Luke. This may be evidence that Luke had before him some document in Aramaic which was difficult to translate into idiomatic Greek. But the passage also contains a large number of words and phrases characteristic of Luke's own writing, and possibly the explanation of its curious construction is to be looked for in a different direction. The nearest thing in Luke's writing to this almost ungrammatical heaping of clause upon clause (which is one of the peculiarities of this speech) is to be found in the songs of worship which he has put in the mouths of Zechariah, Mary and Simeon at the beginning of his gospel; and in the rest of the New Testament the closest parallel is in some passages of certain letters (such as the opening of Ephesians and Colossians) where the writer adopts the devotional language of liturgical prayer, and perhaps even incorporates phrases from prayers already used by the Christian church. This is the style of Peter's speech here. Whether or not some of the phrases are those that were actually used in the church by the time Luke was writing, the atmosphere of the speech is distinctly Christian and devotional. Peter is, as it were, thinking aloud, and the language he uses is that of the church recalling the great events of the gospel. The summary of Jesus' life is not the usual preacher's reference to his death, resurrection and exaltation, but comes nearer to being a résumé of the gospel narratives that were composed for the instruction of Christians. Peter is meditating on the facts that were known to all Christians
34 —but from a new angle. **'I now see how true it is that God has no favourites'**. This was a maxim to which many liberal Jews in the Dispersion

might have subscribed. Outstanding examples of piety among the Gentiles would surely not go unrewarded, and to say as much as this it was only necessary for Peter to have been particularly impressed by the evident holiness of Cornelius. But even this would normally have been said with a certain reserve: some advantage surely still remained with the Jews. God
sent his word to the Israelites: it was precisely their possession of the 36
revealed word of God which gave the Jews their unique advantage. But there was now the further fact that he had given **the good news of peace through Jesus Christ.** And (this is the critical point reached in Peter's meditation) Jesus Christ is **Lord of all,** Lord not only of the Jews who believe in him, but of men of all races. As Paul puts it in his letter to the Romans (10.12) in words that are very close to these, 'there is no distinction between Jew and Greek, because the same Lord is Lord of all'. However local and Jewish
the story might seem (and Luke once again, by calling it **a gibbet,** makes 39
even the Roman instrument of the cross appear as something allowed for in the Old Testament), its significance, like the message of the greatest of the
prophets, was universal, for **everyone.** This was the startling conclusion to 43
which Peter was being led while he went over in his mind the familiar facts of the gospel story; and as if to confirm this conclusion, before even Peter had finished speaking there came upon all present a dramatic repetition of the experience of Pentecost. But this time, "all present" included Gentiles. They too were manifestly inside, not outside, the group of chosen people. The
next step was a matter of course: **'Is anyone prepared to withhold . . .** 47
baptism from these persons?'

News came to the apostles and the members of the church in 11.1
Judaea. Peter himself had been convinced; but he still had to carry the other leaders of the church with him. As always, it was the practical implications of this new development which caused most concern. Theoretically, most Jews were prepared to believe that their religion was ultimately destined for the Gentiles as well, and it need not have been a great shock to the apostles to hear that **Gentiles . . . had accepted the word of God**; the gospel had merely accelerated a process which until now had lain hidden in the inscrutable purposes of God. But the practical implications of this new development were harder to accept. Were Jewish Christians now to reverse their lifelong attitudes and receive Gentiles as equals into the church and into their
houses? Their question to Peter voiced their immediate scruples: **'You** 3
have been visiting men who are uncircumcised', they said, 'and sitting at table with them!' Peter's answer makes it clear that, far from having taken this questionable initiative himself, he was only obeying a divine summons, the objectivity of which was guaranteed by the parallel experience of Cornelius. One could no more doubt that the Holy Spirit had truly been given to these Gentiles than one could doubt the reality of the apostles' experience on the day of Pentecost. Both were equally fulfilments of

16 the promise of a baptism **with the Holy Spirit** that Jesus had given just
18 before his ascension (1.5). Only one conclusion was possible: **'This means that God has granted life-giving repentance to the Gentiles also'**. How this worked out in practice is the subject of the rest of the book.

After Caesarea, Antioch—the third largest city in the Roman empire, the wealthy and cosmopolitan capital of the Province of Syria. Christianity had of course spread to other places outside Palestine by this time—Luke men-
19 tions **Phoenicia** (the Levantine seaboard north of Caesarea) and **Cyprus**—but it was still a movement confined to the Jewish communities in those countries. The place where the breakthrough to the gentile world was to take place was Antioch. Luke mentions this after he has told the Cornelius story, and so gives the impression that the one followed from the other. So, from a theoretical point of view, it doubtless did; but Luke has to admit that it was not Peter, nor even one of the other Jerusalem apostles, who first
20 **began to speak to Gentiles as well**, but **some natives of Cyprus and Cyrene** (at least one of whom, Lucius, may be mentioned by name in 13.1). In fact, we know from Paul's letter to the Galatians (2.11–14) that when Peter visited Antioch he was not yet wholeheartedly committed to the principle of a gentile church.

Nevertheless, Luke's history is written on the assumption that all major
22 advances were authorized by the Jerusalem church. **Barnabas** had already appeared (4.36) as an early member of that church; he was also certainly known to Luke as a close companion of Paul on the first missionary journey undertaken from Antioch (13.4). This made him the obvious link between the two branches of the church, and Luke even goes so far as to suggest that it was his authority (doubtless again representing the authority of the Jerusalem apostles) which brought to Antioch the most famous of the apostles to the Gentiles, Saul.

26 **It was in Antioch that the disciples first got the name of Christians.** This is of a piece with what Luke has told us about the church in Antioch. So long as all Christians were Jews, to the outside world they appeared simply as a Jewish sect, and there was no need to distinguish them by a particular name; and since all Jews believed in some sort of future Messiah or "Christ", the name "Christian" could never have arisen in Jewish circles as that of those particular Jews who worshipped Jesus (their name for them, in fact, was usually "Nazarenes"). But as soon as the new religion began to spread to non-Jews, some distinctive title for its adherents was necessary, not least for the convenience of the Roman administration, which had to decide how this minority was to be treated. The Jews were granted special privileges for their religion. Should the same be extended to this new sect, even though some of its members were not Jews? We have evidence of this question becoming acute at the end of the century, and it is likely that it

was already an issue at Rome under Nero in the sixties. We do not know whether the government of Syria had already had to tackle the question in Antioch; but it can hardly be an accident that the name given there to the members of this new religion was not Greek but Latin: *Christiani.*

During this period some prophets came down from Jerusalem. 27
The church had received the gift of the Holy Spirit. This gift was manifested in many ways; but ever since Old Testament times its principal manifestation was held to be in the form of prophecy. In theory, all Christians had this gift (2.17–18); but in practice, certain members of the congregation were found to be particularly gifted, and became known as **prophets.** This is by no means the only passage in which these prophets appear: 1 Corinthians 14 provides some detailed information about them, and there are many other scattered references to them in the New Testament. In part they were the successors of the Old Testament prophets: they had the gift of reading the signs of the times and of discerning, more clearly than their contemporaries, the hand of God in the present and the shape of things to come (the prediction of Agabus was clearly of this kind). But they also had a wider rôle: they were able to give inspired direction to the church in matters requiring practical decision, and to give an inspired lead to the prayers and praises of Christian worship. They frequently travelled from church to church, and (so long as their gift could be seen to be authentic) they were received as honoured and authoritative visitors.

It follows that we should probably be wrong to think of Agabus' prediction as merely a case of foreknowledge. The early church lived in earnest expectation of the end of the world and the manifest triumph of Christ. Jesus was remembered to have given some teaching on those historical events of the near future which should be regarded as presages of the end; and it was one of the functions of Christian prophets to relate the facts of contemporary history to this teaching of Jesus, and so to help the church to understand the period in which it was living. Now famines were expected to be one of the 'birthpangs of the new age' (Mark 13.8). Agabus may have heard that there were signs of a bad year's harvest and, seeing it in terms of one of the catastrophes of the time before the end, he may have confidently predicted
that the bad harvest would grow into a **severe and world-wide famine**; 28
alternatively he may have simply foretold the calamity before there was any observable evidence to go by. In either event, we can assume that he interpreted the famine as a sign of the times, and we can even hazard a guess at the reason why he was moved to make such a prophecy. In A.D. 40 the Emperor Caligula had threatened to erect a statue of himself in the Jewish temple. This was almost certainly seen by many Christians as the "abomination of desolation" (Mark 13.14), the decisive desecration which would herald the last days, and it may well have made the Christian prophets in Jerusalem alert to any other developments which belonged to the traditional picture of

this catastrophic age. However this may be, the predicted famine **in fact occurred** (as Luke notes) **in the reign of Claudius.** A single world-wide famine is too simple a picture; but it is certainly true that there was serious food shortage in different parts of the empire during Claudius' reign (41–54), and that between A.D. 46 and 48 conditions were so serious in Jerusalem that a visiting queen from the east, Helena of Adiabene, is reported to have imported corn from Egypt and distributed it to the local inhabitants. The immediate effect of such shortages was to send up the price of food; and the church in Jerusalem, perhaps impoverished by its early experiment in communal living, was highly vulnerable.

29 **So the disciples agreed to make a contribution.** A much more
elaborate contribution from the principal gentile churches in Asia Minor and
Greece was subsequently organized by Paul in order to relieve the poverty of
the Christians in Jerusalem and to express the solidarity of the new churches
with their mother church. Luke does not say much about that great enterprise of Paul's, nor does Paul appear (in the fragment of autobiography
which we possess in Galatians 2) to allow for a contribution organized at
Antioch and delivered to Jerusalem in the way that is described here. Since
Paul is making a careful statement about the journeys he undertook to
Jerusalem, his word must be preferred to Luke's. It is not impossible to
reconcile the two accounts (though it requires considerable ingenuity—see
below on Galatians 2.1). Alternatively, it is reasonable to think that Luke
may have had only scanty information about the reaction of the Antioch
church to Agabus' prophecy, and have simply supposed that, if a contribu-
30 tion was made, it must have been taken **to the elders** (a new name for the
Jerusalem leaders: see below on 15.6) by the two men most closely associated
with the Jerusalem church, **Barnabas and Saul.** This supposition was
certainly in keeping with the close solidarity between the churches which he
has been at pains to emphasize all along.

12. 1 **It was about this time.** Luke was now faced with the historian's problem of a tale of two cities: important things were happening at both Antioch and Jerusalem, and the two chronicles had to be dovetailed together. A modern historian would take the reader into his confidence with a phrase like "we must now go back a few years to see what had been happening at Jerusalem". But Luke's readers were less concerned than we are with exact synchronization. **About this time** was a sufficient indication, even if the events which follow took place a few years earlier than those which have just been recounted.

In fact, **King Herod** (the grandson of Herod the Great, usually called Herod Agrippa) was granted the rule of the whole of Palestine (in place of the Roman governor) in A.D. 41, and died in A.D. 44. This gives us three years in which to place the events recorded in this chapter; whereas the famine men-

tioned in the last chapter can hardly have been earlier than 47, and the prophecy of it earlier than, say, 45 or 46. It seems that on coming to the throne Herod did his best to please his new subjects by actively promoting the orthodox traditions of their religion; and this provides a possible reason —for Luke suggests none—why he should have attacked the growing sect of the Christians (who were doubtless becoming increasingly suspect to the Jewish authorities) and should have gained popular support for doing so. This action is apparently not recorded in order to draw attention to the first
martyrdom of an actual disciple of Jesus (**James, the brother of John**), so 2
much as to provide the occasion for recounting a miraculous event in the life of Peter, and the horrible punishment received by Herod for his treatment of the church.

Both stories, whatever their basis in fact, are typical of the kind of divine protection which many new religions in antiquity claimed to receive when threatened by hostile powers; yet the second story can be confirmed, in all essential details, from the contemporary Jewish historian Josephus, and the first, though it contains elements that are conventional in such stories (such
as the angel, the blaze of light, and the gate opening **of its own accord**) is 10
told with such a wealth of plausible detail that it must either contain genuine historical reminiscences or else be the work of an exceptionally good story-teller. It is dated (like other important events) by a Jewish festival, in this
case that **of Unleavened Bread** (which was almost synonymous with 3
Passover—see above on Mark 14.1). The **military guard,** like a regular 4
Roman guard, was divided into **four squads,** each of which was on duty for one of the four watches of the night. The arrangements in the prison are entirely plausible. And psychologically, Peter's trance-like escape, followed by the sudden realization that he was both alone and free, has the ring of truth. But the author's intention is not to make the episode seem more plausible by playing down its miraculous features, but on the contrary to emphasize that it was a deliverance so staggering as to be almost incredible.
This intention governs the way he tells the rest of the story. The scene is **the** 12
house of Mary, the mother of John Mark. This is the first appearance of Mark, who is soon to play a certain part in the story, and whom a later tradition came to regard as the author of the second gospel. Luke says nothing to introduce him here: he was presumably well known to his readers.[a] The house was substantial: it had a room large enough to hold **a large company . . . at prayer,** and a courtyard in the front separated from the street by an
outer door. The maid (**Rhoda** was a common name for a slave) was pre- 13
sumably just coming out of the house when she heard Peter's voice calling across the courtyard from outside in the street. If so, it is understandable that in her excitement, instead of crossing the courtyard and opening the

[a] John (*Johanan*) was his Jewish name, Mark (*Marcus*) his Latin name. Many Jews took a Roman name as a second name: e.g. Joseph Justus (1.23); Simeon Niger (13.1).

door, she went straight back inside with the news. In this way Luke builds up to the climax. That Peter should have escaped seemed physically so impossible that his friends tried any other explanation first. The maid must
15 be out of her mind. If not, the visitor must be **his guardian angel**—for guardian angels were certainly believed in, and were imagined as a sort of heavenly counterpart to a human person, and so perhaps (should one appear on earth) an angel might be mistaken for the man it protected. It was only when they actually saw Peter for themselves that they were prepared to believe he could have escaped. This was the measure of the miracle which had taken place.

17 **'Report this to James'.** James, the brother of Jesus, was neither one of the original apostles nor one of Jesus' own disciples. Presumably he was converted after the resurrection. From now on, he is evidently the leader of the Jerusalem church. Luke says nothing of how he reached this position, nor of why Peter seems to have been displaced.

Luke then leads the narrative back to Herod. The sudden death of this king, at the height of his powers and in the midst of a successful reign, was a phenomenon which few ancient writers would have thought of attributing to chance. Both Luke and Josephus (our other source of information) agree that
23 it was the result of Herod usurping **the honour due to God**; and Herod's fatal illness (**eaten up with worms** is a popular, not a medical, description) was typical of the gruesome kind of disease of which a tyrant was expected to die. But Luke seems also to have had some precise historical information which Josephus lacked. The cities of Tyre and Sidon lay on the coast to the north of Caesarea, in the province of Syria. They would have possessed sufficient autonomy to negotiate the passage of their food supplies; and there is no reason to doubt Luke's version of the episode.

The church breaks barriers

The missions recorded in this section were all based on Antioch; and a few sentences are devoted to giving some information about the church there.
12. 25 Barnabas and Saul had **returned from Jerusalem, taking John Mark with them.**[a] None of the Jerusalem apostles was resident there, but Luke
13. 1 gives us the names of **certain prophets and teachers**, that is to say, men whose particular gift of inspiration, or whose opportunity to acquire first-

[*a*] There is some uncertainty in the manuscripts about their movements (see the footnote in NEB), perhaps arising from the impression given by Luke's arrangement of his information that they were in Jerusalem during the persecution, which is unlikely. But, granted that the events in chapter 12 in any case took place before Saul and Barnabas' visit to Jerusalem, verse 25 can be seen as a resumption of the Antioch narrative, picking it up from the point reached at 11.30.

hand knowledge of the essentials of the new faith, had raised them to a position of authority in the church. Luke has already told us that some (like **Barnabas**) were natives of Cyprus, and some (like **Lucius**) of Cyrene—though they had come to Antioch from Jerusalem. Among the new names is **Manaen, who had been at the court of Prince Herod.** The phrase which Luke uses may even mean that Manaen had been brought up with Herod Antipas as a companion for the young prince at the court of Herod the Great.

But it was not these men who took the responsibility for the "breaking of
barriers" which was undertaken from Antioch. Luke stresses the point: the
initiative belonged entirely to the Holy Spirit. **While they were keeping a** 2
fast. Fasting as a preparation for a religious experience was taken for granted
in many religions, and particularly among the Jews. The Christians continued
the practice, and indeed it is a recurring pattern, both in Luke's gospel and
in Acts, that prayer and fasting preceded a communication of the Holy
Spirit.[a] **Further fasting and prayer** then preceded the ceremony by which 3
the two missionaries were sent on their way. **They laid their hands on**
them. These words could describe two different rites which were practised
at this time by qualified Jewish teachers. One was pressing the hands heavily
upon another person (an act based on the "ordination" of Joshua by Moses
in Numbers 27.23) by which a scholar might signify that his own authority
had passed into a pupil. The other was the much more ordinary act of
touching another person in order to bless, to heal or to commission. The
church soon gave a new meaning to these solemn acts, seeing them particularly as the means by which the Holy Spirit was transmitted from one
Christian to another. Here, the rite appears to have been performed between
equals, all of whom already possessed the Spirit. It expressed not so much
the authority given to Barnabas and Saul to start on a new mission, as the
solidarity between them and those who remained behind, a solidarity which
kept the missionaries still ultimately dependent upon the church in Jerusalem.

Seleucia was the port which served the city of Antioch. **Cyprus,** after 200 4
years under the Ptolemies of Egypt, was now a Roman province, administered by an official to whom Luke gives the correct Greek title corresponding
to the Latin term *proconsul*, **Governor.** There were large communities of 7
Jews on the island, and it seems that Saul first addressed himself to **the** 5
Jewish synagogues. This was in **Salamis,** the largest town in Cyprus,
which lay at the east end of the island. But the seat of the Roman government
was at the other end, at **Paphos,** and it was there that the first distinguished 6
convert was won from the gentile world. A notable miracle prepared the
way for the conversion of no less a person than the Roman Governor.

Sergius Paulus was a Roman civil servant: an earlier stage in his career 7
is recorded in an inscription discovered in Rome. Luke calls him **an intelli-**

[a] E.g. Luke 3.22; 4.1–2; Acts 9.9,19.

gent man, using a Greek word which has to do not so much with native
6 intelligence as with a capacity for sound judgement. In his retinue was a
sorcerer, a Jew who posed as a prophet. Several people of this kind make
their appearance in the course of Acts, and there is no reason to doubt that
there were many people about who made their living by claiming powers of
magic and second sight. Christianity soon found itself in a serious contest
with all kinds of occultism; and this episode illustrates its superiority to
them. Luke mentions the sorcerer's name in a puzzling way. **Bar-Jesus**
(meaning "son of Yeshua") could well have been a name which Christians
preferred not to use of anyone, let alone a sorcerer; and if he was also known
by some sobriquet that meant "sorcerer", this would have been a more
acceptable name to figure in the story. Unfortunately, the alternative name
8 Luke offers, **Elymas,** is a mystery. The letters do not seem to stand for
any Hebrew or Aramaic word meaning anything like "sorcerer", though
they may disguise some form of a word meaning "to dream". The false
prophets referred to in Jeremiah (23.25; 27.9) were "dreamers"; and "the
Dreamer" could conceivably have been a nickname for the false prophet
9 Bar-Jesus. **Saul, also known as Paul,** is a double name of a different kind.
In his letters, the apostle always refers to himself as Paul; but up to this
point in Acts he has been called Saul. Many Jews used a Roman name in
addition to their own, and often chose one that sounded similar. Normally,
we should assume that the Jew Saul called himself Paul outside Palestine.
But Paul was a Roman citizen, that is to say, he must have possessed from
birth the usual set of three Roman names, one of which was doubtless *Paulus*.
In which case, Saul was an extra name, such as many Roman citizens adopted
in the eastern part of the empire. It was perhaps the only name by which he
was known in Jerusalem. But now that his work had taken him so far afield,
Luke gives him his official name, Paul.

9–11 The scene between these three men is quickly played out. Paul did not question or challenge Elymas' power: he simply showed his own to be stronger.
With a string of biblical phrases (and more than a hint on his own part of a
magician's curse) Paul confronted the sorcerer with a greater authority.
12 **When the Governor saw what had happened he became a believer.**
This is the climax of the story. But it was not just the miracle which persuaded
this distinguished convert: he had been **deeply impressed by what he
learned about the Lord.**

13 **Leaving Paphos.** The journey is summarily reported. Sailing north-west
from Cyprus, the travellers landed on the coast of Asia Minor in the small
and undistinguished Roman province of Pamphylia. Their destination lay a
14 hundred miles inland. **Pisidian Antioch** was a Roman town (though
originally founded, like the other more famous Antioch, by one of the
successors of Alexander the Great) with a substantial Jewish community.
Technically, it belonged to the province of Galatia, and it is possible that

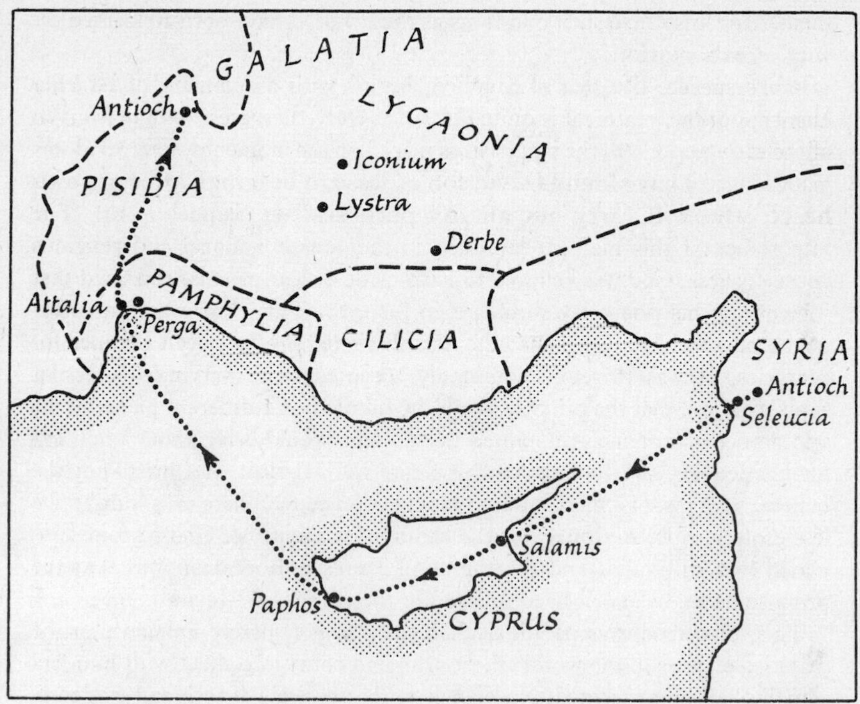

the "Galatians" to whom Paul wrote his letter belonged to this and neighbouring cities.[a] At any rate Paul's visit to it is told in some detail: it sets the pattern for his work and preaching in other cities of Asia Minor.

On the Sabbath they went to synagogue. The procedure was 15
exactly as Luke describes it on the occasion of Jesus' appearance in the synagogue at Nazareth (Luke 4.16–28). Except that the service was probably in Greek instead of Aramaic, the synagogue abroad followed the same order as the synagogue in Palestine, and it was entirely natural that a learned visitor (as we know Paul to have been) should have been invited to give an address after the readings from Scripture. Indeed, we can probably hazard a guess at the kind of address that was expected of him. The phrase,
'by way of exhortation', has a technical sound. Some passage (we are not 15
told which) had just been read from the prophets; and the full meaning of Old Testament prophecies was a subject of constant and earnest speculation. Were there any signs in contemporary history that God's promises to his people were about to be fulfilled? Were there any oracles in Scripture which could help the faithful to trace the hand of God in the world around

[a] See below, p. 598. It is conceivable that the 'bodily illness' which Paul himself says originally brought him to Galatia (Gal. 4.13) was a bout of malaria caught in the low-lying and unhealthy coastal plain of Pamphylia.

them? Any answer to such questions as these would have been welcomed **by way of exhortation.**

16–22 Paul's speech, like that of Stephen, begins with a summary of Israelite
history; but the treatment is quite different. Only the barest outline is given
of the early period: all the emphasis is placed on the moment when David was
22 made king: "**I have found David son of Jesse to be a man after my own
heart, who will carry out all my purposes**" (1 Samuel 13.14). The
importance of this moment lay deep in the Jewish national and religious
consciousness. God was believed to have made a clear promise to David that
23 someone of his **posterity** would reign for ever. This clearly had not happened on the historical plane: the Jewish monarchy had been defunct for
centuries. It was therefore commonly accepted, with varying degrees of
sophistication, that the promise would be fulfilled on a different plane by the
appearance of a divinely appointed Person who would bring about a new era
for his people. The Jews called this figure the Messiah, or Christ. For the
benefit, perhaps, of a more cosmopolitan audience Paul here calls him by the
less esoteric title, **saviour.** But the meaning is the same. God's promise to
David was still valid; and the theme of Paul's **exhortation** was that the
promise had now at last been fulfilled in the person of—**Jesus.**

This, of course, was paradoxical. Jesus was not merely unknown to the
majority of Jews in the world: those who had come in contact with him had
actually had him executed. Nevertheless, that entirely Jewish and evidently
25 inspired figure, John the Baptist, had barely reached **the end of his course,**
preparing for a successor far greater than himself, before the heralded person
29 himself appeared—and that person was Jesus; and even the death on **the
gibbet** could now be seen, not as a proof that Jesus was an ordinary criminal,
but as the fulfilment of old prophecies that had long been misunderstood.
27 The Jews of Jerusalem **did not recognize him.** Even their condemnation
28 of him was, by their own standards, an aberration: **they failed to find
grounds for the sentence of death.** Therefore their conduct did not
necessarily either discredit Jesus or disqualify the Jewish nation from being
the destined recipient of God's promise. It could still be said, by Paul, a Jew
26 in the company of Jews,[a] that '**we are the people to whom the message
of this salvation has been sent**'.

'David died and was buried and his tomb is here to this very day.' So, in his first speech after Pentecost, Peter clinched the argument that the historical David himself could not have been the person in whom great prophecies of

[a] And of course proselytes, some of whom would have been present in any synagogue, and who seem to be allowed for in the words, '**others among you who revere our God**'. This phrase was used to describe pious people in general, Jews and non-Jews alike. It is evidently Luke's intention to present Paul's speech here as primarily an appeal to the Jews, which was followed by an appeal to non-Jews only after it had been rejected by the Jews. The phrase here cannot be meant to draw attention to non-Jews in the audience, but only to allow for the presence of some proselytes in the synagogue.

immortality and eternal dominion would be fulfilled (2.29). The same might
have appeared to be true of Jesus: '**they took him down from the gibbet** 29
and laid him in a tomb'. But it was not so. '**God raised him from the** 30
dead'. And the proof of this was, first, the presence of **witnesses** (among 32
whom, strangely, Luke does not let Paul count himself: the familiar message
is told very much as one of the original apostles might have told it), and
secondly, the fulfilment of Scripture. The first text cited is from Psalm 2. 33
Since the opening verses of this psalm had been so clearly fulfilled by the manner of Jesus' trial and execution (see above, 4.25–6), another verse of it could now be invoked to prove that, far from being merely the condemned criminal which he appeared, Jesus was God's **son**. The second text, though clear enough in the original Hebrew, was mysterious in the Septuagint Greek
version (quoted here): '**I will give you the blessings promised to David,** 34
holy and sure' (Isaiah 55.3). What were these "blessings"? In the Greek, the phrase is even more obscure than it appears in this translation. It means "the holy things". What holy things? To solve a puzzle of this kind, it was a usual technique to introduce another text where the same word or phrase
occurred. Hence the third quotation in this series (Psalm 16.10) which, 35
literally translated, runs, "thou wilt not give thy holy one to suffer corruption". This verse has already been shown to apply to Jesus in an earlier speech in Acts (2.27). It also contains two of the same words ("give" and "holy") as the quotation from Isaiah. Therefore (by this method of reasoning) the "holy things" or **blessings** in the Isaiah passage must also be a reference to Jesus, who was thereby proved to have been promised to "you",
that is, to the Jewish people. '**It is through him that forgiveness of sins is** 38
now being proclaimed to you'—forgiveness of sins, that ultimate restoration of a perfect relationship with God which was the highest aspiration of Jewish religion, and which is here expressed in terms that seem to introduce, for a moment, the real Paul of the letters: '**everyone who has faith** 39
is acquitted'. The sermon ends with a quotation from Habakkuk 1.5, which 41
is a warning that, for all that the promise was intended for the Jews, it could still be forfeited if, instead of believers, they showed themselves to be **scoffers.**

Many Jews and gentile worshippers. The last phrase, in the Greek as 43
well as the English, is ambiguous. It could be meant to include Gentiles who simply attended the synagogue and were only loosely connected with it. But its more natural meaning is "devout proselytes", that is, men of gentile origin who had undergone circumcision and were now members of the Jewish community. This meaning also suits the structure of the narrative better. On this first Sabbath, conversions among non-Jews would have been
out of place. It was a week later, as a result of the **jealous resentment** of the 45
Jews, that Paul and Barnabas took the decisive step of turning **to the** 46
Gentiles. The scene is described impressionistically. **Almost the whole** 44

city suggests a great open-air meeting, perhaps in the theatre; but in fact the setting must still be the synagogue. The Jews had now turned against the Christian preachers, whose message was acclaimed instead by the Gentiles. Who these Gentiles were, and what opportunity they had had to listen to the preaching and prepare themselves for their joyful acceptance of it, are questions Luke does not answer. His concern is simply to present the typical pattern of Jewish rejection followed by gentile acceptance, a pattern which was to be exemplified again and again in Paul's journeys, and which was foreshadowed even in the ministry of Jesus (see especially Luke 4.14–30).
51 **They shook the dust off their feet**—a Jewish gesture,[a] addressed to the
45 Jews, and an answer to the Jews' own **violent abuse.** But this was far more
than a personal reaction of impatience. The pattern was throughout divinely
46 ordained. '**It was necessary that the word of God should be declared**
to you first'—necessary, that is, on several counts: the whole story had started among the Jews; Jesus himself had taught that the Jews should be addressed first; Jesus was the Jewish 'saviour'; and the Jewish people were the obvious inheritors of all that the Old Testament had promised. But after rejection by the Jews, the necessity of an approach to the Gentiles was equally
47 strong. It was implied in a prophecy of Isaiah (49.6), '**I have appointed**
you to be a light for the Gentiles' (a prophecy already used by Luke at the beginning of his gospel, 2.32: the Jews took it to describe the ultimate destiny of their people, Christians saw it as decreeing an immediate task which, if the Jews refused it, they were to perform themselves); and it was predestined by God: it could now be said of Gentiles, and not only of Jews,
48 that some of them were **marked out for eternal life.** In view of the
immense growth of the church in gentile lands by the time he wrote, Luke could safely credit Paul with these tremendous assertions on the occasion of his first deliberate "turning to the Gentiles".

14. 1 **At Iconium.** This city lay nearly a hundred miles south-east of Antioch, in the same Roman province of Galatia. Luke has little to say about Paul's work there, beyond the fact that it followed the pattern established at Antioch; and he hurries on to Paul's arrival in cities south and east of
6 Iconium, **Lystra and Derbe**; for Paul's visit to Lystra was marked by a
sensational event.

8 **At Lystra sat a crippled man.** The description of the healing falls into line with similar stories in the gospels and with Peter's miracle in Acts 3. Fixing his eyes on him, and using a formula borrowed from the Old Testa-
10 ment (it can hardly be an accident that the words, '**Stand up straight on**
your feet' are an exact quotation of Ezekiel 2.1), Paul effected the cure in
11 the manner of an authoritative exorcist. But the reaction of **the crowds**
introduces us to a different world altogether. The city had the outward appearance of a typical Greco-Roman town in Asia Minor. The official

[a] See above on Matthew 10.14.

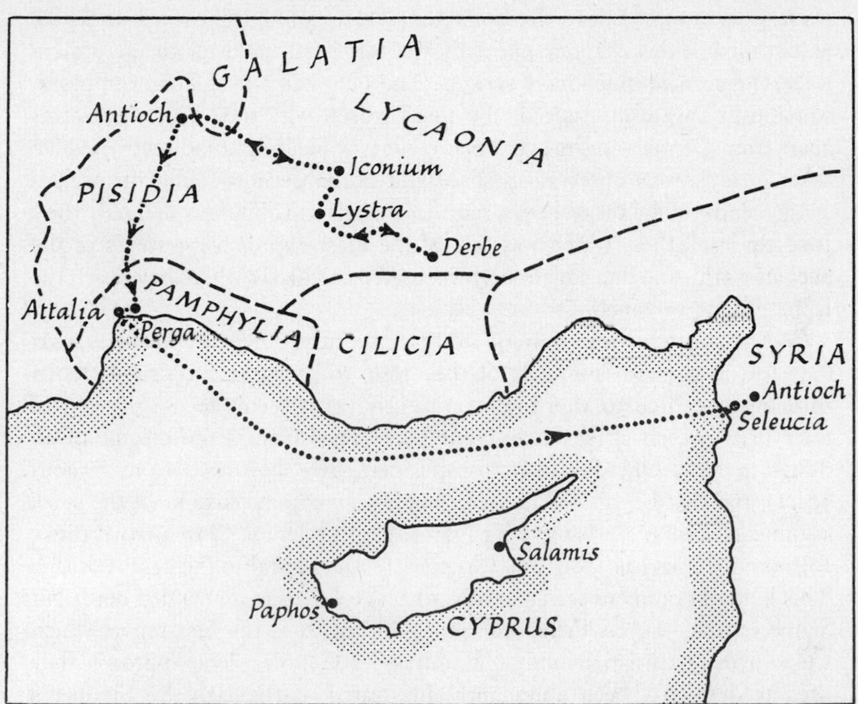

languages were Latin and Greek, and the official religion included the cult
of the main Greek deities such as Zeus (in this translation called by his
Roman name, **Jupiter**), carried on in temples that were doubtless built in 12
the Greek style, one of which lay just outside the walls and close to the
monumental **gates** of the city. But among themselves the inhabitants still 13
spoke their native language, and doubtless it was their own ancestral gods
whom they continued to worship under the forms of the Greek religion.
Seeing the miracle that Paul had performed, they did not (as Jews, or other
more sophisticated Roman citizens, would have done) think of Paul and
Barnabas as men specially endowed by God with miraculous powers. More
credulously, they thought their visitors must be gods themselves, walking
the earth in a way that had formed the subject of countless pagan myths (and
of one in particular that was set in their own part of the country). Paul, the
spokesman, must be **Mercury**, the messenger of the gods. And since the 12
king of the gods was believed often to disguise himself as a human traveller
(in order to test the hospitality which people offered to strangers), Barnabas
could well be **Jupiter** himself. Accordingly, they hastened **to offer sacrifice.** 13
But their shouts were all **in their native Lycaonian.** It was some time 11
before Barnabas and Paul realized what was happening.

They tore their clothes. A non-Jew might have reacted simply with a 14 modest disclaimer. But to **the apostles** (as Paul and Barnabas are unexpectedly called in this chapter: normally the title is reserved for the Jerusalem leaders) it seemed much more serious. The Jews had a deep horror of pagan worship in any form. Indeed, the main reason why they kept themselves apart from Gentiles was to avoid any contact which might indirectly involve them in idolatrous observances. Paul and Barnabas now found themselves at the centre of an act of pagan sacrifice. Their sensibilities outraged, **they tore their clothes,** which was one of the most expressive gestures of the ancient world, and one which the Jews used particularly when they heard the name of God profaned.

15 **'We are only human beings, no less mortal than you'.** This was what
18 they had to get across quickly, if they were **to prevent the crowd from
offering sacrifice to them.** But curiously (as it seems to us) the rest of
their brief speech strikes a different note. That God is the creator of all
15 things (a basic Old Testament proposition, here borrowed from Exodus
20.11), and that he can be known through his creation, was one of the stock arguments used by Jewish writers against pagan religion. '**Turn from these follies to the living God**' was a typical Jewish appeal to the gentile world. This kind of argument seems hardly what the situation demanded here; but in the scheme of Acts the speech is significant. It is the first report which Luke gives of Christians publicly addressing Gentiles. The approach they used to Jews has been abundantly illustrated, particularly by Stephen's speech (chapter 7) and Paul's first speech (chapter 13). Their approach to a fully non-Jewish world will be represented in detail by Paul's speech in Athens (chapter 17). What we have here is a fragment of the same argument. This, so far as Luke could see, was the way Paul and Barnabas *must* have spoken to the pagan crowds in Lystra.

But however pagan the city, the pattern (so at least Luke believed) was the
19 same. **Jews from Antioch and Iconium came on the scene,** and set in
motion that hostile reaction against the church which it seemed to be the destiny of the Jews to provoke. Paul barely escaped with his life—after which his work in the region is only summarily described. The return journey was
23 used for consolidating the new churches. **They also appointed elders for
them in each congregation. Elders** sounds like an official title, and indeed it soon became the name of one of the three orders of ministry in the church. How much of this technical meaning Luke intended when he used the word here, we cannot be sure. He may have meant no more than that some of the senior members of each congregation were entrusted with the responsibility of leadership.

25 **Attalia** was the main port on this part of the coast of Asia Minor. On their
return, Paul and Barnabas reported back to the church in Antioch. A decisive new stage had been reached: Christianity had now been preached direct to the Gentiles. But this (Luke insists once more) was no personal decision. It

was something that God had done through them. Its implications for the 27
church at large are the subject of the next chapter.

Christianity was born as a Jewish religion. Jesus was a Jew, and there is more than a hint in his teaching that he intended his message, at least primarily, for Jews. His followers were also Jews, and for some years their work consisted entirely of convincing their fellow-Jews that the Jesus whom they had personally followed was the Messiah, or Christ, whom all Jews were awaiting. They expressed their message in entirely Jewish terms. Indeed, one of their strongest arguments was that the recent facts of which they were witnesses provided the essential clue to understanding the Jewish scriptures. One could hardly come to Christ unless one started from the Old Testament. It followed that the Jesus whom they proclaimed was the saviour, first and foremost, of the Jewish people.

Yet by the last decades of the first century A.D. (when Acts was probably written) the majority in the church consisted of Gentiles. How had this happened? On a practical level, the process is not hard to understand. There were a large number of Gentiles in the Greek-speaking world who were well acquainted with Judaism. They found in the Jewish faith a pure and exalted conception of God, combined with a high and exacting ethic, such as they seldom found in the many religious cults of Greece and Asia Minor. But they also found in the Jews a disturbing exclusiveness. They were welcomed to listen in the synagogue, but they were not permitted to share the social life of the Jewish community, and the only way in which they could advance further was by submitting to what they could only regard as a barbarous rite—circumcision—and by taking upon themselves all those details of ritual observance which made up the Jewish way of life. By contrast, the Christian church seemed to offer them a religion at least as pure and as exacting, but with none of the racial exclusiveness of Judaism.

However, for the original Christians of Jewish descent, this matter of the admission of Gentiles to the church raised questions of deep principle. As Jews, they had been brought up to believe that theirs was a uniquely privileged race to which God had promised exceptional blessings. Were they now to accept Gentiles as members of the same elect community as themselves? All their lives they had shunned social contact with Gentiles, lest they should unwittingly be involved in pagan worship. Were they now to sit down beside Gentiles at table? They had always regarded the Law of Moses as their one defence against the prevailing immorality of the heathen world. Were they now to allow the Christian community to be one in which this Law was no longer regarded as binding? These questions were brought to a head at different times in different places. At Antioch, for instance, the question of table-fellowship seems to have been the most urgent one, since almost from the beginning there was a large number of Gentiles in that church. In Jerusalem, on the other hand, where a gentile Christian was a rare phenomenon, the question was rather one of principle: should Gentiles be admitted to the church? Should the Christian mission be carried into gentile lands? Some of the phases of this controversy are mentioned in Paul's letter to the Galatians. Luke presents it, perhaps a little schematically (since the details of his narrative are difficult to reconcile with Paul's account), as an issue that was debated and settled once and for all at a meeting in Jerusalem. Church historians have come to call this meeting the Council of Jerusalem. It may be calculated to have taken place at a date not much more than a year before or after A.D. 49.

The main point of principle—whether or not Gentiles should be admitted to the church—had already been settled by the incontrovertible fact that the gift of the Holy Spirit, which was the distinctive possession of the Christian community, had been imparted in full measure to Gentiles as well as Jews. This is the decisive point made by Peter in his speech at the council, and it was doubtless this, in reality, which made it impossible for the original Jewish churches to close their doors altogether to gentile converts. But there were still the more practical questions to be settled of table-fellowship and the application of the Mosaic Law. On these they had some precedents to guide them. Very similar questions were being debated in orthodox Jewish circles. One school believed that there was literally no salvation for mankind apart from the Jewish people, and that the only hope for a Gentile was to undergo the rite of circumcision, enter the Jewish community, and lay upon himself the full observance of the Law of Moses. But another school of thought was more liberal. According to this, God must be believed to accept the piety and good works of those Gentiles who genuinely turned from paganism to worship the true God, even if they did not take the ultimate step of integration with the Jewish community through circumcision. It was doubtless this more liberal opinion which led to the welcoming of Gentiles in the synagogues, and along with it went a much more flexible attitude towards social intercourse between Gentiles and Jews. But this attitude, though it was more humane and accommodating, still involved laying certain obligations and restrictions upon those Gentiles who wished to be associated with the religion of the Jews. They must, of course, give up every kind of pagan worship; they must also observe the Sabbath and the major Jewish festivals; they must keep certain rules about forbidden foods; and they must accept certain basic moral principles which could be deduced from the Law of Moses. Nevertheless, according to this school of thought, it was not necessary for them either to be circumcised or to adopt in full the Jewish way of life. The advocates of this attitude were able to find some precedent for it in the Old Testament, and doubtless they had already drawn up some kind of code regulating the conditions to be observed by gentile adherents to the synagogue. Unfortunately, we do not know exactly what such a code would have consisted of at this date. But it is fairly clear (despite considerable obscurities in Luke's account) that the decision of the Christian council in Jerusalem was modelled on a code of this kind.

Now certain persons who had come down from Judaea. These 15. 1
evidently represented the strictest party among Jewish Christians. Their
teaching was that of the first school of thought mentioned above: **those who
were not circumcised in accordance with Mosaic practice could not
be saved.** At first sight it may seem surprising that such an illiberal point of
view should have been represented in the Jerusalem church. But Luke has
already mentioned that the Pharisees were sympathetic to the church, and
among the Pharisees were to be found some of the most exclusive groups in
Judaism. When, therefore, Luke tells us that there were by now Christians
of the Pharisaic party in Jerusalem, we can understand how the adherence 5
of people of such a background could have led to a movement to exclude
uncircumcised Gentiles from the church. At any rate, it was the appearance
of this strict view in Antioch which caused a deputation, including Paul and
Barnabas, to leave for Jerusalem. They took the route southward along the
coast, and established on the way that they had the wholehearted support of
the Jewish Christian churches outside Jerusalem. Luke emphasizes that all
differences of opinion on the matter were confined to Jerusalem; again,
when we compare his account with Galatians 1–2, we can see that he has
somewhat simplified the picture.

The apostles and elders held a meeting. The structure of the Jeru- 6
salem church had evidently changed since it first appeared as a group of
twelve apostles leading a growing multitude of new converts. In chapter 6
Luke described the appointment of seven additional ministers; the terms he
now uses allow for a further development. Alongside the original apostles
(of whom at least one was dead, and others may have been dispersed), there
were now **elders.** The Greek word, transliterated into English, is *presbyters*,
from which the word "priest" is derived; and it is true that the order of
Christian priesthood had its origins in the presbyters of the early church.
Once again, however, we cannot be sure how far Luke is here using the word
in a technical sense. It could mean simply "the senior men", the persons,
that is, who would naturally be expected to assume responsibility in the
church once the original group of apostles began to be dispersed.

From the letter to the Galatians, one would have expected that it was Paul who presented the case for gentile Christianity. But Luke, seeing Jerusalem as the pivot of the church's activity, has placed the beginning of the gentile mission, not in Paul's recent journeys from Antioch, but in Peter's experience in the house of the centurion Cornelius. Peter, therefore, appears as the spokesman for the liberal point of view, and he bases his argument on that same episode (which is more fresh, perhaps, in the memory of the reader of Acts than it would have been in the minds of Christians some ten or fifteen

8 years after the event), in which God showed his approval of the Gentiles '**by
giving the Holy Spirit to them, as he did to us**'. His language seems to
reflect the arguments subsequently used by the gentile church in its controversies with Jewish synagogues. To Jewish scruples that non-Jews must
be held at a distance because they were ritually "impure", Christians could
9 reply that God had '**purified their hearts by faith**'. To Jewish reliance on
the Law of Moses as the one bulwark against pagan immorality, the Gentiles
10 retorted that it was an intolerable '**yoke**'. Salvation (this is very much the
11 language used by Paul) was only '**by the grace of the Lord Jesus**'.
13 **James summed up.** In the early chapters of Acts, Peter is represented
as indisputably the leader of the church—which is what, indeed, Jesus had
predicted. But subsequently (we do not know why) the leadership seems to
have passed to one who was not one of the original Twelve, but who perhaps
possessed a special claim to it, James the brother of Jesus. Luke tells us
nothing about this change; but his narrative accurately reflects the changed
situation. It is James who now makes the speech which forms the basis of
the church's policy, and it is James who appears as the leader of the church in
the next scene which takes place at Jerusalem (21.18). His speech bears right
at the beginning a touch of local colour: he calls Peter, not even by his original name in its Greek form (Simon), but by the form which the name would
14 have had in his native language (**Simeon**). James, Luke wishes us to understand, was speaking in Aramaic. But this impression is artificial, for the
speech as it stands could never have been composed in any language other
than Greek. The first point made in it is that the evidence of Peter is a
16–18 fulfilment of Scripture. The passage quoted is Amos 9.11–12 (along with a
fragment from Jeremiah 12.15), and it runs here very much as it does in the
Septuagint translation of the Old Testament into Greek. But it happens that
at this point the Septuagint translators misread the Hebrew original. Among
other mistakes, they took what in Amos is an oracle about "the remains of
17 *Edom*" as an oracle about "**the rest of mankind**" (*adam*). This mistaken
translation suits James' argument perfectly. But the historical James is unlikely to have known this Greek version, and in any case he certainly could not have exploited it in a speech purporting to be in Aramaic. It is clear that Luke possessed no transcript of the speech originally made by James. Instead, he followed the historian's convention of composing the kind of speech which he believed James would have made. There is no reason why Luke should have noticed that his Greek text of Amos diverged so strikingly at this point from the Hebrew original.

The principle, then, that Gentiles were intended by God to be admitted to the church was established both by the facts of the Christian mission and by Old Testament prophecy. The church must move in the direction indicated by the more liberal Jewish thinkers; the strict attitude of the Pharisaic party was untenable. But there remained the question of what obligations

should be placed upon these gentile converts. Granted that they were neither to be circumcised nor to be subjected to the full Law of Moses, it was still axiomatic (from the Jewish point of view) that some rules should be laid upon them in order to make sure that when they became Christians they would make a clean break with pagan morals and pagan idolatry, and in order to ease the scruples which pious Jewish converts were bound to feel at having free social intercourse with them. The formula suggested doubtless owed something to the Old Testament itself: certain clauses of the Mosaic Law were expressly said to be binding upon non-Israelites resident in Palestine (for instance, the prohibition on "eating blood" instead of kosher meat, Leviticus 17.10). This provided a precedent for elaborating a "gentile code". Such a code was bound to include a reference to those two aspects of the pagan way of life which the Jews found particularly repellent: idolatry
and sexual immorality. According to the main text of the NEB, these were 20
the precise points covered by James' proposal. But, as the footnotes show, there is considerable disagreement among the manuscripts at this point, and we cannot be sure exactly what terms Luke intended to be included.[a]

(**'Moses, after all, has never lacked spokesmen'.** The last sentence 21
of James' speech is obscure. If James' proposal seemed to some too liberal, he might be answering them by pointing out that the Gentiles in question always had the opportunity to hear and observe more of the Law of Moses if they wished. If on the other hand it seemed too strict, he could be saying that anything less would be inconsistent with a proper respect for the Law which was in fact publicly read **in every town** in the Jewish dispersion. This seems to be an occasion when we are now too far removed from the world of Luke's time to be able to catch the tone of voice of the speaker.)

With the agreement of the whole church. Luke conceives the council 22
on the model of a Greek democratic assembly: speeches are made (on this occasion all on one side), the matter is put to the vote, and a resolution is recorded. Of the envoys, nothing more is known of **Judas Barsabbas** (who may of course have been a brother of the Joseph Barsabbas mentioned in 1.23); **Silas** appears again in the next chapter. Both are Jewish names; but among Romans Silas might well have been known as Silvanus, and we meet a Silvanus in Paul's letters to the Thessalonians and in 1 Peter.

They . . . gave them this letter to deliver. This is one of the few 23
occasions when an actual document is quoted in the New Testament. It has the form and style of the many official letters which have survived written

[*a*] The word "blood" is ambiguous. It could refer to blood in meat (in which case it seems unnecessary to mention it as well as **anything that has been strangled**), or else, in Greek as in English, it could mean murder. But murder comes oddly in this list, which is mainly concerned with ritual observances; and the variations in the manuscripts may be due to a desire to make the list more general, more ethical, and more in line with the moral prohibitions of fornication and murder. Some manuscripts even add a form of the Golden Rule to the list.

on papyrus or recorded in inscriptions. But, as with speeches, so with letters: if a historian had not access to the original document, he felt perfectly free to compose the kind of letter which would have been written under the circumstances. The fact that this letter is written in careful and idiomatic Greek, combined with one or two phrases from the Greek Old Testament, suggests that in its present form it is more likely to be a composition of Luke than of the Jerusalem apostles. Moreover, it ties in with the episode at Antioch with which the chapter began (and which appears to have been forgotten in the meantime) in a way that suggests the hand of a skilful historian. At the same time, Luke may well have seen some document of the kind, and have reproduced, for instance, its address to gentile Christians in **Antioch, Syria, and Cilicia,** despite the fact that he has not yet mentioned the founding of any churches outside Antioch itself. In any case, the letter serves his purpose well. It repeats (with that slight stylistic variation he is fond of) the formula which was the most important result of the episode, and it allows him to emphasize once again that this whole matter of the Christian mission to the Gentiles was by no means the personal decision of certain church leaders, but the direct result of divine guidance. By slightly modifying
28 a familiar official phrase, he can write, **'It is the decision of the Holy Spirit, and our decision'.**

31 **When it was read, they all rejoiced at the encouragement it brought.** On the practical level, this was understandable: the immediate crisis had been resolved. But Luke twice uses a word, **encouragement,** which suggests a little more than this. It is the same word as is used of Paul's great speech at Pisidian Antioch (where it is translated 'exhortation', 13.15), and had an almost technical meaning. Specifically, it was the encouragement which came from being able to show that the great prophecies of the Old Testament were being fulfilled in contemporary events. This could well have been the kind of encouragement given by **Judas and Silas, who were prophets themselves.** We may imagine them, not merely communicating the Jerusalem decision, but demonstrating how it fulfilled the many Old Testament prophecies which stated that the people of Israel would one day, in some manner, be "a light that will be a revelation to the heathen" (Isaiah 42.6, quoted in Luke 2.32).

Paul leads the advance

Throughout the first half of Acts, the progress of the Gospel has been represented as an advance by the whole church, directly authorized by the leaders in Jerusalem, or at least conducted under the supervision of the daughter-church in Antioch. But now the picture changes. The protagonist is Paul and Paul alone, and his movements are no longer dependent on the decisions of a central authority. To this extent, Luke's narrative suggests a new initiative in the Christian mission, aptly described by the heading, *Paul leads the advance.*

Paul began with what we should now call a pastoral visit—'**to see how** 36
our brothers are faring in the various towns where we proclaimed
the word of the Lord'. This second visit included a journey through the
country lying between Antioch and central Asia Minor (**Syria and Cilicia**), 41
which was mentioned during the discussions in Jerusalem (15.24), even though Luke does not record Paul's original mission to it. Meanwhile Barnabas and John Mark revisited Cyprus. Luke has to admit that this was not by any means the result of an amicable agreement to work in separate
areas, but was preceded by a sharp **dispute.** This is the only case of serious 39
disagreement which Luke records in the history of the early church (Paul's letters are very much more candid). Doubtless the crisis at Antioch was too vivid a memory to be passed over. A dispute at Antioch between himself and Barnabas also rankled in Paul's memory (Galatians 2.11–14); but in Paul's account it turned on the question of Jewish observances, and his real opponent was Peter. If the same dispute is behind Luke's narrative (and it is difficult to think that there were two such notable disputes between Paul and Barnabas at Antioch), Luke has made it turn on the much less explosive issue of the personal reliability of John Mark.

Timothy is well known to us from many references to him in Paul's **16.** 1
letters. But the information that Paul **circumcised him, out of considera-** 3
tion for the Jews, is unexpected. Paul was strongly opposed to any pressure exerted upon gentile Christians to receive circumcision—this was the principal theme of his letter to the Galatians; and in one place he strongly repudiated the allegation that he ever advocated circumcision (Gal. 5.11). On the other hand, he continued to lay himself personally under the obligations of a strict Jewish way of life, and it may be that Timothy presented something of a special case. The son of a Jewish mother, even if his father was a Gentile, technically counted as a Jew, and was therefore obliged to be circumcised. Timothy's family had doubtless drifted away from the Jewish faith (Luke's narrative in 14.19 suggests that there was no Jewish community at Lystra), and the obligation to circumcise him had never been carried out. At Lystra he was probably regarded as a Gentile. But once he began travelling with Paul to cities where there were synagogues, his position might have become more difficult: he would have been recognized as a Jew who had failed to observe one of the most basic commandments. It may have been for a reason such as this that Paul, as a special case, **took him and circumcised him.**

They travelled. From being a pastoral visit, the journey soon turned 6
into a new missionary venture; but Luke insists that it was still carried out
strictly under divine guidance. **They were prevented by the Holy Spirit**

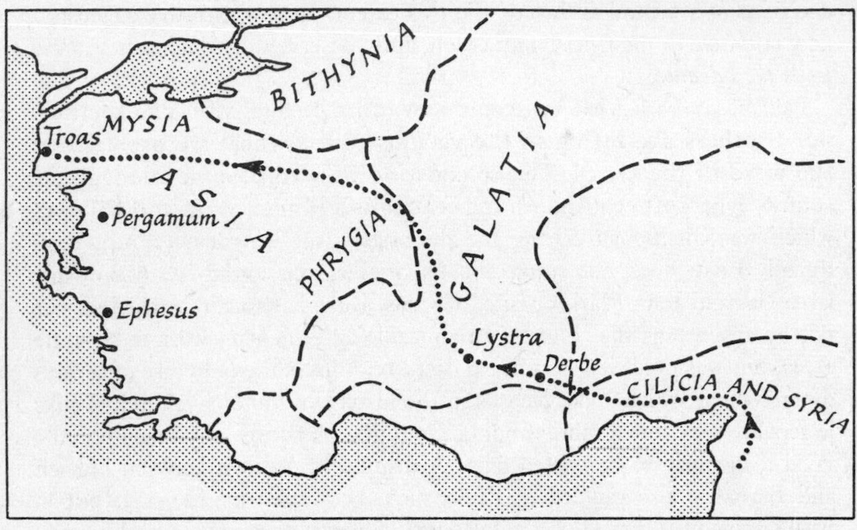

from delivering the message in the province of Asia. The logical sequel to the work done so far might have seemed to be to press on to the great Greco-Roman cities in the heart of the province of Asia, such as Ephesus and Pergamum, where there were substantial Jewish communities and where the missionaries could expect to find a ready hearing among Greek-speaking citizens who were already interested in the Jewish religion. Instead, the Spirit led them further into the interior of Asia Minor. From there, their obvious objective would have been the Hellenistic cities on the shores of the Black Sea, in Bithynia (where there were in fact Christian churches well before the end of the century). But before they got there, their real destina-
8 tion was revealed to them: the port of **Troas** on the Aegean coast. This was a long journey—at least 500 miles—and must have taken many weeks. In the course of it, there must have been occasions when the gospel was preached and churches founded (18.23). But Luke is here giving only the briefest summary, to prepare for a dramatic new phase in the mission; and the few geographical details he offers are only a rough guide to the route actually taken by Paul and his companions. [a]

Divine prompting this time took the form of a dream-vision: it led to their

[*a*] Which may in fact be all that Luke was able to give, unless he knew the country well. In any case, some of his expressions in this paragraph are ambiguous (see footnotes in NEB). On Galatia, see below, p. 598. Phrygia lay to the west of Galatia, and most of it was inside the province of Asia. But Paul and his companions did not go to Asia. Either, therefore, they went through some **Phrygian region** outside the borders of Asia (so the main text of NEB) or else **Asia** is used here, not for the Roman province, but for a smaller area round the great cities near the coast. **They skirted Mysia** is also difficult, since it is hard to see how they could have reached Troas without going through Mysia (hence another possible rendering in the footnote).

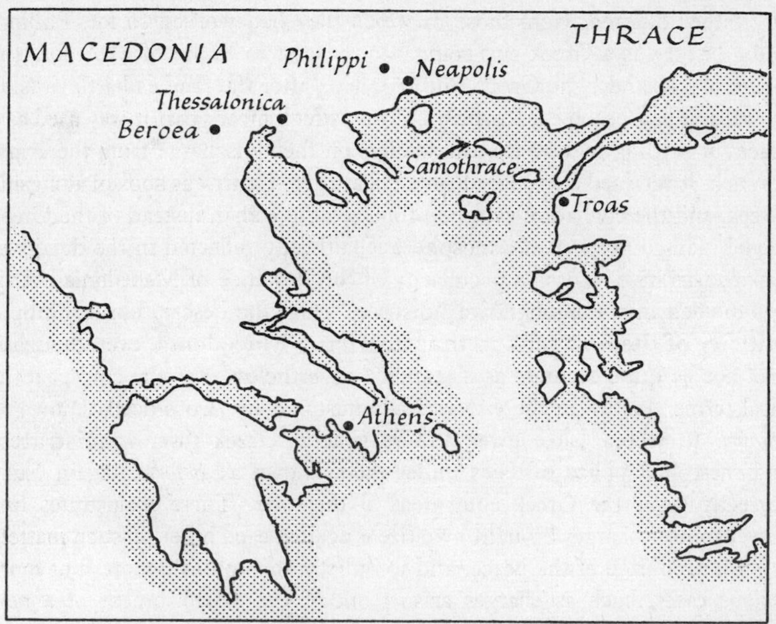

getting a passage to Macedonia. The narrative now becomes noticeably 10
precise about travel movements and ports of call; and at the same time it unexpectedly drops into the first person: **we at once set about getting a passage.** The writer seems suddenly to have joined the party, to leave it again as suddenly two paragraphs later, and to reappear briefly on two subsequent occasions. This "we" is a puzzle. On the face of it, the author seems either to have been present much of the time, but by carelessness to have alluded to the fact only haphazardly, or else to have been present only for short periods, and to have discreetly drawn attention to himself whenever appropriate. But there may also be more subtle reasons. Luke may have had access to some travel diary (whether his own or someone else's) and have dropped almost unconsciously into the first person when he used it as a principal source; or else he may have been more sensitive than we are to the literary convention that a good travel story ought to be vouched for by the writer who tells it. Whatever the explanation, a clear point is gained: the writer shows himself to have some personal knowledge of the events described, and thereby substantiates the claim he made at the beginning of his work (Luke 1.1–4) to give his readers 'authentic knowledge'.

Troas—the island of **Samothrace**—**Neapolis** (the port serving Philippi): 11
this was the most direct sea-route, but their ship set a remarkably straight and swift course if it accomplished the crossing (as Luke implies) in a mere
two days. From Neapolis, the road inland to **Philippi** could have been 12
covered in a few hours. Once there, the travellers found themselves in a

city rather different from those in which they had worked so far. Philippi had a history as a Greek city going back at least to Philip of Macedon, the father of Alexander the Great. But in 42 B.C., after the famous battle outside its walls, it had become **a Roman colony**, which meant that it was used as a place for settling regular Roman soldiers on their discharge from the army. As such, it retained a strongly Roman character. Latin was spoken alongside Greek, and the civil administration followed the Italian instead of the Greek model. This difference of atmosphere is faithfully reflected in the details of Luke's narrative. It was a peculiarity of the Province of Macedonia that it was divided into administrative "districts", and the description of Philippi as **a city of the first rank in that district of Macedonia**, even though it may not be quite accurate as it stands,[a] nevertheless uses the correct technical terms. Justice in the city was administered by two officials known as
20 *duoviri*, to whom Luke gives a more general Greek title, **magistrates**;
35 and these had police **officers** under them known as *lictores:* again Luke
correctly gives the Greek equivalent of this title. These magistrates had
power to hear charges brought by citizens against each other on such matters
20 as a **disturbance** of the peace, and to inflict minor punishments; but more
serious cases, such as charges arising out of the establishment of a new religion,[b] had to be referred to the capital of the province, in which case the accused, if they could not offer surety for themselves (for instance, if they were travellers), would be held in prison until their case could be heard. But Paul possessed the Roman citizenship, and was therefore exempt from the summary justice of local magistrates. In this first encounter between the Roman government and the church, the government was publicly shown to be at fault. The point was important if it was one of Luke's intentions to show that the Christian religion at no time constituted a threat to law and order in the Roman empire.

However, for most of the chapter these official institutions remain in the background. The story begins, as usual, with Paul seeking out the local Jewish community. But this appears to have been very insignificant. Only
13 some **women** gathered on the Sabbath, and a rather unexpected phrase of
Luke's suggests[c] that there was not even a regular synagogue, but only an agreed **place of prayer** by the river (which was over a mile outside the city,

[a] The Greek is awkward at this point, and the manuscript reading uncertain. It is possible that Luke gave the city its correct administrative title, but that this was misunderstood and distorted by copyists.

[b] We are surprised to hear that the customs of Jews or of any other race or religion were in themselves **illegal** for Romans. It was not the customs, but certain activities they led to, which were normally punishable. But a Roman colony may have been particularly anxious to maintain the Roman way of life, and Luke's version of the charge may reflect the spirit of the place rather than the legal code that was actually in force.

[c] But we cannot be sure: **place of prayer** is a phrase often used (though not elsewhere by Luke) to describe a synagogue building; and the manuscript reading is not certain.

unless a smaller stream is meant). **Lydia** may or may not have been Jewish.
Her native city, **Thyatira,** in that part of Asia Minor also known as Lydia, 14
was famous for its purple-dyeing industry. **Purple fabric** was a great luxury, and any dealer in it was likely to be well off, and to have a house large enough to accommodate guests. As a result of her conversion and her hospitality, the Christian missionaries became established; and we know from Paul's letter to the Philippians that in the course of their stay they built up a loyal and flourishing church.

But Luke hurries on to the end of their visit. The immediate cause of this
dramatic episode was **a slave-girl who was possessed by an oracular** 16
spirit. Most cases of spirit-possession in the New Testament are set in a Jewish context; but this spirit was **oracular,** that is to say, it performed fortune-telling in the style of the great Greek oracle at Delphi, and it used
pagan language about God—**the Supreme God**—just as in a notable case 17
of pagan possession recorded in the gospels (Luke 8.28). But spirits of any
kind could be exorcised **in the name of Jesus Christ.** In a pious Jewish 18
community such an exorcism would have caused awe and rejoicing; but pagans saw less evil in the presence of spirits, and their reaction was frankly materialistic.

The release of Paul and Silas—a miracle comparable with the release of Peter in chapter 12—is told in the manner such stories demanded. There
are touches of exaggeration (the **inner** prison, **all** the doors burst open, **all** 24, 26
the prisoners found their fetters unfastened); there are conventional features (the prayers and singing answered by an earthquake—compare 4.31); and there is an irrational haste in the jailer's movements which adds greatly to the drama of the story, but which would have been odd behaviour for someone officially responsible for the whole jail. But the point, for Luke, was that Paul and Silas were miraculously released (as was to be expected when God was so clearly behind their work), and he told the story in the way that came most naturally to him. He was also able to make the episode something more than merely spectacular: it resulted in the conversion of the
jailer **and his whole family.** [a] 33

They now travelled by way of Amphipolis and Apollonia—that is to 17. 1
say, they took the Via Egnatia, the great Roman road which led right across northern Greece to the Adriatic. After a few days' travelling they reached the most important city in Macedonia, **Thessalonica.** We know something of their work there from Paul's letters: Paul spent long enough in the city to found an important church (1 Thess. 1.6–10), to sustain himself by doing manual work (2 Thess. 3.8), and to receive contributions to his physical

[a] This passage has been much used in discussions on the question whether, in the early church, children and infants were baptized as well as adults. But the phrase is too general to decide the question.

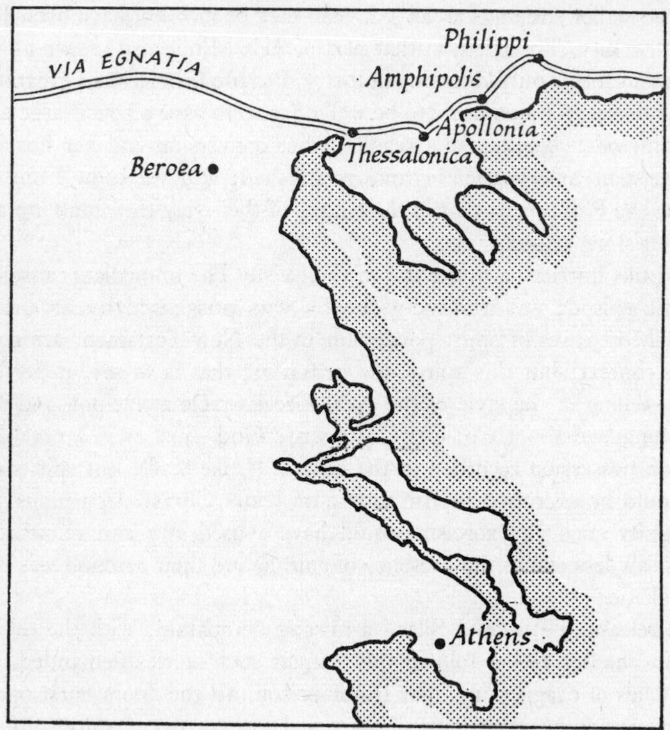

needs from Philippi, a hundred miles away (Philippians 4.16). It is evident, then, that Luke has telescoped his narrative, so that what was really a stay of several months reads like a short visit of a week or two. Moreover, while Paul tells us that the Christians in Thessalonica were persecuted by their pagan fellow-citizens (1 Thess. 2.14), Luke maintains that on this occasion the real instigators of the trouble were the Jews. In any case, Paul's work there
2 conformed to the usual pattern: first (**following his usual practice**) he
addressed himself to the synagogue; but the fruit of his preaching was to be
4 seen in the conversion of **a great number of godfearing Gentiles and**
a good many influential women, with the result that the Jews soon launched a jealous attack upon him. This attack was more subtle than any which Paul had experienced in Asia Minor. Thessalonica was a "free city", which meant that its courts had more freedom of jurisdiction than in most cities of the Roman empire (Luke may well have known this, since he knew
6 the unusual name by which **the magistrates** were known in Thessalonica:
politarchs). If the machinery of justice could be turned against Paul and Silas
5 there, much damage might be done. The first plan was to bring them **before**
the town assembly, where, in a kind of public inquisition, specific charges could be formulated. But, since they could not be found, all that could be

done was to bring a certain **Jason** (who could have been either a Greek or a 6
Jew who had assumed a Greek name) and certain others before the magistrates. The charges were calculated to arouse Roman apprehensions. '**Men
who have made trouble all over the world**' was the kind of language
the Emperor Claudius had made fashionable when he instituted punitive
measures against the Jews (he had accused them of "stirring up a universal
plague throughout the world"): these Christians, therefore, with their
Jewish type of religion, might be a recrudescence of the same evil. '**They** 7
all flout the Emperor's laws'—we do not know what this accusation was
based on, but it sounded damaging enough. '**And assert that there is a
rival king, Jesus**'. This was the hardest charge of all for Christians to
answer, for Jesus had been condemned and executed as a **king**, and it was
not always easy to explain that Jesus' kingship was not of this world. *Prima
facie*, therefore, there was a serious case against these men. But the men
could not be found. The magistrates took the only course open to them.
They bound over Jason—the phrase is technical, meaning that Jason had 9
to guarantee the good conduct of his guests. It would suit both the safety
of Paul and Silas and the convenience of the local government if they left
the city (for the jurisdiction of one city did not extend to another). Which is
what they were immediately persuaded to do.

Beroea (today called Verria) lay off the trunk road, some fifty miles from 10
Thessalonica. Exactly the same pattern was repeated, except that the
Jewish opposition was not local (for the Jews there were **more civil**) but 11
was stirred up by the same Jewish instigators who had caused trouble in
Thessalonica. Once more, Paul prudently left the area. Luke is in error
about Timothy's rather complicated movements. In fact he accompanied
Paul to Athens, and subsequently returned to Thessalonica (1 Thess. 3.1–2).

At Athens he was exasperated to see how the city was full of idols. 16
This was a characteristic Jewish reaction to the city which was still the cultural and intellectual centre of the ancient world; and Paul's speech to the
Athenians is for the most part an attack such as any courageous and educated
Jew might have made on the beliefs and practices of paganism. Athens, since
its subjugation by Rome in the previous century, had lost all vestiges of its
former political power; but its art and architecture were still an impressive
monument to its past glory, its streets continued to be embellished by the
lavish buildings of munificent patrons, and the sheer abundance of its temples
and altars and statues, even compared with other flourishing Greco-Roman
cities, could well have **exasperated** the sensibilities of a pious Jew seeing it
for the first time. To this extent the scene is absolutely true to life. Nevertheless we cannot be sure that Luke had actually been to Athens himself or
that he had any detailed information about Paul's activity there. The things
he tells us about Athens are the things that any educated person knew about
it. Its fame now rested, first on its university, and secondly on the many

religious cults which flourished there, and which even Roman Emperors
found occasion to attend. These cults certainly gave the Athenians the
22 reputation of being, **in everything that concerns religion, . . . uncommonly scrupulous.** As far as public observances such as sacrifices and
festivals were concerned, the Athenian religious institutions were zealously
maintained, and offered a serious object of attack to any convinced mono-
theist. But the religion of an educated Greek was something a good deal
more sophisticated; and this he learnt, not by frequenting the temples, but
by furthering his education in that other institution for which Athens was
famous, the schools of philosophy. It was philosophy rather than religion
(though the dividing line was hard to draw, since many philosophies included a substantial amount of theology) which moulded the principles and
ideals of educated Greeks and Romans. The Stoic view of life was the most
popular, and had become almost the official philosophy of the Roman
empire. It strongly affirmed the moral values of respectable Roman citizens,
and it provided powerful intellectual arguments for a belief in God. But its
vitality was due in part to the continual dialogue which went on between its
exponents and the leaders of other philosophical schools. Athens was the
17 centre of this dialogue. Philosophers met constantly **in the city square,**
under the great colonnaded porticos built by foreign kings and benefactors.
21 It was doubtless often said, somewhat cynically, that **the Athenians in
general and the foreigners there had no time for anything but talking
or hearing about the latest novelty.** But this was a surface impression.
Luke also knew (as, again, every educated person knew, whether or not he
had been there) that serious philosophical issues were constantly discussed.
He presents Paul's appearance as a challenge to all that Athens stood for,
to its religion and its philosophy, its temples and its university.

How was Paul equipped to address himself to such people? On the one
hand the severe monotheism he had inherited from his Jewish upbringing
commended itself to many serious-minded Greeks, and would have been
familiar enough to his audience—though of course Paul was now a Christian,
18 and was expounding this monotheism in terms of **Jesus and Resurrection,**
a name and a concept which were both so alien in sound that his hearers
simply assumed that he must be a **propagandist for foreign deities.** On
the other hand, he possessed, like many educated Jews, a smattering of
Greek philosophical terms and concepts, such that he could present his
beliefs in the kind of language his hearers could understand. They, for their
part, would sense that this was very superficial philosophy, and Luke, using
a rare and expressive Greek word, says that they called him a **charlatan**—
the original word suggests a bird picking up seeds wherever it can find them
—and their first impression of Paul was perhaps of a man mouthing philosophical jargon without much understanding of what it meant.

19 **So they took him and brought him before the Court of Areopagus.**

Areopagus is the name of a small hill ("Mars' Hill") near the Acropolis in Athens. In classical times, a select city council met there, and took its name from it; but, though it had great prestige, its actual power was insignificant. It was only under Roman rule that it became the most important assembly in the government of Athens. It was still called the Areopagus, but it now met in some part of 'the city square', close to the main civic buildings. It is possible that this council, or some committee of it, was in control of the teaching of philosophy, and that it was normal for a new teacher to be presented to it for its approval. But even if Luke had no certain information about what happened to Paul in Athens, it is not difficult to see why he should have chosen the Areopagus as the setting for Paul's self-defence. He knew that this was the name for the most important civic assembly at Athens; and he knew that the hill where it met (or, at least, used to meet) was the site of a historic Athenian tribunal. By using the word, he achieved his purpose of placing Paul at the very centre of the city's life.

In his preaching, Paul usually began with the Old Testament: rightly interpreted, the Jewish scriptures could be shown to proclaim the coming of one who would be the Saviour, not of the Jews only, but of all men; and that Saviour had now come in the person of Jesus. But this approach was only possible when his hearers were either Jews or else Gentiles who were already familiar with the Jewish religion. How was Paul to address himself to Athenian intellectuals, who knew nothing of these things, and who were accustomed to seek God, not by meditating on the history of a particular race, but by means of philosophical speculation? Luke (whether or not his information went back to Paul himself) had his own answer to this (for Paul's only other recorded speech to a gentile audience—that at Lystra, 14.15–17—follows exactly the same pattern as this one): Paul used the same language and arguments as had already been worked out by Greek-speaking Jews to commend the Jewish religion to men whose culture was Greek. Two points were frequently made in such Jewish apologetic. First, the statues and images and diverse cults of paganism were unworthy of the nature of God:
God '**does not live in shrines made by men . . . we ought not to** 24, 29
suppose that the deity is like an image in gold or silver or stone'.
Secondly, even though the Jews alone had received in their scriptures the one authentic revelation of the true God, all men could have some intimation of his nature, and indeed the poets and philosophers of Greece had often come near to the truth about him: 'he has not left you without some clue
to his nature' (14.17), '**he is not far from each one of us**'. These points 27
could of course be supported by quotations from the Old Testament. But they were also implied by some widely held tenets of philosophy (indeed, Paul would probably have carried the Stoics in his audience with him until he reached the specifically Christian part of his argument); and Paul's speech, in the manner of sophisticated Jewish preachers, is a subtle mixture

24 of the two. Thus: God '**created the world and everything in it**'. This is
the theme of the opening of Genesis, and a recurrent motif in Hebrew
poetry (compare especially Isaiah 42.5, where many of the same expressions
occur); but Stoic philosophers also proclaimed that God was the creator of
25 all. Again, '**it is not because he lacks anything that he accepts service
at men's hands**'. This criticism of the temple sacrifices occurs often in the
prophets and psalms (compare especially Psalm 50.12); but it was also a
26 commonplace of Greek philosophy. '**He created every race of men of one
stock.**' Hebrew thought conceived this truth mythologically: all human
beings were descended from Adam, who was created by God; but from their
philosophical standpoint, the Stoics laid equal stress on the unity of mankind. '**He fixed epochs of their history and the limits of their territory.**' The Jews, again, invoked certain myths: God created the world in a
certain number of "days", and laid down a plan for its history which could
be reckoned in "weeks" of years; moreover (a myth which lies under the
surface of parts of the Old Testament), in the course of creation he had
subdued the forces of chaos and pushed back the sea so that it should not
trespass upon the **limits** of inhabited **territory**. But the Stoics, though they
did not share these myths, believed equally strongly in the succession of
epochs and in the providential ordering of the earth's surface which made
some parts fit for human habitation. In all this, Greek philosophy and Jewish
religion stood so close together that we cannot always tell which phrase
belongs to the Old Testament, and which to current philosophical jargon.

But Jewish preachers went further than this. The sages of ancient Greece
were of course inferior to Moses, but they often had glimpses of the truth,
and could be quoted to support the Jewish case. Even the supreme pagan
deity had a name, Zeus, which (in one of its grammatical inflections) suggested "to live", just as the name of the God of Israel suggested "to be";
28 it was therefore self-evident to Jews and pagans alike that '**in him we live
and move, in him we exist**', just as both believed (though in somewhat
29, 28 different senses) that all men are '**God's offspring**'. '**Some of your own
poets have said**'. The quotation is in fact from a poet-astronomer of the
third century B.C. named Aratus; but this does not show that either Paul or
Luke was well read in Greek literature. The verses were quoted by at least
one other Jewish writer, and the line in question was doubtless proverbial
long before Aratus included it in his poem. It was probably just another stock
example of the kind of old Greek wisdom which, Jewish preachers argued,
showed that all men had some intimation of the true God.

But from this point the argument could go in one of two ways. If God had left all men with 'some clue to his nature', then (so one school would argue) the guilt of the Gentiles was all the more evident. They could not plead ignorance; they must bear the full severity of God's judgement on them—this is the line taken by Paul in the first chapter of Romans. Alternatively, a

more liberal and optimistic conclusion could be drawn. The fact that God had revealed himself, even if only partially, to the whole of mankind surely meant that he must intend something better for them than damnation. Even now, if they turned to the pure worship of the God of Israel, the Gentiles
could still be saved. This is the tone of the speech here: '**As for the times** 30
of ignorance, God has overlooked them'. '**Repent**'—this appeal must often have been heard from Jewish preachers: in their mouths it meant, Turn away from the idolatrous religion and debased morals of the pagan world, and accept the austere worship and ethic of the Jewish faith. But Paul proceeded differently: he offered as a motive for this repentance some precise information about the imminence of the Last Judgement and began to prove his argument, not by general considerations, but by a particular fact, the
raising of a man from the dead. At this, **some scoffed**, and no wonder. 32
Philosophy could hardly entertain such a dubious manner of proof. It was, as Paul subsequently wrote to the Corinthians, 'folly to Greeks' (1 Cor. 1.23).

Paul's argument, then, is of a kind that may often have been heard in Jewish propaganda: this was how an educated Jew addressed educated Greeks on the subject of his religion. Only in the last few words is any reference made to the new factors introduced by Christianity. Paul may indeed have adopted this style of preaching on occasion (though from his letters we should hardly have guessed it); but Luke certainly believed—perhaps in the light of the subsequent experience of Christian preachers—that this was the kind of argument which Paul would have used when addressing the Athenians. At any rate, he has certainly used his literary skill to make the form of the speech appropriate to the occasion. It contains a number of expressions and idioms which belonged to the speech of cultivated Greeks; and it makes brilliant use of a technique still used in sermons, that of starting from an
object familiar to the audience. No **altar bearing the inscription "To an** 23
Unknown God" has in fact been found, and probably none existed bearing exactly this wording. But it was well known that, especially in Athens, altars were occasionally erected to nameless gods when none of the "known" gods seemed to be the appropriate one to pray to in a particular emergency; and this was perhaps a sufficient cue for Luke's vivid introduction to the theme of the whole speech: '**What you worship but do not know—this is what I now proclaim**'.

However, some men joined him and became believers. Paul's visit 34
to Athens was not a failure, but neither was it a great success: he left behind him individual converts, but we do not hear of the existence of an Athenian church before the middle of the next century. The university city cannot have offered an easy opening for Paul's message. It was otherwise with
Corinth, which was no longer a Greek city in the sense that Athens was, even **18.** 1
though it was now the administrative capital of the Province of Achaia. Corinth had been virtually destroyed in the wars of the second century B.C.,

and lay deserted until it was refounded as a Roman colony by Julius Caesar. Its new citizens were more Roman than Greek; but its atmosphere was essentially cosmopolitan. It was a great trading centre. Ships from the east unloaded at the Isthmus rather than make the risky voyage round the Peloponnese. Their cargoes were then carried across and re-embarked in the gulf of Corinth. With this trade came settlers from all over the Mediterranean. There was a substantial Jewish community, there were cults of eastern deities (involving, it was said, much immorality). Corinth, in short, was more like the cities which Paul knew in Asia Minor than like Athens. His work there produced a very flourishing church, of which we gain a vivid picture in 1 Corinthians.

2 Luke's narrative touches Roman history at two points. **Claudius had issued an edict that all Jews should leave Rome.** This is confirmed by an independent historian, Tacitus. Claudius' reign (41–54) began with a declaration of a policy of toleration towards the Jews and their worship. But later—possibly as a result of divisions within the Jewish community caused by the arrival of Christianity in Rome—the Emperor moved against them. **Priscilla** (a diminutive form of Prisca) and **Aquila** we know to have been a well-to-do couple (see below on Romans 16.3), and were perhaps prominent enough at Rome to fall immediate victims to Claudius' edict. They may indeed already have been Christians. The second point of contact with secular
12 history is the reference to the proconsul **Gallio.** This person is well known. He was the elder brother of the philosopher and dramatist Seneca, and he is proved by an inscription to have been **proconsul** (the correct title for the governor of a Roman province) of Achaia around A.D. 52. These two historical cross-references make it certain that Paul's arrival in Corinth can be dated between A.D. 49 and 51.

3 **They were tent-makers.** Cloth of goat's hair, used for tents and coats, was one of the industries of Paul's native Cilicia. The same trade may have been possible in Corinth; alternatively, the Greek word may bear the more general meaning it often had in antiquity, "leather-worker". It may seem surprising that a man as learned as Paul should have practised such a trade; but Jewish scholars received no payment for their services to the community, and often supported themselves in quite humble professions. Paul, moreover, prided himself on being financially independent; and the reason why, after
5 the arrival of Silas and Timothy, he **devoted himself entirely to preaching** was probably that these men brought with them contributions from other churches towards his physical needs.

Given this slower and more settled pace, the progress of Paul's work in Corinth followed the usual pattern. First he preached in the synagogue; but on the Jews' refusal to accept that Jesus was the Messiah whom they expected, he solemnly absolved himself of any further responsibility towards them, and
6 turned **to the Gentiles.** But this time the usual reaction was delayed. Some

distinguished Jews became converts, such as **Crispus, who held office in** 8
the synagogue; and in a vision Paul was instructed not to make his usual
rapid departure, but to "settle down" and consolidate the new church.

A serious clash with the Jewish leaders was of course inevitable, but when
it eventually came it left Paul and his church for the first time unharmed.
This was entirely due to the attitude of the Roman government; and Luke
seems to present the distinguished Roman administrator as a typical representative of what he took the correct Roman policy to be. Far from being a
public menace, Christianity deserved to leave the government quite **un-** 17
concerned.

The grandiose rostrum from which the proconsul gave his judgement
(which is the literal meaning of the word here translated **court**) has been 12
excavated in the Agora, or main square, of Corinth. It was for Gallio to
decide whether the charges brought against the defendant constituted an
offence under Roman law. The Jews' charge against Paul could have done so,
since certain kinds of religious proselytizing were certainly **against the law** 13
in the Roman sense. But, in the mouths of Jews, "the law" usually meant the
Jewish law; and so Gallio preferred to take it. This allowed him to decline to
hear the case. What followed sounds like a riot; but once the case was handed
back to the Jews, they were certainly empowered to administer **a beating** to 17
one of their own number if they could prove an offence. If Sosthenes was
now a Christian—and a Christian Sosthenes is mentioned in the opening of
1 Corinthians—it would doubtless have been possible for them to frame a
charge against so prominent a renegade, and to carry out the sentence in the
public square of Corinth, within sight of the proconsul's rostrum. Alternatively, the **general attack on Sosthenes** may have been simply a case of
popular anti-semitism.

After this long stay in Corinth, **Paul set sail for Syria.** The capital of 18
Syria was Antioch, whence Paul had originally set out on his travels (15.36),
and the direct route would have been to the port of Seleucia which served
Antioch. But Paul may well not have found at **Cenchreae** (the port on the
east side of the Isthmus of Corinth) a ship due to make the journey. **Ephesus,** 19
at any rate, was a natural stage on it. Luke mentions that for some reason
Paul made a personal visit to the synagogue there, apparently without
attempting to start a Christian group (for this comes in the next chapter).
Paul is kept moving on his journey. But this seems to have involved a considerable detour. There were many ports nearer to Antioch than **Caesarea.** 22
But Caesarea served Jerusalem, and "going up" from Caesarea was almost
a technical expression for taking the road up into the mountains to Jerusalem. Is this what Paul did? We cannot be sure: but there is perhaps a hint
in Luke's statement that **at Cenchreae he had his hair cut off, because** 18
he was under a vow. Solemnly cutting off one's hair was a religious act in
more than one culture in antiquity, but the Jews practised a particular form

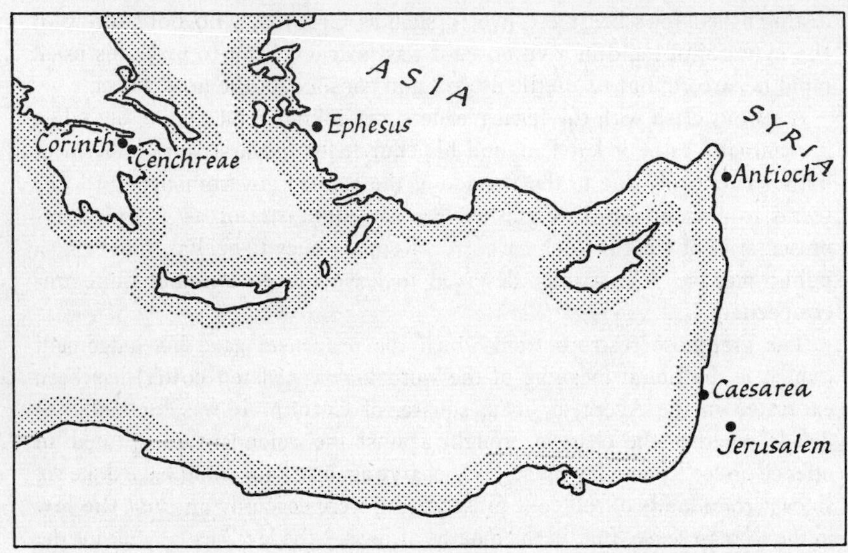

of it. It was open to any individual to lay himself under a vow to keep himself ritually clean, to abstain from wine, and to allow his hair to grow for the duration of the vow (these three disciplines were based on Numbers 6). Vows of this kind were taken for various periods, never for less than a month, but sometimes for much longer; thus, a man might take the vow until he had completed a particular enterprise—it was a way of strengthening his own resolution and (it was believed) of acquiring merit in the eyes of God. When the period of the vow was completed, the growth of hair was cut off and presented, along with other offerings, at the temple in Jerusalem. This procedure is described more clearly below in 21.24, but the reference here can hardly have any other meaning than that Paul had made some vow of this kind before or during his travels, and that his embarkation at Cenchreae marked the moment when the vow came to an end. He was now free to cut his hair and to drink wine; but he still had to make the prescribed offerings in Jerusalem. This would explain his circuitous route to Antioch via Caesarea and Jerusalem; but Luke seems to have mentioned it mainly to show that Paul, for all his contact with Gentiles, still abode by traditional Jewish observances.

Luke has only one more stage to record in Paul's missionary activity. Paul founded no more new churches; but he spent some years building up churches
23 which already existed. Some of these, such as those in **the Galatian country** and in **Phrygia**, he had founded himself (16.6); but in Ephesus, where he was to be active for some time, he found Christianity already established. This presented a new situation in the pattern of Paul's work;

and Luke endeavours to clarify Paul's original relationship with this important church by describing the curious and incomplete form of Christianity which prevailed there before Paul's arrival, and the necessary corrections introduced by Paul.

Until now, each Christian church had been founded either by, or under the
authority of, one of the Jerusalem apostles or by Paul himself; and the
legitimacy of each new serious departure in missionary policy had been
proved by an irrefutable manifestation of the gift of the Holy Spirit (2.4;
8.16–17; 10.44). So, at any rate, Luke seems to have understood the history
of the early church. But Christianity at Ephesus began rather differently.
Among the first missionaries there, Luke mentions only Priscilla and Aquila,
who came from Rome, and **Apollos, an Alexandrian.** The situation was 24
irregular; the Ephesian church needed to be brought into relation with the
Christian tradition which stemmed ultimately from Jerusalem. This is
precisely what Paul did, and the model for his action seems to have been an
episode such as the foundation of the church in Samaria (8.4–17): others
could preach the gospel, but only the apostles themselves (of whom Paul
now counted himself one) could bestow the gift of the Holy Spirit. But in
this case the matter was more complicated. There had been Christians in
Ephesus at least since the arrival of Priscilla and Aquila (18.18). Since then,
Paul had returned by sea to Antioch, and had **travelled through the** 19. 1
inland regions till he came to Ephesus, a long journey that must have
lasted several months. During all this time, was the Christianity that was
flourishing in Ephesus such that the converts were still without that gift
which was the distinctive mark of any Christian community, the Holy
Spirit? Luke says that it was, and suggests that the reason had to do with
their baptism. In the gospel story, two kinds of baptism are mentioned, that
of John the Baptist (which was simply an expression of repentance) and that
of Jesus (which was carried out by his followers and conferred the Holy
Spirit). That the Christians in Ephesus were still without the Spirit is
explained by the fact that their baptism was only of the first kind. Luke
describes how Paul put this right with the appropriate act of laying on his
hands; and he accounts for the rise of this anomalous situation by the activity
of a certain preacher named Apollos who, at least until he was instructed by
Priscilla and Aquila, **knew only John's baptism,** and had presumably 18. 25
started to build up the church on an inadequate foundation.

This explanation is logical; but when examined more closely it raises
difficulties. We are familiar with Apollos from 1 Corinthians 1–3. Luke's
description of him, **an Alexandrian by birth, an eloquent man, power-** 24
ful in his use of the scriptures, suggests a well-known type. It was at
Alexandria that Jewish scholars made the most consistent attempt to interpret the Old Testament in terms of Greek philosophy. In the voluminous
works of Philo we possess an impressive example of this; but there were

certainly others who followed the same method, and Apollos was doubtless one of them. This would have made him a very different kind of preacher from Paul, whose understanding of his ancestral religion, and whose interpretation of the scriptures, was seldom expressed in purely philosophical terms; and the disagreement between the two men, which can be detected in 1 Corinthians, may well have arisen from this difference of background. But did Apollos also start with a serious misapprehension about Christian baptism and about the gift of the Spirit? There is nothing in 1 Corinthians to suggest it; indeed, it is not easy to imagine what sort of Christianity it could have been which left out two such essential elements. Moreover, Luke's account seems barely consistent with itself. How could Apollos have
25 been **instructed in the way of the Lord,** and yet still be in need of being
26 "taken in hand" by Priscilla and Aquila? And why did Priscilla and Aquila,
who had known Paul well in Corinth, not give the necessary instruction about the Holy Spirit long before Paul arrived in Ephesus? It is possible that Luke has put together his narrative out of recollections which were originally quite separate: first, Apollos was a distinguished preacher, at Ephesus and then at Corinth, who presented the gospel in a much more Hellenized form than Paul, and who was therefore regarded by some (as we know from 1 Corinthians) as belonging to a different "party". Secondly, the followers of John the Baptist may have had a longer history than the gospel narratives suggest, and Paul could well have converted a group of them to Christianity while he was in Ephesus. It may have been out of such fragments of historical material that Luke constructed his somewhat schematic account of Paul's part in the shaping of the church at Ephesus.

19. 8–9 **He attended the synagogue . . . some proved obdurate.** Given this new start in the history of the Christian community, Luke is able to show that even at Ephesus Paul's work conformed to the usual pattern: first an approach to the Jews, and only when that had failed a wider mission to the Gentiles. The transition is emphasized by a vivid detail. The synagogue was the centre, not only of Jewish worship, but of that whole culture and education which the Jews strove so hard to keep intact from the influence of pagan customs and beliefs. Over against it stood a number of magnificently endowed buildings (such as still dominate the ruins of Ephesus) devoted to instruction
9 in philosophy and general education in Greek culture. When Paul **withdrew**
his converts from the synagogue and began **to hold discussions daily in the lecture-hall of Tyrannus,** the significance of the move was apparent: he was no longer preaching a religion intended only, or even mainly, for Jews.

10 **This went on for two years.** Ephesus was the most important city in which Paul had yet worked. It was the commercial capital of the Roman Province of Asia, which embraced the whole of the western part of Asia Minor with its many wealthy cities; it was an important port and a great religious and cultural centre. Having been rebuilt on a grand scale during the

Roman period, it had a population of perhaps a quarter of a million. Clearly it presented an important field for mission. Luke says summarily that **the whole population of the province of Asia, both Jews and Gentiles, heard the word of the Lord.** This grandiose claim is not wholly exaggerated. We hear from Paul's letters (Colossians 4.13) of three cities inland from Ephesus where churches were founded (of which Colossae was one); and by the time the Revelation was written, six other great cities in the province had churches. What Luke does not mention (either because he did not know about it or else because he saw no reason to record it) is that during this time Paul also visited Corinth. In short, his activity must have been intense.

Luke, however, describes this period, not with a list of achievements, but
with a series of anecdotes. **Through Paul God worked singular miracles.** 11
Paul—and this is perhaps why Luke mentions it—was not to be imagined as in any way inferior to the other apostles in supernatural power: what Peter could do with his shadow (5.15) Paul could do through even indirect contact with his body. The following paragraph leaves Paul for a moment, and describes the power of the new religion itself over all its competitors (Ephesus was proverbially a centre of magical traditions). Exorcism in particular, though it was esteemed more reputable than magic, used unmistakably magical techniques. It consisted of discovering the name and power of the demon, and then "adjuring" it (a technical term) by the name
of some superior power. **A Jewish chief priest,** by virtue of his office, was 14
privileged to utter the sacred name of the true God (which was religiously avoided by all other Jews). The sons of such a person, by making unscrupulous use of this secret knowledge, might well have had some success as exorcists, since this divine Name was believed to have unique power. But they would doubtless have used many lesser names besides; and hearing of the potency of a certain "Jesus" in this connection, they would naturally have added his name to their repertory. Luke's anecdote is a dramatic pendant to the stories of exorcism in the gospels. There, the spirits had recognized in Jesus an exorcist of supreme authority. Here, while still
recognizing the same authority (**'Jesus I acknowledge'**) the spirit chal- 15
lenges the irresponsible use of that authority, and demonstrates the reality of its own power (and by implication the power of Jesus whom it acknowledges) by a typical manifestation of violence, such that (like the crowds which
witnessed Jesus' miracles) **they were all awestruck.** From the historical 17
point of view, the only difficulty in the story is that we know of no Jewish
chief priest called Sceva (a Latin name)—but the exorcists' father may well 14
have been an impostor also. In any case, Luke has successfully conveyed an atmosphere of charlatanry. Exorcism practised without due authority yielded before the authentic power of the new religion. As for ordinary magic, its practitioners publicly repudiated their arts in one of those orgies

of book-burning by which great cities of the Roman empire periodically attempted to hold in check the superstitious credulity of the time. By the
19 equivalent standard adopted in the NEB, the **total value** of the books was between two and three thousand pounds.

21 **When things had reached this stage.** The phrase is a significant one. Christ was triumphant in the province of Asia; Paul's work here was done. It was no longer a matter of being harried from place to place by the Jewish opposition; Paul was now free to take the initiative himself. Accordingly, he **made up his mind**[a] **to visit Macedonia and Achaia**; and, as if to emphasize his freedom to make his own plans, it is recorded that he sent on
22 ahead **two of his assistants.**[b] All this dispels in advance any sense of compulsion which might have been conveyed by the episode which follows. At the same time, a hint is given of the inexorable destiny which is to deter-
21 mine Paul's movements for the rest of Acts: **'I must see Rome also'.**

23 **The Christian movement gave rise to a serious disturbance.** We know from Paul's letters that his stay in Ephesus was by no means peaceful. He underwent a nearly fatal illness—if that is what is meant by Paul's enigmatic words in 2 Corinthians 1.8–9—and he was involved in some public demonstration which nearly cost him his life (1 Corinthians 15.32). One would have expected Acts to fill in the details; but in fact Luke's narrative is either concerned with a quite different disturbance, or else it deliberately gives the episode another direction. Either way, it is a fitting climax to this part of Acts: the confrontation between Christianity and the greatest religious cult of Asia Minor. For Ephesus' most famous possession was its temple to
24 Artemis (in Latin, **Diana**), which had been rebuilt in the fourth century B.C. and was one of the architectural wonders of the ancient world. To the Ephesians, Artemis was far more than the huntress-goddess of classical Greek mythology. She was the greatest divinity in Asia, and represented the power of fertility. She was worshipped at countless shrines in the countryside, and her temple was a place of the greatest sanctity and wealth.

This temple was served by dignitaries with various exotic titles, one of which was a Greek word meaning literally "temple-makers"; and an inscription proves that one of these "temple-makers" around this time was named Demetrius. It is possible that Luke knew Demetrius' official title, but misunderstood it and inferred that he was **a silversmith who made silver shrines of Diana.** Equally, Demetrius may have been another man of the same name who was really a silversmith, for the manufacture of small models of temples was quite common, and it may only be accident that no such models of the Ephesus temple have been found. In any case, this Demetrius was one

[a] Or, was "led by the Spirit". The Greek could mean either; but the point is the same. No human authority interfered.

[b] This may or may not be the mission referred to in 1 Corinthians 4.17; 16.10. A rather distinguished Erastus is mentioned in Romans 16.23; but the name was not uncommon.

whose interests were directly affected by any falling away in the observance of the cult of Diana. His harangue to his fellow-workers has a prophetic ring: very soon after Luke wrote, a Roman governor in Asia Minor was to complain that, as a result of Christianity, the pagan temples were becoming
deserted. But in his summary of Paul's **propaganda** he borrows the 26
language, not of Christianity, but of Judaism: '**gods made by human hands are not gods at all**' was one of the stock phrases of the Jewish attack upon pagan idolatry. This is the first touch by which Luke allows an agitation which could have been (and may in fact have been) a serious blow for the Christian church to read like an outburst of popular anti-Jewish feeling, in which the Christians were ultimately barely involved.

They seized Paul's travelling-companions . . . and made a con- 29
certed rush with them into the theatre. This theatre is still well preserved. In the course of the first century A.D. the stage buildings underwent massive alterations, and we should probably imagine them surrounded by scaffolding. But the auditorium, an immense semicircle cut into the hillside, with tier upon tier of seats holding over 25,000 people, must have appeared very much as it does today. It was the natural place, not only for drama, but for any large meeting of the city populace; and once the crowd had assembled there, it was for any orator who could be found to explain the emergency and suggest a course of action. Demetrius had mysteriously disappeared (Luke has let him make his speech at an earlier stage), and the only attempt at giving
some direction to the proceedings was made by a certain **Alexander**, who 33
was presumably a spokesman for the Jewish attitude towards the official religion of Ephesus. But his appearance was the cue for a burst of frank anti-semitism. It is easy to imagine how the endless chanting of the crowd would have affected any Jews who happened to be present. The church, on the other hand, seems to have been barely represented. Paul himself was
absent. As Luke observes, **even some of the dignitaries of the province** 31
(Luke uses a technical title mainly reserved for men entrusted with responsibility for the official religion) were sufficiently favourable to Christianity and to Paul to make sure that he should not get implicated. If any of Luke's readers had heard of a riot at Ephesus, and had jumped to the conclusion that it was Christians who were responsible, Luke was careful to correct such a damaging misapprehension.

But there was another side to the affair. Ephesus still retained its old Greek constitution, under which an assembly of the citizen body had the power of a parliament. This power was allowed to them somewhat grudgingly by their Roman rulers, and in fact came to an end a few generations later; and the rest of the scene is played out under the shadow of the stern power of Rome. The assembly of rioters could easily have been misconstrued in official quarters as an abuse of democratic power; and the speech of the senior city
magistrate (whom Luke correctly calls by his official title of **town clerk**) is 35

devoted entirely to avoiding this danger. Emergency assemblies (such as this had become) could be called only when serious danger threatened the life of the city; and no such danger could be alleged. The official mythology of Ephesus was surely unassailable: some symbol or image of the goddess was venerated which, it was believed, **fell from heaven** (we know this to have been the case in some Greek cults, though we have no other evidence it was so at Ephesus), and the city therefore possessed the unique honour of being **temple-warden** of her cult. Moreover, no damage was alleged to have been done to the holy places. There could therefore be no emergency, and the speech ends by outlining the proper course of action which should be taken if someone had a serious grievance. For civil disputes between individuals,
38 regular **assizes** were held before the Roman governor (the *proconsul*); any
39 **further question**—that is, anything affecting the community as a whole—
could be brought in due course before **the statutory assembly**, the citizen body at one of its regular meetings. The speech fits the occasion admirably: this is exactly how we should expect the Ephesian town clerk to have warned the people against conduct which might lead the Romans to deprive them of their privileges. But that, in Luke's narrative, is the end of the story; and the implication is unmistakable. The whole thing was trumped up, the mob had been irresponsibly roused, and it all came to nothing. The only people seriously implicated were the Jews; the Christians were actually under official protection. There was no more than this to the famous incident at Ephesus. The church was perfectly on the right side of the law. It was only incidentally that anyone could say that "the Christian movement had given rise to a serious disturbance".

20. 1 **Paul . . . set out on his journey to Macedonia.** Ephesus to Thessalonica was a long and complicated journey, whether by sea or land; but Luke gives us none of the details. His narrative of Paul's movements is remarkably vague until the mysterious "we" suddenly reappears in verse 5; whoever is speaking (see above on 16.10) seems to have spent the interval at Philippi, and now to rejoin Paul and his party when they call at Philippi on their way. After this the travel diary is as detailed as usual. But for the previous three
2 months spent in **Greece**, we have to draw upon Paul's own letters, from
which (especially Romans 15.22–6) it is fairly certain that his destination in Greece was Corinth, and that at least one of his motives for the subsequent voyage to Jerusalem, if not the most important one, was to pay over the financial contributions which he had so painstakingly collected from his various churches for the needs of the church in Jerusalem. This throws some
3 light on the **plot** that was **laid against him by the Jews.** If Paul had sailed
with all the money on a ship plying direct from Corinth to a port in **Syria**, he would have been very vulnerable. His return by way of **Macedonia**, though it was much longer, had so many different stages (not to mention the

perhaps deliberate splitting up of the party at certain points) that a planned ambush would have been much more difficult. However, Luke says nothing of all this. The purpose of the last part of Acts is simply to show the stages by which Paul reached Rome. It seems significant that the members of Paul's escort are all listed under the countries they came from. They may in fact have been emissaries of the various churches, entrusted with the collection. But again, Luke says nothing of this. In his narrative their names and countries simply reflect the geographical extent of Paul's missionary work.

(**Sopater** may or may not be the Sosipater mentioned in Romans 16.21. 4
Aristarchus has been mentioned in 19.29. **Secundus** is unknown. **Gaius the Doberian,** if this reading is correct, would be the Gaius of 19.29; for Doberus was in Macedonia. But if the usually accepted reading, "the Derbaean", is correct (see the NEB footnote), this would be another Gaius, and be more naturally paired with **Timothy,** who came from Lystra: Lystra and Derbe were neighbouring cities in central Asia Minor. **Tychicus** (Colossians 4.7; 2 Timothy 4.12) and **Trophimus** (21.29) were **Asians,** by which Luke probably means Ephesians.)

We ourselves set sail from Philippi after the Passover season. The 6
dating, as usual in Acts, is by the great Jewish festivals; and in fact the seasons fall exactly as one would expect. The **three months** Paul spent in Greece were presumably in mid-winter, when sea-voyages were seldom risked. Sailings were resumed in the spring, and Paul would have embarked at the earliest opportunity, had he not changed his plans and spent some weeks going north to Philippi. This brought him to **the Passover season,** which fell each year some time in March or April, and left him another six weeks
before the next great festival for the rest of the voyage to Jerusalem (**he was** 16
eager to be in Jerusalem, if he possibly could, on the day of Pentecost). Even allowing for changing ships once or twice, this was quite a feasible programme, given normal Mediterranean conditions in early summer.

On the Saturday night. Literally, "on the first day of the week". If 7
Luke was using the Jewish way of reckoning days from sunset to sunset, then the first day of the week began on Saturday evening, and the NEB is accurate. But he may equally well have been using the Roman reckoning (midnight to midnight), in which case it was Sunday night. In either case we can probably see the point of Luke mentioning it. By the time Luke wrote, if not long before, Christians regularly held their **assembly for the breaking of bread** once a week, on Sunday, the day of the resurrection, in the early morning or in the evening.

It is hard to be sure whether this incident at Troas is intended to read like
a miracle. Falling **from the third storey to the ground** would not neces- 9
sarily have been fatal (the house, like many others we hear of in antiquity, had a ground and two upper storeys); and the version in the NEB seems to

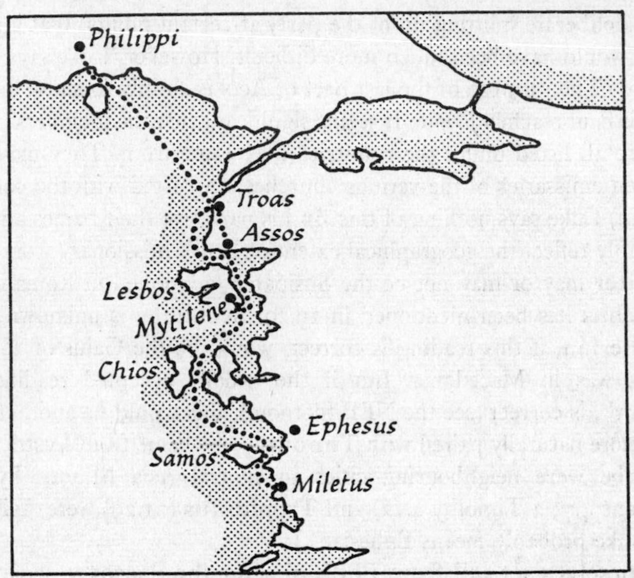

assume that it was not, and that Paul administered some kind of first aid. But
10 the Greek is not so clear. Literally, it has "was picked up dead" for **was picked up for dead,** and "there is life in him" for '**there is still life in him**'. If these details are pressed, we are confronted with a feat which would place Paul in the very first rank of miracle-workers: raising from the dead.

13 **Troas** and **Assos** lay on opposite sides of a promontory: the main party
went round by ship, Paul for some reason crossed by land. After that, the
ship made its way south, stopping each night at one of the islands that lie off
14 the coast of Asia Minor: Lesbos (of which **Mitylene** was the capital),
15 **Chios** and **Samos.** Calling at Ephesus would have involved a substantial
delay, and Paul had deliberately chosen a ship which followed a direct course to Palestine. However, there was one more port of call on the mainland, the historic city of **Miletus.** This marked Paul's final departure from the province of Asia, and Luke records it as a moment of great solemnity.

17 **The elders of the congregation** at Ephesus could hardly have been summoned to Miletus in less than four or five days (the distance by road may have been as much as forty miles); but Ephesus had been the scene of Paul's longest single period of continuous work, and his desire to say a formal farewell is perfectly plausible. If his ship had to spend a few days in the harbour anyway, it would have been natural for Paul to take advantage of the opportunity to make contact with his friends. At the same time, Luke clearly had a historian's interest in the scene. He had reached the end of Paul's missionary work. It was the moment for summing up what had been achieved before beginning what was to be a very different chapter in Paul's

life. A convenient pretext for such a summing up lay ready to hand. Ancient writers liked to put into the mouths of their heroes a farewell speech. Luke had done this for Jesus in his gospel (22.21–38). In this brief pause at Miletus he now had the opportunity to do the same for Paul. Some such scene may well have taken place, and Luke himself may have been present. But we must at least allow for the possibility that, as a conscious literary artist, he deliberately elaborated it in order to fix in the reader's mind a clear picture of Paul's personality and achievements.

A hint of this is provided right at the outset. The description of Paul's
activity **in the province of Asia** rings absolutely true of the pattern which 18
was followed in church after church that he founded, and indeed can be
substantiated in many of its details from Paul's own letters. **The machina-** 19
tions of the Jews have been a recurring theme; but, curiously enough, one
place where Luke has mentioned no such "machinations" is—Ephesus!
Clearly Luke has generalized: Paul's whole missionary experience is the
subject here. Similarly with Paul's glimpse of the future. This is an accurate
foretaste of the story Luke still has to tell, and yields a vivid picture of the
sense both of divine guidance (**constraint of the Spirit**)[a] and of personal 22
self-sacrifice which strengthened Paul as he neared Jerusalem. How did
Paul know in advance of his **imprisonment and hardships**? Luke provides 23
the answer (and illustrates it below, 21.7–14): prophets, moved by the Holy
Spirit, had foretold these things to him **in city after city.**

One word more. The speech so far has been a portrait of Paul; but in 25
what follows the real subject is the church for whose benefit the portrait is
being painted. This church may be Paul's own foundation in Ephesus; or it
may be the church of Luke's day, a generation later, to which Luke is
deliberately addressing a summary of the principles which governed Paul's
work. In either event we are in a difficulty, for we cannot do more than guess
at the issues which caused the saying or the writing of such sensitive words.
'I here and now declare that no man's fate can be laid at my door'. 26
Who was accusing Paul of this? In the original, the word for **fate** is even
stronger: it means "death". The early Christians regarded expulsion from
the church as tantamount to death; and in Corinth, at least, Paul had occasionally recommended expulsion (1 Corinthians 5.5). Is such a case in mind
here? Alternatively, is it the fate of the Jews in general which is meant, to
whom Paul had said, 'Your blood be on your own heads!' (18.6)? Or is it
some subsequent bitter schism in the church, for which the ultimate blame is
being "laid at the door" of some ambiguity in Paul's original teaching? We
do not know. However, in what follows the case is perhaps a little clearer.
'Savage wolves will come in among you and will not spare the flock'. 29

[a] The same Greek word is used for the "Spirit" of God and the "spirit" in man—distinguishing one from the other by a capital letter is a modern convention. Hence the alternative translation in NEB. For the relation between the two "spirits", see below, p. 521.

The metaphor is obvious enough, and was used by Jesus himself. A few generations later than Paul's time, it was used frequently in Christian writings, and always meant heretical teachers. Paul may well have foreseen the emergence of such teachers; but by the time Luke wrote they were a reality, and amid the conflicting loyalties within the contemporary church it may
31 have been useful to record Paul's single-minded devotion **for three years, night and day,** to the building up of the church in Ephesus. Paul's farewell at
28 Miletus could also be read as a timeless warning to **the shepherds of the church**—which, in the Greek, is much more than a metaphor: the phrase translated "shepherd in charge" contains the word which was soon to become the official title of the senior minister in the church: *episkopos*, bishop.

33 **'I have not wanted anyone's money or clothes for myself'.** On the face of it this is an even stranger piece of self-defence: why should Paul have been accused of such a thing? Yet there are hints in his letters that his enemies were not above casting suspicion on his handling of the money collected for the church in Jerusalem. Moreover, we know that a fierce debate raged round the issue whether or not a preacher was entitled to be supported by the church. On this, Paul's own view was that in general it was proper to give a minister his board and lodging, even though in his own case he preferred to decline it. In support he quoted a saying of Jesus that 'those who preach the Gospel should earn their living by the Gospel' (1 Corinthians 9.14). But here,
35 it is Paul's personal example of **hard work** at a manual trade which is held up as an example to the church, and this too is supported by a proverb-like saying attributed to Jesus (though it was certainly said by others besides him), "**Happiness lies more in giving than in receiving**". Paul's financial independence was one of the many ways in which his example was to be followed by the churches; and with this, somewhat unexpectedly, the speech comes to an end.

Even if the later interests of the church have coloured the composition of this speech, its tone is still faithful to the sadness, the foreboding, and the sense of inexorable purpose with which Paul must have taken leave of his churches; and Luke allows the same tone to permeate his brief account of the remaining stages of the voyage. The ship ran easily before the prevailing north-westerly wind, and made the usual stops on its way round to the
21. 1 mainland port of **Patara.** A different ship—possibly a larger one—then took the travellers on the much longer stage across the open sea from Patara to the coast of Palestine (the narrative here has some good nautical terms).
3, 7 They stopped at two ports, **Tyre** and **Ptolemais,** before they reached Caesarea; and at each they found Christian churches to greet them (though
8 their foundation has not been mentioned in Acts). At **Caesarea** there were already links with the past: **Philip the evangelist, who was one of the**
10 **Seven** (6.5; 7.4–13), and a **prophet named Agabus** (11.28) who, in a scene
11–14 reminiscent of the Old Testament (e.g. Isaiah 20), brings to a climax the

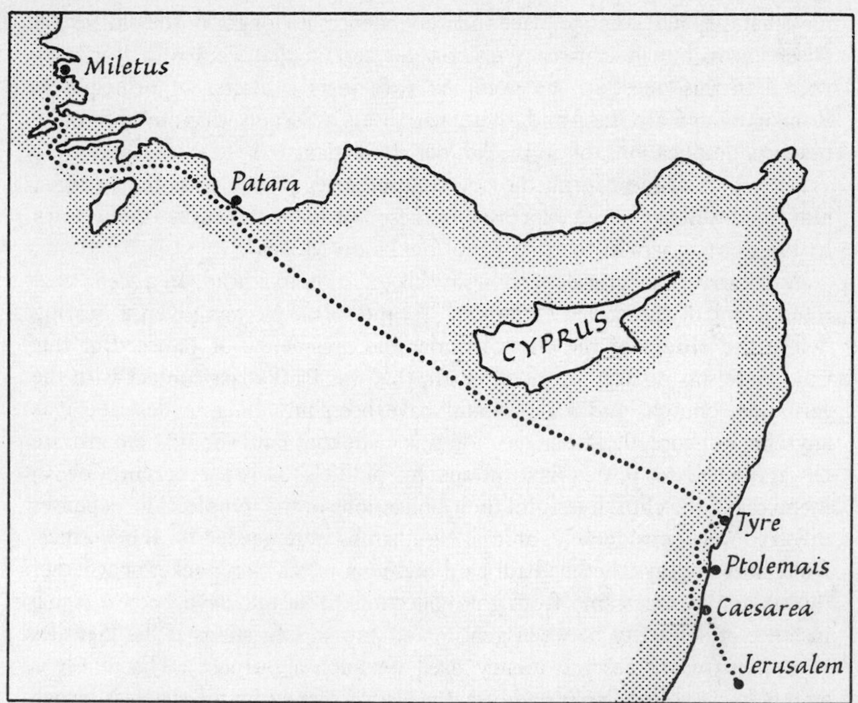

series of prophetic warnings by which the tension of the journey has been built up.

So we reached Jerusalem. The main purpose of this visit we know from 17
Paul's letters: to hand over the collection which had been raised in the gentile churches for the needs of the Jewish church in Jerusalem. Luke seems to have known about this collection and alludes to it below in 24.17. Its purpose was twofold: to express the solidarity of the gentile churches with the parent Jewish church, and to bring assistance to the impoverished Christians in Jerusalem. One aspect of this purpose is in fact dealt with in Luke's narrative, even though for some reason he makes no mention of the collection itself.

The solidarity between Jewish and gentile churches was once again threatened. On a previous occasion (chapter 15), the question had been how far, and under what conditions, Gentiles could be admitted to the church without at the same time becoming full Jewish proselytes. But this had been settled by a decree (which is mentioned again here). The new cause of dissension was the question of the proper conduct of Jews who had become Christians. How far was it right for them to abandon the strict Jewish way of life in order to live in close community with their gentile fellow-Christians? How far was the full observance of the Jewish Law still binding upon them,

now that they had come to place their confidence, no longer in the old Jewish observances, but in Christ? We know for certain that Paul was deeply involved in this question: he grappled with it as a matter of principle in Romans and Galatians; and there had been a serious dispute about the practical implications of it in Antioch (Galatians 2.11–14; see above on 15.39). In its crudest form, the objection of strict Jewish Christians against
21 him could well have been expressed in these words: **'you teach all the Jews in the gentile world to turn their backs on Moses'.**

Paul's arrival in Jerusalem brought this question to a head. In a scene very reminiscent of the earlier "council" (chapter 15), he was given a hearing
18 before **the elders** of the church under the presidency of James. But this time there was no argument—after all, this was Paul's last contact with the Jerusalem church, and Luke would have been unwilling to describe it as anything but cordial. The suggestion was made that Paul should demonstrate his allegiance to Jewish institutions by publicly assisting certain Jewish members of the church to fulfil their obligations in the temple. The expenses involved were considerable: at least eight lambs were needed for the sacrifice. Luke does not say whether Paul paid these out of his own pocket or whether the money in fact came from the collection (it would have been a signal instance of solidarity between gentile and Jewish Christians if the Gentiles were prepared to see the money used for such a purpose). His object is simply to show that Paul's conduct was visibly correct by the strictest Jewish standards. The four men under vow may have been in real financial distress.
24 By **paying their expenses** Paul may have rescued them from an embarrassing situation—this kind of help was highly regarded by the Jews as an act of kindness. Further, by publicly associating himself with the ritual, Paul would have given ample proof that he was still **a practising Jew** himself.

26 The exact details of the **ritual of purification** seem a little confused. A
23 **vow** of this kind has already been mentioned (18.18). It was temporary, and was terminated by shaving the head and making an expensive offering at the temple. During the period of the vow, it was necessary to remain ritually "clean"; unless they had become "unclean" by accident (which would have meant that they had to follow elaborate rules of purification before they could complete their vow), the four men were ready to enter the temple as soon as the offering was available. Paul, on the other hand, had just returned from abroad, and was therefore by definition "unclean". Before he could bring the men's offering to the temple, he had to go through a simple ritual of purification, once on the third day after his arrival, and once on the
26 seventh day. Only thus could he be present for **the offering** to **be made.** Luke's narrative makes it sound as if the four men under a vow had also to be purified **with** Paul. On the basis of what we know, this seems unlikely. Either Luke has expressed himself obscurely, or he was not certain himself

about the details of the observance. But on one point he is clear and convincing. For his part in the ritual, Paul was obliged to make two visits to the
temple. The second of these, at the end of **the seven days**, was to be critical. 27

From Jerusalem to Rome

The remainder of Acts is taken up with Paul's conflict with the Jews in Jerusalem, his appearance before the Roman authorities, and the events which led up to his arrival as a prisoner in Rome. The trouble began in the temple; and we can fill in a number of details. The central and highest part of the temple area consisted of buildings and open courts which only Jews could enter. Surrounding these was a large colonnaded terrace which was open to all. Round the inner part ran a balustrade, on which were fixed prominent notices in red letters forbidding entry to all Gentiles on pain of death. The rumour that Paul had deliberately introduced a Gentile past this barrier was the immediate cause of the disturbance. Such an act would have
been regarded as outrageous. The statement that **the whole city was in a** 30
turmoil may not be more than slightly exaggerated.

The crowds which thronged this temple area, particularly at festival seasons, often gave rise to riots. For this reason, the main Roman garrison in
Jerusalem (consisting of a **cohort** of about a thousand men) was stationed in 31
the Antonia fortress, which had been built by Herod the Great in a commanding position at the north-west corner of the temple area, with its own flight of steps leading down into the colonnaded terrace. A force of soldiers was always on duty there to cope with public disorders. Luke's description of the riot fits these arrangements at every point.

The Roman officer naturally assumed that Paul was yet another of the insurrectionaries who constantly aggravated the burden of keeping the peace
in Judaea. We know that there was in fact an **Egyptian** who had led a large 38
following **into the wilds** about ten years previously with a view to organizing an attack on Jerusalem; and we also know that many murders were committed in Jerusalem by Jewish **terrorists** during the years immediately preceding the Jewish Revolt of A.D. 66, particularly during festivals. The historical distinction between the two movements has been obscured by Luke's narrative. But the purpose of Paul's dialogue with the commandant is to show how far he was from any such movement. A mere insurrectionary would presumably have been an uneducated Jew, unable even to speak Greek correctly. Paul, by contrast, was able to conduct a highly polished conversation in Greek, and as for his upbringing, he could point with pride to his citizenship of one of the leading university cities of the east: Tarsus in
Cilicia—'**no mean city**', as Paul adds, using the idiom of a well read man. 39

These advantages were apparently sufficient for him to obtain **permission to speak to the people.**

22. 1 **'Brothers and fathers'.** The suspicion that Paul had brought a pagan into the sacred precincts of the temple had been the immediate cause of the riot. This was of course unfounded; but it was a symptom of a much more fundamental grievance against Paul which, according to Luke's narrative, was beginning to obsess the Jews in Jerusalem and which eventually left the Roman administration with no choice but to send Paul to Rome for trial. This grievance arose, quite simply, from the fact of Paul's missionary work among the Gentiles. Christian Jews had come to accept this (though Luke allows us to see some of the difficulty they had in doing so); but to ordinary people in Jerusalem it could appear only as a dangerous and shameless attack upon the whole idea of a single and exclusive Jewish religion. Paul's speech (which has clearly been written up by Luke to elucidate this first direct confrontation between Paul and the Jews) is a **defence** against any such interpretation of his work. From the very outset, it stresses Paul's complete solidarity with the Jewish people. Luke even notes the language it was spoken in: not Greek (for, although this was the common language of Jews throughout the world, and the language in which Paul wrote his letters and worked out his theology, it was also the language of that whole pagan culture from which the Jews were so anxious to protect their own traditions), but
21. 40 **the Jewish language** (which, for this purpose, presumably meant Aramaic).
The speaker was in every sense a Jew, by birth, by upbringing, and by his
22. 3 education at the feet of one of the most famous of Jewish scholars, **Gamaliel.**
5 He could even call upon **the High Priest and the whole Council of Elders** to testify to his service in trying to stamp out the Christian movement.
There had followed his conversion, which has already been narrated once in
Acts (9.1–19). Luke lets the story be repeated here (with a few minor
variations of detail and style); but the ending has a significant new twist. The
12 **man called Ananias,** who was Paul's first personal contact in Damascus, is described as **a devout observer of the Law and well spoken of by all the Jews of that place.** That is to say, even Paul's experience of the risen Jesus did not separate him from the company of the strictest Jews; indeed, the new turn in his life was something that could be analysed (as it is here) according to the traditional patterns of Jewish religion. So much so, that he expected his work to be among his former Jewish friends. But his natural expectations were overruled by a vision in the temple (this has not been mentioned before, and is not very easy to fit into the known history of Paul's
21 early years as a Christian). **"Go, for I am sending you far away to the Gentiles".**

But all this made no difference. Paul may have been as Jewish as any of his hearers, and have received his divine summons in the very temple he was accused of desecrating; but a deliberate mission to the Gentiles was still

incompatible with the traditional Jewish faith, and the moment he referred
to it the uproar began again. To the Roman officer it was clear enough that
Paul, for whatever reason, constituted a threat to public order, and he was
fully entitled to take police action and **examine him by flogging.** And 24
there the matter would have ended, but for Paul's revelation (dramatically
held back to this moment by the narrator) that he was a Roman citizen.

Men and women who were citizens of Rome by birth enjoyed certain
privileges when they travelled or lived abroad in any part of the empire. They
were exempt from most of the taxes paid by provincials, and on any criminal
charge they normally had the right to be tried at Rome, and to be protected
from any summary execution of justice on the spot. These privileges constituted a valuable reward which could be given to provincials for services
rendered to the state, and it was a perquisite of the Emperor to confer the
citizenship on anyone he wished. In due course, certain professions and offices
began to entitle a man to apply for the citizenship. In particular, officers in
auxiliary regiments could often obtain it, and indeed had to do so, if they
were to rise to the rank of commanding officer in charge of a cohort (*tribunus
militum*). It is therefore no surprise that this particular officer had done so,
nor that he had had to pay **a large sum** in bribes to get his name high enough 28
on the list. On becoming a citizen, he had correctly added the name of the
reigning Emperor, Claudius, to his own name (23.26); indeed, his full
Roman name now marked him as a Roman citizen. Paul's position was
different: he was a citizen **by birth.** This means that his father, in Tarsus,
had acquired the citizenship in some way before he was born. Nevertheless
Paul, at least when among Jews, lived as a Jew (and presumably dressed as a
Jew) and was known, not by his full Roman name, but only by his last name,
Paul (or Saul). In order to enjoy the privileges of citizenship, he had to claim
them, and even if necessary prove his right to them by producing a document
or consulting the municipal archives at Tarsus. This is the claim he makes
here; and it gives a sensational new turn to the proceedings.

After this, the commandant clearly had to proceed carefully. He could not
discharge his prisoner, for fear of further riots; on the other hand, he could
not inflict a warning punishment himself because of Paul's status as a Roman
citizen. His only course was to try to get the Jews to present their grievance
against Paul in an intelligible form. This is the point of the following scene.
The Jewish **Council**—the Sanhedrin—had only limited powers under the 30
Roman government, but it was still an autonomous body with its own meeting place (somewhere in or near the temple precinct) and its own rules of
procedure. It must have been as the official deputy of the Roman Governor
(who was in Caesarea) that the commandant **ordered the chief priests and
the entire Council to assemble.** He presumably hoped that they would
act as assessors in the case. But proceedings took an unexpected course. Why

23. 2 did the High Priest order Paul to be struck on the mouth? For speaking out
of turn? For not using a sufficiently respectful form of address? For making
5 a statement he regarded as untrue? And why had Paul '**no idea that he was**
High Priest' (for so far as we know it was always the High Priest who
presided)? Because he was short-sighted? Or because he thought the man's
conduct unworthy of his high office? These questions can be answered only
by guesswork; possibly Luke had to construct the scene out of scanty information. But he was able to make two points: first, the court proceeded
illegally in allowing the prisoner to be struck before the verdict (compare
Leviticus 19.15: "You shall do no injustice in judgement"); secondly, Paul's
3 retaliation was in the manner of a prophet: '**God will strike you**'. In fact,
Ananias was murdered a few years later. Luke may have known this and seen
Paul's speech as an inspired prophecy; if so, it became even more impressive
if Paul uttered it as it were blindfold, without realizing who it was he was
speaking to—this is a possible explanation of the episode. At the same time,
Paul's curious unawareness was also his defence against what he recognized
5 to be a clear infringement of the Law (Exodus 22.28), "**You must not**
abuse the ruler of your people". Both in Paul's opening statement, and
despite the formal offence involved in prophesying the priest's death, Luke
was anxious to show that Paul was correct by the Jewish law, and was a man
1 **with a perfectly clear conscience.**

It is certainly true that the Jewish Council at this period consisted of two
6 clearly defined parties. **The Sadducees** were the conservative and aristocratic element; they still exercised considerable power in Jerusalem, but
they were being gradually displaced by the influence of the Pharisees. **The**
Pharisaic party included many **doctors of the law** who held seats in the
Sanhedrin. Alongside the social and cultural differences between them, there
were differences of religious doctrine. The Sadducees accepted as binding
only what was literally stated in the Law of Moses; the Pharisees, on the
other hand, recognizing that this Law was now archaic, professed to have a
tradition of interpretation which enabled them to lay bare its true meaning.
One result of this was that they claimed to be able to support from Scripture
the widespread belief in **the resurrection of the dead**, whereas the
Sadducees, finding no such support for it in their literal interpretation of
Scripture, regarded the belief as false. Luke adds that they also denied the
8 existence of any **angel, or spirit.** This we did not know, but it follows from
what has been said. The Pharisees claimed that their tradition of interpretation was sometimes confirmed by a heavenly apparition; and this of course
the Sadducees disbelieved.

How far a session of the Sanhedrin would in fact have degenerated into a tumultuous dispute between these parties on a matter of doctrine is hard to say. But in the early chapters of Acts Luke has already shown that the Pharisees had much in common with Christianity, and the fact that the heart

of Paul's message was a particular form of the **hope of the resurrection of** 6
the dead, and that his activity had been inspired by a vision like that of **an** 9
angel or spirit (such as the Pharisees believed in as endorsing their own teaching), might well have commended him to the Pharisaic party, and enabled him to exploit the inherent rivalries within the Sanhedrin. At any rate, there was no formal judgement forthcoming to help the commandant; meanwhile Paul was strengthened by a divine intimation that all his vicissitudes were only the stages of a process which would eventually bring him to Rome.

Unless he were to release him unconditionally, the commandant now had no choice but to remit Paul's case to the only person in Judaea who had the right to hear a serious criminal charge against a Roman citizen, the Roman Governor. If he still had any doubt about it (or if Luke's readers were still wondering why the Roman authorities acted as they did), all doubt was
dispelled by the story of the Jews' **conspiracy**. The discovery of the plot 13
led the Romans to take exceptional security measures: Paul was given an
enormous escort—according to Luke, who fills his account with technical 23
military terms,[a] it amounted to half the total garrison of Jerusalem; and the two-day journey to Caesarea, where the Governor resided, was begun during the night, so that by daylight the party was well over half-way from Jerusalem
to Caesarea, at **Antipatris**. There is certainly a touch of exaggeration in all 31
this. Antipatris was more than 35 miles from Jerusalem. The soldiers,
starting **three hours after sunset**, could hardly have got so far by dawn 23
the next day, and the infantry certainly could not have made the return journey within twenty-four hours of setting out. Similarly, Paul's escort seems out of all proportion to the danger of ambush by forty conspirators. But if Luke wanted to give an impression of military strength and urgent preparation being displayed by the Roman authorities for Paul's protection,
he has succeeded vividly; and by adding the text of an accompanying letter 25-30
from Lysias, he has made the whole episode sound formally correct according to official Roman procedure.

It was the policy of the Roman Empire at this period to allow routine matters of administration and jurisdiction to be carried out by local courts and institutions; but serious capital charges, and any case which affected the maintenance of public order, were always heard before the provincial Governor himself. In such cases, the charge was brought by private accusers, and the defendant was given an opportunity to reply. When he had heard the evidence (which was often presented by professional advocates), the Governor, usually with the assistance of a bench of magistrates, decided for himself what kind of offence was involved. If the defendant was an ordinary subject, he then pronounced verdict and sentence; but if the prisoner was a Roman citizen, the case might have to be referred to Rome.

[*a*] One of these terms occurs nowhere else in Greek literature until five centuries later, and we do not know its meaning. **Light-armed troops** or "spearmen" are only guesses.

The official residence of the Governor of Judaea was the palace built by
Herod at the port of Caesarea. Normally, the Governor would probably have
dealt with cases arising in Jerusalem on the occasion of one of his visits there;
but Luke has just shown the reason why it was necessary to take special
measures in Paul's case. Granted these exceptional circumstances, the Gov-
35 ernor's reaction was entirely correct by the usual procedure. **'I will hear
your case,' he said, 'when your accusers arrive.'** The commandant in
Jerusalem had correctly instructed Paul's accusers to go down to Caesarea
30 and **state their case**; and preparations were made for a formal hearing of
both sides. The Governor himself, Antonius Felix, cuts a shabby figure in
the pages of other historians of the time. Provincial governors were normally
Romans of good family; but Felix was the son of a slave or a freedman, and
had won his position entirely through influence at the Emperor's court. He
was governor of Judaea approximately from A.D. 53 to 55, and his period of
office was marked by considerable popular unrest. Luke hints at his venality
(24.26); but in other respects Felix's conduct of the case appears to conform
exactly with what was expected of a Roman Governor.

24. 1 **Five days later** the accusers duly arrived, bringing with them a professional
advocate. Luke's description of the hearing uses the correct legal terminology,
and the two speeches are elegant miniature specimens of formal advocacy,
complete with the compliments with which it was the rule for such speeches
10 to begin (Paul's **'for many years you have administered justice in this
province'** may be a courteous exaggeration, though Felix seems to have held
some position of authority in the province before he became Governor). The
words in which the Jewish advocate brought his charge are carefully chosen.
5 **'We have found this man to be a perfect pest, a fomenter of discord
among the Jews all over the world.'** This was the language of contemporary anti-semitism (see above on 17.6); it was exactly what was needed to
make the Governor uneasy about Paul as a potential threat to public order
(and so to the record of his own tenure of office). But Paul's reply showed
this up as mere rhetoric. The original disturbance in the temple was alleged
18 by **some Jews from the province of Asia,** who had now disappeared.
Paul was on strong ground when he said that if this charge were to be sustained the original accusers would have to be present: we happen to know
that the Roman government was becoming increasingly impatient of in-
formers who failed to appear in person to substantiate their charges. More-
17 over, his own reason for being in the temple at that time was exemplary—**'I
came to bring charitable gifts to my nation and to offer sacrifices'** (a
hint that Luke knew about Paul's collection from the gentile churches, even
though he does not explicitly mention it). As for the other charge, of being
5 **'a ringleader of the sect of the Nazarenes'**, there was nothing sinister in
this. Even the Jewish Council had found it to be mainly concerned with a

belief, a form of which many of them held themselves, in '**a resurrection** 15
of good and wicked alike'. There was nothing in this to make Paul suspect
of disrespect towards Jewish religious and moral traditions. The grandiose
charges of his opponents were simply not proven.

'**When Lysias the commanding officer comes down**', **he said**, '**I** 22
will go into your case.' This was still correct procedure: Lysias was the
one available independent witness of the charge that Paul constituted a threat
to public order, and nothing more could be done until his evidence was
heard. However, two years later Paul was still in prison. This was not unheard
of: provincial governors were not obliged to do prompt justice, and there
must have been many temptations to delay. But Luke perhaps wishes to
drop a few hints about the reason. **Drusilla, who was a Jewess,** was the 24
sister of King Agrippa II, and had left her former husband in order to marry
the Roman Governor, who was a Gentile. Paul's discourse about **morals,** 25
self-control, and the coming judgement may have touched on this affair
(much as John the Baptist had lectured Herod Antipas on a similar mis-
alliance), and so have **alarmed** Felix. On the other hand, Luke represents
him as sympathetically interested in Christianity, and also as hoping to pick
up a bribe (which was of course illegal, but was not uncommonly done).
These conflicting interests could well have encouraged him to prevaricate
until the end of his term of office. He could then either quickly settle the
matter by releasing Paul, or else pass the case on to his successor. In the end,
self-interest prevailed. A retiring governor could always be accused at Rome
by provincials whom he had misgoverned; and Felix may well have had
reason for **wishing to curry favour with the Jews.** 27

Little is known about Porcius **Festus**, beyond the bare fact that he succeeded **25.** 1
Felix as Governor of Judaea around A.D. 55 or 56. In this narrative he stands,
as his predecessor did, for the correct Roman attitude towards a case such
as Paul's. It was natural that the Jews, having failed with his predecessor,
should make a renewed attempt to have Paul brought out of custody as soon
as the new Governor arrived; it was equally natural that Festus should insist
on a renewed formal hearing at his own residence in Caesarea. This hearing
was as inconclusive as the previous one. What was Festus to do? The clue to
his otherwise rather strange suggestion that he should after all hold the trial
in Jerusalem is probably the fact that the Governor did not preside in court
alone, but had **advisers** whom he could consult. Paul's case appeared to turn 12
on questions of Jewish law and religion. If he transferred the hearing to
Jerusalem, he could presumably have some members of the Sanhedrin as his
advisers, and so be better briefed to form a judgement. But this, of course,
would have been to load the proceedings heavily against Paul, and Paul
was fully within his rights to refuse. As a Roman citizen, he was entitled to
ask for the trial to be held at Rome. This was the moment to claim the

privilege. It did not take Festus long to establish that this was a legitimate claim, and that it must be granted. His only remaining responsibility was to
13 draft a report to go with the prisoner. The **courtesy visit** of some Jewish royalty gave him the opportunity to get some expert assistance in this difficult task.

20 For the Roman Governor was, as he admitted himself, "out of his depth".
16 On the question of procedure he was perfectly clear in his own mind: "**It is not Roman practice to hand over any accused man before he is confronted with his accusers and given an opportunity of answering the charge**"—this we know to have been the correct attitude for any provincial Governor to adopt. Therefore it would have been wrong for him to have handed Paul over to the Jews. But Paul's case would now have to be heard in Rome, and Festus would be expected to forward some account of the charges against him. Unfortunately, these appeared to turn upon
19 '**certain points of disagreement . . . about their peculiar religion**'.[a]
Festus' language betrays his frank bewilderment; and his confession of this to Agrippa is doubtless typical of the difficulty which was long felt by Roman administrators when they had to try to understand the exact relationship between Christianity and Judaism, and the disputes which often broke out between the two.

13 **Agrippa and Bernice** are the most distinguished persons yet to have appeared in Acts. Agrippa II, a great-grandson of Herod the Great, had been a youthful companion of the Emperor Claudius, and his influence at court obtained for him various kingdoms in the Middle East. Bernice, his sister, married two other petty kings of Herod's family in succession, and ultimately became the mistress of the Emperor Titus. At this time they were both quite young—well under thirty—but they were already famous and
23 influential. Luke makes the most of this. They **came in full state . . . accompanied by high-ranking officers and prominent citizens.** Paul's last speech of self-defence before he reached Rome was made to the very greatest in the land. In their presence, even the Roman Governor was careful
25 to use correct and deferential language when referring to the Emperor—**His**
26 **Imperial Majesty . . . our Sovereign.**[b] The ostensible occasion of the meeting was to hold a **preliminary enquiry** before despatching the prisoner to Rome. But in the end nothing came of it which could have been of much use to the Governor; and in fact Luke lets it be the opportunity for Paul to make the last and most elaborate statement of his position, no longer to the Roman Governor (who had confessed that it was beyond him), nor to the Jews of

[*a*] This seems an insulting way to refer to the Jewish religion, which was the religion of Agrippa himself. But this may be the translators' fault. Luke puts into Festus' mouth the kind of language any Roman might have used about a religion he did not understand, and his words need not have sounded offensive.

[*b*] This title began to be used in the reign of Claudius. The reigning Emperor was now Claudius' successor Nero.

Jerusalem (who were now his sworn enemies), but to someone who occupied a
middle position between the two, a person of Jewish background but owing
allegiance to the world of high Roman society rather than to the leaders of
Judaism, a sympathetic **expert in all Jewish matters**, who was neverthe- **26.** 3
less not thereby committed to taking the side of Paul's Jewish enemies. This
illustrious person and his distinguished retinue were the audience for Paul's
final presentation of the new faith which was now penetrating sophisticated
society throughout the eastern part of the empire and was no longer—if it
ever had been—what could be described in a Greek idiom as a '**hole-and-** 26
corner business'.

A legitimate development of the Jewish religion—this is how Paul presented Christianity. Yet his speech was carefully adapted to its cultured
audience. It began with the usual polished compliments, and then turned at 2–3
once to Paul's own relationship with Judaism. '**I belonged to the strictest** 5
group in our religion'. As a Pharisee, he could hardly be criticized on
matters of Jewish observance; and moreover he was committed, through the
traditional Pharisaic approach to the scriptures, to expecting God's promises
to the legendary **twelve tribes** of Israel to be fulfilled in terms of a new age 7
initiated by resurrection (a difficult concept for non-Jews: Paul perhaps
deliberately spelt it out for some of his hearers as the proposition **that God** 8
should raise dead men to life). It was only on the character and timing of
this new age that Christians differed from the majority of the Jews.

This difference, however, was critical, so much so that Paul had begun by
working **actively against the name of Jesus of Nazareth** (and there 9
seems to be an element of rhetorical exaggeration in his description of this
activity when compared with Luke's earlier account of it, 7.58; 9.1–2). Only
his experience on the road to Damascus led him to see the truth. This experience is related here for the third time in Acts. There are, as usual, slight
variations in the details (this seems to be a deliberate feature of Luke's style).
In particular, the audience is told explicitly that the supernatural voice spoke
in the Jewish language [a] (though in order to bring home to them the force of 14
the voice's message, it is put for their benefit in the form of a Greek proverb,
"**It is hard for you, this kicking against the goad**"). But the important
change is in the sequel. There is no mention of the temporary blindness, of
Ananias, of Paul's baptism and the other practical consequences. Instead, the
voice outlines Paul's future mission in language drawn partly from Old 16–18
Testament prophecies (compare especially Jeremiah 1.7; Isaiah 35.5; 42.7,
16) and partly from the formulas which Christians soon began to use when
confessing their faith (compare Colossians 1.13–14; Ephesians 2.1–2). The
experience, we know from Paul himself, convinced him that his primary

[*a*] This doubtless means Aramaic. It could have been inferred by the reader from the spelling of Paul's name, which both here and in the other two accounts appears in its Aramaic form, *Saoul*. But the dignitaries of Caesarea might have missed this point.

20 mission was to **the Gentiles** (Galatians 1.16; 2.8), and he ends his autobiography by giving a very summary sketch of his missionary work. It was this approach to the Gentiles which had caused the Jewish opposition. But even this could be seen as a fulfilment of the great prophecies of the Old
22 Testament. **'I assert nothing beyond what was foretold by the prophets and by Moses'**. Christianity was a legitimate development of the Jewish religion. More, it was its necessary end and culmination.

In its essentials, this whole argument turned on the interpretation of Old Testament prophecies. This was too much for Festus, who is made to intervene impatiently just when Paul has made his decisive point. But Paul had his eye on Agrippa, who could be assumed to be following the argument.
27 **'Do you believe the prophets?'** Of course, all Jews did. It was just a question of how one understood them. The difference between Jews and
28 Christians could be reduced to this one point. **Not much** was needed to **make a Christian** of a Jew. If Agrippa saw this, so should any Jew. This is the point of the whole scene, the point which Luke probably especially hoped would be grasped by his Roman readers. Paul ultimately arrived at Rome as a prisoner. Was he therefore a criminal? The highest authorities in Judaea had found no substance in any criminal charges against him. Every-
32 thing turned on the interpretation of the Jewish scriptures. **'The fellow could have been discharged, if he had not appealed to the Emperor'.**

27. 1 **When it was decided that we should sail for Italy.** The responsibility of escorting Paul on the long journey to Rome was given to a military officer, **a centurion named Julius, of the Augustan Cohort.** (The privileged title **Augustan** was given to some detachments of the Roman auxiliary forces, including one known to have been in Syria during the first century A.D.). He had a squad of soldiers with him (27.30), and his task was to secure a passage for the whole party on any ship which was going in the right direction. This particular centurion seems to have been correct and courteous towards Paul.
3 He **very considerately** allowed Paul substantial freedom of movement, both at the first stop (Sidon) and later in the journey. He also apparently
2 consented to Paul bringing some friends with him: **Aristarchus,** who has been mentioned before (19.29), and the person (perhaps the author) who lies behind the mysterious "we" which reappears here from 21.17.

The route of the sea-journey was determined entirely by the course of any available ship, and the courses which the ships took can only be understood in the light of the fact that the prevailing wind in the eastern Mediterranean comes from the north-west. If, as on this occasion, the ultimate destination also lay north-west, then for any sailing ship the course was bound to involve considerable detours and a lot of tacking. From Caesarea, the first stage was
2 made in **a ship of Adramyttium** (a port near Troas, in north-west Asia Minor) **bound for ports in the province of Asia.** This was the right

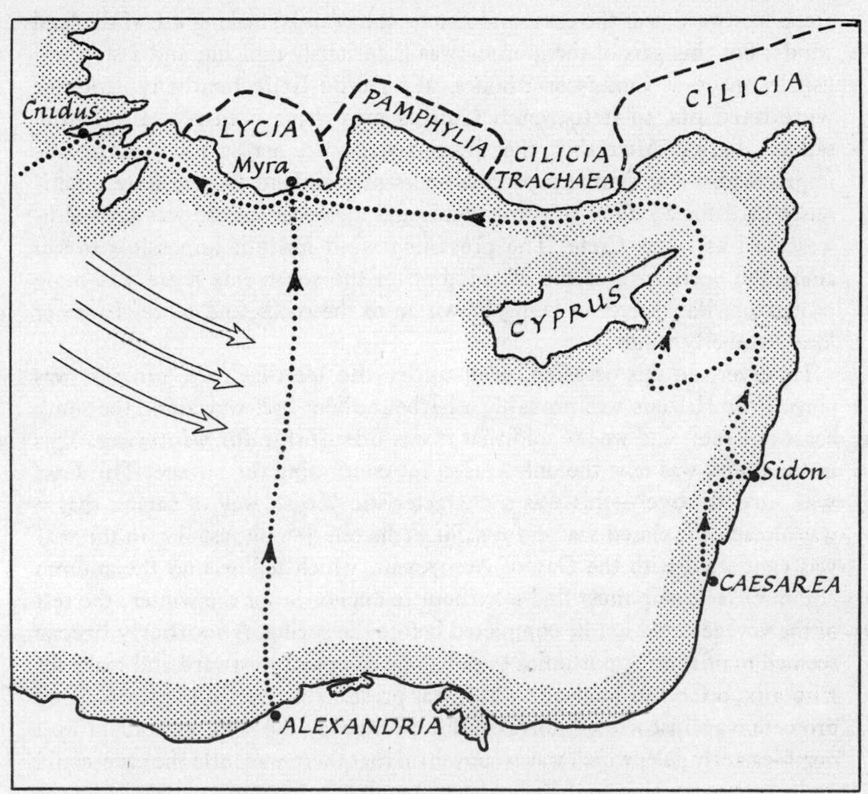

direction (north-west) but there could be no question of sailing straight
across the sea into a head wind. The closest course the ship could set was due
north, leaving Cyprus on the left (**under the lee of Cyprus,** which gave 4
some protection), until it reached the southern coast of Asia Minor, **off the** 5
coast of Cilicia and Pamphylia. It could then take advantage of different
winds coming off the land, and sail or tack westwards, not too far from the
coast, but avoiding the deep bays and inlets, and so, in a sense, **across the**
open sea. In this way it reached an important port in the south-west corner
of Asia Minor, **Myra in Lycia.**

It was nothing out of the ordinary to find in Myra **an Alexandrian vessel** 6
bound for Italy. Rome was provisioned largely by corn from Egypt, which was carried by a fleet of large transport ships. But, once again, the course of these ships was determined by the wind. To sail directly north-west across the open sea was normally impossible. The prevailing wind came from precisely that quarter, and so the ships, sailing as close to the wind as they could, were forced to go due north from Alexandria to the coast of Asia Minor. Myra was one of the ports they could reach: from there, they would

creep westward near the coast and among the islands, making use of the land
winds; but this part of the journey was notoriously difficult, and a stop was
7 usually made at Cnidus or Rhodes. **We made little headway, and we
were hard put to it to reach Cnidus** must have been typical of many
sailors' diaries. After this, the direct route west across the Aegean was impracticable (the southern promontories of mainland Greece were notoriously hard for a sailing ship to round) and an easier course was set southwestward as far as Crete. The prevailing wind made it impossible to sail along the north side of the island, but on the south side there was more protection, less danger of being blown on to the rocks, and more chance of local southerly winds.

However, on this occasion, even **under the lee of Crete,** progress was
8 slow. **Fair Havens** was probably a harbour about half-way along the south
12 coast of Crete; and we are told that it was **unsuitable for wintering.** This
9 unsuitability was now the only reason for continuing the voyage. **The Fast
was already over**—this was a characteristic Jewish way of saying that it
was already the closed season for sailing (the one Jewish fast-day in the year
was connected with the Day of Atonement, which fell around the autumn
equinox). The ship must find a harbour to anchor in for the winter; the rest
13 of the voyage could not be completed before the spring. **A southerly breeze**
seemed to offer an opportunity to sail along the coast westward and make for
12 **Phoenix, a Cretan harbour** which was presumably known to provide good
protection against winter storms.[a] But on the way the ship was caught by a
north-easterly gale, which was so powerful that there was little the crew could
do but allow the ship to drift before it, keeping as far north as possible so as
17 to avoid ending up on the notorious quicksands of **Syrtis,** off the coast of
north Africa. After a fortnight's severe battering in the open sea,[b] the ship
struck land at Malta, some five hundred miles to the west. It was clumsily
beached, and broke up on the shore. No lives were lost.

Reduced to this bare outline, the story is unremarkable. Despite the storm,
the ship actually followed the usual course taken by transports from Alexandria,
and in the long run the only difference for the passengers was that
they wintered in Malta (another regular port of call on the route) instead of
in Crete. But a severe storm in a sailing vessel, ending in shipwreck, is not
the kind of experience that is quickly forgotten, and if Luke was one of the
party, this is sufficient reason why he should have filled out the narrative
with so much detailed description. The chapter abounds in what were
17 evidently nautical terms, not all of which we can understand. "Undergirding"
the ship, for instance, is assumed to mean "frapping", i.e. passing

[a] The site of this harbour has been identified with some probability close to Cape Myros in S.W. Crete. Exact identification is difficult, since the coastline has altered as the result of severe earthquakes.

[b] The **Sea of Adria** (verse 27) included, not just the modern Adriatic, but the open sea between Greece and Sicily.

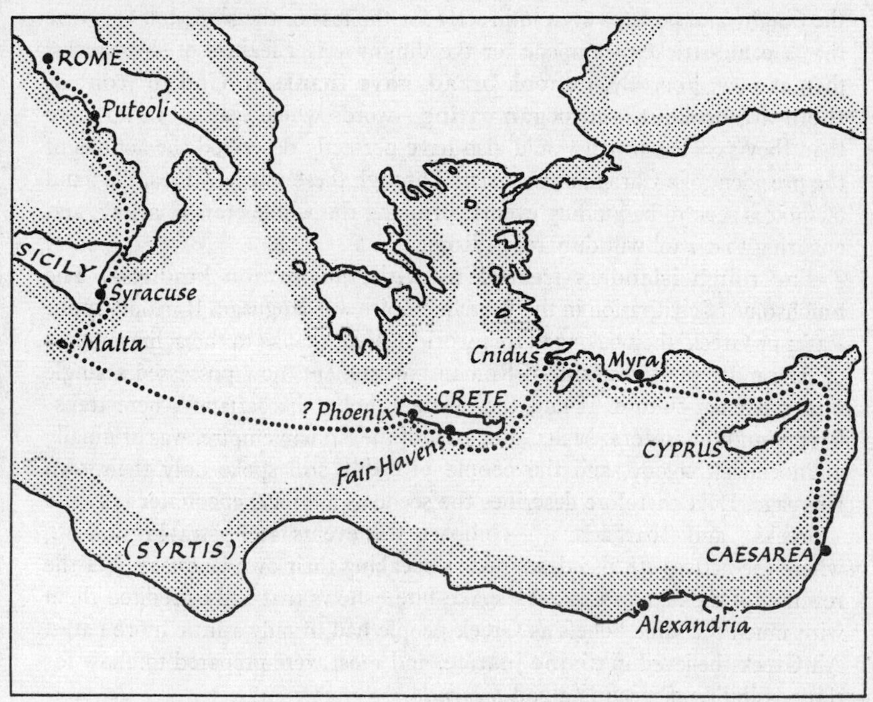

heavy ropes under the ship and tightening them on a windlass to protect the hull from strain in a heavy sea; and when **they lowered the mainsail and let her drive**, the effect was presumably to reduce the amount of sail to the minimum needed to keep the ship on any sort of course (for to have run straight in front of the gale at any speed would have taken them straight south-west towards **the shallows of Syrtis**, whereas in fact they succeeded in drifting more or less due west). But we cannot be sure that this is the correct meaning of the various terms. Moreover, it is not certain that Luke had so much technical knowledge himself. He may simply have wished to colour his narrative with whatever terms he thought appropriate, without checking them with a professional sailor.

Nevertheless, while most writers who described a storm at sea made the most of its horror, Luke's narrative is of exemplary sobriety. There is no exaggeration, no dramatizing. The whole personal interest is concentrated on Paul, who made some unexpected interventions. First, he appeared
simply to offer amateur advice—'**this voyage will be disastrous**'—and 10
was very naturally overruled by the professionals. Secondly, he had a vision, 23–6
and was able to encourage the ship's company. Thirdly, he caused the 31–2
soldiers to interfere in the sailors' use of the dinghy—rightly or wrongly: if he was wrong about the sailors' intentions, he was responsible for the loss of

the dinghy and perhaps even indirectly for the loss of the ship; but it is true
that a panic-stricken stampede for the dinghy was a feature of shipwrecks,
35 then as now. Fourthly, he **took bread, gave thanks to God in front of
them all, broke it, and began eating**—words which may mean no more
than they say, but which would also have perfectly described the actions of
the president of a Christian eucharist. Through these interventions, the hand
of God is seen to be guiding events, bringing the whole crew to safety, and
ensuring that Paul will duly reach Rome.

28. 2 **The rough islanders treated us with uncommon kindness.** The
touchstone of civilization in the Roman empire was language. If people spoke
Latin or Greek, they belonged to a world which, thanks to the achievements
of Alexander the Great and of Roman government, now possessed a single
Greco-Roman culture. If not, they were simply "barbarians", here translated **rough islanders.** Malta, now part of the Roman empire, was originally
a Phoenician colony, and the people probably still spoke only their own
language. Luke therefore describes the scene as a typical encounter between
"Greeks" and "barbarians"—compare the events at Lystra in 14.8–18,
where the natives are also described as speaking their own language. Yet the
reaction of the natives to Paul's snake-bite [a] shows that Luke credited them
with much the same beliefs as Greek people had, if only a little more naïve.
4 All Greeks believed in **divine justice,** and most were prepared to allow for
6 the possibility of meeting a god *incognito.*

7 **The chief magistrate of the island**: we know from inscriptions that
Luke, here as elsewhere, has used the correct title for this official. **Publius**
was one of the standard Roman first names, and we cannot identify him further. The almost casual miracle of the snake-bite is capped by a series of
8–9 healing miracles well in the tradition of Jesus himself.

11 **Three months had passed.** The season for sea voyages opened in
February or March. There was then no difficulty in getting a passage: Malta
lay on the usual route between Alexandria and Rome, and the *Castor and
Pollux* was presumably another of the corn transports which had **wintered
in the island** and was now ready to leave. (The name of the ship was
typical: Castor and Pollux were twin gods, protectors of ships at sea, and
particularly revered in Egypt.) It was an easy tack across the prevailing wind
12, 13 to **Syracuse,** and on up to **Rhegium** (actually a straight course; but to a
passenger it might seem like "sailing round" Sicily). After that, a following
wind gave them a good speed—about 5 knots—up the coast of Italy to
Puteoli, near Naples. This—now called Pozzuoli—was the principal port
serving Rome until very shortly after this date. The last lap of the journey
was by road along the Appian Way, a march of less than a week. Paul found

[*a*] Vipers do not hang on the hand they bite; but this is what Luke says. Perhaps it is simply his way of making it clear that, however difficult it might be to see usually, on this occasion everyone distinctly saw the snake biting Paul, so that there could be no doubt about the miracle.

himself already in the company of Christians, and parties **came out to meet** 15
him at two towns along the way.

When we entered Rome. The last section of the book has the effect of 16
summing up Paul's final position with regard to the Romans on the one hand,
the Jews on the other. **Paul was allowed to lodge by himself with a**
soldier in charge of him, and an impressive picture of the consideration
shown to him by the Roman authorities is built up throughout this chapter.
Even though he was technically in custody, he was able to pursue his work of
preaching and teaching **without hindrance**—the word was often used in 31
legal documents and is placed emphatically at the end of the closing sentence
of the book. It may well be intended as a final proof to Roman readers that
Paul was at no time regarded by the authorities as a serious criminal, and that
therefore (by implication) the religion which he preached must not be
imagined to constitute any sort of threat to public order.

The Jews, on the other hand, behaved true to form. We know that there
was a large and influential Jewish community at Rome, grouped around a
number of synagogues. What is described here is a formal confrontation
between its leaders and Paul; and it is carefully shown that Paul started with
an absolutely clean sheet: no information had yet reached Rome to his
discredit, and he for his part had no **accusation** to bring against them. His 21, 19
efforts to convert them should have had every chance of success. But no,
without reaching any agreement among themselves they began to 25
disperse. This was tantamount to rejecting the gospel. There could be no
explanation but that this was the will of God; and this explanation lay ready
to hand in a passage of Isaiah (6.9–10) which had been used by Jesus himself 26–7
in somewhat similar circumstances (see above on Mark 4.12). The scene was
a further justification—if any was needed—of what had been the principle
of Paul's whole missionary work: '**this salvation of God has been sent to** 28
the Gentiles'.

He stayed there two full years. We have every reason to believe that 30
Paul was put to death in Rome, and there are allusions in letters by him or ascribed to him to at least one period of imprisonment and to his own uncertainty as to the outcome of his trial. But we have no means of knowing either the date of his death or its immediate cause: it may have followed the trial to which the events in Acts have been tending, or Paul may have been acquitted and released and then imprisoned again on a new charge. In any event, given the distance between Jerusalem and Rome, it could well have been many months before his accusers arrived, and there is no reason to doubt Luke's statement that things dragged on for a full two years. The only serious question is why Luke ends his story at this point. To our minds it seems to leave matters very much in the air. We would dearly love to know what happened to Paul, and since it is likely that Acts was written well after

Paul's death, we find it hard to forgive Luke for not telling us about it. It is possible, of course, that he planned, or even wrote, a continuation; but it may also be true that our modern presuppositions about how the book ought to end are mistaken. Luke has described the progress of the church from its first beginnings in Jerusalem to its world-wide presence a few decades later. He has explained the constant Jewish opposition to it, and has justified the consideration so often shown to it by the Roman government. He has now described how its greatest missionary finally reached the capital of the empire,
technically a prisoner, but in fact able to continue teaching and preaching
31 **quite openly and without hindrance.** And he may well have felt that, if
he was to leave these momentous facts clearly impressed upon the minds of his readers, this was the right place to end.

LETTERS

LETTERS

The first thirteen letters in the New Testament are (or purport to be) from the correspondence of Paul. They tell us, as letters should, who was the writer and to whom they were written. In Acts, we possess a brief biography of Paul which (as we can see when we read Paul's own letters) tells us only some of the facts and is not always perfectly accurate. But from this biography, and from occasional pieces of information scattered in the letters themselves, we can make a rough outline of Paul's travels, and gain some picture of the circumstances which caused him to stay a relatively brief time in each of the churches which he founded and to keep in touch with them afterwards by correspondence. In the case of the letters to Corinth, we can be more specific: these letters were written while Paul was in Ephesus some time between A.D. 51 and 54. For the rest, we do not know for certain where and when they were written, beyond the fact that none of them is likely to have been written earlier than A.D. 45 or later than A.D. 65 (when Paul was probably martyred). Nor do we know when and how they were collected, and how far, if at all, they were rearranged by a subsequent editor. Some of them may even have been written by imitators after his lifetime. But these questions are relatively unimportant. The essential thing is that we possess in these letters a number of unquestionably authentic documents which bear witness to the first generation of the church's existence.

For the most part the letters were addressed to churches, and were probably intended to be read aloud to the assembled congregation. They were all elicited by particular questions which had arisen, and they cannot be understood unless an attempt is made to picture the circumstances of the recipients, to understand the arguments which Paul had to refute, and to lay bare the presuppositions which Paul shared with his converts. But the result of such an enquiry is not merely a better understanding of a particular crisis or difficulty in the progress of the early church. It was a part of Paul's genius that he saw the wider implications of each problem he was confronted with, and his treatment of them often involved an exposition of fundamental doctrines of the Christian faith. The letters are real letters, and the issues they deal with belong to a particular period in the history of the church. Yet they have a depth and generality which has given them an interest far beyond their own time and place; indeed they soon became, and have justly remained, among the primary documents of the Christian faith.

The character of the remaining letters is somewhat different. The letter to Hebrews is hardly a "letter" at all, but a treatise by an unknown writer addressed to an unknown church or group of Christians. The other seven are all (in some sense) "letters" but, though the name of the writer is usually mentioned, it is true of most of them that we do not know whom they were written to. Consequently it has been customary, since early times, to refer to them as the "General" (or "Catholic") letters. The letters of John (and indeed the Revelation, which is also in the form of a letter) are real letters, in that they were clearly addressed to readers in a particular area, and in each case the author had some personal acquaintance with those to whom he was writing. But the letters of James, Peter and Jude, being apparently addressed to almost any Christians who might read them, are letters only in a rather special sense. James and 1 Peter may have been what we would now call encyclicals, written from the centre of authority to Christian churches at large; while 2 Peter and Jude are, at most, "open letters", that is to say, treatises for the general reader dressed up (as was commonly done by ancient writers) in the form of a letter. With them, we can perhaps see Christian writing beginning to conform to contemporary literary models. But for the rest, the LETTERS of the New Testament seem to have given new life and content to the hackneyed conventions of Greek letter-writing. Like the gospels, they represent something startlingly new and original in the literature of their time.

THE LETTER OF PAUL TO THE ROMANS

The Gospel according to Paul

From Paul. A typical Greek letter in the ancient world began: "From 1. 1
so-and-so . . . to so-and-so, greetings (*chairein*)". The Jews had their own variation on this, in that instead of saying "greetings" they liked to say "peace" (*shalom*). A combination of the two is found in most of the New Testament letters.

Paul's letters are all real letters, addressed to particular people or churches, and they all make use of the conventional form of opening, even if (as here) they cram a great deal of extra Christian matter into the simple framework. But Paul also makes one very significant change in the formula. Instead of "greetings" (*chairein*), he writes "grace" (*charis*). This is almost a pun: the two words are derived from the same stem; and the NEB tries to bring this
out by rendering the one word *charis* both by **I send greetings** and by 7
Grace . . . to you. This may originally have been a conscious twisting of a conventional expression to make it yield a rich Christian meaning—a device that Paul is very fond of. Whether Paul invented this one, or simply adopted it as an already accepted form of greeting between Christians, we cannot say. It occurs in the opening of many other New Testament letters.

In the Greek, the whole of the first seven verses forms one long sentence: 1–7
"Paul . . . to all of you in Rome . . . grace and peace . . .". But this sentence
is broken into by a massive parenthesis, sparked off by the word **Gospel**, and 1
going on to explain what Paul means by his apostleship. The NEB translators have deliberately refashioned the sentence and broken it up into a number of shorter sentences. By doing so they have undoubtedly made it easier to read. But they have also obscured its original shape, which not only revealed Paul as a letter-writer using the conventional form of opening, but also allowed one to hear the strikingly solemn ring of verses 3 and 4, which are often, for this reason, thought to be a fragment of an early Christian confession or creed, inserted by Paul (with perhaps a few minor alterations) into his opening greeting. This confession makes two statements about Christ.
On the human level he was a particular man, a descendant of King David, 3
and therefore qualified according to current Jewish doctrine to be the expected Messiah or Christ. **On the level of spirit**—that is to say, not as a 4
matter of empirically verifiable fact like his ancestry, but in a manner which presupposed the activity of the Holy Spirit making this reality known to

believers—he was the **Son of God**, as was declared by[a] a mighty act of glorious vindication, when, after the apparent defeat and humiliation of the crucifixion, he **rose from the dead.**

5 **The privilege of a commission.** The Greek means literally "grace and apostleship", two almost technical Christian terms. "Grace" is undoubtedly a kind of **privilege**; but in Paul's thinking it stands for a great deal more. The whole of God's gracious dealings with his people, as recorded in the Old Testament, could be described by a single Hebrew word of which there is no exact Greek or English equivalent but which is usually translated "mercy". These gracious dealings had now reached a climax in the story of Jesus Christ; and to describe this transcendently gracious gift from God to men, along with all the acts of divine mercy which had led up to it in the course of the history of the Jewish people, Paul used another Greek word which stressed still more the free generosity of God: *charis*, of which one of the usual meanings was "grace" or "favour". At the same time, the effect on a believer of this tremendous sign of God's favour towards him was a new power, a new quality of living, a new radiance of personality; and this too could be expressed by the same word *charis*, a word which was also often used to mean "grace" in the subjective sense of "graciousness". All these ideas are present in the single word here translated **privilege.** "Apostleship" too, though it was indeed a **commission**, was also a great deal more. The root meaning of the word *apostolos* was one "sent out" on a mission; the word was already used in Jewish circles for the accredited emissaries of the High Priest in Jerusalem. It belonged to the calling of all Christians that they were "sent out" to preach the Gospel; but this was true to a particular degree of that original group of men who had witnessed the resurrection and who had received an explicit **commission** to undertake the founding of the first Christian communities. Paul, though the circumstances of his calling had been exceptional, was nevertheless soon recognized as one of these original apostles; but what marked off his apostleship from that of other apostles was that it was to **men in all nations**, which meant (the explosive element in Paul's work) to non-Jews.

8 **Let me begin by thanking my God.** Most of Paul's letters proceed straight from the opening greetings to an expression of thanksgiving for the vitality of the church to which he was writing. The only peculiarity here is that the church at Rome was not one which he had founded or for which he had a personal responsibility. He had not yet been to Rome, and he had not met the church there. His thanks were for the good report which he, like everyone else, had heard about them; and his prayers for them, and his longing to see them, were a natural expression of his desire to be more closely associated with a Christian community which had sprung up at the centre of the civilized world.

[*a*] Or possibly, declared after: the preposition in the Greek is ambiguous. See the footnote in NEB.

Nevertheless, Paul did feel a certain urgency in addressing himself to the
Romans. **I have often planned to come . . . in the hope of achieving** 13
something among you. Not that Paul could have added to his own successes by preaching to the already existing Roman church; but he could hope to "have some fruit" (the literal meaning of the Greek words), not only in strengthening those who were already Christians, but in encouraging a greater inclusiveness of membership, and settling, once and for all, the problem he had already met with in his own churches: the relationship, within a single Christian community, of Jews and non-Jews. In this sense he was
under obligation to Greek and non-Greek. 14

This conflict between Jewish and gentile Christians, which was the first great crisis the church had to undergo, was the ostensible occasion of the letter to the Romans, and can be overheard in every chapter of it. Yet Paul characteristically did not treat this problem on a practical level, as if it were merely a question of how these people were to live together amicably. He saw in it a threat to the central truths of the Christian faith. It could only be
solved by a defence of the cardinal proposition that the Gospel was **for** 16
everyone who has faith. But this in turn raised still wider issues. A Jew would instinctively feel that God had made special promises to his own people: how then could Gentiles be admitted to salvation without making God seem to abandon his promises and be "unrighteous"? To answer this, Paul had to speak, not only of the **faith** of the believer, but of God's
"righteousness", here rendered **God's way of righting wrong.** The guid- 17
ing Old Testament text for his discourse, which contains the two principal terms in question, was Habakkuk 2.4: '**he shall gain life who is justified** (i.e. whose wrong is righted) **through faith**'.

For we see divine retribution revealed. This sentence, and the sentence 18
before, both contain the word **revealed,** and each expresses a complementary side of God's activity towards men. God is just, and the positive side of this justice, the way in which God "justifies" (or "rights the wrongs" of) those who believe, is revealed in Jesus Christ. This is the theme of the *Gospel according to Paul,* and is more fully explained later in the letter. But meanwhile there is also a negative side to this justice: **divine retribution.** In the Greek, this is more personally expressed as the "wrath of God". But the meaning is probably much the same. If God is righteous, the consequences of men's unrighteous deeds must necessarily be visited upon them. The important point for Paul's argument is that this in fact happens, that this side also of God's justice is **revealed.** It makes little difference whether this is represented in English as a personal activity of God (God's "wrath"), or as the working out of an inexorable law of **retribution** (see below on Revelation 6.16, pp. 805–6). What matters for Paul is the empirical reality of the consequences of human sin.

For proof of the reality of this **divine retribution**, Paul had only to draw
on the widely shared presuppositions of both Greek philosophy and Jewish
religion. It was common ground to both Jewish and Greek thinkers that the
prevailing immorality of contemporary society was connected with the rejection of pure religion. The existence of God was axiomatic (verse 19). Only
21 **misguided minds** could fail to recognize the creator in his works, and the
28 inevitable consequence of that failure was a **depraved reason**, which led
them **to break all rules of conduct** (literally, "to do what is not fitting", a
Stoic cliché). The long list of vices in verses 29–32 has many parallels in the
religious and philosophical literature of the ancient world.

So much was common ground. But Paul, a Jew, instinctively brought still
severer criticism to bear on the gentile world. Two features of Greek life
in particular shocked the Jews: first, the crude idolatry associated with the
innumerable statues of deities—which were not in fact taken too seriously
by the majority of educated Greeks, but were regarded with horror by the
23 Jews as **exchanging the splendour of immortal God for an image
shaped like mortal man** (an allusion to Psalm 106.20: for this primal sin
had been committed also by the people of Israel); and secondly, the Greeks'
acceptance of unnatural and promiscuous sexual relationships, which had no
counterpart in Jewish culture. These, from the Jewish point of view, were
the characteristic vices of the gentile world. Any Gentile who sought the
fellowship of a Jewish synagogue had to make an explicit renunciation of
them. Paul sketches them somewhat luridly: but he is only giving a characteristically Jewish turn to an argument which would have been widely
recognized as valid. The excesses and perversions of pagan worship and
pagan morality were clear evidence that divine retribution was at work in the
pagan world.

2. 1 **You therefore.** This sudden turning upon an imaginary Jewish reader is,
and is meant to be, a surprise. Up to this point, Paul would have carried any
Jew with him in his argument; and he goes on to make one more point with
2 which a Jew ought to have agreed. **It is admitted** (that is, "we (the Jews)
recognize", as the original has it) **that God's judgement is rightly passed
upon all who commit such crimes as these.** Wrongdoing inexorably
attracts punishment from God—witness the quotation from Proverbs (24.12),
6 **he will pay every man for what he has done.** From these premises Paul
draws the (to us) obvious conclusion that the Jews would be punished by
God for their offences just as much as the Gentiles.

But normally a Jew would not have seen it like this at all. He believed that
17 because he possessed the Law of Moses and bore the **name of Jew**, he had a
certain immunity from the consequences of divine judgement, and had
privileges, both now and on Judgement day, which a Gentile could never
1 have. He assumed that, equipped with the Law, he could **sit in judgement**
4 on the rest of the world; and that the marks of God's **kindness, tolerance**

and **patience** which he found in the history of his own people were evidence
that God judged the Jews less severely than others. He could **rely upon the** 17
law, both as a moral and religious guide for himself and ultimately for all
men **(the very shape of knowledge and truth),** and also as an assurance 20
that God would reserve for him a place in the promised kingdom.

Paul makes a violent attack on this position. Deeper arguments against the Jewish sense of privilege and immunity will come later in the letter. Paul's manner at this point is rhetorical and sweeping. The Jews themselves have committed crimes they condemn others for (verses 21–3); their own conduct
brings their religion into disrepute (verse 24—a quotation from Isaiah 52.5).
God has no favourites. His only criterion is how far a man has carried out 11
the precepts of his law, precepts which are written in the conscience of many
Gentiles just as much as in the scriptures of the Jews.

The Jew bore in his body a physical sign of the privileges and immunities he believed in: circumcision. Without this sign, he could never qualify for blessedness; with it, he could never be consigned to eternal punishment.
Paul, though himself brought up as a strict circumcised Jew, now denied any
such power to an outward rite. **Circumcision has value, provided . . .** 25
No proviso was envisaged by the Jews. Paul, with the distinction which is so obvious to us between "true Jews" and others, between external marks and inward qualities, was saying something quite un-Jewish, quite new—so new,
in fact, to Jewish ears that it would be asked, on what authority did Paul say
this? The answer was—could only be—the authority of Jesus Christ: **So my** 16
gospel declares.

Then what advantage has the Jew? The series of questions which 3.1
follow may have been put to Paul by objectors who misunderstood the implications of what has just been said—indeed verse 8 is evidence for the existence of a faction who thought that Paul's attitude to the law encouraged licence and libertarianism; or it may simply go with the jerky, dialectical style which Paul adopts in this and the following chapter, a style of which we have another example in the "diatribes" (popular lessons in philosophy) of a near-contemporary of Paul, the Stoic philosopher Epictetus. In any case, Paul is agitated by a difficult problem in which he feels personally involved:
if the broad argument of chapter 2 is sound, then **what advantage has the**
Jew? Great, in every way, answers Paul in verse 1. **Are we Jews any** 9
better off? No, not at all, he says in verse 9—and it is impossible to clear
him altogether of inconsistency.[a] Nevertheless, the verses dispose of some
too-easy solutions to the problem. The Jews, after all, have the Law of Moses
(the oracles of God), which is a revelation of the justice and faithfulness of 2
God—and the fact that the Law has not been kept, and perhaps could never be kept, is no reason for tearing it up and starting afresh with the Gospel: it

[a] The punctuation and meaning of verse 9 are uncertain; but the inconsistency belongs to the whole context.

belongs to the very justice and faithfulness of God that the Law should con-
4 tinue valid. **God must be true.** Every word of the Law is a revelation of God
and has eternal validity. No human circumstances, no observed facts of
human history, can affect the truth of God's word. It is always human beings
who are in the wrong, not God. If God were, as it were, put **on trial,** and
confronted with all the sinfulness present in his creation, he would still be
shown to be in the right, he would still **be vindicated** (the quotation is from
Psalm 51.4).

The Jews, then, have both the responsibility and the privilege of closer
access to the revealed will of God, and no amount of failures on their part
can make any difference to the fact that what they have received in their
history and in their scriptures is an authentic revelation of God's righteous-
9 ness. But again, this privilege contains no security. The Jews are no **better**
19 **off.** Scripture itself (which Paul, as a Jew, can refer to as **all the words of**
10–18 **the law,** though in fact he has just given us a cento of quotations mainly
from the Psalms)[a] shows that the **whole world** (i.e. Jews as well as Gentiles)
is **exposed to the judgement of God.** The Jews have the apparent advantage of knowing how God wills men to act; but the effect of this is only to
20 give them **the consciousness of sin.** In the words of Psalm 143.2, **'no**
human being can be justified in the sight of God'. The defence that
one has **kept the law** is as hollow as any other; it may be a sufficient pretext
27 for **human pride** but it makes no difference to the essential unrighteousness
of man before God. The Jews are no better off than anyone else. The problem
is just as acute for them as for the rest of mankind: how is it possible for
sinful men to have any continuing relationship with a just God?

21 **But now.** There is now (this is Paul's 'Gospel') a new answer worked out
independently of law, yet (as will be shown in chapter 4) consistent with
the scriptures. **God's justice**—or, as we might say, a new way of understanding how a just God can yet have dealings with universally sinful men—
has been brought to light by the creation of a new status for men. God
remains just; but a function of his justice is that he has the means of giving
to men, despite their sin, the possibility of a status which is equivalent to that
of the just. Once this status is accepted, God's justice no longer involves
inevitable retribution for sin. In this sense, his justice can now be shown to
22 be (among other things) a **way of righting wrong.**

How has this happened? The short answer is **through faith in Christ**
for all who have such faith. What this means will be given fuller treatment
in chapters 5–8; for the present, Paul merely hints, briefly and somewhat
24 obscurely, at three metaphors. (i) It was an **act of liberation**—a word which
evoked the act of God by which the people of Israel had been delivered from

[a] See above, pp. 3–4, on this use of the term "law" for the scriptures as a whole. The texts quoted here are: Psalms 14.1–3; 53.2–4; 5.9; 140.3; 10.7; 36.1; and Isaiah 59.7–8.

their bondage in Egypt: the sinner is similarly "liberated" from the bonds
which his sins lay upon him; (ii) Christ was a **means of expiating sin**— 25
again (in the original) a technical word, describing the function of Jewish
sacrificial worship, and possibly referring specifically to the cover of the Ark
which had a particular function in the ceremonies of the Jewish Day of
Atonement (see Exodus 25.17–22); and (iii) in this realm of ideas, Christ's
was a **sacrificial death,** though this again is no more than a metaphor: his
sacrifice was **effective** (unlike the temple sacrifices) only **through faith.**

All this, of course, touches the nerve of the Gospel: it totally reverses the
status of man before God, and opens up wholly new possibilities of godly and
joyful living. But here it is introduced with a limited purpose, and has a
logical place in the argument: it is to show how it is possible for God still to
be just and yet to have dealings with men who can be shown to deserve
condemnation. It is "theodicy"—that is to say, the object of enquiry is not
man but God, and the purpose of the argument is **to demonstrate his** 26
justice. The justice revealed in **law** (the law of Moses) is shown, by this new
factor, still to hold good for God, even though all men will not now receive
the punishment they justly deserve for their sins. So: **we are placing law** 31
itself on a firmer footing.

If it be true that God is one. That **God is one** was a proposition recited 30
by a Jew every day in his prayers. It was the distinctive affirmation of the
Jewish faith, the one truly monotheistic religion known to the ancient world.
But even for the Jews, this affirmation was not without its difficulties. When
they thought of God, they thought of him as the God of Israel, the God of
their fathers. He was the God who had a special relationship with the Jewish
people, a relationship that had been demonstrated again and again in the
course of Jewish history. But if he was the one and only God, it could not be
the case that he was **the God of the Jews alone.** He was the creator of all 29
men, and therefore he must be in some sense **the God of Gentiles also.**
This was where the difficulties began; for it seemed obvious to Jewish
thinkers that the Gentiles neither acknowledged the true God nor received
from him the gracious treatment bestowed upon the Jews. In what sense,
then, was he the God of the Gentiles? The question was embarrassing, and
received a variety of answers. But on Paul's premises it was perfectly simple.
Once it was recognized that the Jews could appeal to no special relationship with God, there was no difficulty in seeing how God was the God
of Jews and Gentiles alike. For both, the only possible relationship
with God was established **in virtue of their faith** (or, by a very slight 30
change of phrase which is no more than a matter of style, **through their**
faith).

What, then, are we to say about Abraham? We know that the shocked **4.** 1
reaction of the Jew to any suggestion that he had no privilege in the sight of

God was, 'We have Abraham for our father' (Matthew 3.9; John 8.33). Instinctively, he would introduce into the argument his physical descent from Abraham. The figure of Abraham was the foundation of all Jewish religious thinking. To Abraham, and through Abraham to his descendants, God had given a promise in the form of a "covenant": if a "son of Abraham" kept his part of the covenant (i.e. observed the law), he could look forward to the "inheritance" which had been promised from the beginning to the Jewish people. This 'advantage' of the Jew was axiomatic; the story of Abraham guaranteed it. And Paul, himself physically a "son of Abraham" (**our ancestor in the natural line**) now turns to answer this inevitable Jewish protest.

To demonstrate his superiority to any Gentile, a Jew had only to quote from Genesis, chapters 15 and 17. These chapters showed how Abraham had received a blessing (15.5–6; 17.7–8), and proved that this blessing would pass to all his descendants, on condition that they were duly circumcised (17.10–14). Why had Abraham received this signal blessing? Subsequent Jewish interpretation took the line that it was because Abraham had spontaneously carried out all the precepts of the law (even though these were written down only in the time of Moses, many generations later), and that, to receive the blessing in full, his descendants must do the same. And "descendants" was understood quite literally. The strictest schools of Jewish thought admitted only physical descendants, to the exclusion of all non-Jews. A more liberal school conceded that Gentiles, by becoming proselytes, might also have some share in the blessing; in which case, the fact that Abraham was circumcised so late in life was taken as a sign that, in some sense, he was the "father" of all those who, like him, observed the whole law, even if they were gentile converts and were circumcised only late in life.

It was this second view which Paul, as a Jew, probably once held himself;
but he now develops it in a highly original way. He starts from a text taken
3 from the same chapters of Genesis, '**Abraham put his faith in God, and
that faith was counted to him as righteousness**' (15.6). But his interpretation is quite different from the usual Jewish one. He concentrates
attention on the single expression, '**counted to**'. This, he argues, would not
be an appropriate word for the payment of wages that had been earned or of
a reward that had been deserved. True, the verb itself, in Greek as in English,
does not settle the matter. But it was a recognized technique among Jewish
scholars to determine the meaning of a word in one place in Scripture by
reference to its meaning in another place. So here: Paul quotes Psalm
6 32.1–2 (**David** was assumed to be the author of all the psalms in the Old
7 Testament), '**Happy is the man whose sins the Lord does not count
against him**'. In this text, the word "count" cannot mean "pay as a reward
for certain acts". The subject is a sinner; yet he is **happy** (the Greek word is
sometimes translated 'blest'). Clearly he cannot have earned this blessed-

ness; what must have happened is that God, instead of "counting his sins
against him" (which would be "counted" in the sense of "paid a just
reward") counted to him **as a favour** a happiness which he had certainly 4
not deserved by any deeds of his own. And this gives the sense of **counted** 3
in the Genesis passage. Abraham had not done anything to deserve his
righteousness: God had counted him righteous as a favour in response to
his **faith.** The conclusion drawn from this passage by Paul is thus the exact
opposite of that which was usually drawn by Jewish thinkers. It was not
Abraham's acts of obedience, but only his **faith,** which made him the great
prototype of all whom God counts righteous.

Secondly, Paul attacks the idea that it is necessary to be a physical descendant, or even a circumcised proselyte, in order to have Abraham as one's
"father". Abraham's fatherhood must be understood (as some Jews already
partly realized) not literally but metaphorically: he is the prototype of a
particular kind of relationship with God, **he is the father of all who have** 11
faith. This gives the key to a passage (Genesis 17.5) which had always given
trouble to Jewish expositors: **I have appointed you to be father of many** 17
nations. So long as fatherhood was understood literally 'in the natural line',
this was bound to be a puzzling verse; it could only be taken to indicate a
gracious extension of "sonship" to those Gentiles who became proselytes
and received circumcision—that is, who followed Abraham in keeping the
whole law. But if this "holding by the law" were the criterion for sonship,
there would be no advantage in having Abraham for father; for, as has been
shown already, **law can bring only retribution**: the fact that all break the 15
law prevents **those who hold by the law** from being **heirs,** indeed they 14
have the same status as everyone else: the only difference for the Gentiles is
that, having **no law,** they cannot even recognize their transgressions as a 15
breach of law. No, having Abraham as "father" is only of use if the fatherhood is understood metaphorically. He is **father of all who have faith . . .** 11
so that righteousness is 'counted' to them. Indeed it is arguable that
Abraham's decisive act of faith took place when he was **yet uncircumcised** 12
precisely in order to demonstrate that he was the prototype for all, circumcised and uncircumcised alike.

Abraham's "faith" can be more sharply defined: it was faith in the power
of God to perform a specific and seemingly impossible act, the birth of a son 18–22
in their old age to Abraham and his wife Sarah (Genesis 15–18). The God in
whom men must have faith is a god who does the seemingly impossible. He
makes the dead live (as in the resurrection of Christ), and he **summons** 17
things that are not yet in existence as if they already were (as at the
creation). Abraham's true "sons" are those who have faith in a miraculous
act: in God having **raised Jesus our Lord from the dead.** The significance 24
of this act was already prefigured in the Old Testament: **he was given up** 25
to death for our misdeeds (an allusion to Isaiah 53.12); its newly revealed

significance is [a] that it has secured our status as just before God: it has "justified" us.

5. 1 **Therefore, now that we have been justified through faith.** So far the argument has moved on a somewhat theoretical plane. Paul's concern has been strictly theological: to show how it is possible to hold two apparently incompatible beliefs: (i) that God is just, (ii) that he does not condemn all men, even though 'there is no just man, not one'. He has been presenting his 'Gospel' as a newly revealed solution to this problem: 'Now God's justice has been brought to light' (3.21).

But now Paul passes from theological implications to practical consequences. The new status which is given to 'all who have faith' brings with
4 it peace, hope, and an ability to undergo the **test** of persecution; and its
reality is guaranteed by an experience which is evidently taken for granted in
5 the churches to which Paul writes: that of **the Holy Spirit.**

How has Christ's death and resurrection procured such tremendous consequences for Christians? This act of God in Christ may perhaps be under-
6 stood as comprising two stages. One stage is already completed: **Christ died for the wicked.** That one man's death could have consequences of this order was not an unintelligible idea. Innocent and pious men had been martyred for their faith in the course of Jewish history (particularly during the Maccabean wars in the early second century B.C.), and Jewish thinkers had begun to interpret their deaths as a vicarious sacrifice. These exceptional acts of heroism could be understood as being on behalf of others. But the beneficiaries, so to speak, of these sacrificial deaths were always thought of as the righteous people of God: those who by their own piety were trying to hasten the kingdom of God were assisted in their efforts by the heroism of certain of their forbears which would predispose God to act in favour of his people. In this sense (perhaps) there had been examples in Jewish history of
7 the proposition that **for a good man one might actually brave death.**
But Paul's argument has shown that there are no "good men". Christ's sacrificial death for others cannot be explained as an act of heroic piety enhancing the general piety of others: it is entirely isolated, it is for **the wicked**, for men who are **yet sinners.** The only possible explanation of it
8 is that it was **God's own proof of his love towards us.** But if this is the
true explanation, and God has indeed shown his love towards us, it follows
10 that we have now been **reconciled** to God—a new word, used in place of the
forensic terms "justified", "made righteous". Moreover, we can now
11 **exult in God**—a word (in the Greek) with a touch of pride and confidence
about it (it is translated 'pride' in 3.27): we can now be sure that God,

[*a*] According to the probable meaning of the Greek. The rendering in the footnote of NEB represents a more natural translation of the Greek words, but yields a less satisfactory sense. See below, pp. 794–5.

instead of being inexorably severe to us in judgement, will be 'on our side' (8.31). All this has been effected by Christ's sacrificial death. It now belongs to the past; it is the first stage of God's act in Christ.

But this first stage is immediately followed by a second, which is not past
but present, and which involves our response to what Christ has done for us.
After having been reconciled by Christ's death, we shall be **saved by his** 10
life—a continuing process which transforms the life of the believer. More
will be said about this second stage in the following chapters. The important
point for the present is that the two stages cannot be separated.

To return to the first stage: Paul offers an interpretation of the historical event of Christ's death and resurrection in terms of the story of Adam. One is tempted to ask, did he think of this story as history or as myth? But this is probably not a fair question. A Jew would not have doubted for a moment that the opening chapters of Genesis contain a true record of creation; on the other hand, he would not have shared our interest in the science of history, and therefore would have been more interested in the meaning of the story than in its historicity. Moreover, a general, almost mythological, interest was already built into the story, in that in Hebrew the name Adam means "man", and so one finds, in Jewish literature of about the same period as Paul, generalized and almost psychological interpretations of the story, such as this one from the book known as the Apocalypse of Baruch: "Each of us has been the Adam of his own soul".

Paul's use of the story shows the same ambiguity—it is both a universal
parable and a particular event in history. It is universal, in that **through one** 12
man (Adam) **sin entered the world**; for the main current of Jewish teaching was not that Adam's physical nature had been changed after his disobedience, so that his descendants literally inherited sin and death from him
(though it is possible Paul believed this, and his language in verse 12 has
given rise to severe doctrines of "original sin"), but that in Adam could be
seen the primal representative Man, whose sin was the sin of all humanity.
To this extent, Adam was a timeless and universal figure of myth. But Adam
was also a particular man of a particular time; he represented a particular
stage, as it were, of man's history. Adam's sin was the first sin: the sin of
disobedience. It was only later that the Law of Moses was given as a kind of
paradigm of all possible cases of disobedience (**Law intruded into this** 20
process to multiply law-breaking). The function of the law was to mark
a new stage in man's history by breaking down the sin of Adam into all its
possible varieties. But Paul wishes to set "sin" in a wider context than that
of actions prohibited by the Jewish law. He goes back to the first stage, the
master-sin of Adam. Even in the early period from **Adam to Moses**, when 14
the law had not yet **intruded** (a word by which Paul probably intends to 20
relegate the law to a subordinate place in the sweep of his universal anthro-
pology), all men were already the successors of Adam in that their lives

were conditioned by sin (whatever its precise form) and terminated by death.

But the function of Adam in Paul's argument is not merely to explain sin,
14 it is also to explain Christ. **Adam** (man) **foreshadows the Man who was**
to come. If Adam is the type of every sinner, Christ is the type of the new
humanity which God has "justified" despite its sin. This explanation leans
towards the universal Adam of myth. But Christ is not in any sense myth:
15 he is a particular person, **the one man, Jesus Christ.** And so, when the
parallel between Adam and Christ is being worked out, Adam too is treated,
18 like Jesus, as a particular historical figure, and the **one misdeed** of the one
can be compared with the **one just act** (or, perhaps better, the "act which
rights the wrongs of others" and issues **in a verdict of acquittal**) of the
other. So particular are the two events that a kind of arithmetical comparison
is possible, showing the immense excess of God's grace which was needed to
balance the equation.

And yet the whole force of this excursus into what, for us, is simply Jewish
mythology lies not in its being reduced to particular events and figures of
history, but in its universal application. "Adam" is man—all of us. The
condemnation passed upon Adam resulted in his death. Because of all men's
17 solidarity with Adam—Adam is all men—**death established its reign.** But
14 the new Adam, **the Man who was to come,** is related to us in the same
way. Christians have the same solidarity with Christ as mankind in general
18 with Adam. With Christ they receive **acquittal** instead of condemnation,
life instead of death. The way this solidarity is achieved is the subject of the
next chapter.

It has been suggested that the act of God in Christ can be understood as
comprising two stages: the first is already completed, and consists of the
historical events of Christ's death and resurrection; the second follows from
his continuing activity among men. To concentrate on the first of these
stages at the expense of the second is to open the way to a serious misunderstanding. It is to suggest that the new status, which is acquired through faith
in Christ, lays no moral obligations on the believer, that he will be "just"
whatever he does, indeed that the more he sins the more striking a demonstration he will give of the "righteousness" of God who, despite everything,
"justifies" him. It seems to lead to the shocking conclusion that a Christian
6. 1 may **persist in sin, so that there may be all the more grace.**

The charge that Paul's preaching was libertarian, and simply did away with the old moral restraints without providing any new ones, seems often to have been made during his lifetime; and indeed Paul laid himself open to it. He appeared to devalue the Jewish law, and yet not to put any new moral code in its place. It is true that his letters contain substantial sections devoted specifically to moral instruction; but even so, the emphasis is usually upon the reality of a Christian's new status before God, the freedom of the

Christian life, and the fact that **God gives freely,** not in reward for conduct 23
or actions of a particular kind, but solely in response to the believer's faith.
It is easy to see how such a presentation could have been misconstrued, and
Paul have been accused of encouraging Christians to **persist in sin.** 1

Paul here answers the charge. He has already tried to show that he is not devaluing the law ('we are placing law itself on a firmer footing', 3.31), and in any case the Christians have of course a moral code of their own. But the real answer lies in the fact that it is impossible to separate the two stages of salvation, the historical fact of "justification" from its present consequences.
This can be vividly illustrated by the rite of baptism. **Have you forgotten,** 3
Paul asks, referring to an experience all the Roman Christians will have had
(or perhaps it is better to keep the literal meaning of the original, "Do you
not know", for it is far from certain that they would ever before have thought
of their baptism in quite this way)—**have you forgotten that when we**
were baptized into (the NEB adds **union with**) **Christ Jesus we were**
baptized into his death? The symbolism here would have needed no
explanation. Baptism involved complete immersion: the new convert
stepped down into the river or pool and the waters closed for a moment over
his head. It was a ritual death: he **died with Christ.** This was the first stage 8
of salvation. But, of course, you could not stop there! A second stage followed.
The convert did not remain under water to drown, any more than Christ
remained in the tomb. **If we have become incorporate with him in a** 5
death like his, we shall also be one with him in a resurrection like
his. The newly baptized emerged from the water to set his feet **upon the** 4
new path of life. The second stage of salvation is present and continuing;
it involves an "incorporation" with Christ who, **living as he lives,... lives** 10
to God. And this union with Christ lays a new ethical foundation for
life.

The second stage of salvation, then, takes the form of a new kind of life
for the Christian, in which deliberately committing sin makes no sense. We 2
died to sin: how can we live in it any longer? We might now express this
change by saying that a person has been morally converted, he is psychologically different, and his former sinful way of life no longer holds any attraction for him. But to a person of Paul's background, a psychological analysis of this kind would not have seemed to do justice to the seriousness of man's moral predicament. Paul recognized the fact that there is an irrational element in moral conduct which leads a man to do wrong even when he clearly sees what is right and is determined, in principle, to adhere to it. To do justice to this irrational element in terms of moral philosophy or of a simple psychology is not easy; and many of Paul's contemporaries saw the issue, not as a matter of the psychological make-up of the individual, but as a struggle played out between objective forces of good and evil, fighting for control of a man's personality. To put it crudely, it was as if a person sinned,

not through some fault of his own, but because of some external force of evil working upon him.

Exactly how this struggle was thought of varied from one culture to another, and even within Judaism there were different views. One school imagined two conflicting impulses in man, another represented man as subject to a good and a bad "spirit". But all these approaches to the problem of moral failure had in common a tendency to personify moral concepts, and to think in terms, not of habits and dispositions, but of objective powers to which the personality is subject. There are clear examples of this tendency in
9 the present passage. That Christ **is never to die again** is a simple statement
of fact. But this can be personified: **he is no longer under the dominion of death,** where the point could perhaps be brought out by writing Death with a capital letter. To say that a man will die is doubtless equivalent to saying that a man is under the dominion of Death; but the second formulation implies that there is a personified power, "death", which holds man in subjection. Similarly with sin. "Sin" means simply a certain kind of action.
6 To be **the slaves of sin** may be no more than a metaphor: certain kinds of
conduct, if they become habitual, can "enslave" a person. But with a sen-
12 tence like, **Sin must no longer reign in your mortal body, exacting**
obedience to the body's desires, the language is no longer merely metaphorical: "sin" has become personified. It is an objective force working upon the moral life of the individual. It could now be spelt with a capital letter: Sin.

This tendency to think of external personified forces influencing a man's moral actions explains some of the language in which Paul has tried to express the consequences of Christ's death and man's participation in that death. By our solidarity with Christ, there is a sense in which we "die" (one
6 might say, **the man we once were** dies, or **the sinful self** dies); and this
7 "death" affects our relationship with "Sin". **A dead man is no longer**
answerable for his sin. This was a commonplace in Jewish thinking. Either "sin" was imagined in a law-court demanding his due, but once a man was dead and was no longer there to answer in court, sin got no redress; or, since death is the "wage" of sin, once this was paid there could be no further penalty. Either way, sin lost its power over men at the moment
11 of death; and since Christians have died with Christ, they are now **dead to**
sin and are liberated from it.

To put it another way—a way which brings us closer to the argument that
1 it is absurd to imagine that a Christian can **persist in sin.** Sin may be
12 imagined, not as a claimant in a law-court, but as a king over the **mortal**
16 **body,** as a **master** to whom men are enslaved. Paul has established that all
men are sinners, therefore all are slaves of sin. Once again death—the ritual death undergone with Christ—liberates us from this master. The expression of sin's mastery was the law. Now that the slavery to sin is ended, the law

ceases to be binding. But this was exactly the argument of Paul's critics. What was there instead of the law to control Christians' conduct? The answer lay in a consistent application of the same analysis of moral conduct. Man
is not morally autonomous. His body is **at the disposal** of whatever power 13
is in control. If sin loses its mastery, some other power must take its place. For Christians, there could be no doubt what this power would be: **put yourself at the disposal of God.**

To a Jew, "putting oneself at the disposal of God" meant only one thing: observing the law. But Paul has shown that the law is an expression of the mastery of sin. Therefore Christians must have some other means of making sure that their conduct conforms to God's will. In fact, of course, they have a moral code of their own. Paul seems to be referring to such a code when he
mentions a **pattern of teaching.** Precisely what it consisted of at this date 17
we do not know. Presumably it was based partly on the ethical teaching of Jesus, and partly on existing moral standards. But it must certainly have been sufficiently specific and comprehensive to refute the charge that Christians, because they no longer observed the Law of Moses, were now living in a
state of **moral anarchy.** By obeying this new pattern of teaching, they 19
could acknowledge the control of God in their lives.

It follows, then, from this whole analysis of moral conduct that the act of God in Christ cannot consist merely in liberation from the mastery of sin. That stage must be followed by another. The mastery of sin gives place to a new mastery. A crude way of stating it would be that one has been freed from
one slavery only in order to enter another. At least (it could be said) **when** 20
you were slaves of sin, you were free from the control of righteous-
ness. What was the gain of being freed from sin if it meant being **bound** to a 22
new service? The answer is obvious: it lies in the rewards attached to each;
in the one case **death,** in the other **eternal life.** 23

Union with Christ, not only **in a death like his,** but **in a resurrection** 5
like his—this is the mechanism by which we achieve the status of "just" before God, this is the process which, since it embraces the two stages of
salvation, issues in our **being at the disposal of God, as dead men raised** 13
to life. This is Paul's answer to those who accuse him of abolishing the law, and, with the law, all moral standards. Through union with Christ, we are
freed from the commands of sin; but equally, we are **bound to the** 22
service of God.

Paul adds a further illustration of the way in which the death of Christ entails our liberation. A wife's legal duty to her husband is terminated by the husband's death. Similarly, a man's legal duty to observe the Jewish law is terminated by his own death (this was a familiar Jewish cliché); and a
Christian, by being **identified with the body of Christ,** has "died", and 7.4
has therefore had his legal duty terminated. In each case a death is necessary, and the result of that death is the possibility of a new relationship—this is

presumably the point of comparison, for in other respects Paul's example manifestly does not work out, and no amount of subtle interpretation will make it do so.

But this illustration raises again the awkward question, which recurs throughout the letter, of the continuing validity of the law. It was said
4 earlier (6.2) that 'we died to sin'. It is said now that we have **died to the law.**
7 Does this make **the law identical with sin**? Paul has already had to make good the claims of the Mosaic law to be an authentic revelation of the justice of God (chapter 3). He has now to clarify the connection between law and sin, lest his argument should seem to lead him to the paradoxical conclusion that the law given by God has been wholly harmful in its effects.

That there is a connection between law and sin is admitted. Sinful passions
5, 7 are **evoked by the law,** in that **except through law I should never have become acquainted with sin. For example**—and two views are possible about what Paul's example consists of. One view is that he is referring to his own boyhood: the full obligations of the law were not laid upon a Jewish boy
9 until he was thirteen years of age. **There was a time** would then refer to those early years in which the law did not have to be fully observed. To that extent it could perhaps be said that a boy under thirteen was **fully alive.** But this explanation is somewhat forced. The other view, which seems more probable, is that the example depends, once again, upon the figure of Adam (who is all men, and so "I"). Between Adam and Moses there was a stage when the law did not yet exist: "I lived (on this view **I was fully alive** would not be a correct translation) in the absence of law". But the commandment of the Law of Moses, "Thou shalt not covet", was in fact already given to Adam in the particular form, "thou shalt not eat of the fruit of the tree".
8 Adam's reaction (and so "my" reaction) was to have **all kinds of wrong desires** (literally the same word, "coveting"). Sin, this time personified as
11 the serpent, **found its opportunity** in this commandment and **seduced** me (in the person of Adam: a clear allusion to Genesis 3.13). Sin is therefore not "identical with law": law is merely the opportunity for sin. Thus Paul can
13 still maintain that the law is good. It was sin that **used a good thing to bring about my death.**

The tendency to personify **sin**, which was already apparent in the previous
17 chapter, now becomes explicit: **it is no longer I who perform the action, but sin that lodges in me.** Sin has become an independent source of action, an *alter ego* in conflict with my true self, and the next few verses passionately portray the symptoms of man's moral struggle in terms which are as comprehensible to modern psychology as they were to both Jews and Greeks in the ancient world. It is only the root cause of this struggle which is identified as a demonic entity named **sin.**

This sudden essay in psychology is not entirely unprepared. It follows upon a distinction, alluded to already in this chapter and worked out more

fully in the next, which was widely accepted among Jews: the distinction
between "flesh" (here translated **my unspiritual nature** or **our lower** 18, 5
nature) and **spirit.** This distinction was not a way of dividing up man into his component parts (like body and soul), but of defining the kind of motives, conduct and ambitions of which he is capable. "Flesh" covers the whole range of human conduct which is governed by merely selfish motives. Its propensities may be grossly sensual (such as fornication) or subtly emotional and intellectual (such as idolatry and party-intrigues: see the list in Galatians 5.19–21). It is man's **lower nature** in so far as it covers all that is purely human and that is in no way open to the influence of God. But its opposite is not a "higher (unselfish, altruistic) nature". Its opposite is **spirit,** which is the name for everything in man which responds to the Spirit of God. Spirit can be physical, or emotional, or intellectual. To be "spiritual" is simply to leave room in one's life for a response to the commands and initiatives of God. Now these two terms are distinct, but they are not themselves in conflict. They merely define the area in which a conflict might take place. Paul has to go further than this to find the protagonists in the struggle which he experiences within himself. On the one side, he suggests, is the "I" which is spiritual (i.e. which has responded, however imperfectly, to the promptings of God); and on the other is that power which seems so often to gain control of the rest of my nature: **sin.**

All this is characteristically Jewish psychology. Paul goes a little way towards translating it into terms which a Greek reader would find easier to understand. He allows that the "spiritual nature" is roughly equivalent
to the **inmost self** which is the place of **reason**; whereas the principle of the 22
"flesh" can be expressed as the **law that is in my members.** To this extent, 23
the conflict can be put in terms familiar to Greek-speaking readers, as between the reason and the unreasonable impulses of the body. But Paul does not linger in this terminology; for the Jewish way of seeing the matter is essential when it comes to understanding the Spirit of God (chapter 8).

It seems to follow from the whole run of the chapter that Paul here uses the first person as a way of describing the general condition of men: "I" is every man. But there can be little doubt that Paul is also writing from experience. Every man's struggle is Paul's own struggle. It has often been felt that this creates a difficulty. The analysis (it is said) is appropriate enough in general, but not to a converted Christian, who has surely been liberated from
this body doomed to death. Therefore, if Paul is offering us autobiography, 24
it must belong to his experience before his conversion; he would describe his present state quite differently. The difficulty is to reconcile this view with
the last sentence of the chapter, **I . . . am yet . . . a slave to the law of sin,** 25
and critics have been led to suggest that this sentence must have been displaced in the manuscripts from its correct position a few lines higher. But this is an arbitrary solution. It is better to recognize (for it is consistent both

with Christian experience and with Paul's argument) that a continuing moral
conflict is a part even of the liberated life of the Christian. Paul had reason for
uttering the warning, 'so sin must no longer reign in your mortal body'
(6.12). It is not the reality of the struggle, but its consequences, which have
been changed. And this change is fully momentous enough to warrant the
exclamation, **Thanks be to God!**

8. 1 **The conclusion of the matter is this.** This phrase stands for two Greek
particles, which serve to mark the point which the argument has reached: it
can now be taken as agreed that **there is no condemnation for those who
are united with Christ Jesus.** The fact is established; but how has it
happened? So far, two explanations have been given: one drawn from
mythology (solidarity with Adam superseded by solidarity with Christ:
chapter 5), and one from the rite of baptism ("dying" to sin in Christ:
chapter 6). A third explanation is now offered on the basis of the distinction,
2 made in the last chapter, between 'spirit' and 'lower nature' ("flesh"): **in
Christ Jesus the life-giving law of the Spirit has set you free from the
law of sin and death.** A new kind of living is the result, and indeed the
proof, of our justification.

This is not to say that, by choosing to live in a certain way, we are able to
procure our justification. To think this would be to forget the first stage of
3 salvation, the fact that it was God who took the initiative **by sending his
own Son.** It is true that we benefit from this act of God in so far as, by faith,
1 we become **united with Christ Jesus.** But our faith is only the subjective
side of our salvation; the matter still has an objective side to it. Quite independently of us and our response, something has been done for us by God.

Precisely what God did, and how God's deed affects mankind, is not easily
said in a single sentence. Previously, Paul has made use of metaphors from
the Jewish sacrificial system (3.21–6). He does the same here. Jesus was sent
3 **as a sacrifice for sin**—which is probably [a] an allusion to the Old Testament
"sin offerings" that were offered to expiate inadvertent transgressions of the
law (Leviticus 4). Further, he was sent **in a form like that of our own
sinful nature.** The effect of this (if we may apply the argument that is
worked out in Galatians 3) was to undermine the authority of sin—and here,
once again, "sin" becomes an independent personification of the powers of
evil. Until then, sin had invariably dragged the lower nature with it into
death and condemnation. Its claim on the lower nature, never having been
contested, could be regarded as legally established. But now, by raising Christ
from the dead, God has given a decisive demonstration that condemnation
and death are not the inevitable verdict and sentence passed on the descendants of Adam. By this one great exception, the hitherto uncontested claim of
3 sin has been shown to be groundless: God has **passed judgement against
sin.** And this reverses our whole situation, even our relationship to the law.

[*a*] Though not certainly: the footnote in NEB offers another possible translation.

Before, our lower nature, being governed by sin, made it impossible for us
to obey the law, and so the law could do us no good: **our lower nature
robbed it of all potency.** But now the claim of sin that it could always
bring us into condemnation has been disposed of, and the law can become,
what it always was potentially, a means of promoting right conduct in us and
so of securing our acquittal; **so that the commandment of the law may** 4
find fulfilment in us.

The nature of the Christian's 'union with Christ' may now be more
precisely defined in terms of the distinction made earlier between 'spirit'
and 'lower nature'. The NEB here makes use of modern idioms such as
level and **outlook**; but it is important to bear in mind the meaning of the 5
original Jewish distinction. It is not a question of the 'lower nature' as contrasted with a "higher" one; it is a matter of whether a man's horizon is
entirely limited by his own interests, or whether he is open to the influence
of God. And now that the possibility of being influenced by God is so
enormously enhanced by 'union with Christ' (or: **Christ . . . dwelling** 10
within you), the 'level of the spirit' becomes all-important. A Christian's
whole life is now lived on this **level**, because it is here that union with Christ
takes effect. Or, to put it less subjectively, when you are on that level, **God's** 9
Spirit dwells within you. And conversely, **if a man does not possess the
Spirit of Christ, he is no Christian.**

Christ . . . dwelling within you is more than a metaphor. If we are now 10
directed by the Spirit, this is not a case of remote control. A new power is 4
now master within us, and this within the visible and tangible "us": our
body. Christianity is not "spiritual" in the sense of involving only a part of
us. It involves the whole of our body, that is, the whole of ourselves; in our
wholeness, we can either live on the level of our lower nature (in which case
the body follows its natural bent, its **base pursuits**) or of the spirit. And this 13
body of ours, which can become a **dead thing** through sin, can equally, by 10
the **indwelling Spirit,** receive **new life.** 11

The Roman Christians did not have to be told to believe in the Spirit; they
had experienced it, and not least when they prayed. In Aramaic, **Abba** was an 15
intimate and familiar way of saying "father". It would normally have seemed quite unnatural to address God in this way. God is too great to be treated with such familiarity. The most a Jew would allow himself was the somewhat less personal and proprietary form, "Our Father". But the Christians, when they prayed, found themselves crying **Abba.** They would hardly have done this of their own accord: it must therefore have been the Spirit which inspired them to do so. And the Spirit would only have inspired them to do this if it was correct—i.e. if God really were the Father of each one of them, and they his sons. Now in Jewish law a man could always adopt a son simply by calling him "my son". In this sense, the Spirit **makes us sons.** (Paul here uses the technical Greek word for adoption.) If we can correctly call

God "father" (and the Spirit assures us we can), God must have called us (and adopted us as) his "sons".

The cry **Abba** was uttered by Jesus himself in a moment of suffering
17 (Mark 14.36). It can be uttered by us, but only under the same condition: **if**
we share his sufferings. Not that Paul needed to bid Christians of that
18 time to go out and look for sufferings. They had enough in the **sufferings we**
now endure. But these sufferings are transformed by hope, hope of what is
19 **in store for us.** There is a splendour to come, as yet unrevealed, which will
20 transfigure not only ourselves (revealing us as **God's sons**), but **the universe**
itself. The writer of the Adam story in Genesis painted on a large canvas;
not only the condition of mankind, but the evident disharmony of nature
itself, was the result of Adam's sin: "Cursed is the ground because of you"
(Gen. 3.17). And the concomitant of the ultimate union of Adam-humanity
with Christ will be the restoration of the whole universe to its intended
splendour. This is the scale of the Christians' hope, the majestic context in
25 which we are called to **show our endurance.** [a]

24 **For we have been saved, though only in hope.** "Though only" is an
addition by the translators, making Christian salvation sound somewhat
remote and hypothetical. What Paul is saying here is that, however great the
benefits which a believer enjoys already from the act of God in Christ, there
is a greater future still to come. Consequently, one of the distinctive marks of
Christian living is **hope.** Now anyone who lives in hope is looking forward
to a future more glorious than the present; the present is at most a shadow of
23 what is to come. We are not yet fully God's **sons,** our **whole body** is not yet
fully set free from the dominion of sin. This condition, along with the sufferings and persecutions which inevitably beset the very existence of a Christian
25 community, calls for **endurance.** But this endurance is made easy by the
Christian **hope.**

For we do not merely live in hope. The Spirit is already experienced as a
23 present reality, as **firstfruits of the harvest to come.** If a further example
of this experience is needed, it is the miraculous subvention given to those
28 whose very weakness paralyses their prayer. Indeed, the Spirit **in every-**
thing . . . co-operates for good with those who love God. [b] But this is
29 not the result of their loving God. Once again, the initiative is God's. **God**
knew his own before ever they were. Logically, this has a negative side:
those whom God did not know as his own are presumably without hope. But
possibly Paul is not thinking of this logical corollary here. His words may be

[*a*] This seems, at least, a likely interpretation of this difficult passage. The words, **because of him who made it so** (if they are a correct interpretation of the original), are intelligible if they allude to Adam; and the clue to Paul's conception of a universal restoration seems to lie in the Genesis story. But more than one interpretation is possible, as the NEB footnotes show.

[*b*] This Greek phrase is highly ambiguous. See the alternative rendering given in the NEB footnote.

intended simply to guard against any suggestion that the initiative is ours
and not God's. The emphasis is all on the believer's union with Christ,
which can now be expressed in yet another way: if we have been "adopted"
as God's sons, we have been **shaped to the likeness of his Son,** and our 29
union with him is that of brothers **among a large family.** All this **splen-** 30
dour flows from that first moment of our salvation, when God **justified** us.

With all this in mind. The whole section ends with a direct application 31
of theology to life. If God has done all this for us, what, even in the difficult
situation of the Roman Christians, can any longer cause alarm? It is God
who **pronounces acquittal**: there is no authority in heaven or earth that 33
can reverse this verdict. **Christ . . . pleads our cause**; with such an advocate 34
(this is a new metaphor) we are safe in any court. In the words of a psalm
(44.22), **we are being done to death for thy sake all day long**: the 36
persecution we receive identifies us with the long line of righteous sufferers
who fill the pages of Scripture. But these sufferers could merely hope; now,
overwhelming victory is ours—not only over the persecution of men, but 37
over the psychic and inhuman forces of the universe, over the **heights** and 39
depths of astrology, metaphysics, and popular superstition.

The purpose of God in history

The *Gospel according to Paul* has now been stated: salvation is for all, through faith in Christ, 'quite independently of law'. But it was one thing to state this magnificent impartiality of God as a theoretical proposition of theology; it was quite another to bring the matter down to a personal level and admit that
it involved a moral and spiritual condemnation of one's **natural kinsfolk.** 9. 3
Yet this, from the Jewish point of view, was the inevitable implication of
the universal Gospel of Christ; and Paul, personally caught in the logic of
his own argument, makes no attempt to hide his feelings: **in my heart** 2
there is great grief and unceasing sorrow. What had become of the divine promises made to the Jews? 'Has God rejected his people?' In the short term, the problem was insoluble, and the anguish remained. But in the larger context of world history, an answer might yet be found. Hence the translators' heading for the next three chapters, *The purpose of God in history.*

The list of the Jews' privileges (verses 4–5) is impressive: they had all the
riches of the Old Testament; they had the promises once made to their own
people; and they had the continuing institutions of their religion. Not only
that, but the **patriarchs** themselves, so it was believed, had by their impec- 5
cable obedience built up a balance of credit with God on which their physical
descendants could still draw; and now it was one of themselves whom God

had appointed to fulfil that rôle of world saviour which for several centuries
they had associated with the title Messiah (Christ). Rich indeed was this
inheritance—and Paul breaks off to utter, like any good Jew, his recognition
5 of the goodness of God. **May God, supreme above all, be blessed for
ever! Amen.** [a]

Yet the Jews had rejected their own Messiah, and salvation had gone elsewhere. What then had gone wrong? Had God gone back on his promises?
Was the glory and the privilege an illusion all the time? Was the Old Testa-
6 ment a fraud? No, this was inconceivable: **it is impossible that the word
of God should have proved false.** And indeed one way out of the difficulty
was suggested by Scripture itself.

7 **Not all descendants of Israel are truly Israel.** Paul has already shown
himself ready to make a distinction on general grounds between 'true Jews'
and those who are Jews only 'in externals' (2.28–9). He now invokes the
narrative of Genesis to prove that mere physical descent from Abraham was
not a sufficient condition for claiming the name of Jew. Abraham had two
sons, Isaac and Ishmael. But the Ishmaelites were not true Jews (even though
Ishmael was Isaac's elder brother). Only the descendants of Isaac were
8 **reckoned as Abraham's descendants.** And since Isaac was a child of
promise (for Sarah was past the age of child-bearing, and God had to
intervene, with the promise of a miracle, before she could give birth to Isaac
—Genesis 18.14), the principle of promise, rather than natural genealogy,
was introduced into the Jewish race from the start.

However this argument was a little precarious. Ishmael's mother was a slave-girl (Hagar), and this in itself was a good enough reason for declaring her offspring not to be "truly Israel", as compared with that of Abraham's free-born wife Sarah. A better example was furnished by the next generation. Isaac and Rebekah had two children (who were in fact twins), yet only one
of them, Jacob, was regarded as a Jewish patriarch (Genesis 25). The other,
13 Esau, was **hated** by God, and the Edomites (his presumed descendants) duly
became the object of centuries of Jewish hatred. This second example was
11 decisive proof that **God's purpose** did not work through the ordinary laws
of heredity, but was **selective.**

But this last example, if it proved the point in question, opened up new
problems. If God could choose one of a pair of twins and reject the other,
12 **even before they were born,** one must ask: does God abide by any prin-
14 ciple, or is he entirely capricious? **Is God to be charged with injustice?**
The answer to this is twofold. The key to God's purpose is not caprice but
15 **mercy.** God singles out men (and nations) on whom he **will show mercy**

[*a*] It is uncertain how the text of verse 5 should be punctuated. The most natural run of the words is that given as the first alternative in the footnote; but it is usually thought unlikely that Paul would have so baldly used the title "God" of Christ, and this is avoided by assuming that the last few words form a separate sentence.

(Exodus 33.19), and this singling out inevitably appears unjust and capricious
to those who are not so singled out, but are used as the necessary villains, so
to speak, in the drama of God's merciful purposes. An example is Pharaoh,
whom God deliberately made **stubborn** (Exodus 9.12,16) in the interests 18
of a greater design.

A second answer is also possible, one that is aimed especially at anyone who feels that this apparent capriciousness of God undermines all moral responsibility. This answer received its classic expression in the prophets (Isaiah 29.16; 45.9; Jeremiah 18.6): the creator, like the potter, can do what he likes with his creatures; it is not for them to call him unjust, for only he, and not they, know the purpose for which he created them. But Paul does not develop this somewhat obscurantist conception; he merely uses the metaphor in order to take his previous answer a little further. God's mercy does not always take the form of an immediate action: it may be worked out over a long period and with far-reaching and splendid consequences, which
can even result in a "very patient toleration" of those who have been
assigned parts as villains of the piece, **those vessels . . . due for destruction.** 22

The metaphor also serves to lead back into the point at issue. God's purpose is selective, and the principle of his selection is mercy; and these
propositions, having been demonstrated from the Old Testament, are now
applied to the case of the Christian church: **such vessels are we.** Two 24
verses of Hosea (2.23; 1.10), which originally expressed God's changing 25–6
judgement on the people of Israel, are quoted (as they are in 1 Peter 2.10) to
the advantage of gentile Christianity: God's selective purpose has now
embraced men **whom he has called from among Gentiles**; and that tiny 24
minority of the Jewish race which has also entered the church appears to
give effect to the important principle to be found in Isaiah, that God's
purpose will be achieved even if **only a remnant shall be saved** (Isaiah 27
10.20–2).

From the Jewish point of view, this selection of the Gentiles could hardly
be expected to make sense. It was they, the Jews, who had **made great** 31
efforts after a law of righteousness; and they had noticed the apparent
lack of moral effort on the part of the Gentiles. But they had made the fatal
mistake of supposing that their end could be attained by virtue of these
efforts alone; that (in their own theological language) salvation could be
obtained by **deeds.** They had failed to reckon with the one essential element 32
in the quest for a relationship with a just and merciful God: **faith.** Their
attitude, in fact, was well illustrated by a composite image which the early
church built up from two passages of Isaiah (28.16; 8.14—the same com- 33
bination occurs in 1 Peter 2.6). A piece of masonry, left lying on the ground
by the builders, may seem at first sight to be no more than an obstacle to
stumble over; looked at more closely, it may be recognized as the stone which
will one day crown the whole structure, the 'main cornerstone'.

God is just and God is selective. These apparently incompatible propositions have now been reconciled, in that God's selectivity has been shown to be determined, not by caprice, but by that side of God's righteousness which is his mercy. It must now be asked, is there no way in which this merciful treatment may be earned?

One obvious way of earning it would seem to be religious zeal, and this the
10. 2 Jews had in abundance. **To their zeal for God I can testify.** However,
their zeal for God had turned into a zeal for correct observance of the law, in
3 the belief that such observance would be a **way of righteousness,** i.e. a
means of establishing a relationship with God. The uselessness of this way
has already been sufficiently demonstrated. But there is a further point:
4 **Christ ends the law.** This phrase deliberately exploits the ambiguity of the
word "end" (*telos*). Christ puts a temporal end to the law, in that he opens
a new era in which observance of the law is no longer the decisive criterion.
But he also brings law to its destined "end"—that is, he fulfils the law—in that
he has dethroned the power ("sin") which 'robbed the law of all potency' (8.3).
From now on, that which **brings righteousness** is not observance but **faith.**

The difference between observance and faith can be illustrated by a con-
5 trast latent in the Old Testament itself. Compare Leviticus (18.5), **'The
man who does this shall gain life by it'** (where the emphasis is on
"doing"), with Deuteronomy 30.11–14,

> "The commandment which I lay on you this day is not too difficult for you, it is not too remote. It is not in heaven, that you should say, Who will go up to heaven for us . . . nor is it beyond the sea, that you should say, Who will cross the sea for us to fetch it and tell it to us? . . . but the word is near you: it is upon your lips and in your heart."

There is at least a hint here that something is given to men before ever
they start "doing" anything; and Paul adapts this passage to the Christian
experience. The appearance of the Son of God on earth is something which
6 has happened: no effort is needed on our part **to bring Christ down.** The
7 resurrection has happened: there is no action we have to take **to bring**
8 **Christ up from the dead.** All that matters is the **word of faith** on the lips
9 and in the heart, the **confession** (as it might be, when on trial as a Christian)
that **'Jesus is Lord'.** This word of faith is something utterly different from
the long and exacting discipline of "doing" the law. Yet it guarantees that one
11 will be **saved from shame** (a phrase from Isaiah 28.16, meaning that one
will not be put hopelessly to shame when confronted with God's righteousness)—and it is a possibility for everyone. What had been enunciated as a
13 general principle by the prophet Joel (2.32)—**everyone who invokes the
name of the Lord will be saved**—now has a new and startling meaning:
the word **Lord** in the Old Testament often conceals a reference (so the first

Christians took it) to the Lord Jesus Christ. So here: everyone who invokes
the name of the Lord Jesus will be saved. **There is no distinction between** 12
Jew and Greek.

In verse 14 Paul appears to meet, somewhat abruptly, a possible objection. It might be said that the Jews—perhaps it was true of the majority of the Jews in Rome—have had no chance to hear the Gospel. There may have
been no one to **spread the news** (almost a technical term, in the Greek, for 15
preaching the Gospel); or, if there has, he may have seemed to the Jews to lack the authority of a proper **commission,** such as would be given to one of their own number by a formal act of the authorities in Jerusalem. But (to take the last point first) there is evidence in Scripture (Isaiah 52.7) that
those who bring **good news** authenticate themselves (their feet are **welcome** 15
or "beautiful"); and to answer the first point, Psalm 19.4 ('**Their voice has** 18
sounded over all the earth . . .') can be taken as a prophecy that the outreach of the gospel-preaching is to be universal: the Jews must have heard it (or at any rate they soon will have). The fact is, not that they have not heard,
but that **not all have responded to the good news.** And this failure to 16
respond, with its threatening consequence that salvation may go to others, is
foreshadowed in many passages of Scripture. Paul quotes three: Isaiah 53.1; 19–21
Deuteronomy 32.21; and Isaiah 65.1–2.

I ask then, has God rejected his people? The argument of these chapters **11.** 1
would seem to entail that he has. But at this Paul recoils. **I cannot believe it!**—the phrase ("God forbid!" in older versions) occurs again in verse 11 (**Far from it!**) and above at 3.6 and 3.31 (it is translated differently each time in NEB): it is one which Paul uses to repel what he feels to be an outrageous conclusion. And in fact there were two ways out of the difficulty. One has already been alluded to (9.24–9): the biblical doctrine that so long
as a '**remnant**' of faithful people continued to exist, God's promises to the 5
Jewish people could still be fulfilled even if the majority had shown themselves unworthy. This doctrine was illustrated by **the story of Elijah** (1 2
Kings 19): it made no difference if the entire nation seemed to have gone
after false gods, so long as there were **seven thousand men** left who were 4
still faithful. The principle now had a new application. God had not **rejected** 1
his people, since a tiny '**remnant**' of them had accepted Jesus Christ— 5
among whom was Paul (**I am an Israelite myself**). But this remnant, 1
unlike the previous "remnants" in Jewish history, was **selected by the** 5
grace of God. It had done nothing to deserve its selection; it must not be
imagined that the salvation of this **selected few** had been earned by the 7
merits and **deeds** of the Jewish people. This would be entirely contrary to 6
Paul's Gospel: **grace would cease to be grace.**

But this "remnant" explanation accounted only for that small number of Jews who, like Paul, had become Christians. The question still remained,

what of all the rest? It was true (as has been shown earlier) that any doctrine
of the divine selection of some necessarily implied the rejection of others;
and there were abundant prophecies in Scripture of the fate in store for those
7 who were **made blind to the truth** (Paul quotes two: Isaiah 29.10 and
Psalm 69.22–3). But Paul was still not disposed to accept that the failure of
11 all except a small remnant meant the **complete downfall** of the rest of the
Jewish people. **Because they offended, salvation has come to the
Gentiles**; it was true that the universal scope of the Gospel might never
have been grasped had it not been thrown out by the exclusive religious
system of the Jews. But this need not be the end of the matter. A chain
reaction had been set up, and this would ultimately impinge again on the
Jewish nation which, despite itself, had started it. The effect of gentile
Christianity would be **to stir Israel to emulation**; and the result of this
12 would eventually be **their coming to full strength.**

This line of thought suggested a second explanation; and possibly Paul
was constrained to put it forward, not merely by his natural feelings, but by
a patronizing and complacent attitude that had been taken up by the gentile
Christians over against the Jewish community. Therefore he addressed his
13 second answer specifically to them. **I have something to say to you
Gentiles.**

This answer depended upon taking a long enough view of history. It was
only in the short term that it appeared that salvation had simply passed from
Jews to non-Jews. In the long term, it was impossible to suppose that
anything had changed in the destiny of God's chosen people. Of another
people it might be said simply that their history had a brilliant beginning, but
that it all came to nothing. But the early history of Israel was of a different
28 order. The faith of **the patriarchs** was such that, in that one small area of
human history, God could be said to have treated men as truly his **friends.**
This was no ordinary beginning. Just as it was believed that an offering
16 from the **first portion of dough** made holy all the bread that was eaten
(Numbers 15.18–19), and that a tree, once consecrated, does not have to be
reconsecrated each time a new branch grows, but that **if the root is consecrated, so are the branches,** so the evident sanctification of the generation of the patriarchs guaranteed the divinely appointed destiny of their
29 descendants. **The gracious gifts of God and his calling,** so unambiguously bestowed upon a particular race of men, were **irrevocable.** The
answer must be that the present rejection of Israel—the treating of them as
28 God's **enemies** instead of his friends—was temporary. It was merely the
15 preparation for **their acceptance** in the future, even if (when Paul wrote)
this prospect seemed to demand an intervention by God no less miraculous
than that of bringing **life from the dead.**

In such a perspective, both Paul's own work and the status of his gentile
converts could no longer be understood as ends in themselves. Paul knew

himself to be a **missionary to the Gentiles.** But it was only when his work 13
had the effect of stirring **emulation** in the Jews and so hastening the time 14
when the whole Jewish race would be saved that he gave full **honour to that** 13
ministry. As for his gentile converts, their situation had an analogy in
nature. The normal growth of a wild olive tree can be altered by grafting in
shoots from a cultivated olive, so that the tree begins to bear fruit. The
Gentiles were in this situation: they had been **grafted in** among the 17
branches of the parent tree, and they must not imagine that they could either
be independent of that tree or feel superior to it. Moreover, if the analogy
were pressed, it became another vivid parable of God's gracious treatment
of them. The grafting had been **against all nature**: wild olive shoots had 24
been grafted into the cultivated olive, instead of the other way round!
Against all expectation, and entirely owing to the merciful selection of God,
the Gentiles had been given an essential part to play in the ultimate sanctification of Israel. The moral for them, whenever they were tempted to scorn
their unconverted Jewish neighbours, was clear enough: **put away your** 20
pride.

There is a deep truth here (literally, "a mystery") which can only be 25
plumbed by considering the whole sweep of history. First—one recalls
Jesus' words, Mark 13.10—the Gospel has to be preached to all the world,
the Gentiles have to be **admitted in full strength.** Then—though only 26
then—**the whole of Israel will be saved.** This is the ultimate answer to
the agonizing question with which Paul started. But it also provides striking
confirmation of Paul's understanding of God's dealings with men. Had the
Jewish people, instead of rejecting the Gospel, calmly accepted it, it might
have appeared as if their salvation still depended on their own privileged
history. But their present phase of **disobedience** showed that when they 31
ultimately came to **receive mercy** they would receive it on exactly the same
basis as the Gentiles, as a free and gracious gift. In this way only would those
ancient prophecies be fulfilled which appeared to predict the coming of a
Messiah who would deliver and purify the people of Israel: '**From Zion** 26
shall come the Deliverer' (Isaiah 59.20–1).

Paul has reached the end of his argument: and he breaks off once again
(as he did in 1.25) with a brief hymn of praise, for which most of the material 33–6
can be found in the Old Testament (especially Isaiah 40.13). At the end of
this hymn, his hearers will doubtless have responded, **Amen.** 36

Christian behaviour

The last main section of the letter follows not so much on the previous one as upon the main argument which reached its climax in chapter 8. Man's salvation has been procured by the act of God in Jesus Christ; but there is still a response required from the believer, before that salvation can become effectual. In chapter 6, this response was described in terms of continuing solidarity with the risen Christ. Here, it is presented under the metaphor of a
12. 1 **living sacrifice**—not the old ritual sacrifices of the Jewish temple, but
the worship offered by mind and heart, a total dedication of one's very
self, involving a moral and intellectual transformation, and a new capacity to
2 **discern the will of God.** This section on *Christian behaviour* is logically
1 entailed by Paul's analysis of salvation. And so he begins, **Therefore, my**
brothers . . .

The chapter consists of specific moral instructions, delivered with that
particular authority which Paul believed he possessed by virtue of his
3 apostleship (**the gift that God in his grace has given me**). Some of these
instructions were evoked by the special needs of the Christian church. We
know from 1 Corinthians 12 how the 'gifts of the Spirit' (some of them
newly inspired, others a new intensification of existing talents), though they
were one of the marks of an authentic church, tended to lead to rivalry and
disorder. In his first letter to Corinth, Paul had worked out his answer (which
5 is only hinted at here) in terms of being **united with Christ** to **form one**
body. The gifts are to be exercised in the service of all; there is no superiority
3 of one over another; the only criterion of an individual's worth is **the**
measure of faith that God has dealt to each. It makes no difference if
6 some of the 'gifts' are obviously God-given, like **the gift of inspired**
utterance, while others belong to the routine of life, like *diakonia* (here
7 somewhat misleadingly translated **administration**: it means anything from
technical Christian "deaconship" to specific services performed by some
members of the community for others). Whatever they are, they must be
exercised single-mindedly, without pretension.

But by no means all these sentences express a uniquely Christian insight.
Four of them can be found in the Old Testament; three of these are in
16–19 Proverbs (**Care as much about each other as about yourselves**:
3.7; **Let your aims be such as all men count honourable**: 3.4; **If your**
enemy is hungry . . .: 25.21), and the fourth (**Justice is mine . . .**) in
Deuteronomy (32.35). The church did not create an entirely new moral code: it endorsed much that was already well known to both Greeks and Jews. The second half of this chapter is a Christian variation on a theme which Paul's readers, whatever their background, must have heard many times before.

Continuing to propound his code of behaviour, Paul turns to relationships

with the world outside the Christian community. **Every person must** 13. 1
submit to the supreme authorities. Had the Roman Christians been particularly unruly or uncooperative? Or was civil obedience simply one of the standard sub-headings of the Christian moral code? We do not know. But there is no reason to doubt that, until at least the persecution of Nero some 15 years after the date of this letter, the Roman administration had done nothing which would particularly antagonize the Christians; indeed, at this period the main adversary was usually the local Jewish community, and the narrative of Acts shows the Christians often invoking the protection of the Roman government against Jewish attacks. So Paul, somewhat in the manner
of a Stoic philosopher, argues that the authority of the state is a **divine** 2
institution. We do not know how many Jews would have shared his opinion. Philo of Alexandria would probably have been prepared to do so; but inevitably the Jews we hear about most are those who (especially inside Palestine) fanatically opposed the Roman régime. The evidence of the New Testament and of early Christian literature shows consistently that the Christians were deliberately law-abiding; and we observe that Paul takes it
for granted that the Roman Christians **pay taxes**—an aspect of civil obedi- 6
ence towards which their attitude may well have been modelled on that of Jesus himself (Mark 12.13–17).

Obligations towards the state lead into obligations towards society in
general: one's **neighbour.** It was a well-known speculation of learned Jews, 8
how the law could be **summed up.** Jesus, we know, took part in this specula- 9
tion, and reached his own conclusion: love of God, and love of neighbour. Paul, in this context of social behaviour, quotes only the second part of this. All law, so far as it affects society, can be **summed up in the one rule, 'Love your neighbour as yourself'.** If he had wished to summarize the whole of the Ten Commandments, he would doubtless have added "Thou shalt love the Lord thy God".

All this moral admonition has proceeded logically from the argument of chapters 5–8. For good measure, Paul adds a motive for good conduct which was doubtless (as it has been ever since) a more commonplace one in the church than Paul's highly sophisticated reasoning: the nearness of the End.
It is far on in the night; day is near. One might have expected the urgency 12
of this challenge to have decreased as the years passed; yet throughout the New Testament period the same call is sounded again and again: "The end is at hand . . . therefore be sober and alert". Paul is here adopting one of the distinctive notes of Christian moral teaching. Nevertheless, at the end of the
chapter he returns to his deeper argument: **Let Christ Jesus himself be** 14
the armour that you wear—literally, "Put on Jesus, the Christ", which is more than a metaphor: it recalls the language of Christian baptism (Galatians 3.27), a rite which (as has been shown in chapter 6) carries profound ethical consequences.

There were numerous potential sources of friction in a mixed Jewish–gentile community. In particular, full table-fellowship was hard to achieve. A Jewish Christian might now find himself sitting down at table with non-Jews whose meat would certainly not have been slaughtered in the correct Jewish fashion (it might even be pork!). Moreover there was always the danger, for both parties, that any meat bought in the market might be part of an animal which had been sacrificed to a pagan god—and many found it difficult not to feel somehow implicated in pagan worship if this were the case (see below on 1 Corinthians 8). Some members of the community (doubtless mainly Jews) seem to have resolved the difficulty by becoming vegetarians and abstaining from meat altogether, unable to put their consciences or their deeply inbred
14. 2 prejudices to rest in any other way; whereas those who had **faith enough**
(doubtless mainly Gentiles, though some Jews may have come to share Paul's indifference to these matters) ate **all kinds of food.** And similar scruples—or perhaps plain asceticism—seem to have led to different views
21 about **drinking wine.**

A further complication was the observance of religious festivals. One of the main characteristics of a Jewish community, and one of the first things demanded of any Gentile who wished to be associated with it, was the observance of certain **days**—that is to say, the Sabbath and certain annual festivals. Simply by becoming a Christian, a Jew did not necessarily feel himself to be released from such observances; on the other hand, he could
5 no longer regard them as a matter of mechanical obligation. Rather, **every-**
one should have reached conviction in his own mind. The problem was, how could a Jew who conscientiously felt it right to continue such observances live peaceably within a Christian community in fellowship with non-Jews who recognized no such observances?

It seems that the more emancipated section of the community were
2 showing impatience towards those who (in their eyes at least) were **weaker,**
that is, more scrupulous. In principle, Paul was perfectly prepared to agree
14 with them. **I am absolutely convinced, as a Christian, that nothing is**
impure in itself: this was a Christian conviction which probably went back to Jesus himself (Mark 7.17–23)[a] and was of great importance in the early history of the church (Acts 10.15). But it was also true (and too easily overlooked) that **if a man considers a particular thing impure, then to him it is impure.** There were powerful psychological factors involved which meant that those who were fully emancipated must be prepared to show consideration to those who could not yet bring themselves to share the same freedom. Paul urges them to show more consideration on several grounds. (i) Both traditional observances and freedom from such traditions

[a] If the alternative rendering given in the NEB footnote (Second Edition) is correct, Paul is actually referring to some saying of Jesus similar to that recorded in Mark.

may be practised **for the Lord.** A man who observes a Sabbath is bound to 8
have **the Lord in mind in doing so** (for this is the whole point of the 6
Sabbath). Everyone's meal, whether meat is eaten or renounced, is preceded
by the saying of grace—giving **thanks to God**—and this too means that both
he who eats meat and he who abstains from meat **has the Lord in mind.**
Every detail of living can be dedicated to God in this way. If the effect of
Christ dying was that we can even **die for the Lord,** it follows that we must 8
be able to **live for the Lord** in every detail of our lives, whatever religious
customs and traditions we observe. (ii) It is the plain duty of Christians to 10–13
cease judging one another: this is illustrated here by a composite quota- 13
tion from Isaiah 49.18 and 45.23, and Paul may also have had Jesus' words 11
in mind (Matthew 7.1), 'Pass no judgement, and you will not be judged'.
(iii) **The kingdom of God is not eating and drinking,** which was perhaps 17
not quite so obvious to a Jewish believer as it seems to us, since the Jews
were accustomed to visualizing the age to come as a heavenly banquet, for
which the careful purity of their present meals was an essential preparation.
(iv) All such matters must be subservient to that which will **build up** 19
the common life (*oikodomē*, "building up", an important word in Paul's
understanding of the church, see below on 1 Corinthians 14.2–5). (v) Either
course may be right so long as it is followed with **conviction.** A man who has 22
doubts whether or not a religious obligation is binding is without **conviction.**
In Greek, this is the same word as "faith": and since (as Paul has been
arguing) it is only through faith that men are rescued from sin, it follows
that **anything which does not arise from conviction** (i.e. faith) **is sin.** 23
(vi) Finally, an example has been given us by Christ, who **did not consider** **15.** 3
himself. Christ's whole tenor of life fulfilled a pattern adumbrated in such
passages of the Old Testament as Psalm 69.9, '**The reproaches of those**
who reproached thee fell upon me'. The righteous sufferer of that psalm,
in his agonized complaint to God, found that even his religion was being held
against him by his enemies. These words had come true with startling accuracy in the story of Christ. Such a notable fulfilment of one prophecy (and
of the many others which seemed to prefigure the events of Christ's life)
could only mean that all the other promises contained in Scripture would
shortly be fulfilled. This was the source of a Christian's **encouragement** when 5
he studied the Old Testament, this was one of the grounds of his **fortitude.** 4

But in so far as all these problems sprang from the basic difficulty of Jews
and non-Jews accepting one another as religious equals and living in a single
community without prejudice, the ultimate solution could only be found on
the level of the main argument of the letter. Part of the work of Christ was
to maintain the truth of God by making good his promises to the 8
patriarchs—the Jews were not to be abandoned (chapters 9–11); but **at the** 9
same time to give the Gentiles cause to glorify God for his mercy by
giving them a promise of salvation 'quite independently of the law' (chapters

11 1–4). It was the old vision come true: **Gentiles, make merry together**
12 **with his own people** (Deuteronomy 32.43; Paul goes on to quote Psalm
18.49; 117.1; Isaiah 11.1,10). The greatest spur to agreeing in lesser matters
was the great purpose that God was working out for both peoples together.
7 **In a word, accept one another as Christ accepted us.**

14 **My friends.** The letter suddenly becomes personal. Paul is evidently aware
that he may have used more forceful language than would be warranted by
15 the real state of affairs at Rome. **I have written to refresh your memory**—
the sentence sounds deliberately apologetic. Of course the Christians at
14 Rome were people **well able to give advice to one another**; but Paul,
15 **in virtue of the gift I have from God,** was able to speak to them with an
authority which none of them could claim for themselves; and moreover, this apostleship of his, with its special commission to the Gentiles, made it peculiarly incumbent on him to address himself to the problems of churches with a substantial gentile membership.

No one, after having read the narrative in Acts, would question the
19 statement that Paul's apostleship had been exercised **by word and deed, by**
the force of miraculous signs and by the power of the Holy Spirit.
But what of the next sentence? **From Jerusalem as far round as Illyricum.**
The part of the world in fact covered by Paul's preaching (so far as we know from Acts and from his own letters) can be seen on the map. Jerusalem (which he had visited several times since his conversion) and Illyricum represent the geographical limits of his work; but in what sense, after merely having evangelized a few cities and territories in the intervening area, could
he be said to have **completed the preaching of the gospel,** so much so
23 that he had **no further scope in these parts?** Not, clearly, in an exhaustive
geographical sense. The explanation is probably more theoretical. Jesus had said that 'before the end the Gospel must be proclaimed to all nations' (Mark 13.10). Yet in the first century the end was expected quite soon; therefore the proclamation to all nations must have been understood somewhat symbolically: so long as there had been some preaching in each province of the empire, Jesus' prophecy would be deemed to have been fulfilled. Paul may even have thought that the completion of his own preaching at representative points throughout the civilized world would help to bring about the end—hence his determination to reach Spain, which
was regarded as the westernmost part of the world (though there is no
19 certain evidence that he ever succeeded in doing so). In any case, **I have**
completed the preaching of the gospel is probably intended less as
a claim to have covered a continent than as a statement that his work
had advanced the world-wide progress of the gospel **as far round as**
20 **Illyricum.** Paul had never felt it to be his task to **build on another**
man's foundation. The pattern of his own pioneering work was laid

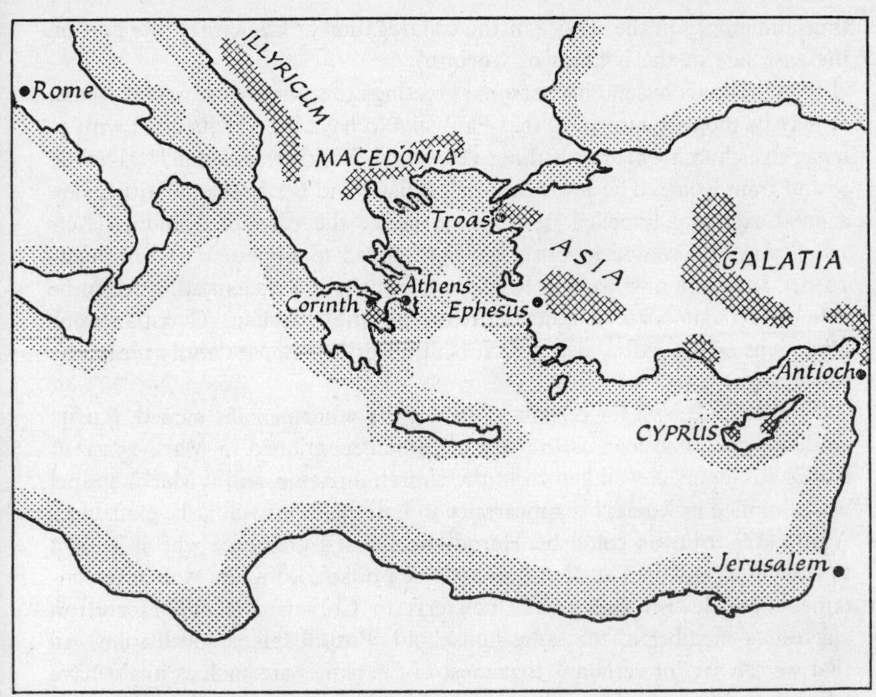

down for him in a prophecy of Isaiah (52.15) which Paul clearly felt was 21
being fulfilled each time he brought the Gospel to a place where it had not been heard before.

But meanwhile he had to complete a task which had occupied him for
some years: the raising of money for **the poor among God's people at** 26
Jerusalem. On this collection, which is mentioned in most of Paul's letters, see especially below on 2 Corinthians 8. It seems that by the time Romans was written the collection had reached a point at which Paul could make plans to deliver the proceeds to Jerusalem in person (which is what the rather
puzzling expression **under my own seal** must amount to). 28

The last paragraph of the section throws a little light on Paul's relations with Jerusalem. The later part of Acts makes it clear that Paul had much to
fear from **unbelievers in Judaea**; but he evidently felt some anxiety also 31
about his reception by the Jerusalem church.

Letters of commendation were as common in the ancient world as they are
now. Paul here commends a certain Phoebe, **who holds office**—that is, she **16.** 1
is a *diakonos*, a word which may already be a technical term, meaning in this case "deaconess" (though the existence of deaconesses at this early period cannot be proved), or may simply be a way of saying that she has given of her

time and money in the service of the congregation at Cenchreae (the port on the east side of the isthmus of Corinth).

Paul proceeds to send his personal greetings to some individuals at Rome. It may be thought surprising that Paul should have been acquainted with so many in a church which he had not yet visited. But there was much travelling
3 to and from Rome. The Jewish couple, **Prisca** and her husband **Aquila,** are
a good example. Expelled from Rome under the edict of Claudius (Acts 18.2), they had settled in Corinth, then moved to Ephesus (1 Corinthians 16.19), and were now back in Rome, apparently in sufficient affluence to be
5 able to accommodate a **congregation at their house** (Christian con-
gregations continued to meet for worship in private houses until at least the third century).

13 Nothing is known for certain of any of the other persons named. **Rufus**
could be the same man as the son of Simon mentioned in Mark 15.21: if Rufus was a person well known to the church in Rome, and if Mark's gospel was compiled in Rome, his appearance in both passages would be explained.
10 Again, **Aristobulus** could be Herod the Great's grandson who is known
to have lived and died at Rome, and whose **household** might well have con-
11 tained both Jewish and gentile converts to Christianity; and **Herodion**
suggests a member of the same household. But all this is speculation. All that we can say for certain is that most of the names are such as might have
9 been met with in any Greco-Roman society, though some (such as **Stachys)**
12, 15 are rare ones; many of them are typical slaves' names **(Persis, Philologus)**;
and the list suggests a socially mixed and cosmopolitan society such as one would expect the church in Rome (though not necessarily only in Rome) to
7 have been. Within it Paul recognizes two **apostles,** both Jews, one with a
Greek name **(Andronicus)** and the other, like Paul, with a Roman name **(Junias,** unless it is Junia, but a woman seems less likely in the context). Evidently he could use the word "apostle" in a wider sense than that implied in the early chapters of Acts (where it denotes one of the Twelve); these two became Christians even before Paul himself, and may have been responsible for the first bringing of the Gospel to Rome.

16 **Greet one another with the kiss of peace.** Literally, "a holy kiss".
But the "kiss of peace" formed part of Christian worship as early as the mid-second century, and may have already been customary in Paul's time. Paul's letters were probably intended to be read to the assembled congregation immediately before the celebration of the eucharist; and this expression may well have been an allusion to a solemn **kiss of peace** which the hearers of the letter were about to exchange with one another.

17–20 After a very direct and personal piece of advice—inspired perhaps by some
specific and disquieting information received from Rome—Paul associates
21 some of his friends with his closest greetings. **Timothy** was one of his most
constant companions; and of his fellow-countrymen, **Lucius** may be the

Lucius of Cyrene of Acts 13.1; **Sosipater** the Sopater of Acts 20.4; and **Jason** the Jason of Acts 17.5–9—but none of these identifications is certain.
Gaius is doubtless the Corinthian of 1 Corinthians 1.14; **Erastus** was 23
evidently an influential person.

The final paragraph sums up much of the argument of the letter in the form of an ascription of praise to God (as in 1.25; 9.5; 11.33); it refers to a
revelation implicit down the ages, but **now disclosed**, in a manner which 25
embraces **all nations**, Jews and non-Jews alike. But it is not certain that it 26
originally formed part of the letter; if one may judge by the style, it may not even be from the hand of Paul. In some manuscripts it occurs at the end of chapter 14, in some at the end of chapter 15, and in some it is omitted altogether. The curious variations in the manuscript tradition over where and how the letter should end (see the footnotes in NEB) suggest that the letter may have existed from the beginning in more than one version, and even (since some manuscripts omit the words 'in Rome' in 1.7,15) that it may have been originally intended for some Christian community other than Rome—possibly Ephesus. But it is also possible that the manuscript tradition suffered derangement at an early stage. In any case there is no serious reason to doubt the traditional view that the letter was destined, at least in the first instance, for the church in Rome.

THE FIRST LETTER OF PAUL TO THE CORINTHIANS

The founding of the church at Corinth by Paul is described in Acts 18; and in Acts 19 it is recorded that Paul subsequently spent some months at Ephesus. These two chapters provide the background of THE FIRST LETTER OF PAUL TO THE CORINTHIANS. The letter was written by Paul from Ephesus (16.8) a certain time after his first visit to Corinth, and deals with a number of practical issues (though such issues often had theological implications) which had arisen there since his departure. But the present letter was not by any means the beginning of the correspondence. Paul had already had occasion to write to the Corinthians once before (5.9), and had received a letter from them (7.1). He had also received information from members of the Corinthian congregation who had visited him at Ephesus (1.11; 16.17). Our FIRST LETTER is therefore Paul's second letter to the Corinthians, and contains both a reply to their letter to him and some comments on the information which he had received. Much of the difficulty of interpreting this letter lies in the fact that we do not possess the earlier stages of the correspondence; it is not always easy to see precisely what questions, complaints or difficulties Paul is answering.

The first six chapters are concerned mainly with some serious matters of *Unity and order in the church* which Paul had heard about through his informants. The remaining chapters appear to answer, one by one, points made by the Corinthians in their letter to Paul.

Unity and order in the church

The opening of the letter, as in Romans, follows the conventional form:
1.1 **From Paul . . . to the congregation of God's people at Corinth . . .**
Grace and peace. But as usual Paul makes this conventional framework
carry a good deal of distinctively Christian matter. In Romans, he adds a long
parenthesis concerning his own apostleship. Here, he is content with only a
brief statement about himself, and inserts instead some words about the
Corinthians, emphasizing two things: that they are not a self-appointed con-
2 gregation, but owe their existence and "dedication" (the word **dedicated** is
perhaps an allusion to their baptism) entirely to the fact that God has called
them (or **claimed** them, as the NEB renders it); and that they are not an
isolated group, but just one part of the universal fellowship of Christians. Paul

also associates with himself as a **colleague** (the Greek word is the same as that usually translated "brother") a certain **Sosthenes**, who appears in Acts 18.17 as a prominent Corinthian Jew.

The greeting is followed by the usual thanksgiving for the state of the church which is being addressed. The Corinthians' conduct comes under a good deal of criticism in the course of the letter; but this does not affect the
fact that they have undoubtedly received great **enrichment** by their con- 5
version, not only intellectually in **knowledge** and in giving **expression** to
that knowledge, but also with regard to their remarkable "gifts". **There is** 7
indeed no single gift you lack—and the word means, not self-cultivated talents and virtues, but those altogether exceptional powers which proceed from the possession of God's Spirit, and which (as we can see from chapters 12–14) were a striking feature of the Corinthian congregation. This enrichment was both **confirmation** of the reality of their faith, and a source of 6
confidence that they would be **without reproach on the Day of our Lord** 8
Jesus—a Day not only of glory but of judgement; and Paul, at least when he wrote this letter, confidently expected this Day to dawn in his own lifetime.

There was no doubt, then, of the Corinthians' gifts; but equally, their present conduct showed serious deficiencies, and Paul begins in a tone of
severity: **I appeal to you.** He has been informed that there are **divisions** 10
and **quarrels** in the Corinthian congregation—at least, that is how he regards 11
the fact (even if the Corinthians did not think it so serious) that the names Paul, Apollos, Cephas and Christ were being used as some kind of party labels. The Corinthians will have known at once what he was referring to;
for us, it has to be guesswork. We have no other evidence that **Cephas** (which 12
is how Paul normally refers to Simon Peter) ever visited Corinth, though equally we cannot say that he did not. **Apollos**, on the other hand, was certainly a well-known person there (3.6; 16.12), and Acts (18.24—19.1) gives this information about him: that he was a scholarly Alexandrian Jew, that he was associated with John the Baptist before he became a Christian, and that he carried on the work of preaching in Corinth after Paul had left. What sort of groups or parties these men could have given their names or their support to, and why another group called themselves **Christ's**, are questions which the names alone do not enable us to answer. But something may be learnt from the way Paul approaches the matter.

Paul does not take the side of any of these groups against the others—not even the one which bears his own name—but instead attacks the whole idea of a divided congregation. Possibly one source of division lay in the circumstances of each convert's baptism: they were attaching importance to the person by whom they had been baptized or the group which had received them at their baptism. If so, Paul could demonstrate the futility of such a distinction by the fact that he personally (even though one of the parties bore his name) did no baptizing—or at least, only in a very few cases, such as

Stephanas and his family, who were among his first converts (16.15). Our
17 second clue is that Paul himself had preached **without relying on the
language of worldly wisdom**; and since the next chapters are devoted to
an attack on this **worldly wisdom** in the light of the Gospel, it is a fair
inference that the **divisions**, whatever the exact significance of the individual
names they bore, were created by too much reliance on different intellectual
formulations of the truth—rather in the manner of the schools of philosophy
which proliferated in cultured Greek cities such as Athens and Corinth.

18 In any case, Paul's concern is to show that the **doctrine of the cross**
supersedes the trivial distinctions which are the essence of **worldly wisdom.**
He uses three arguments.

23 First, look at the doctrine itself—**Christ nailed to the cross.** The learn-
22 ing of the Jews could make nothing of this: **Jews call for miracles,** a
miraculously powerful Messiah, not a crucified one; and so the cross could
23 be only **a stumbling-block** in the way of believing that Jesus was the
22 promised Christ. Equally, for Greeks, who **look for wisdom** (that is to say,
who expect to find the truth expressed in philosophical terms), the claim that
the divine nature could be revealed in an ignominious execution was obvi-
23 ously **folly.** Such a doctrine, in short, did not fit the presuppositions of any
24 intellectual system; yet it was known, **to those who have heard his call,**
to be an authentic revelation of God. Christ, who by any ordinary standard
was a spectacle of weakness and folly, was empirically known by Christians
to be **the power of God and the wisdom of God.** This was God's way of
21 saving the world, not random but **ordained** in God's own wisdom, not
19 unprepared but foretold in a prophecy of Isaiah (29.14). The period of **the
wise** and **the clever** (and these words of Isaiah are probably taken by Paul
as pointing to both the Greek philosophers and the Jewish scholars of his own
20 day) was that of the present **passing age,** which all Jews knew would ultimately be superseded by a more glorious age, but which Christians believed
had only a brief time still to run before the imminent Day of the Lord.

Secondly, look at the intellectual calibre of the Corinthian Christians. If
the doctrine of the cross had been principally an intellectual discovery, the
congregation would hardly have consisted from the beginning of such
undistinguished members as in fact it did. And if it was not because of their
27 own distinction that God had **chosen** them, but rather the reverse, then the
important theological point follows (which, in the original, Paul expresses in
29 a striking Old Testament idiom): **there is no place for human pride in
the presence of God.** The Corinthian Christians have nothing of their own
30 to be proud of. Not only their new **righteousness** (in the specifically
Christian sense expounded in, for instance, Romans 3.21–8), their "consecration" (probably again their baptism) and their freedom, but even their
only true **wisdom,** proceeds from Christ. He is their only source of pride,
the only thing they have to boast of. And since Christ now bears the same

title as the "Lord" of the Old Testament, the words of Jeremiah are appropriate: **'If a man must boast, let him boast of the Lord'** (Jeremiah 31
9.23–4, somewhat freely quoted).

Thirdly, look at Paul himself and the manner of his original preaching. He
had voluntarily renounced all **subtle arguments,** he had made no show of 2.4
rhetoric, and his bearing, far from being confident and persuasive, had been nervous and unsure. There had been nothing that could have made any appeal on the level of worldly wisdom; if Paul **carried conviction,** it could
have been only on the level of the spirit, **the power of God.** 5

The kind of philosophical **wisdom,** therefore, on which the Corinthian Christians were priding themselves and which (we may suppose) was the reason for their divisions, was no qualification for receiving the 'doctrine of the cross'. Yet the word **wisdom** itself was not thereby made obsolete. In the later books of the Old Testament, "wisdom" had assumed great importance as an almost personified attribute of God: it had been present at the creation of the world, it provided a clue both to the pattern of the universe and to the correct ordering of moral behaviour (see especially Job 28; Proverbs 7–9; Ecclesiasticus 24). Furthermore, one of the presuppositions of the many secret pagan rites which flourished in Paul's time was that there existed a secret and esoteric "wisdom" accessible only to initiates (and the
technical Greek word for these initiates occurs here, translated **those who** 6
are ripe for it). In this realm of ideas, Christianity was also a kind of wisdom
—**God's hidden wisdom, his secret purpose**—but not (Paul hastens to 7
add) a wisdom of the ordinary philosophical kind (which would be a **wisdom** 6
belonging to this passing age), nor even a more psychic and esoteric wisdom to do with those demonic powers which were widely believed to influence the course of the world and its rulers (Paul here calls them the
powers that rule the world)[a]—for these very powers had been on the 7
wrong side (so to speak) at the time of the crucifixion, and no wisdom about them could have much to do with God. Yet a kind of wisdom it was, as
Scripture itself had promised (it is not clear whether Paul's quotation is a 9
rough paraphrase of, say, Isaiah 64.4, or is drawn from some lost apocryphal
writing); and it was **revealed,** not through philosophy, the rites of mystery 10
religions, or psychic investigation, but **through the Spirit.**

The point is reinforced by an argument that is partly philosophical, partly psychological. It was a commonly accepted philosophical maxim that among conscious beings only like knows like. In the case of men, only man's
consciousness (here called, for the purpose of the argument, **man's own** 11
spirit) can know **what a man is.** In the case of God, **only the Spirit of God knows what God is.** Man's consciousness, or **spirit,** cannot know

[a] This expression could also mean simply the political rulers, such as the Emperor or Pontius Pilate. But it was a common belief that supernatural powers stood behind temporal rulers. See below, pp. 794–5.

what God is, and no amount of human "wisdom" will help him to do so.
13 But Christians now have a way out of this. They have received **the Spirit,**
that very same Spirit of God which knows what God is; or (to put it in more
16 psychological language) by virtue of their union with Christ they **possess**
the mind of Christ, which gives them insight into the nature of God. Their
13 language about God consequently owes nothing to **human wisdom** (for it
comes **by the Spirit**), and is not subject to human judgement. If a Christian
15 is criticized **by his fellow-men** for his presumption in claiming such know-
16 ledge, and if he is attacked with the scornful words of Isaiah (40.13), '**Who**
knows the mind of the Lord? Who can advise him?', he can answer
that what could be said of the "Lord" of the Old Testament can now be said
of Christ, and—**we possess the mind of Christ.**

3. 1 Christian "wisdom", then, is the possession of those **who have the Spirit.**
But having the Spirit is not only manifested in wisdom, it is manifested also
3 in moral behaviour; and the **jealousy** and **strife** which Paul had heard
about were quite incompatible with this. Such behaviour meant that, far
from being motivated by the Spirit, they were living on the **purely human**
1 **level.** So Paul could not address them as **people who have the Spirit.** The
2 **solid food** of real wisdom was too advanced for them, and Paul had to give
them weaker stuff. Or else (for this is another possible meaning of the Greek
and yields a more logical interpretation) the single-minded concentration
and 'spiritual power' of Paul's original preaching (as described above in
3 2.4–5) was understood by them only **on the merely natural plane,** and so
2 turned out to be no more than **milk to drink, instead of solid food.**

What then of Apollos, Paul, and perhaps others who had influence in the
church at Corinth? If they were not to be party leaders, what was their true
5 rôle? Paul's answer is: essentially subordinate. **We are simply God's**
agents—literally, "deacons", men who have some kind of service to perform. Paul gives two analogies, both quite conventional:[a] gardening and
building. In either case the actual gardeners or builders are not important:
7 all that matters is who gives the growth (**God**), or what the foundation is
11 (**Jesus Christ himself**).

10 Not that this makes the agents' work any less responsible. **Let each take**
care how he builds. The quality of each builder's work will be exposed at
13 the **day of judgement**; and the conventional Jewish imagery of **fire**
associated with the day of judgement is now worked into the building metaphor (even though it does not quite harmonize in every detail). Yet even the
15 poor builder, though all his work may be lost, **will escape with his life** (for
his failure does not exclude him from the company of those who are saved).
On the other hand, there is another side to this building metaphor. It was a

[a] Compare Jeremiah 1.9–10. "Behold I have put my words in your mouth. See I have set you . . . to build and to plant." Paul had this passage much in mind: Galatians 1.15.

Christian commonplace that the church is a new, "spiritual" temple. So
anyone who destroys this building (or begins to destroy it, as the Greek 17
could also mean) will receive, at the same judgement, a far severer sentence—
a hint which brings Paul back to the subject of those who are causing divisions
in Corinth.

Anyone, therefore, who **fancies himself wise** must not merely abandon 18
his philosophical pretensions to eminence in the Christian congregation; if
he is to **gain true wisdom,** he must learn to deem himself what, as a
philosopher, he most despised—**a fool.** Verses from Job (5.13) and a psalm 19, 20
(97.11), though originally directed more against the cunning and the unscrupulous than against the philosopher, are pressed into service to reinforce
the point. Equally, the congregation as a whole must learn where to place
their allegiance: **never make mere men a cause for pride.** 21

Another consequence of the 'divisions' in Corinth was that the Corinthians
inevitably found themselves comparing one leader with another; and it
sounds as if adverse judgements had been passed on Paul. But again, if Paul
and other prominent men in the church are God's 'agents'—you might
call them **subordinates** or **stewards**—then the only person who can call **4.** 1
them to account is their employer, and the only standard by which they will
be judged is whether or not they have been **trustworthy.** Any human 2
judgement at this stage is premature: the divine judgement, the coming of 5
the Lord, is not far off.

All this does not merely concern the apostle Paul and his principal deputy
in Corinth, Apollos. These two are taken only as examples. The principle
that no member of the congregation has any reason to put himself forward
as having special gifts of his own (**What do you possess that was not** 7
given to you?) applies to everyone, and is illustrated by what appears to
have been a proverb. Unfortunately we no longer know what the proverb
meant. The NEB makes a guess at it with the translation, '**keep within the** 6
rules'.

Yet another side-effect of these divisions is that the various party-leaders
derive respect, power, and perhaps even material advantages from their
position. Paul's tone is ironical, and he may be exaggerating the sense of
superiority felt by these men; nevertheless, they offer a poignant contrast
to himself and his real fellow-workers. Not only does Paul's work bring him
insult and deprivation; it brings him an opportunity (which is denied to the
proud Corinthian leaders) of penetrating into the meaning of Christian
discipleship. For curses he returns blessings; for persecution, submission; for 12
slander, words of persuasion and consolation.[a] Such a comparison might 13
well make the Corinthians ashamed; but this is not Paul's main purpose. He
puts himself forward as an **example**, not of superior virtue or asceticism, 16

[*a*] For a classic description of this, see Psalm 35.11–14. The NEB translation, **we humbly make our appeal,** does not quite convey this.

but of the relationship which should hold between 'God's agents' and the
17 congregation. Paul's **way of life in Christ** is not a reference to his own
moral excellence, but to the humble status and rewards which any church
leader should expect to have, and which Paul is trying to establish **in all our congregations.**

The actual situation in the Corinthian church must have been in flagrant
conflict with these principles; and Paul urges them to reform. He bases his
15 appeal on the unique relationship which he has with them, that of **father** as
opposed to **tutor** (on which see below on Galatians 3.24); and he is also
17 sending his most trusted fellow-worker, **Timothy,** to see to the matter in
person. In any case he is confident that the contrast he imagines between
20 himself and the Corinthian leaders, and the **power** which belongs to his own
gifts and authority, will be apparent the moment he is present among them.
It belongs to a 'father' to bring to his children, not only **love and a gentle**
spirit, but (if their conduct deserves it) the **rod** of discipline. It is for them
21 to **choose** which side of their father's nature they wish to see when they
confront him in person.

5. 1 **I actually hear reports.** Divisions and quarrels were only a part of the
disquieting news brought to Paul by his informants. There had also been a
serious case of **sexual immorality.** Both Jewish law (Leviticus 18.8) and
Roman law forbade a man to marry his stepmother; yet the Corinthian
Christians, perhaps mistakenly thinking themselves above the law, were
complacently tolerating such a relationship in their midst. Paul, without
pausing to give reasons why this state of affairs was as unlawful for them as
for anyone else, sternly lays down the procedure to be followed. There can
be no possible reason for hesitation or further delay (in view, say, of alleged
3 mitigating circumstances): **my judgement upon the man who did this**
thing is already given. A solemn assembly of the whole congregation, with
4 an invocation of **the name** and **the power of our Lord Jesus,** must pass
sentence of excommunication; and at that time it seems to have been believed
that exclusion from the church would be followed inevitably by sickness and
5 death (to be inflicted by **Satan,** to use a turn of phrase current since the
Book of Job). This punishment sounds extreme, but in fact it was held to
be the lesser of two evils. The day of judgement was believed to be imminent;
soon it would be too late. Once dead, and his sin punished, a man might still
qualify for the resurrection-life of the **spirit** promised to all Christians;
whereas if he were still alive when the day of judgement came, he would be
classed with 'those on their way to ruin' (1.18).

So much for the sake of the offender. But this act of excommunication was
equally necessary for the church, which might otherwise be corrupted by
the presence of the offender in its midst. A familiar proverb makes the point
6 well enough: **'A little leaven leavens all the dough'**; but Paul develops

the **leaven** idea into a piece of complex Christian imagery. A possible
metaphor for describing the saving work of Christ was furnished by the
Passover. Christ, who was crucified at Passover time, could be seen as the
Passover **sacrifice**, and the Christian life could be described as observing 7
the Passover festival. But—to carry the metaphor still further—the Jewish
Passover festival opened a period when only unleavened bread was eaten.
All the old leaven had to be cleared out and a completely fresh start made in
baking (for, during the rest of the year, a scrap of dough from a previous
baking would be used to leaven the new dough). In the same way, the
Christian "Passover festival" must be observed by making a clean break
from **the leaven of corruption and wickedness.** 8

This leads Paul to mention a point which had come up earlier in the
correspondence. In a previous letter Paul had written that they **must have** 9
nothing to do with loose livers. This had been (perhaps deliberately)
misunderstood by the Corinthians. They had replied that, unless they got
out of the world altogether, they could not possibly avoid such people.
Paul now explains what he meant: he was not talking about the citizens of
Corinth in general, but about people who claimed to be Christians. No such
person must be admitted within the congregation—**you should not even** 11
eat with any such person (which may refer to ordinary social gatherings,
or else, possibly, to the Lord's Supper). An injunction that was frequently
laid upon the Israelite community is in this sense applicable to a Christian
congregation: **Root out the evil-doer from your community** (Deutero- 13
nomy 13.5 and elsewhere).

Paul had also heard of another moral lapse.

Must brother go to law with brother—and before unbelievers? Both **6.** 6
in Jewish communities of the dispersion, and also in some of the religious and
other unofficial societies which abounded in the Greek-speaking world, it
was normal for disputes to be settled within the community, without recourse
to official courts. By taking each other (their own "brothers") to law,
Christians were falling below the standards even of other societies; and
this was all the more inexcusable in that, at the imminent day of judgement,
they were destined to have a place on the tribunal, as it were, with Christ—
to judge the world. And not only the world: since, with Christ, they would 2
have a place superior to all lesser beings, they were even destined **to judge** 3
angels. On these grounds alone, the Christians' conduct was reprehensible;
but Paul characteristically treats the matter on a deeper level. The whole
idea of **going to law with one another** is far **below your standard.** It is 7
the exact opposite of the way Christians should behave to one another. Why 7
not rather suffer injury? Furthermore, any such dispute in court will end
in a verdict being given. One side or the other (even if both are Christians)
will be pronounced **unjust**; and anyone who publicly places himself in one 9

of the traditional categories of wrongdoers[a] will inevitably incur the tradi-
10 tional penalty (failure to **possess the kingdom of God).** It is true that
there are Christians who have once been such people, but who now, by
virtue of their faith, can nevertheless expect to possess the kingdom. But this
is no argument for doing evil now. Such people, since their wrong-doing,
11 **have been through the purifying waters**—they have received baptism
and are enjoying all the tremendous consequences which flow from it: they
have been both **dedicated** and **justified.**
12 **'I am free to do anything'.** These are the next words in the Greek; and
since a Greek manuscript had no quotation marks we cannot be sure who is
speaking. The NEB is probably right to take this as a slogan used by the
Corinthians to justify their behaviour. If so, we reach here the root cause of
the Corinthians' conduct. Christianity is indeed much concerned with freedom—for instance (in Paul's time), freedom from the restraints of the Jewish
12 ceremonial law; and Paul had no wish to deny the truth of the slogan (**no
doubt I am free).** At the same time, Christians have to guard against their
freedom turning into a new slavery to baser things (**I for one will not let
anything make free with me).** Or take another of the Corinthians'
13 slogans: **'Food is for the belly and the belly for food'.** True; neither
food nor belly has much religious importance, and the slogan was a useful
one to employ against religions such as Judaism which insisted on elaborate
food laws. But again, the slogan could be easily misused. If it was intended
so generally that everything to do with the body was regarded as unimportant,
13 or merely **for lust,** then not only did it become a spurious pretext for the
kind of behaviour the Corinthians had been indulging in, but it contradicted
a vital Christian principle. For Christians, the body is far from unimportant:
13 **it is for the Lord.** For

(i) The resurrection, which has already taken place in Christ, and which is
14 promised to all believers (**he will also raise us**), is a resurrection of the body.

(ii) The union of Christians with Christ is not to be understood in a
15 rarefied spiritual or mystical sense, but quite physically: **your bodies are
limbs and organs of Christ.** So much so, that Christians have a new and
powerful reason to shun one of the sins which were most sternly condemned
18, 16 in Jewish ethics: **fornication.** The words in Genesis (2.24), **'The pair shall
become one flesh',** were often interpreted by Jewish scholars (as well as by
Jesus himself—see above on Mark 10.1–12) in a very far-reaching sense,
according to which it was held that sexual intercourse makes two people
physically one. In this sense, fornication affects the body in a way no other
18 sin does: **the fornicator sins against his own body.** And since a Christian's body is united with Christ's body, it follows that for him fornication
is a sin against Christ himself.

[a] On these more or less conventional lists of virtues and vices, see below on Galatians 5, p. 615.

(iii) Not only is the community a temple of the Spirit (3.16), but so also is the individual Christian. And since it was impossible for anyone educated as a Jew to make any distinction (as a Greek might do) between "body" and "soul"—in the Hebrew idiom, an individual could not be conceived of
apart from his body—it followed that a Christian's body is **a shrine of the** 19
indwelling Holy Spirit.

Christians were **bought at a price.** The metaphor is probably from 20
purchasing slaves. The purchaser does not buy only a part of a slave, his "will" or his "soul", as if this were detachable from his body. No, the new master possesses the whole man, and the slave must **honour** him with his body as much as with his mind.

The Christian in a pagan society

And now for the matters you wrote about. Apart from the disturbing 7.1
reports he had heard about Corinthian church life, Paul's main reason for writing seems to have been a letter which he had received from the Corinthians; and the rest of 1 Corinthians is devoted mainly to answering that letter point by point. Precisely why the Corinthians had written, and whether their questions to Paul were in the form of protests against his previous teaching, or genuine requests for guidance, we cannot be sure. But in general, the first few matters on which Paul had to give an answer were practical problems which would naturally beset *The Christian in a pagan society.*

The first topic is relations between the sexes. **It is a good thing for a** 1
man to have nothing to do with women. This general proposition (which, as the subsequent discussion shows, is not as general as it looks: **to have nothing to do with women** is a euphemism for "to avoid sexual intercourse") may be another instance of Paul quoting one of the Corinthians' own slogans (as the NEB footnote allows) and then going on to qualify it; in any case, it was a proposition with which he was in broad agreement. He himself clearly had no wife (though, since he began life as an orthodox and devout Jew, it would be surprising if he had not at one time been married),
and his personal view followed from this: **I should like you all to be as I** 7
am myself. (He also had other less personal reasons for this view, which he gives later on.) On the general principle there does not seem to have been any difference of opinion between Paul and the Corinthians; for the Corinthians clearly held the same view as Paul about sexual intercourse, though probably for more ascetic reasons. What appears to be in dispute is the extent to which the principle should be applied in practice.

First, with regard to marriage itself: both Paul's own feelings and the Corinthians' asceticism point to continence even within marriage. But not

7, 6 everyone has **this gift**, and Paul qualifies the principle **by way of concession**:
2 **because there is so much immorality** (or, "because of the danger of it": the Greek does not necessarily imply that it is happening), normal marital
3–5 relationships are allowable—and Paul prescribes a pattern for them which is in the very best philosophical and religious tradition of the ancient world.

8 Secondly, with regard to **the unmarried and to widows**: Paul again is in general agreement with the Corinthians, and his personal view is clear. They should **stay as I am myself**. But again, there is a danger that this may lead to tension or even immorality; so a similar concession is necessary.

On the other hand, there is one application of the general principle which is definitely not allowable. The ascetic approach might seem to suggest that it would be better for married couples to separate, in which case any 'concession' to married couples would be unnecessary. But against this stands
10 **the Lord's** ruling against divorce (which Paul evidently knew in much the same form as it has in Mark 10, Matthew 19). And although Jesus, when he gave this **ruling**, presumably did not envisage the problems of mixed marriages in which only one partner is a Christian, yet Paul feels justified in extending the prohibition to marriages of this kind. For in the first place, the conversion of one parent makes the whole family into a Christian household, and is bound in some way to involve the other partner (so that a mixed marriage is by no means to be thought of as a pagan marriage, to which, of course, the Lord's ruling would not apply); and secondly, it is always possible
16 that the unbelieving partner may find **salvation** if the marriage continues. The only exception allowed is if the heathen partner (not being subject to
15 the Lord's ruling) **wishes for a separation**. The peace of a Christian household is not to be threatened by a desperate attempt to hold on to a non-Christian partner.

Before going on, Paul digresses a little to place the whole matter in a wider context. At this time, it seems to have been an almost unquestioned belief among Christians that the Day of the Lord, the end of the present age, would occur within the next few years; and this expectation could easily have made Christianity into an anarchic movement if Christians had started to abandon
17 their ordinary occupations and social obligations. Paul's teaching in **all our congregations** had been sternly against this, even with respect to slaves
21 (though whether or not a Christian slave was supposed to seize a legitimate chance of freedom when it came is a detail which the obscurity of Paul's Greek hides from us). Any agitation of this kind would only result in their
23 becoming once more **slaves of men**, and would be incompatible with Christians' real and dearly bought freedom. So in general (and not only with
24 regard to marriage), **each one . . . is to remain before God in the condition in which he received his call.**

25 This principle is relevant when Paul comes to his third topic, **the question of celibacy**. Here (by contrast with the question of divorce) there is no

specific saying of Jesus to appeal to: **I have no instructions from the Lord.** 25
But Paul can give his own **judgement**: although **there is nothing wrong** 28
in marriage, those who are not already committed to it would do better to
remain single. **The time we live in will not last long**; the pressing 29
imminence of the end of this world places a question mark over all human
possessions and institutions—even marriage, which cannot be expected to
continue unchanged into the new age. If they are to take this prospect
seriously, men must be prepared to look upon even marriage as something
provisional—in this sense, **married men should be as if they had no** 29
wives—just as they must have a certain detachment from human grief,
human joy, and **the world's wealth.** At the same time, the imminence of the 31
end must never be a pretext for irresponsible conduct. Again and again in the New Testament the same lesson is drawn from the fact that the end is near: behave with decency (Romans 13.13); have no anxiety (Philippians 4.6); keep awake and sober (1 Thessalonians 5.6); be patient (James 5.7); lead an ordered and sober life (1 Peter 4.7)—and so on through at least the first century of Christian literature. The same applies to the matter in hand:
the best way **to be free from anxious care** is not to take on the commit- 32
ments of married life. Yet even so, Paul is prepared to make his 'concession'.
I have no wish to keep you on a tight rein. Neither the inclination of his 35
own temperament, nor the Corinthians' asceticism, nor even the imminence of the Day, should be allowed to turn celibacy into an absolute rule.

Paul still had one more topic to deal with under this general heading, but we cannot be certain what it was. The Greek word *parthenos* means, literally, "virgin"; but it can also have a wider meaning than this; and on this one page of the NEB it has already been rendered: (i) "celibate" (male or female), and so **celibacy** (verse 25), (ii) **virgin** (verse 28), (iii) **celibate woman** (verse 34). The difficulty is to know what the word means in verse 36. The traditional view, accepted until the end of the last century, was that this paragraph is about the problems of parents marrying off their "virgin daughters" (as in the footnotes in NEB). But this involves severe difficulties of interpretation, and a somewhat easier view, which is adopted in the main
text of NEB, is that *parthenos* here means **partner in celibacy.** It is assumed 36
(on this view) that couples in Corinth were entering into a kind of "spiritual marriage", without either the legal form or the physical reality of normal marriage, and that this experiment had been subject to the inevitable strains of such relationships. Experiments of this kind took place in Christian communities in later centuries; it is not impossible that they had already begun at Corinth. If so, we may suppose that Paul, on his own principles, was not opposed to such spiritual marriages; but if the Corinthians, out of asceticism, thought that it was sinful to turn such a relationship into a real
marriage, Paul's reply was: if anyone finds it necessary to take this course, **he** 37
will do well.

8.1 **Now about food consecrated to heathen deities.** This is the next subject about which the Corinthians had written to Paul, and is one which arose out of the ordinary circumstances of life in a city such as Corinth.

The many temples and altars dedicated to the different gods of Greek religion demanded frequent sacrifices of animals. But only a small part of each animal was actually burnt on the altar; the rest was disposed of in one of two ways. Either an individual, at the time of the sacrifice, might invite his friends to join him in the temple and dine off the "consecrated" meat; or else the meat, after the sacrifice, was returned to the trade to be retailed in the meat-market.

By the ordinary citizen all this was taken for granted: it formed an accepted part both of social life and of marketing arrangements. But for the Jewish community in any such city, this connection of meat with pagan worship could not be a matter of indifference. Indeed, the Jews coined their own word
1 for it, here translated by the phrase **food consecrated to heathen deities,**
and they had a clear policy towards the whole question. Their religion forbade them to join in social gatherings in heathen temples, or indeed to sit at table anywhere with non-Jews; and their scruples about the way in which meat should be slaughtered prevented them in any case from buying meat in the ordinary market, and so protected them from the danger of eating anything that had been contaminated by pagan worship.

What was to be the attitude of non-Jewish Christians? On the one hand, their faith in the one true God (like that of the Jews) was clearly incompatible with any participation in pagan worship; on the other hand, they shared none of the Jews' scruples about eating with Gentiles or about the kind of meat they ate. To have adopted the Jewish policy would have caused them considerable difficulties: it would have cut them off from a great deal of social contact with their non-Christian friends, and would have greatly complicated their shopping in the meat-market. Yet clearly some policy was necessary, if only to demonstrate to non-Christians the seriousness of their monotheistic faith.

Paul deals first with the question of invitations to meals in pagan temples. The Corinthians had taken the line that it was best for them to go on as
1 before, and had used certain arguments in support of this[a] ('We **have**
4 **knowledge**', '**a false god has no existence in the real world**'). With
these arguments Paul was broadly in agreement. The worship of the many "false gods" of the Greeks could be of no significance to Christians, who had
6 superior 'knowledge' of **one God, the Father.** (Here Paul adds some
somewhat metaphysical-sounding attributes—**from whom all being comes,** etc.—which may already have been familiar in the church, and which receive elaboration in the letter to the Colossians). Even though for

[*a*] Once again (see above on 6.12) it is assumed by the translators that some of the sentences in this paragraph are quotations from what the Corinthians said themselves.

many of them (and certainly for Paul) the universe was peopled with supernatural beings such as angels and demons, and so the words '**gods**' and 5
'**lords**' were often on their lips, yet this did not affect the fact that there was
only **one God**, infinitely superior to all such beings. And since pagan worship 6
had no reality for Christians, association with it could do them no harm.

But Paul, though he does not dispute these premises, introduces another
consideration. '**Knowledge' breeds conceit; it is love that builds.** The 1
relationship of love between Christians was far more important than the
intellectual justification of their policy, and the Corinthians' simple solution
to the problem was in danger of becoming a **pitfall for the weak.** Not all 9
their members had reached the same point of enlightened '**knowledge**'.
Long association with heathen practices made it impossible for some of
them to be present at sacrifices without some sense of involvement; for them,
it was better to stay away, and the spectacle of their fellow-Christians openly
sitting down to a meal in a heathen temple might only tempt them to do 10
what they conscientiously felt they ought not to do. Therefore, although
Paul is prepared to agree that nothing to do with food can affect us so far as
God is concerned, yet there may be unfortunate consequences for the
Christian fellowship. It is only **love that builds**: insensitivity may lead to 1
sin. For himself, Paul would rather take the extreme step of becoming a
vegetarian than risk being **the cause of my brother's downfall.** 13

Am I not a free man? Suddenly—and this outburst is so sudden and 9. 1
unexplained that it ought possibly to be regarded as a subsequent addition
to the original draft of the letter—Paul begins to defend himself. Clearly he
has been under some kind of attack; and he addresses at least part of this
chapter against **those who put me in the dock.** He appears to be sensitive 3
on two points: his freedom (which is relevant to the question under discussion), and his right to be called an apostle (which seems to be connected with
his freedom). The fact of his apostolate could hardly be denied by the
Corinthians. It rested ultimately, as with all the apostles, on the fact that
after the resurrection he had had an opportunity actually to **see Jesus our** 1
Lord; and the fruits of his work in Corinth were clear evidence that Paul
had been faithful to the 'commission' he had received to preach the gospel
to the Gentiles (Romans 1.5–6): **you are yourselves the very seal of my** 2
apostolate.

So much, in general terms, the Corinthians could hardly dispute. But the
accusation against Paul seems to have been on a specific point. Paul (as we
are told also in Acts 18.3–4) did not expect the Corinthian congregation to
provide for him, but earned his own living or relied on support from elsewhere.
This he did by personal preference; but it appears that his practice was not
in line with that of **the rest of the apostles.** (Paul adds, **and the Lord's** 5
brothers: we know from the New Testament that one of Jesus' "brothers",

James, became a leader of the Jerusalem church; and there is a later tradition that other relatives subsequently held a position of authority.) They, apparently, felt entitled to support from their congregations, both for themselves and for their wives. This difference of practice between Paul (and perhaps his fellow-worker Barnabas) and the others seems to have provided his opponents with an argument against him. The argument perhaps ran like this: If Paul were a real apostle, he would enjoy the same material privileges as the other apostles. But in fact he has to earn his own living. Therefore he cannot be a real apostle.

Paul attacks both the premise and the conclusion of this argument. The
reason why the other apostles received support from their congregations was
not because of any privilege which belonged to an "apostle" as such, but
8 lay in the kind of work they were doing. Ordinary **human analogies**
showed that such work would entitle anyone to a reward; and indeed the
principle had the authority of Scripture itself—granted a somewhat special-
ized method of interpretation. This method assumed that many passages of
Scripture had a deeper meaning than the literal one. A passage was thought
particularly likely to have such a deeper meaning if its literal sense seemed
inappropriate or unedifying. Paul here applies this method to a passage in
9 Deuteronomy (25.4): '**You shall not muzzle a threshing ox**'. There is no
doubt that this article of the Law of Moses was originally intended to be
exactly what it seems, a humanitarian regulation about the use of domestic
animals in the threshing mill. But the extreme reverence in which the Law
of Moses came to be held by the Jews as the revealed will of God for his
people made this literal sense seem inappropriate; and Paul could say, '**Do
you suppose God's concern is with oxen?**' Evidently there was a hidden
meaning—**of course it refers to us**—yielding a sense which reinforced
Paul's point that work of any kind entitles the worker to a reward. Now
what Paul had been doing was certainly work; so (all questions of apostleship
11 apart) of course he was entitled to a **material harvest**. Furthermore, what
was true of manual work was equally true of religious service. It was true
13 under the temple regulations at Jerusalem; and it was true, on the authority
14 of Jesus himself, of **those who preach the Gospel**. (The **instructions** Paul
refers to were probably something like Jesus' saying recorded in Matthew
10.10, 'The worker earns his keep'. It seems unlikely that Jesus originally
intended his words to be taken in quite this sense, but the early church
evidently took them so.) There could be no question, therefore, but that Paul
had as much right as anyone else to material support. His opponents were
quite wrong on their facts. But they were also wrong in their conclusion. Paul
15 had come to his own decision, and had acted of his own free will. **I have
never taken advantage of any such right, nor do I intend to claim it
in this letter.** His reasons were entirely personal, one might almost say
psychological (he has expressed them somewhat obscurely). But the impor-

tant point was that he felt himself entirely free to follow his own mind on this matter—which brings him back to the question of his "freedom".

Paul's conduct, especially with regard to certain observances laid down in the Law of Moses, and perhaps also with regard to the Gentiles' problem of 'food consecrated to heathen deities', may have seemed, at times, inconsistent (and possibly this inconsistency was at the root of the charges laid against him, and made it the more difficult for him to give a ruling on practical matters of this kind). Paul does not deny this apparent inconsistency; on the
contrary, he justifies it, on the grounds (i) that he is **a free man** (free, that 19
is, like every Christian, from religious ordinances and conventions), (ii) that
he has not been exercising this freedom for its own sake, but **for the sake** 23
of the Gospel. His willingness to accommodate himself to the scruples of
others has brought him even to the point (which would particularly touch
the Corinthians, and shows how they too ought to behave) that he can say,
to the weak I became weak, to win the weak. 22

Not that this can have been easy. A man brought up as a strict Jew could hardly feel indifferent to the principles which had governed his whole upbringing. In the same way, the Corinthians could not expect to be able to accommodate themselves to their more scrupulous fellow-Christians without severe self-discipline. But if athletes (a popular comparison in rhetoric)
were prepared to go into **strict training** for a mere wreath of leaves (the 25
only prize given at the Greek games), how much more should Christians be
prepared to do for a **wreath that never fades**!

You should understand, my brothers. The tone becomes somewhat **10.** 1
more severe. It may be that the Corinthians, with all their "knowledge" and
"freedom", had allowed themselves to slip into a false sense of security.
They believed, as Paul certainly did at the time when he wrote this letter,
that the present world order was rapidly coming to an end: they were the
people on whom **the fulfilment of the ages has come**, they were marked 11
out, as it were, to be the triumphant survivors of the day of judgement, and
they already possessed a supernatural guarantee of their destiny in the rites
of baptism and eucharist. But—**beware! You may fall.** Paul has a warning 12
for them derived from his reading of certain passages of Scripture.

The basic narrative referred to is contained in Exodus 13–17. The people
of Israel (Paul's physical ancestors, but also, in a sense, the spiritual **ances-** 1
tors of Christians), were preserved during their flight from Egypt by means
of certain supernatural events: they were preceded (or "covered", according
to Psalm 105.39) by a **pillar of cloud** (Exodus 13.21), they miraculously
passed through the Red Sea (Exodus 14), they were supplied with the 3
supernatural food of manna (Exodus 16), and were provided with **drink** 4
out of the rock at Horeb (Exodus 17; Numbers 20.11). This narrative had
for a long time been the subject of much scholarly interpretation. Exactly
how the people of Israel had **passed through the Red Sea**, for example, 1

was a question only sketchily answered by the biblical account, and later elaborations of the story made it into a kind of ordeal by water, a symbol (as
2 it seemed to Paul, and perhaps to other Jewish interpreters) of that **baptism**
which was one of the rites by which a proselyte was received into the Jewish
community, **the fellowship of Moses.** To this extent, it could be said that
they all received baptism, a clear foreshadowing of Christian baptism,
though it was baptism, not "into Christ", but **into the fellowship of**
Moses. Similarly, the story of the rock had received considerable elaboration.
It not only provided the people with drink—even in the Exodus account it
4 was clearly a **supernatural rock**—but it came to be thought of, like the
pillar of cloud, as a symbol of the concern of God for his people, which **accompanied their travels** and provided **supernatural drink** in the form of divine wisdom. This kind of speculation made of the rock a powerful symbol of the gifts of God to his people; and Paul was apparently only taking the same line of thought a stage further when he made it stand for the greatest of all God's gifts: **that rock was Christ.** In this way he found clear parallels in the Exodus narrative to the Christian sacraments of baptism and eucharist.

6 **These events happened as symbols**—literally "types", that is to say,
not belonging completely to the past, but pointing forward to some subsequent event. The people of Israel received supernatural blessings; but
5 even so—**the desert was strewn with their corpses** (Numbers 14.16 and
6 elsewhere). Their sins (i) of desiring **evil things** (Numbers 11.34); (ii) of
7 idolatry ('**the people sat down to feast and rose up to revel**' is a quota-
8 tion from the story of the golden calf, Exodus 32.6); (iii) of **fornication**
9 (Numbers 25.1, 9); (iv) of putting **the power of the Lord to the test** (Num-
10 bers 21.5–6); (v) of being disposed to **grumble against God** (Numbers 14.
36–7) were all duly punished—and for the last punishment Paul uses the
biblical expression **the Destroyer** (as in Exodus 12.23). These people, then,
6 were "types" or **symbols**; they pointed forward to those others who would
also receive supernatural blessings (baptism and eucharist), and who would
11 also stand under imminent judgement (**upon us the fulfilment of the**
ages has come). These events of past history were **recorded for our**
13 **benefit as a warning.** No **trial** or **test** will be any excuse for Christians to
commit these sins: punishment is as inevitable as it was for the people of
14 Israel. **So then** (to take from this list the particular sin involved in the
original question (8.10) of 'sitting down to a meal in a heathen temple') **shun**
idolatry.

So much by way of a general warning against associating with heathen worship. Paul now urges a deeper consideration. Christians had their own sacred meal, and they knew this to involve not merely a profound solidarity
16 with each other, but also **a sharing in the blood** and **body of Christ.** This

sharing was doubtless unique; but it was not altogether without analogy. In
the Jewish religion, for instance, the sacrifices made the participants **sharers** 18
in the altar (which is Paul's roundabout Jewish way of saying, sharers in
God). What about pagan sacrifices? Surely the same principle could hardly
apply: if it did, it would seem to imply that an idol was more than an idol,
and had some supernatural existence in which the worshippers could
"share". Paul would have agreed that an idol has no reality; but his argument
is that the real point of resemblance rests, not on that to which the sacrifice
is made, but on the act of sacrificing. The act itself is never, so to speak,
neutral. If it is not offered to God, it becomes demonic. At the receiving end
is not mere nothing, but **demons** (this is proved by Scripture: Leviticus 20
17.7; Deuteronomy 32.17; Psalm 106.37). If a meal partaken of in a heathen
temple were just an empty parody of the Lord's Supper, it might be harmless.
But in fact it is a real involvement with the demonic. It is therefore quite
incompatible with the communion of **the Lord's table**, and is a clear instance 21
of that sin described in Deuteronomy 32.21, "They roused my jealousy with
a god of no account, with their false gods they provoked me"—to which, in
the Greek, Paul's question, **Can we defy the Lord?**, is a clear allusion.[a] It 22
follows that for Christians to join in the temple meals of their pagan friends
is incompatible both with the reality of the Christian eucharist and with the
Old Testament insistence on avoiding idolatry.

Paul is now ready to give a ruling on the remaining questions raised by
'food offered to heathen deities'. He quotes once again (as above, 6.12) the
Corinthians' slogan, '**We are free to do anything**', which in this, as in the 23
matter of sexual morals, is the key to their behaviour; and once again he
accepts it, but qualifies it with the principle that it is still more important
to do what will **help the building of the community** and to show con- 23
sideration for others. **The earth is the Lord's and everything in it** 26
(Psalm 24.1), so that a Christian, when shopping at the meat-market, may
buy anything: no one's conscience is going to be troubled. Equally, Christians may continue to accept invitations to dine at the houses of pagan
friends; their "freedom" allows them to **eat whatever is put before them.** 27
But if on such an occasion the host or a fellow-guest explicitly points out
that the **food has been offered in sacrifice** (the term used here is the one 28
a pagan would have used, not the special Jewish term used above in 8.1),
then it becomes necessary to consider **questions of conscience**, such as the 27
inferences which may be drawn from the Christians' behaviour in public.
The principle of freedom must always be qualified by another, equally 29
important: **give no offence to Jews, or Greeks, or to the church of God.** 32
Paul himself has set an example of this; and, in this matter, Paul is following
Christ.

[a] This is obscured by the NEB rendering. Literally translated, Paul's words mean, "Shall we rouse the Lord to jealousy?"

The next topic is the ordering of public worship. The Corinthians seem to
11. 2 have said in their letter, by way of justifying their own practice, "We have always kept you in mind; we have maintained the tradition you handed on to us". But at the same time they had been permitting women to attend services unveiled. We know very little about the background to this. The Corinthians may have thought that their new Christian principles allowed this (Paul states such a principle in verses 11–12); or they may simply have been continuing ordinary pagan practice—unfortunately, we do not know exactly what this practice would have been. Furthermore, we do not know whether this was something Paul would always have opposed, or whether he had recently changed his mind about it (hence the Corinthians' self-righteous defence). All we can say for certain is that Paul was now giving a ruling against women laying aside their veils; but his arguments are as obscure as the matter in question. They may be tentatively set out as follows:

3 (i) Despite the undoubted equality of the sexes before God (Galatians 3.28), there is still a certain order of precedence: God–Christ–man–woman. (This argument depends on an untranslatable play upon words: **head** is used both literally and metaphorically, and **man,** in Greek, means both "man" and "husband".)

4–6 (ii) An argument from custom: if shaving off the hair is a **disgrace** for a woman, so presumably is taking off the veil.

7–10 (iii) An argument from Scripture: the Genesis account of creation seems to imply the priority of man. In addition, there are **angels** to be reckoned with: either the "bad angels" of Genesis 6, or perhaps good angels such as some may have believed were present at Christian worship. In either case the veil would be important, to ward off the evil angels or to show proper respect to the good ones.

11–12 (Verses 11–12 are parenthetical: a concession that, despite these somewhat conservative arguments, in **Christ's fellowship** there exists a deeper partnership between man and woman.)

13–15 (iv) An argument from **Nature** (of a kind probably borrowed from popular Stoic philosophy): **flowing locks,** and therefore presumably also veils, are "natural" for women.

16 (v) An appeal to universal Christian practice: **there is no such custom among us.**

But Paul has also heard about a much more serious breach of order in the Corinthians' worship. The 'quarrels and divisions' which beset the whole membership of the church are also in evidence at their services; and although
19 there is a sense in which **dissensions are necessary**—in that, before the
Christians can take their place beside Christ at the imminent judgement,
their community will need to have been already sifted out **to show which**
. . . members are sound—yet such things should not be allowed to interfere
20 with worship. The particular abuse Paul has in mind concerns the **Lord's**

Supper—and this is the earliest account we have of the Christian eucharist. It appears that at this stage it was a real supper, supplied by the individual members of the congregation—hence the possibilities of social injustice and selfishness which had so scandalized Paul. But (even if the Corinthians had not fully realized it) it was also much more than this. It was a direct continuation of that supper which the Lord Jesus held **on the night of his arrest**; 23
and the **tradition** which Paul appeals to, and for which he claims the Lord's authority, corresponds essentially with the accounts given by Matthew, Mark and (in one version) Luke. One detail is peculiar to this passage and to the longer text of Luke:[a] the words, '**do this as a memorial of me**'. The precise meaning of the word here translated **memorial** (*anamnēsis*) has been the subject of centuries of discussion; but at least this is clear (and clearer here than in the gospel accounts): that the supper was intended to be continued in the Christian congregation, and that the tone was set by the words
actually spoken on that original occasion; so that to hold the supper was to 26
proclaim the death of the Lord, until he comes. The rite was thus distinguished from any mere love-feast or fellowship meal, such as existed both in the Jewish and in pagan religions; and the consequences of taking
part **unworthily**—that is, in a state in which the partaker **does not discern** 27
that the bread he is eating is **the Body**—were correspondingly serious. 29
Indeed, it appears from this and other passages that, in this early period, all Christians were expected to continue in life and health until the imminent "coming" of the Lord. If any had fallen **sick** or **died**, the explanation might well lie in their irreverent behaviour at the eucharist. Yet even such tokens
of judgement could be beneficial, as a kind of "discipline", to warn other 32
Christians of the consequences of such behaviour, and so to save them **from being condemned with the rest of the world.**

Spiritual gifts

The next topic on which Paul had to answer the Corinthians is indicated by the heading *Spiritual gifts*.

From chapter 14 it is clear that in Corinth there was one mode in particular
in which the reality of the Spirit was experienced, namely **ecstatic utter-** **12.** 10
ance, that is, a form of trance in which the worshipper was inspired to utter words that were either more-or-less unintelligible, or else in a foreign language unknown to the speaker.[b] This experience was apparently so common

[a] See the NEB footnote to Luke 22.19, and above, pp. 286–7.

[b] This has been traditionally rendered, "speaking with tongues". In the NEB it appears as "ecstatic utterance", "tongues of ecstasy", "ecstatic language", etc. The implication of such renderings is not necessarily that the utterances were uncontrolled or meaningless, but that they exceeded the normal powers of men. See above on Acts 2.1–4.

in Corinth that it had become almost a condition of membership, or at least of respect, in the church; and Paul may have had occasion previously to utter some warning about it. The phenomenon was perilously similar to the kind of thing which was known to occur sometimes in pagan worship (**you were swept off to those dumb heathen gods**), and so could not always be distinguished from idolatrous practices. In any case, it did not guarantee the presence of the Spirit. If, for instance, it should take the form of uttering the exact converse of the Christian confession ('**A curse on Jesus!**'), then the
3 utterance clearly could not be **under the influence of the Spirit of God.** But before developing this point further, Paul devotes the next two chapters to putting the question in a wider context. Ecstatic utterance is by no means the only way in which the Spirit is manifested (even if it is the most spectacular). The Corinthians have an altogether too limited conception of the
4 Spirit, and must be introduced to a much richer one: **There are varieties of gifts, but the same Spirit.**

The full Christian experience of the Spirit is highly diversified. Just as, if
5 one follows the example of the Lord's **service**, there is more than one way
6 in which one can serve; and just as, if one recognizes the **work** (literally, "working") of God in anything, one must be prepared to recognize it in everyone and everything; so with the Spirit: there is not just one possible
7 manifestation, but **in each of us the Spirit is manifested in one particular way.** Many different kinds of gifts (which the Corinthians doubtless possessed, but had not associated with the Spirit) are in fact exercised
8, 10 **through the Spirit,** and the Corinthians' particular gift of **ecstatic utterance** does not even come very high on the list.

To drive this point home, Paul uses an analogy which was popular among philosophers of his day: the members of any human society are related to each other like the limbs of a body. The analogy was commonly used to demonstrate the interdependence of the various members; and this is a
24 sufficiently Christian point (especially as it touches the treatment of **humbler** members) for Paul to devote a few lines to it here. But there is another implication. The body-analogy would make no sense if all the members of the society were identical—if they all had the same function or the same
19 gifts. **If the whole were one single organ, there would not be a body at all.** In so far, then, as the Christian community is like a body, there must
4 be, not just one gift, but **varieties of gifts.**

But is the Christian congregation like a body? And if it is, what has this to do with the Spirit? May not the analogy simply show that from the point of view of, say, administrative organization or social status, the congregation does indeed consist of different kinds of people closely dependent upon one another? It may still be the case that the Spirit (as the Corinthians probably believed) manifests itself in one gift only.

By way of answer, Paul shows that the body-analogy is more than a rhetori-

cal commonplace: it applies to the Christian congregation in a quite special
(some would say "mystical") way. When Christians are baptized, they are
brought into a close unity, not only with one another, but with Christ. As a
result, **Christ,** present as he is in a congregation of Christians who have been 12
united with him through baptism, **is like a single body with its many**
limbs and organs. To put it still more boldly: **you are Christ's body.** 27
And if anyone doubts that this involves the Spirit, he need only recall the
circumstances and nature of his baptism. Baptism is **in the one Spirit.** To 13
use another metaphor (which we cannot interpret with certainty: it may come
from water being poured into different channels for irrigation, or into
different cups for drinking), **one Holy Spirit was poured out for all of** 13
us. This means, of course, an end to all racial and social barriers (a point 13
very precious to Paul—see Galatians 3.26–8—though not strictly relevant
here); but it also means that the Spirit is given to **all of us,** not just those who
experience ecstatic utterance. So that the congregation, if it is to be in a true
sense a body, must exhibit **varieties of gifts.** 4

How does this work out in practice? **Within our community God has** 28
appointed, in the first place apostles—and there follows a whole list
of the different offices and gifts which (we may suppose) were in fact exercised in the congregation. Since all these should be present in the community, the situation would be absurd if all the members had one and the same gift and function. Moreover, the gift to which the Corinthians attached so much importance—**ecstatic utterance**—comes right at the bottom of the list. If there was a lack of diversity at Corinth, it was because the Corinthians were not aiming high enough: they were resting content with one relatively unimportant gift.

And now I will show you the best way of all. Over against the Corin- 31
thians' slogans of "knowledge" and "freedom", Paul has had occasion to invoke a still more important principle, that of 'building the community' (10.23) and of showing consideration for all its members (including the weakest). He has already once called this principle, quite simply, 'love' (8.1); and now, in view of the Corinthians' exclusive reliance on one particular gift of the Spirit, he draws out some of its implications. What is this 'love'? It is often felt that the old English word "charity" is still a better translation of the Greek word *agapē*. An almost decisive objection to this (at least in a modern translation) is that in contemporary speech the word "charity" no longer bears its original meaning, and now has the quite different sense of "charitable institutions". On the other hand, it is certainly true that when the early Christians used the word *agapē*, it was a far less common word, and had a far narrower range of meanings, than our modern word "love". Indeed, so far as we can tell, the word did not belong to ordinary speech at all, the commonest expressions being *erōs* (which was predominantly sexual love) and *philia* (friendship). *Agapē* occurred in the Greek version of the

Old Testament; but it seems to have been only among Christians that the word became important, and if we wish to learn its meaning we have to go to the New Testament itself. It occurs most frequently in the gospel and letters of John, where it denotes the self-giving love of God towards man, as expressed in Jesus Christ, and the responding love of man towards God and towards his fellow-men. The word, in fact, is not psychological at all, but is a technical term of the Christian vocabulary. It derives its meaning from the act of God in Christ, and it shows its distinctively Christian character by the fact that it is entirely without self-interest or possessiveness, and is untouched by any of the mixed motives and emotions often associated with the
13. 1 words "love", "friendship" or "affection". Compared with this **love**, not only speaking **in tongues of men or of angels** (the phenomenon of 'ecstatic utterance' which is the immediate subject of these chapters), but the possession of knowledge, the effort of faith, even the ultimate act of self-sacrifice—any one of which, it might be thought, would be sufficient in itself to mark out the true Christian—are relatively insignificant.

4–7 The structure of the next paragraph is slightly obscured in the NEB. It consists of a carefully composed series of short clauses, of each of which the subject is **love**. As a result, **love** seems almost personified—much as, in the later books of the Old Testament, the concept of "wisdom" is almost endowed with an independent existence of its own, and is made to say, for example, "I have counsel, I have sound wisdom, I have insight, I have strength" (Proverbs 8.14—a passage which may have been in Paul's mind here). We do not know—and perhaps there is little point in trying to guess—what led Paul to write in this way. Some have thought that the passage is a portrait of Jesus himself; others, that Paul was showing **love** to be the exact opposite of all those failings for which he had to criticize the Corinthians; others again, that he was using the form of an existing pagan hymn. Whatever the explanation, the passage remains a psychologically perceptive and (so far as we know) brilliantly original description of true Christian motivation.

8 **Love will never come to an end.** The statement meant something slightly different to Paul from what it means to us. Paul did not operate with our modern conception of eternity. His perspective was much shorter. The present world order, he believed, was coming rapidly to an end. His question was not so much, What will last for ever? as, What elements of Christian experience will continue into the new age, and what elements will pass away? He had a criterion to hand. The new age, being a revelation of God and of the sons of God (Romans 8.19), will be characterized by "wholeness":
9 knowledge, prophecy and the like are **partial**, they bear the same imperfect
11 relation to the reality which is to come as **childish** things to adult life, or
12 **puzzling reflections** in the metal mirrors of antiquity to real objects; but
in the new age, knowledge will be whole, **we shall see face to face**. It
follows that all **partial** phenomena, such as the more obvious and sensational

gifts which the Corinthians were so proud of, will come to an end. By contrast, **there are three things that last for ever**: (i) **faith**—which is here 13
used in a quite different sense from verse 2 above, where it denotes an act
of the will (compare the words of Jesus recorded in Matthew 17.20): here
it is "faith" in a large sense, the total self-committal of the person to God,
something which by its very nature cannot be partial, and so will continue
into the future age; (ii) **hope**—which includes the object hoped for (like 'the
hope stored up for you in heaven', Colossians 1.5) and so necessarily belongs
to the coming age; and (iii) **love**. Possibly Paul did not invent this triad, for
it seems to underlie other passages in his letters (1 Thessalonians 1.3; 5.8;
Colossians 1.4–5), and may already have been a motto in the church. But all
three pass the test of "wholeness", and together they form the basic constituents of that part of Christian life and experience which (unlike so much
of what the Corinthians set store by) is of enduring value.[a]

Having talked of 'varieties of gifts' in general, and of that love which is
the greatest of them all, Paul now brings the discussion back to the point
from which it started: the undue importance attached by the Corinthians to
ecstatic utterance. What has been said in praise of love is not intended to
be a depreciation of spiritual gifts altogether: **there are other**[b] **gifts of the** 14. 1
Spirit at which you should aim also. But even among these gifts, the
language of ecstasy cannot be given pre-eminence, for it does not meet the 2
essential requirement (as love supremely does) of building up the community.
By this standard, a higher place is held by the less spectacular but ultimately
more valuable gift of "prophesying"; for **prophecy**, though it was also an
inspired form of utterance, was by definition (unlike the language of ecstasy)
intelligible to its hearers. Ecstatic utterance cannot be of more than limited
value so long as its unintelligibility prevents it from being a gift that will
build up the community. 5

Nevertheless, Paul is careful not to disparage a gift which often so obviously
does proceed from the Spirit. He does not recommend its discontinuance
or suppression, but only that it should be so far as possible accompanied by
the **ability to interpret.** In the absence of such interpretation, ecstatic 13
utterance may be as meaningless as the untutored strumming of a musical 7–9
instrument. Again, praying and praising God is not done entirely by human
thought and effort, but by **the Spirit** within us (Romans 8.15; Galatians 14
4.6); and although this receives striking demonstration if the form taken by
these prayers and praises is **ecstatic utterance** (as Paul knows from his 18

[*a*] It is assumed here that Paul wrote chapter 13 when he wrote the rest of the letter, and that it forms an integral part of the whole; but many feel that the chapter must have had an independent existence of its own before it was incorporated in the letter, and this opinion cannot be proved wrong.

[*b*] The word **other** is a slightly questionable addition by the translators: 'love' is not here classed as one of the gifts of the Spirit, but is a 'way' which is contrasted with all such gifts. The point of the present paragraph is to show what value these gifts nevertheless have.

19 own experience), yet even in his own case he would rather speak **five**
intelligible words. The gifted Corinthians must learn to pray and sing, not
15 only under inspiration, but at the same time **intelligently**, so that one of
their number who is a **plain man** may not feel himself excluded from their
16 worship, but can say his '**Amen**' at the right place. The ultimate significance
21 of the phenomenon can be inferred from Scripture (or **the Law**, as Paul
can loosely call even a quotation from one of the prophets). Paul quotes
Isaiah 28.11–12 in a Greek version otherwise unknown to us. This version
contained the word **men of strange tongues**, which Paul sees as a reference
to 'ecstatic utterance'. In Isaiah, the context (at least in Paul's somewhat
abbreviated quotation) shows that those for whose benefit the phenomenon
22 takes place are **unbelievers**—that is, those who, despite everything, will
never believe. Believers, and those who may still be brought to the faith,
21 must be addressed, not in tongues, but in **prophecies.** It is the searching and
convincing character of prophecy, not the spectacular but unintelligible flow
of ecstatic tongues, which will force from the visitor the scriptural con-
25 fession, '**God is certainly among you**' (Zechariah 8.23).
26 **To sum up, my friends.** Paul is now ready to give specific instructions
about the ordering of public worship. The overriding principle must be
to build up the church; and this dictates a strict control of ecstatic utterances, a careful ordering of different individuals' contributions, and mutual
agreement between those who receive inspiration on how to work peacefully
together. One other instruction is added, of a purely conventional kind:
34 **women should not address the meeting.** It is not clear how this is to be
reconciled with 11.5 above, which seems to envisage women "prophesying".
Either Paul is being inconsistent, or else there is a distinction between
"prophesying" and "addressing the meeting" which we cannot now understand. In any case, the reason is plain: things must be done **as in all congrega-**
tions of God's people, and the Corinthians have no right to assume that they
can set the standard. Moreover, Paul is in touch with all those congregations,
37 and is himself an apostle: he writes with **the Lord's authority.** If it were to
come to the test, anyone who disagreed on a matter such as this would place
38 himself outside the church. **If he does not acknowledge this, God does**
not acknowledge him. [a]

Life after death

15. 12 **How can some of you say there is no resurrection of the dead?** A
statement to this effect must have stood in the Corinthians' letter to Paul,
and he devotes a long chapter to his reply. Once again, we are at a disadvan-

[*a*] Both the meaning and the correct text of this verse are uncertain. The NEB (First Edition) gives a less probable rendering, which has been corrected in the Second Edition.

tage in that we do not possess the whole correspondence, and can only guess at the real nature of the Corinthians' difficulties.

The **resurrection of the dead** is not to be thought of as a general term for any kind of *Life after death.* It was the specifically Jewish doctrine that, at the Last Judgement, all those who had died would be resurrected bodily, in order to receive the appropriate sentence of punishment or reward. The righteous would then receive a new body which would enable them to enjoy the everlasting felicity prepared for them. This doctrine was taken over into Christianity with only slight modifications. Christians believed that their resurrection had already been anticipated, as it were, by the resurrection of Christ (through whom they were able to experience, here and now, something of their future resurrection life), and that in their own lifetime (as most seem to have believed at the time this letter was written) they would experience the general resurrection of all men, when they would share with Christ the office of judging the rest of the world. But in its essentials their belief about life after death was based on the Jewish doctrine of resurrection.

Not all Jews subscribed to this doctrine. We know, for instance, that the
Sadducees roundly denied it, on the grounds that it was not written into the
Old Testament. But it is not likely to have been such ultra-conservative Jews,
now become Christians, who were denying it at Corinth. It is much more
probable that the question was raised by members of the Corinthian congregation who came from a Greek background, and who found the Jewish way of
looking at life after death both crude and improbable. They would have been
accustomed to think of it in abstract and conceptual terms. Immortality of
the soul, for instance, would have been a concept they were thoroughly
familiar with. The Jewish belief in a literal raising up of the physical body
would have made little sense to them; and some of them may well have
thought that it was by no means an essential part of Christianity. Moreover,
the imminence of the Day of the Lord may have made the question seem
somewhat academic. They would still be alive, so they believed, at the end of
the age (unless they forfeited this hope in some such way as Paul refers to
above, 11.30), and some of them evidently imagined that they would pass
unchanged into the new age (if indeed they had not already done so)—a naïve
belief which Paul explicitly refutes with the words, **flesh and blood can** 50
never possess the kingdom of God.

Paul leads into his reply by recalling **the Gospel as I preached it to you.** 2
The salient facts of this Gospel are here laid out with a clarity and precision
which certainly help the argument, but which may also reflect the language
of such summaries of the faith (or "creeds") as were already in use in the
church.

(i) **Christ died for our sins, in accordance with the scriptures.** It 3
was already a basic tenet of the Christian faith that the crucifixion had taken
place according to the will of God, and could be found to have been foretold

in the scriptures. To our minds, Isaiah 53 seems the one passage in the Old Testament which clearly foreshadows this event and offers a clue to its significance. But although this passage was often quoted in the early church (see especially 1 Peter 2.22–5), it is not necessarily the one referred to here. Many other passages seemed now to have gained their true meaning in the light of particular episodes in the suffering, death and resurrection of Christ.

4 (ii) **He was buried.**

(iii) **He was raised to life on the third day, according to the scriptures.** Again, there is no explicit prediction of Christ's resurrection in the Old Testament. But the first Christians were quick to find allusions to it in such passages as Psalm 16.10 (Acts 13.35).

5 (iv) **He appeared to Cephas . . .** One of the qualifications of an apostle
was to have witnessed an appearance of Christ after the resurrection.
Accounts of such appearances occur at the end of Luke's and John's gospels,
and can be used to fill out Paul's summary. But Paul also mentions appearances which are not recorded in the gospels. The most significant of these
7 is the appearance to **James,** the brother of Jesus, who had by now assumed
the leadership of the Jerusalem church, but who was clearly not a disciple of
Jesus before the resurrection. It was presumably this appearance which
turned him from an unbeliever into a church leader (and probably also an
"apostle"—though the language both here and at Galatians 1.19 is ambiguous
on this point). In much the same way, as the last and by far the most dramatic
8 of the series (**an abnormal birth**), Paul also was made an eye-witness and
apostle—the full story is recounted by him in Galatians 1—and his apostleship had been confirmed by the evident success of his efforts; or rather (Paul
10 hastens to add), by **the grace of God working with me.**

Thus the miracle by which Paul became an eye-witness and an apostle was
a part of that single sequence of events which also included the resurrection
of Christ, and which together made up the gospel. Of these basic facts there
11 was only one possible version. **This is what we all proclaim, and this is**
what you believed. It followed that to deny any part of it would be to make
14 **our gospel** (literally, "our proclamation"—the sentence in the original
picks up the language of verse 11) **null and void,** along with **your faith**
(literally, "belief", again picking up verse 11). And this gives Paul his first
12 point against those who say **there is no resurrection of the dead.** His
arguments may be set out as follows.

15 (i) A *reductio ad absurdum.* **If the dead are not raised, it follows that**
Christ was not raised. But this conclusion is incompatible both with the
apostles' basic proclamation and the Corinthians' own belief. Not only that,
but if it were true it would be a doctrine of despair. If Christ were still dead
and buried, there would be no sense in which Christians could now be united
17 with him, and so no release from their **old state of sin**; moreover, Christians
who had died could expect no better destiny than Christ himself, and so

would be utterly lost. Verse 19 is somewhat obscure in the Greek, but its
purpose is clearly to underline the misery of a hope which is bounded by the
limits of human existence. Clearly, then, as applied to Christ, the proposition
that **the dead are not raised** must be false. 16

But this is only half the answer. Christ may have been raised from the dead, but it does not follow that there is a resurrection for others. Christ's resurrection might have been altogether exceptional. Paul still has to prove that "resurrection" is a valid concept for men, and not merely for the Son of God. To do this he uses

(ii) the argument from solidarity. This is essentially the same point as is 20–2
elaborated in Romans 5, though there is a slight difference of emphasis. In
both passages, the skeleton of the argument is the same: just as man's
solidarity with Adam produced (and still produces) death, so our solidarity
with Christ, who has been raised from death to life, procures for us a new
resurrection-life. In Romans, where the subject in hand is Christian living,
this is applied mainly to the present. Here, it is applied to the future: **in** 22
Christ all (by which Paul presumably means, all Christians) **will be**
brought to life. Paul's concern in this paragraph is not with Christian living
in the present age, but with the future hope which he expects very shortly to
be realized. And this leads him into a digression.

The final culmination of history is not to be thought of as a single event,
but as an ordered process, setting **each in his own proper place.** Christ 23
himself is **the firstfruits**—his resurrection, that is to say, is a sure sign of
the imminent resurrection of others, just as the first handful of ripe grain is
a sign of the harvest that must very soon be gathered. The present time is that
brief interval; **afterwards, at his coming,** the promised resurrection will
take place of those (whether dead or still alive) **who belong to Christ. Then** 24
—and we expect further categories, such as those who are not Christians; and
this passage has sometimes been interpreted as if it offered a kind of phased
programme for different classes of men. But in fact Paul moves into entirely
mythological language. Instead of human beings, the subjects become God,
Christ, and those angelic or demonic entities which peopled the universe of
Jewish (and often of Greek) speculation: **every kind of domination,** 24
authority and power, and, finally, the personified figure of **death.** 26

What Paul appears to be doing is working into his scheme of the final 27–8
resurrection a Christian interpretation of two passages from the psalms. The
passages are these:

> "The Lord said to my lord, sit at my right hand until I make your enemies the footstool under your feet" (Psalm 110.1).
>
> "Thou makest him master over all thy creatures; thou hast put all things in subjection under his feet" (Psalm 8.6).

The first of these passages was referred by the Jews to the coming Christ, and was present to the mind of Jesus himself (Matthew 22.44); the second was

also regarded by the early Christians as a prophecy about Christ (Ephesians 1.22; Hebrews 2.6–9). Both seemed to imply a period when the whole created universe would be gradually brought under the lordship of Christ; and Paul conceives of this part of the drama as being played out on a metaphysical
28 stage, with an appropriately metaphysical climax: **God will be all in all.**

After this digression, Paul comes abruptly back to the point with his third argument proving that there is a resurrection of the dead.

29 (iii) An argument from Christian practice. We know nothing more about this custom of **baptism on behalf of the dead**, beyond the fact that various forms of it lingered on in certain parts of the church for some centuries. Presumably, the Corinthians believed that, by a kind of vicarious baptism, they could bring into the promised kingdom relatives and friends who had died before the coming of the gospel. Paul does not comment on this practice; he merely remarks that it presupposed the resurrection.

30–2 (iv) An argument from Paul's own sufferings. If there were no resurrection beyond this life, the old saying (which occurs in Isaiah 22.13, but was of course also a commonplace in both Greek and Latin literature) '**let us eat and drink, for tomorrow we die**' would be a valid philosophy of life, and all that Paul had gone through would be pointless.[a]

Possibly in the series belongs

33–4 (v) a moral argument. The imminence of the day of judgement and resurrection was a powerful spring of Christian moral conduct, and was often invoked to inculcate sobriety, uprightness, decency and the like (see above on Romans 13.12). Those who denied the resurrection were thereby removing this moral pressure, and could have an effect on the **good character** of
33 their fellow-Christians. Paul here quotes a line from a comedy by the Greek playwright Menander, which had doubtless, like many other lines from his plays, become proverbial.

35 **But, you may ask, how are the dead raised?** Even granted the force of Paul's arguments: if there is a resurrection, how is it to be conceived? **In what kind of body?** The Greek mind would still find the bodily aspect of the resurrection difficult to believe in, and we know that the Jews themselves were sometimes puzzled by the question. Accordingly, Paul suggests answers to the difficulty that are drawn from both Jewish and Greek culture.

36–8 (i) The analogy of the seed, which receives a new **body** when it grows into a plant. This analogy was used by Jewish scholars.

39–44 (ii) Ancient medicine recognized different kinds of **flesh**; popular philosophy recognized different kinds of **bodies.**

[*a*] Verse 32 is obscure. Literally it means: "If, in human fashion, I fought with wild beasts at Ephesus, what was the good of it for me?" It is idle to ask whether Paul did in fact have this experience: those who were exposed to wild beasts in the arena did not normally survive to write about it. Either this was a well-known figure of speech—this is the interpretation of the main text in NEB—or else Paul was somewhat exaggerating his own danger (so the footnote).

(iii) The creation story (Genesis 2.7) suggests a distinction between 44–9
animal body and **spiritual body.** This is hard to render in English. When 44
God breathed breath into Adam he made him a "living soul"—meaning
that Adam was now, like the animals, breathing, alive, **an animate being.** 45
But the life given by Christ (**the last Adam**) is on the level of the **spirit**;
and we, by our solidarity with this second Adam or **heavenly man,** will 48
receive a "spiritual" body, as opposed to our old "animal" one.

All these distinctions provide possible ways to conceive of a bodily resurrection. They preclude, either a crudely realistic conception of the coming
age, or the suggestion (apparently made by some Christians in Corinth) that
those who survived to Christ's coming would pass unchanged into the kingdom of God. Paul declares his own convictions on the matter: **I will unfold** 51
a mystery. It is true, some of us will be alive on the Day: **we shall not all**
die. But, whether alive or dead, when the moment comes **we shall all be** 52
changed. A new kind of body will be given to all; and drawing on the conventional Jewish imagery of the last day, as well as on the popular philosophical distinction between **mortal** and **immortal, perishable** and 53
imperishable, Paul paints a vivid picture of how it will all happen.

Two prophecies (Isaiah 25.8 and Hosea 13.14) will then be fulfilled; and 54
the words of the second, '**O Death, where is your sting?**', serve to relate
this whole vision of the future to the present victorious reality of Christian
life. What did the prophet mean by death's **sting**? He meant (so Paul
interprets his somewhat free quotation) that factor in human life to which
death is specifically related (**sin**), and which is seen in its full enormity and
power when its only opposite is **the law.** Over both these (in a manner 56
expounded at length in Romans 5) God **gives us the victory through our** 57
Lord Jesus Christ.

This brings Paul to the end of his argument. It was impossible to do without the concept of resurrection, for it was absolutely basic to the Christian
faith. Nor was there any need to be put off by the crudity with which the
concept was often presented in Jewish circles: many Jews themselves had
worked out a perfectly credible analysis of it, and moreover Christianity had
introduced important modifications. Indeed, resurrection was not merely a
concept any sophisticated person could accept—it was an imminent eventuality. **Therefore, my beloved brothers**—the usual Christian exhortation 58
in view of imminent judgement and glory—**stand firm and immovable.**
As the building metaphor in chapter 3 has made abundantly plain, if it is
in the Lord your labour cannot be lost.

Christian giving

One more question in the Corinthians' letter remained to be answered. We
16. 1 know that Paul had committed himself to raise a **collection** from the
churches which he had founded for the Christian community in Jerusalem.
The necessity for this may have begun with a real shortage of food there
(Acts 11.27–30), and it subsequently became a standing obligation of the
gentile churches towards the parent church in Jerusalem (Galatians 2.10;
Romans 15.26). The question bulks larger in Paul's Second Letter (2 Corinthians 8–9), but it seems that the Corinthians already had queries, if not
complaints, to put to Paul about it. They had been told about the collection,
and had doubtless accepted it in principle; but they were perhaps proposing
to do nothing about it for the time being, and they may possibly have had
doubts (if we may read between the lines of the accusations brought against
Paul later on) about the uses to which Paul was going to put the money.
Paul has apparently already had to give more specific **directions** to another
group of congregations, those in Galatia, and he now repeats them here: the
Corinthians must start laying money aside privately, and (he assures them)
their own representatives will have a part in delivering the money to its
destination.

This leads on to Paul's immediate plans. He is at present at Ephesus
(doubtless the stay described in Acts 19), and plans to stay until after the
8 Jewish feast of Pentecost **(Whitsuntide).** He will then travel, not by the
5 direct route across the sea, but all the way round by land—**by way of
Macedonia**—which will mean that he can hardly be in Corinth before the
autumn, by which time the season for sea travel will be nearly over, and he
6 may stay **perhaps even for the whole winter.**

10 The commendations which follow are more than formalities. **Timothy**
(whose visit was promised above, 4.17) will have the serious and difficult task
of restoring proper order in the church; and (perhaps particularly in view
11 of his youth, compare 1 Timothy 4.12) Paul insists that **no one must slight
12 him. Apollos,** an important figure in the Corinthian church and presumably
particularly popular with the party which bore his name, is refusing to return
at present, and Paul has to apologize for him. It is some indication of the
15 disorder at Corinth that **Stephanas,** one of Paul's first converts, and two
17 other men otherwise unknown to us **(Fortunatus and Achaicus)** have not
been receiving the respect which they deserve in virtue both of their seniority
and of their devoted work. It is indeed their visit to Paul in Ephesus which
has alerted him to the disquieting state of affairs at Corinth, and he finds it
necessary to make a personal appeal for a warm reception for them when they
return.

19 On **Aquila and Prisca** and on the **kiss of peace,** see above on Romans

16.3 and 16.16. As was usual (see below on Galatians 6.11), Paul adds a
greeting in his **own hand**, along with three phrases which may be intended 21
to mark the transition between the reading of the letter to the assembled
church and the beginning of the celebration of the eucharist:
(1) a formula of exclusion from the congregation: **let him be outcast** 22
(literally, *anathema*). Compare Revelation 22.15.

(2) *Marana tha*: a phrase in Aramaic, which doubtless occurred in the prayers of the first Christians. Paul leaves it in the original language—doubtless it was perfectly familiar to his readers; the NEB provides us with what is the most probable translation: **Come, O Lord!** The same prayer occurs at the end of Revelation (22.20), where it is also followed by

(3) the grace. 23

THE SECOND LETTER OF PAUL TO THE CORINTHIANS

We do not know how the First Letter to the Corinthians was received, nor whether Paul paid the visit he promised them. Acts is silent on these questions, and our next letter from the correspondence is so taken up with more recent affairs that the questions raised in 1 Corinthians are barely referred to. Indeed, after that letter was written, Paul's relations with the Corinthian church evidently went through a difficult period. Some member of the church had committed a serious offence, and the Corinthians had failed to punish it in the way demanded by Paul. This had led to a direct challenge of Paul's authority; and Paul, fearing that a personal visit from himself at such a juncture might merely cause pain and embarrassment, sent a stern letter by the hand of Titus; but he was not at all sure how this would be received, and he spent an anxious period of waiting, unable even to carry on with his missionary work in northern Greece, until Titus eventually rejoined him with the news that the Corinthians had yielded.

Paul's side of this story is told in the course of the first two chapters and in part of chapter 7 of 2 Corinthians. At the end of his account of it, he frankly expresses his relief at the way things have turned out, and his tone is as cordial as anywhere in his letters. The difficulty comes when we compare this with the rest of the letter. Apart from two chapters about the raising of funds for the poor in Jerusalem (8 and 9) and an isolated (and almost certainly misplaced) paragraph of moral teaching (6.14—7.1), the remainder of the letter reveals Paul on the defensive: in the earlier chapters he labours to establish the true basis of Christian apostleship, and in the last four chapters he feels himself forced to dwell (even though it is against his principles to do so) on his own superior qualifications for the work; and he concludes with a direct and outspoken attack on his opponents and with a threat to the Corinthians that, unless they own his authority in the meantime, he will be forced to put the matter to the test by confronting them in person.

These differences of mood and purpose are so striking that they demand explanation. In some passages, where Paul seems to change rapidly and repeatedly from one frame of mind to another, the differences can perhaps be explained as due to the tension and agitation which Paul had recently been undergoing, and to the fact that, shortly before, he had endured some torture or illness which nearly cost him his life. But there are certain sections, in particular the last four chapters, which it is hard to believe were written in the same circumstances as produced the serene sentiments of chapter 7; and many critics believe that the only solution to these difficulties is to assume that what we know as the SECOND LETTER OF PAUL TO THE CORINTHIANS is a collection of different letters (or parts of letters) written by Paul at various stages of the trouble with the Corinthians, and assembled by some later editor without regard to the order in which they were originally written.

Whether or not the several parts of the letter were composed at the same time, it is clear that for the most part they were connected with the same crisis. The moment of rebellion against Paul's authority had been accompanied by a many-sided attack on his claim to be an apostle. Men whom Paul calls 'false apostles' (or, with bitter irony, 'superlative apostles') had been alleging that Paul was deficient in eloquence, spiritual gifts and personal authority; that he had been defrauding the church; that he had no letters of recommendation; and even that he was of doubtful ancestry. Precisely who these men were, where they came from and what doctrine they preached, is difficult to determine. Part of the difficulty is caused by a fact which also gives the letter its unique interest and value. Paul seldom comes down to the level of his adversaries to refute them point by point. If he did, we should probably be able to find out more about them. Instead, he takes up an altogether different position, and demonstrates, by implication, the falsity of his opponents' pretensions by an analysis, based on his own experience, of the true nature of an apostle's calling. Hence the heading:

Personal religion and the ministry

The greeting follows the usual form without any notable expansion; but this
time it is addressed, not to Corinth only, but to **all . . . throughout the** 1. 1
whole of Achaia. The Roman province of Achaia, of which Corinth was the
capital, included the whole of Greece south of Thessaly and Epirus. Did
other churches already exist in this area, apart from Corinth? We have no
reason to think so—unless Paul's preaching in Athens (Acts 17) had led to
the growth of a Christian community there. It is therefore likely that the
greeting was simply intended to embrace all the members of the Corinthian
church, including any who were normally resident outside the capital.
Praise be to (or, as it is sometimes translated, "Blessed be") **the God** 3
and Father of our Lord Jesus Christ—a stereotyped beginning which
occurs also in Ephesians and in 1 Peter, and which is a Christian adaptation
of the commonest of all Jewish prayers, "Blessed be God, who . . .". The
particular attribute of God which Paul dwells on here is: **whose consolation** 4
never fails us. He comforts us (the same word, in the Greek, as "consoles": it occurs nine times in this short paragraph)—and this "comforting",
or "consolation", is more than a pious phrase: it is a datum of specifically

Christian experience and, as the letter will show, is an important factor in the life of the apostle and of his churches.

According to Jewish religion, God was certainly a "God of consolation". But this "consolation" took certain precise forms: the prophets, the Messiah, the ultimate destiny of Israel—these things were "consoling" because they gave grounds for hope, and it is hope which makes bearable the tribulations of the present. God's consolation, therefore, took the form of fixing the eyes of the sufferer on a promised future reward. This conception is often found in the New Testament; compare Romans 15.4 (where, however, the same Greek word is translated "encouragement"). But in this passage, and again and again throughout the letter (though not in the previous one), the real substance of God's consolation is taken out of the future and brought into the present. It is seen to consist, not of hope merely, but of a present experience. How does this happen?

5 An answer is suggested by verse 5. **As Christ's cup of suffering overflows, and we suffer with him.** This is a deliberate paraphrase of the Greek; literally, the sense is, "As Christ's sufferings overflow with respect to us", and the meaning of this very compressed phrase may be somewhat similar to Paul's statement in Colossians 1.24, 'this is my way of helping to complete . . . the full tale of Christ's afflictions still to be endured'. The sufferings which Christians endure are not an adventitious calamity which might have been avoided, but a necessary part of their destiny; there is indeed a definite quota of sufferings which has to be undergone before the end of the world comes. These sufferings form a continuous series with the sufferings of Christ himself, who is in some way implicated in them—**we suffer with him**; and this implication of Christ in the sufferings of Christians alters the whole nature of Christian consolation, which now consists, not merely in the hope of a greater destiny after the sufferings are over, but of a personal consciousness of the presence of Christ in the sufferer. The experience of suffering "with Christ" already contains its own consolation; in this sense, **through Christ our consolation overflows.** Moreover, this
new kind of consolation is an experience Christians can communicate to each
6 other. For the Christian, therefore, **distress** and **consolation** are two sides
of the same experience. Whichever way it is looked at, such an experience is
a source of inspiration for others. Paul's sufferings may thus be of positive
help to the Corinthians; and yet the Corinthians should not be in any real
need of help, for so long as their suffering is related to Christ's suffering, they
7 already have their experience of consolation. So Paul can write: **our hope
for you is firmly grounded.**

It is in this perspective that Paul wishes the trials he has recently gone
8 through to be seen. We do not know anything about what he calls **the
trouble that came upon us in the province of Asia.** If it was anything
to do with the disturbance in Ephesus narrated in Acts 19.23–41, then the

author of that account must have been unaware of the true seriousness of the crisis for Paul. But Paul's language is very general; all we can say is that, whether it was illness or persecution, it had clearly been a harrowing experience, and one from which Paul had learnt his own spiritual lesson. His escape had been due to God alone, and his continued safety would depend on the prayers of his friends. There was nothing in his deliverance for which
he could properly take any credit himself. It had been a **gracious favour,** 11
to which the only possible response was **thanks** to God from all who had
been praying for it.

There is one thing we are proud of. The Greek word *kauchēsis* had a 12
larger range of meanings than any corresponding English word. Its normal usage was pejorative, to express any kind of boasting, over-confidence or excessive pride. But there was also a perfectly proper kind of pride or confidence which arose from the consciousness that God had done great things for his people, or even (as here) from a sense of one's own integrity; and this too could be called *kauchēsis*. Paul uses the word a great deal in this letter. His opponents had evidently been behaving in a way well described by the first group of meanings: they had been boasting of advantages or of superior talents which were either fictitious or irrelevant, and their excessive *kauchēsis* was one of the main objects of Paul's attack. On the other hand, Paul had a consciousness of the commission which God had given him, and of his own integrity in carrying it out, which furnished him with a genuine *kauchēsis* of his own to set against the inflated and objectionable *kauchēsis* of his opponents. The word is thus made to do duty for the attitude of both sides in the dispute; and in addition it derives a still more serious meaning from being projected into the context of the ultimate judgement to be passed on man.
On **the Day of our Lord Jesus,** Christians were to come before God 14
supported by each other; it would be the relationship which held between them on earth which would enable them to stand with a certain pride or confidence (*kauchēsis*) before God. What mattered far more than the present misunderstanding between Paul and his friends in Corinth was the deep relationship between them which would come to light on the last day.

Meanwhile, however, there was misunderstanding in plenty. People had been reading between the lines of Paul's letters (verse 13), and in particular had been criticizing his plans and his changes of plan. We last heard of Paul's plans at the end of 1 Corinthians (16.5): 'I shall come to Corinth after passing through Macedonia—for I am travelling by way of Macedonia'. We cannot say for certain whether or not this plan had been carried out before the present letter was written; but in any event Paul certainly paid a visit to Macedonia. From Ephesus, there were two possible routes. He could either have gone mainly by land round the Aegean; or have crossed the sea to Corinth and then proceeded north, either overland, or up the coast by ship. The second route was the one he had decided to take, in order to have a

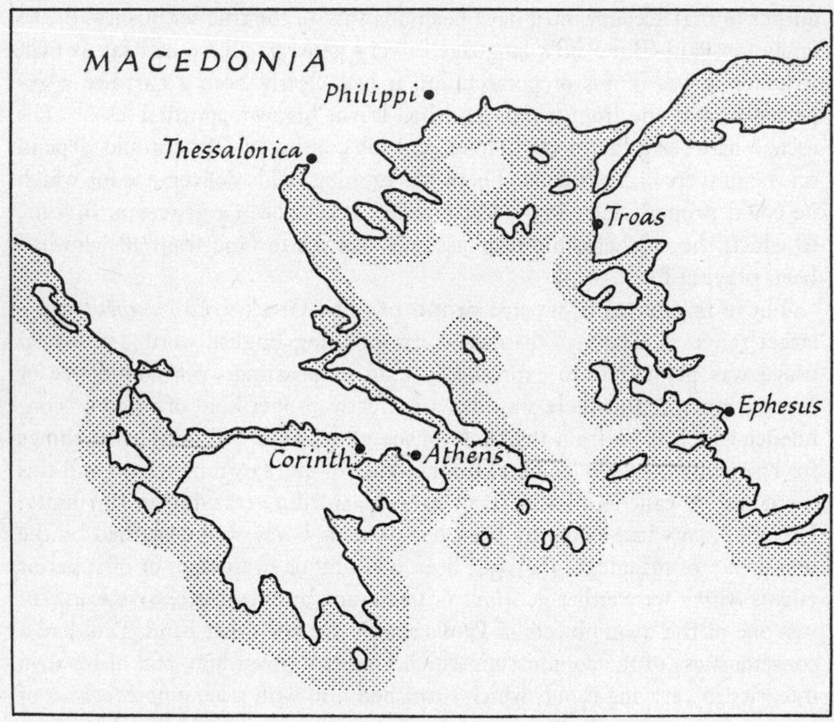

chance to see the Corinthians both before and after his journey to Macedonia
15 —to give them **the benefit of a double visit.** For some reason (the text
does not allow us to be sure what the reason was) all this had exposed Paul
to the charge of irresponsibility; people were criticizing him, perhaps
because he had proposed an ambitious alteration to his previous plan, or
perhaps because he subsequently had not fulfilled his promises.

Paul does not answer this charge by defending any particular plan or course of action. Instead, he sets about refuting the suggestion that his plans or activities in general depended on his own whim or his own interests.
17 **Do I, when I frame my plans, frame them as a worldly man might?**
The "worldly man's" planning consists of reviewing various possible courses
of action, and saying **'yes' and 'yes'** to some and **'no' and 'no'** to others.
18 In order to choose the best combination, his reasoning will involve **an
ambiguous blend of Yes and No.** But this, Paul protests, was not his own
manner of procedure at all. The project, for instance, to go all the way to
Macedonia was not adopted as a result of weighing alternatives and balancing
yes's against no's; it was a command of God, to which only one response was
19 possible: **Yes.** And even this response was not comparable with the worldly
man's decision to adopt the best available course of action, for it was directly

inspired by God himself. Just as Christ Jesus' whole being was **the Yes** 20
pronounced upon God's promises, so Christians, by virtue of having
been baptized into union with Jesus (for which **guaranteed** and **anointed**
are doubtless metaphors) and of possessing the Spirit (for which **seal** and 22
pledge are certainly metaphors) are taken up into this affirming response of
Jesus. Their very '**Amen**' at worship is an expression of their solidarity with 20
Christ Jesus in giving glory to God; and so (if we may round off Paul's
argument for him) their actions and plans, far from being inspired by
"worldly" motives or calculations, are simply their response to the commands of God, which they now make by virtue of their intimate relationship
with Christ.

Nevertheless, Paul did in fact change his plans. **I did not after all come** 23
to Corinth. How was this to be squared with what has just been said?

It was out of consideration for you. In 1 Corinthians Paul insists more
than once that, in anything affecting the relationship between Christians,
there is one overriding principle, which may be called 'love', or 'building
up', or concern for the 'weak'. And so here: this was the principle which
had made him act with apparent irresponsibility. If it had been necessary for
him to go to Corinth to give instruction in the faith, doubtless he would have
gone at once, since this was a task which could not be delayed. But this had
never been the case—**your hold on the faith is secure enough.** And since 24
the only other object of his visit would have been their mutual pleasure—
we are working with you for your own happiness—then to have undertaken it at that moment would have been pointless, since such was the
estrangement between them that it could have resulted only in pain and
bitterness for both sides.

Instead, therefore, Paul wrote them a **letter.** Unless (as some believe) 2. 3
2 Corinthians 10–13 originally formed part of it, we do not possess this letter,
and we know nothing more about it than can be inferred from this chapter
and from chapter 7 below. It was written, we learn, **out of great distress** 4
and anxiety, so much so that Paul was unable to settle down **to preach the** 12
gospel at Troas, or to find any relief in Macedonia (7.5) until he had received
an answer. What was really at stake (as Paul eventually confesses in 7.12) was
not 'the offender or his victim'—i.e. the specific cause of all the trouble in
Corinth—but whether the Corinthians **fully accepted** his **authority.** The 9
issue must have been a test case: Paul had laid down a certain course to be
followed, and remained in suspense until he knew that he had been obeyed.

This test case was either the same as, or similar to, that on which Paul had
already legislated in 1 Corinthians 5. A certain **offender** had been sentenced 7
by **the general meeting** to some penalty which could now be alleviated 6
only **by a formal act.** If the procedure was similar to that recommended in 8
1 Corinthians 5, we may suppose that the offender had been excommunicated,
but had now shown signs of penitence, and that instead of being permanently

'consigned to Satan' (1 Cor. 5.5), he could now be forgiven and formally
11 re-admitted. This course would incidentally deprive **Satan** of a victim; and
the authority behind any blow struck at Satan was of course ultimately, not
Paul's, but Christ's.

But this is to anticipate the end of the story. In the last paragraph of this
chapter, Paul recalls something of the relief with which he finally received an
answer to his letter. A chain of metaphors describes the destiny of a Christian
14 missionary. He is a member of **Christ's triumphal procession** (with perhaps the implication that he must expect to be continually on the move);
15 and he is like **incense** which is both a sacrifice to God (offered by Christ)
and also a means of putting men to the test: for, according to whether they
16 react to it as to a **deadly fume** or a **vital fragrance,** men are thereby
divided up into the lost and the saved. A heavy responsibility indeed; and if
Paul's opponents in Corinth had been saying that they were **equal to** such a
calling (or 'qualified', as the same phrase is translated below, 3.5) they must
realize what they were claiming. The most Paul will say about himself is that
his own preaching is free from either mercenary motives or counterfeit
17 arguments (both implications are probably present in the phrase, **hawking
the word of God about**). In declaring the word of salvation and judgement,
Paul does it, so far as is humanly possible, only as the authorized spokesman
of God.

If this is the case it can hardly be necessary for Paul to start all over again
3. 1 producing his **credentials.** And yet he is forced to say something on the
subject, since his opponents (**some people**) had apparently been basing
their claims to authority on **letters of introduction** which they had brought,
we may suppose, from Jerusalem or some other well-established Christian
community.

Characteristically, Paul does not come down to their level. He refuses to discuss whether such letters of introduction gave their possessors any authority which he did not have himself. If any kind of proof were needed that Paul's commission to preach to the Gentiles was a real one, it lay to hand (as Paul was fond of saying: compare 1 Corinthians 9.2) in the very existence of the churches which had grown up as a result of his preaching. These communities, and in particular the church in Corinth, were all Paul could possibly need by way of a "letter of introduction"; and the idea that this was precisely what they were leads Paul into a complex series of metaphors.

3 If they were a **letter,** then it was a letter which had **come from Christ.**
Paul did not write it for himself, it was written by Christ for him to carry,
and it was more permanent and constantly valid than any ordinary letter
because (in the Old Testament phrase) it was "written on his heart". But
this metaphor also suggests another point. The Old Testament knew of a
divine "letter": the laws given by God to Moses, which were written **on**

stone tablets. But this "letter", the Law of Moses, was precisely that old
covenant or old dispensation which, Paul had come to realize, had no power
to save: **the written law condemns to death**—indeed the Old Testament 6
prophets themselves had looked forward to a new dispensation, under which
the law of God would be taken out of the realm of objective commands and
duties, and would become a spontaneous motive of conduct, written **on the** 3
pages of the human heart (see especially Jeremiah 31.31–3; Ezekiel
11.19), and taking effect through the agency of the Spirit. If one may draw
out the implications of the metaphor a little further than Paul does: the
Corinthian church was a document of the new relationship, or **new covenant,** 6
which now holds between God and men, energized by the Spirit, and displayed in human lives. As such, it provided all the "credentials" needed by
the preacher whose preaching brought it to birth (or, who delivered the
"letter"), but it no more argued for any special **qualification** in the 5
messenger than the character of a letter argues for the character of the
postman. If Paul's opponents were laying claim to some special kind of
qualification for exercising authority in the church, the effect of Paul's
metaphor was to show that, in this matter of dispensing the new, spiritual
covenant, no preacher was entitled to **claim anything as his own.**

The metaphor of the two "letters" or covenants—one on stone, the other
in the heart—serves to make a further point. The agent of the first covenant,
which was **engraved letter by letter upon stone,** was Moses; and at the 7
time when the covenant was made, Moses was invested with an unearthly
splendour which was actually visible to those who saw him. The account is
in Exodus 34.29–35:

> "At length Moses came down from Mount Sinai with the two stone tablets of the Tokens in his hands, and when he descended, he did not know that the skin of his face shone because he had been speaking with the Lord. When Aaron and the Israelites saw how the skin of Moses' face shone, they were afraid to approach him . . .
>
> Then Moses put a veil over his face, and whenever he went in before the Lord to speak with him, he removed the veil until he came out. Then he would go out and tell the Israelites all the commands he had received. Whenever the skin of Moses' face shone in the sight of the Israelites he would put the veil back over his face until he went in again to speak with the Lord."

Yet, despite the splendour of its inauguration, the divine testimony turned
(as we might say) from law into legalism, and became (in Paul's language)
the dispensation under which we are condemned. Its efficacy was of 9
short duration, the splendour **was soon to fade.** There was now a new 11
dispensation, **under which we are acquitted. How much greater,** then, 9
must be the splendour of this new dispensation, what a radiance there must

be in the face of the messenger who brought such a "letter"—and much of
2 Corinthians is concerned to show that this was indeed the case. Paul's
ministry, for instance, had been attended by reverses and tribulations of
various kinds, and his opponents had apparently been fastening on these as
evidence that he lacked divine authority. But, unlike the splendour of the
divine presence on Sinai, which was with Moses only briefly, the splendour
11 of the Spirit was with Christians continuously; it is **the splendour of that
which endures.** Therefore no physical adversity could affect the fact that,
18 all the time, a Christian is being transfigured into the likeness of Christ, **from
splendour to splendour.**

13 The same chapter of Exodus yields a further point. Moses **put a veil
over his face.** Christians, on the contrary, have no need to conceal the
12 splendour given to them by the constantly indwelling Spirit; they can **speak
out boldly.** But more than this: the veil over Moses' face was also a symbol
that the original hearers of the law did not understand its true meaning. Why,
for instance, had the Jews not recognized Jesus as the fulfilment of all that
14 was written in Scripture about the coming Messiah? Because **their minds
had been made insensitive.** The veil symbolized the fact that the Jews had
never yet grasped the true interpretation of Scripture. All that they had ever
seen in it was **the old covenant**—indeed, Paul is bold enough to call
Scripture itself **the old covenant** (the Old Testament), so setting a fashion
which has been universally followed to this day (see above, p. 4). For
Scripture is not self-explanatory: all that the unaided human mind can read
there is the old covenant, and this is **abrogated** only in Christ—or (as the
Greek may also be translated)[a] "the veil is abolished only in Christ", that
is to say, only in the light of Christ does Scripture yield its true meaning.

And there is yet another point to be made. According to the Greek version
of the Septuagint (slightly adapted to his purpose by Paul), one verse from
16 the passage quoted above reads: '**whenever he turns to the Lord the veil
is removed**' (Exodus 34.34). Now Christians were already accustomed to
seeing, in Old Testament statements about "the Lord", prophetic references
17 to Jesus Christ. By the same technique, Paul can say that **the Lord of whom
this passage speaks is the Spirit.** The original subject of the sentence in
Exodus was of course Moses. But if the sentence is taken out of context
(which seemed quite legitimate to an interpreter like Paul, who was prepared
to find prophecies and deeper meanings hidden in any text of the Old
Testament) it sounds quite general, and can even be rendered (as the NEB
footnote has it) "when one turns to the Lord the veil is removed". The text
then becomes a prophecy of the "new covenant" under which Christians
now live. Christians have the Spirit always with them. Not merely, therefore,
18 do they constantly **reflect . . . the splendour of the Lord** but, having
"turned to the Spirit", they have had the "veil" removed—that is to say,

[a] See the footnote in NEB (Second Edition).

they have been cured of the insensitivity of their minds, they can read Scripture aright, and they are released from the slavery of the law. **Such is the influence of the Lord who is Spirit.**

Paul's authority, then (unlike, we may suppose, the authority being claimed
by his opponents), does not depend upon any 'qualification' of his own, but
upon a **commission** (literally, a "service") with which he has been en- 4. 1
trusted by God. It does not need to be proved by subtle arguments (**We** 2
neither practise cunning nor distort the word of God—again doubtless
a glance at Paul's opponents, as in 2.17 above). Nor—and this is a point
which is about to be developed—is it rendered in any way questionable by
the sufferings which the bearer of the commission has to endure. Despite
every tribulation—**we never lose heart.** Paul's conduct, in fact, both with 1
regard to his methods of preaching and with regard to the chequered course
of his ministry, has been entirely candid: **only by declaring the truth** 2
openly do we recommend ourselves. The reason why some of his hearers
have not believed is not (as perhaps the opposition was saying) because of
any distortion on his part, but because of their blindness—or rather, because
Satan (**the god of this passing age**) has blinded them and set them **on the** 4. 3
way to perdition. And it is real blindness; for the **light** which God ori- 6
ginally created out of darkness (Genesis 1.3), and which had always served as
a powerful symbol of the coming of salvation to Israel (Isaiah 9.2), is now
gloriously present **in the face of Jesus Christ** as the **light of revelation.**

Paul now addresses himself more directly to the criticism that the personal
reverses he has suffered are evidence that his authority cannot be from God.
The human body is at best a frail thing, standing under the daily possibility
of death, as breakable as **pots of earthenware.** But such frailty is inevitable:
it is not an argument against the validity of a man's philosophy of life. On the
contrary, it is the very survival of the body under adverse circumstances, it is
the preservation of faith and hope despite all afflictions, which offers the most
convincing testimony of the truth of a man's beliefs. And more than this:
the Christian, when he suffers, enters into still closer union with Christ; or,
to put it the other way round, the external blows which reduce a Christian's
body more and more to the condition of a corpse (an idea which is included
in the meaning of the word here translated **death**) are nothing else but the 10
means by which Christ becomes fully manifested in the persons of his followers. For just as the full manifestation of Christ embraced not merely his
suffering, but suffering followed and transformed by new **life**, so the sufferings of Christians are the necessary context, so to speak, in which **the life of** 11
Jesus also may be revealed in this mortal body of ours.

Thus death is at work in us: the whole paragraph has been an essay in 12
expressing the complex phenomenon of suffering transforming the body of
the Christian sufferer with new life. One would expect the second half of the

sentence to complete the picture: "but at the same time life is at work in us". Unexpectedly, Paul writes **and life in you.** It is as if (though we cannot be sure of his meaning) Paul feels that there is after all a simpler explanation of his own sufferings: they are part of what is necessary to procure **life**—that is, solidarity with Christ, true Christian living—for his converts. Perhaps after all one need not strain one's imagination to understand how **death** and **life,** suffering and splendour, can coexist in the same person, for it is only in exceptional cases, such as that of Paul himself, that Christian suffering reaches such a pitch. Let it rather be said that the extreme suffering of a few is the necessary price that has to be paid for the new and splendid life of the Christian community as a whole. **Thus death is at work in us, and life in you.**

13 **'I believed, and therefore I spoke out'** (Psalm 116.10, in the Greek Septuagint version). The Christian can have more than the confidence of the psalmist. The sufferings which he incurs by his boldness of speech enable him to enter the sufferings of Christ and thereby assure him of being ulti-
14 mately brought by God **to his presence,** along with all other Christians—for this destiny is not reserved for exceptional cases, such as apostles and martyrs, but is the process by which all Christians, in the solidarity of their prayer and thanksgiving, are being prepared for the glory to come.

The usual way for a pious man of Jewish background to explain the sufferings of the righteous was to express the conviction that God would reward the sufferer in the next life. This, too, was Paul's usual way of putting it (Romans 8.18; 1 Corinthians 15.30–2), and indeed Jesus often used the same kind of language himself. But in this letter the thought has been moving towards a conclusion which is more easily formulated in terms of Greek than of Hebrew psychology. It remains true, of course, that present sufferings will be made good in the future (verse 17); but Paul now realizes (perhaps for the first time) that they are also rewarded in the present, by a deep transformation which takes place within the Christian as he enters into the sufferings of Christ. To use terminology which goes back to Plato and which was a
16 commonplace of Greek philosophical language, **though our outward humanity is in decay, yet day by day we are inwardly renewed.** Or
18 (to use another very common Greek antithesis), **our eyes are fixed, not on the things that are seen, but on the things that are unseen.** Paul's sufferings are signs of the invisible renewal taking place within him.

The passage which follows is a particularly difficult piece of Greek, and has been interpreted in various ways. It is possible to find in it a number of ideas, which are somewhat alien to Paul's traditional beliefs, about the fate of the individual immediately after death, and the danger (or advantage) of an interim period of "nakedness" between death and the general resurrection. It is quite possible that Paul shows an interest in such ideas here; but they lie rather wide of the argument as it has developed so far, and the following attempt to interpret the passage assumes that the subject is still

the possible effect on Paul's authority and reputation of his continued weakness and suffering.

The body, Paul has already admitted, is a frail thing. We have our treasure
in pots of earthenware, and you must not judge the truth of the gospel by
what you see happening to a man's body. But suppose—and perhaps at this
time Christians were not reckoning with the possibility seriously enough,
since the majority of them expected to live to see the Day of Christ—suppose
we do not just nearly die, but that the all-too-breakable earthenware is actually broken! Suppose (to change the metaphor) **that...the earthly frame** 5. 1
(the Greek word suggests a "temporary tent-dwelling" which was a notion
of Greek religious philosophy) **that houses us today should be demol-
ished**: we are already in possession of something which makes even that
danger insignificant. What is this possession? It can of course only be
described metaphorically. For instance, it can be called **a building which
God has provided**; and the words **not made by human hands** suggest a
building of a particular kind. For Christians, the old temple worship at
Jerusalem had given way to that of the new temple, which was the church;
and they were fond of saying that this temple, unlike the one at Jerusalem,
was 'not made with hands' (Mark 14.58; Acts 7.48; Hebrews 9.11). It
looks, then, as if Paul's first way of describing the Christian's most precious
possession is by a metaphor suggesting the life and worship of the church.
But then the metaphor changes: it is also something which can be **put on** 2
like a garment. Even this is not quite what it seems. For "putting on" is
an almost technical expression for the act of a Christian when, for instance at
baptism, he accepts Christ as his Lord (Romans 13.14; Galatians 3.27). Thus
the **heavenly habitation**, which is already our possession, emerges from
this mass of images as nothing less than Christ himself as he is known in the
earthly life and the heavenly worship of the church.

But in whatever terms it is described, and despite the immense consolation
and assurance which flow from it, this inestimable possession does not for
one moment protect the believer either from the moral consequences of his
own acts or from the physical dangers which surround him. **In this present** 2
body we do indeed groan: we are still exposed to pain and threatened with
death and judgement; and the reason why this continues to oppress us is that
we cannot yet be sure that our "putting on" of Christ has been complete.
Therefore, if we suddenly die, we may be found not to have put anything on
at all, but to be in the same condition as any other sinner before God's
judgement seat: **naked.**[a] We need time to be sure that our "putting on" of 3
Christ has taken effect, and so we do not wish to be deprived of our present
body too soon: **rather our desire is to have the new body put on over it.** 4

[*a*] Verse 3 presents a difficult problem for the translator. The interpretation above is reconcilable with the NEB rendering, but receives more support from a rendering on these lines: "if, that is, we shall indeed find ourselves clothed, and not naked".

We yearn for the inner transformation and renewal of our inner selves (described in 4.16 above) to be complete before the dissolution of the outward man, **so that** (as Paul has expressed it before in 1 Corinthians 15.53) **our mortal part may be absorbed into life immortal.**

And yet this is perhaps to overstress the ambivalence and insecurity of
5 it all. **God himself has shaped us for this very end.** Christians are "God's
people", their faith assures them of their immortal destiny, and their own
6 experience gives them proof of it: **as a pledge of it he has given us the
Spirit. Therefore,** despite all dangers and uncertainties, **we never cease to
7 be confident.** Since **faith is our guide,** and not the things we see,[a] we do
not judge by appearances or set any store by the safety of our persons; for,
whether or not we die before this is accomplished, our destiny is close union
8 with Christ, and indeed we would actually prefer to die (**we . . . would
rather leave our home in the body**) so long as this meant that we would
go to live with the Lord. "So long as"—and this is the great condition, the
essential factor which prevents our salvation from being in any way auto-
10 matic: **we must all have our lives laid open before the tribunal of
9 Christ. We therefore make it our ambition, wherever we are, here**
(i.e. alive when Christ comes again) **or there** (i.e. already dead), **to be
acceptable to him.**

It has often been noted that the foregoing paragraphs display a certain inconsistency. At one moment, 'we do indeed groan'; at the next, 'we never cease to be confident'. Why does Paul's mood seem to swing so rapidly from one extreme to the other? It is possible that the reason was personal and psychological: because of his private troubles and his anxiety over his churches, his confidence ebbed and flowed even while he was writing the letter. But it may be that the apparent inconsistency is only an extreme form of a tension always present in the Christian life. On the one hand, there is a legitimate assurance of salvation: Christians have received baptism, they are 'God's people, incorporate in Christ' (Philippians 1.1), they experience the Spirit as a 'pledge' of the full glory and liberation which is to come. On the other hand, all this does not diminish the individual's responsibility to walk worthily in the new way, to follow the promptings of the Spirit, and to make all his conduct 'acceptable' to Christ. The ultimate standards of moral action still apply to him, and so all his confidence and assurance must ever be tinged with a serious consciousness that he still stands subject to the judgement of God.

11 **With this fear of the Lord before our eyes we address our appeal to
men.** What Paul has suffered, what dangers he has encountered, what
weaknesses and apparent inconsistencies he has found himself limited by—
nothing of all this provides material for judging his performance as an apostle.

[a] So the footnote in NEB. The rendering of the verse in the main text must be understood as simply a repetition of the idea in the preceding sentence.

All the judging must be done by God, and to this judgement the apostle is
exposed as much as anyone else. But once this accountability is accepted, and
once it is realized that **to God our lives lie open**, then there can be no
possible grounds for practising any deception towards men. **This is not** 12
another attempt to recommend ourselves to you—Paul is not trying to
produce new considerations which will make the Corinthians think better of
him, but rather to help them to look, not at the messenger, but at the message,
and to understand what kind of mission and activity is a proper ground for
pride (*kauchēsis*, see above on 1.12). They will then have a standard by
which to measure both the pretensions of his opponents (**those whose**
pride is all in outward show), and the allegedly extravagant and abnormal 13
behaviour of Paul. It is, in fact, the only possible standard which can be
applied to Christian living in general. The purpose and result of Christ's
death (which was undergone out of **love** for men, and therefore **leaves us** 14
no choice but to respond to it in this way) was that men **should cease to** 15
live for themselves, and should live for him who for their sake died
and was raised to life. Their lives, therefore, like Christ's life, are not to be
judged by **worldly standards**, such as power, eloquence and wisdom, but 16
only by the extent to which they are dedicated and transparent, lived in the
service of God and man—a kind of existence to which man cannot aspire
unaided, but which is part of the **new order**, or new life,[a] which he enters 17
when he becomes **united to Christ.**

To put it in another way: any 'qualification' possessed by the preacher
or the apostle is as much the **work of God** as is the message he bears. The 18
thing which has happened in Christ, and the change which has thereby
become possible in the relationship between God and men, is here described
(unusually) as **reconciliation**; and reconciliation is set in motion by a 18
messenger or an embassy from the other party. **We come therefore as** 20
Christ's ambassadors—and Paul gives a specimen, in the last two verses
of this chapter, of the kind of appeal which the ambassador is empowered to
make: God allowed Christ (though innocent of sin) to become in some way
implicated with **the sinfulness of men** (the metaphor may be sacrificial— 21
see the footnote in NEB), so that men, by their union with him, might be
taken up into Christ's inherent state of "righteousness" or "justification"
(here translated **goodness**) before God.

Such an appeal is evidently intended for the world at large, not for an already Christian congregation. Paul may of course have felt that there were some members of the Corinthian church who could attend to it with advantage, but its main purpose seems to be to stand as a demonstration of Chris-

[*a*] It is not clear from the Greek whether Paul is describing the effect of union with Christ entirely in terms of the individual believer, or whether he also has in mind the whole new order of things which is presaged by Christ and which is partly realized each time a new person comes to Christ. Hence the alternative renderings in the NEB footnotes.

tian preaching and of the function of the Christian preacher. For he addresses
6. 1 the Corinthians as **sharing in God's work.** They have this task—or **grace**
—just as much as Paul has, and they must not allow any sophistical arguments
about, say, the "proper qualifications", to lull them into letting it **go for**
2 **nothing.** To use the inspired words of Isaiah (49.8), **the hour of favour,**
the day of deliverance, is the present. The embassy, the appeal, should be
on its way.

These chapters have accumulated many arguments to show (with reference
to Paul's opponents) what a true apostle is not like, what his authority does
3–10 not depend on, and what his success must not be judged by. In conclusion,
Paul adds a more positive characterization of God's servants, painting in a
few distinctive traits by which they may be recognized. And yet these
marks too are ambiguous; everything the Christian does is of its very nature
open to misunderstanding. The impressive paradoxes of Paul's description
arise out of the very ethos of the Christian life: men of two worlds, poor and
yet rich, suffering and yet triumphant.

All this has involved self-examination and self-exposure, an elaborate
demonstration that Paul has nothing to hide and nothing to apologize for.
12 If there is still **constraint** in his relations with the Corinthians, it must be
on their side, and can be dispelled only if they too follow his example and
13 **open wide** their hearts.

Problems of church life and discipline

There is now an abrupt break in the argument, marked in the NEB by a new heading. The short section 6.14—7.1 seems to have no connection with what comes before or after it, and if it were omitted the letter would run on quite naturally from 6.13 to 7.2.

Furthermore, the content of this short paragraph is unexpected. It consists of a piece of dogmatic moral instruction for Christians, couched in
14 strikingly Jewish terms. **Do not unite yourselves with unbelievers; they**
are no fit mates for you. The metaphor is of setting two different beasts,
say an ox and an ass, under the same yoke together, and the application
intended is probably to the question of mixed marriages between Christians
and non-Christians. But the language seems to be inspired less by the practical inconveniences of such unions as by a Jewish type of horror at contact
with heathendom and idolatry. The "unbeliever" is not regarded (as he is
in 1 Corinthians 7) as a person who might still be influenced for good, but as
14, 15 an embodiment of **wickedness** and **darkness,** indeed as **Belial** himself (a
16 current Jewish word for Satan). The Christian, on the other hand, is **the**
temple of the living God (an idea found elsewhere in Paul); and a veritable

mosaic of scriptural phrases (drawn from Leviticus 26.12, Isaiah 52.11 and 16–18
elsewhere) is used to stress the incompatibility of the two. The paragraph
ends, in terminology which sounds a little unlike Paul (the phrase **flesh or** 7. 1
spirit, for instance, does not seem to bear the precise technical sense he
usually gives to these two words), with a general exhortation to avoid defilement, which certainly has a Christian application, but which again sounds strangely exclusive and Jewish in tone.

In view of this, it is hard to allay the suspicion that the paragraph did not originally belong here, and has been incorporated by accident at this point. Where it originally belonged, and whether indeed it is by Paul at all, are probably unanswerable questions. One possibility, among many others, may be mentioned: that it is a fragment of the letter to which Paul refers in 1 Corinthians 5.9, when he writes, 'In my letter I wrote that you must have nothing to do with loose livers'.

Paul now picks up the point reached in 6.13. **Do make a place for us in** 2
your hearts! The whole burden of the letter so far has been that Paul has
nothing to hide or be ashamed of. If there has been any misunderstanding,
it must be due, not to him, but to them—'any constraint there may be is in
yourselves' (6.12). And yet, though it has been necessary for Paul to clear
himself in this way, he has no wish merely to shift the blame on to them.
I do not want to blame you. Too much is at stake for that, the identity of 3
his destiny with theirs, his **pride** in them, and the **consolation** which is part 4
of their common experience—both these words recalling the opening of the
letter.

But to return to the misunderstanding itself: Paul picks up his account of
the incident from the point where he broke off at 2.13. There he explained
the extreme anxiety he had felt while waiting for news of how his stern letter
had been received: he had been able to do no useful work, and had gone on
to Macedonia, where his agitation continued until Titus eventually brought
his report. Now he describes his relief, and seeks to allay any lingering 6–7
bitterness his letter may have caused by pointing out the benefits which 8–13
have proceeded from it, and expressing his own and Titus' joy at the outcome. 13–16

Feeling, perhaps, that relations between himself and the Corinthians were now at last sufficiently cordial for the question to be reopened, Paul turns to the matter of the collection which he was raising from all his churches for the "poor" Christians at Jerusalem. He has already alluded to this at a previous stage in the correspondence (1 Corinthians 16); at that time it seems that the Corinthians had already agreed to it in principle, but were being slow in doing anything practical about it; and during the period[a] of misunder-

[a] The twice-repeated phrase **last year** (8.10 and 9.2) is the nearest indication we have of how long this period lasted. Unfortunately we do not know at what time of year this letter

standing we may assume that the matter had to be shelved. But now the time was ripe to raise it again, and Paul devotes the next two chapters to it. As usual when it is a question of money, Paul writes with considerable embarrassment (for a notable example, see the concluding paragraphs of the letter to the Philippians). Typically, he never actually refers to the collection in so
8. 1, 4 many words, but only talks vaguely about the **grace of generosity,**[a] the
generous service, the 'promised bounty' (9.5) and so forth; and he leads
1 into the subject obliquely by holding up as an example the **congregations**
in Macedonia. These congregations—we may take it that Paul is referring to churches such as those at Thessalonica and Philippi—could have asked for exemption in view of their adverse circumstances; but, far from doing this, they had begged to be allowed to take part. This so encouraged Paul
6 that he decided to send Titus back to Corinth to **bring this work of generosity also to completion.**

8 **This is not meant as an order**; but Paul presents it as a powerful obligation on grounds both of the Christian faith and of expediency.

(i) It is a Christian obligation, because of the example of Christ himself,
9 who was, in a sense, **generous** (though this translation is a little strained: he had the attribute called in verse 1 the 'grace of generosity', and in his case the idea of "graciousness" was probably the dominant one). That is to say, Christ **was rich** in that he was divine, and **became poor** in that he took human form (the thought is worked out more fully in Philippians 2.5–11); and Christians who profess to follow him and enter the pattern of his existence must at least be ready to do with their material possessions what Christ did with his life.

(ii) It is expedient, because the Christians in Corinth are in fact better off than the Christians in Jerusalem. No heroic sacrifice is being asked of them:
12 **God accepts what a man has; he does not ask for what he has not.**
14 The aim is not extreme self-denial, but simply **equality**, of which an example
15 (of a somewhat ideal kind) may be found in Exodus 16.18: when manna was gathered in the desert, no one had either too much or too little.

There seems to have been criticism about the way in which Paul proposed to handle the actual conveyance of the money to Jerusalem. In 1 Corinthians 16.3 he had to give assurances that representatives of the donor churches would be present; and here he names others who will share the responsibility. Or rather (apart from Titus) he most puzzlingly omits to name them. Who these two men were who were of such high reputation that they would silence all criticism, why Paul leaves them unnamed, and why indeed there
23 should have been **any question about Titus**, are matters quite unknown

was written, nor whether Paul would have reckoned by the Jewish New Year (autumn) or the Roman one (1 January), so that **last year** may mean anything from six to eighteen months previously.

[*a*] If this is what the Greek means. For an alternative translation see the footnote in NEB.

to us. But the Corinthians presumably knew who was being referred to; when the men arrived they would have the opportunity of showing that they could come up to the level of the other churches (and of Paul's expectations) with their contribution.

About the provision of aid for God's people, it is superfluous for 9. 1
me to write to you—an unexpected sentence, which would come more
naturally if Paul had not been writing about precisely this throughout the
previous chapter. This may be just another indication of his embarrassment;
or he may mean that he has no need to go over the actual purpose of the
collection again, for the Corinthians had evidently grasped this when they
showed their eagerness to help. Indeed, so good was their initial response,
that Paul is able to hold them up as an example to the Macedonians (**I tell** 2
them that Achaia had everything ready last year), in much the same
way as he is holding up the Macedonians as an example to the Corinthians.
But that initial response has still to bear fruit; and Paul finds it far from
superfluous to remind them of what they have promised.

The reminder is supported with a string of proverbs and quotations from Scripture. Verses 6 and 7 are a neat adaptation of Proverbs 22.8 which runs (according to the Greek version of the Septuagint),

"He who sows meanly shall reap evils
and shall receive the punishment of his deeds.
A man who is cheerful and generous is blessed by God . . ."

And to the objection that in some circumstances one may not have the means
to give to the poor, there is again an answer in Scripture. In the words of
Psalm 112.9, the **benevolence** (which is the same word as "righteousness") 9
of the generous giver **stands fast for ever**—that is, his claim to stand before
God is lasting; and the God who recognizes this claim is also he who provides **seed for sowing and bread for food** (Isaiah 55.10), and so will 10
himself **swell the harvest of your benevolence** (Hosea 10.12). Besides all
this, the Corinthians' contribution will be a **proof** of the strength of their 13
faith and of the reality of their Christian commitment, a sign of the **grace** 14
which God has imparted; it will therefore do good, and be a cause for
thanksgiving, far beyond the usefulness of the money itself.

Trials of a Christian missionary

At this point there is a sharp change. The preceding chapters were evidently written when relations between Paul and the Corinthian church had become once again confident and affectionate. The tone was serene, and even the somewhat delicate subject of the collection could be broached without fear of causing offence. But with the beginning of chapter 10 it is as if such a period of calm and reconciliation had never been. Paul seems to be reduced, once again, to defending himself against damaging imputations and mounting a fierce attack against his opponents.

Thus the connection of these last four chapters with the rest of the letter is mysterious. It is true that Paul's moods change unpredictably, and we must never expect his letters to follow an altogether ordered and logical course; but to fit these bitter and tortured paragraphs into the same situation as elicited the warm sentiments of chapter 7 is a task which can be achieved only by straining the interpretation of Paul's words. We seem forced to accept one of two alternatives: either these chapters stand in their correct place, but were added as a kind of postscript on receipt of fresh and disturbing news from Corinth; or else they do not belong here at all, and are a fragment of some other letter. Many believe, in fact, that they originally formed part of the letter written 'in great sorrow' between 1 and 2 Corinthians, an answer to which Paul awaited with such agitation when he was in Macedonia (7.5–7), and that a subsequent editor placed them in their present position. The chapters clearly belong somewhere in Paul's correspondence with the Corinthians, but precisely where we cannot say. Meanwhile, it is best to interpret them as an independent section, provoked by circumstances the details of which we can no longer recover. The NEB very properly gives them a separate and fairly general heading: *Trials of a Christian missionary.*

The first charge Paul has to refute is that he lacks the force of personality
10. 1 which is to be expected in a man who possesses real authority: **so feeble**
(you say) when I am face to face with you (the NEB is doubtless right to
add the words, **you say,** though they are not in the Greek: the sentence
looks like an accusation which someone is making against Paul). His immediate response is to appeal to the example of Christ himself, whose
distinctive characteristic was, not force of personality, but **gentleness** and
that kind of **magnanimity** which was the exact opposite, we may suppose,
of the bearing of Paul's opponents. On the heels of this follows another
2 accusation: Paul is charged with **moral weakness** (or "worldliness", if the
alternative rendering in the footnote is correct). We have already seen one
example of what might be meant by weakness or worldliness: the alleged
irresponsibility with which Paul conceived and changed his plans (1.15–17).
Here the specific charge was probably different, but we do not hear what it
3 was, because Paul spares it no further words. In one sense all men are **weak**;
but in this particular battle Paul claims to possess **divinely potent** weapons,
beside which the sophistries of his opponents are seen to be really **weak.**
Armed with these, Paul can exercise authority as much over intellectual
pretensions as over cases of practical disobedience.

Paul now moves to the attack. One of the slogans of his opponents seems

to have been, "We belong to Christ". In reply, Paul challenges them to explain the meaning of this slogan. In what sense could they possibly "belong to Christ" more than he does himself? The point, again, seems to have been the question of personal authority. It was being said that an apostle who really "belonged to Christ" would have obvious power and authority as a speaker, whereas Paul was reduced to exerting his authority at one remove,
so to speak, **by the letters he writes.** We know that the Corinthian church 9
set great store by public manifestations of the Spirit (see above p. 563). A man was recognized as a true Christian if he possessed the gift of spontaneous and ecstatic utterance, and a man whose "inspiration" only took the form of letters composed in his study may have seemed of doubtful authority compared with a truly "spiritual" speaker. If this was his adversaries' insinuation, Paul indignantly repudiates it. **When I come, my actions will show** 11
the same man as my letters showed in my absence. If he has been sparing of this authority so far, it has been out of his usual concern for the
Corinthians' well-being as a church. His authority is **to build you up, not** 8
pull you down.

But it is only momentarily that Paul condescends to come down and fight
on his adversaries' own ground. If he were to accept their **standard of** 12
comparison, he might quite possibly not measure up to it—he might be found lacking in many things which they regarded as essential qualifications for holding authority. But what is the validity of this "standard"? It has none. It merely shows that they **measure themselves by themselves**: it is they who have decided what the standard is to be, and whether a given person measures up to it. Paul's claim, by contrast, depends on no such subjective standard. His authority proceeds, not from qualifications of his own which,
by human standards, make him superior to others, but from a **commission** 14
with which he has been entrusted. Even this, it seems, had been misrepresented. His opponents appear to have been saying that it was they who were really responsible for the growth of the church in Corinth and that Paul's **commission,** if he had one, did not extend to Corinth at all; in
interfering there, he was acting beyond his **proper sphere.** In reply, Paul 15
can simply point to the fact that he was **the first to reach Corinth in** 14
preaching the gospel of Christ. And if, as he hopes, the Corinthian church becomes more firmly established, he will be able to go further on
from there, still without trespassing on **another man's sphere.** All this 17
boasting of his opponents is beside the point. The only proper ground for boasting (*kauchēsis* again, see above on 1.12) is not what we do ourselves, but what the Lord does through us. (Verse 17 is a quotation from Jeremiah 9.23–4.)

Nevertheless, even though it was beside the point to claim any personal qualifications for the task of preaching the gospel, and even though it would
have been almost **folly** (in view of all that has been said) for Paul to try to **11.** 1

'recommend himself', yet he could not resist pointing to certain things within himself which in any normal contest would have shown him to be the equal of his opponents. He was not, after all, only concerned about his own status; he had an anxious concern and affection for the Corinthian church,
2 which he thought of as **betrothed . . . to Christ** (much as an Old Testament
prophet saw Israel as "betrothed" or "married" to God), but now in
3 danger of seduction, like Eve, away from its **single-hearted devotion.**
We cannot tell how real this danger of seduction was, but Paul presumably
had reason for his fears. At any rate, if some other preacher was trying to
modify Paul's gospel, saying that Jesus was not like that at all, or that the
spirit which the Corinthians thought they had received was not the real
Spirit, then the Corinthians were apparently not reacting against such
4 suggestions with the firmness they should: **you manage to put up with**
that well enough. Such preachers, to have had such success, must indeed
5 be **superlative apostles**! But had they in fact any excellence which Paul
did not possess? Perhaps they had one: a facility for rhetorical speech with
6 which Paul did not pretend to compete (**I may be no speaker**). But this
was no substitute for the **knowledge** which Paul possessed and which he
had always taken care to impart fully to the Corinthians.

Before pursuing the 'folly' of listing some of his own qualifications, Paul
turns aside to defend himself against yet another accusation, that of making
7 **no charge for preaching the gospel of God.** This has already formed the
subject of a substantial section in 1 Corinthians (chapter 9), where it appeared
that Paul's unwillingness to conform to the usual practice was exploited as a
reason for doubting his official authority. Here, the attack seems to have been
taken a stage further. It was known to the Corinthians that, although Paul
9 was receiving no maintenance from them (**I sponged on no one,** he says,
using a colloquialism which may have been current in his native dialect), he
8 was in fact **accepting support** from other congregations in Macedonia (this
is referred to in Philippians 4.10–18). What did this mean? Why was he
prepared to accept support from one congregation and not another? Did it
not suggest that Paul lacked confidence in the Corinthians? Paul protests:
11 **Is it that I do not love you? God knows I do.**

In 1 Corinthians, Paul admitted that his attitude in this matter was an
entirely personal one, and gave his reasons for holding to the principle of
financial independence. Here he hints at a further point of principle:
7 **lowering myself to help in raising you.** The word translated **lowering**
has the same root as that rendered 'feeble' in 10.1, and contains, again, an
implicit appeal to the example of Christ, who 'humbled himself' (Philippians
2.8—another form of the same word). Besides, the activities of his opponents
had now furnished him with a further practical reason for continuing in the
same way. If he were once to start accepting money from the Corinthians, it
12, 13 would put him and his apostleship **on the same level** as the **sham-apostles**

(who presumably were drawing a stipend), whereas in fact the difference
between them is as great as the difference between Christ and Satan. If Satan
even **masquerades as an angel of light** (as was affirmed by Jewish writers 14
contemporary with Paul), then, as surely as Paul himself is an agent of God,
his opponents may well be Satan's **agents,** heading for an **end their deeds** 15
deserve.

Paul now allows himself the 'folly' of a **little boast.** If the Corinthians 16
are **so wise** that they can put up with the arrogant and insulting behaviour 19
of his opponents (he permits himself this much irony), then surely they
can **bear with** a mild piece of folly from Paul—indeed, perhaps this was
what they meant by saying that he had been **weak** (10.1): he had not 21
behaved with the insolence of his opponents! Paul is ready to **admit the**
reproach.

Now for the moment of **bravado.** Paul can meet any opponents (and 21
perhaps he is selecting extreme hypothetical cases, perhaps he has certain
people in mind) on their own ground. If they boast of being Jews, they
cannot be more Jewish than Paul himself (on these particular titles to
Jewishness, see below on Philippians 3.5–6). If they claim to be **servants of** 23
Christ, then let them show what they have endured in his service—for in
this matter Paul can certainly **outdo them.** With a lack of modesty of which
he is painfully aware (**I am mad to speak like this**) Paul gives an impressive catalogue of the conditions of his service—and had circumstances not
forced this confession out of him, we should never have known more than
half the afflictions he endured. From the Jews he had received the maximum
penalty short of death: **thirty-nine strokes.** (In Deuteronomy 25.2 the 24
number prescribed is forty, but we know from subsequent Jewish tradition
that 39 was the usual number—perhaps to avoid breaking the law by accidentally giving one too many!—and that the punishment was most frequently given for an offence against the rules of religious purity.) By the
Romans, despite his Roman citizenship which should have protected him,
he was three times **beaten with rods**: one of these occasions is recounted in 25
Acts 16.22. By the Jews again he was **stoned,** a punishment which usually
resulted in death; and it is clear from Acts 14.19 that once at least Paul barely
escaped with his life.

The list is impressive enough. For good measure, Paul adds the **anxious** 28
concern which his responsibility for so many scattered churches constantly
caused him. He ends with a particularly memorable incident, which is also
recorded in Acts (9.24). **King Aretas** was king of the Nabataeans, a desert 32
people, from about A.D. 9 to 39. His capital was at Petra, deep in the desert
towards the Red Sea, but his empire certainly extended as far north as the
region of Damascus, so that it is not improbable that he should have had some
sort of **commissioner** in the city. On the other hand, although Damascus
had been under Roman control from the conquests of Pompey in the previous

century until the death of the Emperor Tiberius in A.D. 37, its history between A.D. 37 and 60 is somewhat obscure, and it is perfectly possible to accept the implication of this passage that at the beginning of this period it came under Nabataean control. Had it been administered by the Romans when this incident took place, Paul (who was a Roman citizen) would hardly have been exposed to the danger of arrest by the representative of a foreign power.

12. 1 **I shall go on to tell of visions and revelations.** Continuing his 'little
boast', and still with the same awareness that, although he feels obliged to do
it, **it does no good** and is indeed inconsistent with his declared intention,
2 Paul mentions a certain supernatural experience. **I know a Christian man**
—doubtless Paul means himself, but this oblique form of speech is not just
modesty: it goes with the recognition that the subject of such an experience
is not quite the same person as one's everyday self. Paul cannot even say
what form it took, whether **in the body** (the experience of being lifted bodily
into another world for a while, which was attributed to the Old Testament
figure of Enoch, and later on to a Rabbi who lived a short time after Paul),
or **out of it** (the more common type of interior vision); therefore, though the
vision was certainly authentic and could be "boasted about" as an enrichment of human experience, Paul is not prepared to take credit for having
5 been the subject of it—**I will not boast on my own account.** What was
the vision? Paul uses the conventional language of visionaries. A Jewish
seer, writing of his experiences, would often describe them as a kind of
progression through a series of "heavens", sometimes three, sometimes four,
4 sometimes seven, of which the last would offer the ultimate vision of **paradise.** Here Paul merely summarizes the experience. We do not know
2, 4 whether his **third heaven** was the same as his **paradise** or merely an
intermediate stage which he had reached in an earlier vision; but his final
vision was the authentic, incommunicable (and so **secret**) mystical experience. Paul is not prevented from talking about this by doubts about the reality
6 of the vision. On the contrary, **if I should choose to boast . . . I should be
speaking the truth.** But this kind of evidence, being necessarily unverifiable,
ought not to be invoked when one is forming **an estimate** of a person; nor
ought the visionary to allow himself to feel elated by his experience. Paul
was saved from any such temptation in a particularly brutal way.

7 **I was given a sharp physical pain.** We have no means of telling the
nature of Paul's affliction. The word he uses means literally (as the footnote
in NEB explains) a "stake" or "thorn"—something, that is, which pierces
the flesh. The metaphor is thus vague enough to cover almost any kind of
illness, and that it came as **Satan's messenger** means only that it was
serious enough to seem to have a malignant existence of its own (the idea
goes back ultimately to the Book of Job). But whatever it was, and whatever

humiliation it had brought Paul in the past, he could now see it as a further
protection against the temptation to set too high a value on his own remarkable gifts. Indeed, it is one of the main contentions of the letter that outward
vicissitudes offer no criterion for judging the validity of the gospel; on the
contrary, they serve to display its power. **When I am weak, then I am** 10
strong.

Apart from the foolishness of this 'little boast', it was also of course quite
irrelevant to the point at issue. If any evidence were needed of the apostle's
status, it should have been looked for, not in the man himself, but in the
fruits of his work: **my credentials should have come from you.** What- 11
ever may have been Paul's personal shortcomings (**even if I am a nobody**),
the very existence of the Corinthian church, and the supernatural experiences
of its members (which had thrown up some of the practical problems with
which Paul had to concern himself in 1 Corinthians), were the sufficient
marks of a true apostle. To produce such results, Paul must have given 12
them everything he had to give. Was there anything they did not receive
from their founding apostle—except perhaps the privilege of giving material
support to that apostle? And by way of this ironical exception Paul returns
to the charge he has already dealt with once in chapter 11, but which still
seems to rankle in his mind: that he had refused financial assistance from the
Corinthians.

Paul sees himself as the Corinthians' 'father' (1 Corinthians 4.15), and 14
this gives him another argument for refusing their money. Children should
not spend money on their father, but the father may spend all he has, his
very self, on his children. Why should such a token of a father's love result
in him being **loved the less**? 15

Paul had never asked for money: that was common ground. Various
inferences had been drawn from this, which Paul had shown to be false.
But there was still one particularly damaging suggestion to attend to. Paul's
refusal to appeal directly for money was, it had been said, simply a **trick**: he 16
must have been recouping his expenses through his assistants. Paul evidently
regarded this suggestion as so obviously unfounded that it was sufficient to
ask the direct question, **Did Titus defraud you?** Presumably the reputation 18
which Titus enjoyed among the Corinthians was sufficient to scotch any
rumour that he had been a deliberate agent of fraud. The language Paul uses
here is very similar to that in chapter 8 (verses 6 and 16–18), where the subject was the collection for the Jerusalem church. Was the present accusation of fraud perhaps aimed at Paul's arrangements for administering this collection? It is tempting to think so; but the chronological sequence of these various references to the matter is so uncertain that we cannot do more than guess.

All this "boasting" and self-justification may have given the impression

that what Paul is mainly concerned about is his own reputation at Corinth.
19 But this is not so. **We are speaking in God's sight, and as Christian men,**
and Paul's only interest in the whole matter is what he has already shown in
1 Corinthians to be an overriding principle governing relations between
Christians—**to build you up** (an almost technical expression, see above on
1 Corinthians 12.31). He hopes that this letter will be effective in putting an
end to the misunderstanding and personal intrigues, with all their pernicious
consequences, which have been caused by his opponents. The only alternative left is a personal encounter, which may be unpleasant for both sides,
either because Paul will have to fulfil his threat of exercising his disciplinary
power (10.1–6), or else because God may choose to make him once again
21 "Christ-like", that is: **humiliate** him in their presence, make him once
again 'feeble' (10.1) and 'downcast' (7.6), so that he has to 'lower himself'
(11.7)—all forms of the same Greek word, and all bearing overtones of the
humiliation of Christ, through which God makes his ultimate appeal to men.

If this second possibility—of humiliation—has been correctly interpreted
(the whole paragraph is singularly ambiguous), it must be confessed that
Paul immediately loses sight of it again. His present purpose, after all, is to
move the Corinthians to repentance before he meets them face to face (13.10);
and even though, when it comes to the point, God may still prevent him from
exerting his authority, and allow him, as before, to show his strength only in
weakness and humiliation, he cannot afford to dwell on this possibility now,
13. 3 for fear of blunting the edge of his warning. It is true that the **Christ who**
speaks through Paul **died on the cross in weakness,** and may therefore
be recognized in a person's weakness as much as in a person's strength; but
4 Christ also rose from the dead and **lives by the power of God.** Paul's
service to the Corinthians must therefore include both elements, the
weakness of the dying Christ, and the power which belongs to those who
now **live with him**; and Paul warns the Corinthians that, just as a third
witness may be decisive in showing a man guilty (Deuteronomy 19.15), so his
1 **third visit** must be expected to be accompanied by a decisive demonstration
of his power—unless, meanwhile, his present warning takes effect.

This double-sided manifestation of the presence of Christ is also the key
to the next paragraph. Christ may be present among Christians either in
their weakness and tribulations, or in their deeds of power: the one may be
a sign of his presence just as much as the other. So far as the Corinthians are
5 concerned, the question (whether **Jesus Christ is among you**) must be
answered with reference both to their tribulations and to their achievements.
It is possible (though Paul thinks it unlikely) that put **to the test** they would
fail on both counts; but what is more important is that they should apply the
same test to Paul, and be able to recognize Christ's presence in him as much
because of his weakness as because of his strength—and Paul very much
10 hopes (in the interests, once again, of the overriding principle of **building**

up) that he may be spared the unpleasantness of giving a demonstration of
strength: **we are well content to be weak.** 9

On the **kiss of peace**, see above on Romans 16.16. Once again, the ending 12
seems to contain echoes of the church at worship. The last sentence is one of the very few "trinitarian" formulae in the New Testament (placing together God, Jesus and the Holy Spirit), though each element of the formula occurs
separately in other places. **Fellowship in the Holy Spirit** is the translators' 14
choice out of several possibilities. In Greek, the phrase means something like "common participation in the Holy Spirit", with perhaps a hint that this participation creates in itself a new kind of community or **fellowship** among Christians. No single translation can do justice to the richness of the phrase.

THE LETTER OF PAUL TO THE GALATIANS

This letter, like the letters to the Corinthians, was evoked by a particular crisis in the relations between Paul and one of the churches he had founded. Something had been going wrong for some time before the letter was written, and this was not the first time that Paul had intervened (4.16). There was pressure from outside the church and there were factions within it, and the atmosphere was such that charges of various kinds had been levelled at Paul by his opponents. So much, at least, is evident from the letter; but, since this letter is the only record we now possess of the various exchanges which took place, a great deal remains mysterious, and it is impossible to reconstruct with any certainty the precise circumstances to which the letter alludes, and the arguments and accusations which Paul had to meet. In addition, many of the sentences from which we might have hoped to learn something are written in unusually ambiguous idioms; and the difficulty of the Greek has in places produced significant discrepancies in the texts offered by the earliest manuscripts.

We cannot even be sure who THE GALATIANS were. Since the third century B.C., when an invasion of Gauls (in Greek: *Galatai*) from central Europe had finally secured an area for settlement in the centre of Asia Minor, "Galatia" had been the name currently used for the territory of these invaders. But in 25 B.C. the Roman Province of Galatia was created out of lands which included not only the original Galatian territory, but also (for political reasons) parts of Pisidia and Lycaonia to the south. So that, from the point of view of the official Roman administration, it became correct to call the cities near the coast, such as Derbe, Lystra, Iconium and Antioch, "Galatian".

We know nothing from Paul's own letters of his movements in the central part of Asia Minor. Acts provides a somewhat vague report of a journey by Paul through 'the Galatian region' during his second missionary journey (16.6; 18.23); but it gives much fuller information about Paul's work in the southern cities during his first journey (13–14), so that although these cities could only technically be called "Galatian", it is possible and in many ways tempting to think that it was to their inhabitants that the letter was addressed.

Bound up with this uncertainty about the destination of the letter is the question of its date. If north Galatia was its destination, then it must have been written some time after the events of Acts 16–18, which bring us down to at least A.D. 52. On the other hand, if the cities to the south were the home of Paul's "Galatian" churches, then it could equally well have been written

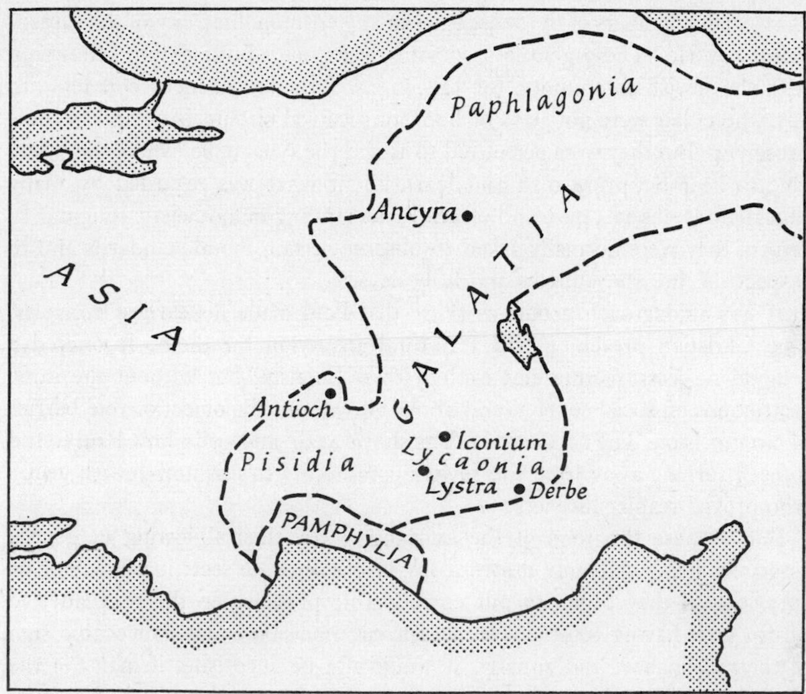

several years earlier, indeed it could be Paul's earliest extant letter. And this wide range of possible dates makes it difficult to relate the incidents mentioned in the letter to other known episodes in Paul's life. Even the fragments of autobiography in chapter 2 present difficulties; for some of the same events are recorded in Acts, and there are serious discrepancies between the two accounts which make it exceedingly hard to fit these events into the history of the early church.

To some extent, the main argument of the letter stands on its own, and all the circumstances do not have to be reconstructed before it can be understood. Nevertheless, it may be helpful to read the letter with some picture of the Galatian church and its difficulties in mind, even though any reconstruction is bound to be somewhat speculative. It appears that the Galatian church, though subject to pressure from the Jewish side, consisted mainly of Gentiles. Even those who had already yielded to Jewish pressure were apparently not Jews by birth, but had recently become proselytes (6.13). On the other hand, the argument of the letter, with its detailed references to the Old Testament, can have been intelligible only to people who were already familiar with the Jewish religion and Jewish traditions. Where were such Jewish-minded Gentiles to be found? One answer may be suggested. They were to be found, in considerable numbers, as associate members of the synagogue in any cosmopolitan city of the Greco-Roman world. These gentile associates were not admitted into fellowship with the Jewish community, for Jewish law forbade full social contact with any who either were not Jews or had not received circumcision and become proselytes. But they were permitted to attend the synagogue, where they were able to hear Scripture read and learn about what was regarded by many educated Greeks as a pure and ethically demanding monotheistic religion. In return, they were normally asked to observe certain moral standards and to respect the Jewish Sabbaths and holy days.

It was among such people as these that Paul made his earliest converts. The Christian preaching had a natural attraction for them. It offered a religion no less exacting and exalted than Judaism, but without the same restrictions on social contact, and above all without the objectionable barrier of circumcision. The narrative of Acts shows again and again how Paul found himself turning away from the Jewish community to this non-Jewish group who proved readier listeners.

But suppose the Jews of the synagogue saw their following of gentile associates being suddenly drawn away into a separate sect: it would not be surprising if they began to put considerable pressure on the renegades to return and, having returned, to accept circumcision as an irrevocable sign of their allegiance; and equally, it would not be surprising if many of the Christians, subjected to persecution from this quarter, felt tempted to purchase a quiet life at the price of accepting the synagogue's conditions. These would, after all, only oblige them to certain outward observances; they would still be free among themselves (so at least they believed, and this view seems quite plausible when we consider the very wide range of beliefs held at that time by law-abiding Jews) to confess Jesus as Lord.

Such was the situation, or something like it, which elicited Paul's letter. To his converts, it seemed merely a practical issue, concerning outward observances. But to Paul it appeared as a challenge to his presentation of the Christian faith. And so he addressed them, not on the level of practical expediency, but of theological truth. His argument rose above the local dispute between church and synagogue, and has been justly prized throughout the history of Christianity as a classic formulation of some of the central truths of the Christian faith. The translators have seized on two of its principal themes in giving it the general heading, *Faith and freedom*.

Faith and freedom

The opening of the letter follows the usual convention (see above on Romans 1. 1
1, where the words **apostle** and **commission** are also discussed). The
nature of Paul's apostleship comes under discussion later in the letter, and
Paul may be deliberately stressing his credentials at the outset. But this is
no more than a hint of what is to come. The greeting itself is conventional
enough, apart from one attribute of Christ which deserves notice: he died to
rescue us out of this present age of wickedness. For Paul, the effect of 4
Christ's self-sacrifice **for our sins** was not merely to cancel the effect of past
misdoings, but to open up a new kind of existence: the new age looked
forward to by Jewish thinkers had already begun, and presented an immediate
alternative to **this present age of wickedness.**

I am astonished. The letter has to deal with a crisis, and comes straight 6
to the point. Certain persons have been recommending a **different gospel.**
Not that any gospel is possible other than the **gospel of Christ**: the gospel
is the good news that Christ—that is, the Messiah expected in the Jewish
religion—has come, and to deny this would be to deny the possibility of any
gospel at all. No, these persons have been **trying to distort the gospel**; 7
that is, they have been misrepresenting its practical implications. And this
is just as serious: they **shall be held outcast.** The word is *anathema*—"a 8
curse on him", as the same word is rendered in 1 Corinthians 12.3.

Strong language—which might be appropriate to **canvassing for men's** 10
support in favour of one religious group or political party over against
another. But Paul is not interested in groups or parties. **Whose support do**
I want but God's alone? The gospel comes from God, it is **no human** 11
invention, and the account which follows of how Paul came by this gospel
is intended both to demonstrate its divine origin (which raises it above
parties) and also to establish the validity of Paul's apostleship which, as he
said at the beginning, was conferred on him not by man but by God.

The story of Paul's conversion is told, with slight variations, three times
in Acts (chapters 9, 22 and 26). Here, it is told more briefly (for it was not
new to the Galatians, verse 13), but with a certain emphasis on two points:
first, that it was an experience comparable with the call of an Old Testament
prophet, not random but predestined (verse 15 contains allusions to Isaiah 15
49.1 and Jeremiah 1.5); and secondly, that the call, as in the two Old Testament passages, was specifically a call to preach **among the Gentiles.** The 16
revelation was both **to** Paul and to a wider public **through** Paul (so the NEB
makes explicit a possible ambiguity latent in the Greek preposition *en*). It
was also so clear and compelling that it did not need either confirmation or
elucidation by the Jerusalem apostles; and Paul (this incident is not mentioned
in Acts) **went off at once to Arabia,** possibly to begin preaching, but more 17

likely for a period of withdrawal and meditation. (The word **Arabia** could denote anywhere from the desert in the immediate neighbourhood of Damascus to the shores of the Red Sea. Much of it was the kingdom of Aretas, king of Petra, who is mentioned in 2 Corinthians 11.32.)

18 **Three years later.** This must be the visit described in Acts 9.26–30, for both accounts presuppose that this was Paul's first visit to Jerusalem after his conversion. The two accounts disagree on several points—enough to show that the author of Acts did not have access to this letter, but not enough to discredit Acts altogether. Paul might well see no reason to mention here some of the more embarrassing incidents mentioned in Acts, and the author of Acts may not have known exactly what the situation was in Jerusalem three years after Paul's conversion, and exactly whom Paul did and did not see. At any rate, Paul says that his motive for the journey was to **get to know**
Cephas. [a] The exact sense of the verb here translated **to get to know** is
disputed. It may mean, "to get information from him". The impression
given, in any case, is of a private visit. Apart from Peter, Paul saw only
19 **James the Lord's brother,** who was soon to become the leader of the
Jerusalem church, and who seems here (though the Greek is as indecisive
as the English) to be counted as one of the apostles. The Acts narrative certainly gives the impression of a much more public visit; but the other
apostles may in fact have been away from Jerusalem at this time, and for the
purpose of Paul's argument it was the church leaders who mattered. The
20 point being emphasized by Paul and reiterated with an oath (**before God I**
am not lying), is that despite this visit he had remained entirely independent
21 of the Jerusalem church, and that on his return to Tarsus in **Cilicia** (Acts
22 9.30) and Antioch in **Syria** (Acts 11.25) he **remained unknown . . . to**
Christ's congregations in Judaea. That is to say, whether or not the
tumultuous episode of Acts 9.29 actually took place, Paul's first visit to
Jerusalem was essentially (so far at least as the church leaders were concerned) a private one, and not such as to damage his claim that, in these early
years, he acknowledged no dependence on the Jerusalem church.

2. 1 **Next, fourteen years later.** Attempts to reconstruct the history now run into difficulties. The next visit recorded in Acts (11.30; 12.25) is the mission of Paul and Barnabas to Jerusalem with an emergency contribution from Antioch 'for the relief of their fellow-Christians in Judaea' in a time of famine. Since Paul here is also clearly describing his **next** visit, the two should correspond, and in fact they can be made to do so without serious violence to either. The identification, however, has the somewhat unwelcome consequence that Paul's conversion must have taken place not less than 15 years (which is what, by Greek inclusive reckoning, two periods of 3 and 14 years amount to) before the famine of A.D. 46–48—i.e. only a year or so after the Crucifixion; and also that, if this letter then fails to mention the "coun-

[a] Paul's usual name for Simon Peter: the only exception is at 2.7 below.

cil" of Acts 15 which has such a bearing on its subject, the most likely explanation is that it was written before the council took place (probably around A.D. 49), in which case it will be the earliest of Paul's extant letters, and will be separated by several years from the letter to the Romans, which in some ways it closely resembles. The alternative is to assume some error in the order of events in Acts, and to identify this visit to Jerusalem, as described in Galatians, with the council of Acts 15, with which indeed it has some striking resemblances. But in this case there are also serious differences between the two accounts, and it becomes difficult to understand the incident in Galatians 2.11–14 if the decision on this question recorded in Acts 15 had already been taken. Either way, complete harmonization is impossible.

There is a further difficulty presented by Paul's own account. The words
was not compelled to be circumcised are as ambiguous in the Greek as 3
they are in English: it is impossible to be sure whether Titus was in fact circumcised or not. Moreover, in the next sentence, it is not quite clear whether Paul is referring to something which happened during the visit or something which happened subsequently; and the obscurity of his words has caused the further complication of a number of variants in the manuscripts (see notes [*d*] and [*e*] in the NEB).

Despite these difficulties, it is possible to see the point which Paul is making in recalling these events. Paul's gospel was 'no human invention' but something received directly 'through a revelation' (1.11–12). From the
outset, it was addressed **to the Gentiles**, and its proclamation was to that 2
extent independent of the mission to the Jews being conducted by the Jerusalem leaders; indeed, this gospel was given to Paul quite independently of them (this is the reason for Paul's emphasis on the unofficial nature of his first visit, 1.18–24). The climax of the argument is reached with the second visit (2.1–10). This time, Paul took with him a Greek named Titus, perhaps as a living example of what had hardly yet been seen at Jerusalem—a non-Jewish, uncircumcised Christian! (Titus, either then or subsequently, became the subject of pressure from a party within the church which could not yet conceive of a society composed of both Jews and non-Jews; who were
shocked by what Paul called **the liberty we enjoy in the fellowship of** 4
Christ Jesus; and who could see only one solution to this new problem, namely that of making all non-Jewish members acceptable to a Jewish community by having them circumcised—a solution which Paul could only call
bondage.) His object was **to make sure that the race I had run, and** 2
was running, should not be run in vain—not in the sense that anything could be wrong with his own proclamation of the gospel, for he 'received it through a revelation of Jesus Christ' (1.12); but rather (presumably) to forestall the danger of the Jerusalem church falling out of sympathy with what he was doing, in which case their common cause would be imperilled

by disunity. In the event, the Jerusalem leaders accepted the situation: they
6 **did not prolong the consultation** (if that is what the difficult Greek word
means) but agreed on a partnership. Paul and Barnabas were entrusted with
9 the mission to the Gentiles, while **they went to the Jews.** The only condition was that the new gentile churches should express their loyalty to Jerusalem by sending financial relief—a collection which we know Paul subsequently took very seriously (Romans 15.25–7; 2 Corinthians 8), and which he may even have begun already. [a]

With this narrative, Paul has sought to establish the following points: (i) that his original call and his own special mission were received directly from God by a revelation, and not from the Jerusalem church; (ii) that for many years he worked quite independently of the Jerusalem church, most of whom had never even met him; (iii) that his visit three years after his conversion was private and exploratory only; (iv) that when he finally went to Jerusalem to coordinate his work with that of the other apostles, the legitimacy of all his previous missionary activity among the Gentiles was recognized, and he was encouraged to continue working on the same lines and with the same independence as before, with the single proviso that he should raise funds for the relief of the Christians in Jerusalem. All this is stated with great emphasis; and it can be presumed that Paul was concerned to answer a party in Galatia which questioned his right to take important decisions independently of the Jerusalem church.

Paul's mission to the Gentiles, even though it was recognized as legitimate by the whole church, nevertheless had embarrassing practical consequences. These consequences may hardly have been experienced at first in Jerusalem (where a non-Jewish Christian would have been a rarity) but presented an acute problem wherever (as in a city such as Antioch) the young church was likely to consist of both Jews and non-Jews. How could these two distinct groups be expected to form a single congregation? And in particular, how could Jews, who had been brought up to regard sitting at table with non-Jews as a serious sin, now take part in the Lord's Supper of a gentile church? Paul's own experience in such churches had convinced him that the solution
4 was what he called **the liberty we enjoy in the fellowship of Christ**
Jesus; and Peter, perhaps encouraged by his experience at the house of
12 Cornelius (Acts 10), adopted this liberty when he visited Antioch: **he was**
taking his meals with gentile Christians. But (in theory at least) there
was another solution: if all non-Jewish Christians were to be circumcised,
it would then be permissible for the Jewish Christians to eat with them, and
14 the problem would disappear. This solution, **that Gentiles must live like**
12 **Jews,** was seriously envisaged by a party at Jerusalem (where **James** was
now the leader), and the arrival of some of this party at Antioch precipitated
the crisis described in verses 11–14.

[a] The Greek tense is again ambiguous; see the footnote to this verse in NEB.

Paul rejected this solution outright, not merely because it would soon have
been impracticable anyway, but because of his conviction that **their conduct** 14
did not square with the truth of the Gospel. Circumcision must not be
regarded merely as a matter of practical expediency in a mixed community;
on the contrary, Paul saw it as an act charged with theological significance.
The following chapters are a sustained attempt to alert the non-Jewish
Galatians to the danger of taking this question of circumcision too lightly.

But first Paul has something to say about the proper attitude of Jewish
Christians (like himself) to circumcision.[a] **We ourselves are Jews by** 15
birth, and therefore have been circumcised. But now, like all Christians,
we too have put our faith, no longer in such things as circumcision (**what** 16
the law demands) but **in Jesus Christ.** Being **justified** is a human impossibility (this is argued in detail in Romans 3: here Paul simply adduces,
as a proof from Scripture, Psalm 143.2). God has now made it possible—but
not **by such deeds** as circumcision.

If now. Popular Jewish theology (as can be seen from many passages in 17
the gospels) regarded the Gentiles as, by definition, "sinners"; and any
Jews who flagrantly transgressed the law were relegated to the same category
—indeed, some pious Jewish circles regarded the majority of their fellow-
countrymen in Palestine as **sinners.** The same accusation could be made
(and presumably was made) against Jews who had become Christians and
were now committing such unlawful acts as taking their meals with Gentiles.
If so, it would seem to follow (granted this somewhat technical meaning of
"sin") that **Christ is an abettor of sin.** But this technical meaning of "sin" 17
and "law" is now a thing of the past for the Christian. What *is* sin (i.e. real
transgression of the law) is building up again the old system of observances,
when in fact the Christian has **died to law** by being **crucified with Christ.** 19, 20
To continue to believe that, after this, there is saving value (**righteousness**) 21
in keeping the law, would be to **nullify the grace of God** now revealed in
Jesus Christ. What appears, in Jewish eyes, to be a "sinful" disregard of the
law is in fact the new life, entered upon by dying with Christ to the law, and
governed, no longer by law, but by **faith in the Son of God.** 20

Paul now turns to the Galatians. They have **been bewitched,** that is to say, 3. 1
they are evidently under a sinister kind of pressure to adopt Jewish observances (things essentially **material,** to do with keeping the ceremonial law) 3
and have already partly yielded. Paul appeals to the most certain fact of their
Christian experience: they have received the Spirit; and he asks them twice
over whether this experience has been the result of **keeping the law** or of 2

[*a*] It is possible (for there are no inverted commas in a Greek manuscript) that verses 15–21 (or some of them) are a continuation of Paul's reply to Peter. The NEB translators, along with most English versions, have rejected this possibility. In any case, Paul's remarks are addressed to Jewish Christians, real or hypothetical.

3 **believing the gospel message.** This second clause, **believing the gospel message,** is a paraphrase. Literally, the Greek means "having faith in what you heard" (as contrasted with the **keeping** of the law), and it is important to keep this literal meaning in mind; for if the answer to Paul's question is "having faith" (which of course it is—the question is a rhetorical one),
7 then Christians are **men of faith,** and therefore **Abraham's sons.**

Why does Paul introduce Abraham at this point? When addressing non-Jewish Christians, he could surely have used the simpler argument that, in Christ, they had no need of Jewish ordinances such as circumcision, and therefore no need of the Abraham mythology either. But for Paul to have abandoned this mythology, and all the theology which went with it, would not have been so easy. Like every Jew, Paul regarded Abraham as the key figure in the history of mankind. Abraham was the symbol of God's concern for men, it was Abraham who embodied the proposition that God can deal with men in terms of a promise, a covenant, an assurance of salvation. All this had been expressly given to Abraham. And not merely to him: through him, to his descendants—the Jews.

So, at any rate, it seemed to the Jews. But this conclusion was hard to reconcile with the (to Paul) incontestable fact that non-Jews, by becoming Christians, had entered into at least as rich a relationship with God as the Jews had ever enjoyed. A non-Jew would probably therefore have been tempted to jettison the premises, and abandon the whole argument as irrelevant. But Paul could not jettison the premises, for they were written into the Old Testament record, which, as a Jew, he knew to be a true revelation of God's dealings with men. Instead, he chose to reinterpret the Abraham story in another way. The relevant passage is Genesis 12–17. In the course of these chapters it is repeatedly stated that God made his promise to Abraham and to his "descendants" (*sperma*, 'issue'), but that his descendants would inherit the promise only on condition that they were duly circumcised: "Any uncircumcised male who is not circumcised in the flesh of his foreskin shall be cut off from his people" (Genesis 17.14). The meaning of these chapters seems quite clear: the promise was made only to the physical descendants of Abraham, and only to them on condition that they were circumcised. Taken literally, they could mean nothing else.

But Paul opens up a new line of interpretation altogether when he takes
7 these texts to be referring, not to Abraham's "descendants", but to **Abraham's sons.** This harmless-looking alteration has considerable significance. A "descendant" of Abraham could only mean one who was literally of the family, that is, a Jew: but a "son" of Abraham could have a wider meaning. A common idiom in Palestine was to speak of (for instance) a "son of peace", meaning a "peaceful man". Equally it was an acceptable Greek idiom to speak of a "son of Plato", meaning a Platonic philosopher. So, a "son of Abraham" could mean: an Abraham-like man. Paul's point is this: God's

promises were not made just to Abraham's physical descendants, but to sons of Abraham, that is, to any Abraham-like man.

But if physical descent does not count, what is the criterion for recognizing an Abraham-like man? Paul answers: his faith. To prove this, he takes an isolated text (a procedure which seemed less shocking to Jewish scholars of his time than it does to us) from the same chapters of Genesis: Abraham
put his faith in God, and that faith was counted to him as righteous- 6
ness (Gen. 15.6). Paul's understanding of this verse is developed at length in Romans 4. Briefly, it may be said that he regards it as the clue to understanding Abraham. What secured for Abraham his status as "just" before God (his **righteousness**)? Not any outward act of obedience, but simply faith; and Abraham's true "sons" are those who, confronted by the promises of God in the form of the Gospel of Christ, also have faith. This puts an end to all superiority based on membership of the Jewish nation. The Gospel which evokes the faith of the Christian now is equivalent to the promise which evoked the faith of Abraham then—and Paul presses into the service
of this interpretation another verse from the same chapters of Genesis: **In** 8
you all nations shall find blessing (18.18), which makes his point for him all the more cogently in that he quotes it with the usual word "tribes" replaced by **nations** (*ethnē*, which is also the usual Greek word for "Gentiles"). The Jews normally took this verse to mean simply that all tribes would acknowledge that Abraham was blessed; but Paul, by a slight manipulation, turns it into a prophecy that (as he devoutly believes is already happening) the Gentiles will come to share in Abraham's blessing.

Having shown the cardinal significance of faith, Paul now goes back to
his original rhetorical question and picks up the other half of it: **keeping the** 2
law. From the Jewish point of view, **obedience to the law** was the obvious 10
road to salvation—and this was the course being urged upon the Galatians. But not only is reliance upon the law incompatible with faith in Christ—'if righteousness comes by law, then Christ died for nothing' (2.21)—but law itself has terrible penalties attached to it; **for Scripture says** (Deuteronomy 27.26). **'A curse is on all who do not persevere in doing everything that is written in the Book of the Law'**; and since Paul takes it for granted that no one succeeds in doing all that is written in the Book of the Law, it follows that, so far as the law goes, everyone is cursed. The law can never be a means to righteousness (or "justification"), which must come, if at all, in some other way. How then does it come? The answer is given by one of
Paul's favourite proof-texts from Scripture, Habakkuk 2.4: '**he shall gain** 11
life who is justified through faith' (see above on Romans 1.17). This way of faith is incompatible with the way of law; for law's emphasis is entirely
on "doing"—**he who does this shall gain life by what he does** (Leviticus 12
18.5)—and since, as we have seen, no one ever can "do this", the only result of the law is to put a curse on everyone.

This curse was broken by Christ. According to the law (Deuteronomy
13 21.23) Christ's death on the cross rendered him **an accursed thing**; yet
Christ was shown (by the resurrection) not to be accursed in God's eyes, but
on the contrary righteous. Thus, by Christ, the law was discredited, and
along with the law that legalistic interpretation according to which it was
thought that the blessing of Abraham could be extended only to the Jews.

But here an objection could be made. Paul's case against the law had
rested so far on his interpretation of the figure of Abraham. But, so far as
the law was concerned, the decisive figure was surely not Abraham but
Moses. The promises made to Abraham may have been only provisional: the
final dispensation of God was not revealed until the law was given to Moses.
Paul's answer to this objection involves a play upon the Greek word *diathēkē*,
15 which normally meant **will and testament** but which, in the Septuagint
translation of the Old Testament, was used in the special sense of the
17 **covenant** made by God with his people. Taking the word in its usual sense
15 of **will,** Paul first points out that once a will **has been duly executed,** and
the testator is dead, no alteration can be made. Therefore, since God's
promise to Abraham was called "a will" (or "covenant") then it could not
be altered by the subsequent dispensation of the law of Moses. True, God
does not die, and can hardly be thought of as making wills. But from the fact
17 that the same word could do duty for both, Paul infers that the **testament,
or covenant** given by God to Abraham had at least this in common with a
"last will and testament" in ordinary life, that it could not be invalidated by
subsequent legislation.

(The argument is interrupted by a parenthesis which seems bewildering
to a modern reader, since it involves a highly technical form of argument.
In the so-called "allegorical" method of interpreting Scripture, which Paul
occasionally adopted (see below on 4.24), the hidden or "spiritual" meaning
of a text was held to be at least as important as the literal meaning. One of
the signs which was believed to indicate the presence of such a hidden
meaning was a noun occurring in the singular when a plural noun might
16 have been expected (or vice versa). Now in fact the word '**issue**' here was
perfectly intelligible as a collective description of the physical descendants
of Abraham. But Paul (somewhat arbitrarily, as it seems to us) chose to regard
this noun as a less natural expression than the plural, '**issues**', and therefore
as an indication that there was a hidden meaning. By this method of interpretation (which would have been regarded as legitimate by many Jewish
scholars) he was able to declare: **the 'issue' intended is Christ.** The point
becomes important at the end of the chapter.)

19 **Then what of the law?** Paul has been arguing that salvation depends
neither on physical descent from Abraham, nor on obedience to the (subsequently enacted) law, but only on faith; and he is now ready, in the light
of this, to reveal to the Galatians the true seriousness of what they would be

doing if they came to accept the Jewish attitude towards the law. But first, he has to guard against an apparent implication of his argument: **what of the law?** It would almost seem as if the law has been by-passed altogether, and lost its whole value and function. Exactly as in the letter to the Romans (7.7–13), Paul feels the necessity to show that the law still has a purpose, and here he suggests a number of answers:

(i) **It was added to make wrongdoing a legal offence**—a somewhat 19
obscure sentence in the Greek, but it probably suggests one possible function for the law, that of helping to draw the line between right and wrong.

(ii) **It was a temporary measure,** now suspended, but historically sig- 19
nificant.

(iii) **It was promulgated through angels.** This is not stated in the Old Testament; but that angels were present at the law-giving on Sinai was an accepted tradition in Paul's time; and this circumstance is apparently taken to indicate the subordinate place of law. Similarly, **there was an intermediary**—meaning, of course, Moses; and Paul again takes the mediating function of Moses (for reasons as obscure as in the case of angels) to be a sign of the law's inferiority to the new dispensation.

(iv) **The law was a kind of tutor.** In the ancient world the tutor (*paida-* 24
gōgos) was a slave who was put in charge of his owner's children, to accompany them back and forth from school and generally to supervise their conduct. The children owed obedience to this tutor until they came of age; and Paul finds the analogy with the law so striking that he develops it further at the beginning of chapter 4.

For reasons such as these Paul is able to claim that the law has, or at least has had, a necessary function, and is not invalidated by the new state of
affairs brought about through Christ. **Does the law, then, contradict the** 21
promises? No, never! On the contrary, it is the very verdict passed on mankind by the law (and by **Scripture** which embodies the law), that men
are everywhere **in subjection to sin,** which shows that **the ground on** 22
which the promised blessing is given must be something quite different, namely, **faith in Jesus Christ.**

The whole argument can now be summed up and applied to the Galatian crisis. The traditional Jewish interpretation of 'Abraham' and 'the law' created barriers and divisions among men: only the physical descendants of Abraham—the Jews—could inherit the promises made to Abraham, and only those who acknowledged obedience to the whole of the law of Moses—that is to say, Jews and proselytes—could hope to escape the severity of God's judgement upon the rest of mankind. But Paul has now shown that the true sons of Abraham (and so his real 'issue') are not sons by birth or nationality, but sons because they have a comparable faith; and equally, the law itself, by its own limitations, points to the necessity of faith. Faith is therefore the sole criterion: the old divisions and barriers have been super-

seded. Any attempt to re-create them (for instance, by adopting the essentially divisive and exclusive rite of circumcision, as the Galatians were
27 showing signs of doing) is a denial of this new unity in faith, this **union** with
Christ into which they have been baptized (the **garment** metaphor belongs
26, 28 to the language of baptism). For **you are all** (and this **all** is very emphatic,
and is placed twice over at the beginning of the sentence in the Greek) **you are all sons of God . . . you are all one person in Christ Jesus.** The old distinction between **Jew and Greek** has been abolished—indeed, as if this were not enough, Paul enlarges on his theme far beyond the point required by the argument: *all* distinctions, whether social (**slave and freeman**) or even natural (**male and female**), are abolished by this new unity in Christ.

One further point rounds off the argument. Paul has demonstrated earlier (by some highly technical reasoning) that the phrase, Abraham's 'issue', has a hidden meaning, namely 'Christ'. But Christians are **all one person in**
29 **Christ.** Therefore they too are the true **'issue' of Abraham** to which the
promise was made.

The incompatibility of this new faith with any kind of reliance upon the
law can be illustrated still further. Paul has already talked of the law as a
24 **kind of tutor.** He now picks the idea up again. Before Christ we were
4. 1 "minors", and so (since we were under a tutor) **no better off than a slave.**
But this slavery can take different forms. The Jews' slavery was obvious
enough: it was slavery to the law. But non-Jews also were in slavery; and
3 Paul is writing for them when he says, **We were slaves to the elemental**
spirits of the universe,[a] that is, to those elements of pseudo-philosophy,
astrology or even sheer superstition which governed the lives of all but the
most enlightened, and from which they needed the release offered by the
5 coming of Christ as surely as did **the subjects of the law.**

And if the reality of this release needs further proof, an argument is to
hand from Christian experience. If you find that your prayer (or rather, the
6 prayer of the Spirit praying within you) is addressed to God as **'Abba'** (an
intimate word for **'Father'**), then this proves that you are God's son, and
7 **if a son, then . . . an heir,** due for release from all tutorship and all dominion
from outside. There is a fuller treatment of this theme in Romans 8.14–17.

[*a*] The meaning of this phrase is a puzzle. The argument would run most simply (since the Jewish law would then be the subject throughout) if the second alternative translation in the NEB footnote could be adopted, "elementary ideas belonging to this world", a phrase which could at least include the ordinances of the law. But the Greek words mean literally "elements of the natural world" (the first alternative translation), a scientific or philosophical term for the basic constituents of the physical universe, also used sometimes to refer to the stars. Enlightened minds would hardly have thought of these as imposing slavery; but popular belief may well (and we have evidence for this at a later period) have regarded these "elements" as the agents of spiritual or demonic powers to which mankind is subject. It is assumed here that Paul's thought embraces two distinct kinds of "slavery", both of which are brought to an end by Christ: slavery to the law, and slavery to superstition.

In which case—**how can you turn back?** The pagan's submission to 9
superstitious beliefs (**beings which in their nature are no gods** or 8
beggarly spirits of the elements) is equivalent to the practical obligations 9
imposed by the synagogue to keep special **days and months and seasons** 10
and years (the Sabbaths, new moons and holy days of Jewish observance).
Even if the Galatians' previous servitude was of the former kind, their
present intention to adopt Jewish observances is no advance, but merely a
relapse into similar **service all over again.** If they persevere, they will 9
nullify their newly obtained freedom, and all Paul's pains will be **labour** 11
lost.

Put yourselves in my place. The letter now becomes more personal, and 12
the passage is obscure mainly because we do not know enough of the circumstances to be able to understand the allusions. In addition, the Greek is particularly difficult and ambiguous. Even the first words raise a question. **Put yourselves in my place . . . for I have put myself in yours.** Literally, the Greek means, "Become as I am, for I too as you". The NEB interpretation may be right; but equally Paul may be making the same point here as in 1 Corinthians 9.22 ('I have become everything in turn to men of every sort'): just as he, Paul, has exercised the freedom to behave like a non-Jew ("I as you"), so the Galatian Christians should, with the same freedom, resist the pressure being put upon them to behave like Jews. There follows a reference to Paul's previous visit (and again, as the footnotes show, the Greek is too ambiguous for us to be sure which visit he means, or how many visits there had been). Evidently Paul had been forced by an illness to abandon some more ambitious journey and to preach to the Galatians instead; but his illness had not been held against him, either (as appears to have happened at Corinth, see above, p. 581) as a means of discrediting the gospel, or as a pretext for withholding hospitality. On the contrary, their welcome had been cordial, and contrasted sharply with the present relations between them, which Paul seems to have recently rendered even more strained by
being frank with them. 16

There follows a brief reference to the party which is putting pressure on the Galatians—presumably the advocates of greater allegiance to the synagogue; but it is impossible to be sure exactly what Paul is accusing them of here. Their approaches have been deceitful, and advantage may have been taken of Paul's absence; and their success is sufficient for Paul to be at his
wits' end. That is about as much of the picture as we are allowed to see. 20

At any rate, the Galatian Christians have already gone some way towards
subjecting themselves to the Mosaic law (**you who are so anxious to be** 21
under law), and Paul now mounts a direct attack on this attitude out of **the Law** itself (for **the Law** was the correct name for the whole of the first five

books of the Old Testament). The passage referred to consists of those chapters in Genesis (16–21) which tell the story of Abraham having children,
23 first by his slave, Hagar, and then (late in life, and so **through God's promise**) by his free-born wife, Sarah. Normally, this story was taken quite straightforwardly: the Jews regarded themselves as descended from Abraham and Sarah, and despised the tribes supposed to be descended from Abraham's union with Hagar. But Paul turns this usual interpretation upside down, and makes the Jews the descendants of Hagar, the Christians the descendants of Sarah.

24 He achieves this feat by treating the story as **an allegory**, that is to say, by taking each character in it as a symbol of something else. The key to this symbolism is the antithesis, slavery: freedom. Hagar was a slave woman, and this made her appropriate to symbolize the law, and the covenant given with it on Sinai, which (as the argument of chapter 4 has shown) was a kind of
25 slavery; and also **the Jerusalem of today,** which, either because it was under Roman occupation (this would be one of Paul's rare political allusions), or else because it was still governed in the main by the Mosaic law, was also **in slavery.** All three are linked by the common tie of slavery: they belong "in the same column" (a metaphor which underlies the Greek word trans-
26 lated **represents** in verse 25). On the other side stands, first, Sarah (**the free woman**); secondly, the new covenant of freedom (which Paul does not
24 explicitly mention, but his reference to **two covenants** shows that he has it
26 in mind); and, thirdly, **the heavenly Jerusalem,** which can be shown to belong to this column by the fact that Isaiah, when using language entirely appropriate to a childless wife such as Sarah (54.1), was in fact prophesying a new Jerusalem of the future (54.11–12). So two columns emerge:

slavery	*freedom*
Hagar	Sarah
Sinai: covenant of the law	new covenant
Jerusalem of today	New Jerusalem

Thus, by an allegorical interpretation of Scripture (a method Paul seldom used, but which was brought to a fine art, for example by Philo of Alexandria), Paul finds further support for the conclusion reached in chapter 3. The true sons of Abraham are those who live under the new covenant of faith and are members of the new Jerusalem; the Jews, by comparison, are still labouring under the slavery of the law, and are no better off than the "Hagarenes" and other tribes supposedly descended from Hagar.

Paul scores one further point from the same narrative in Genesis, though this time by a more direct application of the biblical text. The sequel of God's miraculous promise to Sarah was the birth of a son, Isaac, who, having
28 been born as the result of a **promise** rather than in the normal course of nature, could be called (since "promise" and "spirit" belong closely to-

gether in Paul's mind) **the spiritual son** as opposed to Hagar's son, **the** 29
natural-born son. Now our existing texts of Genesis (21.9) do not say
that Hagar's son **persecuted** the boy Isaac; they say that he "played with
him" or "laughed at him". But the Hebrew word is a little obscure, and it
seems that Jewish scholars were becoming accustomed to taking the word
to mean "persecuted", which then gives more point to Sarah's request to
Abraham which follows in Genesis: **'Drive out the slave-woman and her** 30
son . . .' And this gives Paul one more proof that he is correct in identifying
the Christians with the descendants of Sarah, the Jews with those of Hagar;
for just as Hagar's son **persecuted** Isaac, so the Jews are now persecuting 29
the Christians. **You see then, my brothers . . . our mother is the free** 31
woman. The correspondence has been established by two separate arguments. **Christ set us free,** and so placed us in the "freedom" column. **5.** 1
The moral is inescapable: **refuse to be tied to the yoke of slavery**
again.

But possibly the Galatians did not think of it as "slavery" at all. To them, the issue may have seemed to be one merely of keeping out of trouble by agreeing to certain conditions. Even if these conditions did include the irksome rite of circumcision, they were still only binding themselves to certain outward observances. They could still hold their Christian beliefs as before, and it would surely be a gross exaggeration to call this **slavery.**

But if this is what they thought, they had been grievously (perhaps even
deliberately) misinformed. The real situation was that **every man who** 3
receives circumcision is under obligation to keep the entire law. The
circumcised proselyte was as much subject to every detail of legal observance
as was the born Jew, so that everything said above about the 'slavery' of the
law would apply to the Galatians, if they were circumcised, just as much as
to the Jews—and Paul proceeds, in a few emphatic sentences, to recapitulate 4–6
the great argument of chapter 3.

Paul has been addressing the whole congregation; but the blame for the
present state of affairs did not necessarily rest with all of them. Proverbially
(**'a little leaven . . .'**) even one man might be sufficient to "unsettle their 9
minds", and he would be the one who ultimately **must bear God's judge-** 10
ment. As for the suggestion (we assume it was made by his opponents) that
Paul himself was **still advocating circumcision**: something in Paul's past 11
may have given colour to the accusation (such as the circumcision of Timothy
recorded in Acts 16.3), but it could be scotched by a simple observation of
fact. It was being claimed by some of the Galatians (see below on 6.12) that
accepting circumcision was a way of "escaping persecution"—presumably
persecution from the Jews. But Paul was **still persecuted,** his preaching
was still a **stumbling-block** (as he describes it himself in 1 Corinthians 1.23).
Evidently, then, he could not be advocating circumcision now, even if he had
in fact urged it in one particular case in the past.

13 **You, my friends, were called to be free men.** This is not a general
statement about the human race, like "Man is born to be free". It refers to a
particular moment of liberation. The freeing of slaves was a familiar feature
of Paul's world. It was often done, both by Jews and pagans, under the guise
of a religious act: the ransom money was paid to the owner through the
treasury of the temple or the synagogue, so that it could be said that God
had "bought" (or **called**, as here) a slave into freedom. This procedure
offered a ready analogy to Christian experience. In so far as it was
accepted that living under the law (or, for a pagan, under the 'elemental
spirits') was a kind of slavery, then the liberation which had been
gained through Christ could aptly be likened to a slave's acquisition of
freedom.[a]

But the use of this metaphor also points to a difficulty. The Jews thought
of their law as their one bulwark against the general immorality of the pagan
world; and the Christians to whom Paul was writing had been for some time
associated with the synagogue and so had come to accept the standards of
moral behaviour which the law imposed on them. But now, remove the
restraint of the law, and what was to prevent these people from immediately
relapsing into their immoral ways? The very frequency with which Paul had
21 to utter warnings about this (**I warn you, as I warned you before**) suggests
that such accusations, if they were made from the Jewish side, were not
without foundation. Paul may have been right in theory when he argued that
observance of the law had no value; but morally, the position was a dangerous
one. And so now, as a consequence of his whole argument, he has to turn his
13 attention to moral questions. **Do not turn your freedom into licence for
your lower nature.**

If, for the Christian, the law was now superseded, what was there to take its place? What was there now to guide behaviour and enforce moral standards? Paul has two answers to this. The first is very brief, and somewhat paradoxical. The old slavery has gone, and been replaced by...another slavery! The new slavery is **to one another in love**—and this is nothing other than a summing up of **the whole law**. The same point is made more fully in Romans 13.8–10.

The second answer is more far-reaching. It presupposes an analysis of
16 human conduct in terms of **the Spirit** and the **lower nature** (the "flesh")
which is worked out at greater length in Romans 7 (see above p. 521).
This analysis is a matter of faith rather than psychology, for **the Spirit** is
not as it were a source of inspiration which anyone can draw on at will, but is
a gift of God directly dependent upon the acknowledgement of Jesus as Lord.
Once received, it becomes a new and dominant factor in moral conduct, and
works against **the desires of your lower nature.** It offers, in fact, an

[a] This metaphor may also underlie 5.1: 'Christ set us free, to be free men.' Also perhaps 3.13: 'Christ bought us freedom.'

empirical answer to the question, what guide and motive in moral conduct will take the place of the now obsolete law?

Lists of virtues and vices were a standard rhetorical device in the ancient world, and we possess many examples of them, both serious and flippant. We should probably not look in these verses for any distinctively Christian moral insight: Paul's list can be paralleled from both pagan and Jewish sources, and indeed these show that he drew on both. What is distinctive is the source
of these virtues: they are the **harvest** (or "fruit") of the Spirit—that is to 22
say, not the result of high moral aspirations or of strict legal discipline, but a
consequence of accepting the new guidance and dynamic which is now
available to **those who belong to Christ,** who have **crucified the lower** 24
nature, and who find themselves in the grip of a new kind of motivation
altogether. This view of the Spirit seems to be Paul's own. Whereas (for instance in Acts) the Spirit is on the whole the source of supernatural guidance, prophecy, ecstatic utterance or other somewhat exceptional powers, here it is seen as responsible for much less sensational and more ordinary qualities; it is indeed the distinctive motivation for the whole of the Christian's moral conduct. The qualities and excellences which flow from it make
ordinary civil restraints superfluous: **There is no law dealing with such** 23
things as these.

The lists of vices and virtues are followed by some specific moral instructions. Again, we should probably not expect them all to be distinctively Christian. Several of these somewhat jerky sentences are
known to be proverbs (**a man reaps what he sows,** for instance), 6. 7
and others have a proverbial ring; and verse 6 simply reiterates a 6
principle which seems to have been generally accepted in the early church
(as elsewhere), that teachers should be paid. Paul is not working out a
new moral standard; he is recommending an already accepted one, but
with this difference: the motivation is to be quite new—once again, **the** 8
Spirit.

You see these big letters? The clearest evidence about the mechanics of 11
Paul's correspondence comes in 2 Thessalonians 3.17. Like other letter-writers, such as Cicero and Augustine, he seems usually to have dictated his letters and then added a greeting in his own hand (which was perhaps strikingly large). This time, he adds, not so much a greeting, as a final urgent appeal, in which he drops the veiled and tactful manner of the rest of the letter and comes directly to the point, thus allowing us to gain a clearer glimpse of the danger threatening the Galatian church than any we have had up to now.

At last he names his opponents: they were **those who do receive circum-** 13
cision—that is to say, not Jews (who would have been circumcised at birth),
but Gentiles who had yielded to Jewish pressure and had only recently been

circumcised.[a] Even they, Paul argues, had still not realized the full implications of their action, and that it entailed a **thoroughgoing** obligation to
12 observe every article of the law (5.3). Their only object had been **to escape**
persecution for the cross of Christ, which they hoped apparently to
achieve if they could satisfy the local Jewish community both by receiving
16 circumcision themselves and by **trying to force circumcision** on their
fellow-Christians. If they succeeded, the church would no longer present to
the synagogue the spectacle of a dissident and supposedly lawless group, but
a **fair outward and bodily show** of men who had accepted an irrevocable
and outward act of allegiance to the Jews, even while professing their
13 Christian beliefs. Here would be something for them **to boast of!**

The word **boast**[b] recalls Paul to one of his deepest theological convictions.
14 A Christian has no ground for boasting save **the cross of our Lord Jesus**
Christ. None of the old distinctions and observances retains any ultimate
15 validity. 'There is no such thing as Jew and Greek' (3.28): **the only thing**
that counts is new creation!

And so Paul's greeting to this torn and harassed church is a partial one.
16 His blessing (the usual Jewish one of **peace and mercy**) can only be upon
those who **take this principle for their guide,** and who thereby qualify,
not as the outward, but as the true, **Israel of God.**

17 The **marks** on Paul's body could mean almost any distinctive scar. The meanings of the Greek word include a soldier's tattoo, a leopard's spots, and a brand burnt on the skin of a runaway slave. We shall probably never know whether Paul meant the scars of his labours (vividly described in 2 Corinthians 11.23–7), the "brand" of his Christian baptism, or a merely figurative and internal scar; but whatever he meant, he probably intended it to be understood as the antithesis of that all-too-physical mark which his opponents were advocating, and which indeed was the practical issue to which the whole letter is devoted: circumcision.

[*a*] It would of course greatly simplify the argument if Paul's opponents were in fact Christian Jews; but the force of the Greek participle, both here and at 5.3, is only faithfully rendered by a phrase like "those who receive circumcision", that is, non-Jews who are becoming proselytes by being circumcised.

[*b*] The Greek word is difficult to translate. See above on 2 Corinthians 1.12.

THE LETTER OF PAUL TO THE EPHESIANS

Paul knew the church at Ephesus well. He spent more than two years there (Acts 19–20)—longer than he spent in any other single city during his missionary work. One would therefore expect his letter to this church to be particularly intimate and personal. But in fact this "Letter to the Ephesians" is the least personal of all those attributed to Paul. It contains no hint that the writer was personally acquainted with his correspondents—indeed the impression given by such verses as 1.15 and 3.2–4 is that he had never met them; and it seems impossible to believe that the letter was really written by Paul to his friends at Ephesus. A further peculiarity of the letter is that, compared with the majority of Paul's letters, it is about nothing in particular. There is, of course, plenty of solid teaching in it about the church, about the unity of all Christians, about the institutions of marriage and slavery, and about the fight against supernatural powers; but, even if one may occasionally suspect a particular danger or heresy to have been in the writer's mind, there is no point at which the letter is clearly addressed to a specific situation or problem. The tone is throughout general, never particular, and in fact the letter reads more like a circular letter or homily than like a document from a missionary's correspondence. Add to this the fact that the words 'at Ephesus' in the first verse are omitted in a number of manuscripts, and may therefore have been added at a much later date, and it is difficult to resist the conclusion that originally the letter was never intended for this or any other particular church, but that the writer, using the form of a letter (as was not unusual in antiquity), was in fact composing a treatise of general interest to Christians, wherever they might be.

The letter purports to have been written by Paul from prison (1.1; 3.1; 6.19–22). But this does not necessarily settle the question of authorship. In antiquity, the writing of literary works under the name of a distinguished master was not regarded in quite the same light as it would be now. It might be felt, for instance, that certain ideas of the master's which he had not committed to writing but which were remembered by his disciples ought to be given wider circulation; and for this purpose a book might legitimately be written under the master's name and so far as possible in his style. A generation or so later, when the circumstances surrounding the production of the book had been forgotten, it might be included, in all good faith, among the collected works of the master. Many such cases are known from antiquity, and several of the New Testament writings may have originated in this way. Among the letters attributed to Paul, Ephesians is one of those which, since early in the last century, has most frequently come under a similar suspicion.

There are a number of minor peculiarities in the letter—its formal structure, its vocabulary, its style—which distinguish it from the other letters of Paul. But the one really remarkable feature is its relationship with Colossians. Several paragraphs are almost identical; only Colossians, out of all the New Testament letters, offers any parallel to the extraordinarily elaborate style of Ephesians; and the number of verbal resemblances is so great that the author of Ephesians must either have had Colossians fresh in his mind or had an actual copy of it in front of him.[a] There are also frequent reminiscences in Ephesians of other passages in Paul's writings. Now these facts, however curious, do not make it impossible that Paul was the author; but another widely held explanation of them is that the letter was composed by an early Christian writer who was steeped in Paul's works and whose ideas were only a slight development of those which Paul had expressed in his letter to the Colossians.

The result, however, is by no means slavish imitation. The writer of this letter, whether it was Paul or another, may have drawn freely on the language of Colossians, but he made it carry a new and different message. What is said here about the church—its nature and its place in the divine ordering of the universe (*The glory of Christ in the church*)—is unique in the New Testament, and there are many other passages in which, though the language is more-or-less familiar, the thought is striking and original. The questions raised by the origin and purpose of this letter, the strangeness of its style and its curious ties with Colossians, are ultimately of little importance beside the richness of the ideas which find expression in it.

The glory of Christ in the church

The greeting, which follows the usual Christian pattern (see above on Romans 1.1), does little more than name the writer and the recipients. The
1.1 writer is described as an **apostle of Christ Jesus, commissioned by the will of God**—a status which receives fuller treatment in the opening verses of Galatians; and the recipients are called **believers incorporate in Christ Jesus.** Where the English has **incorporate in**, the Greek has simply "in". But the conception of believers being "in" Christ is a rich and complex one, and is most easily understood in terms of Paul's doctrine that Christians are 'limbs of Christ's body' (1 Corinthians 12.27). The NEB translators have introduced the expression **incorporate in** to draw out this meaning.

[a] This, of course, is not the only possible explanation. Theoretically, Ephesians might have been written first, and Colossians modelled upon it. But that Ephesians was written later than Colossians is on the whole the easier hypothesis.

Praise be to the God and Father of our Lord Jesus Christ. This 3
Christian adaptation of one of the commonest of Jewish religious phrases
("Blessed be God, who . . .") seems to have become already a stereotyped
expression in the church (it occurs in identical words at 2 Corinthians 1.3
and 1 Peter 1.3). In 2 Corinthians 1 the burst of praise is evoked by the
experience of God's 'consolation' given in this present life to Christians
undergoing tribulation. Here the motive is a promise of a different kind:
spiritual blessing in the heavenly realms. Christians have a great destiny,
to be fulfilled not only on earth but in heaven. That is to say (and this is an
important theme of the letter), they are to share in Christ's ascendancy over
all supernatural powers which may be held to influence life on earth: they
are to take their place above all such beings **in the heavenly realms.**

This high destiny is expressed in terms borrowed from the language used
by the Jewish people about themselves. To the Jews, it was axiomatic that
they had been chosen from all other races in the world to receive a unique
inheritance; and when they reflected on the question when the act of divine
choice took place, it seemed logically necessary to push this moment of
choosing as far back in history as possible—indeed, even beyond its beginnings. But then, in the formless time before the world was created, how could
God have made a choice? What object could have existed for God to point
to and say, That is what I choose? One answer was found in the figure of the
Messiah. The Messiah was thought of as a divinely appointed person of the
future, whose main function would be to usher in the new age of Israel's
glory. That such a person should at some future moment make his appearance and fulfil his prescribed destiny was intended by God from the beginning. Indeed, God had determined who this person was to be. As later Jewish
scholars were to put it, the "name of the Messiah" was one of the things
which existed before the world began. But if God had chosen the Messiah
before the world was founded he must also have chosen the people whom 4
that Messiah was to deliver. There was a sense in which God had chosen
Israel "in" the Messiah.

All this could be given a Christian interpretation. Jesus was the Messiah
(that is, the Christ), and Christians were the true Israel. It was as represented
by Christ that God, even before history, had chosen his new people for their
destiny: **In Christ he chose us before the world was founded.** 4

A description of this destiny is attempted first in Jewish terms: **to be
dedicated, to be without blemish,** is a metaphor drawn from the temple
sacrifices—Christians were to be made by God (what they could never be
otherwise) all that a victim needs to be if it is to be acceptable;[a] they were
to be **accepted as his sons**—though no longer because, like the Jews, they 5
belonged to a particular nation which was accustomed to regard God as its

[a] The phrase, to be full of love, is a little strange in this sacrificial context, and another possible translation is given in the footnote.

7 "father"; they were to have **release**, which was one of the commonest
expressions of the Jews for the removal of all the obstacles, physical and
political as well as spiritual, which prevented them from fulfilling what they
believed to be their true destiny (and this was always understood to involve
an unmerited act of God by which **sins** would be **forgiven**); and they were
8 to have full **wisdom and insight.** This last gift moves beyond the strictly
Jewish horizon. It was the promise of every religion and every philosophy to
provide insight into the pattern and purpose of the universe, and Christianity
was soon challenged to do the same. Its answer was that the Christ who was
now revealed to Christians had existed since before the world began, and had
9 represented all along the **hidden purpose** of God. He contained within
10 himself the principle of **unity** and completeness which was manifest already
in the comprehensiveness and universality of the new people of God—the
church, Christ's body—but was also to be revealed in the whole **universe.**

In Colossians, this last point is worked out on a cosmic and metaphysical
scale. In Ephesians, the concern is more with a particular application of it.
One of the most flagrant cases of disunity in the universe was seen by this
writer to be the racial intolerance which existed between Jews and non-Jews;
and one of the most dramatic changes brought about by Christ was the
removal of this barrier. The Jews (with whom this author appears to identify
11 himself when he says **we**) had long looked forward to a glorious fulfilment of
their destiny, and associated this fulfilment with the coming of a Messiah (a
Christ); but they had always thought of this as something reserved for themselves alone, to the exclusion of all other nations, and so their expectations
had had the effect of merely accentuating the religious and social exclusiveness of their culture. But the newly revealed Christ cut right across this
13 distinction. Gentiles (**you too,** to this writer) were now to share the heritage
as much as Jews—indeed both alike were already experiencing a new force
in their lives which was a guarantee of their future destiny: **the seal of the
promised Holy Spirit.** This reversal of an age-old prejudice seemed to
this author one of the most significant moments in the 'hidden purpose'
of God.

The whole of the last two paragraphs consists, in the Greek, of one continuous sentence. The pivot is the opening formula, 'Praise be to God, who . . .', and the rest is an elaborate conglomeration of subordinate clauses, loosely attached together and creating, more by accumulation than by any logical sequence, a sense of the magnitude of the blessings for which God is to be praised. As such, it presents the most extreme example in the New Testament of a style which also appears elsewhere (particularly in Colossians), and which doubtless originates in the language of worship: its somewhat general and repetitive phrases build up a strongly devotional atmosphere. The thanksgiving is followed (as so often in New Testament letters) by a prayer, which is a little more personal, though it continues in somewhat

the same richly loaded style, and is still in fairly general terms. Yet it is noticeable that the gifts which are prayed for seem concentrated around one
of the points which has come up in the previous section, namely **wisdom.** 17
Usually, such prayers are more diverse, and have a practical slant; but here, the prayer (which draws on some of the language of the great paragraph which precedes it) is entirely for a certain kind of knowledge. The reason for this may be that the author has in mind a situation somewhat similar to that which elicited the letter to the Colossians. There may have been a tendency in the church to suggest that Christ offered only limited power and limited knowledge, and that there were other powers and other mysteries abroad which could not be mastered without stronger resources than Christ alone could supply. To which this author replies by appealing (as the early Christians loved to do) to the first verse of Psalm 110: 20

> "The Lord says to my lord:
> 'Sit at my right hand, till I make your enemies your footstool.'"

and to Psalm 8.6: 22

> "Thou hast put all things under his feet."

These words, they believed, declared the truth about Christ. They proved that his place was above all other powers, not only in the present order of the
universe, but also (in the terminology they had taken over from the Jews) **in** 21
the age to come. Not that Christ is thereby removed in lofty majesty from
creation: on the contrary, he is organically related to it through **the church,** 22
which is his body. Indeed, it is by means of the church that he fills the universe and explains its mystery—such seems to be the drift of the last sentence of the chapter, which (at least to modern ears) seems more impressive in sound than precise in meaning.

Time was . . . The following paragraph reads almost like a summary of the 2. 1
main theme of Romans. Not only Gentiles (again addressed as **you**) but Jews as well (**we too**), by reason of the standard of moral conduct they all displayed, lay under the dreadful judgement of God (Romans 1–2). And yet,
even when we were all in this condition (Romans 5.8), God **brought us to** 5
life with Christ (Romans 6.11), not because of anything we had done or
deserved, but entirely **by his grace** (Romans 3.24). **There is nothing for** 9
anyone to boast of (Romans 3.27–8); but on the other hand, we are now
under obligation to **devote ourselves to the good deeds for which God** 10
has designed us (Romans 8.12). All this is familiar Pauline theology; yet at two points it breaks new ground.

(i) Both Romans and Ephesians describe the general state of mankind, as it was before the advent of Christ, in straightforward moral and psychological
terms. **We all lived our lives in sensuality, and obeyed the promptings** 3

of our own instincts and notions is language typical of both letters. But
Ephesians also adds another dimension, which is only hinted at in Romans.
3 Immorality is thought of not only as endemic in man (due to **our natural
condition**) but as originating outside, inflicted by demonic powers. Such
2 powers were believed to exist in the space immediately above the earth (**the
air**), and their **commander** was, of course, Satan. The means by which
Satan and his underlings worked upon men was through an evil **spirit** which
inclined them to immorality (a similar idea is prominent in the Dead Sea
Scrolls); and although the effect was psychological, the ultimate cause was
often thought to be a personified form of evil working upon men from outside. This conception is of some importance later in the letter.

6 (ii) **In union with Christ Jesus he raised us up.** This is exactly the same
point as is made in Romans 6.5–11, where it is the intimate solidarity of
Christians with Christ, not only in his death but in his resurrection, which
explains the new life they now enjoy, and gives them a sure hope for the
future. But here the idea is taken a stage further. Our union with Christ
6 extends beyond the resurrection to the ascension: **he . . . enthroned us
with him in the heavenly realms.** This is what releases us from the
'spiritual powers of the air' just mentioned: by our solidarity with Christ,
we occupy a place far superior to theirs.

The magnitude of the change brought about by Christ can be seen from
another point of view. Gentiles were not only (in Jewish eyes) proverbially
prone to moral laxity, they suffered from a radical disadvantage. When the
11 Jews called the Gentiles '**the uncircumcised**' they meant far more than
the empirical fact that Gentiles (unlike Jews) belonged to a culture in which
circumcision was not practised—though Jewish Christians had now learnt
that this was nothing after all but **an outward rite.** They meant that the
Gentiles were deprived of all those ultimate advantages and privileges which
the Jews deemed themselves to possess—even the Gentiles' worship of many
12 'gods' and many 'lords' (1 Corinthians 8.5) left them ultimately in **a world
without hope and without God.** With regard to the coming judgement,
the Jews believed that their only ground of confidence was membership of
the **community of Israel**—and this was barred to Gentiles. There was no
means by which (according to a common Jewish interpretation of Isaiah
13 57.19) those who were **far off** could be brought **near.** But the shedding of
Christ's blood had changed all this. Christ, being the proclaimer (verse 17)
15 and maker (verse 15) and very essence (verse 14) of peace, had **broken down
the enmity which stood like a dividing wall between them.** It has
sometimes been thought that the key to this metaphor is the balustrade in
the temple area in Jerusalem which marked the point beyond which Gentiles
must not go (see above on Acts 21.29). But this is probably too recondite.
Another figure of speech was the "wall" with which the Jews protected and
defined the exclusive identity of their people—the observance of the Law of

Moses. If this was the "wall" referred to here, then we can understand the point of saying that Christ **annulled the law with its rules and regulations.**

The result was a completely new community, a new solidarity between men who had formerly been deeply estranged. Gentiles, who had always been
made to feel, in their relations with the Jews, like **aliens in a foreign land,** 19
had now become **fellow-citizens with God's people.** The resultant community could be described as a building, still in progress from its inception
by the **apostles** and (doubtless Christian) **prophets,** founded upon[a] Jesus 20
Christ, and superseding the Jewish temple as the **spiritual dwelling for** 22
God.

It is, then, one particular result of the work of Christ which receives emphasis
in this letter: **that through the Gospel the Gentiles are joint heirs with** 3.6
the Jews. But this is also the key to the career of Paul. It is clear from the letter to the Galatians (1.15–16) that Paul's experience on the road to
Damascus (his **revelation**) was not merely a personal conversion to Christ, 3
but included an explicit commission to work among the Gentiles. **I have** 4
already written a brief account of this—these words perhaps refer to some other letter of Paul's which contained this important piece of autobiography. On the face of it, the new gospel was as Jewish as the environment out of which it came, and it was at first (even for the church) difficult to believe that it was addressed to anyone but the Jews. Paul's commission, to preach to the Gentiles, would have seemed quite incompatible with the special destiny of the Jews as revealed in the Old Testament, were it not for what was called earlier in the letter the 'hidden purpose of God' or, as here,
the **secret of Christ**—that is, the newly created possibility, at best only 4
dimly presaged in Scripture, **but now . . . revealed by inspiration to his** 5
dedicated apostles and prophets, of the Gentiles sharing in the inheritance, the community and the promises hitherto reserved for the Jews. It was the proclaiming and bringing about of this new state of affairs which had been Paul's particular task and privilege, and it was this, inevitably, which had led him into the fiercest opposition and the acutest sufferings. It was
because of this, even now, that Paul was a **prisoner.** 1

But here, as so often, the letter is less concerned with immediate consolation for present sufferings than with the ultimate destiny of Christians in the
realms of heaven (a frequent and characteristic phrase in Ephesians). And 10
the startling thought now appears that **this hidden purpose** (the adoption 9
of the Gentiles) is not only something to be proclaimed and experienced on
earth, but is also, as part of **the wisdom of God in all its varied forms,** 10
still to be made known at the supernatural level **to the rulers and authori-**

[*a*] Or perhaps built upon: as the NEB footnote shows, there is slight ambiguity about the "cornerstone" metaphor.

ties in the realms of heaven; and this (since the church has a footing in that supernatural world) is to be done **through the church.**

In the light of this high destiny, the prayer for the church, begun in 1.17
and since somewhat interrupted, is resumed and concluded with greater
15 precision. It is addressed to **the Father, from whom every family in**
heaven and on earth takes its name—a solemn phrase which, in the
Greek, exploits the fact that "father" and "family" are both words derived
16 from the same root; and it asks again that, along with **strength and power,**
which are needed not only in the endurance of physical trials but also in the
formation of that **inner being** which is the real reward of endurance (2
Corinthians 4.16), Christians may be endowed with a love that will make them
aware of the true dimensions of **the love of Christ**, and may be able to take
part in that ultimate unravelling of the secrets of the universe which is here
19 again, as in 1.23, impressively rather than clearly expressed in terms of the
fullness of God himself. The prayer ends with an elaborate ascription of
glory to God.

4.1 **I entreat you, then.** The remainder of the letter, like the final section of
many of Paul's letters, consists almost entirely of moral exhortations. Ephesians is exceptional only in that between the opening prayers and thanksgivings (which are greatly extended in this letter) and the concluding ethical
passages there are no paragraphs devoted specifically to doctrinal or practical
questions; and the absence of any central section concerned with specific
problems is the strongest reason for thinking that this letter, unlike all those
which are certainly to be attributed to Paul, was written without any particular church or any particular situation in mind. On the other hand, the
first part of the letter, despite its somewhat diffuse and devotional character,
contains a fair amount of solid doctrine, and reverts again and again to the
theme of the new unity between men (especially men of different races)
3 which has been made possible in Christ. This theme of unity—**the unity**
which the Spirit gives—leads naturally into the first exhortation: an attitude of humility and peaceableness is essential if this new possibility of unity
is not to be frustrated by ordinary human shortcomings. Indeed, this unity
is not merely desirable in itself: unity of worship and unity of worshippers
is a reflection of the oneness of God himself, who (according to a conven-
6 tional religious formula which occurs also in 1 Corinthians 8.6) **is over all**
and through all and in all.

But what will this new community be like? Must unity mean uniformity?
Are all its members to have the same function and the same gift? The
answer to this question is already familiar from 1 Corinthians 12. The one
Spirit has a variety of gifts to impart, and the unity of a Christian community
11 consists in the interdependence of different gifts and offices, enabling **some**
to be apostles, some prophets, some evangelists, some pastors and

teachers (evangelists and pastors are an addition to the list in 1 Corinthians
12.28, reflecting perhaps a slight change in the needs of the church). The
point is proved, as so often, by a quotation from Scripture, though the 8
application is a little complicated. Psalm 68.18 runs, in both the Greek and
Hebrew versions:

> "Thou didst ascend into the heights
> with captives in thy train
> having received gifts among men."

These words were doubtless addressed originally to a victorious king returning to Jerusalem; but Jewish tradition had come to interpret them as referring to Moses ascending Mount Sinai in order to receive the Law, and in so doing it seems to have made current a version of the text somewhat closer to that which is quoted here, substituting "given" for "received". According to this text and interpretation, the "gifts" became, not the tribute of conquered nations, but the blessings proceeding from the Law. Now the point which the text is quoted to prove is that Christ gave, not one gift, but a variety of gifts to his people; and the proof lies in the words **he gave gifts to men.** But first it has to be shown that the subject of the verse is neither a king of Israel, nor Moses, but Christ; hence the importance of the first words of the quotation. **He ascended** suggests a previous descent. Who could be meant, who had both descended and ascended, if not Christ? For Christ,
having been from the beginning up above with God, came down to **the** 9
lowest level of the heavens-and-earth universe[a] before ascending once again
to that position of supremacy which has already been described in 1.20–3.
Given this way of thinking, and given this method of interpretation, the
passage could be claimed, like many others in the Old Testament, to be a
prophecy of Christ; as such, it proved that the church had received, not just
one uniform gift for all, but a variety of **gifts.** 11

The quality of men bound together in such a unity and exercising their
gifts in close interdependence is shown above all in their maturity. Their
personality must develop towards the new possibilities revealed for humanity
in Christ, and they must grow out of their childish susceptibility to **every** 14
fresh gust of teaching. The most powerful metaphor at the writer's command for expressing the unity and vitality of such a community (though for
Paul it is usually more than a metaphor, as is clear from 1 Corinthians 12.13)
is once again that of Christ's **body**; and the language here is an elaboration 12
(though with a slightly different slant) of the same metaphor as it is worked
out in Colossians 2.19.

This then is my word to you. The moral exhortations now continue in 17
earnest. There are striking similarities between the language of these paragraphs and that of other passages in the New Testament, and many of the

[a] If it is thought likely that a writer of this date would have known the later doctrine of a "descent into hell", the words may bear the meaning given in the footnote in NEB.

sentiments can also be paralleled in Jewish and Greek literature. The explanation appears to be that the early church, needing an ethical code which could be taught to new converts whatever their background, drew on a number of different sources. Some rules of conduct went back to the teaching of Jesus, or were forged out of distinctly Christian principles; others had long been a part of Jewish education and were recognized by Christians as still valid for themselves; others, again, were the common property of the civilization of the time. All these strands were woven into the Christian ethical tradition, without any attempt to label each according to its origin. The resultant code, consisting both of radically new demands and of long-accepted standards, was endorsed by the Christian community as representing its own distinctive way of life; and in this sense the whole code, or any
17 part of it (whatever its origin), could be urged **in the Lord's name.**
Give up living like pagans. The letter, it is clear (1.12–13), is addressed by a Jewish Christian writer to Gentile Christians. With regard to Gentiles, the prevalent Jewish assumption was that, having no respect for the Jewish law, and having no strict moral code of their own, Gentiles were bound to fall into the vices characteristic of a pagan civilization. So here: verses 18–20 use the conventional language of Jewish attacks on the pagan way of life, and the tone is similar to that which Paul adopts, for the same purpose, in the first chapter of Romans. But the Christian way of life (for all that Jewish anti-
20 Christian propagandists might say) was not like this. **That is not how you learned Christ**—which appears, from what follows, to mean that the act of accepting Christ as Lord—which is, in fact, the moment of baptism—involves not only a course of instruction in **the truth as it is in Jesus,** but a "laying aside" of the old nature and a "putting on" of the new, so that the whole pattern of life is changed. The language here is all familiar from what Paul says about baptism in passages such as Romans 6 and Colossians 3.
26 The next exhortations follow no particular order. **Do not let anger lead you into sin** is an allusion to Psalm 4.4 (the roughness of the Semitic way of expressing this, "Be angry and do not sin", is softened in this translation).
30 **Do not grieve the Holy Spirit of God** is an Old Testament idiom (Isaiah 63.10), but takes on a special meaning for Christians, since their baptism (also called a **seal** in 1.13) places them in a new relationship with the Spirit, as well as giving them a foretaste and guarantee of their future destiny. In verses 4.32—5.2 the example of Christ himself is appealed to, with an allusion to the sacrificial language of passages such as Exodus 29.18 and Psalm 40.7. In verses 4.29 and 5.5 some curiously un-Greek expressions (which can hardly be reproduced in translation) suggest a Hebrew original. These verses are a good example of the diverse origins of Christian moral teaching.
At verse 6, however, the writer seems to have a specific danger in view:
5.6 **shallow arguments** suggest a rival religion or rival philosophy; and one may hazard a guess at the character of this rival from the "darkness" which

seems to go with it. It is possible that what are being attacked are certain rites and doctrines which were clothed in secrecy and so attracted (as Christianity itself subsequently attracted) suspicions of immoral practices.
Now as Christians you are light—and the supporting quotation is not, 8
this time, from any known part of Scripture, but is doubtless (as indicated
by the NEB rendering, which inserts the word **hymn**) a fragment of a very 14
early Christian hymn. Immediately after this, the paragraph returns to general moral exhortation, and comes in two places (16 and 19–20) very close to Colossians (4.5 and 3.16).

At verse 21, the injunctions fall into a distinctive pattern. A regular topic of moral teaching in antiquity was the domestic relations between different classes of persons—husbands and wives, fathers and children, slaves and masters; and this teaching tended to be set out in a more or less stereotyped form. The New Testament writers more than once appear to make use of this conventional form, adding to it new implications drawn from the Christian faith (see below on Colossians 3.18). So here: under the general
heading, **Be subject to one another** (which was a guiding principle in 21
Christian communities: Galatians 5.13, 1 Corinthians 16.16), a Christian version of this conventional type of teaching is introduced, beginning with the category of wives and husbands.

Wives, be subject to your husbands as to the Lord. As to the Lord 22
is the important phrase. The Christian experience of subjection and obedience to Christ is the pattern which wives should follow in their behaviour towards their husbands. But (it could be asked) does the analogy hold? Does what applies to the relationship of Christians to Christ apply also to the relationship of wives to their husbands? The answer is simple and logical. The Christian, as a member of the church, is a part of that body of which Christ is the head (4.16). His obedience to Christ is therefore the obedience which the body owes to the head. But it was an accepted figure of speech (as we can see from 1 Corinthians 11.3, though we do not know where the idea
came from) that **the man is the head of the woman.** It follows that the 23
wife's obedience to her husband is also the obedience which the body owes to the head. Therefore what applies to Christians' obedience to Christ must also apply to wives' obedience to their husbands.

The converse relationship, that of husbands to wives, needs a different model, since "subjection" (at least in antiquity) could hardly describe it.
Again, a new Christian experience is appealed to: **love your wives, as** 25
Christ also loved the church and gave himself up for it. The point is taken further than is required by the argument: Christ's death made possible Christian baptism (Romans 6) which, by virtue of the cleansing and (perhaps)
the invocation which accompanied the rite (**water and word**), made the 26
church what it could never be by its own efforts, a sacrifice perfectly acceptable to its Lord (the metaphor in verse 27 contains clear allusions to the

Jewish sacrificial system). But this is by the way. More relevant to the
30 behaviour of husbands is that **that is how Christ treats the church, because it is his body.** But (it could be asked once again) does the analogy hold? Why should husbands behave to their wives as Christ behaved to his body? The answer, this time, is found in that verse of Genesis (2.24) which
31 was the basis of Christ's own view of marriage: '**the two shall become one flesh**'. This shows that the husband's wife is his body, and therefore that what holds of Christ's treatment of his body, the church, holds also of the
32 Christian husband's treatment of his body—his wife. **It is a great truth that is hidden here.** Christ's relationship with his church has deeper and richer implications than this; but here it serves the purpose of casting a new and brilliant light upon married life.

6. 1–3 Children's subjection to their parents is to be grounded in the fifth commandment (Exodus 20.12). Fathers' behaviour to their children, on common
4 sense and the principles of **a Christian upbringing.** For slaves, the fact that
6 all Christians are now **slaves of Christ** is an encouragement to behave, even in literal slavery, with full responsibility; and masters are exhorted to humanity on the strength of the basic Old Testament proposition
9 (2 Chronicles 19.7) that, at least with regard to social class, God **has no favourites.**

10 **Finally then, find your strength in the Lord.** All the exhortations so far have been to action which a man may take on his own initiative, as a response to the new demands of Christ, or as an attack against the weaknesses of his own nature. But this writer (as has already appeared above, 2.1–2) does
12 not think of evil merely as a human and psychological phenomenon. **Our fight is not against human foes, but against cosmic powers.** Evil is an objective and external fact, a superhuman force which bears upon men from outside and brings them into compulsory subjection. In unsophisticated Jewish religion (as we can see from the gospels) this force was identified quite simply with Satan and his attendant demons. But the popular philosophies and religions of the time offered to the more cultivated thinker a wide range of concepts for describing this objective and personified power of evil. There was the late Jewish myth of fallen angels; there was the popular world-view which saw the space between heaven and earth as peopled with spiritual beings, some benign, but mostly malignant and in revolt against God; and there were the doctrines of astrology, which invested the heavenly bodies with ineluctable power over the lives of men. This author draws freely on such concepts. In 2.2 he talks of 'the spiritual powers of the air'.
12 Here, he paints a still more sombre picture of men pitted **against cosmic powers, against the authorities and potentates of this dark world, against the superhuman forces of evil in the heavens.** The letter began, it is true, with a vision of the ultimate destiny of the church raised, in unity with its Lord, to a position high above these supernatural powers; and this

great destiny is in course of fulfilment. Yet meanwhile the powers are still
abroad, and the Christian, like all men, is exposed to their influence. For
this, his own strength is inadequate, and he is urged to **put on all the** 11
armour which God provides. The metaphor is magnificently worked out;
and by means of the last term in the exhortation—**pray for me**—a gentle 19
transition is made to the personal remarks at the end of the letter.

Verses 21–2 are almost identical with Colossians 4.7, on which see below.

THE LETTER OF PAUL TO THE PHILIPPIANS

The events which accompanied Paul's first visit to Philippi are dramatically told in Acts 16 and are also referred to by Paul, with some indignation, in 1 Thessalonians (2.2). Despite this violent beginning, the Philippian church had evidently taken root and flourished; and although Paul was only able to pay it one, or possibly two, subsequent visits (Acts 20.2; 2 Corinthians 2.13), it more than once provided him with generous financial support, and its record of faith and loyalty elicited this, the warmest and most affectionate of Paul's surviving letters.

The city of Philippi was an important one, being the first station on the Egnatian Way leading from Asia to the Adriatic (see the map on p. 464). Along with the indigenous Greek inhabitants, it contained many families from Italy who had been settled there by the Romans during the first century B.C. These families now constituted a considerable Latin element, and had given the city a distinctly Roman character. There was also a Jewish community, too small, it seems, to have been able to build itself a prominent synagogue (Acts 16.13), but able none the less to exert some pressure upon the Christians.

It is clear from the text that when Paul wrote this letter he was in prison, awaiting trial. The traditional view is that this captivity was at Rome, and that Philippians, like Colossians and Philemon, therefore belongs to the last period of Paul's activity; and this provides a reasonable explanation of the circumstances which are alluded to in the letter. On the other hand, the journey from Philippi to Rome was a long one, and the mail must have taken several weeks; yet messengers had passed between Paul and the Philippians at least twice before this letter was written (2.25–6); and since we do not know the details of earlier imprisonments (such as Paul alludes to in 2 Corinthians 11.23), we cannot rule out the possibility that the letter was written from a place much nearer to Philippi, such as Ephesus, at an earlier period in his life.

The apostle and his friends

The opening of the letter follows the usual convention (see above on Romans 1.1), and does little more than name the sender and the recipients; but there
1.1 is one remarkable addition: **including their bishops and deacons.**

The Greek words used here for **bishops** and **deacons** are the same as those which subsequently became the names of established orders of ministry within the church; but in Paul's time their meaning may have been somewhat different. It was not until early in the second century that a threefold ministry of bishops, presbyters (priests) and deacons was established in any part of the church, and it did not become universal until the beginning of the third. During the first decades of the church's existence the organization seems to have been much less uniform. According to Acts, the church in Jerusalem was governed, first by the apostles, and then by "elders"; in Corinth, there do not seem to have been any clearly defined offices at all; and only in the letters to Timothy and Titus do the titles "bishop" and "deacon" reappear. The most we can say is that some sort of precursors of the later bishops and deacons had already been established at Philippi.

Thanksgiving for the record of the church to which he is writing and a
prayer for its continuing progress stand at the beginning of many of Paul's
letters: the pattern is the same in Colossians, in Ephesians, and elsewhere.
The tone here is particularly warm. **The part you have taken in the work** 5
of the Gospel may be a reference specifically to the material contributions
made by the Philippian church (4.15–16); but Paul at once goes on to indicate
other reasons for his gratitude—the general progress of the Philippians, their
solidarity with him in his present critical circumstances, and his conviction
that their faith is such as to last unshaken until the imminent Day of Christ.
And so Paul longs to see them, **with the deep yearning of Christ Jesus** 8
himself—not, that is to say, as if Paul imagines his own emotions to be
similar to those of Jesus, but rather with that depth of feeling which is due to
the unique relationship which now holds between Christians (and especially
between Paul and his converts) who are **incorporate in Christ Jesus.**[a] 1

Meanwhile Paul was in prison. The word *praetorium* (here rendered
headquarters) might have been hoped to yield some indication of where 13
exactly Paul was; but unfortunately the word has several possible meanings.
If Paul was in Rome, it would probably imply that he was under the custody
of the Praetorian Guard, that is to say the Emperor's household troops; if he
was in a provincial capital, it would mean the official residence of the Roman
governor (these possibilities are allowed for in the NEB footnote). In any
case, his imprisonment might have been regarded by many as a serious
check to the progress of the gospel. Paul, on the contrary, could show that it
had been in the main a source of encouragement, and even if some of his
personal rivals had taken advantage of his absence in prison to advance their
own reputation—**what does it matter? One way or another . . . Christ is** 18
set forth.

But Paul was not merely in prison, he was on trial for his life. Job, brought near to the point of death by his misfortunes, had been anxious above all

[a] The detailed interpretation of this passage is a little obscure—see the footnotes in NEB; but the general sense is clear enough.

that he should not die in disgrace: convinced of his innocence, his most earnest prayer was, not for an escape from death, but for this innocence of his to be recognized. "The issue of it all will be my salvation", he said, "in that no deceit shall come into God's presence" (Job 13.16 in the Greek version of the Septuagint). Job's only concern was to maintain the justice of his
19 cause. Paul, by alluding to this verse (**the issue of it all will be my deliverance**) placed his own ordeal in the same light: the important thing was not whether he lived or died, whether he was released or condemned,
20 but only that he should **have no cause to be ashamed**, and that, whichever way the human judgement went, the truth of Christ should **shine out clearly.** He was so sure that this would happen that the imminent possibility of death did not affect his mood: **Yes, and rejoice I will.**

But suppose he was in fact to die, had he personally no fear of death? Paul was not one to take lightly the seriousness of the judgement which must follow death, nor was he disposed to assume too easily that his future destiny was assured (3.12–14). But at the moment of writing his consciousness of
21 union with Christ was so intense (**to me life is Christ**) that, brushing aside all theoretical schemes of the after-life (such as that in 1 Corinthians 15), he seems to have envisaged his own death as an immediate escape into a still
25 closer relationship with Christ; and only the obligation he felt to **stand by** his churches kept alive in him a desire to be spared.

The following paragraphs (1.27—2.18) amount to a brief sermon addressed
27 to the Philippians, of which the theme is: **let your conduct be worthy of the gospel of Christ**; and a number of different arguments are used. First, the Christian life is painted in the colours of a battle: **contending as one man for the gospel faith.** The longer the battle lasts (and Paul did not expect it to last very long) the clearer will become the line of demarcation between the opposing forces, and on the day of judgement the essential thing will be to be found standing on the right side of the line. Those who have
28 remained faithful—**without so much as a tremor**—can be assured of their salvation; whereas those who have been opposing the Gospel will be able to infer from the very faithfulness of the Christians that what they have been opposing is indeed the truth, and so will be convinced, even before the judgement, that they are on the wrong side of the line, **that their doom is sealed.** (The same point is made more elaborately and more ruthlessly in 2 Thessalonians 1.6–10). Paul's first visit to Philippi (Acts 16.16–24) was a notable demonstration of the kind of opposition which Christians must expect, and which the Philippians may still have been having to face.

2. 2 Paul's second argument is a highly personal one. **Fill up my cup of happiness.** Life in Christ is an experience binding men and women closely together; if it is real at all, it inevitably makes the Christian particularly sensitive both to the excellences and to the shortcomings of his fellow-Christians.

So Paul begs that his own happiness may be increased by the mutual love and personal humility of the Christians at Philippi.

Thirdly, there is the example of Christ himself—or rather (following the
main text in NEB as opposed to the footnote) there is a vital implication of
the Christian's **life in Christ**. The passage which follows has a marked 5
poetic quality in the Greek, and a kind of symmetry of construction which
suggests that it may have been a transcription of an existing poem. Not that
Paul could not rise to great heights of eloquence himself; but the poetical
form, combined with certain peculiarities of diction, suggests that the passage
may be, not a piece of original Pauline thinking about the nature of Christ,
but a fragment of a hymn which had come to be used in the worship of the
earliest Christian communities. If so, Paul is quoting from this hymn, perhaps
with slight modifications, in order to press home the point of his sermon.

The theme of the hymn is the humility and obedience of Christ; but these
are not thought of as marks of Jesus' character that might be illustrated by
known episodes from his earthly life, but rather as clues to the understanding
of who Jesus was and what he did. The story is taken up (as at the beginning
of John's gospel) long before his human birth. Christ **humbled himself,** 8
not just by his demeanour on earth, but in a more significant, almost metaphysical, sense, in that he willingly and deliberately exchanged[a] his rightful
equality with God for the **nature of a slave**—that is, for a human existence 7
exposed to everything which might befall such an existence: not death only,
but the extreme humiliation of **death on a cross.** This, beyond anything 8
which a merely human being could perform, was supreme obedience,
supreme humility; as a result of it (**therefore** is emphatic in the Greek, 9
beginning the second strophe of the poem and thereby showing that this was
the important thing about Jesus, the key to his nature and work, the point
at which divinity and humanity touch) **God raised him to the heights** and
gave him the paramount honour which, in Isaiah (45.23), God reserves for
himself: "To me every knee shall bow, every tongue shall swear". Yet this 10
exalted position, above all earthly, infernal and even heavenly beings, was no
usurpation by Jesus: it was still **to the glory of God the Father.** 11

All this has theological and metaphysical implications; but the passage betrays no interest in these. It may also owe much to the ideas which were

[*a*] The meaning of verse 7 is not clear. The most natural sense of the Greek words is that at some specific moment Jesus could have made himself equal with God, but chose not to. Such a moment could perhaps be thought of in the context of the myth of Adam, whose sin was precisely to "snatch at equality with God" (Genesis 3.5): Christ, the Second Adam (Romans 5), could be seen to have resisted the identical temptation. Alternatively, the words may be taken in the sense given by the footnote in NEB: "He did not prize his equality with God"—that is to say, having always been equal with God, he was prepared to forgo this equality in order to assume the nature of a slave. Both interpretations presuppose that Christ existed before he became man; the first describes this pre-existence in terms of a myth, the second in terms of an eternal metaphysical relationship with God. But many other interpretations are possible.

implicit in Jesus' use of the title Son of Man, or to the "suffering servant" motif in Isaiah 53—not to mention more remote antecedents which have been suggested by scholars; but these lie so far beneath the surface that they can no longer be clearly distinguished. What is before us is a brief poetical statement, such as a hymn or an act of worship might have contained—perhaps an example of the way in which the earliest Christians sought to explain to themselves the significance of the life and work of Jesus. They studied it, not so much for instances of divinely inspired virtue, as for traces of the grand design which underlay it—the obedience and self-humiliation of a divine being who had abandoned his status of equality with God, descended to the depths of human suffering and ignominy, and only then been restored to his rightful place in the whole created universe. It was obedience on a divine and cosmic scale, the supreme obedience of Jesus Christ, to
12 which Paul was appealing when he wrote, **So you too, my friends, must be obedient.**

Obedient to what? When Paul was present in Philippi it may have seemed easy enough to grasp this obedience as obedience to the apostle's personal authority. But the real object of the Christian's obedience was perhaps seen more clearly now that he had left them. The motive of their new life was now experienced as having nothing to do with Paul's authoritative
13 personality. **It is God who works in you**—yet in such a way that he allows complete freedom of response. However paradoxical it might seem (in view of the initiative which God had undoubtedly taken) it remained true that **you must work out your own salvation in fear and trembling.**

The last section of this short sermon, like the first, is conceived in the light of the coming day of judgement. When that day comes, the Christians must be sure that their conduct has been such as to place them in the right camp:
15 not (as the scriptural phrase has it, Deuteronomy 32.5) **in a warped and crooked generation,** but as **faultless children of God.** Thus, not only do they already have a radiance and a message which distinguishes them from all other men,[a] but, on that same day of judgement, they will stand to the credit of Paul himself when he too is called to account for his career. Paul
17 may die before that day; but his death (in a metaphor probably based on pagan sacrifices as much as on anything Jewish or Christian) will be only a part of that sacrifice which they are making themselves: it need neither separate him from them, nor impair their mutual joy.

Two envoys were to maintain contact between Paul and the Philippian
19 church. One, **Timothy,** had already been entrusted with a delicate mission to Corinth (1 Corinthians 4.17), and is here given an eloquent testimonial;
25 the other, **Epaphroditus,** belonged to the Philippian church, and we know

[a] This is an approximate paraphrase; the precise bearing of the metaphor in verse 15 is a little obscure.

nothing about him and his misfortunes beyond what we read about him here
and at 4.18.

And now, friends, farewell. This looks like the end of the letter; but there 3. 1
is still a serious issue to be dealt with which causes Paul to change his mind
and continue; and by way of transition he adds some rather colourless words
(**to repeat what I have written . . .**) which may in fact have been something
of a commonplace, a trite way of apologizing for returning to a familiar topic
(the Greek words form an almost perfect line of verse).

Beware of those dogs. Whenever a Jew said this, he was usually express- 2
ing his contempt of non-Jews (much as Jesus did, though somewhat more
politely, in Matthew 15.26). But Paul here turns the expression round, and
flings it back at those Jews, or their sympathizers among the Christians, who
were endeavouring to impose upon the church the necessity of accepting the
rite of circumcision (which Paul, with an untranslatable play upon words,
sarcastically calls **mutilation**).

The pressure being exerted upon the church at Philippi must have been
similar to that which provoked a major crisis in Galatia. In both churches the
trouble was caused by those who "insisted on circumcision". But there is a
difference. In Galatia, the pressure seems to have taken the form of a threat
of actual persecution by the synagogue; here, there is a suggestion of a more
subtle kind of propaganda. **We are the circumcised**, says Paul; and we 3
can probably overhear the attacks of the outraged Jewish community, who
would be taunting the Christians and saying, "you do not have circumcision,
you have no temple and no sacrifices, you have no religious tradition in which
you can put your confidence". To which Paul replies, "we are the true
circumcised, we have all the things you are so proud of—but not in the same
sense as you have them; and in any case the essence of our religion is that we
put no confidence in anything external". (For other examples of this
propaganda, see Colossians 2.11; 1 Peter 2.5–10.)

If this was the answer of the ordinary non-Jewish Christian, it may well
have seemed to the Jews somewhat evasive, as if, lacking the advantages
which the Jews believed in, the Christians were reduced to pretending that
they possessed the equivalent in their new religion. In Paul's mouth, on the
other hand, the argument was formidable. He, if anyone, could argue from
strength:

(i) **circumcised on my eighth day**—the regular time for this ceremony 5
(compare the circumcision of Jesus, Luke 1.59), without which no male
could be regarded as a member of the Jewish people;

(ii) **Israelite by race**—that is, both parents born Jews;

(iii) **of the tribe of Benjamin**—there is slight evidence that a certain
distinction, or some exceptional purity, was held to belong to this tribe;

(iv) **a Hebrew born and bred**—the word **Hebrew** may be slightly more specific than the commoner word "Jew": it may mean either that the family came from Palestine (and there is an early tradition that Paul's parents had moved to Tarsus from Gischala in Galilee), or that, unlike most Greek-speaking Jews of the Dispersion, they still knew Hebrew (see the footnote in NEB).

So much for his ancestry. His conduct and way of life, before his conversion to Christianity, were equally irreproachable from the Jewish point of view:

6 (i) his **attitude to the law** was that of the Pharisees, who considered that no part of the law was outmoded, but that it was all capable of interpretation in such a way as to be manifestly practicable, and who went to great pains to bring their lives into conformity with its detailed requirements;

(ii) **in pious zeal, a persecutor of the church**—that is, ruthlessly opposed to any apparent deviation from Jewish orthodoxy;

(iii) **in legal rectitude, faultless.**

Paul, therefore, could meet his Jewish opponents on their own ground. For sheer Jewishness, he could stand comparison with any inhabitant of Palestine, a fact he did not hesitate to exploit to the full whenever he found himself in dispute with the Jewish authorities. But this Jewishness of Paul also had its ambiguous side. Despite the strength and consistency of his Jewish upbringing, he was also capable of behaving, when in gentile company, exactly as if he were a Gentile himself (as he tells us himself, 1 Corinthians 9.19–23). Such adaptability was exceedingly un-Jewish; and his Jewish opponents may well have asked, was he or was he not going to continue to call himself a Jew? Equally, his Christian friends may have wondered whether, despite all this talk of "putting no confidence in anything external", Paul was still in fact "relying" on his parentage, his circumcision, and his Pharisaic education. To this question Paul gives an unequivocal answer: he has only mentioned these things for the purpose of the argument, in order to silence the taunts which the Jews were aiming at uncircumcised Christians.
7 His real opinion of them he expresses in violent language—**all such assets**
8 **I have written off . . . I count it so much garbage.**

What was it that Paul regarded as of such overwhelming value that he was prepared to write off all the advantages of race and upbringing which his fellow-Jews set such store by? It is not sufficient to answer, his Christianity, for his opponents evidently thought of Christianity as a system of beliefs which could be held in addition to reliance upon the "externals" of the Jewish religion, whereas Paul was thinking of something which replaced all
9 these. Part of the answer was **the righteousness which comes from faith**
in Christ, a conception which is not explained here, but which is familiar from Romans and Galatians, and which excluded all "reliance upon the law" and confidence in externals. But Paul also gives another, much more
8 surprising, answer: **all is far outweighed by the gain of knowing Christ**

Jesus my Lord. Only here does Paul speak in such intimate and personal terms of "knowing his Lord"; and we must ask, in what sense did Paul "know" Jesus? Not, it seems, in the sense that he was acquainted with Jesus on earth—if he had ever in fact seen Jesus, he attached no importance to it.[a] His "knowledge" was more of the kind associated with many popular forms of religion, in which the supreme object of all rites and ceremonies was to "know" the deity in a mystical sense. For Paul, this meant not so much knowledge about God as a relationship with him, such that "to know God" was almost equivalent to "being known by him" (Galatians 4.9, where the same word "know" is translated 'acknowledge' in the NEB). It involved an experience (whether personal and unique, as on the Damascus road, or more generally conveyed through other experiences, as seems to be implied in
Romans 6) of the **power**—the reality and efficacy—of Jesus' resurrection, a 10
sense of solidarity with Jesus in suffering, and the hope of ultimately sharing in the glory.

In certain Greek religions the devotees were promised "knowledge" as a result of certain initiations, having attained which they would be "perfect". Paul's momentary use of the language of such religions might have aroused a similar expectation; after initiation by baptism, the Christian might feel
himself to have **reached perfection.** But of course this was not so—not even 12
in Paul's case, though he, under the imminent threat of martyrdom, could plausibly claim to have followed Christ to the end. No, **it is not to be thought that I have already achieved all this.** Yet the analogy of initiation into a "mystery religion" was not without its value. In the Christian life, some will
be more **mature** than others—Paul deliberately uses another form of the 15
technical word which is translated **reached perfection** in verse 12. Those who have not yet got so far may still **think differently**, but so long as their progress is maintained, they too will soon reach the point at which **God will make plain** to them what at present is known only to those **who are mature.**
Meanwhile, there is no excuse for anyone to slacken his efforts: **let our con-** 16
duct be consistent with the level we have already reached.

Agree together, my friends, to follow my example. Without explana- 17
tion, Paul's example might have been somewhat ambiguous. He seemed ready enough to make a point of his pure Jewishness, but equally ready to feel himself free from Jewish regulations; and he used language about "knowing" Christ which could suggest that he belonged to a special class of initiates and had already achieved perfection. But now, having forestalled any such misunderstandings, Paul could safely offer himself as an example to his converts, some of whom, to his deep chagrin, had been placing a disastrously licentious interpretation upon the gospel principles of "freedom" and "knowledge".

[*a*] This is often thought to be the meaning of 2 Corinthians 5.16. The NEB renders this verse to yield a somewhat different sense; but in any case Paul's silence about the earthly Jesus is notable.

19 Their behaviour amounted to having their minds **set on earthly things;**
20 whereas Paul thinks of Christians as, **by contrast . . . citizens of heaven,**
which means, not that the body, with all its appetites and shame, is irrelevant
to Christian ethics (which was the usual excuse for licentious behaviour
among Christians), but on the contrary that the existing body is the material
out of which **our deliverer** will fashion us a new body on the Day of his
4. 1 coming. **Therefore, my friends** (the almost inevitable sequel to any mention of that Day, see above on Romans 13.12), **stand . . . firm!**
2 There follows a brief paragraph on domestic matters: a quarrel between
3 two women in the church, an appeal to an unknown **comrade** to help in
settling it, and a reference to other faithful members of the church, **whose
names are in the roll of the living** (a conventional expression: see below
on Revelation 3.5).

4–9 And here the letter appears to be coming to an end, with a series of more or
less unconnected exhortations and expressions of affection. But a further
10–20 section is added (it may possibly have been originally a separate letter altogether, placed at this point by an editor) by way of thanking the Philippians
for their financial contribution. The passage is very laboured. There can
be no doubt that the Philippians had made generous contributions for Paul's
support during his earlier travels (2 Corinthians 8.14), and had now sent a
fresh present with Epaphroditus. It is also clear from the Corinthian letters
that Paul could not have managed without such support. But Paul seems to
have been afraid that, if he thanked them profusely now, he might either give
the impression that their previous gifts had been inadequate, or else that he
still wanted more; so he goes out of his way to deny both, and at the same
time shows considerable embarrassment at having to accept anything at all.
Hence the protestations that, personally, he could stand any degree of poverty
11 (**I have learned to find resources in myself**, a cliché of popular philosophy), and hence perhaps also the rather surprising piling-up of technical
17, 18 business terms (**the profit accruing to you . . . my receipt . . . I am paid
in full**) in order to conceal his embarrassment behind a formal mode of
speech. To round it off, he describes the Philippians' gift, not just as a piece
of ordinary generosity, but in the cult-language of the Jerusalem temple as
18 **a fragrant offering, an acceptable sacrifice, pleasing to God.**

While Paul was in prison (whether at Rome or elsewhere) the people he
saw most of were presumably soldiers and junior civil servants (many of
whom would have been technically slaves of the Emperor). Evidently
Christianity had already spread to many of those who belonged to the
22 **imperial establishment.**

THE LETTER OF PAUL TO THE COLOSSIANS

Outside this letter, there is no explicit reference to the city of Colossae in the New Testament; and from the letter itself it is clear that Paul had never been there. The church had been founded by an assistant of Paul's named Epaphras, who appears to have been a native of the city; and, to the question when this took place, the most likely answer is provided by the account in Acts of Paul's stay at Ephesus. His work there 'went on for two years, with the result that the whole population of the province of Asia, both Jews and pagans, heard the word of the Lord' (19.10). Colossae, with Laodicea and Hierapolis, made up a group of three small cities some 100 miles inland from Ephesus, in the valley of the river Lycus. We know that Christian communities had taken root in all three of them (4.13), and the obvious time for this to have taken place is during Paul's activity at Ephesus.

From the last sentence of the letter it appears that Paul was writing from prison, and it has been traditionally assumed that the imprisonment referred to is that which Paul underwent while awaiting trial in Rome. As with Philippians, this cannot be regarded as certain; but in any case the question hardly affects the interpretation of the letter. Wherever Paul was, he had received a visit both from the original founder of the church (Epaphras), and from Onesimus, a runaway slave from Colossae, about whom Paul also wrote a letter to the slave's former master, Philemon. He was clearly in constant touch with this church, and had many personal acquaintances among its members (4.10–17). It was as the result of fresh news brought by Epaphras that he felt the need to write this letter.

The trouble which had overtaken the Colossian church was not so much practical (as in Corinth) as doctrinal. The Christians in Colossae had been exposed to 'hollow and delusive speculations' (2.8) and the immediate purpose of the letter is to warn them of the dangers of such ideas and to strengthen their understanding of the true faith. It is probably in answer to these 'speculations' that Paul develops a conception of the nature and work of Christ which is on a grander scale, and has wider metaphysical implications, than any other passage in the New Testament. The only other writing which comes near to it is the letter to the Ephesians: but this has in other respects such remarkable similarities to Colossians that it seems necessary to assume that the one is in some way dependent on the other (on the relationship between the two letters, see above p. 618).

The centre of Christian belief

After the opening greeting,[a] the letter proceeds with the usual thanksgivings and prayers. But in this letter (as in Ephesians) the prayer is greatly extended; indeed the language of almost the whole of the first chapter has a devotional ring, and even the great theological statements which it contains on the place of Christ in the universe are set in the framework of the prayer. This devotional intention may explain the style of the chapter, which is diffuse and elaborate to a degree that is rare in the New Testament.

The immediate subject for thanksgiving is the reputation of the church at
Colossae: its members had shown clear evidence of possessing that same
1.4, 5 triad of Christian virtues—**faith, hope** and **love**—which appears in the
great thirteenth chapter of 1 Corinthians. But the Colossian church was not
alone. Its progress must be seen in the context of the world-wide spread of
the gospel. And the preacher who first brought this gospel to Colossae on
7 Paul's **behalf**[b] had now been able to report back to Paul the news of some
tangible act of love (such as, perhaps, a contribution to the needs of the church
at Jerusalem, which Paul had urged in all his churches) which fully entitled
the Colossian church to an honourable place among the new churches of
Christendom.

The prayer itself is very similar to that in Philippians (1.9–11). The
religion of those speculative thinkers who had been troubling the church in
Colossae was, apart from anything else, too theoretical; and Paul here insists
9 that **spiritual understanding,** which was admittedly indispensable, must
10 nevertheless go together with **active goodness of every kind.** Equally
11 practical, doubtless, was the prayer for **ample power,** which means not so
much fortitude of character as endowment with those exceptional powers
which are the gift of the Spirit (1 Corinthians 12.10).

12 And then they were **to give thanks**; and the normal form which thanksgiving takes in worship and devotion is that of a recital of the gracious acts and attributes of God. Thus, the remarkable passage which follows is essentially a summary of the benefits given by God to men in the person and work of Christ. The sequence of short clauses, which are all grammatically bound together in a single movement of thanksgiving and praise, and show traces of deliberate symmetry and rhythmical pattern, dwells upon the paramountcy of Christ in the church and in the universe. But in the course of it the thought extends far wider than the usual range of New Testament conceptions of Christ, and opens up a cosmic perspective; and the language

[*a*] On **commissioned,** see on Romans 1.1. On **our colleague Timothy,** see on 2 Corinthians 1.1. On **incorporate in Christ** see on Ephesians 1.1.

[*b*] The information about Epaphras is a little uncertain, since there is doubt about the correct reading of the Greek text: see the footnote in NEB.

draws on the vocabulary both of Jewish and of Greek speculation to an extent otherwise unexampled in Paul. There are many possible reasons for this somewhat exceptional language: it may have been already adopted into the devotion of the church; it may be a conscious reaction against the speculations of the heretics; it may be an adaptation of originally non-Christian concepts to the needs of Christian theology; or it may be a combination of several of these. Equally, it may simply be the result of Paul searching for means to express something with more far-reaching metaphysical implications than he normally ventures upon. But whatever the explanation, the passage represents a significant advance in the direction of that kind of doctrine of Christ which was later worked out by the Christian Fathers.

To give thanks to the Father who has made you fit to share the 12
heritage of God's people. This is the first of God's gracious acts for which
thanks are to be offered, and it seems to spring from a wholly Jewish
approach. If the Colossians were (as seems likely) mainly Gentiles, then one
way of expressing the magnitude of God's graciousness would be to say that
he had made available to them the heritage promised (and promised only)
to his own people, the Jews. But if this is Paul's point of departure, he immediately changes direction by adding the words, **in the realm of light.** The
exclusive Jewish conception of a world divided between the Jews (who have
an assured prospect of future life) and the rest of mankind (who have no such
prospect) is replaced by an impartial picture of the whole of mankind
existing up to the present time in **the domain of darkness,** but now 13
offered rescue through Christ. This is ordinary philosophical imagery. But
the 'realm of light' is the **kingdom** of God's **dear Son**—which is the imagery of the Gospel; and the result of this rescue is expressed in terms more
characteristic of traditional Jewish theology than of Paul's own thinking:
release (the same word as 'act of liberation' in Romans 3.24) and forgiveness 14
of sins.

So far, the language used of Christ has kept well within the concept of a divine Redeemer who enters the world in order to "rescue" those who believe in him. But now the interest broadens. Christ is to be understood not only in the context of redemption but in that of creation; he is Lord, not only of his own followers, but of the whole universe.

He is the image of the invisible God. This is an unmistakable allusion 15
to Genesis: the first man was created "in God's image", and Christ is the
perfect example of what all men were created to be. But the sentence implies
more than this; for the moment one says **invisible God,** one is talking
philosophy of religion, and the question arises, if God is invisible, how can
he be known? Paul's answer is given elsewhere: he can be known in his
creation. 'His invisible attributes . . . have been visible . . . to the eye of
reason, in the things he has made' (Romans 1.20). And if such a philosophy
of religion is now to be brought into harmony with faith in Christ, it will

follow that Christ himself, if he is indeed God's image, must stand behind the created universe, either (like the figure of Wisdom in Jewish literature) because he is conceived of as having assisted at the moment of creation, or (like the divine rational principle believed by Stoic philosophers to underlie the visible world) because he is the key to understanding the universe—and either or both of these lines of thought are suggested here by the phrases
16 beginning **in him . . . through him . . . for him . . .** All of which is of
15 more than theoretical importance. It gives Christ **the primacy**[a] **over all created things**, and in particular over those beings which in popular belief occupied a sphere much superior to men (though inferior to God) and from
16 which indeed men must expect protection by any true saviour—**thrones, sovereignties, authorities, and powers.** (On these beings, see above on Ephesians 6.12.)

It is a little surprising, amid these tremendous conceptions, to find the
18 interest suddenly focused upon that comparatively small entity, **the church**; yet it is true that one aspect of Christ's supremacy over all things is his supremacy over his church. In 1 Corinthians 12 Paul describes the church as Christ's body, in order to express the unity of its individual members who perform different functions within the single Christ-filled organism. But here the same metaphor is used in a different way: Christ does not so much fill the church as preside over it, as the head presides over the body. The means
18 by which he achieved this supremacy was the resurrection: having been **the first to return from the dead**, he is now the head of that community to which the same resurrection is promised and already in some measure imparted. But death, in Paul's thought, is sometimes personified as a cosmic power (1 Corinthians 15.26); and Christ's victory over death, by the resurrection, is again of cosmic significance. For the universe, despite its origin in the act of a single creator, is now a place of strife and alienation, not only on a human level, but also on the level of those superior powers already mentioned which are in rebellion against God; and the paradoxical con-
19 ception is advanced that he in whom **the complete being of God, by God's own choice, came to dwell**, and who underlies and presides over the whole created universe, is also, through his sacrificial death, an instrument of reconciliation between God and the warring elements in creation.

21 **Formerly you were yourselves estranged from God.** The Colossians themselves (or is the language intended to embrace all who have been converted?) were objects of the same great act of reconciliation. They (like all non-Jews in Jewish eyes, like all mankind in Paul's eyes) were formerly God's **enemies**; and the reconciliation, even if it has a cosmic dimension, has the immediate consequence for them that at the imminent Last Day, instead of being inevitably condemned for their evil deeds, they will now, by virtue of

[a] Admittedly rather a vague word: it can mean the first in time, the first in rank, or simply the first in God's estimation. See the footnote in NEB.

Christ's self-sacrifice, be "presented" before God with the same innocence
and perfection as marked the divine victim himself. **Only you must con-** 23
tinue—and, as usual after any reference to the imminent end, the necessary
inference is drawn (see above on Romans 13.12): **continue . . . firm.**

The thanksgiving, with its recital of the gracious acts of God, has touched upon immense concepts. A transition is now made to the more personal prayers and aspirations of Paul and his churches. The Gospel is already (in a sense) world-wide. One part of its fruit is the Colossian church, one agent of its growth is Paul. All this is a sign that God's purpose is advancing: the end is not far off. But, before the end can come, certain things must happen. In particular (so the Jews commonly believed, and so Jesus appears to have
taught) there are **afflictions** which have to be endured—not indefinitely, 24
but until the ordained quota of afflictions has been exhausted. This is the meaning of Paul's own sufferings: they are part of that quota of sufferings which the church must bear before the end can come, and which it is privileged to bear in fellowship with Christ (Philippians 3.10). Since (Paul believed) this quota is fixed, it follows that the more he suffers himself the less others will have to suffer. In this sense, he suffers **for the sake of . . . the church.** So: **it is now my happiness to suffer for you . . . to complete, in my poor human flesh, the full tale of Christ's afflictions still to be endured.**

This is an incidental consequence of Paul's mission. His real task, **assigned** 25
to him by God (for the divine origin of his commission is one of the things
Paul is most certain of) can be expressed thus: **to announce the secret.** The 26
Greek word is *mystērion*, literally "mystery"; but it is used in a distinctive
sense. To a Greek thinker, the things of God were indeed a "secret", and
could be plumbed only by a sustained course of speculative enquiry, perhaps
accompanied by certain rites of religious initiation. The secret was thus
destined always to remain secret, accessible only to those who had received
the necessary instruction and initiation (and Paul is perhaps playing on this
idea when he uses the almost technical word **mature** in verse 28—see above 28
on Philippians 3.8–16). But the God of the Old Testament was never "secret"
in this sense. He revealed himself in a multitude of ways, and if men failed
to understand, it was not because of their lack of sophisticated religious
knowledge, but because of their blindness, or their hardness of heart. When,
therefore, towards the end of the Old Testament period, the word *mystērion*
was taken into the Jewish religious vocabulary, it acquired a new meaning.
There were indeed things about God which were "secret", but these were
not attributes of his nature known only to the initiated: they were stages in
his purpose for the world which had not yet been revealed. An inspired
visionary might occasionally be given a glimpse of this purpose; but in
principle it remained secret until such time as it would be God's pleasure to
disclose it. It was something **hidden for long ages and through many** 26

generations; but (unlike the Greek idea of a *mystērion*) it was not intended
always to remain hidden from all except a few initiates: it was now—and
27 this is the Gospel—disclosed to God's people, **to whom it was his will to
make it known.** And the particular aspect of this secret which is stressed
here is that God's purpose (against all expectations from the Jewish side) was
working itself out **among all nations**, and that even of a non-Jewish community such as the church at Colossae it could be said: **Christ in you, the
hope of a glory to come.**

2.2 Thus Paul's prayer for the Colossians comes to this: that they may **grasp
God's secret. That secret is Christ himself**, and if they know Christ,
they need have no anxiety to explore other avenues of knowledge besides;
3 for **in him lie hidden all God's treasures of wisdom and knowledge.**
This needed to be said; for clearly the Colossian church was in danger of
4 **being talked into error by specious arguments.** What these arguments
were will have to be inferred from the paragraphs which follow, when
counter-arguments are advanced. Meanwhile Paul assures the church at
Colossae—and the nearby church at Laodicea—of his lively concern for their
welfare. If the local agitators had been suggesting that Paul's teaching could
be disregarded since it came from a man who had no real connection with the
churches concerned, Paul was ready to reply that, on the contrary, he knew
5 all about them: **I am with you in spirit.**

Two indications of the heretics' teaching can be gleaned from the following section.

8 First: it was **based on traditions of man-made teaching.** The Christian faith itself was based on a "tradition", which consisted principally of
6 the essential truths about Jesus (**Jesus was delivered to you as Christ
and Lord**), but also included a new interpretation of Scripture in the light
of Christ. The heretics, however, even if they accepted this tradition, seem
not to have understood its importance. Whatever the precise meaning of the
8 phrase, **the elemental spirits of the universe** (see above on Galatians 4.3),
it clearly belonged to the vocabulary of a speculative type of religion far
removed from Christianity; and it is a reasonable guess that Paul's opponents,
even if they did interpret Scripture in the light of Christ, nevertheless used
their interpretation as material for constructing a system in which Christ held
only a secondary place. In reply, Paul recapitulates the great affirmations of
9 chapter 1. **It is in Christ that the complete being of the Godhead
dwells embodied.** Precisely what is meant by **embodied** here is a theological puzzle, but the intention of the phrase is clear: there is nothing in
heaven or earth with a power or an importance equal to Christ's. Any true
8 tradition must therefore be **centred . . . on Christ.**

Secondly: we seem once again (as in Philippians 3.3) to overhear the slogans of Jewish anti-Christian propaganda. "You have not even been

circumcised," this propaganda seems to have run, "therefore you cannot
have a share in the world to come"; to which the Christian reply was, "We
have indeed been circumcised, but **not in a physical sense**". The Christian 11
equivalent—**Christ's way of circumcision**—was baptism, and Paul could
apparently take for granted the analysis of baptism which he develops in
detail in Romans 6: it involved **being divested** of the lower nature, being
buried with Christ, and so **raised to life with him.** The Colossian Chris- 12
tians, being Gentiles, had formerly been even further from salvation than the
Jews; they were "dead", not merely **because of their sins,** but because they 13
were **uncircumcised** (Paul seems prepared to concede this to his Jewish
opponents).[a] But now, by the Christian equivalent of circumcision (which
was of course something far greater than circumcision), God had made them
alive with Christ. In a brilliant metaphor, Paul relates all this to the cross.
The sinner (that is, all men), having failed to render what was due to God
and to fulfil what was required by God's law, was in the position of a debtor,
whose **bond** is unquestionable evidence of his indebtedness. The effect of 14
the crucifixion was to **set aside** this evidence, and so to restore the broken
relationship between man and God. Not only this: the cross was also the
instrument of that victorious act of reconciliation, already alluded to in the
previous chapter, by which the **cosmic powers** were reduced to the status 15
of captives, abjectly following some Roman general who, having returned to
Rome after victories abroad, would march through the streets at the head of
a triumphal procession.[b]

What had these two tendencies, one towards religious and philosophical
speculation, the other towards Jewish propaganda, to do with each other? On
the face of it, very little. But almost at once the same combination occurs
again. **Allow no one therefore to take you to task . . .** The Colossian 16
Christians were being molested by those who insisted on the observance of
Jewish food-laws[c] and festivals, which were no more than a shadowy
anticipation of Christian institutions; these molesting persons seem then to
have been Jews. Yet in the very next sentence we hear of **people who go in** 18
for self-mortification and angel-worship, and try to enter into some
vision of their own. These latter people could hardly have been Jews in the
orthodox sense. The Jews did not normally think of their regulations as **self-**

[a] The word **morally** in verse 13 has no equivalent in the Greek and has been introduced by the translators in order to suggest that what the Colossians had lacked (in Paul's view) was "moral circumcision", i.e. Christian baptism. But the Greek phrase most naturally means physical circumcision; in which case it has to be assumed that Paul was conceding to the Jewish party that, before the coming of Christ, the Gentiles were in fact "dead" compared with the Jews.

[b] The Greek of verse 15 is obscure and ambiguous. The NEB footnote suggests a number of possible renderings.

[c] We know of no Jewish laws about drink, and **drink** may be mentioned here for no other reason than that "food and drink" is as natural an expression in Greek as it is in English.

mortification, and although of course they believed in angels, strict Jewish circles looked with disfavour on anything approaching angel-worship. Again,
20 in verse 20, Paul refers a second time to **the elemental spirits of the universe,** and then goes on immediately to talk about orthodox rules of ritual purity. Since, three times over, the language of Jewish ordinances and the language of speculative religion are brought so closely together, it seems necessary to conclude that Paul's opponents were people who were interested in both. How could this have been so? It is time to draw together the scattered clues which the letter affords as to the identity and beliefs of these heretics.

It is evident, in the first place, that they were intellectuals: Paul has to warn the Colossians against their 'specious arguments' and 'delusive speculations'. The objects of their thinking were such things as 'the elemental spirits of the world'; and the importance they attached to supernatural beings of one kind or another can be seen from the fact that, to answer them, Paul had to insist again and again on the supremacy of Christ in the universe, his victory over the 'cosmic powers', and his central position in the whole pattern of creation. Clearly, his opponents were much preoccupied with those powers and influences which (it was widely believed) inhabit the regions between heaven and earth and exercise a demonic influence over the lives and destinies of men; and among these beings they assigned to Christ a subordinate place.

We know what this kind of speculation led to from the systems of the so-called "gnostic" thinkers, who arranged all these beings, along with a series of philosophical abstractions, in a kind of ascending hierarchy, and accounted for the origin of this hierarchy by means of an elaborate mythology. Christ and the Creator usually held a place, but by no means the highest place, in the hierarchy. Salvation was held to consist in an ascending scale of knowledge (*gnōsis*) by which the soul could be released from subjection to the forces operative at the lower end of the hierarchy and rise to the freedom of the superior beings.

Our evidence for the existence of speculative systems of this kind is all at least a century later than the writing of this letter. How much of this type of thinking had already developed in Paul's time we do not know; but that the speculations of his opponents ran on somewhat similar lines is in itself quite likely. And if it is asked where such thinkers found the materials for their speculative constructions, the answer is (of course): all over the place—in science, in astrology, in philosophy, in religion. In particular, they were interested in the Jewish scriptures, which furnished them with many figures and events which could be incorporated in their mythology. How did they get to know these scriptures? One way was to hear them read in the synagogue. And they could only hear them read in the synagogue if they were either Jews themselves, or else Gentiles whom the Jews permitted to attend

the synagogue in return for observing certain Jewish regulations such as those
relating to sabbaths and festivals. This, apart from any interest they may
have had themselves in ascetic practices and **self-mortification,** would 18
explain their concern for **the observance of festival, new moon, or** 16
sabbath.

If this is correct, it is possible to gain a clearer picture of the troublemakers
at Colossae, and to understand why Paul had to warn the Colossians not only
against such speculations but also against the observance of Jewish ordinances. His opponents, taking advantage of his failure to visit Colossae and
of his alleged lack of interest in the churches of that area, had been trying to
use the Gospel of Jesus Christ as just one element in a larger speculative
system of their own, and had been encouraging the Christians there to make
such gestures of conformity with the demands of the Jewish law as would
entitle them to attend the synagogue regularly, and so to acquire a deeper
knowledge of the Old Testament and of traditional Jewish interpretations
of it. The mistake here (Paul replies) is twofold. First: **such people, burst-** 18
ing with the futile conceit of worldly minds, lose hold upon the
Head. Paul's conception of the church as Christ's body is rich in applications. In 1 Corinthians 12 it explains how a variety of people with a variety
of gifts can create a harmonious and unified society; in 1.18 above it explains
the relationship of the Christian community to him who is also supreme over
all created things; and here it suggests that belonging to the church, as to a
living and growing organism, is an actual source of power and knowledge,
making superfluous all the speculative efforts of the heretics.

The second mistake is that of attaching any importance to ritual ordinances
about handling, tasting and touching. The appeal here may be to a saying of
Jesus: 'Do you not see that nothing that goes from outside into a man can
defile him, because it does not enter into his heart but into his stomach, and
so passes out into the drain?'; on which Mark comments, 'Thus he declared
all foods clean' (Mark 7.18–19). The words Paul uses are different; but the 22
phrase, **things that must perish as soon as they are used,** makes the same
point, and the verse of Isaiah (29.13, following the Greek version of the
Septuagint), to which he alludes with the words **merely human injunctions**
and teaching, is also quoted in the same context in Mark (7.8). At any rate,
Paul seems (though the Greek is obscure at this point) to be rejecting these
ordinances for much the same reason as Jesus does. He admits that such
practices have a certain spurious air of usefulness. But in reality they are **of** 23
no use at all in combating sensuality.

With that, Paul moves away from the complex topics into which the
heretics have drawn him, and allows the rest of the letter to take the form of a
straightforward sermon on moral behaviour. The link with what goes before
is baptism. In baptism, Christians **died** and were **raised to life with** 3. 3, 1
Christ; they have **discarded** (the same almost technical Greek word as 9

'being divested' in 2.11) **the old nature . . . and have put on the new nature,** and this moment in their lives (as Paul is careful to insist when he gives the matter full treatment in Romans 6) lays moral duties upon them to which, in view of ordinary human weakness, Christian preachers have to return again and again.

1 **Aspire to the realm above.** This is the age-old religious picture of a
higher and lower "world", and of man free to choose between them. But
here it is crossed with a distinctively Jewish or Christian conception. The
Jews (and the Christians after them) tended to think not in spatial terms
(higher and lower) but in temporal terms (the present age, the age to come).
For Christians, the "age to come" has already dawned (which could also be
expressed by saying, they already have access to the **realm above**); but it is
not yet fully present and visible. Therefore the new life they already possess
3 by their baptism is still **hidden.** Its full manifestation must await the time
4 when **Christ, who is our life, is manifested.**

Nevertheless, "higher" and "lower" are convenient moral terms; and
5 some kinds of behaviour so obviously **belong to the earth** that there is no
6 need to explain why, because of them, **God's dreadful judgement is
impending.** The lists of virtues and vices which appear in Paul's letters are
usually fairly conventional, and the fact that here they occur in regular groups
of five is perhaps a further sign that he is making use of a stereotyped form of
moral exhortation. Yet, in what he says on the positive side, there is a distinctive Christian ring, and a frequent appeal to the example and challenge of
10 Christ. In Christ, the **image of the Creator** has taken on a new and vivid
meaning; baptism not only brings moral regeneration, but also (as the great
argument in Galatians 3 labours to prove) breaks down the old divisions
11 between men, whether of race (**Greek and Jew, circumcised and uncircumcised**), education (**barbarian** means without Greek culture,
Scythian is typical of the totally illiterate), or social rank (**slave and freeman**); and **love** has an obvious and acknowledged supremacy in the
Christian life.

Just as there were commonly accepted lists of virtues and vices in the
ancient world, so (it seems) there was a widely recognized code of behaviour
to be observed between different classes of people in the home—wives and
husbands, fathers and children, masters and slaves. Christian writers made
18 use of this, sometimes simply endorsing it (**that is your Christian duty . . .
20 the Christian way**), sometimes working some specifically Christian teaching
into it. In Ephesians, the section on husbands and wives is elaborated to reveal
a new conception of the relationship (5.22–33); here, as in 1 Peter 3, it is the
relationship of masters and slaves which is placed in a distinctively Christian
24 light. **Christ is the Master whose slaves you must be**—and the implications of this for slaves are developed more fully in 1 Corinthians 7.21–4. Here,

the more conventional point is made that, since both masters and slaves **have a Master in heaven,** neither can use their position as a pretext for dishonest behaviour.

The way to the oxymoron, **make the secret plain,** has been prepared by 4. 4
what was said about this peculiar "secret" above. Paul, now in prison,
needs the prayers of his fellow-Christians, not just for survival, but for using
every opportunity of turning his predicament to good (how this can happen
is described in Philippians 1.12–18). Four disconnected sentences of exhorta- 5–6
tion follow, which again (as at the end of Galatians, 6.7–10) have a somewhat
conventional sound.

Of the people with whom Paul was in touch while in prison, two, **Tychicus** 7
and **Aristarchus,** had been his companions on his last journey from Greece 10
to Palestine (Acts 20.4). Another, **Onesimus,** was a runaway slave, and is the 9
subject of the Letter to Philemon. **Mark** appears to have been reconciled 10
with Paul after the dispute recorded in Acts 15.37–9. **Jesus Justus** is other- 10
wise unknown: like Paul (Saul), he had both a Jewish name (Jesus) and a
Roman name (Justus). **Epaphras** has already been mentioned (1.7). He 12
seems to have been the first to bring the Gospel to Colossae, and to have had
somewhat the same kind of relationship with the church there (and with the
neighbouring churches of Laodicea and Hierapolis) as Paul had with his
own churches. **Luke, the doctor,** is the Luke to whom the third gospel and 14
Acts are traditionally ascribed. **Demas** is otherwise unknown. **Nympha,** 15
which in Greek is a feminine name, is indistinguishable in some of its cases
from the masculine name Nymphas, and there is consequently some uncertainty in the manuscripts about this person's sex. She (or he) was evidently
a well-to-do person with a house large enough to accommodate the meetings
of the congregation. The following sentence indicates that some of Paul's
letters were intended to be used to some extent as circular letters. **Archippus** 17
was a common name, and we know nothing about this person, nor the duty
entrusted to him.

On greetings in Paul's **own hand,** see above on Galatians 6.11. 18

THE FIRST LETTER OF PAUL TO THE THESSALONIANS

Thessalonica was the capital of the Roman province of Macedonia. It stood, like Philippi, on the Via Egnatia—the great road across northern Greece which linked Rome with the East—and its population, though predominantly Greek, included a Jewish community (Acts 17.1).

Since much of the letter is taken up with Paul's personal recollections of
his visit to Thessalonica, it is possible to reconstruct most of the circumstances from his own words. The account in Acts (17–18) adds little to our
knowledge, and is not always consistent with what Paul says himself; but it
does help us to decide the place and (within certain limits) the date of
1. 1 writing. If Acts can be trusted, the only time when **Paul, Silvanus, and
Timothy** were all together was during Paul's 18-month stay in Corinth
(Acts 18.5);[a] and this period, since it followed soon after Paul's visit to
Thessalonica, seems an appropriate one for the writing of a letter which is
so full of vivid reminiscences. If this is correct, and the letter was written
while Paul was in Corinth (say in the year 50 or 51), then it has some claim
to being the earliest of Paul's surviving letters, indeed the earliest writing in
the New Testament.

Hope and discipline

The first three chapters consist, in effect, of the usual thanksgiving leading
into prayer, though the sequence is broken by a long section of personal
reminiscence and self-vindication, and the prayer itself is not reached until
3.11. The thanksgiving is, first, for the evident fruits of Paul's preaching
among the Thessalonians, who had already exhibited the characteristic
Christian triad of **faith, hope and love** (1 Corinthians 13.13; Colossians
1.4–5). Such results proved that the preaching was not just an exhibition of
5 one individual's powers of persuasion, but was **in the power of the Holy
Spirit**; and to have produced them, the preachers must have had a more
than human authority: **that is the kind of men we were at Thessalonica.**
And secondly: the Thessalonians' subsequent loyalty to their new faith,
which was worthy of Paul himself (or rather, he hastens to add, worthy of
6 **the Lord**), had achieved widespread fame. The news was in many mouths.

[a] In Acts, Silvanus is called by the Semitic form of his name, Silas.

As a gentile community, they had taken the decisive step (as seen from the
Jewish-Christian point of view) of turning **from idols**; and in the phrases 9
which follow we may perhaps be reading a more or less stereotyped summary 9–10
of the main tenets of their new faith.

After the violent end to his stay in Philippi (Acts 16), Paul, to continue his
missionary work, had travelled on to Thessalonica (17.1–4). This information
from Acts is confirmed by Paul's own words to the Thessalonians: **after all** 2. 2
the injury and outrage which to your knowledge we had suffered at
Philippi, we declared the gospel of God to you. But Paul adds to our
knowledge when he goes on to remind the Thessalonians of the conditions
under which he had worked among **them—a hard struggle it was.** The
language indeed becomes so pointed that one suspects he was anxious to
scotch some insinuation that had come to his ears about his conduct at
Thessalonica; or it may just be that he is contrasting his own methods with
those of travelling philosophical teachers who were proverbially suspect of
working for a **base motive.** At any rate, he makes it clear that at Thessa- 3
lonica he had adhered strictly to his normal practice, which (as we know from
frequent references to the matter in the Corinthian correspondence) was to
make himself self-supporting, either by working **for a living,** or else by 9
securing contributions from existing churches. But it seems that this policy,
by comparison with that of other apostles, tended to arouse criticism. It was
suggested, on more than one occasion, that Paul must be lacking in confidence
and authority if he did not claim the financial support due to him as an
apostle. Paul was evidently sensitive on this subject, and devoted a surprising
amount of space to it in his letters; and it may have been the same anxiety
which made him say here: **as Christ's own envoys we might have made** 6
our weight felt. In this case he defended his practice on the grounds of the
particularly intimate relationship—that of **nurse,** or **father,** towards children 7, 11
—which had grown up between himself and the Thessalonians, and to which
indeed the tone of the whole letter bears witness.

However, the real proof of the authenticity of the preaching was to be
seen, as always, in its results: **you received it, not as the word of men,** 13
but as what it truly is; and in consequence the Thessalonian church had
already had its taste of persecution. There is some discrepancy here from the
account in Acts (17.5–9), where it is clearly stated that the opposition came
from the Jewish colony in Thessalonica. Possibly this was so in the early
stages, or possibly the writer of Acts deliberately made his account conform
to the pattern which he regarded as characteristic for the foundation of Paul's
churches—immediate opposition from the Jewish community, followed by a
rapid spread of the gospel in the gentile population. However this may be,
the opposition the Thessalonians had to meet when this letter was written
came from their **countrymen,** who were following the example set by the 14
Jews in Palestine. And in terms which may owe something to the age-old

15 language of anti-semitism (**enemies of their fellow-men**), Paul breaks off
to deliver a prophetic denunciation of his own people—in marked contrast
to his more reflective treatment of the matter in Romans 9–11.

According to Acts, Paul was forced by the Jews to leave Thessalonica by
night and take refuge in the neighbouring city of Beroea. From there he went,
first to Athens, and then to Corinth, while Timothy and Silvanus (Silas)
remained behind at Beroea until they received Paul's command to join him
in Corinth (17.15; 18.5). Paul's own evidence shows this to be not quite
accurate. Timothy did not stay in Beroea, but accompanied Paul to Athens;
3. 1 but such was Paul's anxiety that by this time he could **bear it no longer.**
He had been forced to leave Thessalonica at a few hours' notice. He had had
no news about the church there, how far it had taken root or withstood the
troubles it was involved in when he left. He had not been able to take any
2. 18 of the opportunities which presented themselves to return (**Satan thwarted
us**—the phrase could mean anything from missing a boat to encountering
malicious obstruction), and had finally sent Timothy instead. Moreover, his
anxiety was not just that of any man for his friends: it had a still more serious
aspect, in that Paul knew himself to be accountable to God for the churches
he had founded, and any neglect on his part would be severely judged by the
19 Lord **at his coming.** The good news which Timothy brought on his return
3. 9 caused him correspondingly intense **joy**, and prompted him to write the
present letter.

11–13 After this long digression, the prayer for the church is at last resumed, and
13 rounded off with another glance into the future—**when our Lord Jesus
comes.** This "coming" would of course entail judgement. In the Old
Testament (as in Zechariah 14.5, to which this verse doubtless alludes) God
was sometimes thought of as coming to pass judgement, not alone, but in
company with beings who were already (as it were) on the right side of
judgement and could take a part in it. Who these creatures were—whether
righteous men or supernatural spirits—remained an open question among
interpreters of the Old Testament. But the idea fitted well into the Christians'
expectation of the Lord Jesus coming **with all those who are his own**—for
Christians were promised a place on the tribunal at the last great assize
(1 Corinthians 6.3).

4. 1 A short section is now devoted to **the tradition of the way we must live
to please God.** It is clear from the New Testament that a tradition of this
kind was developed in the early years of the church in order to clarify and
where necessary supplement the moral demands of Jesus. This was particularly necessary in view of the traditional Jewish prejudice that the Gentiles,
having no "law" in the Jewish sense, had nothing to prevent them from
leading immoral lives. Christians had to show that they lived by a moral

standard at least as exacting as that of the Jews. One of the commonest of
Jewish charges against gentile morals was that of sexual impurity: and this
Paul takes up here, warning the church to avoid fornication, **not giving** 5
way to lust like the pagans who are ignorant of God (the last phrase is
scriptural, as in Psalm 79.6; Jeremiah 10.25). The reason he gives here
(though there were many others he might have given, compare 1 Corinthians
7) is that the **holiness** attributed to and demanded of Christians necessarily 7
implies mastery over the **body.** [a] Impurity has of course social consequences 4
which would be intolerable in a Christian community, [b] but the real objection
is not social but religious: **anyone therefore who flouts these rules is** 8
flouting, not man, but God.

Another danger about which Paul has to sound a warning is one which
seems to have arisen from the Christians' earnest expectation of an early
return of Christ. More will be said about this in the following paragraphs.
Meanwhile, the danger referred to is that of reacting to the prospect of the
imminent end of the world by giving up normal work and social obligations,
as things belonging to a world order that is passing away. There are signs
that the churches found themselves having to support a number of such
people. Paul's advice is: **let it be your ambition to keep calm and look** 11
after your own business.

The question now to be discussed is not the general and perennial one of the
destiny of **those who sleep in death,** but a particular and urgent one 13
precipitated by the unexpected death of some members of the church at
Thessalonica. The first generation of Christians believed that the Lord's
coming would take place in their lifetime, and that they would then be given
a place beside him in judging the world. The premature death of some of
their number was not allowed for in this scheme. When it happened, it could
sometimes be explained as the result of some sin or blasphemy which the
dead man had committed—this explanation was apparently accepted in the
church at Corinth (1 Corinthians 11.30). But at Thessalonica evidently no
such explanation offered itself, and the Thessalonians must have conveyed
to Paul their unhappy question: could they be sure that those of the faithful
who had already died would still share their own glorious destiny?

Paul's answer is, first, quite general. **You should not grieve like the rest of men, who have no hope.** This, of course, was an overstatement.

[*a*] The word translated **body** means literally "vessel", or "utensil". There are grounds for thinking that this was an idiomatic way of talking about the human body, as opposed to the soul which the body "contains"; but it is also possible that the phrase here translated **his body** originally stemmed from a Jewish phrase which was a euphemism for "intercourse with a woman".

[*b*] There is doubt about the meaning of verse 6. The Greek word translated (in the main text) **this matter** could also bear the meanings indicated in the footnote, in which case we should have to understand Paul as wishing to allude to a wider range of offences than merely sexual ones.

The majority of Jews believed in a future life; and a number of popular Greek religious and philosophical schools taught some kind of life after death. But it was certainly true—and to this the gravestones of the period bear eloquent witness—that in any Greco-Roman city such as Thessalonica most ordinary people shared the traditional Greek view of a dark and formless underworld in which the dead enjoyed at best a bleak and shadowy existence; and very few would have had any belief in an after-life comparable in intensity with that of the Christians. By contrast, the Christian faith was centred upon the resurrection of Jesus, as a result of which those who believed in him were assured of sharing a glorious life after death. **We believe that Jesus died and rose again; and so it will be for those who died as Christians.** It followed, not from any particular scheme of the last things, but from the fundamental doctrine of Christianity—Christ's resurrection—that Christians who had died would themselves rise to a new and glorious life.

But although this was certainly true in principle, it was still far from clear
just how the future was to be envisaged. The majority of Christians (it was
15 then believed) would be **left alive until the Lord comes.** What about the
minority who had prematurely died? How would they too be able to take
their rightful place in the final drama?

The answer still moves within the somewhat naïve (as it seems to us)
framework of the Thessalonians' question, which was in fact a legacy from
16 Jewish religion (**archangel's voice** and **God's trumpet-call** were conventional features of Jewish expectation, and are taken for granted by Paul:
15 compare 1 Corinthians 15.52). It also goes back, in some sense, to **the Lord's**
word—though we cannot be sure whether Paul is referring specifically to the
promise which Jesus was understood to have made that some Christians
would certainly be left alive **until the Lord comes** (Mark 9.1), or else to
some more general teaching of Jesus about the end. At any rate, the basic
scheme was certainly endorsed by Jesus: the Lord would shortly come to
hold his judgement of the whole world, and Christians, instead of being
among the multitude of those who were to be judged, would take their
places as a kind of tribunal at the side of the judge. It would make no difference that some had already died. In the words of the Old Testament prophecy
alluded to in 3.13, the Lord would come 'with all those who are his own'.
Christians already dead and Christians still alive would alike be caught up
to take part in judging the world where that judgement was most naturally
17 thought of as taking place: **in the air.** [a]

Given that Christians expected the end so soon, it is not surprising that

[a] A further Old Testament idea which may play its part here is that of the Son of Man who, when he comes to the last judgement, will gather his chosen to be with him (Daniel 7; Mark 13.27). This would give point to the alternative rendering of verse 14 (as given in the footnote) which is in any case much the more natural translation of the Greek.

there should have been speculation about exactly when it would happen—
about dates and times. Such speculation existed even among the Jews, and 5. 1
was strongly discouraged by responsible thinkers. Jesus, too, recognized the
force of this temptation, and warned against it (Luke 17.20). It was true that
the Day would be preceded by certain signs and portents; but not in the
sense that anyone could use them to calculate the date and make plans accordingly. On the contrary, it was destined to be sudden. It would come, as Jesus
had said himself (which is what Paul may mean by a phrase which in the
Greek has a slightly technical sound, **you know perfectly well**), **like a** 2
thief in the night—and Paul adds two other descriptions of its suddenness
which, whatever their origin, were probably equally familiar to his readers:
first, that when there is talk of **peace and security** (which were almost 3
official slogans of the Roman empire), **all at once calamity is upon them**;
and secondly, the simile of birth-pangs. And the proper response to this
threatened suddenness is expressed, as so often, in terms of light, wakefulness
and sobriety, with a brief allusion to the metaphor of heavenly armour which
is so brilliantly developed in the last chapter of Ephesians.

Among the miscellaneous injunctions with which, as so often, the letter
closes, it is notable that Paul, as in 1 Corinthians 16, makes an appeal for
proper respect to be paid to the leaders of the local church; and these leaders
are described in two terms which belong inseparably, if paradoxically,
together in the concept of Christian ministry—service (here appearing as
working so hard) and leading. There is also a reference to another topic to 12
which Paul had to pay attention in Corinth (and we have seen that there is
reason to believe this letter was written from Corinth)—the proper management of **inspiration** and **prophetic utterances.** [a] 19, 20

On the **kiss of peace,** and on the general character of the ending, see 26
above on Romans 16.16.

[*a*] 1 Corinthians 12. If the alternative rendering (given in the footnote) is correct, it may possibly (in view of certain verbal similarities) be an allusion to a saying of Jesus which is not recorded in the gospels, but which seems to have been known to some early Christian writers: "Be good bankers, rejecting some things but retaining what is good".

THE SECOND LETTER OF PAUL TO THE THESSALONIANS

The greeting is almost identical with that of 1 Thessalonians, and suggests that the two letters must have been written from the same place and within a short time of each other. They are indeed very similar—so similar, in fact, that it has often been doubted whether they could originally have been intended for the same congregation, or even whether they could both have been written by the same author: for how, it is said, could anyone have written two letters within a short space of time to the same people, and used whole paragraphs in the second letter which are taken almost verbatim from the first? At the same time, there are notable differences between the two letters. The treatment of questions about the end of the world runs on somewhat different lines, and in the second letter the tone is throughout a little more severe. The problem is to explain both the similarities and the differences.

Various explanations have been proposed. One is that Paul, soon after writing the first letter, received news from Thessalonica which caused him to write off again at once, while phrases from the first letter were still running in his mind. Another is that the two letters were originally written to go by the same messenger to two different (though probably neighbouring) congregations. A third is that the letter was written by an imitator who was anxious to give circulation to a somewhat stricter doctrine of the coming judgement than Paul himself had expressed.

All these explanations are plausible, but none of them is fully convincing. It is not impossible, in any case, to take this letter as what it purports to be, Paul's second letter to the Thessalonians. He had heard (not long after writing his previous letter) about the irresponsible behaviour of some members of the Thessalonian church (3.11), and deemed it necessary to correct some mistaken ideas which were current about the coming of Christ (2.1–2); and the fresh news he had received may sufficiently account for the different tone of the second letter. As for the similarities, it is important to notice that they are concentrated in two contexts: first, in the greetings and prayers—for which a fairly conventional and stereotyped vocabulary was already emerging; and secondly, in the section on the necessity (felt even by the apostle) to work for a living—a topic to which Paul reverts a number of times in his letters, and for which he tends in any case to use a standard terminology.

Hope and discipline

The initial section of thanksgiving and prayer contains echoes of the first
letter: the Thessalonians' **faith** and **love**—though the triad is not completed 1.3
with '**hope**'—are again singled out. But the section is much shorter, and a
reference to **persecutions** leads Paul off into a discourse on the **justice of** 4
God's judgement. This judgement follows the pattern laid down in the
first letter. It is described in traditional language, with free use of the Old
Testament. Christ will have the central position, accompanied by **his own** 10
and surrounded by the traditional **fire** of divine judgement. This judgement 7
will **balance the account,** at present so intolerably upset by those who, with 6
apparent impunity, persecute the church. For they, along with all those
who will not obey the gospel of our Lord Jesus, will receive the punish- 8
ment the prophets foretold (compare Isaiah 2.10,19–21; 66.5 with the
details of this passage). The view that all who reject the gospel will inevitably be damned was not often expressed so crudely either by Paul or by
the church at large; but the language here may be the result of a particularly
intense experience of persecution.

And now, brothers, about the coming of our Lord Jesus Christ and 2.1
his gathering of us to himself. This doctrine was discussed, in much the
same terminology, in the first letter, and was presumably now common
ground between Paul and the Thessalonians. But it had apparently undergone a new and dangerous interpretation: some people were **alleging that** 2
the Day of the Lord is already here. One can see how the teaching of
Paul, and indeed that of the church as a whole, could easily have given rise to such an interpretation. The Day was proclaimed to be imminent; signs of its coming had already appeared; Christians, under the influence of the Spirit, were having experiences which were recognized as a foretaste of the age to come. It would not have been difficult to promote the view that the decisive event—the Day—had already happened. A sudden surge of those remarkable experiences of the Spirit which were a feature, say, of church life at Corinth, or a sensational increase in the membership of the church, might easily (in conjunction with **some oracular utterance** or **some letter purporting to come** from Paul) have tipped the balance for those who had only a limited and parochial conception of the Day; then, thinking that the final act of history had been completed, they would presumably abandon their normal occupations and wait for God to bring down the curtain on the drama.

Paul's answer is not (as might have been expected) that the present bears no resemblance to the conditions which will prevail on that climactic Day; instead, he explains that the Day cannot have come yet, since certain things

have got to happen first. He had already given some teaching about these
5 things in the course of his original preaching at Thessalonica (**I told you
this while I was still with you**)—and this is the cause of most of our difficulties. The language used on such matters tends in any case to be somewhat cryptic, and when, in addition, Paul is not attempting to give any fresh teaching, but is merely reminding his hearers of something he has told them already, it is hardly surprising if we are now unable to follow him.

The background to the paragraph is not too hard to reconstruct. The Day is a day of judgement; and one reason why the judgement cannot yet come is that it is not yet sufficiently clear on whom the judgement should fall. The reception or rejection of the gospel is a preliminary criterion. As we have seen, those who reject it and persecute the church have already secured their condemnation. But this criterion is not sufficient; it leaves too many borderline cases. If men, confronted by the good (in the form of the gospel), merely remain indifferent, it could be that they have not yet been put seriously to the test; their indifference is hardly decisive proof of their guilt, in which case they are not yet ready for judgement. It is envisaged, therefore, that there will be an intensification of evil, a stepping-up of calamities, under which men will more quickly show their true nature. In particular—and here a concept is borrowed, perhaps, from popular Jewish mythology—men will be exposed, not merely to the challenging truth of the gospel, but also to a
9 positive force of deception—**all the powerful signs and miracles of the
Lie**—which will lead astray all who are not fully committed to the truth, and
so will draw a clear line between those who will be saved and those who are
lost. When this process is complete, the time will be ripe for them all to be
12 **brought to judgement.**

So much is reasonably clear; but Paul fills out his picture of the future with a more complex mythology, only part of which is familiar from contemporary Jewish writings. It was a frequent theme of so-called "apocalyptic" writers that immediately before the End there would be a final and decisive confrontation between the forces of good and the forces of evil, in which evil would be represented by a single supernatural individual and would reach, in that individual, an unprecedented pitch of intensity. This is
3 the context of such phrases as **the final rebellion, the man doomed to**
4 **perdition, the Enemy**; and it is probable that the threat of the Emperor
Caligula, in the year 40, to set up a statue of himself in the holiest part of the
Jewish temple had given fresh actuality to the old prophecy (Ezekiel 28.2;
Daniel 11.36) that this personification of wickedness even **takes his seat in
the temple of God.** Furthermore, there are faint traces in the Old Testament (Amos 9.3; Job 7.12) of an ancient myth (not uncommon in other
middle-eastern religions) that this evil monster had existed since the beginning
6 of the world, and was held in imprisonment (or "restraint") until **the proper
time**; and this idea reappears elsewhere in the New Testament (Revelation

20.2). But even if this myth was in Paul's mind (which is far from certain)
it does not take us very far, for we are still left without any clue to the meaning of the cryptic expression, **the restraining hand**, and its more personal 6
complement, **the Restrainer.** Since early centuries it has been suggested 7
that Paul is referring to the rule of law maintained by the Roman empire. But
Paul is deliberately expressing himself in a way that only the Thessalonians
could have understood. Without the explanation he had given them, we shall
never know for certain what he meant.

The thanksgiving and the prayer which follow are strongly reminiscent of the 13–17
previous letter (especially 1 Thess. 3.11–13). On the concept of being chosen
from the beginning of time, see above on Ephesians 1.4.[a] 13

We hear that some of your number are idling their time away. 3. 11
Whether this was the result of the particular misapprehension about the
End which was dealt with in chapter 2, or whether it was merely a manifestation of ordinary human nature, Paul takes the opportunity of appealing
once again to the example he set himself: he always preferred to work for his
own living **rather than be a burden** (a phrase which is almost a cliché in 8
this context: compare 1 Thessalonians 2.9; 2 Corinthians 11.9), and his
motive for so doing was **not because we have not the right to main-** 9
tenance—a point on which he was sensitive—**but to set an example.** To
clinch the matter he presses into service what looks like an old proverb: **the** 10
man who will not work shall not eat.

On greetings in Paul's **own hand** see above on Galatians 6.11. The 17
reference earlier (2.2) to 'some letter purporting to come from us' perhaps
explains his anxiety to authenticate his own letters in this way.

[a] Unless the true reading is that given in the footnote, which is a different but easily intelligible metaphor.

THE FIRST LETTER OF PAUL TO TIMOTHY

The three letters which follow are addressed, not to churches, but to two of Paul's colleagues, Timothy and Titus; but this does not mean that they were originally part of a personal correspondence. On the contrary, Timothy and Titus are addressed, not just as friends and partners in Paul's missionary activity, but as men who hold long-term responsibility in their respective churches of Ephesus and Crete, and to whom it is natural to send instructions about the correct ordering of the church. They are addressed, in fact, in their capacity as established pastors; and these three letters, which are noticeably similar in tone and presuppose similar situations in the churches to which they were written, have been known since the eighteenth century as the "pastoral" epistles.

The letters purport to have been written by Paul and were accepted as genuine by the church from at least the end of the second century. But in recent times their authenticity has been questioned. The language and style can be seen on a first reading to be different from that of the other letters attributed to Paul; the structure and the concerns of the churches addressed seem to reflect a somewhat later stage of development than one would expect to find in the period of Paul's main correspondence; and indeed the writer's presentation of the Christian faith has an unexpectedly steady, settled quality. For all these reasons it is widely believed that the letters must have been written by an imitator some decades after Paul's death, with the purpose of adapting the Pauline message to a somewhat different situation in the church, and of giving the authority of the apostle to a form of church organization which had not yet developed when Paul was alive but which (it was perhaps felt) he would certainly have approved of had he lived to see it.

An explanation of this kind has been suggested for the origin of the letter to the Ephesians (see above p. 617); but there the problem is very much simpler. That letter consists, in effect, of a treatise, given the form of a letter only by the addition of brief opening and closing greetings and of a very small amount of personal matter. Here, however, there is a comparative wealth of personal details. If these three letters were not written by Paul himself, the imitator must have been anxious to make his work look as convincing as possible by introducing (either from imagination or from some source now lost to us) fragments of the kind of private correspondence which Paul might have been expected to exchange with his friends. However, if this is really what happened, it is all the more puzzling that these details do not fit at all easily into the biography of Paul as we can reconstruct it from the other letters and from Acts. To take only the most obvious examples: nothing is known from the New Testament of any journey made by Paul to Crete, nor of a winter spent (or intended to be spent) on the Dalmatian coast at Nicopolis (Titus 3.12); there is no period in Paul's missionary work up to his imprisonment in Rome which would allow for Timothy assuming long-term responsibility for the church at Ephesus; and the vivid personal touches in 2 Timothy 4 are impossible to reconcile completely with the known events in Paul's life immediately preceding his trial at Rome. If, therefore, the letters are the work of an imitator, this writer must either have invented fresh episodes in the life of Paul without caring to match them with what could be known from existing letters, or else have assembled fragments of real biographical value with so little regard for their true sequence that the picture as a whole is a different one from that which emerges from the other documents.

These details are, of course, no less of a problem if the letters are genuine. The traditional explanation is that Paul must have been released after the imprisonment at Rome which is recorded at the end of Acts, have travelled widely for a few years, and then have been once more imprisoned, tried, and put to death. Outside these letters there is virtually no evidence that Paul had this spell of freedom. If, therefore, the letters were written by an imitator, we cannot assume that he did, and the personal details remain as baffling as ever. On the other hand, if they are genuine, we must write a further chapter to the life of Paul; and it is arguable that the undoubted differences of style and content between these and the other letters of Paul are due to the fact that Paul wrote the Pastorals somewhat later in his life.

There is one other possibility to be mentioned. There can be little doubt that when Paul wrote his other letters he had the help of a secretary; and since verbatim dictation of a work as long as, say, the letter to the Romans would have taken several days, it is possible that the secretary was occasionally given a fair amount of freedom in the actual composition. Now at least one of the Pastorals (2 Timothy) was written from prison, where writing or dictation might well have been difficult. If Paul, for these letters, used a different secretary, and was forced to give this secretary only the outlines of what he wished to say, then the result could well have been such as to raise doubts in the minds of modern readers whether the author can have been Paul himself.

Church order

From Paul. A private letter in antiquity almost invariably opened with the 1.1
briefest formula: "From so-and-so, to so-and-so, greeting." All the letters of Paul are unusual in that he greatly elaborates this basic formula and inserts a fair amount of Christian matter in it—the opening of the letter to

the Romans is a notable example. But not only are these openings all, by the
standards of the time, unusually long; they also vary considerably from one
letter to another. Normally it was only in the greetings of his more formal
letters addressed to whole churches that Paul emphasized his authority as an
apostle; in the more personal letters, such as Philippians, 1 and 2 Thessalonians, and of course Philemon, he came nearer to the usual convention
of writing simply, "From Paul to so-and-so". It is therefore all the more
surprising to find the formal manner reappearing in the letters addressed to
Timothy and Titus. It is a clear sign that from the outset the real people
being addressed are the churches over which these "pastors" preside.

3 **When I was starting for Macedonia, I urged you to stay on at**
Ephesus. The only departure of Paul from Ephesus to Macedonia of which
we know anything from other sources is that recorded in Acts 20.1–5. But
that Paul then left Timothy in Ephesus is hard to reconcile either with the
account in Acts or with Paul's own letters to the Corinthians, and either this
detail is inaccurate, or else it belongs to that later period of Paul's activity to
which these letters (if they are genuine) must be assigned. In any case, the
danger which Timothy was to resist is one which reappears several times in
the Pastorals in much the same form, and may have been prevalent in many
4 churches at the time these letters were written. It arose from **studying those**
interminable myths and genealogies. It will appear from what follows
that the trouble-makers, though they probably were not Jews themselves
(unlike those in Crete, Titus 1.10), were interested in the Jewish scriptures,
and their **myths and genealogies** (the phrase is a familiar and not too
precise one in the polemical language of philosophers of the time) may well
have been similar to the fantastic mythologies which later speculative
thinkers constructed out of Old Testament materials (see above on Colossians
2). A true interpretation of Scripture, by contrast, presented it as a consistent
and unified message, designed **to make known God's plan for us**; and to
understand this plan, it was necessary to have, not intellectual ingenuity, but
only **faith.**

In 1 Corinthians 13 Paul describes 'love' as the greatest of all God's gifts,
exceeding in value even those spectacular manifestations of the Spirit which
had so excited the members of the church in Corinth. Here the analysis is
5 tamer and less original: **love** is described as a necessary psychological consequence of a certain kind of behaviour and belief. The phrase **a good**
conscience is not nearly so frequent in the New Testament as its currency
in English would lead one to expect, and it occurs only in the later letters.
Indeed the idea was something rather new in Greek moral thought. "Conscience" itself, in a fully moral sense, was a concept which appeared only a
century or two before the time of Christ, and it was normally used in the
"bad" sense, as equivalent to the consciousness of having done wrong. Its
opposite (the consciousness of not having done wrong) did not play an impor-

tant part in moral analysis until later times, and its emergence in the Christian moral vocabulary is more likely a relic of the Jewish concern for "cleanness" from any acts that were regarded as impure or sinful. A biblical phrase for this is used here—**a clean heart**; and doubtless **a good conscience** meant very much the same. It is hard to see how this slightly meritorious feeling can be reconciled with Paul's characteristic emphasis on the total incapacity of man to abide by God's commandments—but the underlying thought here is clearly the paramount necessity of sincerity. What the erroneous teachers
were guilty of was its opposite, hypocrisy. **They set out to be teachers of** 7
the moral law. The translators have inserted the word **moral** (which is not in the Greek), but in doing so they have not made the writer's meaning clearer; for the essence of a "moral" law is that, being an inner principle of behaviour instead of an external code of written commandments, it assists towards sincerity and discourages hypocrisy. It is possible that these teachers believed themselves to be expounding such a principle, and were guilty of hypocrisy in doing so. But it is perhaps more likely that they were taking as their rule of life an actual code of law, such as the Jewish law itself, and proclaiming this to be an adequate guide to good conduct. But of course the function of a code of law is only to define indictable offences. **Good citizens,**
who do not commit such offences, are not helped by it. Indeed, they may 9
actually be affected by it the other way; for (and this is the classic objection to any such law being used as an ultimate standard of moral conduct) they may be encouraged by it to feel that, since they have not transgressed it, their behaviour is irreproachable. It is by living, in this sense, "within" the law that people may fall into that kind of insincerity which the author is attacking here.

The possibility of a good conscience, the description of the law as **an** 8
excellent thing—these sentiments would have come strangely from the author of the letter to the Romans. There are also two phrases in this paragraph which seem to belong especially to the language of the Pastorals. One is
the wholesome teaching, which occurs frequently in these letters but in 10
no other New Testament book. It was a common enough phrase in the mouths of moral philosophers, but seems (at least for Paul) a curiously tame
way of describing the revolutionary truths of the gospel. The other is **God in** 11
his eternal felicity. This rather ornate translation of a single Greek adjective at least brings out the fact that the expression is unusual in the New Testament—it belongs rather to the language of the Greek-speaking synagogue (as does **the King of all worlds** a few verses below). It is small 17
details such as these which build up the impression that the Pastorals, compared with the other letters of Paul, stem from a somewhat different cultural and religious background.

When Paul refers to his own conversion in other letters, he does so in order to justify his status as an apostle. Here the intention seems to be more general: Paul's conversion is put forward for the inspiration and encourage-

ment of all who enter the church. It did not matter what outrages they had committed in the past, provided only that (unlike, say, the persistent heretics,
13 who had had their chance of learning the truth) they **acted ignorantly in unbelief.**

15 **Here are words you may trust.** This phrase occurs at least three times in the Pastorals, and its function seems to be to alert the reader to the fact that the writer is quoting a familiar piece of Christian doctrine. The only difficulty is that, since Greek manuscripts had nothing corresponding to inverted commas, it is not always clear which words belong to the quotation and which belong to the writer's commentary. Here, however, it is fairly clear that the quotation is '**Christ Jesus came into the world to save sinners**'. It was presumably a sentence much used in the worship or the teaching of the church, and is quoted here to show how Paul's conversion
16 was **typical** of Christ's patience with **all who were in future to have faith in him.**

We have no other information about the circumstances of Timothy's first association with Paul, though Acts 13.1–3 may be an example of the kind of
18, 20 **prophetic utterance** which is meant here. Another of **Hymenaeus'** errors is mentioned in 2 Timothy 2.17. About **Alexander** we know nothing, unless he is the copper-smith of 2 Timothy 4.14. Consigning **to Satan** presumably involved excommunication: see above on 1 Corinthians 5.5.

2. 1 **First of all, then.** The next two chapters turn from the danger of heretical teaching to questions of *Church order*. There is nothing surprising in the
2 early Christians having offered prayers **for sovereigns and all in high office** (the word **sovereigns** is probably meant to include both the Roman Emperor and the vassal kings, such as the Herods, whom the Romans allowed to reign in eastern territories). Even though there were moments when the church had cause to regard the Roman administration as an agent of the devil, it was always conscious of the great benefits, in the form of a **tranquil** and **quiet life,** which the power of the empire afforded, and was glad to follow the example of the Jews, who regularly offered prayers (and even, in the temple, sacrifices) for the welfare of the Emperor. We happen to possess a prayer [a] which was used by Christians towards the end of the first century, and which includes the words, "Give them, O Lord, health, peace, concord and stability, that they may exercise without offence the rule thou hast entrusted to them".

Such prayers were not only good in themselves: they helped to combat an
4 exclusiveness which all too easily crept into Christianity. God's **will it is that all men should find salvation.** Taken out of context, this statement raises acute difficulties. It is hard to reconcile both with the observed facts that many men obviously do not find salvation, and also with the realization,

[a] First Letter of Clement, chapter 61 (written from Rome about A.D. 96).

which occasionally comes to the surface in the New Testament, that some men are apparently not intended to be saved. But here the purpose of the statement is probably not so much to lay down a general truth as to answer those who took the view that some classes of men were *a priori* outside the scheme of salvation. The Jews, for example, believed this of non-Jews, and the kind of speculative thinkers who are alluded to in these letters tended to believe it of all who could not qualify for salvation by pursuing the right kind of "knowledge". Christians, by contrast, were to think of salvation as in
principle available to all; and so there was good reason to pray **for all** 1
men.

For there is one God. The point is supported with a sentence which looks 5
like a fragment of an early creed. Concise formulations of this kind normally come into existence when there is some heretical tendency abroad which needs to be refuted. Is there a particular heresy in mind here? The significant words seem to be **one mediator.** Much religious speculation in the first and second centuries after Christ was concerned with the question of "mediators" between the supreme, inaccessible God and the earth-bound existence of human beings. Jewish writers often described Old Testament figures such as Moses or Enoch in this way (there is a striking example in Galatians 3.19), or thought of supernatural beings like angels, or abstractions like "wisdom", as fulfilling this function; and more philosophically minded thinkers postulated a whole series of such entities mediating between God and man. It is against such a background that we should probably seek to understand the significance of the unusual phrase **one mediator** (whether it was the writer's own or, as suggested, a quotation from an existing creed). The rest of the passage uses normal New Testament vocabulary. The word translated
win freedom means literally "ransom" and may go right back to some 6
words of Jesus (Mark 10.45: 'to give up his life as a ransom for many'). **Proof of the divine purpose** represents an attempt by the translators to make sense of the single Greek word *martyrion*, "testimony".

We are now given a few glimpses of the customs of the early church. Jews and Greeks alike normally prayed with hands "lifted up"; and the Christians evidently did the same. They also accepted with little modification the place accorded to women in ancient society. It is true that the context here seems to be that of the meetings of the congregation for worship; but what is said about women's conduct and dress is very much the kind of thing which was a commonplace among popular teachers of the time, and most of the language is applicable to the status of women generally as this was understood in the time of the writer. This somewhat inferior status was taken for granted; but possibly the new freedom and importance which was being accorded to women in Christian congregations made it necessary to reaffirm the conventional view from time to time. Two traditional Jewish arguments are adduced, based on the narrative in Genesis 3. Adam and Eve, in Jewish

thinking, were conceived of both as individual historical persons and as type-figures representing the whole human race (see above on Romans 5.12). So here: as a matter of history Adam was created first, but (since Adam is also representative Man) this priority over women is shared by all his male
14 descendants. Equally it was Eve who first yielded to the **deception** of the serpent; but all women, since they necessarily share Eve's propensity to evil, must take second place. Yet there is one thing—this was a commonplace of both Greek and Jewish thought—which gives women a unique status:
15 **motherhood** (literally, "childbirth"). This goes some way to compensate for their Eve-like susceptibility; and, taken in this sense, **she will be saved through motherhood** is a fairly obvious statement. But in Christian language "saved" means a great deal more than this, and the writer hastens to avoid misunderstanding by adding the qualification that for Christian salvation other things of course are necessary.[a]

3. 1 **There is a popular saying: 'To aspire to leadership is an honourable ambition'.** This is an unusual interpretation of the Greek text and demands a few words of explanation. In a number of manuscripts the first phrase is identical with that in 1.15, 'Here are words you may trust'; and this phrase appears to be one which the writer regularly uses to indicate that he is quoting some well-known article of faith. But at this place the formula seems inappropriate. Neither the paragraph which precedes it nor the one which follows it contains the kind of quotation one would expect. However, other manuscripts offer the formula in a slightly different form: **There is a popular saying.** For various reasons the NEB translators believed that this is more likely to be the correct reading here; and this reading also has the advantage that it gives a more suitable lead into the quotation (if it is one) which follows, '**To aspire to leadership is an honourable ambition**'; for this certainly sounds much more like a **popular saying** than an article of the Christian faith. The difficulty is that the Greek word translated **leadership** is anything but a "popular" one: it never occurs in this sense in secular Greek, and it is very unlikely that it would have figured in a **popular saying.** The NEB rendering is therefore not fully satisfactory, and the verse remains exceedingly puzzling. At any rate, the important point for the writer was the appearance in the saying of a word for **leadership** (*episkopē*) which was a form of the Greek word that had already become a technical term for an official of the church, *episkopos* (bishop). The
2 play upon the word is reflected in the NEB by the translation, **Our leader, therefore, or bishop.** From the general saying about leadership the writer

[a] It is perhaps the very awkwardness with which, in the Greek, the Christian sentiment is tacked on to the Jewish commonplace which makes these words difficult to translate with any certainty (see the alternative renderings in NEB). The Latin fathers, feeling a difficulty, saw in them a reference to Mary, who by giving birth to Christ could be said to have raised womanhood to a new level of sanctity; and other interpretations are possible. That given in the text is the one which seems to suit the context best.

finds that he can move easily to the character required by a particular kind of leader, namely a Christian bishop.

The chapter goes on to give a list of the qualities which are to be expected
both in the bishop and in the **deacons** (another word which by this time had 8
become a technical title in the church: in ordinary Greek usage it meant one who performs comparatively menial duties such as waiting at table). It can be seen at once that there is very little difference between the two lists; and in fact the qualities in both of them are very similar to those which would normally have been looked for in the holder of any responsible office in the ancient world. In other words, what we are being given is not (what we might have hoped for) a picture of the specific offices of bishop and deacon, with the duties and resources required of these ministers, but a fairly conventional account of what the men ought to be like who are entrusted with any responsible office whatever in the church. The only obscurity is in the words
faithful to his one wife: we cannot be sure whether this is aimed at marital 12
unfaithfulness, at a tendency to marry again after the first wife's death (which Paul certainly tried to discourage at Corinth, 1 Corinthians 7.27), or even at polygamy. There is also a slight ambiguity in verse 11. The Greek word
translated **their wives** means literally "women". In Greek this would be a 11
perfectly natural way of referring to the deacons' wives (so the main text in NEB), but it could also be taken to mean, "if they are women" (i.e. deaconesses, so the footnote).

These qualities, though applicable in many walks of life, are mentioned
here to show **how men ought to conduct themselves in God's house-** 15
hold. This is a new image for the church; but it leads easily (since the Greek for household is the same as the Greek for house) into the more familiar idea of the church as a "building". The building which the church is most often said to replace is the Jewish temple at Jerusalem. But here it is just possible that another building is in mind. The temple of Artemis at Ephesus was one of the largest and most famous buildings of antiquity (it became one of the "wonders of the world") and will have been for most Ephesians the most impressive religious monument in their experience. This too the church replaces; and the classical architecture of that temple may possibly have suggested to the writer the two architectural terms **pillar and bulwark.**

The chapter ends with what was probably a familiar summary of the
mystery of our religion. The lines have a discernible rhythmical pattern; 16
and since each phrase looks more like a statement of belief than an attempt to advance fresh teaching, it seems likely that the writer is quoting an existing hymn or creed rather than composing something new. Each line is a succinct statement about Jesus Christ, and the stanzas can be set out in groups of two or (as here) three lines each. (i) **Manifested in the body** is a clear description of Jesus' earthly life; **vindicated in the spirit** is a little more allusive.

Outwardly, Jesus' life and work appeared a failure, a failure which could be interpreted as God's judgement passed against Jesus. But the Christian faith was that this was not so. God did not condemn Jesus; he accepted him and endorsed his acts. By the resurrection and exaltation of Jesus, and by the power now released in the church, God **vindicated** him. Yet this vindication was only apparent (as we say) to the eye of faith. Jesus was not yet vindicated in such a way that 'every eye shall see him' (Revelation 1.7)—that belonged to the future. Meanwhile, he was vindicated **in the spirit**—that is to say (and here a number of interpretations are possible) that it was only "by the spirit" that men could know that God had vindicated him (1 Corinthians 2.10–16); or, that men were led to believe that God had vindicated him by the mighty acts performed by the Holy Spirit through the church; or again, that it was in the spiritual sphere, not yet in the fully visible and material sphere, that the vindication had taken place. **Seen by angels** possibly continues this thought. Many of the supernatural powers, Paul believed, apparently drew the wrong inference from the crucifixion (see above on 1 Corinthians 2.8), and the vindication needed also to be "seen" by them. (ii) The second three lines sum up the mission of the church. It was Paul's constant source of pride and confidence that the gospel had now been preached, not to the Jews only, but **among the nations,** and that Jesus' prophecy of a world-wide proclamation was already, in a sense, nearing fulfilment (see above on Romans 15.19). The complement to this was Jesus' present ascendancy in the universe: **glorified in high heaven.**

4. 1 **The Spirit says expressly.** When the early church found itself confronted by persecution, heresy and counter-propaganda, it did not regard these things as either unexpected or intolerable. Christ had said that such things were bound to happen before the end could come (Mark 13.7); and the church therefore tended to see its tribulations as a necessary part of the ordained pattern of history which would immediately precede the end. It was moreover a fairly common theme of contemporary Jewish "apocalyptic" writing that the final age of world history would be marked by a kind of intensification of evil. Thus although we cannot identify in any known writing the prophecy alluded to here, we can recognize, in outline, a belief which was widely held both inside and outside the church, and which found expression in many writings believed to have been inspired by **the Spirit.** This view of the ultimate course of history tended naturally to be expounded in vivid and mythological terms. It was believed, not simply that men of their own nature were likely to get worse and worse, but that objective forces of evil would progressively assume control over men's minds and bodies. The phrase rendered **in after times** was almost a technical term for this final age, which would be characterized by **subversive doctrines inspired by devils** (compare 'all the powerful signs and miracles of the Lie' in 2 Thessalonians

2.9) and by the fact that some men would already have become committed
servants of the devil, a **sign** having been branded on their **conscience** (the 2
word here is equivalent to "consciousness"), or even—in the more picturesque language of the Revelation (7.3)—on their foreheads.

When, therefore, the church was overtaken by some crisis, the correct approach was not just to hope that it would soon blow over, but to see in it one of the predicted signs of the times—and this attitude prevailed right through the New Testament period (see 1 John 2.18 for a late example). And so here: the "erroneous doctrines" of certain trouble-makers, which were mentioned at the beginning of the letter (1.3), were not just a passing threat to the peace of the church, but were to be seen in the same serious context; and the nature of this menace (assuming that the heretics in this chapter are the same persons as those referred to earlier) is now sketched in for us in
more detail. They **forbid marriage and inculcate abstinence from** 3
certain foods. Those philosophies which regarded everything in the material world as evil, and saw the liberation of the soul from all earthly limitations as the only purpose of life, tended naturally to discourage their followers from assuming the cares of married life. Detailed descriptions of such philosophies and of their followers are available to us only from the second century A.D., but it is intrinsically probable that the interest in 'myths and genealogies' discussed above had a similar tendency and carried with it the same kind of asceticism. This seems, at any rate, a more likely explanation of why these men "forbade marriage" than pressure from the Jewish side, for the Jewish attitude to marriage was distinctly positive, and only one Jewish sect is known of which discouraged it. **Abstinence from certain foods** is more difficult to pin down: there were so many possible motives for it. It could have been another instance of asceticism inspired by philosophy; but equally, it could have been the influence of any religion, such as Judaism, which held certain foods to be ritually unclean. Whatever form it actually took in Ephesus, it is attacked in this letter in terms that would be appropriate to a polemic against Jewish ordinances. It is stated in Genesis (1.31)
that God saw that his creation was good; and this statement is invoked as 4
making invalid the detailed prohibitions of the Law of Moses. **Believers** 3
who have inward knowledge of the truth—i.e. Christians—may partake of any food, provided only (as in Romans 14.6; 1 Corinthians 10.30) that they say grace. And grace, according to Jewish custom, and doubtless also among
Christians, included a verse of Scripture. Thus the food was **hallowed by** 5
God's own word and by prayer.

On such matters Timothy (like Paul himself on similar topics, as in 1
Corinthians 7) was not to exercise strict authority, but was to give **advice,** 6
like a **good servant.** (The word for **servant** is the same as that rendered 'deacon' above: although it had already become an official title in the church, it could still be used in its ordinary Greek sense.) The advice was to spring,

not from any new Christian insight, but (and this is characteristic of the atmosphere of the Pastorals) from the **sound instruction which you have**
7 **followed.** By contrast, the teaching of the heretics sounded like **godless myths, fit only for old women**—the last phrase being a stock term of abuse that had long been used by rival philosophers against each other. **Keep yourself in training for the practice of religion.** The athletic metaphor was a commonplace, but this writer also sees its dangers. On the one hand, the heretics were turning this **training** into an excessive asceticism; and on the other hand, athletic achievement tended to take an unduly prominent part in the Greek system of education, and serious-minded pagan thinkers were often induced to point out its limitations in terms very similar to those used here.

9 **Here are words you may trust.** The phrase, as usual, clearly indicates a quotation; but once again it is hard to be sure which words should be put in inverted commas. The sentence which follows may well be the saying referred to (the footnote in NEB gives another possibility), amplifying the idea of the
10 Christian's 'training'. On **Saviour of all men**, see above on 2.4.

The following paragraphs return to questions of church order, and afford a glimpse of the circumstances in which Timothy had to learn to exercise his authority. It is possible that seniority was normally regarded as a qualification for leadership (this would partly account for the emergence of the word "elder" as a title in the church); in which case Timothy's youth would have made it harder for him to get his authority accepted. His normal duties
13 included **public reading of the scriptures,** preaching **(exhortation)** and **teaching,** and his authority stemmed from the fact that he had originally
14 been commissioned with the **laying on of hands.** There are several descriptions in Acts of the ceremony by which hands were laid on a Christian minister to commission him for a particular task—on occasion **under the guidance of prophecy,** as in Acts 13.1–3. It was with the same gesture that Moses commissioned Joshua (Numbers 27.22–3) and the people of Israel commissioned the Levites (Numbers 8.10); and the church, inspired perhaps by these precedents, and perhaps also by the similar "ordination" of Rabbis which was by this time an accepted institution among the Jews, had come to recognize the rite as one which conferred a **spiritual endowment** on its ministers. Nevertheless, we must not too hastily read back into this passage the form which was subsequently taken by Christian "ordination". For one thing, 2 Timothy 1.6 refers to an occasion when Paul alone laid hands on Timothy, without the **elders as a body** being present; for another, the Greek of this passage is capable of another interpretation altogether (see the footnote in NEB). Here, once again, the exact details of early church order are accidentally withheld from our curiosity.

5. 1 **Never be harsh with an elder.** The word here seems to connote, not an official of the church, but any elderly man over whom Timothy, himself

much younger, may have had to exercise his authority. The question of
widows is more complicated. Women married young in the ancient world:
they were free to do so straight after puberty, and there was a correspondingly
high risk of them being widowed quite early in life. Often they would marry
again, or they might have grown-up children to support them. But equally
often they fell into real poverty. In addition, they had no adequate protection
at law and their difficulties made them proverbially unfortunate members of
society. The charitable support of needy widows was of concern to both
Jewish and Christian communities, and indeed was held to be one of the most
meritorious activities of religious people (compare James 1.27). But for any
community which took this responsibility seriously it was essential to discriminate between those widows who were really in need and those who had
other means of support; and to this the writer turns first. It was the prime
duty of a widow's relations to **make provision** for her, not only on social 8
grounds, but because this was in the spirit of the Fifth Commandment (**for** 4
this God approves); whereas any widows who had no such means of support were to be treated as widows "in the full sense" (or, granted the **status** 3
of widow, as the NEB somewhat formally expresses it). The church, in any
case, would be well rewarded for such charity, since the widow would have
abundant time for prayer.

In verse 9 we learn that there was a **roll** on which widows' names were 9
entered; but judging by the qualifications required, and by the fact that some
sort of commitment or **troth** to Christ is alluded to, it looks as if this was 12
not so much a roll of those who genuinely needed support from the church as a
distinct "order" of widows entrusted with specific duties. This is the only
reference to such an institution in the New Testament, but there is some
evidence for its existence in the following centuries, and the conditions for
belonging to it are rather what one would expect for such an order—being
over sixty, or having **washed the feet of God's people** (a customary act of
hospitality in the eastern part of the empire). The paragraph as a whole is a
little complicated only because it refers to widows in three senses: (i) in the
ordinary sense of any bereaved wife; (ii) **in the full sense** of the term, that 3
is, widows in genuine need of support; and (iii) the **roll** of those widows who 9
were given responsible tasks in the church.

The writer then turns again to **elders**; but this time they clearly cannot 17
be just "older men", but are persons who have specific duties and receive a
regular **stipend.** We learn with surprise that they are also to be paid according to merit. Paul uses the same passage of Scripture, '**You shall not** 18
muzzle a threshing ox' (Deuteronomy 25.4) to support the principle that
'those who preach the Gospel should earn their living by the Gospel' (1
Corinthians 9.14), but says nothing there about "double stipends": his
concern is whether it is right for them to be paid at all. The other saying
quoted here—'**the worker earns his pay**'—was used by Jesus (Luke 10.7).

But this writer is not necessarily thinking of Jesus' teaching: the sentence has a proverbial ring, and may have been endorsed, rather than invented, by Jesus.

One of Timothy's responsibilities was evidently that of arbitrating between members of the church. Elders were doubtless particularly vulnerable because of their public position, and they were entitled to at least the protection customary under Jewish law: more than one witness was necessary to substantiate a charge (Deuteronomy 19.15). But once a charge was proved, they (or indeed any Christian: it is hard to know exactly whom verse 20
21 applies to) must be judged with all severity and **impartiality.** One way of avoiding scandal was of course to exercise great care in the choice of those who were to be ordained in the first place, and from the text it appears that powers of discretion rested with Timothy. But once again this detail of church order is made uncertain by an ambiguity in the Greek: see the alternative rendering in the footnote in NEB.

23 **Stop drinking nothing but water.** Whether it was a personal trait of Timothy's or the influence of the over-ascetic heretics which prompted this warning we do not know. The medicinal qualities of wine were well known in antiquity. As Plutarch aptly put it, "the most useful of drinks and the pleasantest medicine".

6. 1 The reason why Christian slaves must **count their own masters worthy of all respect** is obvious enough: insubordination would profit no one. But
2 **if the masters are believers** the matter is clearly more delicate. Slaves may find it difficult to think of the same individuals both as the masters whom they must obey and at the same time as **their Christian brothers.** The key to their difficulty is the **service** which Christians are in all circumstances to offer to each other (Galatians 5.13).

3 **If anyone is teaching otherwise.** With the heretics once again in mind, the writer contrasts **good religious teaching** with the intellectual extravagances
4 of those whose real concern is at the level of **verbal questions and quibbles.** He has, indeed, a still more damning criticism to make. Their ultimate motive is no better than that of any free-lance wandering philosopher: they
5 hope to make money out of their teaching—**they think religion should yield dividends.** Such a mercenary attitude needs no refutation; but the idea of **dividends** puts the writer in mind of what was probably a current
6 philosophical maxim about religion in general (the phrase, **the man whose resources are within him,** was a familiar one in the language of Stoic
7–10 teachers); and the critique of wealth which follows includes a number of more or less proverbial sayings.

11 **But you, man of God.** The remainder of the letter consists of a personal address to Timothy who, by virtue of his particular office and responsibility, merits the title given to Moses, Samuel and many other Old Testament

figures, **Man of God**—unless it is meant in a more mystical sense, in so far
as any Christian, by virtue of his incorporation into Christ, has become a man
enjoying a special relationship with God. **Run the great race of faith.** This 12
phrase is familiar in its traditional form, "Fight the good fight"; but the
Greek word (*agōn*) means, not a battle, but a competition, and the metaphor,
like many others in the New Testament, derives from athletics. **You confessed your faith nobly before many witnesses.** To what occasion does
this refer? Timothy's ordination? A trial in which he was arraigned for his
faith? Possibly; but the moment at which every Christian had publicly to
"confess his faith" was his baptism, and it is probably of the vows he made
at his baptism that Timothy is being reminded. The word **confession** is 13
picked up in an appeal to the example of Christ. If the translation, **before
Pontius Pilate,** is correct, the allusion is to Jesus' bearing at his trial; on the
other hand, the Greek words could also mean, "in the time of Pontius Pilate"
(which reappears as "under Pontius Pilate" in the Apostles' Creed), in which
case the reference is a general one to Jesus' passion and death. The ultimate
motive of Christian steadfastness is here, as so often in the New Testament,
the expectation of the imminent coming of Christ in glory—**until our Lord** 14
Jesus Christ appears—and if it was asked (as perhaps it was being increasingly asked) when that appearing would come to pass, the answer given
was essentially the answer given by Jesus himself: in God's **own good time.** 15
And in a string of phrases which very probably derive from the worship of 15–16
Greek-speaking synagogues, God is praised with the traditional attributes
both of the Lord of the Old Testament and of the divinities of Hellenistic
religions.

After some conventional thoughts on wealth, the letter ends with a per- 17–19
sonal postscript (in the manner, for instance, of Galatians 6.11–18), under- 20–21
lining the most urgent point in the letter. (On the metaphor underlying **that
which has been entrusted to you,** see below on 2 Timothy 1.12.) Just as,
in the following century (when this kind of thinking became more powerful
and systematic) many religious systems claimed to offer a kind of "knowledge" which would enable the soul to rise above the realm of earthly things,
so, we may assume, the false teachers in Ephesus made similar claims for
their own speculations. In so doing, they **shot far wide of the faith.**

THE SECOND LETTER OF PAUL TO TIMOTHY

Character of a Christian minister

The greeting is very similar to that of the first letter, and has the same unexpected appearance of formality; but the usual prayer for the recipient
which follows has a personal warmth which is sustained throughout this
letter. There is a natural tie between the two men even in the piety they have
inherited. Paul has the traditions of worship (which here means not only
what is done in church or synagogue, but the whole fashioning of a life in the
1.3 service of God) which came to him from his Jewish **forefathers** and which
are supplemented and perfected, rather than replaced, by his Christian
5 devotion; while Timothy has the example of his mother and grandmother,
who may indeed have been converted to Christianity when Timothy was still
young, or who may equally have been models of that traditional Jewish piety
which Christianity inherited and only partly modified (we know from Acts
16.1 that Timothy's mother was Jewish).

Timothy's faith and piety, then, had for long been habitual to him. In
addition, he had received, by the laying on of hands, both a commission and
6 a **gift** to enable him to perform that commission.[a] But this too, for all its
supernatural origin, was something which (as modern experience will
endorse) could in due course be taken for granted and lose its potency unless
constantly "stirred up" by an effort of the will; and to assist this process of
"stirring up" the writer devotes a few words to the **Spirit** which is imparted
with the gift. As is explained, for instance, in Romans 8, the function of the
Spirit in human conduct is to provide a new motive, and the kind of behaviour
7 which it inspires is not **craven** ('slavery' in Romans 8.15) but **strength,
love, and self-discipline**; and this relates the gift to that aspect of the Chris-
8 tian life which really demands such strength: fearless **testimony to our
Lord.**

To what does a Christian testify? The main headings of his testimony are
set out in terms which can be paralleled in (or may in fact be drawn from) other
9 Pauline writings. (i) The phrase, **not for any merit of ours but of his own
purpose and his own grace,** is a basic Pauline proposition; (ii) the long
perspective of this salvation, beginning **from all eternity** and now manifested
in a decisive revelation, is familiar from Ephesians and Colossians (though the
10 words used in this translation, **now at length brought fully into view,** must
not be taken to exclude a still more complete revelation which is promised for

[a] On the question of Timothy's "ordination" see above on 1 Timothy 4.14.

the future); and (iii) 1 Corinthians 15 provides a full commentary on **he has broken the power of death.** The only word which belongs to a slightly different world of ideas is **Saviour.** This was soon to become a standard title of Christ, just as it already was of the gods of many contemporary religions and indeed of great benefactors such as the Roman Emperor. But it was never used by Christ of himself, and it is rare in Paul. Its occurrence here (and twice in the Letter to Titus) may be an example of the way in which Christianity, which was at first preached in the exclusive idiom of Palestine, gradually accepted the terminology of a more cosmopolitan society.

The **Gospel,** which Paul has a special charge to proclaim, and which is 11
the cause of his **present plight,** is here described under a new metaphor 12
(which is also hinted at in 1 Timothy 6.20). Both Greek and Roman law
defined the conditions under which a sum of money or a valuable object
might be placed on deposit with another person: the man who accepted the
deposit was obliged to keep it intact and return it on demand. The Gospel
is such a "deposit". It has to be "kept safe"—that is, untainted by deviations
of doctrine—and held in readiness for **the great Day.** Thus both Paul and
Timothy (and presumably their successors) have the responsibility to **keep**
safe what has been put in their charge,[a] or to **guard the treasure** (both 14
phrases are the same in the original). Faith in God will enable them to do it.

Nothing further is known about **Phygelus and Hermogenes. Onesi-** 15, 16
phorus had evidently shown particular loyalty to Paul during Paul's imprisonment (or one of his imprisonments). It is not clear whether he was still
alive. If not, this is the first example of Christian prayer for the dead (for
which there is plenty of evidence a century or two later). The prayer itself 18
looks conventional—the clumsy double use of **the Lord** suggests that the
writer is somewhat carelessly adapting a traditional (perhaps Jewish) formula.

The metaphor of the "deposit" is taken up once more. Timothy received
the deposit of 'sound teaching' (which he now has to entrust to others) on a
solemn occasion, **in the presence of many witnesses.** What was this **2.** 2
occasion? Possibly his baptism; but more probably the rite of commissioning
or "ordination" which had placed him in a position of special responsibility.
The devotion required of him is illustrated by three examples which were
doubtless proverbial: the soldier must be completely **at his commanding** 4
officer's disposal, the athlete cannot qualify for a prize unless he has 5
undergone a certain period of intensive training, a farmer can lay first claim 6
to his crop only if he has been working on the land himself.

The **theme** of the gospel, from which the sound teaching flows, can be 9
summed up in a number of ways. **Jesus Christ, risen from the dead, born** 8
of David's line, is one way (Romans 1.3–4 contains a similar formulation);
another way is to state the consequences of Christ's work for those who

[*a*] The Greek can also mean that there is something (i.e. the church) which has been put into God's charge. See the footnote in NEB.

11 believe in him. **Here are words you may trust.** This phrase usually
introduces a quotation; and from the structure of the following verses it
seems that we are being given, once again, a fragment of an early hymn which
puts together, without much sense of logical connection, a number of familiar
Christian ideas. '**If we died with him, we shall live with him**' is reminis-
12 cent of Paul's exposition of baptism in Romans 6; '**if we endure, we shall
reign with him**' is similar to Romans 8.17 and reminiscent of Luke 22.28–9.
If we deny him, he will deny us recalls a saying of Jesus (Matthew 10.33);
but here this seems on the face of it to be contradicted by the last two lines.
However there is a difference, more clear in the Greek than can be expressed
13 in English. **If we are faithless** does not mean, if we renounce our faith,
but rather, if we waver in our faith. When this happens to us (as it is bound
to) we can be sustained by the thought of the faithfulness of God, who has
made us a promise in Christ, and cannot allow it to come to nothing without
"denying himself".

Timothy's constancy, devotion and firm hold on sound teaching are now set
in a context which makes them specially relevant. In the first letter the
heretical thinkers who were causing trouble in the church were characterized
by their interest in 'myths and genealogies' and by their tendency to indulge
in unnecessary ascetic practices. Here they reappear in much the same guise:
14 Timothy has to resist those who are **disputing about mere words** and
16 indulging in **empty and worldly chatter.** Two such people are named (one
of whom, Hymenaeus, was mentioned in 1 Timothy 1.20) and their error
18 is described: they are **saying that our resurrection has already taken
place.** Many people who were accustomed to Greek ways of thinking must
have found the Christian picture of the after-life (which the Christians had
inherited from the Jews) both strange and naïve, and have been tempted to
reformulate it in more congenial terms. Paul had to face precisely this
difficulty in 1 Corinthians 15. Here, the proposed reinterpretation probably
took its start from the experience of baptism. Christians, when they were
baptized, "rose" with Christ. This, in orthodox Christian teaching, was no
more than a foretaste of that future "resurrection" when Christians would
rise in bodily form to sit beside Christ at the Last Judgement. But the heretics
perhaps hoped to avoid the apparent naïvety of this doctrine by concentrating
on the foretaste to the exclusion of the future consummation. They held that
what was meant by "resurrection" was simply the new quality of life which
flowed from conversion and baptism, and that it was therefore unnecessary
to believe in what they felt to be a primitive concept of future "resurrection".
For their purpose, it was sufficient to point to the experience they had had
already. All that a sophisticated Christian could expect to understand by the
word "resurrection" had already taken place.

The writer attacks this view, not by seeking to refute it (as Paul might

have done in the earlier letters), but by appealing to the strength and dura-
bility of the church which is entrusted with the true tradition. In a metaphor
which appears frequently in the New Testament, the church is likened to a
building of which God has laid **a foundation,** and of which Christians are 19
the stones. The building is imagined as bearing inscribed upon it the text,
'The Lord knows his own'. This comes from the story of Korah (Numbers
16.5), who was the Old Testament prototype of all apostates; and the words,
spoken as a threat by Moses to Korah, were an appropriate warning to any
Christian who was tempted to depart from the sound teaching entrusted to
the church. A second "inscription" is added, this time more freely con- 19
structed out of biblical phrases, and expressing a more general warning to
those who belong to the building; and the metaphor is then given a new
twist. The building is now a **great house,** and the Christians are the various 20
utensils in it. Given their place on the shelves, so to speak, it is up to them
(presumably, in this context, by the consistency of their beliefs)[a] to make
themselves **of use to the Master.** 21

A personal word for Timothy: being young, he is subject to **wayward** 22
impulses; but he is also warned, once more, against **foolish and ignorant** 23
speculations—not, this time, because of the errors of doctrine they lead to,
but because of their moral consequences. The kind of discipline he must be
prepared to exercise is that appropriate to a **servant of the Lord**: its very 24
gentleness may save others from **the devil's snare.** 26

As in the previous letter, the appearance of heresy and immorality is seen,
not as a passing hazard to the progress of the young church, but as a necessary
feature of **the final age of this world.** The sketch of human depravity 3.1
which follows is written in terms which were probably quite conventional;
on the other hand, the subversion of some of the women in the congregation
is a detail which may well be drawn from the actual experience of the
church. **Jannes and Jambres** are the names which tradition gave to two of 8
Pharaoh's magicians, who performed miracles identical with those of Moses
(Exodus 7.11), but were powerless to avert the fate ultimately coming
upon Egypt—**their successes** were **short-lived.** 9

The **persecutions and sufferings** that are mentioned here seem to 11
belong to the earlier period of Paul's work (Acts 13.50; 14.5–6, 19). Timothy's
home was in the region of Lystra (Acts 16.1), and he might well be expected
to remember what Paul suffered there.

From early childhood you have been familiar with the sacred 15
writings. The Old Testament was as normative for the early Christians as it was for the Jews. Admittedly, the Christians had a new revelation by which to interpret it, and often drew quite new inferences from it. But the New Testament itself provides clear evidence that they regarded the Old Testa-

[a] Or, as the Greek could mean, by shunning the company of heretics. See the footnote in NEB.

16 ment as uniquely **inspired** and made use of it for the teaching of both morals
and doctrine.

All these injunctions are now summed up with a fresh note of urgency.
4. 1 **I charge you solemnly by his coming appearance and his reign.** As so
often in early Christian moral teaching, belief in the imminent end of the
world is a powerful stimulus. The period immediately preceding the end is
to be marked by an upsurge of evil and apostasy (see above on 1 Timothy
3 4.1–2); and when this writer says, **the time will come,** he is evidently not
brooding on a distant future, but is pointing to the premonitory signs already
4 manifest in the present. Those who stop their ears to the truth and **turn to**
mythology do not merely represent a danger which has to be resisted: they
5 are themselves a signal that the crisis is near. Therefore Christians must **keep**
calm and sane at all times.

The letter suddenly becomes very personal—so personal that, if Paul is not
the author of the whole letter, it is often felt that these verses at least must be
a genuine fragment of his correspondence, worked in here by a later writer.
6 The metaphor, **being poured out on the altar,** occurs also in Philippians
2.17; while the athletic comparison, which is common both in Paul and in
other contemporary writers, bears a rather unusual emphasis, not so much
8 on the contest itself as on the reward at the end of it, here called **the garland**
of righteousness: the victor's garland is the symbol that Christians, both
as a result of their own prowess, and also (and still more) owing to the gracious
act of God in Christ, will be counted "righteous"—a destiny (it must be
quickly added) by no means reserved for Paul alone, but promised to all who
confess Christ as their Lord and Saviour, and have **set their hearts on his**
coming appearance.

The main part of the letter has consisted of advice and instructions to
Timothy in Ephesus, and seems to presuppose that he is permanently
established there. Nevertheless, Paul is now anxious for a visit from him.
9 **Do your best to join me soon.** The reason is that Paul has only one companion left; the rest, for one reason or another, have dispersed. It is just
possible to fit all these movements into the period of Paul's first (and only
10–11 recorded) imprisonment in Rome. **Demas, Luke, Mark,** and **Tychicus**
were all with Paul when he wrote Colossians (also from prison), and all but
one of them could by now have left. **Crescens** is otherwise unknown;[a]
Titus had not been heard of for some time, unless his presence in **Dalmatia**
is to be connected with a projected visit of Paul's to Nicopolis, mentioned in
13 Titus 3.12. The only real difficulty is Paul's stay at **Troas.** He can hardly be
referring to the occasion when he was there waiting for news from Corinth,
several years before his imprisonment in Rome (2 Corinthians 2.12); and

[*a*] An early tradition, however, makes him the founder of the church at Vienne, near Lyons in Gaul; and the Greek word **Galatia** can also bear this meaning (see above, p. 598).

none of his recorded journeys subsequently took him to Troas. The easiest explanation would certainly be that Paul made a journey back to Asia after being released from prison, in the course of which he could have visited both Troas and **Miletus.**

Alexander the copper-smith may be the same Alexander as was men- 14
tioned in 1 Timothy 1.20 (where he was already punished with excommunication). The scriptural phrase (2 Samuel 3.39; Psalm 28.4), **Retribution will fall upon him from the Lord,** is sufficient condemnation, but clearly the man is still influential, and Timothy has to be warned against him.

Exactly what stage in the proceedings is indicated by **the first hearing of** 16
my case would be uncertain even if we could be sure that these were genuine words of Paul. It seems unlikely (in view of the closing scenes in Acts) that Paul was left so much **in the lurch** during his first trial in Rome; therefore (on the traditional view) the trial in question must be a second one which, unlike the first, ultimately led to Paul being put to death. Such a trial (according to Roman practice) could well have begun with a preliminary hearing before a magistrate. If this were not decisive (as would appear to have been the case here) the hearing would be adjourned for a fuller trial; and Paul looked forward to this more public occasion as an opportunity for
making **the full proclamation of the Gospel for the whole pagan world** 17
to hear—in Philippians 1.12–18 he expresses very much the same idea.
Meanwhile, the immediate danger had passed—Paul was **rescued out of** 18
the lion's jaws. And the Lord will rescue me: nothing that men could do to him could in any case prevent him from entering into the **heavenly reign** of Christ.

Prisca and Aquila: see above on Romans 16.3. 19

Onesiphorus: already mentioned at 1.16 above.

Erastus: possibly the same as in Romans 16.23. 20

Trophimus: an Ephesian, according to Acts 20.4; 21.29.

Eubulus, Pudens, Linus and **Claudia** are not mentioned elsewhere in 21
the New Testament, though there is an early tradition that the second bishop of Rome, after Peter, was named Linus.

THE LETTER OF PAUL TO TITUS

Training for the Christian life

We know nothing of a journey by Paul to Crete, nor of the founding of a church there, but by the time this letter was written there was clearly a settled Christian community on the island. The letter is addressed to Titus, whom we know from other letters and from Acts to have been one of Paul's principal assistants, and to have been entrusted with missions of some delicacy. Here, although he still seems to be regarded as surprisingly young and inexperienced, he is in charge of the church in Crete, and the letter, though addressed to him, is clearly intended for the church as a whole. For the most part, its tone is not personal but formal and authoritative.

This formality is stressed at the outset by the long parenthesis which
1. 1–4 interrupts the normal structure of the greeting, **From Paul ... to Titus** (see
above on Romans 1.1), and which rehearses the qualifications of the writer
to give authoritative instructions to the church. It is not clear from the Greek
1 whether the writer means that an apostle is specially **marked** by his commission to preach (so the main text in NEB), or that his apostleship is
discharged in bringing these distinctive notes of the Christian faith to others
2 (so the alternative rendering); in either event, God's purpose, **promised**
long ages ago (an idea developed in Ephesians, see above on Eph. 1.4) is
3 fulfilled in the **proclamation which was entrusted** to the apostle, by
virtue of which the apostle now has authority to give instruction to the
church.

4 **True-born son** was a favourite expression of Paul's for his converts; see
above on 1 Corinthians 4.15.

The historical situation we are to imagine is that Paul, after preaching the
gospel in Crete and making a number of converts, left to Titus the task of
5 organizing the young church and appointing its leaders. The **tests** which he
then prescribed are repeated here, presumably to serve as a guide in all
future appointments. The qualities desired in candidates for office are very
similar to those listed in 1 Timothy 3 and are of a general character: this is
the sort of man that anyone who holds responsibility of any kind in the
church ought to be. The only difficulty in the paragraph is that at the outset
it is concerned with the appointment of elders, but two verses later is speak-
6 ing of a **bishop**. Do both these names denote the same office? This supposition would make good sense of the present passage, but would raise
difficulties elsewhere. In 1 Timothy, for instance, the bishop is treated quite

separately from the elders; and in the subsequent order of the church the
bishop and the elders (presbyters) were clearly differentiated. It is possible
that the confusion arises from the phrase **institute elders.** On the face of it, 5
one would expect this to mean, institute men to the office of "eldership".
But it could also mean, institute "elders"—i.e. responsible men, who were
usually among the older members of the church—to certain offices in the
church, and in particular to the office of bishop.

There are all too many . . . Just as in Ephesus one of the main responsi- 10
bilities of the leader of the church was to protect his congregation from the
influence of teachers who wove elaborate speculative systems out of a combination of Old Testament and Christian materials (see above on 1 Timothy
1.4), so in Crete Titus is warned against a similar danger, that of his people
lending their ears to Jewish myths and commandments of merely 14
human origin. Here, **Jewish myths** clearly cannot mean any part of the
Old Testament, for no Christian would ever have thought of the Old
Testament as anything but a divinely inspired book. The phrase must be
an allusion to fanciful interpretations of the Old Testament such as we find
in later Jewish literature or in the systems of the so-called "gnostic" thinkers
of the following century. As for **commandments of merely human** 14
origin, these were probably rules of asceticism and ritual purity devised by
these thinkers for themselves—rules which the Christians could disregard
on exactly the same grounds as they disregarded orthodox Jewish ordinances:
to them, **all things are pure** (as Paul had said in Romans 14.20, perhaps 15
appealing to a word of Christ, Mark 7.15), whereas if once the mind is
tainted alike in reason and conscience, no ascetic rules of any kind have
the slightest value.

To this extent (and also because they do it **all for sordid gain,** compare 11
1 Timothy 6.5) the trouble-makers in Crete are very similar to those described in 1 Timothy. But there are two respects in which they are unlike the
heretics in Ephesus. First, they are **Jewish converts**—that is to say, having 10
been converted from Judaism, they are now presumably dissatisfied with
Christianity, and propose to construct their own more ambitious religious
philosophy; and secondly, they are Cretans—and Cretans are proverbially
liars! The proverb in question was originally a line of verse attributed to 12
Epimenides, a philosopher of the sixth century B.C. He is here called a
prophet, doubtless because it was felt he had rightly predicted the national
character which the Cretans would still have some centuries later. Certainly
the Cretans generally had a bad reputation, and the writer assumes that this
is another reason why the Cretan church is in trouble.

As in the other pastoral letters, the defence to be presented against these subversive influences is not (as it might have been in an earlier letter of Paul) a pugnacious counter-attack or even a careful restatement of Christian beliefs, but simply that sound hold on Christian essentials which is once

13, **2.** 1 again called **sane belief . . . wholesome doctrine** (both **sane** and **whole-**
some are translations of the same Greek word, which is characteristic of the
pastoral letters, see above on 1 Timothy 1.10). And, since this **wholesome**
2. 1–10 **doctrine** is as much ethical as theoretical, the writer goes on to give a
picture of the Christian way of life as it is to be lived out by different groups
within the Christian community. This kind of systematic presentation of
Christian duties is familiar from other New Testament letters (see above on
Colossians 3.18) and occurs frequently in early Christian literature. In
Ephesians and Colossians, however, the groups singled out are those
represented in a domestic household—husbands, wives, children and slaves.
Here, the groups are those to be found in the congregation as a whole—the
older men, the older women, the younger men and the slaves. As so often, the
qualities demanded of them (as of the church's leaders in 1 Timothy) are
those which were expected of respectable people anywhere in the Greco-
2 Roman world. Only occasional touches, such as the **faith, love and endur-**
ance of the older men, betray a specifically Christian insight.

Yet even if these moral ideals were nothing out of the ordinary, there was
something quite new about Christian motives. In Paul's earlier letters this
11 new factor was called simply the Spirit; here, it is the **grace of God** which
has dawned upon the world. There, the Spirit was described as working
directly upon a man, assuming control, as it were, of his conduct, and bringing forth a "harvest" of qualities to which, unaided, men could hardly aspire.
Here, the metaphor is less dramatic, and perhaps appropriate to a more
gradual evolution of the Christian character. The grace of God is thought of
12 as something by which **we are disciplined.** The word was a basic one in
the Greek theory of education, according to which education was a process
by which the naturally unruly body and mind were trained and disciplined
until they functioned according to their true potentiality. This discipline was
of course imparted by tutors—and the psychological effect of the grace of
God is here seen as fulfilling precisely the tutor's function, providing a
constant stimulus to endeavour, and training mind and body in habits of
temperance, honesty, and godliness. A further motive is suggested by
the phrase, **the present age,** which always implies, in both Jewish and early
Christian literature, that the present order is temporary, and will be succeeded
by that more perfect age promised long ago by God. Christians now had
their own vision of this future age, and expected it to dawn very soon, and its
imminence was frequently invoked as a spur to calm, sober and vigilant
13 conduct. It would be the moment when the splendour of **our great God and**
Saviour Christ Jesus will appear[a]—and the following summary of the
14 achievement of Christ is full of scriptural reminiscences. **To set us free**

[*a*] There are very few instances in the New Testament of Christ actually being called God: though closely associated with God the Father, he is usually also distinguished from him. This consideration makes many translators favour the other possible rendering which is given in the footnote.

from all wickedness is the "ransom" metaphor used by Jesus (Mark 10.45); and **to make us a pure people marked out for his own** expresses the Christian understanding of the church as the new Israel, the people for whom the Old Testament promises were ultimately destined (the allusion here is to such passages as Exodus 19.5, Deuteronomy 14.2 and Ezekiel 37.23).

Remind them to be submissive to the government and the authori- 3. 1
ties. This was the normal Christian attitude: see above on Romans 13.1.

These are words you may trust. Each time this phrase occurs in the 8
Pastorals, it seems to point to a quotation or article of belief well known to
the church. Here, the passage referred to must be the paragraph which 1–8
immediately precedes. On more than one occasion (see, for instance, the first
chapter of Romans, or Colossians 3.5–7) Paul used what may seem almost
excessively sombre colours to portray the state of mankind before its redemption through Christ; and the same vivid contrast seems very soon to have
entered the ordinary vocabulary of the early church. The contrast serves to
throw into high relief the **kindness and generosity of God our Saviour** 4
(words which were more often used of human benefactors than of God, and
which may be another instance of the church coming under the influence of
the language of a cosmopolitan society). Inspired only by his own mercy
(**not for any good deeds of our own**), God had overlooked the years of 5
unregeneracy, and the moment when this act of mercy became effective for
the individual believer was the moment of baptism, **the water of rebirth.**
The idea of "rebirth", whether of the individual or of the whole universe, to
a better kind of existence, was quite a common one. When the Christians
adopted it, they made it more specific by relating it to **the water** of baptism
and to the **Spirit** which made the rite effective.

It was Christ's command that those who sinned in a moral sense should be
treated with great patience (Matthew 18.15–17 is the severest passage on the
subject). But if a man, after two warnings, showed himself still a heretic, then
this was no ordinary sin: the man was one of the predicted and inevitable
signs of the last times, an instrument in the hands of the devil. Therefore
only one course was possible—**have done with him.** 10

On Paul's intention to spend the winter at Nicopolis, see the introduction 12
to 1 Timothy (p. 661). **Artemas** and **Zenas** are not otherwise known;
Tychicus appears in 2 Timothy 4.12; **Apollos** may well be the famous 13
preacher of Acts 18.24. The letter was evidently to serve as a letter of
recommendation for two travelling Christians, who may have been its
bearers.

THE LETTER OF PAUL TO PHILEMON

A runaway slave

A runaway slave, in the Greek world, might take refuge in the house of someone whom he had met at his master's, and beg his new protector not to send him back. If he made a good impression, he might be a cause of some embarrassment to his protector, who would either have to keep the slave against the wishes of his former master, or send him back to certain punishment; and if the two men were friends, this might be a genuinely difficult decision. We happen to possess two letters of the Latin writer Pliny which are concerned with precisely this dilemma. Pliny, like Paul, solved it by sending back the culprit with a carefully worded letter in which he asked his friend to receive the slave kindly. This letter of Paul's is of exactly the same kind.

Yet it is not entirely personal. It appears to have been written at the same
time as the letter to the Colossians, and the greetings at the beginning and
1 end (with the addition only of an otherwise unknown **Apphia** and of
Philemon himself) make mention of almost the same names. It looks,
then, as if Philemon lived at Colossae; and this is confirmed by the statement
in Colossians (4.9) that Onesimus was also a native of that city. In writing to
Philemon, therefore, Paul writes to him not merely as an individual friend
but as a member of the Colossian church; and, like his letter to that church,
his letter to Philemon opens with thanksgiving and prayer, using indeed a
number of the same phrases (compare especially Philemon 4–6 with Colossians 1.3–9).[a]

8 The transition to personal matters is made in verse 7. Writing **in Christ**
as an apostle to a member of a church, Paul could have used a tone of
authority—**I might make bold to point out your duty.** But he prefers to
put the matter as tactfully as he can, and even puts off mentioning the
culprit's name as long as possible. He refrains from invoking the power of
9 an apostle, or even the gentler persuasion of an **ambassador . . . of Christ
Jesus.**[b] The complication here, which makes this a very different case from
that of most runaway slaves, is that Paul has converted Onesimus to Chris-
10 tianity (a process which Paul more than once compares to becoming **father**

[*a*] Verse 6 is no more intelligible in the Greek than in the English.

[*b*] The Greek word for **ambassador** is almost indistinguishable from that which means "old man"; hence the rendering given in many translations—"Paul, an old man, a prisoner of Christ Jesus". It is possible to make sense of "old man" by making it point forward to the word **father** in verse 10.

of a child, as in 1 Corinthians 4.15). This makes it harder for Paul to part with him, since he now has a personal tie with him, and his conversion has
made him, as his name would suggest, **now useful indeed.** (There seems to 11
be a pun on the Greek word *onēsimos*, "useful", though Onesimus was a common name for slaves.) But Paul would not wish to keep him without Philemon's consent, and so he adopts the only other possible course, that of
sending him back. The remainder of the letter is a plea for humane treat- 12
ment of him, not however on grounds of common humanity, but for the much more serious reason that, having become a Christian, Onesimus is now
more than a slave . . . a dear brother. Paul even offers to make good any 16
property which Onesimus, in his flight, may have stolen from his master—though, as an apostle to a Christian convert, he hardly expects this to be required!

Philemon's answer to Paul's letter is not preserved, and we do not know the sequel. Early in the second century there was a bishop of Ephesus named Onesimus; but that it was the same Onesimus, duly reformed and reinstated, and growing up to a position of authority in the church, is no more than an intriguing possibility.

A LETTER TO HEBREWS

As early as the second century A.D. this writing was referred to by ancient authors under the title, "To Hebrews". If, at that date, they knew any more about it—who was its author, why it was written—they have not told us. Indeed, even the title tells us nothing we could not have inferred for ourselves. Whoever was originally intended to read this letter must have been thoroughly familiar, not only with the Jewish religion, but with current Jewish techniques of interpreting the Old Testament: without a thoroughly "Hebrew" background, no one could possibly have followed the argument. It would seem to follow that the first readers were therefore "Hebrews"—that is, Jews or proselytes—who had been converted to Christianity. This conclusion is by no means certain: they could equally well have been Gentiles who had spent many years attending a Jewish synagogue before they became Christians (like the recipients of Paul's letter to the Galatians: see above, pp. 599–600). The traditional title, TO HEBREWS, is therefore not certainly correct. But, so far as it goes, it represents a reasonable guess.

It is less obviously appropriate to call the work A LETTER. It is true that it ends, as letters should, with some personal greetings; but at the beginning, where one normally looks for at least some indication of who is writing and to whom, there is nothing of the kind. The work begins like a treatise, and there are only a few moments in the course of it when the tone is sufficiently personal to give the impression of a man writing to his friends. If it is a "letter" at all, it is only a letter in that rather special sense (more familiar in antiquity than it is now) of a literary work intended for general circulation but adopting the conventional form of a letter. At most one might say that the treatise may have been inspired by particular circumstances, and was perhaps sent to a particular congregation after a personal conclusion had been added to serve as a kind of cover note.

Who wrote it? Until the fourth century A.D. many people were ready to confess that they did not know. It was perhaps by way of taking the line of least resistance that the church began to attribute it to Paul. The only other letters in the New Testament as extended as this one were by Paul, and the argument in Hebrews is on a scale that would have been worthy of the author of Romans. Nevertheless, there are great differences, in both style and content, between this and the authentic letters of Paul, and it is only the somewhat uncritical tradition of the church (which in any case has not always been in agreement on the matter) which provides any basis for continuing to regard Paul as the author. Other candidates have been proposed: Barnabas was suggested in the third century, Apollos in more recent times. But there is virtually no evidence, and one can do little more than guess.

The letter itself gives little away. The recipients have already undergone persecution and have the prospect of more coming to them; and they are warned several times of the danger of falling away from the faith. But this was a situation which must have been characteristic of many Christian congregations during the first few decades of their existence. As for the author, perhaps the most distinctive thing about him is his approach to the Old Testament. He uses a method of interpretation which we know to have been particularly highly developed among Jewish scholars at Alexandria. But even this is not sufficient to identify him as an Alexandrian; for he had considerably more respect for the literal meaning of Old Testament texts than did Philo (the only Alexandrian Jew who has left us extensive examples of this method), and in any case this kind of interpretation was by no means confined to Alexandria. Even Paul, who was educated in Jerusalem, occasionally made use of it. For all we know, he could have been a Jewish Christian who lived in any city of the empire where the dominant language was Greek.

Around A.D. 96 the letter was quoted by Clement of Rome. Can we say how much earlier than this it was written? Much of it consists of a discussion of the Jewish sacrificial system, and the light it throws upon the sacrifice of Christ. On the face of it, this should make it easy to tell whether the author wrote before or after A.D. 70, when the temple in Jerusalem was destroyed and the Jewish sacrificial system came to an end. But even this clue leads nowhere. The author had an academic mind. If he wished to know the details of the work of the priests in Jerusalem, he did not for a moment consider the ritual which was performed in his own day in the temple there: he simply went to his library and consulted the Law of Moses, which laid down the pattern of priestly service which still regulated all that was done in Herod's temple. The actual continuance of this ritual in his own day seems to have held not the smallest interest for him (in this respect he was a typical Jew of the Dispersion). Even if he was writing shortly after it came to an abrupt end with the fall of Jerusalem, it is quite possible that he would not have referred to the fact. We can draw no conclusions from his silence. He drew the entire inspiration for his argument from his study of the Old Testament. From the narrative in the Book of Exodus he gained his overpowering sense of the seriousness and awesomeness of the presence of God; and out of the detailed regulations in the Law of Moses concerning the arrangement of the sanctuary, and the office and function of the high priest, he developed his doctrine—the most systematic and suggestive in the New Testament—of *Christ divine and human.*

Christ divine and human

1. 1 **When in former times God spoke to our forefathers.** The opening
paragraph is a carefully composed piece of Greek. The details of its style and
vocabulary show that the author was by no means merely a Jew who happened to write in Greek, but a man well educated in Greek culture. Nevertheless, he took for granted in his readers a number of distinctively Jewish
presuppositions. The most fundamental of these was an understanding of
world history entirely conditioned by the Old Testament: at a certain time
in the past, God had revealed himself to men by means of the Law given to
Moses on Sinai. This Law, which was the unique possession of the Jewish
people, guaranteed to them a significant rôle in history. It gave them a
detailed moral and religious code by which to regulate their lives; and it
contained the promise of a glorious destiny for those who observed it. The
perfect keeping or "fulfilment" of this Law was the state of affairs for the
2 sake of which the world was created, the **final age** towards which all history
was tending.

But the empirical facts of history and human psychology made it impossible to think of this Law in isolation. The Jewish people down the centuries had failed to observe it; and the individual Jew was well aware that it demanded of him a standard of moral and ritual correctness to which he could not easily aspire. He needed some indication of how the divine imperatives of the historic Law of Moses could be accommodated to the actual circumstances of a Jew living many centuries later. He looked, in short, for God's guidance on the way the Law was to be observed, and on the sense in which it could still be understood as giving the clue to the history of mankind and the meaning of the universe.

Such guidance had in fact been given. God had not been silent since the
time of Moses. It was true that people differed about the way in which God
had spoken. The Pharisees, for example, believed that God himself inspired
that learned tradition of interpreting Scripture which they practised themselves; in Alexandria, on the other hand, it was through the insight of Greek
philosophy that thoughtful Jews sought to discern the contemporary meaning
of their ancient Law. But on one aspect of the question they were mostly
agreed. There had been a period in Jewish history (roughly, from the
establishment of the monarchy to the return from exile, the tenth to the sixth
centuries B.C.) when the divine guidance had been clothed in a particularly
1 challenging form. God spoke **through the prophets** who, by the oracles
they uttered, and by the example of their lives, demonstrated the kind of
religion and the kind of morality which the Law was intended to evoke.

It is to this stage in God's dealings with his people that the writer refers in his opening words. After the Law itself, the prophets had represented the most powerful and important phase in God's revelation. But it had taken place (all would agree) **in fragmentary and varied fashion.** Nobody could claim that it had been final and exhaustive. By contrast, Christians could now point to a revelation which, though it by no means superseded the original Law of Moses (for this too was the authentic word of God), gave a new and decisive turn to the relationship between man and God, and showed for the first time the true meaning of much in Scripture which had previously been indeterminate or obscure. Old truths could now be seen in a new light.

This the final age. The present age was at some time to give place to a 2
more glorious future age—this was the usual Jewish way of looking at history. But the coming of Christ seemed to Christians to be an event of such a decisive kind that they could only think it marked the transition between the two ages. They must now stand at least at the threshold of **the final age.** For there was no longer anything partial or fragmentary in the revelation of Christ. The Son was **heir to the whole universe.** Until you know who the heir is to be, you cannot understand why the father shapes the inheritance as he does; but as soon as the heir is known, you can see the purpose of each detail of what he is to inherit. Now that we know who is to be **heir** to the universe we can, for the first time, understand the purpose of the universe itself, a purpose which has in fact been there from the beginning, since it was **through** Christ—that is to say, with reference to him as to the guiding principle of creation—that God **created all orders of existence.**

To be so completely involved in the nature of all created things, this Son
must be almost indistinguishable from God himself—and the writer uses a
metaphor of light and a metaphor from the minting of coins to express this 3
near-identity. Yet he was distinct: he **brought about the purgation of sins,** a highly individual act, which this writer will go on to explain in terms of the function of a priest; and at a definite moment in time **he took his seat at the right hand of Majesty on high**—a clear allusion to the first verse of Psalm 110, a verse which this writer, along with the early church as a whole, regarded as an inspired description of the destiny which Jesus fulfilled after his resurrection from the dead: "The Lord said unto my Lord, 'Sit at my right hand until I make thy enemies thy footstool'".

One point in this sketch of the destiny and status of Christ is taken up for
special treatment: **raised as far above the angels, as the title he has** 4
inherited is superior to theirs. Why is Christ's superiority to the angels so important? We can only suppose that among the readers of this letter were some who were inclined to place angels too high on the scale of heavenly beings, and who failed to see that Christ was far superior to all such intermediaries between man and God. We know that in some sections of Judaism people went so far as to worship angels and had to be rebuked for it by the orthodox; and such people, when they became Christians, may have been

tempted to think of Christ as just "another angel". Alternatively, it was an accepted doctrine among Pharisaic Jews that God might send 'an angel or spirit' (Acts 23.9) in order to reveal or to endorse a new interpretation of Scripture; and it may have been suggested that the particular revelation which Christians had received, having been given to them by one, Jesus, who was probably an angel, was only one of the many such fragmentary revelations which pious men had received since the close of the period of the prophets. Whatever the reason, the writer now devotes the first part of his argument to proving that Christ is immeasurably superior to any angel.

5 **God never said.** All Jewish scholars took it for granted that the whole of the Old Testament was inspired, and that any individual passage, whatever its original context, could be regarded as an authentic utterance of God through the Holy Spirit. Among Greek-speaking Jews, the version used was almost always the Septuagint, that is, the Greek translation of the Hebrew text which had been made in Alexandria in the third century B.C. This translation was not regarded as in any way less inspired or authoritative than the original Hebrew. It was believed to have been made under divine guidance, and every syllable of it was revered as a vehicle of the word of God. Interpreters therefore felt fully justified in concentrating on minute points of the Greek text, and in using the same techniques of interpretation as were used on the Hebrew text by scholars in Palestine. When this writer expounds his own deeply serious and original understanding of the nature of Christ by means of what seems to us a highly artificial approach to Scripture, he is only following a method widely accepted among his Jewish contemporaries.

5 **God never said to any angel, 'Thou art my Son'.** This is the pattern of the following argument. Words spoken to angels are compared with words spoken to the Son, and the difference between them shows the inherent superiority of the Son. This procedure was quite straightforward so far as angels were concerned: there were a number of texts explicitly about angels. But what about the Son, the Christ? This was more difficult; for the Old Testament writers did not directly foretell the Christ whom Christians worshipped; they merely used language—sometimes about God, sometimes about particular persons known to them—which later generations came to regard as prophetic of a Messiah who was still to come in the future, and which Christians now saw to be completely fulfilled and explained by the person of Jesus Christ. It is to such passages as these that the writer appeals. His readers must have been already accustomed to reading these texts as prophecies about the Messiah, even if they had not yet taken the further step of applying them to Jesus Christ. Without this clue, they could hardly have followed the argument.

'Thou art my Son; today I have begotten thee' (Psalm 2.7). The words are echoed in the gospel account of Jesus' baptism, and the whole psalm is one of those which seemed to the early church to have been most startlingly fulfilled by Jesus. The fact that it was originally addressed to an actual king of Israel was not important: its real meaning was now finally disclosed by Christ.

'I will be father to him, and he shall be my son' (2 Samuel 7.14). This was part of God's promise to King David, transmitted by the prophet Nathan. On the face of it, the promise was no more than a metaphor: God intended to show particular favour to one of David's immediate descendants. But we know (from the Dead Sea Scrolls) that at least one Jewish sect had no hesitation in reading the text as a prophecy about the "son of David" whom the Jewish race still awaited, the Messiah, the Christ. This writer evidently assumed that his readers were used to taking it in the same way.

'Let all the angels of God pay him homage' (Psalm 97.7). In the 6
original Hebrew, this verse reads "Bow down, all gods, before him"—the poem is about the absolute supremacy of God compared with the worthless idols of the pagans. In the Greek version, the Septuagint translators, bothered perhaps by the implication that there exist such things as other "gods", rephrased the verse in the form given here. But in both versions it is God himself whom angels (or gods) must worship—there is nothing whatever about the Son. To see the force of the argument here, we have to read on. Verse 11 of the same psalm runs (in the Greek), "Light dawns for the righteous". This was regarded in many Jewish circles as almost a technical expression for the coming of the Messiah. Therefore (so the argument must have run) if the end of the psalm was about the Messiah, so were the earlier verses. **'Let all the angels of God pay him homage'** was a prophecy about Christ. If so, there could be no question about Christ's superiority to the angels.

Of the angels he says—and the verse quoted (Psalm 104.4) needs no 7
commentary. **But of the Son**—and another psalm-text follows (45.6–7) that 8
was again, like Psalm 2, originally addressed to an actual king. This was court poetry: the king was literally praised to the skies, so much so that it appears he was actually given the terrific title "God".[a] But the kings of Israel had never lived up to this high vocation; and these words of Scripture were therefore believed to refer to a figure of the future. Who this figure was is
given away by the last line of the quotation. **'By anointing'**—who was 9
anointed? Why, the Messiah, the Christ (which literally means The Anointed One). Christ, therefore, was given the highest title of all: God.

'By thee, Lord, were earth's foundations laid of old' (Psalm 10
102.25–7). This, to us, is the most puzzling of the series. The original psalm speaks of God the creator—the context and the language leave no possible doubt about this. But for Christians, the word "Lord" was ambiguous. God

[a] Whether this is really so has been uncertain almost since the psalm was written. Ultimately, it is a question of punctuation (and there was no punctuation to speak of before the time of Christ). A different punctuation yields the meaning given in the NEB footnote.

was Lord, but so was Jesus Christ. There is slight evidence to be found in small details of the Septuagint translation of the psalm that this part of it was already, in the century or so before Christ, being interpreted as a prophecy about the coming Messiah. If so, it is a little easier to understand how the Christians felt able to take the "Lord" of these verses as referring to Christ instead of to God the creator. This, at any rate, must have been the interpretation held in common between this writer and his readers. On the basis of this interpretation, he could use the quotation to prove the superiority of Christ to the angels.

13 **'Sit at my right hand until I make thy enemies thy footstool'**
(Psalm 110.1). There was no doubt in the minds of Christians that this
referred to Christ. Had not Jesus himself used it of the Messiah (Mark
12.35–7)? And did it not explain where Christ had gone to be after the resurrection? With this quotation, already alluded to in verse 3 above, the series
of proof texts is rounded off. They all show (given a certain method of
interpretation) the decisive superiority of Christ. The angels, by comparison,
14 are **but ministrant spirits**—this follows from Psalm 104 already quoted;
and possibly the experiences of the earliest Christians, such as those described in the first chapters of Acts, caused the writer to add that these angels
are **sent out to serve, for the sake of those who are to inherit salvation.**
2. 1 **Thus we are bound to pay all the more heed.** It is characteristic of this
author frequently to bring his argument round to a point where it bears
directly upon the way of life of his readers. Angels, it has been shown, are far
inferior to Christ. But there was a **word spoken through angels**, which
was none other than the Law of Moses itself (a tradition, later than the Old
Testament, held it to have been transmitted to Moses by means of angels).
2 This was a law which had to be obeyed: any **transgression or disobedience**
met with due retribution. How much more binding, therefore, was a word
3 **announced through the lips of the Lord himself**?—a word of **deliver-**
ance, certainly, but still to be obeyed with all the submission due to a divine
command. Of course, it could be said that the angels, through whom the
original law was spoken, were also witnesses to it: this gave it high authority.
4 But here again the Gospel was not at all inferior: to it too **God added his**
testimony through the remarkable events which marked the early years of
the Christian church.

But it was not sufficient to demonstrate the superiority of Christ to all
powers under God. This Christ was also the Jesus who suffered and died on
earth. The two aspects are held together in a quotation from another psalm
6 (Psalm 8.4–6). **'What is man, that thou rememberest him?'** The psalm
is in praise of the dignity given by God to man: this is its clear meaning. But
to our author it was open to question whether a passage of Scripture meant
only what it appeared to mean on the surface. Any curious inconsistency in
the language could be regarded as a clue which might lead to discovering a

deeper meaning underneath. And so here: '**Thou didst put all things in** 7
subjection beneath his feet'. If by "man" were meant human beings in
general, this would be simply untrue. **In fact we do not yet see all things** 9
in subjection to man. Therefore a particular "man", or "son of man",
must be meant. Who was this? The psalm offered a further clue: it was
someone who was '**for a short while lower than the angels**' (the original 7
probably meant "a little lower", but **for a short while lower** was a possible
translation). This sounds a hard riddle—but not for Christians. **In Jesus. . .** 9
we do see one who both had his moment of suffering and death (**lower**
than the angels) and then went on to be **crowned now with glory and**
honour at the right hand of God; since his tasting of death took place, not
by way of a tragedy or a defeat, but **by God's gracious will.** [a]

Jesus, then, was superior to the angels; yet there was a period when he was **lower** than they, a period which involved suffering and death. This much has been proved from Scripture. But it has still to be shown what was the meaning and purpose of this suffering. The clue was that he should **stand for us all.** The image that is now to be elaborated, and which will give the key to this part of Jesus' work, is the image of a priest.

To perform the function of a priest at the temple in Jerusalem did not demand any qualities of character or spirituality: it was only necessary to be a member of the appropriate family, and to be without any physical deformity. The purpose of the priesthood was to perform all the rites connected with the sacrifices in the temple. This the priests did on behalf of the people as a whole, and in order to do it they underwent ablutions and rites of cleansing, so that, when they performed their ritual duties, they would be ritually pure, or "perfect".

If Jesus was to be likened to such a priest, he must be shown to have
fulfilled similar conditions. First, he must have been able to represent others,
to **stand for us all.** This he could do only if he had as much solidarity with
the people whom he represented as the Jewish priestly families had with the
rest of the Jewish race. It was axiomatic that a **consecrating priest and** 11
those whom he consecrates are all of one stock. Did Jesus, a being 'far
above the angels', have this solidarity with men? He did; and this is proved
again by some quotations from Scripture. The force of these quotations
depended on knowing the Christian interpretation of them. The first, '**I will** 12
proclaim thy name to my brothers' (Psalm 22.22), is from a psalm which
was actually quoted by Jesus on the cross, and contained many exact
prophecies of the passion. No Christian could doubt that the speaker in the
whole of the psalm was Christ. Therefore the psalm proved that Christ had

[a] The variant, "apart from God", is found in some manuscripts. It may have been hard for some copyists to accept that the crucifixion happened by God's gracious will, and this would explain the change. Yet "apart from God" also makes good sense. Christ went to his death deliberately, of his own personal will, even if it was in fact God's will that he should die.

human **brothers.** In much the same way, several of the verses in the eighth
chapter of Isaiah seemed to contain clear allusions to the Christ who was to
come ("Emmanuel", "the rock of stumbling"). Therefore, if verses 17 and
13 18 of that same chapter included the words 'I will wait for the Lord . . . **I will
keep my trust fixed on him . . . Here am I, and the children whom
God has given me'**, it could be inferred that Christ was the speaker, that
his relationship with God was based, like that of any man, on **trust,** and that
his relationship with other men was as close as that of **children** in the same
family. All this showed that his solidarity with men was at least as great as
that of a priest with his people.

Secondly, Jesus must have been made ritually pure or **perfect.** Was he so
10 prepared? He was—not by any ritual act, but **through sufferings,** an idea
which breaks out of the conventional priest-imagery altogether. No such
experience was demanded of the Jewish priest, indeed rather the opposite.
The difference can be seen most clearly in the case of the high priest on the
annual Day of Atonement. For a week before this day, the high priest had to
isolate himself from all social contacts lest any chance meeting should make
him ritually "unclean". He had to be, so far as possible, totally insensitive
to personal or family ties, so that no private concerns should interfere with
his performance of the great ritual act upon which, once a year, the whole
Jewish people depended for its sense of the continuing favour of God. Jesus'
priesthood was totally different. Instead of being dispassionate and aloof, he
17 was **merciful and faithful.** His solidarity with his brothers involved
entering into the darkest corners of their experience; he was not just their
10 priest, he was also their **leader who delivers them,** by treading the path of
14 human life and death, and so breaking **the power of him who had death
at his command, that is, the devil** (this is the author's one major excursion
into the mythological manner of speech which is exemplified in Romans
6.12–19). His solidarity with men meant far more than being able to stand
17, 18 **before God** on their behalf: it meant that he could **help those who are
meeting their test now,** up to, and even through, the moment of death. It
was true, his function could be defined like that of the high priest, as being
17 **to expiate the sins of the people.** But the means by which he did this
were such as to give new content altogether to the concept of priesthood.

3. 1 This high priest was **faithful**—a new idea, and one that plays an important part in the letter. For an illustration of what this means, the reader is referred to a passage in Numbers (12.7–8), where God is speaking of Moses: "Not so my servant Moses: he is faithful in my whole household. I will speak to him mouth to mouth." But here the passage is quoted in indirect speech, which makes the pronouns look ambiguous: "Not so his servant Moses: he was faithful in his whole household. He would speak to him mouth to mouth." Quoted thus, "faithful in his household" might be misunderstood to mean that Moses was faithful in his own household; so the

writer has first to dispose of this possible misunderstanding. Every house
(or household: the Greek word is the same) has its owner, and "his house"
could certainly mean "the owner's house", i.e. (in this case) "Moses'
house". But it is also true that **every house has its founder.** "His house" 4
can therefore mean "the founder's house", and since **the founder of all is**
God, "his house" in this case must mean God's house, **God's household** 2
(which is how the NEB translation renders it in the first place; but the Greek
has the slightly ambiguous "his household", and it is essential to know this
in order to follow the argument of verse 4).

This little misunderstanding disposed of, it is possible to use Moses'
"faithfulness in God's household" **as a** pointer to the nature of Jesus'
faithfulness. Jesus of course was superior to Moses, both as the founder of a
house is superior to its owner, and also as **a son** is superior to **a servitor.** 6, 5
But Jesus also has a household (**we are that household of his**), and this 6
household is the setting, so to speak, in which he exercises his faithfulness,
just as God's household was the setting in which Moses exercised his own
(lesser) faithfulness. This gives some idea (though more about this will
follow) of the sense in which Jesus, the High Priest, is **faithful.**

Therefore. In the Greek, the connection is emphatic: Christ is faithful; 7
we have become Christ's partners (this follows from what has been said 14
about his solidarity with us); **therefore** we must not be **faithless.** Characteristically, the writer turns the argument into a moral one; and he marks
the transition by means of a long quotation from Psalm 95. The second line 7–11
of this yields an immediate moral lesson: '**do not grow stubborn**'. But the 8
bearing of the rest of it on Christian belief and conduct depends, again, on a
detailed and technical process of interpretation.

Who, I ask, were those who heard and rebelled? It was essential to 16
fix exactly who was referred to in each of the verses of the quotation before
the passage could be interpreted. It was obvious enough that those **who . . .**
rebelled were the whole of the desert generation, whose various "rebellions"
are described in the Book of Exodus. But to whom, then, were the verses
addressed? This was a more difficult question, and could be answered only
when the whole passage was considered. The key was in the last words:
'**they shall never enter my rest**'. This implied, surely, that someone else 11
would. The obvious candidates were the very next generation, those whom
Joshua had brought into the promised land (which was often described by
the same word, **rest**). But the psalm under consideration implied that the **4.** 8
"rest" still had not been entered when the psalm was written, and the psalm
was spoken **through the lips of David after many long years,** that is, 7
some centuries after the time of Joshua. **The rest referred to,** therefore, 3
must have meant something other than the historical possession of the promised land. What it meant could be shown from another passage of Scripture,

4 '**God rested from all his work on the seventh day**' (Genesis 2.2). It
might be thought that this referred only to God's own "rest" which he had
3, 5 been enjoying **ever since the world was created.** But the words, '**They
shall never enter my rest**', showed that this "rest" did not belong only to
9 God, but was also a future reality intended as a kind of **sabbath rest** for
the people of God. The psalm, therefore, was addressed to the future
inheritors of this "rest". The option to enter it was still open.

It only remained to ask, what were the qualifications for entering? This could be answered from the psalm itself. It was said of the desert generation,

3. 10 **'Their hearts are for ever astray;**
They would not discern my ways'.

19 In other words, **we perceive that it was unbelief which prevented their
entering.** The opposite, belief (or faith, the same word), was the particular
attribute of those who believe in Christ, who are partners with the faithful
high priest. This faith would guarantee their entering so long as they held
4. 11 fast to it, and did not **fall by following this evil example of unbelief.**
Once again, the writer brings his argument round to a point of direct moral
exhortation.

12 **For the word of God is alive and active.** The word, in this brief poem,
12–13 may be taken to embrace the whole of the divine revelation: the original Law
given to Moses, the sporadic guidance given by the prophets, and the
definitive revelation given in the Son. As such, it is of the strongest moral
force and penetration. Any kind of failure to conform to it is still as serious
as it ever was.

14 **Since therefore we have a great high priest.** Once a year the Jewish high priest **passed through** the outer sanctuary which any priest could enter, on through the curtain beyond it, and into the Holy of Holies itself. This "passing through" was the great moment of his priesthood, it was the act for which the high priesthood existed. The high priest of Christians has
similarly **passed through**—but further still, **through the heavens,** to the
15 throne of God himself. Yet he is still in contact with men, **because of his
likeness to us.** Both by the measure of his sympathy with those who are
tested every way, and also by his perfect access to God, he fulfils all the
16 functions of an ideal priesthood. **Let us therefore boldly approach the
throne of our gracious God.**

The shadow and the real

It has been shown that the category of the actual Jewish high priest was far
transcended by Jesus; but there were still one or two more points of correspondence to be brought out. The high priest was **taken from among men** 5. 1
and appointed their representative before God. That is to say, every
candidate for the high-priesthood had to belong to a particular family, and
was duly **appointed**: no one could seize the office for himself. Now it was
known that Jesus did not belong to the high-priestly family (which traced its
descent back to **Aaron**). Did he therefore seize the high-priesthood, instead 4
of being **called by God,** as Aaron and his descendants were? On the contrary, the two psalm verses which form the basis of the whole argument 5, 6
(2.7 and 110.4) show that he became both Son and priest by direct appointment from God. Secondly, the high priest was very much a man like other
men, **beset by weakness,** and therefore bringing his prayers and sacrifices 2
before God out of the same situation as that of those whom he represented.
Was there anything to correspond to this in Jesus' life? The writer tells us
that there was. **In the days of his earthly life he offered up prayers and** 7
petitions, with loud cries and tears, to God. The image is still that of a
priest, "offering up" his prayers for himself and others, but it is filled out
here with what seems to be a historical reminiscence. The gospels do not
report any episode in Jesus' life which exactly fits this description. Jesus
prays in a general way in the manner of a high priest in John 17, and in Luke
22.32 he refers to a prayer which he has offered for one of his disciples. But
the only place where an actual struggle in prayer is described is in the episode
at Gethsemane. There, we can well imagine that he prayed **with loud cries**
and tears; and there are a number of points of contact between Luke's
account of this episode (22.39–46) and these verses in Hebrews. But the
natural meaning of the statement in Hebrews that **his prayer was heard** is
that, being threatened with death, Jesus prayed, and was delivered in answer
to his prayer. In Gethsemane, on the other hand, his prayer was not answered
in this sense: he was not delivered "from death". It is only by assuming
that the prayer alluded to here was a prayer to be delivered, not from
death itself, but from the consequences of death (as the NEB suggests
by taking "from death" to mean **from the grave**) that the two descriptions
can be made to match. Possibly some other episode was in the writer's
mind, which happens not to be recorded in the gospels; or possibly he
was thinking of Jesus' **humble submission** on the cross, and of the
prayers which Jesus **offered up** just before his death. But this uncertainty
does not affect the point being made: **he learned obedience in the** 8
school of suffering, a jingle of Greek words which had become something
of a cliché, but which throws light on an apparently paradoxical point

made earlier: it was not by ritual ablutions, but by suffering, that Jesus was
9 **perfected** as a priest.

11 **About Melchizedek we have much to say.** This mysterious figure who suddenly appears and as suddenly disappears in the narrative of Genesis 14, provoked much speculation among Jewish scholars, and the writer is to devote a substantial section of his work to him. But first, he breaks off in order to ask whether his readers are any longer fit for a lesson of this kind. The deeper meaning of Scripture (so at least it soon came to be held among Christian scholars in Alexandria) could only be known to those who had advanced some distance in the knowledge of God. Mere beginners had to
12 remain at the level of the literal meaning of the text, **the ABC of God's**
oracles. [a] Jewish boys, for example, were not expected to understand and
obey God's Law until they were 13 years old. Under that age, they could not
14 be expected **to discriminate between good and evil.** Were the readers of
this letter in danger of reverting to a similar moral infancy?

6. 1 **We ought not to be laying over again the foundations.** It is tantalizing to try to discover from this passage exactly what the foundations consisted of, and how new converts to Christianity were given their first instruction. The difficulty is that we do not know whether these particular converts were Jews or Gentiles before they became Christians. If they were Jews, then the
foundations were presumably distinctive Christian doctrines—but although
2 **laying-on-of-hands** sounds sufficiently like the rite by which Christians received the Holy Spirit, **cleansing rites** is a curious way to describe Christian baptism. If they were Gentiles, then much of the initial instruction must have been indistinguishable from the teaching that was given to any Gentile interested in Judaism—and nothing in the list is so obviously Christian that it could not also describe a course in the elements of the Jewish faith. To either faith, most of these things were fundamental. But the writer is concerned for a **maturity** which took all this for granted and pressed on to a higher stage of knowledge.

It is not that his readers have never reached this stage. On the contrary,
4, 5 having **once been enlightened,** there is a risk they may **have fallen away.** How could you tell whether in fact a Christian had **fallen away**? Not, usually, by anything he said about his own faith or lack of faith (for this kind of introspective reflection on religious belief was less common in antiquity than it is now), but by his moral conduct, which might suddenly seem not to square with the beliefs he professed, or even (the real danger which seems to be constantly at the back of the writer's mind) by the fact that he had actually repudiated his allegiance to the church. In the early days of the church, such

[*a*] This phrase, like much in this section, is ambiguous. It might equally well mean the elementary truths of the Christian gospel. But it is very similar to a phrase used by Paul of the Old Testament (Romans 3.2), and at this date the basic document of the Christian faith, as of the Jewish faith, was still the Old Testament.

lapses posed a problem. Christians were people who, having been baptized,
had been forgiven their sins and had entered a new life. It made no sense for
them to start sinning again. Yet Christians did sin, and it was hard to know
what to do about it. After their baptism, was further repentance and forgiveness possible? Should the offender be expelled from the church, or should he
be pleaded with until he repented? Different answers to these questions
are given by different New Testament writers, and it was some time before
it became generally accepted that the pattern of inevitably sinning and
repeatedly being forgiven is inherent in the Christian life, even after baptism.
It was perhaps natural that the question should have presented itself somewhat differently in the early years of Christianity, when the end of the world
was expected to come within most people's lifetime, and when the church
was thought of as the community of those who would automatically enter the
promised new age. At any rate, this writer adopts (both here and elsewhere
in the letter) an attitude that is more stringent than is to be found anywhere
else in the New Testament: **it is impossible to bring them again to** 6
repentance. Moreover, he does not seem to feel it necessary to argue the
point. He merely supports it with an illustration somewhat in the manner of
a parable of Jesus. Earth that does not bear a crop is **worthless and God's** 8
curse hangs over it.

The warning is a strong one; and the writer mitigates it a little by pointing
to the good things in his readers' record. (All this is very general: it could be
a recollection of specific acts on the part of certain Christians, or it could be
merely a general compliment such as any writer might have paid to any
church. It helps us very little as we try to picture the Christians to whom the
letter was written.) It is a matter of, **through faith and patience . . .** 12
inheriting the promises; and this leads on to a more positive kind of
encouragement. Can God's promise be relied on? Obviously, yes. But to
make assurance doubly sure, **God . . . guaranteed it by an oath** (the words 17
of the oath are from Genesis 22.16–17). Admittedly it was an unusual oath, 14
for it did not say what it was that it was being sworn by. But this was because
there is nothing greater than God, and therefore nothing other than himself
by which God can swear. **Here, then, are two irrevocable acts**—both a 18
promise and an oath[a]—**in which God could not possibly play us false.**
This hope is **like an anchor**—an obvious enough metaphor; but it becomes 19
startling when it is combined with another that is drawn from the image of
the high priest on the Day of Atonement entering the Most Holy Place. **It**— 20
the anchor, the priest, Jesus himself—**enters in through the veil.**

This Melchizedek. The relevant verses of Genesis are as follows: "After 7. 1
Abram's return from the rout of Kedorlaomer and his confederate kings . . .

[a] This is an unusual rendering. The Greek could also mean, "two unalterable things", i.e. God's oath, and that by which God swore, God himself.

Melchizedek King of Salem brought out food and wine. He was priest of God Most High. And he blessed him . . . And Abram gave him a tithe of all the spoil." (14.17–20.) Nothing is known about Melchizedek beyond what is stated in these verses, which seem to preserve some recollection of an ancient pre-Israelite king of "Salem" (probably Jerusalem), whose religion included the worship of a "God most high" (and so was not too far removed from that of the Jews) and who was permitted by custom to be both king and priest. This enigmatic figure gave Jewish interpreters some trouble. It was almost an axiom of many Old Testament writers that the same person could not be both priest and king: the priesthood went back to Aaron himself, and was instituted in the Law of Moses; but the kingship was a later creation, and the king must not presume to claim the rights of a priest. The appearance of this Melchizedek, who was both a king and "priest of God Most High", was therefore something of an embarrassment to them. To this writer, on the
other hand, he was a godsend. He wished to present Jesus under the image of
14 a priest. But Jesus did not come from a priestly family (**our Lord is sprung**
from Judah, a tribe to which Moses made no reference in speaking of priests), and he was also in some sense a king. How could he be a priest? The answer was given by the precedent of Melchizedek.

The point is made by means of a careful commentary on the text in Genesis. First, what could be gathered about Melchizedek himself?

(i) He was certainly a king: this was proved, both by his name (which, in
2 Hebrew, suggested '**king of righteousness**'), and by his title, **king of**
Salem (which was also suggestive, since *salem* was a form of the word *shalom*, meaning peace).

(ii) Nothing is said anywhere in the Old Testament about his ancestors, his birth or his death. At least, that is how we would put it. But to interpreters accustomed to seeing significance in the smallest details of the sacred text, another principle suggested itself: there must have been some reason for not
mentioning these things, and the reason could only be that they did not
3 exist. By this principle, Melchizedek had **no father, no mother, no**
lineage; his years have no beginning, his life no end. In short, a unique and exceptional king-priest, whose function in the Old Testament narrative could now at last be understood: he pointed forward to Christ (**He is like the Son of God**).

Secondly, two actions of Melchizedek are recorded: he received a tithe from Abraham, and he gave Abraham his blessing. Each of these was significant.

(i) The priests and the Levites—all those who served the sanctuary in Jerusalem—were entitled to receive a tenth part of all agricultural produce.
This tithe was laid down in the Law: it was a right which certain of the
5 **descendants of Abraham** had over the rest. Melchizedek was certainly not
one of these privileged descendants; yet he apparently had the right to tithe Abraham (who represented the entire Jewish people that was to come, in-

cluding the Levites). This demonstrated a greatness far exceeding that of any regular priest.

(ii) A similar greatness was proved by the blessing he gave Abraham; for
beyond all dispute the lesser is always blessed by the greater. Mel- 7
chizedek was greater than Abraham himself! Moreover, as we have seen,
Genesis says nothing about Melchizedek's death; from this it could be
inferred (by the same principle as before) that **Scripture affirms him to be** 8
alive. This put him in a different class altogether from **men who must die.**

This commentary on the text of Genesis had proved that being a king, and
having no priestly ancestry, did not disqualify Melchizedek from being a
priest of exceptional dignity. But could this be applied to Jesus? Would
there ever be such a priest again? The answer was given by the one other
text in the Old Testament which mentions Melchizedek (Psalm 110.4): 17

"The Lord has sworn and will not go back on his word,
'Thou art a priest for ever, in the succession of Melchizedek'."

This text had apparently been spoken by the Holy Spirit to some successor
of King David, long after the promulgation of the Law of Moses. It proved,
therefore, that a priest of this exceptional type was to be expected in the
future. In other words, the precedent of Melchizedek was valid for Jesus.
But this text had another implication: the new priesthood would supersede
the existing one. And, since the existing Levitical priesthood was an integral
part of the Law of Moses, this could only mean that the Law itself was to be
superseded. In fact, however, this was bound to happen anyway: for the Law
(like the Levitical priesthood) **brought nothing to perfection.** 18

Two more phrases in the psalm are significant. (i) **'A priest for ever'**— 17
that is, no longer a series of men succeeding one after the other to the office
according to **a system of earth-bound rules,** but a perpetual priest, with 16
all that the phrase implies in terms of effectual representation of men before
God: Jesus **is always living to plead on their behalf.** (ii) **'The Lord has** 25, 21
sworn'. An oath was given to the successor of Melchizedek, but not **when**
those others were made priests: another proof of the superiority of Jesus'
priesthood and therefore of the new **covenant** of which he is **the guarantor.** 22

Such a high priest does indeed fit our condition—and here it is not a 26
question of Jesus' "qualifications" (these—his suffering, his solidarity with
human beings—can now be taken for granted), but of his present status. Just
as the high priest in Jerusalem was separated from all possible contact with
"sinners" for a week before he was called on to perform the great ritual of
the Day of Atonement, [a] so Jesus is **separated**—in the sense that his place is

[a] There was a daily ritual at which the ordinary priests offered sacrifices for the people, and an annual ritual at which the high priest offered sacrifices **first for his own sins and then for those of the people** (verse 27). Both these rituals seem to be in mind when the writer says that Jesus **has no need to offer sacrifices daily.**

now in heaven, far away from all that might profane the presence of God.
This might seem a fatal separation from those whom Jesus' priesthood was
27 intended to save. But no, Jesus **offered up himself**, his great act was a
28 priestly act, making him **perfect now for ever**, and setting him in heaven as
the representative of mankind.

8. 1 **Now this is my main point.** The difficulty in the idea that one person
could be both priest and king has been resolved by means of the figure of
Melchizedek. But a further difficulty remains. The same psalm which contains the reference to Melchizedek begins with the words, "Sit at my right hand until I make thy enemies thy footstool" (110.1). Since all the verses of the psalm must be addressed to the same person, it follows that Christ, the Melchizedek-type priest-king, is now in heaven, with a rôle that looks more kingly than priestly. In what sense is he still a priest? Priests surely belong to the sanctuary on earth (whether the Tent of the Book of Exodus, or the
actual temple in Jerusalem which was its successor). But Jesus cannot belong
4 there—**there are already priests who offer the gifts which the Law
prescribes**—and in any case his place is now in heaven. He is certainly still
3 a priest: for the condition of priesthood, that one **must have**[a] **something
to offer,** was certainly fulfilled in his case. What kind of "sanctuary" can there possibly be in heaven for this new high priest to be able to exercise his priesthood there?

The answer is in another verse of Exodus (25.40). On Sinai, Moses had
been given detailed instructions about the construction and furnishing of the
Tent in which God was to be worshipped. The instructions ended with
5 these words: **'See to it that you make everything according to the
pattern shown you on the mountain'.** The literal-minded reader would take these words at their face value: Moses was to follow carefully the instructions he had just been given. But Jewish scholars, brooding on the word 'pattern', found a great deal more in it than that. Moses, they felt, must have been "shown the pattern" of an ideal sanctuary, of which the earthly sanctuary which he actually constructed was no more than an imperfect copy. Scholars whose background was Greek and philosophical imagined this ideal sanctuary to be a kind of microcosm of the universe, and in the actual details of Moses' Tent (and subsequently of the temple) they found symbols of the great principles underlying the physical world; while those whose culture was more narrowly Jewish assumed that the ideal sanctuary was one which God would institute on earth in the new age, the present sanctuary being but a kind of rough draft of that which was to come.

This writer comes somewhere between the two. The terms he uses to

[*a*] Or "must have had". The Greek is ambiguous, and does not make it clear whether the writer is thinking of the offering of himself which he once made on the cross, or the offering of prayers he still makes as a priest.

describe the relationship between the earthly and the heavenly sanctuaries
are terms borrowed from Greek philosophy—**copy and shadow**, symbol 5
and reality (9.24), shadow and no true image (10.1): this kind of distinction
between appearance and reality goes back ultimately to Plato. But the realities he describes in these terms are not philosophical at all. For him, the
heavenly sanctuary is not an abstraction, but a real sanctuary with a real
priesthood. And this answers the question how Jesus can be thought of as a
"priest" in heaven.

Before this answer is worked out in detail, there is one more point to be
made. It has been said already that a new priesthood involved a new code of
law (for the old Law included the regulations for the old priesthood). But the
Law was only an expression of the "covenant" made between God and men.
It followed that the new priesthood of Christ implied a new covenant, to
replace the old—and this too could be confirmed by Scripture. Jeremiah had 8–12
spoken of a '**new covenant**' (31.31–4). This phrase alone proved that the
original covenant was never intended to last for ever.

Like the temple in Jerusalem, and indeed like many ancient sanctuaries in
the Middle East, the sacred Tent described in Exodus consisted essentially
of two rooms, separated by a curtain (**the second curtain**). The outer room **9.** 3
—**the Holy Place**—was entered directly (again through a curtain) from the 2
courtyard outside. The inner room—**the Most Holy Place**—had no outside 3
door, and could be entered only from the outer room. The outer room contained the articles necessary for the regular services during the year (including
the golden altar of incense: it is strange that this writer seems to think of 4
this altar in the inner room—unless he is speaking of it as a necessary adjunct
of the inner room, though not actually inside it). The contents of the inner
room were more mysterious, for they were seldom seen. Originally they were
trophies of Israel's earliest history. By the time of the Jerusalem temple they
had mostly disappeared.

On these we cannot now enlarge. For many Jewish thinkers, each of 5
these objects had a deeper meaning. But this writer has no time for such
detailed interpretations. Instead, he concentrates upon just one feature of the
material sanctuary, its arrangement in the form of an outer room and an 1
inner room, a first tent and a second tent. It is this which he describes as
symbolic, pointing to the present time. The Most Holy Place, where 9
God was believed especially to dwell, was separated from the faithful by an
outer sanctuary given over to the ritual of **offerings and sacrifices.** But this
ritual brought people no closer to the presence of God: it concerned only
ritual cleansing and **outward ordinances.** It constituted, in effect, a per- 10
manent barrier between the inner sanctuary and the people: so long as the
old priestly system remained in force, it merely kept people at a distance from
God. If it was intended that there should be freer access to the divine pres-

8 ence, then it could be said that the **way into the sanctuary** remained still
unrevealed. If at all, it was trodden only by the high priest, once a year,
after sacrifices that were incapable of effecting lasting reconciliation with God.
11 **But now Christ has come.** The question from which this discussion
started was, in what way could Christ be thought of as a "high priest" in
heaven? The answer has been suggested by an appraisal of the existing
temple-arrangements (described rather as they are laid down in the Book of
Exodus than as they may actually have existed at Jerusalem in the writer's
9 own day). These arrangements were defective—they could not **give the**
worshipper inward perfection. But then, they were only a copy of the
'pattern' shown to Moses on the mountain (8.5). This meant that they
pointed forward to a new and better kind of sanctuary altogether. This was
the sanctuary where Christ would exercise his high-priesthood; and the fact
that this new high priest had now come showed that the old sanctuary was
obsolete, and the new one in operation.

Yet there were important analogies between the old and the new. The old
functioned by means of animal sacrifices. In the new, Christ sacrificed him-
12 self: **the blood of his sacrifice is his own blood.** A priest sacrificing
himself is of course a paradoxical idea—it almost tears apart the whole priest-
metaphor. But there are three ways in which this paradox can be shown to
be significant.

(i) The sacrifices of the old sanctuary were not by any means useless: they
13 did at least restore **external purity (the sprinkled ashes of a heifer** were
the means of cleansing what was thought to be the most serious "impurity"
of all, that caused by contact with a dead body). Christ's sacrifice was clearly
something far more potent than this. If animal sacrifices cleansed the body,
14 Christ's sacrifice must **cleanse our conscience.**

15 (ii) Some sacrifice was necessary for the **new covenant.** This argument
(like that of Paul in Galatians 3.15–18) depends on a kind of pun. The
covenant made by God with his people was rendered into Greek by the
word which usually meant "will" or **testament.** This made it appear as
17 though the covenant, like a will, could only come into force **after a death.**
Now of course God does not die. But the original covenant was in fact sealed
by death—the death of sacrifices: to this extent it was like a "testament". In
which case the new covenant must also be established by a death. Here was
another way of expressing the meaning of the death of Christ.

(iii) The sacrifices which took place in the earthly sanctuary were not
23 meaningless: they presupposed **better sacrifices** in the sanctuary in heaven,
they **cleanse the copies of heavenly things.** The heavenly sanctuary,
therefore, is still a real sanctuary with a real sacrifice; but that sacrifice, the
sacrifice of Christ himself, is able to do all that the high priest's sacrifice
could never do.

27 The old realities remain: **it is the lot of men to die once, and after**

death comes judgement. But that which before made death and judgement
to be feared—**men's sins**—has now been cancelled by Christ's offering (just 28
as acts causing ritual impurity were cancelled by the offerings of the Levitical
priests); and the judgement itself will be transformed, for it will be the
moment when Christ himself **will appear a second time . . . to bring
salvation to those who are watching for him.**

For the Law contains but a shadow, and no true image. The argument 10. 1
so far has not borne directly upon the Law: it has merely suggested that a
new kind of priesthood itself implies a new Law and the end of the old. But
now it can be shown that the Law, of its own nature, belongs to the world of
shadows, not of reality (to make use once again of the familiar philosophical
distinction). The Law **provides for the same sacrifices year after year.**
What clearer proof could there be that these sacrifices are useless? Each time
they are offered, prayers of confession are said in which, year after year, the
same sins **are brought to mind,** as if the sacrifice of the previous year had 3
had no effect at all. Clearly this could not be the ultimate state of things—
and the proof, once again, is found in Scripture itself: Psalm 40.6–8.

At his coming into the world, he says. Who says? This enigmatic 5
introduction belongs, once again, to the kind of private language which scholars like this writer, whether Jewish or Christian, felt able to use when interpreting Scripture. Psalm 40 was originally the utterance of a pious worshipper who had been mercifully delivered from misfortune, and who saw that his sense of gratitude to God must be expressed in the form of something more personal and demanding than the prescribed ritual of sacrifices and offerings. But to those accustomed to find deeper meanings in Scripture the psalm was full of suggestive phrases. '**Here am I . . . I have come**'. Who had come? Why, he who "was to come", the Messiah. But the Messiah had not yet come. Therefore the psalm must be a prophecy, it contained the words he would say when he finally did come. All this chain of reasoning is presupposed in the highly condensed phrase, **at his coming into the world, he says.**

(Traces of this reasoning are to be seen in the Septuagint translation of
the psalm into Greek, which is the version always used by this writer. The
original Hebrew version was probably intended to mean: "as it is written
for me (to do) in the scroll (the Law), I have come to do thy will". But by
rendering this, '**as it is written of me**', the Septuagint translators implicitly 7
identified the speaker with one whose coming was foretold in Scripture. They
seem also to have frankly misunderstood the sentence they rendered '**But thou** 5
hast prepared a body for me'. The original meant something like, "thou
hast given me attentive ears". However, this mistranslation yielded a valuable
point to the Christian interpreter.)

Many of the prophetic writings protested against undue importance being

attached to the ritual of sacrifice—Jesus himself quoted Hosea 6.6, 'I require
mercy, not sacrifice' (Matthew 9.13). But taken as an authoritative utterance
of him "who was to come into the world", these verses of Psalm 40 were
more than a protest: they actually "annulled" the former Law with its
system of sacrifices, and established a new dispensation, under which the
10 one sacrifice was **the offering of the body of Jesus Christ.** In that offering,
the will of God took the form of an obedient self-sacrifice; and the effects
of this sacrifice were such that by it we too **have been consecrated.**

This offering, unlike its shadowy counterparts in the old system, was
once and for all. This finally removes the difficulty of conceiving of a
single person being both priest and king at the same time. A priest's place is
at the altar, a king's is on his throne: how could Christ be both? The answer
12 is now quite simple. First, **Christ offered for all time one sacrifice for
sins**; then, **he took his seat at the right hand of God.** The two acts
followed each other, and we do not have to try to imagine them taking place
simultaneously. Now at last we know how to put together the two verses of
Psalm 110 which have been running right through the letter: "Sit at my
right hand, until I make thy enemies thy footstool" and "Thou art a priest
for ever, in the succession of Melchizedek".

15 **Here we have also the testimony of the Holy Spirit.** One more text
ties up the argument (Jeremiah 31.33–4). This text has already been quoted
17 to prove that there will be a new covenant (8.7–13). It ends, **'and their sins
and wicked deeds I will remember no more at all'.** The promise of a
new covenant has now been fulfilled, in which case this last line must have
been fulfilled also. It follows that the old system of making sacrificial
18 **offerings for sin** no longer has any function.

Take a final glance at the old system. What you see in the outer room are the
arrangements for ritual cleansing by sprinkled blood and water ablutions.
Beyond that is the curtain through which, once a year, the high priest enters
the inner sanctuary. All this is now superseded: the sprinkling is in the heart,
22 the ablutions are the **pure water** of baptism (presumably), and the way
20, 19 **through the curtain** has been opened by the **blood of Jesus.**[a] **So let us
22 make our approach in sincerity of heart**—the metaphor is still that of
the sanctuary, but here the writer characteristically changes his tone of
voice: no longer doctrinal teaching, but moral exhortation. And without so
much as a pause for breath, he comes straight to a particular point where his
25 readers had been at fault—**staying away from our meetings.** There is
probably more to this than mere slovenliness in attendance at church.

[a] It is not clear, in this rush of metaphor, whether it is the way or the curtain which is described as the **flesh** of Jesus. In solidarity with him, we either burst through the limitations of flesh to the life beyond (in which case his flesh is the curtain); or else, united with him, we come to be where he now is (in which case his flesh is the way).

Staying away suggests (in the Greek, if not in the English) a failure to stand firm with fellow-Christians in times of adversity—and a sketch of such times follows a few lines further on. This was serious, not least in view of the **Day drawing near**: for, while those within the church would undoubtedly be saved, those outside must expect the full severity of God's judgement.

The seriousness of this judgement is a fixed point in both the Jewish and
the Christian faith. **A fierce fire which will consume God's enemies** is a 27
typical Jewish phrase for it, but both the idea and the imagery were taken
over unchanged into Christianity. For the Christian, as for the Jew, **a**
terrifying expectation of judgement remains if he falls away from his
faith or his obedience. The author of this letter differs from other New
Testament writers only in the greater stringency with which he regards any
such apostasy or moral laxity in Christians. **If we wilfully persist in sin . . .** 26
no sacrifice for sins remains. In other parts of the New Testament a
distinction is made between (for instance) the sin against the Holy Spirit and
all other sins (Mark 3.29), or between sins that are and are not deadly (1
John 5.16–17). Does this writer attach the same condemnation to all sins?
His language, here and elsewhere, suggests that he does. Nevertheless, the
sins which he actually mentions here are of a particular kind. They consist of
having **trampled under foot the Son of God, profaned the blood of the** 29
covenant . . . and affronted God's gracious Spirit. We might today be
inclined to give these words a psychological meaning, and to interpret them
as a kind of secret and interior disloyalty to the faith. But they were probably
originally intended in a much more exterior sense. Under conditions of
persecution (such as are about to be described) one had to be visibly either in
the church or out of it; and if one stood away from it, one would be forced to
renounce it altogether in words that amounted to blasphemy and sacrilege.
For such apostasy, God remained as severe a judge as he had ever been under
the old system of the Law of Moses. There were plenty of texts in the Old
Testament to underline this severity. Two are quoted here, from Deutero- 30
nomy 32.35–6.[a]

Remember the days gone by. The Christian churches did not escape 32
persecution for long—the description here is presumably typical of what they
suffered. Under persecution, Christians needed **endurance** and **faith.** 36, 39
Faith is one of the themes of the letter, and is about to receive fuller treatment: it is a deep and many-sided attitude. But the easiest way for an early
Christian writer to encourage it was to point to the imminence (as it was then
believed) of the end of the world and of the vindication of the righteous. This
suggested a text which was in fact often appealed to in Jewish circles to
encourage those who were tempted to doubt the promises of God (Habakkuk 37–8

[a] The first is quoted also in Romans 12.19—for a rather different purpose. In each case the quotation is something of a paraphrase of the original: perhaps it had become almost a proverb.

2.3–4). This text also contained some suggestive words about faith—words which (somewhat differently understood) played an important part in the reasoning of Paul (see above on Romans 1.17).

A call to faith

11. 1 **And what is faith?** For us, the word has become very technical. We feel forced to ask, faith in what? And the answer will usually be expressed in specifically religious terms—faith in God, faith in Christ. So, indeed, the word is used by Paul: for him, it takes on its full meaning only when it denotes the relationship which should exist between a Christian and Christ. But for this writer, the word is much more general. He does not reflect on all the different kinds or objects of "faith" which are open to man. He reduces the question to a choice between clear alternatives. One alternative is thoroughgoing materialism: you base your life entirely on conditions as you see them here and now; you do not concern yourself with any metaphysical realities lying behind appearances, nor with any expectations of a future state of affairs better than the present; everything you do is a calculated response to the tangible world around you. The other alternative is simply faith: for the sake of **hopes,** which you believe to have **substance,** and of **realities** you **do not see,** but of which you are **certain,** you live a totally different kind of life from that of the materialist. Because you believe that there will be some ultimate, other-worldly reward, you are prepared to endure exile, suffering, even death. Your decisions are no longer made on the basis of material advantage in this world; you set your heart on realities which are known only to faith.

In some circles these basic questions presented themselves rather differently. The alternative to materialism was not always thought of as faith in a future heaven or an underlying reality. The most widely followed philosophy of the time—Stoicism—taught a complete detachment from worldly things, and offered the philosopher an inner peace and security far superior to anything that could be gained from the comfort and enjoyment of the senses. Here, the antithesis was not between materialism and faith, but between materialism and detachment. Similarly, Paul's experiences as a Christian led him to discover that the reason for present sufferings was not merely the promised reward in heaven, but rather the sense of intimacy with Christ, the inner transformation of the person, which was effected by the suffering itself. Here again, the issue was not so much between materialism and faith, as between the values of this world and the values of an experience which embraced both this world and the next.

But for less sophisticated Jewish thinkers the choice was quite simple.

Either the visible world is all that is, or else God exists, God makes demands on men, and God rewards the men who are faithful to his demands. There were only the two alternatives, materialism or faith. Not that faith was an easy alternative. It was all very well to say that God rewards those who are faithful to his demands: was this borne out by the facts? The Old Testament was full of stories of men and women who had made great sacrifices rather than disobey the will of God; and every Jew felt inspired by the example of the heroes and martyrs of the Maccabean period, who had steadfastly faced torture and death rather than abandon the religion of their forefathers. But had these people received their vindication and their reward? The answer was no—not yet. The alternative to materialism was the persistent faith of the Jewish people that the promises made by God would ultimately be fulfilled, that God would pronounce his universal judgement and vindicate his elect, and that the men of faith would then receive their rightful reward. The present was the time when this faith was tested: the time of ultimate vindication and reward still lay in the future.

Christians inherited the same view of the alternative between material rewards and faith. If they were being persecuted, they would have the same temptation to opt for the easier way out. But no, they must have "endurance" and "faith", and the classic examples of this faith were all those great figures in the history of the Jewish race who had unswervingly adhered to the will of God in the face of all the discouragements that materialistic common sense
or ruthless enemies could devise. **It is for their faith that the men of old** 2
stand on record. But there was a difference. For the Jewish heroes the
reward lay still in the future: **they did not enter upon the promised** 39
inheritance. But for Christians the period of reward had come so close that it had already partly begun. They still needed faith—that is the point of this whole section—but whereas previous generations could only see a distant prospect of reward, Christians stood on the very threshold.

Accordingly, this writer did not have to look for his examples of faith in the fresh annals of the Christian church. He could point to any of the great figures of the past who had consistently obeyed the commands of God rather than the promptings of expediency. He could search the Old Testament for them; or he could read a lesson from that more recent period when Jewish history seemed to have attained its summit of nobility and glory, the Maccabean resistance to the paganizing oppression of Antiochus Epiphanes. In point of fact, he probably did not need to work out his own list of heroes. Jewish writers were fond of singing the praises of the great names of their history, and he could borrow from the work of others. This list happens to be far the longest example in the New Testament (the letter of James, in a somewhat similar passage (2.21–6), mentions only Abraham and Rahab), but it is less ambitious than that, for example, in Ecclesiasticus 44–50.

Open the Bible at the beginning, and you find these men of faith on almost

every page. As the story progresses, their faith becomes more explicit: it is a positive response to a particular command or promise of God. But at the beginning it is simply the recognition that behind the created world stands God. The first words of the whole Bible are a statement of this faith: "In the beginning God created heaven and earth". This is the ultimate and basic faith held in common by all those **men of old** who are about to be mentioned and by their successors down to the present day. To put it in slightly more
3 philosophical terms: **By faith we perceive that the universe was fashioned by the word of God, so that the visible came forth from the invisible.**

4 The list begins with **Abel.** "The Lord received Abel and his gift with favour; but Cain and his gift he did not receive" (Genesis 4.4–5). Genesis gives no explanation of God's preference; a certain arbitrariness seemed characteristic of God's dealings with men at this early stage in human history. But later Jewish thinkers were not content to leave it at that. There must have been something about Abel and his offering which made God accept Abel without accepting Cain. Our author assumes without question that this something was faith: **through faith his goodness was attested.** In the Genesis narrative, God subsequently says to Cain, "Your brother's blood that has been shed is crying out to me from the ground". This may explain the choice of words here: **through faith he continued to speak after his death.**

"Having walked with God, Enoch was seen no more, because God had taken him away" (Genesis 5.24). This enigmatic verse gave rise to much legend and speculation. Evidently Enoch, like Elijah, did not die. Why was he spared the normal fate of men? Genesis said only that he "walked with
5 God"—or **pleased God,** as it appeared in the Greek version always used by this writer. What exceptional character or quality was there here to explain such a prodigious exception to the general rule? Differing answers were given; but our author again takes it for granted that it was faith, for **without faith it is impossible to please him.**

7 **Noah**: again there has been a shift of emphasis. In Genesis (6–9) Noah represents the means by which God allowed the world of living things to survive the punishment that was to be inflicted on the entire human race. But later thinkers began to reflect on the response of Noah himself. He had been given the apparently absurd command to build a huge ship in the middle of dry land. That he did so was proof of amazing faith in God's command. And as it turned out, he was right and **the whole world** was wrong.

8 **Abraham**: it was traditional to think of Abraham as the subject of a whole series of "tests", by means of which God made him the perfect progenitor of the Jewish race. The last and most demanding of these was the command
17, 18 to sacrifice Isaac (Genesis 22), **of whom he had been told, 'Through the line of Isaac your descendants shall be traced'** (Gen. 21.12). This was

the supreme test of faith: Abraham passed it, and was rewarded with
promises of a unique destiny. Besides this, our author mentions two more of
Abraham's acts of faith: his obedience when called to leave his native country 8
(Genesis 12.1, 4), and his acceptance of a nomadic existence. This acceptance, 9
which characterized not only Abraham but the whole of his family and his
people, was a clear sign of living by faith and not by self-interest. **If their** 15
hearts had been in the country they had left, they could have found
opportunity to return. But in fact they were sustained by God's promise
of a land of their own in the future. Indeed our author goes further and
spiritualizes this promise: ultimately their faith was not even in something as
tangible as that part of the earth's surface they were to inherit, but in the
remote vision of a perfect society, **the city with firm foundations, whose** 10
architect and builder is God.

(One more Abraham example is given: both **Sarah** and Abraham were 11
past the age for begetting and bearing children when Isaac was born;
nevertheless God promised them a tremendous posterity (**numerous as the** 12
stars etc., Genesis 22.17 and elsewhere). In point of fact, Genesis records
that both Abraham and Sarah laughed at this promise instead of believing it
(17.17; 18.12). But what Jewish thinkers remembered was that their race
was the result of a supernatural promise made to Abraham and Sarah, who
in the end accepted their responsibility, and thereby gave another example
of faith.)

Isaac: the interest of Isaac's two blessings in Genesis 27 depends upon 20
the deception that had been played upon him by Jacob: this is the dramatic
climax of the scene. But it could still be said that Isaac could not have given
his blessing at all unless he had believed in his vision of the future.

Jacob: the same goes for Jacob's blessing of **each of Joseph's sons** 21
(Genesis 48). (The detail that he was **leaning on the top of his staff** is an
echo of a different incident (Genesis 47.31), where in fact the word **staff** is a
misreading by the Septuagint translators: the correct Hebrew word means
"bed".)

Joseph: every man wishes to be buried in the place where his own people 22
live. Joseph's desire to be buried in Palestine (Genesis 50.24–5) was a clear
proof of his faith in God's promise to Abraham that his people would one
day return there.

Moses' **parents**: in the Hebrew version of Exodus only his mother is 23
credited with defying the king's edict (2.1–3). But in the Greek version of
the Septuagint, and in subsequent tradition, both parents take the credit.

Moses is cited for three acts of faith. It is true that he soon abandoned his 24
status as **the son of Pharaoh's daughter**, in order to take up the cause of
the Hebrews; but according to Exodus, the immediate cause of this was the
fear of being caught after killing an Egyptian (2.11–15). However, this writer
takes a longer view. Ultimately, Moses preferred to share the still obscure

25 destiny of his own people **rather than enjoy the transient pleasures of**
26 **sin**; and this was a typical decision of faith. The choice was a sharp one: **the**
treasures of Egypt were proverbial; **the stigma that rests on God's**
Anointed had now been sensationally exemplified in the crucifixion of Jesus
Christ, but was an idea with a long history: Psalm 69.9 and Psalm 89.51
were both passages which recognized that a righteous man—even one whom
God has chosen and **Anointed**—might have to bear a stigma; and the destiny
27 which lay before Moses could be regarded in the same light. Seeing **the**
invisible God is of course a contradiction in terms. Moses, it is true, was
spoken to by God "face to face" (Exodus 33.11); but the Bible hardly concedes that he could actually have seen God—at most he could have seen God's "back", but certainly not his "face" (Ex. 33.23). God is invisible—this was an axiom to Jewish saints and Greek philosophers alike. None of Moses' experiences fundamentally altered the fact that he acted on the evidence, not of sight, but of faith.

Three more episodes from the saga of national history are adduced as
28, 29 examples of faith: the Passover, the crossing of the Red Sea, and the fall of
30 Jericho. Last in the list of individuals—and somewhat surprisingly—comes
31 **Rahab.** The story of Rahab is in Joshua 2. She was a prostitute and a heathen
—two serious disqualifications for appearing in a list of the honourable figures of Jewish history. But again, later speculation fastened upon the fact that she, alone of **the unbelievers** of that time, had made a true confession of faith: "the Lord your God is God in heaven above and on earth below" (Joshua 2.11). Rahab became the prototype of all who turned to the Jewish faith from paganism; she began to appear in the ancestry of King David himself (Matthew 1.5), and to be revered as the mother of prophets and priests. Her popularity in Jewish tradition sufficiently explains her appearance in the series here.

32 **The stories of Gideon, Barak, Samson, and Jephthah** are in the Book
of Judges; those of **David and Samuel** in 1–2 Samuel. In the earliest period
their exploits were mainly in the form of achievements against overwhelming
33 odds: **through faith they overthrew kingdoms . . . their weakness was**
turned to strength. (An allusion to two notable miracles, one of Elijah (1
Kings 17), one of Elisha (2 Kings 4), seems to be slipped in with the words,
35 **women received back their dead raised to life.**) Later, faith was more
characteristically shown in the resistance of the pious to all threats and
tortures which might have made them abandon their ancestral faith. The
literature of this later period began with the Book of Daniel: Daniel himself
33 **muzzled ravening lions** (Daniel 6), Shadrach, Meshach and Abednego
quenched the fury of fire (Daniel 3). In the Maccabean wars, there were countless heroes of the faith whose fortitude became enshrined in history and legend, and who soon inspired a whole literature of martyrdom. Even the great prophets of the Old Testament began to be credited with feats of

endurance and martyrs' deaths (like Isaiah, who, legend said, was **sawn in** 37
two). With so many examples to choose from, the writer could do no more
than summarize: **Time is too short . . . to tell the stories.** 32

The author of one of the psalms, appalled and bewildered by the fact that so often the wicked appear to flourish, had been tempted to abandon his faith. A sudden thought brought him up short:

> "Yet had I let myself go on talking in this fashion,
> I should have betrayed the family of God." (Psalm 73.15)

The fact that so many people in the past had chosen God, not the world—
—that is, had shown faith—was one of the strongest supports an individual
could have in making the same choice himself. All these figures of the past
had "witnessed" to the decision of faith being the right one. And so now:
with all these witnesses to faith around us like a cloud, we Christians 12. 1
should not falter for a moment in choosing the way of faith rather than the
way of compromise.

But then the metaphor changes. The "witnesses" become a dense crowd
of spectators seated round a stadium, while the athlete throws off **every**
encumbrance and stands straining at the starting line, inspired by the
example of one who has run the race with surpassing **resolution: Jesus, on** 2
whom faith depends from start to finish. The **witnesses** have not yet 1
received the prize, their faith has not yet been vindicated. But Jesus inspires,
not merely as one of those who had the resolution to make the choice of faith,
but as one whose faith has now been triumphantly justified. It was for the
sake of what **lay ahead**[a]—which could be grasped only by faith and hope—
that he took the bitter alternative and **endured the cross, making light of**
its disgrace. But (unlike all previous witnesses) he has already taken
possession of what lay ahead. To quote Psalm 110.1 again, he **has taken his**
seat at the right hand of the throne of God.

For Christ, the cost of this steadfast and uncompromising faith in the
face of **such opposition from sinners** was death. The Christians' **struggle** 3, 4
against sin—which probably means both the struggle against their persecutors and the struggle within themselves against the impulse to betray their faith—is not yet so serious: **you have not yet resisted to the point of shedding your blood.** Their endurance has not yet had to be anything out of the ordinary. There are places in the New Testament where the problem of suffering is tackled in a deep and original way: Christian suffering is a sharing of Christ's suffering, a renewal of the inner man, an element of true discipleship. But this author is content to use an old and familiar argument

[*a*] The Greek of this sentence can be taken in two ways. Some will feel that Christ can hardly be said to have suffered **for the sake of the joy that lay ahead of him,** and that the rendering given in the NEB footnote is preferable.

to explain the relatively mild suffering which his readers have undergone.
7 **Can anyone be a son, who is not disciplined by his father?** But we are
5–6 God's sons: therefore we must expect discipline. The argument makes use of
proverbial Hebrew wisdom (Proverbs 3.11–12) and Greek moralizing
11 (**Discipline, no doubt, is never pleasant**); it ends with some vivid biblical
12, 13 imagery (Isaiah 35.3 and elsewhere) and allows us perhaps a glimpse of a
typical situation within the church. There was a **disabled limb**—temptation
had already been at least partly yielded to by some; but this did not concern
15 only individuals. A single renegade could be a **bitter, noxious weed**
growing up to poison the whole (the phrase is taken from Deuteronomy
29.18). The health and peace of the whole church was at stake.

No middle position was possible. To abandon the church was to relapse
into paganism and to join the society of Gentiles which was proverbially
16 (at least in Jewish eyes) **immoral** and **worldly-minded** (a word which, in
the original, includes the idea of profanity and idolatry). Where, in the Bible,
could one find an example of such a lapse? The figure of Esau suggested
17 itself. **He sold his birthright** (Genesis 25.31–4)—which was tantamount
to renouncing his membership of the people of God—and later tradition
painted him in the colours of the most persistent immorality. Moreover, **he**
found no way open for second thoughts, his apostasy was irrevocable;
in this too he could serve as a warning to the Christian apostate, for whom
likewise (as this writer has already twice insisted) there was no possibility of
repentance.

18 **Remember where you stand.** The fact of God is to be taken seriously. No
matter who you are—Jew or Christian—you stand exposed to the majesty
29 of his presence and the clarity of his justice. **Our God is a devouring fire,**
and there is no escaping from him. How then is man to stand at all in this
terrifying neighbourhood of the divine? Hear first the answer of Judaism.
God gave his Law on Sinai: obey that, and you need not fear God's judgement.
But this hardly removes the terror. Read the description of that
tremendous law-giving (Exodus 19.12–13,16; Deuteronomy 4.11): even
21 Moses said, **'I shudder with fear'** (Deuteronomy 9.19).

22 Hear now the answer of Christianity. Instead of Sinai, **Mount Zion and**
the city of the living God, heavenly Jerusalem, a symbol of the ultimate
and glorious society which God will one day bring into being. God is no
longer an awesome presence, keeping all creatures at their distance by the
blazing fire of his sovereignty. He now holds court in heaven, surrounded
22 first by **myriads of angels** (his dedicated worshippers since the beginning of
23 time), then by **the first-born citizens of heaven** (again, perhaps,
angelic beings, or else the great Old Testament recipients of God's first
promises to men), then by **the spirits of good men made perfect** (for
some, in more recent times, had lived in such perfect obedience that they

could surely hold up their heads before God). But is this heavenly and holy
society, this great symphony of consecrated worship, any more accessible to
the ordinary human being than the **blazing fire of Sinai**? Yes, because of 18
Jesus, the mediator of a new covenant. Sinai, and the Law proclaimed 24
there, has been superseded. Jesus has been killed, and his blood, instead of
crying for vengeance like Abel's, is a means (like the **sprinkled blood** of
the old ritual) of making others pure and admitting them to the presence
of God.

Is this really so? Does this ideal state of affairs exist? Scripture gives no
explicit promise of it, but there are many texts which prove it by implication.
Haggai 2.6 is one: **'Yet once again I will shake not earth alone, but** 26
the heavens also'. If heaven and earth—the whole world of appearance—can
be "shaken" in a final cosmic catastrophe, there must be some reality which
endures, a **kingdom** which is **unshakable**: it only makes sense to talk of 28
transience if somewhere there is permanence to measure it by.

Let us therefore give thanks to God—yes, but God is still to be taken
seriously, he is to be worshipped **with reverence and awe.** The old covenant may have gone, but there is a new one; the old Law may have been
superseded but there is still **One who speaks from heaven.** We may have 25
new privileges in the face of the realities of majesty and judgement, but those
realities still remain. It is still awesomely true, as it was when Moses spoke
the words (Deuteronomy 4.24), that **our God is a devouring fire.** 29

Never cease to love your fellow-Christians. A series of more or less 13. 1
unconnected moral injunctions occurs towards the end of several New Testament letters. Those in this letter are not specifically Christian: they belong
to the common stock of the moral teaching of antiquity. **Remember to** 2
show hospitality. This was a virtue highly esteemed by both Jews and
Greeks, and there were stories in the literature of both which showed how
dangerous it might be to neglect it: in Genesis 18–19 Abraham and Lot
offered solicitous hospitality to their mysterious visitors, who did indeed
turn out to be angels; and in Homer it was a commonplace that a stranger
from over the mountains might always be a god in disguise. **Remember** 3
those in prison: again, this was a duty taken for granted in popular Stoic
ethics, and for much the same reasons as are given here; and it features in
the list of "acts of kindness" which Christians must do for each other in
Matthew 25.31–46. **Marriage is honourable.** Adultery and unnatural 4
affections were regarded by all Jews as among the most crying sins of the
pagan world: they never felt any doubt that **God's judgement will fall on**
fornicators and adulterers. Do not live for money: this again was a 5
philosophical ideal—**be content with what you have** is a phrase that owes
something to the Stoic principle of "self-sufficiency". It was also strongly
endorsed by Jesus on the grounds that God provides all that is needful. The 6

two quotations here make much the same point. The first is a paraphrase of a
7 passage like Joshua 1.5; the second is from Psalm 118.6. **Remember your leaders.** This again seems to have been one of the regular topics of Christian ethics. It occurs in similar contexts elsewhere (Galatians 6.6; 1 Thessalonians 5.12) and is developed further in verse 17 below.

8 **Jesus Christ is the same yesterday, today, and for ever.** This sounds like the kind of phrase that Christians must have used in church. It was perhaps more natural to make this affirmation about God: so, in Revelation (1.8), God is he 'who was and who is and who is to come'. Here it is boldly transferred to Jesus Christ, perhaps with the difference that **yesterday** means not "existing from eternity", but "he who was among us on earth such a short time ago".

9 The series of unconnected[a] injunctions continues. **Do not be swept off your course by all sorts of outlandish teachings.** Here we have no idea what the writer was attacking. **Outlandish teachings,** from the point of view of people steeped in Jewish and Christian traditions, must refer either to a fringe sect of Judaism or to some frankly pagan cult or philosophy; and **scruples about what we eat** must refer to a particular kind of abstinence[b] practised by such people. More we cannot say: though these "teachings" sound a little like movements which we hear of elsewhere in the New Testament (see above on 1 Timothy 4.3).

10 **Our altar.** The moral tone is suddenly supported by a piece of argument. During much of the letter, the writer has had in mind, as an image of Christ's sacrifice, the ritual of the Day of Atonement, performed once a year by the Jewish high priest in the Holy of Holies. Part of the ordinance of this ritual runs as follows (Leviticus 16.27): "The two sin-offerings, the bull and the goat, the blood of which was brought within the veil to make expiation in the sanctuary, shall be taken outside the camp and destroyed by fire. . . "
Here was another respect in which the old ritual foreshadowed the new
12 spiritual reality: like the sacrificial victims in that ceremony, **Jesus also suffered outside the gate.** It might seem more natural to say "outside the city" or "outside the walls", where Jesus was in fact crucified. But this writer is meditating all the time, not on the actual sacrifices as they took place in the temple at Jerusalem, but on the description of the ritual as it stands in the Law of Moses. That description presupposed a nomadic people, whose sanctuary was still a tent and whose dwelling was still an encampment; the

[a] The NEB implies that in this instance there is a connection by inserting the word so (which is not in the Greek). But there is little logical progression from verse 8 to verse 9, unless it is that, if Jesus Christ is unchanging, Christian doctrine must also be protected from **outlandish teachings.**

[b] This is the NEB interpretation. But the original Greek is still less precise. Literally, it means "from the grace of God, and not from things eaten". The exponents of these outlandish teachings could have been recommending, not abstinence, but eating a certain kind of food, or even consuming a certain kind of sacrifice.

temple and city of Jerusalem lay in the future. It was that original ritual
which Jesus fulfilled; and so this writer goes on, **Let us then go to him** 13
outside the camp. Indeed, the picture of those early worshippers living
under canvas, their possession of lands and cities still a promise for the
future, suggested another point of comparison: Christians too **have no** 14
permanent home, but we are seekers after the city which is to come.
Our Jerusalem is a heavenly one. The exhortation may be a perfectly general
one: to follow Christ, to share his **stigma,** and renounce attachment to 13
material things; but if in fact these Christians were Jews who were now
finding themselves excluded from the Jewish community to which they had
always belonged, there would be a sharper point in the words, **Let us then go to him outside the camp.**

It may be, indeed, that these Christians were under attack from non-Christian Jews, on the grounds that, in their new religion, they had no temple, no priesthood and no sacrifices. Their answer would have been, they had these things, only in a different sense from the Jews (and this answer would have been greatly strengthened by much of the argument of this letter): they had a definitive high priest in Jesus, they had a sanctuary, not in the world of appearances, but in the reality of heaven, and their sacrifices
were such as the prophets[a] had so often recommended, not living victims, 15
but praise, kindness and sharing one's possessions—**for such are the** 16
sacrifices which God approves. It could even be said that they had an
altar of another kind from that used by **the priests of the sacred tent.** On 10
the other hand, it is far from certain that these particular Christians were
under attack from the Jewish side, and the paragraph reads just as well as
an elaboration of the symbolism which the writer found in the biblical
description of the worship of the desert generation. To the sacrificial victims
slaughtered by those worshippers corresponds the **sacrifice of praise** of the
Christians; and in so far as it can be said that Christians have an **altar,** the
prototype is not the daily altar-sacrifice of the old rite (which the priests
were permitted to eat afterwards), but that one sacrifice in the year—on the
Day of Atonement—**from which the priests of the sacred tent have no**
right to eat, since the victims were carried outside to be burnt—a clear
symbol of Jesus, who also **suffered outside the gate.**[b] 12

Obey your leaders. Obedience within the church was another regular 17
topic in the group of moral exhortations which tended to be gathered at the
end of New Testament letters (compare 1 Corinthians 16.16; 1 Thessalonians 5.12; Romans 16.19). The tireless concern and sense of ultimate responsibility of Christian leaders comes vividly out of Paul's letters (compare especially 2 Corinthians 11.28; 1 Thessalonians 2.19–20).

[*a*] There is an echo here of Hosea 14.2 and Psalm 50.14 (a psalm which expresses a criticism of reliance on ritual sacrifices very much in the manner of the prophets).

[*b*] This is the interpretation implied by the NEB footnote.

18 **Pray for us.** These words are perfectly conventional, and bring us little closer to the personality of the author.

20 **May the God of peace.** Some kind of prayer, again, belongs to the end of such a letter. This one is strong and solemn: the **Amen** at the end of it was probably echoed by those who heard it read. It uses ideas that have been worked out earlier in the letter—**blood of the eternal covenant,** making **perfect**—but also introduces a new one—**the great Shepherd of the sheep**—which was perhaps already familiar to the readers: it occurs again in 1 Peter 5.4.

22 **I beg you, brothers.** These final verses are the only ones written in the style of a personal letter. They tell us nothing about the author, and very little about the time and place at which he wrote. Indeed they are so general that it would not have been difficult for a later editor to add them to the original treatise in order to give it the appearance of a letter, so that we cannot even be sure that the little they tell us is authentic. **Bear with this exhortation.** This reads like a conventional apology for length. But the word **exhortation** is somewhat technical: it often means a demonstration of the bearing of certain passages of Scripture on contemporary events (see above on Acts 13.15). This is exactly what the foregoing letter has consisted of. Doubtless it was intended, like other New Testament letters, to be read
during the worship of the church: perhaps it was not exactly what the
23 worshippers expected! **Our friend Timothy has been released.** There is a
famous Timothy in the New Testament, the friend of Paul. If this is the same one, it is news to us that he was ever in prison. But there may well have been other people called Timothy.

24 **Greetings to you from our Italian friends.** Again, this means nothing to us. But there is one frail link by which this letter can be attached to a known fact of history. Clement of Rome, writing to the church in Corinth in about the year A.D. 96, quoted the Letter to Hebrews. This makes it seem likely that the letter was written to Christians in Rome; in which case it would have been natural for the writer, wherever he was, to convey the greetings of Italian friends to their kinsmen.

A LETTER OF JAMES

From James. The name was a common one (it was the Greek equivalent of 1. 1
the Hebrew name Jacob), and there are at least five men who bear it in the New Testament alone. But this James writes with authority, and has apparently no need to explain who he is: his mere name is enough to command attention. Only one of the men called James in the New Testament held such a prominent position in the church: this was James, the brother of Jesus, who became the leader of the church in Jerusalem.

But can the letter really be from his hand? It is true that originally it owed its place in the New Testament to the belief that its author was indeed this James; but this belief was only adopted slowly by the church, and was frequently called into question. To many, the letter has always seemed to speak too little of Christ to be the work of one of the first Christian leaders; and the style, which uses a number of sophisticated Greek expressions, is one with which it is hard to credit a Jew brought up (as Jesus and presumably his brothers were) in Galilee. The writer was almost certainly a Jew himself; but his religious and social presuppositions are more characteristic of Jews outside Palestine than of the Judaism of Jerusalem. It is not impossible that the writer was Jesus' brother; but it is perhaps easier to imagine him as the leader of an almost exclusively Jewish community of Christians in some other city of the Roman empire, writing some time after the death of James the brother of the Lord.

The letter is addressed to **the Twelve Tribes dispersed throughout the world**; similarly 1 Peter is 'to those of God's scattered people who lodge for a while in Pontus, Galatia, Cappadocia, Asia, and Bithynia'. Both these phrases contain the word *diaspora* which, then as now, was a technical term for the Dispersion, that is, the Jewish people scattered outside Palestine. But it is clear from 1 Peter (and to a lesser extent from James) that the letters were intended, not for Jews as such, but for Christians. That is to say, the word *diaspora* is used metaphorically: the Christian church was the New Israel, the true successor of the historic Jewish nation. Therefore, just as it was possible to describe the church in terms of the legendary Twelve Tribes of Israel, so it was possible to think of its widely scattered members in terms of a new "dispersion", *diaspora.* Now the old *diaspora*—the Dispersion of the Jews—looked to Jerusalem as its spiritual centre, and received from it periodic exhortations to remain true to the ancestral faith and to observe the cycle of religious festivals according to a calendar that was still regulated there. These exhortations took the form of circular letters, emanating from Jerusalem and addressed to the Jewish people, either in certain areas (such as Egypt), or else throughout the world. Three such letters are in the

Apocrypha: the "Letter of Jeremiah" and the two letters prefixed to 2 Maccabees. Two of these (see especially 2 Macc. 1.1–5; 2.17–18) have a number of words and ideas in common with the opening of 1 Peter. It is quite possible that Jewish Christian leaders, moved by the Spirit to address their fellow-Christians at large, and aware of possessing a certain authority over the whole church, deliberately chose the form of a Jewish encyclical letter in order to convey their message to the new *diaspora*, the scattered Christian churches. Such a letter would have seemed to demand, as its author, someone of a status equivalent to that of the leader of the Jewish nation in Jerusalem. Either James or Peter would have been an obvious choice.

These letters, then, may be pseudonymous. But that is not to say that they were not written in good faith. The author of James may well have had means of knowing the kind of teaching which the real James would have given and, having an authoritative message for his fellow-Christians, would have found it natural to claim the authority of one of the great apostles of the past. James is among the most Jewish, and the least obviously Christian, of the writings of the New Testament. It has kept its place there because (whether or not it should be attributed to the apostle) it has been felt by most (though not all) Christians to be an authentic document of the life of some part of the Christian church during the first formative half-century or so of its existence.

Practical religion

2 **My brothers.** This paragraph is typical of the style and ethos of the whole
letter. There is no real progression of thought: one topic leads to another
quite casually, and sometimes the connection is suggested by no more than
4–5 a single word (the occurrence of **falls short** in two consecutive sentences is a
good example). The topics are for the most part commonplaces of Jewish
moral instruction, with an occasional phrase or illustration borrowed from a
2 more cosmopolitan society: that **trials** are good for the character, that
5 **wisdom** (in the Jewish sense of conformity to the will of God rather than
in any sophisticated philosophical sense) is given by God to those who
sincerely desire it, and that prayer must be full-hearted and unwavering, are
sentiments which can all be found in (for instance) Wisdom (11.9), Proverbs
6 (2.6) and Ecclesiasticus (1.28; 2.1–5), while the simile of a **heaving sea
ruffled by the wind** belongs to the common stock of Greek literary metaphors. Indeed, the teaching throughout would have seemed unexceptionable
to a wide section of Jewish society, and it has even been thought that the
"letter" was a Jewish writing, simply adapted to Christian use by the
1 addition of **the Lord Jesus Christ** (1.1; 2.1). Nevertheless, there are
certain phrases which sound more Christian than Jewish; there are several

almost unmistakable allusions to sayings of Jesus; and even in this paragraph, the teaching of Jesus himself on prayer is almost perceptible in the background (Mark 11.23–4; Matthew 7.7–11). The most likely explanation is that when Christianity took root among solidly Jewish communities the social and moral life of those communities continued very much unchanged: the traditional morality of the synagogue needed only slight adjustment to bring it into line with Christian principles. To such a community of Jewish Christians this writer belonged.

The brother in humble circumstances . . . the wealthy brother. 9–10
Evidently the church consisted of both; and evidently there was a tendency for worldly values to reassert themselves, and for the wealthy to receive respect on the basis of their social position. To oppose this tendency, the writer could draw upon a critique of such distinctions which he inherited from the Old Testament. In certain strands of Jewish religious thought, "poor" had become almost synonymous with pious, "rich" with ungodly and oppressive (see above on Matthew 5.3). True religion, according to this tradition, was preserved by the poor; and in a new age, God would make this apparent by "lifting up" the poor and humble, and "bringing low" the wealthy and proud. This reversal of ordinary social values (which was apparently part of Jesus' message) was earnestly believed in by Christians. The influence and allurement of riches naturally threatened to blur this insight; but reflection on the transitoriness of material possessions helped to keep it clear. Isaiah (40.6–7) had used the suddenness with which (in Palestine) spring vegetation can be turned brown by summer heat as a vivid illustration of the transitoriness of human life. The same metaphor would serve for riches.

Happy the man who remains steadfast under trial. This is a return 12
to the first topic of the letter (1.2–4). But the word for **trial** also meant
"temptation"; and this association of the two ideas led the writer to deal
with an excuse which people often made when they succumbed to temptation, **'I am being tempted by God'.** The idea was as old as Homer, and 13
expressed a fatalistic acquiescence in human limitations. In Jewish literature,
a good example of it is in Ecclesiasticus 15.11–12. But essentially, such
fatalism was alien both to Judaism and to Christianity. This writer here uses
an argument which is again a play upon words. The Greek for **untouched**
sounded like "untempted": everyone agreed that God was **untouched by**
evil; therefore God could have nothing to do with "temptation". The real
cause of temptation was **lust**, a psychological concept familiar to anyone who 14
knew something of popular Hellenistic philosophy.

Make no mistake. Exactly the same phrase is used by Paul in Galatians 16
(6.7) to introduce a proverb, and in 1 Corinthians (15.33) to introduce a popular saying quoted from the Greek comic poet Menander. Here, the words, "All giving is good and every gift perfect" make up an almost perfect line of Greek verse. It looks as if the writer is quoting part of a familiar

17 proverb and then, by taking the grammar in a slightly different way (**All
good giving instead of "All giving is good") and by adding the words
comes from above, adapting it to the Jewish aphorism that God is the
author of all good things. The word **above** was perhaps sufficient to bring
to mind a common Jewish notion of God, **Father of the lights of heaven**;
and this gave rise to the further thought that, unlike the heavenly bodies
which rise and set and go into eclipse, with God **there is no variation.**

That God (in various ways, such as through the Law) "declared the truth",
18 and that his people were **a kind of firstfruits**, were ideas that would have
been familiar to any Jew. But the particular combination of these ideas here
has an un-Jewish sound, whereas it perfectly expresses the Christian convictions that (i) God has declared **the truth** in the gospel, (ii) he has given
men new **birth** through baptism, (iii) that the church is **a kind of firstfruits** of humanity (Revelation 14.4). This is one of the verses where the
21 Christian tone seems unmistakable. The same goes for **the message planted
in your hearts, which can bring you salvation**, which can hardly mean
anything but the gospel, though it is embedded in a sequence of traditional
25 moral injunctions. The same probably also goes for **the perfect law, the
law that makes us free.** It is true that some Jewish thinkers (affected
perhaps by the prevalent philosophical notion that a true philosophy makes a
man free) regarded the Jewish Law as a means towards moral and spiritual
freedom; but most Jews were more conscious of their Law as a "yoke", and
it was with a sense of relief that Christians claimed that their own rule of life
made them free of it. But of course it did so only if it was taken seriously.
23 The case of **a man who listens to the message but never acts upon it** is
as old as morality itself, though it receives a particularly vivid illustration in
the Sermon on the Mount (Matthew 7.24–7).

26 **A man may think he is religious.** Most Jews would have agreed that
mere attendance at religious ceremonies was inadequate: serious concern for
27 charitable work (**to go to the help of orphans and widows in their
distress** was one of the most typical of Jewish "good works"), and an earnest
effort to adhere to one's own way of life uninfluenced by the contamination
of the secular world, were essential components of any true religion. Exactly
the same was true of Christianity.

2. 1 **You must never show snobbery.** This is too facile a translation. Snobbery is a matter of social behaviour; but the Greek word has a much more serious application. Primarily it suggests the favouritism and partiality shown by a bad judge in a law-court. If Christians showed this kind of partiality they were deliberately conforming themselves to a society where in fact the influence of the rich did subtly affect the course of justice and the settlement of disputes. They were assimilating themselves to the many who **judge by false standards.** This was a more serious matter than **snobbery.**

The basic argument against such behaviour was one that has been touched
on already (1.9–10). **Has not God chosen those who are poor?**—the 5
faith of the "poor" in the Old Testament, that they were the chosen of God, had now been decisively endorsed by Jesus. This made it unthinkable that the church should begin to reproduce the structure of secular society and allow special prestige and power to the rich. But there was also a more practical reason for resisting this tendency. **Are not the rich your oppressors?** 6
However desirable such people might appear as visitors and members of the congregation, they represented a class which (society being organized as it was) could constantly be seen in the rôle of plaintiffs in the law-courts, claiming against debtors, evicting tenants, suing for compensation, in short using its influence to further its own interests under the cloak of the law. In all such cases, the defendants were usually "the poor". Moreover, many of the rich might even have a grudge against Christianity as such, and seek to
pour contempt upon the Christians' conviction that they, as much as any 7
pious Jew, bore an **honoured name by which God** had **claimed** them. Such people had a class solidarity. Christians might welcome them into the church; but they must not welcome the social distinctions and injustices they represented.

It was against the whole Jewish tradition to select any particular commandment from Scripture and call it **the sovereign law.** It was an axiom of Jewish 8
interpreters that all individual laws were of equal weight. True, some laws were more general than others and could be regarded as basic principles which implied a whole series of particular laws; but this was a question of logical arrangement, not of a greater or lesser degree of importance attaching to the laws themselves. From the strict Jewish point of view, it was correct to regard **'Love your neighbour as yourself'** as a law which in fact summed up a great many other laws, but not to suggest that other laws were therefore less binding than this one. Jesus, we know, was prepared to discuss the academic question, 'which is the greatest commandment in the Law?' (Matthew 22.34–40) and to give an academic answer; and the church, following his example, continued to regard **'Love your neighbour as yourself'** as a summary of the whole Jewish Law. But to anyone untrained in this strict Jewish tradition, it seemed natural to take such a principle, not as a technical summary of the Jewish Law, but as a general moral rule which in fact replaced the detailed commandments of the Law of Moses. There are signs of this beginning to happen in Mark's account of Jesus' teaching on the subject (see above on Mark 12.28–34); but here, the process is clearly complete. The Christians had taken this single commandment from Scripture, and made it into what philosophers called **the sovereign law,** a universal moral principle which allowed them to dispense with the detailed ordinances of the Jewish legal code.

Up to a point this was excellent, and fully in line with Jesus' moral teach-

ing. But it also had the danger of breeding a certain moral insensitivity. Certain sins, which a Jew would avoid because they were explicitly forbidden in the Law, might be committed by Christians simply because they did not
9 realize they were sins. Such a sin was the partiality (**snobbery**) of which the
writer has been complaining. A good corrective was to take a fresh look at the detailed commandments in the Law, the same law from which in fact Christians had culled their general principle, "Love your neighbour as yourself" (Leviticus 19.18). A few verses earlier in Leviticus (19.15) came the sentence, "You shall not pervert justice, either by favouring the poor or by subservience to the great". The two laws came almost as close together as two of the Ten Commandments; no one would think of making any dis-
11 tinction of seriousness between **adultery** and **murder** (both were in theory
punishable by death); and even when the punishments were less severe, from the religious point of view a man was just as much a sinner whatever transgression he had committed. To break **one single point** of the law was equivalent to **breaking all of it**. This characteristically Jewish reverence for the Law in all its details had its dangers, and was justly criticized by Jesus. But there was a useful lesson to be learnt from it. "Loving one's
12 neighbour" was no excuse for "perverting justice". The Christian **law of**
freedom made no less extensive moral demands than the Jewish Law of Moses.

"Talking of judgement" (a modern idiom which exactly expresses the
13 connection between this verse and the last), it was as true in Christian as in
Jewish thinking that the man who shows mercy will receive mercy. To put this old truth in the form of a memorable epigram: **Mercy triumphs over judgement.**

That the Christian faith entailed an absolute duty to help one's fellows was a truth immediately grasped by the church; but precisely why the one followed from the other was not so obvious. There was no easy logical connection between the conviction that Jesus was the Christ and the duty to love and serve one's fellow-men; and different New Testament writers worked it out in different ways. For Paul, the key to the matter was the solidarity of Christians with Christ and with each other: Christians form a "body", and each member of the body shares the concerns and the burdens of all the other members. For the author of John's gospel the explanation lay in Jesus' love for his disciples which must necessarily be reflected in their love for each other. But these were somewhat sophisticated answers to the question. To anyone familiar with Jewish morality, a much simpler line of thought suggested itself. The Jews set great store by "good deeds", and Jewish thinkers had many arguments to show that good deeds were an essential part of the Jewish faith, and were what would principally save a man at the Last Judgement. Jesus himself took much of this attitude for granted. And it was not difficult to show that, if good deeds were essential to the practice of the Jewish faith, they must equally be an integral part of the Christian way of life.

This writer's first argument is an appeal to common sense. If a Christian is seen treating his fellow-Christians without even the ordinary consideration
which any good man would show to his fellow-men, **what use is it for a** 14
man to say he has faith? (A more sophisticated version of the same argument can be seen in 1 John 3.17.) Anyone could see that his religion
meant nothing, that his Christian faith was **a lifeless thing.** 17

But someone may object. At first sight one wonders who could possibly 18
have objected to such an obvious proposition. A "faith" which has absolutely
no effect on one's actions is certainly **a lifeless thing.** But perhaps the objec- 17
tion did not sound quite so implausible to the original readers of the letter. There were plenty of religious philosophies about in the Greek-speaking world which concentrated entirely upon intellectual "knowledge" of God (which was, after all, a kind of "faith"), and paid no attention to morals or "good deeds". Moreover, Paul's great argument in Galatians 3 that the basis of Christian salvation is, not good deeds, but "faith" (by which, of course, Paul meant a great deal more than a mere profession of religious belief) may have made a considerable impact in the church, and have lingered on in the over-simplified form (which Paul would never have held) that good deeds were irrelevant, and that "faith" (of any kind) was all that mattered. Either of these tendencies might have thrown up an objection to the common-sense
proposition that **faith, if it does not lead to action . . . is in itself a** 17
lifeless thing.

However, it is not really necessary to look so far afield for an explanation of this paragraph. In logic, it was possible to drive a wedge between faith and good deeds: the one did not seem logically to imply the other. But this writer had an ingenious argument on the other side. To introduce it, he deliberately adopted the style of a popular lesson in philosophy (technically known as a
"diatribe"). In this style, **someone may object** was a standard way of 18
introducing a possible objection which the writer wished to demolish in order to put his own position in a clearer light. The brief dialogue which follows is wholly artificial and imaginary. It is a typical example of the way in which philosophical teachers liked to make a point.

The point which this writer wished to make is quite clear. Every day the Jews began their prayers with the statement of faith that "the Lord is our God, the Lord is one" (Deuteronomy 6.4). Theoretically, it could be argued that this "faith" was enough to save a man: there was no need of good works as well. To this it could be replied that even devils believe this much (as is taken for granted in, for instance, Mark 1.24). But devils, far from being
"saved", actually **tremble** before God. Therefore **faith like that** could not 19
be sufficient to save a man.

18 This point is led up to by a short dialogue between the writer and the imaginary objector. The style of this is exactly what we should expect in a fragment of popular philosophical argument, and the general drift is clear enough: the objector is allowed to sharpen his thesis that faith can exist without good deeds before having it decisively refuted by the point about devils. But the details are hopelessly obscure. Greek manuscripts at that time had no quotation marks and little punctuation, and it is impossible to tell from the language alone where the interjections of the objector begin and end, and how the sentences should be distributed between the two speakers. Either the writer's brief excursion into this style was somewhat unsuccessful, or else an early copyist so muddled the text that we can no longer follow it.

After this the argument becomes more straightforward. The Jews cherished
the memory of great figures of the past who had acted, not from ordinary
human and materialistic motives, but from "faith" (see above on Hebrews
11). The greatest of these figures was Abraham, and the most spectacular
21 example of his faith was his readiness to offer **his son Isaac upon the altar**
(Genesis 22.9–12). True, the way Scripture talked about this "faith" of
23 Abraham was perhaps open to misunderstanding. **'Abraham put his faith
in God, and that faith was counted to him as righteousness'** (Genesis
15.6), taken in isolation, could be held to imply that it was Abraham's state of
mind, not his particular actions, which was important and made him **'God's
friend'** (Isaiah 41.8)—and indeed in Romans 4 Paul exploited this very
ambiguity in order to demonstrate the importance of "faith" (in the special
sense in which he understood it). But a moment's reflection was sufficient to
show that certain actions were necessary to prove that Abraham really had
22 this attitude, to prove **the integrity of his faith**. And the same went for any
25 of the other heroes of Jewish history, such as **Rahab** (see above on Hebrews
11.31), who were celebrated for their faith. Ultimately, they were all justified
not just by a form of belief—**faith in itself**—but by their actions.

3. 1 **We who teach.** In the church, as in the synagogue, teachers were important
and respected. Their prestige attracted many to follow the same career; but
it was necessary to remind the aspirants of the frightening responsibility
they would bear and which **not many** were fit to undertake. The writer can
speak with authority as a teacher himself (the one thing we know for certain
about him); and he bases his warning on a weakness which is common to all
2 men (for **a perfect character** in this respect hardly exists) but which is
particularly serious for teachers: the uncontrollable nature of the tongue.
5 Plenty of similes were available to illustrate **a small member** that has
3–4 great influence: the bridle of a horse, the rudder of a ship. These were
commonplace comparisons, and perhaps the writer did not pause to consider
that they did not fit his argument perfectly: bridles and rudders are used for
constructive purposes, whereas what he wanted to illustrate was the tongue

as a destructive influence. But his third simile—**the tiniest spark** producing 5
a blaze—was perfectly to the point, and led into a whole chain of images.
The tongue is not just like a fire; it is **in effect a fire.** What then does it 6
burn? Human life was called by some thinkers (especially those who believed
in the reincarnation of the soul in one body after another) a "cycle" or
wheel. Borrowing this phrase, and thinking rather literally of a wooden or
metal wheel, our author could combine it with his fire-metaphor, and say
that the tongue **keeps the wheel of our existence red-hot.** Normally, fire
purifies. But not so the tongue, which is the quintessence of **wickedness,**
with a touch of hell-fire about it.

Out of the same mouth come praises and curses. To a Jew, cursing 10
was something occasionally demanded as a religious duty, and the phenomenon would not necessarily have worried him. But to a Christian, cursing was always evil, and this fickleness of the tongue seemed something unnatural, something which (as Stoic philosophers liked to put it) prevented a man from being true to his own nature even to the extent that water or plants are true to theirs. The tongue seemed to offend, not just against morals, but against natural law.

Who among you is wise or clever? Being a follower of a new religion 13
almost inevitably meant claiming to know the answers to old questions, to have a deeper understanding of God and the world (for which **clever** is an inadequate translation). The dangers of this kind of intellectual "wisdom" are the subject of the first few chapters of 1 Corinthians. There, Paul seeks to meet them by a radical critique of philosophical wisdom as such. Here, the writer is content to insist that Christian wisdom must never be purely intellectual, and must be accompanied by **modesty**; otherwise it leads (as
Paul saw so clearly) to **bitter jealousy and selfish ambition,** and shows 14
itself to belong to the sphere of the world, of the senses, and even of demons.
By contrast, there exists a true wisdom which Christians can legitimately
aspire to, **the wisdom that comes from above** (a conventional Jewish way 15
of saying, "the wisdom that comes from God"). The characteristics of that
wisdom are listed in many Jewish writings (compare especially Wisdom
7.22–5). One of them is peacemaking; and this leads to a general maxim
about **peacemakers** (which is somewhat less laboured in the original than 18
it appears in this translation).

What causes conflicts and quarrels among you? It was a common- 4. 1
place of moral philosophy that it is the **aggressiveness of bodily desires** 2
which is the root cause of human conflicts and quarrels. This writer agrees, and adds a brief piece of psychological analysis which was probably equally familiar to his readers:[a] the point was valid as a general observation about

[a] There are several possible ways of punctuating the Greek in verse 2. The NEB translation follows that which seems to fit the argument best.

human nature, and there would have been no need to object that there were hardly likely to be members of the Christian church who were **bent on murder.** The argument begins to bear on religion with the mention of prayer. It was firm Christian doctrine that prayers are answered; but in the face of the fact that some prayers are not answered, it was necessary to define the conditions which prayer must fulfil if it is to be successful. There are traces of this in the gospels (see above on Mark 9.29). Here, the failure of
3 certain prayers is put down to praying **from wrong motives.** This is another of the evil effects of bodily **pleasures**: they pervert even a man's prayers.

But alongside this psychological analysis of the dangers of bodily desires, an important insight into the matter was offered by the religion of the Bible. In the Old Testament, the most serious sin of the people of Israel was their tendency to desert the worship of the one true God and to compromise with the polytheistic faiths of their pagan neighbours. This sin came to be called "idolatry", and in the Greco-Roman world the Jews remained as sensitive as ever to the danger of their own religion being contaminated by the many different cults which were popular in the civilized world around them. At the same time, they came to realize that the worship of the statues of pagan gods was not the only danger. Equally serious was the inclination to worship the worldly values which went with paganism. Some even went so far as to say that the real meaning of "idolatry" was nothing other than greed for money
4 (Colossians 3.5). In a word, **love of the world is enmity to God**; or, as Jesus himself put it, 'You cannot serve God and Money' (Matthew 6.24). Just as idolatry, in the Old Testament, was often described as the unfaithfulness of a wife to her husband, so those who pursue worldly values could be called **false, unfaithful creatures.**

Yet another of the many psychological explanations of sin which were familiar to both Jewish and Christian thinkers was one in terms of a "spirit" in man which begins its life in all innocence and is capable of responding to promptings of the Spirit of God, but is liable to be corrupted by evil desires or malicious spirits. This psychology does not occur in the Old Testament, but was explored by later Jewish thinkers; and the quotation
5 here given[a] from "**Scripture**" probably comes in fact from some lost writing of a more recent period, which was perhaps for a short time included among the books of the Old Testament. According to this analysis of human behaviour, the effect of Christ's death and resurrection on a Christian was that a new factor was now active within him which cancelled out the evil

[*a*] As they stand, the Greek words of this quotation are almost untranslatable. Two lines of approach seem possible: (i) "The spirit which dwells (or, which God has made to dwell) in us longs jealously (for us)"; (ii) "God longs jealously for the spirit which he has made to dwell in us". Some form of one of these alternatives is found in most English translations. The NEB adopts a third rendering, which makes good sense and fits well into the context, but does somewhat more violence to the Greek.

forces to which man's spirit was exposed. This new factor was called **grace,** 6
which was **stronger** than **envious desires.** The concept was a new one; but
the word itself could be found in the Septuagint translation of the Old
Testament, for instance in Proverbs 3.34: **'God . . . gives grace to the
humble.'** And this led naturally to another injunction: **Be submissive** 7
then to God.

The remaining sentences in the paragraph are all broadly relevant to the
same theme, but have little connection with one another. Doubtless they
were the kind of injunctions often used in Christian teaching. To our ears,
an unexpected note is struck by **Be sorrowful, mourn and weep,** but this 9
may be partly because we do not immediately catch the biblical overtones.
It is the tone of an Old Testament prophet, addressing the proud, the arrogant and the wealthy, and prophesying their speedy discomfiture. The writer adopts this tone to ridicule the easy complacency and cheerfulness of the wealthy. God is about to bring about a reversal of social values. The only way to be sure of salvation is to join the ranks of the "poor" who make up
the church. **Humble yourselves before God and he will lift you high.** 10
This writer may have a certain bias against the rich as such (5.1–6); but basically he has the faith which underlies Jesus' own beatitudes.

Brothers, you must never disparage one another. This Christian 11
society lived under the Jewish law, of which God was the **lawgiver,** and any serious offence would be dealt with according to that law. But there was always a temptation for one individual to censure another's conduct, even when there was no legal offence involved. At its mildest, this might be simply a matter of "disparagement", but equally it could take the much more serious form of slander (the Greek word translated **disparage** would cover both). Slander was regarded by the Jews as a very serious sin, even though it was not expressly forbidden in the law. Here, the obvious point is being made that anyone who passes unfavourable judgements on another, whether trivial or serious, is arrogating to himself the function of the law and so
judges the law. Who are you to judge your neighbour? was a note which 12
had been sounded by Jesus and which was often reiterated in Christian preaching. It was an explicit challenge to the natural propensity of human beings to **judge** one another all the time.

'Today or tomorrow'. The sentence is in conversational Greek, and is 13
evidently the kind of thing that was often heard in the street. Possibly it was sometimes heard also in the Christian congregation. At any rate it gave the writer the cue for a little sermon. Underlying it was a certain over-confidence,
or **boasting,** which showed that the speaker had forgotten his human 16
condition. **What you ought to say is: 'If it be the Lord's will'.** Greeks 15
and Romans in fact constantly said, "If it be God's will", as do Muslims today; but (so far as we know) it was not a common expression among the

Jews. For once the Christians could learn a moral lesson, not from their Jewish ancestors, but from their heathen neighbours.

5. 1 **Next a word to you who have great possessions.** A critique of riches
could be pitched in more than one tone of voice. There was, first, the simple
3 point that all worldly possessions are precarious and transient: **fine clothes**
can become **moth-eaten,** and **silver and gold,** though if understood literally
as metals they are imperishable, if understood metaphorically as wealth can
shrivel into nothing and be subject to **decay**—this was a piece of ancient
wisdom, though it also occurs in the teaching of Jesus (Matthew 6.19–20).
But the moralist could also adopt a sharper tone. When the rich get richer, it
usually means that the poor get poorer: the amassing of wealth involves
4 injustice and extortion. Depriving a workman of his wages was a social
injustice very strongly condemned in the Old Testament (Jesus' use of the
proverb, 'The worker earns his pay', may have originally been simply an
endorsement of this traditional piece of social morality); yet cases were
probably known of it happening, and it could be used as a typical example of
the injustices committed by the rich, which would bring their own inevitable
3 retribution. Moreover, the **very rust** of their hoarded wealth (which should
have been distributed as alms) was a symbol of the fiery punishment which
their meanness would earn them at the Last Judgement. All this belonged to
the traditional repertory of the moralist.

But here the writer is speaking in the tone, not so much of a moralist, as of
a prophet. It had been the faith of the righteous "poor" in the past that God
would one day vindicate their cause against the rich, that he would "lift up"
the poor, and "bring low" the proud and wealthy (1.9–10). This faith was
now burning with new intensity among Christians, who confidently expected
some such reversal of social values to take place very soon. Their present
situation was that which had been well described in the Wisdom of Solomon
(2.10–20), where the rich were made to say, "Down with the poor and
honest man! . . . he is a living condemnation of all our ideas . . . let us con-
6 demn him to a shameful death". Against them, the poor could offer **no**
resistance. But the moment had almost arrived when they could say, The
5 day of reckoning (or **the day for slaughter**[a] to use a lurid Old Testament
expression) **has come.** The tone is prophetic; the tense of the warning is no
longer future but present.

8 **The coming of the Lord is near.** Again and again in the New Testament
(and to a lesser extent in Jewish literature, as in Habakkuk 2.3) the expectation of an imminent new age, accompanied by judgement, is evoked as one

[*a*] The Greek is very compressed. It means literally, "You have fattened your hearts in the day" (or "a day") "of slaughter". The NEB translation is bold, but may be correct. Alternatively, the day of slaughter may be the eventual elimination of the poor which the rich have been working for in order to increase their own possessions. Many interpreters have seen a reference to the suffering of Christ in this passage; but the context suggests a more general meaning.

of the main reasons for living a life of sobriety, watchfulness and purity.
Here the particular quality in mind is **patience under ill-treatment,** and 10
the warning is filled out with two other illustrations. The first is that of **the** 7
farmer looking for the precious crop his land may yield. In Palestine
and Syria, all farming depends on the rainfall. After the long dry summer, nothing can be done until the autumn rains have moistened the ground sufficiently for ploughing and sowing. This usually happens in about October, but sometimes is delayed until late November, and the patience of the farmer can be sorely tested as he waits. The season of rains then lasts until March or April; but a successful crop depends on some good showers after the fine weather has begun. So **the autumn and spring rains** were as much a proverbial preoccupation of the Palestinian farmer as the monsoon for the Indian; if this writer did not know the fact from experience, he could have read the phrase in the Old Testament (Deuteronomy 11.14).

(Before the second illustration, the writer reminds his readers that the
Lord is also **the Judge,** and—as he has said earlier (4.11)—"blaming" one's 9
brother, like "disparaging" or accusing him, too easily leads into "judging" him, which is a sure way of falling under the judgement of the one true Judge. At this point, the teaching of Jesus (Matthew 7.1–2) seems to lie very near the surface.)

The second **pattern of patience under ill-treatment** is provided by 10
the prophets who spoke in the name of the Lord. That many of the prophets were persecuted and martyred does not appear from the Old Testament, but was a traditional belief in the time of Christ (see above on Matthew 23.30). Their names occurred in lists of Jewish heroes, as also did
that of **Job.** The main part of the Book of Job, as it now appears in the Old 11
Testament, consists of a highly wrought debate in the course of which it can hardly be said that Job always **stood firm.** But this debate was evidently the creation of a great thinker and literary artist, who attached it somewhat loosely to the simple folk-tale which is told in the first and last chapters. In this tale, Job was afflicted by many misfortunes, but **stood firm,** and was rewarded **in the end.** It is clearly the Job of the folk-tale, rather than of the literary work, who is in mind here. The point is clinched by two quotations from Scripture: **'We count those happy who stood firm'** (Daniel 12.12), and **'the Lord is full of pity and compassion',** a formula which occurs in many places (e.g. Psalm 103.8).

Above all things, my brothers. If this sentence occurred in a logically 12
constructed argument, we should have to conclude that the prohibition of swearing was the most important thing the writer felt he had to say. But in fact it is an isolated injunction, with no connection with the rest of the chapter, and we can probably take **above all things** with a pinch of salt. The author is simply asking his readers to pay special attention to the danger of swearing.

In Judaism, swearing was a serious matter. If one swore an oath, one must be believed; and if one was found to have sworn falsely, the punishment was severe. Yet swearing is very natural, particularly in moments of anger; and although it was a rule of the Law that all oaths must be by the name of God (Deuteronomy 6.13), it was thought that it made the consequences less serious if one said '**by heaven**' or '**by earth**' or used some other phrase which referred only obliquely to God. It was not difficult to demonstrate the casuistry of this (Matthew 5.33–7): all oaths expose the swearer to judgement (since no man can always be certain that his oath is true, or will be fulfilled); therefore it is better to avoid swearing altogether. The formulation here is slightly different from that of Jesus (Matthew 5.33–7), and indeed Jesus was not the only Jewish or pagan thinker who held this point of view. But it is likely that this writer took his prohibition of swearing from the teaching of Jesus rather than from any other source, since on the whole the Jews regarded oaths as a necessary feature of their legal system, and as a natural (even if undesirable) habit of ordinary speech.

13 **Is anyone among you in trouble?** The vivacious style is once again that
of a popular lesson in moral philosophy: this is how people of a certain
14 persuasion ought to live. But the answer to the question, **Is one of you ill?**
breaks right out of these conventional generalities and gives us a glimpse of the organization of the early church. Visiting the sick and praying for them (or **over** them) was a highly esteemed act of charity among the Jews; the relatives and friends of a sick man recognized that they had a clear duty to visit him. In this case the initiative rested with the visitor. But there were also certain people whom the patient might actually **send for**, such as a noted man of prayer or a physician—though this last was a comparatively late development: Jewish religion regarded sickness as a consequence of sin; the only cure, therefore, lay in the forgiveness of God, and the only proper course for the sick man was to throw himself upon God's mercy; the first and only positive thing which is said about the physician in the whole Bible is in Ecclesiasticus 38.1–15 (written around 180 B.C.); and even there the diagnosis and the cure are closely associated with prayer. Healing, that is to say, was still essentially a religious act; and there was at least one Jewish sect in the time of Christ—the Essenes—which practised both the arts of medicine and what we would now call "spiritual healing".

Evidently the early church had a similar approach to sickness and had its own ministry of healing. Jesus had actually healed sick people; and his followers continued to exercise this power of healing, in which the main
14 constituent (as in the stories in Acts) was the invoking of **the name of the**
Lord. We learn from this passage that the responsibility for responding to the sick man's call lay with **the elders of the congregation**; and that, just as Jesus himself used the outward gestures of magical or quasi-medicinal cures (Mark 7.33; John 9.6), so the church used **oil** as part of its rite of

healing (there is another reference to this in Mark 6.13). It is also a presupposition of this passage (as of many of the accounts of Jesus' healing
miracles) that sickness is the result of sin, and that any recovery is conditional upon one's being forgiven. **Therefore,** says this writer, **confess** 16
your sins to one another—this is essential if prayer for healing is to work.
Another condition for success (for perhaps it was already necessary to have
some explanation ready in case of failure) was that the prayer should be made
by **a good man.** But this was by no means setting an impossible condition
(the tone of the passage leaves little doubt that its readers would have agreed
that this procedure, if taken seriously, was likely to succeed). One of the great
historical examples of faith, **Elijah** (about whom many details were supplied 17
by popular tradition rather than by the Bible) was after all **a man with**
human frailties like our own.

The last topic of this letter (as of 1 John) is the problem of Christians defecting from the church. The seriousness of this can be gauged from other passages in the New Testament (1 Corinthians 5.1–5; Hebrews 10.26–31), where a basic Christian presupposition comes to the surface: inside the church was salvation and eternal life, outside was death and condemnation.
Bringing back a straying brother was therefore **rescuing his soul from** 20
death. It was possible to think of the apostate as an agent of the devil, and to dismiss him with hatred. But more often the "straying" was not so serious, and Christian love dictated a different course. Here, as in 1 Peter 4.8, an old proverb was relevant:

> "Hatred stirs up strife,
> But love cancels innumerable sins."
>
> (Proverbs 10.12)

THE FIRST LETTER OF PETER

1.1 **From Peter, apostle of Jesus Christ.** There is only one Peter in the New Testament, and the letter purports to come from his pen. This in itself does not settle the matter. The Second Letter of Peter makes the same claim, but the church has always, and for good reason, hesitated to accept it as the work of the apostle. The first letter bears much better credentials: it breathes the authentic spirit of early Christianity, and it expounds the central principles of the faith with a seriousness and authority comparable with that of Paul. Nevertheless, it is not easy to see how it could have been written by the Galilean fisherman who was a disciple of Jesus. It is composed in polished Greek, such as could hardly have been commanded by a Jew who had not spoken Greek as his first language since childhood; and the frequent allusions in it to persecution seem to presuppose a relationship between church and state a great deal more tense and dangerous than anything which is alluded to in the letters of Paul, or which seems probable much before the end of the first century A.D. Peter was almost certainly martyred in A.D. 64. It is possible that there were local outbreaks of persecution before that date in Asia Minor; or that Peter was assisted in writing the letter by Silvanus (5.12), who was doubtless fluent in Greek. But to rely too much on these possibilities is to indulge in special pleading. A somewhat easier explanation of the facts is that the letter was written by a person of considerable standing in the church, who felt inspired to address his fellow-Christians, and found it natural to invest his letter with the authority of the apostle Peter.

The calling of a Christian

God's scattered people. If the letter stands in the tradition of the encyclicals which were issued from Jerusalem to the Jews of the Dispersion (see above, pp. 719–20), then we would expect to find, in its opening sentences, Christian equivalents to the kind of language with which a Jewish leader would have greeted his own people. The author is writing to Christians scattered over a large area: **Pontus** (and **Bithynia**: the two districts formed one province), **Galatia, Cappadocia** and **Asia** were four Roman provinces which between them covered the whole of Asia Minor apart from the small coastal strip south of the Taurus mountains. Unlike the Jews, the Christians had no common nationality (the majority of those addressed here seem to

have been Gentiles, see below on 1.14), but only a common loyalty, which transcended any earthly allegiance and made them feel lightly attached (as a philosopher might have said) to the physical conditions of life, like people who only **lodge for a while** in the countries of their birth. Yet they were not just so many individuals who happened to share a common faith: they were bound together in a solidarity that was no less powerful than the strong
national consciousness of the Jews. Like them, they were **chosen of old in** 2
the purpose of God the Father; like them, they were **hallowed to his service**—though not now by participation in the cult at the temple in Jerusalem, but in a way that affected their inmost being: **by the Spirit**; and, like them, they were **consecrated with the sprinkled blood.** Here the NEB gives only a free paraphrase. The Greek, translated literally, runs as follows: "to obedience and sprinkling of the blood of Jesus Christ". This, though it hardly bears logical analysis, gives a clue to what was in the author's mind. When Moses received the Law from God at Sinai and read it to the people, they replied, "we will be obedient", and Moses "took the blood and flung it over the people" (Exodus 24.7–8). This was the "covenant" made between God and Israel. Christians had now entered a new covenant, effected by the blood of Christ. Moreover, **sprinkled blood** was also an element of the regular Jewish sacrificial ritual (Leviticus 4.6; 5.9; 16.14). To a Christian, the phrase now suggested the sacrifice of Jesus on the cross, which a believer shared by being "sprinkled" with water at his baptism.

The inheritance to which we are born. This was another traditional 4
Jewish expression, now transformed into a Christian concept. The "inheritance" of the Jews was thought to be, first of all, a peaceful and prosperous existence in the land of Palestine; with the advance of religious ideas and the increasing insecurity of the Jewish state, it was reinterpreted as a reward promised to the Jewish people in a future age, or even in the after-life. But however it was conceived, it represented a conviction, common to all Jewish people, that they were reserved for a unique and privileged destiny in the ultimate purposes of God. Christians now believed that this destiny
had passed to them. Its full realization must await **the end of time**; mean- 5
while they were **under the protection** of God so long as they had faith—this was one of the many possible ways of putting into words what the Christian faith meant to them. Another was **new birth into a living hope,** a way of describing the Christian experience which appears in several strands of Christian thinking (Titus 3.5; John 3.1–8), and which seemed particularly appropriate to Christian baptism. A third was **salvation**, a concept common to many religions, but understood by Christians as something both present and future: to put it almost as a paradox, it was **even now in readiness and will be revealed at the end of time.**

All these concepts, in part distinctively Christian, in part adaptations of Jewish ones, are worked into an opening which carries the usual form of

2 Christian greeting (**Grace and peace to you**) and the very common
3 exordium, **Praise be to the God and Father of our Lord Jesus Christ**
6 (2 Corinthians 1.3; Ephesians 1.3). Only with the mention of **trials of many**
kinds does the letter become more personal. We can guess (in the light of
clearer hints later in the letter) that these trials consisted of persecution from
the Roman authorities. It was an old discovery of Jewish wisdom that tribula-
7 tion can purify the character like an **assayer's fire** (Wisdom 3.6; Ecclesiasticus 2.5); this author takes the idea one stage further. Compared with a
Christian's faith, even gold—the precious residue from the refiner's furnace
—can be called **perishable**. The second piece of encouragement is more
8 distinctively Christian. **You have not seen him, yet you love him.** A
modern reader thinks at once of Jesus on earth: how easy to **love him** if (like Peter) one had actually **seen him**. But in the letters of the New Testament there is very little harking back to Jesus' presence in Galilee and Jerusalem. The Jesus who is longed for is the Jesus who is at present known only by faith but who will one day be revealed in his glory so that all men may see him for what he is. At that final revelation, a Christian will know he belongs to Christ and will be united with him. Meanwhile, his relationship with Christ is one of trust and love. Even this is enough to transport him **with a joy too great for words.** [a] Christian salvation belongs, not only to the future, but also to the present.

A third source of encouragement for Christians was the fact that they
could find the death and resurrection of Christ, and the great consequences
which followed, foretold in Scripture. Sayings of the prophets, which had
for so long seemed to point to some future event, now took on their definitive
meaning in the light of the Christian experience. Some, indeed, though
spoken by the prophets themselves in the first person, seemed so perfectly
11 fulfilled by Christ that one could talk of **the spirit of Christ in them** (a
good example is the quotations in Hebrews 2.12–13, on which see above).
Those prophets were inspired to cast their utterances in the form of oracles
about the future. To understand them, Christians were no longer dependent
12 upon the efforts of learned interpreters. They now had **preachers** who
brought, with the gospel, the key to all that had been foretold in the past. Even **angels**, who traditionally had access to the secret purposes of God, did not have that perfect understanding of the pattern of human history which was now the possession of Christians.

13 **Therefore.** The readers have been bidden to fix their eyes upon what is to come, the salvation which is to be revealed. As so often in the New Testament, a reference to the end of time has a serious moral corollary: **be mentally stripped for action, perfectly self-controlled**—the warning

[a] The NEB omits a word in this sentence. In full, the Greek means "with unutterable and glorious joy", i.e. the joy is invested already with some of the glory which awaits Christians in the future.

can be paralleled from many other passages (see above on Romans 13.12).
Here it is joined with a reference to the past, which throws precious light on
the background of the readers of this letter. **The desires you cherished in** 14
your days of ignorance. This is how a Jewish writer might have spoken
to gentile proselytes: while the Jews had the Law to show them what kind of
moral conduct was demanded of men, Gentiles lived in "ignorance", and
so were given to the fulfilment of unnatural desires (Romans 1.18–24). The
same tone could be used when speaking to Christian converts from paganism:
they too had emerged from a life of ignorant immorality into one governed
by the Law of Christ. But no Christian would have spoken like this to converts from Judaism. The Jews were never in **ignorance**, nor would it have
occurred to any Christian to talk of the **empty folly** of their **traditional** 18
ways. Their Law was still the most complete guide to conduct the world had
known. The readers of this letter, then, (or most of them) had been pagans
before they became Christians.

Christianity was a new and distinctive way of life, totally different from
paganism, but different also from Judaism. Yet much of its ethos was
inherited from the Jews. It aspired, like the Jewish faith, to form in its
adherents a standard of "holiness", a character which would bring them
closer to God. Both faiths found inspiration in a passage such as Leviticus
19.2: "You shall be holy; for I the Lord your God am holy". 16

'Our Father'. This address to God,[a] which rose spontaneously to the 17
lips of Christians through the inspiration of the Spirit (Romans 8.15) and
which was originally taught them by Jesus himself (Luke 11.2), was such an
intimate form of prayer that it could easily breed over-confidence. It was true
that Christians were "God's sons" in a very real and intimate sense; but it
was also true (and the two truths had somehow to be held together) that God
was still what he had always been, **the One who judges every man**
impartially on the record of his deeds. Christians had reason for confidence about their fate at the Last Judgement; and yet that Judgement
retained as much seriousness as ever.

The writer's purpose, as we can see by now, is principally a moral one: he
is exhorting his readers to live by the standards of their faith, and warning
them of the consequences of licentious behaviour. To do this, he reminds
them of important articles of their belief, or of expressions (such as '**Father**')
which were constantly on their lips, and then draws out the implications of
these for moral conduct. Another such expression was "ransom", the price
paid for a man's **freedom.** This was an Old Testament metaphor, often 18

[a] The NEB is perhaps misleading here. The Greek has simply 'Father', which suggests (as in Luke's version of the Lord's Prayer) the Aramaic word *Abba*: this was the distinctive Christian prayer, an intimate address to God. '**Our Father**', the form found in Matthew, was probably an assimilation to a form of address which Jewish Christians would have found more acceptable (see above on Matthew 6.9). There is little reason to think that the author of 1 Peter meant 'Our Father' instead of 'Father'.

used in the church (1 Corinthians 6.20; 1 Timothy 2.6) and probably by Jesus himself (Mark 10.45) as a means of describing the effect of Jesus' death. A prisoner ransomed or a slave freed simply by the payment of a sum of **gold or silver** might not feel under any strong obligation to behave himself
19 afterwards. But if the ransom was a man's life—**the price was paid in**
precious blood—then it would be unthinkable to put such an expensive freedom to immoral uses. Surely Christians were in precisely this situation: their freedom had been bought by Christ's **blood**, a death which could be understood, both as the payment of a ransom for mankind, and also as a sacrifice of **a lamb without mark or blemish**, a perfect offering for the sins of men such as the temple sacrifices could never be.

20 **Predestined . . . manifest.** These two statements (particularly in the
Greek) sound like something which Christians may often have said or sung
21 —there is a hymn on similar lines in 1 Timothy 3.16. **Through him you**
have come to trust in God. If the Christians so addressed were pagans before their conversion, this was an apt description of what had happened to them. Through Christ, they had learnt for the first time what it was **to trust in God.** But even Jewish converts, whose ancestral religion was also based on "trusting in God", had now come to a new "trust". Previously, their trust had constantly been, so to speak, in spite of appearances: it had often seemed that it was the godless who flourished, and there was little to show that the "trust" of those who believed in God was justified. But Christ had changed all that: **God . . . raised him from the dead and gave him glory.** After that, no Christian could doubt that God was on the side of his own. There existed a new and convincing ground for **faith and hope.**

22–3 **You have purified your souls . . . You have been born anew.** These expressions would be particularly appropriate to people who had recently been baptized (for the language, compare 1 Corinthians 6.11; Titus 3.5), and it is quite possible that parts of the letter were originally written to be read aloud when a baptism of converts had just taken place. In any case, the symbolism of baptism seems to have been much in the author's mind, and one of his main purposes was to remind his readers of the kind of conduct which necessarily followed from their baptism and their Christian profession.
22 So here: baptism implies that Christians should **love one another.** If the
matter were put in the form of a logical proof, the argument might run like
this: it is agreed that baptism is a kind of "rebirth"; now this rebirth is
23 through the **word of God**, and the word of God, as a passage of Isaiah
25 proves (Isaiah 40.6–7), **endures for evermore**, it is immortal, whereas
human beings are mortal; the rebirth of baptism must therefore be quite different from mortal birth: it must have to do with immortality, and the new life to which it leads must have immortal characteristics; one immortal characteristic (if we may complete the argument from 1 Corinthians 13.8–13) is love; therefore, **love one another.**

That religious truth to the newly converted is like milk to a new-born
infant—milk that is **pure**, unlike the devious natural instincts of the heart, 2. 2
and **spiritual**, appropriate to the mind or the soul and not to the natural
appetites—was a common enough metaphor in both the Jewish and the Greek
world. In the second century A.D. it was even worked into the symbolism
of Christian baptism: the newly baptized were given milk and honey to
drink. The Bible is full of such sensuous imagery. Psalm 34 is much in this
writer's mind throughout the letter. Here he quotes verse 8: "Taste then 3
and see that the Lord is good".

So come to him, our living Stone. In isolation, this seems a very strange 4
expression; but the author goes on to show how he arrived at it. Jesus himself
was remembered to have quoted Psalm 118.22, "The stone which the builders
rejected has become the main corner-stone", as an illustration of the dramatic
reversal which would follow his rejection by his own people (Mark 12.10);
and the idea of a stone which might either be **a corner-stone** for the faith 7
of the believer or **a stone to trip over** for those who refuse to believe was 8
furnished by putting together two texts from Isaiah, 28.16 and 8.14 (the fact 6
that the same combination of texts occurs in Romans 9.33 suggests that these
passages were frequently quoted together in the early church). In this sense,
a "living stone" was an eloquent image for the Christ who continued to be
the basis of life for those who believed, but to make still more confounded the
destiny of those who refused to believe.

Come, and let yourselves be built, as living stones, into a spiritual 5
temple. The metaphor of a living stone suggests to the writer another image
which had wide currency among Christians: the church was a **spiritual
temple**, replacing the one of masonry in Jerusalem, its members were
living stones, and the sacrifices offered in it were **spiritual sacrifices.**
That is to say, it replaced the old institutions of Judaism; and yet it was not a
totally new society, without a past. The author writes to Christians as a High
Priest might have written to the Jewish people: the church constituted a
"nation" just as Israel did; indeed it was the first true embodiment of the
ideal which from the beginning had been set before the Jewish people.
Royalty and priesthood, in Jewish history, had always been vested in certain
individuals; but these individuals exercised it as representatives of the people
as a whole, a people which believed itself to be "chosen" from among other
nations as a special kind of "kingdom", and to have the task of offering a
unique "priestly" service to God. All these ideas were present in passages
such as Exodus 19.6; 23.22; Isaiah 43.20–1 (which are alluded to here). They 9
found their fulfilment in the new community of Christians; but, paradoxically, this community was largely composed of men and women who, being
Gentiles, had long been regarded by the Jews as automatically disqualified
from playing any such rôle in history. Yet even this paradox could be
illuminated from the Old Testament. Hosea, in his vivid representation of 10

the infidelity of the chosen race, had talked of Israel being called by God "Not-my-people", and of the possibility that, when it repented, "Not-my-people" would once more be called "My people" (Hosea 1–2). The Gentiles had always been "Not-my-people": it could be seen as the true fulfilment of Hosea's prophecy when, by entering the Christian church, they became "My people".

Dear friends, I beg you. Moral exhortations fill a substantial part of most New Testament letters. They were, of course, a necessary element of any religious teaching, and the exhortations here (directed to servants, wives and husbands in turn) follow the same conventional pattern as in Colossians and Ephesians. But it may also be true that moral behaviour was something about which Christians were particularly sensitive. Their faith enabled them,
16 whatever their circumstances, to **live as free men.** For those of Jewish background, this meant a new flexibility with regard to the Law of Moses; for those of pagan background, it may have meant a new freedom from superstition, heathen customs and social distinctions. It was not difficult for their enemies to allege that this freedom was in fact simply **a screen for wrongdoing**; and should there turn out to be any substance in these allegations, it could result in Christians being brought before a civil court, where awkward questions might be asked about their religious beliefs. This author had serious reason for devoting so much of his letter to these matters.

11 **Abstain from the lusts of the flesh which are at war with the soul.** This was a cliché of popular ethics, and was as old as Plato. It was not, properly speaking, a correct Christian or Jewish way of putting it: in Paul, for example, "spirit", not "soul", constitutes man's higher nature. But here the writer was not concerned to give a Christian doctrine of man, but to tell his readers how to behave, and he used the current moral jargon of his time. Nevertheless, the reasons he gave were specifically Jewish and Christian. **As aliens in a foreign land**: so the Jews described their hold upon life and property (Leviticus 25.23; Psalm 39.12). All they possessed belonged ultimately to God, and they must never presume to make free with it, but must behave becomingly in the eyes of their Lord. And not only of their
12 Lord: also of the Gentiles by whom they were surrounded, the **pagans** (the Greek word is that which the Jews used of non-Jews in general). Here, the thought is applied to the present circumstances of Christians. **They malign you as criminals now.** Christians, for one reason or another, were getting a bad name. It was part of their faith that they would ultimately be shown to be in the right and their persecutors in the wrong. But this could hardly happen before God's final **assize.** Meanwhile, they must keep their own record absolutely clean.

13 **Submit yourselves.** It was not only Christians who advocated civil obedience; and when the writer adds, **for the sake of the Lord,** he is probably saying no more than that this duty also applied to Christians

(compare the way in which, in Ephesians and Colossians, other widely
accepted moral principles are endorsed as elements of the Christian way of
life; see above on Colossians 3.18). **The sovereign** was the Roman Emperor, 14
the **governor** was the Emperor's deputy with whom Christians in Asia
Minor had most contact: he administered justice in criminal cases, and
promoted public rewards (such as statues and testimonials) for those who
served the state well. For Christians, as for anyone else, **good conduct** was 15
the only sure way to silence calumny. The demands of Christian conduct
even in a pagan and hostile society could be summed up in a variation on an
old proverb: "My son, fear God and the King" (Proverbs 24.21). 17

Servants, accept the authority of your masters. The Christian move- 18
ment embraced people of widely different social classes, and included slaves and household servants. Christianity was consequently a potential source of social friction and unrest, and it may have been partly to avoid the danger of disturbances that one of the articles of the Christian domestic code was addressed specifically to **servants.** There is a similar warning in both Ephesians (6.5–8) and Colossians (3.22–5), and in each case it is supported with a distinctively Christian piece of teaching. Here, it is the cue for one of the most profound passages in the letter. The situation in mind was one of the perennial topics of comedy and casuistry: a servant under a master who
is **perverse.** Christian teaching goes along with that of many moralists: one
must be obedient even if, having **behaved well,** one has to **suffer for it.** 20
But in recommending this difficult course, our author has a motive to offer of great power: the servant's situation is exactly that of Christ himself, and through such a situation the Christian draws closer to his Lord.

Christ . . . thereby left you an example; it is for you to follow in 21
his steps. The idea that Christians are to follow the example of Christ has become a commonplace of Christian teaching, but this is one of the very few places where it occurs in the New Testament. For the most part, early Christian writers concentrated on Christ's death and resurrection; Christian conduct was ultimately based on the implications of these fundamental facts. But this writer appeals to a slightly earlier moment in the story: Jesus' trial.
For the most part he does not describe it directly: **He committed no sin,** 22–4
he was convicted of no falsehood . . . he carried our sins . . . by his wounds you have been healed, are all phrases which occur in Isaiah 53, the chapter describing the death of a nameless Suffering Servant which was found by the early church to throw precious light on the meaning of Jesus' suffering and death. If Christians were to follow the example of Christ, what they must have most in mind was the manner in which Christ himself followed a pattern of suffering which was laid down for him, so to speak, in the Old Testament. At the same time our author works in something new (which he may either have witnessed himself, or have heard or read about at second
hand). **When he was abused he did not retort with abuse, when he** 23

suffered he uttered no threats, but committed his cause to the One who judges justly are words with no precedent in the Old Testament: the author knew what had actually happened at Jesus' trial. Moreover, it was common knowledge that the trial had been followed by the crucifixion, a penalty not allowed for in the Old Testament. But at a stretch one could call
24 the cross **the gibbet,** which did appear in Scripture (Deuteronomy 21.23); and (doubtless for this reason) Christians soon began to use this scriptural word for the crucifixion. Thinking, then, of Christ as the Suffering Servant, one could fill in a gap which is left in that chapter of Isaiah. It is not said there, though it seems to be implied, that the Servant was actually killed. How did he meet his death? Presumably, on **the gibbet.** By adding this detail, the writer completes the scriptural prototype which found its final expression in Christ. With a slight strain of grammar, he inserts his addition after Isaiah's words, **he carried our sins.** The resulting phrase is compressed and suggestive: **he carried our sins to the gibbet.**

25 **You were straying like sheep.** The metaphor of straying sheep (standing for a people who have lost their sense of moral direction, and so fallen into sin) appears for a moment in Isaiah 53. This author takes it a stage further. The opposite of straying sheep is a compact flock purposefully following its shepherd. Jesus was such a **Shepherd** (the idea is worked out in John 10, but occurs also in Hebrews 13.20, and was doubtless familiar to Christians). He was also a **Guardian**: the word is that which was subsequently used as a title for the highest order of ministry in the church (*episkopos*, bishop), but it already had a long history as a word for describing God's care for his flock. Jesus, the Shepherd, had now assumed God's historic guardianship of his own people.

3. 1 **In the same way you women must accept the authority of your husbands.** A section on wives forms part of the exhortations in Ephesians and Colossians, and there is a similar paragraph in 1 Timothy 2.9–15. The topic was conventional, and it was a commonplace among Christians, as among other moral teachers, that wives should be submissive to their husbands, and that they should concentrate on inward beauty rather than
3 **outward adornment.** To this our author adds, first, a particular reason for submissiveness. If a husband was a non-believer (and the problem of "mixed marriages" between Christians and non-Christians seems to have been as actual here as it was in Corinth), then the proper attitude of the wife was neither to seek a separation nor to assume any kind of superiority, but
2 to persevere in **chaste and reverent behaviour** by which the husband
1 might be **won over.** Secondly, just as it was possible to regard Christian men as "sons of Abraham" by reason of their Abraham-like faith (see above
6 on Galatians 3.7), so Christian women could be called **children** of Abraham's wife **Sarah** if they imitated Sarah's obedience to her husband. For us, who have only the Old Testament to go by, and not the subsequent traditions

and legends by which Jewish readers interpreted it, the argument seems far-fetched; for in fact the only place in the Old Testament where Sarah refers to her husband at all is Genesis 18.12, where (though admittedly she calls him '**my master**') she is being anything but obedient. But Sarah, like other Old Testament figures, had since come to be regarded as a model of virtue. As such, she was a suitable figure for Christian wives to emulate by doing good (and also apparently by showing **no fear**; but why the author adds this is mysterious. The Greek words are reminiscent of Proverbs 3.25, a chapter which is alluded to again in 5.5; but this hardly explains their occurrence here. Possibly wives of non-Christian husbands are once again in mind, who might well have had reason to fear the consequences of following their new faith.)

The series is completed by a brief word to **husbands**, which again (like 7
Paul's treatment of the same theme in 1 Corinthians 7.3–6) stands in the
very best tradition of Greek and Jewish domestic morals.

To sum up. In conclusion, a general exhortation is given to the church as 8
a whole on the kind of life Christians should seek to live together. The
church did not attempt to evolve a completely new code of values: many
passages in the Old Testament which offered a definition of the righteous life
could serve as examples. Psalm 34 was one of these: it has already been
quoted once (2.3), and here several verses are given (13–17). It enunciates the 10–12
basic standards of the common life; upon this basis, Christians could build
their own distinctive society, of which one of the principles was **Do not** 9
repay wrong with wrong (as in 1 Thessalonians 5.15; Romans 12.17) but
on the contrary—and the positive side of this reflects the teaching of the
Sermon on the Mount (Matthew 5.43–8)—**retaliate with blessing.**

Who is going to do you wrong if you are devoted to what is good? It 13
is possible that cases had occurred of Christians abusing the moral freedom
which seemed to belong to their religion and thereby finding themselves
taken to court on criminal charges. If so, they deserved their punishment;
but in any case, it was vital that in all matters of civic life Christians should
keep their **conscience clear.** Even when giving an account of their beliefs, 16
they must indulge in no superior attitudes or violent demonstrations, but
must make their **defence with modesty and respect.** Simply by being 15
conscientious and peace-loving citizens, they could silence calumny and
keep out of harm's way.

But of course that was only a part of the matter. Christians might well find
they had to **suffer** for their **virtues** (a translation which suggests a certain 14
moral complacency: the Greek says simply that they might suffer "for
doing right"). It is probable that at the time of writing it was already, under
certain circumstances, a criminal offence to practise the Christian religion
(though it remained the responsibility of their fellow-citizens to institute
legal proceedings against Christians, and this may not have happened often).

In any case, it was impossible for Christians to identify themselves completely with the pagan society in which they lived: they were people called out of it to bear witness to a particular faith and a particular way of life. In this respect they could read the pattern of their situation in a passage of Isaiah (chapters 6–9, a passage which, through its reference to Emmanuel, to the virgin bearing a son, and to a stone that was both a cornerstone and a stumbling-block, seemed rich in intimations of Christianity). In the course of that passage, the prophet encourages the people of Jerusalem to dissociate themselves from the panic of the leaders of the state, whose motives are dictated by fear and a desire to compromise, and to "hold the Lord in
reverence, and let him be your fear" (Isaiah 8.13 in the Greek version of the
15 Septuagint). Our author here adapts the words of Isaiah to his purpose of
describing the Christian community as a people necessarily independent of
the secular state, and therefore necessarily in danger of suffering for its
beliefs—which amounted (so long as their conscience was clear) to suffering
17 **for well-doing.** What was the philosophy which would support them in
this situation?

One answer could be given immediately, which was simply an echo of
14 Jesus' teaching (Matthew 5.10): **If you should suffer . . . you may count
yourselves happy.** But the strength and courage with which Christians
faced persecution was inspired by more than this bare statement. It followed
from their whole understanding of the new situation created by Christ. This
could be stated quite simply in terms that were already familiar to Christians.
18 **Christ . . . died for our sins once and for all . . . the just . . . for the
unjust** is a statement which forms the basis of Paul's great argument in
Romans 6. But there was another way of putting it, which is hinted at else-
18–22 where, and is developed with a good deal of elaboration here. The passage is
solemn, allusive, and stylized; its opening and its ending may be another example of an early Christian hymn, such as seems occasionally to be quoted in the New Testament (its opening is strikingly similar in form to the hymn in 1 Timothy 3.16); and its theme would again make it appropriate to an occasion when Christian baptism was fresh in people's minds. But taken as a whole it amounts to a statement of the efficacy of Christ's death and resurrection in the light of a particular approach to the problem of evil and of human sin.

When a man does wrong, there often seems something irrational about his conduct: he knows what he ought to do, but for some reason he does not do it. In Jewish thinking, various explanations were offered for this apparent failure of human reason. One was what we should now call a psychological one: it was an evil impulse within a man, a destructive constituent of his nature, which caused him to sin. If Christ had "saved" us, it must therefore be by having effected some change in our nature which altered the balance of power (so to speak) within us, and enabled us to resist the evil impulse.

But another explanation was also popular, which located the cause of human sin and human misfortune outside a man, in the realm of objective evil powers and demonic forces. Man sinned because he was forced to, and if he were to be saved from sin, it followed that Christ would have to have defeated and disarmed the evil spirits which were the ultimate cause of the human predicament.

This was in fact one of the ways in which the Christian proclamation was expressed: Christ had overcome the forces of evil. But people who took seriously the existence of the world of spirits and demons (and most of the original readers of this letter will have taken it for granted) were almost bound to accept at the same time a certain amount of mythology. These spirits were not timeless elemental forces: they had a history, and their history explained their present activity. A popular version of this history was that the spirits had originally been in heaven, that they had "fallen" soon after the creation of the world, and had wrought such havoc on earth that God was compelled to put an end—by means of the Flood—to the generation of human beings whom they had corrupted, and to restrain all but a small
number of the spirits by having them "bound" or **imprisoned** beneath the 19
earth. On that occasion, God had nevertheless saved **a few persons** from 20
the consequences of the spirits' influence by bringing them **to safety through the water.** He had **waited patiently,** in the hope that someone would be found who had not deserved the fate incurred by mankind in general; and that person was Noah with his family. But the descendants of Noah were still subject to a certain amount of evil influence from these spirits. It remained for Christ to administer the *coup de grâce.*

In the body he was put to death. This seemed like a victory for the 18
forces of evil, an assertion of the supremacy of Death. But—**in the spirit**[a] **he was brought to life.** Death was made impotent by his resurrection: in that moment the forces of evil were overwhelmed. All that remained was to inform them of the fact, and Christ is imagined as doing precisely this: **in the spirit he went and made his proclamation to the imprisoned**
spirits. As a result, **Christ . . . entered heaven after receiving the** 22
submission of angelic authorities and powers. The issue in the realms of angels and spirits was decided. But how did this affect human beings? How were they to be rescued from the still continuing consequences of the
long activity of these spirits on earth? The answer was **prefigured** by the 21
story of Noah itself. Safety was available once again through water, this time **the water of baptism.**[b]

[*a*] According to 1 Cor. 15.44–6 there was a sense in which resurrection must necessarily be **in the spirit,** even though strictly speaking it was a bodily resurrection; but the language here may be a reflection of a view held by more Hellenized Jewish writers, that the souls, or spirits, of the righteous are in the hand of God, though their bodies lie in the grave (Wisdom 3.1).
[*b*] The definition offered of baptism in verse 21 is puzzling. The first part of it—**not the washing away of bodily pollution**—is in line with much New Testament teaching. But

(This interpretation knits the passage into its context, and does reasonable justice to the very compressed and allusive language. But many other interpretations are possible. The most famous, and one of the oldest, is that which connects this passage with the Christian doctrine of Christ's "descent into hell": Christ, on this view, used the period of 2½ days during which he was buried to visit the underworld and "make his proclamation" (i.e. preach the gospel) to "the imprisoned spirits" (i.e. the dead), who thus had the opportunity to repent.)

4. 1 **Remembering that Christ endured bodily suffering.** This seems to be a third approach to the problem of the suffering of Christians. That Christ's suffering (and not merely his death and resurrection) has power to help a Christian in adversity is an idea already worked out earlier (2.18–25). Here it is related to what has just been said by means of the proposition, **When a man has thus endured bodily suffering he has finished with sin.** As a general statement, this is obviously untrue. To make sense of it, we must read into it a good deal of Christian meaning, perhaps along the following lines: the suffering a Christian endures (as a Christian) is suffering for the sake of Christ, suffering which is therefore to be identified with Christ's own suffering, a suffering which is a kind of "death" to which a Christian commits himself at baptism; and at his baptism (as the previous passage made clear) **he has finished with sin.** At any rate, the Christian profession meant a complete break with the licentiousness (as Jews and Christians always saw
4 it) of pagan life. Pagans might **vilify** this attitude. They might accept that there was an ultimate moral judgement which would demand a reckoning from every man, but when they saw Christians still exposed to the common lot of death, and especially perhaps when they saw them suffering and dying for their faith, they might ask sarcastically what use their Christianity had been to them. What was the point of it, if believers died all the same?
6 **Why was the Gospel preached to those who are dead?** To this, Christians replied that, **although** (granted) **in the body they received the sentence common to men,** their faith was gloriously justified in that they shared the victory over death, the resurrection, the "being brought to life in the spirit" (3.18) of Christ himself: they were **alive with the life of God.**

(This last sentence is again open to different interpretations: that **the Gospel was preached to those who are dead** is reminiscent of 3.19, 'Christ made his proclamation to the imprisoned spirits', and it may be

the second part—**the appeal made to God by a good conscience**—seems to contradict the usual Christian understanding of baptism as something given by God, whether or not the convert has a "good conscience", and to be quite irrelevant to the context. The Greek sentence is very compressed, and its meaning is uncertain. The word translated "appeal" also occurs in the sense of "response" or "undertaking". If this is the meaning here, we may understand that baptism is the response a Christian makes to Christ's victory, committing himself "with a good conscience" to God.

possible to work out a connection between the two. Nevertheless, the Greek words themselves fit more easily into the interpretation given above.)

The end of all things is upon us. This conviction is voiced again and 7
again in the pages of the New Testament. In literal terms, it was not justified: the end did not come. Yet there is little evidence that this delay disturbed the faith of the church. The serious expectation that the present was about to give place to a new age was characteristic of Christianity throughout at least the first century of its existence and has remained so (though usually in a less naïve form) ever since. Moreover, the New Testament writers were careful to draw the right consequences from it. It must not be thought of as a pretext for irresponsible excitement or for failure to fulfil one's social responsibilities. On the contrary, it was a spur to prudent and moral behaviour. Almost every time it is mentioned in the New Testament it leads into an exhortation to vigilance and sobriety. **You must lead an ordered and sober life** is a typical example.

What follows provides a distinctive portrait of the Christian community. 7-11
Love, hospitality, service, were three key-words of Christian life. Most of the ideas can be found in Paul's letters (hospitality, Romans 12.13; the use of varied gifts, 1 Cor. 12; Christians as stewards, 1 Cor. 4.1–2, Titus 1.7): they were doubtless a common factor in Christian teaching throughout the early
church. This writer adds one piece of proverbial wisdom: **love cancels** 8
innumerable sins. In isolation, this sounds like a weighty statement about the power of love to procure the forgiveness of a sinner. But in fact it should probably be taken in its original context:

> "Hatred stirs up strife,
> but love covers all offences"
> (Proverbs 10.12).

In this form, the proposition is a simple one: in an atmosphere of hatred, the smallest offences are magnified; in an atmosphere of love they are immediately overlooked, covered, cancelled. The proverb certainly circulated in the early church (it occurs also in James 5.20). It may even have been used by Jesus himself. In any case, it served the purpose well of supporting the exhortation
to keep your love for one another at full strength. 8

The fiery ordeal that is upon you. What is this? Earlier references to 12
persecution have suggested that it was, at most, a possibility to be taken seriously. Here it seems to have broken out in earnest. It is possible the writer has just heard of the crisis, and hastily adds a postscript to his letter
(the previous verse, with its **Amen**, might have been intended to be the end 11
of the letter—compare the ending of Jude—but there are many more cases where this kind of formula occurs in the middle of a letter). On the other hand, it is hard to be sure how literally we ought to take **the fiery ordeal.**

In our minds, it arouses a picture of arson and violence, and even perhaps of the Emperor Nero burning Christians alive. But if it is taken as a metaphor, it need be nothing so dramatic. At the beginning of the letter, the writer commented on the apparently minor tribulations of the church and pointed out that 'even gold passes through the assayer's fire'. The analogy was a very old one, and provided one of the ways in which innocent sufferers could see some meaning in their sufferings. Following the same line of thought, the writer may still have only sporadic and relatively mild persecution in mind when he calls it a **fiery ordeal.**

The reason given for encouragement under the ordeal is similar to one
13 given previously (2.18–25): **it gives you a share in Christ's sufferings.**
14 **Count yourselves happy**—this is reminiscent of Jesus' words, 'How blest
(the same word, in the Greek, as **happy**) you are, when you suffer insults . . .
for my sake' (Matthew 5.11), and seems to be supported also by a reference
to Jesus' promise that when Christians found themselves under attack **the**
Spirit would tell them what to say (Mark 13.11).

Once again, the point is made that Christians must not lay themselves
open to any charges which might legitimately be punished by the state,
16 except that of being **a Christian.** This time the argument appears to be
based on a passage of Malachi (3.1–5): "Suddenly the Lord whom you seek
will come to his temple . . . Who can endure the day of his coming? . . . He is
like a refiner's fire . . . he will purify the Levites and cleanse them like gold
and silver . . . prompt to testify against sorcerers, adulterers and perjurers."
17 The "temple" of the Lord is now his **household** (one word in Greek does
for both)—that is, the Christian church. The "Levites" who served the
Jerusalem temple have been replaced by a new priesthood (2.5) which is
12, 17 now undergoing "the refiner's fire", **the fiery ordeal.** The **judgement**
which was the theme of Malachi's prophecy is now about to begin, and it
will follow the pattern which Malachi foretold. Those in **God's own house-**
15 **hold** will be the first to be exposed if they are found guilty of **murder, theft,**
or sorcery or **infringing the rights of others.** This is sufficient warning
to Christians; for those outside the church it is still more sombre. As a verse
18 of Proverbs puts it (11.31), **It is hard enough for the righteous to be**
saved; what then will become of the impious and sinful? Christians
19 need not fear: **their Maker will not fail them.** But even so, their salvation
will be conditional upon their **doing good.**

5. 1 **And now I appeal to the elders of your community.** The letter has already had one section addressed to different groups within the community. It now has another, and this time the distinction is between **the elders** and **the younger men.** This was perhaps a more natural grouping than it would seem now: most of the Greco-Roman cities of Asia Minor had highly organized guilds and associations of "older men" and "younger men", and a similar tendency to form separate societies within the whole may have been

present in the church. It was also doubtless true of the church, as of most institutions, that the responsibility for leadership lay mainly in the hands of the elders (or some of them). At any rate, it is no surprise that this appeal to **the elders** is concerned with their exercise of responsibility.

The author writes as a **fellow-elder.** His authority to write such a letter must in fact have been due to a position of considerable respect in the church at large; but he prefers to dwell on the dignity and responsibility which he holds in common with other "elders". **A witness of Christ's sufferings** would be a particularly appropriate description of Peter while present at the trial of Jesus (and so would come naturally from the pen, either of Peter himself, or of a writer wishing to invest his letter with the authority of the historical Peter). But it also had a more general meaning. **Christ's sufferings** were continued in the church (Colossians 1.24), and a **witness** of them might be anyone who was personally involved in those sufferings and who believed (like any Christian) that they would be more than compensated for by **the splendour that is to be revealed.**

Christian leaders are **shepherds**, pastors: the church took the metaphor 2
from the Old Testament and enriched it with overtones which had in fact
sounded through much of the teaching of Jesus (see above on John 10). The
pattern for their shepherding was set by Christ himself, **the Head Shep-** 4
herd. In practice, the task was doubtless onerous, and some may have been
inclined to undertake it only under **compulsion**; it commanded a stipend, 2
and some may have been attracted by the money; and it bestowed a particular
rank and sphere of influence which some may have coveted as an opportunity
for **tyrannizing** over others. Such motives were the opposite of those which 3
should animate Christian elders.

The particular subordination demanded of the **younger men** (by custom 5
in any society) was no more than an example of that **humility towards**
each other which should characterize all members of the church. Humility
had already been often commended in the Old Testament (there is a quota- 6
tion here from Proverbs 3.34), but it came into its own as a general principle
of human relationships only in the Christian church.

Awake! be on the alert! Not only violence, but also stealth and deceit, 8
were the weapons of the church's enemies. Now, at the end of the letter,
these enemies are finally identified as agents of **the devil**, who is active
wherever the Christian church exists. The pattern is everywhere the same.
The writer closes in words that recall his opening (1.6). In the present, **brief** 10
suffering; but in the future, a share in the unimaginable glory of Christ.

I write you this brief appeal through Silvanus. Writing a letter in 12
antiquity usually meant dictating it to a member of the household or a pupil,
and then entrusting it to a personal messenger. Silvanus (which is the Latin
form of the name which appears as Silas in Acts) was a companion of Paul's;
he is mentioned in the opening of the letters to the Thessalonians, and he

may have assisted Paul in one of these ways. We did not know that he was also a companion of Peter's. Whether he was or not, the name could easily have suggested itself to a writer who wished to imagine whom Peter would
13 have had as a secretary at that time. **Mark** was also (for a time) a fellow-worker with Paul. A later tradition has it that he was with Peter in Rome, and stood in a relationship to him which could well have been metaphorically described as being Peter's **son.**

Greetings from her who dwells in Babylon. A Jewish "Letter to the Dispersion" would properly have come from Jerusalem. But at a certain moment in the history of the Jewish people, its leaders had all been taken into exile in Babylon. During that period, they had to address their fellow-Jews "from Babylon". The actual city of Babylon had ceased to be important long ago; but it still stood in the minds of Jewish people as the archetype of any great pagan city, and in the first century A.D. there was only one city which obviously deserved the name: Rome (see below on Revelation 17). The writer of this Letter to the Christian Dispersion was presumably in Rome. Everyone would have known what he meant when he mentioned **Babylon.**

Her who dwells . . . chosen by God. This soon established itself as a formula for conveying greetings from one church to another (compare 2
14 John 1,13). On the **kiss,** see above on the similar phrase in Romans 16.16.

THE SECOND LETTER OF PETER

In the course of this letter, extensive use is made of phrases and ideas which appear in the Letter of Jude; there is a reference to the letters of Paul, which seems to presuppose that there existed already a collection of them, bearing the authority of Scripture (3.15–16); and the apostles are referred to as 'your apostles' (3.2), as if they were figures already remote from the circle of the writer. All this (quite apart from the general style of the letter) would have been barely conceivable in the lifetime of Peter the apostle. There can be little doubt that the letter is one of those which appear to have been written after the death of their supposed authors, and which supported their claim on the attention of Christians by invoking the authority of one of the apostles. It was referred to by no ancient writer before the third century A.D., and was only hesitantly accepted by the church into the canon of the New Testament. It may well have been written as late as the first half of the second century A.D.

The remedy for doubt

From Simeon Peter. The apostle was usually called Simon, the Greek 1. 1
equivalent of the Hebrew or Aramaic name Simeon. By using the form
Simeon, the writer may have wished to give a particularly Palestinian flavour
to the opening. But there may also have been another reason. Simeon was one
of the original patriarchs of Israel; and a popular form of Jewish writing
since about the end of the second century B.C. seems to have consisted of
"testaments", or farewell discourses, attributed to a patriarch just before
his death, but containing moral instruction appropriate to the time of writing.
This was evidently one of the sources of inspiration for our author. Peter is
represented as being about to die **very soon**; and just as in Jewish works of 14
this kind the patriarch was made to recall some of the events of his life
(recorded in the Old Testament) before proceeding to the message he had to
give, so Peter is represented as harking back to a significant moment in his
own life (recorded in the New Testament), his presence on **the sacred** 18
mountain when Jesus was transfigured (Matthew 17.1–8). Formally, the
document begins as a letter; but the convention is not kept up: there are no
personal greetings and no salutation at the end. The model the writer had
before him was not so much a "letter" as a "testament"; and he may have
felt it particularly appropriate to introduce Peter as **Simeon,** the name also
borne by one of the patriarchs.

Nevertheless, if the literary model was Jewish, the language reflects a
culture shaped more by Greek religion. There is no longer the diffidence
1 which a purely Jewish writer might have felt in calling Jesus **God** alongside
the one true God, or in giving him the title of **Saviour**, which was borne both
by pagan gods and by rulers (see above on 2 Timothy 1.10); **faith** is no
longer something imparted by God and active in believers, but is a **privilege**
which an apostle could say that he shared with his fellow-Christians; phrases
3 like **divine power, true religion, splendour and might,** belong to the
vocabulary of Hellenistic religious thought; and the process of escaping
4 **corruption** and coming to **share in the very being of God** was recognized
to be the object of many philosophies in the Greek-speaking world. The chain
of virtues in verses 5–7 is a rhetorical device found in both Jewish and Greek
literature. In short, the style is that which might be expected of an educated
Hellenistic Jew.

As for this writer's understanding of Christianity, it has already a certain
conventional rigidity compared with that of the first generation of Christians.
11 For him, the **kingdom of our Lord and Saviour Jesus Christ** evidently
means a blessed state in the future, to which Christians may qualify for
admission by the cultivation of a certain kind of behaviour: a Paul or a John
would hardly have described the distinctive elements of Christian living in
terms merely of an expectation of better things to come in the after-life.
Again, he seems no longer to share the exhilaration of the early church in its
discovery that Old Testament prophecies were now fulfilled in the person
and destiny of Christ. For him (and this is a point to which he returns at the
end), Scripture, including what we should now call the New Testament,
may have been one of the sources of the church's faith, but was also dangerous
20 material in the hands of undisciplined interpreters: **no one can interpret**
any prophecy of Scripture by himself. To his mind, the significance of
the Transfiguration lay not in its implications for understanding the nature
and earthly activity of Christ, but in the dogmatic pronouncement given on
17-18 that occasion by **a voice from heaven** that Jesus was God's **Son** (Matthew
17.5). In the face of heretics who were inclined to belittle the status of Jesus,
he appealed to what he took to be a fully authoritative statement, proceeding
from **the sublime Presence.**

2.1 **But Israel had false prophets.** When the church found itself confronted
with the problem of **false prophets** (see above on Matthew 7.15), it was
guided, not only by the predictions which Jesus had made on the subject,
but by precedents in the Old Testament. It suited this writer's purpose to
see **false teachers** as part of the same predestined ordeal which the church
was bound to have to face. Having thus identified the enemy, he proceeded to
attack it in a way characteristic of the later books of the New Testament, that
is to say, not by arguing with his opponents, but by representing them as

such a serious danger to Christianity that his readers must cease to have
anything to do with them. This technique makes it impossible for us to gain
any clear picture of these false teachers. The writer is not afraid to exaggerate
and to generalize; he accuses them of being dissolute, mercenary and in-
subordinate—but these accusations were so commonly levelled at heretics
that they do not much help us. The situation is complicated by the fact that
throughout this chapter the writer seems to have had before him the Letter
of Jude.[a] Many of the phrases used there appear again here, and most of the
Old Testament examples are the same. The only specific charges against the
heretics concerning their teaching which are made in the whole chapter are
taken verbatim from Jude: **disowning the . . . Master, they flout authority** 1, 10
and **insult celestial beings** (on which see below on Jude 8). Even these
charges, therefore, must have been of a fairly general nature, if more than
one writer could take them up and use them in a letter intended generally
for the support of his fellow-Christians.

Having identified the heretics as the predicted diabolical enemies of the
church, it was not difficult to find traditional colours in which to paint their
inevitable retribution. For his first example, he follows Jude in quoting the
myth of fallen **angels**; but like the author of 1 Peter (3.18–20) he adds that 4
of the flood, and draws a contrast between the **world of old** and **Noah,** 5
preacher of righteousness. The traditional **object-lesson** of Sodom and 6
Gomorrah again comes from Jude, but the contrast with **Lot, who was a** 7
good man, is another of his own additions (and to us a surprising one, since
the natural inference to be drawn from the story in Genesis 19 is that Lot
was far from good, and that it was only Abraham's intercession which saved
him; but Lot was another of the Old Testament figures whom later tradition
included in a list of the righteous). The clearest case of dependence on Jude 10–11
is in verses 10–11: the language is almost the same, but this writer, just as he
drops all reference to the Book of Enoch, also leaves out the (perhaps, to
his mind, not sufficiently well-attested) story of Michael's restraint when
disputing with the devil over Moses' body (Jude 8–9). Without that story,
it is hard for the reader to make any sense of the statement that **angels . . .** 11
employ no insults. His last example, that of **Balaam,** is an expansion of 15
the reference in Jude, based on the story in Numbers 22.

Apart from these examples, the language is mainly a more lurid version of
the attack in Jude. **To carouse in broad daylight** represented a degree of 13
profligacy which deeply shocked an oriental. Exactly what the misdemeanour
at table amounted to is impossible to tell with certainty, though it is tempting
to accept the alternative reading recorded in the NEB footnote, and to see here,
as in Jude 12, some allusion to irreverent behaviour at Christian 'love-feasts'.

[a] This is of course not certain: Jude may have copied 2 Peter. But some literary dependence is undeniable, and it is on the whole easier to imagine the author of 2 Peter expanding and generalizing what he found in Jude, than the author of Jude sharpening the point of what he found in 2 Peter.

22 The writer ends the section with two proverbs which, if taken strictly,
suggest that he thought there was something inevitable about the apostasy
of these heretics. These proverbs usually illustrated the truism that whatever
you do to nature it reverts to its old self. The heretics (he seems to be saying)
19 were originally such **slaves of corruption** that it was almost inevitable they
should have returned to their old ways.

3. 1 **This is now my second letter.** Possibly the writer had composed a previous
treatise which is now lost; possibly he had read 1 Peter (though he makes no
other allusion to it). Or possibly the phrase (like that in Jude 3) was simply
meant as a conventional apology for not covering the whole of the subject.
In any case, it was characteristic of the style of a "testament", not to propound new teaching, but to recall to its readers **what you already know,**
2 and to remind them of **commands** already **given.** For a Christian writer,
this meant an appeal, first to **God's own prophets** of the Old Testament,
and secondly to the tradition handed down by the **apostles** (from whom,
despite his opening claim to be writing as an apostle himself, this writer feels
himself so far removed as to call them **your apostles**).
3 **In the last days there will come men who scoff at religion and live
self-indulgent lives.** That the church would have to contend with an
intensification of both heresy and immorality was accepted by Christians as
a necessary part of the divine purpose; the ordeal was a pre-ordained element
of **the last days,** the period in which the church now believed itself to be
living. To this extent, the statement simply echoes others which occur elsewhere in the New Testament (see especially 1 Timothy 4.1). But here, the
writer sees an important connection between heresy and immorality. One of
the arguments most commonly invoked for moral and sober behaviour
among Christians was the imminence of the Last Judgement, the coming of
the Lord, and the end of the world. "The Lord is at hand . . . therefore be
11, 14 sober, be vigilant" is a recurrent theme in the New Testament, and is
reiterated here. It followed that any who doubted or denied the imminence
of the end lacked an important moral motive and were particularly liable to
3, 4 **live self-indulgent lives.** The scoffing question, **'Where now is the
promise of his coming?'** had to be dealt with, not just as a doctrinal error,
but as a source of moral recidivism.

The promise of his coming suggests to a Christian reader the glorious return of Jesus Christ. This had apparently been predicted by Jesus himself, and was earnestly expected by his followers to take place within their own lifetime. But now, a whole generation of Christians had been **laid to their rest.** What could be more natural than that people should **scoff** at a religion which made such promises, and regard the new faith as discredited when they were not fulfilled?

And yet, so far as we can tell, this is not how it worked out. The books of the New Testament were written during a period which covers nearly the first century of the church's existence. Paul's earliest letters show that he confidently expected the end within his own lifetime; yet there is little evidence in those books which were written, say, fifty years later that its unexpected delay seriously troubled the faith of Christian people. They still believed in an imminent consummation of history; but they seem to have been so conscious of the new dimension which their religion added to their lives in the present world order, that they were able to accept without flinching the apparent extension of the time during which that world order was to continue. Indeed, this is the only place in the New Testament where the question, '**Where now is the promise of his coming?**' is explicitly raised.

It may be that in the second or third generation of the church the question did indeed become acute for some people, and that we ought not to be surprised to find it discussed in a letter which probably belongs to a comparatively late period. But it remains strange that the writer does not attempt to answer it by appealing to the promise of Jesus himself, or to the consistent expectation of the church. On the contrary, his answer is in very general terms; and in fact it is possible that the question was itself a more general one. **His coming** is a phrase which was certainly used of the return of Christ;
but it could also mean **the coming of the Day of God**, that is, the Last 12
Judgement and the end of the world. **Our fathers**, again, could certainly have meant the previous generation of Christians; but in any Jewish environment it was a technical term for the patriarchs of the Old Testament. In which case, the scoffers' question may have been a general attack on the basic view of history which is presupposed in the Old Testament and in all subsequent Jewish and Christian thinking. History, in that culture, was always pictured as one great and developing movement leading towards the final judgement of God and the establishment of a new age. It may have been this whole conception which the scoffers, influenced perhaps by Greek philosophical thinking, intended to call into question when they pointed to the
huge span of Israel's history and observed that **still everything continues** 4
exactly as it has always been since the world began.

If so, this writer's counter-arguments become more comprehensible. He points out, first, that the scoffers had a false view of the historical facts
recorded in the Bible itself. **The water of the deluge** represented a pre- 6
liminary (and nearly decisive) judgement on the world by God, by which he allowed it to revert to the element out of which it had been created. This near-destruction of the world was a clear warning that a still more drastic act
of God lay in the future. True, there existed an assurance **by God's word** 5
that there would be no second flood (Genesis 9.11). But this only meant that
the end would take place, not by water, but by **burning**. To a Jew, this 7
"burning" naturally represented **the day of judgement when the godless**

will be destroyed. But it was a widely held belief, both in eastern religions and in western philosophy, that the universe would ultimately be destroyed by water and fire. One half of this popular prediction had already been fulfilled by the flood. It followed that destruction by fire must still lie in the
10, 12 future. **The elements will disintegrate in flames . . . that day will set the heavens ablaze**—these propositions were accepted by many thinkers who reflected on the probable end of the world. The scoffers were factually
4 incorrect when they said that **everything continues exactly as it always has been since the world began.** They had overlooked the fact that the first stage of the destruction of the world had already taken place in the time of Noah.

8 The second argument sounds more philosophical: **with the Lord one day is like a thousand years and a thousand years like one day.** To us, this seems self-evident. God's time-scale, we say, is not ours. In the measureless span of eternity, the few thousand years of human history have little significance. It is possible that this was what the writer meant here. It was absurd, he may have been saying, to complain that the end had not come after only a few centuries, when by God's reckoning only a few days had passed. But if this is what he meant, it would have taken much of the force out of his
12 injunction to **look eagerly for the coming of the Day of God.** If one might have to reckon with tens of thousands of years of history still to come,
14 it would be difficult to **look forward** to the end with such intensity that it
11 kept one's life **devout and dedicated.** In fact, few people in antiquity, and certainly no one with any Jewish education, would have contemplated anything of the kind. History, it seemed to them, had lasted some three or four thousand years. How much longer would it continue? The question was often pondered, whether by philosophers, religious men or astrologers, and the answer given usually presupposed a total duration for world history (or at least this cycle of it) of not more than about seven thousand years. The answer depended upon what unit, so to speak, God used in imposing his arithmetic upon history. Many Jewish thinkers found the clue in Psalm 90.4,
8 which could be taken to mean, in Greek or Hebrew, "In thy sight **a thousand years are like one day**". From this the inference could be drawn (as it appears to be drawn here, even though it is stated in the same breath as the verse from the psalm) that God's unit, God's "day", is a thousand years: **with the Lord one day is like a thousand years.** How many "days" did God's plan allow for? The answer to this could be read off from the account of the creation in Genesis. There could be no doubt that creation was based on a seven-day "week". Seven thousand years was therefore the absolute maximum for world history. But seven thousand years seemed a long time. History had hardly been running for as long as that. There was certainly no cause for "scoffing" that the end had not yet come. At the same time, there was no justification for banking on a further delay. At some stage God

might 'cut short the time' (Mark 13.20). In view of this, it was perfectly
possible that the end might come tomorrow—**unexpected as a thief**, as 10
Christ himself had said (Matthew 24.43–4; 1 Thessalonians 5.2).

For a Jew, the question could never be academic: the end, with its traditional *mise-en-scène* of fiery chaos among the heavenly bodies, meant
judgement. Still less could it be so for a Christian, who now could see new
substance in God's age-old **promise** to his people, and could look forward to 13
the inauguration, through Christ, of **new heavens and a new earth, the
home of justice.** The end was an object of faith and hope, and the longer
one had to wait for it, the more natural it became to complain that **the Lord** 9
is slow in fulfilling his promise. The complaint was as old as Habakkuk
(2.1–5), who had replied to it by simply stressing the need for faith. Another
answer, which could also be found in the Old Testament, was that the delay
was nothing but God's **patience**, allowing time for more people to repent 15
before the day of judgement. This answer—that **our Lord's patience with
us is our salvation**—was in fact used by Paul, as this writer points out
(Romans 2.4). Moreover, a third answer was becoming popular in Jewish
circles around this time: the end was delayed because not enough people
were living god-fearing lives, so that it was possible to **hasten it on** by 12
keeping one's own conduct irreproachable.

We might agree that Paul's letters contain **some obscure passages**, and 16
our reaction would probably be to wish that he had expressed himself more clearly. But until the rise of a critical approach to Scripture in recent centuries, an obscurity was not necessarily regarded as a defect. On the contrary, it might be a sign that the passage contained a particularly rich and subtle meaning, which it was the task and privilege of the qualified interpreter to unravel. This was the positive side. But here, the writer is more concerned with the danger of heretical teachers interpreting these passages in such a way as to support their own doctrine. Instead of finding salvation there, they would **misinterpret to their own ruin.**

THE FIRST LETTER OF JOHN

Recall to fundamentals

1. 1 **It was there from the beginning.** This is not how one would expect any
letter, ancient or modern, to begin; nor is there any greeting at the end to make
up for the lack of one at the beginning (as there is in Hebrews, the only other
New Testament "letter" which begins so abruptly). Clearly, the document
is not a letter in the ordinary sense. Nor, apparently, is it a "letter" in the
literary sense (that was so common in the ancient world) of a piece of religious
or philosophical writing dressed up in the form of a letter: for such "letters"
always had at least the conventional greetings at the beginning and end.
This writer starts straight in on his subject, and at first sight he appears to
be writing a treatise or a sermon. Yet a few lines further down he begins a
2. 1 new paragraph with the words, **My children, in writing thus to you.**
There is nothing conventional or literary about this: we are reading a real message written to a real congregation. A pastor is appealing to his flock; and for some reason he does not make his appeal in person, but writes it down and sends it to them. It is as if we are overhearing a conversation which has already been going on for some time. The writer takes a great deal for granted in his readers, and uses a characteristic idiom of his own which was doubtless familiar to them, but would have sounded strange and esoteric to the outside world. This is an essentially private piece of writing; today we have to find our way about in it as best we can.

The main thing which this writer seems to have taken for granted in his readers is a knowledge of the gospel according to John. The opening of the letter contains unmistakable allusions to the opening of the gospel, and the whole argument centres round words like "light", "life", and "love", which only yield their full Christian meaning to someone who has studied them in John's gospel. On every page the style and the idiom are constantly reminiscent of the larger work; and it is not surprising that ever since the end of the second century A.D. the church has assumed (in the absence of any indication in the document itself) that this "letter" is from the pen of the author of the gospel.

Yet the tradition is by no means certainly correct. It is impossible to regard the letter as simply a kind of extension of the gospel. Certain small points of style and thought are different; the idiom has a very much less Jewish flavour than the gospel (there is virtually no reference to the Old Testament); and the situation envisaged is not at all the same as that to which the gospel was

addressed. The gospel was written explicitly 'that you may hold the faith' (20.31); its purpose was to help men to believe in Jesus Christ. But, in the letter, that faith is assumed. 'It is addressed to those who give their allegiance to the Son of God' (5.13). The issue now is the danger of schism and heresy within the church; the purpose is no longer a proclamation of something new, but (as the NEB puts it) a *Recall to fundamentals.* This is reflected even in the writer's way of addressing his people. Sometimes he writes in his own person: the writer is "I", the whole church to which he is writing is "you". But sometimes he is so conscious of a division in the church between those who are faithful and those who hold false beliefs, that he deliberately identifies himself with one party against the other. "We" then becomes the
true church, "you" the dissidents; and the purpose of the letter is **that you** 1. 3
and we together may share in a common life. It is not impossible to imagine the author of the fourth gospel addressing himself to such a situation, say at the very end of his life; but it is perhaps more likely that the letter was written, not by the evangelist himself, but by the leader of a church in which the fourth gospel had already been known and studied for some time.

Our theme is the word of life. In the Greek, this paragraph consists of a 1
string of short phrases, loosely connected together in a way that can be represented in English only by a liberal use of dashes and brackets. To bring out the sense, the NEB has broken it up into short sentences, and has isolated this one phrase in order to provide a kind of centre of gravity for the whole complex of ideas. In itself, **the word of life** is a vague expression. It seems to promise, if anything, a philosophical discourse. But a reader familiar with John's gospel would at once give it a more specific meaning. Jesus himself was "life", he was also "the Word"; and moreover the transmission of that "life" to new members of the church involved an exposition of who and what Jesus was, an exposition which could also be called **the word of life.** Such a reader, that is to say, would expect to hear about Jesus. But there was more than one way of hearing about Jesus. The task of a gospel was to portray the person of Jesus during his earthly life—and this, for the readers of this letter, had already been done by the gospel according to John. This writer had nothing to add to that. But the Jesus who was known from that gospel was continuous with the Christ who still enlivened the faith of Christian believers: in an important sense, Jesus was still present among Christians in the church (and in part this letter seems to have been written as an answer to those who questioned this continuity, and who did not see much importance in the historical Jesus for the reality of their religious faith). It is from this point of view that the writer now proposes to speak about Jesus. The **word of life** is no longer concentrated entirely in the story of one person, but is diffused, so to speak, in the experience of Christians. This experience, though rooted in the historical Jesus, is something still developing. It can therefore

no longer be defined (as in the gospel) in purely personal terms, as a certain "he" who made the whole experience possible; it is now a more complex phenomenon, involving a certain amount of abstraction: it is an "**it**".

This new point of view imposes a different time-scale. In the gospel, the person of Jesus was there 'when all things began'. A similar phrase is used here: **It was there from the beginning**; but the subject of the sentence is no longer just the person of Jesus, but the total experience of the church of which Jesus was the origin. The "beginning" of that experience was the moment when Jesus first began to be fully believed in—perhaps the resurrection, perhaps the first preaching by the apostles. If any heretics were claiming that they had a new experience more important than that which was shared by all members of the church, it was sufficient to answer that what the church believed in was no second-hand discovery made by the present generation, but **was there from the beginning.**

Let us assume that the letter was written around the end of the first century A.D. Few, if any, Christians survived who had actually seen Jesus. In the fourth gospel, the testimony of eye-witnesses is of great importance. But
2 in the letter, the perspective has changed. **We have seen it and bear our testimony** is not a claim to have actually seen Jesus; it is still about "it", that is, about that **life . . . made visible** which began with the appearance of Jesus on earth but which is still continuing in the form of a prolongation of his presence on earth in the experience of the church. Each generation of Christians receives its inheritance from the previous generation: every Christian has a tremendous solidarity with all those Christians who have gone before. In this sense, every Christian feels himself one with those individuals who originally "saw", "heard" and "touched" Jesus. But since then, Jesus has been experienced in the church in ways almost as tangible; and it is to this experience, which began as a personal apprehension of the earthly Jesus, and continues as an awareness of Jesus' continuing presence among them, that the Christians of this writer's generation **bear** their **testimony.**

5 **Here is the message.** Again, the form of this "message"—**God is light** —sounds abstract and philosophical, and devoid of that particularity which usually goes with statements of Christian belief. It is true that the reader is doubtless expected to have in mind those great statements in the fourth gospel to the effect that Jesus is the light of the world. But this writer goes on to show that he understands this proposition in a quite particular way. He is not attempting to offer a definition of the nature of God, but is drawing out an implication of what was in fact quite a common religious idiom. On a physical level, human existence is conditioned by alternating periods of darkness and light. By night, a man has to grope and guess. By day, he can see and explore to the full the possibilities of life. In religion, the same contrast suggests itself. Without God, a man is groping in darkness. With God, he can see where he is going. And so: **God is light.** But the same contrast also

suggests itself in ethics: immoral behaviour is walking in darkness, moral
behaviour is walking in light. If the two metaphors are now brought together,
an important point is made against anyone who thinks that religious knowledge can be had without moral reform: **if we claim to be sharing in his** 6
life while we walk in the dark, our words and our lives are a lie. Not
that one can "walk in the light" just by intending to: Christians are not
people who claim they can be good just by turning over a new leaf. On the
contrary: **we are being cleansed from every sin by the blood of Jesus.** 7
Neither pretending to be without sin, nor pretending that sin does not matter,
is compatible with the particular message which this writer has for his congregation, that **God is light.**

My purpose is that you should not commit sin. The danger does not 2. 1
seem to have consisted in the ordinary temptations of the flesh—though a
few fairly conventional warnings about these occur later on—but in the
insidious view that sin does not matter. We can guess who it was who held
this view. **The man who says, 'I know him'** is a familiar character in the 4
history of the early church. "Knowing God" (*gnōsis*) was the professed ideal
of a very popular kind of religious philosophy, which took many different
forms and adopted many different speculative systems, but which always
tended to represent the true aim of life as an attempt to free oneself from the
evil environment of the visible world by means of "knowledge" of the real
and the good. In this kind of religion—which is often called by the general
term Gnosticism—to "know God" was to be saved; and since this salvation
was held to consist in rising above the realm of earthly things to a knowledge
of purer things above, it was not unusual for these "gnostics" to regard the
body and its passions as quite unimportant, and to pay no attention to
morality. It was certainly true of some of them that, on their principles, sin
did not matter. These were evidently the kind of people who were menacing
the unity of the church to which this letter was written. It was to check the
spread of their influence that the author found it necessary to say, **my** 1
purpose is that you should not commit sin.

But should anyone commit a sin. It was one thing to discourage a
religious doctrine which might lead to immorality. It was quite another thing
to pretend that Christians, any more than anyone else, were immune from
the danger of committing sin. The church was not a community of people
who never sinned (which would be impossible) but of people who had reason
to believe that their sins were no longer a permanent source of estrangement
from God. The conviction that, in Christ, something had happened which
fundamentally affected man's relationship with God, was characteristic of
Christians right from the beginning. It was not easy to put into words, and
a number of different metaphors were used. One which was well accepted in
the church (though it is not actually used in John's gospel) was drawn from
the Jewish sacrificial system, and this author alludes to it twice: **We are** 1.7

2. 2 **being cleansed from every sin by the blood of Jesus . . . He is himself
the remedy for the defilement of our sins. Another was the image of the
Last Judgement, where **one to plead our cause** (an "advocate") will appear
on behalf of Christians. This advocacy, in John's gospel, is one of the rôles
of the Spirit. But here (following another line of thought which is also hinted
at in the gospel, 14.16) the "advocate" is Jesus himself.

3 **Do we keep his commands?** Granted that religion and morals were not
separable (as the heretics were claiming), the mark of true religion was
obedience to God. In the Jewish religious tradition this was taken for
granted. The revelation of God to men took the form of a Law which they
must obey, and it was axiomatic that anyone who professed to stand in any
relationship with God must **keep his commands.** At first the church
unquestioningly adopted the same attitude. All Christians were bound at
least by the moral standards of the Law of Moses: this obligation was presupposed in the teaching of Jesus as recorded in all the gospels, including
that of John. But here we seem to have moved a long way from the Jewish
tradition. The readers of this letter seem to have been more used to philosophical preachers than Jewish Rabbis; and here, for almost the first time in
Christian literature, the ultimate moral standard appealed to is, not the Law
6 of Moses, but the example of Christ: **whoever claims to be dwelling in
him, binds himself to live as Christ himself lived.**

The essence of this example is love. When Jesus gave his disciples the
command to love one another, it was, in a sense, something new (John 13.34).
To this writer, surveying the growth of Christianity from its origins, it was
7 already old: it was **the message which you heard at the beginning.** It
was the kind of conduct that had always been demanded of Christians. To
use again the metaphor of light and darkness, it was this that constituted
"dwelling in light". Yet there was more to it than metaphor. Loving one's
brother was a part of that whole new experience of living which was indeed
so new that it could be described as the beginning of that "new age" to
which so many religious thinkers had looked forward. In the language of
8 that traditional expectation, it could be said that **the darkness is passing
and the real light already shines.** The present was a new age; and a
command which had so much to do with the inauguration of that new age
must itself be, in some sense, **new.**

12 **I write to you, my children.** Thus the writer frequently addresses his
readers. But, to our surprise, he now singles out two groups within the
13 congregation, **fathers** and **young men,** to speak a special word to each;
13–14 and then he repeats the whole pattern again, with only very slight changes
in what he has to say. Why he does this we do not know; the message for
each group is not obviously appropriate only to them (though it may be that
the young men, having stronger passions, could be said to have scored a
greater victory over the devil—**the evil one**—by mastering them). Nor does

the section play any clear part in the argument: it comes after a point that is
complete in itself, and before a piece of perfectly conventional philosophical 15–17
wisdom (though **he who does God's will stands for evermore** is drawn 17
from the store of Jewish or Christian apophthegms). The readers are, and have always been, Christians. The distinctive things they live by are the forgiveness of sins, the knowledge of the Father and the Son, and a will and capacity to resist evil. Here, these propositions are simply woven into a balanced refrain.

You were told that Antichrist was to come. The church inherited a 18
characteristic way of looking at history. The present age was nearing its end, and God would shortly bring into existence a new age fraught with blessings for his elect people. But before that could come to pass, there would be a period of intensified tribulation. The forces of evil would make a last desperate stand, the elect would be subjected to unprecedented trials, and the violence of this final struggle would be such as to leave those who survived with no more opportunity to compromise: events would show which side they were on, and by the time the hour struck for the Last Judgement the sheep would have already been effectively divided from the goats. In this picture, the forces of evil tended to be personified in the form of some monstrous being, who was destined to have a brief spell of power and freedom before his final overthrow; and when, in a period of particular distress, Jewish visionaries represented the events of their own time as signs of the imminent end, they were not slow to identify the nation or ruler particularly responsible for their sufferings with that dreadful Being in whom, in the last days, the power of evil was to be concentrated.

The church (doubtless following the example of Jesus himself) made use of the same mythology and adapted it to specifically Christian beliefs. It seldom regarded its own vicissitudes as mere strokes of ill-fortune that might soon give place to better times. Instead, it interpreted them as necessary features of that climactic stage of history in which Christians were now living. Jesus Christ had inaugurated the kingdom of God; its full realization could not be far distant, the promised new age was dawning. Inevitably, therefore, the present age would see those grievous portents of the end which had been expected for so long. Each new adversity could be understood as a fulfilment of ancient visions.

For Christians, therefore, as much as for Jews, it was natural to regard any particularly virulent adversary of the church as a manifestation of those intensified forces of evil which were expected to make their appearance in the last days. Here, a slightly different line is followed, in that it is the heretics within the church who are **Antichrist**. The term was a new one, but it clearly represented the traditional monster of Jewish mythology, the personification of the evil forces ranged against the true Christ. This figure, the writer was

saying, must now be understood in a new way, not as a single king or emperor, but as a type: **now many antichrists have appeared.** The heresy
of these men was one of the characteristics of the age. Their function was to
26 **mislead** (so that the faith of the elect should be fully tested before the end),
and their presence within the church was the means by which it was to be made clear, even before the Last Judgement, who belonged, and who did not, to the fellowship of those who were to be saved. The church, in any case, firmly believed that this was the last hour. This belief enabled them to identify the enemies in their midst as necessary actors in the drama. Having
18 identified them, they were confirmed in their belief: this **proves to us that**
this is indeed the last hour.

To this writer, then, it seems that those who held heretical views were not people who had merely gone slightly wrong in their beliefs and needed to be corrected: they were "antichrists", personifications of evil whose task was the predicted one of making clear, in the last days of the present age, that
19 **not all in our company truly belong to it.** Strong language: what had
these people done to deserve it? It has already appeared that, with their indifference to questions of conduct, they constituted a threat to the morals of the church. We are now told where their doctrine was wrong: they denied
22 **that Jesus is the Christ.** It is difficult, at first, to imagine how people who
denied this could ever have been Christians; but from hints later in the letter we can piece together the kind of beliefs they held. They were Christians in the sense that they believed the Christ had come; but for them, "the Christ" was only a mythological symbol for a spiritual reality. The man Jesus was no essential part of their faith; at most he was an example of a general truth, a lay figure in a drama that must be played out ultimately in terms of philosophical abstractions. What their way of looking at things hardly allowed for was a proposition as starkly concrete as that which the church proclaimed, that 'Jesus Christ has come in the flesh' (4.2). They denied that **Jesus is the Christ** in the sense that they denied that the great abstract concepts they associated with the Christ could be identified with a person as particular and human as Jesus.

The apostle Paul would have attacked this error with argument, and shown why the heretics were wrong. This writer also had his arguments: the heretics did not care about morality, and no doctrine which gave rise to immoral conduct could possibly be correct; moreover, as was clear from John's
23 gospel, **to deny the Son is to be without the Father**—as Jesus himself
said, 'No one comes to the Father except by me' (John 14.6). But his main line of attack is one more characteristic of some of the later writings of the New Testament: no argument is necessary; the truth is in the keeping of the church; those who are in the church can be sure that what they are taught is the truth; those who separate themselves from the church separate themselves also from the source of truth. Here, this is expressed in unusual

language. **You, no less than they, are among the initiated.** The word 20
here for "initiation" means literally "an anointing" or "chrism" (see the footnote in NEB). A possible explanation of this surprising expression is that Christians were already beginning to refer to their baptism as (metaphorically) the "anointing" by which they were brought into solidarity with Christ, the Anointed One (see 2 Corinthians 1.21); moreover it was through baptism that they received the Spirit, which (as John's gospel puts it, 14.26) would 'teach them everything', so that (as this writer puts it) they
would **need no other teacher.** But the heretics had (presumably) also been 27
baptized: why could they not also claim the same guarantee of the truth of their doctrines? The answer must be that this writer intends, by "anointing", not just the moment of baptism, but that subsequent experience of the Spirit's guidance and of solidarity with the Son which, though it certainly followed baptism, also depended on the Christian remaining within the company of the church. Why does he call this experience by a name, "anointing", which suggests a once-for-all act of initiation? The answer may be that the heretics themselves, like certain gnostic sects in later years, practised a special rite of "anointing" which they believed guaranteed them access to the knowledge which they sought. If so, this writer is saying in effect that Christians have just as good an "anointing": as a consequence of
their baptism and continuing fellowship in the church, they can **learn all** 27
they **need to know.**

Let us assume that the heretics were saying that the important thing is to "know" God: what the body does—what people call "sin"—does not matter. Our author has not yet finished with this dangerous error. It was a familiar turn of speech to call a man metaphorically someone's "child" if his character and conduct were like those of his "father". For example, anyone who called himself a "child of Abraham", as the Jews did, ought to behave as Abraham did (John 8.39). In the same way, since most religions allowed that men are in some sense "God's sons", it followed that, since God is righteous, his "sons" must be righteous too. If one wished to define what
this sonship meant, one could say, quite generally, **that every man who** 29
does right is his child. Conversely, **the man who sins is a child of the** 3. 8
devil (and here, as in John 8.44, there is a hint of another possible way of understanding what Christ has done: man sins because an external force of evil, the devil, makes him sin; Christ, by overthrowing the devil and **undoing the devil's work,** has rescued man from sin).

So much followed from common speech, and was already a serious argument against the heretics. If they said that sin did not matter, how could they claim (as they presumably wished to claim) to be "children of God"? But in the Christian vocabulary (which the heretics presumably shared) the term,
God's children, meant a great deal more. Not only John's gospel, but the 9
teaching of Jesus as recorded in all the gospels, made much of this. Being a

"child of God" meant having a new relationship with God through Jesus
Christ. It was a new status, a new kind of living, which was not man's by
right, but which had been given to Christians through the sheer grace of
1 God: **How great is the love that the Father has shown to us!** One way
of describing what this meant for a Christian was offered by the traditional
picture of the last things: at the Last Judgement (which, for Christians,
involved the definitive appearance of Christ) Christians, by virtue of their
2. 28 faith in Christ, would be **confident and unashamed.** But this writer has
3. 1 a much bolder definition of Christian "sonship" to offer than this. **God's
children** is not something we are called automatically, or will be called only
at the last day. [a] It is something **we are—here and now.** This must not be
imagined as a crudely obvious change in a man's appearance or character:
even Jesus himself was not recognized by **the godless world** (a clear
allusion to the argument of John's gospel). Rather it is a new intimacy with
God: Christians (just as much as the heretics) claim to "know" God, and
this, on the familiar philosophical principle that "like knows like", means
that already in the present life, and much more hereafter, [b] Christians are
2 **like him,** they have something new in common with God. Sometimes this
"something" is called the Spirit, sometimes it is described in terms of union
with Christ, or of a just status before God. Here, a term is borrowed from
9 popular philosophy: it is **the divine seed.**

This was more than mere words. Describe it how they would, Christians
knew that something had happened to them, and that what had happened
brought them closer to God. But being closer to God necessarily involved
being further from that which is abhorrent to God, namely sin. There could
be no dispute about what this meant. "Sin", admittedly, was a religious
term; but its consequences were indistinguishable from ordinary wrong-
4 doing: **Sin, in fact, is lawlessness.** This was the final answer to those who
were saying that moral conduct does not matter. That new closeness, or
likeness, to God which went with being a Christian was totally incompatible
9 with an immoral life. To put the matter in its simplest form: **A child of
God does not commit sin.**

All this was logical enough, and was a powerful argument against the heretics. But as a full description of the Christian life it needs considerable qualification. It may be true that the new kinship with God which comes from being a Christian is incompatible with sin; but the fact is that of course Christians go on sinning—indeed it has already been said with great emphasis that 'if we claim to be sinless, we are self-deceived and strangers to the truth' (1.8). Any analysis of the Christian life has to do justice to two

[a] Grammatically, the Greek allows of more than one interpretation. See the footnote in NEB.

[b] This seems to be the drift of verse 2. But the Greek is not clear, and indeed a slight change of punctuation makes it yield the somewhat different sense given in the second footnote to this verse in the NEB.

apparently contradictory facts. One is that the Christian is no longer subject to the power of sin; the other is that Christians, like everyone else, continue to sin. The tension between these two facts is resolved only by the conviction that, when a Christian sins, his sin, though just as serious as anyone else's, is nevertheless something which can be cancelled out because of Jesus Christ. The writer does not enlarge on the nature of this cancellation here; but he
makes two allusions to it: **everyone . . . purifies himself, as Christ is pure** 3
—where the metaphor is drawn from cultic sacrifices believed to "purify"
the worshipper; and, **Christ appeared . . . to do away with sins.** 4

The contrast in this section has been between doing right and committing
sin. But the Christian commandment is not just that we should do right, but
that we should love one another; and the opposite of this is not just sin, 11
but active hatred. The Bible likes to paint things in black and white. Just as
Jesus rated anger on a level with murder, so this writer makes the choice as
sharp as possible: love or hate. And, **everyone who hates his brother is a** 15
murderer.

Is the choice really so brutal? Is the alternative to love nothing less than
murder? Two examples seem to support this extreme use of language. The
first example comes from the Old Testament. It is written there (Genesis 4)
that God accepted Abel's offering, but not Cain's, after which Cain murdered
his brother Abel. But no explanation is given for the beginning of the feud;
nothing is said to show why God preferred Abel's offering. Subsequent
Jewish tradition, not content with this silence, filled in the reason: Abel was
just, Cain was unjust. As this writer puts it, Cain's **actions were wrong,** 12
and his brother's were right. Abel then began to figure in lists of Jewish
saints (as in Hebrews 11.4), Cain in lists of villains. From such a list (since
he does not elsewhere refer to the Old Testament at all) this writer may have
drawn his example. It suited his purpose admirably. Cain was a sinner; in
the phrase used earlier (3.8), **a child of the evil one.** His was a perfect
example of wrongdoing leading to murder: he **murdered his brother.**

The second example is only hinted at. **Do not be surprised if the world** 13
hates you. By the time this letter was written, there was a sharp division
between the church and the world. The church was persecuted and some of
its members had been killed. The antithesis of love and murder may not have
been overdrawn. Inside the church was mutual love; outside was a hatred for
Christians which had been known to lead to martyrdom.

In John's gospel the new life experienced by Christians was shown to be
as different from the old as life is from death. This writer uses the same
dramatic imagery: **we for our part have crossed over from death to** 14
life. In this sense the new life is **eternal life.** It was possible, of course, to
misunderstand the "love" which made such life possible, since this was a
word to which Christianity had given a new meaning. Some might be tempted
to think of it as a mere emotion, a superficial **matter of words or talk.** But: 18

16 **it is by this that we know what love is: that Christ laid down his life
for us.** Nothing less was demanded of Christians—though (the writer adds,
with an eye to the more prosaic routine of daily life) it need not always take
such a sensational form: it comes into action just as much when there is
17 simply a **brother in need.**

The reality of a Christian's love, then, is the test of his religion, the ultimate appeal of his conscience, the ground of that relationship with God which, in the fourth gospel, is marked by free access to him in prayer (16.23–4), a sense of unity with him (17.21), and the objective experience of the
18–24 Spirit (20.23). Here, all this is compressed into a few verses, with the result
that the Greek is in places exceedingly obscure (see the footnotes in NEB).

4. 1 **Test the spirits.** In the early church, as we can see it in the pages of the New Testament, Christians were distinctly aware of having received a new power, or a new quality of living, which they called the Spirit. The name came from the Old Testament, where it described the phenomenon of a man acting or speaking in a way which showed that the initiative was not his own, but God's. The classical manifestation of this Spirit was prophecy: a man was inspired to proclaim his insight into present or future events, and his words, though they were still the personal utterances of an individual prophet, were recognized to have the authority of an oracle proceeding from God. Similarly in the church: the fact that the Spirit was once more active was proved most spectacularly by Christians speaking words which were evidently supernaturally inspired (although, as Paul argued, there were many other ways in which the Spirit might be experienced—see above on 1 Corinthians 12). The reality and objectivity of this experience was denied by no one; and yet, like everything in the Christian life, it was ambiguous. Just as, in the Old Testament, warning had to be given against prophets whose words seemed to be supported by every sign of supernatural inspiration, yet whose message must be rejected because it was pernicious (Deuteronomy 13.1–4), so, in the church, there was a danger of **prophets falsely inspired**, and warnings against them appear in many early Christian writings. This, again,
could be understood as one of the tribulations to which the church would
6 necessarily find itself exposed in the "last days". A **spirit of error** was one
of the things which would seek to shake the faith of the elect, and would separate the sheep from the goats in readiness for the Last Judgement. Only those whose faith was sound and sure would remain safely within the fold. This spirit of error would take the form of a spurious manifestation of the real Spirit, it would ape the Spirit of truth which inspired authentic prophecy
among Christians. Indeed, this was one of the ways in which the ultimate
3 personification of evil would manifest itself: **This is what is meant by
'Antichrist'.** Behind it all was the devil, and normally men were very much in the devil's power. But Christ had overcome the devil, therefore Christians

need not fear the devil's agents: **you have the mastery over these false** 4
prophets.

How were these false prophets to be identified? They gave themselves away only if what they said was contrary to the Christian faith. That faith,
the writer has argued, depended on the proposition **that Jesus Christ has** 2
come in the flesh. A version of Christianity which did not do justice to the full humanity of Jesus, and to the identity of that Jesus with the Christ, could not possibly be proclaimed by a true prophet; and that, it seems, was precisely the doctrine which was being preached by the heretics, who denied 'that Jesus is the Christ' (2.22). Once their doctrine could be shown to be false, it made no difference if they supported it by means of apparently supernatural prophetic utterances: on the contrary, the very power of their prophesying showed them up in their true rôle as agents of a personified spirit of error, as manifestations of Antichrist. The fact that they were widely listened to was nothing for Christians to be alarmed by. It was merely another instance of the mysterious truth that the **world** did not accept Jesus, and still does not accept his followers.

Dear friends, let us love one another. This is more than a general 7
remonstrance. Christianity disclosed a new concept of "loving", and seems almost to have coined a new word for it (*agapē*). It meant something very demanding: following the example of Christ, if need be to the point of laying down one's life for another. It is one of the themes of this letter; but so far, in chapter 3, it has been introduced in a rather negative way: a Christian must love, because not to love is to sin, and a sinner cannot know God. But now this love is commended more positively. **Love is from God**; therefore loving is in effect the medium by which we come to know God. This could easily be misunderstood. There was a widely accepted philosophical sense in which men could be said to "love God". Men have an urge to know more about God, to seek him and to find ultimate satisfaction in the sense of having drawn near to him. This could be called "loving God"; and in this sense, the
statement that **God is love** was something with which the heretics, with 9
their passion to "know God", might very well have agreed. But the Christian answer to this was that the love of God is shown, not in man's response to God, but in what God has done, historically, for man (just as, in the Old Testament, God's attributes are always defined by reference to concrete interventions of God in the lives of men). If one is to be sufficiently like God to know something of God, one must have something of that love in oneself
which God had towards men when he sent **his son as the remedy for the** 10
defilement of our sins. God cannot be directly known by the evidence of
the senses: **God has never been seen by any man.** Nevertheless, there is 12
an empirical experience which brings a man close to God: **God . . . dwells in us if we love one another.** Doubtless much more is necessary besides if God is to dwell in us. But this insight into the nature of God was a powerful

8 argument against the moral indifference of the heretics: **the unloving know nothing of God.**

13 **Here is the proof.** The doctrine that God is love, and that we come into a close relationship with him by loving him and loving each other, is one that might conceivably have been put forward on philosophical grounds alone, and thus have been exposed to correction or refutation by philosophical arguments. But Christians did not merely believe in it as something inherently probable: they had two proofs which were rooted in objective experience. One proof was their own experience of **the Spirit**: something objective must have happened to bring this new force into their lives. The
14 other was the original encounter of Christians with that Jesus who was **the saviour of the world**, an encounter so vividly remembered and so faithfully handed down to subsequent generations that this writer could say (much as he said at the outset) **we have seen for ourselves, and we attest.** It was on the basis of these objective facts, and not as a result of abstract speculation,
16 that Christians had **come to know and believe the love which God has for us.**

Consider the traditional picture of the Last Judgement. Man appears before God, who is totally other, utterly just and good. Immediately, he is made bitterly aware of his own sin and inadequacy; he knows that his whole life (apart perhaps from a few gracious moments which may speak in his favour) has disqualified him to receive anything but a stern verdict; and so, in those moments of life when he takes stock of all this beforehand, man is necessarily afraid. But suppose now that God is after all not perfectly other; suppose that there is something in common between the love with which
19 God **loved us first** and the love towards God and our brother with which we
17 respond to God's love. It will follow that, by virtue of this love, **even in this world we are as he is.** At the Last Judgement, we shall not come before One who is totally other, terrible and transcendent, but One with whom we already share something essential. Our past life, instead of being mercilessly held up to the objective standard of God's justice, will be seen to have embodied already something of God's own love. And so we shall **have confidence.** Meanwhile, we need no longer live our present life with a fear
18 of ultimate consequences, the **fear** which **brings with it the pains of judgement**; to the extent that we love, and that God already dwells in us, the verdict on us at the Last Judgement is settled in advance. Apprehension gives place to confidence: **perfect love banishes fear.**

21 **He who loves God must also love his brother.** From the emphasis placed on this **command**, it seems likely that the heretics were denying it. With their indifference to moral conduct, they were prepared to talk about "loving God" without recognizing that this involved a corresponding attitude of love towards their fellow-Christians (which is what the word **brother** usually means in early Christian writings). Our author seems to have three

arguments to bring against this attitude (though he deploys them so briefly, and with so little care for logical order, that the passage is obscure):

(i) a straight argument from psychology: **If he does not love the brother** 20
whom he has seen, it cannot be that he loves God whom he has not seen;

(ii) an appeal to the teaching of Christ: **this command comes to us** 21
from Christ himself;

(iii) an argument by analogy: **to love the parent means to love his** 5. 1
child. This is an observation (perhaps an optimistic one, but with at least a measure of justification) about ordinary human life. But Christians are God's children: to claim to love God therefore involves loving his children, our fellow-Christians.

To love God is to keep his commands. A writer more conscious of 3
Jewish traditions would have agreed, but would have meant something different. God's **commands** were given in the Law, and keeping the Law was the way in which man expresses his love towards God. But this Law was made **burdensome** by the fact that the devil—or perhaps (less personally) **the godless world**—continually placed obstacles in the path of the man who tried to keep it. This writer's thinking is the same, except for one important point. The **commands** are no longer those of the Law of Moses, but of Jesus Christ; and they are no longer burdensome **because every child of God is victor over the godless world.** It was a standard article of Christian belief that Christ, on the cross, had overcome the devil, or (in the language of John's gospel) had 'conquered the world' (16.33). And those who believed in him shared in his victory.

This is he who came with water and blood. This is clearly symbolic 6
language, unintelligible to outsiders, full of meaning to those within the church, for whom **water** and **blood** had come to stand for profound realities: **water** meant baptism, the rite by which they had become Christians and received the Spirit; **blood** was the sacrificial death of Christ, which Christians made their own in the wine of the eucharist. In the life of the church, these were continuing realities: they were a part of the Christians' objective experience which, along with the general **witness** of the Spirit, assured them of the truth and saving efficacy of their faith. But they were not merely spiritual experiences: they were rooted in two decisive historical events, the baptism and the crucifixion of Christ. The heretics, it seems, disbelieved in the full humanity of Christ; and one form which such disbelief certainly took in early centuries was the view that the man Jesus became united with the divine Christ at his baptism, but that the crucifixion involved only Jesus, the divine Christ (who could not suffer) having left him before it took place. If this was the kind of heresy which the author of this letter had to contend with, we can understand his insistence that Jesus Christ **came, not by water alone, but by water and blood.** But this is guesswork: all we can say for

certain is that he must have had some reason for insisting so much. In any case he quickly returns to his main point. Water, blood and Spirit are objective realities in the church. As such, they are **witnesses** to the historical facts on which the Christian faith is based. In a Jewish court of law, witnesses were subjected to two tests. First, did they agree with each other? Secondly, were they the kind of people whose word could be trusted? The **witnesses**
8 to the Christian faith pass both these tests: the **three are in agreement**;
9 and as for their reliability, **this threefold testimony is indeed that of God himself.**[a]

In English, the word "witness" is ambiguous: it can mean the person testifying, or the testimony he gives. The NEB has made this paragraph
10 slightly more confusing by using it in both senses. **God's own witness** does not mean a person giving evidence, but the testimony which is given. The
11 content of this testimony (or **witness**) is given at the end: **that God has given us eternal life**—this is the fundamental theme of the whole letter. It was proclaimed right at the beginning (1.1); and a final reference to it here rounds off the argument. But the original subject of this paragraph is, not the content of the testimony, but the way it is given. How does God "give his testimony" to the facts of the Christian religion? We have seen: through those objective signs of his presence—his "witnesses"—which are experienced by Christians in the form of baptism, eucharist and the Spirit. It follows that to accept this testimony is to let it become part of one—the
10 Christian **has this testimony in his own heart**; to reject it is to make God out **to be a liar.**

13 **This letter . . . is addressed to those who give their allegiance to the Son of God.** It has used language of the utmost severity about those who have deviated from the true faith; it has even called them personifications of evil, 'Antichrist'. It would have made for a clear and simple picture if a line could have been drawn between these heretics and those who had remained faithfully within the church. But the reality was more complicated: the line of division was blurred. There were Christians who were neither fully in the church nor definitely out of it. In this situation Christians had a clear duty to pray for their wavering brothers—for the efficacy of Christian prayer, given certain conditions, is taken for granted in this letter (3.22), as in John's gospel and indeed in many traditions of Jesus' teaching (Mark 11.24). If the
16 sin was **not a deadly sin**—that is to say, if the **brother** had not yet definitively separated himself from the church, which was the community of

[a] In verse 7, after the words 'For there are three witnesses', the Authorised Version of the English Bible has the following insertion: "that bear record in heaven, the Father, the Word and the Holy Spirit; and these three are one. And there are three that bear witness on earth." This insertion occurs in no early Greek manuscript, but appears occasionally, from the fourth century onwards, in manuscripts of Latin translations of the Bible. It is now universally agreed to be a relatively late interpolation into the Latin text.

those who have **life**—then there was hope for the sinner. On the other hand,
there is such a thing as deadly sin: a man might have gone so far in the
way of heretics that his sin was no longer just a case of **wrongdoing** such 17
as could be remedied through forgiveness and cleansing (1.7; 2.2), but
placed him irrevocably outside God's family, in the realm of "death".
It was no part of a Christian's duty to pray for a return of those who
were in such open opposition to the church that they could be called
'Antichrist'.

(This is an interpretation which knits the passage into the context of the letter as a whole; but the writer may have had something quite specific in mind to which we no longer have the key. Jesus' saying about the sin against the Holy Spirit (Mark 3.28–9) shows that some sort of grading of sins into forgivable and unforgivable sins was known to early Christianity; and the problem of Christians who committed the grave sin of apostasy was a serious one for, for instance, the writer of the letter to Hebrews. However, the systematic classification of sins into "venial" and "mortal" is a much later development, and is hardly anticipated in this passage.)

Nevertheless, apart from these borderline cases for whom the Christian
could pray, the line between the church—the children of God, **God's** 19
family—and **the whole godless world** was sharply drawn. Outside, men
were by definition sinners; they lay **in the power of the evil one** (for it did
not come naturally to think of a life without God as neutral: it exposed a man
to all the forces of evil that are rampant in the world, and from which there
is only protection for the Christian in so far as **it is the Son of God who** 18
keeps him safe). Inside was the community of those who were not sinners
(in the sense explained earlier) and who had all the knowledge, the experience
of reality, which the heretics had been claiming as their own.

We know . . . We know . . . We know . . . These sentences serve to sum 18–20
up the main points made in the letter. But there could hardly be a more
unexpected ending than the words, **My children, be on the watch against** 21
false gods. It is the kind of thing which was said again and again by strict
Jewish writers: the worship of **false gods** was what the Jews found most
horrifying in their heathen neighbours, and they insistently tried to protect
themselves (and all who sympathized with Judaism) from the dreaded
contagion of it. In the early years of Christianity the same warning had to be
sounded: the images of pagan gods which adorned every Greco-Roman city
were a source of danger as much to the pure religion of the Christian as to
that of the Jew. But it was essentially a warning for the simple: more sophisticated spirits, whether of Greek or of Jewish background, did not attach
much importance to images and statues. God, they knew, was known by the
mind and the heart, not by the senses. And so the old cry of Jewish propaganda—**be on the watch against false gods**—was reinterpreted, by more
cultured writers, as a warning against the "false gods" of things such as

money or ambition. At the same time, the word used for these **false gods**—*eidōla*, idols—was a technical term of popular Platonic philosophy: it meant the transient appearance of things as opposed to eternal realities. The letter has been speaking the language of cultured people more at home, probably, in the jargon of philosophy than in the catchphrases of Jewish religion. To them, all the pretensions, all the seductive "knowledge", of the heretics could be caricatured, in a parting shot, as mere appearance, **false gods.**

THE SECOND LETTER OF JOHN

Truth and love

The Elder to the Lady. In form, this is exactly the way any letter was 1
expected to begin: "From A to B, greetings". Indeed, unlike THE FIRST
LETTER, this and THE THIRD LETTER are more like the actual letters of
their time than almost any other writing in the New Testament. They are
both of the right length to fill one side of a sheet of papyrus, they both have a
beginning and end typical of the conventions of letter-writing in the ancient
world. Yet there is a difference between them. THE THIRD LETTER is part
of a correspondence between individuals, and was clearly written personally
to its recipient; but THE SECOND LETTER, though it uses exactly the same
conventions, puts them to a different use. It is not a private letter at all, but
an open one. And the salutations and greetings (as in the letters of Paul)
are made to carry a load of Christian teaching.

To this extent, the letter is artificial, and its artificiality can be seen at once
in the opening. The **Lady**, if a real lady, would have a name. But this lady
has only **children and a Sister.** The symbolism is obvious: just as, on a 13
Roman coin, a lady goddess often represented a nation or a city (our own
Britannia was one of these), so, for a Christian writer, a Lady could stand for a
particular church, her Sister for a neighbouring church. It is the same convention as in 1 Peter 5.13: in each case the symbolic lady is called **chosen** 1
by God. No Christian reader would have doubted what was meant.

Thus the formula, "From A to B", is turned into a symbolic device for
addressing an open letter to a church. The same is done with the rest of the
formula: "greetings". Not only is the usual Greek word (*chairein*, greeting)
replaced by its Christian equivalent (*charis*, **grace**) and combined with two 3
other solemn words—**mercy, and peace**—but the whole phrase is transformed from a conventional expression of good wishes into a statement of
Christian hope: **Grace, mercy, and peace shall be with us.** And into this
framework is worked a brief variation on two themes which are dominant in
1 John, and which the NEB has chosen for the heading: *Truth and love*.

The whole salutation, then, (like that of many of Paul's letters) is a piece of
conscious literary artifice. What then of **the Elder**? Is this also a pen-name 1
for some well-known person? We might be tempted to think so, were it not
that the opening of 3 John, which is not in the least artificial, uses exactly
the same term, 'the Elder'. To the first readers of the letter, this was evidently sufficient to identify the author: it must therefore have been a fairly

distinctive title. Now by the end of the first century A.D. the word "elder" (*presbyter*) had become a title for one of the orders of ministry in the church. Every church had its "elders", who came next in seniority after the bishop. By this time, no church leader could have referred to himself simply as "the Elder"—there were too many elders in each church for this to be a distinctive title. Indeed, from the very first appearance of "elders" in the church, there seems always to have been more than one of them in each place. However, this was not the only use of the word. A man became "an elder" (or "senior"), not just as an official status, but by reason of advancing years. In the church in the New Testament period, it was a distinction in itself to be old enough to have met some of the original eye-witnesses to the events of Jesus' life. Early in the second century, a certain Bishop Papias knew of a John whom he called "the Elder", evidently meaning that this John had been a Christian long enough to remember the first generation of Christians. The same John may or may not have been the author of this letter; but in any case the most likely explanation of the title, "the Elder", is that it was borne by a man of great seniority in his own church, whose advanced years made him a unique contact with the early days of Christianity, and who thereby possessed the authority to write the two letters which begin, **The Elder.**

Did the writer of this letter also write 1 John and the gospel of John? That he did has been the tradition of the church since early times. But there are the same difficulties here as have been mentioned in connection with 1 John. In particular, the letters are not so much an extension of the thought of the gospel, as its subsequent application to particular situations in the church; and 2 John is at one remove further from the gospel, in that it applies, not the thought of the gospel itself, but the formulation of it which we find in 1 John.
5 Thus the first exhortation, to **love one another,** is compounded almost
entirely out of the teaching in 1 John 2.6–8; and the description of the
7 **deceivers** matches the treatment of the same theme in 1 John 2.18–19. As in
1 John (2.22–3; 4.2), the point at issue between the author and the heretics is
9, 7 the **doctrine of the Christ**; the **deceivers** (almost a technical term, as in
1 John 2.26, where it is translated, 'those who would mislead you') did not recognize that the abstract figure of Jewish mythology, the Christ, was identical with the Jesus who had come **in the flesh** (or could be known **as coming,** as this letter puts it, probably without much difference of meaning). The only new point added here is that such a doctrine is characteristic of
9 **one who runs ahead too far.** The heretics are too progressive, and the author implies that the true doctrine of the church is something relatively stable and unchanging. We can overhear a certain anxiety (similar to that expressed in the letters to Timothy and Titus) to preserve the church's heritage intact against the onslaught of adventurous thinkers.

In 1 John much has been said about the danger which is constituted by

such a heretic. Now, for the first time, we are told what action must be
taken: **do not welcome him into your house or give him a greeting.** 10
This sounds less than Christian; but we must remember the background.
Heresy was not seen by the church at this time as something which it could
contain and influence for good, but as a manifestation of those intensified
forces of evil which must be expected to assail the faithful during this critical
stage of history. There were of course Christians who were borderline cases,
wavering between truth and error: these it was proper to pray for (1 John
5.16). But on the whole, the heretics betrayed their true colours, and could
be identified as malicious opponents of the church, as **the Antichrist, the** 7
arch-deceiver. They were particularly dangerous when they descended upon
a church from the outside. Giving hospitality to travelling fellow-Christians
was an absolute duty in the church; and any visitor who was a "prophet"
had a special claim on such hospitality. The problem of the abuse of this
hospitality by "false prophets" soon became pressing; and it is perhaps
understandable that when (as in this case) there was a clear criterion which
showed whether the teaching of such a visitor was heretical, and when the
heresy in question had manifested itself as a diabolical menace to the church,
it seemed right to make the position absolutely clear: **do not welcome him** 10
into your house or give him a greeting.

THE THIRD LETTER OF JOHN

Trouble in the church

1 **The Elder to dear Gaius.** The opening, the prayer for Gaius' health, the
expression of pleasure at news recently received: all these can be paralleled
in numerous private letters in Greek which have been preserved on papyrus
in the sands of Egypt. The author is writing as men constantly wrote to their
friends in the ancient world. At the same time, he is **The Elder**—a senior
and distinguished Christian (see above on 2 John)—writing to one whom he
4 calls one of his **children,** that is (if we may assume that he uses the figure
of speech in the same way that Paul does), to a man whom he converted
himself to Christianity or who belongs to his own flock. The Christian term
he chooses around which to compose his greeting is one that has occurred
again and again in these three letters: **the truth.**

The writer is in touch with some fellow-Christians who have been making
a missionary journey and who depend for their sustenance (as the rule was
7 in the church) not on the **pagans** to whom they have been preaching but on
the hospitality of Christians in the neighbourhood. Gaius has been host to
some of these, and has treated them so well that the report of it has come back
6 to the Elder. It only remains to **help them on their journey** (which
presumably involves a certain expense)—and this is one of the reasons for
writing the letter. Another is the common one of sending a testimonial. This
is for a certain Demetrius. The testimonial tells us little about him; somewhat
8 obscurely, the writer once again works in his theme-word, **truth.**

Hospitality to travelling Christians, letters of commendation from one church to another: these things were part of the normal life of Christian communities. That they were subject to abuse we know from the previous letter and from many other references in early Christian literature. It would not be surprising if some church leaders occasionally erred too far in the direction of forestalling abuses, and deprived deserving Christians of hospitality to which they were entitled; and this could well have led to friction between the leader of the church which refused hospitality and the church from which the travellers came. The Elder, it seems, had written a letter commending some of his own people to the leader of another church named Diotrephes; but his letter had not been heeded, and his people had been treated much as he had himself recommended that heretics should be treated in 2 John (10–11). Exactly how the two men stood to each other we do not know. The Elder was clearly an authority in his own church, but may

not have been equally respected elsewhere; Diotrephes he calls a **would-be** 9
leader, a word which was certainly intended to be derogatory, but is not
very precise:[a] Diotrephes was probably really the leader, but is being criticized for arrogance and spitefulness. What would in fact have happened when
they confronted each other we do not know. It is possible that this conflict
between them was characteristic of a period in the history of the early church
when the leadership of men like the Elder, whose memory reached back to
the first generation of Christians, was passing to an elected hierarchy of
younger men; but this is guesswork. In any case, the Elder is not asking
Gaius to take any action. He is merely citing the case of Diotrephes as an
example which is emphatically not to be followed. By his conduct, Diotrephes has shown himself up as an **evil-doer,** which means (according to 11
the argument of 1 John) that he is one who **has never seen God.**

The ending of the letter, like the beginning, uses the conventions of the 13–14
age, and repeats a whole sentence (which was doubtless also a letter-writer's
convention, then as now) from the ending of 2 John.

[*a*] See the footnote in NEB (Second Edition).

A LETTER OF JUDE

The danger of false belief

1 **From Jude . . . brother of James.** What has been said above about JAMES
applies equally to JUDE: the writer is evidently claiming to be that Jude (so
called in English Bibles, presumably to distinguish him from Judas the traitor,
though in the Greek the names are the same) who appears in Mark 6.3 and
Matthew 13.55 as the brother of Jesus. With his eye, possibly, on the opening
of the letter of James, he identifies himself discreetly as the brother of that
James who became the leader of the Jerusalem church.

Like the author of James, this writer was probably a Christian of Jewish
origin, writing in idiomatic Greek but drawing freely on the stock of a
Jewish education. This is hardly the background to be expected of a native
of Galilee; moreover the situation to be combated—*The danger of false
belief*—and the arguments used are characteristic, not of the first generation
of Christians, but of the church as we get to know it through the later
17 writings of the New Testament. Indeed, the injunction to **remember the
predictions made by the apostles** points to a time when the apostles themselves were dead. The period around A.D. 100 is the one which seems to fit
the letter best; and it must be assumed that it was written under the name of
Jude in order to give wide circulation and weighty authority to the contents.
1 **To those whom God has called.** The address is quite general, and there
is no salutation at the end. Evidently the document is a "letter" only in the
literary sense; it is intended for any Christian who may read it. One of the
conventions of such writing was to begin with the imaginary circumstances
3 which caused the letter to be written. So here: **I was fully engaged in
writing to you about our salvation . . . when it became urgently
necessary to write at once.** Nevertheless, this letter appears to have been
4 inspired by particular circumstances. **Certain persons** had **wormed their
way in,** the church was being influenced by the views of a certain group,
and the writer saw in this influence such an insidious danger to the faith that
he felt moved to warn his fellow-Christians at large about the real nature of
this movement.

What was the movement? We are badly placed to discover, for the author's
concern was not to describe it accurately, but to caricature it. His readers
knew whom he was attacking; his task was to portray these people in such
dark colours that faithful Christians would no longer be tempted to yield to
their influence; consequently his language is allusive and probably exag-
19 gerated. (The distinction **between spiritual and unspiritual persons** may
be an allusion to Paul's psychology or to distinctions made by "gnostic"

thinkers; but the Greek is very obscure.) Certain features stand out from his
attack: they could be accused of licentious sensuality, and of **disowning** 4
Jesus Christ. At first sight, it seems difficult to imagine how such people
could have called themselves Christians at all. But similarly radical heretics crop up in other parts of the New Testament, and it looks as if the movement attacked here is one form of a tendency that must have been widespread during the first century of the church's existence: the tendency to try to incorporate Christ in an elaborate metaphysical system which would lead to a more perfect "knowledge" of God. This often involved an indifference towards the world of the senses, and took the form, either of extreme asceticism, or of frank immorality. The name subsequently given to the exponents of such beliefs was "gnostics".

The writer does not attempt to argue with them—and this is one of the
features of this letter which betray a comparatively late date for it. The
church now possessed **the faith which God entrusted to his people once** 3
and for all; it was no longer something to be explored and developed, but
something to be defended against all attempts to adulterate it. The church was the community of people to whom this faith had been entrusted. As members of it, Christians were assured of salvation; and some might have thought that (as was broadly speaking the case with the Jewish religion) so long as a man complied with the demands and the profession of the church in essentials it did not matter if he held somewhat unorthodox beliefs. But this was not so: Christians were not safe regardless. If their belief and their behaviour were not worthy of their calling, they would still be exposed to God's judgement; indeed, such an eventuality was allowed for in the providence of God. There existed **men whom Scripture long ago marked** 4
down for the doom they have incurred.

Paul, to make the same point, invoked an example from Old Testament
history. Some of **the people of Israel,** even after their spectacular deliver- 5
ance out of Egypt, showed themselves **guilty of unbelief,** and were de-
stroyed. Similarly Christians, despite their own deliverance, were always liable to apostasy and punishment (1 Corinthians 10.1–12). This writer uses the same argument, and elaborates it with other examples. The myth of fallen angels, starting from Genesis 6.1–4, but worked up into a complex scheme by later Jewish tradition (see above on 1 Peter 3.20), provided another
warning: if even angels, who had seen God himself, could have been **not** 6
content and fallen under judgement, how much more the members of the
church! Thirdly, there was the example of **Sodom and Gomorrah,** which 7
was particularly relevant to the alleged immorality of the heretics; this again was proverbial, and was much elaborated in later Jewish writings.

To defile the body, to flout authority, and to insult celestial beings. 8
One might have hoped that these three charges would have been specific
enough to afford a clear picture of the heretics. The first item is almost

certainly another allusion to sexual immorality; but the second is ambiguous.
It could mean a disrespect for certain heavenly powers, or a disparagement of
the Lordship of Christ (as in verse 4), or (as it is rendered here) a disrespect
for the authority of church leaders. The third is equally mysterious, and can
be understood only in the light of the argument in verse 9. There was a
9 Jewish legend that, when Moses died, **the archangel Michael** was about
to take charge of his body, but was challenged by the devil, who claimed that,
since Moses had murdered an Egyptian (Exodus 2.11–12), his body, like any
other murderer's, belonged to the devil. This was to "insult" Moses. But
such **insulting words** were characteristic of the devil. The archangel would
not use such language, even when addressing the devil himself. Far less was
8 it permissible for Christians to **insult celestial beings** in this way. We have
to assume that the heretics' philosophy reserved only a humble rank for
beings such as angels which, according to the orthodox Jewish or Christian
view, occupied a place in heaven inferior only to God and Christ. This is not
improbable: demotion of angels was a feature of some "gnostic" systems in
the second century A.D.

11 **Cain** was now a proverbial example, not just of murder, but of every kind of wickedness (see above on 1 John 3.12). **Balaam,** originally guilty of disobedience to God (Numbers 22), had become a traditional model of arrogance and malice. And **Korah** was remembered for his rebellion against Moses and Aaron (Numbers 16), and provided in addition a stern example of the **doom** awaiting the heretics.

12 It is uncertain whether **love-feasts** is simply another name for the
Christian eucharist, or whether the church celebrated other solemn meals of
a religious character to express the solidarity of its members with each other.
The behaviour of the heretics, at any rate, is reminiscent of that of certain
people in Corinth (1 Corinthians 11.16–22). Their actions are a caricature
of Christian "shepherding". Their futility can be described in well-worn
images of clouds that bring no rain to a thirsty land, or trees that bear no
fruit in an orchard. Their bombastic protestations have no more substance
13 than **fierce waves of the sea**; and their destiny is that of the planets, which
some Jewish thinkers imagined to be **stars that have wandered from their
course** and are heading for a place of punishment in **blackest darkness.**

14 **Enoch.** The quotation is from the Book of Enoch, a work which was compiled during the second and first centuries B.C., and was never accepted into the canon of the Old Testament. Much of it is in the form of a **prophecy,** that is, of visions which Enoch, **the seventh in descent from Adam** (Genesis 5.21–4) is alleged to have been given of the future. The book was evidently familiar to this writer (he alludes to it in other places besides this one); and that the heretics seemed to be fulfilling Enoch's prophecy was yet another reason for condemning them. (This reliance on a Jewish writing which was never part of Scripture was the main reason which prompted

some sections of the early church to deny the letter of Jude a place in the New Testament.)

In fact, however, it did not need the dubious authority of "Enoch" to identify these men. Again and again New Testament writers told their readers to see in such heretics, not a chance hazard for the church, but a predicted
and unmistakable feature of the final age. Examples of such **predictions** 18, 17
are 1 Timothy 4.1; 2 Tim. 3.1–5; Acts 20.29. This writer betrays himself as belonging to a later generation when he cites such a warning at second hand.

It was always hard to draw the line between those who must be shunned because their heresy was irrevocable and those who might still be saved. Two other New Testament letters (James, 1 John) close with advice on this subject, and we evidently have a glance at the same topic here. But the obscurity of the writer's Greek makes it impossible to be sure what line he was taking.

Now to the One. The style of the ending is similar to that of Romans. 24
Here, as there, it may be a fragment of the kind of language which was actually used in the worship of the church.

THE REVELATION OF JOHN

THE REVELATION OF JOHN

THE REVELATION. So far as we know, this had never before been the title 1. 1
of a book. The idea behind the title is of course as old as religion itself: there have always been certain men and women who have claimed that in the course of some supernatural experience divine mysteries were "revealed" to them; and the religions of Greece and Rome, as of Palestine and Egypt, produced numerous books in which the writer (whether under his own or an assumed name) claimed to have fallen into a trance, to have seen inexpressible visions, and to have been instructed by heavenly voices, apparitions or angels in the meaning of the mysteries he had seen and heard. To this extent, no one who read Greek would have found anything surprising in the appearance of such a book in a collection of early Christian literature. Nevertheless, this book, though it was written in Greek, owed more to Jewish religion and culture than it did to the Greco-Roman world. To a Jewish thinker, the ultimate mystery to be revealed was not (as it might have been to a Greek philosopher or mystic) the reality lying behind the appearance of the physical world, or the destiny of the individual soul, or even (as was widely believed in an age much afflicted with astrology) the pattern inexorably fixed on history by the movements of the stars. The ultimate mystery, for the Jews, was the future—the state of affairs for which creation had been destined by God, and which alone gave meaning to the present. Partial glimpses of that future had been vouchsafed to the prophets of the Old Testament, who had used them as precious clues by which to interpret the significance of the times in which they lived. More recently (that is to say, since the second century B.C.), Jewish books had been written which worked up these partial glimpses into more elaborate pictures: the visionary authors believed themselves to have inherited an insight into the future which had originally been possessed by great figures of the past such as Enoch or Moses, but which could only now be divulged, since only now had history reached the moment at which they were destined to be fulfilled. This type of writing (usually called "apocalyptic", from *apokalypsis*, "revelation") began in earnest with the Book of Daniel, a collection of stories and visions, which, though associated with a national hero of the remote past, was written in such a way as to seem to throw light on the sensational vicissitudes and rebellions of the Jewish people under their Hellenistic rulers at the time of writing (second century B.C.). But it gained immediate popularity, and a number of books were soon written under the names of famous figures of Old Testament history which claimed to divulge the emerging pattern of a new age, and so to illuminate the times through which the writers were living.

Nevertheless, even among the Jews these books attracted only a limited public. Their language seemed too naïve, and their outlook too rigidly nationalistic, to appeal to the more sophisticated and cosmopolitan Jews of the Dispersion. For Christians, on the other hand, this kind of writing assumed great importance. The conditions which had made the visions of Jewish seers so partial and tantalizing were now dramatically altered. The new age, which for them had lain in an imprecise future, was now inaugurated by Jesus Christ; and the difficult and subjective process of elucidating old and mysterious oracles had given place to direct and authoritative teaching. Jesus himself had shown the way; Paul and other New Testament writers no longer felt any doubt about the basic shape of things to come; and here, at the end of the New Testament, is offered nothing less than the definitive **revelation given by God to Jesus Christ.** Christians were in a position to complete and to supplement the fragmentary insights of their predecessors. There existed now, not just dreams and oracles and visions, but an authoritative and final **revelation.** The claim contained in the first words of the book was as new as the religion which made such a book possible.[a]

To the modern reader, this book may well appear as the most obscure in the New Testament. Ultimately, the reason for this is that the task which it attempts is one which stretches language to its limits, and the writer's prose has for the most part the freedom and scope of visionary poetry. But a more immediate reason for this strangeness is that the author used the forms of speech and imagery which came naturally to him for the purpose, but which to us seem exotic and desperately allusive. His idiom starts from the language
3 of the prophets: indeed he calls his book a **prophecy** (and himself God's
1 **servant,** a traditional title of a prophet), and the great visions of his pre-
decessors—particularly Ezekiel—were constantly present to his mind. His imagery is drawn from the accumulated stock of visionary pictures which Jewish seers had been elaborating ever since the composition of the Book of Daniel. Whatever the nature of his visionary experience may have been, his description of it was conditioned by the literary resources which he had inherited. The work is one of extreme originality and power; but its shape is determined by the logic of the traditional elements out of which it is composed.

Who was the person who describes himself by no other name or title than
1 **John**? We know nothing about him beyond the very little which he reveals
of himself in the book. A tradition that goes right back to the second century

[a] The title which stands at the head of the page, THE REVELATION OF JOHN, stands at the beginning of all the manuscripts (sometimes with the addition of "the theologian", rendered in the Authorized Version as "the Divine"). But it is unlikely to have been put there by the author, who carefully defines, in his opening words, the nature of his book. The new circumstance was not that a certain John had suddenly been privileged to see what no one had ever seen before, but that Jesus Christ had come to reveal all things, a revelation of which it happened that John was chosen to be the human recipient. To this extent the traditional title, The Revelation of John, is inexact. It was probably simply prefixed to the work as a convenient way of referring to the title and the author.

A.D. identifies him with the author of the gospel and letters of John. Certainly he writes to the churches of Asia with considerable personal authority, and in view of certain echoes of the language of the fourth gospel it is probable that both works arose in the same part of the world. One might not have expected there to be more than one "John" who exercised such influence; but since both the style and the content of the Revelation are totally different from that of John's gospel (and indeed from anything else in the New Testament), it is hard to believe that the same man wrote both. The most which the evidence allows us to say is that the work was written (probably in about the last decade of the first century A.D.) by a Jewish Christian who was familiar with some of the ideas contained in John's gospel, who was held in respect by certain churches in Asia Minor, and whose name was John.

Yet even though we know so little about the author, we can catch something of the mood in which the book was written. John had **borne witness,** 2
a phrase which was beginning to take on a heavy meaning: Christians "witnessed" to their faith at the risk of their lives, and their final "witness" might be sealed with their death. John, as we shall see, was now in exile: he had already, at some cost, **borne witness.** And in writing his book he had a serious purpose. He had no intention of merely satisfying the idle curiosity of his readers. His book was meant to be read aloud, presumably during the
worship of the church. It carried no less authority than the word of God 3
itself, of which Jesus had said, 'Happy are those who hear the word of God and keep it' (Luke 11.28). Like so much of the exhortation found in the New Testament, it received its urgency from the fact that the final stages of history, expected for so long, had now been precipitated by the coming of Christ: **the hour of fulfilment is near.**

A message from Christ to the churches

The form of what John had to impart was still further conditioned by the circumstances in which he wrote. Whatever the eventual circulation of his book might be, he intended it in the first instance for certain churches which were known to him personally. Consequently, he began with exactly the
address and salutation which would have been normal in any letter: **John to** 4
the seven churches in the provinces of Asia. Grace be to you and peace. But in Christian letters, these conventional greetings were often transformed into something more significant by being made to express the great truths of the faith. So here: John first works in (with, in the Greek, an apparently deliberate disregard of grammar) a solemn formula, based perhaps on Exodus 3.14 ("I am what I am") but extended into the present and the future to take account of the Creator's necessary involvement in all stages of

history: **him who is and who was and who is to come.** Next (his mind
already forming a visual image of the court of heaven) he speaks of **seven
spirits before his throne**—archangels, he might have called them, since it
was angels who (in the Jewish picture of heaven) stood closest to God; but
angels were spirits, and "spirits" were an intelligible symbol for the Spirit
5 of God. Finally, he invokes **Jesus Christ**, and robes him with titles that had
their literary origin in Psalm 89.27, but which were now full of Christian
meaning (**faithful witness,** John 18.37; 1 Timothy 6.13; **first-born from
the dead,** Colossians 1.18; **ruler of the kings of the earth,** Romans 14.9).
This indeed is characteristic of the style of Revelation. The Old Testament
is never explicitly quoted, but phrases from it occur in every paragraph. Thus,
6, 7 **a royal house, to serve as the priests** is from Exodus 19.6, **coming with
the clouds** from Daniel 7.13, and the rest of verse 7 from Zechariah 12.10.
But these allusions are not mere padding from a literary source: along with
5 specifically Christian phrases (**him who loves us**—a characteristic expres-
6 sion of John's gospel—**freed us from our sins, his God and Father**), they
are combined in a texture that is fresh and distinctive.

8 **Says the Lord God.** This is how an Old Testament prophet spoke; and
3 the book calls itself a **prophecy.** But Alpha and Omega are the first and last
letters of the Greek, not the Hebrew, alphabet. God is first and last: the idea
is Hebrew as much as Greek (Isaiah 44.6), but it appears here in Greek dress.
This writer (it appears from his grammar) thinks in Hebrew, but he writes
for readers who know only Greek.

9 **I was on the island called Patmos.** This was evidently exile. We know
that the Roman Emperor banished political enemies to lonely islands, and a
provincial governor could do the same. Patmos lies off the coast of Asia
Minor, a small and thinly populated island. How much special **suffering**
10 and **endurance** were involved in John's exile we do not know. **It was on
the Lord's day.** This is the first time the expression occurs in literature: it
soon became the standard one for Sunday, the day which Christians celebrated as the weekly festival of the resurrection of Jesus Christ, as opposed
to Saturday, the Sabbath of the Jews. **I was caught up by the Spirit**: John,
even if he was now separated from all his fellow-Christians, would be most
susceptible to such an experience when that day came round.

This is all that the author says about himself and the circumstances in
which he saw his vision. From now on he is completely controlled by what
11 he saw and heard. **'Write down what you see on a scroll'.** This was a
command to set to work in earnest: John was not merely to take notes (which
he would have done on wax tablets or possibly a parchment notebook), but
was to compose a document that would fill a scroll of papyrus. This was then
to be sent **to the seven churches.** These cities all lay in an approximate
circle, between 25 and 50 miles from each other. Why John was to write to just
these seven (when there were certainly others in the area which were at least

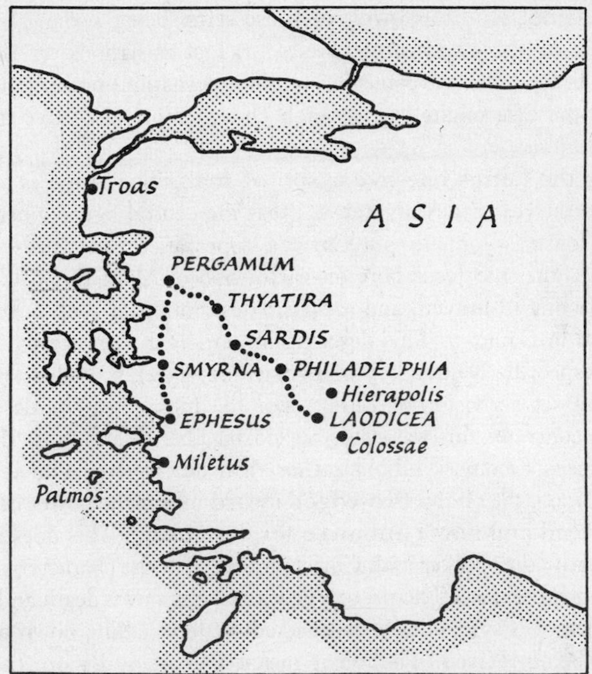

as important) we do not know. His mind certainly worked in sevens, and seven messages to seven churches fit well into the plan of the work. It is also true that a messenger, charged with delivering a message to each of these churches, would most conveniently have started from Ephesus, and the main roads would have brought him to each of them in the order in which they are mentioned. But beyond this, the selection of these seven seems arbitrary: it may just have happened that these were the particular churches for which John had a message.

I saw seven standing lamps of gold. In the outer room of the temple in 12
Jerusalem stood a great golden candlestick with seven branches. In any
Jewish prophet's vision of heaven, the same "standing lamp" naturally
tended to appear (as it does in Zechariah 4). But John saw, not one, but seven
separate lamps—a symbol with a **secret meaning** which is explained at the 20
end of the chapter: each stood for one of the churches which, for these
Christians, now replaced the Jerusalem temple. And of course, not only
these seven: seven was a perfect number, representing the totality of all the
churches in the world. With this symbol is combined another. **In his right** 16
hand he held seven stars. These were perhaps the planets: they signified
dominion over all the nations of the world. But they too had a secret meaning. Stars, in ancient religion, were not inanimate. They were governed by

angels or spirits. And the angels of these stars, being seven, also signified
20 **the angels of the seven churches**—for, just as nations, or their rulers,
were held to be under the control of some supernatural power (an angel or a
demon as the case might be), so each church must also have its angel in
heaven.

13 **Among the lamps one like a son of man.** The vision is a Christian
vision, and the reader already guesses that the central figure must be Christ
himself. How was John to put Christ's appearance into words? The clue
was perhaps the title Jesus bore on earth, Son of Man: this title implied a
glorious destiny in heaven, and a classic description of such a Son of Man
lay to hand in Daniel 7. This description, enriched with details from other
passages (especially Daniel 10.5–6; Ezekiel 9.2; 43.2), provided the frame in
which John set his vision of Christ. For the most part, the description is
visual and concrete: this was what he looked like. But towards the end the
16 words perhaps become symbolic rather than descriptive. The **seven stars**
mean dominion, the **sharp two-edged sword** means the power of his word.
18 **'I was dead and now I am alive for evermore'.** This does more than
merely identify the speaker with Christ: it describes the characteristic pattern
of Christian experience. The prototype was Christ's own death and resurrec-
17 tion, and here it is symbolically re-enacted by John falling down **as though
dead** and being revived. Though it meant a great deal more than this, it
meant at least that Christ had 'conquered death' (1 Corinthians 15.26, 57),
18 or (to use a slightly different image) that Christ now held **the keys of Death
and Death's domain.** This was a datum of the Christian faith: its implications for the churches were now to be spelled out.

2. 1 **'To the angel of the church at Ephesus write'.** John has been told to
write down what he sees and 'send it to the seven churches' (1.11). Accordingly, the book begins and ends in the form of a letter addressed to a group of
churches. But just as a letter to a particular church might single out one class
of people within that church for a special message (1 John 2.12–14), so this
letter has a special message for each of the churches within the group. Each
of these messages contains a warning appropriate to the condition of the
church addressed: the actual circumstances of Christians in, say, Ephesus or
Smyrna seem to have been vividly in the author's mind while each message
was being composed.

Yet in each case the message is addressed, not to the church itself, but to **the angel** of the church. "Angel" originally meant "messenger", and it is conceivable that here it is simply an enigmatic way of referring to the leader of each church, who would have the task of imparting John's message to the congregation. But elsewhere in the Revelation angels are always angels, and so they should be here. In that case, why warn an angel about the dangers of heresy or inertia? The clue probably lies in a way of thinking much influenced by astrology. Stars controlled the destiny of men. But the stars in their turn were controlled by spirits or angels. We have been told that the seven stars in John's vision were 'the angels of the seven churches' (1.20). Therefore what happened in these churches would ultimately depend on the angels who controlled the seven stars. It made no practical difference whether the Spirit spoke to the church on earth or its **angel** in heaven; and it was more in keeping with the tone of the rest of the book that the messages should be written as if addressed to heavenly beings.

Ephesus properly stands first in the list. It was the first port of Asia, its largest and most prosperous city, and the place where the courier would have begun his journey. The church there had much to its credit; but the standard applied to it was not just a general one of moral and religious excellence. The question was, How had it withstood the particular trials which were destined to appear in the "last days"? One of these was the visitation of false prophets
or (as they are called here) false **apostles,** men who tried to claim authority 2
for their teaching, not just because it was inspired, but because of their supposed position in the historic church. This proved to be a menace to the church in many places, and is mentioned in many early Christian writings; but it was always understood as one of the necessary tribulations which had been foretold by Christ himself (Mark 13.22). Against this danger, the Christians in Ephesus had shown a firm front; they had also resisted heresy, which
took the form in some of these churches of **the practices of the Nicolaitans** 6
(on which see below, p. 795). But against another danger that had also been
foretold (Matthew 24.12) they had been less vigilant: losing their **early love.** A 4
church which failed in this important respect would cease to be a church, its members would be no better prepared for judgement than those outside. For these times must be seen as a deadly struggle against the forces of evil: heresy and disaffection within, persecution outside, were all manifestations of a
single demonic enemy. The destiny of Christians was to be **victorious** 7
(1 John 5.4–5). The reward for victory was the whole range of blessings traditionally associated with the after-life. Here, an image is used that was common to many religions: **the right to eat from the tree of life.**

Travelling due north from Ephesus, the messenger would have reached
another of the great ports of Asia Minor, **Smyrna.** It was a prosperous and 8
beautiful city, and it is possible that the famous sky-line of its public buildings, encircling a table mountain that rises sheer out of the plain, put into the
writer's mind the phrase, the **crown of life.** We get the impression of a 10
struggling Christian community, rich only in the possession of its faith, and
persecuted by the Jewish population. **Those who claim to be Jews but** 9
are not. It would be in keeping with John's style if this were a play upon words. True Jews (as Paul would have said) were those who recognized Jesus Christ: those who did not were no longer "the Lord's synagogue" (Numbers 16.3) but a monstrous perversion of it—**Satan's synagogue.**

Alternatively, those behind the persecution may have been renegade Christians who had become Jewish proselytes, and so only "claimed" to be Jews. (This was apparently the situation in Galatia: see above on Galatians 6.13.) We can glimpse the kind of persecution involved: the Jews, by informing on Christians, could have had them brought before a Roman court as apparently disloyal citizens. To test their loyalty, the court could have ordered them to go through the motions of sacrificing to the image of the Emperor. As Christians they would of course have refused; and since they did not enjoy the privilege of the Jews to practise their own religion and to abstain from pagan worship, they would have been liable to punishment. A famous case of this took place a few decades later in Smyrna, when the aged bishop Polycarp was burnt to death on refusing to participate in the worship of the Emperor, and the Jewish community turned out in force to watch. Some-
10 thing less than martyrdom seems to have been the experience here. **For ten days you will suffer cruelly. Ten days** was a way of saying a short period (Daniel 1.12,14): the author did not envisage a long persecution, or one pushed to extremes. But there was always the danger of a Christian yielding to the pressure of his persecutors and compromising his faith by performing the required act of pagan ritual. The Christians of Smyrna are warned, **only be faithful till death.** The alternatives for them are not just death or survival. Through faithfulness they can have **life** in the full sense which that word has in John's gospel. Even if this involves the ultimate penalty on earth,
11 the martyr is safe from that **second death** which (as in 20.14) means the verdict passed at the Last Judgement on those who, because of their misdeeds, have lost their claim to share in the life of the age to come.

12 **Pergamum** was the most impressive city of Asia Minor. It had been the capital of the most wealthy of the successors of Alexander the Great, and the centre of a substantial empire. With its temples, its immense altar to Zeus (one of the wonders of the ancient world: its foundations are still visible, and cover an area about 40 yards square; its famous sculptures are in a museum in Berlin), its library, its theatre and civic buildings, all built on the terraced summit of a rocky hill that dominates the country for many miles around, it was a monument of Hellenistic culture and wealth. All this passed to the Romans in 133 B.C.; but the city, though shorn of its power, kept something of its ceremonial splendour. The Roman governor made it his principal residence, and the cult of the Roman Emperor received its first sanctuary in Asia when a temple in Pergamum was dedicated to Augustus. In most matters of ceremony and law, Pergamum was the visible centre of Roman power in Asia.

13 John calls it the place where **Satan has his throne.** Many things may have contributed to this image: the mountain on which the city was built, the great altar in its midst, the palace where the Roman governor lived in state. But it was more than an image. The pagan rulers who surrounded the

small Jewish nation were not thought of (at least in Jewish religious writing) as merely human powers. They were ultimately controlled by demonic forces; in the last analysis, they could be overthrown, not by armies of men, but only by God himself: the real contest was between God and the devil. Behind the Roman power (according to this way of thinking) stood Satan himself. Where this power was focused in the person of the Roman governor and in the cult of the official Roman religion, it was not just a metaphor to say that "Satan had his throne".

The Roman governor had the power of life and death over all his subjects
who were not Roman citizens. Technically, this was known as *jus gladii*, the
right of the sword. John was delivering a message from **One who has the** 12
sharp two-edged sword proceeding from his mouth (1.16). That is to say,
the word of Christ stood over against the authority of Rome. To what extent
did the two come into conflict? Part of the difficulty of interpreting the
Revelation is that we have very little evidence on the matter. There seems to
have been no systematic persecution; but it was doubtless possible to get
Christians brought before the Roman courts, and once there they might be
challenged to participate in the official ritual of offering sacrifice before the
statue of the Emperor. Under some such pressure one Christian in Pergamum, **Antipas,** had lost his life rather than compromise with his faith. 13
The rest are complimented on **holding fast.**

But the real danger came, not from the state, but from those same
Nicolaitans who have already appeared at Ephesus (2.6). They were 15
evidently a heretical group within the church. We know nothing more about
them. Irenaeus, writing about a hundred years later, states that they were
followers of the Nicolas of Antioch who is mentioned in Acts 6.5. This may
be correct, but it tells us nothing about the nature of the heresy. The readers
of the letter must have known all about it; but presumably they were not
sufficiently aware of its dangers, and John uses a parallel from the Old
Testament as a caution. The well-known story of Balaam and his ass is
immediately followed in Numbers 25 by an account of how the people of
Israel were seduced by Moabite women into performing acts of heathen
worship. A single verse later in Numbers (31.16) alludes to the fact that it
was Balaam who instigated these women; and the story of how he did so was
much elaborated in later traditions. When John referred to **the teaching of** 14
Balaam, this story will have come to the minds of his readers. The result
of Balaam's teaching had been that the Israelites were led to compromise
with heathen religions. The result of the Nicolaitans' teaching (John must
be saying) might be that Christians would be led to compromise with the
demands of the official religion of Rome.

Manna had been the supernatural food of the people of Israel in the wil- 17
derness (Exodus 16), and it was natural to assume that it would also be the
food of the elect in heaven. Some traditions existed which went further: the

manna of the future would be literally the same as that eaten by the desert generation. A piece of it (so such stories ran) had been **hidden** in some place on earth, and would be brought out at the beginning of the new age.

John's second image for the prize of constancy is more obscure. Small stones were used for many purposes: as voting papers in a ballot, as tickets for admission to a large entertainment, as counters for calculating, as tokens, as charms. A white stone could mean acquittal or election (the opposite of our "blackball"), it could be a sign of good fortune or a badge of success. Any stone with writing on it could have various religious or magical uses. Thus acquittal after trial, victory over persecution, admission to heaven, the power of a "name" over evil—any or all of these ideas may have been evoked by the idea of **a white stone.**

18 **Thyatira.** The courier carrying the letter must now be imagined as taking the important road which led south-east from Pergamum through the remaining four cities to which the letter is addressed. Thyatira, though it had had an important political history in the Hellenistic period, was an undistinguished place in Roman times, and seems to have been mainly a centre of industry and commerce. There is a reference to its purple dyes in Acts 16.14, and there is evidence that it had a remarkable number of trade guilds: **burnished brass** is a translation of a word which occurs nowhere else in Greek literature—possibly the bronze-smiths of Thyatira were familiar with it.

Like the church in Pergamum, this church had a good record, but was
20 threatened from within. **You tolerate that Jezebel.** The heresy once again
is painted in Old Testament colours. Jezebel's worst crime had been that of
introducing foreign cults; "fornication" was a standard biblical metaphor
for deserting the worship of the one true God. In true prophetic style, John
22 carries the metaphor through: the heresy is a harlot, she has **lovers** and
23 **children** who will all be involved together in her punishment. This is again
deliberately strong language: the Christians in Thyatira are being warned of
the seriousness of the danger they are in. As in Pergamum, so here: it is hard
to know what actual doctrines or practices lie behind the biblical language.
20 **Fornication** almost certainly stands for a permissive attitude towards
associating with pagan cults. On the other hand, **eating food sacrificed to**
idols could mean exactly what it says. We know that this was an issue in the
24 church at Corinth (1 Cor. 8), and it may be significant that the phrase, **on you I will impose no further burden,** is one which was used in an instruction to Christians about the extent to which they must separate themselves from pagan society (Acts 15.28): John may be saying that they must keep away from all pagan sacrifices, but that they need not adopt the social exclusiveness of a strict Jewish community. There is one further clue to the nature of the heresy: **what they like to call the deep secrets of Satan.** It is possible that they prided themselves on their thorough acquaintance with

pagan religion, and that they called this **the deep secrets of Satan.** But it is more likely, and more in keeping with John's style, that the phrase is a deliberate parody of one of their doctrines. The 'depths of God's own nature' (1 Corinthians 2.10) were something into which Christians claimed to have insight through the Spirit. The heretics may have claimed a still better insight, which John ridiculed by calling it an experience of **the deep secrets of Satan.**

Amid all this metaphor and word-play, what are we to make of **the woman** 20
who claims to be a prophetess? Is this yet another symbol for the heretic
group? Possibly. Yet the problem of people claiming to be prophets was a familiar one in the church. It is likely that the heresy was in fact led by a woman of this kind, and that the phrase, **that Jezebel,** was intended as an opprobrious nickname.

To him who is victorious. This, like all the messages, ends with a 26
promise. The words come from Psalm 2.8–9. They were originally addressed to a king of Israel, by way of promising him victory in his battles. But for a long time the psalm had been regarded as a prophetic description of the destiny of the Messiah who would one day come to inaugurate an age of glory for his people. The church then seized on the passage as a statement of the ultimate sovereignty of Jesus Christ, a sovereignty in which (as Jesus had promised) Christians were destined to share.

I will give him also the star of dawn. What this stands for in John's sym- 28
bolism is revealed only at the very end of the book (22.16): it is Christ himself.

Sardis had the most illustrious history of any city of Asia Minor. It was 3. 1
the capital of the Lydian kingdom, and in the sixth century B.C., under Croesus its king, it was the centre of luxury and power in the entire Mediterranean world. By Roman times the power had departed; and an earthquake in A.D. 17 destroyed most of its buildings, which were only restored through the generosity of the Roman Emperor. Compared with Pergamum or the great ports on the coast, it must have seemed something of a backwater.

To this setting of past glory and present decline, the church in Sardis
presented a parallel. **Though you have a name for being alive, you are** 1
dead . . . I have not found any work of yours completed. A phenomenon 2
that was to be common enough in the later history of the church appears already in the pages of the New Testament: the original zeal has departed, and only an apparently flourishing exterior remains. The reprimand takes the form (as so often in the New Testament) of a reference to the imminent
reckoning, the "coming" of Christ. **I shall come upon you like a thief** 3
are words attributed to Jesus himself in the gospels (Matthew 24.43) and are used by Paul for just the same purpose (1 Thessalonians 5.2). In view of this constantly impending "coming" (however it is interpreted), the tone of Christian morality must always be, **wake up,** "keep awake" (Matthew 24.42).

Both priests in sanctuaries and Roman citizens in ceremonial processions
wore robes of white: similarly this colour of innocence and purity is for those
5 who will be admitted to heaven. **The roll of the living**, too, had its counterpart on earth. To be on the roll of citizens in a city meant to enjoy its privileges; so, to the people of Israel, to be on "God's roll" meant to be sure of
inheriting the people's promised destiny. Heaven, now, was the destiny of
Christians, but not by right or predestination: they could still be struck off.
But the reward they awaited was to be on the **roll of the living.** They would
achieve it, so long as they lived faithfully on earth; Jesus would then
acknowledge them before his Father—a clear allusion to another saying of
Jesus (Matthew 10.32).

7 **Philadelphia** was the next substantial city on the route. It had been
founded in the second century B.C. by Attalus II Philadelphus, one of the
kings of Pergamum, as a vantage-point for the further spread of Greek
culture into the interior of Asia Minor; but it had been one of the worst
victims of the earthquake of A.D. 17, from which it never fully recovered.

We learn something of the church there through the way the message is
composed. The beginning of each of these messages takes an element from
the description of Christ in 1.12–20. For Philadelphia, the phrase selected is
'I hold the keys of Death and Death's domain'; but the metaphor of a key
immediately goes its own way and governs the imagery of most of the
message. First, it recalls a passage of Isaiah (22.22): "I will lay the key of the
house of David on his shoulder; what he opens no one shall shut and what he
shuts no one shall open". When this was first written, it was a prophecy that
a certain Eliakim would become the king's chief minister in the government
of Jerusalem. But it came naturally to a Christian writer to see more in it
than this: it was a prophecy which became true and meaningful only when
7 fulfilled by Jesus Christ. Moreover the word **key** suggested a door; and a
"door", in Christian language, was almost a technical expression for an
opportunity for spreading the gospel (it is used in the Greek of 1 Corinthians
16.9; 2 Corinthians 2.12; Colossians 4.3). The church, though **small**, had a
8 great missionary task to perform: **look, I have set before you an open door.**

9 The danger to this church, as in Smyrna, came from **those of Satan's
synagogue**—again, either Jews, or gentile Christians who had joined the
synagogue. The Jews had always believed that ultimately the tables would
be turned in their favour: their enemies and oppressors would one day
recognize that the Jews were after all God's **beloved people** and would
come and fall down at their feet (such language is characteristic of Isaiah,
60.14; 49.23; 45.14 and elsewhere). But Christians now believed themselves to be the "true Israel". They could invoke the same prophecies in
their own favour, even against those who were, or claimed to be, Jews
themselves.

10 **I will also keep you from the ordeal.** This ordeal, or "test", is what

Christians must constantly pray to be spared ('Do not bring us to the test', in the Lord's prayer (Matthew 6.13), uses the same Greek word). Doubtless it can take many forms in the experience of each individual; but in the early church, the decisive "test" was thought of as an element in the final stage of history, the ordeal that was **to fall upon the whole world and test its inhabitants.** The main part of the book is in fact a description of this ordeal as something coming simultaneously, in a moment of time, to all the inhabitants of the earth. But this did not take away from the seriousness of local and particular ordeals that might fall upon individuals and churches—only, they must always be seen as part of, or at least as signs of, that ultimate ordeal from which God had promised that his elect would be saved.

A pillar in the temple of my God. One of the ways in which Christians 12
conceived of the church, whether they were thinking of its empirical existence and structure on earth or of its ultimate destiny in heaven, was as a building composed of living stones, a spiritual temple replacing the old one of masonry in Jerusalem. To be firmly knit into the fabric of this building, like a **pillar,** was to be sure of salvation. On such a pillar might be written the name of the city's founder, or the name of the city itself—the imagery leads the mind to the **new Jerusalem** that is described in chapter 21. But the **name,** including the **new name** of Christ, was something that might be written on a Christian here and now, like a charm against the forces of evil.

Laodicea, Hierapolis and Colossae formed a cluster of cities in a valley 14
about a hundred miles inland from Ephesus. When Paul wrote his letter to the new church at Colossae, he asked that it should be read also to 'the congregation at Laodicea' (Colossians 4.16). It can hardly be an accident that John's phrase, **the prime source of all God's creation,** echoes Paul's words in Colossians 1.15: either Paul's letter was still being read in Laodicea, or else the kind of language it used had become part of the usual Christian vocabulary in those cities.

Laodicea was renowned for its wealth, its wool industry, and its medical school. The church, it seems, had identified itself with the city's fame and prosperity, and so had lost hold of its own distinctive values. Instead of its
material wealth it should have **gold refined in the fire**—which, in the 18
church, was usually a metaphor for suffering and martyrdom. Instead of the glossy woollen garments which were the pride of Laodicean industry, it should have the **white clothes** of innocence and purity. And instead of that eye **ointment** which was a well-known product of the Laodicean medical school, it should find something which would improve its spiritual vision.

All these symptoms of accommodation to the secular world are summed
up in a single vivid image: **you are lukewarm, neither hot nor cold.** The 16
figure of speech may already have been (as it is now) proverbial. But the metaphor was perhaps quite precise. The hot water of the neighbouring hot springs of Hierapolis was good; and cold spring water was good. But luke-

warm water was only of use (so ancient doctors said) to make one vomit. So here: **I will spit you out of my mouth.**

19 **All whom I love I reprove and discipline.** This was a piece of proverbial wisdom (Proverbs 3.12—see above on Hebrews 12.5–11), one of the stock answers to the problem of evil: suffering is imposed by God on those whom he loves in order to test and strengthen their character. The converse must then also be true: if those whom God loves are not suffering, there must be something wrong with them. The comfortable existence of the church in Laodicea was a sign of a dangerous inertia. The message is stern and urgent: **Be on your mettle therefore and repent.**

14 The message comes from **the Amen.** This was a Hebrew word with which the Christian congregation was accustomed to express its participation in worship. There was a sense in which Christ could be thought of as an "Amen" to the promises of God (the idea is worked out by Paul in 2 Corinthians 1.19–20). But the word "Amen" itself (whatever it originally meant in a phrase like "the God of Amen" in Isaiah 65.16) was usually understood to mean "in truth": this is the force of it when it occurs in a characteristic phrase of Jesus, 'In very truth (*Amen*) I say to you'. Christ, then, was truth, **the faithful and true witness,** who would vindicate his followers at the final judgement by making a true confession on their behalf.

20–2 The joys of the age to come were often pictured both as a heavenly banquet and as a period of world dominion for the elect. Both these images are used here, but with a mass of Christian meanings. Christians must be ready for the return of their master at any time, 'ready to let him in the moment he arrives and knocks' (Luke 12.36). But the heavenly feast is anticipated by that supper which Christians already celebrate in the eucharist; Jesus "comes", here and now, to anyone who hears his voice and **opens the door.**

The opening of the sealed book

4. 1 **After this I looked.** So far John's vision has been of a single being, 'one like a son of man', and the setting, in so far as it has been sketched in at all, has been suggested by the great seven-branched candlestick which stood in the temple at Jerusalem. Now the scene shifts: the central figure, though he is not named or described, is evidently God himself. John was writing freely of what he had seen; yet his imagery was still controlled by things seen or heard of on earth. At the beginning of his vision he was in the outer room of the temple, the Holy Place, where a priest entered every day to offer incense and tend the sacred lights. Facing him in that Holy Place there was a curtain over the door leading to the Most Holy Place, the mysterious inner sanctuary where God himself was believed especially to dwell, and where only once a year the high priest was privileged to enter. John was now about to penetrate further: **before my eyes was a door opened in heaven.** What lay beyond the door in the innermost sanctuary of the temple? In recent centuries, probably nothing at all. The sacred objects which once were kept there had disappeared with the destruction of Solomon's temple in 586 B.C., and the Most Holy Place was simply a room of darkness and mystery. But John's imagination was nourished, not by the actual temple as he may have known it in Jerusalem, but by the traditions preserved in the Old Testament (in this respect he stands close to the writer of the letter to Hebrews). According to these, the Most Holy Place contained the Ark, a wooden chest in which were placed the stone tablets of the Law (Exodus 25.10–22). This was the symbol of God's presence, his "throne" (Isaiah 6.1; Ezekiel 43.7). Over it stood statues of winged sphinx-like creatures, the "cherubim" of the original sanctuary (Exodus 25.18–20) and of Solomon's temple (1 Kings 6.23–8).

But these were only the raw materials. Out of them John forged something
new. As in Ezekiel's vision (Ezekiel 1), the cherubim become **four living** 6
creatures; but here each one has its own personality.[a] As in Isaiah's vision
(Isaiah 6), these creatures sing the praises of God; but here their praise is
not enough, and another biblical picture becomes fused with that of the
temple: "The Lord of hosts has become king on mount Zion and in Jerusalem, and shows his glory before their elders" (Isaiah 24.23). The inner
room of the temple becomes the heavenly throne-room, where God holds
court among the angels and spirits who worship him. The twenty-four families of priests who officiate in the outer room of the temple are replaced by
twenty-four elders, the seven-branched candlestick by **seven flaming** 4, 5
torches, the seven spirits of God (perhaps the traditional seven archangels,
perhaps simply a numerical symbol for the single Spirit of God); and one
more feature of Solomon's temple, the huge basin (or "sea") of bronze
(1 Kings 7.23–6) which stood in the courtyard and served for ablutions, but
which may also have been symbolic of the primordial ocean from which all
creation began, reappears transformed into **what seemed a sea of glass,** 6
like a sheet of ice.

Then I saw . . . a scroll. Scrolls of papyrus were used for a variety of 5. 1
purposes—books, letters, legal documents. But there can be little doubt what sort of scroll is meant here. A contract or a will was sometimes written out in full on one side of a sheet of papyrus; the sheet was then rolled up to form a scroll and tied round with narrow papyrus strips. Each witness added his seal to secure the knots, and a brief summary of the contents was written on the outside of the roll so that it could be identified without being unrolled. Examples of this have actually been recovered from the sands of Egypt. The

[a] These four creatures have become traditional symbols of the four evangelists. But this was the idea of later commentators.

first thing suggested to John's readers by a scroll with several seals **and with writing inside and out** would certainly have been a legal document of this kind. If such a scroll were produced in a law-court, only a respected and qualified person could break the seal and use it as evidence. Christians thought of Christ as their "advocate" in the heavenly court, ready to produce decisive evidence on their behalf. It was in this sense that they would have
2 recognized Christ as the one who was **worthy to open the scroll.**

But since, in real life, a scroll could be other things besides, so in the vision there were many possible meanings of the symbol. Those of John's readers who were familiar with Ezekiel's vision would have been expecting a scroll containing "dirges and laments and words of woe" (Ezekiel 2.10): and here, sure enough, the seer was about to witness events that were all written beforehand in the book of God's purposes, and the opening of the book was a symbol that this inexorable sequence of events was about to begin. In a synagogue, again, the president would take one of the leather scrolls of the Old Testament from its case, and present it to some qualified person who would "come up" and read and expound it. In exactly this way, Jesus had once accepted a scroll of the scriptures in synagogue at Nazareth, and had declared that the words he read from it were now fulfilled in his own person (Luke 4.16–21); and it was part of the Christian faith that only in the light of Christ could the Old Testament be understood, only through him could the secrets of the scrolls of Scripture be known. None of these analogies must be pressed too hard. This scroll was no ordinary one. It had no less than seven seals, and the breaking of each seal, not the reading of the contents, was the signal for a spate of catastrophes on earth. Nevertheless, all these ideas may have been present in the background.

5 The being who had **won the right to open the scroll** is described first in two Old Testament phrases which were often taken to be prophetic descriptions of the Messiah: **the Lion from the tribe of Judah** (Genesis 49.9) and the **Scion of David** (Isaiah 11.1). But John's own vision of him takes a new and startling form: **a Lamb with the marks of slaughter upon him.** Jesus, according to John's gospel, was called by John the Baptist 'the Lamb of God', and was crucified while the Passover lambs were being slaughtered in front of the temple. Moreover, some New Testament writers saw in Jesus the fulfilment of the mysterious oracle in Isaiah 53 about one who was "led like a lamb to the slaughter". To this extent, the idea of Jesus as a Lamb was not wholly new; but it was at most a metaphor that helped to throw light on the purpose of his death. Here, the metaphor has turned into a vivid picture. The Messiah whom Jewish writers thought of as a Lion now appears as a Lamb. To us, the animal suggests weakness, the helplessness of Jesus' unresisting progress to the cross. But, just as the cross was also a symbol of victory, so John's image of the slaughtered lamb bears the conventional marks of power and knowledge. Throughout the Old Testament,

a horn is a symbol of power: in the visions of Zechariah (1.18) and Daniel (7.7–8; 8.3), horns appear on the heads of the beasts which have a temporary dominion over the world. Writing in the same tradition, John portrays the Lamb as a ram with **seven horns,** the number seven representing (as usual) totality, total dominion; and the **seven eyes,** perhaps suggested by another vision of Zechariah in which the seven lamps on the golden lampstand represent "the eyes of the Lord, which range through the whole earth" (4.10), stand, he tells us, for **the seven spirits of God**—for Jesus and the Spirit are ultimately one.

Even if features of the synagogue and the law-court crowd in for a moment
with the appearance of the scroll, the scene is still the heavenly temple. The
elders, like psalmists, each **had a harp,** and like temple priests they **held** 8
golden bowls full of incense, which were a readily understood symbol (as
in Psalm 141.2) for **the prayers of God's people.** But the essence of their
worship was **a new song.** The traditional language of praise was not enough: 9
the Lamb was a new object of worship in heaven who had effected something quite new on earth, and a new set of concepts was needed. Each phrase
of the song could be elaborated from other pages of the New Testament: the
idea of **purchase** by blood combines that of sacrifice with that of a ransom
(Mark 10.45); **men of every tribe and language** represent the universality
of Christ's work, far transcending the traditional nationalist emphasis of
Jewish religion; and the **royal house,** serving as **priests,** is a picture of the 10
church that is elaborated in 1 Peter 2.9–10. But John is not concerned here
with the working out of these concepts. He uses them only as headings
under which to arrange the praise of Christ. When the circle of worshippers
widens to include, first the myriads of angels who throng the courts of heaven, 12
and then the whole order of created things, the words of the song become 13
more general. The object of worship is still God with the Lamb. But the
language is such as might have been heard at the procession of a Roman
Emperor or in the temple of a pagan God: it is the universal language of
praise.

Then I watched as the Lamb broke the first of the seven seals. Heaven, 6. 1
for this writer (and indeed for the whole tradition of Jewish writers in which he stands) is not a place remote from the world, whose occupants live a life of undisturbed felicity and praise. It is in heaven that the future of the world is prepared; a revelation of heaven is a revelation of the secret destinies which are working themselves out in the affairs of men. What the writer sees are symbolic actions—the breaking of seals, the blowing of trumpets, the pouring of bowls—which are the heavenly counterparts of predestined events on earth. These symbols come in groups of seven; and the seventh of each group prepares for the next sevenfold catastrophe. The visions, that is to say, proceed according to their own logic, and fill out a pattern imposed

upon them from the beginning. Yet they never lose contact with the course of events on earth.

And so here: the breaking of the seals is the signal for the first cycle of calamities. These John could have inferred, both from his own prophetic understanding of contemporary events, and from his inherited presup-
8 positions about the destined course of world history. **Sword, famine, pestilence and wild beasts** were traditional scourges by which God was believed to punish a disobedient world (Ezekiel 14.21). To symbolize these in heaven, a vision of Zechariah suggested itself (1.8; 6.1–8), in which sometimes four horses, sometimes four chariot teams of different-coloured horses, were sent to patrol the earth. But instead of simply fitting these to the four traditional scourges, John appears to have worked in some allusions to con-
2 temporary history. A horse whose **rider held a bow** represented the cavalry of the Parthians. This nation constituted a recurring threat to the eastern frontier of the Roman empire, and won an important battle against Rome in A.D. 62. Mounted bowmen formed the most distinctive and dreaded part of the Parthian army. The **white horse** and the **crown** (or victor's garland) symbolized the victory of these forces. To this extent, John made the traditional scourge of the **sword** come alive in the possibility of successful barbarian incursions into the territory of the Roman empire.

But the **sword** could also mean civil war: that fellow-citizens would slaughter one another was one of the grisly predictions which belonged to the traditional Jewish picture of the last days. There had been a bitter experience of this in the last stages of the Jewish rebellion which ended with the sack of
4 Jerusalem in A.D. 70. For this, **another horse, all red,** was a fitting symbol.

Food shortages afflicted the Middle East several times during the first
6 century, and made for very high prices. **A quart** of wheat flour was an average ration per man per day. A **whole day's wage** (literally a *denarius*, as in Matthew 20.2) would have been a prohibitive price for all but the rich; working men would have had to make do with **barley-meal**—but they would have survived, if it did not go on too long; and since serious damage would not be done to **the olive and the vine** (which take years to replace), this was the kind of famine which people could bear, the kind of famine which was known to happen—and in which Christian prophets discerned the signs of the critical times that lay ahead (see above on Acts 11.27–8).
8 **Another horse, sickly pale; and its rider's name was Death.** John has made a rough equation between each of the first three horses and the afflictions already experienced by his contemporaries. The fourth horse is a more general symbol; it stands both for the other three and for all the traditional scourges that were to come. And whereas perhaps any of the other three might have been avoided by most people, cumulatively they would inevitably take their toll, to the extent of **a quarter of the earth.**

All these were calamities which might be encountered in the ordinary run

of history. John and his readers were not the first to experience such things: their significance lay only in a certain intensification which made it possible to see them as movements in the final drama of the world. But there was also a more particular calamity which had begun to oppress the minds of Christians. Persecution of the church had already resulted in martyrdoms: men
had been **slaughtered for God's word and for the testimony they bore.** 9
This raised two questions. First, what was the point of their death? Jewish writers, reflecting on the persecution of the saints of their own faith (particularly the heroic martyrdoms of the Maccabean period), had for some time been describing them as a "sacrifice", that is to say, a means by which the suffering of a few could ward off the suffering of the many. Christians soon seized on the same idea (see Paul's use of it in Philippians 2.17); and John represents it here by filling out his description of heaven with one more feature of the Jerusalem temple, the great altar which stood before it and on which animals were sacrificed, their blood (in which the life was thought to dwell) running **underneath the altar.** The sacrifice of these martyrs was the reality symbolized by the old Jewish ritual.

Secondly, when and how would they be vindicated and avenged? This question appears to be distinctly at variance with Christian principles; but it arose out of what may be described as a distinctively Jewish approach to the problem of evil. It is a fact that the righteous suffer, and often suffer for their beliefs. If a righteous man meets misfortune and death, the world may judge him to have been a hypocrite or a victim of self-delusion; but if the God in whom he believes is just, surely he is bound to save a man who has faithfully served him. If he does not, either the man is not what he claims to be, or God is not just. This dilemma afflicted many pious men as they prepared to meet their deaths amid the taunts of their enemies. If they must die, they prayed for vindication, either now or in the future. If God were just, he must turn the tables, so to speak, on their persecutors. He must force them to acknowledge that their victims were right and that they were wrong. This would doubtless involve something not unlike revenge: it would only be by suffering some of the pain which they had inflicted themselves that the unrighteous would be brought to see their error. But (at least at its best) this longing for vindication was not simply the very human desire to be avenged. It was a postulate of faith: the God whom the sufferer believed to be just must surely, at some stage, be seen to be just. In the end he must surely come down on the side of those who had served him faithfully, whatever the consequence for their enemies.

This way of thinking must be borne in mind through much of the bloody imagery of the Revelation. It throws some light, for example, on the phrase
which occurs later in this chapter, **the vengeance of the Lamb.** The Lamb, 16
we know, is Christ; and Christ, surely, is not to be thought of as taking **vengeance** on his enemies. But this word **vengeance** is not quite so per-

sonal in the New Testament as it is in ordinary speech. In Romans 1.18, for example, the same Greek word is translated 'retribution', and probably means, not the personal wrath or revenge of God, but the inevitable consequences of men's evil deeds in any world which is ultimately subject to divine justice. If God was in Christ, and men nevertheless crucified him, their total opposition to God must surely one day be made clear to them. This terrifying reversal might be called (according to these presuppositions) **the vengeance of the Lamb.**

And so here: it is promised that the martyrs would indeed be vindicated—
11 but not yet; the period of waiting would be **a little while longer** (an almost
technical expression in this kind of writing: see above on John 16.16). There was positive value in these sacrifices, and there were more of them to come (the idea of a **tally**, or quota of sufferings, that must be completed before the end could come, occurs also in Colossians 1.24). Meanwhile, the martyrs could already enjoy their rightful place in heaven: they were given their **white robe** of purity, victory and service.

12 **There was a violent earthquake,** and at the same time a cataclysm in
the heavens. The sky was thought of (by poets, if not by astronomers) as a
kind of tent stretched over the earth, from which the heavenly bodies were
suspended. These heavenly bodies controlled the seasons, and much else, on
14 earth. If they fell, there would be chaos. In this vision, the sky itself **vanished.**
A man reading a scroll of papyrus would hold one end in each hand; when he had finished reading, he would roll it up and put it away. It would be like this with the sky: instead of being stretched out overhead, it would be **rolled up,** leaving nothing in its place.

At this point, the reaction of all classes of mankind (which here include
15 such suggestive titles as the **magnates** of eastern kingdoms and the **mar-**
shals of the Roman army) is painted in colours freely drawn from the Old Testament: compare Isaiah 2.10; Hosea 10.8; Joel 2.11. They recognize, at
last, that such things are not just an inexplicable catastrophe of nature, but
16 constitute God's judgement upon themselves. It is the **vengeance** of God,
the great day for which Christians have been praying, when men can no longer deceive themselves about the iniquity of their own deeds.

The church in Asia Minor may have experienced something of these things during the last decades of the first century A.D. But it also experienced periods of peace and comparative security. The secular mind would think of these periods as a return to normal; but to a prophet, who saw in contemporary events the signs of that final stage in history when the tribulations of mankind
would necessarily be intensified, they might have seemed abnormal, an
7. 1 exceptional **holding back** of an inexorable process of destruction. Why
were there such pauses? The breaking of the seventh seal is delayed for a moment in order to glance at this question. The end, Jesus had warned, would come suddenly, 'like a thief in the night'; and yet certain things were

destined to happen first—the gospel had to be preached throughout the
world, the number of the elect had to be filled up. That is to say, an interlude
of peace must be understood, not as a time for relaxation, but as a merciful
extension of the time in which men might avoid the retribution to come by
declaring themselves unambiguously to be on the side of the church, to be
God's **servants.** An image lay to hand in Ezekiel's vision (9.3–4) of a man, 3
armed with pen and ink, being instructed by God, "Go through the city,
through Jerusalem, and put a mark on the foreheads of those who groan and
lament over the abominations practised there". Those who were so marked
would be spared from the imminent catastrophe. John uses the same image,
but replaces the ink-mark by a **seal**: being "sealed" seems already to have been
an accepted Christian metaphor for becoming a Christian (Ephesians 1.13).

From all the tribes of Israel there were a hundred and forty-four 4
thousand. To speak of the actual Jewish people as "the twelve tribes of Israel" would have been sheer antiquarianism: the tribal organization had disappeared at a very early stage in Old Testament history, and in the New Testament period only three of the tribes retained any distinct identity. But the Christian church was encouraged by at least one saying of Jesus (Matthew 19.28) to think of itself as the "new Israel", the true embodiment of the People of God to whom the Old Testament promises had been made. It was natural, therefore, to describe it in terms, not of contemporary Judaism, but of an ideal Israel such as could be discerned in the earlier books of the Old Testament. The order, and even the names, of the twelve tribes vary in the Old Testament lists. John's order is different from any of them, and he omits Dan (perhaps because there was by now a legend that Antichrist would arise from the—extinct—tribe of Dan). But his meaning is expressed in easy symbolism. The church is the new Israel, its members are a perfect multiple of the twelve tribes of remote history.

Yet even while a pause is being made to fill up the predetermined complement of the people of God, there is the hard fact to be reckoned with that
Christians **from every nation, of all tribes, peoples, and languages** 9
have lost their lives. Why have they not been spared? Part of the answer has
already been given: their deaths are effective as a sacrifice (6.9). But a further
answer is provided by a vision of the existence upon which they have entered
in heaven. This magnificent scene is built out of Old Testament materials: 9–17
the motif of the dialogue with **one of the elders** from Zechariah 4.1–5, the 13
description of the martyrs' felicity from Isaiah 49.10; 25.8 (to mention only 16
a few). But at the centre of it stands a Christian affirmation clothed in startlingly paradoxical symbolism: **they have washed their robes and made** 14
them white in the blood of the Lamb. The martyrs' death was stained
with blood. They now have white robes, obtained, not by their own heroism
or their own righteousness, but because of their faith in Christ crucified:
the blood of the Lamb.

The sequence of breaking the seven seals has been interrupted by a moment of insight into two facets of the history of the church: the time graciously allowed for completing the roll of the new people of God on earth, and the glorious destiny of those who meet suffering and death in the meantime.[a] The sequence is now resumed: one more seal is still to be broken, the last. And that, one would have thought, would be the end of the drama: after the earth had received such punishment, what more could still be in store?
8. 1 And so, with **the seventh seal,** one expects the final cataclysm. It does not
come. Instead **there was silence in heaven for what seemed half an**
hour. The climax of this series of seven turns out to be the overture to a
further series. For this is John's method. The Revelation contains three of
these cycles of seven signals in heaven answered by seven catastrophes on
earth. It is hardly possible to set them end to end, as if John were writing a
consecutive history of the future of the world. Rather he is composing sets of
variations on a single sevenfold theme. And so here: the seventh seal is the
cue for a new development altogether, this time announced by the archangels
2 —**the seven angels that stand in the presence of God**—by means of
seven trumpets.

That there were periodic spells of silence in heaven was assumed by Jewish
theologians: how otherwise could the prayers of men ever be heard amidst
the continual worship which surrounds the throne of God? How, in any case,
do human prayers ever reach the ears of God? A time-honoured metaphor
gave the answer: they rise to heaven like incense—and this took the mind,
once again, to the temple in Jerusalem, where every day, morning and
3 evening, a priest entered the Holy Place and offered incense on **the golden**
altar; at the same time, one of the seven Levites appointed for the task
blew a blast on his trumpet that could be heard (men said) as far away as
Jericho. These are the elements (or some of them) out of which John built his
description of this dramatic moment in heaven. And he adds one thing more:
the prayers were **the prayers of all God's people.** As such, they were
5 answered. How did they know? Because God gave the usual sign: **peals of**
thunder, lightning, and an earthquake. A similar sign is given in Acts
4.31.

The powers of darkness conquered

6 **Seven trumpets.** In Jerusalem, a trumpet was blown at regular times to
announce a religious service or festival, but also at exceptional times (like
church bells before the age of sirens and radio) to announce any natural

[a] This is clearer in the Greek, which means literally "those who are passing through the great ordeal", rather than (with NEB and other versions) who have passed through (verse 14).

calamity. The first four angels' trumpets are the signals for natural, but not yet supernatural, catastrophes: a third of the world suffers, the disasters are as severe as anyone can conceive. They certainly merit their place among the portents of the end; but they do not yet exceed the bounds of human experience.

As before, John mingles the language of the Bible with recollections of 7–12
recent events. Three of the plagues which Moses brought upon Egypt—hail,
blood and darkness (Exodus 7–10)—form the framework; fire is added,
perhaps from Joel 2.30, the blazing mountain from Jeremiah 51.25. The
poisoning of rivers and streams in a time of great heat was a calamity prophesied already by Jeremiah (9.15; 23.15) and taken up in more recent Jewish
writing. **Wormwood** is a bitter plant, and was thought to be poisonous: this 11
would be the immediate cause; but the remote cause (in an age given to
astrology) would be assumed to be the influence of an evil star.

Did such things happen? If, as is likely, Revelation was written after A.D.
79, when the sudden eruption of Vesuvius completely engulfed the city of
Pompeii with molten lava, filled the air with sulphurous dust, and destroyed
the ships in the gulf of Naples, then John's readers, from the reports they
had heard of the catastrophe, would have had no difficulty in picturing **what** 8
looked like a great blazing mountain being **hurled into the sea.** John
was not the only Jewish writer whose imagination was kindled by that event.

The cry of an eagle—**Woe**, a syllable which in the Greek (*ouai*) sounds 13
not unlike the call of a bird—accompanied each of the last three trumpet
blasts. This extra note of terror goes with an extra dimension of evil which
attends these final plagues: demonic forces are joined to the effects of natural
disasters. Here the images melt into one another. First, **a star that had** 9. 1
fallen—but the stars were believed to be controlled by angels or spirits, one
of whom, descending with the star, could unlock **the shaft of the abyss.** 2
This is the geology of myth: in the primordial conflict between God and
chaos, the unwanted waters of the ocean, along with destructive elemental
forces, were finally imprisoned far beneath the earth; their only escape
was through a single shaft to which God held the key. To open this shaft was
to threaten the earth with a new onslaught from the forces of destruction
which had been so long suppressed. What rises first is **smoke**; but the cloud
of smoke turns into a cloud of locusts—a swarm of these creatures can look
like a cloud against the sun. Locusts—as the prophet Joel noticed in his
terrifying description of a plague of them (2.4–5)—have something in their
appearance that makes one think of horses; so, in John's vision, they turn
into almost human cavalry, the metallic sound of their wings being **like the** 9
noise of horses and chariots rushing to battle. Indeed, they become
centaurs; and since, in the east, the Centaur (Sagittarius) of the zodiac was
sometimes depicted, not only with the traditional bow (**equipped for** 7
battle) and long hair (**like women's hair**), but with the tail of its neigh-

9 bouring sign Scorpio (**they had tails like scorpions**), it is possible that
what started in John's mind as one of Moses' plagues on Egypt—the locusts
—became fused (through Joel's description of them as horses) with a more
sinister influence suggested by a sign of the zodiac, able to afflict men
5 instead of green things, and lasting the full **five months** which lie between
the beginning of the period of Scorpio and the end of the year. That is to say,
these are not locusts at all, but demons in insect form, marching under one
11 of the signs in the heavens. They have a king, **the angel of the abyss,** the
power who commands all the suppressed evil of the universe, Satan, the
devil. Shunning his name, John gives an equivalent, **the Destroyer.** (In
Hebrew, this equivalent, **Abaddon,** occurs in Job 26.6 and other places in
the later books of the Old Testament.)

13 **The sixth angel.** The ceremony in heaven consists of a trumpet blast, **a
voice coming from between the horns of the golden altar** (it was a
characteristic of altars in Israel that they had a "horn", or vertical projection,
14 at each of the corners), and the release of **the four angels held bound at the
great river Euphrates.** These last angels form the immediate link, so to
speak, with events on earth. The kingdoms of the world were believed to be
ultimately controlled by supernatural powers—angels, spirits or demons.
The river Euphrates was now the eastern frontier of the Roman empire; it
had also been for centuries the north-east frontier which separated Syria and
Palestine from the Assyrian, and subsequently the Parthian, empires. The
most dreaded enemies of Israel had always come "from the north", and
awesome descriptions of these northern warriors occur frequently in the Old
Testament prophets. The menace had reasserted itself in recent times: the
Parthians had inflicted humiliating defeats on the Romans in 53 B.C. and
again in A.D. 62. Their immense forces of cavalry—mounted bowmen who
19 shot with deadly accuracy both when charging and when retiring (**the
power of the horses lay in their mouths, and in their tails also**)—had
become a symbol of the incalculable military power of the barbarian hordes
of the east that were constantly threatening the frontiers of the Roman
empire. To the Romans, the Parthians constituted a military problem. To
a visionary of the Jewish tradition, who was convinced of the imminent fall
of Rome as a punishment by God for the iniquities of Roman rule, they
represented one of the most obvious means by which this fall would be
brought about. It was not that the Parthians were not yet strong enough to
attack: the delay was rather to be understood as another instance of God
deliberately holding back the forces of destruction until the predestined
moment. That moment, in John's vision, had now come. The image of the
Parthian cavalry is elaborated into a free description of mythological beasts,
representing the innumerable horsemen and deadly weapons of the nations of
the east.

20 **The rest of mankind.** The attack from the east might destroy the Roman

empire, but would it affect the fundamental paganism of Greco-Roman culture? To the Jew (and also to the Christian) the most offensive thing about this civilization was its polytheism, its multitudinous statues and temples, and the unashamed materialism which went with so much of pagan religion. To cover all this, Jewish writers used the one word "idolatry", and applied to it all the polemics they found in the Old Testament against religions which (unlike the pure worship of the Jews) seemed to be directed towards **gods their hands had fashioned.** (Psalm 135.15–17 seems to be particularly in mind here, but there are many similar passages in the Old Testament.) They also saw in their pagan neighbours a permissiveness towards certain vices which were particularly abhorrent to Hebrew culture,
especially **sorcery** and **fornication.** Any real change of heart in the world 21
at large must surely involve a change of heart over these basic things. The purpose of this revealing of 'divine retribution' (Romans 1.18) was to encourage such a change of heart. But John, having seen no such change resulting from the calamities of his own lifetime, realized that even the intensified tribulations of the future would not alter the basic propensities of human nature.

All this time John has enjoyed the supreme privilege of the seer. From his
vantage-point in heaven, he has witnessed both the preparation of the
scenario by God and its acting out on earth. He has had full insight, not only
into the pre-ordained course of history, but into its meaning within the grand
purposes of God. But now, in the heavy and ominous pause which precedes
the final trumpet blast, John finds himself once more on earth, his powers of
vision provisionally limited like those of other prophets. Before, when he
saw a **mighty angel** and a scroll, he was in heaven, and he was allowed to **10.** 1
witness both the unsealing of the scroll and the corresponding events on
earth. But now he is on earth—as it might be on Patmos—and he sees a
second **mighty angel coming down from heaven.** The building up of
thunderclouds as seen across the sea could well have suggested his description
of this angel, and when at last the thunder comes, it is the voice of God
himself, roaring like a lion (the metaphors were traditional: Psalm 29.3–9; 3
Hosea 11.10; Amos 1.2). But not all that a man hears of God is communicable.
Paul, in an experience of paradise, heard 'words so secret that human lips
may not repeat them' (2 Corinthians 12.4). John, likewise, is forbidden to 4
write down the thunderous words of God. Instead, he has to be content with
partial understanding, a **little scroll.** He is after all one of God's **servants** 2, 7
the prophets. He stands alongside other Christian prophets in the succession
of the great prophets of the Old Testament. The question mark which had
always hung over the prophecies of these men was not so much, Was their
vision true? but, How much longer would it be before it came to pass? To
John, along with all the prophets, is now given the confirmation their work

cried out for: **'There shall be no more delay'.** (The angel's manner of
6 swearing the great oath is modelled on Daniel 12.7.)

9 **'Take it, and eat it'.** As a metaphor, the word of God that tastes sweet in the mouth is common enough in the Old Testament. The more elaborate picture of a prophet actually eating the words of a book before prophesying occurs in Ezekiel 3.1–3, and is closely reproduced here. The book of destiny can never be read straight off. It has to be digested and meditated before it can be communicated. The experience, for the prophet, is precious. As Ezekiel put it, "It was in my mouth as sweet as honey". But the message
10 to be imparted was a heavy one; and John adds, **my stomach turned sour.**

11. 1 **I was given a long cane, a kind of measuring-rod.** After the destruction of Solomon's temple in 586 B.C., two prophets, Ezekiel (40.3) and Zechariah (2.1–2), received visions of measurements being taken for a new temple: for each, it was a symbolic assurance that the religious life of Israel would soon be re-established. Not long before John was writing, the temple had been once again totally destroyed by the Romans. In the tradition of the great prophets, John received a vision of its imminent replacement.

But John was a Christian prophet, and the new temple which Christians looked forward to was not a localized masonry structure, but a body of people, the church. For them, "temple" and "altar" had become metaphors: the new temple created by Christ consisted only of **the worshippers.** Yet one feature of the old temple could not be absorbed, even as a metaphor, into the new. In Jerusalem, the central area containing the temple building itself and the immediately surrounding courtyards was accessible only to Jews: it was thought too holy to be profaned by gentile visitors. But the immense terrace around this area, though still part of the temple and under the authority of the priests, was open to all: Gentiles could enter freely, and mingle with Jewish worshippers. This arrangement was symbolic of the relationship between Judaism and the world. In the Roman empire, the Jewish religion was officially sanctioned, and Jewish worship continued peacefully in gentile cities, sometimes actually attended by gentile sympathizers. Quite different was the situation of the new temple—the church—in the pagan world. In
2 this period of intensified tribulation, the **Gentiles** (a word by which Jewish Christians often meant "non-Christians") would continue to be implacably opposed to the new Israel with its new temple (the Christians and their church). Persecution was mounting. There was no **outer court** where Christians and non-Christians could mingle peacefully together.

For any observer, whether Jewish or Christian, the sack of Jerusalem in A.D. 70 was the end, not only of a nation, but of a religious ideal. That God had given the heathen permission to **trample the Holy City underfoot** (as the writer of Isaiah 63.18 had described a previous sack of Jerusalem, and as Jesus himself had prophesied, according to Luke 21.24) could only constitute a divine judgement upon his own people. This débâcle had taken place in

recent memory when John wrote. The shrine of the worship of the true God had been extinguished. What was to take its place? The answer was the Christian church. But no city, or building, or institution, now enjoyed the respect from the pagan world which Jerusalem and its temple had once received. The church had gone, so to speak, underground: the heathen were trampling the whole world with no respect for any place set apart to the God of Israel, who was also the God of Christians. Christians now, like the Jews in the war of A.D. 66–70, saw their very identity threatened. It was the time that had been foretold of great tribulation. How long would it last? John was writing to his suffering fellow-Christians. His purpose was the same as that of many Jewish writers before him: to give his readers hope and courage; and he used the same idiom. What they had to express was their conviction that the period of distress was finite; it had an end set to it, therefore it could last only a certain time, a given number of years, months and days. But not, obviously, a random number: God had imposed a pattern on time when he created the week of seven days. Any significant period of history must be reckoned in sevens, or in a fraction of seven. Daniel, predicting the length of oppression under Antiochus Epiphanes, had opted for a half-week—"a time, two times and half a time" (12.7). What were these $3\frac{1}{2}$ "times"? Days, months, years? Probably Daniel deliberately left the symbol open. The point was that it was certainly finite, and would certainly be the kind of period which would betray, even in the arithmetic of its units, the providence of God. John here
uses the same idiom. **Forty-two months . . . twelve hundred and sixty** 3
days sounds more precise than Daniel's formula. But it represents the same symbolic half-week of years; it is any period that is moving swiftly to its end in God's predetermined time-scale.

If everything holy is to be trampled underfoot, how will the church survive? With no prospect of establishing itself visibly against the onslaughts of its persecutors, what will be the manner of its existence? Here John's images melt into each other. The first function of the church will be to bear witness—witness to the facts of Jesus' life, death and resurrection, and witness to the continuing presence of Christ in his church. Witness, in a Jewish court, had normally to be borne by not less than two persons; the church is therefore pictured in the form of **two witnesses.** Its heavenly counterpart, we know, is a set of lamps (1.12), like the seven-branched candlestick that stood by the door of the inner sanctuary of the temple. Think of the church
as two witnesses, and you may think of **two lamps**; but better still, think of 4
the two olive-trees which Zechariah in his vision (4.3–14) saw on either side of the lampstand, representing the two "anointed ones" who, as king and priest, were to lead the people of God (Christians, John said at the beginning (1.6), are both kings and priests). This is how they might appear in heaven: on earth, they appear as two typical prophets, calling unceasingly for repentance,
and **dressed in sackcloth.** Yet they are more than ordinary prophets. They 3

6 have the attributes of Moses and Elijah—Moses, who had **the power to turn**
water to blood and to strike the earth at will with every kind of
5 **plague** (Exodus 7–12), Elijah, who was a man of **fire** (2 Kings 1; Ecclesias-
6 ticus 48.1–3), and had **the power to shut up the sky** (1 Kings 17). They
stand, that is, for the Law and the prophets, for the rule of life the church
proclaims and the inspiration by which it is led. Yet even this witness of the
7 church will not prevail. **The beast that comes up from the abyss**—the
superhuman force of evil which has been held in check until this moment—
8 **will defeat and kill them.** Indeed they will suffer the last indignity of being
9 refused burial, and will lie exposed to the gaze of their enemies throughout
the three days when, people said, the soul might still return to the body (see
above on John 11.39). The city which allowed such a thing could well be
8 given a name of proverbial notoriety, like **Sodom** (or **Egypt**, the place of
Israel's bondage before the time of Moses). Jerusalem itself had crucified
Jesus, and so branded itself as **Sodom**; similar things could happen in any
city. The conscience of the world, it would seem, had been finally eliminated.
The voice of God was silenced for ever. Or so people would think.

But Christians knew that this was all part of the destiny of the Son of Man —the destiny of Jesus himself, the destiny of those who followed him, the destiny even of Elijah when he returned to earth before the End (according at least to one version of the Elijah saga).[a] In the pattern of this destiny, the triumph of the world was only apparent. Christians believed that the victims were raised to life again and vindicated. So far, this was only faith: in the eyes of the world, they were dead, their trust in God obviously betrayed, their profession vain. But one day—the great day with which John's vision is concerned—it would not be so. That God was on their side, that their death was not defeat, would be proved to all the world by a visible "resurrection" and "ascension", accompanied by terrible natural calamities. Then at last
13 men would be forced to believe. Accordingly, in John's vision, **the rest in**
terror did homage to the God of heaven.

15 **Then the seventh angel blew his trumpet.** This is evidently the climax,
the end towards which the whole series of trumpets (and the briefer series of woes which double the last three trumpets) have been tending. Yet this end is not accomplished in a moment. It is not a shapeless cataclysm effacing all that has gone before, but a reasoned judgement upon the whole of history. To be understood, its several aspects have to be explained. This is the function of the second half of the Revelation.

It is in John's manner to describe first what takes place in heaven, before

[a] This version seems to be alluded to by Jesus in Mark 9.13, where he refers to it as Scripture. It was perhaps the same lost writing which gave the length of the drought as $3\frac{1}{2}$ years, instead of the 2 years given in the Old Testament (1 Kings 18.1). This writing was apparently known both to Luke (4.25) and to the author of the letter of James (5.17). In 1898 a fourth-century Coptic work was discovered which appears to be based on an older writing of exactly this kind.

revealing the corresponding events on earth. This time, it is a hymn of praise. 17–18
God is king and has always been so; but his kingship has not been fully recognized on earth. Christians, like Jews, pray 'Thy kingdom come', not doubting for a moment that God is already on his throne, but expressing their faith that his kingship will one day be manifest, not just to those who worship him, but to all mankind. The seventh trumpet is the signal that this has at last come about; and its immediate consequence is a burst of praise from the worshippers: what they have been praying for has at last come to pass.

Some of the words for such a hymn were suggested by Psalm 2, which was originally the triumphal enthronement-song of a king of Israel, the "anointed king" of the Lord, but which seemed to the early church to contain numerous prophecies of Christ; others by other psalms (see especially Psalm 115.13). The essential elements of this final establishment of God's kingship are all there: the Last Judgement takes place, the righteous are recompensed for what they have suffered at the hands of the wicked, and the destructive forces of evil that have long seemed to hold the field are themselves finally destroyed.

Another way of putting this was simply to imagine the splendour of God fully revealed to all men on earth. Suppose you were in the temple in Jerusalem, and had before you the curtain which hid from view the dark inmost sanctuary where God was thought to dwell, the Most Holy Place. The curtain, the darkness, the mystery symbolized the effort of faith required to believe in the lordship of God. But imagine now the curtain removed, the darkness turned to light, so that the divine presence was visible to all; and then transfer this vision from the Jerusalem temple of history to the eternal
realities of heaven. **God's temple in heaven was laid open.** In the old 19
days, that innermost sanctuary had contained the original **ark of his covenant,** the symbol of God's faithfulness towards those who perform his will. It is this aspect of God, at the moment of judgement, which is placed before the eyes of men.

Next appeared a great portent in heaven. No one in antiquity who 12. 1
looked at the night sky saw a mere mass of undifferentiated stars. Each constellation had its name, and the regularity of the movements of the heavenly bodies was known and understood. Indeed it was essential to understand them. It had long been realized that the rising or setting of certain stars was a sign of the beginning of certain seasons, a signal for ploughing or harvesting; and in the last two centuries before Christ the notion that events on earth are controlled by the movements of the heavenly bodies grew into a complex astrological science which exercised a powerful hold on people's minds. John's vision of portents in heaven corresponding to portents on earth was no more than an extension of this widespread way of thinking.

But each constellation also had its own character. Named after some god or hero in Greek mythology, each presented a still shot, so to speak, from an old story: Orion for ever bore his sword, Andromeda her chains. The timeless myths of classical antiquity were all caught in action as eternal pictures in the heavens.

A classical writer, therefore, when describing the night sky, involuntarily borrowed images from pagan mythology. These were the familiar terms in which the sky was known, and the regularity of the stars was a sign and guarantee of the orderly succession of events on earth. Conversely, any prophet who foresaw a major interruption of the normal course of history must necessarily envisage a significant dislocation of the heavenly bodies. Moreover, if the prophet were a Christian, he would also be disposed to find in the constellations, not a reminder of pagan myths, but images suggesting the actual course of Christian history. In his hands the current language of astrology would be subtly transformed. But his readers would know their map of the heavens as well as we know the map of Europe. A **woman** in heaven would have suggested the Virgin of the zodiac as naturally as the "heel" suggests to us the south of Italy.

It is likely, therefore, that John's description of **a woman robed with the sun** was suggested at least in the first instance by the Virgin of the zodiac in the season when the sun rises in that constellation. In a complete chart of the zodiac, sun, moon and stars would belong equally to all the signs; but in the period of Virgo, it would have been natural to think of **the moon beneath her feet** (for the moon rises in the same quarter as the sun) and **a crown of twelve stars** indicating her sovereignty in the heavens. Who, then, was this **woman** in the sky? Pagan writers connected Virgo with various myths; but John, a Jewish Christian, drew upon the Old Testament. One figure suggested itself, the Daughter of Zion. This of course was not a real person at all: it was the personification of an idea, a poetic code-name, both for the inhabitants of Jerusalem itself and for that ideal of society cherished by the great prophets. One day (they believed) the people of Israel, or a part of it, would become fully obedient to the will of God and fully responsive to the demands of its high destiny. A nucleus of pious men would at last be established in Jerusalem worthy of the great promises which God had made to the Jewish people. This nucleus they often called the Daughter of Zion.

"Writhe and groan, O Daughter of Zion, like a woman in travail", the prophet Micah had cried (4.10), seeing the citizens of Jerusalem carried off into exile in Babylon, and with them the hope of a perfect nation of the future. And the same metaphor could be elaborated: if her suffering was like birth-pangs, it would bring forth a child (Isaiah 66.7–9), the suffering would be the very process which brought forth the perfect community. So far the Old Testament: but for Christians the image took on new life. The church was

the true Israel, the community in which God's ancient promises were destined to be fulfilled. In the Daughter of Zion they saw themselves, in her
birth-pangs their own tribulations. **In the anguish of her labour she cried** 2
out to be delivered. John sees in the Sign of the Virgin a still shot, as it
were, from the continuing drama of the sufferings of the church on earth.

But this was only the beginning of John's interpretation. The Daughter of Zion now symbolized the new community which was founded by the death and resurrection of Christ; but she still represented also the historic people of God out of which Christ himself had been born: she had already given birth to one momentous child—so momentous, that there must surely have been a major change among the heavenly bodies to signal so great a revolution in human affairs. Matthew's gospel expresses this astrological necessity in the story of the new star recognized by astrologers from the east (2.1–2). John puts it more dramatically in terms of a mythical conflict in heaven
between Virgo on the one hand, and on the other **a great red dragon** 3
(perhaps Hydra, or Serpens) with a tail sweeping through the sky, as in a
vision of Daniel (8.10). The myth itself was almost universal. Again and again, in classical and oriental literature, we read of an infant god or infant hero whom some power of evil tries to eliminate at the moment of birth, but who is snatched away and kept safe until he is of an age to fulfil his glorious destiny. The myth was true of Jesus: in a literal way, it was acted out in the story of Mary and Joseph's flight to Egypt in Matthew 2.13–15; in a more fundamental sense, it was fulfilled when Jesus, through the crucifixion and the resurrection, was snatched from the power of the devil, and was established as the one (to quote Psalm 2 again) who was **destined to rule all** 5
nations with an iron rod. But **the woman herself**—even if, to our minds, 6
Virgo seems to be turning into the Virgin Mary, the actual mother of Jesus—
still represented the people of God. That people (now the church) was to live in **the wilds** during a spell of persecution which would last (as we have been told earlier) for a symbolic period of 3½ years, **twelve hundred and sixty days.** All this mythology—now rendered true and actual in the facts of Christian history—John reads off from the symbolic constellations in the sky.

Then war broke out in heaven. John now looks beyond the visible sky 7
to the real **heaven** where the ultimate destiny of the world was to be decided.
The archangel Michael was believed to be the heavenly patron of Israel, and so, by extension, of the new people of God. The final contest between the church and the pagan world was to reach such a pitch of intensity (this is the very kernel of John's vision of the future) that no Christian would think of it merely as an issue between men and men. Behind each side stood supernatural forces, and the real war would be fought out **in heaven.** The idea of a final battle between Michael and Satan was an old one (Daniel 12.1); John had only to combine it with the myth of the dragon. The dragon was a

9 serpent, the **serpent of old**, who tempted Eve and so **led the whole world**
astray, that is, **Satan, or the Devil.** In a sense, of course, Satan was always
active on earth; some believed that he had been **thrown down** from his
original place in heaven at the beginning of the world's history. But even so,
this was nothing to the ravages he would cause on earth in the last days. His
original fall (if it took place) had been no more than a rehearsal for his decisive
overthrow at the end.

In a strict chronological scheme, this would make difficulties. The devil is
defeated, yet he is still at work; the victory should be final, yet there still
seems to be more fighting to come. One must ask, why this repeated prolongation of the battle? The answer lies in the whole conception of the
Revelation. The book was based on the proposition (which was taken for
granted in a great deal of early Christian thinking) that sin, persecution and
error were not just permanent elements of the human condition which men
could be helped to overcome by faith in Christ, but were caused by supernatural forces, and that what Christ had done for men could be described in
terms of his victory over those forces: if Christ had defeated the devil, the
devil could no longer cause men to sin. Now this was precisely what Christ
had done on the cross; and his followers, through their solidarity with him,
were now immune from the fatal consequences of sin. Nevertheless, error,
sin and death were still rife in the world. That is to say, the devil had been
defeated, but he could still do a great deal of damage in defeat. Consequently,
John's vision of *The powers of darkness conquered* had to allow for various
stages in his final elimination. The first stage was his expulsion from the
10 heavenly court, where, in his rôle of **accuser**, he had been trying to bring
11 evidence against Christians. His expulsion was caused not only by **the**
sacrifice of the Lamb (the crucifixion) but by the **testimony** of all those
against whom Satan found he had no charge to bring, since they had been
willing to die rather than compromise their Christian profession—**they did**
not hold their lives too dear to lay them down. (This is the cue for
another triumph-song in heaven.) But there was still another stage to come
of the devil's defeat, his death-throes, so to speak, in his place of punishment.
12 **'Woe to you, earth and sea, for the Devil has come down to you in**
great fury'.

To describe this stage, John returns to his star-myth of the woman and the
dragon. When we last heard of the woman (who is now the church), she had
6 **fled into the wilds.** The story is picked up again at the same point, John
14 adding only that she reached her refuge by means of **two great eagle's**
wings. (Virgo was often depicted with wings in art; or perhaps the idea is
that another constellation, Aquila, came to her aid.) [a] As for the picture of
16 the earth swallowing **the river which the dragon spewed from his**
mouth, it is hard to be sure at this point whether John is interpreting

[a] Translated literally, the Greek reads, "she was given the two wings of the great eagle".

patterns among the stars or working into his vision a phenomenon he had actually seen, such as a river disappearing underground. The important thing, in any case, is the explanation John offers of the tribulations of the church: they represent the last spasms of the devil's fury.

He took his stand on the sea-shore. All that the church suffered was 13. 1
ultimately traceable to the devil; but the dragon himself was in a sense too general a figure to stand for the particular kinds of suffering which the church had to undergo. These could be represented more vividly as the work of the devil's agents: in the drama of the devil's final overthrow there were lesser forms of evil on his side. Accordingly, John imagines the dragon on the sea-shore, calling up an assistant from the sea.[a]

Then out of the sea I saw a beast rising. It was a general belief that behind the rulers of heathen powers stood demonic forces. The churches in Asia Minor (like John himself, exiled to Patmos) were under Roman rule, and if they suffered, it was in Roman courts, in Roman prisons, and (if it came to that) by Roman executioners. Rome, therefore, was the devil's agent, and John had next to show how Rome itself would be involved in the devil's ultimate fall. There were doubtless many good things—such as peace, stability, and ease of travel—which were due to Roman rule. But there were also certain aspects of it which seemed to Christians so monstrous that they were bound in the end to bring fearful punishment on Rome. These are the aspects which are portrayed in John's imagery.

John's vision starts, once again, from the Book of Daniel (7.1–7). Daniel in his "visions of the night . . . saw four huge beasts coming up out of the sea", the last with ten horns; and later he was told that the four beasts signified four successive empires, and the ten horns ten kings who reigned over the last of these empires. John here combines the characteristics of the four beasts into one, for only one empire, that of Rome, was now of significance in world history. He keeps the **ten horns**: he tells us in 17.12–13 that these are ten of the vassal kings whom the Romans allowed to rule in their name over parts of the east; and he adds **seven heads**, representing (we learn again in 17.9–10) both the seven hills of Rome and seven Roman Emperors.
One of its heads appeared to have received a death-blow; but the 3
mortal wound was healed. It seems that the career of Nero, advancing through the murder of his own relatives, and apparently ending with suicide in A.D. 68, had struck particular horror into many minds, and a superstition persisted that he had not died at all, but had fled to the Parthians east of the Euphrates and would one day return at the head of an immense army. In any event, his death had been followed by a period of civil war, when the future of the empire itself had seemed in doubt. These events were enough to have

[a] Some manuscripts offer a reading which makes John say of himself, "I stood by the sea-shore" (see the footnote in NEB); but this, though it is easier to interpret, is less likely to be correct.

caused a memorable break in the normal succession of "heads", a scar which might well show on the mythical monster which represented the empire.

5 We are still in the period of $3\frac{1}{2}$ years, **forty-two months**, the symbol of the time during which the church's suffering was to last. Throughout that time, Rome would have **the right to reign.** Throughout that time, therefore, there would be a continuance of that particular feature of Roman imperial policy which caused the greatest offence to Jewish and Christian sensibilities.
6 The beast **opened its mouth in blasphemy against God, reviling his name and his heavenly dwelling.** We know what this means. Beginning with Julius Caesar, Roman Emperors had been "deified", that is, given the status and worship due to a god, usually after their death, but more recently even during their lifetime. Their official titles began to include the word "divine": *Augustus* itself, when rendered into Greek, meant "worshipful". In most of the cities to which John was writing, temples had been built to these "deities"—a mockery of the **heavenly dwelling** of the one true god. All this, to the passionately monotheistic Jews, caused the greatest scandal. But the Jews were permitted to practise their own religion in peace. They were not forced to assent to the worship of an emperor. Not so the Christians. Any of them who found themselves in a court of law might be put to the test and bidden to offer sacrifice to a statue of the Roman Emperor. Refusing to do so, many of them lost their lives. Indeed, this ordeal could be
8 regarded as decisive for a man's salvation. Only those in the **roll of the living** would pass the test. The rest would consent to worship the beast. For
10 them, the prophetic judgement was appropriate that was once made by Jeremiah upon his own contemporaries (15.2): there would be no escape from the violent end their conduct merited. The only way to salvation lay in **the fortitude and faithfulness of God's people.**

The policy of fostering an emperor-cult came ultimately from the Emperor himself, that is, from the distant source of authority which (to John) lay far
1 across the sea (**out of the sea I saw a beast rising**). But its execution lay in the hands of local officials, whether the Roman provincial governor himself or the regional councils responsible for the organization of the cult. These administrators were doubtless a still more vivid source of horror and fear to the churches than the policy itself, and could be aptly represented by
11 **another beast, which came up out of the earth.** John packs into this
13 symbol some of the actual dangers to which the church was exposed. **It worked great miracles, even making fire come down from heaven to earth before men's eyes.** This is a clear reference to Elijah (1 Kings 18.38), the first of the prophets; and false prophets (who might even perform miracles as part of their deception) were one of the hazards which the church had to expect. They would add their delusive influences to complicate the agonizing decision which Christians had to make in the face of demands to conform to the cult of the Emperor. The pressures of contemporary society,

as well as the decrees of the Roman administrators, are all gathered into the symbol of the second beast.

One of the ways in which a ruler impressed his sovereignty most vividly on the minds of his subjects was by the issue of a coinage bearing his image and his title. Throughout the Roman empire, every transaction of buying and selling, if it involved the use of money, meant handling imperial coins. The ordinary citizen constantly held in his hand a head of the Emperor surrounded by an inscription giving his titles, including what seemed to many the blasphemous one AUGUSTUS, which in Greek read ΣΕΒΑΣΤΟΣ, "worshipful". This was grist to the mill of John's imagination: holding a coin
was like being **branded with a mark**, not only on the **right hand**, but in a 16
more sinister sense on the **forehead**, a diabolical counterpart to the 'seal' on the forehead received by God's own people (7.3).

The letters of both the Greek and the Hebrew alphabets served as numerals, and it was a well-known technique to add up the letters composing a proper name. The result could be used as a code-number; or else (according to the popular number-symbolism of the time) a new meaning could be found in a
name by working out its **numerical value**. John is clearly doing the second 18
here: the letters in the inscription on a Roman coin could be made to add up to 666. Unfortunately we neither know how he got this answer, nor what he believed it meant. None of the names of the Roman Emperors of the first century A.D. gives the right figure in Greek, though if Hebrew letters are in mind "Nero Caesar" can be made to add up to the right figure. An abbreviated form of Domitian and his titles would also do so in Greek—but this is a long shot, and it is better to confess that we do not know how John arrived at the figure. As for the figure itself, the cluster of sixes doubtless has some significance; but again, we no longer have the clue to the principles of John's symbolical arithmetic.

Visions of the end

In one sense, the whole of the Revelation consists of *Visions of the end*: John was shown 'what must happen hereafter' (4.1). But the end had turned out to have many phases: it was the key to so much of human history, and to so many of the mysteries of God, that it had to be described in its separate aspects if its meaning was to be understood. But there was one end-moment, so to speak, of which men had a particularly vivid picture in their imaginations, so vivid, indeed, that it perhaps seemed to them to express all that really needed to be said about the end. The proposition expressed by this picture was a simple one: at the Last Judgement the righteous would be rewarded, the unrighteous would be punished. Any visual picture which represented both parts of this proposition necessarily brought on to a single canvas both the reward and the punishment; and Jewish writers of a certain mentality drew the naïve (and as it seems to us immoral) conclusion from this juxtaposition that one of the joys of the blest in heaven would be the spectacle of the torments now inflicted on those who were once their enemies and persecutors, and that an additional torment of the wicked would be the sight of the righteous, whom they had once despised, now enjoying their heavenly reward.

After the completion of all those events which, in the traditional scheme, were due to come to pass before the Last Judgement could take place, John was now ready to present his own picture of the end. He was too sophisticated a writer to include the motif of the righteous gloating over the condemned. But, if there was to be a Last Judgement at all, some condemned there must be. No representation could do justice to the seriousness of God's sentence upon the wicked unless it depicted a dreadful punishment for them. To this extent, John was bound by the conventions within which he wrote. The resultant scene has an element of horror from which the Christian reader
14. 10 may recoil. Words like **wrath** and **vengeance**, when applied to God, seem incompatible with the revelation of God's love and mercy in Jesus Christ. Yet, just as the idea of God "choosing" certain men logically implied that others were not "chosen" and were therefore apparently victimized for the sake of those who were, so the idea of God rewarding the righteous logically implied a very much less happy future in store for those who persevered in wickedness. Biblical language tends to paint in black and white. The opposite of reward is punishment. Using such language, and inheriting such a tradition, John was perhaps less free than a modern writer would be to temper the necessary terror of God's ultimate judgement with faith in his ultimate mercy.
1 **On Mount Zion stood the Lamb.** The right-hand side of the picture (so to speak)—the place of those acquitted by God's judgement—was often represented as a new Jerusalem. Mount Zion, originally the hill on which the oldest city of Jerusalem had been built, became, even in the Old Testament, a symbol for an ideal city of the future. The new feature in John's vision was the Lamb standing there—new, that is to say, because this was a new rôle for the Lamb: he was now to be king among his own people in heaven. In the words of Psalm 2 (which was doubtless still running in John's mind), "I have enthroned my king on Zion my holy mountain". **With him were a hundred and forty-four thousand**: this symbolic number has already appeared in chapter 7; it represents the ideal complement of the new Israel, who bore the names of Christ and God on their foreheads instead of the
3 name of the beast. They alone could join in the worship of heaven. They **had been ransomed**—this metaphor for obtaining salvation through Christ has occurred already in 5.9 ("purchase" and "ransom" translate the same Greek word). But there is also a hint that their own lives and deaths were to
4 benefit others: if they were the **firstfruits ofhumanity** it should follow that

a still greater harvest was to come; if they were **faultless,** this meant that 5
(like an animal at the altar) they were fit to be a sacrifice for others. What was
it in their conduct which produced these great consequences? We should say,
their faith in Christ. But John has very much in mind the ordeal he has just
been describing, so he says, **no lie was found in their lips**—they did not
compromise their allegiance to Christ with so much as a word of homage
to pagan gods. **They follow the Lamb wherever he goes**—this is a 4
straightforward description of Christian discipleship. More puzzling is the
sentence, **These are men who did not defile themselves with women,
for they have kept themselves chaste.** This has almost always been taken
literally, as if John, in the middle of his sweeping description of universal
judgement, suddenly chose to concentrate on that very small section of the
church which practised celibacy. But, apart from other difficulties, this is
hardly in keeping with John's elaborately symbolic style. He had just described the great company of the faithful as the new Israel. In its formative
days the Israel of history, when organized for war, believed it should maintain its army in ritual and sexual purity (Deuteronomy 23.9–10; 1 Samuel
21.5). Here was another symbol. In the Bible, any contact with pagan worship
was called "fornication". It was doubtless from this, even under compulsion
to worship the Roman Emperor, that the righteous had **kept themselves
chaste.**

An angel flying in mid-heaven. One side of the judgement-picture is 6
complete, the other—more gruesome—side is still to be painted. But John
has something to place in between. All that has gone before is preparation for
this judgement, and logically the verdict on each human being must now be
given. But, in defiance of such logic, John seems to introduce a last chance.
The final catastrophes of history may be significant of God's judgement on
the world. But **an eternal gospel** is still proclaimed up to the very last
minute. A constructive reaction is still possible: **'Fear God and pay him** 7
homage'. By calling the angel's warning a **gospel,** John can only mean that
it is always open to mankind to be saved until the moment when judgement
is passed. Between his two panels of reward and punishment, he sets a last
opportunity of choice.

Indeed, the choice is made easier. **'Fallen, fallen is Babylon the great'.** 8
Babylon, the greatest enemy of Israel in the past, was a Jewish and Christian
code-name for the greatest city in the contemporary world: Rome. It was
Rome which seemed ultimately responsible for the oppressive paganism of
civilization. It was **she who had made all nations drink of the fierce wine
of her fornication**—a tumbled combination of Old Testament metaphors
which compresses into a few words both the allurement of paganism and its
terrible consequences. The ultimate fall of Rome seemed inevitable to anyone
who stood in the tradition of Jewish seers (John elaborates the theme later).
Meanwhile, here was a new factor in the circumstances leading up to God's

judgement. When Rome fell, mankind would see the hollowness of all she stood for. Then perhaps they would find it easier to acknowledge God and escape condemnation.

Finally, the other side of the picture: the punishment of those who, despite
10 everything, continue to worship the beast and its image. **The wine of God's wrath, poured undiluted into the cup of his vengeance** may be good Old Testament language (Isaiah 51.17; Psalm 75.8; Jeremiah 25.15), but it sounds strange in a Christian book. Yet, as was said above, retribution for evil deeds is a concept which is still valid for Christians. Since his justice demands it, God allows it; the writer startles us only by personifying it as the **wrath or vengeance** of God.

This whole vision might be understood as a commentary on a text which
13 John is now explicitly told to communicate to his churches: "**Happy are the dead who die in the faith of Christ**". In the face of losses from among their number, this was what they most needed to hear. Paul, after giving to the Corinthians his own vision of the end, summed up in these words: 'Therefore, my beloved brothers . . . work for the Lord always, work without limit, since you know that in the Lord your labour cannot be lost' (1 Cor. 15.58). John has now seen for himself the promised rest which follows the labour; and he can offer what is virtually the same reassurance. Christians' labour cannot be lost; "**they take with them the record of their deeds**".

But this simple picture far from exhausted the repertory of images which John had inherited for describing the Last Judgement. Another vital element was Daniel's vision of the vindication of the righteous: "I saw one like a son
14 of man coming with the clouds of heaven". This **one like a son of man** was now, to any Christian writer, Jesus himself; and Jesus had connected his "coming in the clouds" with a final harvesting: 'Then they will see the Son of Man coming in the clouds with great power and glory, and he will send out the angels and gather his chosen from the four winds, from the farthest bounds of earth to the farthest bounds of heaven' (Mark 13.26–7). This suggested a new piece of imagery for the (so to speak) right-hand side of the picture, the gathering of the righteous into the harvest of their reward. What of the other side?

> "Let all the nations hear the call to arms
>   and come to the Valley of the LORD's Judgement . . .
> Ply the sickle, for the harvest is ripe;
>   come, tread the grapes,
> for the press is full and the vats overflow;
>   great is the wickedness of the nations". (Joel 3.12–13)

It is possible that, in John's mind, the two harvesting images both stood for the same horrifying reality on the left-hand side of the picture: the ultimate judgement on the obdurately wicked. But it seems, nevertheless, as if John

was deliberately keeping them separate by allotting the grain-harvest to
one like a son of man (whom we must guess to be Christ), the grape-
harvest to **another angel** (even though Christ himself is said to tread the 17
winepress later on, 19.15); that is to say, he was still elaborating the
traditional picture of the Last Judgement, with the gathering-in of the elect
on one side and the destruction of the wicked on the other. At any rate, he
leaves us in no doubt about the meaning of the second image. The order is
given by the angel **who has authority over fire** (where perhaps the more 18
literal rendering, "over *the* fire", would be correct, since the **fire** involved is
certainly the traditional fire of punishment). The **winepress of God's** 19
wrath is still clearer: the metaphor is worked out in Isaiah 63.1–6. We might
say, more squeamishly, that God "allowed" the wicked to be punished. But
the imagination of a Hebrew was both more vivid and more logical. If God
"allowed" it, then he took full responsibility for it, and could just as well be
pictured as carrying it out himself. If the punishment was like a winepress,
this was not a concession made by God to inexorable principles of justice,
it was a working out of God's own justice, it was the **winepress of God's
wrath.**

John adds a further grisly detail that was already probably traditional in
this context. **The winepress was trodden outside the city**: the "Valley of 20
the Lord's Judgement" in Joel's vision (quoted above) was often imagined
as the Kedron valley which separates Jerusalem from the Mount of Olives.
This valley is in fact at the head of a long *wady* which winds down through
the mountains for many miles until it reaches the Dead Sea. In the summer
it is dry; but after a spell of heavy rain in the winter it can be a raging torrent.
The immense winepress outside Jerusalem is imagined as discharging its
gory liquid down the valley in such quantities that horsemen could only just
ford the stream—an image that was used by Jewish rabbis to describe the
horror of the sack of Jerusalem by the Romans in A.D. 70. John unexpectedly
adds, **for two hundred miles.** (**Around** is a word gratuitously added by the
NEB. It is hardly right: Jerusalem would never have been imagined as set
in a plain that could be filled with blood. Jerusalem is high in the mountains,
and the blood would flow down valleys.) In one of Ezekiel's visions (47.1–12),
great springs of fresh water rose from under the temple in Jerusalem, filling
the valleys, sweetening the stagnant Dead Sea, and flowing on south through
the desert towards the Red Sea, some two hundred miles away. John may
have been consciously suggesting a gruesome parody of this theme; but in
any case his interest was probably, once again, in numbers. **Two hundred
miles** is a correct but prosaic translation. John actually says, "sixteen
hundred stades". We can guess that this number (which contains the square
of 4) seemed significant to him, even though we no longer possess the clue
to his arithmetical symbolism.

Then I saw . . . seven angels with seven plagues. In what manner 15. 1

John saw them is about to be told. But to the reader of the Old Testament the word "plagues" suggested, not just natural calamities, but a scourge visited on a particular people for the ultimate benefit of others. Through Moses, plagues had afflicted the Egyptians to the benefit of the people of Israel. These **last plagues of all**, which symbolized the final phase of God's judgement upon the earth, were to follow a similar programme. Immune from
2 them now were **those who had won the victory over the beast**: they stood **beside the sea of glass**, which was described earlier as part of the landscape of heaven (4.6), but which was now **shot with fire**, perhaps suggesting that it was also a sea of ordeal, like the Red Sea through which the original Exodus had taken place. Their reaction to the plagues was like the song of Moses after the deliverance from Egypt (Exodus 15): Moses saw in that deliverance something which redounded to the glory of God and filled
3 whole nations with awe. It was also **the song of the Lamb**, since the deliverance had been entirely through Christ; and the greater the deliverance, the more effect could be expected on the nations who witnessed it: when those who served God (and not the beast) were delivered, it was a revelation of
4 God's **just dealings**. Plagues were necessarily visited on someone; some people must suffer from them. But in biblical thinking (even if there is logically little room for the thought at this stage in the Revelation, since one wonders who is left to be an onlooker), the justification for such afflictions was the effect they had on others. To put it in thoroughly scriptural language (and the whole song is a tissue of Old Testament phrases), '**All nations shall come and worship in thy presence, for thy just dealings stand revealed**'.

The plagues, then, were to be no orgy of indiscriminate destruction, but an expression of God's justice: and this determines the symbolism which follows. John repeats from chapter 4 the dramatic image of the opening of the door or curtain that concealed the innermost sanctuary of the temple (or, if one thought of the ideal description in Exodus rather than of its actual
5 realization in Jerusalem, of the **Tent of Testimony**). But this time the feature of that sanctuary which is most in his mind is the Ark of the Covenant, containing the tables of Law which Moses wrote at the dictation of God. This Law was the definitive expression of God's justice; and the final vindication of God's justice involved the punishment of those who disobeyed. Hence the mission of the seven angels, symbolically described as the pouring
7 of **seven golden bowls full of the wrath of God.**

A further series of seven may cause surprise at this point, when everything seems to be tending towards its final end. But for John (as for any biblical writer) the end meant judgement; and the ultimate judgement on mankind must be seen to be appropriate to the various atrocities which mankind had
16. 6 committed. The point is made explicit after the third bowl: '**they shed the blood of thy people...and thou hast given them blood to**

drink. Even **the angel of the waters** admits the justice of this, who is the 5
representative in heaven of that element on earth; and of course **the altar** 7
agrees, which is soaked with the blood in question (6.9). The point becomes
still more obvious as the plagues proceed from the physical elements of the
earth to specific political entities: doom, if it is to be seen as a function of
God's justice, must be analysed into its component parts. But there is also
an artistic reason for a further series of seven. It allows the writer scope to
take as his model the plagues visited on Egypt (**sores,** waters **turned to** 2, 3–4
blood, darkness, frogs and **hailstones,** all occur in Exodus 7–10), and it 10, 13, 21
also enables him to match the effects of the seven trumpets (8.6—11.15) with
another intensified series: previously, repentance was still possible; but this
time men only **cursed the God of heaven for their sores and pains,** for 11
now the moment had come for executing justice, not for launching yet
another appeal for repentance.

After the first four general plagues, which affect the natural environment
indiscriminately (though with a certain rough justice, the mark of the beast
turning to sores, the shedding of blood leading to drinking it, and possibly the
burning of Christians by Nero being rewarded with a burning sun), the
punishments become focused on political entities. The **darkness** of the 10
Egyptian story is here visited on **the throne of the beast,** which we know
from chapter 13 to mean the cult of the Roman Emperor: possibly the darkness is an allusion to the period of anarchy and disputed succession which
followed the death of Nero in A.D. 68. The **great river Euphrates,** as in the 12
trumpet series, is the eastern frontier where Parthian troops were constantly
thought to be massing for a final assault upon Rome. Part of the necessary
preparation for the end was the removal of this natural barrier, so that **the
way** might be open **for the kings from the east.** For perhaps it was not
easy to conceive of the final visitation of God's justice taking place simultaneously in widely distant places. One needed to be able to imagine the
kingdoms of the world gathered together for the purpose. What would
produce this extraordinary and comprehensive gathering? Why, a great
battle involving everyone, **the great day of battle of God the sovereign** 14
Lord. But of course the kings and emperors would not naturally commit
themselves to this all-or-nothing confrontation on a gigantic battlefield. To
get them there demonic powers of persuasion would be needed. True to the
character of the contending powers (13.14), out of their mouths came **devils,
with power to work miracles,** and so **to muster all the kings of the
world.** Where would this great battle take place? What site more natural
than one of the great and tragic battlefields of Jewish history, Megiddo
(Judges 5.19; 2 Kings 9.27; 23.29): Zechariah, in his own prophecy (which
was much meditated on by John), used this evocative name (12.11); but
John, perhaps to make his geography more solemn and mysterious, calls it
Armageddon, and tells us this is Hebrew. We can construe the word: 16

harmegiddo means "Mount Megiddo". We protest: Megiddo is (as battlefields must be) in a plain, the great plain between Samaria and Galilee. Only Mount Carmel is in the neighbourhood. Perhaps John simply wished to work in Carmel as well, with its association of the punishment of idolatrous worship (1 Kings 18).

15 (**'That is the day when I come like a thief!'** This saying of Christ has already been referred to in 3.3. Christ's "coming" can mean many things, even—apparently—Armageddon. But whatever it means, the message is the same: be prepared, stay awake.)

17 **'It is over!'** Three syllables of a Greek word (which suggest by their
sound—*ge-gŏ-nen*—a clap of thunder) bring the drama to a close. Everything
was now on a cosmic scale. People in Asia Minor had experienced cata-
18 strophic earthquakes, but this one was **like none before it in human history, so violent it was.** They had suffered from terrible hail, but not from
21 **hailstones, weighing perhaps a hundredweight.** Mountainous islands
had been known to disappear in the Aegean through volcanic eruptions, but
this was to be a complete redrawing of the map of the world.

Yet even the series of seven plagues did not give John scope to show
exactly how God's justice was visited upon the greatest offenders. In par-
19 ticular, he needed to emphasize that **God did not forget Babylon the
great**—always the symbol for the city of Rome—but made her **drink the
cup which was filled with the fierce wine of his vengeance.** After the
general description of the end of the kingdoms of the world, the next two
chapters provide as it were a close-up of this particular scene of the drama.

17. 1 **'Come, and I will show you the judgement on the great whore'.** The Old Testament prophets, contemplating the capitals of the east at their moment of greatest influence and wealth, were the first to establish this metaphor in literature. Nineveh (Nahum 3.4), Tyre (Isaiah 23.16–17), even Jerusalem itself in its moments of religious infidelity (Isaiah 1.21), were each described as a **whore**: the word suggested both a spiritual permissiveness and promiscuity, contrasting with Israel's uncompromising worship of the one true God, and a state of material luxury, contrasting with the simplicity and austerity of living that went with obedience to the Jewish faith. It epitomized the paganism, the idolatry, and the affluence based on social injustice, which so forcibly struck the Jewish people when they contemplated their powerful neighbours. To some, these features of a great city might have seemed a symbol of lasting power. But the prophets knew better: these things were essentially sinful, and attracted inexorably the judgement of God. Their writings contain elaborate prophecies of the inevitable downfall of such cities—prophecies which were fulfilled as the splendour of each one passed away and gave place to another.

Contemplating the Rome of his own day, John stood in the tradition of

these prophets. From Isaiah (21.1, 9), he took the pattern of a vision seen in
the wilds, at the end of which the cry is heard, '**Fallen, fallen is Babylon** 3, **18.** 2
the great.' From the great oracle in Jeremiah about the fall of the historical
Babylon (51.6–14), he took the image of a woman holding a **gold cup**, making **17.** 4
drunk **men all over the world** and having her seat by the "many waters" 2
of the Euphrates (**enthroned above the ocean** is a free translation, which 1
obscures the reference to Jeremiah's image; though John draws more than
Jeremiah does out of the image by making the waters stand for **an ocean of** 15
peoples and populations, nations and languages). But John was not
merely working, like a prophet, with powerful metaphors. He did not just
describe Rome as a whore, he had a vision of an actual whore which he then
interpreted as Rome. He **saw her mounted on the beast** that he had seen in a 3
previous vision (chapter 13): he saw her clothes, of which the colours and the
magnificence recalled those of the Roman Emperor; and he saw a name
written on her forehead, just as (we are told) it was the impudent custom 5
of harlots in Rome to advertise themselves by wearing their name on a band
across their foreheads. The name was '**Babylon the great**'—Babylon,
which long after the fall of its empire remained the prototype of any great
imperial city. In John's day, the rôle of Babylon was manifestly played by
Rome, and Rome had all the classical attributes of such a city. She also had a
new one, of particular horror to Christian readers: she was **drunk with the** 6
blood of God's people and with the blood of those who had borne
their testimony to Jesus. In the manner of the author of Daniel 7, John 7
tells us his own astonishment at the vision and records the interpretation
given to him by an angel. '**I will tell you the secret of the woman**'. To a
certain extent, there was of course no secret. The woman was Rome, and the
beast she was riding (as we know from 13.1–8) was the dynastic succession of
Caesars who had blasphemously assumed the title, "god". The details of the
symbolism were easy to read. But this did not exhaust their meaning. There
was still a **secret** hidden among the familiar attributes of Rome which it was
important for John's readers to know.

For example, they may have known what the beast was; what they did not
know was that it could be described as one **who was once alive, and is** 8
alive no longer, but has yet to ascend out of the abyss. That is to say,
the empire was the embodiment of an old myth, the myth that the monster of evil and chaos, which had been subdued when the earth was created, and would remain imprisoned in the abyss for most of the world's history, would have a brief period of terrible freedom before the end. The beast symbolized a fearful pattern in the destiny of Rome: her present power was as nothing to the absolute power and absolute terror she would wield in the last phase of her history, to the astonishment of all mankind except those who (being Christians) understood these things and were invulnerable in Christ.

Or again: **the seven heads are seven hills on which the woman sits.** 9

One hardly needed to be told this. Everyone knew that Rome was built on
10 seven hills. But—**they represent also seven kings** (or emperors: the Greek word would be the same for both). That is to say: the succession of the emperors conformed to John's pattern of symbolic numbers; it was finite, and was moving rapidly towards the end of the series. It was not in the style of this kind of writing to make exact historical predictions, and it is unlikely that John was committing himself by saying, for example, that Domitian or Trajan was to be the last or the last but one.[a] What he was almost certainly doing was saying that the series, like the periods of world history, would inevitably fall into a pattern of seven—a symbolic "week"—and that (however it worked out exactly) the end would not be slow in coming. Moreover, the pattern was to show a significant variation. John has already given a hint (13.3) that he shared the prevalent, almost superstitious, awe at the memory of the reign of Nero. Nero would return; he was, so to speak, a
11 microcosm of the mythical beast **that once was alive and is alive no longer,** but is still to have its period of destructive freedom before the end. John turns this popular dread of a re-incarnation of Nero to the advantage of his scheme: the series of Roman Emperors will be brought to an end by an anarchic power such as this, **an eighth—and yet he is one of the seven, and he is going to perdition.**

12 **The ten horns you saw are ten kings.** The beast in Daniel's vision had ten horns, each signifying a king (7.24). The same detail fits John's vision, since the Romans allowed vassal kings to hold territories in the eastern part of the empire, and these kings also, like the Emperor, tended to adopt blasphemous-sounding titles like "saviour" or even "god". They were therefore a fitting element in the total character of the beast; and so long as the empire lasted, they would necessarily share Rome's policy towards Christians.

How would the whore meet her end? In pictorial terms, she would receive
16 the traditional punishment of the adulteress: stripping and humiliation (Hosea 2.3)—but she was also a city, so she would be pillaged and burnt to ashes. In political terms, she would succumb to an eventual revolt of all the eastern kingdoms against the western tyranny. Their subjection to Rome, after all, had been unnatural, and would last only so long as was necessary for God's overriding purpose to be fulfilled.

It remained only to return from symbols to reality, and to describe the ruin of the city itself. John may never have seen Rome; but he will have known of its size and splendour, and will have been aware what a fantastic
18. 16 picture of destruction was involved in his prophecy that **in one hour so much wealth should be laid waste.** Once more, he drew heavily on

[a] There had certainly been more than seven Emperors by the time John wrote. It would be possible to bring the seventh down to his time by omitting some from the list (such as the three contending Emperors of A.D. 68–9); but no identification is fully satisfactory, and it is unlikely that John intended one.

passages of Isaiah, Jeremiah and Ezekiel, describing the doom of earlier
cities. The picture of ruins infested by beasts and demons is from Isaiah 2
13.20–1; the warning to **come out** before it is too late from Jeremiah 51.6; 4
the notion of divine justice paying the city back in her own coin occurs often 6
in the prophets, and the **double** payment is suggested by Isaiah 40.2; the 7
boasting words followed by retribution are a theme of Isaiah 47.7–9; the idea 7–8
of the lament of kings, merchants and sea-captains is worked out in Ezekiel 9–19
27; and the casting of a stone into the water as a symbol of the city's final end 21
is modelled on Jeremiah 51.63. None of these passages is quoted verbatim. They are merely the materials out of which John created his own tremendous picture of the sudden doom of the greatest city the world had ever known. It made no difference that these materials did not fit the stage reached in John's drama: logically, there should no longer have been any kings or merchants surviving to raise a lament about the fall of Rome. But a lament was what John needed in his picture, and the mourners were an artistic necessity. The total effect of his description was quite properly more important to him than a rigid adherence to the formal progression of the drama.

A vast throng in heaven. The worship in heaven, which John becomes **19.** 1
aware of at intervals throughout the book, is partly timeless, partly an
appropriate response to the events taking place. In this chapter there are both
elements. **Alleluia**, a Hebrew phrase that occurs in some of the psalms 2
and means "praised be God", became a formula of Jewish and then of
Christian worship. The same goes for **Amen** (the two occur together in 4
the Hebrew at the end of Psalm 106); and another of the responses of the
heavenly worship takes the form of a psalm-verse, '**you that fear him, both** 5
great and small' (Psalm 115.13). It was natural to think of the heavenly
liturgy as using the language in which God had for centuries been praised
on earth. But there is also a note in the singing which belongs to the moment
reached in the drama. '**He has condemned the great whore**'—it is the 2
manifestation of God's justice which has called forth the hymn of praise. To us, justice and vengeance seem two different and incompatible things, and we are shocked when the hymn goes on, '**and has avenged upon her the blood of his servants**'. But the notion may have seemed less crude to John. The suffering of the righteous was for Hebrew thought the nub of the problem of evil. If those who inflicted it seemed to escape any penalty, it became agonizingly difficult to continue to believe in the absolute justice of God: somehow, some time, God must surely come down on the side of his righteous servants, either by bringing their persecutors to recognize their error, or else (if that failed) by inflicting on them an answering punishment. This ultimate punishment—the decisive execution of God's justice when all appeals for repentance had failed—was seen as a kind of necessary "vengeance", an inescapable corollary of the justice of God.

The last stanza of the hymn introduces a fresh group of images which

7 dominate much of the rest of the book. **The wedding-day of the Lamb** is
strong Old Testament imagery. Ideally, God's relationship with his people
was always intended to be like that of bride and bridegroom—perfect mutual
trust and fidelity. That relationship was at last to be realized in the union of
Christians with Christ. For the wedding, the bride must have white clothes,
signifying innocence. But, in the sight of God, no human beings can be
8 innocent: if they have white clothes it is because they have **been given** them.
We have been told earlier how Christians have obtained them—through the
sacrifice of Christ. (Hence it is tempting to think that the explanatory note,
that they signify **the righteous deeds of God's people**, betrays the hand
of a later editor who had a less firm grasp on Christian essentials than John.)
9 The **wedding-supper** itself would be how Christians might conceive of that
spiritual banquet prepared for them in heaven—the image runs through
much of the teaching of Jesus. **"Happy are those who are invited to the wedding-supper of the Lamb!"** might sound, in another context, simply like a Christian version of a religious truism: it is good to be one of those who are saved. But here it belongs to a series of statements which John is explicitly told to **write** for the reassurance of the churches, and an additional note of authority is given, **'These are the very words of God'**. Evidently the statement struck a solemn chord in the Christian mind. Perhaps we can guess why. When Christians celebrated the Lord's supper on earth, they thought of it as a kind of foretaste of the heavenly banquet they would ultimately share with Christ. The words of the angel to John may have sounded like an authoritative confirmation of their faith that those who took part in this supper on earth would certainly be **invited to the wedding-supper of the Lamb** in heaven.

10 **At this I fell at his feet to worship him.** Of course it was wrong to worship angels. **'It is God you must worship'.** But here, as in a repetition of the same little scene in 22.8–9, John appears to draw a further point from it. It was possible to make too many distinctions in the church, to regard bearing **testimony to Jesus** (even at the risk of one's life) as something quite different from moments of prophetic inspiration, and to give greater honour to **the prophets.** John seems to be saying that there is no distinction. It is all one. Even the prophecy of an angel is on a level with the testimony of those who witness by their lives. The church must not become a competitive society, awarding honours to one gift rather than another: Christians must turn their eyes, not upon one another, but always upon God.

11 **There before me was a white horse.** The reader is well aware by now that
at the centre of John's heaven is the ineffable presence of God himself, and
associated with him is the ascended Christ, who also shares the ultimate
12 mystery of God (**written upon him was a name known to none but**
himself). In much of the Revelation this figure of Christ is in the back-

ground, and we are kept in mind of him only by the worship with which he is surrounded. But from time to time he comes to the front of the stage, clothed in a form which gives expression to some aspect of his status and influence. Most often he is the Lamb: the image serves to keep Christ's sacrifice continually before the reader's mind. In this chapter there is a new symbol, that of a white horse and its rider. The name, **Faithful and True**, referring back to a previous description of Christ (3.7), is enough to tell us whom the symbol represents.

A white horse signifies a conqueror: the aspect of Christ which is now 11
to be revealed is his sovereignty over all nations. Christians believed that Christ was the fulfilment of the prophecy of Psalm 2:

> "I have enthroned my king on Zion my holy mountain . . .
> I will give you nations as your inheritance,
> the ends of the earth as your possession.
> You shall break them with a rod of iron . . ."

Yet he fulfilled it in a totally unforeseen way. Temporal power he firmly rejected (it is described as a temptation of the devil in Matthew 4, Luke 4),
and he won his victory only through his own death (of which his **garment** 12
drenched in blood is probably meant as a reminder: it also made white
the **fine linen, clean and shining**, of his followers, 7.14). So, when his 15
sovereignty finally becomes manifest at the end, the crudely military language
of the psalm has to be reinterpreted. The rider bears on his head **many** 12
diadems. The diadem—a jewelled band across the brow—was the mark of an oriental king (as distinct from the wreath worn by the Roman Emperor); two diadems were occasionally worn to signify the possession of two kingdoms. The rider's **many diadems** show him to be a universal ruler. But the
sword of his conquest is (as in 1.16) a sword proceeding **from his mouth**: 15
it is (as one of his names testifies) the **Word of God**, an instrument, that is 14
to say, not of military power, but of righteous judgement—the metaphor is used in Hebrews 4.12, and is doubtless present also when John's gospel introduces Jesus under the single concept of 'the Word'. For another prophecy has to be kept in mind along with Psalm 2:

> "He shall judge the poor with justice
> and defend the humble in the land with equity;
> his mouth shall be a rod to strike down the ruthless
> and with a breath he shall slay the wicked." (Isaiah 11.4)

It is true that his kingship inevitably involves the condemnation of those
inexorably opposed to him—he has to **tread the winepress of the wrath** 15
and retribution of God (see above on 14.19). But the weapons of his rule are always and only those by which he has won his victory on the cross. It is only these which have won for him the title that, in the Old Testament, was

16 reserved for God: **'King of kings and Lord of lords'.** (John is perhaps
thinking of a statue inscribed with the subject's name when he says, a little
obscurely, **on his robe and on his thigh there was written the name.**)
The figure of the conquering rider is now added to the picture that was
begun in chapter 16 of all the nations of the earth mustered for battle at
Armageddon. The battle turns into a final encounter with Christ; and John
lets his imagination work on the scene of the battlefield when it is all over (he
was inspired by a similar vision in Ezekiel 39.17–20). The feast of the
17 vultures was **God's great supper,** a terrible parody of the wedding-supper
of the Lamb. Such was the inevitable end of the human combatants. But
20 their ranks had been led by demonic agencies, the **beast** and the **false
prophet,** for whom a special place of destruction was reserved, **the lake of
fire with its sulphurous flames.**

Yet even now, there were still aspects of God's justice which had been left out of John's scheme. Divine justice must not only be done, it must be seen to be done. If the obdurate enemies of God, who continued until the end to inflict suffering on the righteous, were to be punished simply by being consigned to death and oblivion, this still left a certain unfairness in the reckoning: were those who had been unjustly deprived of recognition, and even of their basic human rights, to be given no recompense, no vindication, before the end of the world? To put it another way: even in the present age, Christ was proclaimed to be Lord; he had a rule, or kingship, which, though denied by the world, was nevertheless real, and was to be shared with his followers. To a cynic who questioned the reality of this lordship, it was natural to reply: "You may not see it now, but one day you will". Christians were destined to be kings and priests (1.5). To give substance to these titles, it was necessary to look forward to a future period of history, when the physical rule of kings and armies would give place to a different kind of authority, vested in the persons of Christians and acknowledged by those who had previously despised it. But John's drama seemed not to have allowed for this stage: the forces of evil had been steadily gathering momentum until their final overthrow; and now (we would have thought) the world had come to an end. It was too late for a Christian epoch.

It was perhaps to meet this objection that John, just before describing the end of the world, slipped in a Christian millennium. The theme was not a new one. In the Old Testament, hopes of a new age in which God's people would enjoy a just, peaceful and prosperous existence under the rule of an "Anointed One" (Messiah, Christ) were concentrated upon some future period of history; and, if it were once established, there seemed no reason why this glorious kingdom should ever end. But with the disappearance of the physical possibility of such a destiny for Israel (after about the second century B.C.), and with the growth of a belief in resurrection and a glorious after-life, this ideal kingdom of the Messiah was increasingly thought of as a

transcendent reality, to be brought into existence only after the end of the world. Yet a hankering for the old ideal of a restored and purified political kingdom remained; and some thinkers tried to combine the two beliefs by postulating a limited period of Messianic kingship on the old model, followed by the Last Judgement and the definitive reward of the blest. We can also see some further reasons which may have led John to find a place for such a period in his scheme. First, he was able to draw out of it a new application of the old myth of the chained monster (see above on 9.1): the reign of Christ
would be untroubled even by the seductive power of the devil, for **that** 20. 2
serpent of old, which men thought had been imprisoned in the abyss since the creation, had in fact been at work throughout recorded history, and his real "chaining" must lie in the future. Secondly, he seems to have shared the view of certain Jewish thinkers that when God created the world in six days each day corresponded to a thousand years, and therefore the last thousand would be the world's Sabbath, the glorious period to which all history was tending. Thirdly, and most important, it allowed him to include a detail of Ezekiel's vision (38–9) which perhaps seemed to fill a serious gap in his own presentation. Again and again, in Israel's history, conquering armies had approached Palestine from the north, and had been recognized by the prophets as instruments in the hand of God, punishing the Hebrew people for their sins. But in the Messianic era, the function of a great invading army would be different: no longer to punish Israel, but to demonstrate, by its own unlooked-for defeat, the inviolability of the people of God. Ezekiel had called these invaders by the already almost legendary name of "Gog, from the land of Magog". John made them sound even more legendary by calling
them **the hosts of Gog and Magog**: they represented the final spasm of the 8
Devil's power, and their defeat was his final elimination.

To this extent John was guided by precedent. Yet it is still difficult not to feel that, by including this episode, he seriously interrupted the logical progression of the drama. Moreover, he had to make some adjustments to the Jewish scheme to make it fit its Christian context. Jewish writers, thinking of the Messianic kingdom as a future period of history, longed to be alive when that period should begin, but recognized that the enjoyment of it might be reserved for others. For Christians this conclusion would have been impossible: it was a firm article of belief that it would make no difference having died; all Christians were to share in Christ's reign (see above on 1 Thessalonians 4.13–18). Therefore John had to introduce the complication of two deaths and two resurrections. The first death would be the natural death of all men in their own generation, from which Christians alone would be resurrected in order to enjoy the millennium. The second resurrection would be at the moment of the Last Judgement, when all the dead of the past would rise to hear their sentence, and those who were condemned would be consigned to a second death, this time without reprieve.

After this interlude, John was at last ready to round off the history of the world with its traditional climax, the Last Judgement. The reality of this final verdict cast by God upon the life of every human being was not doubted by any Christian (even though it received considerable re-interpretation in the fourth gospel), and the imagery in which it was pictured remained fairly constant: John had little new to add, and he made his account quite brief. All the dead had been placed by Death in the shadowy underworld of Hades
—this was the almost universal belief of the ancient world. The only excep-
13 tions were those who had died at sea (there was some speculation about
exactly what happened to the bodies of the shipwrecked). But all alike were
brought for a judgement that was based upon the carefully kept record of
their deeds. It only remained to dispose of those personifications of physical
14 death, **Death and Hades**. They too were cast into the fiery oblivion reserved
for all the wicked. As Paul put it (1 Corinthians 15.26), 'the last enemy to be
abolished is death'.

21. 1 **Then I saw a new heaven and a new earth.** The Hebrew prophets never imagined that one day things might take a turn for the better, and that mankind would slowly progress towards a new age. The events around them were significant, not of man's progress towards better things, but of God's judgement on men's sins. The world was not as God intended it to be; but nor would it become so merely by human efforts. What was needed was a new act of creation. The age to come was something which could only be brought about by God.

John had now reached this point in his vision. Justice having been done on all those elements of the world order which constituted an offence against the will of God, the decks could be cleared, so to speak, for a new created order. **The first heaven and the first earth had vanished**—we might have thought it would be sufficient to do away with the earth; but the ancient picture of the universe was integrated by astrology. Events on earth were governed by movements in heaven. Doing away with one meant doing away with the other, and a newly created earth would require a new heaven to regulate its destiny. Moreover, the earth was thought of as hemmed in on all sides by the sea, and as resting on waters imprisoned underneath it. This element, in the old order, was the place of the chaotic forces of evil. In the new order it had no function. So: **there was no longer any sea.**

So much was easy to state negatively: it was easy to see what would not belong to the new order. But John's task was now the positive one, of describing what *would* belong to it. In this he was influenced, as always, by those who had written before him. The new age, however different it might be from the present, was never thought of as a completely fresh start. There were elements in the present which pointed forward to it, and which would in fact be incorporated in it. The ideal of human life—God dwelling among

his people, and his people living with the purity and justice demanded by God—had for centuries been symbolized by the city of Jerusalem. In Jerusalem there was a great precinct around the central sanctuary which only those could enter who were members of the chosen people and who had been cleansed from ritual impurity; and around that was a still larger precinct, which people from any nation could enter, in order to catch at least a glimpse of the holiness of God. Around this precinct again stretched the city, the capital of a people whose lives were orientated towards the God who was worshipped in the temple in their midst. In theory, the city was a microcosm of God having his dwelling among men. In practice (as the prophets were quick to notice) it was nothing of the kind: the worship might be hypocritical, the people disobedient. More than once both city and temple had been destroyed (and both stood in ruins when John was writing). But the old ideal remained; whether one were a Jew or a Christian, one's vision of man's
ultimate destiny was likely to be clothed in the forms of **the holy city, new** 2
Jerusalem. Some even said that the historical city of Jerusalem was a copy of the true Jerusalem existing in heaven. Therefore it was not even necessary to envisage a new work of creation. All that was necessary was for the archetype to come **down out of heaven from God.**

Given this almost inevitable frame for his final tableau, John proceeded characteristically by allowing his imagination to work on the material he found in the prophets. The first source of his inspiration was Isaiah 65.17–19:

> "For behold I create new heavens and a new earth
> Former things shall no more be remembered
> Nor shall they be called to mind . . .
> For I create Jerusalem to be a delight
> And her people a joy . . .
> Weeping and lamentation
> Shall never again be heard in her."

These verses dominate John's first paragraph; what he adds to them is the
principle which governs the whole vision: '**Now at last God has his dwel-** 3
ling among men!'—the fulfilment of a hope expressed again and again in the Old Testament (e.g. Ezekiel 37.27; Zechariah 8.8: **dwelling** is a suggestive word, see above on John 1.14), but stated in its most generous form: not among men of one particular race or allegiance, but quite generally **among men.**

Before proceeding with his description, John has one more very important
thing to say to his readers. '**Write this down**': this phrase always announces 5
some message that is to reassure the churches; and so it does here. The joys of the new Jerusalem are not a theoretical reality of the distant future: in one thunderous word it is declared that "they have happened" (*ge-gŏ-nen*,

as in 16.17: the NEB rather spoils the effect with a wordy paraphrase,
6 **'Indeed they are already fulfilled'**). That is to say: just as in certain
respects the new Jerusalem was anticipated by the old, so the vision of
'God-with-us', which can be fully realized only in the future age, is nevertheless anticipated in present Christian experience. All that was said at the
beginning of the Revelation about the nature of God (**the Alpha and the**
7 **Omega,** 1.8) and the reward of the **victor** ('I will acknowledge him as
mine', 2.7), is already true; what remains to be told is only its perfect fulfilment in the new Jerusalem. To use an image hinted at earlier (7.16), and
6 worked out in detail in John's gospel (4.7–15), **'A draught from the
water-springs of life will be my free gift to the thirsty'.** How much of
humanity was ultimately destined to share these blessings is a question which is never directly answered (though there are suggestive hints scattered through the book). But there would always be an irreducible remainder of
8 those for whom the **second death** was reserved. Partly, they were those
whose courage failed them, the apostates from the church, **the cowardly, the faithless**; partly they were those who were irremediably committed to the (from the Jewish and Christian points of view) characteristic vices of the pagan world.

9 **'Come, and I will show you the bride'.** The poetry of John's final
vision must be allowed to speak for itself: what determined his choice of words was what he actually saw, and his recollections of the visions of previous writers served only to impose a certain pattern on his writing. It is not difficult to trace the sources of his imagery; but in every case he has used his sources so freely that the result is entirely his own.

(i) The city was to accommodate the true Israel, a re-embodiment of the
12 legendary **twelve tribes.** This gave it a twelvefold arrangement such as
had been worked out by Ezekiel (48.30–5); it was only necessary to add the
fact that there was a further very important "twelve" in Christian history,
14 **the twelve apostles of the Lamb.**

(ii) The city would be of immense size—necessarily, to accommodate the number of its citizens. This necessity struck many Jewish writers, who were prepared to extend the boundaries of the new Jerusalem as far, if need be, as
Damascus. John's dimensions, if taken literally, would make the city the size
16 of a continent (**twelve thousand furlongs** = 1,500 miles), and perhaps that
would not be too big. But John's numbers are usually symbolical, and his choice of twelve thousand was doubtless determined mainly by the twelves of the previous paragraph. **The city was built as a square**: this gave it a kind of mathematical perfection; to be "foursquare" was to have an ideal shape, or (metaphorically) a sound character. John takes the idea a stage further when he adds a third dimension, **its length and breadth and height being equal.** A cubic city strains our imagination. The essential thing was doubtless the mathematical symmetry; but we probably need not think of

anything quite so improbable as a cube of masonry: Jerusalem was always imagined as a "city set on a hill", and John may well have had in mind the picture of a city spreading up the slopes of a mountain so high that in the end the height of it equalled the breadth. This also eases the problem of the walls,
a mere **one hundred and forty-four cubits high** (about 200 feet), sufficient 17
for an ordinary city, but not for a cubic continent. All this is established with
a gold measuring-rod. The convention of an angel revealing dimensions 15
by measuring them out before the eyes of the seer is in Zechariah 2.1 and Ezekiel 40 (see above on 11.1). Some kings of the east had their own special measures, slightly larger than the norm. But the angel, John tells us, was
using ordinary **human measurements.** 17

(iii) An exiled prophet in the sixth century B.C., prophesying the restoration of the ruined city of Jerusalem to a state of ideal peace, justice and prosperity, had written:

> "Now is the time when I set your stones in finest mortar
> And your foundations in lapis lazuli:
> I will make your battlements of jasper
> Your gates of garnet,
> All your boundary stones shall be jewels". (Isaiah 54.11–12)

The theme lent itself readily to elaboration. Another essay in it—written some 300 years before the Revelation—can be found in Tobit 13.16–17. John's description stands in the same tradition, though here it is combined with the symbolic twelvefold structure of the city. A further recollection which may have run through John's mind is that of the "breast-piece" (a kind of shallow box) which was attached to the high priest's garments, and which was studded with twelve precious stones, each different stone symbolizing one of the twelve tribes of Israel (Exodus 28.15–21). As for the gates made each
from a single pearl, the comparatively recent pearl-trade from the Red 21
Sea had prepared the oriental mind to imagine the possibility of ever larger pearls: the brilliantly white masonry of some of Herod's buildings in Jerusalem could have suggested, if one half closed one's eyes, the shimmering brightness of immense pearls.

(iv) **I saw no temple in the city.** A large part of Ezekiel's vision, which 22
was so much in John's mind, had been taken up with the details of a new temple replacing the one which had recently been destroyed in Jerusalem. It was this which would set the standard, so to speak, for the purity and holiness of the nation. In John's time, the temple was once again in ruins; but in his vision of the new Jerusalem, John dared to extend the holy precinct over the whole city. All that the temple stood for would be diffused throughout every part of it; there would be no need for a central shrine, any more than a lamp is needed when the sun is shining. The barrier excluding anything **unclean** would no longer be set up around a small temple courtyard, 27

but would be at the city boundaries: for all the citizens would be in a constant state of holiness. In the old Jerusalem, access to the sanctuary of God was reserved for those who specially cleansed themselves from the ways of the world. In the new, there would be no need of any such preparation: the inhabitants would live perpetually in the presence of God.

(v) Ezekiel dreamed of a restored Jerusalem making the desert fertile by
a river of water that flowed from under the temple: on either side would
22. 2 grow trees bearing fruit every month of the year, and leaves "for healing"
(47.1–12). The picture was already an ideal one; but John has (as we would
1 say) spiritualized it still further. The river is **of the water of life**, such as
2 Jesus promised to his followers (John 4.14), the trees are each a **tree of life**,
such as grew in the Garden of Eden (Genesis 2.9), and are reserved for the
faithful followers of Christ (Revelation 2.7).

However much the reader may have been carried along by the sequence of John's visions, he will find himself at some stage pausing to ask, But is all this true? The promise of a new Jerusalem for those who are enduring persecution from a contemporary Babylon is encouraging only if it can be confidently believed. Moreover, since the vision is not just of some ultimate reality outside space and time, but of a process already taking shape in history, it will cease to excite and console if its fulfilment seems to belong only to a remote future. John needs to leave his readers with a strong impression of both the authenticity and the immediacy of what he has been imparting.

In strict logic, there could be no greater authority than that carried by the
vision itself. John had heard the voice of Christ and of angels. If he wrote
these things down, he ought to be believed. But would he be? Moses, after
his first vision of God, had the same doubt: "But behold, they will not
believe me or listen to my voice, for they will say, 'The Lord did not appear
to you'" (Exodus 4.1). On that occasion, God promised to support Moses
with certain miracles. In part, John was aware of similarly supernatural
support. No one doubted that the prophesying which could be heard in
Christian communities was divinely inspired; and what John had heard
from an angel was simply a development of that stream of prophecy to which
6 his readers already gave credence. **'The Lord God who inspires the
prophets has sent his angel'**.

But there is a further way in which it is only human (even if not entirely
logical) to emphasize the truth of what one says, and that is by swearing that
it is true. John had received the revelation from Christ himself, and it was
natural to end by once more invoking the name of Christ as a guarantee of
its truth. He does so by means of titles which, at the beginning of the book,
belonged to God himself (1.8), but which, by the end of the drama, are
13 shared also by Christ: **'I am the Alpha and the Omega, the first and the
last, the beginning and the end'**.

As for the immediacy of the vision's fulfilment, this was the really new thing about it. The pattern for it had been the visions in the Book of Daniel; but Daniel was a legendary figure of the sixth century B.C.: the oracles ascribed to him were intended to illuminate contemporary history for the readers of the book some four hundred years later; and so Daniel was told, "You must keep the vision secret, for it points to days far ahead" (8.26). In the same way, later Jewish writers, when ascribing their visions to figures of the distant past, explained that the writings had been "sealed up" until the time that they would become relevant and actual. John's situation was the opposite. The times of which he saw the fulfilment had already begun. So
the conventional injunction is reversed: **'Do not seal up the words of** 10
prophecy in this book, for the hour of fulfilment is near'.

Another constant feature of Christian (as of Old Testament) prophecy was its serious moral tone. It was never intended either to satisfy idle curiosity about the future or to breed complacency by dwelling on the joys in store for the elect. What it read in the future was always, in some form or another, a judgement on the present: its immediate message, therefore, was the necessity of vigilance and faithfulness here and now. Hence the strong moral note
sounded here: **Happy is the man who heeds the words of prophecy** 7
contained in this book! The Last Judgement would draw the line finally between the good and the bad; but the line was already being sketched in. The ultimate division could be described in terms of John's vision of the new
Jerusalem: inside would be those **who wash their robes clean; outside** 14
are dogs—this was Jewish language for pagans, taken over into Christian parlance to describe all who persevered in the notorious sins of heathendom. Before the end, there would doubtless be many opportunities for repentance. But if Christians looked around them now, they could see the materials for
judgement already being assembled, the attitude of **the evil-doer** already 11
beginning to harden. The message of the prophecy must be taken to heart as a solemn warning to the **good man to persevere in his goodness.** The coming of Christ, however confidently it might be yearned for by Christians,
contained always a threat as well as a promise. He would come **to requite** 12
everyone according to his deeds.

'It is God you must worship'. The little episode of John's misdirected 9
worship of an angel (19.10) is repeated, perhaps to help the transition from the writing and reading of a message addressed to particular churches to the act of worship in which those churches must share. There are signs at the end of some of Paul's letters that they were read out when the church was assembled, and that the ending was intended to be the signal for the congregation to begin the service. In the same way, when one reaches the end of Revelation, it is as if the music of praise has already started. The worship is antiphonal; that is to say, to each of the sentences spoken by the leader, the congregation makes its response. The leader may be speaking in his own

person, bidding the people to prayer and praise, or he may be using scriptural language and hallowed phrases of worship, in which case the real speaker is understood to be God or Christ. Either way, there is no need to distinguish: it is all part of a single act of worship. If there seems to be an almost bewildering change of speakers in these last few verses, this atmosphere of worship must be kept in mind.

This is more than speculation. The end of 1 Corinthians contains, first, an injunction to separate from the congregation anyone who is there for dishonest reasons ('if anyone does not love the Lord, let him be outcast'); secondly a formula of prayer, given in the original Aramaic (*Marana tha*, 'Come, O Lord!'); and thirdly, the grace. Exactly the same three elements
18 occur here. First, a **warning**: prophecies of this kind were the easiest material for an unscrupulous impostor to tamper with; therefore, on any occasion when this book was read, it was particularly false prophets who must be threatened with exclusion from the congregation and thereby with the loss of their right to the Christian inheritance hereafter; secondly, the same
20 formula of prayer (though given only in Greek, **Come, Lord Jesus**); and
21 thirdly, **the grace.** The form of worship is evidently the same in each case; and here the language of worship pervades the whole section. Jesus bears
16 titles such as befit the object of worship, **the scion and offspring of David** (a variation on the expression in 5.5), **the bright star of dawn** (as in 2.28).
17 He offers, in the very moment of being worshipped, **the water of life.** Above all, in this book devoted to assuring Christians of the destiny which awaits
20 them, Jesus is heard voicing the greatest assurance of all: **'Yes, I am coming soon!'** And the response of all who are moved by the Spirit to lead the
17 congregation, the response of the whole church on earth (**the bride**), the response of **each hearer,** is that of a people prepared and expectant: **'Come!'**

INDEX